AUDITING

THE ART AND SCIENCE OF ASSURANCE ENGAGEMENTS

CANADIAN ELEVENTH EDITION

ALVIN A. ARENS

PricewaterhouseCoopers Auditing Professor

Michigan State University

RANDAL J. ELDER

Syracuse University

MARK S. BEASLEY

North Carolina State University

INGRID B. SPLETTSTOESSER-HOGETERP

York University

Pearson Canada
Toronto

Library and Archives Canada Cataloguing in Publication

Auditing: the art and science of assurance engagements / Alvin A. Arens . . . [et al.].—Canadian 11th ed.

Canadian 3rd–Canadian 7th eds. published under title: Auditing: an integrated approach. Canadian 3rd. ed. written by Alvin A. Arens, James K. Loebbecke, W. Morley Lemon. Canadian 4th ed.–Canadian 7th ed. written by W. Morley Lemon, Alvin A. Arens, James K. Loebbecke. 8th Canadian–10th Canadian eds. published under title: Auditing and other assurance services / Alvin A. Arens . . . [et al.]

Includes index.
ISBN 978-0-13-505467-3

1. Auditing—Textbooks. I. Arens, Alvin A.

HF5667.A93 2011   657'.45   C2009-904856-6

ISBN 978-0-13-505467-3

Vice-President, Editorial Director: Gary Bennett
Editor-in-Chief: Nicole Lukach
Sponsoring Editor: Carolin Sweig
Executive Marketing Manager: Cas Shields
Developmental Editor: John Lewis
Production Editor: Imee Salumbides
Copy Editor: Susan Bindernagel
Proofreader: Michael Arkin
Production Coordinator: Lynn O'Rourke
Compositor: MPS Limited, A Macmillan Company
Art Director: Julia Hall
Interior Designer: Opus House Inc./Sonya V. Thursby
Cover Designer: Kerrin Hands
Cover Image: John Rensten/Getty Images

1 2 3 4 5   13 12 11 10

Printed and bound in the United States of America.

Contents

Preface

Welcome to the Canadian Eleventh Edition of *Auditing: The Art and Science of Assurance Engagements*. It is with great pleasure that I bring forward this eleventh edition, after having discussed with numerous practitioners the impact of the international auditing standards that are being adopted here in Canada. Practitioners highlighted the fact that many of these standards represent work that is already being done but is being codified and organized in a different way. Accordingly, this text represents a major shift to further clarify the risk-based model, where the audit work conducted is a response to identified risks.

What's New to This Edition?

- More practice, more examples, and more stories help illustrate the assurance material.
- Up-to-date information about auditing standards in transition—New icons and text boxes highlight the changes that are occurring as Canada incorporates new international standards.
- Concept Check questions—Concise review questions appear at the end of each major chapter section and test the reader's understanding of the section material. Solutions to the Concept Check questions are provided on the textbook's Companion Website.
- ACL audit software—Students will be able to download a trial version of this widely used audit software from the Premium Companion Website. ACL software is used by professional auditors to extract and analyze data on clients' computerized systems. ACL Problems in the text show students how audit software is used to perform specific types of audit tests.
- CondoCleaners.com—A running case with discussion questions about a small company, CondoCleaners.com, has been added to focus attention on the auditing needs of small businesses.
- Chapters are organized in a new order to facilitate progressive learning; details are provided below.

Students want more practical information and practice to illustrate the assurance material that can, at times, be quite technical. *Auditing*, Canadian Eleventh Edition, therefore contains more stories and practice questions that relate to small and large businesses at home or from the international business perspective. We are currently living in a period of shifting standards, when some International Standards on Auditing (ISAs) have been adopted as Canadian Auditing Standards (CASs), while others are being reviewed, and the revision of the *CICA Handbook* from the Canadian Institute of Chartered Accountants continues.

To guide students and instructors throughout this change, *Auditing*, Canadian Eleventh Edition, focuses on the required standards and audit practices. A cross-referenced appendix of new as well as prior standards, available on the Companion Website, facilitates finding the exact standards that you need.

Objectives

This book is intended for use in a first auditing course, for one-semester or two-semester instruction at the undergraduate or graduate level. Using a risk-based approach, this text focuses on the auditor's decision-making process. It is important to keep the underlying objective in mind—the need to collect evidence to enable the auditor's statement of opinion with respect to financial statements (and other types of information, as discussed in the later chapters). Assessing and documenting the risks associated with the client's business and the various components of the financial statements allows the auditor to target the fieldwork to specific objectives called audit assertions. If a student in auditing understands the objectives to be accomplished in a given audit area, the circumstances of the engagement, and the decisions to be made, he or she should be able to determine the appropriate evidence to gather and how to evaluate the evidence obtained.

The title of this book reflects the reality that auditing goes beyond financial statement auditing to other assurance services. Auditing is an art, as it requires considerable use of professional judgment, but it is also a science, resting upon a solid frame of technical skills and knowledge of multiple disciplines, including accounting, tax, and information systems. In incorporating substantial new material on risk assessment and corporate governance, my primary purpose is to integrate the most important concepts of financial statement auditing and the general assurance engagement framework. Electronic commerce, non-profit businesses, and many topics that engage professional judgment are highlighted by Problems and new, specialized boxes: Auditing in Action, Audit Challenge, and New Standards.

Organization

This text is divided into five parts.

Part 1, The Auditing Profession (Chapters 1–4)

We begin with explaining the importance of assurance services, including auditing, and differentiating accounting from auditing. Then we talk about the different types of accountants and what they do. In Chapter 2, we move to the role of public accounting firms and other organizations, such as the Office of the Auditor General of Canada, in doing audits. We show how the Sarbanes–Oxley Act, Canadian and international quality control standards, and the Canadian Public Accountability Board have resulted in methods that produce high-quality audits. Chapter 3, Professional Relationships, reflects the fact that professional rules of conduct govern the behaviour of the public accountant in the context of relationships with corporations, other business entities, and the users of reports. Independent standards using a threat-based model are applied to public and non-public engagements. Threats to independence and the way these are mitigated with good quality-control practices are thoroughly examined. Part 1 concludes with Chapter 4, which presents an investigation of the auditor's legal liability and the profession's response.

Part 2, The Audit Process (Chapters 5–13)

This section has been adapted to international terminology, whereby the audit process phases are grouped into three sections: Risk Analysis, Risk Response, and Reporting. Chapter 5 allocates eight phases to those three sections, integrating international standards with Canadian practice and standards. It explains the auditor's and management's responsibilities and the key role of the audit committee in corporate governance. Transaction cycles are explained with the help of the annual report and financial statements of Hillsburg Hardware Limited, a fictitious public company located in eastern Canada. Chapter 6 discusses evidence decisions and the general concepts of evidence accumulation. The risk-based audit approach with its large investment in up-front planning and the concepts of materiality and the audit risk model are covered in Chapter 7. Chapter 8 focuses on the development of a client risk profile in the context of the business environment. Chapter 9, Internal Controls and Control Risk, uses the components of internal control that are consistent with international standards.

Corporate Governance and Entity-Level Controls, the new Chapter 10, provides a basic discussion of enterprise-wide risk-management processes, crucial to auditors who must conduct their audit using a risk-based approach. After explaining the role of the auditor in assessing corporate governance, more advanced topics, such as information technology governance and the effect of advanced information systems on the audit, are included. Chapter 11, Fraud Auditing, and examines the nature of fraud and the auditor's responsibilities with respect to fraud. Chapter 12 provides an overall risk-based audit plan, linking planning to assertion-based audit programs, and Chapter 13 discusses sampling concepts relevant to the audit process.

Part 3, Application of the Audit Process to the Sales and Collection Cycle (Chapters 14 and 15)

These chapters apply the concepts from Part 2 to the audit of sales, cash receipts, and the related income statement and balance sheet accounts, using further details from Hillsburg Hardware Limited as examples. In Chapter 14, the audit procedures for sales and cash receipts are related to internal control and audit objectives for tests of controls. Chapter 15 continues to use audit objectives and the results of internal controls tests to formulate tests of details of balances. Students will learn to apply audit sampling to the audit of sales, cash receipts, and accounts receivable by incorporating sampling into the appropriate test, showing the design, conduct, and evaluation of the sample.

Part 4, Application of the Audit Process to Other Cycles (Chapters 16–20)

Each of the chapters in Part 4 deals with a specific transaction cycle or part of a transaction cycle in much the same manner as Chapters 14 and 15 deal with the sales and collection cycle. Each chapter is meant to demonstrate the relationship of internal control and tests of controls for each broad category of transactions to the related balance sheet and income statement accounts. Cash in bank is the first chapter studied, since the audit of cash balances is related to most other audit areas.

Part 5, Completing the Audit and Offering Other Services (Chapters 21–24)

Completion of the audit depends on evaluating whether sufficient audit evidence has been gathered, in the context of the client risk profile and the audit risk model, to enable provision of an opinion on the financial statements. This final phase is explained in Chapter 21. Chapter 22 describes audit reports and variations to such reports. The chapter has significant changes due to the adoption of international standards resulting in a longer and more specific audit report. The impact of electronic filing is considered, as are events discovered after the report date. Chapter 23 focuses on review and compilation engagements, a common service for small- and medium-sized businesses, both profit-oriented and non-profit-oriented. It also describes other types of assurance engagements, such as a report of assurance with respect to internal control over financial reporting, required by public companies under Section 404 of the Sarbanes–Oxley Act of 2002 in the United States. The final chapter, Chapter 24, covers services performed most often by governmental and internal auditors, including risk assessment and systems control design, training and education on risk management and internal controls, specialized audits such as operational audits, and financial statement audits.

Chapter Outline

Each chapter contains the following:

- Learning objectives, listing the concepts that you should be able to address after reading the chapter.
- An opening vignette discussing a real-world topic to highlight a theme and the importance of the chapter. Each vignette describes the importance of the topic to auditors and provides questions to think about the topic further.

- A list of *CICA Handbook* sections referenced in the chapter, targeting additional readings.
- Figures and tables to illustrate, summarize, or clarify topics covered.
- **NEW!** Auditing in Action, Audit Challenge, and New Standards boxes identifying relevant challenges to auditors, successes and research, key current topics, further cases and questions, or recent events in the area.
- **NEW!** An icon (CAS) highlights discussions of new standards in the text.
- Essential terms defined in the margin and presented in boldface in the running text, for easy reference.
- **NEW!** Concept Check questions placed at the end of each major chapter section, testing and reinforcing the section material.
- A summary expanding upon the learning objectives.
- Review questions for students to assess comprehension of chapter material.
- Discussion questions and one or two professional judgment problems offering real-world topics to which chapter content can be applied.
- **NEW!** Discussion questions about a small company, CondoCleaners.com, to focus attention on the needs of small business.
- **NEW!** ACL Problems that show students how audit software is used to perform specific types of audit tests. A trial version of the software can be downloaded from the text's Companion Website.

Student Resources

COMPANION WEBSITE *Auditing: The Art and Science of Assurance Engagements*, Canadian Eleventh Edition, is supported by a Premium Companion Website at **www.pearsoned.ca/arens** that truly reinforces and enhances the text material.

Here you will find additional information about ISAs, self-test quizzes, and additional chapter review material, including:

- **NEW!** ACL audit software available for download.
- **NEW!** An integrated case, Pinnacle Manufacturing, containing questions and detailed financial statements for Chapters 6, 8, 10, 12, and 13.
- **NEW!** Internet problems that encourage using the Internet to research additional material for discussion and presentation in class.
- **NEW!** Answers to the Concept Check questions.

To enhance your use of these materials for self-study, we have also provided you with a function known as Grade Tracker. With Grade Tracker, the results from the self-test quizzes you take are preserved in a grade book. Each time you return to the Companion Website, you can refer back to these results, track your progress, and measure your improvement. You can log on to the Companion Website using the Student Access Code that comes packaged with every copy of *Auditing: The Art and Science of Assurance Engagements*, Canadian Eleventh Edition.

COURSESMART CourseSmart goes beyond traditional expectations, providing instant, online access to the textbooks and course materials you need at an average savings of 50 percent. With instant access from any computer and the ability to search your text, you will find the content you need quickly, no matter where you are. And with online tools such as highlighting and note-taking, you can save time and study efficiently. See all the benefits at **www.coursesmart.com/students**.

Instructional Support Materials

INSTRUCTOR'S RESOURCE CD-ROM The Instructor's Resource CD-ROM contains a rich collection of materials to facilitate the teaching of the course. Some of the materials presented on the CD-ROM can also be downloaded from a secure password-protected instructor's area of the Pearson Canada online catalogue. The CD-ROM includes the following items:

Instructor's Resource Manual and Transparency Masters The Instructor's Resource Manual assists the instructor in teaching the course more efficiently. The features include instructions for assignments, practical examples to help the students understand the material, and helpful suggestions on how to effectively teach each chapter. This manual includes numerous enlarged transparency masters, including key tables and figures from the book.

Instructor's Solutions Manual This comprehensive resource provides detailed solutions to all the end-of-chapter review questions, multiple choice questions, problems, and cases.

Pearson MyTest and TestGen A comprehensive testbank of questions has been prepared to accompany the new edition. The questions are rated by difficulty level, and the answers are referenced by section. The test bank is presented in a special computerized format known as Pearson TestGen. It enables instructors to view and edit the existing question, add questions, generate tests, and print the tests in a variety of formats. Powerful search and sort functions make it easy to locate questions and arrange them in any order desired. TestGen also enables instructors to administer tests on a local area network, grade the tests electronically, and prepare the results in electronic or printed reports. Issued on the Instructor's Resource CD-ROM, the Pearson Test-Gen is compatible with PC and Macintosh systems.

PowerPoint Slides Electronic colour slides are available in Microsoft PowerPoint. The slides illuminate and build on key concepts in the text.

Image Library The Image Library is an impressive resource that helps instructors create vibrant lecture presentations. Almost all figures and tables in the text are included and organized by chapter for convenience. These images can easily be imported into Microsoft PowerPoint to create new presentations or to add to existing ones.

COURSESMART CourseSmart goes beyond traditional expectations–providing instant, online access to the textbooks and course materials you need at a lower cost for students. And even as students save money, you can save time and avoid any hassle by using a digital eText that allows you to search for the most relevant content at the very moment you need it. Whether it is evaluating textbooks or creating lecture notes to help students with difficult concepts, CourseSmart can make life a little easier. See how when you visit **www.coursesmart.com/instructors.**

COMPANION WEBSITE The Companion Website prepared for this textbook includes an exciting new function: Class Manager. This feature gives you the ability to quickly and easily monitor student progress on quizzes and other website activities in an online gradebook. A variety of browse and search functions are available and allow you to quickly find any particular activity or student.

Ask your Pearson Canada sales representative about how to obtain an Instructor Access Code for the Companion Website. Once you have logged into the website, you can begin using Class Manager by clicking on the Class Manager tab on the home page and creating a new class. Follow the on-screen instructions to generate a Course ID to distribute to your students. When students register for the website using their access code, they will be given the option to join a class; at this point, they can input the specific Course ID that you have given them.

Students can also use the Companion Website's Grade Tracker function to record and review their own progress on the self-graded quizzes. This function is available even if you decide not to use Class Manager.

TECHNOLOGY SPECIALISTS Pearson's technology specialists work with faculty and campus course designers to ensure that Pearson technology products, assessment tools, and online course materials are tailored to meet your specific needs. This highly qualified team is dedicated to helping schools take full advantage of a wide range of educational resources by assisting in the integration of a variety of instructional materials and media formats. Your local Pearson Canada sales representative can provide you with more details on this service program.

Acknowledgments for the Canadian Eleventh Edition

Our world is changing. This text reflects some of those changes in the rapid pace of standards shifts in the external auditing profession. The feedback and assistance from individuals both inside and outside the profession, with different perspectives, have spurred on my creativity and reinforced the knowledge that we are all different and bring a broad spectrum of skills to the work we do.

I would like to thank the following individuals who contributed their time and energy in sharing their opinions and best practices, helping make this book representative not only of sound theory but of the actual work done in the field of audit and assurance:

Salvatore V. Bianco, PricewaterhouseCoopers LLP
Daniel D'Archivio, PricewaterhouseCoopers LLP
Aldo DiMarcantonio, York University
Rukshana Dinshaw, Soberman LLP
Stuart Hartley, FocusROI Inc.
Sandra Iacobelli, York University
Mark Lam, BDO Dunwoody LLP
Linda M. Lister, Ernst & Young LLP
Tony Stanko, Hydro One
Astra Williamson, Salvation Army
Larry Yarmolinsky, Internal Audit Division, Government of Ontario
Cecilia Yung, Sears Canada

Thanks are also due to the following reviewers for their valuable feedback:

Betty Wong, Athabasca University
Merridee Bujaki, University of Ottawa
Greg Caers, Ryerson University
Kenneth J. Caplan, Ryerson University
Ralph Cecere, McGill University
Bailey Church, University of Ottawa
Susan Ferris, CGA-Canada
John Kurian, CGA-Canada
Julie McDonald, University of Toronto Scarborough
Michael A. Perretta, Sheridan College
Linda A. Robinson, University of Waterloo
Sandra M. Robinson, Concordia University
Joan Wallwork, Kwantlen University College

In addition, I thank all the editorial and production staff at Pearson Canada for putting together a high-quality product, including Gary Bennett, Vice-President, Editorial Director; Carolin Sweig, Sponsoring Editor; Nicole Lukach, Editor-in-Chief; John Lewis, Developmental Editor; Imee Salumbides, Production Editor; and Lynn O'Rourke, Production Coordinator.

This book is dedicated to my family—Jake, Pat, and Mike—who did the extra chores around the house and cooked dinner while I worked late. Thank you; without your love and support this book would not have been possible.

Ingrid B. Splettstoesser-Hogeterp

A Great Way to Learn and Instruct Online

The Pearson Canada Companion Website is easy to navigate and is organized to correspond to the chapters in this textbook. Whether you are a student in the classroom or a distance learner, you will discover helpful resources for in-depth study and research that empower you in your quest for greater knowledge and maximize your potential for success in the course. An access code, packaged with this textbook, is required to log on to the Companion Website.

Companion Website

[www.pearsoned.ca/arens]

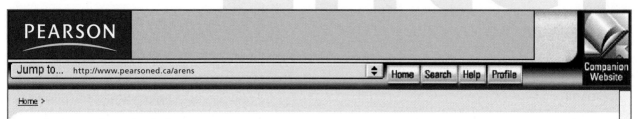

PEARSON

Jump to...   http://www.pearsoned.ca/arens   ◆   Home | Search | Help | Profile   Companion Website

Home >

Companion Website

Auditing: The Art and Science of Assurance Engagements, Canadian Eleventh Edition, by Arens, Elder, Beasley, and Splettstoesser-Hogeterp

Student Resources

The modules in this section provide students with tools for learning course material. These modules may include:

- Chapter Objectives
- Chapter Summaries
- Web Destinations
- Self-Test Quizzes
- Internet Exercises
- Application Exercises
- Answers to Concept Check questions
- Glossary Flashcards
- PowerPoint® Presentation Slides

In the quiz modules students can send answers to the grader and receive instant feedback on their progress through the Results Reporter. Coaching comments and references to the textbook may be available to ensure that students take advantage of all available resources to enhance their learning experience.

Instructor Resources

This module links directly to additional teaching tools. Downloadable PowerPoint® Presentations and an Instructor's Manual are just some of the materials that may be available in this section. Instructors can also use the Class Manager function to assign marks for participation or for quiz scores.

A trial version of ACL audit software is also available for download from the Companion Website.

1

The auditing profession

Who are auditors and why are they important? These first four chapters provide background for performing financial statement audits, which is our primary focus. This background will help you understand why auditors perform audits the way they do.

Our book begins with a description of assurance services, including auditing, and the role of accountants, public accounting firms, and other organizations in doing audits. The chapters in Part 1 emphasize the regulation and control of public accounting through auditing and ethical standards and discuss the legal responsibilities of auditors. We also present a detailed discussion of audit reports, which are the final products of audits.

1

The demand for an auditing and assurance profession

Don't all accountants do the same thing? No, not really. There are well-trained accountants who do only accounting, accountants who do auditing (public accountants or internal auditors), and accountants who have many other specializations, such as financial planning or forensics. This chapter will talk about many different types of accountants. You can use this information to help you consider the focus that your accounting career will take.

STANDARDS REFERENCED IN THIS CHAPTER

CICA Standard

CAS 210 – Agreeing the terms of audit engagements (previously Section 5110 – Terms of the engagement)

LEARNING OBJECTIVES

1 Identify the components of an audit and explain why there is a demand for audits. Differentiate accounting from auditing.

2 Describe assurance services. Distinguish audit engagements from other assurance and non-assurance services.

3 Describe the different types of accountants and what they do.

Prevention versus Detection

Fines, fines, everywhere fines—it seems that the amounts are going up and up. Sample fines for lack of compliance include Microsoft Corp. (2008, US$1.15 billion, for non-compliance with a 2004 antitrust order), DaimlerChrysler (2007, US$30 million for lack of compliance with U.S. fuel-efficiency standards) and York International Corp. (also 2007, with respect to the U.S. Foreign Corrupt Practices Act of 1977). These fines illustrate situations where organizations were caught engaging in non-compliance with regulations or laws. It seems that management of these organizations engaged in willful practices that violated the stated standards or laws.

Compliance pertains to acting in accordance with laws and regulations. It is particularly important directly where lives can be at stake, such as with food products. In the summer of 2008 alone, large food recalls occurred in Canada, including a recall of sandwich meats due to high counts of listeria and several brands of cheeses in Quebec due to increases in salmonella infections.

IMPORTANCE TO AUDITORS

Auditors of every kind are expected to conduct their work in accordance with assessed risks. External auditors provide an opinion on financial statements, which includes assessing the likelihood of financial failure, while internal auditors are expected to help assess compliance with regulations, such as those described above. Yet internal auditors within an organization have only as much authority as is given to them by the corporate governance of the organization. We will discover that auditors must assess that "tone at the top" as an important part of their audit.

WHAT DO YOU THINK? ❓

1. Is it possible to audit an organization where management is deliberately trying to deceive the auditors?
2. How are fines for non-compliance an indicator of lack of management integrity?
3. What could auditors do to bring potential non-compliance with laws or regulations to the attention of management?

Sources: 1. Burch, Susan, "Auditing for compliance," *Internal Auditor*, December 2008, p. 53–56, 59. 2. Lorigia, Paola, "Cheese products recalled in Quebec," *Toronto Star*, August 30, 2008, p. A3. 3. Lorigia, Paola, "Tainted meat list grows," *Toronto Star*, August 30, 2008, p. A3.

continued >

PROFESSIONAL accountants provide examinations of controls, audit financial statements, and help businesses be more successful. As businesses become more complex and need more reliable information, auditors play a vital role, both in providing assurance on information other than financial statements and in providing business advisory and tax services. For example, businesses and consumers who use information technology and electronic communication networks such as the internet to conduct business and make decisions need independent assurances about the reliability and security of electronic information. Auditors are valued because of their technical knowledge and independence in providing assurances, as well as their competence and experience in assisting companies to improve operations. Auditors often make and help implement recommendations that improve profitability by enhancing revenue or reducing costs, by including the reduction of errors and fraud, and by improving operational controls.

❶ Nature and Relevance of Auditing

To audit effectively, you need to learn the rules and procedures—the science—of auditing, after you have studied accounting, tax, and management information systems. In addition, you need to practise this knowledge in a variety of situations and gain experience in the real world. The defined practice of **auditing**, below, includes several key words and phrases.

> Auditing is the accumulation and evaluation of evidence about information to determine and report on the degree of correspondence between the information and established criteria. Auditing should be done by a competent, independent person.

We will now look at each of these key phrases in turn.

INFORMATION AND ESTABLISHED CRITERIA To do an audit, there must be information in a verifiable form and some standards (criteria) by which the auditor can evaluate the information. Information can and does take many forms. Auditors routinely perform audits of quantifiable information, including companies' financial statements and individuals' federal income tax returns. Auditors also perform audits of more subjective information, such as the effectiveness of computer systems and the efficiency of manufacturing operations.

The criteria against which information is evaluated vary depending on the information being audited. For example, in the audit of historical financial statements by public accounting firms, the criteria are generally accepted accounting principles. To illustrate, this means that in the audit of RONA Inc.'s (**www.rona.ca**) financial statements, Raymond Chabot Grant Thornton LLP, the public accounting firm (see **www.rcgt.com**), determines whether RONA Inc.'s financial statements have been prepared in accordance with generally accepted accounting principles. **Canada Revenue Agency auditors** use the provisions of the Income Tax Act to audit tax returns. In the audit of RONA's corporate

Auditing—the accumulation and evaluation of evidence about information to determine and report on the degree of correspondence between the information and established criteria.

Canada Revenue Agency auditor—an auditor who works for the Canada Revenue Agency and conducts examinations of taxpayers' returns.

tax return by the Canada Revenue Agency, the Income Tax Act, rather than generally accepted accounting principles, would provide the criteria for assessment.

For more subjective information, such as auditing the effectiveness of computer operations, it is more difficult to establish criteria. Typically, auditors and the entities being audited agree on the criteria well before the audit starts. For a computer application, the criteria might, for example, include the absence of input or output errors.

ACCUMULATING AND EVALUATING EVIDENCE **Evidence** is defined as any information used by the auditor to determine whether the information being audited is stated in accordance with the established criteria. Evidence takes many different forms, including oral representation of the auditee (client), written communication with outsiders, and observations by the auditor. Certain evidence (from a third party) is considered more reliable than other evidence (from the client). It is important to obtain a sufficient quality and volume of evidence to satisfy the audit objectives. The process of determining the amount of evidence necessary and evaluating whether the information corresponds to the established criteria is a critical part of every audit. It is the primary subject of this book.

> **Evidence**—any information used by the auditor to determine whether the information being audited is stated in accordance with established criteria.

COMPETENT, INDEPENDENT PERSON The auditor must be qualified to understand the criteria used and competent to know the types and amount of evidence to accumulate to reach the proper conclusion after the evidence has been examined. The auditor also must have an independent mental attitude. The competence of the individual performing the audit is of little value if he or she is biased in the accumulation and evaluation of evidence.

Auditors reporting on company financial statements are often called **independent auditors**. Even though an auditor of published financial statements is paid a fee by a company, he or she is normally sufficiently independent to conduct audits that can be relied on by users. Absolute independence is impossible, but auditors strive to maintain a high level of independence to keep the confidence of users relying on their reports. Although **internal auditors** work for the company, they usually report directly to the audit committee to help maintain independence from the operating units being audited.

> **Independent auditor**—a public accountant or accounting firm that performs audits of commercial and non-commercial entities.

> **Internal auditor**—an auditor employed by a company to audit for the company's board of directors and management.

REPORTING The final stage in the audit process is the **auditor's report**—the communication of the findings to users. Reports differ in nature, but in all cases they must inform readers of the degree of correspondence between information and established criteria. Reports also differ in form and can vary from the auditor's opinion usually associated with financial statements to a simple oral report in the case of an audit of a small department's effectiveness.

> **Auditor's report**—the communication of audit findings to users.

Figure 1-1 summarizes the important ideas in the description of auditing by illustrating an audit of an individual's tax return by a Canada Revenue Agency auditor.

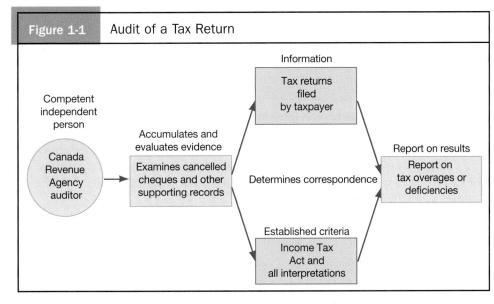

Figure 1-1	Audit of a Tax Return

Practitioners Performing British Columbia Ministry of Small Business and Revenue Tax Audits

In addition to income taxes, organizations and consumers pay a host of other taxes. These may include hotel taxes, food taxes, provincial sales tax, and goods and services tax. In British Columbia, the Ministry of Small Business and Revenue (MSBR) conducts audits of a selection of these taxes, as explained in the video referenced below. In 2006/7 the MSBR conducted over 185,000 audits! A single auditor, normally a qualified accountant with specialized tax training, will work with a small business, evaluating the processes used by the organization for collecting

and remitting taxes, as well as the actual amounts collected, looking for potential errors. The auditor follows a structured process.

Sources: Ministry of Small Business and Revenue, "Annual Service Plan Report, 2006/7," www.bcbudget.gov.bc.ca/Annual_Reports/2006_2007/sbr/sbr.pdf, Accessed: July 10, 2008. Ministry of Small Business and Revenue, "Consumer Tax Audits," www.sbr.gov.bc.ca/individuals/Customer_Service/Audit/audits.htm, Accessed: July 10, 2008.

The objective is to determine whether the tax return was prepared in a manner consistent with the requirements of the Income Tax Act. The auditor examines supporting records provided by the taxpayer and from other sources, such as the taxpayer's employer. After completing the audit, the Canada Revenue Agency (**www.cra-arc.gc.ca**) auditor will issue a report to the taxpayer assessing additional taxes, advising that a refund is due, or stating that there is no change in the status of his or her return.

Distinction between Auditing and Accounting

Many financial statement users and members of the general public confuse auditing and accounting. The confusion occurs because most auditing is concerned with accounting information, and many auditors have considerable expertise in accounting matters. The confusion is increased by giving the title "public accountant" to individuals of any accounting designation who performs the external audit function.

Accounting–the recording, classifying, and summarizing of economic events in a logical manner for the purpose of providing financial information for decision making.

Accounting is the recording, classifying, and summarizing of economic events in a logical manner for the purpose of providing financial information for decision making. The function of accounting is to provide certain types of quantitative information that management and others can use to make decisions. Accountants must have a thorough understanding of the principles and rules that provide the basis for preparing the accounting information. Accountants also help to develop the systems used to record an entity's economic events in a timely way and at a reasonable cost.

When auditing accounting data, the concern is with determining whether recorded information properly reflects the economic events that occurred during the accounting period. The auditor is not simply auditing data but must look at the organization's planning methods and risks, including its strategies and economic niches, as discussed further in Chapter 8. Since the accounting rules are the criteria for evaluating whether the accounting information is properly recorded, any auditor involved with these data must also thoroughly understand the rules, such as generally accepted accounting principles (GAAP) for the audit of financial statements. These principles are constantly evolving as business practices and standards change—Canada is currently moving to adopting international financial reporting standards as its GAAP. Throughout this text, the assumption is made that the reader has already studied generally accepted accounting principles.

Economic Demand for Auditing

Businesses, governments, and not-for-profit organizations use auditing services extensively. Publicly accountable organizations, such as businesses listed on securities exchanges or large not-for-profit organizations, are legally required to have an annual financial statement audit.

A brief study of the economic reasons for auditing highlights why auditing is so necessary. Consider a bank manager's decision to make a loan to a business. The decision will be based on such factors as previous financial relations with the business and the financial condition of the business as reflected by its financial statements. Assuming the bank makes the loan, it will charge a rate of interest determined primarily by three factors:

1. *Risk-free interest rate*. This is approximately the rate the bank could earn by investing in Canada Treasury Bills for the same length of time as the business loan.
2. *Business risk for the customer*. This risk reflects the possibility that the business will not be able to repay its loan because of economic or business conditions such as a recession, poor management decisions, or unexpected competition in the industry.
3. **Information risk.** This risk reflects the possibility that the information upon which the business decision was made was inaccurate. A likely cause of the information risk is the possibility of inaccurate financial statements.

> **Information risk**—the risk that information upon which a business decision is made is inaccurate.

Auditing has no effect on either the risk-free interest rate or business risk. It can have a significant effect on information risk. If the bank manager is satisfied that there is low information risk, the risk is lowered and the overall interest rate to the borrower can be reduced. For example, assume a large company has total interest-bearing debt of approximately $1 billion. If the interest rate on that debt is reduced by only 1 percent, the annual savings in interest is $10 million. Many lenders such as banks require annual audits for companies with large bank loans outstanding.

As society becomes more complex, there is an increased likelihood that unreliable information will be provided to decision makers. There are several reasons for this: remoteness of information, bias and motives of provider, voluminous data, and the existence of complex exchange transactions.

Managers of businesses and the users of their financial statements may conclude that the best way to deal with information risk is simply to have it remain reasonably high. A small company may find it less expensive to pay higher interest costs than to increase the costs of reducing information risk (e.g., by having an audit).

For larger businesses, it is usually practical to incur such costs to reduce information risk. There are three main ways to do so:

1. The user may go to the business premises to examine records and obtain information about the reliability of the statements.
2. Management is responsible for providing reliable information to users. Users may evaluate the likelihood of sharing their information risk loss with management.
3. An independent audit is performed. This is most common way for users to obtain reliable information.

In addition to understanding accounting, the auditor must also possess expertise in the accumulation and interpretation of audit evidence. It is this expertise that distinguishes auditors from accountants. Determining the proper audit procedures, the number and types of items to test, and evaluating the results are tasks that are unique to the auditor.

concept check

C1-1 List and explain the five key elements of the definition of auditing.

C1-2 Explain the difference between accounting and auditing.

C1-3 Describe the economic reasons for conducting an audit.

② Assurance and Non-Assurance Services

Figure 1-2 on the next page reflects the relationship between assurance and non-assurance services. Audits, reviews, reports on the effectiveness of internal control over financial reporting, and attestation services on information technology are all examples of attestation services, which are a subset of assurance services. Management consulting services, depending upon their purpose, could be assurance or non-assurance, while tax and bookkeeping services are non-assurance services.

New Standards: More Acceptable Financial Reporting Frameworks?

Canadian accountants are used to using GAAP as their criteria (reporting framework) for assessing financial statements. However, multiple criteria may be used in the future. In response to the globalization of business, the Canadian Institute of Chartered Accountants (CICA) has adopted international auditing and assurance standards for use in Canada. They are being called CASs, "Canadian Auditing Standards," and in the transition period, there will be both the existing *CICA Handbook* sections and the new CASs in the *CICA Handbook*.

As an example, CAS 210, Agreeing the terms of audit engagements, is based upon the international standard numbered 210 of the same name. (Auditing standards are discussed further in the next chapter.) This standard indicates that there are multiple financial reporting frameworks available, and one of the tasks of the auditor is to assess whether the framework used by management is acceptable. The exact nature of these multiple reporting frameworks that would be considered acceptable in Canada is still being finalized.

Assurance Services

Assurance engagement—a service where a written communication is provided expressing an opinion about the reliability of an assertion made by another party; also called "assurance service."

Assurance engagements, or **assurance services**, are independent professional services that improve the quality of information for decision makers. The assurance engagement is an assurance service in which the auditor issues a report about the reliability of an assertion prepared by another party. Individuals who are responsible for making business decisions seek assurance services to help improve the reliability and relevance of the information used to make their decisions. Assurance services are valued because the assurance engagement provider is independent and is perceived as unbiased with respect to the information examined.

Assurance services can be performed by auditors or by a variety of other professionals. For example, companies that perform television ratings are performing an assurance engagement. BBM Canada (**www.bbm.ca**), a non-profit television rating organization, and Nielsen Media Research Canada (**www.nielsenmedia.ca**) conduct television rating studies. These organizations provide assurance that a specified number of viewers are watching the identified television shows. Another example of a company that provides assurance services is the Canadian Council of Better Business

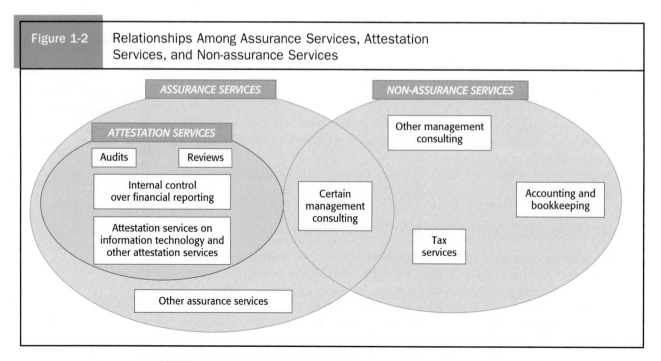

Figure 1-2 Relationships Among Assurance Services, Attestation Services, and Non-assurance Services

Bureaus (CCBBB, see **www.ccbbb.ca**). The CCBBB collects information about Canadian businesses. Some of the information is not verified (and so would be considered equivalent to a compilation engagement, discussed below), while other information, such as details about current business scams, are verified, providing assurance regarding the specifics of those illegal activities.

The need for assurance is ongoing. Auditors have provided assurance services for years, particularly about historical financial statement information. Accounting firms have also performed assurance services related to lotteries and contests to provide assurance that winners were determined in an unbiased fashion in accordance with contest rules. More recently, auditors have been expanding the types of assurance services they perform, such as assurance engagements about company financial forecasts, website controls, and the security of information. The demand for assurance services is expected to grow as the demand for forward-looking information increases and as more real-time information becomes available through the internet.

A large category of assurance services provided by accounting firms is attestation services. The **attestation service** or engagement is a particular form of assurance service in which the auditor issues a report about the reliability of any information provided by one party to another. Here, we use five categories to discuss attestation services:

Attestation service—a special form of assurance engagement, such as a financial statement audit, in which the auditor issues a report about the reliability of any information provided by one party to another.

1. Audit of historical financial statements.
2. Review of historical financial statements.
3. Attestation on internal control over financial reporting.
4. Attestation services on information technology.
5. Other attestation services that may be applied to a broad range of subject matter.

AUDIT OF HISTORICAL FINANCIAL STATEMENTS Audits of historical financial statements are a major service provided by many of the larger public accounting firms. In an audit of historical financial statements, management asserts that the statements are fairly stated in accordance with GAAP. The responsible other party is the client who is making various assertions in the form of published financial statements. The auditor's report expresses an opinion on whether those financial statements conform with Canadian generally accepted accounting principles or with another appropriate disclosed basis of accounting. External users of financial statements rely on the auditor's report for their decision-making purposes.

Publicly traded companies in Canada are required to have audits. Auditor reports can be found in any public company's annual financial report, and many companies' audited financial statements can be accessed via the internet from System for Electronic Document Analysis and Retrieval (SEDAR) at **www.sedar.com**. This website, developed by the Canadian Securities Administrators (CSA) and CDS Inc., a subsidiary of the Canadian Depository for Securities Limited, has been available since 1997. It contains public filings, such as annual reports, management discussion and analysis, and press releases from public companies. Most public companies also have a website where copies of financial statements are posted. However, **www.sedar.com** is particularly useful for examining information about public companies that do not have a website, such as Jannock Properties Limited, headquartered in Streetsville, Ontario.

The auditor's report on financial statements is carefully worded to provide information to users (as discussed further in Chapter 22). The report describes the financial statements being audited, the responsibility of the auditors and management, and briefly describes how an audit is conducted before providing the auditor's opinion.

Many public companies voluntarily contract for audits to provide assurance to investors and to facilitate access to capital. Many privately held companies also have annual financial statement audits to obtain financing from banks and other institutions. Government and not-for-profit entities often have audits to meet the requirements of lenders or funding sources.

External users, such as shareholders and lenders, who rely on those financial statements to make business decisions, look to the auditor's report as an indication of the statements' reliability. They value the auditor's assurance because of the auditor's independence from the client, expertise, and knowledge of financial statement

Figure 1-3   Relationships Among Auditor, Client, and External Users

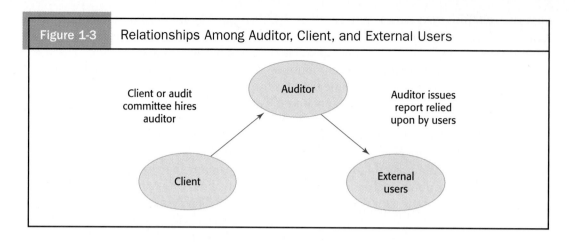

reporting matters. Figure 1-3 illustrates the relationships among the auditor, client, and financial statement users.

REVIEW OF HISTORICAL FINANCIAL STATEMENTS Many smaller, non-public companies want to issue financial statements to various users but do not wish to incur the cost of an auditor's report. A review, which provides a much lower degree of assurance than an audit, is usually conducted in such a situation. For a review, management also asserts that the financial statements are fairly stated in accordance with GAAP, the same as for audits. As moderate assurance is provided, the public accountant (PA) is required to do considerably less work than in an audit so the resulting cost is less. Reviews are discussed in more detail in Chapter 23.

ATTESTATION ON INTERNAL CONTROL OVER FINANCIAL REPORTING For an attestation on internal control over financial reporting, management asserts that internal controls have been developed and implemented following well-established criteria. Section 404 of the Sarbanes-Oxley Act in the United States requires publicly listed companies to report management's assessment of the effectiveness of internal control. The Act also requires auditors to attest to the effectiveness of internal control over financial reporting. This evaluation, which is integrated with the audit of the financial statements, increases user confidence about future financial reporting because effective internal controls reduce the likelihood of future misstatements in the financial statements. Canadian subsidiaries of U.S. companies and Canadian companies selling publicly listed shares in the United States would be subject to these requirements.

ATTESTATION SERVICES ON INFORMATION TECHNOLOGY One of the major factors affecting the demand for other assurance services is the growth of the internet and electronic commerce. Concern over privacy and security of information on the internet has slowed the potential growth of electronic commerce. In addition, the volume of real-time information available on the internet is shifting the need for assurance from historical information at a point in time, such as financial statements, to assurances about the privacy and reliability of processes generating information in a real-time format. For example, many business functions, such as ordering and making payments, are conducted over the internet and directly between computers using electronic data interchange (EDI). As transactions and information are shared online and in real time, there is an even greater demand for assurances about computer controls surrounding information transacted electronically and the security of the information related to the transactions. Auditors can help provide assurance about these functions.

To respond to the growing need for assurance related to business transacted over the internet, the American Institute of Certified Public Accountants (AICPA) and the Canadian Institute of Chartered Accountants (CICA) developed two products.

Table 1-1	Principles for *WebTrust* and *SysTrust* Services	
***Trust* Principles**	**Description of Assurance**	
Online privacy	Provides assurance that the system protects the privacy of personal information provided by individuals, such as social security numbers	
Security	Provides assurance that access to the system and data is restricted to authorized individuals	
Processing integrity	Provides assurance that transactions are processed completely and accurately	
Availability	Provides assurance that systems and data will be available to users when they need them	
Confidentiality	Provides assurance that information designated as confidential is protected	
Certification authorities (*WebTrust* only)	Provides assurance on the adequacy and effectiveness of controls used by certification authorities with responsibility for verifying electronic transactions	

1. The *WebTrust* service is an electronic seal affixed to a website to assure the user that established criteria related to business practices, transaction integrity, and information processes have been met. The seal is a symbolic representation of the Public Accountant's report on management assertions about its disclosure of electronic commerce practices.
2. *SysTrust* provides assurance on information system reliability in areas such as security and data integrity. The accountant evaluates a company's computer systems using *Trust* Services principles and criteria, as shown in Table 1-1, and determines whether controls over the system exist. The accountant then performs tests to evaluate the controls and prepares a report covering the specific period of the tests.

OTHER ATTESTATION SERVICES Accountants may also prepare special reports for clients where the auditor provides an opinion on financial information other than financial statements or on compliance with an agreement or regulations. For example, an auditor might provide an opinion on the sales at a Shoppers Drug Mart in a Saskatoon shopping mall because the store's rent is based on sales and the owner of the mall requires an audit opinion.

OTHER ASSURANCE SERVICES There are almost no limits to the types of services that auditors can provide. A survey of large Certified Public Accountant (CPA) firms, performed by the AICPA Special Committee on Assurance Services, identified more than 200 assurance services currently provided.

auditing in action 1-3
Research Evaluates Relevance of Web Assurance Seal Services (WASSs)

How do web assurance seal services (WASSs) such as those provided by WebTrust (**www.webtrust.org**), TRUSTe (**www.truste. org**), or BBBOnline (**www.BBBonline.org**) add value? Academic researchers such as Yujong Hwang and Dan Kim believe that value is related to the perception of web quality and what they term "e-trust" (consisting of integrity, benevolence, and reliability). If the quality of the website is high, then enjoyment occurs for the user, improving e-trust. If quality is low, then anxiety occurs, reducing e-trust. WASSs can help to improve the perception of the quality of a site, but the use of a WASS is only one of

several other variables (such as the ability to control private information and depth of content) that affect a user's intention to purchase from a site. Academic research can help organizations design their privacy practices and their websites to promote e-trust and increase customer intentions to purchase.

Sources: Hwang, Yujong and Dan J. Kim, "Customer self-service systems: The effects of perceived web quality with service contents on enjoyment, anxiety, and e-trust," *Decision Support Systems*, 43, (2007): p. 746–760. Kim, Dan J., Charles Steinfield, and Ying-Ju Lai, "Revisiting the role of web assurance seals in business-to-consumer electronic commerce," *Decision Support Systems*, 44, (2008): p. 1000–1015.

"It will never happen here—our data will not be disclosed!" Unfortunately, it can happen, and it has. In January 2007, a laptop was stolen from the vehicle of a research physician working with the Toronto Hospital for Sick Children. The laptop contained unencrypted names, medical information, and identification information from about 2,900 patients of the hospital. This led to a public outcry and an order from the Ontario Information and Privacy Commissioner for the hospital to develop and implement policies that protected electronic information, including forbidding removal of information that could be read.

Accountants could help organizations like hospitals to design and test privacy policies. A privacy assurance engagement includes examining how information is used, accessed, stored, and retrieved. For example, how are passwords managed, or is information encrypted when stored on removable devices or transmitted to remote locations?

CRITICAL THINKING QUESTIONS

1. What are some of the ways that information could leak out of the hospital? These are called risks of data exposure.
2. Identify the skills that would be required of a professional team called upon to do a privacy assurance engagement at the Hospital for Sick Children.
3. Link the skills needed to the professional designations that would be held by the team members. What types of auditors could complete a privacy assurance engagement?

Sources: 1. Ferenc, Leslie, "Secure patient data, Sick Kids told," *Toronto Star*, March 8, 2007, www.TheStar.com/News/article/189670, Accessed: October 3, 2007. 2. Parker, Robert G., "Private practices," *CAmagazine*, November 2004, p. 28–34. 3. Spence, Bob (Communications Coordinator), "Stolen laptop sparks order by Commissioner Cavoukian requiring encryption of identifiable data: Identity must be protected," News Release, March 8, 2007, www.ipc.on.ca, Accessed: October 3, 2007.

NON-ASSURANCE SERVICES Accounting firms perform numerous other services that generally fall outside the scope of assurance services. Some of these are related to financial statements, while others would be considered financial planning or management advisory services.

COMPILATIONS A compilation involves the accountant preparing financial statements from a client's records or from other information provided. A compilation is much less extensive than a review, and the cost is much less. No assurance is provided by a compilation.

TAX SERVICES Accounting firms prepare corporate and individual tax returns for both audit and non-audit clients. In addition, sales tax remittance, tax planning, and other aspects of tax services are provided by most firms.

MANAGEMENT ADVISORY SERVICES Management advising includes services such as retirement planning and personal financial planning. Most accounting firms also provide services that enable businesses to operate more effectively, including simple suggestions for improving accounting systems, help with marketing strategies, computer installations, and pension benefit consulting. The firm offering these types of services needs to be aware of independence rules that prohibit the provision of some of these services to audit clients, as discussed in Chapter 3.

ACCOUNTING AND BOOKKEEPING SERVICES Some small clients lack the personnel or expertise to prepare their own subsidiary records. Many small accounting firms work with accounting software packages to help clients record their transactions. Often such clients proceed with a compilation engagement.

When a PA conducts a review or an audit after bookkeeping work, he or she must take care to ensure that independence rules are properly followed. In particular, the PA must ensure that all transactions and journal entries are approved by management during the bookkeeping engagement.

Types of Audits

Auditors perform three primary types of audits, as illustrated by examples in Table 1-2.

1. Financial statement audits.
2. Compliance audits.
3. Operational audits.

Table 1-2	Examples of the Three Types of Audits			
Type of Audit	Example	Available Evidence	Information	Established Criteria
Financial Statement Audit	Perform annual audit of Trans-Canada Corporation's financial statements	Documents, records, and outside sources of evidence	TransCanada Corporation's financial statements	Canadian generally accepted accounting principles
Compliance Audit	Determine if bank requirements for loan continuation have been met	Financial statements and calculations by the auditor	Company records	Loan agreement provisions
Operational Audit	Evaluate whether the computerized payroll processing for subsidiary H is operating economically, efficiently, and effectively	Error reports, payroll records, and payroll processing costs	Number of payroll records processed in a month, costs of the department, and number of errors made	Company standards for economy, efficiency, and effectiveness in payroll department

FINANCIAL STATEMENT AUDITS A **financial statement audit** is conducted by public accountants to determine whether the overall financial statements (the information being verified) are stated in accordance with specified criteria. Normally, the criteria are generally accepted accounting principles, although it is also possible to conduct audits of financial statements prepared using the cash basis or some other basis of accounting appropriate for the organization. The financial statements most often included are the balance sheet, income statement, statement of retained earnings, and statement of cash flows, including the notes to the financial statements.

Effectively completing the financial statement audit requires a strategic systems audit approach. The auditor must have a thorough understanding of the entity and its environment. This holistic, top-level understanding includes knowledge of the client's industry and its regulatory and operating environments, including external relationships such as those with suppliers, customers, and creditors. In addition, the auditor considers the client's business strategies, processes, and measurement indicators for critical success factors related to those strategies. This analysis helps the auditor identify risks associated with the client's strategies that may affect whether the financial statements are fairly stated.

COMPLIANCE AUDITS The purpose of a **compliance audit** is to determine whether the auditee is following specific procedures or rules set down by a higher authority. A compliance audit for a private business could include determining whether accounting personnel are following the procedures prescribed by the company controller, reviewing wage rates for compliance with minimum wage laws, or examining contractual agreements with bankers and other lenders to be sure the company is complying with legal requirements. In the audit of governmental units such as school boards, there is increased compliance auditing due to extensive regulation by higher government authorities. In virtually every private and not-for-profit organization, there are prescribed policies, contractual agreements, and legal requirements that may call for compliance auditing.

Results of compliance audits conducted by internal auditors are generally reported to someone within the organizational unit being audited rather than to a broad spectrum of users. Management, as opposed to outside users, is the primary group concerned with the extent of compliance with certain prescribed procedures and regulations. When an organization wants to determine whether individuals or organizations that are obliged to follow its requirements are actually complying, the auditor is employed by the organization issuing the requirements. An example is the

Financial statement audit—an audit conducted to determine whether the overall financial statements of an entity are stated in accordance with specified criteria (usually GAAP).

Compliance audit—(1) a review of an organization's financial records performed to determine whether the organization is following specific procedures, rules, or regulations set down by some higher authority; (2) an audit performed to determine whether an entity that receives financial assistance from a federal or provincial government has complied with specific laws and regulations.

auditing of taxpayers for compliance with the Income Tax Act—the auditor is employed by the government to audit the taxpayers' tax returns.

OPERATIONAL AUDITS An **operational audit** is a review of any part of an organization's operating procedures and methods for the purpose of evaluating economy, efficiency, and effectiveness. The auditor provides recommendations to management for improving operations. An example of an operational audit is evaluating the efficiency and accuracy of processing payroll transactions with a newly installed computer system. Another example, for which most accountants would feel less qualified, is evaluating the efficiency and accuracy of, and customer satisfaction with, the distribution of letters and packages by a company such as Canada Post (**www.canadapost.ca**). An example of an economy issue is whether goods and services are obtained at the best prices.

Because of the many different areas in which operational effectiveness can be evaluated, it is impossible to characterize the conduct of a typical operational audit. In one organization, the auditor might evaluate the relevance and sufficiency of the information used by management when acquiring new capital assets, while in a different organization the auditor might evaluate the efficiency of the paper flow in processing sales. Operational audits can include the evaluation of organizational structure, computer operations, production methods, marketing, and any other area in which the audit team is qualified, such as the quality of health care services provided. We look at operational auditing in greater depth in Chapter 24.

concept check

C1-4 Explain the difference between assurance and non-assurance engagements, providing an example of each.

C1-5 List and describe three types of audits, giving an example for each. Why is each type of audit important?

③ Professional Accountants and Their Work

Professional Accounting/Auditing Organizations

Auditors are trained professionals, frequently coming from the accounting profession. Various organizations perform auditing functions—external and internal—in Canada. Selected organizations, the designations awarded by the organizations, and the manner of qualifying for the designations are described below. These organizations require that individuals have a university degree and obtain relevant work experience. Each organization conducts research and develops, monitors, and comments upon standards relevant to its members. Because of the dynamic nature of business environments, each organization offers continuing education programs, providing the opportunity for members to specialize in particular areas such as taxation, information systems, management consulting, or business valuations. Professional organizations in many of these specialized areas offer specific programs of study leading to further specialist designations.

The **Canadian Institute of Chartered Accountants** (CICA, see **www.cica.ca**), in consultation with an advisory board and others, sets the private- and public-sector accounting and auditing standards which must be followed by public accountants in Canada. It is one of the three major accounting organizations in Canada providing a professional designation relating to accounting and auditing, and it is the umbrella organization of the provincial institutes and *ordre* that regulate the CA profession in Canada. Members of the CICA are **chartered accountants** (CAs). The educational requirements for becoming a CA vary among provinces, with a common experience requirement of 30 months. All provinces require that an individual, to qualify as a CA, pass a national uniform examination administered by the CICA.

The **Certified General Accountants Association of Canada** (CGAAC, see **www.cga-online.org**) also provides a professional designation relating to accounting and auditing. CGAAC is the umbrella organization of the provincial associations that regulate the CGA profession in Canada. The use of the title "**certified general accountant**" (CGA) is awarded by CGAAC. Experience requirements are set at a minimum of two years in a combination of intermediate and senior positions in accounting or finance. Individuals, depending upon educational background, must pass a variety of subject-based examinations, with a capstone national examination.

Finally, there is the **Society of Management Accountants of Canada** (SMAC, see **www.cma-canada.org**), which provides a professional designation relating to accounting and auditing and regulates the CMA profession in Canada. The SMAC administers the **Certified Management Accountant** (CMA) program, leading to the CMA designation. Students must pass examinations in required subject areas, pass a uniform national examination, and meet experience requirements.

For an accountant to work as a public accountant, that is, do the work to assess financial statements and provide an opinion upon them, the person must complete the requirements of both an accounting designation (CGA, CMA, or CA) and the licensing for public accounting. Requirements for a public accounting licence vary by province.

Internal auditors and operational or compliance auditors may be accountants or come from any area of specialization, such as information systems, actuarial science, or psychology, before moving into the audit field. Internal auditors have a professional organization, the Institute of Internal Auditors (IIA, see **www.theiia.org**), and a professional designation, "certified internal auditor" (CIA). The designation is earned by passing a set of examinations that are administered internationally by the IIA and by meeting experience requirements.

The Information Systems Audit and Control Association (ISACA, see **www.isaca.org**) awards the Certified Information Systems Auditor (CISA) designation to individuals passing an international examination and meeting experience requirements.

Both the IIA and ISACA have several classes of members, including associates and educational members, who can join the association to have access to publications and educational material but who would not be permitted to use the CIA or CISA designation until they had completed the necessary examination and experience requirements.

Types of Auditors

What type of auditing would you like to specialize in? Financial statement audits are conducted by public accountants skilled in accounting and auditing. Compliance audits also require skill in legislation, regulations, or policies that are being audited, as well as knowledge of controls-related processes. Operational audits may require a multidisciplined specialist team that understands clearly the organizational and operational facets under audit. Operational and compliance audits are often conducted by governmental and internal auditors. Depending upon their work experience and training, professional accountants have the skills to conduct all of these audits.

Of course, other specialized careers such as management accounting, finance or financial planning, business valuation, taxation, information systems, and forensic accounting are available to professional accountants and auditors by building upon their initial professional qualifications (see Figure 1-4 on the next page).

Next, we briefly discuss four types of auditors. They are public accountants, government auditors, Canada Revenue Agency auditors, and internal auditors. Throughout the text, we will frequently talk about the roles of specialist auditors, such as that of the tax expert when reviewing a financial statement audit, the information systems specialist when assessing information systems functions, and the forensic auditor when assessing fraud risks and conducting fraud audits.

PUBLIC ACCOUNTANTS Public accounting firms have, as a primary responsibility, the performance of the audit function on published financial statements of all publicly traded companies and most other large companies. Such an audit is known as an attestation engagement because the auditor attests to the fair presentation of the financial statements. If the audit is due to a size requirement, or required by law, the audit is a statutory audit. Because of the widespread use of audited financial statements in the Canadian economy, as well as businesses' and other users' familiarity with these statements, it is common to use the terms "auditor" and "public accounting" *firm* synonymously even though there are several types of auditors. Another term frequently used to describe a public accounting firm is "independent auditors."

Society of Management Accountants of Canada (SMAC)—one of the three major accounting organizations in Canada providing a professional designation relating to accounting and auditing; umbrella organization of the provincial societies that regulates the CMA profession in Canada.

Certified Management Accountant (CMA)—one of three professional designations in Canada relating to accounting and auditing.

Figure 1-4   Use of Professional Accountant Skills

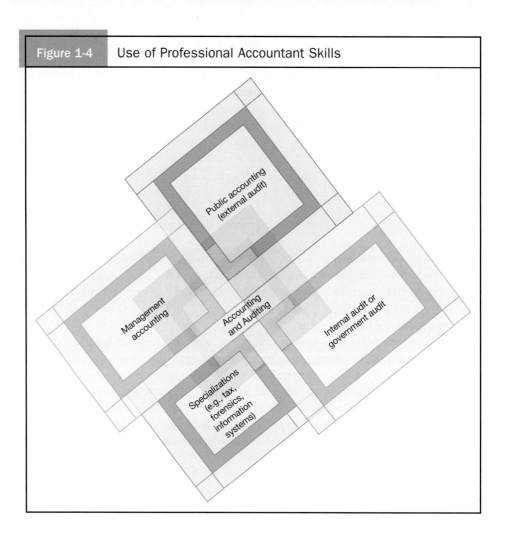

Canadian provinces restrict the audit attest function to one or more of chartered accountants, certified general accountants, or certified management accountants licensed in that province. Most provinces require a licence to perform an attest audit. The two bodies whose members perform most of the attest audits in Canada are the CICA and the CGAAC. The terms "public accountant," "external auditor," and "auditor" are used frequently throughout this book to describe an individual who is licensed to perform the audit attest function.

Most young professionals who want to become public accountants start their careers working for a public accounting firm. After they become public accountants, many leave the firm to work in industry, government, or education. These people may continue to be members of a professional body but may lose their right to practise as independent auditors. CAs and CGAs must meet licensing requirements to maintain their right to practise in most provinces. It is common, therefore, to find people who are CAs or CGAs but who no longer practise as independent auditors.

Auditor General—responsible for auditing federal and provincial ministries, departments, and agencies, including Crown corporations.

GOVERNMENT AUDITORS The Government of Canada and the various provincial governments have **Auditor Generals** who are responsible for auditing the ministries, departments, and agencies which report to that government. These government auditors may be appointed by a bipartisan legislative committee or by the government in that jurisdiction. They report to their respective legislatures and are responsible to the body appointing them. The primary responsibility of the government audit staff is to perform the audit function for government. The extent and scope of the audits performed are determined by legislation in the various jurisdictions. For example, in 1977, the federal parliament revised existing legislation by passing the Auditor General Act to require the Auditor General to report to the

House of Commons on the efficiency and economy of expenditures or whether value for money had been received.

In 1984, the House of Commons passed Bill C-24, which amended the Financial Administration Act with respect to Crown corporations.[1] The implications are significant for auditors in public practice and in the government. Included among its stipulations are the following:

1. Internal audits that look at financial matters or compliance with regulations and audits that look at whether or not the operations are conducted in an efficient, effective, and economic manner, are required.
2. External audits of the financial statements are required.
3. Special examinations of efficiency, effectiveness, and economy must be carried out every five years.

The audit responsibilities of these government auditors are much like those of a public accounting firm. Most of the financial information prepared by various government agencies and, in some cases, by Crown corporations is audited by these government auditors before the information is submitted to the various legislatures. Since the authority for expenditures and receipts of government agencies is defined by law, there is considerable emphasis on compliance in these audits.

An example of audit work in the public sector is the evaluation of the computer controls of a particular purpose within a governmental unit. For a financial application, this could include access controls (quality of management supervision, segregation of duties) and controls executed both by human beings and by computer systems.

In many provinces, experience as a government auditor fulfills the experience requirement for a professional designation. In those provinces, if an individual passes the professional examination and fulfills the experience stipulations of the particular professional organization, he or she may then obtain the professional certification.

CANADA REVENUE AGENCY AUDITORS The Canada Revenue Agency has as its responsibility the enforcement of the federal tax laws as they have been defined by Parliament and interpreted by the courts. A major responsibility of this agency is to audit the returns of taxpayers to determine whether they have complied with the tax laws. The auditors who perform these examinations are referred to as Canada Revenue Agency auditors. These audits are solely compliance audits.

It might seem that the audit of returns for compliance with the federal tax laws would be a simple and straightforward problem. However, tax laws are highly complicated, and there are hundreds of volumes of court interpretations. Taxation problems could involve individual taxpayers, sales tax, goods and services tax, corporate taxes, or trusts. An auditor involved in any of these areas must have expertise in the applicable taxes to conduct the audit. The tax returns being audited vary from the simple returns of individuals who work for only one employer and take the standard tax deductions to the highly complex returns of multinational corporations.

INTERNAL AUDITORS Internal auditors, many of whom are members of the IIA, are employed by individual companies to audit for management, much as the Auditor General does for Parliament. The internal audit group typically reports directly to the audit committee of the board of directors or a senior executive.

Internal auditors' responsibilities vary considerably, depending upon the employer. Internal audit staff size can range from one or two to hundreds of employees, each of whom has diverse responsibilities, including many outside the accounting area. In recent years, many internal auditors have become involved in operational auditing or have developed expertise in evaluating computer systems. They also provide

---

[1] The interested reader is referred to A Director's Introduction to the Audit and Special Examination Provisions of the Financial Administration Act (as amended by Bill C-24), published by the Canadian Comprehensive Auditing Foundation, from which this material is taken.

assistance in evaluating new systems prior to implementation and in assessing risks within the organization.

Modern internal auditing takes a proactive business advisory approach in contrast to traditional operational- and compliance-based audits. The need to emphasize consulting is evident from the definition of internal audit provided by the Institute of Internal Auditors (**www.theiia.org**): "an independent, objective assurance and consulting activity designed to add value and improve an organization's operations. It helps an organization accomplish its objectives by bringing a systematic, disciplined approach to evaluate and improve the effectiveness of risk management, control, and governance processes."

To operate effectively, an internal auditor must be independent of the line functions in an organization but will not be independent of the entity as long as an employer-employee relationship exists. Internal auditors provide management with valuable information for making decisions concerning the efficient and effective operation of its business. Users from outside the entity, however, are unlikely to want to rely on information verified by internal auditors because of their lack of independence (explained further in Chapter 3). This lack of independence is the major difference between internal auditors and public accounting firms.

Preventing Information Systems Failure

In addition to considering compliance with regulations and legislation, auditors can help organizations consider effective practices for the implementation or change of their information systems. This starts at the top, for example, by assessing internal risk management practices for the business and by reviewing systems development practices or the effectiveness of information security policies. Some questions to be asked are: How do these policies guide the implementation of information systems? If there is a failure in compliance with legislation, would that lead an auditor to believe that there were also failures in other internal processes, such as information systems implementation or security?

concept check

C1-6 List and describe three professional accounting organizations in Canada.

C1-7 Which professionals could conduct the audit of a company that manufactures automobiles? Provide examples of the types of assurance or non-assurance engagements they could conduct for this company.

Summary

1. *What is an audit?* An audit is an engagement where evidence collection and evaluation are used to assess client information, such as a financial statement, using specific criteria, such as GAAP (generally accepted accounting principles). The results are reported by independent professionals.

   Why is there continued demand for audits? Audits provide added value to information since they provide independent assurance where the user of the report is remote from the provider, where the provider may be biased, or where data audited are voluminous or complex.

   What is the difference between accounting and auditing? Accounting involves the actual preparation of underlying records, whereas auditing helps determine whether that recorded information reflects actual economic events.

2. *What are the different types of engagements completed by auditors?* An audit is an attest engagement, a subset of

assurance engagements. For an attest engagement, the client prepares the materials (such as the financial statements), and the auditor provides a written report on them, whereas for an assurance engagement, the auditor may actually prepare the report (such as comments on lottery processes).

3. *What type of work do accountants complete?* Audits and assurance engagements are conducted by accountants and other professionals. Public accountants (PAs), who audit financial statements as well as conducting these other engagements, can be either CGAs, CMAs, or CAs in Canada. Although some CMAs provide assurance services, most CMAs are financial management professionals. CIAs and internal auditors often do operational audits and help management assess risks. There are also many specialist designations, such as the CISA.

Review Questions

1-1 Your local veterinarian is complaining about all of the "accountants" he has had to work with—the government has been in to look at his income taxes, the bookkeeper has been sick so he has had to hire someone else, and now you are coming in to do an audit. Using the definition of an audit, explain to the veterinarian what you will be doing with the financial statements.

1-2 Explain what is meant by determining the degree of correspondence between information and established criteria. What are the information and established criteria for the audit of Glickle Ltd.'s tax return by a Canada Revenue Agency auditor? What are they for the audit of Glickle Ltd.'s financial statements by a public accounting firm?

1-3 Describe the nature of evidence the Canada Revenue Agency auditor will use in the audit of Glickle Ltd.'s tax return.

1-4 In the conduct of audits of financial statements, it would be a serious breach of responsibility if the auditor did not thoroughly understand accounting. However, many competent accountants do not have an understanding of the auditing process. What causes this difference?

1-5 Describe the different types of assurance engagements that could be provided for a hospital.

1-6 What are the differences and similarities among audits of financial statements, compliance audits, and operational audits?

1-7 List five examples of specific operational audits that could be conducted by an internal auditor in a manufacturing company.

1-8 Using a law firm as an example, describe the different audit, attestation, and assurance services that could be provided to the firm, with examples.

1-9 Explain why auditors need to be knowledgeable about e-commerce technologies.

1-10 Briefly describe the accounting organizations that exist in Canada and identify the professional designations they award. What roles do these organizations play for their members?

1-11 What are the major differences in the scope of the audit responsibilities for public accountants, auditors from the Auditor General's office, Canada Revenue Agency auditors, and internal auditors?

1-12 Distinguish the following three risks: risk-free interest rate, business risk, and information risk. Which one or ones does the auditor reduce by performing an audit?

Discussion Problems

1-13 Daniel Charon is the loan officer of the Georgian Bay Bank. Georgian Bay Bank has a loan of $540,000 outstanding from Regional Delivery Service Ltd., a company specializing in the delivery of products of all types on behalf of smaller companies. Georgian Bay's collateral on the loan consists of 20 small delivery trucks with an average original cost of $45,000.

Charon is concerned about the collectibility of the outstanding loan and whether the trucks still exist. He therefore engages Susan Virms, public accountant, to count the trucks, using registration information held by Charon. She is engaged because she spends most of her time auditing used automobile and truck dealerships and has extensive specialized knowledge about used trucks. Charon requests that Virms issue a report stating:

1. Which of the 20 trucks is parked in Regional's parking lot on the night of June 30.

2. The condition of each truck, using the categories poor, good, and excellent.

3. The fair market value of each truck using the current "blue book" for trucks, which states the approximate wholesale prices of all used truck models based on the poor, good, and excellent categories.

REQUIRED

a. Identify which aspects of this narrative fit each of the following parts of the definition of auditing:
   (1) Information.
   (2) Established criteria.
   (3) Accumulates and evaluates evidence.
   (4) Competent, independent person.
   (5) Report of results.

b. Identify the greatest difficulties Virms is likely to face doing this assurance engagement.

1-14 Vial-tek has an existing loan in the amount of $1.5 million with an annual interest rate of 9.5 percent. The company provides an internal company-prepared financial statement to the bank under the loan agreement. Two competing banks have offered to replace Vial-tek's existing loan agreement with a new one. First National Bank has offered to loan Vial-tek $1.5 million at a rate of 8.5 percent but requires Vial-tek to provide financial statements that have been reviewed by a public accounting firm. Second National Bank has offered to loan Vial-tek $1.5 million at a rate of 7.5 percent but requires Vial-tek to provide financial statements that have been audited. The controller of Vial-tek approached a public accounting firm and was given an estimated cost of $12,000 to perform a review and $20,000 to perform an audit.

REQUIRED

a. Explain why the interest rate for the loan that requires a review report is lower than that for the loan that does not require a review. Explain why the interest rate for the loan that requires an audit report is lower than the interest rate for the other two loans.

b. Calculate Vial-tek's annual costs under each loan agreement, including interest and costs for the public accounting firm's services. Indicate whether Vial-tek should keep its existing loan, accept the offer from First National Bank, or accept the offer from Second National Bank.

c. Assume that First National Bank has offered the loan at a rate of 8 percent with a review, and the cost of the audit has increased to $25,000 due to new auditing standards requirements. Indicate whether Vial-tek should keep its existing loan, accept the offer from First National Bank, or accept the offer from Second National Bank.

d. Explain why Vial-tek may desire to have an audit, ignoring the potential reduction in interest costs.

e. Explain how knowledge of e-commerce technologies and a strategic understanding of the client's business may increase the value of the audit service.

1-15 The list below indicates various audit, attestation, and assurance engagements involving auditors:

1. An auditor's report on whether the financial statements are fairly presented in accordance with GAAP.
2. An electronic seal indicating that an electronic seller observes certain practices.
3. A report indicating whether a governmental entity has complied with certain government regulations.
4. A report on the examination of a financial forecast.
5. A report on the effectiveness of internal control over financial reporting.
6. A review report that provides moderate assurance about whether financial statements are fairly stated in accordance with GAAP.
7. A report on compliance with a royalty agreement.
8. A report about management's assertion on the effectiveness of controls over the availability, reliability, integrity, and maintainability of its accounting information system.
9. An evaluation of the effectiveness of key measures used to assess an entity's success in achieving specific targets linked to an entity's strategic plan and vision.

REQUIRED

a. For each of the services listed above, use Figure 1-2 to indicate which type of service the item represents.
b. Justify your response.

1-16 Consumers Union is a non-profit organization that provides information and counsel on consumer goods and services. A major part of its function is the testing of different brands of consumer products that are purchased on the open market and then reporting the results of the tests in Consumer Reports, a monthly publication. Examples of the types of products it tests are mid-sized automobiles, residential dehumidifiers, canned tuna, and boys' jeans.

REQUIRED

a. In what ways are the services provided by Consumers Union similar to assurance services provided by public accounting firms?

b. Compare the concept of information risk introduced in this chapter with the information risk problem faced by a buyer of an automobile.
c. Compare the causes of information risk faced by users of financial statements as discussed in this chapter with those faced by a buyer of an automobile.
d. Compare the ways users of financial statements can reduce information risk with those available to a buyer of an automobile.

Professional Judgment Problems

1-17 A small, but expanding, specialty home-products retailer recently implemented an internet portal that allows customers to order merchandise online. In the first few months of operation, their internet site attracted a large number of visitors; however, very few placed orders online. The retailer conducted several focus-group sessions with potential shoppers to identify reasons why shoppers were visiting the website without placing orders. Shoppers in the focus group made these comments:

1. "I am nervous about doing business with this retailer because it is relatively unknown in the marketplace. How do I know the product descriptions on the website are accurate and that the stated return policies are followed?"
2. "I am reluctant to provide my credit card information online. How do I know the transmission of my personal credit card information to the retailer's website is protected?"

3. "Retailers are notorious for selling information about customers to others. The last thing I want to do is enter personal information online, such as my name, address, telephone number, and e-mail address. I am afraid this retailer will sell that information to third parties and then I'll be bombarded with a bunch of junk e-mail messages!"
4. "Websites go down all the time due to system failures. How do I know the retailer's website will be operating when I need it?"

REQUIRED

Discuss whether this situation provides an opportunity for PAs to address these customer concerns. How could a PA provide assistance?

1-18 A large conglomerate is considering acquiring a medium-sized manufacturing company in a closely related industry. A major consideration by the management of the conglomerate in deciding whether to pursue the merger is the operational efficiency of the company. Management has decided to obtain a detailed report based on the intensive investigation of the operational efficiency of the sales department, production department, and research and development department.

REQUIRED

a. What professionals could the conglomerate hire to conduct the operational audit? What skills should be present in the audit team?

b. What major problems are the auditors likely to encounter in conducting the investigation and writing the report?

Case

1-19 It is your first day in auditing class, and your instructor has explained how grades are going to be earned and recorded. Attendance (worth 5 percent) is going to be tracked with sign-in sheets, while discussion marks (again up to 5 percent) can be earned by means of several options: taking up a text book question, bringing in a current article or video for discussion, or talking about a change in auditing standards. There are also a group term paper with a presentation, a midterm examination, and a final examination. The instructor will record grades in spreadsheets and post preliminary results (with truncated student numbers). Then you are asked some questions about your grades that you were never asked before. The purpose of these questions is to help you integrate the current class materials and to think about auditing in the context of something that is important to you.

REQUIRED

a. Who are the stakeholders who would be concerned if your grades are wrong?

b. Which grades are at the most risk of being incorrect, and which stakeholders would be most affected by errors in those grades? Answering this question is part of a risk assessment process.

c. What could you or the instructor do to prevent errors in the grades? This step is known as risk response or risk mitigation.

d. What steps would you take to audit your grades? What types of audit engagement do these steps belong to?

Ongoing Small Business Case: Thinking about CondoCleaners.com

1-20 Jim and Cecilia were having lunch at the public accounting firm cafeteria downtown and discussing the future. They had both been recently promoted to managers, with incomes approaching six figures. Cecilia and her husband had recently purchased a house, while Jim had accumulated a sizable nest egg, living with his parents. They were talking about the "departed ones"—their peers who had left the firm and were working as internal auditors or executives or had started their own business. Others had stayed with the firm but were now working as specialists rather than in auditing. Jim had an idea that had been in the back of his head for two or three years—what about an online cleaning business? There were so many large condominium towers near the office—people could book their cleaning appointment online and then have the cleaning done within two or three days. Cecilia smiled, "I don't think I would take that kind of risk, having just committed to a mortgage, but I regret not using my skills in starting a new business."

REQUIRED

Using the definition of auditing, identify the types of skills that Jim and Cecilia have acquired at the public accounting firm. How would these skills translate into being able to run your own business? What types of skills might Jim need to run this new business?

2

The public accounting profession

As we saw in Chapter 1, public accountants (PAs) add value to information by providing assurance. What are the processes that help ensure that PAs do a good job? What is the difference in organizational structure between the large public accounting firms that earn over a billion dollars per year in Canada and the sole practitioner who works with small businesses? Future management accountants will use the information in this chapter to work with professional accounting firms. Future auditors (external, internal, government, or specialists) can use the chapter to see how quality assurance is maintained.

LEARNING OBJECTIVES

1 Describe the organizational structure of public accounting firms.

2 Discuss the market forces that help ensure that audit and assurance engagements are completed to high standards of quality. Describe the organizations involved in the development and maintenance of Canadian GAAS (generally accepted auditing standards) for public accountants. Explain how these standards are enforced.

3 Identify the characteristics of quality control for financial statement audits. Explain how quality control is monitored, including the role of the CPAB (Canadian Public Accountability Board).

STANDARDS REFERENCED IN THIS CHAPTER

CICA Standards

Section 5021 – Authority of auditing and assurance standards and other guidance

AuG-21 – Canada–U.S. reporting differences

CSQC-1 – Quality control for firms that perform audits and reviews of financial statements, and other assurance engagements (previously GSF-QC – General standards of quality control for firms performing assurance engagements)

CAS 200 – Overall objectives of the independent auditor, and the conduct of an audit in accordance with Canadian Auditing Standards (previously included aspects of Section 5100 – Generally Accepted Auditing Standards)

CAS 220 – Quality control for an audit of financial statements (previously Section 5030 – Quality control procedures for assurance engagements)

New Computer System Results in Errors and Accounting Clean-up

If you have stayed at a hotel, you may have used software provided by Guest-Tek Interactive Entertainment Ltd. (Guest-Tek). The company provides telecommunications solutions (hardware, software, and support) to hoteliers. Services include telephone, internet, video-on-demand, and high-definition television. You would expect that such a high-technology company would also have excellent in-house systems. Unfortunately, after installing an enterprise-wide accounting system in fall 2006, financial reporting was stalled.

The company issued press releases saying that it would delay filing of its quarterly financial statements for December 2006 and its annual financial statements of March 31, 2007. It voluntarily issued a cease-trading order for management and insider shareholders. The Alberta Securities Commission issued a cease-trading order for all shares on June 29, 2007, as financial statements still failed to appear. It was almost a year later, in December 2007, that shares resumed trading after financial results were prepared.

Problems deepened as the company announced that prior financial statements would be restated. Inventory quantities and costs entered into the new system had been inaccurate, resulting in misstated inventory. Then, as these errors were investigated, problems in the 2006 financial statements were found in the way inventory was valued, in the allocation of purchase costs between years, and in the way that revenue was recognized. Prior years' deficits were increased by over $2.1 million; management reissued the 2006 financial statements, and the auditors withdrew and reissued their audit report.

IMPORTANCE TO AUDITORS

These problems illustrate the impact of volume and complexity of data—mistakes can be hard to find and extremely time consuming to correct. Incorrect entry of information results in unreliable information being processed by computer systems (i.e., the "garbage-in, garbage-out" concept), potentially magnifying the impact of errors. Conversely, new computer systems that provide more detail than old systems may help to pinpoint errors that could not be detected with older, less sophisticated accounting systems. It could be that these errors made it difficult for the auditors to conduct their audit of the financial statements. By having an audit team consisting of auditors who understood both the industry and the information systems, the auditors were able to effectively audit the financial statements.

WHAT DO YOU THINK? (?)

1. What can professional accountants do to help prevent or detect errors in information systems processing?

continued >

2. How can public accountants ensure that they have the skills to detect material errors in financial statements?

3. From this case and your knowledge of information systems, what risks arise when organizations implement new information systems? How could these risks affect financial statement results?

Sources: 1. Guest-Tek Interactive Entertainment Ltd., "Form 51-102F3, Material Change Report," filed February 14, 2008, www.sedar.com, Accessed: July 23, 2008. 2. Guest-Tek Interactive Entertainment Ltd., "Amended Management's Discussion and Analysis for Quarter and six months ending September 30, 2006," www.sedar.com, Accessed: July 23, 2008. 3. Guest-Tek Interactive Entertainment Ltd., "Amended Consolidated Financial Statements for Years ended March 31, 2006 and 2005," www.guest-tek.com/, and Guest-Tek Interactive Entertainment Ltd., homepage, Accessed: July 23, 2008.

MISTAKES happen. They happen in everyday life, in the preparation of financial statements and in the conduct of an audit engagement. Actions and procedures should be in place to prevent high-risk or large errors from happening—auditing can help verify that such controls are functioning effectively. We learned in the first chapter that auditing plays an important role in society by reducing information risk and adding assurance to information, and that audit firms provide non-assurance services such as management consulting to their clients. Our story about Guest-Tek illustrates problems that occurred with the preparation of financial statements. Professional accountants and auditors helped to track down the problems, resolve them, and establish new procedures to ensure the accuracy and integrity of the information.

➊ Organization of Public Accounting Firms

Public Accounting Firms

There are currently more than 1,000 public accounting firms in Canada. These firms range in size from a sole practitioner to the more than 5,400 professional staff employed by Canada's largest public accounting firm, Deloitte & Touche LLP (internationally Deloitte Touche Tohmatsu, see **www.deloitte.com**). Four size categories can be used to describe public accounting firms: "Big Six" international firms, other international or national firms, large local and regional firms, and small local firms.

INTERNATIONAL FIRMS How many "big" firms are there? In terms of revenue, the top three firms each earned Canadian revenues over $1 billion. These firms, plus three others, make up the Canadian firms with more than 1,500 employees. Nine Canadian firms had more than 100 partners, and many regional firms have national and international affiliations.[1]

---

[1] Jeffrey, Gundi, "Top six busy despite slowdown," *The Bottom Line*, 25(4), 2009, p. F1, F3.

The six largest accounting firms in the world, referred to as the "Big Six," are Deloitte & Touche LLP, KPMG (www.kpmg.com), PricewaterhouseCoopers (www.pwcglobal.com), Ernst & Young (www.ey.com), Grant Thornton (www.grantthornton.com), and BDO Dunwoody (www.bdo.ca).[2] They audit most of the 1,000 largest companies in Canada. Their gross revenues ranged from $340 million to over $1.4 billion for 2009.[3] These firms have offices that range in size from several hundred professionals in Toronto to smaller offices with fewer than 20 people.

These international firms are so large because they need to be able to serve all major international cities as the globalization of businesses increases. For example, if a Canadian company has branches in the United States, Brazil, and Spain, the public accounting firm doing the audit needs, in each of those countries, auditors who are familiar with that country's laws, accounting practices, and auditing standards. Each of the Big Six now has the capability to serve all major international markets.

NATIONAL FIRMS Several other firms in Canada, such as Collins Barrow (www.collinsbarrow.com), PKF Canadian firms (www.pkfnan.org), and BHD Association (http://accountantsca.com), are referred to as national firms because they have offices in most major cities. Their revenues range from $66 million to more than $132 million.[4]

These firms perform the same services as international firms and compete directly with them for clients. In addition, each is affiliated with firms in other countries and therefore has an international capability.

LARGE LOCAL AND REGIONAL FIRMS There are fewer than 30 public accounting firms with professional staffs of more than 50 people. Some have only one office and serve clients primarily within commuting distance. Others have several offices in a province or region and serve clients within a larger radius. These firms compete with other public accounting firms, including the Big Six, for clients. Many of them become affiliated with associations of public accounting firms to share resources for such matters as technical information and continuing education. Firms in this category have revenues that range up to $46 million.[5]

---

[2] *The Bottom Line*, April 2005, p. 12.

[3] Ibid, p. 12.

[4] Ibid, p. 12.

[5] Ibid, p. 14

audit challenge 2-1

Top-Quality Service East and West

Forty-seven partners and 136 professionals comprise the newly formed AC Group, a group of independent small firms which share specialist resources in the provinces of New Brunswick, Nova Scotia, and Prince Edward Island. These include business valuation, litigation support, estate planning, and WebTrust, as well as audit, accounting, and tax services.

The executive officer of the association, Robert Caswill, told *The Bottom Line*, a business periodical for accountants, that the organization plans to stay eastern, composed of local small business service offices, rather than looking for members outside the region.

Contrast this to Meyers Norris Penny, ranked seventh in Canada (with $210 million in revenue), with all of its offices in the four western provinces. This firm has close to 600 personnel (partners and staff) providing all the services of the AC Group, plus capabilities for public company audits. This firm intends to expand, and is looking for potential members all across Canada.

CRITICAL THINKING QUESTIONS

1. What qualities would each of these firms be looking for in potential new member offices?
2. How would these organizations ensure that consistent, high-quality work is provided by each member office?
3. What type of company would you prefer to work for—one that provides service to only small businesses, or one that has a greater breadth of clientele, from small- to medium-sized and public companies?

Sources: 1. The AC Group, www.acgca.ca, Accessed: July 24, 2008. 2. Graham, Penelope, "Seed of a new idea blossoms quickly," *The Bottom Line,* 24(4), 2008, p. 17. 3. Jeffrey, Gundi, "Growing western powerhouse looks east," *The Bottom Line,* 24(4), 2008, p. 20. 4. Jeffrey, Gundi, "Optimism despite trouble in the U.S.," *The Bottom Line,* 24(4), 2008, p. 13. 5. Meyers Norris Penny, www.mnp.ca, Accessed: July 24, 2008.

SMALL LOCAL FIRMS Most of these public accounting firms have fewer than 25 professionals in their single office. They perform audits and related services primarily for smaller businesses and not-for-profit entities, although some do have one or two clients with public ownership. Many small firms are resigning from these public company audits due to the need to register with the **Canadian Public Accountability Board** (CPAB).

Canadian Public Accountability Board (CPAB)—an oversight organization for the audit of publicly listed businesses that includes practice inspections.

Structure of Public Accounting Firms

The organization and structure of public accounting firms can vary depending on the nature and range of services offered by the firm. Three main factors influence the organizational structure of all firms:

1. The need for independence from clients. Independence permits auditors to remain unbiased in drawing conclusions about their clients' financial statements.
2. The importance of a structure to encourage competence. The ability of the structure to encourage competence permits auditors to conduct audits and perform other services efficiently and effectively.
3. The increased litigation risk faced by auditors. In the last decade, firms have experienced increases in litigation-related costs. Some organizational structures afford a degree of protection to individual firm members.

The organizational form used by many public accounting firms is that of a sole proprietorship or a partnership, although some provinces allow special-purpose limited liability partnerships or professional corporations. In a typical firm, several CAs or CGAs join together to practise as partners, offering auditing and other services to interested parties. The partners normally hire professional staff to assist them in their work. Competence is encouraged by having a large number of professionals with related interests associated in one firm, which facilitates a professional attitude and continuing professional education.

The organizational hierarchy in a typical public accounting firm includes partners, managers, supervisors, seniors or in-charge auditors, and assistants, with a new employee usually starting as an assistant and spending two or three years in each classification before achieving partner status. The titles of the positions vary from firm to firm, but the basic structure is the same in all. When we refer in this text to

Table 2-1	Recent Surveys Conducted by Deloitte and KPMG

Deloitte Touche Tohmatsu

2007 Global Venture Capital Survey (500 venture capitalists)
2007 Global Security Survey (169 financial institutions)
2007 TechTalent Pulse Survey Report: "Coming of Age" (60 technology and telecommunications organizations)

KPMG

Global Corporate Capital Flows 2008/09 to 2013/14 (300 multinational companies)
2008 Key Issues for Rising National Oil Companies (8 corporations plus archival research)
C-Suite 2008 Survey on Carbon Tax and Environmental Measures (over 150 chief executive officers, chief financial officers, and chief operating officers)

Sources: www.deloitte.com and www.kpmg.com, Accessed: July 24, 2008.

the auditor, we mean the particular person performing some aspect of a financial statement audit. It is common to have one or more auditors from each level on larger engagements.

E-Commerce and Public Accounting Firm Operations

Like all industries, public accounting firms are using the internet to market their services. Firms of all sizes use the internet to highlight such things as office locations, affiliations, service lines, and industry specializations and to provide reference tools and materials to existing and potential clients. Firm websites feature news and insights about business issues, such as updates on changes in tax laws and interactive forms to determine which type of retirement account to choose. Firms also conduct research of interest to their clients, potential clients, and the general public. Table 2-1 provides examples from the top two Canadian public accounting firms.

Public accounting firms use the internet to connect their global professional staff and to take advantage of online resources and databases. These resources are useful to PAs for staying current on emerging business and standards-setting issues. Databases such as Standard and Poor's Net Advantage Database and the Goldman Sachs Research Database provide extensive industry-specific information and coverage of companies. PAs use these on a subscription basis to stay current on industry developments and to obtain industry data useful for auditing and consulting.

concept check

C2-1 How do the structures of small and large public accounting firms differ?

C2-2 How can the internet be used to facilitate client services and internal communication for public accounting firms?

❷ Responding to the Public Call for High-Quality Audits

High-profile failures, such as Enron and WorldCom, and frequently restated financial statements, such as those by Nortel and Guest-Tek, help explain why there is an increasing focus on standards and upon high-quality audits.

Professional Accounting Organizations

High-quality audits adhering to professional standards are promoted by professional organizations that serve as umbrella organizations for their members. Depending upon the organization, they coordinate the examination processes, provide for continuing education activities, fund research projects, produce relevant publications, and engage in standard setting and peer review processes.

RESEARCH AND PUBLICATIONS Each association has some form of monthly (or bi-monthly) newsletter or national magazine. For example, in its role as representative of the CAs in Canada, the CICA publishes a wide range of materials. These include the monthly *CAmagazine* (**www.camagazine.com**), accounting and auditing research studies, and the biannual *Financial Reporting in Canada*. The CICA coordinates the

Uniform Evaluation exam and publishes the Board of Evaluators' Report on each year's exam. It also coordinates the common activities of the provincial institutes and *ordre*.

The Certified General Accountants Association of Canada (CGAAC) plays a similar role in the professional lives of CGAs, as does the Society of Management Accountants of Canada for CMAs and the Institute of Internal Auditors for CIAs. For example, CGAAC publishes *CGA Magazine* (**www.cga-canada.org**), SMAC publishes *CMA Magazine* (**www.managementmag.com**), and ISACA publishes *Information Systems Control Journal* (**www.isaca.org/journal**). In addition, each association administers exams and provides professional guidance and continuing professional education. They also conduct research and publish materials of interest to their members and students.

CONTINUING EDUCATION The professional organizations are active in continuing professional education, sponsoring seminars, and developing and providing material for use by their membership. The CICA established six specializations for Chartered Accountants, in cooperation with other professional organizations. The ISACA also has specialized designations in information systems security and governance.

ESTABLISHING STANDARDS AND RULES The CICA has been given the authority by the Canada Business Corporations Act and the various provincial incorporating acts to set accounting and auditing standards that must be followed by public accountants doing audits of companies chartered under one of those Acts. This is done by stating that the financial statements should be prepared in accordance with the standards as set out in the *CICA Handbook*. In this role, the CICA supports research by its own research staff and, through grants, by others. It also sets the standards, which are called "Recommendations" and are codified in the *CICA Handbook*, and proposes guidelines and rules for members and other public accountants to follow. The *CICA Handbook* is a four-volume set, with two volumes on accounting and two on assurance.

Regulatory Influences on the Financial Statement Audit Process

Figure 2-1 uses the definition of auditing to illustrate components of the financial statement audit process. The figure shows key management actions, standards, and

| Figure 2-1 | Management and Public Accountant (Auditor) Roles During the Conduct of the Financial Statement Audit |

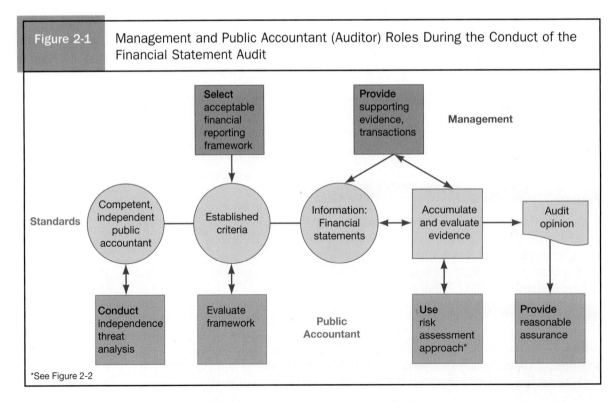

*See Figure 2-2

Canada Has Embraced CASs

Canadian accounting and auditing standards are moving toward conformity with international standards because of an increasingly global business environment and a desire for efficiency in the standard-setting process. The CICA website has documents explaining how the ISAs (International Standards on Auditing) in effect as of December 15, 2009, have been adopted as Canadian Auditing Standards, CASs, and provides a reconciliation document between previous *CICA Handbook* section numbers and the new CASs. Canadian standards are being renumbered in conformity with the ISAs. These CASs are effective for the audits of financial statements for periods that end after December 14, 2010. This means that organizations with a December 2010 year-end will have their audits conducted using the new CASs.

The CICA website (**www.cica.ca**) has a menu item titled "Canadian Standards in Transition" devoted to the transition to international standards. It contains the above-noted reconciliation document as well as current information about the conversion, reasons for the change, and frequently asked questions (FAQs) about ISAs and CASs. Similar information is available from the CGA Canada website's assurance section, **https://www.cga-pdnet.org/en-CA/Pages/default.aspx**.

The ISAs already adopted focus on standards for the audit of financial statements. Some current Canadian standards combine guidance for the audit of financial statements and other types of assurance engagements. This means that the existing Canadian auditing standards will likely be rewritten to provide separate guidance for financial statement audits and other engagements. In the meanwhile, we will be using both *CICA Handbook* section numbers and CAS numbers.

The CICA uses the terms *CICA Handbook—Assurance* or *Assurance Handbook* to refer to assurance standards. CASs have been placed in Part I of the *Assurance Handbook*. Part II contains the remaining sections, called Other Canadian Standards—Engagement Standards (or OCSs). For convenience, we will use *CICA Handbook* when talking about any of the CICA Standards.

Canadian auditing standards are issued by the Auditing and Assurance Standards Board (AASB), which is composed of volunteers appointed by the Auditing and Assurance Standards Oversight Board (AASOB) and from the business community.

The conversion to CASs brings with it changes in terminology and a reorganization of Canadian standards, expected to be completed in the coming years. Each CAS is organized into the following sections: Introduction, Objective, Definitions, Requirements, Application, and Other Explanatory Material.

auditor actions. This figure helps us see regulatory influences on the component parts of the audit.

The process of establishing Canadian regulations has been influenced by the introduction of the Sarbanes-Oxley Act in the United States.[6] Some of these influences are shown in Table 2-2.

Table 2-2	Influence of Sarbanes-Oxley Act on Canadian Regulations
Sarbanes-Oxley Requirement	**Effect on Canada**
Creation of the PCAOB (Public Company Accounting Oversight Board) to oversee listed company auditors and develop audit standards	Implementation of the CPAB to oversee Canadian audit professionals
Listed company management to certify the accuracy and completeness of financial statements	Same requirements implemented in Canada
Listed company management to certify existence of adequate internal controls and describe material changes to internal controls	Similar requirements implemented in Canada
Auditors required to provide an opinion on management's certification of internal controls	Not implemented in Canada
Increased independence requirements for auditors	Revisions of national and provincial rules of professional conduct for CAs and CGAs

---

[6] See www.gpo.gov/fdsys/pkg/PLAW-107publ204/content-detail.html.

It is important to consider these external influences as we talk about the nature of auditing, for it is in the eyes of external users and regulators that independence is assessed. Walking through the definition in Figure 2-1, we see that an independence threat analysis using the rules of professional conduct (explained further in Chapter 3) helps identify when a public accountant (or auditor) is independent. Prior to developing the financial statements, management will select an acceptable financial reporting framework. As explained in Chapter 1, this framework is usually GAAP. The auditor is required to assess whether the framework selected by management is suitable, using Canadian GAAP and international GAAP to make that assessment. For U.S. reporting, the auditor will also need to be familiar with U.S. GAAP.

When preparing the financial statements, management ensures that appropriate evidence exists to support the numbers and other information in the financial statements. Sarbanes-Oxley in the United States and regulatory reporting requirements in Canada provide the clout to make management directly responsible for the financial statements. International Standards on Auditing (ISAs) and proposed CASs state that the auditor can conduct the audit only if management agrees to provide this supporting evidence.

ISAs and Canadian auditing standards require that the audit be conducted using a risk assessment approach. Part 2 of this text explains the risk assessment audit approach in detail, but an overview is provided in this chapter (see Figure 2-2). First, the auditor must identify potential risks of material misstatement in the financial statements. Based upon these risks, the auditor will provide a risk response, which includes the design and execution of the evidence-gathering process to assess the likelihood of these material misstatements actually occurring. Canadian and international standards describe quality-control methods and actions that the auditor should undertake during this process. The auditor continually evaluates evidence to enable preparation of the audit report. The audit report (discussed further in Chapter 22) is an opinion, not a guarantee, that provides reasonable assurance that the financial statements are free of material misstatement.

We will be examining CICA **Assurance Recommendations** throughout this text. Assurance Recommendations are issued by the **Auditing and Assurance Standards Board** (AASB), as explained in *CICA Handbook* Section 5021 and in the Part I Preface to the CASs in the Assurance section of the *CICA Handbook*. These

Assurance Recommendations—a framework for the auditor to use to assist him or her in the conduct of an audit engagement; the rules underlying the audits and related-services activities carried on by public accountants; the italicized portions of the *CICA Handbook*. They are issued by the Auditing and Assurance Standards Board.

Auditing and Assurance Standards Board (AASB)—a committee of the CICA that has the responsibility for issuing Assurance Recommendations and Assurance and Related Services Guidelines.

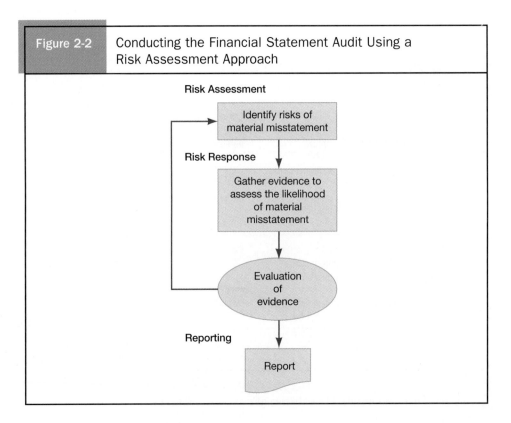

| Figure 2-2 | Conducting the Financial Statement Audit Using a Risk Assessment Approach |

Risk Assessment

Identify risks of material misstatement

Risk Response

Gather evidence to assess the likelihood of material misstatement

Evaluation of evidence

Reporting

Report

recommendations are the rules underlying the audits, assurance engagements, and related services activities carried out by public accountants. Assurance Recommendations are the italicized portions of Sections 5000 to 9200 and Sections PS 5000 to PS 6420 of the *CICA Handbook*, and the statements in Part I CAS standards that use the statement "the auditor shall." Sections preceded by "PS" are specific to audits of public sector companies. These are considered to be authoritative rules.

We will also use **Assurance and Related Services Guidelines** issued by the AASB. These Guidelines do not have the authority of Assurance Recommendations and are either interpretations of existing Recommendations or the views of the AASB on a particular matter of concern. An example is Assurance and Related Services Guideline 43 (AuG-40) issued in December 2005, titled "Audit of policy liabilities of insurance companies."

Assurance and Related Services Guidelines—interpretations of Assurance Recommendations or views of the Auditing and Assurance Standards Board on particular matters of concern; less authoritative than Assurance Recommendations.

Ways Public Accountants Are Encouraged to Perform Effectively

Because public accounting firms play an important social role, it is essential for the management of those firms and their professional staff to conduct themselves appropriately and provide high-quality audits and other services. The various professional organizations (CICA and CGAAC) and other outside organizational influences have developed several mechanisms to increase the likelihood of appropriate audit quality and professional conduct. These are summarized in Figure 2-3 and discussed in the remainder of this and subsequent chapters. The codes of professional conduct of the various accounting bodies have a significant influence on members and are meant to provide a standard of conduct for members who are in public practice. The codes and related issues of professional conduct are examined in Chapter 3. Legal liability is studied in Chapter 4. Shaded circles indicate items discussed in this chapter.

Generally Accepted Auditing Standards

Auditing or assurance standards are general guidelines to aid auditors in fulfilling their professional responsibilities in the audit of historical financial statements. They include consideration of management honestly providing relevant evidence; professional qualities such as competence and independence; evidence; and reporting requirements.

The broadest auditing standards available are the **generally accepted auditing standards** (GAAS) discussed in CAS 200 (comprising material that corresponds to Sections 5090, 5095, and 5100). These general standards are not sufficiently specific

Generally accepted auditing standards (GAAS)—eight auditing standards, developed by the CICA, consisting of the general standard, examination standards, and reporting standards; often called auditing standards.

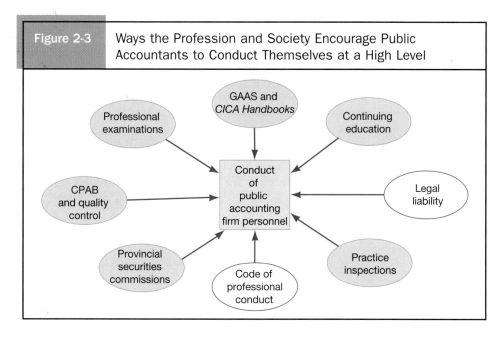

| Figure 2-3 | Ways the Profession and Society Encourage Public Accountants to Conduct Themselves at a High Level |

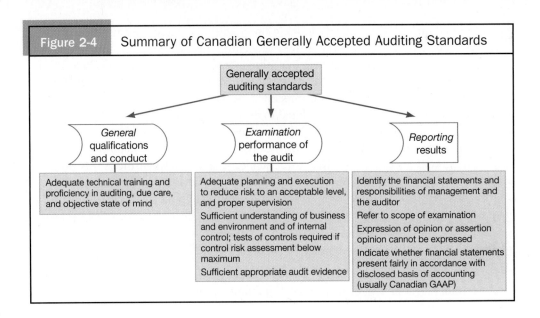

Figure 2-4   Summary of Canadian Generally Accepted Auditing Standards

to provide any meaningful guide to practitioners, but they do represent a framework for further discussion of detailed standards. These underlying principles of GAAS have been summarized in Figure 2-4. We discuss them below briefly and expand upon them throughout the text. GAAS comprises all standards that have been adopted by a particular country. In Canada, they comprise *CICA Handbook* Sections, CAS standards, and generally accepted auditing practices used by firms.

GENERAL: QUALIFICATIONS AND CONDUCT This standard stresses the important qualities the auditor should possess. In addition to technical competence obtained by a formal education in auditing and accounting, practical experience and continuing professional education are aspects of competence. The auditor must be technically qualified and experienced in those industries in which the auditor has clients. Recent court cases clearly demonstrate that in any case in which the public accountant or the accountant's assistants are not qualified to perform the work, a professional obligation exists to acquire the requisite knowledge and skills, suggest someone else who is qualified to perform the work, or decline the engagement.

The general standard involves due care in the performance of all aspects of auditing (discussed further in Chapter 4). Simply stated, this means that the auditor is a professional responsible for fulfilling his or her duties diligently and carefully. As an illustration, due care includes consideration of the completeness of the working papers, the sufficiency of the audit evidence, and the appropriateness of the auditor's report. As a professional, the auditor must not be guilty of negligence or bad faith, but he or she is not expected to make perfect judgments in every instance.

To conduct the audit effectively, the auditor must be free of bias. The importance of an objective state of mind and independence was stressed earlier in the definition of auditing. The Rules of Professional Conduct of the various provincial institutes of CAs and the *ordre* as well as CAS 200 stress the need for independence and the adherence to ethical standards (discussed further in the next chapter). The rules of conduct of CGAAC also stress the need for independence of CGAs engaged in public accounting. The Canada Business Corporations Act (CBCA), which is similar to several of the provincial incorporating Acts, also requires the auditor to be independent. Public accounting firms are required to follow several practices to increase the likelihood of independence of all personnel. For example, there are established procedures for larger audits that utilize an audit committee whenever there is a dispute between management and the auditors that facilitate the auditors' independence from management. Specific methods to ensure that auditors maintain their independence and professional rules of conduct are studied in Chapter 3. The internal and external auditors usually report to the audit committee. An audit committee is a subcommittee of the board of directors of a company. So that the audit committee can provide effective oversight, the audit committee members must be independent, that is, be composed of directors not belonging to management, also strengthening audit independence. Audit committees are discussed further in Chapter 3.

EXAMINATION: PERFORMANCE OF THE ENGAGEMENT These standards require that the auditor conduct the audit using a risk-based approach, taking into account the potential for material misstatement (which includes errors or fraud) in the financial statements. Part 2 of this text discusses the components of the audit risk model as well as audit responsibilities and objectives, relating these to the auditor's objective of obtaining reasonable assurance that the financial statements are free of material misstatement.

To provide an opinion requires planning, understanding the client's business, and gathering sufficient evidence, as discussed in Part 2. Overall, the engagement should be well planned and executed, with proper supervision of assistants, to ensure an adequate audit. Supervision is essential in auditing because most of the field work or examination is done by less experienced staff members.

A strategic and risk-based approach means that the client must be assessed in the context of the business environment and the corporate governance process. Are the client's accounting systems and internal controls sufficient to generate reliable financial information? If the auditor is convinced that the client has excellent controls that provide reliable data and safeguard assets and records, then the amount of audit evidence to be accumulated can be significantly less than for a system that is not adequate. In some instances, the controls may be so poor as to preclude reliance on the data in the records and an audit may not be possible.

The decision as to how much and what quality of evidence to accumulate for a given set of circumstances requires professional judgment. A major portion of this book is concerned with the study of evidence accumulation and the circumstances affecting the amount needed.

To assist the auditor, the CBCA specifies the auditor's qualifications in Section 161 but also provides the auditor with statutory rights and responsibilities. These give the auditor the right to attend shareholder meetings and the right to have access to the necessary records, information, and explanations necessary to conduct the audit. These rights afford the auditor the access necessary for completion of the audit.

REPORTING: RESULTS Specific wording is required in the auditor's report (explained in Chapter 22). The report describes the auditor's responsibilities, management's responsibilities, the financial statements that were audited, the scope of the engagement, and the auditor's opinion. If the standard opinion cannot be provided, standards explain when and how the report should be modified.

Auditing Requirements

Recommendations in the *CICA Handbook* are the most authoritative requirements for public accountants performing financial statements audits of companies incorporated under the various federal or provincial incorporating Acts or listed on one of the Canadian stock exchanges. As the *CICA Handbook* is redrafted in conformance with international standards, requirements are identified by using the word 'shall' rather than having italicized recommendations. PAs are required by their rules of professional conduct to follow the Recommendations of the *CICA Handbook*. The Recommendations are a framework for the auditor to use to assist him or her in the conduct of the audit engagement. The framework is built upon the generally accepted auditing standards.

Auditing standards in the United States are issued by the American Institute of Certified Public Accountants (**www.aicpa.org**) and the Public Company Accounting Oversight Board (PCAOB, see **www.pcaobus.org**), as described in New Standards 2-2 on the next page. The AICPA is the umbrella organization for the CPA designation and the state CPA associations.

Standards from the PCAOB in the United States

The Sarbanes-Oxley Act of 2002, signed into law on July 30, 2002, is considered by many observers to be the most important legislation affecting the American auditing profession since the 1933 and 1934 Securities Acts. The Sarbanes-Oxley Act was triggered by the bankruptcies and alleged audit failures involving Enron and WorldCom. The provisions of the Act apply to publicly held companies and their audit firms.

This Act established the Public Company Accounting Oversight Board (PCAOB), appointed and overseen by the Securities and Exchange Commission (SEC). The PCAOB provides oversight for auditors of public companies, including establishing auditing, ethics, independence, and quality control standards for public company audits and performing inspections of the quality

controls at audit firms performing those audits. These activities were formerly the responsibility of the AICPA. The U.S. Auditing Standards Board (ASB) is still responsible for issuing pronouncements on auditing matters for all entities other than public companies. Although the PCAOB is responsible for setting standards, existing auditing standards remain in effect for public companies until the PCAOB develops specific guidance.

The PCAOB regularly issues new standards that have an impact on SEC registrants, including Canadian companies which file on the SEC. The most recent standards (effective with 2008 year-ends) concern internal control reporting and pre-approval of non-audit services by the audit committee.

Although GAAS and the Assurance and Related Services Recommendations are the authoritative auditing pronouncements for members of the profession, they provide less direction to auditors than might be assumed. There are almost no specific audit procedures required by the standards; and there are no specific requirements for auditors' decisions, such as determining sample size, selecting sample items from the population for testing, or evaluating results. Some practitioners believe the standards should provide more clearly defined guidelines for determining the extent of evidence to be accumulated. Such specificity would eliminate some difficult audit decisions and provide a line of defence for a public accounting firm charged with conducting an inadequate audit. However, highly specific requirements could turn auditing into mechanistic evidence gathering, devoid of professional judgment. Simply filling in long checklists without considering the unique requirements of the client result in an audit that is not responsive to risks identified. The use of professional judgment to identify risks and clearly tailor the engagement to those risks results in a better quality audit.

Standards published by the CICA and other standard-setting bodies (i.e., GAAS) should be looked upon by practitioners as minimum standards of performance, rather than as maximum standards or ideals. Any professional auditor constantly seeking means of reducing the scope of the audit by relying only on the standards, rather than evaluating the substance of the situation, fails to satisfy the spirit of the standards. At the same time, the existence of auditing standards does not mean the auditor must always follow them blindly. If the requirement of a Recommendation is impossible to perform, the auditor might adopt some other course of action that allows adherence to the spirit of the Recommendation. If the amount involved is immaterial, it is also unnecessary to follow the standards. However, the burden of justifying departures from the standards falls upon the practitioner.

When the *CICA Handbook* is silent on an issue, the auditor must turn to other authoritative sources. These include the Statements on Auditing Standards (SASs) issued by the AICPA, the ISAs issued by the International Federation of Accountants, textbooks, journals, and technical publications. Materials published by the CICA, mentioned earlier in the chapter, such as audit technique studies, are particularly useful in furnishing assistance on specific questions.

International Auditing Standards

The CICA, the CGAAC, and the SMAC are members of the International Federation of Accountants (IFAC, see **www.ifac.org**), a body that seeks to harmonize auditing standards on a worldwide basis. IFAC, through the International Auditing and Assurance Standards Board (IAASB), issues International Standards on Auditing and International Auditing Practice Statements (IAPSs) for the guidance of accountants in member countries. ISAs are standards and are authoritative, while IAPSs provide guidance and are not authoritative. Now that Canada has adopted the ISAs, our standard-setters will start taking a look at the IAPSs for potential adoption. Those adopted will become CAPS, or Canadian auditing practice statements. Prior to adopting international standards in Canada, the CICA issues exposure drafts explaining how the standards will be changed (if at all) and solicits feedback. Feedback is used to further revise exposure drafts and determine whether the proposed standard is acceptable.

In addition, the provincial securities commissions are members of the International Organization of Securities Commissions (IOSCO, see **www.iosco.org**). IOSCO members are concerned with securities that are issued by a company in one country and sold in a second country. For example, shares of Vale Inco Limited (**www.inco.com**), a Canadian corporation owned by a Brazilian company, are traded on the Toronto Stock Exchange (under the jurisdiction of the Ontario Securities Commission [OSC, see **www.osc.gov.on.ca**]) and on the New York Stock Exchange (under the jurisdiction of the U.S. Securities and Exchange Commission [SEC, see **www.sec.gov**]); Inco's shares are said to be "cross-listed." Both the OSC and the SEC are members of IOSCO. IOSCO members are concerned about International Auditing and Assurance Standards as they have to decide on the quality, sufficiency, and appropriateness of evidence collected and the report issued for audits of financial statements submitted to them for cross-listing.

A Canadian auditor must conduct an audit of a Canadian or foreign company in accordance with Canadian GAAS (i.e., follow the *Handbooks*) and may, in addition, conduct the audit in accordance with international GAAS (i.e., the ISAs or the GAAS of another country such as the United States). Canada's adoption of international auditing standards facilitates the efficient completion of such international engagements. The auditor may report that the audit was conducted using Canadian and foreign GAAS. It is important to note that Canadian GAAS would be the floor in this case, and differences in the two standards may need to be identified.

Where there are reporting differences between Canadian GAAS and the ISAs or foreign GAAS, the auditor should follow Canadian reporting standards. An example is the Auditing Guideline 21, "Canada–United States Reporting Differences." AuG-21 requires the auditor to issue an auditor's report in compliance with Canadian GAAS and to also issue a separate comment explaining the conflict between the reporting standards.

The *Handbooks* take precedence over the ISAs when there is a conflict. A Canadian auditor who is engaged to conduct an examination in accordance with International Standards on Auditing would consult the most recent version of the ISAs.

concept check

C2-3 What are the factors that contribute to the competence of the PA?

C2-4 List the ways that the accounting professions and societies promote effective financial statement engagements.

C2-5 Identify three organizations involved in standard setting for the PA profession.

③ Quality Control

For a public accounting firm, **quality control** comprises the methods used to make sure that the firm meets its professional responsibilities to clients. These methods include the organizational structure of the public accounting firm and the procedures the firm sets up. For example, a public accounting firm might have an organizational structure that assures the technical review of every engagement by a partner who has expertise in the client's industry.

A public accounting firm must make sure that generally accepted auditing standards are followed on every audit. Quality controls are the methods used by the firm that help it meet those standards consistently on every engagement. Quality controls are therefore established for the entire public accounting firm and all the activities in which the firm is involved; GAAS require that these standards are applied to each engagement on an individual basis.

Quality control—methods used by a public accounting firm to make sure that the firm meets its professional responsibilities.

Timing and Detail Changes in Quality Control Processes

CSQC-1 (Canadian standard on quality control, which replaces GSF-QC) and CAS 220 (Quality control for an audit of financial statements, which replaces *CICA Handbook* Section 5030), the Canadian versions of the equivalent international standards, apply to assurance engagements for financial statements. GSF-QC *CICA Handbook* quality control standards also apply to other types of assurance engagements. Keep an eye out for forthcoming *CICA Handbook* sections that will clarify requirements for

non-financial statement engagements. Changes in CSQC-1 include the timing of quality control reviews (to occur before the audit opinion is issued), and a requirement for more specific documentation about independence, consultation, and assessment of evidence. The changes also codify monitoring of quality control procedures and procedures for dealing with complaints.

Elements of Quality Control

The new *CICA Handbook* Section CSQC-1 (formerly GSF-QC) describes general standards of quality control that are applied to firms performing assurance engagements. These are described in Table 2-3, where the general components of quality control are listed under a series of headings called elements of quality control.

CAS

These standards clarify the minimum policies and procedures that firms should have in place. PAs need to ensure that they adequately apply quality control to each audit engagement. For example, there are specific procedures to help ensure that differences of opinion on an engagement are brought forward and cleared before finalizing the engagement. We will be looking at these quality control procedures in more detail when we talk about the various phases of the audit engagement throughout this text.

Quality control standards complement the independence rules that are in place for PAs in response to increased demands for public accountability. After the Sarbanes-Oxley Act of 2002 was passed in the United States, creating the PCAOB, a similar body was implemented in Canada, called the Canadian Public Accountability Board (**www.cpab-ccrc.ca**). Rather than being legislated, the CPAB was created by the provincial securities commissions, the Office of the Superintendent of Financial Institutions, and the CICA. The CPAB's purpose is to help improve the public's confidence in independent auditing. This is accomplished by promoting high-quality audits. The CPAB has developed an oversight program that involves regular inspections of those public accounting firms that audit Canadian public companies.[7] One of the items absent from the CPAB's mission statement is the development of auditing standards. This is a key difference between the Canadian and American approaches. Although the CPAB will provide feedback to the standard-setting process, it is leaving these up to the CICA and coordination with international standard-setting bodies.

Public accounting firms that audit companies called "reporting issuers" are required to register with the CPAB and are subject to a quality control inspection by the CPAB. (This inspection process is discussed further in the next section.) The term "reporting issuers" is used to describe entities, such as profit-oriented businesses and mutual funds, that have raised capital from the public, are listed on a Canadian stock exchange, and are required to file annual audited financial statements with their listing exchange.

At the time of writing, there were 270 registered firms on the CPAB website. (About 200 were Canadian; the others came from around the world.) These include both CGA firms and CA firms.

Public accounting firms that do not audit reporting issuers are not subject to the quality control inspection by the CPAB but are still required to have quality control standards in

---

[7] Source: Canadian Public Accountability Board, www.cpab-ccrc.ca, Accessed: July 28, 2008.

Table 2-3   Elements of Quality Control at the Firm Level

Element	Summary of Requirements
1. Leadership and responsibilities within the firm:	An organizational culture that provides audit quality should be present. Quality control procedures should be developed, documented, implemented, and communicated. Management within a firm should ensure that qualified personnel monitor and address non-compliance with quality control procedures. A firm should establish a formal code of conduct that includes procedures for individuals to disclose differences of opinion and any inappropriate conduct.
2. General ethical requirements:	The general ethical principles of integrity, objectivity, professional competence and due care, confidentiality, and professionalism should be addressed at the policy level, promoted by firm personnel, and monitored.
3. Independence:	Policies and procedures should be developed, communicated, and monitored to ensure that the firm complies with the independence guidelines. Areas to be addressed are extent of non-assurance services provided to audit clients, documentation of independence evaluations, partner rotation (where required), fee policies, partner compensation, and effects of litigation.
4. Client acceptance or continuance:	Documentation of annual risk assessment processes should be present, including an evaluation of a potential client's management integrity and auditor competence and independence.
5. General human resource policies:	Adequate hiring policies (and documentation of their implementation) that ensure competence and integrity of personnel should be in place. Ongoing professional development of personnel should exist, with assignment to work that matches employee competence, and performance evaluation related to audit quality.
6. Extent of professional development:	Employees should be adequately trained in the skills needed to conduct audits. Both instructors and attendees are to be evaluated, with documentation of that evaluation.
7. Engagement performance:	Adequate processes and procedures should be in place to ensure that the audit is conducted in accordance with GAAS, that quality control procedures are followed for each engagement, and that the audit is appropriately documented. These include the use of software tools, supervision, review of work, use of internal or specialist consultation, and processes for handling differences of opinion.
8. Engagement quality control review:	Quality control review is to take place during the engagement and monitoring should occur after engagement completion. Policies in place should include use of second or independent partner review, technical review, documentation, and compliance with quality control processes. Processes should exist for following up internal and external complaints.
9. Documentation:	Policies should address extent of documentation, whether retained in hard copy or electronic format, file retention, storage, security and back-up for audit documentation, correspondence, policies, and procedures.

Practice Inspection Comes Calling

For a CA or CGA functioning as a sole practitioner or working for a small public accounting office, the provincial practice inspectors will likely come to review audit files every three years, depending upon the province where the practice office is located. If the office does not conduct audits, the PA may not see them at all—the practice inspection team will ask to have the files sent to them for review. Inspections are conducted by qualified PAs, either CAs or CGAs, licensed by the same provincial association as the practitioner.

If the office is licensed to have articling students, the inspectors will review the ability of the office to provide sufficient, appropriate hours to the students, as well as the quality control procedures. Then, they will review the quality control manual, a sample of client files, and ask questions. The report will be discussed with the PA before being finalized.

If the inspectors find any files or quality control procedures unsatisfactory, the PA may be required to revise processes, attend training courses, or have more frequent practice inspections (that the PA would have to pay for).

Sources: 1. The Institute of Chartered Accountants of BC, *News and Views*, February 2008, www.ica.bc.ca/pdf/nnv_2008feb.pdf, Accessed: July 28, 2008. 2. The Institute of Chartered Accountants of Ontario Practice Inspection Program, January 2008, www.icao.on.ca, Accessed: July 28, 2008.

place. Quality control needs to be considered during all phases of the engagement, including client acceptance, continuance, planning, and execution of the engagement.

The quality control procedures that a public accounting firm employs will depend on the size of the firm, the number of practice offices, and the nature of the practice. The quality control procedures of a 150-office international firm with many complex multinational clients would vary considerably from those of a five-person firm specializing in small audits in one or two industries.

PRACTICE INSPECTION One of the ways in which the PA profession in Canada has dealt with quality control is through the establishment of practice inspections. The purpose of all practice inspections is to ensure the existence of, and adherence to, quality control standards. These inspections may be administered by professional associations, provincial institutes, *ordre*, or the CPAB.

Practice inspections may be conducted by accounting bodies independently of the CPAB. Practice inspection for CAs, for example. is administered by the provincial institute or *ordre* and is usually mandatory for CAs in public practice. A practice inspection of each practice unit (usually an office but it could be each partner in the office) is normally completed every three years but could be yearly if the practice unit is found not to maintain the level of practice standards set forth by the provincial practice inspection committee.

CPAB practice inspections may be conducted by a provincial accounting body, with the CPAB providing direction and reviewing the results. CPAB inspections are conducted annually for audit firms that have 50 or more reporting issuers. Audit firms having fewer reporting issuers may be inspected once every three years.

The CPAB publishes an annual report summarizing its findings, organized by size of firm. For example, the March 2009 report, available from the CPAB website, reveals that for the period ended December 2008, there were inspections of the six largest public accounting firms in Canada, recurring inspections of 15 other firms, and 21 follow-up inspections. The report states that, of the 123 files reviewed by the CPAB from the top six national firms, five audits had significant deficiencies, one set of financial statements was not in accordance with GAAP, and some financial statements might require restatements. Concerns cover a number of areas, such as the documentation of quality monitoring, consultations, and quality control reviews. These are the same areas where the implementation of international standards differ from Canadian standards. CPAB also noted in its major findings that excellent work was also present in the files that it selected for review.[8]

A Provincial Practice Inspection Committee does have sanctions it can impose. These include reinspection the following year and referral to the Professional Conduct

---

[8] Source: Canadian Public Accountability Board, www.cpab-ccrc.ca, Accessed: July 28, 2008.

Committee, whose powers include requiring the member to take courses, removing the practice unit's right to train students, and expelling the member from their professional Institute and forfeiting the member's right to use the appellation Chartered Accountant or Certified General Accountant.

The CPAB could impose additional sanctions or restrictions such as engaging an independent monitor or limiting the right to audit reporting issuers. It could also make the inspection reports public but would do so only if the member firms were not addressing the recommendations for improvement.

Practice inspection can be beneficial to the profession and individual firms. The profession gains if reviews result in practitioners doing higher-quality audits. A firm can also gain if the practice inspection improves the firm's practices and thereby enhances its reputation and effectiveness and reduces the likelihood of lawsuits. Of course, practice inspection is costly. There is always a trade-off between costs and benefits.

Provincial Securities Commissions

Securities regulation in Canada is a provincial matter; therefore, companies that issue securities in Canada must abide by rules promulgated by the provincial securities commissions. The national umbrella organization, the Canadian Securities Administrators (**www.csa-acvm.ca**), sets policies to which the member commissions agree to adhere. The **provincial securities commissions** are responsible for administering the purchase and sale of securities within their jurisdictions.

Copies of the actual policy statements, which may include questions and answers and multimedia presentations about them, are available at the websites of the following provincial securities commissions' sites: British Columbia Securities Commission (**www.bcsc.bc.ca**), Alberta Securities Commission (**www.albertasecurities.com**), Ontario Securities Commission (**www.osc.gov.on.ca**), and l'Autorité des marches financiers (**www.lautorite.qc.ca/index.en.html**).

More specifics on some of these rules will be discussed in subsequent chapters. The CSA was responsible for the rule that required listed companies' auditors to participate in the oversight program of the CPAB. It also implemented the requirement that the listing company's Chief Financial Officer and Chief Executive Officer provide certification of annual and interim financial statements (as well as the accompanying management discussion and analysis and information forms filed with the exchanges). Another recent requirement is that every listed company must have an audit committee, with specifics about the composition and responsibilities of those audit committees. We will be discussing how CSA requirements affect the audit process in subsequent chapters.

Securities and Exchange Commission

Since many Canadian companies sell their stocks and borrow money in the United States, they must meet the requirements of the **Securities and Exchange Commission (SEC)**. It is therefore appropriate to review the functions and operations of that body.

The overall purpose of the SEC, an agency of the U.S. federal government, is to assist in providing investors with reliable information upon which to make investment decisions. To this end, the Securities Act of 1933 requires most companies planning to issue new securities to the public to submit a registration statement to the SEC for approval. The Securities Exchange Act of 1934 provides additional protection by requiring the same companies and others to file detailed annual reports with the commission. The commission examines these statements for completeness and adequacy before permitting a company to sell its securities through the securities exchanges.

Although the SEC requires considerable information that is not of direct interest to CPAs, the securities acts of 1933 and 1934 require financial statements, accompanied by the opinion of an independent certified public accountant, as part of a registration statement. Specific reports, for example, interim financial information, changes in officers or directors, and certain related-party transactions also need to be filed.

Since large CPA firms usually have clients that must file one or more of these reports, and since the rules and regulations affecting filings with the SEC are extremely complex, most CPA firms have specialists who spend a large portion of their time making sure their clients satisfy all SEC requirements.

The SEC has considerable influence in setting generally accepted accounting principles and disclosure requirements for financial statements as a result of its authority for specifying reporting requirements considered necessary for fair disclosure to investors. The SEC has power to establish rules for any CPA associated with audited financial statements submitted to the commission. Even though the commission has taken the position that accounting principles and auditing standards should be set by the PCAOB or the profession, the SEC's attitude is generally considered in any major change proposed by the Auditing Standards Board or equivalent U.S. standard setting bodies.

The SEC requirements of greatest interest to CPAs are set forth in the commission's Regulation S-X and Accounting Series Releases, and Accounting and Auditing Enforcement Releases. These publications constitute important regulations, as well as decisions and opinions on accounting and auditing issues affecting any CPA dealing with publicly held companies.

concept check

C2-6 What are the different ways that quality control is established and enforced for public accounting firms in Canada?

C2-7 Why is it important that PAs have high-quality financial statement audits?

Summary

1. *How are public accounting firms organized?* Most accounting firms are set up as sole proprietorships or partnerships, although some are set up as limited liability partnerships.

   What are some of the largest public accounting firms? The six largest firms are Deloitte Touche Tohmatsu, KPMG International, PricewaterhouseCoopers, Ernst & Young, Grant Thornton, and BDO Dunwoody.

2. *What market forces ensure that audit and assurance engagements are completed to high standards of quality?* The biggest threat is that a public accounting firm will be forced out of business due to legal liability. Provincial securities commissions and the CPAB are now involved to ensure that the quality of audits is high. Completion of audits to high ethical standards helps maintain the positive image of auditors. The use of technology in auditing, just as information technology has been adopted by other businesses, helps ensure the effective and efficient completion of audits.

   Which organizations develop and maintain the standards that public accountants use? In Canada, public accounting standards are the responsibility of the CICA. The CICA develops standards in consultation with many organizations and groups: other accounting organizations in Canada, CPAB, securities and exchange commissions, international and other national standard-setting organizations, individual PAs, and the business community.

   How are these standards enforced? Quality control inspections called practice inspections are conducted by the professional associations, the provincial institutes/ *ordre*, and the CPAB.

3. *What is quality control, and how is it monitored?* Quality controls are methods used by a public accounting firm to ensure that it meets its professional responsibilities. Table 2-3 describes some of the characteristics of quality control. Public accounting firms are required to have a quality control manual and to monitor and enforce their quality procedures. Feedback from practice inspections, such as those of the CPAB, help monitor quality controls so that public accounting firms can engage in continuing improvement.

Visit the text's website at www.pearsoned.ca/arens for practice quizzes, additional case studies, and international standards information.

Review Questions

2-1 What are the advantages and disadvantages of practising as a large public accounting firm rather than a small one?

2-2 What major characteristics of the organization and conduct of public accounting firms permit them to fulfill their social functions competently and independently?

2-3 Research the rules in your province with respect to accounting firm structure. Are LLPs permitted? What is the primary difference between a public accounting firm organized as a partnership and an LLP? Why would a public accounting firm choose to organize as an LLP?

2-4 How can a PA use the internet to assist the PA practice?

2-5 Although the *CICA Handbook* standards provide general guidance, the application of these standards is dependent upon particular circumstances. In practice, a professional accountant may encounter situations where *CICA Handbook* standards do not exist or may not apply. Since there is no substitute for the exercise of professional judgment in the determination of what constitutes fair presentation and good practice, it has been suggested that too much effort is being directed toward the development of standards. Discuss the issues raised in the above statements. (Adapted from the CICA)

2-6 What benefits do organizations such as the CICA, CGAAC, and SMAC provide to their members?

2-7 What role does the *CICA Handbook* have in the professional activities of public accountants in Canada?

2-8 Distinguish between generally accepted auditing standards and generally accepted accounting principles, and give two examples of each.

2-9 Explain how an objective state of mind and due care contribute to a PA's qualifications to conduct a financial statement audit.

2-10 How did business failures by Enron and WorldCom affect quality control procedures for public accounting firms in Canada and the United States?

2-11 How has Sarbanes-Oxley affected the Canadian regulatory environment for PAs?

2-12 What is the role of the CPAB?

2-13 Describe the role of International Standards on Auditing. Discuss whether a PA who conducts an audit in accordance with generally accepted auditing standards simultaneously complies with international standards on auditing.

2-14 What is meant by the term "quality control" as it relates to a public accounting firm?

2-15 State what is meant by the term "practice inspection." What are the implications of the term for the public accounting profession?

Discussion Problems

2-16 For each of the following procedures that are taken from the quality control manual of a public accounting firm, identify the applicable element of quality control from Table 2-3 on page 37 and explain why the procedure is important for the audit engagement.

a. Appropriate accounting and auditing research requires adequate technical reference materials. Each firm professional has online password access through the firm's website to electronic reference materials on accounting, auditing, tax, and other technical information including industry data.

b. Each audit engagement of the firm is directed by a partner and, in most instances, a manager of the firm. On every engagement, an attempt is made to maintain continuity of at least a portion of the personnel.

c. Audit engagement team members enter their electronic signatures in the firm's engagement management software to indicate the completion of specific audit program steps. At the end of the audit engagement, the engagement management software will not allow archiving of the engagement file until all audit program steps have been electronically signed.

d. At all stages of any engagement, an effort is made to involve professional staff at appropriate levels in the accounting and auditing decisions. Various approvals of the manager or senior accountant are obtained throughout the audit.

e. No employee will have any direct or indirect financial interest, association, or relationship (for example, a close relative serving a client in a decision-making capacity)

not otherwise disclosed that might be adverse to the firm's best interest.

f. Each office of the firm shall be visited at least annually by review persons selected by the director of accounting and auditing. Procedures to be undertaken by the reviewers are illustrated by the office review program.

g. Existing clients of the firm are reviewed on a continuing basis by the engagement partner. Termination may result if circumstances indicate that there is reason to question the integrity of management or its independence, or if accounting and auditing differences of opinion cannot be reconciled. Doubts concerning whether the client-auditor relationship should be continued must be promptly discussed with the director of accounting and auditing.

h. Individual partners submit the nominations of those persons whom they wish to be considered for partner. To become a partner, an individual must have exhibited a high degree of technical competence; must possess integrity, motivation, and good judgment; and must have a desire to help the firm progress through the efficient dispatch of the job responsibilities to which he or she is assigned.

i. Through the continuing employee evaluation and counselling program and through the quality control review procedures as established by the firm, educational needs are reviewed and formal staff training programs modified to accommodate changing needs. At the conclusion of practice office reviews, apparent accounting and auditing deficiencies are summarized and reported to the firm's director of personnel.

2-17 A local PA, who has been in practice for several years, recently met with representatives of an internet service provider that is interested in developing a website for the PA's practice. The PA has been reluctant to develop an internet site but is willing to learn more about the types of information and resources that PAs often provide on their internet sites before making a final decision.

REQUIRED

a. Describe the types of resources and weblinks that PAs often provide on their websites.

b. State reasons why public accounting firms invest resources in creating sophisticated internet sites.

c. Discuss how the internet site can be a useful tool for a public accounting firm's accounting and auditing practice.

2-18 The following comments summarize the beliefs of some practitioners about quality control and practice inspection:

Quality control and practice inspection are quasi-governmental methods of regulating the profession. There are two effects of such regulation. First, it gives a competitive advantage to national public accounting firms because they already need formal structures to administer their complex organizations. Quality control requirements do not significantly affect their structure. Smaller firms now need a more costly organizational structure, which has proven unnecessary because of existing partner involvement on engagements. The major advantage smaller public accounting firms have traditionally had is a simple and efficient organizational structure. Now that advantage has been eliminated because of quality control requirements. Second, quality control and practice inspection are not needed to regulate the profession. Elements of quality control have always existed, at least informally, for quality firms. Three things already provide sufficient assurance that informal quality control elements are followed without practice inspection. They are competitive pressures to do quality work, legal liability for inadequate performance, and a code of professional ethics requiring that PAs follow generally accepted auditing standards.

REQUIRED
a. State the pros and cons of these comments.
b. Evaluate whether control requirements and practice inspection are worth their cost.

Professional Judgment Problem

2-19 The Mobile Home Manufacturing Company is audited by the public accounting firm Rossi and Montgomery. Mobile Home has decided to issue stock to the public and wants Rossi and Montgomery to perform all the audit work necessary to satisfy the requirements for filing with the OSC. The public accounting firm has never had a client go public before.

REQUIRED
a. What are the implications of Rossi and Montgomery accepting the engagement?
b. List the additional issues confronting the auditors when they file with the OSC as compared with dealing with a regular audit client.

Case

2-20 Raymonde, the owner of a small company, asked Holmes, a public accountant, to conduct an audit of the company's records. Raymonde told Holmes that an audit is to be completed in time to submit audited financial statements to a bank as part of a loan application. Holmes immediately accepted the engagement and agreed to provide an auditor's report within three weeks. Raymonde agreed to pay Holmes a fixed fee plus a bonus if the loan was granted.

Holmes hired two accounting students to conduct the audit and spent several hours telling them exactly what to do. Holmes told the students not to spend time reviewing the controls but instead to concentrate on proving the mathematical accuracy of the ledger accounts and summarizing the data in the accounting records that supported Raymonde's financial statements. The students followed Holmes' instructions and after two weeks gave Holmes the financial statements, which did not include footnotes. Holmes reviewed the statements and prepared an unqualified auditor's report. The report did not refer to generally accepted accounting principles.

REQUIRED
Briefly describe each of the generally accepted auditing standards and indicate how the actions of Holmes resulted in a failure to comply with each standard. Organize your answer as follows: Brief Description of GAAS; Holmes' Actions Resulting in Failure to Comply with GAAS.

(Adapted from AICPA)

Ongoing Small Business Case: Planning for CondoCleaners.com

2-21 As a professional in the practice of giving advice, Jim knew when he had to ask questions, too. He called a lawyer friend of the family who owned a cleaning business at the other end of the country and was suitably cautioned, "It's very competitive, and you don't make much money. You'll have to succeed on volume. You're an accountant—crunch some numbers on what you expect!" Jim also talked to his family and peers at work, finding out that people who used cleaning services were primarily working couples or the elderly. Finally, he used the services of a local university marketing class to do some market research for him. This was totally new for Jim—as an experienced auditor, how could his skills help him in running a cleaning business?

REQUIRED
How is running an accounting business similar to running a cleaning business?

3

Professional relationships: The role of ethics and independence

The public accountant (PA) is a professional who works with the audit committee, board of directors, management, and other professionals such as lawyers. In addition to providing a high quality of work, the PA is expected to be free from bias and to behave in an ethical manner. In this chapter, we will look at some of the issues and rules affecting the professional accountant's behaviours in relationship with others.

Rules of professional conduct are regularly updated by all accounting professions, and qualified accountants are expected to abide by these rules whether they work in public accounting, in industry, in education, or in the not-for-profit sector. As a potential PA, it is important that you understand how these rules govern your relationships with your fellow members and potential clients. If you will be working as a management accountant, specialist, or internal or government auditor, you will still be bound by the rules of the professional accounting organizations you are a member of. Some of those rules are discussed in this chapter.

STANDARDS REFERENCED IN THIS CHAPTER

CICA Standards

CAS 220 – Quality control for an audit of financial statements (previously Section 5030 – Quality control procedures for assurance engagements)

CSQC-1 – Quality control for firms that perform audits and reviews of financial statements and other assurance engagements (previously Introduction and GSF-QC – General standards of quality control for firms performing assurance engagements)

LEARNING OBJECTIVES

1 Describe ethics and their relevance. Acquire tools to work through an ethical conflict (known as an ethical dilemma).

2 Explain how PAs are different from other professionals. Examine the role of a code of professional conduct in encouraging public accountant ethical behaviour.

3 Analyze the threats to independence. Discuss how the auditor's relationship with the audit committee affects independence. Identify some of the key rules of professional conduct and how are they enforced.

WorldCom Illustrates Auditor Responsibility

"Oh my!" Gene Morse was stunned. He stared at the computer screen in his cubicle, unable to believe that he had found an unsupported entry for $500 million in computer acquisitions. He immediately took his discovery to his superior Cynthia Cooper, vice-president for internal audit at WorldCom. "Keep going," directed Cooper. Her team of internal auditors kept digging. As they pursued the trail of fraud, the internal audit department was obstructed at every turn. Senior management greeted them with hostility, told them to delay their audit, and even had the information systems group restrict their access to information.

Yet the auditors were able to obtain evidence that the company had recorded billions of dollars of regular fees paid to local telephone companies as capital assets. This accounting trick allowed the company to turn a $662 million loss into a $2.4 billion profit in 2001. In June 2005, the company announced that it had inflated assets by $3.8 billion, the largest accounting fraud in history.

IMPORTANCE TO AUDITORS

Major frauds often begin at the top, and such was the case at WorldCom. Bernie Ebbers, WorldCom's founder and CEO, had told Cooper not to use the term "internal controls," claiming that he did not understand it. However, Cooper fought for more respect and more resources for the internal audit department. It was Cooper's right to contact and work directly with the audit committee as well as the courage and ethics of the internal audit department that allowed the fraud to be revealed. The right to report to the audit committee should be part of internal auditors' charter.

WHAT DO YOU THINK? (?)

1. How do poor attitudes toward internal controls contribute to mismanagement and fraud?
2. How does access to the audit committee help the PA conduct an effective financial statement audit?
3. Should other accountants and employees within the organization have access to the audit committee for reporting control or operational violations?

Sources: Adapted from 1. Carozza, Dick, "An interview with Cynthia Cooper," *Fraud Magazine,* March/April 2008. 2. Cooper, Cynthia, "A dark cloud descending," *Fraud Magazine,* March/April 2008. 3. Ripley, Amanda, "The night detective," *Time,* December 30, 2002. 4. Pulliam, Susan and Deborah Solomon, "Uncooking the books: How three unlikely sleuths discovered fraud at WorldCom," *The Wall Street Journal,* October 20, 2002, p. A1.

continued >

HOW do you feel when someone disagrees with you? Are you able to sit back and discuss things reasonably? Have you ever prepared a tax return and included figures that were unsubstantiated? This would be against the rules of professional conduct. Do you believe there are "grey" areas of behaviour—where you are uncertain how you might behave in a given circumstance? Now is a good time to decide what you think is ethical and what is not.

In the previous chapter, we discussed the nature of auditing and the demand for audit and other assurance services. The value of the audit report and the demand for audit services depend on public confidence in the independence and integrity of PAs as they conduct their work. This chapter discusses ethics and independence and other ethical requirements for qualified accountants under professional rules of conduct. We will provide some comparison of IIA rules, which will be described further in Chapter 24.

① Ethical Behaviour is a Cornerstone of Trust

What Are Ethics?

Ethics can be defined broadly as a set of moral principles or values. Each of us has such a set of values, although we may or may not have considered them explicitly. Philosophers, religious organizations, and other groups have defined, in various ways, ideal sets of moral principles or values. Examples of prescribed sets of moral principles or values at the implementation level include laws and regulations, church doctrines, codes of business ethics for professional groups such as CAs, CGAs, and CMAs, and codes of conduct within individual organizations such as accounting firms, corporations, and universities.

> **Ethics**—a set of moral principles or values.

An example of ethical principles is included in Table 3-1 on the next page. These principles were developed by combining principles from the Josephson Institute of Ethics (a non-profit organization focused on ethical quality) with ethical standards published by both an international coaching organization and a technical journal. A search of the internet will reveal thousands of sites with published ethical standards.

It is common for people to differ in their moral principles or values and the relative importance they attach to these principles. These differences reflect life experiences, successes and failures, and the influences of parents, teachers, religious organizations, and friends.

NEED FOR ETHICS Ethical behaviour is necessary for a society to function in an orderly manner. It can be argued that ethics is the glue that holds a society together. Imagine, for example, what would happen if we could not depend on the people we deal with to be honest. If parents, teachers, employers, siblings, co-workers, and friends all consistently lied, it would be almost impossible for effective communication to occur.

The need for ethics in society is sufficiently important that many commonly held ethical values are incorporated into laws. However, many of the ethical values found

<table>
<tr><td colspan="2">**Table 3-1**   Illustrative Ethical Principles</td></tr>
<tr><td colspan="2">The following list of ethical principles incorporates characteristics and values that many people and organizations associate with ethical behaviour.</td></tr>
<tr><td>Trustworthiness</td><td>Be honest and reliable. Honour your agreements or promises, and do not intentionally mislead others. Be reliable—do your best to fulfill your commitments. Declare conflicts of interest. Act promptly to disclose hazards.</td></tr>
<tr><td>Respect</td><td>Be civil, courteous, and accepting of others, understanding the many differences that exist among people. Be unbiased in your decision making.</td></tr>
<tr><td>Responsibility</td><td>Be accountable for your own actions and aware of the actions of those you are supervising. Keep confidential information confidential. Use resources wisely and economically. Do not use the work of others without declaring the source. Identify your own competence levels and act within that competence.</td></tr>
<tr><td>Fairness</td><td>Judge actions and individuals on their merits, considering the equality of individuals and with regard for due process and transparency.</td></tr>
<tr><td>Caring</td><td>Act out of a positive intention to do no harm or to minimize harm. Be concerned for others, showing benevolence when it is within your ability to do so.</td></tr>
<tr><td>Citizenship</td><td>Obey laws, and assist others in obeying laws, including the reporting of offenders. Help your society function by participating in voting, volunteer work, and the conservation of resources.</td></tr>
</table>

Sources: 1. ASME Technical Journals, www.asme.org, Accessed: January 6, 2005. 2. International Coach Federation, www.coachfederation.org, Accessed: January 6, 2005. 3. The Josephson Institute, www.josephsoninstitute.org, Accessed: January 6, 2005.

in Table 3-1 cannot be incorporated into laws because of the judgmental nature of certain values. This does not imply, though, that the principles are less important for an orderly society.

WHY PEOPLE ACT UNETHICALLY Most people define unethical behaviour as conduct that differs from what they believe would have been appropriate given the circumstances. Each of us decides what constitutes ethical behaviour. It is important to understand what causes people to act in a manner that we decide is unethical.

There are two primary reasons why people act unethically: the person's ethical standards are different from those of society as a whole, or the person chooses to act selfishly. In many instances, both reasons exist.

The Person's Ethical Standards Differ from General Society's Extreme examples of people whose behaviour violates almost everyone's ethical standards are drug dealers, bank robbers, and larcenists. Most such people feel no remorse when they are apprehended because their ethical standards differ from those of society as a whole.

Many far less extreme examples exist where others violate our ethical values. When people cheat on their tax returns, treat other people with hostility, lie on employment applications, or perform below their competence levels as employees, most of us regard that as unethical behaviour. If the other person has decided that this behaviour is ethical and acceptable, there is a conflict of ethical values that is unlikely to be resolved.

The Person Chooses to Act Selfishly The difference between ethical standards that differ from general society's and acting selfishly is illustrated in the following example: Person A finds a briefcase in an airport containing important papers and $1,000. He tosses the briefcase and keeps the money. He brags to his family and friends about his good fortune. Person A's values probably differ from most of society's. Person B faces the same situation but responds differently. He keeps the money but leaves the briefcase in a conspicuous place. He tells nobody and spends the money on a new wardrobe. It is likely that Person B has violated his own ethical standards, but he has decided that the money was too important to pass up. He has chosen to act selfishly. What would you do? Shouldn't the briefcase and its entire contents be returned? Consider Person C who returns the entire briefcase and gets a reward of $500.

This example shows that unethical behaviour often results from selfish behaviour. Political scandals result from the desire for political power; cheating on tax returns and expense reports is motivated by financial greed; performing below one's competence and cheating on tests are typically due to laziness. In each case, the person knows that the behaviour is inappropriate but chooses to do it anyway because of the personal sacrifice needed to act ethically.

An **ethical dilemma** is a situation a person faces in which a decision must be made about appropriate behaviour. A simple example of an ethical dilemma is finding a diamond ring, which necessitates deciding whether to attempt to find the owner or to keep it. A far more difficult ethical dilemma to resolve is the following one; it is the type of case that might be used in an ethics course:

Qin Zhang is the senior auditor in-charge of the September 30, 2009, financial statement audit of Paquette Forest Products Inc., a forest products company that produces lumber and paper products in northern Manitoba. The company employs 375 people and is the main employer in the remote town of Duck Lake, Manitoba; the other businesses in Duck Lake provide goods and services to Paquette Forest Products and its employees. In the course of the audit, Qin discovers that the company has had a number of failures of the equipment that removes the sulphuric acid from the paper production process, and as a result, thousands of litres of untreated water have been dumped into the Loon River and Duck Lake. Qin learns that the cost of replacing the equipment so that no further spills are likely is much more than the company can afford and that if ordered to replace the equipment by the environment ministry, the company would be forced to cease operations. What should Qin do?

Auditors, accountants, and other business people face many ethical dilemmas in their business careers. Dealing with a client who threatens to seek a new auditor unless an unqualified opinion is issued presents a serious ethical dilemma if an unqualified opinion is inappropriate. Deciding whether to confront a supervisor who has materially overstated departmental revenues as a means of receiving a larger bonus is a difficult ethical dilemma. Continuing to be a part of the management of a company that harasses and mistreats employees or treats customers dishonestly is an ethical dilemma, especially if the person has a family to support and the job market is tight. Deciding whether or not to report the negligence of a supervisor to a partner is a problem young staff accountants may face.

RATIONALIZING UNETHICAL BEHAVIOUR There are alternative ways to resolve ethical dilemmas, but care must be taken to avoid methods that are rationalizations of unethical behaviour. The following are commonly employed rationalization methods that can easily result in unethical conduct:

1. *Everybody does it.* The argument that it is acceptable to falsify tax returns, cheat on exams, or sell defective products is commonly based on the rationalization that everyone else is doing it and therefore it is acceptable.
2. *If it's legal, it's ethical.* Using the argument that all legal behaviour is ethical relies heavily on the perfection of laws. Under this philosophy, one would have no obligation to return a lost object to its owner unless the other person could prove that it was his or hers.
3. *Likelihood of discovery and consequences.* This philosophy relies on evaluating the likelihood that someone else will discover the behaviour. Typically, the person also assesses the severity of the penalty (consequences) if there is a discovery. An example is deciding whether to correct an unintentional overbilling to a customer when the customer has already paid the full billing. If the seller believes the customer will detect the error and respond by not buying in the future, the seller will inform the customer now; otherwise the seller will wait to see if the customer complains.

Auditing Courses Reflect Real-World Problems

How would you feel? I was sitting down to mark my introductory auditing assignments, where students were asked to compare current *CICA Handbook* standards to exposure drafts and international standards. After about four assignments, I read something familiar, and sure enough, the student had copied material without quoting or referencing the source. After another three assignments, it happened again, then again, and again. Out of a total of close to 60 students in two classes, close to 20 had plagiarized—copied material into their assignments without stating the source—even after being warned in writing and verbally in class not do so.

After discussion with the university's Undergraduate Program Director and the Academic Council Office (which is responsible for academic honesty issues), I decided to spend time in the class explaining to students how academic honesty issues are prosecuted. I was given approval to give the students the choice of either following the normal process or of doing additional work: attending a seminar on plagiarism, completing an essay and an online tutorial on plagiarism, and redoing their assignment properly.

I also initiated an active discussion with students about how to prevent plagiarism in their group assignments and how this lesson about plagiarism could be used in the future. Students should be accurate about their written and verbal representations, such as assignments and resumes, as well as when they write up audit working papers. My own opinion is that if students plagiarize in class and cannot follow academic honesty policies here, then they will likely not follow rules of conduct when they are working. As students, you need to understand that the penalties in an academic environment are far less severe than they would be in the "business world."

From I. Splettstoesser-Hogeterp

CRITICAL THINKING QUESTIONS

1. How does this incidence of classroom plagiarism serve as a lesson for auditing practice for accounting students?
2. As a future practitioner, now a student, how can you contribute to an improved ethical environment in the classroom?
3. Research the actions that your school takes to prosecute plagiarism and discuss this with your classmates.

RESOLVING ETHICAL DILEMMAS In recent years, formal frameworks have been developed to help people resolve ethical dilemmas. The purpose of such frameworks is to help a person identify the ethical issues and decide on an appropriate course of action based on the person's own values. The six-step approach that follows is intended to be a relatively simple approach to resolving ethical dilemmas:

1. Obtain the relevant facts.
2. Identify the ethical issues from the facts.
3. Determine who is affected by the outcome of the dilemma and how each person or group is affected.
4. Identify the alternatives available to the person who must resolve the dilemma.
5. Identify the likely consequence of each alternative.
6. Decide on the appropriate action.

An illustration is used to demonstrate how a person might use this six-step approach to resolve an ethical dilemma.

ETHICAL DILEMMA Bryanx Longview has been working for six months as a staff assistant for De Souza & Shah, public accountants. Currently he is assigned to the audit of Reyon Manufacturing Corp. under the supervision of Karen Van Staveren, an experienced audit senior. There are three auditors assigned to the audit, including Karen, Bryan, and a more experienced assistant, Martha Mills. During lunch on the first day, Karen says, "It will be necessary for us to work a few extra hours on our own time to make sure we come in on budget. This audit isn't very profitable anyway, and we don't want to hurt our firm by going over budget. We can accomplish this easily by coming in a half hour early, taking a short lunch break, and working an hour or so after normal quitting time. We just won't write that time down on our time report." Bryan recalls reading in the firm's policy manual that working extra hours and not charging for them on the time report is a violation of De Souza & Shah's employment policy. He also knows that seniors are paid bonuses instead of overtime, whereas staff are paid for overtime but get no bonuses. Later, when Bryan discusses the issue with Martha, she says, "Karen does this on all of her jobs. She is likely to be our firm's next audit manager. The partners think she's great because her jobs always come in under budget. She rewards us by giving us good engagement evaluations, especially under the cooperative attitude category. Several of the other audit seniors follow the same practice."

Resolving the Ethical Dilemma Using the Six-Step Approach

RELEVANT FACTS There are three key facts in this situation that deal with the ethical issue and how the issue will likely be resolved:

- The staff person has been informed that he will work additional hours without recording them.
- Firm policy prohibits this practice.
- Another staff person has stated that this practice is common practice for Karen and also for other seniors in the firm.

Ethical Issue The ethical issue in this situation is not difficult to identify.

- Is it ethical in this situation for Bryan to work additional hours and not record them?

Who is affected, and how is each affected? There are typically more people affected in situations where ethical dilemmas occur than might be expected. Table 3-2 on the next page describes the key persons involved in this situation.

Consequences of Each Alternative In deciding the consequences of each alternative, it is essential to evaluate both short- and long-term effects. There is a natural tendency to emphasize the short term because those consequences will occur quickly, even when the long-term consequences may be more important. For example, consider the potential consequences if Bryan decides to work the additional hours and not report them. In the short term, he will likely get good evaluations for cooperation and perhaps a salary increase. In the longer term, when other ethical conflicts arise, what will be the effect of not reporting the hours this time? Consider the following similar ethical dilemmas Bryan might face as he advances in his career:

- An audit firm supervisor asks Bryan to work three unreported hours daily and 15 each weekend.
- An audit firm supervisor asks Bryan to initial certain audit procedures as having been performed when they were not.
- Bryan concludes that he cannot be promoted to manager unless he persuades assistants to work hours that they do not record.
- Management of a client informs Bryan, who is now a partner, that either the company gets an unqualified opinion for a $40,000 audit fee or the company will change auditors.
- Management of a client informs Bryan that the audit fee will be increased by $25,000 if Bryan can find a plausible way to show an increase in earnings by $1 million.

Note how each dilemma is more serious than the one preceding it; the penalties that Bryan would face if he were caught grow more severe as the dilemmas grow more serious. In short, if Bryan agrees to work the additional hours and not report them, he has put himself on a slippery slope that becomes ever steeper.

Appropriate Action Only Bryan can determine the appropriate option to select in the circumstances after considering his ethical values and the likely consequences of each option. The attitudes of audit management (partners, managers, and supervisors) can support audit staff to come forward with standards problems, just as the "tone at the top" of corporations helps management prevent errors and fraud. At one extreme, Bryan could decide that the only relevant consequence is the potential

Table 3-2	Persons Involved in Bryan's Ethical Dilemma
Who	**How Affected**
Bryan	Being asked to violate firm policy. Hours of work will be affected. Pay will be affected. Performance evaluations may be affected. Attitude about firm may be affected.
Martha	Same as Bryan.
Karen	Success on engagement and in firm may be affected. Hours of work will be affected. Bonus will be affected.
De Souza & Shah	Stated firm policy is being violated. May result in underbilling clients in current and future engagements. May affect firm's ability to realistically budget engagements and bill clients, thus violating quality control procedures as specified in auditing standards. May affect the firm's ability to motivate and retain employees. Could result in the firm's being sued for not following labour laws with respect to payment for overtime.
Audit staff assigned to Reyon Manufacturing Corp. in the future	May result in unrealistic time budgets. May result in unfavourable time performance evaluations. May result in pressures to continue practice of not charging for hours worked.
Other staff in De Souza & Shah	Following the practice on this engagement may motivate others to follow the same practice on other engagements, resulting in a poor ethical climate at the firm.
Bryan's available alternatives	• Refuse to work the additional hours. • Perform in the manner requested. • Inform Karen that he will work the additional hours and will charge the additional hours to the engagement. • Talk to a manager or partner about Karen's request. • Contact the designated whistle-blowing partner. • Refuse to work on the engagement. • Quit working for the firm. Each of these options includes a potential consequence, the worst one likely being termination by the firm.

auditing in action 3-1
Helping Out the Whistle-Blower

Poor Bryan—in our ethical dilemma example, he is stuck in a quagmire of individuals who are not following his firm's policies. There is help in professional standards, though. Quality control standards explain how situations of non-compliance with the firm's system of quality control should be handled to avoid reprisals.

Recording time worked accurately is a firm policy that directly affects the quality of planning for an engagement, which would affect the ability of the firm to conduct a high-quality audit. Employees need a risk-free way to report peer pressure or other forms of violations such as field work disputes. This could be accomplished by having a designated standards partner available for anonymous discussion or having a toll-free number or third-party organization to handle the complaints and then notify the appropriate individuals in the organization for action.

The firm needs to establish a protocol, provide clear, risk-free reporting mechanisms, and have an oversight group or individual track and resolve items reported. The oversight group needs to have sufficient authority to query and resolve items that are brought to its attention. For example, with prompt action, Bryan's partner on this engagement could be asked to visit the client at 5:30 p.m. and remind Karen that the firm is taking a solid stand on its time recording policies given its current quality control standards.

Sources: 1. Murdock, Hernan, "Early warning system," *Internal Auditor*, August 2003, p. 57–61. 2. Moulton, Gary, "Safe disclosure," *CAmagazine*, October 2003, p. 20–27.

New Canadian audit standards CAS 220, Quality control for an audit of financial statements, and CSQC-1, Quality control for firms that perform audits and reviews of financial statements and other assurance engagements have additional requirements. The engagement partner is expected to monitor engagements for compliance with firm policies and procedures, checking for procedures to enable compliance and looking for potential non-compliance. The firm should also provide training, communicate policies to employees, check for non-compliance, and take remedial action when non-compliance is discovered.

impact on his career. Most of us would conclude that Bryan would be an unethical person if he followed that course. At the other extreme, Bryan can decide to refuse to work for a firm that permits even one supervisor to violate firm policies. Talking to a designated standards partner or manager who helps deter such inappropriate practices by reporting to the partners involved would help both Bryan and the firm in improving both employee morale and the quality of firm work.

concept check

C3-1 What are the six ethical principles that many people and organizations associate with ethical behaviour?

C3-2 Describe an ethical dilemma. How does a person resolve an ethical dilemma?

❷ Professional Ethics and Principles of Conduct

Special Need for Ethical Conduct in Professions

Our society has attached a special meaning to the term "professional." A professional is expected to conduct himself or herself at a higher level than most other members of society. For example, when the press reports that a physician, clergyperson, member of Parliament, CA, CGA, or CMA has been indicted for a crime, most people feel more disappointment than when the same thing happens with people who are not labelled as professionals.

The term "professional" carries a responsibility for conduct that extends beyond satisfying the person's responsibilities to himself or herself and beyond the requirements of our society's laws and regulations. This responsibility is to the public, to the client, and to fellow practitioners and includes honourable behaviour even if that means personal sacrifice. A CA, CGA, or CMA in public practice is a professional who carries that responsibility.

The underlying reason for a high level of professional conduct by any profession is the need for public confidence in the quality of service by the profession, regardless of the individual providing it. For the professional PA, it is essential that the client and external financial statement users have confidence in the quality of audits and other services. If users of services do not have confidence in physicians, judges, or PA, the ability of those professionals to serve clients and the public effectively is diminished.

It is not practical for users to evaluate the performance of professional services because of their complexity. A patient cannot be expected to evaluate whether an operation was properly performed. A financial statement user cannot be expected to evaluate audit performance. Most users have neither the competence nor the time for such an evaluation. Public confidence in the quality of professional services is enhanced when the profession encourages high standards of performance and conduct on the part of all practitioners.

Increased competition sometimes makes public accounting firms more concerned about keeping clients and maintaining a reasonable profit. Because of the increased competition, many public accounting firms have implemented philosophies and practices that are frequently referred to as "improved business practices." These include such things as improved recruiting and personnel practices, better audit quality control practices, effective office management, and tailored advertising and other promotional methods. Public accounting firms are also attempting to become more efficient in doing audits in a variety of ways, for example, through the use of computers, effective audit planning, and careful assignment of staff.

New standards for obtaining and renewing PA licences in many provinces (such as a minimum number of annual hours in provision of assurance services) mean that detailed engagement record keeping is crucial. For those accounting students who do not want to work in public practice, other types of work experience in industry are now possible.

DIFFERENCE BETWEEN PUBLIC ACCOUNTING FIRMS AND OTHER PROFESSIONALS
Public accounting firms have a different relationship with users of financial statements than most other professionals have with the users of their services. Lawyers, for example, are typically engaged and paid by a client and have the primary responsibility to be an advocate for that client. Public accounting firms are engaged by management for private companies and the audit committee for public companies and are paid by the company issuing the financial statements, but the primary beneficiaries of the audit are statement users. Often, the auditor does not know or have contact with the statement users but has frequent meetings and ongoing relationships with client personnel.

It is essential that users regard such public accounting firms as competent and unbiased. If users were to believe that such public accounting firms do not perform the valuable service of reducing information risk, the value of and demand for those firms' audit and other attestation reports would be reduced. This provides incentives for public accounting firms to conduct themselves at a high professional level.

Ways Professional Accountants in Public Practice Are Encouraged to Conduct Themselves Professionally

There are several ways in which society and the public accounting professions encourage those in public practice to conduct themselves appropriately and to do high-quality audits and related services. Figure 3-1 shows the most important ways. Several of these were discussed in Chapter 2, including GAAS requirements, the Recommendations of the *CICA Handbook*, professional examinations, quality control,

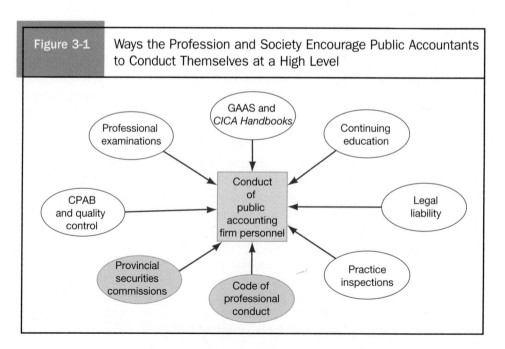

| Figure 3-1 | Ways the Profession and Society Encourage Public Accountants to Conduct Themselves at a High Level |

Table 3-3	For Whom the Bell Tolls

Examples of Sanctions That Can Be Imposed Against PAs or Firms When Standards Are Violated
Publication of the name(s) of the violator(s) and the nature of the convicted offence
Sanctions from regulatory bodies such as the CPAB, OSC, or the SEC (e.g., refusal to accept new publicly listed clients for a period of time)
Refusal to renew PA licences for individuals or firms (with the CPAB)
Increased frequency of peer review
Appointment of an external monitor
Fines and/or payment of costs such as legal fees
Requirements to change quality control procedures
Mandatory education
Suspension of designation (e.g., CA, CGA, or CMA) or expulsion from the professional association

the CPAB and provincial securities commissions, practice inspection, and continuing education. The ability of individuals to sue public accounting firms also exerts considerable influence on the way practitioners conduct themselves and audits. Legal liability is studied in Chapter 4.

The code of professional conduct of the PA's respective accounting body also has a significant influence on the practitioner. It is meant to provide a standard of conduct for members of that body. When professionals do not adhere to the standards of their profession, they are subject to a variety of potential sanctions. Table 3-3 explains that many of these are related to public release of information about the actions of the accountant, which is why the table is called "For Whom the Bell Tolls."

Code of Professional Conduct

A code of conduct can consist of general statements of ideal conduct or specific rules that define unacceptable behaviour. The advantage of general statements is the emphasis on positive activities that encourage a high level of performance. The disadvantage is the difficulty of enforcing general ideals because there are no minimum standards of behaviour. The advantage of carefully defined specific rules is the enforceability of minimum behaviour and performance standards. The disadvantage is the tendency of some practitioners to define the rules as maximum rather than minimum standards. A second disadvantage is that some practitioners may view the code as the law and conclude that if some action is not prohibited, it must be ethical. A practitioner must consider the intent of the code in addressing whether a particular action is acceptable or not.

A professional code of conduct serves both the members of the body promulgating the code and the public. It serves members by setting standards the members must meet and providing a benchmark against which the members will be measured by their peers. The public is served because the code provides a list of standards that the members of the body should follow and helps determine expectations of members' behaviours. Yet such a code will be followed only in an organization with the appropriate organizational culture, as explained in Auditing in Action 3-2 on the next page.

At present, most PAs in Canada are either CAs or CGAs. The provincial institutes and Quebec *ordre* of chartered accountants determine the rules of professional

Research on Commitment Helps Explain Violations

Can you do the audit of an organization that you are marketing with? As explained in the next section, this could be a self-interest threat, because your own financial results are linked with those of the organization. One of the top international accounting firms was barred from accepting new SEC clients for six months as it both audited PeopleSoft Inc. as well as marketed and installed the software. The firm maintained that it was not violating the rules, yet this clearly violated the appearance of objectivity of the firm.

Tyler, Dienhart, and Thomas talked about the 'command and control' versus the 'values and integrity' approach to ethical compliance. In a values and integrity model, employees are encouraged to comply with ethical processes because they understand the goals of the processes, and they believe that they are fair. This encourages employees to come forward with what they believe are ethical violations. In the command and control model, as advocated by strict rules, employees are less likely to comply with rules and may not come forward with potential violations.

The most important finding discussed in Tyler et al.'s article was the fact that organizational culture is the most important variable in ethical compliance—more important than the type of ethical compliance program. This means that organizations that are focused on profits to the exclusion of anything else send the message to employees that ethics do not matter. Perhaps something like this happened at the accounting firm involved—the profits from software sales and installation were considered more important than independence.

Sources: 1. Morris, Floyd, "Big auditing firm gets 6-month ban on new business," *The New York Times*, April 17, 2004, www.nytimes.com/2004/04/17/business/17ERNS. html, Accessed: September 14, 2008. 2. Tyler, Tom, John Dienhart, and Terry Thomas, "The ethical commitment to compliance: Building value-based cultures," *California Management Review*, 50(2), Winter 2008, p. 21-51.

conduct for members and students of that provincial institute or *ordre*. The provincial institutes and *ordre* have harmonized their rules of professional conduct so that, generally, the same set of rules applies to all CAs in Canada. Certain rules (e.g., confidentiality, which is discussed below) apply to students as well as to members. All of the rules apply to members in public practice, while a smaller number also apply to members who are not engaged in the practice of public accounting.

The rules of conduct for certified general accountants are determined by the CGAAC and apply to all CGAs and CGA students in Canada; the provincial associations are charged with administering the code and have the power to amend and add to this national code of conduct. The principles and rules of conduct apply to all members, although certain rules are specific to public practitioners. We will restrict the remainder of our discussion to rules of conduct of British Columbia CGAs and Ontario CAs (as examples of provincial rules of conduct).

Generally the codes of conduct have attempted to accomplish both the objectives of general statements of ideal conduct and of specific rules. For example, the Rules of Professional Conduct of the Institute of Chartered Accountants of Ontario (ICAO) have principles that are stated in broad terms, the rules themselves, and additional guidance on the rules, called "interpretations." The ICAO, the Certified General Accountants Association of British Columbia (CGA-BC), and other organizations such as the IIA, provide discussions of current issues and examples of how to deal with particular ethical issues through regular newsletters sent to members. Figure 3-2 is illustrative of this. The structure is listed in order of increasing specificity: The principles provide ideal standards of conduct, whereas rules of conduct are more specific, and the interpretations or examples are very specific.

PRINCIPLES OF PROFESSIONAL CONDUCT The principles generally are characteristics that the professional body deems desirable in its members. An organization is judged by the behaviour of its members; therefore, one principle would be that members behave in a way that enhances the reputation of all the members. Members should act ethically and in a way that will serve the public interest. For example, CGA-BC at **www.cga-bc.org** talks about "safeguarding and advancing the interests of society," while the ICAO at **www.icao.on.ca** talks about "conduct[ing] . . . in a manner

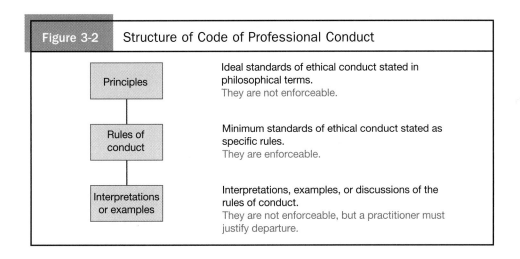

Figure 3-2 Structure of Code of Professional Conduct

Principles	Ideal standards of ethical conduct stated in philosophical terms. They are not enforceable.
Rules of conduct	Minimum standards of ethical conduct stated as specific rules. They are enforceable.
Interpretations or examples	Interpretations, examples, or discussions of the rules of conduct. They are not enforceable, but a practitioner must justify departure.

which . . . serve[s] the public interest." Both CGAs and CAs are also told that they should not use confidential information for their own benefit and to avoid, and where unavoidable to disclose, conflicts of interest. When the courts discipline or convict a member of a profession, the profession's reputation suffers along with that of the member. It is a mistake to think that only the member loses his or her reputation in such a situation.

Other common principles are that members act with integrity and due care in the performance of their professional activities; that they maintain (i.e., keep current) their professional competence; that they do not undertake work for which they lack the necessary competence; and that they behave in a professional way toward colleagues. The accountant must maintain confidentiality with respect to the affairs and business of the client. There is one principle that relates more specifically to PAs: The accountant should ensure that he or she maintains an independent or objective state of mind when providing assurance services (e.g., audits or reviews) for clients.

A careful examination of these ethical principles will indicate that most are applicable to any professional, not just professional accountants. For example, physicians should behave in a way that is not discreditable to their profession; they should act ethically and in a way that serves the public interest; and they should exercise integrity and due care. Physicians should maintain their professional competence and behave in a professional way toward their colleagues. They should not breach their clients' confidentiality. One difference between auditors and other professionals, as discussed earlier, is that most professionals need not be concerned about maintaining independence.

These principles will be explored more fully in the remainder of this chapter.

EXAMPLES OF RULES OF CONDUCT The discussion that follows will consider some of the more important rules of conduct followed by PAs in Canada. A student interested in obtaining a particular professional designation (e.g., CA, CGA, or CMA) should refer to and become familiar with the specific rules of conduct of the provincial and national body to which he or she seeks admission.

As was mentioned previously, while all the rules discussed below apply to members of the professional accounting bodies in public practice, some of the rules discussed do not apply to members who are not engaged in the practice of public accounting.

Figure 3-2 indicated that while principles may not be enforceable, the rules of conduct are. For that reason, the rules of conduct of the accounting bodies are stated in more precise language than the principles can be. Because of their enforceability, the rules are often called Rules or Code of Professional Conduct.

At what level do practitioners conduct themselves in practice? As in any profession, the level varies among practitioners. Some operate at high levels, whereas others operate as close to the minimum level as possible. Unfortunately, some also conduct themselves below the minimum level set by the profession and are subject to disciplinary action.

APPLICABILITY OF THE RULES OF CONDUCT The rules of conduct for CAs and CGAs specifically state that while the rules are for all CAs and CGAs, respectively, certain rules, because of their nature, may apply only to members who are in public practice.

It would be a violation of the rules if someone did something on behalf of a member that would have been a violation if the member had done it. An example is a banker who states in a newsletter that Johnson and Able, public accountants, have the best tax department in the province and consistently get large refunds for their tax clients. This is likely to create false or unjustified expectations and is a violation of both the CA and CGA rules of conduct.

A member is also responsible for compliance with the rules by employees and partners.

DEFINITIONS A few definitions must be understood to minimize misinterpretation of the rules to be discussed shortly.

- Client—the person(s) or entity that retains a member or his or her firm, engaged in the practice of public accounting, for the performance of professional services.
- Firm—a proprietorship or partnership engaged in the practice of public accounting, including individual partners thereof.
- Member—a member of the Canadian Institute of Chartered Accountants (and a provincial institute or *ordre*) or of the Certified General Accountants Association of Canada (and a provincial association) or of the Society of Management Accountants of Canada (and a provincial association).
- Practice of public accounting—representing oneself as a PA and at the same time performing for a client one or more types of services rendered by PAs.

SUMMARY OF THE BASIC COMPONENTS OF A CODE OF CONDUCT The intent of the next section is to discuss several rules of conduct that are fundamental to the practice of public accounting. As such, they are found in differing forms and to differing degrees in the rules of professional conduct of qualified accountants. It must be pointed out that the rules of conduct governing the behaviour of these groups of professionals are much more extensive and detailed than the ensuing discussion. For more detail, refer to the specific rules of conduct of these associations.

③ Professional Rules of Conduct for the Public Accountant

Independence

Generally, the rules of conduct promulgated by the accounting bodies require their members who are engaged in the practice of public accounting to be independent when they perform certain functions. For example, the rules require that auditors of historical financial statements be independent. **Independence** (impartiality in performing professional services) is also required for other types of attestation engagements such as review engagements.

Independence in auditing means taking an unbiased viewpoint in the performance of audit tests, the evaluation of the results, and the issuance of the auditor's report. If the auditor is an advocate for the client, a particular banker, or anyone else, he or she cannot be considered independent. Independence must certainly be regarded as the auditor's most critical characteristic. The reason that many diverse users are

concept check

C3-3 Explain the need for a code of professional ethics for PAs. In which ways should the PAs' code of ethics be similar to and different from those of other professional groups such as lawyers or dentists?

C3-4 List the three parts that may be part of the structure of a code of professional conduct, and state the purpose of each.

C3-5 What is meant by the statement, "The rules of professional conduct of a professional accounting organization should be regarded as a minimum standard?"

Independence—impartiality in performing professional services.

willing to rely upon the professional PA's reports as to the fairness of financial statements is their expectation of an unbiased viewpoint.

Not only is it essential that professional PAs maintain an independent attitude in fulfilling their responsibilities, but it is also important that the users of financial statements have confidence in that independence. These two objectives are frequently identified as "independence in fact" and "independence in appearance." **Independence in fact** exists when the auditor is actually able to maintain an unbiased attitude throughout the audit, whereas **independence in appearance** is the result of others' interpretation of this independence. If auditors are independent in fact but users believe them to be advocates for the client, most of the benefit of the audit function will be lost.

Independence in fact—the auditor's ability to take an unbiased viewpoint in the performance of professional services.

Independence in appearance—the auditor's ability to maintain an unbiased viewpoint in the eyes of others.

The Threats to Independence

In response to financial statement and management frauds, the CA provincial and *ordre* professional codes of conduct have adopted very specific rules of conduct with respect to independence. The CGA national rules are general, with provinces articulating more specific requirements. These rules are considered a foundation for providing public trust, since objectivity in an engagement relies upon auditor independence.

When deciding to accept a client or to continue an existing engagement, the PA is required to examine five threats to independence: self-interest threat, self-review threat, advocacy threat, familiarity threat, and intimidation threat. The PA is to assess threats when they exist and document the safeguards that were used to reduce the threats to an acceptable level. Table 3-4 lists and defines these threats to independence with examples. Table 3-5 on the next page describes safeguards that the firm can implement to either eliminate the threats or reduce them to an acceptable level.

Table 3-4	Threats to Independence
Threat to Independence (defined)	**Examples**
Self-interest threat—when the member could receive a benefit because of a financial interest in the client or in the financial results of the client or due to a conflict of interest.	The firm or member owns shares in or has made a loan to the client. The client fees are significant in relation to the total fee base of the PA or of the firm.
Self-review threat—when the PA is placed in the position of having to audit his or her own work or systems during the audit.	The reasons for this could be that the PA prepared original data or records for the client as part of a bookkeeping engagement or was an employee or officer of the organization. The PA could also have designed and implemented an accounting information system used to process client records.
Advocacy threat—when the firm or member is perceived to promote (or actually does promote) the client's position, that is, the client's judgment is perceived to direct the actions of the PA.	The PA is acting as an advocate in resolving a dispute with a major creditor of the client. The firm or PA is promoting the sale of shares or other securities for the client or is receiving a commission for such sales.
Familiarity threat—occurs when it is difficult to behave with professional skepticism during the engagement due to a belief that one knows the client well.	There is a long association between senior staff and the client (e.g., being on the engagement for 10 years). A former partner of the firm is now the chief financial officer of the client.
Intimidation threat—the client personnel intimidate the firm or its staff with respect to the content of the financial statements or with respect to the conduct of the audit, preventing objective completion of field work.	The client threatens to replace the audit firm over a disclosure disagreement. The client places a maximum upon the audit fee that is unrealistic with respect to the amount of work that needs to be completed.

Table 3-5	Safeguards to Independence

Safeguard Category	Examples
Created by the profession or provided in legislation or securities exchange regulation	Education and training provided by the professional accounting body. Practice review provided by the professional accounting body or by the CPAB.
Provided by the client	A qualified, independent audit committee. A corporate code of ethics that provides for disclosure and resolution of conflicts. Competent client personnel.
Available within the firm's systems and procedures	Firm policies and procedures that promote awareness and ensure compliance for independence. Rotation of senior personnel on client engagements.

Self-interest threat—a threat to independence where the member has a financial interest in the client or in the financial results of the client.

Advocacy threat—a threat to independence where the firm or member is perceived to promote (or actually does promote) the client's position.

Self-review threat—a threat to independence where the PA is in the position of having to audit his or her own work during the period.

Familiarity threat—a threat to independence that occurs when it is difficult to behave with professional skepticism during the engagement.

Intimidation threat—a threat to independence that occurs when the client intimidates the public accounting firm or its staff with respect to the content of the financial statements or with respect to the conduct of the audit.

Listed entity—an entity whose debts or shares are listed on a stock exchange and that has market capitalization and total assets greater than $10 million.

It is obvious that some of the threats affect overall independence. If you own shares in your client's business (**self-interest threat**) or are trying to help them obtain financing (**advocacy threat**), you stand to gain from the result of the financial statement audit.

Some people have more difficulty seeing the impact of the other threats. The **self-review threat** means that you are auditing your own work. Imagine that you have assisted the client in designing an information system that calculates the costs for an inventory system. The new system seems to be working well, and there are excellent reports that track inventory movement and out-of-stock situations. However, during the design phase, you neglected to put in controls to highlight when the system creates a negative inventory situation, either due to clerical error or programming error.

What would you do during the audit? Perhaps you would be less likely to point out this error to the client in a management letter because it would imply that you did not properly perform your work during the system design. Alternatively, you might not detect the system inadequacy during your analysis of internal controls; you believe that it is such an excellent system that you do not need to complete a detailed analysis of internal controls. This example shows how a self-review threat can be very dangerous to the completion of a quality audit engagement.

With a **familiarity threat**, it may be that you were the audit junior on a job, worked as an assistant, then were promoted to supervisor and manager, and are now a partner. You have worked with the client for 15 years, and it seems that you know the strengths and weaknesses of all of the employees, juniors and executives alike. You may take it for granted that they are doing their jobs just as well this year as they did last year. However, you do not know that the controller is going through a messy divorce and the vice-president of finance has started gambling. They are both short of money, which gives them an incentive to manipulate the records and steal money from the company. The actual financial manipulation could lead to **intimidation threat**—where the senior accounting personnel expect you to overlook their manipulation or you may lose the audit. You have known these individuals for 15 years and think of them as friends, so what is a little financial statement manipulation among friends?

The independence rule situations listed in Table 3-6 help prevent independence threats from occurring. Some rules apply to all assurance engagements (e.g., financial statement audit and review for businesses of all sizes), while others apply only to an entity listed on a stock exchange with total market capitalization greater than $10 million, called a **listed entity**.

In addition to the specifics described in Table 3-6, where the member or firm is not allowed to complete the engagement, there are situations where only the person affected is to be excluded from the engagement team. These are situations where the student or member:

- Has made a loan to or guarantees a loan to the client.
- Has an immediate family member as a director, officer, or employee who can exert control over the engagement or who is in an accounting role.

| Table 3-6 | Applicability of Independence Rules |

Independence Rule Situation	Prohibited Engagements if Situation Applies During Term of Engagement			
	Audit of Listed Entity	Audit of Non-listed Entity	Other Assurance Engagement (e.g., review)	Non-assurance Service
Has direct or indirect financial interest	X	X	X	X
Exerts control over the entity	X	X	X	
Has a loan from or has a loan guaranteed by the entity (except in normal course of business; e.g., a bank)	X	X	X	
Has close business relationship	X	X	X	
Engagement staff accepted financial-related position at client within the last year	X			
Member of firm is officer or director	X	X	X	
Management decisions were made	X	X	X	
Prepared or changed originating source data or journal entry without management approval	X	X	X	
Accounting or bookkeeping services provided	X			
Valuation services provided	X			
Actuarial services provided	X			
Internal audit services provided	X			
Financial information systems design or implementation provided	X			
Expert opinion or service provided	X			
Legal services provided	X	X	X	
Human resources for senior positions provided	X			
Corporate finance services provided	X	X	X	

Note: Not all situations are listed. Please consult the rules of conduct at www.cga-bc.org, or your provincial PA association for more details.

new standards 3-2
Broadening "Listed Entity"

The rules of conduct of provincial professional organizations in Canada currently define a listed entity with a size test, that is, there must be a market capitalization greater than $10 million. However, proposed Canadian standards would shift to the definition used in CAS 220: simply an organization that has capital listed on a stock exchange (or that is marketed by such a stock exchange). This likely means that all public company financial statement audits would have a high level of restrictions on the additional services that can be provided by PAs (see Table 3-6). Even though this new definition is included in the CAS, each accounting association would need to modify its own rules of conduct to bring them in alignment with the new CAS.

- Was an employee with the client in a financial oversight position during the duration of the audit.

At the engagement level, independence rules for listed clients include the mandatory rotation of senior personnel (with reinstatement provisions after two years) as follows: the engagement partner and quality control partner after five years; other partners who provide more than 10 hours of service after seven years. All services to a listed client must be approved by the audit committee.

A practical way for a PA to document the independence rules for each engagement is to fill in a checklist. A checklist actively states that the rules have been followed for the engagement and clearly identifies action taken where threats exist, with a conclusion stated for each engagement. This helps ensure that the assessment of independence is part of the quality assurance process for each engagement.

It seems from the above-mentioned list that it would be difficult for a PA to provide comprehensive services to a client! What if you work for a small practice where the bulk of the work is accounting, bookkeeping, and review engagements? How is your work affected? Assuming that you and the other members of the firm have adequately addressed the five threats to independence, the primary practical concerns would be familiarity and self-review. There should be periodic change of staff at a client, where possible, and all transactions and journal entries should be discussed with and approved by the client before being processed.

Independence is far broader than simply preventing a financial interest, such as owning shares in a client. For the PA to be truly independent, all five threats must be considered and addressed for each engagement.

INDEPENDENCE THREAT ANALYSIS As you will see in the next part of this text, public accounting firms must actively assess their ability to conduct an engagement prior to accepting (or renewing) the engagement. This means having policies and procedures in place to identify any new threats to independence, training employees, and monitoring the policies and procedures. If the current processes are not working (for example, employees may be investing in an organization unaware that it is a client of the firm), then new practices may be needed, such as having employees sign a form which lists every client, perhaps on a quarterly basis, stating that they do not have any investments in those organizations. These new practices are an example of remedial action. Then, prior to accepting each engagement, audit management (such as the partner and the manager) is required to evaluate, in writing, the independence of the firm and the staff assigned to the engagement. This formal **independence threat analysis**, or assessment of independence threats, for a particular engagement forms part of the documentation for the engagement.

AUDIT COMMITTEE An **audit committee** is a selected number of members of a company's board of directors who provide a forum that is independent of management for both external and internal auditors. Most audit committees are made up of three to five or sometimes as many as seven directors. Incorporating Acts generally require that the audit committee must comprise independent outside directors (i.e., not part of company management). Access to an active audit committee by internal and external auditors is one of the indicators of a healthy corporate governance structure.

A typical audit committee decides such things as which public accounting firm to retain and the scope of services the public accounting firm is to perform. The audit committee also meets with the public accounting firm to discuss the progress and findings of the audit and helps resolve conflicts between the public accounting firm and management. At least annually, the auditor should inform the audit committee in writing of the following items: the level of the auditor's independence; all relationships between the auditor and his or her related business or practice and the entity and its related entities; and the total fees charged (separating out audit and non-audit

---

Independence threat analysis—assessment of independence threats for a particular engagement.

Audit committee—selected members of a client's board of directors, who provide a forum for the auditors to remain independent of management.

services). The audit committee should also work directly with the internal auditors, approving their strategic plan and discussing their findings with them. The internal auditors should also be required to clarify the level of their independence.

Most organizations that have debt or securities listed on a Canadian or American stock exchange (regardless of size) are required to have an audit committee consisting of at least three independent members who are also directors of the organization. Members of the audit committee are also required to be financially literate.

The auditor has the right to attend meetings of the audit committee and to call meetings if he or she feels they are necessary. Directors who become aware of any misstatements in issued financial statements must notify the auditor and the audit committee of the misstatements.

AIDS TO MAINTAINING INDEPENDENCE The accounting profession and society, especially in the past decade, have been concerned about ensuring that (1) auditors maintain an unbiased attitude in performing their work (independence in fact) and (2) users perceive auditors as being independent (independence in appearance). Many of the elements shown in Figure 3-1 and other requirements or inducements encourage PAs to maintain independence in fact and appearance. Those elements that have a close relationship to independence are now briefly summarized.

Legal Liability The penalty involved when a court concludes that a practitioner is not independent can be severe, including criminal action. The courts have certainly provided major incentives for auditors to remain independent. Legal liability is discussed in Chapter 4.

Rules of Professional Conduct The existing rules of conduct restrict PAs in their financial and business relationships with clients.

Generally Accepted Auditing Standards The general standards require the auditor to maintain an objective state of mind in all matters related to the assignment.

Public Accounting Firm Quality Control Processes Most public accounting firms establish policies and procedures to provide reasonable assurance that all personnel are independent. Effective training, monitoring, and remedial action with respect to these processes help ensure compliance.

Audit Committee An audit committee, as was recently discussed, can help auditors remain independent of management.

Shopping for Accounting Principles Management may consult with other accountants on the application of accounting principles. Although consultation with other accountants is an appropriate practice, it can lead to a loss of independence in certain circumstances. For example, suppose one public accounting firm replaces the existing auditors on the strength of accounting advice offered but later finds facts and circumstances that require the public accounting firm to change its stance. It may be difficult for the new public accounting firm to remain independent in such a situation. The Auditing and Assurance Standards Board issued Section 7600, "Reports on the Application of Accounting Principles," setting out requirements that must be met when a public accounting firm is requested to provide a written opinion on the application of accounting principles or auditing standards by a party other than the client (also discussed in Chapter 23). Such an opinion would be issued for specific circumstances or transactions relating to an audit, review, or compilation client of another public accounting firm. It applies if the PA is asked to provide a generic or hypothetical opinion on the application of accounting principles.

The purpose of Section 7600 is to minimize the likelihood of management following the practice commonly called "opinion shopping," which could result in a potential intimidation threat to independence. Primary among the requirements is that the consulted or "reporting" accounting firm should communicate with the entity's incumbent accountant to obtain all the available facts to form a professional judgment on the matters the firm has been requested to report on.

Approval of Auditor by Shareholders The Canada Business Corporations Act and other incorporating Acts require shareholders to approve the selection of a new auditor or the continuation of the existing one. Shareholders are usually a more objective group than is management. It is questionable, however, whether shareholders are in a position to evaluate the performance of previous or potential auditors.

CONCLUSION Regardless of the rules of conduct of the various accounting bodies, it is essential that the PA maintain an unbiased relationship with management and all other parties affected by the performance of the PA's responsibilities. In every engagement, including those involving management, advisory, and tax services, the PA must not subordinate his or her professional judgment to that of others. Even though pressures on the PA's objectivity and integrity may be frequent, the long-run standing of the profession in the financial community demands resisting those pressures. If the conflicts are sufficiently serious to compromise the PA's independence, it may be necessary for the public accounting firm to resign from the engagement.

Confidentiality

The rules of conduct for PAs state that members shall not disclose any confidential client information or employer information without the specific consent of the client or employer. The rules also prohibit using **confidential** or **inside information** to earn profits or benefits.

Confidential or **inside information**—client information that may not be disclosed without the specific consent of the client except under authoritative professional or legal investigation.

The rule against disclosure does not apply if the member is called upon to disclose the information by the courts. Communication between auditor and client is not privileged as it is between lawyer and client; a court can require a PA to produce all files and documents held, including confidential advice provided. For this reason, the auditor must take care with information put into the file, recognizing that the file could appear as a court document. The rule against disclosure also does not apply if the member's professional body requires the confidentiality rule to be waived in connection with the body's exercise of its duties (e.g., when an auditor is called upon to produce working papers in connection with the disciplinary process or when an auditor is required to produce files as part of practice inspection).

While the rules of professional conduct with respect to confidentiality are quite clear, as you will discover in Chapter 4, the auditor may be confronted with a situation where he or she must choose between confidentiality and other rules of conduct or another course of action. A situation is described where an auditor has two clients who deal with each other; the auditor must choose between violating the rule respecting confidentiality or the rule respecting association with false or misleading financial information. (Although an auditor may decline clients who could result in a potential conflict of interest, organizations who previously may not have had business relationships may initiate these after the auditor has accepted the engagements.) Chapter 4 also illustrates the conflict that arises when an auditor has information about one client that could be beneficial to a second client. This demonstrates how auditors face ethical dilemmas where they cannot rely on the rules of conduct to provide a solution.

NEED FOR CONFIDENTIALITY During an audit or other type of engagement, practitioners obtain a considerable amount of information of a confidential nature, including officers' salaries, product pricing and advertising plans, and product cost data. If auditors divulged this information to outsiders or to client employees who have been denied access to the information, their relationship with management would become strained and, in extreme cases, would cause the client harm. The confidentiality requirement applies to all services provided by public accounting firms, including tax and management services.

Ordinarily, the public accounting firm's working papers can be provided to someone else only with the express permission of the client. This is the case even if a PA sells his or her practice to another public accounting firm or is willing to permit a successor auditor to examine the working papers prepared for a former client. Permission is not required from the client, however, if the working papers are subpoenaed by a court or are used as part of practice inspection. If the working papers are subpoenaed, the client should be informed immediately. The client and the client's lawyer may wish to challenge the subpoena.

Maintenance of the Reputation of the Profession

The rules of accounting bodies in Canada require their members to behave in the best interests of their profession and the public. This means accountants should not take advantage of the trust placed in them. An accountant should not be publicly critical of a colleague (i.e., by making a complaint about the colleague's behaviour to their professional body or by being critical, as a successor auditor, to the new client) without giving the colleague a chance to explain his or her actions first.

Actions by a member of a professional body—in law, medicine, or any other profession—reflect not only on the member but also on the body. For example, a lawyer who steals trust monies sullies not only his or her own reputation but also that of the law profession; the theft brings all lawyers into disrepute. Reputation is affected by anti-social behaviour such as harassment and discrimination, since such behaviour is considered abhorrent, resulting in professional disciplinary actions. Therefore, it is essential that an accountant behave in an exemplary manner as a member of the professional body.

Integrity and Due Care

The rules of conduct for professional accountants require members to act with integrity and due care. Integrity is one of the hallmarks of the profession. One of a professional accountant's most important assets is his or her reputation for honesty and fair dealing; if users of financial statements audited by or prepared by an accountant do not believe in the practitioner's honesty or fairness, the value of the financial statements or the audit is diminished. The professional accountant's behaviour with clients, colleagues, employers, and employees must be above reproach.

Due care in the performance of duties is also a hallmark of a professional. The PA has a legal duty of care to certain users of financial statements, as will be seen in Chapter 4. Due care means the application by a professional of a level of care and skill in accordance with what would reasonably be expected of a person of his or her rank and training.

Competence

A PA has a responsibility to maintain his or her professional competence. The rules of conduct require practitioners to maintain competence; similarly GAAS state the necessity of "adequate technical training and proficiency in auditing." The public expects that all professionals will strive to keep abreast of the latest techniques and methodologies.

Members are encouraged to keep current in a variety of ways. The various institutes and the *ordre* of chartered accountants have practice inspections (discussed in Chapter 1) over a three-year period of all public practice units. Certified general accountants and many CAs, such as those in Ontario, are required to attend a certain number of continuing professional education courses a year. Primarily, however, it is a PA's professionalism that dictates that he or she keep current.

The auditor is required, explicitly by the general standard of GAAS, and implicitly by the rules of conduct of the various professional accounting bodies, to have the

auditing in action 3-3
Practice Firm Argues About Lawsuit Disclosure

ABCD LLP, a medium-sized regional CA firm, was contacted by Amy, the corporate controller of a public company, about conducting the audit of Model Manufacturing Limited (MML). Amy had attended several external training events with members of the firm and was known to the partners of ABCD LLP. ABCD conducted a due diligence investigation and was informed by MML about the existence of a defective products lawsuit that was being vigorously defended. The lawsuit was disclosed in MML financial statements but had not been accrued. ABCD accepted the audit engagement, and upon corresponding with MML lawyers, found that a judgment had actually been issued against MML for $400,000, which should have been accrued in the previous quarterly financial statements. ABCD argued about the disclosure with MML, which finally agreed to accrue the amount when the lawyers supported ABCD's request. ABCD was so disenchanted with MML management's attitude about disclosure that it resigned after having completed the current year's audit engagement.

technical knowledge and competence necessary to conduct the audit. This is especially true as businesses—and accounting for them—increase in complexity. An auditor should not undertake an audit of a client unless that auditor has both knowledge of that client's business and industry and of the technical aspects of the audit. For example, the audit of an insurance company requires knowledge of auditing the policy reserves that form a significant part of the insurance company's liabilities. Many larger accounting firms form industry specialization groups within the firm that are responsible for all audits within their specialty.

An audit firm should decline a new audit if the firm either lacks or does not have access to the technical knowledge required to complete the audit. Similarly, an auditor within a firm should ensure that he or she has access to the technical knowledge required to complete the audit.

Adherence to GAAP and GAAS

Professional accounting bodies require their members in practice as PAs and working in industry not to associate with false or misleading information or to fail to reveal material omissions from financial statements. PAs can lose faith in management when information is withheld, as described in Auditing in Action 3-3, and it then becomes difficult to complete the audit engagement. Users of financial statements prepared by or audited by professional accountants are entitled to believe that the financial statements are complete and fairly present the financial position of the company, to believe that the financial statements are not false and misleading, and to rely on the integrity of the accountants involved.

Given that public trust of professional accountants does exist, if an accountant betrayed this trust and provided a clean opinion on financial statements known to be misleading, users would accept the statements as correct and would suffer a loss. Discovery that the PA was associated with false and misleading financial information or failed to reveal a material fact would destroy the accountant's reputation for integrity.

PAs are required to comply with professional standards when preparing and auditing financial statements. These standards would include the standards of the professional body but, more importantly, GAAP and GAAS as set out in the *CICA Handbook*. As you learned in Chapter 1, the Canada Business Corporations Act and the incorporating Acts of many of the provinces require financial statements to be prepared according to GAAP as specified by the *CICA Handbook* and also require the auditor's report to be in accordance with the standards of the *CICA Handbook*. The Canadian Securities Administrators, who set policy for the securities commissions and stock exchanges in Canada, also specify the *CICA Handbook* as the source of GAAP.

Advertising and Solicitation

A profession's reputation is not enhanced if the members openly solicit one another's clients or engage in advertising that is overly aggressive, self-laudatory, or critical of other members of the profession or that makes claims that cannot be substantiated. As a consequence, the professional accounting bodies in Canada either explicitly or implicitly prohibit solicitation of another PA's client and advertising that is not in keeping with the profession's high standards.

Responding to a request for information from a client of another public accounting firm is not solicitation, nor is responding to an invitation to tender from another firm's client. Rather, solicitation is approaching the client of another public accounting firm to convince him or her to switch to one's own firm; it is a targeted act of seeking a specific professional engagement.

Advertising that is in good taste is acceptable. It may include complimentary material about the accounting firm but should not claim any superior skills or make promises that cannot be kept (e.g., a promise that certain favourable results will be achieved). Advertising is a general process of informing potential users of the availability of services.

There has been a gradual change over the past few years as the rules regarding solicitation and advertising have been made less stringent. As a consequence, advertising in various media is much more common. There is an increased emphasis on marketing and more competitive pricing of services. Many public accounting firms have developed sophisticated advertising for national journals read by business people and for local newspapers.

Has the quality of audits become endangered by these changes? The existing legal exposure of PAs, the disciplinary processes of the professional accounting bodies, practice inspection requirements, and the potential for interference by the securities commissions and government have kept audit quality high. In the opinion of the authors, the changes in the rules have caused greater competition in the profession but not so much that high-quality, efficiently run public accounting firms have been harmed.

Other Rules

Breaches of the Rules The rules of conduct of the professional accounting bodies require members who are aware of a breach of the rules by another member to report that member to the profession's discipline committee after first advising the member of the intent to make a report. The bodies are self-regulating. It is important that the member be notified of the intent to report the breach in case there are mitigating circumstances of which the reporting member is not aware.

Contingent Fees The charging of a fee based on the outcome of an audit, such as the granting of a loan by a bank, could easily impair the auditor's independence. Contingent fees are prohibited for audits, reviews, and any other engagements that require the auditor to be objective.

Communication with Predecessor Auditor The rules of conduct of the PAs and incorporating Acts such as the Canada Business Corporations Act require a (potential) successor auditor, prior to accepting an appointment as auditor, to communicate with the incumbent auditor to inquire if there are any circumstances of which the incumbent is aware that might preclude the successor from accepting the appointment. The successor would ask the potential client to authorize the incumbent to provide the information requested. If the client refuses to do so, the successor should be reluctant to accept the appointment because it is likely that the client is hiding something.

The rules also require that the incumbent respond to the successor's request and be candid in responding. The communication between the incumbent and the successor is important because it prevents a successor from unknowingly accepting an appointment that might, if all the facts were known, be rejected. For example, if the incumbent resigned after finding that management of the client was dishonest and was engaged in fraud, it is unlikely any public accounting firm would accept the client if the incumbent passed on that knowledge. In short, the required communication protects prospective successors, and thus the profession, from getting involved with undesirable clients. Review of the previous auditor's working papers is an important part of the audit process, as discussed further in audit planning.

Professional Liability Insurance In several provinces, members practising public accounting are required to carry professional liability insurance. Two issues arise that can cause confusion: defining public accounting and the extent of work being done without remuneration.

For example, during tax season, individuals may prepare tax returns for family and friends at no charge. Since basic advice such as maximization of RRSP contributions is often included, this process is considered to be practising public accounting. However, if only a limited number of returns are being prepared for no remuneration, a public practice is not being carried on. If more than a handful of returns are being prepared and fees are being charged, either on a full- or part-time basis, then professional liability insurance is required.

Other Rules The rules of conduct of the professional accounting bodies include many more rules than have been described here; an aspiring professional accountant should be aware of the rules of conduct of the professional body of which membership is sought. The rules not covered, and those described above, may be categorized as general rules, rules that deal with protection of the public, rules that deal with relations with other accountants, and rules that relate to the conduct of a professional practice.

Enforcement

The rules of conduct for CAs are established and administered provincially. The rules of conduct for CGAs are promulgated by CGA-Canada. The provincial CGA associations have the power to add rules and have the responsibility for enforcing the rules.

As described in Table 3-3, the various professional bodies have the power to impose penalties ranging from public censure in the body's newsletter or requiring courses to be taken to upgrade skills to levying fines or expulsion. CPAB has the power to restrict a firm's ability to audit a listed entity. As previously mentioned, the professional accounting bodies are self-regulating; that is, they have the responsibility for developing their own rules of conduct and for disciplining members who violate the rules. There is a danger that the public will perceive the disciplinary process as not being as stringent as it should be and that there is a reluctance to punish members who break the rules. This issue is being dealt with by including laypersons on the disciplinary committees and by the inspections supervised by CPAB. Information is also available to the public about findings of the discipline committees and actions taken by them.

concept check

C3-6 What are the five threats to independence? Describe each and provide an example.

C3-7 List three categories of safeguards to independence. Provide an example of each.

C3-8 Why are contingent fees prohibited for financial statement audits?

Summary

1. *What are ethics and why are they important?* Ethics are broad moral principles or values that help guide our behaviour and establish trustworthy, responsible, and fair relationships.

   How can I work through an ethical conflict (known as an ethical dilemma)? A six-step framework that walks through information collection, analysis, and a decision is provided in the chapter (see page 48).

2. *How are PAs different from other professionals?* The clients of PAs are individuals as well as management of corporations. In addition, PAs have a responsibility to users of financial statements such as shareholders and creditors. This is a more expanded responsibility than that of other professionals.

   What is the role of a code of professional conduct in encouraging PA ethical behaviour? Such a code of conduct can have general statements of ideal conduct and specific rules that define unacceptable behaviour.

3. *What are the threats to independence?* There are five areas where independence must be considered: self-interest, self-review, advocacy, familiarity, and intimidation.

How does the auditor's relationship with the audit committee affect independence? The audit committee can help the auditor remain independent of management by making the auditor retention decision, approving the services provided by the PA, discussing the audit progress and findings, and by helping to resolve conflicts between the public accounting firm and management.

What are some of the key rules of professional conduct and how they are enforced? There are rules of professional conduct covering independence, confidentiality, maintenance of the reputation of the profession, integrity and due care, competence, adherence to professional standards, and advertising and solicitation. Rules of conduct are enforced by the professional accounting associations and by CPAB.

Visit the text's website at **www.pearsoned.ca/arens** for practice quizzes, additional case studies, and international standards information.

Review Questions

3-1 Using Table 3-1, explain how a professional accountant would embody each of the illustrated ethical principles.

3-2 When analyzing an ethical dilemma, why is a structured approach helpful?

3-3 How does the presence of a whistle-blowing process improve quality control and independence at a public accounting firm?

3-4 Distinguish between independence in fact and independence in appearance. State three activities that may not affect independence in fact but are likely to affect independence in appearance.

3-5 Why is an auditor's independence so essential?

3-6 What is an independence threat analysis? When and why should it be completed?

3-7 Many people believe that a PA cannot be truly independent when payment of fees is dependent on the management of the client. Explain a way of reducing this appearance of lack of independence.

3-8 The auditor's working papers usually can be provided to someone else only with the permission of the client. What is the rationale for such a rule?

3-9 The rules of conduct of PAs require them to report a breach of the rules of conduct by a member to their profession's disciplinary body. What should they do before making such a report?

3-10 After accepting an engagement, a PA discovers that the client's industry is more technical than at first realized and that he or she (i.e., the accountant) is not competent in certain areas of the operation. What should the PA do in this situation?

3-11 Identify and explain factors that should keep the quality of audits high, even though advertising and tendering are allowed.

3-12 For what types of engagements are contingent fees acceptable as charged by professional accountants?

3-13 Why is it so important that a successor auditor communicate with the incumbent before accepting an appointment as auditor? What should the successor do if the incumbent does not reply?

Discussion Questions and Problems

3-14 Trish Mulcahy, a new junior in your office, says that she does not understand why she cannot work on the audit of a company that is a client of your firm and that is owned by her uncle. Trish says she knows she must have an independent attitude and she will; her relationship to the owner is not important.

REQUIRED
What would you say in answer to her question? Would you let her work on the audit?

3-15 The following situations involve the provision of non-audit services. Indicate whether providing the service is a violation of the rules of professional conduct for PAs. Explain your answer.

a. Providing bookkeeping services to a listed entity. The services were preapproved by the audit committee of the company.

b. Providing internal audit services to a listed entity that is not an audit client.

c. Designing and implementing a financial information system for a private company.

d. Recommending a tax shelter to a client that is a publicly held listed entity. The services were preapproved by the audit committee.

e. Providing internal audit services to a listed entity audit client with the preapproval of the audit committee.

f. Providing bookkeeping services to an audit client that is a private company.

3-16 Each of the following scenarios involves a possible violation of the rules of conduct. Indicate whether each is a violation and explain why if you think it is.

a. John Brown is a PA, but not a partner, with three years of professional experience with Lyle and Lyle, Public Accountants, a one-office public accounting firm. He owns 25 shares of stock in an audit client of the firm, but he does not take part in the audit of the client and the amount of stock is not material in relation to his total wealth.

b. In preparing the corporate tax returns for a client, Phyllis Allen, a PA, observed that the deductions for contributions and interest were unusually large. When she asked the client for backup information to support the deductions, she was told, "Ask me no questions, and I will tell you no lies." Phyllis completed the return on the basis of the information acquired from the client.

c. A private entity audit client requested assistance of Kim Tanabe, a PA, in the installation of a computer system for maintaining production records. Kim had no experience in this type of work and no knowledge of the client's production records, so she obtained assistance from a computer consultant. The consultant is not in the practice of public accounting, but Kim is confident of her professional skills. Because of the highly technical nature of the work, Kim is not able to review the consultant's work.

d. Five small Moncton public accounting firms have become involved with an information project by taking part in an interfirm working paper review program. Under the program, each firm designates two partners to review the working papers, including the tax returns and the financial statements, of another public accounting firm taking part in the program. At the end of each review, the auditors who prepared the working papers and the reviewers have a conference to discuss the strengths and weaknesses of the audit. They do not obtain the authorization from the audit client before the review takes place.

e. George Thorty, a PA, was having a matrimonial dispute with his wife, and he got so angry that he threatened to kill her. His wife obtained a court injunction requiring that he stay away from her home and place of work. George violated the injunction and was sent to jail after being found in contempt of court.

f. Bill Wendal, a PA, set up a casualty and fire insurance agency to complement his auditing and tax services. He does not use his own name on anything pertaining to the insurance agency and has a highly competent manager, Renate Jones, who runs it. Bill frequently requests Renate to review with the management of an audit client the adequacy of the client's insurance if it seems underinsured. He feels that he provides a valuable service to clients by informing them when they are underinsured.

g. Michelle Rankin, a PA, provides tax services, management advisory services, and bookkeeping services and conducts audits for the same private company client. She requires management to approve, in writing, transactions and journal entries. Since her firm is small, the same person frequently provides all the services.

3-17 Each of the following situations involves possible violations of the rules of conduct that apply to professional accountants. For each situation, state whether it is a violation. Where there is a violation, explain the nature of the violation and the rationale for the existing rule.

a. Mario Danielli is the partner on the audit of a boating club. He is also a member of the board of directors, but this position is honorary and does not involve performing a management function.

b. Martha Painter, a CA, was appointed as the trustee of the So family trust. The So family trust owned the shares of the So Manufacturing Company, which is audited by another partner in Martha's office. Martha owns 15 percent of the shares of the So Manufacturing Company and is also a director of the company, in the position of Treasurer.

c. Marie Godette, LLB, has a law practice. Marie has recommended one of her clients to Sean O'Doyle, a PA. Sean has agreed to pay Marie 10 percent of the fee Sean receives from Marie's client.

d. Theresa Barnes, a CA, has an audit client, Choi, Inc., which uses another public accounting firm for management services work. Theresa sends her firm's literature covering its management services capabilities to Choi on a monthly basis unsolicited.

e. Alan Goldenberg leased several vehicles from his friend Norm. Norm said that he would give Alan a $200 commission for each referral. Alan referred to Norm several clients who were interested in leasing vehicles. After a few months, Alan was pleased to receive a cheque for $3,000 in the mail. Several of his clients had decided to change automobile leasing companies.

f. Edward Golikowski completed for his client financial projections that covered a period of three years. Edward was in a hurry and inadvertently stated that they covered five years; so he redid the client's calculations, rather than checking assumptions and doing field work, even though he attached an assurance report.

g. Marcel Poust, a PA, has sold his public accounting practice, which includes bookkeeping, tax services, and auditing to Sheila Lyons, a PA. Marcel obtained permission from all audit clients for audit-related working papers before making them available to Sheila. He did not get permission before releasing tax- and management services-related working papers.

3-18 The Canada Business Corporations Act requires all companies incorporated under it to have audit committees.

REQUIRED
a. Describe an audit committee.
b. What are the typical functions performed by an audit committee?
c. Explain how an audit committee can help an auditor be more independent.
d. Your friend's mother, who is chair of an audit committee of a large publicly traded company, knows that you are studying auditing and has asked you for advice on how she can make the audit committee she chairs more effective. Your response should consider both sides of each recommendation you make.

3-19 Diane Harris, a PA, is the auditor of Fine Deal Furniture, Inc. In the course of her audit for the year ended December 31, 2008, she discovered that Fine Deal had serious going concern problems. Henri Fine, the owner of Fine Deal, asked Diane to delay completing her audit.

Diane is also the auditor of Master Furniture Builders Ltd., whose year end is January 31. The largest receivable on Master Furniture's list of receivables is Fine Deal Furniture; the amount owing represents about 45 percent of Master Furniture's total receivables, which, in turn, are 60 percent of Master Furniture's net assets. The management of Master Furniture is not aware of Fine Deal's problems and is certain the amount will be collected in full.

Master Furniture is in a hurry to get the January 31, 2009, audit finished because the company has made an application for a sizable loan from its bank to expand its operations. The bank has informally agreed to advance the funds based on draft financial statements submitted by Master Furniture just after the year end.

REQUIRED
What action should Diane take and why?

3-20 Marie Janes encounters the following situations in doing the audit of a large auto dealership. Marie is not a partner.
1. The sales manager tells her that there is a sale on new cars (at a substantial discount) that is limited to long-established customers of the dealership. Because her firm has been doing the audit for several years, the sales manager has decided that Marie should also be eligible for the discount.
2. The auto dealership has an executive lunchroom that is available free to employees above a certain level. The controller informs Marie that she can also eat there any time.
3. Marie is invited to and attends the company's annual Christmas party. When presents are handed out, she is surprised to find herself included. The present has a value of approximately $200.

REQUIRED
a. Assuming Marie accepts the offer or gift in each situation, has she violated the rules of conduct?
b. Discuss what Marie should do in each situation.

3-21 The following are situations that may violate the general rules of conduct of professional accountants. Assume in each case that the PA is a partner.
1. Simone Able, a PA, owns a substantial limited partnership interest in an apartment building. Juan Rodriquez is a 100-percent owner in Rodriquez Marine Ltd. Juan also owns a substantial interest in the same limited partnership as Simone. Simone does the audit of Rodriquez Marine Ltd.
2. Horst Baker, a PA, approaches a new audit client and tells the president that he has an idea that could result in a substantial tax refund in the prior year's tax return by application of a technical provision in a tax law that the client had overlooked. Horst adds that the fee will be 50 percent of the tax refund after it has been resolved by Canada Revenue Agency. The client agrees to the proposal.
3. Chantal Contel, a PA, advertises in the local paper that her firm does the audit of 14 of the 36 largest drugstores in the city. The advertisement also states that the average audit fee, as a percentage of total assets for the drugstores she audits, is lower than that of any other public accounting firm in the city.
4. Olaf Gustafson, a PA, sets up a small loan company specializing in loans to business executives and small companies. Olaf does not spend much time in the business because he works full time in his public accounting practice. No employees of Olaf public accounting firm are involved in the small loan company.
5. Louise Elbert, a PA, owns a material amount of stock in a mutual fund investment company, which, in turn, owns stock in Louise largest audit client. Reading the investment company's most recent financial report, Louise is surprised to learn that the company's ownership in her client has increased dramatically.

REQUIRED
Discuss whether the facts in any of the situations indicate violations of the rules of conduct for professional accountants. If so, identify the nature of the violation(s).

Professional Judgment Problem

3-22 Joseph Smith was the chairman and chief operating officer of Maximum Software Limited, providing software solutions to companies in Manitoba. Joseph owned 40 percent of the company and had several silent partners who sat on the board of directors but did not participate in the company's operations. The chief financial officer of Maximum was Barbara Black, who had been with the company since its inception 10 years ago.

Joseph was short of money, so he created a fictitious company and requested that Barbara send monthly cheques of $10,000 to this company, called Network Best, for consulting fees. Barbara agreed since Joseph approves the invoices.

The controller, Samuel Chu, was a single parent with three children. Samuel did a normal credit check on Network Best and told Barbara that the company did not exist and the invoices should not be paid. Barbara berated Samuel and told him to keep quiet or he would lose his job. Joseph billed amounts through Network Best for three years.

REQUIRED

Assuming that all of the individuals described are qualified accountants, what rules of professional conduct were violated? What should Barbara or Samuel have done?

Cases

3-23 Gilbert and Bradley formed a corporation called Financial Services, Inc., each man taking 50 percent of the authorized common stock. Gilbert was a public accountant and a member of one of the professional accounting bodies in Canada. Bradley was a CPCU (Chartered Property Casualty Underwriter). The corporation performed auditing and tax services under Gilbert's direction and insurance services under Bradley's supervision. The opening of the corporation's office was announced by an 8-cm, two-column "card" in the local newspaper.

One of the corporation's first audit clients was Grandtime Corp. Grandtime had total assets of $600,000 and total liabilities of $270,000. In the course of his examination, Gilbert found that Grandtime's building, with a book value of $240,000, was pledged as security for a 10-year term note in the amount of $200,000. The client's statements did not mention that the build-

ing was pledged as security for the note. However, as the failure to disclose the lien did not affect either the value of the assets or the amount of the liabilities and his examination was satisfactory in all other respects, Gilbert rendered an unqualified opinion on Grandtime's financial statements. About two months after the date of his opinion, Gilbert learned that an insurance company was planning to loan Grandtime $150,000 in the form of a first mortgage note on the building. Realizing that the insurance company was unaware of the existing lien on the building, Gilbert had Bradley notify the insurance company of the fact that Grandtime's building was pledged as security for the term note.

REQUIRED

Identify and discuss the ethical implications of those actions by Gilbert that were in violation of the rules of conduct.

3-24 Barbara Whitley had great expectations about her future as she sat at her graduation ceremony in May 2008. She was about to receive her Master of Accountancy degree, and the following week she would begin her career on the audit staff of Green, Thresher & Co., a public accounting firm. Things looked a little different to Barbara in February 2009. She was working on the audit of Delancey Fabrics Ltd., a textile manufacturer with a calendar year end. The pressure was enormous. Everyone on the audit team was putting in 70-hour weeks, and it still looked as if the audit would not be done on time. Barbara was doing work in the property area, vouching additions for the year. The audit program indicated that a sample of all items over $10,000 should be selected, plus a non-statistical sample of smaller items. When Barbara went to take the sample, Jack Bean, the senior, had left the client's office and could not answer her questions about the appropriate size of the judgmental sample. Barbara forged ahead and selected 50 smaller items on her own judgment. Her basis for doing this was that there were about 250 such items, so 50 was a reasonably good proportion of such additions. Barbara audited the additions with the following results: The items over $10,000

contained no errors; however, the 50 small items contained a large number of errors. In fact, when Barbara projected them to all such additions, the amount seemed quite significant.

A couple of days later, Jack Bean returned to the client's office. Barbara brought her work to Jack in order to inform him of the problems she found, and got the following response: "My God, Barbara, why did you do this? You were supposed to look only at the items over $10,000, plus 5 or 10 little ones. You've wasted a whole day on that work, and we can't afford to spend any more time on it. I want you to throw away the schedules where you tested the last 40 small items and forget you ever did them."

When Barbara asked about the possible audit adjustment regarding the small items, none of which arose from the first 10 items, Jack responded, "Don't worry, it's not material anyway. You just forget it; it's my concern, not yours."

REQUIRED
a. In what way is this an ethical dilemma for Barbara?
b. Use the six-step approach discussed in the chapter to wresolve the ethical dilemma.

Ongoing Small Business Case: Quitting the Firm to Start CondoCleaners.com

3-25 Jim has been thinking about CondoCleaners.com for the last three months now. He has been a bit distracted at work and has had some difficulty concentrating, as he has started organizing a request for proposal for his new website and for a market study to help him plan his approach. After discussions with the firm's personnel partner, he decided to give the firm four months' notice, rather than leaving in the middle of a busy season. The firm is sorry to see him go and has said that there will always be a job there for him. Jim is wondering if he should ask the current client he is working on, a marketing company, to complete a market survey for him.

REQUIRED

Explain why or why not Jim should use the services of his firm's audit client for the CondoCleaners.com market study. What other quality control or independence issues are caused by Jim's proposed new business?

4

Legal liability

Why can the auditor be sued when a business goes bankrupt? Isn't it management's responsibility to run the business? In this chapter, we will explore terminology associated with legal liability, and look at how lawsuits and legislation have framed the public accounting legal environment. Future management accountants will learn how some of these same liability issues affect management, while potential public accountants will identify actions that they can take to mitigate the likelihood of lawsuits. Internal or government auditors and specialists are often involved in the development of assurance reports, so mitigation actions are relevant to them as well.

STANDARDS REFERENCED IN THIS CHAPTER

CICA Standards

Section 5020 – Association

Section 9200 – Compilation engagements

LEARNING OBJECTIVES

1 Identify the public accountant's sources of legal liability. Explain how this liability is related to a distinction between business failure and audit failure. Describe the financial statement auditor's fiduciary responsibility and the money-laundering reporting requirements of the public accountant.

2 Explain why the accountant does not have the right of privileged communication. Define selected concepts and terms associated with the auditor's legal liability. Describe actions the public accountant should take if a client sues him or her.

3 Describe the groups of individuals or organizations, in addition to the client, who can sue the auditor. Explain how the auditor would defend against such suits. Consider whether the auditor can go to jail because of criminal liability.

4 Examine conditions where the auditor may consider disclosure of confidential information. List the actions that individual accountants and the profession can undertake to mitigate the risks of legal liability.

5 Identify the actions that accountants should take to determine which legislation has an impact on their work. Link those actions to standards of continuing education, quality control, and engagement completion.

UQAM Real Estate Development Criminal Investigation

The cost of the science pavilion started out at $95 million in 2003 but was estimated to end at $217 million (up 128 percent) in late 2007. The classroom and parking complex was estimated at $333 million in March 2005, skyrocketing to costs of $529 million as of early 2008 (an increase of 59 percent) for only a partial completion. These costs and the resulting liquidity problems at the Université du Québec à Montréal (UQAM) resulted in the Quebec National Assembly requesting a special report from the Auditor General of Quebec (AGQ), which was tabled in June 2008.

Normal mismanagement does not result in a criminal investigation. However, the AGQ report identified that individuals responsible for the real estate development acted outside of their authority, approving changes to the construction projects without executive approval and providing reports that were inaccurate and incomplete to the Board of Directors and the Board of Governors of UQAM. The AGQ also stated that the revenue forecast (prepared by a firm of public accountants) for one of the projects provided inappropriate credibility for the projected costs and revenues associated with the parking–classroom complex.

IMPORTANCE TO AUDITORS

Auditors need to look at controls present at an organization as well as at what is missing. For example, the AGQ report described an absence of UQAM executive oversight for these projects, such as lack of discussion by the audit committee and executive decisions without detailed supporting documentation and discussions. Regulatory authorities also were stated as not following up on apparent reporting problems on a timely basis, which potentially could have stopped this project from becoming too large.

WHAT DO YOU THINK?

1. What should be the role of executive management in approving large transactions such as building projects?

2. There is no profit or loss in this case, but taxpayers will end up paying for these buildings. Who would be sued and by whom to recover excess interest costs?

3. Should accountants be held liable for errors or problems with financial projections that are based upon management estimates and assumptions?

Sources: 1. Adapted from Auditor General of Quebec, "Report of the Auditor General of Quebec to the National Assembly concerning the special audit carried out at the Université du Québec à Montréal," June 2008, www.vgq.gouv.qc.ca/default-EN.aspx, Accessed: September 16, 2008. 2. Curran, Peggy, "Cops to probe UQAM expenses; Bungled real estate development," *Montreal Gazette*, August 26, 2008, p. A10. 3. Millan, Luis, "Blistering report on financial woes," *The Bottom Line*, 24(8), July 2008, p. 5, 7.

continued >

PUBLIC accountants (PAs) provide assurance in a variety of reports about financial information. Users of these reports could sue the PA if they believed there was a material representation that caused them a loss. How do you feel about legal liability? Does it worry you that you might be sued if you become a public accountant? How does it feel to know that you might be called upon to be an expert witness? Legal liability (and its consequences) can be significant and is the reason accountants carry liability insurance—to enable them to conduct their work in a professional manner and deal with lawsuits from clients and others. Sound quality control practices and adherence to independence rules and other professional standards and rules of conduct assist firms in preventing lawsuits.

This chapter discusses the nature of legal liability of public accountants. **Legal liability** is the professional's obligation under the law to provide a reasonable level of care while performing work for those he or she serves. First, the reasons for increased litigation against public accountants are discussed. Then, specific legal responsibilities related to financial loyalty and money laundering are described. This is followed by a detailed examination of the nature of the lawsuits and the sources of potential liability. Significant lawsuits involving public accountants that relate to the various issues are presented in summary form. You will note that the cases discussed come from the United States, the United Kingdom, and Canada; the legal systems in all three countries (except in Quebec, whose private law is based on French civil law[1]) are based on English common law; as a consequence, when judges in all three countries hand down decisions, while they have no obligation to follow decisions in the other countries, they will often refer to those decisions in the course of giving their own judgments. The options available to the profession and individual practitioners to minimize liability while meeting society's needs are presented. We close by looking at the importance of awareness of current legislation for accountants in management and public accounting.

 ## Appreciating the Legal Environment

Changed Legal Environment

Legal liability—the professional's obligation under the law to provide a reasonable level of care while performing work for those he or she serves.

Common law—laws developed through court decisions rather than through government statutes; also called "judge-made law" or "case law".

Professionals have always had a duty to provide a reasonable level of care while performing work for those they serve. Audit professionals have a responsibility under **common law** to fulfill implied or expressed contracts with clients. They are liable to their clients for **negligence** and/or breach of contract should they fail to provide the services or should they fail to exercise due care in their performance. Auditors may also be held liable under the tort of negligence or provincial securities Acts to parties other than their clients in certain circumstances. The precise legal definition of the auditor's third-party liability continues to evolve. (Third parties are people who do not

---

[1] Smyth, J. E., D. A. Soberman, and A. J. Easson, *The Law and Business Administration in Canada*, Seventh Edition, (Toronto: Prentice Hall Canada Inc., 1995), p. 46–47.

74   PART 1 | THE AUDITING PROFESSION

have a contract with the auditor.) The position of the Supreme Court of Canada at the time of writing remains that the auditor owes a duty of care to third parties who are part of a limited group of persons whom the auditor knows will use and rely on the audit, and that the auditor's knowledge extends to the purpose or transaction for which the financial statements would be used.

Negligence—failure to exercise reasonable care in the performance of one's obligations to another.

Note the use of the term "evolve" here; in Canada, as in other countries, lower courts are presenting other definitions. You will see further discussion of this shortly. Finally, in rare cases, auditors have also been held liable for criminal acts. A criminal conviction against an auditor can result only when it is demonstrated that the auditor acted with criminal intent.

As described in Chapter 1, professional accountants perform a variety of services in addition to financial statement audits. As independent advisors, they may prepare financial statements or financial projections. As accountants, they may record transactions, prepare payroll, make tax or remittance payments, or handle other parts of the accounting functions. This may trigger a duty of loyalty to the client and additional government reporting requirements with respect to money laundering.

A relatively new area of liability is fiduciary duty. Fiduciary duty suits are a growing body of Canadian law that has affected accountants and may also affect auditors. **Fiduciary duty** results when a party (such as an accountant) has an obligation to act for the benefit of another, and that obligation includes discretionary power. It has also been called a "duty of loyalty." The Supreme Court of Canada case of *Robert L. Hodgkinson v. David L. Sims and Jerry S. Waldman* (File No. 23033, 1997) summarized many of the then-current definitions of a fiduciary. On page 385 of the case, the court indicates that "the hallmark of a fiduciary relationship is that one party is dependent upon or in the power of the other." It then looks to three conditions: (1) the fiduciary has the ability to exercise discretion or power, (2) discretion or power can be unilaterally exercised, and (3) the beneficiary is peculiarly vulnerable. The court then goes on to say that this is not an absolute test. It is not further discussed in this text since in an ordinary auditor–client relationship, no fiduciary duty would arise.[2]

Fiduciary duty—a party (such as an accountant) has an obligation to act for the benefit of another, and that obligation includes discretionary power.

A PA conducting a financial statement audit would not have any fiduciary duty as the PA is not acting on behalf of the organization or its stakeholders but is providing an opinion on the financial statements. The situations where an accountant is making payments on the client's behalf to a tax authority or is appointed as a trustee for an estate are examples where fiduciary duty could arise. A professional accountant acting as an officer or director of an organization would have a fiduciary duty to shareholders.

Canadian PAs are required to have controls in place to identify and track suspicious transactions and comply with the reporting requirements of the Proceeds of Crime (Money Laundering) and Terrorist Financing Act (PCMLTFA), which came into effect in 2001 and has had several revisions. This reporting needs to take place if the PA is doing specific work on behalf of the client (called triggering activities) that triggers the requirements of the Act. These activities are (1) receipt or payment of funds (e.g., tax payments or employee remittance payments), (2) purchase or sale of assets (e.g., marketable securities or real estate), or (3) transferring cash or securities (e.g., using electronic funds transfer to make employee remittances). If you engage or your firm engages in these activities, then cash transactions of $10,000 engage or more must be reported to FINTRAC (the Financial Transactions and Reports Analysis Centre of Canada). You would also be expected to have systems in place to help identify clients who might be terrorists and to identify suspicious transactions over $3,000. More information is available on the FINTRAC website (**www.fintrac-canafe.gc.ca**) and professional accounting websites. Penalties for PAs (and others) for failing to follow the requirements of the PCMLTFA include up to five years in jail and/or a fine of up to $2 million.

In addition to reporting requirements, there are also criminal offences associated with money laundering. Part XII.2 of the Criminal Code, Bill C-61, is known

---

[2] See also: Paskell-Mede, Mindy, "Fiduciary duty," *CAmagazine*, April 2004, p. 43–44, 49.

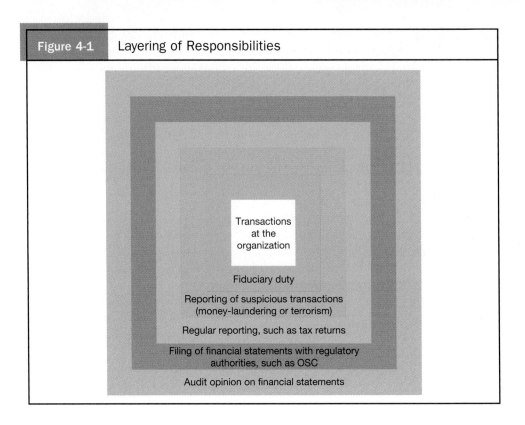

Figure 4-1	Layering of Responsibilities

Transactions
at the
organization

Fiduciary duty

Reporting of suspicious transactions
(money-laundering or terrorism)

Regular reporting, such as tax returns

Filing of financial statements with regulatory
authorities, such as OSC

Audit opinion on financial statements

informally as the "proceeds of crime" legislation. In *R. v. Loewen* (1996), an accountant was convicted of laundering $125,000. The accountant stated to an undercover officer that he had a "few companies" through which he could move money. He then transferred the money through various accounts, retaining a commission. If this accountant were a professionally designated accountant, actions by the accountant's professional organization would have followed, likely expelling the accountant from the organization.

This case clearly demonstrates the accountant committing a criminal act. However, the legislation also applies to individuals who accept property (including fees), should they know or be willfully blind to the fact that the property was obtained illegally. Such individuals could be charged with possession or laundering. This is an additional incentive for accountants to be cautious when they have any doubts regarding management integrity.

Figure 4-1 shows how responsibilities are layered upon the basic transaction processing of an organization. If something goes wrong with any of the layers, problems could arise. Decision makers are counted on to effectively process and organize transactions (a duty of loyalty). They are also expected to report suspicious transactions. Management accountants help ensure that accurate information is present in the underlying transactions in order to effectively prepare reports such as tax returns and financial statements. The latter are provided to regulators and are also audited by PAs. This figure helps show how auditors and regulators rely upon management in the conduct of their responsibilities.

Sources of auditors' legal liability in assurance engagements are the main focus of this chapter. They are shown in Table 4-1, along with the other potential claims or charges we have discussed. An example of a potential claim from each source is listed.

In recent years, both the number of lawsuits and the size of awards to plaintiffs have significantly increased in both Canada and the United States, although the increase in the United States has been more significant because of a number of factors, including the more litigious climate in that country. Many of the lawsuits brought against auditors are brought by third parties. There are no simple reasons for this increase, but the following are major factors:

Table 4-1   Major Sources of Auditors' Legal Liability

Source of Liability	Example of Potential Claim or Charge
Assurance Engagements	
Client—liability to client under common law	Client sues auditor for not discovering a defalcation during the audit.
Third party—liability to third parties under common law	Bank sues auditor for not discovering materially misstated financial statements.
Liability under provincial securities acts	A purchaser of stock issued by a company sues the auditor for not discovering materially misstated financial statements in a prospectus.
Criminal liability	Court prosecutes auditor under the Criminal Code of Canada for knowingly issuing an incorrect auditor's report.
Other Requirements	
Fiduciary duty—one party has an obligation to act for the benefit of another, and that obligation includes discretionary power	An accountant acting as trustee for a client invests in inappropriate investment vehicles and otherwise squanders the assets of the trust.
Proceeds of Crime (Money Laundering) and Terrorist Financing Act—obligation to report cash transactions and suspicious transactions and maintain control systems to track same	Five years in jail and/or a fine of up to $2 million for non-reporting of cash transactions over $10,000 or suspicious cash transfers
Criminal offence of possession or laundering	Transfer to legitimate organizations of money that was known to be proceeds of illegal activities, resulting in criminal charges.

- The growing awareness of the responsibilities of public accountants by users of financial statements.
- An increased consciousness on the part of the provincial securities commissions regarding their responsibility for protecting investors' interests.
- Increased market volatility, resulting in losses to third parties such as shareholders and institutional investors.
- The greater complexity of auditing and accounting due to such factors as the increasing size of business, the sophistication of computer-based systems, and the intricacies of business operations.
- Society's increasing acceptance of lawsuits by injured parties against anyone who might be able to provide compensation and who appears to be at least partially responsible for the loss. This is frequently called the "deep-pocket" concept of liability.
- The willingness of public accounting firms to settle their legal problems out of court in an attempt to avoid costly legal fees and adverse publicity rather than resolving them through the judicial process.
- The difficulty courts have in understanding and interpreting technical accounting and auditing matters.

DISTINCTION AMONG BUSINESS FAILURE, AUDIT FAILURE, AND AUDIT RISK Many accounting and legal professionals believe that a major cause of lawsuits against public accounting firms is the lack of understanding by financial statement users of the difference between a business failure and an audit failure and between an audit failure and audit risk. These terms are first defined, then followed by a discussion of how misunderstanding in the differences between the terms often results in lawsuits against auditors.

Business failure—the situation when a business is unable to repay its lenders or meet the expectations of its investors because of economic or business conditions.

Audit failure—a situation in which the auditor issues an erroneous audit opinion as the result of an underlying failure to comply with the requirements of generally accepted auditing standards.

Audit risk—the risk that the auditor will conclude that the financial statements are fairly stated and an unqualified opinion can therefore be issued when, in fact, they are materially misstated.

Fraud—a false assertion that has been made knowingly, without belief in its truth, or recklessly without caring whether it is true or not.

Due care [during an audit]—is completing the audit with care, diligence, and skill.

Business Failure A **business failure** occurs when a business is unable to repay its lenders or meet the expectations of its investors due to economic or business conditions such as a recession, poor management decisions, or unexpected competition in the industry. The extreme case of business failure is filing for bankruptcy. As stated in Chapter 1, there is always some risk that a business will fail.

Audit Failure An **audit failure** occurs when the auditor issues an erroneous audit opinion as the result of an underlying failure to comply with the requirements of generally accepted auditing standards (GAAS). For example, the auditor may have assigned unqualified assistants to perform audit tasks, and because of their lack of competence and inappropriate supervision, they fail to find material misstatements that qualified auditors would have discovered.

Audit Risk **Audit risk** is the risk that the auditor will conclude that the financial statements are fairly stated and an unqualified opinion can therefore be issued when, in fact, they are materially misstated. As will be shown in subsequent chapters, auditing cannot be expected to uncover all material financial statement misstatements. Auditing is limited by sampling, and certain misstatements and well-concealed **frauds** are extremely difficult to detect; therefore, there is always some risk that the audit will not uncover a material financial misstatement, even when the auditor has complied with GAAS.

Most accounting professionals agree that in most cases when an audit has failed to uncover material misstatements, and the wrong type of audit opinion is issued, a legitimate question may be raised as to whether the auditor exercised due care. A PA who exercises **due care** is completing the audit with care, diligence, and skill. If the auditor failed to use due care in the conduct of the audit, then there is an audit failure. In such cases, the law often allows parties who suffered losses as a result of the auditor's breach of duty of care owed to them to recover some or all of the losses linked to the audit failure. It is difficult in practice to determine when the auditor has failed to follow due care because of the complexity of auditing. It is also not always clear who has a right to expect the benefits of an audit because of the evolving nature of the law.

The difficulty arises when there has been a business failure but not an audit failure. For example, when a company goes bankrupt or cannot pay its debts, it is common for statement users to claim there was an audit failure, particularly when the most recently issued auditor's opinion indicates the financial statements were fairly stated. This conflict between statement users and auditors often arises because of

auditing in action 4 - 1
Benefits from Research in Predicting Organizational Failures

Remember that one of the principles in GAAP is "going concern"—that an organization will be there in the coming financial year. Auditors use ratios and financial modelling to help them assess the likelihood of business failure. Some of these financial models were first derived by researchers and tested against publicly available information about organizational failure and success. According to Statistics Canada, there were over 6,000 bankruptcies in 2007 alone, so analytical tools that help predict business failure are a welcome adjunct to the auditor's toolbox.

Dionne, Laajimi, Mejri, and Petrescu compared the results of three sets of calculations in their ability to predict bankruptcy defaults among Canadian public corporations. The authors used a model that examined stock market data (which predicted

61 percent of the defaults correctly), one that used financial statement data only (86 percent accuracy for defaults), and a combined or hybrid model that used both financial statement and stock market data (97 percent accuracy for defaults). What was most interesting was that splitting the time period studied in half resulted in a 100 percent accuracy prediction rate for defaults for the period 1996–2004. PAs can certainly use this kind of help when assessing the going-concern assumption!

Sources: 1. Dionne, Georges, Sadok Laajimi, Sofiane Mejri, and Madalina Petrescu, "Estimation of the default risk of publicly traded companies: Evidence from Canadian data," *Canadian Journal of Administrative Studies*, 25, 2008, p. 134–152. 2. Statistics Canada, "Bankruptcies, by industry, by province and territory," 2008, www40.statcan.gc.ca/l01/cst01/econ11a-eng.htm, Accessed: September 22, 2008.

It is a difficult scenario—management fraud occurs and the financial statements are misstated. The business fails, and the bank or creditors lose money because asset accounts had been inflated. You think that is the worst—then management (who committed the fraud) turns around and sues the auditor. Luckily, the courts will not allow someone who benefited from a criminal action (e.g., fraud) to sue an auditor and recover money as part of the consequences of his or her fraud. Misleading the auditor includes deliberately withholding documentation. Even though the financial statements are misstated, the auditor relied upon management to prepare those financial statements.

A similar concept applies to directors. If directors rely upon the advice of management in making their decisions, they will not always be held liable for losses related to their decisions based upon that reliance.

CRITICAL THINKING QUESTIONS

1. How does management benefit from withholding information from auditors?
2. What effect does the absence of evidence have on the auditors?
3. How can lack of relevant disclosure affect the shareholders of a company?

Sources: 1. Paskell-Mede, Mindy, "Judging ill-gotten gains," *CAmagazine*, November 2002, p. 33–34. 2. Paskell-Mede, Mindy, "Obligated to reveal," *CAmagazine*, September 2007, p. 55, 57. 3. Rose, Jan, "Directors make mistakes," *CAmagazine*, November 2003, p. 36–38.

what is referred to as the expectation gap between users and auditors. An **expectation gap** is the conflict between what some users expect from an auditor's report and what the auditor's report is designed to deliver; some users believe that an auditor's report is a guarantee for the accuracy of the financial statements, although the report is, in fact, an opinion based on an audit conducted according to GAAS. Most auditors believe that conducting an audit in accordance with GAAS is all that can be expected of auditors. Many users believe auditors guarantee the accuracy of financial statements, and some users even believe the auditor guarantees the financial viability of the business. Fortunately for the profession, the courts continue to support the auditor's view.

> **Expectation gap**—the conflict between what some users expect from an auditor's report and what the auditor's report is designed to deliver; some users believe that an auditor's report is a guarantee for the accuracy of the financial statements, although the report is, in fact, an opinion based on an audit conducted according to GAAS.

❷ Legal Terms Affecting PAs and Their Clients

Legal Concepts Affecting Liability

The public accountant is responsible for every aspect of his or her public accounting work, including auditing, taxes, management advisory services, and accounting and bookkeeping services. Section 5020 of the *CICA Handbook*, "Association," helps explain the public accountant's involvement with an enterprise and with information issued by that enterprise. (There is no equivalent CAS proposed for Section 5020.) For example, if a public accountant negligently failed to properly prepare and file a client's tax return, the public accountant can be held liable for any penalties and interest the client was required to pay plus the tax preparation fee charged.

Most of the major lawsuits against public accounting firms have dealt with audited or unaudited financial statements. The discussion in this chapter deals primarily with these two aspects of public accounting. The areas of liability in auditing can be classified as (1) liability to clients, (2) liability to third parties under common law and statute law, and (3) criminal liability. Several legal concepts apply to these types of lawsuits against public accountants: the prudent person concept, liability for the acts of others, and the lack of privileged communication.

PRUDENT PERSON CONCEPT There is agreement within the profession and the courts that the auditor is not a guarantor or insurer of financial statements. The auditor is

> **concept check**
>
> C4-1 List the sources of legal liability of a PA.
>
> C4-2 Explain when a PA has a fiduciary duty to a client.
>
> C4-3 How does Canadian money-laundering legislation affect a PA?

expected only to conduct the audit with due care. Even then, the auditor cannot be expected to be perfect.

The standard of due care to which the auditor is expected to be held is often referred to as the **prudent person concept**. This is the legal concept that a person has a duty to exercise reasonable care and diligence in the performance of his or her obligations to another.

LIABILITY FOR ACTS OF OTHERS The partners of a public accounting firm may have **joint and several liability** if a suit for tort or negligence is brought against the partnership. In other words, each partner may be held liable in a civil action for the tort or negligent actions of each of the other partners and employees in the partnership. Ontario provincial legislation has given accounting firms the ability to reduce their liability by forming **limited liability partnerships (LLPs)**. This is an organizational structure whereby only the person who does the work, those who supervise that person, and the firm itself are liable, but not other individual partners within the firm. In the absence of fraud or actual knowledge, only the person who did the work and those who supervised that person, as well as the firm itself, would be liable. The auditor can also be held responsible for damages of others using the concept of joint and several liability. If an auditor is partially responsible but none of the other defendants has assets or insurance, then there will be an attempt to collect all damages from the auditor.

The partners may also be liable for the work of others on whom they rely. The groups an auditor is most likely to rely on are other public accounting firms engaged to do part of the work, internal auditors, and specialists called upon to provide technical information. Where a primary–secondary auditor relationship exists, the primary auditor would be entitled to rely upon the work of the secondary auditor, assuming that the primary auditor had conducted sufficient quality control work with respect to that secondary auditor. If the auditor proved that there was appropriate reliance on the work of a specialist, there would be an extremely strong defence that the auditor was not negligent and would not be liable to the plaintiff, assuming that GAAS were followed.

LACK OF PRIVILEGED COMMUNICATION Public accountants do not have the right under common law to withhold information from the courts on the grounds that the information is privileged. A court can subpoena information in an auditor's working papers. Confidential discussions between the client and auditor cannot be withheld

new standards 4-1
Effects of Changed Rules for Civil Liability

Effective December 31, 2005, the Ontario government enacted legislation as part of its Investor Confidence Initiative (comprising Bill 198, 2002; Bill 145, 2004; and Part XXIII.1 Ontario Securities Act) that both increases legal liability and reduces the amounts that auditors could be liable for. The legislation provides that both initial and secondary investors could sue (with court permission) where they relied upon information that was misrepresented (such as incorrect financial statements). Changes that would affect public accountants are proportional liability (they could be sued for only the portion for which they are judged to be at fault) and a cap on liability based upon a formula that is the greater of $1 million or the earnings from the client (and its affiliates) for the 12 months preceding the misrepresentation. These changes mean that more parties could sue

the auditor but that the amount for which he or she would be liable would be less. The cap on liability does not apply if the defendant knew about the misrepresentation or failed to make known the misrepresentation on a timely basis.

An important aspect of this legislation is that the plaintiff does not need to prove that he or she relied upon the false information but only that there was a loss. Lawsuits could use these regulations, and similar legislation in other provinces, to "fast track" their claims.

Sources: 1. DiLieto, Rossana, Jean-Paul Bureaud, William J. Braithwaite, Peter Jervis, and G. Wesley Voorheis, "Preparing for Secondary Market Civil Liability," www.apgo.net/newsletters/2005-12/dwo_20051117_market-disclosure.pdf, Accessed: November 11, 2009. 2. Morgan, Brian, "New liabilities," *CAmagazine*, June/July 2003, p. 34-36.

from the courts. In the very specific situation where an accountant prepares documentation as a result of a lawyer's request to be used in existing or potential litigation, that documentation could be considered privileged (e.g., *Cineplex Odeon v. MNR* *[Ministry of National Revenue]*, 1994), as could confidential legal information provided by a client.

Definitions of Legal Terms

The material in the rest of the chapter can be studied more effectively if the most common legal terms affecting public accountants' liability are understood. Take a moment to review the terms in Table 4-2. Be sure to note the distinction between joint and several liability and separate and proportionate liability. In Canada, unless the charges are brought under provincial civil liability legislation (see New Standards 4-1), joint and several liability applies.

Gross negligence—lack of even slight care that can be expected of a person, tantamount to reckless behaviour.

Table 4-2	Legal Terms Affecting PA Liability
Legal Term	Description
Terms Related to Negligence and Fraud	
Negligence	Failure to exercise reasonable care in the performance of one's obligations to another. For auditors, it is in terms of what other competent auditors would have done in the same situation.
Tort action for negligence	A legal action taken by an injured party against the party whose negligence resulted in the injury. A typical negligence action against a PA is a bank's claim that an auditor had a duty to uncover material errors in financial statements that had been relied on in making a loan.
Gross negligence	Lack of even slight care that can be expected of a person, tantamount to reckless behaviour.
Contributory negligence	When a person injured by a public accountant's negligence has also been negligent, and this negligence has also caused or contributed to the person's loss or injuries. A common example of such negligence is failure to give a public accountant information requested during the preparation of a tax return. The client later sues the accountant for improper preparation of the return. The court may hold that there was contributory negligence on the part of the client, and any damages that the client is awarded would be reduced in proportion to the amount that the client's own negligence was responsible for the loss. This defence is also used to reduce the effects of joint and several liability.
Fraud	A false assertion that has been made knowingly, without belief in its truth, or recklessly without caring whether or not it is true. An example is an auditor giving a standard (unqualified) opinion on financial statements that will be used to obtain a loan when the auditor knows the financial statements contain a material misstatement.
Constructive fraud	Existence of such recklessness that, even though there was no actual intent to defraud, a court will impute or construe fraud to the action. For example, if a public accountant failed to follow most of the generally accepted auditing standards, he or she may be found to have committed constructive fraud even though no intent to deceive statement users has been proven. (This concept has been used in foreign court cases but has not been used in Canadian cases. It is therefore not discussed further in this chapter. We will focus instead on negligence and fraud.)
Terms Related to Contract Law	
Breach of contract	Failure of one or both parties in a contract to fulfill the requirements of the contract. An example is the failure of a public accounting firm to deliver a tax return on the agreed-upon date. Parties who have a relationship that is established by a contract are said to have privity of contract. There can be privity of contract without a written agreement, but an engagement letter defines the contract more clearly.

continued >

Table 4-2	Legal Terms Affecting PA Liability (*Continued*)

Legal Term	Description
Third-party beneficiary	A third party who does not have privity of contract but is known to the contracting parties and is intended to have certain rights and benefits under the contract. A common example is a bank that has a large loan outstanding at the balance sheet date and requires an audit as a part of its loan agreement.
Other Terms	
Common law	Laws developed through court decisions rather than through government statutes; also called "judge-made law" or "case law". An example is an auditor's liability to a bank related to the auditor's failure to discover material misstatements in financial statements that were relied upon in issuing a loan. Common law is always evolving as new precedents are set by the courts.
Statutory law	Laws and regulations that have been passed by a Canadian government body, either federal or provincial. The Canada Business Corporations Act is an important statutory law affecting auditors of companies incorporated under its jurisdiction.
Civil action	An action between individuals such as those that may be brought for breach of contract or tort.
Criminal action	An action brought under a provision of criminal statute law, for example, the Criminal Code of Canada.
Joint and several liability	The assessment against a defendant of the full loss suffered by a plaintiff, regardless of the extent to which other parties shared in the wrongdoing. For example, if management intentionally misstates financial statements, an auditor can be assessed the entire loss to shareholders if the company is bankrupt and management is unable to pay.
Separate and proportional liability	The assessment against a defendant of that portion of the damage caused by the defendant's negligence. For example, if the courts determine that an auditor's negligence in conducting an audit was the cause of 30 percent of the loss to a defendant, only 30 percent of the aggregate damage will be assessed to the public accounting firm.

Separate and proportional liability—the assessment against a defendant of that portion of the damage caused by the defendant's negligence.

Liability to Clients

The term "client" refers to the entity being audited and not to its owners or shareholders. Although the shareholders vote to appoint the auditors, the contract is between the enterprise and the auditors. In effect, shareholders are third parties and are discussed further, together with liability to other third parties, on page 90.

Lawsuits against public accountants from clients vary widely, including such claims as failure to complete an audit engagement on the agreed-upon date, inappropriate withdrawal from an audit, failure to discover a **defalcation** (theft of assets), and breach of the confidentiality requirements of public accountants. These lawsuits are relatively rare, and they do not receive the publicity often given to third-party suits. *Cameron v. Piers, Conrod & Allen* (see Figure 4-5 on page 86) is a case in this area.

Defalcation—theft of assets.

A typical lawsuit involves a claim that the auditor did not discover an employee defalcation as a result of negligence in the conduct of the audit. The lawsuit can be for breach of contract, a **tort action for negligence**, or both. Tort actions can be based on ordinary negligence or fraud. Note that, while, it might sound odd for plaintiffs to claim under both breach of contract and negligence, the way each is proven and the amount of damages available under each might be different. By claiming under both, the plaintiff is covering all bases. The plaintiff cannot, however, be awarded damages twice for one event or loss.

Tort action for negligence—a legal action taken by an injured party against the party whose negligence resulted in the injury.

The principal issue in cases involving alleged negligence is usually the level of care required. Although it is generally agreed that nobody is perfect, not even a professional, in most instances, any significant misstatement will create a doubt regarding competence. In the auditing environment, failure to meet GAAS is often strong evidence of negligence. An example of an audit case raising the question of negligent performance by a public accounting firm is the case of *Haig v. Bamford et al.* (see Figure 4-8 on page 88). The reader should remember from the study of GAAS in Chapter 2 that determining due care and the amount and type of evidence to be obtained on an audit are subjective decisions. In a suit where negligence by an auditor was alleged, the court would hear evidence from one or more expert (auditing) witnesses as to the decision they would have reached in similar circumstances. From this evidence, a judge or jury would decide what the typical public accountant would do and, therefore, what the accountant being sued should have done.

The question of level of care becomes more difficult in the environment of unaudited financial statements (i.e., a review or compilation) in which there are few accepted standards by which to evaluate performance. An example of a lawsuit dealing with the failure to uncover fraud in unaudited financial statements is the Multi Graphics case, summarized in Figure 4-2 on the next page. Figure 4-3 (also on the next page) addresses a key standard of review engagements (plausibility, Chapter 23) in *Italian Gifts v. Dixon*, 2000.

AUDITORS' DEFENCES AGAINST CLIENT SUITS FOR NEGLIGENCE The public accounting firm normally uses one or more of six defences (see Table 4-3 on page 90) when there are legal claims of negligence by clients: lack of duty to perform the service, absence of misstatement, no damages, absence of negligence, absence of causal connection, and **contributory negligence**.

Lack of Duty The **lack of duty to perform** the service is a legal defence under which the professional claims that no contract existed with the plaintiff; therefore, no duty existed to perform the disputed service. For example, the public accounting firm might claim that errors were not uncovered because the firm did a review engagement, not an audit. A common way for a public accounting firm to demonstrate a lack of duty to perform is by use of an engagement letter.[3] Many litigation experts believe well-written engagement letters are one of the most important ways public accounting firms can reduce the likelihood of adverse legal actions.

Kuziw et al. v. Abbott et al. (see Figure 4-4 on page 85) illustrates reliance with a lack of duty.

Absence of Misstatement Prior to addressing negligence, the defendant accountants could provide evidence that the financial statements were in accordance with GAAP, that is, that there were no material errors. Thus, even if the auditors had been negligent, the appropriate financial statements would not have differed from those on which the plaintiff relied. Therefore, no grounds exist for suing the auditors, since the financial statements appropriately portray the financial situation of the organization and there was an **absence of misstatement**.

No Damages (or Reduced Damages) It is possible that the financial statements were misstated and that the audit was negligently performed but that the plaintiff did not suffer any damages. This was one of the issues addressed by the Supreme Court of Canada in the case of *Hercules Managements Ltd. v. Ernst & Young* (see Figure 4-10 on page 89). A third party, the shareholders, claimed damages, but the Supreme Court

Contributory negligence—a legal defence under which the professional claims that the client failed to perform certain obligations and that it is the client's failure to perform those obligations that brought about the claimed damages.

Lack of duty to perform—a legal defence under which the professional claims that no contract existed with the plaintiff; therefore no duty existed to perform the disputed service.

Absence of misstatement—the financial statements appropriately portray the financial situation of the organization.

---

[3] Two types of letters that are commonly used by auditors to reduce potential liability to clients are an engagement letter and a management representation letter. An engagement letter is a signed agreement between the public accounting firm and the client identifying such items as whether an audit is to be done, other services to be provided, the date by which the work is to be completed, and the fees. The representation letter documents oral communication between auditors and management and states management's responsibilities for fair presentation in the financial statements.

Figure 4-2	466715 Ontario Limited Operating as Multi Graphics Print & Litho v. Helen Proulx and Doane Raymond (1998)[4]

Doane Raymond (now Grant Thornton) carried out review engagements between 1985 and 1993 for Multi Graphics Print and Litho for an annual fee of about $1,500. Helen Proulx, the sole bookkeeper, commenced fraudulent activity in 1988, when she was given signing authority. Shortly afterwards, a computerized ACCPAC Bedford system was installed. The fraud involved Helen Proulx preparing cheques to herself, signing and cashing them (the cheques were recorded as payable to suppliers or to reimbursement of petty cash), pocketing money from C.O.D. orders, issuing fictitious invoices, and pocketing the difference between amounts recorded and amounts actually deposited. Over $100,000 was stolen. The owners signed cheques over $1,000 and did not handle mail or review source documents or bank statements.

When the fraud was discovered, Multi Graphics sued the accountants, claiming that the accountants ought to have known of the control problems at Multi Graphics and should have alerted the owners to the related dangers. The accountants countered by saying that they were retained to provide review services. The engagement letter explicitly described a review engagement and stated that there was no responsibility to consider internal controls or to detect fraud. The accountants were not consulted on issues of internal controls, the change in the computerized accounting system, or the change in signing authority.

The court ruled in favour of Doane Raymond, finding that the accountants had fulfilled their professional and contractual obligations, and that the agreement between the parties specifically excluded responsibility to detect fraud and error. The court added that the duty of care in a review engagement would not create the obligation to go any further than the accountants did.

Figure 4-3	Italian Gifts v. Dixon (2000)[5]

Dixon, a chartered accountant firm, was hired to conduct a review engagement for Italian Gifts. The firm did not detect an under-remittance of sales taxes with a corresponding over-remittance of income taxes. In one particular month, only $1.68 in sales taxes was remitted on more than $19,000 of sales. The client was claiming damages that included the penalties and interest on the unremitted sales tax, as well as income tax overpayments that could not be recovered, interest on overpaid income taxes, and professional fees.

Two lower courts had rejected this claim for three reasons:

1. No duty was owed, since the client was not relying on the accountants for tax remittances.

2. The nature of a review engagement would not have included the duty of preparing sales tax remittances.

3. The bookkeeping [review engagement] function was not of a nature to require an analysis of the remittances.

The Ontario Court of Appeal overturned this rejection, stating that the accountants' failure to inquire into the plausibility of the sales tax remittances fell below the standards set out in the *CICA Handbook*. This reference reinforces the importance of this CICA publication. A simple analysis (calculating sales tax as a percentage of sales, for example) would have revealed the inadequacy of these amounts. An engagement letter with exclusions for responsibility for the detection of errors and irregularities was not considered an acceptable defence, due to the accountants' negligence.

Given the client's own errors, which caused the original problem, and that clients are clearly responsible for their own financial statements, the Court of Appeal reduced the damages by 50% due to contributory negligence.

stated that the damages were suffered by the corporate entity itself rather than by the shareholders. Thus, those plaintiffs (the shareholders) had no standing in law to claim the damages.

---

[4] Kulig, P., "Doane Raymond absolved of wrongdoing," *The Bottom Line*, November 1, 1998, p. 14; and Trial judgment, Ontario Court (General Division), 95-CU-87608, August 20, 1998.

[5] Paskell-Mede, Mindy, "A limitation of liability," *CAmagazine*, November 2000, p. 47–48. Note that there is no equivalent CAS proposed for Section 9200.

Absence of Negligence This is a legal defence under which the professional claims that the disputed service was properly performed; an auditor would claim that the audit was performed according to GAAS. Even if there were undiscovered unintentional misstatements (errors), intentional misstatements, or misrepresentations (fraud and other irregularities), the auditors would argue that they were not responsible if the audit was properly conducted. This occurs because there was an **absence of negligence**. The public accounting firm is not expected to be infallible.

It is likely that the courts will accept the *CICA Handbook* as evidence of appropriate standards of behaviour for the auditor, but it is possible that the courts could decide that an auditor who complied with the *Handbook* had been negligent. Such circumstances would be rare, but they could occur if the court thought the auditor had complied with the letter and not the spirit of the rules, or if GAAP were not sufficiently informative.

Requiring auditors to discover all material misstatements would make them insurers or guarantors of the accuracy of the financial statements. The courts do not require that. *Cameron v. Piers, Conrod & Allen* (see Figure 4-5) is an example of a case where the public accountant was not negligent; the court ruled that the auditor had satisfied the prudent person concept.

Absence of Causal Connection To succeed in an action against the auditor, the client must be able to show that there is a close causal connection between the auditor's breach of the standard of due care and the damages suffered by the client. For example, assume an auditor failed to complete an audit on the agreed-upon date. The client alleges that this caused a bank not to renew an outstanding loan, which caused damages. A potential auditor defence is that the bank refused to renew the loan for other reasons, such as the weakening financial condition of the client. The case of *Kuziw et al. v. Abbott et al.*, discussed in Figure 4-4, illustrates **absence of causal connection** — the legal defence under which the professional contends that the damages claimed by the client were not brought about by any act of the professional; the court

Absence of negligence—a legal defence under which the professional claims that the disputed service was properly performed; an auditor would claim that the audit was performed according to GAAS.

Absence of causal connection—a legal defence under which the professional contends that the damages claimed by the client were not brought about by any act of the professional.

<table>
<tr><td>Figure 4-5</td><td>*Cameron v. Piers, Conrod & Allen* (1985)[6]</td></tr>
</table>

Piers, Conrod & Allen (PCA) were the auditors for Cameron Limited and its subsidiary, Kentville Publishing Company Limited. The year end of the latter company was October 31, while that of the former company was December 31. Kentville was run by a competent accountant who was in frequent contact with and highly regarded by the owner of Cameron Limited.

PCA was unable to gain access to Kentville books for the year ended October 31, 1979, until several months after the year end.

The auditor from PCA and his staff went to the offices of Kentville and did what work was considered necessary to complete the audit of Cameron. At that time, there was no indication of any serious problems at Kentville. The Cameron December 31, 1979, financial statements were issued with an unqualified opinion. The notes to the financial statements indicated that the accounts of Kentville and other subsidiaries were not consolidated but were carried at cost.

Subsequently, the manager of Kentville was hospitalized. It was discovered that the reports that the manager had been giving to the owner of Cameron and to the auditor were not accurate.

Cameron Limited sued PCA on the grounds that PCA had been negligent in evaluating Cameron's investment in Kentville as at December 31, 1979. The court found (sustained on appeal) that the auditor had not been negligent in that he had exercised reasonable care and skill in attempting to evaluate Cameron's investment in Kentville.

ruled that the purchaser, Kuziw, did not rely on an incorrect auditor's report but rather had decided to purchase Graf-Tech based on other information.

Contributory Negligence A defence of contributory negligence means that the public accounting firm claims that part or all of the loss arose because of the claimant's own negligence. For example, suppose the client is the claimant and argues that the public accounting firm was negligent in not uncovering an employee theft of cash. A likely contributory negligence defence is the auditor's claim that the public accounting firm informed management of a weakness in the internal controls that enhanced the likelihood of the fraud, but management did not correct it. Management often does not correct internal control weaknesses because of cost considerations, attitudes about employee honesty, or procrastination. The auditor is unlikely to lose this suit, assuming a strong contributory negligence defence, if the client was informed in writing of internal control weaknesses. Figure 4-3, *Italian Gifts v. Dixon*, is an example of contributory negligence.

concept check

C4-4 How could the changing legal environment in Canada increase or decrease auditor liability?

C4-5 Explain the difference between joint and several liability and proportional liability.

C4-6 Can the auditor withhold information from the courts? Why or why not?

③ Liability to Non-Clients

Liability to Third Parties under Common Law

A public accounting firm may be liable to third parties if a loss was incurred by the claimant due to reliance on misleading financial statements. Third parties are those with whom the auditor did not enter into a contract and include actual and potential shareholders, vendors, bankers and other creditors or investors, employees, and customers. A typical suit might occur when a bank is unable to collect a major loan from an insolvent customer. The bank will claim that misleading audited financial statements were relied upon in making the loan and that the public accounting firm should be held responsible because it failed to perform the audit with due care. Understanding when the auditor will be held liable calls for an understanding of the continuing evolution of this area of the law.

---

[6] Rowan, Hugh, Q.C., "Stymied by management: A case of negligence?" *CAmagazine*, April 1986, p. 80–87.

Figure 4-6 *Ultramares Corporation v. Touche* (1931)

The creditors of an insolvent corporation (Ultramares) relied on the audited financials and subsequently sued the accountants, alleging that they were guilty of negligence and fraudulent misrepresentation. The accounts receivable had been falsified by adding to approximately $650,000 in accounts receivable another item of over $700,000. The creditors alleged that careful investigation would have shown the $700,000 to be fraudulent. The accounts payable contained similar discrepancies. The court held that the accountants had been negligent but ruled that accountants would not be liable to third parties for honest blunders beyond the bounds of the original contract unless they were third-party beneficiaries. The court held that only one who enters into a contract with an accountant for services can sue if those services are rendered negligently.

The court went on, however, to order a new trial on the issue of fraudulent misstatement. The form of certificate then used said, "We further certify that subject to provisions for federal taxes on income the said statement in our opinion presents a true and correct view of the financial condition." The court pointed out that to make such a representation if one did not have an honest belief in its truth would be fraudulent misrepresentation.

EVOLUTION OF LIABILITY The leading precedent-setting auditing case in third-party liability was a 1931 U.S. case, *Ultramares Corporation v. Touche*. It established the traditional common law approach known as the Ultramares doctrine. The case has been cited many times in England and Canada. It is summarized in Figure 4-6.

The key aspect of the Ultramares doctrine is that ordinary negligence is insufficient for liability to third parties because of the lack of privity of contract between the third party and the auditor. The judge commented that it would be inappropriate to hold the auditors liable to third parties in the circumstances, since this would open the doors to indeterminate liability of an indeterminate amount to an indeterminate number of people. The case was followed by other jurisdictions on the basis of the policy considerations underlying this judgment. In addition, Ultramares also held that if there had been fraud or **constructive fraud**, the auditor could be held liable to more general third parties.

Traditionally, third parties in Canada were in a position similar to those in the United States: they were effectively prevented from suing successfully for negligent misstatements if they had no contract with the auditor. The situation began to change in 1963 with an English case, *Hedley Byrne & Co. Ltd. v. Heller & Partners Ltd.* (see Figure 4-7). Although the case was English, not Canadian, and did not deal specifically with accountants, it contained very real implications for them. In the United Kingdom, it was viewed as the long-awaited statement about the law of negligent misstatement, and it came from the most senior court of that country, the House of Lords. All common law countries were interested in its outcome. The defence of lack of privity enunciated in Ultramares was said by the House of Lords to be no longer relevant. The notion of foreseeable third parties was introduced as a possible test of the extent of duty. The law lords said that those uttering negligent misstatements may be liable

Constructive fraud—conduct that the law construes as fraud even though there was no actual intent to deceive; considered to be so reckless that the courts decide it is tantamount to fraud.

Figure 4-7 *Hedley Byrne v. Heller & Partners* (1963)

Hedley Byrne was an advertising agency that was about to incur a liability for advertising for a client. They asked their bankers to find out from the client's bankers, Heller & Partners, if the client was credit-worthy. Heller replied in the affirmative to the banker, who passed the information on to Hedley Byrne, and so Hedley Byrne, a third party, incurred the liability. Subsequently, the client was unable to pay its accounts, and Hedley Byrne sued Heller & Partners for negligence.

Heller & Partners had issued a disclaimer together with their opinion and thus the House of Lords ruled in their favour. However, with respect to the lack of privity, the Lords found that not to be a bar to success by the plaintiff, Hedley Byrne. Some of the law lords argued that despite the lack of privity, Heller owed a duty of care to Hedley Byrne and that Heller should have foreseen that Hedley Byrne would rely on their statement about the client.

Scholler Furniture & Fixtures Ltd. needed additional working capital and approached Saskatchewan Economic Development Corporation (SEDCO) for further advances. SEDCO agreed to grant the advances, provided Scholler would produce satisfactory audited financial statements for the fiscal period ended March 31, 1965.

Scholler told his accountants, Bamford et al., that he needed audited financial statements for SEDCO, his bank, and a potential but then unknown investor. The statements were prepared with an auditor's report appended and shown to Haig who invested $20,000.

Subsequently, the company again floundered, and investigation revealed that the financial statements included $28,000 of revenue received in advance as earned revenue; the corrected statements showed that the company had lost money and not earned a sizable profit as shown by the earlier statements. It was discovered that Bamford et al., although they were told an audit was required and although they appended an auditor's report, had not done an audit.

Later Haig advanced additional funds but the company went into receivership. Haig sued the accountants for negligence and sought to recover both his original investment and later advance.

The Supreme Court, in their decision, concurred with lower courts that Bamford et al. had been negligent. As regards the extent of the duty of care on the part of the accountants to third parties, the court said there were three possible tests:

1. Foreseeability of the use of audited financial statements by the plaintiff.

2. Actual knowledge of the limited class who will rely on the audited statements.

3. Actual knowledge of the person who will rely on the audited statements.

The appropriate test was deemed to be #2. The court decided that Haig was entitled to recover his original investment from the auditors because he had relied on the financial statements that had been negligently prepared. He was not entitled to recover subsequent investments because he made them on the basis of his own information.

to third parties but did not make clear precisely under what circumstances. Courts in a number of countries have been grappling with the issue ever since.

The Supreme Court of Canada decided the next case of importance on this issue in 1976. The case was *Gordon T. Haig v. Ralph L. Bamford et al.* (see Figure 4-8).

This case confirms the finding in *Hedley Byrne v. Heller* that lack of privity is not necessarily a valid defence. However, the Supreme Court decided it should not consider the foreseeability test (i.e., test #1), as it was not relevant to the particular circumstances. Instead, the narrower test of actual knowledge of the limited class was deemed to be appropriate, that is, in Canada, persons making negligent misstatements (in this case, auditors) are potentially liable to all those third parties who were members of a limited group of whom the auditors had knowledge at the time the audit was performed and to whom the audited financial statements were issued. For example, the test of actual knowledge would apply if an auditor were asked to give an opinion on financial statements to be shown to several local banks for purposes of obtaining a loan. The narrowest of the three tests, that the auditor must know the actual individual, was rejected as being too narrow.

At about the same time, another case of interest was unfolding; it was *Toromont Industrial Holdings Limited v. Thorne, Gunn, Helliwell & Christenson*. This case, summarized in Figure 4-9, reached its final resolution in the High Court of Justice in Ontario. The Toromont case raises several interesting issues. The judgment, which referred both to *Hedley Byrne* and a lower court decision on *Haig v. Bamford*, confirmed the broadening of an auditor's liability to third parties known to be using the audited financial statements. In the case of *Toromont v. Thorne*, Toromont was able to

---

[7] The *Haig v. Bamford* case was first decided in a lower court in 1972 for the plaintiff. The decision was appealed and reversed by the Saskatchewan Court of Appeal in 1974. Haig appealed that decision and was successful in the Supreme Court of Canada in 1976.

Figure 4-9	*Toromont v. Thorne et al.* (1975)

Toromont proposed to acquire all of the shares of Cimco Ltd. for cash and Toromont shares. The purchase price was based on Cimco's assets, liabilities, and financial position. Prior to purchase, a partner of the accounting firm that did Toromont's audit talked to a partner of Thorne, Cimco's auditors, about the work the latter had done with regard to the December 31, 1968, financial statements. Cimco's financial statements at this point were in draft form. In other words, Thorne et al. were aware of Toromont's interest in the financial statements prior to their being issued.

The court decided that the financial statements did present fairly the financial position at December 31, 1968, but that the auditors, Thorne et al., had been negligent in their performance of the 1968 audit. The reasons given were as follows:

1. They did not obtain sufficient evidence about certain contracts.

2. They relied too heavily on oral evidence from management.

3. They did not adequately check the system of internal control in force although they relied on it.

4. The accounts included goodwill with respect to a company sold two years previously.

The court concluded that Thorne et al. had been negligent and that Toromont did have a right of action as Thorne knew Toromont would be relying on the financial statements. The court, however, also concluded that Toromont did not suffer any loss from the negligence, and so the case was dismissed.

prove that Thorne et al. owed a duty of care to Toromont and that Thorne et al. had been negligent in the performance of that duty, but Toromont was not able to prove that it suffered a loss. As a consequence, Toromont did not succeed.

In 1997, in *Hercules Managements v. Ernst & Young*,[8] as mentioned earlier, the court ruled that the auditors had no special knowledge that the shareholders planned to use the financial statements for investment decisions and that there was no privity of contract. The auditors relied on Caparo in their defence that they owed no duty of care to the shareholders. Figure 4-10 describes this case further and shows that the Supreme Court of Canada agreed with the lower court.

Figure 4-10	*Hercules Managements Ltd. v. Ernst & Young* (1997)[9]

Hercules Managements Ltd. and other shareholders of Northguard Acceptance Ltd. (NGA) and of Northguard Holdings Ltd. (NGH) sued Ernst and Young in 1988 after both NGA and NGH went into receivership in 1984. The plaintiffs argued that the audit reports for the years 1980, 1981, and 1982 were negligently prepared and that the shareholders suffered financial losses due to reliance on these reports.

This action was dismissed both by the Manitoba Court of Queen's Bench and by the Manitoba Appeal Court on the grounds that (1) the defendants did not owe the plaintiffs a duty of care and (2) the claims should be brought by the corporations and not by the shareholders individually, since a shareholder cannot succeed for a reduction in value of equity, even if a duty of care were owed, because the loss of equity is really the loss suffered by the company.

In May 1997, the Supreme Court of Canada generally agreed. The court said audited financial reports call for "a duty of care" by auditors when they are used "as a guide for the shareholders, as a group, in supervising or overseeing management." Thus, there appears to be no direct liability to the shareholders for any reduction in the value of their equity.

This case has entrenched the principle of "no general auditor liability" where this might give rise to an indeterminate amount of such liability in the absence of any evidence that the auditor knew of a specific purpose, other than corporate governance, to which the financial statements would be put. Such liability, though, could be legislated, as described in New Standards 4-1 on page 80.

---

[8] Paskell-Mede, Mindy, "What liability crisis?", *CAmagazine*, May 1996, p. 47–48.

[9] Mathias, Philip, "Auditors not legally liable to investors, top court rules," *Financial Post*, May 24, 1997, p. 3; and Paskell-Mede, Mindy and Don Selman, "Point, counterpoint," *CAmagazine,* September 1997, p. 39–40.

Table 4-3	**Six Auditor Defences Against Third-Party Suits**

Defence	Description
Lack of duty to perform (also known as duty of care)	Liability is limited to foreseeable known users.*
Absence of misstatement	Also known as "no error"—the financial statements as relied upon are accurate in all material respects.
No damages	Even though the financial statements were misstated and the audit was negligently performed, the plaintiff did not suffer any damages.
Absence of negligent performance	The auditor conducted the audit in accordance with GAAS.
Absence of causal connection	a) It is irrelevant that the financial statements are materially misstated, as the user did not rely upon them, or b) the auditor is liable only for losses due to fraud after a time when they could or should have detected the fraud.
Contributory negligence	The party suing is also negligent.

*This defence is subject to legislation. For example, in Ontario, it is proposed that auditors would have liability to investors, which is presently not the case under common law.

AUDITOR DEFENCES AGAINST THIRD-PARTY SUITS The defences available to auditors in suits by clients are also available in third-party lawsuits (see Table 4-3).

The previous section outlined the lack of duty of care defence. As the preceding discussion has suggested, the court, in *Ultramares*, limited the auditor's liability for negligence to parties being in privity with the auditor. *Hedley Byrne* introduced the notion of the auditor having a duty of care to foreseeable third parties; *Haig v. Bamford* narrowed the responsibility for duty of care by the auditor to the limited class whom the auditor actually knew would use and rely on the financial statements. The more recent cases in both the United Kingdom and Canada suggest that we now know that the limited class is to be defined in relation to the known purpose of the financial statements and that, therefore, each case should be decided on its own factual context. The class that the auditor is liable to is also subject to legislation. As explained in the previous section, secondary investors (those who purchase shares after an initial offering) can now also sue auditors under provincial legislation without needing to prove reliance on the information.

The second defence in third-party suits, absence of misstatement, is also known as "no error" in the financial statements. Thus, a plaintiff's damages would be inappropriately calculated because the financial statements on which they relied would have been accurate.

In no damages, the third party did not suffer a loss due to reliance—the loss may have occurred for other reasons, such as poor management or a worsening economic environment.

Next is non-negligent performance. If the auditor conducted the audit in accordance with GAAS, there is a strong inference of no negligence. Recognize, however, that non-negligent performance is difficult to demonstrate to a court. Proving lack of negligence normally involves a debate between experts hired by both sides. The judge, who is a layperson with respect to accounting and auditing, then assesses the credibility of the experts from both sides in order to make an independent decision based upon legal, accounting, and auditing concepts.

Absence of causal connection in third-party suits has two variations. The first occurs when there is a material misstatement in the financial statements, the second when there is a defalcation at the client or plaintiff's place of business. When there is a misstatement in the financial statements, the defence usually means non-reliance on the financial statements by the user. For example, assume the auditor can demonstrate that a lender relied upon an ongoing banking relationship with a customer, rather than the financial statements, in making a loan. The fact that the auditor was negligent in the conduct of the audit would not be relevant in that situation. In the case of a defalcation, the auditors would not be liable for the entire loss caused by the culprit (e.g., if there had been a certain amount of defalcation that had already taken place before the auditors could have been expected to detect it). Normally, the auditor is held liable only for additional fraud committed after the first date on which the whistle could have been blown. Another good example of "no causal connection" arises in tax cases where the client is required to pay additional taxes. The accountant would not be liable to reimburse the client for taxes paid but only for the interest and penalties, since nothing could have been done legitimately to avoid payment of the taxes.

Finally, it is possible to find contributory negligence if it could be said the claimants were themselves negligent, say, by ignoring other relevant information. It would be more common, however, for the auditor to defend on one of the other bases outlined above.

Criminal Liability

Fraud by anyone can be a criminal act, and the perpetrator can be subject to criminal prosecution.[10] The criminal action would be brought by the Attorney General; conviction of a professional accountant for criminal liability would likely result in a charge of criminal misconduct by the professional accountant's institute (or *ordre*). **Criminal liability for auditors** is the possibility of being found guilty under criminal law for defrauding a person through knowing involvement with false financial statements.

For example, if the auditor of a company gave an unqualified auditor's report on the company's financial statements knowing that inventory was grossly overvalued, it is possible the auditor would be found guilty of criminal fraud and could be sued in a civil action.

Suppose in this case that inventory was to be valued at the lower of cost or market but the auditor deliberately did not include drastic decreases in market value that occurred in the second month following the balance sheet date. Failure to reflect all the information in the auditor's possession in the financial statements would make them misleading despite their being in accordance with GAAP. This occurs when there are multiple alternatives under GAAP or where GAAP requires limited disclosure. The auditor could be judged guilty of fraud.

While there are almost no Canadian cases involving fraud, there have been several U.S. cases. Fraud, however, is interpreted more liberally in the United States. There the term "fraud" is used in civil cases, when errors in financial statement disclosures that benefit management or others occur. Although not great in absolute number, these U.S. fraud cases damage the integrity of the profession, both in Canada and the United States, due to their high profile and reduce the profession's ability to attract and retain outstanding people. On the positive side, these court actions encourage practitioners to use extreme care and exercise good faith in their activities.

The leading case of criminal action against CPAs is *United States v. Simon*, which occurred in 1969. In this case, three auditors were prosecuted for filing false financial statements of a client with the government and held to be criminally liable. The consequences for these three men were significant. They lost their CPA certificates under the U.S. Rule 501 of the Code of Professional Conduct (acts discreditable) and were forced to leave the profession. *United States v. Simon* has been followed by three

Criminal liability for auditors—the possibility of being found guilty under criminal law; defrauding a person through knowing involvement with false financial statements.

---

[10] Section 338 of the Criminal Code of Canada.

additional major criminal cases. In *United States v. Natelli* (1975), two auditors were convicted of criminal liability for certifying the financial statements of National Student Marketing Corporation that contained inadequate disclosures pertaining to accounts receivable.

In *United States v. Weiner* (1975), three auditors were convicted of securities fraud in connection with their audit of Equity Funding Corporation of America. Equity Funding was a financial conglomerate, the financial statements of which had been overstated through a massive fraud by management. The fraud was so extensive and the audit work so poor that the court concluded the auditors must have been aware of the fraud and were therefore guilty of complicity. In Canada, these auditors would likely have been found guilty of negligence.

In *ESM Government Securities v. Alexander Grant & Co.* (1986), a U.S. case, it was revealed by management to the partner in charge of the audit of ESM that the previous year's audited financial statements contained a material misstatement. Rather than complying with professional and firm standards in such circumstances, the partner agreed to say nothing in the hope that management would work its way out of the problem during the current year. Instead, the situation worsened, eventually to the point where losses exceeded $300 million. The partner was subsequently convicted of criminal charges for his role in sustaining the fraud and was handed a 12-year prison term. In this case, the partner personally benefited from the fraud and would likely also have been found guilty of fraud in Canada.

In the United States, the Sarbanes-Oxley Act of 2002 made it a felony to destroy or create documents to impede or obstruct a federal investigation. Under the Act, a person may face fines as well as imprisonment of up to 20 years for altering or destroying documents. These provisions were adopted following the *United States v. Andersen* (2002) case described in Figure 4-11, in which the government charged Andersen with obstruction of justice for the destruction and alteration of documents related to its audit of Enron. This case is another example of criminal liability in the United States.

Several practical lessons can be learned from these cases:

- An investigation of the integrity of management is an important part of deciding on the acceptability of clients and the extent of work to be performed.
- Independence in appearance and fact by all individuals on the engagement is essential, especially in a defence involving criminal actions.
- Transactions with related parties require special scrutiny because of the potential for misstatement.
- Generally accepted accounting principles cannot be relied upon exclusively in deciding whether financial statements are fairly presented.

Figure 4-11   *United States v. Andersen* (2002)—Criminal Liability

In this case, the government charged Andersen with destruction of documents related to the firm's audit of Enron. During the period between October 19, 2001, when Enron alerted Andersen that the SEC had begun an inquiry into Enron's accounting for certain special-purpose entities, and November 8, 2001, when the SEC served Andersen with a subpoena in connection with its work for Enron, Andersen personnel shredded extensive amounts of physical documentation and deleted computer files related to Enron.

The firm was ultimately convicted of one count of obstruction of justice. The conviction was not based on the document shredding but on the alteration of a memo related to Enron's characterization of charges as non-recurring in its third-quarter 2001 earnings release, in which the company announced a loss of $618 million.

As a result of the conviction, Andersen was no longer able to audit publicly traded U.S. companies. The conviction was overturned in May 2005 by the U.S. Supreme Court because the instructions provided by the jury were too broad. The victory was largely symbolic since the firm effectively ceased operations after the original conviction.

- Good documentation may be just as important in the auditor's defence of criminal charges as in a civil suit.

- The potential consequences of the auditor knowingly committing a wrongful act are so severe that it is unlikely that the potential benefits could ever justify the actions.

concept check

C4-7 Describe the third parties that could sue an auditor, and explain why they would sue the auditor.

C4-8 Why is third-party liability evolving?

C4-9 When can auditors be held criminally liable?

4 Auditor Confidentiality and Liability Prevention

Conflict Between Confidentiality and Association with False and Misleading Information

The issue here is whether a public accountant has greater responsibility for the rule of professional conduct regarding confidentiality or for the rule regarding association with false and misleading financial information. Effective quality control procedures, including independence threat analysis, can help avoid this type of conflict. Yet, due to a changing business environment, not all conflicts can be avoided.

Consider the following scenario that could easily occur in a public accounting firm. PA & Co., public accountants, is the auditor for both BG Construction Inc. (BG) and Carter Building Supplies Ltd. (CBS). BG, whose year end is January 31, 2009, owes a large amount of money to CBS, whose year end is February 28, 2009. Suppose an audit of BG is completed but the statements have not been issued. As BG's auditor, you are concerned about whether the company will be able to continue to operate or will become insolvent.

As auditor of BG, you are aware during your audit of CBS that a material asset of CBS (the receivable from BG) may be worthless. How do you ensure that CBS's February 28, 2009, financial statements are not misleading? There is a conflict between the confidentiality due BG and the association with CBS's financial statements (potentially false and misleading if the receivable from BG is not reserved) if you provide a clean opinion. If the auditor cannot persuade BG to disclose the problem to CBS either directly or through the issue of BG's financial statements, the auditor should probably resign from the CBS audit to avoid being associated with misleading financial statements. The BG confidentiality issue is a common problem because a public accounting firm often has clients who conduct business with one another.

Consolidata Services, Inc., described in Figure 4-12, addresses the question of public accounting firms' responsibility to inform users when they have information normally considered confidential under the public accounting profession's rules of conduct.

Figure 4-12	*Consolidata Services, Inc. v. Alexander Grant & Company* (1981)

Consolidata Services Inc. was a payroll services company that prepared payroll cheques and disbursed payroll monies to clients, employees, and taxing authorities. The CPA firm's relationship with Consolidata involved tax work rather than auditing or accounting services. In addition, the CPA firm recommended the payroll services to existing clients, and Consolidata, in return, recommended the CPA firm to its clients.

In a meeting between representatives of the CPA firm and Consolidata, it was determined that Consolidata was insolvent. After discussion with its legal counsel, the CPA firm requested that Consolidata notify its customers about the insolvency, but management refused to do so. The president then informed the CPA firm that he had resigned. The CPA firm informed management of its intent to inform its customers of Consolidata's insolvency. Consolidata requested the CPA firm to wait 10 days to enable them to borrow money to correct their solvency problem.

The CPA firm's partners decided to call all 12 of its clients that used Consolidata's payroll services to advise them not to send in any more money. No one informed Consolidata's other 24 customers.

The client sued for negligence and breach of contract for breaking an obligation of confidentiality. The court found in favour of Consolidata Services, Inc. in the amount of $1.3 million.

Figure 4-13	*Transamerica Commercial Finance Corporation, Canada v. Dunwoody & Company and F. S. Hirtle* (1996)[11]

Dunwoody and Company was the auditor for the years ended January 31, 1984 to January 31, 1987, for a Toyota car dealership called Robin Hood Holdings Ltd. The partner responsible for the engagement was F. S. Hirtle, named as a co-defendant. Transamerica financed the Toyota dealership by providing a credit line of $1.1 million, $500,000 of which was for used vehicle inventory and $200,000 for a capital loan.

Because of decreasing liquidity, Robin Hood Holdings Ltd. engaged in dubious financial practices. For the year ending January 31, 1986, the company used intercompany financial transfers to obtain unauthorized borrowing from the bank (known as "kiting"). Dunwoody, the auditors, detected this, advised the client in writing to discontinue this practice, and ensured that the financial statements accurately reflected cash balances. In January 1986, Transamerica conducted a surprise vehicle inventory and found several used vehicles missing. The vehicles had already been sold.

This resulted in a credit review, and a representative of Transamerica held a meeting with the auditors in March 1987 while the audit was in progress. During this meeting, Hirtle discussed financial reorganization issues with Transamerica but did not disclose the kiting (which continued) or the fact that during the audit, two fictitious vehicles were discovered in inventory. The auditors again warned Robin Hood Holdings Ltd. to discontinue the kiting.

Transamerica concluded that credit should continue to be extended but that Robin Hood required careful monitoring (which Transamerica did not do). In January 1988, the auditors discovered 15 to 20 fictitious vehicles and continuing financial irregularities. After consulting with legal counsel, Dunwoody advised that it would not be providing Robin Hood with an auditor's opinion.

Transamerica put Robin Hood into receivership, operated the dealership in an attempt to reduce its losses, and eventually sold it as a going concern. Transamerica calculated its losses at over $1 million and sued Dunwoody to recover these losses on the basis that Dunwoody should have disclosed the financial irregularities and the fictitious inventory in March 1987.

Both the Supreme Court of British Columbia in 1994 and the Court of Appeal for British Columbia dismissed the plaintiff's action, awarding the defendant some costs. The courts found that the defendant owed a professional duty of confidentiality to its client. They also found that the plaintiff did not rely on the defendants and that its losses arose solely from its own business and management decisions made during the course of its dealings with Robin Hood.

A recent Canadian case, *Transamerica Commercial Finance Corporation*, addressed this issue in the context of an auditor's responsibility to disclose normally confidential information to a major creditor when the financial statements are not misstated. This case is outlined in Figure 4-13.

In the Consolidata Services case, the information had or would have had a significant effect on the plaintiff client or other clients of the same CPA firm. The CPA firm revealed to other clients certain confidential information that had been obtained during a conference with Consolidata Services, Inc. The CPA firm did so on the advice of legal counsel and contended it had a professional duty to inform other clients and help them avoid losses. This points to a dilemma facing public accounting firms in both Canada and the United States. It is difficult to do the "right thing" even when there are good intentions.

The Transamerica case illustrates how accountants could be in possession of information that would be important for creditors in lending decisions. In this particular case, it supports the view that the auditor is justified in maintaining client information as confidential when the financial statements are not misleading. However, it is always important for the auditor to obtain legal advice, as the courts have also found that the auditor may need to violate confidentiality, as shown in an older case, *Fund of Funds v. Arthur Anderson* (1977).

---

[11] Trial judgment, Supreme Court of British Columbia, No. C902491 (February 18, 1994), and trial judgment, Court of Appeal for British Columbia, CA018550 (April 18, 1996).

The Profession's Response to Legal Liability

There are a number of things the CICA, the CGAAC, and the public accounting profession as a whole can do to reduce the practitioner's exposure to lawsuits. The instituting of practice inspection by the provincial institute, CPAB, and *ordre* of members in public practice (discussed in Chapter 2) is one positive step in recognizing the additional responsibility that the public demands of professionals. Some of the others are discussed briefly.

1. *Conduct research in auditing.* Continued research is important in finding better ways to do such things as uncovering unintentional material misstatements and management and employee fraud, communicating audit results to statement users, and making sure that auditors are independent. Significant research already takes place through the professional accounting associations, public accounting firms, and universities. For example, the University of Waterloo Centre for Information Systems Assurance (UWCISA, see **www.arts.uwaterloo.ca/ACCT/ uwcisa**) has a variety of research and educational activities, including information systems assurance research.

2. *Set standards and rules.* The CICA must constantly set standards and revise them to meet the changing needs of auditing. New Canadian Auditing Standards, revisions of the rules of conduct of the various professional accounting bodies, and other pronouncements must be issued as society's needs change and as new technology arises from experience and research. Auditing in Action 4-2 provides an example of the role of standards.

3. *Set requirements to protect auditors.* The CICA and CGAAC can help protect public accountants by setting certain requirements that better practitioners already follow.

4. *Establish practice inspection requirements.* The periodic examination of a firm's practices and procedures is a way to educate practitioners and identify firms not meeting the standards of the profession.

5. *Defend unjustified lawsuits.* It is important that public accounting firms continue to oppose unwarranted lawsuits even if in the short run the costs of winning exceed the costs of settling.

6. *Educate users.* It is important to educate investors and others who read financial statements as to the meaning of the auditor's opinion and the extent and nature of the auditor's work. Auditors do not test 100 percent of all records and do not guarantee the accuracy of the financial records or the future prosperity of the company. This means that there still could be errors or other misstatements in the financial statements.

auditing in action 4-2
How Are the Standards of the Forum of Firms Related to Nortel?

Nortel Networks Corp. has been in the news for many years, starting with the summer of 2004 and the early part of 2005, as financial statement misstatements were discovered—apparently because executives needed specific figures to obtain their management bonuses. Since Nortel stock is traded on many exchanges around the world, it is considered an international audit.

The Forum of Firms (FOF) is a small group of international public accounting firms that perform audits of financial statements of international companies where financial statements may be used in multiple countries. These firms are required to comply with international auditing standards. They also identify audit practice issues, discuss best practices, and offer a voluntary global inspection program—cooperation on an international scale intended to improve the quality of audit engagements.

Sources: 1. Bruser, David, "Nortel targets bogus bonuses," *Toronto Star*, July 3, 2004, p. D1, D10. 2. Hamilton, Tyler, "Driving from a profit to a loss," *Toronto Star*, January 13, 2005, p. D1, D7. 3. "The Forum of Firms" and "Transnational Auditors Committee," www.ifac.org, Accessed: September 25, 2008.

7. *Sanction members for improper conduct and performance.* One characteristic of a profession is its responsibility for policing its own membership. The professional accounting bodies have disciplinary procedures that are designed to deal with the problems of inadequate performance by members.

8. *Lobby for changes in laws.* If the risk exposure of auditors to legal liability becomes too high, insurance will either be prohibitively expensive or unobtainable, and self-insurance is not an option. If the risk exposure does start to approach an unacceptable level, governments should be lobbied at least to ensure viable insurance coverage exists. Lobbying can produce results such as the June 1998 law permitting limited liability partnerships (LLPs) in Ontario and the more recent provincial legislative changes providing for secondary investor suits with liability ceilings.

The Individual Professional Accountant's Response to Legal Liability

Practising auditors may also take specific action to minimize their liability. Most of this book deals with that subject. A summary of several of these practices is included at this point.

1. *Deal only with clients possessing integrity.* The auditor needs to be alert to risk factors that may result in lawsuits. There is an increased likelihood of having legal problems when a client lacks integrity in dealing with customers, employees, units of government, and others. A public accounting firm needs procedures to evaluate the integrity of clients and should dissociate itself from clients found lacking.

2. *Hire qualified personnel and train and supervise them properly.* A considerable portion of most audits is done by young professionals with limited experience. Given the high degree of risk public accounting firms have in doing audits, it is important that these young professionals be qualified and well trained. Supervision of their work by more experienced, qualified professionals is also essential.

3. *Follow the standards of the profession.* A firm must implement procedures to make sure that all firm members understand and follow the Recommendations of the *CICA Handbook* and other authoritative sources of GAAP and GAAS, their profession's rules of conduct, and other professional guidelines.

4. *Maintain independence.* Independence is more than merely financial. Independence in fact requires an attitude of responsibility separate from the client's interest. Much litigation has arisen from a too willing acceptance by an auditor of a client's representation or of a client's pressures. The auditor must maintain an attitude of healthy professional skepticism.

5. *Understand the client's business.* The lack of knowledge of industry practices and client operations has been a major factor in auditors failing to uncover errors in several cases. It is important that the audit team be educated in these areas.

6. *Perform quality audits.* Quality audits require that appropriate evidence be obtained and appropriate judgments be made about the evidence. It is essential, for example, that the auditor evaluate a client's internal controls and modify the quantity and quality of evidence obtained to reflect the findings. Well-documented and monitored quality control procedures help provide quality audits.

7. *Document the work properly.* The preparation of good working papers helps in organizing and performing quality audits. Quality working papers help an auditor defend an audit in court.

8. *Obtain an engagement letter and a management representation letter.* These two letters are essential in defining the respective obligations of client and auditor. They are helpful especially in lawsuits between the client and auditor and also in third-party lawsuits.

9. *Maintain confidential relations.* Auditors are under an ethical and sometimes legal obligation not to disclose client matters to outsiders.

10. *Carry adequate insurance.* A public accounting firm needs to have adequate insurance protection in the event of a lawsuit. Although insurance rates have risen considerably in the past few years as a result of increasing litigation, professional liability insurance is still available to all public accountants.
11. *Seek legal counsel.* Whenever serious problems occur during an audit, a public accountant would be wise to consult experienced counsel. In the event of a potential or actual lawsuit, the auditor should immediately seek an experienced lawyer.

concept check

C4-10 Who should respond to the audit profession's legal liability? Why?

C4-11 Why is international cooperation important in the limitation of legal liability?

⑤ Legislation and the Assurance Engagement

In the preceding sections of this chapter we discussed professional legal liability after the completion of an engagement. There are many other times when legislation has an impact on the PA. In this section we will talk about tax legislation, the Personal Information Protection and Electronic Documents Act (PIPEDA), and the importance of knowing the legislation that affects your client when conducting a financial statement audit.

Impact of Tax Legislation

There is an old saying that the only certainties are "death and taxes," yet the impact of taxes can be far from certain. We have municipal property taxes, sales and excise taxes, estate taxes, and income taxes for both the province and the country. PAs often decide to specialize in one or more forms of these taxes, performing quality control for the financial statement audit or doing special investigations and calculations for clients. Errors in tax calculations or assumptions can be large, resulting in refunds, enormous debts, or misstatements in the financial statements. This explains why most firms require a quality control tax person's sign-off of the client's tax returns before the financial statements are released for printing. Large errors can result in the loss of the client, liability for unpaid interest or penalty, or lawsuits. PAs need to be aware of recent tax rulings that might affect their clients, since a clarification of tax law could result in the ability to refile or change a tax return. For example, Moulton[12] reported in 2008 that about 2,200 taxpayers could be affected by a clarification of the term "contingent liability" when deducting expenses.

Many of the functions in an organization are impacted by the proper treatment of taxation. Organizations need to collect and remit payroll taxes and withholdings, collect and remit provincial sales taxes and the goods and services tax, and correctly record their transactions so that they can calculate income tax. As a PA, you will be asked to identify potential risks of error at your client before examining client systems to identify key controls that mitigate those risks. Knowing your client's profit objectives, for example, can help determine whether there is a risk of over- or understatement of income taxes, which will affect the types of audit tests that you design.

Impact of Privacy Legislation

Besides Canada's federal privacy legislation, PIPEDA, there are also provincial privacy Acts and privacy protection provisions in provincial health-care Acts. International organizations would also be subject to the privacy legislation of their trading partners (suppliers and customers). Some countries have stricter legislation than Canada's, while others have less comprehensive legislation. Most legislation embodies basic principles of data collection, data accuracy, and data confidentiality. For example, only authorized individuals should have access to data for legitimate business purposes, and data should be retained only as long as they have a business purpose.

---

[12] Moulton, Donalee, "Taxpayer wins 12-year court battle," *The Bottom Line*, September 2008, p. 5.

We will talk about some examples in Chapter 10, when we discuss corporate governance and entity-level controls. As an example here, consider that employees should be trained about privacy, be asked to annually sign a privacy policy document, and that privacy adherence should be monitored with violations resulting in remedial action.

As a public accountant, you would include in your engagement letter a statement that you would keep client data confidential, securing your working paper files so that data stored in the files stay private. This means that your office should have appropriate security, as should your filing cabinets and your computer systems, so that only authorized individuals have access to client data files. It would be a public relations and legal liability disaster should client data files that you used for audit testing be leaked to the internet, resulting in investigations by Canada's Privacy Commissioner! As part of your client risk assessment, you will consider your client's data management policies and practices, which include privacy policies.

Some PAs specialize in privacy assurance engagements, helping clients assess their privacy practices and implement policies and procedures for effective privacy management in their organizations. Privacy is part of a well-run organization, and needs to be considered together with effective security over information systems, appropriate authentication of users, and carefully designed individual access rights. All of these systems need to be working to help ensure privacy.[13]

Other Legislation and Audits

Think about other legislation that affects clients of financial statement audits. These include labour laws, municipal bylaws, expropriation laws, environmental laws, consumer safety laws, and numerous others. As an interested observer, you might become aware of these laws only when your client violates them and is on the front page of the newspaper. However, as a PA, assessing financial statement risks includes assessing fraud risks and the procedures in place at your client for assessing its own risks. This means that the client should be aware of the legislation that impacts it and communicate this information to you, its auditor. If the client does not have an effective risk assessment or quality control mechanism (for example, to prevent toxins from entering the food production system), then the auditor would need to carefully assess the going concern ability of the client if it were fined and sued for violations of health and safety regulations.

As part of their training, PAs will learn about effective risk management processes so that they can assess these at their client. Audit quality control procedures include updating checklists used with clients to include questions about relevant new legislation that affects all clients, and asking clients about their own processes in adhering to the laws in their jurisdictions, whether they be local, national, or international. Engagement completion will include communication with the client's lawyers to determine the status of lawsuits so that disclosure can be included in financial statements, or the financial records adjusted where judgment has occurred either for or against the client.

In this text, we will also learn about risk management from the perspective of the financial statement audit. Risk assessment helps identify risks of misstatement. A variety of audit procedures form the audit responses that can be taken to deal with the identified risks. Evaluation of the audit responses is a continuing process throughout the audit as well as at the end of the engagement, as team members communicate with each other and document the results of their field work.

concept check

C4-12 How can federal income tax legislation affect the financial statement audit?

C4-13 Why does the auditor need to consider environmental legislation during a financial statement audit?

---

[13] If you are interested in learning more about privacy and privacy assurance engagements, there is a free guide available at www.cica.ca/research-and-guidance/research-activities/recent-publications/public-interest/item12973.aspx called *Privacy Compliance: a Guide for Organizations and Assurance Practitioners*, developed jointly by the CICA and the AICPA.

Appendix 4A
Securities Legislation

In Chapter 2, it was pointed out that a number of Canadian companies were listed on American stock exchanges or sold securities in the United States or both and that these companies were therefore subject to the requirements of the U.S. Securities Act of 1933 and the Securities Exchange Act of 1934. The following discussion pertains to the civil liability of accountants under a typical Canadian securities act—the Ontario Securities Act—and relevant U.S. acts.

Ontario Securities Act Part XXIII, Civil Liability, deals with liability for misrepresentation in a prospectus. It applies not only to auditors but also to issuers, those selling securities, underwriters, and directors. Auditors are not referred to directly but are described in Section 130(1) as those "whose consent has been filed pursuant to a requirement of the regulations but only with respect to reports, opinions, or statements that have been made by them." The section states that the purchaser who purchases the security based on the prospectus is deemed to be relying on representations with respect to that prospectus. Thus, the issue of privity would be automatically dealt with in the event that the purchaser sued the auditor or others.

Section 130(8) goes on to state that all persons or companies specified in the first section are jointly and severally liable, but the amount recoverable (specified in the next paragraph of the Act) would not exceed the price at which the securities were offered to the public.

Section 131 specifies the same deemed reliance, liability, and amount recoverable in the context of a take-over bid circular.

U.S. Laws

SECURITIES ACT OF 1933 This Act deals with the information in registration statements and prospectuses. It concerns only the reporting requirements for companies issuing new securities. The only parties that can recover from auditors under the 1933 Act are original purchasers of securities. The amount of the potential recovery is the original purchase price less the value of the securities at the time of the suit. If the securities have been sold, users can recover the amount of the loss incurred.

The Securities Act of 1933 imposes an unusual burden on the auditor. Section 11 defines the rights of third parties and auditors. These are summarized as follows:

- Any third party who purchased securities described in the registration statement may sue the auditor for material misrepresentations or omissions in audited financial statements included in the registration statement.
- The third-party user does not have the burden of proof that he or she relied on the financial statements or that the auditor was negligent or fraudulent in doing the audit. The user must prove only that the audited financial statements contained a material misrepresentation or omission.
- The auditor has the burden of demonstrating as a defence that (1) an adequate audit was conducted in the circumstances or (2) all or a portion of the plaintiff's loss was caused by factors other than the misleading financial statements. The 1933 Act is the only U.S. common or statutory law where the burden of proof is on the defendant.
- The auditor has responsibility for making sure the financial statements were fairly stated beyond the date of issuance, up to the date the registration statement became effective, which could be several months later. For example, assume the audit report date for December 31, 2009, financial statements is

February 10, 2010, but the registration statement is dated November 1, 2010. In a typical audit, the auditor must review transactions through the audit report date, February 10, 2010. In statements filed under the 1933 Act, the auditor is responsible to review transactions through the registration statement date, November 1, 2010.

Although the burden on auditors may appear harsh, there have been few cases tried under the 1933 Act.

SECURITIES EXCHANGE ACT OF 1934 The liability of auditors under the Securities Exchange Act of 1934 frequently centres on the audited financial statements issued to the public in annual reports or submitted to the SEC as a part of annual 10-K reports.

Every company with securities traded on national and over-the-counter exchanges is required to submit audited statements annually. There are obviously a much larger number of statements falling under the 1934 Act than under the 1933 Act.

In addition to annual audited financial statements, there is potential legal exposure to auditors for quarterly (10-Q), monthly (8-K), and other reporting information. The auditor is frequently involved in reviewing the information in these other reports; therefore, there may be legal responsibility. However, few cases have involved auditors for reports other than auditor's reports.

SEC SANCTIONS Closely related to auditors' liability is the SEC's authority to sanction. The SEC has the power in certain circumstances to sanction or suspend practitioners from doing audits for SEC companies. Rule 2(e) of the SEC's Rules of Practice says:

> The commission may deny, temporarily or permanently, the privilege of appearing or practising before it in any way to any person who is found by the commission: (1) not to possess the requisite qualifications to represent others, or (2) to be lacking in character or integrity or to have engaged in unethical or improper professional conduct.

In recent years, the SEC has temporarily suspended a number of individual CPAs from doing any audits of SEC clients. It has similarly prohibited a number of CPA firms from accepting any new SEC clients for a period, such as six months. At times, the SEC has required an extensive review of a major CPA firm's practices by another CPA firm. In some cases, individual CPAs and their firms have been required to participate in continuing education programs and to make changes in their practice. Sanctions such as these are published by the SEC and are often reported in the business press, making them a significant embarrassment to those involved.

FOREIGN CORRUPT PRACTICES ACT OF 1977 Another significant congressional action affecting both CPA firms and their clients was the passing of the Foreign Corrupt Practices Act of 1977. The Act makes it illegal to offer a bribe to an official of a foreign country for the purpose of exerting influence and obtaining or retaining business. The prohibition against payments to foreign officials is applicable to all U.S. domestic firms, regardless of whether they are publicly held or privately held, and to foreign companies filing with the SEC.

Apart from the bribery provisions that affect all companies, the law also requires SEC registrants under the Securities Exchange Act of 1934 to meet additional requirements. These include the maintenance of reasonably complete and accurate records and an adequate system of internal control. The law significantly affects all SEC companies and may affect auditors through their responsibility to review and evaluate systems of internal control as a part of doing the audit.

Summary

1. **What are a public accountant's sources of legal liability?** Public accountants could be liable to clients and third parties such as shareholders and debt holders.

   How is this liability related to a distinction between business failure and audit failure? Financial statement users might confuse business failures, for example, due to bankruptcy, with an audit failure, where an audit was not conducted in accordance with GAAS, resulting in more frequent lawsuits.

   Does the financial statement auditor have a fiduciary duty? No. As explained on page 75, the PA would need to have discretionary power over funds to have a fiduciary duty.

   Does the PA have reporting obligations with respect to potential money-laundering? In some cases, yes. Page 75 describes triggering activities (basically receipt and disbursements of funds under certain conditions) that would require a PA to report financial transactions to FINTRAC.

2. **Do accountants have the right of privileged communication?** No. Accountants must disclose their working papers to the courts when subpoenaed.

   What other concepts or terms are associated with auditor's legal liability? The prudent person concept (pages 79–80) is an important concept, as are distinctions between negligence and fraud (page 81) and distinctions between contract and common law (pages 81–82).

   What should auditors do if a client sues them? With the assistance of legal counsel, assuming the conduct of an audit in accordance with GAAS, the auditor would likely pursue one of the defences listed in the chapter commencing on page 83.

3. **Who else can sue the auditor, besides the client?** Non-clients such as actual and potential shareholders, vendors, bankers, creditors, investors, employees, and customers can sue an auditor.

   How would the auditor defend against such suits? The auditor would use a series of defences used with clients, summarized in Table 4-3 (page 90).

   Can the auditor go to jail because of criminal liability? Yes, though this would likely occur only where the auditor was deliberately involved with materially incorrect financial statements and intended to mislead.

4. **If the auditor has access to confidential information that would help a different business avoid financial hardship, can this information be disclosed?** No. The auditor has a duty to hold client information confidential. It can be disclosed only with client permission.

   What are individual accountants and the profession doing to respond to legal liability? Individual accountants can undertake many actions (listed on pages 96–97) to help prevent lawsuits. The profession has made changes in the recent past, including the formation of the Forum of Firms, participation with the CPAB, and numerous activities such as research (see pages 95–96).

5. **What should auditors do to determine the impact of legislation on the financial statement audit?** Auditors need to discuss with management the organization's risk assessment process, including identification and requirements of legislation for their business.

   How does the need to understand relevant legislation affect the audit process? Auditors need to have sufficient training to understand the legislation, identify sources of relevant legislation, and have checklists in their documentation to remind them to consider relevant legislation. Once relevant legislation is identified, the auditor incorporates consideration of the legislation into the planning and conduct of the audit.

   Link those actions to standards of continuing education, quality control, and engagement completion. Quality control, supervision, and clear documentation help auditors incorporate the results of their findings into their audit process.

Visit the text's website at **www.pearsoned.ca/arens** for practice quizzes, additional case studies, and international standards information.

Review Questions

4-1 The legal environment in which a public accountant in Canada operates is changing. Discuss some of the reasons for the changes.

4-2 Distinguish between business risk and audit risk. Why is business risk a concern to auditors?

4-3 How does the prudent person concept affect the liability of the auditor?

4-4 A partner in a public accounting firm may be held liable for errors in the work of others. Identify at least two groups of such others and explain why the partner might be liable.

4-5 Differentiate between criminal action and civil action.

4-6 A common type of lawsuit against public accountants is for the failure to detect a defalcation. State the auditor's responsibility for such discovery. Give authoritative support for your answer.

4-7 What is meant by "contributory negligence"? Under what conditions will this likely be a successful defence?

4-8 Is the auditor's liability affected if the third party was unknown rather than known? Explain.

4-9 Distinguish among the auditor's potential liability to the client, liability to third parties under common law, and criminal liability. Describe one situation for each type of liability in which the auditor could be held legally responsible.

4-10 In what ways can the profession positively respond and reduce liability in auditing?

4-11 In what ways can an individual public accountant positively respond and reduce liability in auditing?

4-12 Describe two types of legislation that could affect the financial statement audit; explain why there is an impact.

Discussion Questions and Problems

4-13 Helmut & Co., a public accounting firm, was the new auditor of Mountain Ltd., a private company in the farm equipment and supply business.

In early February 2009, Helmut & Co. began the audit for the year ended December 31, 2008. The audit was to be run by Frost, a senior who had just joined Helmut from another firm. Frost was to be assisted by two juniors.

Sara Mountain, the president of Mountain Ltd., approached Frost and said that the Bank of Trail was prepared to increase its loan to Mountain upon receipt of the 2008 financial statements.

The juniors were assigned the accounts receivable and inventory sections, both of which were significant in relation to total assets, while Frost concentrated on the income statement and the remaining balance sheet accounts. The audit was finished quickly, and after a cursory review of the file and statements by Martin Helmut, senior partner of Helmut & Co., the signed auditor's report was appended to the financial statements, which were delivered to Mountain, which, in turn, sent them to the bank.

The bank increased the loan significantly principally on the basis of the very successful year the company had enjoyed despite the fact that the farm supply business was depressed. Several months later, Mountain Ltd. made an assignment in bankruptcy. The trustee found that many accounts receivable were still outstanding from the balance sheet date and that inventory on hand included substantial quantities of obsolete and damaged goods that had been included in the year-end inventory at cost. In addition, the year-end inventory amount included inventory that had been sold prior to the year end.

Bank of Trail sued Helmut & Co. for negligence.

REQUIRED

Discuss Helmut & Co.'s defence. Is lack of privity a defence in this case? Was Helmut & Co. negligent? Explain your answer fully.

4-14 Watts and Williams, a firm of PAs, audited the accounts of Sampson Skins, Inc., a corporation that imports and deals in fine furs. Upon completion of the audit, the auditors supplied Sampson Skins with 20 copies of the audited financial statements. The firm knew in a general way that Sampson Skins wanted that number of copies of the auditor's report in order to furnish them to banks and other potential lenders.

The balance sheet in question was misstated by approximately $800,000. Instead of having a $600,000 net worth, the corporation was insolvent. The management of Sampson Skins had doctored the books to avoid bankruptcy. The assets had been overstated by $500,000 of fictitious and nonexistent accounts receivable and $300,000 of nonexistent skins listed as inventory when, in fact, Sampson Skins had only empty boxes. The audit failed to detect these fraudulent entries. Martinson, relying on the audited financial statements, loaned Sampson Skins $200,000. He is now seeking to recover his loss from Watts and Williams.

REQUIRED

State whether each of the following is true or false, and give your reasons:

a. If Martinson alleges and proves negligence on the part of Watts and Williams, he will be able to recover his loss.

b. If Martinson alleges and proves constructive fraud (i.e., gross negligence on the part of Watts and Williams), he will be able to recover his loss.

c. Martinson does not have a contract with Watts and Williams.

d. Unless actual fraud on the part of Watts and Williams can be shown, Martinson cannot recover his loan.

e. Martinson is a third-party beneficiary of the contract Watts and Williams made with Sampson Skins.

4-15 The public accounting firm of André, Mathieu & Paquette (AMP) was expanding very rapidly. Consequently, it hired several junior accountants, including Jim Small. The partners of the firm eventually became dissatisfied with Jim's production and warned him that they would be forced to terminate him unless his output increased significantly.

At that time, Jim was engaged in audits of several clients. He decided that to avoid being fired, he would reduce or omit entirely some of the standard auditing procedures listed in audit programs prepared by the partners. One of the public accounting firm's clients, Newell Corporation, was in serious financial difficulty and had adjusted several of the accounts being examined by Jim to appear financially sound. Jim prepared fictitious working papers in his home at night to support the purported completion of auditing procedures assigned to him, although he, in fact, did not examine the adjusting entries. The public accounting firm rendered an unqualified opinion on Newell's financial statements, which were grossly misstated. Several creditors, relying on the audited financial statements, subsequently extended large sums of money to Newell Corporation.

REQUIRED

Would the public accounting firm be liable to the creditors who extended the money because of their reliance on the erroneous financial statements if Newell Corporation should fail to pay them? Explain.

(Adapted from AICPA)

4-16 Jan Sharpe recently joined the public accounting firm of Spark, Watts, and Wilcox. On her third audit for the firm, Jan examined the underlying documentation of 200 disbursements as a test of purchasing, receiving, vouchers payable, and cash disbursement procedures. In the process, she found 12 disbursements for the purchase of materials with no receiving reports in the documentation. She noted the exceptions in her working papers and called them to the attention of the audit supervisor. Relying on prior experience with the client, the audit supervisor disregarded Sharpe's comments, and nothing further was done about the exceptions.

Subsequently, it was learned that one of the client's purchasing agents and a member of its accounting department were engaged in a fraudulent scheme whereby they diverted the receipt of materials to a public warehouse while sending the invoices to the client. When the client discovered the fraud, the conspirators had obtained approximately $70,000, of which $50,000 was recovered after the completion of the audit.

REQUIRED

Discuss the legal implications and liabilities of Spark, Watts, and Wilcox as a result of the facts just described.

4-17 In confirming accounts receivable on December 31, 2009, the auditor found 15 discrepancies between the customer's records and the recorded amounts in the subsidiary ledger. A copy of all confirmations that had exceptions was turned over to the company controller to investigate the reason for the difference. He, in turn, had the bookkeeper perform the analysis. The bookkeeper analyzed each exception, determined its cause, and prepared an elaborate working paper explaining each difference. Most of the differences in the bookkeeper's report indicated that the errors were caused by timing differences in the client's and customer's records. The auditor reviewed the working paper and concluded that there were no material exceptions in accounts receivable.

Two years subsequent to the audit, it was determined that the bookkeeper had stolen thousands of dollars in the previous three years by taking cash and overstating accounts

receivable. In a lawsuit by the client against the public accountant, an examination of the auditor's December 31, 2009, accounts receivable working papers, which were subpoenaed by the court, indicated that one of the explanations in the bookkeeper's analysis of the exceptions was fictitious. The analysis stated the error was caused by a sales allowance granted to the customer for defective merchandise the day before the end of the year. The difference was actually caused by the bookkeeper's theft.

REQUIRED

a. What are the legal issues involved in this situation? What should the auditor use as a defence if sued?
b. What was the public accountant's deficiency in conducting the audit of accounts receivable?

4-18 Marino Rossi, a public accountant, audited the financial statements of Newfoundland Rugs Ltd. Cooke, the president of Newfoundland Rugs, told Marino that the company was planning a private placement of company bonds to raise $500,000 of needed capital. The audit proceeded smoothly, and the audited financial statements were issued.

Unbeknownst to Marino, several significant receivables represented consignment accounts and not receivables, but Cooke had persuaded the companies involved to sign the receivable confirmations Marino had sent out, indicating they agreed that they owed the balances reported at the balance sheet date. In addition, a large number of rolls of low-

quality interior carpeting had been classed as first quality. The effect of these two fraudulent acts resulted in a profit of $150,000 (instead of a loss of $480,000) and a positive net worth (instead of a negative net worth).

Newfoundland Rugs borrowed the money on the private placement and then went bankrupt several months later.

REQUIRED

a. Could the private-placement lenders succeed in a suit against Marino? If so, what must they prove?
b. What defence would Marino use?

Professional Judgment Problem

4-19 Jackson is a sophisticated investor. As such, he was initially a member of a small group that was going to participate in a private placement of $1 million of common stock at Clarion Corporation. Numerous meetings were held between management and the investor group. Detailed financial and other information was supplied to the participants. Upon the eve of the completion of the placement, it was aborted when one major investor withdrew. Clarion then decided to offer $2.5 million of Clarion common stock to the public, registered with the OSC. Jackson subscribed to $300,000 of the Clarion public stock offering. Nine months later, Clarion's earnings dropped significantly, and as a result, the stock dropped 20 percent beneath the offering price.

Jackson sold his shares at a loss of $60,000 to Chang. Jackson seeks to hold liable all parties who participated in the public offering, including Clarion's accounting firm of Allen, Dunn, and Rose. Although the audit was performed in conformity with auditing standards, there were some relatively minor misstatements subsequently discovered in the financial statements that accompanied the share registration documents. It is believed by Clarion and Allen, Dunn, and Rose that the claim is without merit.

REQUIRED
a. What will be the likely basis of Jackson's suit?
b. What are the probable defences that might be asserted by Allen, Dunn, and Rose? Will the defences succeed?
c. If, subsequent to Chang's purchase of the shares at $240,000, a material misstatement was discovered in the financial statements, would your answers to questions (a) and (b) change? If Chang then lost $80,000 upon disposal of his shares, what suit would be available to Chang?

Case

4-20 In late 1998 and early 1999, Your Best Magnets Inc. (YBM) offices in New York and Toronto were raided by the U.S. Organized Strike Force and the Royal Canadian Mounted Police. Records were seized, and the public company and its officers were charged with money laundering. The company has since been delisted and court proceedings continue. One newspaper article showed the flow of a single YBM transaction of $2.3 million being split into different amounts, moving among 10 different banks and as many different companies. Connections were shown with Russian organized crime.

Delskiny and Lather, CPAs, the auditors of YBM, were subpoenaed to appear before a grand jury in the United States.

REQUIRED
a. What are the auditor's normal responsibilities during an audit engagement with respect to assessing management integrity?
b. How does the assessment of management integrity tie in to the nature of evidence to be collected during the audit?
c. Assume that one of the directors of YBM was a member of Russian organized crime, known to local and international police forces but not publicly known. What is the auditor's normal responsibility regarding detection of criminal affiliations of directors?
d. How does the crime affiliation of directors or other management affect the fair presentation of financial statements?
e. The company's financial statements in 1996 showed $13.6 million worth of North American magnet sales—a figure that exceeded total magnet imports to the continent that year. YBM officials created fictitious sales lists and destroyed banking records. Auditors identified questionable transactions, demanded explanations from management, and received supporting evidence. A clean auditor's report was issued in 1996. Discuss the potential legal liability of the auditors should it be discovered that several sales on the sales lists were to fictitious companies.

Ongoing Small Business Case: CondoCleaners.com and the Law

4-21 Jim is in the process of organizing, the business details for his business, getting a website established, and preparing marketing documentation. To save money, he has decided to do the initial cleaning himself until he has enough business to hire staff. He did some of his training at home, substituting himself for the cleaning service that his parents used. Then, he asked friends of his family if he could clean their places. He investigated cleaning products and how they could be used and determined how quickly he could work.

REQUIRED
What legislation will Jim need to be concerned with when setting up his business? How will the legislation affect his website development process and the way that he runs his business?

2

The audit process

Part 2 presents the strategic audit process. The figure on the opposite page shows how the chapters in this book are organized in the context of eight audit phases. This eight-phase model starts with risk assessment (introduced in Chapter 3). To conduct risk assessment, you need to understand audit responsibilities and objectives (Chapter 5), the nature of audit evidence (Chapter 6), the concepts of materiality and risk (Chapter 7), and a framework for audit planning and documentation (Chapter 8). Key risks that the auditor assesses include those with respect to controls (Chapter 9), as well as corporate governance and entity controls (Chapter 10) and fraud risks (Chapter 11).

It is essential to understand the material in these chapters because the information will be used extensively throughout the rest of the book. Chapter 12 summarizes and integrates audit planning and audit evidence. You will use these planning concepts throughout the rest of the book.

Many of the concepts throughout the remainder of the book are illustrated with examples based on Hillsburg Hardware Limited. The financial statements and other information from the company's annual report are included in the insert on pages 147–162.

5

Audit responsibilities and objectives

Now that you have an understanding of the environment within which an auditor functions, we can begin to look at the specifics of the financial statement audit. Management accountants will often be involved in preparing documents for the public accountant (PA) prior to the conduct of the financial statement audit, while internal or operational auditors may assist in working paper preparation or actual audit testing. Specialists may assist in the audit in a variety of roles—so all types of accountants can benefit from knowing their responsibilities with respect to the audit.

LEARNING OBJECTIVES

1 Describe the objective of conducting an audit of financial statements. Explain the difference between management and auditor responsibilities with respect to the financial statements and the discovery and correction of material misstatements or illegal acts.

2 Examine the preplanning steps that the auditor completes before accepting the financial statement audit engagement. Document the importance of an engagement letter.

3 List the eight phases of a financial statement audit and provide an overview of the audit process.

4 Show how financial statements are divided into cycles. Describe the relationship between the cycle approach and the financial statement audit. Explain relationships among the cycles and between the cycle approach and entity-level controls.

5 Describe management assertions about financial information. Relate management assertions to general transaction-related audit objectives and general balance-related audit objectives.

STANDARDS REFERENCED IN THIS CHAPTER

CICA Standards

CAS 200 – Overall objectives of the independent auditor, and the conduct of an audit in accordance with Canadian auditing standards (previously included aspects of Section 5100 – Generally Accepted Auditing Standards)

CAS 210 – Agreeing the terms of audit engagements (previously Section 5110 – Terms of the engagement)

CAS 240 – The auditor's responsibilities relating to fraud in an audit of financial statements (previously Section 5135 – The auditor's responsibility to consider fraud)

CAS 250 – Considerations of laws and regulations in an audit of financial statements (previously Section 5136 – Misstatements – illegal acts)

Section 5090 – Audit of financial statements – an introduction

Section 5110 – Terms of the engagement

Section 5136 – Misstatements – illegal acts

Here Come the Audit Detectives!

Lawsuits, lawsuits everywhere! Risks of management fraud! What do you do? You either send away your risky client or you send in the audit detectives, auditors who are experts in forensic investigation.

In 2007, the top four firms in Canada earned about $4.3 billion (while the top four U.S. firms earned $31.2 billion). Estimates of the percentage of market capitalization audited by these firms ranges between 95 percent and 98 percent. There are risks with these audits, though. As of late 2004, research statistics indicated that the top four accounting firms were dropping clients considered to be high risk. For example, Audit Analytics reported that, in the first three quarters of 2004, the top four accounting firms resigned from 157 audits. The reasons for these resignations do not have to be stated by the firms, but a likely conclusion is that the engagement was high risk or could affect the firm's perception of independence.

Auditors may also have resigned from clients due to stiffer independence requirements. In 2002, based on information filed with the SEC, public company payments to their accountants included 51 percent for non-audit work, while such non-audit payments had dropped to 21 percent by 2007.

Figure 5-1 on page 109 shows a summary of the audit process and the chapters where we study that process in the remainder of this text. Risk assessment guides the audit process and continues throughout the entire financial statement audit as the results of field work are reviewed and assessed.

IMPORTANCE TO AUDITORS

For those high-risk engagements that a public accounting firm decides to keep, it is necessary to assign additional expertise to the audit team to evaluate risky or complex information. Such assignment does not necessarily mean that the auditor suspects fraud, but it helps ensure that high-quality evidence is obtained for areas that are difficult to audit or that could involve professional judgment due to the need for estimates or evaluation. *The Globe and Mail* reported, in November 2004, that at least two Canadian accounting firms—KPMG, and Deloitte and Touche—were using forensic auditors on audit teams to help evaluate risks. The Office of the Auditor General of Canada also has specialized forensic auditors who assist with the risk assessment and the evidence-gathering process for high-risk engagements.

WHAT DO YOU THINK?

1. Should auditors specializing in fraud be assigned to every financial statement audit? Why or why not?

2. Would assigning auditors specializing in fraud increase the auditors' liability for these engagements? Why or why not?

3. How can the use of audit specialists justify an increase in audit fees?

continued >

Sources: 1. "Advisory Committee on the Auditing Profession Final Report to the U.S. Department of the Treasury," October 6, 2008, www.treas.gov/offices/domestic-finance/acap/docs/final-report.pdf, Accessed: November 7, 2008. 2. Crosariol, B., "Audit detectives walking the beat at accountancies," *The Globe and Mail*, November 29, 2004, p. B13. 3. Jeffrey, G., "Optimism despite trouble in the U.S.," *The Bottom Line*, April 2008, p. 13. 4. Jensen, B., "Bob Jensen's threads on professional practice, fees, choosing accountants, financial advisors and consultants," www.trinity.cdu/rjensen/fees.htm, Accessed: February 26, 2005. 5. Interview with: Rick Smith, Assistant Auditor General, Office of the Auditor General of Canada, January 13, 2005. 6. Katz, David M., "Since Sarbox, non-audit fees dove from 51% to 21%," CFO.com, May 7, 2009, www.cfo.com/printable/article.cfm/13634614, Accessed: August 10, 2009.

Forensic auditors are PAs who have had training in fraud detection and gathering of documentation, often obtaining a professional designation such as Certified Fraud Examiner (CFE). Does this sound exciting to you? Although the possibility of tension and secrecy is present, sifting through information to support potential fraud requires meticulous attention to detail and skills in information technology, as discussed further in Chapter 11. Think about what might make an audit engagement risky, and keep your ideas in mind as we go through the next few chapters. Risk assessment is a process that continues throughout the entire financial statement audit.

Before beginning the study of how to conduct an audit, it is necessary first to understand the objectives of an audit and what the auditor should do prior to accepting an audit engagement. Then, we look at the eight phases of the financial statement audit before considering how the financial statements are divided into cycles to facilitate the audit process, looking also at the relationships among the cycles. Management makes assertions (both implied and explicit) when preparing financial statements. The auditor uses these assertions to derive audit objectives. Knowledge of assertions and audit objectives help the auditor decide which audit tests to conduct (both to evaluate risks and as a risk response process), as discussed in the next chapter.

1 The Objective of the Audit—Management and Auditor Responsibilities

Objective of Conducting an Audit of Financial Statements

CAS 200 (formerly contained in part in Section 5090) of the *CICA Handbook* explains that the purpose of the financial statement audit is to express an opinion on the financial statements. This opinion is an assessment of whether the financial statements are presented fairly, in the context of materiality (discussed in Chapter 7), using Canadian generally accepted accounting principles (GAAP) as the criteria for assessment.

Auditors accumulate evidence to enable them to reach conclusions about whether financial statements are fairly stated in all material respects and to issue an appropriate auditor's report.

Figure 5-1 Summary of the Audit Process

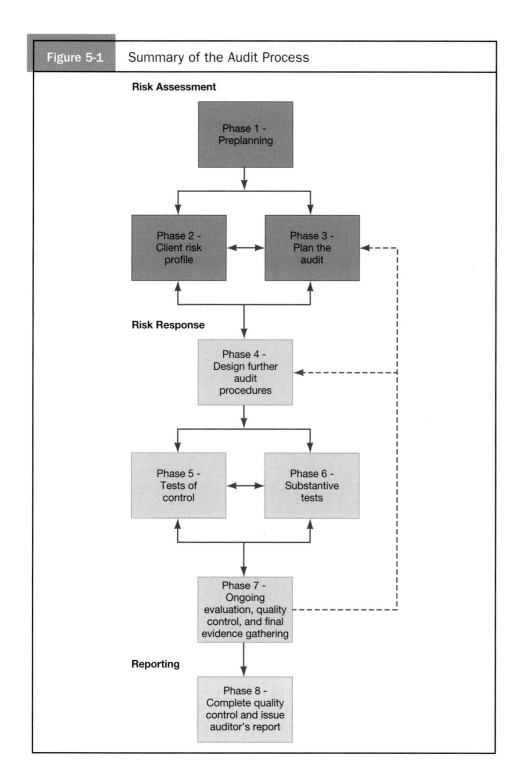

Risk Assessment

Phase 1 - Preplanning

Phase 2 - Client risk profile

Phase 3 - Plan the audit

Risk Response

Phase 4 - Design further audit procedures

Phase 5 - Tests of control

Phase 6 - Substantive tests

Phase 7 - Ongoing evaluation, quality control, and final evidence gathering

Reporting

Phase 8 - Complete quality control and issue auditor's report

new standards 5-1
Multiple Financial Frameworks!

CAS 200—Overall objectives of the independent auditor, and the conduct of an audit in accordance with Canadian auditing standards—par. 3, talks about an applicable financial reporting framework rather than Canadian GAAP. Paragraph 5 adds that the reasonable assurance about the absence of material misstatement needs to consider both fraud and error. Having an acceptable financial reporting framework by management is considered to be a precondition for the auditor to accept an audit engagement (described further in CAS 210, par. A2-3.)

When, on the basis of adequate evidence, the auditor concludes that the financial statements are unlikely to mislead a prudent user, the auditor gives an audit opinion on their fair presentation and associates his or her name with the statements. If facts or evidence discovered subsequent to their issuance indicate that the statements were not actually fairly presented, the auditor is likely to have to demonstrate to the courts or regulatory agencies that the audit was conducted in a proper manner and reasonable conclusions were drawn. Although not an insurer or a guarantor of the fairness of the presentations in the statements, the auditor has considerable responsibility for notifying users as to whether or not the statements are properly stated. If the auditor believes the statements are not fairly presented or is unable to reach a conclusion because of insufficient evidence or prevailing conditions, the auditor has the responsibility to notify the users through the auditor's report.

Management's Responsibilities

The responsibility for adopting sound accounting policies, maintaining adequate internal control, and making fair representations in the financial statements rests with management rather than with the auditor. The primary responsibility for internal control and the financial statements appropriately rests with management given that the entity's transactions and related assets, liabilities, and equity are within the direct knowledge and control of management throughout the year. In contrast, the auditor's knowledge of these matters and internal control is limited to that acquired during the audit.

In recent years, the annual reports of many public companies have included a statement about management's responsibilities and relationship with the public accounting firm. The insert on pages 147–162 presents a report of management's responsibility by the management of a large retail hardware distributor, Hillsburg Hardware Limited. The first paragraph states management's responsibilities for the fair presentation of the financial statements, and the second paragraph discusses management's responsibilities with respect to internal control. The third paragraph comments on the audit committee, the board of directors, and their role with respect to the financial statements.

CAS Management's responsibility for the fairness of the representations (assertions) in the financial statements carries with it the privilege of determining which disclosures it considers necessary. These responsibilities are described in detail in *CICA Handbook* CAS 210, Agreeing the terms of audit engagements (previously covered, in part, in Section 5110). Although management has the responsibility for the preparation of the financial statements and the accompanying footnotes, it is acceptable for an auditor to draft this material for the client or to offer suggestions for clarification. In the event that management insists on financial statement disclosure that the auditor finds unacceptable, the auditor can either issue an adverse or qualified opinion or, as a last resort, withdraw from the engagement. Reporting is discussed further in Chapter 22.

The Canadian Securities Administrators (CSA), Canada's securities regulators, have filed rules that impose requirements similar to those of the U.S. Sarbanes-Oxley Act of 2002 for most companies listed on Canadian stock exchanges. The chief executive officer (CEO) and chief financial officer (CFO) of such companies must certify annual and interim financial statements as well as management discussion and analysis (MD&A) and certain information forms that are filed with the stock exchanges. Management is required to certify that it has reviewed the documents, that they do not contain any misrepresentations or material omissions and present fairly the financial condition of the company, and that disclosure controls and procedures or internal control over financial reporting have been designed, evaluated, and disclosed. If companies do not adhere to these rules, they will not be allowed to sell their shares or debt via Canadian stock exchanges.

Auditor's Responsibilities

Paragraph 5090.05 of the *CICA Handbook* states:

> "The auditor should plan and perform an audit with an attitude of professional skepticism, recognizing that circumstances may exist that cause the financial statements to be materially misstated."

Similar words are used in CAS 200 (par. 15). The financial statement audit process is discussed in this chapter, describing eight phases.

The requirement for an attitude of skepticism does not mean that the auditor should plan and conduct the audit with an attitude of disbelief or of distrust in management. As shown in Table 5-1, management has many important responsibilities that, in most cases, management performs well and conscientiously. Rather, **professional skepticism** means that the auditor should not be blind to evidence that suggests that documents, books, or records have been altered or are incorrect. The auditor should not assume that management is dishonest, but the possibility of dishonesty must be considered. The concept of reasonable assurance indicates that the auditor is not an insurer or guarantor of the correctness of the financial statements.

There are several reasons the auditor is responsible for reasonable but not absolute assurance. First, most audit evidence results from testing a sample of a population, such as accounts receivable or inventory. Sampling inevitably includes some risk of not uncovering a material misstatement. Also, the areas to be tested; the type, extent, and timing of those tests; and the evaluation of test results require significant judgment on the part of the auditor. Even with good faith and integrity, auditors can make mistakes and errors in judgment. Second, accounting representations contain complex estimates, which inherently involve uncertainty and can be affected by future events. Third, fraudulently prepared financial statements are often extremely difficult, if not impossible, for the auditor to detect, especially when there is collusion among management.

The *CICA Handbook*, in CAS 240, The auditor's responsibilities in relation to fraud in an audit of financial statements (formerly Section 5135, The auditor's responsibility to consider fraud), details how the auditor should utilize professional skepticism when considering the risk of the financial statements containing material error or fraud and other irregularities. CAS 240 distinguishes between two types of misstatements, errors and fraud and other irregularities. An **error** is an unintentional misstatement of the financial statements, whereas **fraud and other irregularities** are intentional. Two examples of errors are a mistake in extending price times quantity on a sales invoice and overlooking older raw materials in determining lower of cost or market for inventory.

For fraud and other irregularities, a distinction can be drawn between "theft of assets," often called "**defalcation**" or "**employee fraud**," and "fraudulent financial

Professional skepticism—the auditor should not be blind to evidence that suggests that documents, books, or records have been altered or are incorrect. The auditor should not assume that management is dishonest, but the possibility of dishonesty must be considered.

Error—an unintentional misstatement of the financial statements.

Fraud or **other irregularity**—an intentional misstatement of the financial statements.

Defalcation or **employee fraud**—theft of assets.

Table 5-1	Management and Auditor Responsibilities
Management's Responsibilities	**Auditor's Responsibilities**
• Adopt sound accounting policies.	• Use professional skepticism.
• Maintain adequate internal control.	• Conduct the audit using a risk-based approach.
• Make fair representations in the financial statements.	• Conduct the audit to provide reasonable assurance about material misstatements.
• Acknowledge its responsibilities to the auditors.	• Consider fraud and error.
• Provide documentation and information for the audit process.	• Issue a management letter if weaknesses are encountered that could result in a material error.
	• Issue an appropriate report.

reporting," often called "management fraud." Employee fraud also includes corruption, such as managers or others taking bribes or having the corporation pay for personal expenses. One way of characterizing the difference is that employee fraud is perpetrated against the company, whereas management fraud is perpetrated for the apparent benefit of the company. An example of theft of assets is a clerk taking cash at the time a sale is made and not entering the sale in the cash register. An example of fraudulent financial reporting is the intentional overstatement of sales near the balance sheet date to increase reported earnings. In the case of the former, the company loses the money stolen; in the case of the latter, the company appears more profitable and, presumably, its stock rises in price.

It is usually more difficult for auditors to uncover fraud and other irregularities than errors. This is because of the intended deception associated with fraud and other irregularities. The auditor's responsibility for uncovering fraud and other irregularities deserves special attention. Not only the auditors but also professional accountants employed by management should be alert to errors fraud, and other irregularities. These issues are also discussed in Chapter 11. *CICA Handbook* Section 5110.14 describes specific responsibilities of the auditor (i.e., keeping the client's information confidential, maintaining independence, and communicating [where required] with management or the audit committee).

MANAGEMENT FRAUD **Management fraud** is inherently difficult to uncover because (1) it is possible for one or more members of management to override internal controls, and (2) there is typically an effort to conceal the misstatement. Instances of management fraud may include omission of transactions or disclosures, fraudulent amounts, or misstatements of recorded amounts. Careful examination of journal entries and other adjustments made by management may help to identify risks of management fraud.

Audits cannot be expected to provide the same degree of assurance for the detection of material management fraud as is provided for an equally material error. Concealment by management makes fraud more difficult for auditors to find. The cost of providing equally high assurance for management fraud and for errors is economically impractical for both auditors and society.

Factors indicating potential management fraud Due to criticism of the profession resulting from auditors' non-discovery of several large management frauds, auditors

> **Management fraud**—a fraud or other irregularity resulting in fraudulent financial reporting.

---

audit challenge 5-1
When Is It "Worth Bothering?"

After the official interview about corporate governance and management policies, the audit manager, Diane, invited Joe, the corporate controller, out to lunch. Joe started talking about some of his job frustrations.

"It's tough working in a unionized environment. We lose so much due to sick days! This makes it difficult to enforce the rules that we have for segregation of duties, particularly for refund policies. With over 60 different locations where payments or credit card payments are handled, there is a high risk of theft," said Joe.

Diane responded that this was also assessed as high risk by the internal audit department, which had conducted audits of many of the locations in the past year.

"Yes, I know," responded Joe. "But when the internal auditor comes to me with these little thefts of $2,000 while I'm faced

with losses in the hundreds of thousands of dollars due to absenteeism, I don't really feel like prosecuting these little thefts. My heart isn't in it, and I really feel like telling internal audit to drop the whole thing." Diane, at a loss for words, kept eating and then asked, "When would it be worth bothering?"

Source: Based upon an interview with an accountant conducted by I. Splettstoesser-Hogeterp in June 2008.

CRITICAL THINKING QUESTIONS

1. Do you think that this organization should prosecute all thefts or frauds? Why or why not?
2. What might Joe's attitude say about other problems or inefficiencies in the organization?
3. What questions might Diane ask of other financial managers or executives at the organization after her lunch with Joe?

now have greater responsibility for discovering management fraud than they did previously. The most important change has been increased emphasis on auditors' responsibility to evaluate factors that may indicate an increased likelihood of management fraud. These are discussed further in Chapter 11.

EMPLOYEE FRAUD The profession has also been emphatic that the auditor has less responsibility for the discovery of employee fraud than for errors. If auditors were responsible for the discovery of all employee fraud, auditing tests would have to be greatly expanded because many types of employee fraud are extremely difficult, if not impossible, to detect. The procedures that would be necessary to uncover all cases of fraud would certainly be more expensive than the benefits would justify. For example, if there is fraud involving the collusion of several employees that includes the falsification of documents, it is unlikely that such a fraud would be uncovered in a normal audit.

As the auditor assesses the likelihood of material management fraud, he or she should also evaluate the likelihood of material employee fraud. This is normally done initially as a part of understanding the entity's internal control and assessing control risk and fraud risk. Audit evidence should be expanded when the auditor finds an absence of adequate controls or failure to follow prescribed procedures, if he or she believes material employee fraud could exist.

COMPUTER FRAUD Computer fraud consists of fraud conducted with the assistance of computer software or hardware. This could include deliberately programming functions into a computer program so that it incorrectly calculates interest, placing unauthorized employees ("horses") on a computerized payroll system, falsifying an electronic mail message, obtaining "free" long distance telephone services, or creating fraudulent electronic cash transactions.

As with other forms of error or fraud, the auditor cannot be expected to always detect immaterial fraud but should investigate unusual relationships or patterns. Good internal controls spanning the development, acquisition, and use of automated systems help to prevent computer fraud.

ILLEGAL ACTS Illegal acts are defined in the now-replaced *CICA Handbook* Section 5136 as "a violation of a domestic or foreign statutory law or government regulation attributable to the entity under audit, or to management or employees acting on the entity's behalf." CAS 250—Consideration of laws and regulations in an audit of financial statements, the replacement for Section 5136—refers to non-compliance with legislation (par. 11) as occurring when the organization does not comply with laws and regulations that pertain to it. This can happen in error or deliberately and would result in an illegal act. Two examples of illegal acts are a violation of income tax laws and a violation of an environmental protection law. Section 5136 and CAS 250 point out that an auditor's responsibility is to comply with generally accepted auditing standards (GAAS) and, as a result, the auditor may not detect non-compliance or become aware that an illegal act has occurred if management has not disclosed it to the auditor.

> **Illegal acts**—violations of laws or government regulations other than irregularities.

The performance of an illegal act by management or an employee of a company may affect the company (and the financial statements) in a variety of ways. For example, the payment of a bribe by a subsidiary in a foreign country could lead to expulsion of the company and/or expropriation of the company's assets; both the balance sheet and income statement could be affected. Failing to properly dispose of untreated waste products could make the company liable for fines and penalties; the income statement could be affected. Even if the magnitude of the illegal act itself is not material, the consequences could be. The auditor must be interested in illegal acts so that their potential impact may be properly evaluated.

When an illegal act is discovered, the auditor must consider whether such an act is a reflection of the company's corporate culture. Are such acts condoned or encouraged by management? If management does not promote ethical behaviour, the auditor should question management's good faith and consider whether continued association with the client is desirable.

CAS 250 (par. 16) requires that the auditor requests written representation from management (or those charged with governance of the organization) with respect to non-compliance with laws or regulations or possible acts of non-compliance that would affect the financial statements or notes thereto. The section goes on to say that, other than inquiry of management, the auditor should not search for such illegal acts unless there is reason to believe they may exist.

Direct-effect illegal acts Certain violations of laws and regulations have a direct financial effect on specific account balances in the financial statements. For example, a violation of income tax laws directly affects income tax expense and income taxes payable. The auditor's responsibilities under CAS 250 for these direct-effect illegal acts are the same as for errors or fraud and other irregularities. As an example, on each audit, the auditor will evaluate whether there is evidence available to indicate material violations of federal or provincial tax laws. This might be done by discussions with client personnel and examination of reports issued by the Canada Revenue Agency after it has completed an examination of the client's tax return.

Indirect-effect illegal acts Most illegal acts affect the financial statements only indirectly. For example, if a company violates environmental protection laws, there is an effect on the financial statements only if there is a fine or sanction. Potential material fines and sanctions indirectly affect financial statements by creating the need to disclose a contingent liability for the potential amount that might ultimately be paid. This is called an indirect-effect illegal act. Other examples of illegal acts that are likely to have only an indirect effect are violations of insider securities trading regulations, employment equity laws, and employee safety requirements.

Auditing standards clearly state that the auditor provides no assurance that indirect-effect illegal acts will be detected. Auditors lack legal expertise, and the frequently indirect relationship between illegal acts and the financial statements makes it impractical for auditors to assume responsibility for discovering those illegal acts. One of the first things that an auditor would due upon discovering an illegal act would be to consult a lawyer.

There are three levels of responsibility that the auditor has for finding and reporting illegal acts.

- *Evidence accumulation when there is **no reason to believe** illegal acts exist.* Many audit procedures normally performed on audits to search for errors or fraud and other irregularities may also uncover illegal acts. Examples include reading the minutes of the board of directors and inquiring of the client's lawyers about litigation. The auditor should also inquire of management about policies it has established to prevent illegal acts and whether management or the audit committee knows of any laws or regulations that the company has violated. Other than these procedures, the auditor should not search for illegal acts unless there is reason to believe they may exist.
- *Evidence accumulation and other actions **when there is reason to believe** illegal acts may exist.* The auditor may find indications of possible illegal acts in a variety of ways. For example, the minutes may indicate that an investigation by a government agency is in progress, or the auditor may identify unusually large payments to consultants or government officials.

  When the auditor believes an illegal act has occurred, it is necessary to take several actions. First, the auditor should inquire of management at a level above those likely to be involved in the potential illegal act. Second, the auditor should consult with the client's lawyers or another specialist who is knowledgeable about the potential illegal act. Third, the auditor should consider accumulating additional evidence to determine if there actually is an illegal act. All three of these actions are intended to provide the auditor information about whether the suspected illegal act actually exists.
- *Actions when the auditor **knows** of an illegal act.* The first course of action when an illegal act has been identified is to consider the effects on the financial statements,

including the adequacy of disclosures. These effects may be complex and difficult to resolve. For example, a violation of employment equity laws could involve significant fines, but it could also result in the loss of customers or key employees, which could materially affect future revenues and expenses. If the auditor concludes that the disclosures relative to an illegal act are inadequate, the auditor should modify the auditor's report accordingly. The auditor must also ensure that the audit committee or an appropriate level of management has been informed of the illegal act.

The auditor should also consider the effect of such illegal acts on his or her relationship with management. If management knew of the illegal act and failed to inform the auditor, it is questionable whether management can be believed in other discussions.

concept check

C5-1 Is it possible for the auditor to conduct the audit without reliance on management? Why or why not?

C5-2 Why is management fraud harder to detect than employee fraud?

C5-3 How do indirect-effect illegal acts affect the financial statements?

② Before Accepting an Engagement, Preplanning Takes Place

Preplan the Audit

Most preplanning takes place early in the engagement, frequently in the client's office, to the extent that this is practical. **Preplanning the audit** involves the following steps: decide whether to accept or continue doing the audit for the client, identify the client's reasons for the audit, conduct an independence threat analysis, obtain an engagement letter, and select staff for the engagement.

CLIENT ACCEPTANCE OR CONTINUANCE Even though obtaining and retaining clients is not easy in a competitive profession such as public accounting, a public accounting firm must use care in deciding which clients are acceptable. The firm's legal and professional responsibilities are such that clients who lack integrity or argue constantly about the proper conduct of the audit and fees can cause more problems than they are worth. Some public accounting firms may refuse clients in what they perceive to be high-risk industries, such as high technology, health, and casualty insurance, and may even discontinue auditing existing clients in such industries.

New client investigation Before accepting a new client, most public accounting firms investigate the company to determine its acceptability. To the extent possible, the prospective client's standing in the business community, financial stability, and relations with its previous public accounting firm should be evaluated. For example, many public accounting firms use considerable caution in accepting new clients from newly formed, rapidly growing businesses. Many of these businesses fail financially and expose the public accounting firm to significant potential liability.

For prospective clients that have previously been audited by another public accounting firm, the new (successor) auditor is required by the rules of conduct of the institutes and *ordre* of chartered accountants, by the rules of conduct of CGAAC, and by incorporating acts such as the Canada Business Corporations Act to communicate with the predecessor auditor. The purpose of the requirement is to help the successor auditor evaluate whether to accept the engagement. The communication may, for example, inform the successor auditor that the client lacks integrity or that there have been disputes over accounting principles, audit procedures, or fees.

The burden of initiating the communication rests with the successor auditor. Permission must be obtained from the client before the communication can be made because of the confidentiality requirement in the rules of conduct of the professional accounting bodies. The predecessor auditor is required to respond to the request for information. In the event there are legal problems or disputes between the client and the predecessor, the latter's response can be limited to stating that no information will be provided. The successor should seriously consider the desirability of ※

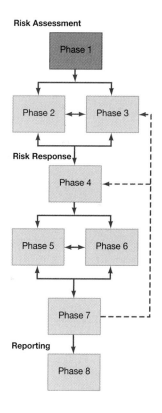

Risk Assessment

Phase 1

Phase 2 ⟷ Phase 3

Risk Response

Phase 4

Phase 5 ⟷ Phase 6

Phase 7

Reporting

Phase 8

Preplanning the audit—actions taken prior to commencing detailed client risk analysis, which involves the following steps: decide whether to accept or continue doing the audit for the client; identify the client's reasons for the audit; conduct an independence threat analysis; obtain an engagement letter; and select staff for the engagement.

accepting a prospective engagement, without considerable investigation, if a client will not permit the communication or the predecessor will not provide a comprehensive response.

Even when a prospective client has been audited by another public accounting firm, other investigations are needed. Sources of information include local lawyers, other public accountants, banks, and other businesses.

Many practitioners take advantage of the Internet as a search tool to learn more about the potential new client and its key operations by studying available client websites and by using search engines for other sites that discuss the potential client. In addition, they use database search tools or customized search engines to examine financial data or recent publications about the client. This information is useful in the client acceptance decision and throughout the audit if the client is accepted.

Continuing clients Considering whether or not to continue doing the audit of an existing client is as important a decision as deciding whether or not to accept a new client. For that reason, many public accounting firms evaluate existing clients annually to determine whether there are reasons for not continuing to do the audit. Previous conflicts over such things as the appropriate scope of the audit, the type of opinion to issue, or fees may cause the auditor to discontinue association. The auditor may also determine that the client lacks basic integrity and therefore should no longer be a client. If there is a lawsuit against a public accounting firm by a client or a suit against the client by the public accounting firm, the firm probably should not do the audit because its independence could be questioned.

Even if none of the previously discussed conditions exist, the public accounting firm may decide not to continue doing audits for a client because of excessive risk. For example, a public accounting firm might decide that there is considerable risk of a regulatory conflict between a governmental agency and a client, which could result in financial failure of the client and, ultimately, lawsuits against the public accounting firm. Even if the engagement is profitable, the risk may exceed the short-term benefits of doing the audit.

As an example, consider Hillsburg Hardware Limited, audited by Berger, Kao, Kadous & Co., LLP (BKK), a firm in Halifax, Nova Scotia. BKK is part of a national association of firms, so it has access to specialists and national standards personnel. Hillsburg has been a client of BKK since the company was formed in 1980. Hillsburg management has generally been easy to work with, although at times there have been minor disagreements. Management turnover is low, and profits have been consistent, although recent earnings have declined in the wake of the current recession. BKK conducted a search on the Internet and found that Hillsburg received positive press, primarily for local charitable work. Discussions with management indicated that the only major issue coming up that would affect the audit would be continuing enhancements to information systems.

Investigation of new clients and re-evaluation of existing ones are an essential part of deciding risk. Assume that a potential client is in a reasonably risky industry and has management that has a reputation of integrity but is also known to take aggressive financial risks. The public accounting firm may choose not to accept the engagement. If the public accounting firm concludes that the client is still acceptable, the fee proposed to the client is likely to be affected. Audits with higher risks will normally result in higher audit costs, which should be reflected in higher audit fees.

IDENTIFY CLIENT REASONS FOR AUDIT Two major factors affecting the appropriate evidence to accumulate are the likely statement users and their intended uses of the statements. It will be shown in Chapter 7 that the auditor is likely to accumulate more evidence when the statements are to be used extensively. This is often the case for publicly held companies (such as Hillsburg), those with extensive indebtedness, and companies that are to be sold in the near future.

The most likely uses of the statements can be determined from previous experience in the engagement and discussion with management. Throughout the engagement, the auditor may get additional information as to why the client is having an audit and the likely uses of the financial statements.

CONDUCT INDEPENDENCE THREAT ANALYSIS The rules of conduct state that an auditor may conduct an audit only if independent. The five threats to independence (i.e., self-interest, self-review, advocacy, familiarity, and intimidation) must be explicitly assessed, and any potential threats described. The auditor then determines whether it is possible to institute safeguards to mitigate the threat (e.g., changing the partner in charge of an engagement to deal with the familiarity threat). If such safeguards can be put into place, or there are no threats, the engagement can be accepted. The auditor would communicate to the audit committee any such threats and how they had been dealt with.

If there are threats without compensating safeguards available, or the safeguards do not adequately mitigate the threat, the engagement must be declined.

OBTAIN AN ENGAGEMENT LETTER A clear understanding of the terms of the engagement should exist between the client and the public accounting firm. The terms should be in writing (Section 5110, ISA 210) to minimize misunderstandings. Management's responsibilities are clarified and clearly agreed upon prior to the auditor being able to accept the engagement. This is done using an engagement letter.

The **engagement letter** is an agreement between the public accounting firm and the client for the conduct of the audit and related services. It should specify whether the auditor will perform an audit, a review, or a compilation, plus any other services such as tax returns or management services. It should also state any restrictions to be imposed on the auditor's work, deadlines for completing the audit, assistance to be provided by the client's personnel in obtaining records and documents, and schedules to be prepared for the auditor. If the client has an internal audit department, it will also specify the role of that department during the audit. It often includes an agreement on fees. The engagement letter is also a means of informing the client that the auditor is not responsible for the discovery of all acts of fraud.

The engagement letter does not affect the public accounting firm's responsibility to external users of audited financial statements, but it can affect legal responsibilities to the client. For example, if the client sued the public accounting firm for failing to find a material misstatement, one defence a public accounting firm could use would be a signed engagement letter stating that a review, rather than an audit, was agreed upon.

Engagement letter information is important in planning the audit principally because it affects the timing of the tests and the total amount of time the audit and other services will take. If the deadline for submitting the audit report is soon after the balance sheet date, a significant portion of the audit must be done before the end of the year. When the auditor is preparing tax returns and a management letter, or if client assistance is not available, arrangements must be made to extend the amount of time for the engagement. Client-imposed restrictions on the audit could affect the procedures performed and possibly even the type of audit opinion issued. An example of an engagement letter for the audit of Hillsburg Hardware Limited is given in Figure 5-2 on page 118. The financial statements for Hillsburg Hardware Limited are included on pages 147–162.

Engagement letter—an agreement between the public accounting firm and the client as to the terms of the engagement for the conduct of the audit and related services.

IDENTIFY STAFF AVAILABLE FOR THE ENGAGEMENT Assigning the appropriate staff to the engagement is important to meet quality control standards in GAAS and to promote audit efficiency.

Staff must, therefore, be assigned with competence and quality in mind. On larger engagements, there are likely to be one or more partners and staff at several experience levels doing the audit. Specialists in such technical areas as statistical sampling, provision of industry expertise, or computer auditing may also be assigned. On smaller audits, there may be only one or two staff members.

A major consideration affecting staffing is the need for continuity from year to year. An inexperienced staff assistant is likely to become the most experienced non-partner

Figure 5-2   Engagement Letter

June 14, 2008

Boritz, Kao, Kadous & Co., LLP
Halifax, Nova Scotia
B3M 3JP

Mr. Rick Chulick, President
Hillsburg Hardware Limited
2146 Willow Street
Halifax, Nova Scotia
B3H 3F9

Dear Mr. Chulick:

The purpose of this letter is to outline the terms of our engagement to audit the financial statements of Hillsburg Hardware Limited for the year ending December 31, 2008.

Objective, scope, and limitations

Our statutory function as auditor of Hillsburg Hardware Limited is to report to the shareholders by expressing an opinion on Hillsburg Hardware Limited's financial statements. We will conduct our audit in accordance with Canadian generally accepted auditing standards and will issue an audit report.

It is important to recognize that there are limitations inherent in the auditing process. Since audits are based on the concept of selective testing of the data underlying the financial statements, they are subject to the limitation that material misstatements, if they exist, may not be detected. Because of the nature of fraud, including attempts at concealment through collusion and forgery, an audit designed and executed in accordance with Canadian generally accepted auditing standards may not detect a material fraud. Further, while effective internal control reduces the likelihood that misstatements will occur and remain undetected, it does not eliminate the possibility. For these reasons, we cannot guarantee that misstatements or other illegal acts, if present, will be detected.

Our responsibilities

We will be responsible for performing the audit in accordance with Canadian generally accepted auditing standards. These standards require that we plan and perform the audit to obtain reasonable assurance about whether the financial statements present fairly, in all material respects, the financial position, results of operations, and cash flows in accordance with Canadian generally accepted accounting principles. Accordingly, we will design our audit to provide reasonable, but not absolute, assurance of detecting fraud, errors, and other irregularities that have a material effect on the financial statements taken as a whole, including illegal acts the consequences of which have a material effect on the financial statements.

One of the underlying principles of the profession is a duty of confidentiality with respect to client affairs. Accordingly, except for information that is in or enters the public domain, we will not provide any third party with information related to Hillsburg Hardware Limited without Hillsburg Hardware Limited's permission, unless required to do so by legal authority, the rules of professional conduct/code of ethics, or to satisfy the requirements of the Canadian Public Accountability Board.

We will communicate in writing to the Audit Committee the relationships between us and Hillsburg Hardware Limited that, in our professional judgment, may reasonably be thought to bear on our independence. Further, we will confirm our independence with respect to Hillsburg Hardware Limited.

The objective of our audit is to obtain reasonable assurance that the financial statements are free of material misstatement. However, if we identify any of the following matters, they will be communicated to the appropriate level of management, including the Audit Committee:

(a) misstatements, other than trivial errors;
(b) fraud;
(c) misstatements that may cause future financial statements to be materially misstated;
(d) illegal or possibly illegal acts, other than those considered inconsequential;
(e) significant weakness in internal control; and
(f) certain related-party transactions.

The matters communicated will be those that we identify during the course of our audit. Audits do not usually identify all matters that may be of interest to management in discharging its responsibilities. The type and significance of the matter to be communicated will determine the level of management to which the communication is directed.

We will consider Hillsburg Hardware Limited's internal control over financial reporting solely for the purpose of determining the nature, timing, and extent of auditing procedures necessary for expressing our opinion on the financial statements. This consideration will not be sufficient for us to render an opinion on the effectiveness of internal control over financial reporting.

continued >

Figure 5-2   Engagement Letter (*Continued*)

Management's responsibilities

Management is responsible for:

(a) The fair presentation of Hillsburg Hardware Limited's financial statements in accordance with generally accepted accounting principles;

Completeness of information:

(b) providing us with and making available complete financial records and related data and copies of all minutes of meetings of shareholders, directors, and committees of directors;

(c) providing us with information relating to any known or probable instances of non-compliance with legislative or regulatory requirements, including financial reporting requirements;

(d) providing us with information relating to any illegal or possibly illegal acts, and all facts related thereto;

(e) providing us with information regarding all related parties and related-party transactions;

Fraud and error:

(f) the design and implementation of internal controls to prevent and detect fraud and error;

(g) an assessment of the risk that the financial statements may be materially misstated as a result of fraud;

(h) providing us with information relating to fraud or suspected fraud affecting the entity involving

   (i) management, (ii) employees who have significant roles in internal control; or (iii) others, where the fraud could have a material effect on the financial statements;

(i) providing us with information relating to any allegations of fraud or suspected fraud affecting the entity's financial statements communicated by employees, former employees, analysts, regulators, or others;

(j) communicating its belief that the effects of any uncorrected financial statement misstatements aggregated during the audit are immaterial, both individually and in the aggregate, to the financial statements taken as a whole;

Recognition, measurement, and disclosure:

(k) providing us with an assessment of the reasonableness of significant assumptions underlying fair value measurements and disclosures in the financial statements;

(l) providing us with any plans or intentions that may affect the carrying value or classification of assets or liabilities;

(m) providing us with the measurement and disclosure of transactions with related parties;

(n) providing us with an assessment of significant estimates and all known areas of measurement uncertainty;

(o) providing us with claims and possible claims, whether or not they have been discussed with Hillsburg Hardware Limited legal counsel;

(p) providing us with information relating to other liabilities and gain or loss contingencies, including those associated with guarantees, whether written or oral, under which Hillsburg Hardware Limited is contingently liable;

(q) providing us with information on whether or not Hillsburg Hardware Limited has satisfactory title to assets, liens or encumbrances on assets, and assets pledged as collateral;

(r) providing us with information relating to compliance with aspects of contractual agreements that may affect the financial statements;

(s) providing us with information concerning subsequent events; and

(t) providing us with written confirmation of significant representations provided to us during the engagement on matters that are

   (i) directly related to items that are material, either individually or in the aggregate, to the financial statements;

   (ii) not directly related to items that are material to the financial statements but are significant, either individually or in the aggregate, to the engagement; and

   (iii) relevant to your judgments or estimates that are material, either individually or in the aggregate, to the financial statements.

Coordination of the Audit

Assistance is to be supplied by your personnel, including preparation of schedules and analysis of accounts, as described in a separate attachment.

Fees

Our fees are based on the amount of time required at various levels of responsibility, plus out-of-pocket expenses (i.e., travel, printing, telephone, and communications) payable upon presentation of billing. We will notify you immediately of any circumstances we encounter that could significantly affect our estimate of total fees.

continued >

| Figure 5-2 | Engagement Letter (*Continued*) |

We appreciate the opportunity to be of service to Hillsburg Hardware Limited. The above terms of our engagement shall remain operative until amended, terminated, or superseded in writing.

If you have any questions about the contents of this letter, please raise them. If the services as outlined are in accordance with your requirements and if the above terms are acceptable, please sign the copy of this letter in the space provided and return it to us.

Yours very truly,

J.E. Boritz
Boritz, Kao, Kadous & Co., LLP
Accepted by:
Title: President
Date: June 21, 2008

concept check

C5-4 Why does the auditor assess clients for acceptability prior to conducting the audit engagement?

C5-5 What are some of the typical reasons that a client wants a financial statement audit?

C5-6 Describe the sections in an engagement letter and explain the relevance of each section.

on the engagement within a few years. Continuity helps the public accounting firm maintain familiarity with technical requirements and close interpersonal relations with the client's personnel. The extent of assistance provided by the client, including work done by the internal audit department, also affects staffing. Throughout the planning and conduct of the audit, the entire team meets to share information and to ensure awareness of risks.

Audit Phases

The financial statement audit is a strategic process—this means that forward planning is conducted with regular ongoing evaluation of work to date so that adjustments can be made to the process as needed in response to findings to date. The goal is to gather sufficient, high-quality evidence to provide an audit opinion. As we discuss the eight phases (shown and described in Figure 5-3 on page 124), keep in mind that these are part of one audit and that in practice the auditor will go back and forth between phases as findings are documented and evaluated.

Think about a recent decision that you made that involved multiple steps, such as deciding which major to select in school. You would have looked at your own preferences, talked to people, gathered information from the internet, and considered the impact on your future job. Some data are easy to gather, some are quantitative (e.g., which courses you would have to take), and some are qualitative (which courses do you like or dislike, and how strongly?). Perhaps when you found out that you would have a low income in one discipline, you changed your strategy and looked at another discipline. Perhaps this even caused you to switch gears totally and start looking at another university.

A strategic audit process is similar. You will see that as we describe decisions to be made during the audit (for example, whether to rely upon internal controls), that the answer can have a major impact upon the actions taken during the audit.

The eight phases of the audit are broken down into three sections: Risk Assessment, Risk Response, and Reporting. In practice, information moves back and forth among these sections and phases, as you will see when we discuss examples. In the **risk assessment** section, the auditor identifies what could go wrong with the financial statements and the approaches for dealing with the risks. Substantial information must be collected and analyzed about the industry, business environment, and client to identify and assess these risks. Then, the auditor moves to **risk response**, whereby specific audit programs and processes are designed and tests conducted to obtain reasonable assurance with respect to the financial statements in the context of assessed risks. Finally, in the **reporting** section, the auditor decides upon the report to be issued, issues the report, and communicates with management and the audit committee.

Risk assessment—the auditor identifies what could go wrong with the financial statements and the approaches for dealing with the risks.

Risk response—specific audit programs and processes are designed and tests conducted to obtain reasonable assurance with respect to the financial statements in the context of assessed risks.

Reporting—the auditor decides upon the report to be issued, issues the report, and communicates with management and the audit committee.

For any given audit, there are many ways an auditor can accumulate evidence to meet the overall audit objectives. Two overriding considerations affect the approach the auditor selects: (1) sufficient, high-quality audit evidence must be accumulated to meet the auditor's professional responsibility, and (2) the cost of accumulating the evidence should be balanced against the quality of the evidence. The first consideration is the more important, but cost optimization is necessary if public accounting firms are to be competitive and profitable. In the remainder of this section, we present an overview of the phases of the audit, which we will discuss further in subsequent chapters.

Risk Assessment

The risk assessment phases are phases where the auditor finds out about the client and the client's industry and business environment. A phrase that describes risks is "what could go wrong?" For example, you would likely not replace your car unless it were old, needed repairs, and you were going on a long trip and wanted to avoid break-downs. Similarly, in the audit engagement, the auditor needs to know "what could go wrong" in the financial statements, the client industry, or business, before tailoring the risk response to those assessed risks. The three phases of risk assessment are preplanning (to decide whether the audit should proceed), client risk assessment (to identify and document risks), and audit planning (to organize documentation and risks into an audit framework and develop a tailored strategic audit approach). Chapters 6 through 12 cover risk assessment and the audit planning process.

PHASE 1—PREPLANNING As explained in the previous section, the auditor first decides whether to accept the new client or continue with the existing client. This is a mutual decision, often following a lengthy proposal and discussion phase for new clients. Only if the decision is to proceed with the engagement does the auditor continue on to the remaining phases of the audit.

PHASE 2–CLIENT RISK PROFILE
Obtain knowledge of the industry and business environment Unique aspects of different businesses are reflected in the financial statements. An audit of a life insurance company could not be performed with due care without an understanding of the unique characteristics of that industry. Imagine attempting to audit a client in the bridge construction industry without understanding the construction business and the percentage-of-completion method of accounting. Neither audit could be effectively conducted without an awareness of the business environment and regulatory environment within which these businesses function. Industries operate within the broader context of the local, national, and international economy and are subject to changes in accounting standards, foreign-exchange rates, interest rates, overall demand, or raw material prices. Prior to looking at the client's financial statements in detail, the auditor needs to develop expectations of client results in the context of the overall business environment.

Obtain knowledge of the client's business What is the business doing and why? Is its business strategy linked with its information systems strategy? What accounting policies were selected and why? These are only some of the questions that the auditor will ask when obtaining or updating knowledge of the client's business. Many organizations will be dealing with changes to accounting policies and practices as they transition to international accounting standards. The auditor will identify transaction streams (also called "cycles," such as sales), nature of information systems, and supporting infrastructure that enable the business to operate. From there, the auditor will identify those systems that are used to record information for the financial statements, which are the focus of greater attention. Potential high-risk areas, such as complex transactions and related-party transactions, will also be identified at this early stage.

Document corporate governance processes and control environment These processes are also known as entity-level controls, as they impact the entire organization.

A positive "tone at the top" helps ensure effective operations. Documenting these processes helps the auditor understand how the business is managed. The auditor will also look for management to have its own risk assessment process that includes risk identification, assessment, and mitigation.

Assess entity-level controls Once documented, the auditor will then need to assess the consistency and impact of the entity-level controls. The auditor may consider questions such as: Are all transaction cycles affected? Does it appear that management is reliable and honest? Are there pressures on management to misstate the financial statements? Does management actively monitor risks both internal and external to the organization and deal with them?

Assess risks of fraud The auditor will ask management whether it has an active fraud risk assessment process and what actions are undertaken when fraud is discovered. Linking these to the quality of entity-level controls and potential pressures on management will allow the auditor to consider the potential for fraud.

Document internal controls and evaluate design effectiveness of internal controls The ability of the client's internal controls to generate reliable financial information and safeguard assets and records is one of the most important and widely accepted concepts in the theory and practice of auditing. If the client has excellent internal controls and they are operating effectively, risks of errors will be low and the amount of audit evidence to be accumulated can be significantly less than when internal controls are inadequate.

Generally accepted auditing standards require the auditor to gain a sufficient understanding of internal control to plan the audit. This understanding is obtained by reviewing organization charts or procedural manuals, by discussions with client personnel, by completing internal control questionnaires and flowcharts, and by observing client activities. Many firms have software that assists in the evaluation process by prompting the auditor to answer specific questions and then providing a summary of the likely effects of the responses on risk. Software also helps the auditor link controls to specific assertions.

Identify significant risks or transactions/accounts that require more than substantive tests Some highly automated systems, such as paperless systems and electronic data interchange, cannot be effectively tested by substantive tests. Once the auditor has documented internal control and considered their design effectiveness, the auditor can identify those controls and assertions that require control testing. The auditor will also consider transactions or events that require special focus, such as complex investments or related-party transactions.

PHASE 3—PLAN THE AUDIT Developing the client risk profile (Phase 2), and planning the audit are two sets of activities that are closely linked and completed in parallel. As information about the client is gathered, it is structured and analyzed as part of an audit planning model, such as the audit risk model (explained further in Chapter 7).

Based upon the purpose of the audit, the projected users, and the business risk of the client (the risk that the client will fail to achieve its objectives, discussed further in Chapter 7), the auditor will determine audit risk, representing the willingness to accept potential material error in the financial statements. The knowledge of the business, industry, and environment will enable the auditor to assess the likelihood of material misstatement in the financial statements as a whole or by assertion before the consideration of internal controls: inherent risk. Using the financial results of the client, the auditor will set preliminary materiality levels.

After the auditor gains an understanding of internal control, he or she is in a position to evaluate how effective controls should be in preventing and detecting errors or fraud and other irregularities, as the auditor must specifically consider the risks of fraud. This evaluation involves identifying specific controls that reduce the likelihood that errors or fraud and other irregularities will occur and not be detected and corrected on a timely basis. Supervisory, managing, or monitoring controls are specifically identified as having important effects. This process is referred to as evaluating control risk, and it is completed by assertion, for each material account or class of transactions.

Using the assessed inherent risks and assessed control risks, the auditor will then determine the risks of material misstatement at the financial statement and assertion levels, which helps identify the depth of audit work required for the individual accounts and transaction streams. On an ongoing basis, these risks and the audit plan are discussed with the audit team, and audit plans modified as required. The nature of these risks and their relationships within the audit risk model are explained further in Chapter 7.

The outcome of the planning process is a strategic audit approach for the audit overall, and for the components of the audit (accounts with potential for material error, or material transaction streams).

Risk Response

The concept of risk response refers to the fact that the audit is designed to respond to identified risks, with audit programs and tests addressing those risks. The four risk response phases are the design of further audit procedures (describing audit tests to be conducted); tests of control (in response to control risk and accounts that require more than substantive tests); substantive tests; and ongoing evaluation, quality control, and final evidence gathering. Chapters 12 through 15 and Chapters 20 and 21 address the risk response process.

PHASE 4—DESIGN FURTHER AUDIT PROCEDURES The audit procedures are prepared to respond to the risks of material misstatement identified in the risk assessment phases of the audit. The auditor considers the balance of different types of tests, the type of sampling to be used to actually conduct the tests, and adding unpredictability (or randomness) to the testing process. The tests are conducted in relationship to the materiality levels determined, dealing with specific risks such as the potential for management bias or override, fraud risks, or complex transactions identified.

PHASE 5—TESTS OF CONTROL Where the auditor has decided to rely upon internal controls, the auditor must test the effectiveness of the controls or rely upon tests of controls conducted in one of the prior two years if the control has characteristics that permit extended reliance. (This concept is discussed further in Chapter 9—controls do not have to be tested every year.) For example, assume that the client's order entry software requires that all amounts over $10,000 must be entered twice. This control is directly related to the accuracy of sales. One possible test of the effectiveness of this control is for the auditor to enter a transaction over $10,000 and observe whether the system requests a second entry. **Tests of controls** are audit procedures that test the effectiveness of control policies and procedures in support of a reduced assessed control risk.

Tests of controls—audit procedures to test the effectiveness of control policies and procedures in support of a reduced assessed control risk.

As the tests are completed, the results are evaluated to determine if there should be any changes in assessed risks or in the design of the audit procedures.

PHASE 6—SUBSTANTIVE TESTS There are three general categories of substantive procedures: analytical procedures, tests of details of balances, and tests of key items. **Analytical procedures** are those that assess the overall reasonableness of transactions and balances using comparisons and relationships. An example of an analytical procedure that would provide some assurance for the accuracy of both sales transactions and accounts receivable is to have the auditor run an exception report (using audit software) of sales transactions for unusually large amounts and compare total monthly sales to prior years. If a company is consistently using incorrect sales prices, significant differences are likely.

Analytical procedures—use of comparisons and relationships to determine whether account balances or other data appear reasonable.

Tests of details of balances are specific procedures intended to test for monetary misstatements in the balances in the financial statements. An example related to the

Tests of details of balances—an auditor's tests for monetary errors or fraud and other irregularities in the details of balance sheet and income statement accounts.

Figure 5-3   The Audit Process

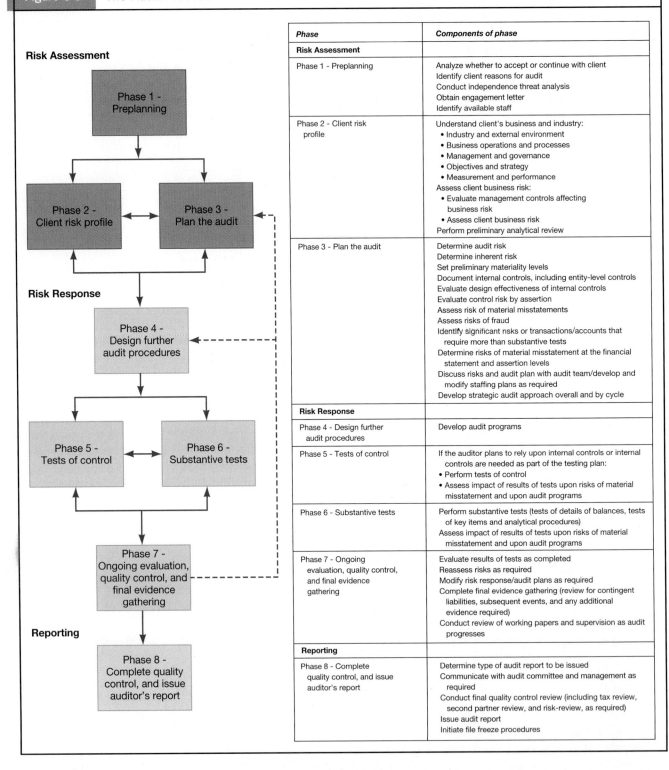

Risk Assessment

Phase 1 -
Preplanning

Phase 2 -
Client risk profile

Phase 3 -
Plan the audit

Risk Response

Phase 4 -
Design further
audit procedures

Phase 5 -
Tests of control

Phase 6 -
Substantive tests

Phase 7 -
Ongoing evaluation,
quality control, and
final evidence
gathering

Reporting

Phase 8 -
Complete quality
control, and issue
auditor's report

Phase	Components of phase
Risk Assessment	
Phase 1 - Preplanning	Analyze whether to accept or continue with client Identify client reasons for audit Conduct independence threat analysis Obtain engagement letter Identify available staff
Phase 2 - Client risk profile	Understand client's business and industry: • Industry and external environment • Business operations and processes • Management and governance • Objectives and strategy • Measurement and performance Assess client business risk: • Evaluate management controls affecting business risk • Assess client business risk Perform preliminary analytical review
Phase 3 - Plan the audit	Determine audit risk Determine inherent risk Set preliminary materiality levels Document internal controls, including entity-level controls Evaluate design effectiveness of internal controls Evaluate control risk by assertion Assess risk of material misstatements Assess risks of fraud Identify significant risks or transactions/accounts that require more than substantive tests Determine risks of material misstatement at the financial statement and assertion levels Discuss risks and audit plan with audit team/develop and modify staffing plans as required Develop strategic audit approach overall and by cycle
Risk Response	
Phase 4 - Design further audit procedures	Develop audit programs
Phase 5 - Tests of control	If the auditor plans to rely upon internal controls or internal controls are needed as part of the testing plan: • Perform tests of control • Assess impact of results of tests upon risks of material misstatement and upon audit programs
Phase 6 - Substantive tests	Perform substantive tests (tests of details of balances, tests of key items and analytical procedures) Assess impact of results of tests upon risks of material misstatement and upon audit programs
Phase 7 - Ongoing evaluation, quality control, and final evidence gathering	Evaluate results of tests as completed Reassess risks as required Modify risk response/audit plans as required Complete final evidence gathering (review for contingent liabilities, subsequent events, and any additional evidence required) Conduct review of working papers and supervision as audit progresses
Reporting	
Phase 8 - Complete quality control, and issue auditor's report	Determine type of audit report to be issued Communicate with audit committee and management as required Conduct final quality control review (including tax review, second partner review, and risk-review, as required) Issue audit report Initiate file freeze procedures

accuracy of accounts receivable is direct written communication with the client's customers. Tests of ending balances are essential to the conduct of the audit because most of the evidence is obtained from a source independent of the client and therefore considered to be of high quality.

Tests of key items focus on specific transactions that could be at risk of material error. For example, the purchase of shares in a subsidiary company may be at risk of incorrect valuation. Similarly, the auditor may choose to examine the activity

Tests of key items—audit tests that focus on specific transactions that could be at risk of material error.

between the company and a related party to ensure that the amounts have been recorded correctly.

There is a close relationship among the general review of the client's circumstances, results of understanding internal control and assessing control risk, analytical procedures, and the substantive tests of the financial statement account balances. If the auditor has obtained a reasonable level of assurance for any given audit objective by performing tests of controls and analytical procedures, the tests of details for that objective can be significantly reduced. In most instances, however, some tests of details of significant financial statement account balances are necessary.

Ongoing evaluation of the effects of substantive tests upon assessed risks and upon the audit programs helps ensure that this close relationship is considered.

PHASE 7—ONGOING EVALUATION, QUALITY CONTROL, AND FINAL EVIDENCE GATHERING
This phase links to the other phases of the audit engagement. As the results of the tests and other information gathered throughout the audit are compiled, audit management (the supervisor, manager, and partner) works with the audit team to assess the impact upon assessed risks and procedures designed as a response. This means that supervision and quality control are ongoing, as working papers are regularly reviewed and unusual items followed up.

After the auditor has completed all the procedures for each audit objective and for each financial statement account, it is necessary to combine the information obtained to reach an overall conclusion as to whether the financial statements are fairly presented. This is a highly subjective process that relies heavily on the auditor's professional judgment. In practice, the auditor continuously combines the information obtained as he or she proceeds through the audit. The final combination is a summation at the completion of the engagement.

Reporting

When the audit is completed, the PA must issue an auditor's report to accompany the client's published financial statements (Phase 8). The report must meet well-defined technical requirements that are affected by the scope of the audit and the nature of the findings. These reports are studied in Chapter 22. Prior to releasing the report, the auditor will conduct final quality control reviews (such as tax, second partner, or risk reviews). The auditor will also issue a management letter and report to management and the audit committee about the outcome of the audit.

concept check

C5-7 What is the relationship between risk assessment and risk response during the financial statement audit?

C5-8 When is quality control conducted during the audit? How does this affect risk assessment?

4 Entity-Level Controls and Financial Statement Cycles

Corporate Governance and Entity-Level Systems

Prior to looking at specific cycles, the auditor will inquire about and document corporate governance systems such as the policies and procedures employed by the board of directors, the audit committee, and senior management. As you will discover in later chapters, actions at the corporate governance level have a significant impact upon the level of risk assigned to the audit of the organization.

There are also many entity-level controls, such as supervision policies and information technology general controls that affect multiple or all transaction cycles. For example, controls over program changes affect all systems that have automated information systems, as do security and access controls. Prior to working with individual transaction cycles, the auditor would document, evaluate, and test (where reliance is warranted) these entity-level controls. Chapter 9 looks at the study and assessment of internal controls, and Chapter 10 discusses corporate governance and entity-level controls.

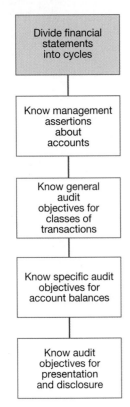

Cycle approach—a method of dividing an audit by keeping closely related types of transactions and account balances in the same segment.

Financial Statement Cycles

Individual accounts and cycles within the audit are assessed using audit assertions. Figure 5-4 explains how these assertions are developed in the context of the objectives of the audit. Dividing the financial statements into smaller segments or components makes the audit more manageable and aids in the assignment of tasks to different members of the audit team. For example, most auditors treat capital assets and notes payable as different segments. Each segment is audited separately but not completely independently (e.g., the audit of capital assets may reveal an unrecorded note payable). After the audit of each segment is completed, including interrelationships with other segments, the results are combined. A conclusion can then be reached about the financial statements taken as a whole.

There are different ways of segmenting an audit. One approach would be to treat every account balance on the statements as a separate segment. Segmenting that way is usually inefficient. It would result in the independent audit of such closely related accounts as inventory and cost of goods sold.

THE CYCLE APPROACH TO SEGMENTING AN AUDIT A more common way to divide an audit is to keep closely related types (or classes) of transactions and account balances in the same segment. This is called the **cycle approach**. For example, sales, sales returns, cash receipts, and charge-offs of uncollectible accounts are four classes of transactions that cause accounts receivable to increase and decrease, all part of the sales and collection cycle. Similarly, payroll transactions and accrued payroll are a part of the payroll and personnel cycle.

The logic of using the cycle approach can be seen by thinking about the way transactions are recorded in journals, data files, or databases and summarized in the general ledger and financial statements. Figure 5-5A shows that flow for manual, paper-based systems. Transactions are written into journals, the totals posted to the general ledger, and financial statements prepared from the general ledger.

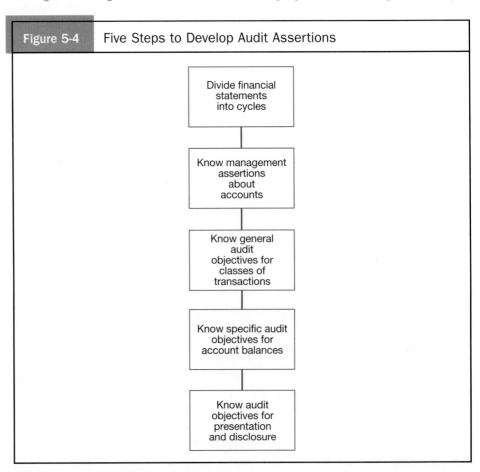

Figure 5-4	Five Steps to Develop Audit Assertions

Figure 5-5B shows the flow for batch processing systems. Transactions are entered into subsystems, resulting in transactions being retained in history files for each subsystem. The transactions are used to update the appropriate master files. Each subsystem is used to print a report summarizing the transactions entered (called a "history report," or often still a "journal"). The general ledger subsystem is used to prepare the financial statements. Figure 5-5C on the next page, which depicts database

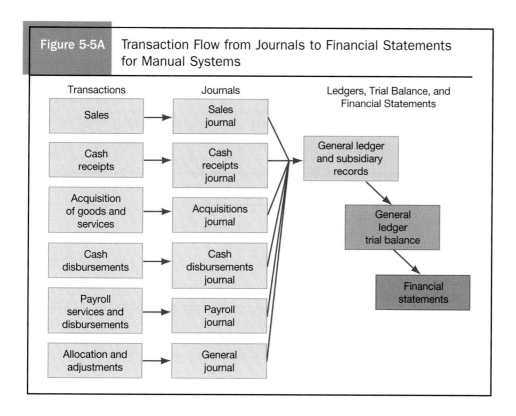

Figure 5-5A Transaction Flow from Journals to Financial Statements for Manual Systems

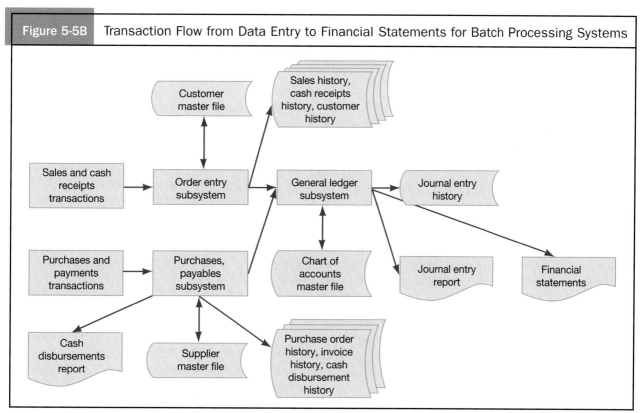

Figure 5-5B Transaction Flow from Data Entry to Financial Statements for Batch Processing Systems

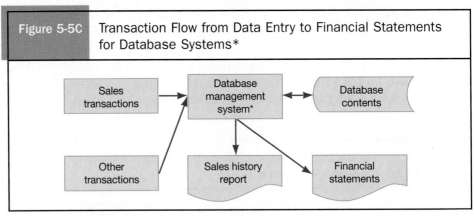

Figure 5-5C Transaction Flow from Data Entry to Financial Statements for Database Systems*

*The structure and complexity depend upon the type of database used.

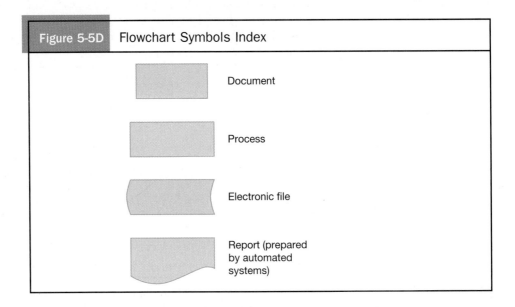

Figure 5-5D Flowchart Symbols Index

Document

Process

Electronic file

Report (prepared by automated systems)

processing, looks deceptively simple since all transactions are updated against a single database containing all company data. Such systems are normally more complex than batch processing systems, however. (Figure 5-5D is a symbol index for the flowcharts used in Figures 5-5A through C.)

To the extent that it is practical, the cycle approach combines transactions recorded in different journals or subsystems with the general ledger balances that result from those transactions.

The following is a list of cycles explained in detail in this text:

• Sales and collection cycle.
• Payroll and personnel cycle.
• Acquisition and payment cycle.
• Inventory and warehousing cycle.
• Capital acquisition and repayment cycle.

Each of these cycles is so important that it is part of the title of one or more chapters in the remainder of this book.

To illustrate the application of cycles to audits, Figure 5-6 presents the December 31, 2008, trial balance of Hillsburg Hardware Limited. The financial statements prepared from this trial balance are included in the insert on pages 147–162. Prior-year figures usually included for comparative purposes are excluded from Figure 5-6 in order to focus on transaction cycles. A trial balance is used to prepare financial statements

Figure 5-6   Hillsburg Hardware Limited Adjusted Trial Balance

HILLSBURG HARDWARE LIMITED
TRIAL BALANCE
December 31, 2008

		Debit	Credit
S,A,P,C	Cash in bank	$ 827,568	
S	Trade accounts receivable	20,196,800	
S	Allowance for uncollectible accounts		$ 1,240,000
S	Other accounts receivable	945,020	
A,I	Inventories	29,864,621	
A	Prepaid expenses	431,558	
A	Land	3,456,420	
A	Buildings	32,500,000	
A	Computer and delivery equipment	3,758,347	
A	Furniture and fixtures	2,546,421	
A	Accumulated amortization		31,920,126
A	Trade accounts payable (1)		4,483,995
C	Notes payable		4,179,620
P	Accrued payroll		1,349,800
P	Accrued payroll expenses		119,663
C	Accrued interest		149,560
C	Dividends payable		1,900,000
A	Goods and services tax payable (net) (1)		235,994
A	Accrued income tax		795,442
C	Long-term notes payable		24,120,000
A	Deferred tax		738,240
A	Other accrued payables		829,989
C	Capital stock		8,500,000
C	Retained earnings		11,929,075
S	Sales		144,327,789
S	Sales returns and allowances	1,241,663	
I	Cost of goods sold	103,240,768	
P	Salaries and commissions	7,738,900	
P	Sales payroll benefits	1,422,100	
A	Travel and entertainment—selling	1,110,347	
A	Advertising	2,611,263	
A	Sales and promotional literature	321,620	
A	Sales meetings and training	924,480	
A	Miscellaneous sales expense	681,041	
P	Executive and office salaries	5,523,960	
P	Administrative payroll benefits	682,315	
A	Travel and entertainment—administrative	561,680	
A	Computer maintenance and supplies	860,260	
A	Stationery and supplies	762,568	
A	Postage	244,420	
A	Telephone and fax	722,315	
A	Rent	312,140	
A	Legal fees and retainers	383,060	
A	Auditing and related services	302,840	
A	Amortization	1,452,080	
S	Bad debt expense	3,323,084	
A	Insurance	722,684	
A	Office repairs and maintenance	843,926	
A	Miscellaneous office expense	643,680	
A	Miscellaneous general expense	323,842	
A	Gain on sale of assets		719,740
A	Income taxes	1,746,600	
C	Interest expense	2,408,642	
C	Dividends	1,900,000	
	(1) These accounts were grouped together on the financial statements	$237,539,033	$237,539,033

Note: Letters in the left-hand column refer to the following transaction cycles: S = Sales and collection, A = Acquisition and payment, P = Payroll and personnel, I = Inventory and warehousing, C = Capital acquisition and repayment.

and is a primary focus of every audit. The letter representing a cycle is shown for each account in the left column beside the account name. Each account has at least one cycle associated with it, and only cash and inventories are part of two or more cycles.

The cycles used in this text are shown again in Table 5-2. The accounts for Hillsburg Hardware Limited are summarized by cycle and include the transaction types that typically appear in each cycle. The following observations expand the information contained in Table 5-2.

Table 5-2	Cycles Applied to Hillsburg Hardware Limited		
		General Ledger Account Included in the Cycle	
Cycle	Transaction Types Included in the Cycle (See Figures 5-5A, B, C)	Balance Sheet	Income Statement
Sales and collection	Sales Cash receipts Journal entries	Cash in bank Trade accounts receivable Allowance for uncollectible accounts Other accounts receivable	Sales Sales returns and allowances Bad-debt expense
Acquisition and payment	Acquisitions Cash disbursements Journal entries	Cash in bank Inventories Prepaid expenses Land Buildings Computer and delivery equipment Furniture and fixtures Accumulated amortization Trade accounts payable Goods and services tax payable Accrued income tax Deferred tax Other accrued payables	Advertising[S] Amortization Auditing[A] and related services Computer maintenance and supplies Gain on sale of assets Income taxes Insurance[A] Legal fees and retainers[A] Miscellaneous general expense[A] Miscellaneous office expense[A] Miscellaneous sales expense[S] Office repairs and maintenance Postage[A] Rent[A] Sales and promotional literature[S] Sales meetings and training[S] Stationery and supplies[A] Taxes[A] Telephone and fax[A] Travel and entertainment—selling[S] Travel and entertainment—administrative[A]
Payroll and personnel	Payroll Journal entries	Cash in bank Accrued payroll Accrued payroll benefits	Salaries and commissions[S] Sales payroll benefits[S] Executive and office salaries[A] Administrative payroll benefits[A]
Inventory and warehousing	Acquisitions Sales Journal entries	Inventories	Cost of goods sold
Capital acquisition and repayment	Acquisitions Cash disbursements Journal entries	Cash in bank Notes payable Accrued interest Long-term notes payable Accrued interest Capital stock Retained earnings Dividends Dividends payable	Interest expense

S = Selling expense
A = General and administrative expense

All general ledger accounts and transaction types for Hillsburg Hardware Limited are included at least once. For a different company, the number and types of transactions and general ledger accounts would differ, but all would be included.

Some transaction types and general ledger accounts are included in more than one cycle. When that occurs, it means the transaction type is used to record transactions from more than one cycle and indicates a tie-in between the cycles. The most important general ledger account included in and affecting several cycles is the general cash account (cash in bank). General cash connects most cycles.

The capital acquisition and repayment cycle is closely related to the acquisition and payment cycle. The acquisition of goods and services includes the purchase of inventory, supplies, and general services in performing the main business operations. Transactions in the capital acquisitions cycle are related to financing the business, such as issuing stock or debt, paying dividends, and repaying debt. The same transaction type is used to record transactions for both cycles, and the transactions are similar. There are two reasons for treating capital acquisition and repayment separately from the acquisition of goods and services. First, the transactions are related to financing a company rather than to its operations. Second, most capital acquisition and repayment cycle accounts involve few transactions, but each is often highly material and therefore should be audited extensively. For both reasons, it is more convenient to separate the two cycles.

The inventory and warehousing cycle is closely related to all other cycles, especially for a manufacturing company. The cost of inventory includes raw materials (acquisition and payment cycle), direct labour (payroll and personnel cycle), and manufacturing overhead (acquisition and payment and payroll and personnel cycles). The sale of finished goods involves the sales and collection cycle. Because inventory is material for most manufacturing companies, it is common to borrow money using inventory as security. In those cases, the capital acquisition and repayment cycle is also related to inventory and warehousing.

RELATIONSHIPS AMONG CYCLES Figure 5-7 illustrates the relationship of the cycles to one another. In addition to the five cycles, general cash is also shown. Each cycle is studied in detail in later chapters.

Figure 5-7 shows that cycles have no beginning or end except at the origin and final disposition of a company. A company begins by obtaining capital, usually in the form of cash. In a manufacturing company, cash is used to acquire raw materials, capital assets, and related goods and services to produce inventory (acquisition and payment cycle). Cash is also used to acquire labour for the same reason (payroll and personnel cycle). Acquisition and payment and payroll and personnel are similar in

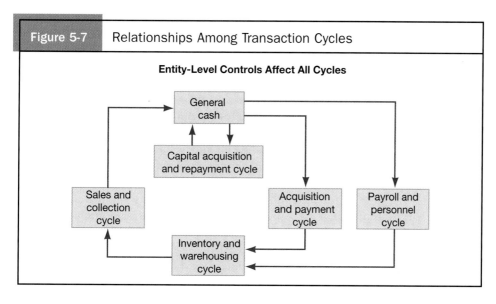

| Figure 5-7 | Relationships Among Transaction Cycles |

Entity-Level Controls Affect All Cycles

Sinks in Cycles

How do sinks relate to audit cycles? An audit senior was working at a client that manufactured a variety of sinks and bathtubs. During her observation of inventory, she found certain colours and brands tucked back in a corner, gathering dust and dirt.

She asked management to transfer inventory data into a spreadsheet so that she could further analyze the impact on the financial statements. It turned out that certain sinks were overvalued in the financial statements. Management made an adjustment and wrote down the value by several thousand dollars.

This meant that in future sales, less cash would be received (as the sinks were worth less). Less revenue and accounts receivable will be recorded in the sales and collection cycle.

The inventory value was written down, reducing the cost of inventory. Coordination with the purchasing department would mean that the company would no longer purchase the colours in question (deep greens and purples) and would purchase other colours instead.

This example shows that a single audit observation (and the resulting journal entry) is linked to several financial statement cycles.

Source: Discussion between an audit supervisor, summer 2008, and I. Splettstoesser-Hogeterp.

---

nature, but the functions are sufficiently different to justify separate cycles. The combined result of these two cycles is inventory (inventory and warehousing cycle). At a subsequent point, the inventory is sold and billings and collections result (sales and collection cycle). The cash generated is used to pay dividends and interest and to start the cycles again. The cycles interrelate in much the same way in a service company, where there will be no inventory, but there may be unbilled receivables.

RELATIONSHIPS AMONG TRANSACTION CYCLES Transaction cycles are of major importance in the conduct of the audit. For the most part, auditors treat each cycle separately during the audit. Although auditors should take care to interrelate different cycles at different times and be aware of the interrelationships among the cycles, they must treat the cycles somewhat independently in order to manage complex audits effectively.

Setting Audit Objectives

Auditors conduct audits consistent with the cycle approach by performing audit tests of the transactions making up ending balances and also by performing audit tests of the account balances themselves. Figure 5-8 illustrates this important concept by showing the four classes of transactions that determine the ending balance in accounts receivable. Assume that the beginning balance of $17,521 was audited in the prior year and is therefore considered reliable. If the auditor could be completely sure that each of the four classes of transactions was correctly stated, the auditor could also be sure that the ending balance of $20,197 was correctly stated. However, it may be impractical for the auditor to obtain complete assurance about the correctness of each class of transactions resulting in less than complete assurance about the ending balance in accounts receivable. In such a case, overall assurance can be increased by auditing the ending balance of accounts receivable. Auditors have found that, generally, the most efficient way to conduct audits is to obtain some combination of assurance for each class of transactions and for the ending balance in the related account.

For any given class of transactions, there are several audit objectives that must be met before the auditor can conclude that the transactions are properly recorded. They are called transaction-related audit objectives (or assertions) in the remainder of this book. For example, there are specific sales transaction-related audit objectives and specific sales returns and allowances transaction-related audit objectives.

Similarly, there are several audit objectives that must be met for each account balance. They are called balance-related audit objectives. For example, there are specific accounts receivable balance-related audit objectives and specific accounts payable

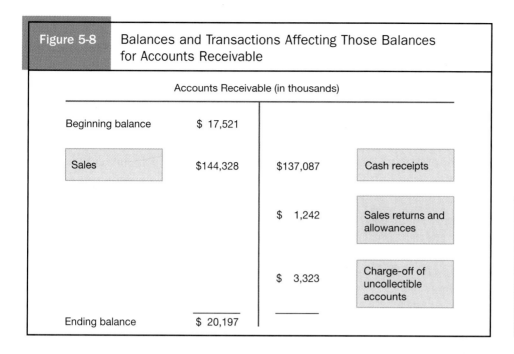

Figure 5-8 | Balances and Transactions Affecting Those Balances for Accounts Receivable

Accounts Receivable (in thousands)

Beginning balance	$ 17,521		
Sales	$144,328	$137,087	Cash receipts
		$ 1,242	Sales returns and allowances
		$ 3,323	Charge-off of uncollectible accounts
Ending balance	$ 20,197		

concept check

C5-9 How do general controls affect cycles?

C5-10 Why does the audit process use cycle?

C5-11 List two typical cycles.

balance-related audit objectives. It will be shown later that the transaction-related and balance-related audit objectives, called **specific audit objectives** or "assertions," are somewhat different but closely related. Throughout the remainder of this text, the term "audit objectives" refers to both transaction-related and balance-related audit objectives.

Before examining audit objectives in more detail, it is necessary to understand management assertions. These are studied next.

Specific audit objectives—transaction-related, balance-related, or presentation and disclosure audit objectives used to tailor the audit process to transactions, events, balances, or disclosures.

Management assertions—implied or expressed representations by management about classes of transactions; related accounts; or classification, presentation, or disclosures in the financial statements.

⑤ Management Assertions and Audit Objectives

Management Assertions

Management assertions are implied or expressed representations by management about (i) classes of transactions or events, (ii) related account balances in the financial statements, and (iii) the classification, presentation, or disclosure of information in the financial statements. As an illustration, the management of Hillsburg Hardware Limited asserts that cash of $827,568 (see Figure 5-6) was present in the company's bank accounts or on the premises as of the balance sheet date. Unless otherwise disclosed in the financial statements, management also asserts that the cash was unrestricted and available for normal use. Similar assertions exist for each asset, liability, equity, revenue, and expense item in the financial statements. These assertions apply to both classes of transactions and account balances.

Management assertions are directly related to generally accepted accounting principles. These assertions are part of the criteria that management uses to record and disclose accounting information in financial statements. Return to the definition of auditing in Chapter 1, on page 4. It states, in part, that auditing is a comparison of information (financial statements) to established criteria (assertions established according to generally accepted accounting principles). Auditors must therefore understand the assertions to do adequate audits.

Assertions about existence or occurrence Assertions about existence deal with whether assets, obligations, and equities included in the balance sheet actually existed on the balance sheet date. For example, management asserts that merchandise inventory included in the balance sheet exists and is available for sale at the balance

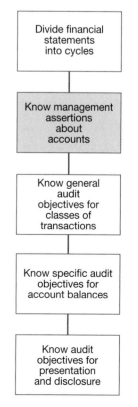

Divide financial statements into cycles

Know management assertions about accounts

Know general audit objectives for classes of transactions

Know specific audit objectives for account balances

Know audit objectives for presentation and disclosure

sheet date. Assertions about occurrence concern whether recorded transactions included in the financial statements actually occurred during the accounting period. Management asserts that sales in the income statement represent exchanges of goods or services that actually took place.

The auditor also needs to address "ownership" (for assets), also called "rights and obligations" (for assets and liabilities). These management assertions deal with whether assets are the rights of the entity and liabilities are the obligations of the entity at a given date. For example, management asserts that assets are owned by the company or amounts capitalized for leases in the balance sheet represent the cost of the entity's rights to leased property and that the corresponding lease liability represents an obligation of the entity.

Assertions about completeness These management assertions state that all transactions and accounts that should be presented in the financial statements are included. For example, management asserts that all sales of goods and services are recorded and included in the financial statements. Similarly, management asserts that notes payable in the balance sheet include all such liabilities of the entity.

The completeness assertion deals with matters opposite from those of the existence and occurrence assertions. The completeness assertion is concerned with the possibility of omitting items from the financial statements that should have been included, whereas the existence and occurrence assertions are concerned with inclusion of amounts that should not have been included.

Thus, recording a sale that did not take place would be a violation of the occurrence assertion, whereas the failure to record a sale that did occur would be a violation of the completeness assertion.

Assertions about measurement, including accuracy, classification, and valuation These assertions deal with whether the asset, liability, equity, revenue, and expense accounts have been included in the financial statements at appropriate amounts and in the proper period. For example, accurate "measurement" asserts that property is recorded at historical cost equal to the invoice amount. Similarly, management states that the correct quantities and prices were used to calculate ending inventory amounts ("mechanical accuracy"). "Valuation" refers to whether an asset or liability is asserted as being recorded at an appropriate carrying value. This involves the use of management judgment to determine whether the value is accurately recorded originally (normally at cost) and whether the current carrying value is appropriate. For capital assets, this includes determining the amount of amortization that should be recorded against the asset and whether the asset value has been impaired or not, thus requiring a writedown. Inventory should be examined for potential obsolescence, and accounts receivable should be assessed for collectability. Management asserts that its estimates and conclusions on valuation are those that should be used for the financial statements.

Classification deals with whether components of the financial statements are properly combined or separated, described, and disclosed. For example, management asserts that obligations classified as long-term liabilities on the balance sheet will not mature within one year. Similarly, management asserts that amounts presented as extraordinary items in the income statement are recorded in the correct accounts.

Assertions about allocation Also known as cut-off, allocation addresses whether transactions are recorded in the correct accounting period. For example, sales should be recorded in the correct period. When shipments of goods are made toward the last day of the fiscal year, management asserts that the shipments are recorded in the correct period, and inventory relieved in the same financial period.

Assertions about financial statement presentation and disclosure The previous assertions are expected to apply to the way that the financial statements and the notes thereto are shown. For example, only transactions that belong to the company should be included (occurrence, rights and obligations), and all relevant information should

Internal auditors also use assertions when they are conducting their audits. An important assertion for accounts payable is existence—you do not want to pay the same invoice twice! Another is accuracy—an invoice for $100 should not be paid as $1,000.

Continuous audits are audits that are taking place (as the name implies) on an ongoing basis, testing transactions as they take place. This is done by embedding audit programs into the processing cycle and having unusual transactions transferred into an audit file, or by having regular reports of unusual transactions sent to the auditors.

In the year ended 2005, internal auditors at the RCMP used continuous auditing techniques to identify accounts payable transactions that should be matched to supporting documentation and ran other types of analyses as well.

The RCMP paid for the audit by discovering over $100,000 worth of duplicate payments that were subsequently recovered.

Pat Ferrell and Seth Davis (2008) described continuous audit techniques that they used when testing for the validity of payments. They searched for matches between employee telephone numbers and supplier telephone numbers, for matches between addresses, and for suppliers within the same postal code as employees.

Sources: 1. Coderre, D., "A continuous view of accounts," *Internal Auditor Journal*, April 2006, p. 25-28. 2. Ferrell, P. and Davis, S., "How an internal audit department maximized its technology," *FRAUD Magazine*, March/April 2008, p. 25-27, 46. 3. ISACA Standards Board, "Continuous auditing: is it fantasy or reality?", *Information Systems Control Journal*, 5, 2003, p. 43-46.

be included (completeness). The disclosures should be correctly classified (in the appropriate accounts) in an understandable way, using language that is clear and portrays the intention of transactions and events. The information should be accurate and valued appropriately (for example, at the lower of cost and net realizable value for inventory).

Transaction-Related Audit Objectives

The auditor's **transaction-related audit objectives** follow and are closely related to management assertions. This is not surprising, since the auditor's primary responsibility is to determine whether management assertions about financial statements are justified. Each general transaction-related audit objective is expressed specifically for transactions or events (such as sales or the shipment of goods). Transaction-related audit objectives are the six audit objectives that must be met before the auditor can conclude that the amounts for any given class of transactions are fairly stated. The general transaction-related audit objectives are: occurrence, completeness, accuracy, classification, timing, and posting and summarization.

These transaction-related audit objectives are intended to provide a framework to help the auditor accumulate sufficient, high-quality audit evidence required by auditing standards and to decide the proper evidence to accumulate for classes of transactions given the circumstances of the engagement. The objectives remain the same from audit to audit, but the evidence varies depending on the circumstances.

A distinction must be made between general transaction-related audit objectives and specific transaction-related audit objectives for each class of transactions. The general transaction-related audit objectives discussed here are applicable to every class of transactions but are stated in broad terms. Specific transaction-related audit objectives are also applied to each class of transactions but are stated in terms tailored to a class of transactions, such as sales transactions. Once you know the general transaction-related audit objectives, they can be used to develop specific transaction-related audit objectives for each class of transactions being audited. Table 5-3 on the next page lists the transaction-related audit objectives (with specific examples) beside the management assertions, as well as providing examples of audit objectives about account balances, and **presentation and disclosure audit objectives**.

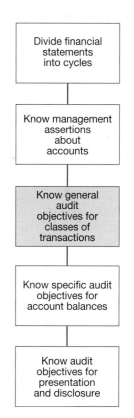

Transaction-related audit objectives—six audit objectives that must be met before the auditor can conclude that the total for any given class of transactions is fairly stated. The general transaction-related audit objectives are occurrence, completeness, accuracy, classification, timing, and posting and summarization.

✕	Audit Objectives about **transactions** or events	Audit Objectives about **transactions** or events	Audit Objectives about **account balances** at the end of the period	Audit Objectives about **account balances** at the end of the period	Audit Objectives about **presentation and disclosure**	Audit Objectives about **presentation and disclosure**
Management Assertion	*General Audit Objective*	*Specific Audit Objective: Sales*	*General Audit Objective*	*Specific Audit Objective: Inventory*	*General Audit Objective*	*Specific Audit Objective: Accounts Payable*
Existence or Occurrence	Occurrence	Recorded sales are for shipments made to non-fictitious customers	Existence	All recorded inventories exist at the balance sheet date (i.e., are real)	Occurrence	Accounts payable balances are for transactions that actually occurred and pertain to the entity
Existence or Occurrence			Rights and obligations (ownership)	Inventories belong to the company (i.e., are not being held on consignment)	Rights and obligations (ownership)	Accounts payable belong to the company (and do not pertain to costs of others, such as management)
Completeness	Completeness	All existing sales transactions are recorded	Completeness	All existing inventory has been counted and included in inventory	Completeness	Disclosures about accounts payables are fully included (e.g., related-party transactions identified)
Measurement	Accuracy	Recorded sales are for the amount of goods shipped and are correctly billed and recorded	Accuracy	Inventory quantities agree with items physically on hand. Prices used to extend inventory cost are materially correct. Extensions of price times quantity are correct, and details are correctly added	Accuracy	The accounts payable balance shown on the financial statements is materially correct
Measurement			Valuation	Inventories have been written down where net realizable value is less than book value	Valuation	N/A
Measurement	Classification	Sales transactions are recorded in the correct account	Classification	Inventory items are recorded in the correct account (e.g., as raw materials, work in progress, or finished goods)	Classification	Accounts payable is correctly grouped as current versus long-term
Measurement	Posting and summarization	Sales transactions are updated correctly to the customer master file, and the posting to the general ledger summed these trans-actions correctly	Detail tie-in	Total of inventory items agrees with the general ledger	Understandability	Financial and non-financial information is clearly shown, indicating the nature of the accounts payable and associated risks (e.g., foreign exchange exposure)
Allocation	Timing	Sales are recorded on the correct dates	Cut-off	Purchases at year end are recorded in the correct period. Sales at year end are recorded in the correct period		

Effective November 18, 2008

General Transaction-Related Audit Objectives

Occurrence—recorded transactions occurred Inclusion of a sale in the sales journal when no sale occurred violates the occurrence objective, as the sale is then fictitious. This objective is the auditor's counterpart to the management assertion of occurrence.

Completeness—existing transactions are recorded This objective deals with whether all transactions that should be included in the journals have actually been included. Failure to record a sale when a sale occurred violates the completeness objective. The objective is the counterpart to the management assertion of completeness.

The occurrence and completeness objectives emphasize opposite audit concerns: occurrence deals with potential overstatement and completeness with unrecorded transactions (understatement).

Accuracy—recorded transactions are stated at the correct amounts For sales transactions, there would be a violation of the accuracy objective if the quantity of goods shipped was different from the quantity billed, the wrong selling price was used for billing, extension or adding errors (perhaps due to program errors) occurred in billing, or the wrong amount was updated to the master file. Accuracy is one part of the measurement assertion, with classification, posting, and summarization also considered part of measurement.

Classification—transactions included in the client's records are properly classified Examples of misclassifications of sales are including cash sales as credit sales, recording a sale of operating capital assets as revenue, and misclassifying commercial sales as residential sales.

Posting and summarization—recorded transactions are updated to the master files and are correctly summarized This objective deals with the accuracy of the transfer of information from recorded transactions to subsidiary records (or master files) and summarization to the general ledger. For example, if a sales transaction is recorded in the wrong customer's record and to the wrong customer in the master file, it is a violation of this objective.

Since the posting of transactions to subsidiary records, the general ledger, and other related master files is typically accomplished automatically by computerized accounting systems, the risk of random human error in posting is minimal. Once the auditor has established that the automated information systems are functioning properly, there is a reduced concern about posting and summarization errors.

Timing—transactions are recorded on the correct dates A timing error (the management assertion of allocation) occurs if transactions are not recorded on the dates the transactions took place. A sales transaction, for example, should be recorded on the date of shipment.

SPECIFIC TRANSACTION-RELATED AUDIT OBJECTIVES The general transaction-related audit objectives must be applied to each material type (or class) of transaction in the audit. Such transactions typically include sales, cash receipts, acquisitions of goods and services, payroll, and others. Table 5-3 on page 136 lists the six transaction-related audit objectives. It includes the general form of the objectives, the application of the objectives to sales transactions, and the management assertions.

Balance-Related Audit Objectives

Balance-related audit objectives are eight audit objectives that must be met before the auditor can conclude that any given account balance is fairly stated. The general balance-related audit objectives are existence, completeness, valuation, accuracy, classification, cut-off, detail tie-in, and rights and obligations.

Balance-related audit objectives are similar to the transaction-related audit objectives just discussed. They also follow from management assertions, and they provide a framework to help the auditor accumulate sufficient appropriate evidence. General

Presentation and disclosure audit objectives—there are seven general audit objectives used to examine the financial statements. These are occurrence, rights and obligations (ownership), completeness, accuracy, valuation, classification, and understandability.

Balance-related audit objectives—eight audit objectives that must be met before the auditor can conclude that any given account balance is fairly stated. The general balance-related audit objectives are existence, completeness, valuation, accuracy, classification, cut-off, detail tie-in, rights and obligations, and presentation and disclosure.

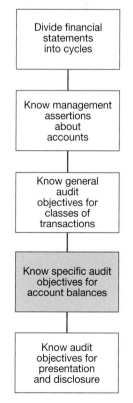

balance-related audit objectives are applied to specific account balances, resulting in specific balance-related audit objectives.

There are two differences between balance-related and transaction-related audit objectives. First, as the terms imply, balance-related audit objectives are applied to account balances, whereas transaction-related audit objectives are applied to classes of transactions such as sales transactions and cash disbursements transactions. Second, there are more audit objectives for account balances than for classes of transactions. There are eight balance-related audit objectives compared to six transaction-related audit objectives. These are also shown in Table 5-3 (see page 136), as are the counterpart management assertions.

Because of the way audits are done, balance-related audit objectives are almost always applied to the ending balance in balance sheet accounts, such as accounts receivable, inventory, and notes payable. Balance-related objectives are also applied to certain income statement accounts. These usually involve non-routine transactions and unpredictable expenses, such as legal expense or repairs and maintenance. Other income statement accounts are closely related to balance sheet accounts and are tested simultaneously (e.g., amortization expense with accumulated amortization, interest expense with notes payable).

When using the balance-related audit objectives as a framework for auditing balance sheet account balances, the auditor accumulates evidence to verify detail that supports the account balance, rather than verifying the account balance itself. For example, in auditing accounts receivable, the auditor obtains a listing of the aged accounts receivable balances from the client that agrees with the general ledger balance (see page 507 for an illustration). The accounts receivable balance-related audit objectives are applied to the customer accounts in that listing.

GENERAL BALANCE-RELATED AUDIT OBJECTIVES

Existence—amounts included exist Inclusion of an account receivable from a customer in the accounts receivable trial balance when there is no receivable from that customer violates the existence objective. Similarly, if the same inventory is accidentally counted twice and thus inventory is inflated, the existence objective has been violated. This objective is the auditor's counterpart to the management assertion of existence or occurrence.

Rights and obligations In addition to existing, most assets must be owned before they can be included in the financial statements. Similarly, liabilities must belong to the entity. Rights are always associated with assets and obligations with liabilities.

Completeness—existing amounts are included Failure to include an account receivable from a customer when the receivable exists violates the completeness objective. Forgetting to count and include certain types of inventory does the same.

The existence and completeness objectives emphasize opposite audit concerns: existence deals with potential overstatement and completeness deals with unrecorded transactions and amounts (understatement).

Accuracy—amounts included are correct An inventory item on a client's inventory listing could be incorrect mathematically (inaccurate) if the number of units of inventory on hand was misstated, the unit price was incorrect, or the total was incorrectly extended due to a programming error. Each of these violates the accuracy objective. Accuracy is one part of the measurement assertion, as are valuation, classification, and detail tie-in.

Valuation (realizable value)—assets are included at the amounts estimated to be realized This objective concerns whether an account balance has been reduced for declines from historical cost to net realizable value. Examples of when this objective applies are considering the adequacy of the allowance for uncollectible accounts receivable and writedowns of inventory for obsolescence. The objective applies only to asset accounts and is part of the valuation assertion.

Classification—amounts included in the client's listing are properly classified Classification involves determining whether items on a client's listing are included in the correct accounts. For example, on the accounts receivable listing, receivables must be separated into short-term and long-term, and amounts due from affiliates, officers, and directors must be classified separately from amounts due from customers. Inventory should be correctly classified by type.

Detail tie-in—transaction details sum to the master files amounts, and subsidiary records (manual or automated) agree with the total in the account balance in the general ledger Account balances on financial statements are supported by details in data files and schedules prepared by clients. The detail tie-in objective is that the details are accurately prepared, correctly added, and agree with the general ledger. For example, individual accounts receivable on a listing of accounts receivable should agree with the customer master file, and the total should equal the general ledger control account.

Cut-off—transactions near the balance sheet date are recorded in the proper period The transactions that are most likely to be misstated are those recorded near the end of the accounting period. It is proper to think of cut-off tests as a part of verifying either the balance sheet accounts or the related transactions but, for convenience, auditors usually perform them as a part of auditing balance sheet accounts.

SPECIFIC BALANCE-RELATED AUDIT OBJECTIVES After the general balance-related audit objectives are understood, specific balance-related audit objectives for each account balance on the financial statements can be developed. There should be at least one specific balance-related audit objective for each general balance-related audit objective unless the auditor believes that the general balance-related audit objective is not relevant or is unimportant in the circumstances. There may be more than one specific balance-related audit objective for a general balance-related audit objective. For example, specific balance-related audit objectives for rights and obligations of the inventory of Hillsburg Hardware Limited could include that (1) the company has title to all inventory items listed, and (2) inventories are not pledged as collateral unless it is disclosed.

Presentation and Disclosure-Related Audit Objectives

In response to the increased demands for clear disclosure in financial statements, audit standards have expanded the level of detail of the examination of the presentation and disclosure of information in the financial statements and accompanying notes. Table 5-3 (on page 136) shows the seven general audit objectives about presentation and disclosure. These are occurrence, rights and obligations (ownership), completeness, accuracy, valuation, classification, and understandability.

Financial statements are summary documents used to communicate information directly to users. For example, an organization may have several cash accounts that show up only as one line on the financial statements. Financial statement audit objectives are different from the transaction or account balance audit objectives, as they are associated with the quality of the information provided in the financial statements. If a complex investment is described in a confusing manner, the reader cannot understand what the business is doing. The underlying purpose of these audit objectives is to assess whether financial information portrays (through the transactions, accounts, and narratives) the actions of the organization in a way that reflects the underlying economic reality of what actually occurred. For example, in the notes in the Hillsburg Hardware Limited financial statements on pages 147–162, there is a clear description of accounting policies used by the business. Table 5-3 (on page 136) relates general and specific audit objectives to management assertions.

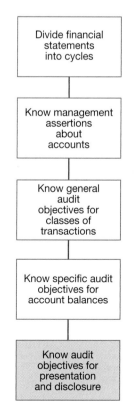

Divide financial statements into cycles

Know management assertions about accounts

Know general audit objectives for classes of transactions

Know specific audit objectives for account balances

Know audit objectives for presentation and disclosure

General Presentation and Disclosure-Related Audit Objectives

Occurrence—disclosed information has occurred Transactions or events that were fictitious or had not been finalized (such as a contract that had not been fully negotiated or signed), and sales made to a non-existent company would be violations of the occurrence objective.

Rights and obligations (ownership)—assets belong to the entity and obligations are owed on behalf of the entity Expenses that were incurred by executives, showing as a liability on behalf of a corporation, would be a violation of the obligations objective. Showing fictitious accounts receivable would mean that the company did not have the rights to collect those funds.

Completeness—relevant disclosures should be included Material future commitments for expenditures such as leases and long-term debt should be included, as should commitments for major purchase or supply contracts, where prices are fixed and bind the organization. The description should be thorough, identifying the different types of information as to both the amounts and other details, such as timing.

Accuracy—information should be mechanically accurate Compilation of information from the underlying general ledger accounts and supporting documents should be mechanically accurate and described correctly. For example, when describing a loan commitment, the amount of the loan should agree to the liability account and the interest rates should agree to interest rates in loan agreements or in the confirmation obtained from the lender.

Valuation—information should be disclosed fairly Generally accepted accounting principles should be described and applied to value assets with the appropriate method and to disclose the nature of complex instruments, such as investments or liabilities in foreign currencies or using sophisticated methods. The credit constraints that started in 2008 with respect to asset-backed paper provide an example of financial instruments that were not supported by underlying assets and are difficult to describe.

Classification—information is appropriately described in the correct accounts Assuming that transactions, events, and balances are in the correct accounts (e.g., current versus long-term debt, and raw materials versus finished goods inventory), the financial statements should appropriately describe those accounts.

Understandability—account balances and related disclosure requirements are clearly presented in the financial statements The auditor will need to assess the financial statements and notes from the perspective of a reasonably informed business user to determine whether the information is presented in a clear way, portraying the events and actions of the organization. For example, industry-specific methods would be shown, as described in the Hillsburg Hardware Limited financial statements (note 2), where vendor allowances and rebates are included in other receivables (see pages 147–162). These types of explanations help the reader to understand the nature of the business transactions included in the accounts.

SPECIFIC PRESENTATION AND DISCLOSURE-RELATED AUDIT OBJECTIVES By looking at each amount or note in the financial statements, the auditor can develop specific presentation and disclosure-related audit objectives. These would be linked to the type of account and the nature of the communication issue. For example, assets might have valuation, classification and understandability as specific audit objectives. Table 5-3 on page 136 provides examples for accounts payable.

RELATIONSHIPS AMONG MANAGEMENT ASSERTIONS AND GENERAL AUDIT OBJECTIVES The reason there are more general audit objectives than management assertions is to provide additional guidance to auditors in deciding what evidence to accumulate.

Table 5-3 illustrates this by showing the relationships among management assertions, the general audit objectives, and specific audit objectives as applied to sales transactions, inventory balances and accounts payable disclosures for a company such as Hillsburg Hardware Limited.

How Audit Objectives Are Met

The auditor must obtain sufficient appropriate audit evidence to support all management assertions in the financial statements. As stated earlier, this is done by accumulating evidence in support of some appropriate combination of transaction-related, balance-related, presentation, and disclosure audit objectives. Table 5-3 (page 136) shows examples of these audit objectives.

The auditor plans the appropriate combination of audit objectives and the evidence that must be accumulated to meet them by following the structured eight-phase audit process shown in Figure 5-3. The risk assessment phases help the auditor identify those assertions where there is the greatest likelihood of misstatement. Then, the risk response phases are used to design further audit procedures which are completed to assess evidence using the assertions. The use of assertions to help organize evidence enables the completion of a high-quality audit with the appropriate audit report.

concept check

C5-12 What are management assertions about financial information?

C5-13 How does the auditor use management assertions during the financial statement audit?

C5-14 What are the three different types of audit objectives? Provide an example of each, for the completeness audit objective.

Summary

1. *What is the objective of conducting an audit of financial statements?* The auditor expresses an opinion about the fairness of presentation of the financial statements.

   Explain the difference between management and auditor responsibilities with respect to the financial statements and the discovery and correction of material misstatements or illegal acts. Management is responsible for designing internal controls to prevent and detect errors, fraud, and illegal acts. These controls should be concerned with errors of all sizes, not just material errors. Auditors are concerned with material misstatements as they consider the financial statements in the context of users. Auditors express an opinion on the financial statements that have been prepared by management.

2. *Describe the preplanning steps that the auditor completes prior to accepting the financial statement audit.* The auditor goes through a client acceptance or continuance decision process, identifies the client's reasons for an audit, and conducts an independence threat analysis.

   Why is an engagement letter important? The engagement letter clarifies the responsibilities of both the auditor and the client and is used to minimize misunderstandings.

3. *List the eight phases of a financial statement audit, and provide an overview of the audit process.* The eight phases are divided into three groups. First there are three risk assessment phases: pre-planning (phase 1); client risk profile (2); and planning the audit (3). This is followed by four risk response phases: designing further audit procedures (4); tests of control (5); substantive tests (6); and ongoing evaluation, quality control, and final evidence gathering (7). The final phase is complete quality control

and issue of the auditor's report (8). These phases allow the auditor to collect sufficient appropriate audit evidence to state an opinion on the financial statements.

4. *Show how financial statements are divided into cycles.* The smaller segments or components are: cash; capital acquisition and repayment; acquisition and payment; payroll and personnel; inventory and warehousing; and sales and collection.

   How is this cycle approach related to the financial statement audit? One aspect of evidence gathering is the auditor testing classes of transactions that are part of the transaction cycles.

   What is the relationship among the cycles? The cycles show that transactions are related to each other, since the cycles interrelate. For example, cash has a role in each of the cycles—payment of sales, purchase of materials, and acquisition of debt.

   What is the relationship between the cycle approach and entity-level controls? Entity-level controls affect all cycles, as the corporate governance structure includes policies and procedures for all transactions.

5. *Describe management assertions about financial information.* Management assertions are implied or expressed representations about classes of transactions and accounts in the financial statements.

   Relate management assertions to general transaction-related audit objectives and general balance-related audit objectives. Transaction-related and balance-related audit objectives follow from and are closely related to management assertions and provide a framework to help the auditor collect audit evidence.

Review Questions

5-1 State the objective of the audit of financial statements. In general terms, how do auditors meet that objective?

5-2 Distinguish between management's and the auditor's responsibilities for the financial statements being audited.

5-3 Distinguish between the terms "errors" and "fraud and other irregularities." What is the auditor's responsibility for finding each?

5-4 Distinguish between management fraud and employee fraud. Discuss the likely difference between these two types of fraud on the fair presentation of financial statements.

5-5 Define the term "illegal act." What is the auditor's responsibility with respect to illegal acts by clients?

5-6 What factors should an auditor consider prior to accepting an engagement?

5-7 What is the purpose of an engagement letter? Explain how it is important to both the auditor and management.

5-8 Identify the eight phases of the audit. Provide an example of an activity completed in each phase.

5-9 Describe what is meant by the cycle approach to auditing. What are the advantages of dividing the audit into different cycles?

5-10 Why are sales, sales returns and allowances, bad debts, cash discounts, accounts receivable, and allowance for uncollectible accounts all included in the same cycle?

5-11 How are entity-level controls related to cycles?

5-12 Distinguish between general audit objectives and management assertions. Why are the general audit objectives more useful to auditors?

5-13 Explain the differences among transaction-related, balance-related, and presentation and disclosure-related audit objectives.

5-14 An acquisition of equipment repairs by a construction company is recorded in the incorrect accounting period. Which transaction-related audit objective has been violated? Which transaction-related objective has been violated if the acquisition has been capitalized as a capital asset rather than expensed?

5-15 A banker found a set of financial statements difficult to read, and the disclosures seemed to be incomplete. Which presentation and disclosure-related objectives have been violated? Why?

5-16 Distinguish between the existence and completeness balance-related audit objectives. State the effect on the financial statements (overstatement or understatement) of a violation of each in the audit of accounts payable.

5-17 Identify the management assertion and general balance-related audit objective for this specific balance-related audit objective: All recorded capital assets exist at the balance sheet date.

Discussion Questions and Problems

5-18 Frequently, questions have been raised regarding the responsibility of the independent auditor for the discovery of fraud (including defalcations and other similar irregularities), and concerning the proper course of conduct of the independent auditor when his or her examination discloses specific circumstances that arouse suspicion about the existence of fraud.

REQUIRED

a. What are (1) the function and (2) the responsibilities of the independent auditor in the examination of financial statements? Discuss fully, but do not include fraud in this discussion.

b. What are the responsibilities of the independent auditor for the detection of fraud and other irregularities? Discuss fully.

c. What is the independent auditor's proper course of conduct when his or her examination discloses specific circumstances that arouse his or her suspicion as to the existence of fraud and other irregularities?

(Adapted from AICPA)

5-19 The classes of transactions and the titles of the journals used for Phillips Equipment Rental Co. Ltd. are shown in the chart on the next page.

REQUIRED

a. Identify one financial statement balance that is likely to be affected by each of the nine classes of transactions.

Classes of Transactions	Titles of Journals
Purchase returns	Cash receipts register
Rental revenue	Cash disbursements journal
Charge-off of uncollectible accounts	Acquisitions journal
Acquisitions of goods and services (except payroll)	Revenue history
Collection of goods and services tax	Payroll journal
Adjusting entries (for payroll)	Adjustments history
Payroll service and payments	
Cash disbursements (except payroll)	
Cash receipts	

b. For each class of transactions, identify the journal that is likely to be used to record the transactions.

c. Identify the transaction cycle that is likely to be affected by each of the nine classes of transactions.

d. Explain how total rental revenue, as cited on the financial statements of Phillips Equipment Rental Co. Ltd., is accumulated in journals and summarized on the financial statements. Assume there are several adjusting entries for rental revenue at the balance sheet date.

5-20 It is well accepted that throughout the conduct of the ordinary audit, it is essential to obtain large amounts of information from management and to rely heavily on management's judgments. After all, the financial statements are management's representations, and the primary responsibility for their fair presentation rests with management, not the auditor. For example, it is extremely difficult, if not impossible, for the auditor to evaluate the obsolescence of inventory as well as management can in a highly complex business.

Similarly, the collectability of accounts receivable and the continued usefulness of machinery and equipment are heavily dependent on management's willingness to provide truthful responses to questions.

REQUIRED

Reconcile the auditor's responsibility for discovering material misrepresentations by management with these comments.

5-21 The following general ledger accounts are included in the trial balance for an audit client, Jones Wholesale Stationery Store.

Income tax expense
Income tax payable
Accounts receivable
Advertising expense
Travel expense
Bonds payable
Common stock
Unexpired insurance
Furniture and equipment

Allowance for doubtful accounts
Inventory
Property tax expense
Interest expense
Amortization expense— furniture and equipment
Retained earnings

Cash
Notes receivable trade
Purchases
Sales salaries expense
Accumulated amortization of furniture and equipment
Notes payable
Property tax payable

Sales
Salaries, office and general
Telephone and fax expense
Bad-debt expense
Interest receivable
Insurance expense
Interest income
Accrued sales salaries
Rent expense
Prepaid interest expense

REQUIRED

a. Identify the accounts in the trial balance that are likely to be included in each transaction cycle. Some accounts will be included in more than one cycle. Use the format that follows:

b. How would the general ledger accounts in the trial balance most likely differ if the company were a retail store rather than a wholesale company? How would they differ for a hospital or a government unit?

Cycle	Balance Sheet Accounts	Income Statement Accounts
Sales and collection		
Acquisition and payment		
Payroll and personnel		
Inventory and warehousing		
Capital acquisition and repayment		

5-22 The following are specific balance-related audit objectives applied to the audit of accounts receivable (a through g) and management assertions (1 through 4). The list referred to in the specific balance-related audit objectives is the list of the accounts receivable from each customer at the balance sheet date.

SPECIFIC BALANCE-RELATED AUDIT OBJECTIVES

a. There are no unrecorded receivables.
b. Receivables have not been sold or discounted.
c. Uncollectible accounts have been provided for.
d. Receivables that have become uncollectible have been written off.
e. All accounts on the list are expected to be collected within one year. *Current vs long term — classification*

f. All accounts on the list arose from the normal course of business and are not due from related parties.
g. Sales cut-off at year end is proper.

MANAGEMENT ASSERTIONS

1. Existence or occurrence
2. Completeness
3. Measurement
4. Allocation

REQUIRED

For each specific balance-related audit objective, identify the appropriate management assertion.

5-23 The following are specific transaction-related audit objectives applied to the audit of cash disbursements (a through f), management assertions (1 through 4), and general transaction-related audit objectives (5 through 10).

SPECIFIC TRANSACTION-RELATED AUDIT OBJECTIVES

a. Recorded cash disbursement transactions are for the amount of goods or services received and are correctly recorded.
b. Cash disbursement transactions are properly included in the accounts payable master file and are correctly summarized.
c. Recorded cash disbursements are for goods and services actually received.
d. Cash disbursement transactions are properly classified.
e. Existing cash disbursement transactions are recorded.
f. Cash disbursement transactions are recorded on the correct dates.

MANAGEMENT ASSERTIONS

1. Existence or occurrence
2. Completeness

3. Measurement
4. Allocation

GENERAL TRANSACTION-RELATED AUDIT OBJECTIVES

5. Occurrence
6. Completeness
7. Accuracy
8. Classification
9. Posting and summarization
10. Timing

REQUIRED

a. Explain the differences among management assertions, general transaction-related audit objectives, and specific transaction-related audit objectives and their relationships to one another.
b. For each specific transaction-related audit objective, identify the appropriate management assertion.
c. For each specific transaction-related audit objective, identify the appropriate general transaction-related audit objective.

AR existence is more risky

5-24 The following are two specific balance-related audit objectives in the audit of accounts payable.

1. All accounts payable included on the list represent amounts due to valid vendors.
2. There are no unrecorded accounts payable.

The list referred to in the objectives is the aged accounts payable trial balance produced using the supplier master file.

The total of the list equals the accounts payable balance on the general ledger.

AP - existence is not risky completeness is risky

REQUIRED

a. Explain the difference between these two specific balance-related audit objectives.
b. For the audit of accounts payable, which of these two specific balance-related audit objectives would usually be more important? Explain.

5-25 The following are eight general balance-related audit objectives for the audit of any balance sheet account (1 through 8) and 10 specific balance-related audit objectives for the audit of property, plant, and equipment (a through j).

GENERAL BALANCE-RELATED AUDIT OBJECTIVES

1. Existence
2. Rights and obligations

3. Completeness
4. Accuracy
5. Valuation
6. Classification
7. Detail tie-in
8. Cut-off

SPECIFIC BALANCE-RELATED AUDIT OBJECTIVES

a. There are no unrecorded capital assets in use.
b. The company has valid title to the assets owned.
c. Details of property, plant, and equipment agree with the general ledger.
d. Capital assets physically exist and are being used for the purpose intended.
e. Property, plant, and equipment are recorded at the correct amount.
f. The company has a contractual right to use of assets leased.
g. Cash disbursements and/or accrual cutoff for property, plant, and equipment items are proper.
h. Expense accounts do not contain amounts that should have been capitalized.
i. Amortization is determined in accordance with an acceptable method and is materially correct as computed.
j. Capital asset accounts have been properly adjusted for declines in historical cost.

REQUIRED

a. What are the purposes of the general balance-related audit objectives and the specific balance-related audit objectives? Explain the relationship between these two sets of objectives.
b. For each general balance-related objective, identify one or more specific balance-related audit objectives.

5-26 The following are seven general presentation and disclosure-related audit objectives (1 through 7) and 10 specific-balance related audit objectives for the audit of payroll and human resource expenses (a through j).

GENERAL PRESENTATION AND DISCLOSURE-RELATED AUDIT OBJECTIVES

1. Occurrence
2. Rights and obligations (ownership)
3. Completeness
4. Accuracy
5. Valuation
6. Classification
7. Understandability

SPECIFIC PRESENTATION AND DISCLOSURE-RELATED AUDIT OBJECTIVES

a. Travel expenses were paid to employees who travelled for the purposes of authorized work activities.
b. Payroll payments were made to employees who existed and worked for the company.
c. Payroll expenses shown on the financial statements are materially correct.
d. All amounts paid to employees who are related parties are disclosed in the financial statements.
e. Stock options paid to employees are clearly described.
f. Payroll expenses are correctly shown by type (e.g., operations, administration, sales).
g. "Golden parachute" agreements and any other costly agreements with management are described clearly in the financial statements.
h. Accrued liabilities for benefits such as employment insurance are included in the accounts.
i. Only valid benefits are paid to employees (i.e., unauthorized benefits are not paid).
j. Payroll expenses are clearly described by type.

REQUIRED

For each general presentation and disclosure-related audit objective, identify one or more specific presentation and disclosure-related audit objectives.

Professional Judgment Problem

5-27 Jane was the audit supervisor in charge of the audit of an advertising agency. Unfortunately, two other audit supervisors in the office resigned and moved on to other positions. Rather than hiring or promoting another supervisor, the firm reallocated clients. Jane was asked to take on some of the other audit clients and spend less time reviewing files and supervising staff. The audit managers and partners were expected to do a more thorough audit review to help compensate for the fewer than usual number of supervisors.

Jane felt harried, and her audit staff at the advertising agency were upset that she had not been present there for several days. There were numerous outstanding questions, and one day the staff left early because they could not go on to some technical issues. The tax provision looked complex, and Jane decided to leave the tax section for the tax area to review.

To Jane's horror, she discovered six months later that the tax provision had been incorrect by over $100,000. The client was upset that the financial statements were materially in error, decided to seek other auditors.

REQUIRED

Using your knowledge of audit standards and the audit process, explain which audit phases were poorly executed in the audit of the advertising agency. Provide suggestions for improvement to help prevent this type of error in the future.

Case

5-28 Rene Ritter opened a small grocery and related products convenience store in 1985 with the money she had saved working as a Loblaws store manager. She named it Ritter Dairy and Fruits. Because of the excellent location and her fine management skills, Ritter Dairy and Fruits grew to three locations by 1990. By that time, she needed additional capital. She obtained financing through a local bank at 2 percent above prime, under the condition that she submit quarterly financial statements reviewed by a public accounting firm approved by the bank. After interviewing several firms, she decided to use the firm of Gonzalez & Fineberg, CGAs, after obtaining approval from the bank.

By 1994, the company had grown to six stores, and Rene developed a business plan to add another 10 stores in the next several years. Ritter's capital needs had also grown, so Rene decided to add two business partners who both had considerable capital and some expertise in convenience stores. After further discussions with the bank and continued conversations with the future business partners, she decided to have an annual audit and quarterly reviews done by Gonzalez & Fineberg, even though the additional cost was almost $15,000 annually. The bank agreed to reduce the interest rate on the $4,000,000 loan to 1 percent above prime.

By 1999, things were going smoothly, with the two business partners heavily involved in the day-to-day operations and the company adding two new stores per year. The company was growing steadily and was more profitable than they had expected. By the end of 2000, one of the business partners, Fred Warnest, had taken over responsibility for accounting and finance operations, as well as some marketing. Annually, Gonzalez & Fineberg did an in-depth review of the accounting system, including internal controls, and reported their conclusions and recommendations to the board of directors. Specialists in the firm provided tax and other advice. The other business partner in the dairy, Ben Gold, managed most of the stores and was primarily responsible for building new stores. Rene was president and managed four stores.

In 2004, the three business partners (now the executive management of the company) decided to go public to enable them to add more stores and modernize the existing ones. The public offering was a major success, resulting in $25 million in new capital and nearly 1,000 shareholders. Ritter Dairy and Fruits added stores rapidly, and the company remained highly profitable under the leadership of Ritter, Warnest, and Gold.

Rene retired in 2008 after a highly successful career. During the retirement celebration, she thanked her business partners, employees, and customers. She also added a special thanks to the bank management for their outstanding service and to Gonzalez & Fineberg for being partners in the best and most professional sense of the word. She mentioned their integrity, commitment, high-quality service in performing their audits and reviews, and considerable tax and business advice for more than two decades.

REQUIRED
a. Explain why the bank imposed a requirement of a quarterly review of the financial statements as a condition of obtaining the loan at 2 percent above prime. Also, explain why the bank did not require an audit and why the bank demanded the right to approve which public accounting firm was engaged.
b. Explain why Ritter Dairy and Fruits agreed to have an audit performed rather than a review, considering the additional cost of $15,000.
c. What did Rene mean when she referred to Gonzalez & Fineberg as "partners"? Does the CGA firm have an independence problem?
d. What benefit does Gonzalez & Fineberg provide to shareholders, creditors, and management in performing the audit and related services?
e. What are the responsibilities of the CGA firm to shareholders, creditors, management, and others?

Ongoing Small Business Case: Transaction Flows at CondoCleaners.com

5-29 Jim is doing preliminary planning to organize transaction flows at CondoCleaners.com. His secure website will use a credit card service to process customer payments, which will be deposited directly into the business bank account. He will pay for expenses using his own credit card or personal cheque, then submit expenses to the company monthly. Once he decides to hire employees, he will initially do the payroll calculations himself, and issue cheques manually.

REQUIRED
a. List the financial statement cycles that will be present at CondoCleaners.com. For each financial statement cycle, list three general ledger accounts that will likely be present at the company.
b. Using Figure 5-5B as a guide, draw a flow diagram showing how sales will be processed at CondoCleaners.com.
c. Describe three specific transaction-related audit objectives that you would use to audit the sales revenue at CondoCleaners.com.

2008 Annual Report

HILLSBURG HARDWARE LIMITED 2008 ANNUAL REPORT

CONTENTS

Rick Chulick, President and Chief Operating Officer

DEAR SHAREHOLDERS: March 29, 2009

We are proud to announce another year of noticeable improvement.

In last year's letter we stated, "We are committed to increasing the efficiency and effectiveness of operations through cost savings and productivity improvements. In addition, we intend to maintain and further develop our customer base through recently implemented post-sale service programs." The operating results in this report demonstrate that our objectives have been achieved, resulting in a net income increase of $740,000 from 2007 to 2008. This amounts to 15 cents per share, a 23.2% increase from last year. Our goal in the current year is to further improve the results of operations and create value for shareholders. In doing so, we will focus primarily on the following three strategic components of our business plan:

1. Post-sale service arrangements designed to further develop and maintain our customer base.
2. Aggressive advertising campaigns that allow us to penetrate markets dominated by national wholesale hardware store chains.
3. Implementation of new warehouse technology designed to increase productivity and reduce stocking and distribution costs.

We will report our progress throughout the year.

Christopher J. Kurran
Chief Executive Officer

Rick Chulick
President and Chief Operating Officer

2

HISTORY

Hillsburg Stores Ltd. began operations in 1980 in Halifax, Nova Scotia, as a retail hardware store chain. On September 25, 1986, Hillsburg merged with Handy Hardware and Lumber Company, which established the concept of selling high-quality hardware through wholesale distribution outlets in 1981, to form Handy-Hillsburg, Inc., a provincial corporation. On June 5, 1990, after spinning off all of its lumber-related assets to Handy Corporation, the company changed its name to Hillsburg Hardware, Ltd. On October 22, 1992, the company reincorporated as a federal company and changed its name to Hillsburg Hardware Limited (heareafter referred to as "the Company"), which trades on the TSX under the symbol "HLSB."

OVERVIEW

Hillsburg Hardware Limited is a wholesale distributor of hardware equipment to a variety of independent, high-quality hardware stores in the eastern part of Canada. The primary products are power and hand tools, landscaping equipment, electrical equipment, residential and commercial construction equipment, and a wide selection of paint products.

More than 90% of the Company's products are purchased from manufacturers and shipped either directly to customers or to the main warehouse in Halifax, Nova Scotia, where shipments are combined to minimize the costs of freight and handling.

Hardware retailers, now more than ever, find it advantageous to purchase from us rather than directly from manufacturers. We make it possible for smaller, independent retailers to purchase on an as-needed basis, rather than in bulk. Moreover, we offer our customers a range of high-quality products that cannot be found at most national chains.

We also offer far more post-sale services to customers than are offered by manufacturers and other national distributors. We simplify the purchasing process by assigning each customer a permanent salesperson. Each salesperson becomes involved in the sales process, and also acts as a liaison between the customer and post-sale service areas. For example, when customers experience technical problems with recently purchased hardware, their salesperson has the responsibility to coordinate both exchanges and warranty repairs with the manufacturer. This process adds value for customers and makes post-sales service more efficient and less problematic. Low turnover and extensive training of our salespeople enhance this service.

To further encourage customer loyalty, each customer is given access to our internal database system—ONHAND (Online Niche-Hardware Availability Notification Database). The ONHAND system lets customers check the availability of hard-to-find products instantly over the Internet. Moreover, the system includes data such as expected restock dates for items that are currently sold out and expected availability dates for items that will soon be introduced to the market.

Because of the two aforementioned processes, we have managed to maintain a repeat-customer base. Nearly 75% of all first-time customers make at least one additional purchase within one year of their first purchase.

Recently, there have been major consolidations in the wholesale hardware industry. We believe this consolidation trend is advantageous to our operations as a distributor of hard to-find, high-quality hardware equipment. The recent consolidation of Builder's Plus Hardware, Inc., one of the top ten largest national hardware store chains, is a case in point. One month after the consolidation, Builder's Plus decided not to carry high-end construction and landscaping equipment in order to focus on what it called the "typical hardware customer."

PRODUCTS

To more effectively manage inventory, we carefully monitor the composition of net sales by category of items sold. The following chart indicates the percentage of net sales by class of merchandise sold during the years 2008, 2007, and 2006:

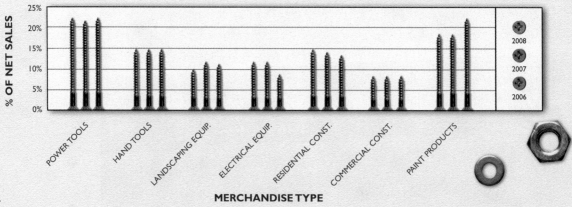

MARKETING PROGRAM

This year, the Company made a significant investment in a new advertising campaign. Various radio, newspaper, magazine, and television advertisements were purchased at the local and regional levels using the Company's new catchphrase, "Hardware for Hard Workers." The new jingle has been partially responsible for the fiscal 2008 increase in sales of 9%.

CUSTOMERS

The majority of our customers are located in Nova Scotia, Prince Edward Island, New Brunswick, and Newfoundland and Labrador. Our current customer base consists of more than 400 independently owned hardware stores. Approximately 25% of our customers make up more than 80% of total sales revenue. To promote long-standing relationships with customers, we offer an array of incentive and customer appreciation programs. Since these programs were implemented in 1997, customer satisfaction ratings have improved steadily in each subsequent year.

SUPPLIERS

We purchase hardware and other products from more than 300 manufacturers. No single vendor accounted for more than 5% of our purchases during fiscal 2008, but our 25 largest vendors accounted for nearly 35%. We currently have long-term supply agreements with two vendors: Mechanical Tools and Painter's Paradise. These agreements are in effect until the end of fiscal year 2009. The combined dollar amount of each contract is not expected to exceed 5% of total purchases for the year.

COMPETITORS

There are other regional wholesale hardware distributors that compete with the Company, but national wholesale hardware store chains dominate the industry. Most of our competitors are not only larger, but have greater financial resources than our company. Ten national chains exist in the geographic area in which Hillsburg Hardware Limited operates. Of the ten national chains, Hardware Bros., Tools & Paint, and Construction City account for a significant portion of the wholesale hardware market share and also carry the hard-to-find and high-quality items we provide. The success of our business depends on our ability to keep distribution costs to a minimum and our customers satisfied through superior customer service.

The chart that follows is a breakdown of market share in the wholesale hardware market by competitor category, including the 2% market share held by the Company. The chart illustrates that we have considerable opportunity for sales growth.

EMPLOYEES

Hillsburg Hardware currently employs 319 individuals. The majority of our employees are involved in day-to-day sales. Because of our marketing and customer relations strategy, we make significant investments in ongoing training and professional development activities. Each year employees are required to attend 75 hours of professional training. Each employee receives a performance evaluation at least four times per year, usually once each quarter. Our turnover is among the lowest in the industry because of our compensation, training, and evaluation programs. We regard our employees as our most valuable asset.

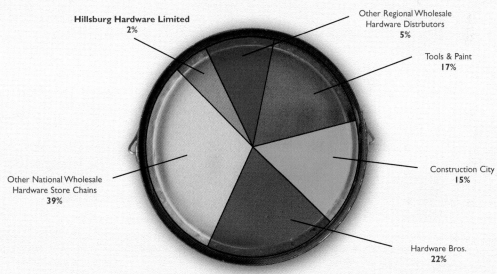

Hillsburg Hardware Limited
2%

Other Regional Wholesale Hardware Distrbutors
5%

Tools & Paint
17%

Construction City
15%

Hardware Bros.
22%

Other National Wholesale Hardware Store Chains
39%

4

PROPERTIES

The Company owns and operates its main warehouse and an administrative office. The main warehouse and administrative office are in the same 475,000 square-foot building. We also rent a second warehouse for $312,000 annually. The building, located in Sydney, Nova Scotia, serves as an off-site storage facility.

LEGAL PROCEEDINGS

On September 3, 2007, a suit was filed in the Municipal Court in Yarmouth, Nova Scotia against the Company. The product liability suit, "*Don Richards* v. *Hillsburg Hardware Limited*" is related to injuries that resulted from an alleged defective design of a tractor manufactured by Silo-Tractor, a Canadian corporation. The suit is currently in pretrial proceedings. In the opinion of our legal counsel, the suit is without merit. We intend to vigorously defend our position.

The Company does not believe any other legal issues materially affect its finances.

EXECUTIVE OFFICERS

The following list provides names and present positions of the Company's officers:

NAME	POSITION
John P. Higgins	Chairman of the Board
Rick Chulick	President and Chief Operating Officer (a)
Christopher J. Kurran	Chief Executive Officer (b)
Avis A. Zomer	Chief Financial Officer
Brandon S. Mack	Vice-President, Sales and Marketing
Mary R. Moses	Vice-President, Merchandising
Vanessa M. Namie	Vice-President, Operations (c)
Joseph A. Akuroi	Vice-President, Quality Assurance (d)

(a) Mr. Chulick has been President and Chief Operating Officer of the Company since November 1993. Mr. Chulick was Chairman of the Board from 1996 to 1998.

(b) Mr. Kurran has been Chief Executive Officer of the Company since September 1999. Prior to his role as CEO, Mr. Kurran was employed from 1990 to 1998 by Trini Enterprises, an industrial distributor.

(c) Ms. Namie has been employed by the Company since its inception in 1992. She has held her current position since 1998 and served as an operations manager from 1992 to 1998.

(d) Mr. Akuroi was Chief Operating Officer and President of Hardware Bros., one of the ten largest wholesale hardware chains in the country, from 1996 to 2001.

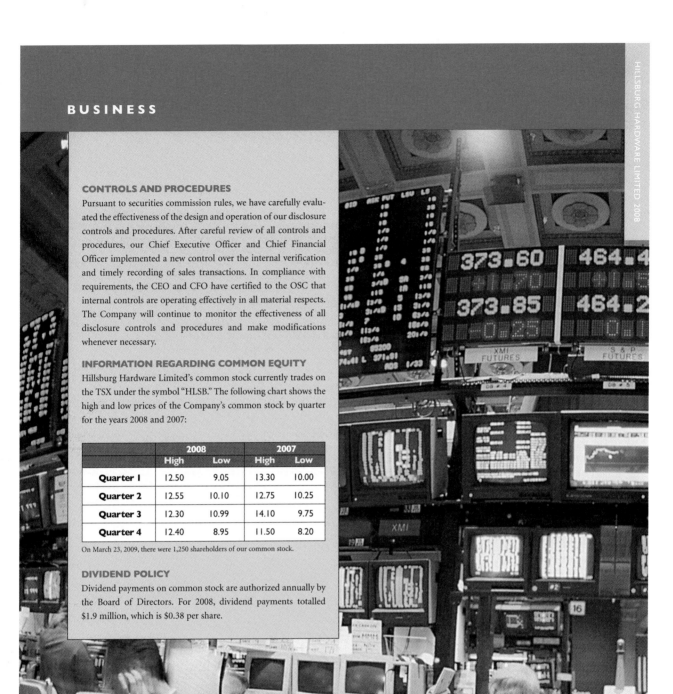

CONTROLS AND PROCEDURES

Pursuant to securities commission rules, we have carefully evaluated the effectiveness of the design and operation of our disclosure controls and procedures. After careful review of all controls and procedures, our Chief Executive Officer and Chief Financial Officer implemented a new control over the internal verification and timely recording of sales transactions. In compliance with requirements, the CEO and CFO have certified to the OSC that internal controls are operating effectively in all material respects. The Company will continue to monitor the effectiveness of all disclosure controls and procedures and make modifications whenever necessary.

INFORMATION REGARDING COMMON EQUITY

Hillsburg Hardware Limited's common stock currently trades on the TSX under the symbol "HLSB." The following chart shows the high and low prices of the Company's common stock by quarter for the years 2008 and 2007:

	2008		2007	
	High	Low	High	Low
Quarter 1	12.50	9.05	13.30	10.00
Quarter 2	12.55	10.10	12.75	10.25
Quarter 3	12.30	10.99	14.10	9.75
Quarter 4	12.40	8.95	11.50	8.20

On March 23, 2009, there were 1,250 shareholders of our common stock.

DIVIDEND POLICY

Dividend payments on common stock are authorized annually by the Board of Directors. For 2008, dividend payments totalled $1.9 million, which is $0.38 per share.

HLSB +12.40

6

To the Shareholders of Hillsburg Hardware Limited

We have audited the accompanying balance sheets of Hillsburg Hardware Limited as at December 31, 2008 and 2007, and the related statements of income, retained earnings, and cash flows for each of the years in the three-year period ended December 31, 2008. We have also audited the effectiveness of Hillsburg Hardware Limited's internal control over financial reporting as at December 31, 2008, in accordance with criteria established in *Internal Control—Integrated Framework*, as issued by the Committee of Sponsoring Organizations of the Treadway Commission (COSO), and management's assessment thereof included in the accompanying report, *Management's Report on Internal Control, 2005*. Hillsburg Hardware Limited's management is responsible for these financial statements, for maintaining effective internal control over financial reporting, and for its assessment of the effectiveness of internal control over financial reporting. Our responsibility is to express an opinion on these financial statements, an opinion on management's assessment, and an opinion on the effectiveness of the company's internal control over financial reporting based on our audits.

A company's internal control over financial reporting is a process designed to provide reasonable assurance regarding the reliability of financial reporting and the preparation of financial statements for external purposes in accordance with generally accepted accounting principles. A company's internal control over financial reporting includes those policies and procedures that (1) pertain to the maintenance of records that, in reasonable detail, accurately and fairly reflect the transactions and dispositions of the assets of the company; (2) provide reasonable assurance that transactions are recorded as necessary to permit preparation of financial statements in accordance with generally accepted accounting principles, and that receipts and expenditures of the company are being made only in accordance with authorizations of management and directors of the company; and (3) provide reasonable assurance regarding prevention or timely detection of unauthorized acquisition, use, or disposition of the company's assets that could have a material effect on the financial statements.

We conducted our audit of Hillsburg Hardware Limited's financial statements in accordance with Canadian generally accepted auditing standards. Those standards require that we plan and perform an audit to obtain reasonable assurance whether the financial statements are free of material misstatement. An audit of financial statements includes examining, on a test basis, evidence supporting the amounts and disclosures in the financial statements. A financial statement audit also includes assessing the accounting principles used and significant estimates made by management, and evaluating the overall financial statement presentation. We conducted our audit of the effectiveness of the Company's internal control over financial reporting, and management assessment thereof, in accordance with the standards established by the Canadian Institute of Chartered Accountants (CICA) for audits of internal control over financial reporting. Those standards require that we plan and perform our audit to obtain reasonable assurance about whether effective internal control over financial reporting was maintained in all material respects. Our audit of internal control over financial reporting included obtaining an understanding of internal control over financial reporting, testing, and evaluating the design and operating effectiveness of internal control over financial reporting, and performing such other procedures as we considered necessary in the circumstances. We believe that our audits provide a reasonable basis for our opinions.

In our opinion, the financial statements referred to above present fairly, in all material respects, the financial position of Hillsburg Hardware Limited as at December 31, 2008 and 2007, and the results of its operations and its cash flows for each of the years in the three-year period ended December 31, 2008 in accordance with Canadian generally accepted accounting principles. Also, in our opinion, management's assessment that Hillsburg Hardware Limited maintained effective internal control over financial reporting as at December 31, 2008, is fairly stated, in all material respects, in accordance with criteria established in *Internal Control—Integrated Framework* issued by the Committee of Sponsoring Organizations of the Treadway Commission (COSO). Furthermore, in our opinion, Hillsburg Hardware Limited maintained, in all material respects, effective internal control over financial reporting as at December 31, 2008, in accordance with criteria established in *Internal Control—Integrated Framework* issued by the Committee of Sponsoring Organizations of the Treadway Commission (COSO).

Because of its inherent limitations, internal control over financial reporting may not prevent or detect misstatements. Also, projections of any evaluation of effectiveness to future periods are subject to the risk that controls may become inadequate because of changes in conditions, or that the degree of compliance with the policies or procedures may deteriorate.

Berger, Kao, Kadous & Co., LLP

Berger, Kao, Kadous & Co., LLP
Halifax, Nova Scotia
March 21, 2009

7

FINANCIAL STATEMENTS

Management's Accountability

To Our Shareholders:

The management of Hillsburg Hardware Limited is responsible for the accompanying Financial Statements and all other information in the annual report. The financial statements have been prepared by management in accordance with Canadian generally accepted accounting principles, which recognize the necessity of relying on some best estimates and informed judgments. All financial information in the annual report is consistent with the Financial Statements.

To discharge its responsibilities for financial reporting and safeguarding of assets, management depends on the Company's systems of internal accounting control. These systems are designed to provide reasonable assurance that the financial records are reliable and form a proper basis for the timely and accurate preparation of financial statements. Management meets the objectives of internal accounting control on a cost-effective basis through the prudent selection and training of personnel, adoption and communication of appropriate policies, and employment of an internal audit program.

The Board of Directors oversees management's responsibilities for financial statements primarily through the activities of its Audit Committee, which is composed solely of Directors who are neither officers nor employees of the Company. This Committee meets with management and the Company's independent auditors, Berger, Kao, Kadous & Co., LLP, to review the financial statements and recommend approval by the Board of Directors. The Audit Committee is also responsible for making recommendations with respect to the appointment and remuneration of the Company's auditors. The Audit Committee also meets with the auditors, without the presence of management, to discuss the results of their audit, their opinion on internal accounting controls, and the quality of financial reporting.

The financial statements have been audited by Berger, Kao, Kadous & Co., LLP, whose appointment was ratified by shareholder vote at the annual shareholders' meeting.

John P. Higgins
Chairman of the Board

Christopher J. Kurran
Chief Executive Officer

Avis A. Zomer
Chief Financial Officer

8

BALANCE SHEET

HILLSBURG HARDWARE LIMITED
BALANCE SHEETS (in thousands)
December 31

ASSETS	2008	2007
Current assets		
Cash and cash equivalents	$ 828	$ 743
Trade receivables (net of allowances of $1,240 and $1,311)	18,957	16,210
Other receivables	945	915
Merchandise inventory	29,865	31,600
Prepaid expenses	432	427
Total current assets	51,027	49,895
Property and equipment		
Land	3,456	3,456
Buildings	32,500	32,000
Equipment, furniture, and fixtures	6,304	8,660
Less: accumulated amortization	(31,920)	(33,220)
Total property and equipment (net)	10,340	10,896
Total assets	$ 61,367	$ 60,791
LIABILITIES AND SHAREHOLDERS' EQUITY		
Current liabilities		
Trade accounts payable	$ 4,720	$ 4,432
Notes payable	4,180	4,589
Accrued payroll	1,350	715
Accrued payroll taxes	120	116
Accrued interest and dividends payable	2,050	1,975
Accrued income tax	796	523
Total current liabilities	13,216	12,350
Long-term notes payable	24,120	26,520
Deferred income taxes	738	722
Other long-term payables	830	770
Total liabilities	38,904	40,362
SHAREHOLDERS' EQUITY		
Common stock (5,000,000 shares issued)	8,500	8,500
Retained earnings	13,963	11,929
Total shareholders' equity	22,463	20,429
Total liabilities and shareholders' equity	$ 61,367	$ 60,791

See Notes to Financial Statements.

9

"We offer our customers a range of high-quality products that cannot be found at most national chains."

INCOME STATEMENT

HILLSBURG HARDWARE LIMITED INCOME STATEMENT (in thousands) Year Ended December 31			
	2008	**2007**	**2006**
Net sales	$143,086	$131,226	$122,685
Cost of sales	103,241	94,876	88,724
Gross profit	39,845	36,350	33,961
Selling, general and administrative expenses	32,475	29,656	28,437
Operating income	7,370	6,694	5,524
Other income and expense			
Interest expense	2,409	2,035	2,173
Gain on sale of assets	(720)	—	—
Total other expense (income)	1,689	2,035	2,173
Earnings before income taxes	5,681	4,659	3,351
Provision for income taxes	1,747	1,465	1,072
Net income	$3,934	$3,194	$2,279
Earnings per share	$0.79	$0.64	$0.46

See Notes to Financial Statements.

STATEMENTS OF RETAINED EARNINGS

HILLSBURG HARDWARE LIMITED STATEMENTS OF RETAINED EARNINGS (in thousands)					
	Common Stock		**Paid-in Capital**	**Retained Earnings**	**Total Shareholders' Equity**
	Shares	**Par value**			
Balance as of December 31, 2005	5,000	$5,000	$3,500	$10,256	$18,756
Net income				2,279	2,279
Dividends paid				(1,900)	(1,900)
Balance as of December 31, 2006	5,000	5,000	3,500	10,635	19,135
Net income				3,194	3,194
Dividends paid				(1,900)	(1,900)
Balance as of December 31, 2007	5,000	5,000	3,500	11,929	20,429
Net income				3,934	3,934
Dividends paid				(1,900)	(1,900)
Balance as of December 31, 2008	5,000	$5,000	$3,500	$13,963	$22,463

See Notes to Financial Statements.

HILLSBURG HARDWARE LIMITED STATEMENTS OF CASH FLOWS (in thousands) Year Ended December 31			
Operating activities	**2008**	**2007**	**2006**
Cash flows provided by (used in) operating activities:			
Net income	$ 3,934	$ 3,194	$ 2,279
Amortization	1,452	1,443	1,505
(Gain) loss on sale of assets	(720)	—	—
Deferred income taxes increase (decrease)	16	(8)	43
Changes in non-cash working capital:			
Trade and other receivables	(2,777)	(393)	(918)
Merchandise inventory	1,735	(295)	(430)
Prepaid expenses	(5)	(27)	(55)
Accounts payable	288	132	76
Accrued liabilities	714	77	142
Income taxes payable	273	23	13
Net cash provided by operating activities	4,910	4,146	2,655
Investing activities			
Capital expenditures	(10,500)	(1,800)	(2,292)
Sale of equipment	10,324	—	—
Net cash used in investing activities	(176)	(1,800)	(2,292)
Financing activities			
Dividend payment	(1,900)	(1,900)	(1,900)
Proceeds (repayments) from borrowings (net)	(2,749)	(423)	1,602
Net cash used in financing activities	(4,649)	(2,323)	(298)
Net increase in cash and cash equivalents	85	23	65
Cash and cash equivalents at beginning of year	743	720	655
Cash and cash equivalents at end of year	$ 828	$ 743	$ 720

See Notes to Financial Statements.

1. DESCRIPTION OF SIGNIFICANT ACCOUNTING POLICIES AND BUSINESS

We are a wholesale distributor of high-quality power tools, hand tools, electrical equipment, landscaping equipment, residential and commercial construction equipment, and paint products. The majority of our customers are smaller, independent hardware stores located in Nova Scotia, Prince Edward Island, New Brunswick, and Newfoundland and Labrador.

Allowance for Doubtful Accounts: Our allowance for doubtful accounts is maintained to account for expected credit losses. Estimates of bad debts are based on individual customer risks and historical collection trends. Allowances are evaluated and updated when conditions occur that give rise to collection issues.

Merchandise Inventory: Merchandise inventory is presented at the lower of average cost or market. To present accurately the estimated net realizable value of the accounts, we adjust inventory balances when current and expected future market conditions, as well as recent and historical turnover trends, indicate adjustments are necessary.

Property and Equipment: Land, buildings, computers and other equipment, and furniture and fixtures are stated at historical cost. Depreciation is calculated on a straight-line basis over estimated useful lives of the assets. Estimated useful lives are 20 to 35 years for buildings and 2 to 10 years for equipment and furniture and fixtures.

Revenue Recognition: Revenues are recognized when goods are shipped, title has passed, the sales price is fixed, and collectibility is reasonably assured. A sales returns and allowance account is maintained to reflect estimated future returns and allowances. Adjustments to the sales returns and allowance account are made in the same period as the related sales are recorded and are based on historical trends, as well as analyses of other relevant factors. Sales are recorded net of returns and allowances in the statements referred to in this report.

Income Taxes: The deferred income tax account includes temporary differences between financial accounting income and taxable income. The account consists largely of temporary differences related to (1) the valuation of inventory, (2) depreciation, and (3) other accruals.

2. OTHER RECEIVABLES

The other receivables balance consists largely of vendor allowances and vendor rebates. When vendor allowances and vendor rebates are recognized (all activities required by the supplier are completed, the amount is determinable, and collectibility is reasonably certain), they are recorded as reductions of costs of goods sold.

3. NOTES PAYABLE

Notes payable for the year ended December 31, 2008 consists of three notes payable to the bank. Each note carries a fixed interest rate of 8.5%. One note for $4,180,000 matures in June 2009 and the other two

mature on December 31, 2011. During 2008, there was an additional note outstanding in the amount of $4,400,000, which was paid off during October 2008.

4. COMMITMENTS

The Company is currently committed to an operating lease that expires in 2012. Rental payments for the remainder of the lease are set at $312,000 per annum.

5. SEGMENT REPORTING

The Company operates in one segment. The breakdown of revenues (in thousands) from different products is listed in the chart below:

SEGMENT REPORTING			
	2008	**2007**	**2006**
Power Tools	$ 31,479	$ 27,557	$ 26,991
Hand Tools	21,463	19,684	18,403
Landscaping Equipment	14,309	15,645	13,494
Electrical Goods	17,170	15,849	11,042
Residential Construction Equipment	21,463	18,372	15,949
Commercial Construction Equipment	11,447	10,498	9,815
Paint Products	25,755	23,621	26,991
	$143,086	**$131,226**	**$122,685**

6. EARNINGS PER SHARE

Earnings per share calculations for 2008, 2007, and 2006 were computed as follows:

Numerators
(net income in thousands): $3,934, $3,194, and $2,279

Denominators
(shares of common stock): 5,000,000
(unchanged for all years)

Diluted earnings per share was the same as basic earnings per share for all years.

12

**Management's Discussion and Analysis
of Financial Condition and Results of Operations**

The following discussion and analysis of the results of our operations and our financial condition are based on the financial statements and related notes included in this report. When preparing the financial statements, we are frequently required to use our best estimates and judgments. These estimates and judgments affect certain asset, liability, revenue, and expense account balances. Therefore, estimates are evaluated constantly based on our analyses of historical trends and our understanding of the general business environment in which we operate. There are times, however, when different circumstances and assumptions cause actual results to differ from those expected when judgments were originally made. The accounting policies referred to in Note 1 to the financial statements, in our opinion, influence the judgments and estimates we use to prepare our financial statements.

RESULTS OF OPERATIONS

For the year ended December 31, 2008, gross profit increased by 9.6% or $3,495,000 from 2007. This increase in gross profit more than offsets the increase in operating expenses from 2007 to 2008 of $2,819,000 or 9.5%. The increase in gross margin largely explains the operating income increase of $676,000.

For the year ended December 31, 2007, gross profit increased by $2,389,000 or 7% from 2006. Total operating expenses increased by $1,219,000 or approximately 4.3% from 2006. The increase in gross profit offset the total operating expense increase, and the net result was a $1,170,000 increase in operating income.

Net Sales: From 2007 to 2008 net sales increased by $11,860,000 or 9%. The increase in net sales can be explained largely by an aggressive advertising campaign that the Company organized during the second half of 2008. Net sales for 2007 increased by $8,541,000 or 7% from 2002, which is consistent with industry-wide average revenue growth of 7% from 2006 to 2007.

Gross Profit: Gross profit as a percentage of net sales stayed relatively stable at 27.68% and 27.70% in 2006 and 2007, respectively, but increased to 27.85% in 2008. The 2008 increase is mostly due to improved vendor incentive programs, our focus on cost containment, and increases in the resale values of certain commodities such as PVC piping material and certain types of metal wiring. While gross profit percentages in the industry have declined somewhat, our position as a niche provider in the overall hardware market allows us to charge premium prices without losing customers.

Selling, General and Administrative Expenses: Selling expenses increased by $1,911,000 or 14.8% from 2007 to 2008 and by $805,000 or 6.7% from 2006 to 2007. As a percentage of net sales, selling expenses

increased by 0.52% since 2007 and decreased by 0.03% from 2006 to 2007. The increase in selling expenses as a percentage of net sales from 2007 to 2008 is due to our new advertising campaign and increased expenditures on sales meetings and training.

General and administrative expenses increased by $908,000 or 5.4% from 2007 to 2008 and by $414,000 or 2.5% from 2006 to 2007. As a percentage of net sales, general and administrative expenses decreased by 0.42% since 2007 and decreased by 0.55% from 2006 to 2003. The overall increase from 2007 to 2008 was caused mostly by unexpected repairs needed to reattach and replace damaged shelving units in our main warehouse building.

Interest Expense: In 2008, interest expense increased by $374,000, or approximately 18.4%, compared to 2007. The increase was due to an overall interest rate increase and the restructuring of debt covenants that are less restrictive but demand higher interest rates. In 2007 interest expense decreased by $138,000 or 6.4% compared to 2006. The 2007 decrease was mainly due to the Company's decision to decrease the level of long-term debt. The average interest rates on short- and long-term debt during 2008 were approximately 10.5% and 8.5% respectively.

LIQUIDITY

During 2008, our working capital requirements were primarily financed through our line of credit, under which we are permitted to borrow up to the lesser of $7,000,000 or 75% of accounts receivable outstanding less than 30 days. The average interest rate on these short-term borrowings in 2008 was approximately 10.5%.

Cash provided by operating activities for 2008 and 2007 was $4,910,000 and $4,146,000 respectively. The change from 2007 to 2008 is primarily due to the increase in net income. Increases in receivables were largely offset by decreases in inventories and increases in payables and other current liabilities. The increase in cash provided from operating activities of $1,491,000 from 2006 to 2007 is largely the result of the increase in net income and smaller increases in receivables and merchandise inventory in 2007 compared to 2006. We believe that cash flow from operations and the available short-term line of credit will continue to allow us to finance operations throughout the current year.

STATEMENT OF CONDITION

Merchandise inventory and trade accounts receivable together accounted for over 95% of current assets in both 2008 and 2007. Merchandise inventory turned over approximately 3.4 times in 2008 and 3.0 times in 2006. Average days to sell inventory were 108.6 and 120.9 in 2008 and 2007 respectively. Net trade receivables turned over approximately 7.6 times in 2008 and in 2007. Days to collect accounts receivable computations were 48.1 and 48.0 in 2008 and 2007 respectively. Both inventory and accounts receivable turnover are lower than industry averages. We plan for this difference to satisfy the market in which we operate. Our market consists of smaller, independent hardware stores that need more favourable receivable collection terms and immediate delivery of inventory. Because we hold large amounts of inventory, we are able to fill orders quicker than most of our competitors even during the busiest times of the year.

OUTLOOK

During 2008 we experienced another year of noticeable improvement. The Company's financial performance can largely be attributed to (1) a continued focus on cost containment, (2) productivity improvements, (3) aggressive advertising, and (4) the implementation of programs designed to enhance customer satisfaction.

During 2009, we will continue to apply the same strategic efforts that improved 2008 performance. We are also implementing a new warehouse information system designed to increase productivity and reduce stocking and distribution costs. Management believes that earnings growth will be primarily driven by (1) continued focus on

customer satisfaction, (2) penetration into markets currently dominated by national wholesale hardware store chains, and (3) the use of technology to attract additional customers and promote more efficient operations.

INFORMATION CONCERNING FORWARD-LOOKING STATEMENTS

This report contains certain forward-looking statements (referenced by such terms as "expects" or "believes") that are subject to the effects of various factors including (1) changes in wholesale hardware prices, (2) changes in the general business environment, (3) the intensity of the competitive arena, (4) new national wholesale hardware chain openings, and (5) certain other matters influencing the Company's ability to react to changing market conditions. Therefore, management wishes to make readers aware that the aforementioned factors could cause the actual results of our operations to differ considerably from those indicated by any forward-looking statements included in this report.

HILLSBURG HARDWARE LIMITED
FIVE-YEAR FINANCIAL SUMMARY (in thousands, except for per share amounts)

BALANCE SHEET DATA:	2008	2007	2006	2005	2004
Current assets	$ 51,027	$ 49,895	$ 49,157	$ 47,689	$ 46,504
Total assets	61,367	60,791	59,696	57,441	51,580
Current liabilities	13,216	12,350	12,173	12,166	9,628
Long-term notes payable	24,120	26,520	26,938	25,432	25,223
Total shareholders' equity	22,463	20,429	19,135	18,756	15,764
INCOME STATEMENT DATA:					
Net sales	$ 143,086	$ 131,226	$ 122,685	$ 120,221	$ 117,115
Cost of sales	103,241	94,876	88,724	88,112	85,663
Gross profit	39,845	36,350	33,961	32,109	31,452
Earnings before income taxes	5,681	4,659	3,351	3,124	1,450
Net income	3,934	3,194	2,279	2,142	994
Cash provided by operating activities	4,910	4,146	2,655	1,811	1,232
Per common share data:					
Net income	$ 0.79	$ 0.64	$ 0.46	$ 0.43	$ 0.22
Cash dividends per share	$ 0.38	$ 0.38	$ 0.38	$ —	$ —
Common shares outstanding	5,000	5,000	5,000	5,000	4,500
KEY OPERATING RESULTS AND FINANCIAL POSITION RATIOS:					
Gross profit (%)	27.85%	27.70%	27.68%	26.71%	26.86%
Return on assets (%)	9.30%	7.73%	5.72%	5.73%	2.86%
Return on common equity (%)	26.49%	23.55%	17.69%	18.10%	9.50%

14

6

Audit evidence

What does an auditor examine to provide assurance about the quality of the financial statements? When has enough information been collected? These are difficult questions, and this chapter examines the nature of evidence that is collected. All types of auditors will make decisions about the types of audit tests they will conduct in response to assessed risks. This chapter provides a toolkit of the different types of evidence and the factors that need to be considered to select high-quality evidence.

LEARNING OBJECTIVES

1 Describe five evidence decisions made during the audit process. Explain the phrase "sufficient appropriate audit evidence."

2 List and explain the seven general methods of evidence collection. Explain the importance of automated audit techniques in supporting the conduct of recalculation and reperformance.

3 Discuss methods used to choose the types of evidence to collect. Describe the times when particular types of evidence collection are mandated.

4 Define analytical procedures. State their role in the evidence collection process. Discuss the purposes of five major types of analytical procedures.

STANDARDS REFERENCED IN THIS CHAPTER

CICA Standards

CAS 315 – Identifying and assessing the risks of material misstatement through understanding the entity and its environment (previously Section 5141 – Understanding the entity and its environment and assessing the risks of material misstatement)

CAS 330 – The auditor's responses to assessed risks (previously Section 5143 – The auditor's procedures in response to assessed risks)

CAS 500 – Audit evidence (previously Section 5300 – Audit evidence)

CAS 520 – Analytical procedures (previously Section 5301 – Analysis)

CAS 505 – External confirmations (previously Section 5303 – Confirmation)

Sometimes the Most Important Evidence is Not Found in the Accounting Records

Crenshaw Properties was a real estate developer that specialized in self-storage facilities that it sold to limited partner investors. Crenshaw's role was to identify projects, serve as the general partner with a small investment, and raise capital from mortgage funds or other lenders such as banks and credit unions. Crenshaw had an extensive network of people who marketed these investments on a commission basis. As general partner, Crenshaw earned significant fees for related activities, including promotional fees, investment management fees, and real estate commissions.

The investments were successful, and business prospered. The value of self-storage facilities increased in line with the real estate market, and values were booming. But sales started to slow down in 2007 and continued slow into 2008.

George Crenshaw received a shock when he went to the bank in mid-2008 to secure mortgages for his next construction project. The bank requested detailed valuations of all of the properties in the Crenshaw Properties portfolio. It also wanted quarterly cash flow reporting, to be reviewed by the company's auditors, and a personal guarantee from George Crenshaw before considering provision of more mortgage funds.

Upon analysis of the valuations and a cash flow statement, the bank declined the mortgage to Crenshaw Properties, saying that the company's margins needed to increase and costs needed to be cut before it would consider lending additional funds. Crenshaw Properties wants to sell off some assets to continue operations, but the depressed real estate market may make this difficult.

IMPORTANCE TO AUDITORS

Crenshaw Properties ran into difficulties in financing because of the international credit crunch triggered by falling real estate values, turmoil in the asset-backed paper market, lower bank liquidity, and a tightening credit market. Lack of financing and decreased real estate values could mean that Crenshaw will no longer be a going concern if it cannot reorganize and cut costs.

As part of their audits in 2007 and 2008, the auditors should have considered the values of the assets held by Crenshaw, with the resultant impact on borrowing capacity and the ability of the company to continue operations.

WHAT DO YOU THINK?

1. What other factors could affect the ability of Crenshaw Properties to continue operations? How would the auditors find out about these factors?

continued >

2. How does general knowledge of the economy help the auditor when conducting the financial statement audit? What about specific industry knowledge?

Sources: 1. Thornton, Grant, "The credit crunch: a practical guide," Fall 2008, www.grantthornton.com, Accessed: November 21, 2008. 2. Trichur, Rita, "BMO, CIBC pull the plug on 40-year mortgages," *Toronto Star*, July 12, 2008, p. B2.

WHAT other types of companies or business activities could be affected by a credit crunch? Virtually every organization uses banking facilities and has debt. The inability to renew debt or borrow money can cripple an organization. As an auditor, you need to think about both the big picture risks involved in a company's operations, as well as the small picture—risks associated with individual transactions and potential errors. Evidence helps the auditor both assess risks and decide upon the likelihood of potential misstatement in the financial statements.

Audit Evidence and Associated Decisions

Nature of Evidence

Audit evidence was defined in Chapter 1 as any information used by the auditor to determine whether the financial statement being audited is stated in accordance with the established criteria. The information becomes a decision tool—it varies widely in the extent to which it persuades the auditor whether financial statements are stated in accordance with generally accepted accounting principles. Evidence includes persuasive information, such as the auditor's count of marketable securities, and less persuasive information, such as responses to questions by the client's employees.

Evidence is gathered in all phases of the audit process—in the risk assessment process, to help the auditor decide where there could be a risk of material misstatement in the financial statements; as a response to risks at the assertion level; and to document quality control, supervision, and overall conclusions about the type of audit report.

AUDIT EVIDENCE CONTRASTED WITH LEGAL AND SCIENTIFIC EVIDENCE The use of evidence is not unique to auditors. Evidence is also used extensively by scientists, lawyers, historians, and many others to support their decisions.

Through television, most people are familiar with the use of evidence in legal cases dealing with the guilt or innocence of a party charged with a crime such as robbery. In legal cases, there are well-defined rules of evidence enforced by a judge for the protection of the innocent. It is common, for example, for legal evidence to be judged inadmissible on the grounds that it is irrelevant, prejudicial, or based on hearsay.

Similarly, in scientific experiments, the scientist obtains evidence to draw conclusions about a theory. Assume, for example, a medical scientist is evaluating a new medicine that may provide relief to asthma sufferers. The scientist will gather

Table 6-1 Characteristics of Evidence for a Scientific Experiment, a Legal Case, and an Audit of Financial Statements

Basis of Comparison	Scientific Experiment Involving Testing a Medicine	Legal Case Involving an Accused Thief	Audit of Financial Statements
Use of the evidence	Determine effects of using the medicine	Decide guilt or innocence of accused	Determine if statements are fairly presented
Nature of evidence	Results of repeated experiments	Direct evidence and testimony by witnesses and party involved	Various types of audit evidence generated by the auditor, third parties, and the client
Party or parties evaluating evidence	Scientist	Jury and judge	Auditor
Certainty of conclusions from evidence	Vary from uncertain to near certainty	Requires establishing guilt beyond a reasonable doubt	High level of assurance
Nature of conclusions	Recommend or not recommend use of medicine	Innocence or guilt of party	Issue one of several alternative types of auditor's reports
Typical consequences of incorrect conclusions from evidence	Society uses ineffective or harmful medicine	Guilty party is not penalized, or innocent party is found guilty	Statement users make incorrect decisions, and auditor may be sued

evidence from a large number of controlled experiments over an extended period of time to determine the effectiveness of the medicine.

The auditor also gathers evidence to draw conclusions. Different evidence is used by auditors than by scientists or lawyers, and it is used in different ways, but in all three cases, evidence is used to reach conclusions. Table 6-1 illustrates key characteristics of evidence from the perspective of a scientist doing an experiment, a legal case involving an accused thief, and an auditor of financial statements. There are six bases of comparison. Note the similarities and differences among the three professions.

Audit Evidence Decisions

CAS 330, The auditor's responses to assessed risks, explains that the auditor needs to link completed audit work to the assessed risks at the assertion level, as well as documenting the conclusions and results of the *audit procedures* (par. 29). Identifying risks helps the auditor determine the appropriate types and amount of evidence to accumulate to be satisfied that the components of the client's financial statements and the overall statements are fairly stated. This judgment is important because of the prohibitive cost of examining and evaluating all available evidence. For example, in an audit of financial statements of most organizations, it is impossible for the public account- ant (PA) to examine the contents of all computer files or available evidence such as cancelled cheques, vendors' invoices, customer orders, payroll time cards, and the many other types of documents and records.

The auditor's decisions on evidence accumulation can be broken into the follow- ing five subdecisions:

1. Which risks could result in a risk of material misstatement (RMM) at the assertion level.
2. Which audit procedures to use (their "nature").
3. What sample size to select for a given procedure (the "extent" of a test).
4. Which particular items to select from the population.
5. When to perform the procedures (the "timing").

IDENTIFYING RISKS BY ASSERTION For each major class of transactions and material general ledger account, the auditor looks at the potential for RMM. Knowledge of the industry, business, and operating procedures at the client will help the auditor complete this assessment. For example, at Hillsburg Hardware, the auditor may decide that risk of obsolescence of inventory (the valuation assertion) is high due to frequent new product announcements and the potential for economic recession, while the risk of accuracy (recording the quantity, cost, and mechanical calculations) is low due to the high quality of information systems and monitoring controls at the company.

AUDIT PROCEDURES An **audit procedure** is the detailed instruction for the collection of a particular type of audit evidence that is to be obtained at some time during the audit. For example, evidence such as physical inventory counts, comparisons of cancelled cheques with cash disbursements, journal entries, and shipping document details is collected using audit procedures.

> **Audit procedure**—detailed instruction for the collection of a type of audit evidence.

In designing audit procedures, it is common to spell them out in sufficiently specific terms to permit their use as instructions during the audit. The auditor will consider manual and automated procedures, depending upon their cost. For example, the following is an audit procedure for the verification of cash disbursements:

- Obtain the cash disbursements report, and compare the payee name, amount, and date on the cancelled cheque with the cash disbursement report.

Several commonly used audit procedure terms are defined and illustrated with examples later in this chapter.

SAMPLE SIZE Once an audit procedure is selected, it is possible to vary the sample size from one to all the items in the population being tested. In the audit procedure above, suppose there are 6,600 cheques recorded in the cash disbursements report. The auditor might select a sample size of 40 cheques for comparison with the cash disbursements report. The decision as to how many items to test must be made by the auditor for each audit procedure. The sample size for any given procedure is likely to vary from audit to audit. Sampling is discussed further in Chapter 13.

ITEMS TO SELECT After the sample size has been determined for a particular audit procedure, it is still necessary to decide the particular items to test. If the auditor decides, for example, to select 40 cancelled cheques from a population of 6,600 for comparison with the cash disbursements journal, several different methods can be used to select the specific cheques to be examined. The auditor could (1) select a week and examine the first 40 cheques, (2) select the 40 cheques with the largest amounts (also known as "key items"), (3) select the cheques randomly, or (4) select those cheques the auditor thinks are most likely to be in error. A combination of these methods could also be used.

TIMING An audit of financial statements usually covers a period such as a year, and an audit is often not completed until several weeks or months after the end of the period. The timing of audit procedures can therefore vary from early in the accounting period to long after it has ended. In the audit of financial statements, the client normally wants the audit completed one to three months after year end.

Audit procedures often incorporate sample size, items to select, and timing. The following is a modification of the audit procedure previously used to include all five audit evidence decisions. (Italics identify the assertion, timing, number of items to select, and sample size decisions.)

- *Occurrence:* Obtain the *October* cash disbursements report, and compare the payee name, amount, and date on the cancelled cheque with the cash disbursements report for a *randomly selected sample of 40* cheque numbers.

> **Audit program**—detailed instructions for the entire collection of evidence for an audit area or an entire audit; always includes audit procedures and may also include sample sizes, items to select, and timing of the tests.

AUDIT PROGRAM The detailed instructions for the entire collection of evidence for an audit area is called an **audit program**. The audit program includes a list of the audit procedures. It usually also includes the sample sizes, items to select, and the timing of the tests. Normally, there is an audit program for each component of the audit (e.g., accounts receivable and sales). An example of an audit program that includes audit procedures, sample size, items to select, and timing is given on page 402 in Table 12-5. The right side of the audit program also includes the audit objectives for each procedure, as studied in Chapter 5.

Most auditors use computers to facilitate the preparation of audit programs. The simplest application of computers involves typing the audit program in a word processor and saving it from one year to the next to facilitate changes and updating. A more sophisticated application involves the use of a specialized program designed to help the auditor think through the planning considerations of the audit and select appropriate procedures using audit program generation software or other audit planning database templates.

Persuasiveness of Evidence

Generally accepted auditing standards (GAAS) require the auditor to obtain sufficient appropriate audit evidence to be able to draw reasonable conclusions on which to base the audit opinion. Because of the nature of audit evidence and the cost considerations of doing an audit, it is unlikely that the auditor will be completely convinced that the opinion is correct. However, the auditor must be persuaded that his or her opinion is correct with a high level of assurance. By combining all evidence from the entire audit, the auditor is able to decide when he or she is sufficiently persuaded to issue an auditor's report.

Persuasiveness of evidence is the degree to which the auditor is convinced that the evidence supports the audit opinion; the three determinants of persuasiveness are sufficiency, appropriateness, and timeliness.

SUFFICIENCY The quantity of evidence obtained determines its **sufficiency** (CAS 500, par. 5[e]). Quantity is measured primarily by the sample size the auditor selects. For a given audit procedure, the evidence obtained from a sample of 50 would ordinarily be more sufficient than that from a sample of 25.

There are several factors that determine the appropriate sample size in audits. The two most important are the auditor's expectation of errors and the effectiveness of the client's internal controls. To illustrate, assume that during the audit of Lau Computer Parts Inc., the auditor concludes that there is a high likelihood of obsolete inventory due to the nature of the client's industry. The auditor would sample more inventory items for obsolescence in an audit such as this than in one where the likelihood of obsolescence was low. Similarly, if the auditor concludes that a client has effective rather than ineffective internal controls over recording capital assets, a smaller sample size in the audit of purchases of capital assets is warranted. Expectation of errors and internal controls and their effect on sample size are critical topics in this book and are studied in depth in subsequent chapters, starting with Chapter 7.

In addition to affecting sample size, the particular items tested affect the sufficiency of evidence. Samples containing population items with large dollar values, items with a high likelihood of error, and items that are representative of the population are usually considered sufficient.

APPROPRIATENESS **Appropriateness** refers to the quality of evidence, that is, to the degree to which the evidence can be considered relevant and reliable. If evidence is considered to be highly appropriate, it is a great help in persuading the auditor that the financial statements are fairly stated. For example, if an auditor counted inventory, that evidence would be more appropriate than if management gave the auditor its own figures. Generally, the more appropriate the evidence, the less evidence is needed. Evidence is appropriate when it is both relevant and reliable.

Appropriateness of evidence depends on the audit procedures selected. Appropriateness cannot be improved by selecting a larger sample size or different population items. It can be improved only by selecting audit procedures that improve either the relevance or the reliability of the evidence.

Persuasiveness of evidence—the degree to which the auditor is convinced that the evidence supports the audit opinion; the three determinants of persuasiveness are the sufficiency, appropriateness, and timeliness of the evidence.

Sufficiency—the quantity of evidence; appropriate sample size.

CAS

Appropriateness—the degree to which evidence can be considered relevant and reliable.

Evidence Needs to Be Complete, Accurate, Precise and Consistent

Whom would you trust more, a used-car salesman, a banker, or your brother? These are the kinds of intangible judgments the auditor needs to make when assessing evidence.

CAS 500, Audit evidence, asks auditors to specifically consider how useful the evidence is that they receive from management and others.

For example, paragraph 9 of CAS 500 asks the auditor to obtain evidence about the accuracy and completeness of information. The auditor might consider the competence of employees or of the preparer of the information or the quality of information systems in that assessment.

The same paragraph also asks the auditor to consider whether the audit evidence is precise enough. This standard is asking about the level of detail. For example, if you confirmed information about debt, you would need to include information about interest rates.

Paragraph 11 of CAS 500 raises the issue of consistency. If management has a different assessment of the outcome of a lawsuit than staff involved in the process or the lawyer, then the evidence will be difficult to assess.

RELEVANCE **Relevant evidence** pertains to the audit objective the auditor is testing. For example, assume the auditor is concerned that a client is failing to bill customers for shipments (completeness transaction-related audit objective). If the auditor selected a sample of duplicate sales invoices and traced each to related shipping documents, the evidence would not be relevant for the completeness objective because it tests for occurrence instead. A relevant procedure would be to compare a sample of shipping documents with related duplicate sales invoices to determine if each shipment had been billed. The reason the second audit procedure is relevant and the first is not is that the shipment of goods is the normal criterion used for determining whether a sale has occurred and should have been billed. By tracing from shipping documents to duplicate sales invoices, the auditor can determine if shipments have been billed to customers. When the auditor traces from duplicate sales invoices to shipping documents, it is impossible to find unbilled shipments.

Relevance can be considered only in terms of specific audit objectives.

> **Relevant evidence**—the pertinence of the evidence to the audit objective being tested.

RELIABILITY **Reliability of evidence** increases when it is obtained from (1) the auditor's direct knowledge, (2) an independent provider, (3) a client with effective internal controls, (4) qualified providers such as law firms and banks, (5) objective sources, or (6) consistent or multiple sources.

> **Reliability of evidence**—evidence is reliable when it is obtained from (1) the auditor's direct knowledge, (2) an independent provider, (3) a client with effective internal controls, (4) qualified providers such as law firms and banks, (5) objective sources, or (6) consistent and multiple sources.

(1) Auditor's direct knowledge Evidence obtained directly by the auditor through observation, reperformance, and inspection is more appropriate than information obtained indirectly. For example, if the auditor observes recent fixed asset additions, notes serial numbers, and calculates the historical cost from original invoices, the evidence would be more reliable than if the auditor relied on documents and calculations provided by the controller.

(2) Independence of provider Evidence obtained from a source outside the entity is more reliable than that obtained from within, assuming that the external party is arms-length from the organization. For example, external evidence such as communications from banks, lawyers, or customers is generally regarded as more reliable than answers obtained from inquiries of the client. Similarly, documents that originate from outside the client's organization are considered more reliable than those that originate within the company and have never left the client's organization. An example of external evidence is an insurance policy, whereas a purchase requisition is internal evidence.

(3) Effectiveness of client's internal controls When a client's internal controls are effective, evidence obtained from the client is more reliable than when controls are weak. For example, if internal controls over sales and billing are effective, the auditor can obtain more accurate and complete evidence from sales invoices and shipping documents than if the controls are inadequate. When considering internal controls, the auditor also considers the likelihood of management override and the pervasive impact of management integrity.

(4) Qualifications of individuals providing the information Even when the source of information is independent, the evidence will not be reliable unless the individual providing it is qualified to do so. For this reason, communications from law firms and bank confirmations are typically more highly regarded than accounts receivable confirmations from persons not familiar with the business world. Also, evidence obtained directly by the auditor may not be reliable if he or she lacks the qualifications to evaluate the evidence. For example, examination of an inventory of diamonds by an auditor who is not trained to distinguish between diamonds and glass would not provide reliable evidence of the existence of diamonds. The auditor needs to consider the qualifications of providers with respect to each source of evidence, whether it be from management, internal auditors, or external specialists.

(5) Degree of objectivity Objective evidence is more reliable than evidence that requires considerable judgment to determine whether it is correct. Examples of objective evidence include confirmation of accounts receivable and bank balances, the physical count of securities and cash, and the adding (footing) of a list of accounts payable to determine if it is the same as the balance in the general ledger. Examples of subjective evidence include communication from a client's lawyers as to the likely outcome of outstanding lawsuits against the client, observation of obsolescence of inventory during physical examination, and inquiries of the credit manager about the collectability of non-current accounts receivable. In evaluating the reliability of subjective evidence, the qualifications of the person providing the evidence is important.

(6) Consistency from multiple sources With respect to a particular assertion, the auditor could use multiple sources of evidence. Consider, for example, obsolescence of inventory at Hillsburg Hardware. The auditor could calculate inventory turnover, review recent purchasing invoices, talk to shipping personnel, and observe physical inventory in the warehouse. If shipping personnel stated that no old stock existed, but the auditor observed old inventory (perhaps dusty or dirty boxes of products), then the auditor would need to investigate further to clarify the inconsistency. Evidence with all sources consistent is more reliable than inconsistent evidence.

TIMELINESS The **timeliness** of audit evidence can refer either to when it was accumulated or to the period covered by the audit. Evidence is usually more persuasive for balance sheet accounts when it is obtained as close to the balance sheet date as possible. For example, the auditor's count of marketable securities on the balance sheet date would be more persuasive than a count two months earlier. For income statement accounts, evidence is more persuasive if there is a sample from the entire period under audit rather than from only a part of the period. For example, a random sample of sales transactions for the entire year would be more persuasive than a sample from only the first six months.

COMBINED EFFECT The persuasiveness of evidence can be evaluated only after considering the combination of sufficiency, appropriateness, and timeliness in the context of the RMM for that audit objective. A large sample of evidence is not persuasive unless it is relevant to the audit objective being tested. A large sample of evidence that is neither appropriate nor timely is also not persuasive. Similarly, a small sample of only one or two pieces of appropriate and timely evidence also lacks persuasiveness. The auditor must evaluate the degree to which all three qualities have been met in deciding persuasiveness.

To illustrate the characteristics shown in Table 6-2, assume an auditor is verifying inventory that is a major item in the financial statements. Generally accepted auditing

	Audit Evidence Decisions and Qualities Affecting Persuasiveness of Evidence
Table 6-2	

Audit Evidence Decisions	Qualities Affecting Persuasiveness of Evidence
Likelihood of risk of material misstatement	Level of assessed risks, by assertion

Audit procedures	Appropriateness
	   Relevance
	   Reliability
	      Auditor's direct knowledge
	      Independence of provider
	      Effectiveness of internal controls
	      Qualifications of provider
	      Objectivity of evidence
	      Consistency of evidence

Sample size	Sufficiency and adequate sample size
Items to select	Based upon sampling methods chosen

Timing	Timeliness
	   When procedures are performed
	   Portion of period audited

standards require that the auditor be reasonably persuaded that inventory is not materially misstated. First, the auditor identifies the RMM for the audit objectives about inventory. For example, there could be a high risk for incompleteness due to many small items that can be easily stolen. The auditor must obtain a sufficient amount of appropriate and timely evidence about inventory. This means deciding which procedures to use for auditing inventory (such as an inventory count conducted by the auditor) to satisfy the appropriateness requirement, as well as determining the proper sample size (based upon risk and statistical tables) and items to select from the population (likely those most easily stolen or of high value) to satisfy the sufficiency requirement. Finally, the auditor must determine the timing of these procedures (such as at the same time as the client conducts an inventory count). The combination of these last four evidence decisions must result in sufficiently persuasive evidence to satisfy the auditor that inventory is materially correct. The audit program for inventory will reflect these decisions.

PERSUASIVENESS AND COST In making decisions about evidence for a given audit, both persuasiveness and cost must be considered. It is rare when only one type of evidence is available for verifying information. The persuasiveness and cost of all alternatives should be considered before selecting the best type or types. The auditor's goal is to obtain a sufficient amount of timely, reliable evidence that is relevant to the information being verified and to do so at reasonable cost. Automated audit procedures can often allow for high volumes of testing at a lower cost than manual testing, as discussed further in Chapter 13.

concept check

C6-1 How is audit evidence similar to legal evidence?

C6-2 List the five evidence decisions that the auditor makes. Explain their relevance to the audit process.

Methods of Evidence Collection

Types of Audit Evidence

The *CICA Handbook* specifies that audit evidence may be obtained through the methods of inspection, observation, inquiry, confirmation, recalculation, reperformance, and analytical procedures. These terms are defined and explained in CAS 500, from par. A7 (previously in Section 5300). Note that *documentation* is no longer considered

How would you feel if you received a tax assessment that was based on incorrect information? Now imagine you were required to pay additional taxes. CIBC's Amicus unit, administering 3,061 customers of President's Choice Financial, sent incorrect tax information to Canada Revenue Agency (CRA), while sending different (correct) information to the customers. The incorrect information sent to CRA stated that the customers had cashed in some of their 2003 RRSPs, resulting in tax reassessments.

How is it possible that computer systems could send different information to two different parties? The *Toronto Star* reported that the cause was the switch from a manual to a computer-based system. This would mean that there was either a large-scale programming error or data entry error.

In November 2007, Air Canada's reservation systems encountered communications problems with airports, so that tickets and tags could not be printed, stranding travellers for over five hours, again affecting "thousands" of customers. The problem was identified as a computer error of some kind, with no further information provided.

CRITICAL THINKING QUESTIONS

1. If a client has problems in delivering services, what is the likelihood that there are also information systems processing errors in the accounting systems?
2. What kinds of checks and balances should be in place when an organization implements program changes?
3. How does the quality of information systems affect your perception of the quality of internal control?

Sources: 1. Laidlaw, Stuart, "Tax error blamed on systems update," *Toronto Star*, January 27, 2005, p. D3. 2. Olive, David, "CIBC is really, really sorry," *Toronto Star*, January 27, 2005, p. D3. 3. Teotino, Isabel, "Airline glitch strands travellers," *Toronto Star*, November 17, 2007, p. A10.

---

a type of evidence collection method, but rather, it can be collected in different ways during evidence gathering.

The order in which these methods are listed and discussed should not be interpreted as signifying the relative strengths of the types or categories of evidence. In other words, the fact that "inspection" appears at the top of the list does not mean that any evidence belonging to that category is automatically stronger than evidence belonging to another category. The quality of each type of evidence, regardless of type, must be evaluated according to the criteria of its type.

Before beginning the study of types of evidence, it is useful to show the relationships among auditing standards, which were studied in Chapter 1, types of evidence, and the five evidence decisions discussed earlier in this chapter. These relationships are shown in Figure 6-1. Note that the standards are general, whereas audit procedures are specific. Types of evidence are broader than procedures and narrower than the standards. Every audit procedure obtains one or more types of evidence.

Inspection—the auditor's physical examination or count of a tangible asset, or inspection of a document.

INSPECTION Inspection (also called "physical examination") is the auditor's inspection or count of a tangible asset or document. This type of evidence is most often associated with inventory and cash but is also applicable to the verification of securities, notes receivable, and tangible capital assets. The distinction between the inspection of assets, such as marketable securities and cash, and the inspection of documents, such as cancelled cheques and sales documents, is important for auditing purposes. If the object being examined, such as a sales invoice, has no inherent value, the source is called documentation. For example, before a cheque is signed, it is a document; after it is signed, it becomes an asset; and when it is cancelled, it becomes a document again.

Inspection, which is a direct means of verifying that an asset actually exists (existence objective), is regarded as one of the most reliable and useful types of audit evidence. Generally, inspection is an objective means of ascertaining both the quantity and the description of the asset. In some cases, it is also a useful method for evaluating an asset's condition or quality. However, inspection is not sufficient evidence to verify that existing assets are owned by the client (rights and obligations objective), and in many cases the auditor is not qualified to judge such qualitative factors as obsolescence or authenticity (net realizable value for the valuation objective).

Figure 6-1 Relationships Among Auditing Standards, Types of Evidence, and the Five Audit Evidence Decisions

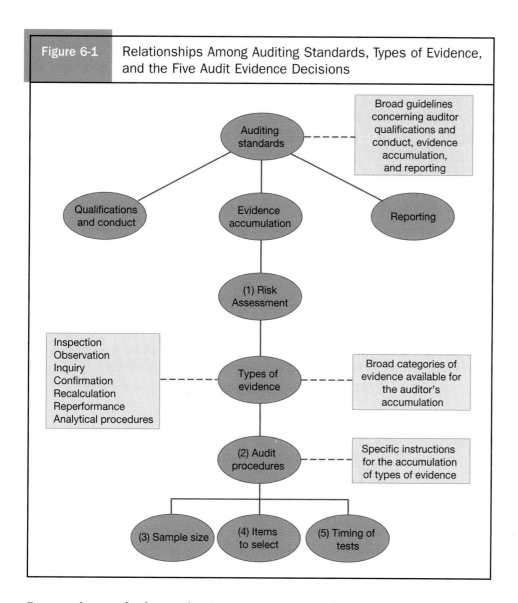

Proper valuation for financial statement purposes usually cannot be determined by inspection.

OBSERVATION **Observation** is the use of the senses to assess certain activities. Throughout the audit, there are many opportunities to exercise sight, hearing, touch, and smell to evaluate a wide range of things. For example, the auditor may tour a plant to obtain a general impression of a client's facilities, observe whether equipment is rusty to evaluate obsolescence, and watch individuals perform accounting tasks to determine whether the persons assigned responsibilities are performing them. Observation is rarely sufficient by itself because there is the risk that the client's personnel involved in accounting activities are aware of the auditor's presence. They may, therefore, perform their responsibilities in accordance with company policy but resume other activities once the auditor is out of sight. It is necessary to follow up initial impressions with other kinds of corroborative evidence.

INQUIRY **Inquiry of the client** is the obtaining of written or oral information from the client in response to questions from the auditor. Although considerable evidence is obtained from the client through inquiry, it usually cannot be regarded as conclusive because it is not from an independent source and may be biased in the client's favour. When the auditor obtains evidence through inquiry, it is normally necessary to obtain further corroborating evidence through other procedures. As an illustration, when the auditor wants to obtain information about the client's method of recording and controlling accounting transactions, he or she usually begins by asking the client how

Observation—use of the senses to assess certain activities.

Inquiry of the client—the obtaining of written or oral information from the client in response to questions during the audit.

internal controls operate. Later, the auditor performs a walk-through and tests of controls to determine if the controls function in the manner stated.

CONFIRMATION **Confirmation** describes the receipt of a written or oral response from an independent third party verifying the accuracy of information that was requested by the auditor. The request is made to the client, and the client asks the independent third party to respond directly to the auditor. Since confirmations come from sources that are independent of the client, they are a highly regarded and often-used type of evidence. However, confirmations are relatively costly to obtain and may cause some inconvenience to those asked to supply them. Therefore, they are not used in every instance in which they are applicable. Because of the high reliability of confirmations, auditors typically obtain written responses rather than oral ones.

Whether or not confirmations should be used depends on the reliability needs of the situation as well as the alternative evidence available. Traditionally, confirmations are not used to verify individual transactions between organizations, such as sales transactions, because the auditor can use documents for that purpose. Similarly, confirmations are seldom used in the audit of capital-asset additions because these can be verified adequately by documentation and physical examination. While confirmations are generally a very reliable form of evidence, the auditor must be aware that the third party providing the confirmation may be careless or may not have the correct information; the auditor should not automatically assume the confirmation is correct, especially if the response is unexpected or contradicts other evidence. In addition, the third party may not be independent of the client.

CAS The *CICA Handbook* (Section 5303) previously required confirmation of accounts receivable except when combined inherent risk and control risk (defined on page 209) and other substantive procedures would provide sufficient appropriate evidence; or when confirmation would be ineffective in providing reliable audit evidence. This requirement existed because accounts receivable usually represent a significant balance on the financial statements, and confirmations are a highly reliable type of evidence about them. CAS 505, External confirmations, does not require confirmations per se but states that external evidence is considered more reliable than evidence obtained from within the organization.

The CAS further states that the use of confirmations needs to be tailored to the risk assessments concluded by the auditor. Practically, this means that confirmations should still be used unless the auditor has alternative high-quality evidence or believes for some reason that the confirmations received would be unreliable. The major types of information that are frequently confirmed, along with the source of the confirmation, are indicated in Table 6-3.

To be considered reliable evidence, confirmations must be controlled by the auditor from the time they are prepared until they are returned. If the client controls the preparation of the confirmation, performs the mailing, or receives the responses, the auditor has lost control and with it independence; thus the reliability of the evidence is reduced.

new standards 6-2
Non-Required Confirmations

ISA 505, External confirmations, does not require the use of confirmations but, rather, provides additional guidance for the auditor to follow when confirmations are used.

For example, negative confirmations are discouraged (negative confirmations ask respondents to reply only in the event of differences).

ISA 505 also requires the auditor to conduct alternative procedures where there are no responses to confirmations, where management refuses permission to send a confirmation, or where results of evidence received are contradictory.

Table 6-3   Information Frequently Confirmed

Information	Source
Assets	
Cash in bank	Bank
Accounts receivable	Customer
Notes receivable	Maker
Owned inventory out on consignment	Consignee
Inventory held in public warehouses	Public warehouse
Cash surrender value of life insurance	Insurance company
Liabilities	
Accounts payable	Creditor
Notes payable	Lender
Advances from customers	Customer
Mortgages payable	Mortgagor
Bonds payable	Bondholder
Owners' Equity	
Shares outstanding	Registrar and transfer agent
Other Information	
Insurance coverage	Insurance company
Contingent liabilities	Company law firm(s), bank, and others
Bond indenture agreements	Bondholder
Collateral held by creditors	Creditor

RECALCULATION **Recalculation** involves rechecking the computations and mathematical work completed by the client during the period under audit. Rechecking of computations consists of testing the client's arithmetical accuracy. It includes such procedures as extending sales invoices and inventory, adding reports and subsidiary ledgers, and checking the calculation of amortization expense and prepaid expenses.

When done manually, recalculation involves selecting a sample of transactions. However, many auditors use computer-assisted audit techniques so that recalculation can occur for a whole class of transactions. For example, in the inventory file, quantity on hand times unit price can be extended, added, and agreed to the general ledger control total.

REPERFORMANCE The redoing of other procedures such as internal controls (i.e., non-mathematical procedures) is called **reperformance**, or **parallel simulation**. This could include rechecking of transfers of information, which consists of tracing amounts to ascertain that when the same information is included in more than one place, it is recorded at the same amount each time. For example, the auditor normally makes limited tests to ascertain that the information in the sales history report has been included for the proper customer and at the correct amount in the subsidiary accounts receivable files and is accurately summarized in the general ledger.

Reperformance relies heavily upon the use of computer-assisted audit tests. The general term **computer-assisted audit tests** (CAATs) is used to describe tests that the auditor conducts using computer software or using the data or systems of the client. The two most common forms of CAATs are the use of test data and generalized audit software.

Test data **Test data** include the use of fictitious transactions to determine whether client programs are functioning as described. For Hillsburg Hardware, test data are used to determine whether the system rejects transactions that it should reject, such as invalid customer numbers, unapproved prices, unapproved credit terms, or invalid

Recalculation—repeating or checking the mathematical accuracy of calculations completed by the client

Reperformance or parallel simulation—the redoing of procedures and internal controls (other than mathematical calculations) of the client by the auditor.

Computer-assisted audit tests (CAATs)—tests that the auditor conducts using computer software or using the data or systems of the client.

Test data—the use of fictitious transactions to determine whether client programs are functioning as described.

dates. This is the most common use of test data for reperformance, since the client data files need not be disrupted and the testing can be performed quickly and efficiently.

Should the auditor wish to determine whether programs are calculating invoice extensions correctly (a test of recalculation), test data that show the expected result would need to be prepared and then entered into the client system. Such a test would result in an invoice being calculated and posted against a client account. A credit transaction would need to be created to reverse this invoice test from the client records (i.e., customer master file, transaction files, general ledger, and inventory files). Some of the inconvenience could be avoided by also establishing a fictitious client, but then the auditor has inserted deliberate fictitious transactions in the client's systems. This is the major drawback of test data. It is also a point-in-time test and verifies that the programs being tested are functioning as tested at the time of the test. The auditor needs to conduct additional tests to determine that these same programs were used during the period under audit.

An **integrated test facility** overcomes the problems with test data by allowing the auditor to use test data in a test environment where it does not affect client accounting records. However, it can be used only with clients who have established such a capability during the initial set-up of their accounting systems.

Generalized audit software Generalized audit software consists of a software package that is used by the auditor to run routines against client data. Two common packages in Canada are Audit Command Language for Personal Computers (ACL-PC) and Interactive Data Extraction and Analysis (IDEA). The auditor obtains a copy of the client data files and runs one or more of the following types of activities against the data file. The examples shown are typical tests that would be run against the customer master file together with open item accounts.

- *Mathematical calculations*: addition of debit and credit amounts, extensions.
- *Aging functions*: aging of the accounts to recreate figures in the aged accounts receivable trial balance.
- *Comparisons*: between the outstanding balance and the credit limit.
- *Sampling*: using random, dollar-unit, interval, or stratification.

Reperformance is also referred to as *parallel simulation*. For example, if the auditor recreates the aged accounts receivable trial balance using client data, this is parallel simulation. This is a dual-purpose test since it ensures the mechanical accuracy of the aging process (a substantive test) while also verifying that the client's aging program is functioning correctly (a controls test).

ANALYTICAL PROCEDURES Analysis is used to identify the components of a financial statement item so that its characteristics can be considered during planning. **Analytical procedures** use comparisons and relationships between financial and non-financial information to determine whether account balances appear reasonable. An example is comparing the gross margin percent in the current year with the preceding year's. For certain audit objectives or small account balances, analytical procedures may be the only evidence needed. For other accounts, other types of evidence may be reduced when analytical procedures indicate that an account balance appears reasonable. In some cases, analytical procedures are also used to isolate accounts or transactions that should be investigated more extensively to help in deciding whether additional verification is needed. An example is comparison of the current period's total repair expense with previous years' and investigation of the difference, if it is significant, to determine the cause of the increase or decrease.

CAS 520 (previously Section 5301) of the *CICA Handbook* states that analytical procedures should be used on all audits to conduct risk assessments and at or near the end of the audit when assessing the financial statements as a whole. For certain audit objectives or small account balances, analytical procedures alone may be sufficient evidence. In most cases, however, additional evidence beyond analytical procedures is also necessary to satisfy the requirement for sufficient competent evidence.

Because analytical procedures are an important part of planning audits, performing tests of each cycle, and completing audits, their use is studied more extensively at the end of this chapter, and in most of the remaining chapters of this book. Normally, specialized software or spreadsheet templates are used to perform analytical procedures.

Internal versus External Documentation

The documents examined by the auditor are the records used by the client to provide information for conducting its business in an organized manner. Since each transaction in the client's organization is normally supported by at least one document or computer file, there is a large volume of this type of evidence available. For example, the client often retains a customer order, a shipping document, and a duplicate sales invoice for each sales transaction. These same documents, whether in paper or electronic form, are useful evidence for verification by the auditor of the accuracy of the client's records for sales transactions. Documentation is a form of evidence widely used in every audit because it is usually readily available to the auditor at a relatively low cost. Sometimes it is the only reasonable type of evidence available.

Documents can be conveniently classified as internal or external. An **internal document** is one that has been prepared and used within the client's organization and is retained without ever going to an outside party such as a customer or a vendor. Examples of internal documents include duplicate sales invoices, employees' time reports, exception reports, and inventory receiving reports. An **external document** is one that has been in the hands of someone outside the client's organization who is a party to the transaction being documented but that is either currently in the hands of the client or readily accessible. In some cases, external documents originate outside the client's organization and end up in the hands of the client. Examples of this type of external document are vendors' invoices, cancelled notes payable, and insurance policies. Other documents, such as cancelled cheques, originate with the client, go to an outsider, and are finally returned to the client.

The primary determinant of the auditor's willingness to accept a document as reliable evidence is whether it is internal or external, and when internal, whether it was created and processed under conditions of good internal control. Internal documents created and processed under conditions of weak internal control may not constitute reliable evidence.

Since external documents have been in the hands of both the client and another party to the transaction, there is some indication that both members are in agreement about the information and the conditions stated on the document. Therefore, external documents are regarded as more reliable evidence than internal ones. Some external documents have exceptional reliability because they are prepared with considerable care and, frequently, have been reviewed by lawyers or other qualified experts. Examples include title papers to property such as land, insurance policies, indenture agreements, and contracts.

When auditors use documentation to support recorded transactions or amounts, it is often referred to as **vouching**. To vouch recorded acquisition transactions, the auditor might, for example, trace from the acquisitions report to supporting vendors' invoices and receiving reports and thereby satisfy the occurrence objective. If the auditor traces from receiving reports to the acquisitions report to satisfy the completeness objective, it would not be appropriate to call it vouching, since this would be reperformance.

It is common, in many companies, for a portion of clients' documentation to be available only in electronic form. For example, many companies use EDI (Electronic Data Interchange—the electronic exchange of standardized business transactions). This change in business practices increases the dependence of organizations on computer-based information systems. Purchase, shipping, billing, cash receipt, and cash

Internal document—a document, such as an employee time report, that is prepared and used within the client's organization.

External document—a document, such as a vendor's invoice, that has been used by an outside party to the transaction being documented and that the client now has or can easily obtain.

Vouching—the use of documentation to support recorded transactions or amounts.

concept check

C6-3 Provide one example of each of the seven methods of evidence collection.

C6-4 Why are CAATs important for recalculation and reperformance?

C6-5 What is the difference between internal and external documentation?

disbursement transactions may be available only in electronic form. Financial statement assertions most affected by EDI are completeness and accuracy. The auditor would also need to assess authorization of transactions, resulting in a need to test automated controls for these objectives.

Other forms of automation, such as image processing systems, whereby documents are scanned and converted into electronic images rather than being stored in paper format, also require changes in audit techniques. Auditors need to assess the strength of such electronic evidence based upon controls in place over changes to such documents, just as they would assess the strength of internal paper documentation.

③ Choosing the Right Type of Evidence

Evidence During Risk Assessment

Risk assessment is used as the basis of targeting field work and other procedures. Yet the risk assessment process itself requires the collection of evidence. CAS 315 requires the auditor to use inquiry (e.g., to ask management about its risk assessment process), analytical procedures (e.g., to consider relationships in the financial statements), as well as observation and inspection. CAS 315 goes on to describe the work that the auditor should complete to obtain an understanding of the entity, its business environment, and systems of internal control. This process is discussed further in Chapter 8.

Reliability of Types of Evidence

The first five criteria for determining the reliability of evidence (independence of provider, effectiveness of controls, auditor's direct knowledge, qualifications of provider, and objectivity of evidence), discussed in the first section of this chapter, are related to the seven types of evidence in Table 6-4. Several observations are apparent from a study of this table.

Table 6-4	Reliability of Types of Evidence Collection Methods				
	Criteria to Determine Reliability				
Type of Evidence	Independence of Provider	Effectiveness of Client's Internal Control	Auditor's Direct Knowledge	Qualifications of Provider	Objectivity of Evidence
Inspection	High (auditor does)	Varies	High	Normally high (auditor does)	High
Observation	High (auditor does)	Varies	High	Normally high (auditor does)	Medium
Inquires of the client	Low (client provides)	Not applicable	Low	Varies	Varies—low to high
Confirmation	High	Not applicable	Low	Varies—usually high	High
Recalculation	High (auditor does)	Varies	High	High (auditor does)	High
Reperformance	High (auditor does)	Varies	High	High (auditor does)	High
Analytical procedures	High/low (auditor does/client responds)	Varies	High	Not applicable	Low

First, the effectiveness of the client's internal controls has a significant effect on the reliability of most types of evidence. For example, automated calculations and procedures from a company with effective internal controls are more reliable than manual calculations because the calculations are more likely to be consistent. Similarly, analytical procedures will not be appropriate evidence if the internal controls that produced the data provide information of questionable accuracy.

Second, both inspection and reperformance are likely to be highly reliable if internal controls are effective. These two types of evidence effectively illustrate that equally reliable evidence may be completely different. Inspection involves examining an asset (such as inventory, or a fixed asset such as equipment) at a point in time, while reperformance can be used to redo work that has occurred throughout the year, such as posting of transactions or comparison of documents.

Third, some types of evidence are rarely sufficient to provide competent evidence to satisfy any objective. From examining Table 6-4 we see that observation, inquiries of the client, and analytical procedures are examples of this.

Cost of Types of Evidence

The two most expensive types of evidence are inspection and confirmation. Inspection is costly because it normally requires the auditor's presence when the client is counting the asset, often on the balance sheet date. For example, inspection of inventory can result in several auditors travelling to widely separated geographical locations. Confirmation is costly because the auditor must follow careful procedures in the confirmation preparation, mailing, and receipt, and in the follow-up of non-responses and exceptions.

Reperformance and analytical procedures are moderately costly. If client personnel locate documents for the auditor and organize them for convenient use, these procedures usually have a fairly low cost. Analytical procedures require the auditor to decide which analytical procedures to use, enter or transfer data to make the calculations, and evaluate the results. Doing so may take considerable time.

When auditors must find the documents themselves, audit techniques can be extremely costly. Even under ideal circumstances, inspection of information and data on documents is sometimes complex and requires interpretation and analysis. For example, it is usually time-consuming to read and evaluate a client's contracts, lease agreements, and minutes of the board of directors' meetings.

The three least expensive types of evidence are observation, inquiries of the client, and recalculation. Observation is normally done concurrently with other audit procedures. An auditor can easily observe whether client personnel are following appropriate inventory counting procedures at the same time he or she counts a sample of inventory (physical examination). Inquiries of clients are done extensively on every audit and normally have a low cost. Certain inquiries may be costly, such as obtaining written statements from the client documenting discussions throughout the audit.

Recalculation can vary in cost. It can be low when it involves simple calculations and tracing that can be done at the auditor's convenience. Costs per transaction are reduced when the auditor's computer software is used to perform these tests after obtaining a copy of the client data files.

Application of Types of Evidence to Evidence Decisions

An application of three types of evidence to the last four evidence decisions for one audit objective is shown in Table 6–5 on the next page. First, review the examples in column 5 of Table 5-3 on page 136. These are the specific balance-related objectives of the audit of inventory for Hillsburg Hardware Limited. The overall objective is to obtain persuasive evidence (sufficient, appropriate, and timely), at reasonable cost, that inventory is materially correct. The auditor must therefore decide which audit procedures to use to satisfy each objective, what the sample size should be for each procedure, which items from the population to include in the sample, and when to perform each procedure.

Table 6-5	Types of Evidence and Decisions for a Specific Audit Objective*			
		Evidence Decisions		
Type of Evidence	Audit Procedure	Sample Size	Items to Select	Timing
Observation	Observe client's personnel counting inventory to determine whether they are properly following instructions	All count teams	Not applicable	Balance sheet date
Inspection	Count a sample of inventory and compare quantity and description to client's counts	120 items	40 items with large dollar value, plus 80 randomly selected	Balance sheet date
Reperformance	Compare quantity on client's perpetual records to quantity on client's counts	70 items	30 items with large dollar value, plus 40 randomly selected	Balance sheet date

*Balance-related audit objective: Inventory quantities on the client's perpetual records agree with items physically on hand.

One objective from Table 5-3 (see page 136) is selected for further study: inventory quantities agree with items physically on hand. Several types of evidence collection methods are available to satisfy this objective. Table 6-5 lists three types of evidence and gives examples of the last four evidence decisions for each type.

Mandated Evidence Collection

 The auditor has substantial discretion in designing audit procedures in response to assessed risks. CAS 330, The auditor's responses to assessed risks, provides specific times when specific types of tests should be conducted as part of the evidence mix.

TESTS OF CONTROLS WHERE SUBSTANTIVE PROCEDURES ARE INSUFFICIENT With highly automated systems, such as electronic data interchange and electronic banking, primary reliance upon accuracy and completeness of transactions could rest with the computer programs functioning correctly. This is an example where substantive

auditing in action 6-1
Research on Security is a Warning to Keep Your Evidence Secure!

Observation by an auditor at a client can be an important indicator of the quality of security controls over client data. For example, if employees share passwords or have their password information written on a piece of paper, access to client data could be easy.

Lineberry described methods of accessing information or circumventing controls: targetting busy times of the day, creating a false sense of familiarity, and appearing to be unconcerned about the outcome.

Auditors could be liable if they are carrying client data on a laptop or in a briefcase, for example, and the laptop or briefcase is stolen.

Simple precautions, such as always securing documents in locked spaces, or returning them to the client, can help prevent auditor liability for potential violations of privacy laws and the resultant possibility of identity theft.

Data stored on laptops (even spreadsheets and Word files!) should be password protected or encrypted, especially if the equipment is used by more than one person (for example, if your laptop is used by more than one family member).

Sources: 1. Barker, Paul, "The perils of privacy," *National Post*, December 10, 2007, www.nationalpost.com, Accessed: March 14, 2008. 2. Lineberry, Stephen, "The human element: the weakest link in information security," *The Journal of Accountancy*, 204(5), 2007, p. 44–49.

procedures alone (for example, recalculation of interest charges) could not provide sufficient evidence with respect to an assertion. CAS 330 par. 8(b) requires that in such cases, the auditor should also design and perform tests of controls.

FINANCIAL STATEMENT CLOSING PROCESS Unfortunately, financial statements are subject to manipulation. If management, or others, choose to misstate financial statements, they could process journal entries that do not have adequate support or authorization. This could result in the financial statements disagreeing with the underlying financial records. Because of these risks, the auditor is required to (a) compare the underlying accounting records (such as subsidiary ledgers or computer files) to the general ledger accounts with reconciliation to the financial statements and (b) review those material adjustments or journal entries and their supporting documentation that are part of the financial statement preparation process (CAS 330, par. 21).

SUBSTANTIVE PROCEDURES REQUIRED FOR MATERIAL RISKS As part of the risk assessment process, the auditor identifies those audit objectives, transactions, and accounts that are prone to a high risk of material misstatement. CAS 330 par. 22 mandates that tests of details (substantive procedures) should be completed for such accounts. For example, if the auditor believes that there is a potential for material misstatement in the bad-debt allowance for accounts receivable (valuation audit objective) and has already conducted detailed analytical review, further specific tests of detail, such as looking at individual accounts for their collectability (e.g., the extent of payments received subsequent to the year end), would be required.

concept check

C6-6 How does the quality of internal controls affect evidence?

C6-7 Describe two audit techniques that the auditor should use to reduce the risk of financial statement misstatement during the financial statement closing process.

Special Terms

Audit procedures are the detailed steps, usually written in the form of instructions, for the accumulation of the seven types of audit evidence. They should be sufficiently clear to enable members of the audit team to understand what is to be done.

Several different terms are commonly used to describe audit procedures. These are presented and defined in Table 6-6 on the next page. To help you understand the terms, an illustrative audit procedure and the type of evidence are shown in the table.

Analytical Procedures and Their Role

Analytical Procedures

Analytical procedures use financial and non-financial data in meaningful comparisons and relationships to determine whether account balances or other data appear reasonable. The results of the analytical procedures help in designing the nature, timing, and extent of other audit procedures so that sufficient appropriate audit evidence may be obtained and the appropriate opinion given in the auditor's report.

For example, the auditor might compare current year recorded commissions expense to total recorded sales multiplied by the average commission rate as a test of the overall reasonableness of recorded commissions. For this analytical procedure to be relevant, the auditor has likely concluded that recorded sales are correctly stated, all sales earn a commission, and there is an average actual commission rate that is readily determined.

CAS 520 provides standards for the use of analytical review. It is recommended that the auditor use analysis in planning the audit, as a substantive procedure, and in the overall evaluation of the financial statements. Advisable actions in the previous Section 5301 (that have become a requirement in CAS 520) are that the auditor evaluate the reliability of the information that is used for the analytical procedures, as well as follow up and corroborate any explanations that management gives when discussing the results.

CAS

Table 6-6	Terms, Audit Procedures, and Types of Evidence	
Term and Definition	**Illustrative Audit Procedure**	**Types of Evidence**
Examine—A reasonably detailed study of a document or record to determine specific facts about it.	Examine a sample of vendors' invoices or data to determine whether the goods or services received are reasonable and of the type normally used by the client's business.	Inspection
Scan—A less detailed examination of a document or record to determine if there is something unusual warranting further investigation.	Scan the sales report, looking for large and unusual transactions. For large sales history files, use audit software to run an exception report for large amounts.	Analytical procedures
Read—An examination of written information to determine facts pertinent to the audit and the recording of those facts in a working paper.	Read the minutes of a board of directors' meeting, and summarize all information that is pertinent to the financial statements in a working paper.	Inspection
Compute—A calculation done by the auditor independent of the client.	Compute the inventory turnover ratios, and compare to previous years as a test of inventory.	Analytical procedures
Recompute—A calculation done to determine whether a client's calculation is correct.	Recompute the unit sales price times the number of units for a sample of duplicate sales invoices, and compare the totals to the client's calculations.	Recalculation
Foot—An addition of a column of numbers to determine if the total is the same as the client's.	Foot the sales history files using audit software, and compare all totals to the general ledger.	Recalculation
Trace—An instruction normally associated with documentation or reperformance. The instruction should state what the auditor is tracing and where it is being traced from and to. Frequently, an audit procedure that includes the term "trace" will also include a second instruction, such as "compare" or "recompute."	Trace a sample of sales transactions from the sales reports to sales invoices, and compare customer name, date, and the total dollar value of the sale. Trace postings from the sales reports to the general ledger accounts.	Recalculation Reperformance
Compare—A comparison of information in two different locations. The instruction should state which information is being compared in as much detail as practical.	Select a sample of sales invoices and compare the unit selling price as stated on the invoice to the master files of unit selling prices authorized by management.	Reperformance
Count—A determination of assets on hand at a given time. This term should only be associated with the type of evidence defined as physical examination.	Count petty cash on hand at the balance sheet date.	Inspection
Observe—The act of observation should be associated with the type of evidence defined as observation.	Observe whether the two inventory count teams independently count and record inventory quantities.	Observation
Inquire—The act of inquiry should be associated with the type of evidence defined as inquiry.	Inquire of management whether there is any obsolete inventory on hand at the balance sheet date.	Inquiries of client

Purposes and Timing of Analytical Procedures

The most important reasons for utilizing analytical procedures are discussed in this section. As a part of that discussion, the appropriate timing is also examined.

UNDERSTANDING THE CLIENT'S BUSINESS In Chapter 8, there is a discussion of the need to obtain knowledge about the client's industry and business. Analytical procedures are one of the techniques commonly used in obtaining that knowledge.

Generally, an auditor considers knowledge and experience about a client company obtained in prior years as a starting point for planning the examination for the current year. By conducting analytical procedures where the current year's unaudited information is compared with prior years' audited information, changes are highlighted. These changes can represent important trends or specific events, all of which will influence audit planning. For example, a decline in gross margin percentages over time may indicate increasing competition in the company's market area and the need to consider inventory pricing more carefully during the audit. Similarly, an increase in the balance in capital assets may indicate a significant acquisition that must be reviewed.

ASSESSMENT OF THE ENTITY'S ABILITY TO CONTINUE AS A GOING CONCERN Analytical procedures are often useful as an indication that the client company is encountering severe financial difficulty. The likelihood of financial failure must be considered by the auditor in the assessment of audit-related risks (discussed further in the next chapter) as well as in connection with management's use of the going-concern assumption in preparing the financial statements. Certain analytical procedures can be helpful in that regard. For example, if a higher-than-normal ratio of long-term debt to net worth is combined with a lower-than-average ratio of profits to total assets, a relatively high risk of financial failure may be indicated. Not only would such conditions affect the audit plan, they may indicate that substantial doubt exists about the entity's ability to continue as a going concern, which would require disclosure in the notes to the financial statements.

INDICATION OF THE PRESENCE OF POSSIBLE MISSTATEMENTS IN THE FINANCIAL STATEMENTS Significant unexpected differences between the current year's unaudited financial data and other data used in comparisons are commonly referred to as **unusual fluctuations**. Unusual fluctuations occur when significant differences are not expected but do exist or when significant differences are expected but do not exist. In either case, one of the possible reasons for an unusual fluctuation is the presence of an accounting error, fraud, or other irregularities. If the unusual fluctuation is large, the auditor must determine the reason for it and whether the cause is a valid economic event, not an error or fraud. For example, in comparing the ratio of the allowance for uncollectible accounts receivable to gross accounts receivable with that of the previous year, the auditor may discover that the ratio had decreased while, at the same time, accounts receivable turnover also decreased. The combination of these two pieces of information would indicate a possible understatement of the allowance. This aspect of analytical procedures is often referred to as attention directing because it results in the performance of more detailed procedures by the auditor in the specific audit areas where errors or fraud and other irregularities might be found.

> **Unusual fluctuations**—significant unexpected differences, indicated by analytical procedures, between the current year's unaudited financial data and other data used in comparisons.

REDUCTION OF DETAILED AUDIT TESTS When an analytical procedure reveals no unusual fluctuations, the implication is that the possibility of a material misstatement is minimized. In that case, the analytical procedure constitutes substantive evidence in support of the fair statement of the related account balances, and it is possible to perform fewer detailed tests in connection with those accounts. For example, if analytical procedure results of a small account balance such as prepaid insurance are favourable, no detailed tests may be necessary. In other cases, certain audit procedures can be eliminated, sample sizes can be reduced, or the timing of the procedures can be moved farther away from the balance sheet date.

Analytical procedures are usually inexpensive compared with tests of details, since they can often be automated. Most auditors prefer to reduce tests of details by doing analytical procedures whenever possible. To illustrate, it may be far less expensive to calculate and review sales and accounts receivable ratios than to confirm accounts receivable. If it is possible to reduce confirmations by doing analytical procedures, considerable cost savings can occur.

The extent to which analytical procedures provide useful substantive evidence depends on their reliability in the circumstances. For some audit objectives and in some circumstances, they may be the most effective procedure to apply. These objectives might include proper classification of transactions, completeness of recording transactions, and accuracy of management's judgments and estimates in certain areas, such as the allowance for uncollectible accounts. For other audit objectives and circumstances, analytical procedures may be considered attention directing at best and not to be relied on for gathering substantive evidence. An example is determining the validity of sales transactions.

CAS

TIMING Analytical procedures are performed principally at any of three times during an engagement. Previously Section 5301 addressed the different uses of analytical procedures. Now there are three CASs: CAS 315 during risk assessment, CAS 330 for use as a general risk response technique, and CAS 520 as substantive procedures. CAS 315 par. 6 requires risk assessment that includes analysis, used in the planning phase as risk assessment procedures to determine the nature, extent, and timing of other auditing procedures to be performed. Use of analytical procedures during planning helps the auditor identify significant matters requiring special consideration later in the engagement. For example, the calculation of inventory turnover before inventory price tests are done may indicate the need for special care during those tests.

Analytical procedures are often done during the testing phase of the examination in conjunction with other audit procedures. For example, the prepaid portion of each insurance policy might be compared with the same policy for the previous year as a part of doing tests of prepaid insurance.

CAS 520 par. 6 states that analytical procedures should be used during the completion phase of the audit. Such tests are useful at that point as a final review for material misstatements or financial problems and help the auditor take a final "objective look" at the financial statements that have been audited. It is common for a partner to do a detailed review of the analytical procedures during the final review of working papers and financial statements. Typically, a partner has a good understanding of the client and its business because of ongoing relationships. Knowledge of the client's business combined with effective analytical procedures is a way to identify possible oversights in an audit.

The purposes of analytical procedures for each of the three different times they are performed are shown in Figure 6-2. The shaded boxes in the matrix indicate that

Figure 6-2	Timing and Purposes of Analytical Procedures

Purpose	(Required) Planning Phase	Testing Phase	(Required) Completion Phase
Understand client's industry and business and assess risks	X		
Assess going concern	X		
Indicate possible misstatements (attention directing)	X		X
Reduce detailed tests		X	

Table 6-7	Example of Comparison of Client and Industry Data			
	Client		Industry	
	2008	2007	2008	2007
Inventory turnover	3.4%	3.5%	3.9%	3.4%
Gross margin percent	26.3%	26.4%	27.3%	26.2%

certain purposes are applicable to a certain phase. Note that purposes vary for different phases of the audit. Analytical procedures are performed during the planning phase for all four purposes, whereas the other two phases are used primarily to determine appropriate audit evidence and to reach conclusions about the fair presentation of financial statements.

Five Types of Analytical Procedures

An important part of using analytical procedures is selecting the most appropriate procedures. There are five major types of analytical procedures. In each case, auditors compare client data with the following:

1. Industry data.
2. Similar prior-period data.
3. Client-determined expected results.
4. Auditor-determined expected results.
5. Expected results using non-financial data.

These procedures are facilitated by many of the firm's software tools that provide direct linkages to client data.

COMPARE CLIENT AND INDUSTRY DATA Suppose you are doing an audit and obtain information about the client and the average company in the client's industry (Table 6-7).

If we look only at client information for the two ratios shown, the company appears to be stable with no apparent indication of difficulties. However, compared with the industry, the client's position has worsened. In 2007, the client did slightly better than the industry in both ratios. In 2008, it did not do nearly as well. Although these two ratios by themselves may not indicate significant problems, the example illustrates how comparison of client data with industry data may provide useful information about the client's performance. For example, the company may have lost market share, its pricing may not be competitive, it may have incurred abnormal costs, or it may have obsolete items in inventory.

The Financial Post Company (**www.financialpost.com**) and Dun & Bradstreet Canada Limited (**www.dnb.ca**) accumulate financial information for thousands of larger companies and compile the data for different lines of business; local credit bureaus compile data for companies in their community. Many public accounting firms purchase these publications for use as a basis for industry comparisons in their audits.

The most important benefits of industry comparisons are that they are an aid to understanding the client's business and are an indication of the likelihood of financial failure. The ratios in Dun & Bradstreet Canada, for example, are primarily of a type that bankers and other credit executives use in evaluating whether a company will be able to repay a loan. The same information is useful to auditors in assessing the relative strength of the client's capital structure, its borrowing capacity, and its likelihood of financial failure.

A major weakness of using industry ratios for auditing is the difference between the nature of the client's financial information and that of the firms making up the industry totals. Since the industry data are broad averages, the comparisons may not be meaningful. Frequently, the client's line of business is not the same as the industry standards. In addition, different companies follow different accounting methods, and this affects the comparability of data. This does not mean that industry comparisons should not be made. Rather, it is an indication of the need for care in interpreting the results.

COMPARE CLIENT DATA WITH SIMILAR PRIOR-PERIOD DATA Suppose the gross margin for a company has been between 26 and 27 percent for each of the past four years but is 23 percent in the current year. This decline in gross margin should be a concern to the auditor. The cause of the decline could be a change in economic conditions. However, it could also be caused by misstatements in the financial statements, such as sales or purchase cut-off errors, unrecorded sales, overstated accounts payable, or inventory costing errors. The auditor should determine the cause of the decline in gross margin and consider the effect, if any, on evidence accumulation.

There are a wide variety of analytical procedures where client data are compared with similar data from one or more prior periods. The following are common examples.

Compare the current year's balance with that for the preceding year One of the easiest ways to make this test is to include the preceding year's adjusted trial balance results in a separate column of the current year's trial balance spreadsheet. The auditor can easily compare the current year's and previous year's balance to decide early in the audit whether a particular account should receive more than the normal amount of attention because of a significant change in the balance. For example, if the auditor observes a substantial increase in supplies expense, the auditor should determine whether the cause was an increased use of supplies, a misstatement in the account due to a misclassification, or a misstatement in supplies inventory.

Compare the detail of a total balance with similar detail for the preceding year If there have been no significant changes in the client's operations in the current year, much of the detail making up the totals in the financial statements should also remain unchanged. By briefly comparing the detail of the current period with a similar detail of the preceding period, it is often possible to isolate information that needs further examination. Comparison of details may take the form of details over time or details at a point in time. A common example of the former is comparing the monthly totals for the current and preceding year for sales, repairs, and other accounts. An example of the latter is comparing the details of loans payable at the end of the current year with those at the end of the preceding year.

Compute ratios and percentage relationships for comparison with previous years The comparison of totals or details with previous years as described in the two preceding paragraphs has two shortcomings. First, it fails to consider growth or decline in business activity. Second, relationships of data to other data, such as sales to cost of goods sold, are ignored. Ratio and percentage relationships overcome both shortcomings. The earlier example about the decline in gross margin is a common percentage relationship used by auditors.

A few types of ratios and internal comparisons are included in Table 6-8 to show the widespread use of ratio analysis. In all cases, the comparisons should be with calculations made in previous years for the same client. There are many potential ratios and comparisons available for use by an auditor. Subsequent chapters dealing with specific audit areas describe other examples. Normally, the auditor will arrange to have trial balance information entered annually into audit software that calculates a range of ratios and comparisons automatically.

Table 6-8	Internal Comparisons and Relationships
Ratio or Comparison	**Possible Misstatement**
Raw material turnover for a manufacturing company.	Misstatement of inventory or cost of goods sold or obsolescence of raw material inventory.
Sales commissions divided by net sales.	Misstatement of sales commissions.
Sales returns and allowances divided by gross sales.	Misclassified sales returns and allowances or unrecorded returns or allowances subsequent to year end.
Goods and services tax payable (current year) divided by goods and services tax payable (preceding year).	Failure to properly accrue the goods and services tax owing at year end.
Each of the individual manufacturing expenses as a percentage of total manufacturing expense.	Significant misstatement of individual expenses within a total.

Many of the ratios and percentages used for comparison with previous years are the same ones used for comparison with industry data. For example, it is useful to compare current year gross margin with industry averages and those of previous years. The same can be said for most of the ratios described in Appendix 6A beginning on page 191.

There are also numerous potential comparisons of current and prior-period data beyond those normally available from industry data. For example, the ratio of each expense category to total sales can be compared with those of previous years. Similarly, in a multi-unit operation (e.g., a retail chain), internal comparisons for each unit can be made with previous periods (e.g., the revenue and expenses of individual retail outlets in a chain of stores can be compared).

Auditors often prepare common-size financial statements for one or more years that display all items as a percent of a common base, such as sales. Common-size financial statements allow for comparison between companies or for the same company over different periods, revealing trends and providing insight into how different companies compare. Common-size income statement data for the past three years for Hillsburg Hardware are included in Figure 6-3 on the next page. The auditor should calculate income statement account balances as a percent of sales when the level of sales has changed from the prior year—a likely occurrence in many businesses. Hillsburg's sales have increased significantly over the prior year. Note that accounts such as cost of goods sold, sales salaries, and commissions have also increased significantly but are fairly consistent as a percent of sales, which we expect for these accounts.

The auditor is likely to require further explanation and corroborating evidence for the changes in advertising, bad-debt expense, and office repairs and maintenance.

- Note that advertising expense has increased as a percent of sales. One possible explanation is the development of a new advertising campaign.
- The dollar amount of bad-debt expense has not changed significantly but has decreased as a percent of sales. The auditor needs to gather additional evidence to determine whether bad-debt expense and the allowance for doubtful accounts are understated.
- Repairs and maintenance expense has also increased. Fluctuations in this account are not unusual if the client has incurred unexpected repairs. The auditor should investigate major expenditures in this account to determine whether they include any amounts that should be capitalized as a fixed asset.

Figure 6-3   Hillsburg Hardware Common-Size Income Statement

HILLSBURG HARDWARE LIMITED
COMMON-SIZE INCOME STATEMENT
Three Years Ending December 31, 2008

	2008		2007		2006	
	(000) Preliminary	% of Net Sales	(000) Audited	% of Net Sales	(000) Audited	% of Net Sales
Sales	$144,328	100.87	$132,421	100.91	$123,737	100.86
Less: Returns and allowances	1,242	0.87	1,195	0.91	1,052	0.86
Net sales	143,086	100.00	131,226	100.00	122,685	100.00
Cost of sales	103,241	72.15	94,876	72.30	88,724	72.32
Gross profit	39,845	27.85	36,350	27.70	33,961	27.68
Selling expense						
Salaries and commissions	7,739	5.41	7,044	5.37	6,598	5.38
Sales payroll benefits	1,422	0.99	1,298	0.99	1,198	0.98
Travel and entertainment	1,110	0.78	925	0.70	797	0.65
Advertising	2,611	1.82	1,920	1.46	1,790	1.46
Sales and promotional literature	322	0.22	425	0.32	488	0.40
Sales meetings and training	925	0.65	781	0.60	767	0.62
Miscellaneous sales expense	681	0.48	506	0.39	456	0.37
Total selling expense	14,810	10.35	12,899	9.83	12,094	9.86
Administration expense						
Executive and office salaries	5,524	3.86	5,221	3.98	5,103	4.16
Administrative payroll benefits	682	0.48	655	0.50	633	0.52
Travel and entertainment	562	0.39	595	0.45	542	0.44
Computer maintenance and supplies	860	0.60	832	0.63	799	0.65
Stationery and supplies	763	0.53	658	0.50	695	0.57
Postage	244	0.17	251	0.19	236	0.19
Telephone and fax	722	0.51	626	0.48	637	0.52
Rent	312	0.22	312	0.24	312	0.25
Legal fees and retainers	383	0.27	321	0.25	283	0.23
Auditing and related services	303	0.21	288	0.22	265	0.22
Amortization	1,452	1.01	1,443	1.10	1,505	1.23
Bad debt expense	3,323	2.32	3,394	2.59	3,162	2.58
Insurance	723	0.51	760	0.58	785	0.64
Office repairs and maintenance	844	0.59	538	0.41	458	0.37
Miscellaneous office expense	644	0.45	621	0.47	653	0.53
Miscellaneous general expense	324	0.23	242	0.18	275	0.22
Total administrative expenses	17,665	12.35	16,757	12.77	16,343	13.32
Total selling and administrative expenses	32,475	22.70	29,656	22.60	28,437	23.18
Operating income	7,370	5.15	6,694	5.10	5,524	4.50
Other income and expense						
Interest expense	2,409	1.68	2,035	1.55	2,173	1.77
Gain on sale of assets	(720)	(0.50)	0	0.00	0	0.00
Earnings before income taxes	5,681	3.97	4,659	3.55	3,351	2.73
Provision for income taxes	1,747	1.22	1,465	1.12	1,072	0.87
Net income	$ 3,934	2.75	$ 3,194	2.43	$ 2,279	1.86

COMPARE CLIENT DATA WITH CLIENT-DETERMINED EXPECTED RESULTS Most companies prepare budgets for various aspects of their operations and financial results. Since **budgets** represent the client's expectations for the period, an investigation of the most significant areas in which differences exist between budgeted and actual results may indicate potential misstatements. The absence of differences may also indicate that misstatements are unlikely. It is common, for example, in the audit of local, provincial, and federal governmental units to use this type of analytical procedure.

Budgets—written records of the client's expectations for the period; a comparison of budgets with actual results may indicate whether or not misstatements are likely.

Whenever client data are compared with budgets, there are two special concerns. First, the auditor must evaluate whether the budgets were realistic plans. In some organizations, budgets are prepared with little thought or care and therefore are not realistic expectations. Such information has little value as audit evidence. The second concern is the possibility that current financial information was changed by client personnel to conform to the budget. If that has occurred, the auditor will find no differences in comparing actual data with the budget, even if there are misstatements in the financial statements. Discussing budget procedures with client personnel is done to satisfy the first concern. Assessment of control risk and detailed audit tests of actual data are usually done to minimize the likelihood of the latter concern.

COMPARE CLIENT DATA WITH AUDITOR-DETERMINED EXPECTED RESULTS A second common type of comparison of client data with expected results occurs when the auditor calculates the expected balance for comparison with the actual balance. In this type of analytical procedure, the auditor makes an estimate of what an account balance should be by relating it to some other balance sheet or income statement account or accounts, or by making a projection based on some historical trend.

An example of calculating an expected value based on relationships of accounts is the independent calculation of interest expense on long-term notes payable by multiplying the ending monthly balance in notes payable by the average monthly interest rate (see Figure 6–4 on the next page). This independent estimate based upon the relationship between interest expense and notes payable is used to test the reasonableness of recorded interest expense.

An example of using a historical trend would be where the moving average of the allowance for uncollectible accounts receivable as a percent of gross accounts receivable is applied to the balance of gross accounts receivable at the end of the audit year to determine an expected value for the current allowance.

COMPARE CLIENT DATA WITH EXPECTED RESULTS USING NON-FINANCIAL DATA Suppose that in auditing a hotel, you can determine the number of rooms, room rate for each room, and occupancy rate. Using those data, it is relatively easy to estimate total revenue from rooms to compare with recorded revenue. The same approach can sometimes be used to estimate such accounts as tuition revenue at universities (average tuition times enrollment), factory payroll (total hours worked times wage rate), and cost of materials sold (units times materials cost per unit).

The major concern in using non-financial data is the accuracy of the data. In the previous illustration, it is appropriate to use an estimated calculation of hotel revenue as audit evidence unless the auditor is not satisfied with the reasonableness of the count of the number of rooms, room rate, and occupancy rate. It would be more difficult for the auditor to evaluate the accuracy of the occupancy rate than the other two items.

Using Statistical Techniques and Computer Software

The use of statistical techniques is desirable to make analytical procedures more relevant. Many auditors use computer software to make statistical and non-statistical calculations easier. These two auditors' tools are discussed briefly.

STATISTICAL TECHNIQUES Several statistical techniques that aid in interpreting results can be applied to analytical procedures. The advantages of using statistical techniques are the ability to make more sophisticated calculations and objectivity.

The most common statistical technique for analytical procedures is regression analysis. Regression analysis is used to evaluate the reasonableness of a recorded balance by relating (regressing) the total to other relevant information. For example, the auditor might conclude that total selling expenses should be related to total sales, the previous year's selling expenses, and the number of salespeople. The auditor would then use regression analysis to statistically determine an estimated value of

Figure 6-4	Hillsburg Hardware Overall Tests of Interest Expense December 31, 2008

Hillsburg Hardware Limited
Overall Test of Interest Expense
12/31/08

Schedule __N-3___ Date
Prepared by __TM___ _3/06/09_
Approved by __JW___ _3/12/09_

Interest expense per general ledger   2,408,642 [1]

Computation of estimate:

Short-term loans:

Balance outstanding at month-end: [2]

Jan.	2,950,000
Feb.	3,184,000
Mar.	3,412,000
Apr.	3,768,000
May	2,604,000
June	1,874,000
July	1,400,000
Aug.	1,245,000
Sept.	1,046,000
Oct.	854,000
Nov.	2,526,000
Dec.	4,180,000
Total	29,043,000

Average ($\div$12) 2,420,250 @ 10.5% [3]   254,126

Long-term loans:

Beginning balance 26,520,000 [2]
Ending balance   24,120,000 [2]
                   50,640,000

Average ($\div$2) 25,320,000 @ 8.5% [4] 2,152,200

Estimated total interest expense   2,406,326

Difference   2,316 [5]

Legend and Comments
[1] Agrees with general ledger and working trial balance.
[2] Obtained from general ledger.
[3] Estimated based on examination of several notes throughout the year with rates ranging from 10% to 11%.
[4] Agrees with permanent file schedule of long-term debt.
[5] Difference not significant. Indicates that interest expense per books is reasonable.

selling expenses for comparison with recorded values, or to assess the profitability of different product lines. Regression and other statistical methods commonly used for analytical procedures can be found in several advanced auditing texts dealing with statistical sampling techniques for auditing.

AUDITOR'S COMPUTER SOFTWARE Computer-based **audit software** can be used to prepare audit working papers and perform extensive analytical procedures as a byproduct of other audit testing. In the past several years, most public accounting firms have implemented a variety of computer software as tools for doing more efficient and effective audits. One feature common to all such software is the ability

Audit software—software used to automate preparation of audit working papers or the analysis of client data files.

Working Paper Document Management

How many documents do you have on your personal computer? You may have several hundred, pertaining to correspondence, courses that you have worked on, or other types of projects. My system has over 60,000 files from different versions of courses and books that I have written over the years.

Audit firms regularly update their forms to reflect current standards and best business practices. It can be difficult to ensure that employees are using the current version, though, if the practice is to download versions onto their personal computer systems.

Best practices require audit firms to have current forms and documents accessible on a central server to audit staff. Employees are required to use only the forms from the central server every time they add a document to the audit file.

This helps to ensure that only authorized employees access current forms (by means of password access) and that only up-to-date forms are used, since they are always obtained from the central server.

Source: Interviews with accounting firms held in summer 2008 by I. Splettstoesser-Hogeterp.

---

to input or import the client's general ledger into the auditor's computer system. Adjusting entries and financial statements are thereby computerized to save time. These are linked to working papers and cross-referenced, saving many hours of tedious working-paper referencing. Some systems also link directly to client data.

The general ledger information for the client is saved and carried forward in the auditor's computerized data file year after year. The existence of current and previous years' general ledger information on the auditor's computer files permits extensive and inexpensive computerized analytical calculations. The analytical information can also be shown in different forms such as graphs and charts to help interpret the data.

A major benefit of computerized analytical procedures is the ease of updating the calculations when adjusting entries to the client's statements are made. If there are several adjusting entries to the client's records, the analytical procedures calculations can be quickly revised. For example, a change in inventory and cost of goods sold affects a large number of ratios. All affected ratios can be recalculated immediately.

concept check

C6-8 Why are analytical procedures an important part of the planning process?

C6-9 How can audit software assist the analytical review process?

Appendix 6A
Common Financial Ratios

Auditors' analytical procedures often include the use of general financial ratios during planning and final review of the audited financial statements. These are useful for understanding the most recent events and financial status of the business and for viewing the statements from the perspective of a user. The general financial analysis may be effective in identifying possible problem areas for additional analysis and audit testing as well as business problem areas for which the auditor can provide other assistance. This appendix presents a number of widely used general financial ratios.

Short-Term Debt-Paying Ability

Many companies follow an operating cycle whereby production inputs are obtained and converted into finished goods and then sold and converted into cash. This requires an investment in working capital, that is, funds are needed to finance inventories and accounts receivable. A majority of these funds come from trade creditors

Figure 6A-1	Short-Term Debt Ratios

$$\text{Current ratio} = \frac{\text{current assets}}{\text{current liabilities}}$$

$$\text{Quick ratio} = \frac{\text{cash} + \text{marketable securities} + \text{net accounts receivable}}{\text{current liabilities}}$$

$$\text{Cash ratio} = \frac{\text{cash} + \text{marketable securities}}{\text{current liabilities}}$$

and the balance comes from initial capitalization, bank borrowings, and positive net cash flow from operations.

The net working capital position of a company is the excess of current assets over current liabilities and is also measured by the current ratio. Presumably, if net working capital is positive (i.e., the current ratio is greater than 1.0), the company has sufficient available assets to pay its immediate debts; and the greater the excess (the larger the ratio), the better off the company is in this regard. Companies with a comfortable net working capital position are considered preferred customers by their bankers and trade creditors and are given favourable treatment. Companies with inadequate net working capital are in danger of not being able to obtain credit.

However, this is a somewhat simplistic view. The current assets of companies will differ in terms of both valuation and liquidity, and these aspects will affect a company's ability to meet its current obligations. One way to examine this problem is to restrict the analysis to the most available and objective current assets. The quick ratio eliminates inventories from the computation, and the cash ratio further eliminates accounts receivable. Usually, if the cash ratio is greater than 1.0, the company has good short-term debt-paying ability. In some cases, it is appropriate to state marketable securities at market value rather than cost in computing these ratios (see Figure 6A-1).

Short-Term Liquidity

If a company does not have sufficient cash and cash-like items to meet its obligations, the key to its debt-paying ability will be the length of time it takes the company to convert less liquid current assets into cash. This is measured by the short-term liquidity ratios (see Figure 6A-2).

The two turnover ratios—accounts receivable and inventory—are very useful to auditors. Trends in the accounts receivable turnover ratio are frequently used in assessing the reasonableness of the allowance for uncollectible accounts. Trends in the inventory turnover ratio are used in identifying a potential inventory obsolescence problem.

When the short-term liquidity ratios (and the current ratio) are used to examine a company's performance over time or to compare performance among companies,

Figure 6A-2	Short-Term Liquidity Ratios

$$\text{Average accounts receivable turnover} = \frac{\text{gross credit sales net of returns}}{\text{average gross receivables}}$$

$$\text{Average days to collect (or number of days' sales in accounts receivable)} = \frac{\text{average gross receivables} \times 365}{\text{gross credit sales net of returns}}$$

$$\text{Average inventory turnover} = \frac{\text{cost of goods sold}}{\text{average inventory}}$$

$$\text{Average days to sell (or average days' sales in inventory)} = \frac{\text{average inventory} \times 365}{\text{cost of goods sold}}$$

$$\text{Average days to convert inventory to cash} = \text{average days to sell} + \text{average days to collect}$$

differences in inventory accounting methods, fiscal year ends, and cash-credit sales mix can have a significant effect. With regard to inventories, a few companies have adopted the LIFO (last in, first out) method. This can cause inventory values to differ significantly from FIFO (first in, first out) values. When companies with different valuation methods are being compared, the company's LIFO value inventory can be adjusted to FIFO to obtain a better comparison.

When two companies have different fiscal year ends, such that one is on a natural business year that corresponds to the business cycle and the other is not, the simple average gross receivables and inventory figures for the former will be lower. This will tend to cause the company with natural business year to appear more liquid than it really is. If this is a problem, an averaging computation with quarterly data can be used.

Finally, the use of net sales per the financial statements in the receivables liquidity ratios can be a problem when a significant portion of sales is for cash. This will be somewhat mitigated when the proportions are fairly constant among periods or companies for which comparisons are being made.

Ability to Meet Long-Term Debt Obligations and Preferred Dividends

A company's long-run solvency depends on the success of its operations and on its ability to raise capital for expansion or even survival over periods of temporary difficulty. From another point of view, common shareholders will benefit from the leverage obtained from borrowed capital that earns a positive net return.

A key measure in evaluating this long-term structure and capacity is the debt-to-equity ratio (see Figure 6A-3). If this ratio is too high, it may indicate the company has used up its borrowing capacity and has no cushion for future events. If it is too low, it may mean available leverage is not being used to the owners' benefit. If the ratio is trending up, it may mean earnings are too low to support the needs of the enterprise. And, if it is trending down, it may mean the company is doing well and setting the stage for future expansion.

The tangible net assets–to-equity ratio indicates the current quality of the company's equity by removing those assets whose realization is wholly dependent on future operations, such as goodwill. This ratio can be used to better interpret the debt-to-equity ratio.

Lenders are generally concerned about a company's ability to meet interest payments as well as its ability to repay principal amounts. The latter will be appraised by evaluating the company's long-term prospects as well as its net asset position. The realizable value of assets will be important in this regard and may involve specific assets that collateralize the debt.

The ability to make interest payments is more a function of the company's ability to generate positive cash flows from operations in the short run, as well as over time. Times interest earned shows how comfortably the company should be able to make interest (and preferred dividend) payments, assuming earnings trends are stable.

Figure 6A-3	Long-Term Debt and Preferred Dividends Ratios

$$\text{Debt-to-equity ratio} = \frac{\text{total liabilities}}{\text{total equity}}$$

$$\text{Tangible net assets-to-equity ratio} = \frac{\text{total equity} - \text{intangible assets}}{\text{total equity}}$$

$$\text{Times interest earned} = \frac{\text{operating income}}{\text{interest expense}}$$

$$\text{Times interest and preferred dividends earned} = \frac{\text{operating income}}{\text{interest expense} + [\text{preferred dividends}/(1 - \text{tax rate})]}$$

Operating and Performance Measurement

The key to remedying many financial ills is to improve operations. All creditors and investors, therefore, are interested in the results of operations of a business enterprise, with the result that a number of operating and performance ratios are in use (see Figure 6A-4). The most widely used operating and performance ratio is earnings per share, which is an integral part of the basic financial statements for most companies. Several additional ratios can be calculated and will give further insights into operations.

The first of these is the efficiency ratio. This shows the relative volume of business generated from the company's operating asset base. In other words, it shows whether sufficient revenues are being generated to justify the assets employed. When the efficiency ratio is low, there is an indication that additional volume should be sought before more assets are obtained. When the ratio is high, it may be an indication that assets are being fully utilized (i.e., there is little excess capacity) and an investment in additional assets will soon be necessary.

The second ratio is the profit margin ratio. This shows the portion of sales that exceeds cost (both variable and fixed). When there is weakness in this ratio, it is generally an indication that either (1) gross margins (revenues in excess of variable costs) are too low, or (2) volume is too low with respect to fixed costs.

Two ratios that indicate the adequacy of earnings relative to the asset base are the profitability ratio and the return on total assets ratio. In effect, these ratios show the efficiency and profit margin ratios combined.

An important perspective on the earnings of the company is what kind of return is provided to the owners. This is reflected in the return (before taxes) on common equity. If this ratio is below prevailing long-term interest rates or returns on alternative investments, owners will perceive that they should convert the company's assets to some other use, or perhaps liquidate, unless return can be improved.

An interesting supplemental analysis is provided through leverage analysis. Here, the proportionate share of assets for each source of capital is multiplied by the company's return on total assets. This determines the return on each source of capital. The result is compared with the cost of each source of capital (e.g., interest expense), and a net contribution by capital source is derived. If this amount is positive for a capital source, it may be an indication that additional capital should be sought. If the leverage is negative from a capital source, recapitalization alternatives and/or earnings

---

Figure 6A-4   Operating and Performance Ratios

$$\text{Earnings per share} = \frac{\text{earnings} - \text{preferred dividends}}{\text{number of common shares}}$$

$$\text{Efficiency ratio} = \frac{\text{gross sales net of returns}}{\text{tangible operating assets}}$$

$$\text{Profit margin ratio} = \frac{\text{operating income}}{\text{gross sales net of returns}}$$

$$\text{Profitability ratio} = \frac{\text{operating income}}{\text{tangible operating assets}}$$

$$\text{Return on total assets ratio} = \frac{\text{income before interest} + \text{taxes}}{\text{total assets}}$$

$$\text{Return on common equity ratio} = \frac{\text{income before taxes} - [\text{preferred dividends}/(1 - \text{tax rate})]}{\text{common equity}}$$

Leverage ratios (computed separately for each source of capital other than common equity, for example, short-term debt, long-term debt, deferred taxes) =

$$\frac{(\text{return on total assets} \times \text{amount of source}) - \text{cost attributable to source}}{\text{common equity}}$$

$$\text{Book value per common share} = \frac{\text{common equity}}{\text{number of common shares}}$$

improvements should be investigated. It is also helpful to use this leverage analysis when considering the debt-to-equity ratio.

The final operating and performance ratio is book value per common share. This shows the combined effect of equity transactions over time.

The use of operating and performance ratios is subject to the same accounting inconsistencies mentioned for the liquidity ratios previously identified. The usefulness of these ratios in making comparisons over time or among companies may be affected by the classification of operating versus non-operating items, inventory methods, amortization methods, research and development costs, and off-balance-sheet financing.

Illustration

Computation of the various ratios is illustrated in Figure 6A-5 using the financial statements of Hillsburg Hardware Limited introduced in Chapter 5.

Figure 6A-5	Ratio Illustration Using Hillsburg Hardware Limited

$$\text{Earnings per share} = \frac{3{,}934 - 0}{5{,}000} = \$0.79$$

$$\text{Current ratio} = \frac{51{,}027}{13{,}216} = 3.86$$

$$\text{Quick ratio} = \frac{828 + 0 + 18{,}957}{13{,}216} = 1.50$$

$$\text{Cash ratio} = \frac{828}{13{,}216} = 0.06$$

$$\text{Accounts receivable turnover} = \frac{143{,}086}{(20{,}197 + 17{,}521)/2} = 7.59 \text{ times}$$

$$\text{Days to collect} = \frac{18{,}859 \times 365}{143{,}086} = 48.11 \text{ days}$$

$$\text{Inventory turnover} = \frac{103{,}241}{(29{,}865 + 31{,}600)/2} = 3.36 \text{ times}$$

$$\text{Days to sell} = \frac{30{,}733 \times 365}{103{,}241} = 108.65 \text{ days}$$

$$\text{Days to convert to cash} = 108.65 + 48.11 = 156.76 \text{ days}$$

$$\text{Debt to equity} = \frac{38{,}904}{22{,}463} = 1.73$$

$$\text{Tangible net assets to equity} = \frac{22{,}463}{22{,}463} = 1.00$$

$$\text{Times interest earned} = \frac{7{,}370}{2{,}409} = 3.06 \text{ times}$$

$$\text{Times interest and preferred dividends earned} = \frac{7{,}370}{2{,}409 + 0/(1 - 0.31)} = 3.06 \text{ times}$$

$$\text{Efficiency ratio} = \frac{143{,}086}{29{,}865 + 10{,}340} = 3.56$$

$$\text{Profit margin ratio} = \frac{7{,}370}{143{,}086} = 0.05$$

$$\text{Profitability ratio} = \frac{7{,}370}{29{,}865 + 10{,}340} = 0.18$$

$$\text{Return on total assets} = \frac{5{,}681 + 2{,}409}{61{,}367} = 0.13$$

$$\text{Return on common equity} = \frac{5{,}681 - 0/(1 - 0.31)}{22{,}463} = 0.25$$

Leverage ratios:

$$\text{Current liabilities} = \frac{(0.13 \times 13{,}216) - 0}{22{,}463} = 0.08$$

$$\text{Notes payable} = \frac{(0.13 \times 28{,}300) - 2{,}409}{22{,}463} = 0.06$$

$$\text{Book value per common share} = \frac{22{,}463}{5{,}000} = \$4.49$$

Summary

1. *What are the five evidence decisions that need to be made?* After identifying the risk associated with audit objectives (1), the auditor needs to select audit procedures (2), choose sample size (3), decide on items to select (4), and determine the timing of the actual conduct of the procedures (5).

   What does the auditor mean by the phrase "sufficient appropriate audit evidence"? The auditor needs to have enough evidence that is relevant to the financial statement accounts to state an opinion on the financial statements.

2. *List and explain the seven general methods of evidence collection.* These are inspection (physical examination of a tangible asset of document); observation (using senses, such as watching); inquiries of the client (obtaining written or oral details); confirmation (written or oral response from an independent third party); recalculation (computing mathematical items such as sales invoices and comparing to client results); reperformance (redoing internal control procedures); and analytical procedures (use of comparisons and relationships).

   Why are automated audit procedures particularly helpful with recalculation and reperformance? Comparisons and calculations are often repeated for thousands of transactions. Having computer assisted audit procedures redo this work for all transactions rather than a sample helps to increase the effectiveness of audit procedures.

3. *How does the auditor choose the type of evidence to collect?* The auditor considers the independence of the provider, the effectiveness of internal controls, the qualifications of the provider (including the auditor), and the objectivity of the evidence in the context of the specific financial statement assertions that are being examined, as well as the overall risk of the engagement and the materiality of the account or balance. The auditor considers multiple sources so that consistency can be assessed among them.

   Describe the times when particular types of evidence collection are mandated. The auditor needs to conduct control tests when substantive procedures are not sufficient, conduct tests of the financial statement closing process, and perform tests of detail when the risk of material misstatement for an account or transaction stream is high.

4. *What are analytical procedures?* They are the use of financial and non-financial data in meaningful comparisons and relationships to assess the reasonableness of account balances or other data.

   What is their role in the evidence collection process? They are used in all phases of the audit, and are required during the planning and completion phases.

   Describe five major types of analytical procedures. Client data can be compared with industry data, prior-period data, client-determined expected results, auditor-determined expected results, or non-financial data.

Visit the text's website at **www.pearsoned.ca/arens** for practice quizzes, additional case studies, and international standards information.

Review Questions

6-1 Discuss the similarities and differences between evidence in a medical test and evidence in the audit of financial statements.

6-2 List the five major evidence decisions that must be made on every audit.

6-3 Describe what is meant by an audit procedure. Why is it important for audit procedures to be carefully worded?

6-4 Describe what is meant by an audit program for accounts receivable. What four things should be included in an audit program?

6-5 Explain why the auditor can only be persuaded with a reasonable level of assurance, rather than convinced, that the financial statements are correct.

6-6 Identify the three factors that determine the persuasiveness of evidence. How are these three factors related to audit procedures, sample size, items to select, and timing?

6-7 Identify the characteristics that determine the appropriateness of evidence. For each characteristic, provide one example of a type of evidence that is likely to be appropriate.

6-8 List the seven types of audit evidence included in this chapter, and give two examples of each.

6-9 What are the four characteristics of the definition of a confirmation? Distinguish between a confirmation and external documentation.

6-10 Distinguish between internal documentation and external documentation as audit evidence, and give three examples of each.

6-11 Explain the importance of analytical procedures as evidence in determining the fair presentation of the financial statements.

6-12 Your client, Harper Ltd., has a contractual commitment as a part of a bond indenture to maintain a current ratio of 2.0. If the ratio falls below that level on the balance sheet date, the entire bond becomes payable immediately. In the current year, the client's financial statements show that the ratio has dropped from 2.6:1 (or 2.6) to 2.05:1 (or 2.05) over the past year. How would this situation affect your audit plan?

6-13 Distinguish between attention-directing analytical procedures and those intended to reduce detailed substantive procedures.

6-14 Gail Gordon, a PA, has found ratio and trend analysis relatively useless as a tool in conducting audits. For several engagements, she computed the industry ratios included in publications by The Financial Post Company and compared them with client ratios. For most engagements, the client's business was significantly different from the industry data in the publication, and the client would automatically explain away any discrepancies by attributing them to the unique nature of its operations. In cases in which the client had more than one branch in different industries, Gail found the ratio analysis no help at all. How could Gail improve the quality of her analytical procedures?

6-15 It is imperative that the auditor follow up on all material differences discovered through analytical procedures. What factors affect such investigations?

6-16 Explain the purpose of common-size financial statements.

Discussion Questions and Problems

6-17 The following are examples of documentation typically obtained by auditors:

1. Vendors' invoices
2. General ledgers
3. Bank statements
4. Cancelled payroll cheques
5. Payroll time cards
6. Purchase requisitions
7. Receiving reports (documents prepared when merchandise is received)
8. Minutes of the board of directors' meetings
9. Remittance advices
10. Signed TD-1s (Employees' Income Tax Withholding Exemption Certificates)
11. Signed lease agreements
12. Duplicate copies of bills of lading
13. Accounts receivable transaction history file
14. Cancelled notes payable
15. Sales invoices history file
16. Articles of incorporation
17. Notes receivable

REQUIRED

1. Classify each of the preceding items according to type of documentation: (1) internal or (2) external.
b. Explain why external evidence is more reliable than internal evidence.

6-18 The following are examples of audit procedures:

1. Review the accounts receivable with the credit manager to evaluate its collectability.
2. Stand by the payroll time clock to determine whether any employee "swipes in" more than one time.
3. Count inventory items and record the amount in the audit working papers.
4. Obtain a letter from the client's law firm addressed to the public accounting firm stating that the law firm is not aware of any existing lawsuits.
5. Extend the cost of inventory times the quantity in an inventory transaction file to test whether it is accurate.
6. Obtain a letter from an insurance company to the public accounting firm stating the amount of the fire insurance coverage on buildings and equipment.
7. Examine an insurance policy stating the amount of the fire insurance coverage on buildings and equipment.
8. Calculate the ratio of cost of goods sold to sales as a test of overall reasonableness of gross margin relative to the preceding year.
9. Obtain information about the system of internal controls by asking the client to fill out a questionnaire.
10. Trace the total on the cash disbursements journal to the general ledger.
11. Watch employees count inventory to determine whether company procedures are being followed.
12. Examine a piece of equipment to make sure a major acquisition was actually received and is in operation.
13. Calculate the ratio of sales commissions expense to sales as a test of sales commissions.
14. Examine corporate minutes of directors' meetings to determine the authorization of the issue of bonds.
15. Obtain a letter from management stating there are no unrecorded liabilities.
16. Review the total of repairs and maintenance for each month to determine whether any month's total was unusually large.
17. Compare a duplicate sales invoice with the sales history file for customer name and amount.
18. Add the sales journal entries to determine whether they were correctly totalled.
19. Make a petty cash count to make sure the amount of the petty cash fund is intact.
20. Obtain a written statement from a bank stating the client has $15,671 on deposit and liabilities of $50,000 on a demand note.

REQUIRED

Classify each of the preceding items according to the seven types of audit evidence: (1) inspection, (2) observation, (3) inquiries of the client, (4) confirmation, (5) recalculation, (6) reperformance, and (7) analytical procedures.

6-19 List two examples of audit evidence that the auditor can use in support of each of the following:
a. Recorded amount of entries in the purchase journal.
b. Physical existence of inventory.
c. Accuracy of accounts receivable.
d. Ownership of capital assets.
e. Liability for accounts payable.
f. Obsolescence of inventory.
g. Existence of petty cash.

6-20 Seven different types of evidence were discussed. The following questions concern the reliability of that evidence:
a. Explain why confirmations are normally more reliable evidence than inquiries of the client.
b. Describe a situation in which confirmation will be considered highly reliable and another in which it will not be reliable.
c. Under what circumstances is the physical observation of inventory considered relatively unreliable evidence?
d. Explain why recalculation tests are highly reliable but of relatively limited use.
e. Give three examples of relatively reliable documentation and three examples of less reliable documentation. What characteristics distinguish the two?
f. Give several examples in which the qualifications of the respondent or the qualifications of the auditor affect the reliability of the evidence.
g. Explain why analytical procedures are important evidence even though they are relatively unreliable by themselves.

6-21 As auditor of Star Manufacturing Corp., you have obtained a trial balance taken from the books of Star one month prior to year end:

	DR. (CR.)
Cash in bank	$ 87,000
Trade accounts receivable	345,000
Notes receivable	125,000
Inventories	317,000
Land	66,000
Buildings, net	350,000
Furniture, fixtures, and equipment, net	325,000
Trade accounts payable	(213,000)
Goods and services tax payable	(22,000)
Mortgages payable	(400,000)
Capital stock	(300,000)
Retained earnings	(510,000)
Sales (net)	(3,130,000)
Cost of sales	$ 2,300,000
General administrative expenses	622,000
Legal and professional fees	3,000
Interest expense	35,000

Notes: There are no inventories consigned either in or out. All notes receivable are due from outsiders and held by Star.

REQUIRED

Which accounts should be confirmed with outside sources? Briefly describe from whom they should be confirmed and the information that should be confirmed. Organize your answer in the following format:

Account Name	From Whom Confirmed	Information to Be Confirmed

(Adapted from AICPA)

6-22 The following audit procedures were performed in the audit of inventory to satisfy specific balance-related audit objectives as discussed in Chapter 5. The audit procedures assume the auditor has obtained the inventory count records that list the client's inventory. The general balance-related audit objectives from Chapter 5 are also included.

AUDIT PROCEDURES
1. Using audit software, extend unit prices times quantity, foot the extensions, and compare the total with the general ledger.
2. Trace selected quantities from the inventory listing to the physical inventory to make sure the items exist and the quantities are the same.
3. Question operating personnel about the possibility of obsolete or slow-moving inventory.
4. Select a sample of quantities of inventory in the factory warehouse, and trace each item to the inventory count sheets to determine if it has been included and if the quantity and description are correct.
5. Using both this year's and last year's inventory data files, compare quantities on hand and unit prices, printing any

with greater than a 30 percent or $15,000 variation from one year to the next.

6. Examine sales invoices and contracts with customers to determine if any goods are out on consignment with customers. Similarly, examine vendors' invoices and contracts with vendors to determine if any goods on the inventory listing are owned by vendors.

7. Send letters directly to third parties who hold the client's inventory and request that they respond directly to us.

GENERAL BALANCE-RELATED AUDIT OBJECTIVES
Existence
Rights and obligations
Completeness
Accuracy
Valuation
Classification
Detail tie-in
Cut-off

REQUIRED
a. Identify the type of audit evidence used for each audit procedure.
b. Identify the general balance-related audit objective or objectives satisfied by each audit procedure.

6-23 The following are eight situations, each containing two means of accumulating evidence:

1. Confirm accounts receivable with business organizations versus confirming receivables with consumers.
2. Physically examine 8-cm steel plates versus examining electronic parts.
3. Examine duplicate sales invoices when several competent people are checking one another's work versus examining documents prepared by a competent person in a one-person staff.
4. Physically examine inventory of parts for the number of units on hand versus examining them for the likelihood of inventory being obsolete.
5. Confirm a bank balance versus confirming the oil and gas reserves with a geologist specializing in oil and gas.
6. Confirm a bank balance versus examining the client's bank statements.
7. Physically count the client's inventory held by an independent party versus confirming the count with an independent party.
8. Physically count the client's inventory versus obtaining a count from the company president.

REQUIRED
a. For each of the eight situations, state whether the first or second type of evidence is more reliable.
b. For each situation, state which of the factors discussed in the chapter affect the appropriateness of the evidence.

6-24 In auditing the financial statements of a manufacturing company, the PA has found that the traditional audit trail has been replaced by an electronic one. As a result, the PA may place increased emphasis on analytical procedures of the data under audit. These tests, which are also applied in auditing visibly posted accounting records, include the computation of ratios that are compared with prior-year ratios or with industry-wide norms. Examples of analytical procedures are the computation of the rate of inventory turnover and the computation of the number of days' sales in receivables.

REQUIRED
a. Discuss the advantages to the public accountant of the use of analytical procedures in an audit.
b. In addition to the computations given in part (c), list five ratios that an auditor may compute during an audit on balance sheet accounts and related income accounts. For each ratio listed, name the two (or more) accounts used in its computation.
c. When an auditor discovers that there has been a significant change in a ratio when compared with the preceding year's, he or she considers the possible reasons for the change. Give the possible reasons for the following significant changes in ratios:
   (1) The rate of inventory turnover (ratio of cost of sales to average inventory) has decreased from the preceding year's rate.
   (2) The number of days' sales in receivables (ratio of average daily accounts receivable to sales) has increased over the prior year.

(Adapted from AICPA)

6-25 Your comparison of the gross margin percentage for Singh Drugs Ltd. for the years 2005 through 2008 indicates a significant decline.

A discussion with Marilyn Adams, the controller, brings to light two possible explanations. She informs you that the industry gross profit percentage in the retail drug industry declined fairly steadily for three years, which accounts for part of the decline. A second factor was the declining percentage of the total volume resulting from the pharmacy part of the business. The pharmacy sales represent the most profitable portion of the business, yet the competition from discount drugstores prevents these sales from expanding as fast as the non-drug items such as magazines, candy, and many other items sold. Marilyn feels strongly that these two factors are the cause of the decline.

	2008	2007	2006	2005
Sales (thousands)	$14,211	$12,916	$11,462	$10,351
COGS (thousands)	9,223	8,266	7,313	6,573
Gross margin	$ 4,988	$ 4,650	$ 4,149	$ 3,778
Percentage	35.1	36.0	36.2	36.5

The additional information shown on the previous page and below is obtained from independent sources and the client's records as a means of investigating the controller's explanations.

REQUIRED
a. Evaluate the explanation provided by Adams. Show calculations to support your conclusions.
b. Which specific aspects of the client's financial statements require intensive investigation in this audit?

Singh Drugs Ltd.

Year	Drug Sales	Non-Drug Sales	Drug Cost of Goods Sold	Non-Drug Cost of Goods Sold	Industry Gross Profit Percentage for Retailers of Drugs and Related Products
2008	$5,126	$9,085	$3,045	$6,178	32.7
2007	$5,051	$7,865	$2,919	$5,347	32.9
2006	$4,821	$6,641	$2,791	$4,522	33.0
2005	$4,619	$5,732	$2,665	$3,908	33.2

6-26 In the audit of Worldwide Wholesale Inc., you performed extensive ratio and trend analyses. No material exceptions were discovered except for the following:

1. Commission expense as a percentage of sales had stayed constant for several years but has increased significantly in the current year. Commission rates have not changed.
2. The rate of inventory turnover has steadily decreased for four years.
3. Inventory as a percentage of current assets had steadily increased for four years.
4. The number of days' sales in accounts receivable has steadily increased for three years.
5. Allowance for uncollectible accounts as a percentage of accounts receivable has steadily decreased for three years.

6. The absolute amounts of amortization expense and amortization expense as a percentage of gross fixed assets are significantly smaller than in the preceding year.

REQUIRED
a. Evaluate the potential significance of each of the exceptions above for the fair presentation of financial statements.
b. State the follow-up procedures you would use to determine the possibility of material misstatements.
c. What do these changes indicate about the overall financial position of Worldwide Wholesale Inc.?

6-27 As part of the analytical procedures of Mahogany Products, Inc., you perform calculations of the following ratios:

Ratio	Industry Averages 2008	Industry Averages 2007	Mahogany Products, Inc. 2008	Mahogany Products, Inc. 2007
1. Current ratio	3.30	3.80	2.20	2.60
2. Days to collect receivables	87.00	93.00	67.00	60.00
3. Days to sell inventory	126.00	121.00	93.00	89.00
4. Purchases divided by accounts payable	11.70	11.60	8.50	8.60
5. Inventory divided by current assets	0.56	0.51	0.49	0.48
6. Operating earnings divided by tangible assets	0.08	0.06	0.14	0.12
7. Operating earnings divided by net sales	0.06	0.06	0.04	0.04
8. Gross margin percentage	0.21	0.27	0.21	0.19
9. Earnings per share	$14.27	$13.91	$2.09	$1.93

REQUIRED
For each of the preceding ratios:
a. State whether there is a need to investigate the results further and, if so, the reason for further investigation.

b. State the approach you would use in the investigation.
c. Explain how the operations of Mahogany Products, Inc. appear to differ from those of the industry.

Professional Judgment Problem

6-28 Your province administers to students in public schools and high schools standardized tests of reading, writing, and mathematics. Reports are produced both by school and for the

province overall describing how students fared in these tests. Recently, the Annual Report of the Office of the provincial Auditor General evaluated this testing process. The report was thorough, describing the process and how it was audited and providing some observations and recommendations. One observation related to the methods of monitoring and comparing student progress. Issues raised were as follows:

- Not enough information is collected in student information systems about student practices such as homework assignment, homework completion, and whether remedial assistance was provided or available.
- There were questions about the accuracy of information recorded about students.
- Concerns were raised about the comparability of data for students from school to school.
- Information systems may not be capable of retaining sufficient student data.

REQUIRED

a. Using the seven different types of evidence listed in Table 6-4 on page 190, identify the evidence that the provincial auditor's office might have collected to reach the conclusions described above. For each type of evidence, explain who would have provided the evidence, and note the level of objectivity of such evidence. Justify your answer.

b. What would be the relevant transaction-related audit objectives considered during this audit? List at least one audit procedure that could have been conducted for each of the transaction-related audit objectives that you consider to be relevant.

Case

6-29 Grande Stores is a large department store chain with catalogue operations. The company has recently expanded from 6 to 43 stores by borrowing from several large financial institutions and from a public offering of common stock. A recent investigation has disclosed that Grande materially overstated net income. This was accomplished by understating accounts payable and recording fictitious supplier credits that further reduced accounts payable. An OSC investigation was critical of the evidence gathered by Grande's audit firm, Montgomery & Ross, in testing accounts payable and the supplier credits.

The following is a description of some of the fictitious supplier credits and unrecorded amounts in accounts payable, as well as the audit procedures.

1. McClure Advertising Credits—Grande had arrangements with some vendors to share the cost of advertising the vendor's product. The arrangements were usually agreed to in advance by the vendor and supported by evidence of the placing of the ad. Grande created a 114-page list of approximately 1,100 vendors, supporting advertising credits of $300,000. Grande's auditors selected a sample of 4 of the 1,100 items for direct confirmation. One item was confirmed by telephone, one traced to cash receipts, one to a vendor credit memo for part of the amount and cash receipts for the rest, and one to a vendor credit memo. Two of the amounts confirmed differed from the amount on the list, but the auditors did not seek an explanation for the differences because the amounts were not material.

   The rest of the credits were tested by selecting 20 items (one or two from each page of the list). Twelve of the items were supported by examining the ads placed, and eight were supported by Grande debit memos charging the vendors for the promotional allowances.

2. Springbrook Credits—Grande created 28 fictitious credit memos totalling $257,000 from Springbrook Distributors, the main supplier of health and beauty aids to Grande. Grande's controller initially told the auditor that the credits were for returned goods, then said they were a volume discount, and finally stated they were a payment so that Grande would continue to use Springbrook as a supplier. One of the Montgomery & Ross staff auditors

concluded that a $257,000 payment to retain Grande's business was too large to make financial sense.

The credit memos indicated that the credits were for damaged merchandise, volume rebates, and advertising allowances. The audit firm requested a confirmation of the credits. In response, Jon Steiner, the president of Grande Stores, placed a call to Mort Seagal, the president of Springbrook, and handed the phone to the staff auditor. In fact, the call had been placed to an officer of Grande. The Grande officer, posing as Seagal, orally confirmed the credits. Grande refused to allow Montgomery & Ross to obtain written confirmations supporting the credits. Although the staff auditor doubted the validity of the credits, the audit partner, Mark Franklin, accepted the credits based on the credit memoranda, telephone confirmation of the credits, and oral representations of Grande officers.

3. Ridolfi Credits—$130,000 in credits based on 35 credit memoranda from Ridolfi, Inc., were purportedly for the return of overstocked goods from several Grande stores. A Montgomery & Ross staff auditor noted the size of the credit and that the credit memos were dated subsequent to year end. He further noticed that a sentence on the credit memos from Ridolfi had been obliterated by a felt-tip marker. When held to the light, the accountant could read that the marked-out sentence read, "Do not post until merchandise received." The staff auditor thereafter called Harold Ridolfi, treasurer of Ridolfi, Inc. and was informed that the $130,000 in goods had not been returned and the money was not owed to Grande by Ridolfi. Steiner advised Franklin, the audit partner, that he had talked to Harold Ridolfi, who claimed he had been misunderstood by the staff auditor. Steiner told Franklin not to have anyone call Ridolfi to verify the amount because of pending litigation between Grande and Ridolfi, Inc.

4. Accounts Payable Accrual—Montgomery & Ross assigned a senior with experience in the retail area to audit accounts payable. Although Grande had poor internal control, Montgomery & Ross selected a sample of 50 for confirmation of the several thousand vendors who did business with Grande. Twenty-seven responses were received, and 21 were reconciled to Grande's records.

These tests indicated an unrecorded liability of approximately $290,000 when projected to the population of accounts payable. However, the investigation disclosed that Grande's president made telephone calls to some suppliers who had received confirmation requests from Montgomery & Ross and told them how to respond to the request.

Montgomery & Ross also performed a purchases cutoff test by vouching accounts payable invoices received for nine weeks after year end. The purpose of this test was to identify invoices received after year end that should have been recorded in accounts payable. Thirty percent of the sample ($160,000) was found to relate to the prior year, indicating a potential unrecorded liability of approximately $500,000. The audit firm and Grande eventually agreed on an adjustment to increase accounts payable by $260,000.

REQUIRED

Identify deficiencies in the sufficiency and appropriateness of the evidence gathered in the audit of accounts payable of Grande Stores.

ACL Problem

Additional ACL problems are in Chapters 8, 11, 14, 15, and 18.

6-30 This problem requires the use of ACL software, which is included in the companion website at **www.pearsoned.ca/arens**. Information about installing and using ACL and solving this problem can be found in the ACL Appendix, also on the companion website. You should read all of the reference material preceding instructions about "Quick Sort" before locating the appropriate command to answer questions a-c. For this problem, start ACL, then click on "Open an existing project," and within the project, open "Sample Project.ACL." Click on the plus sign beside the "Tables" folder, which will reveal a series of files. We will be conducting an inventory review, so click on the plus sign beside "Inventory Review," then click on "Inventory" to open the inventory sample data file. The suggested command or other source of information needed to solve the problem requirement is included at the end of each question.

a. Obtain and print statistical information for both Inventory Value at Cost and Market Value. Determine how many inventory items have positive, negative, and zero values for both Inventory Value at Cost and Market Values (Statistics Command).

b. Use Quick Sort Ascending and Descending for both Inventory Value at Cost and Market Value (Quick Sort). Use this information and the information from part (a) to identify any concerns you have in the audit of inventory.

c. Calculate the ratio of Inventory Value at Cost to Market Value and sort the result from low to high (Computed Fields and Quick Sort). Identify concerns about inventory valuation, if any.

d. What is the potential impact of your findings upon your field work? For example, if you found zero or negative amounts for inventory values, think about how these might arise at an organization. What might negative inventory values tell you about controls over inventory or over inventory data?

Ongoing Small Business Case: Banking at CondoCleaners.com

6-31 Jim has decided to use only one bank account for processing transactions at CondoCleaners.com. He will have sales transactions (credit card deposits from the credit card service provider), payroll and expense cheques, and bank charges.

REQUIRED

a. Describe the internal and external documentation that will be available for the audit of CondoCleaners.com.

b. For each of the seven methods of evidence collection, provide an example of an audit step that you could use for the audit of the cash transactions or balances at CondoCleaners.com.

7

Materiality and risk

We have not "talked any numbers" yet. How does the auditor assess the financial statements to decide what should be tested? What is the model used to organize and assess risks during the audit process? In this chapter, we will explain the audit risk model and how it is used for planning. We will also examine the key concept of materiality. Together with the information of the previous chapter, where we discussed evidence, the concepts of materiality and risk will allow us to move on to Chapter 8, where we will talk about client risk assessment and audit planning. All types of auditors and accountants can benefit from an awareness of materiality to help them assess when to investigate unusual items; risk assessment concepts help identify where the focus of audit procedures or control processes should be.

LEARNING OBJECTIVES

1 State the components of the audit risk model. Explain why the auditor needs to consider client business risk during the financial statement audit. Describe engagement risk in auditing.

2 Describe the factors the auditor considers when assessing inherent risk.

3 Examine how materiality is used to assess the amount of work conducted during an audit engagement. List quantitative and qualitative factors that an auditor considers when setting materiality.

4 Relate the components of the audit risk model to the amount of evidence that should be collected during an audit. Link materiality to the use of the audit risk model. Describe drawbacks associated with the use of the audit risk model during field work assessment.

STANDARDS REFERENCED IN THIS CHAPTER

CICA Standards

CAS 200 – Overall objectives of the independent auditor, and the conduct of an audit in accordance with Canadian auditing standards (previously included aspects of Section 5100 – Generally Accepted Auditing Standards)

CAS 315 – Identifying and assessing the risks of material misstatement through understanding the entity and its environment (previously Section 5141 – Understanding the entity and its environment and assessing the risks of material misstatement)

CAS 320 – Materiality in planning and performing an audit (previously portions of Section 5142 – Materiality and AuG-41 – Applying the concept of materiality)

CAS 450 – Evaluation of misstatements identified during the audit (previously portions of Section 5142 – Materiality)

Section 5095 – Reasonable assurance and audit risk

Explain to Me One More Time How You Did a Good Job, but the Company Went Broke

Maxwell Spencer is a senior partner in his firm, and one of his regular duties is to attend the firm's annual training session for newly hired auditors. He loves doing this because it gives him a chance to share his many years of experience with inexperienced people who have bright and receptive minds. He covers several topics formally during the day and then sits around and "shoots the breeze" with participants during the evening hours. Here we listen to what he is saying.

"Suppose you are a retired 72-year-old man. You and your wife, Minnie, live on your retirement fund, which you elected to manage yourself, rather than receive income from an annuity. You concluded that your years in business gave you the ability to earn a better return than what the annuity would provide.

"So when you retired and got your bundle, you called your broker and discussed with him what you should do with it. He told you that the most important thing was to protect your principal and recommended that you buy bonds. You settled on three issues that your broker and his firm believed were good ones, with solid balance sheets: (1) an entertainment company that was building a series of amusement parks across Canada, (2) a fast-growing alternative energy company, and (3) a major life insurance company. All you have to do is sit back and clip your coupons.

Ah, "the best-laid plans of mice and men" . . . First, the entertainment company went broke, and you can look forward to recovering only a few cents on the dollar over several years. Then the alternative energy company failed, and you might get something back—eventually. Finally, the life insurance company was closed by the government and has to default on all of its outstanding bonds. A recovery plan has been initiated, but don't hold your breath. Your best strategy is to apply for a job at McDonald's. They hire older people, don't they?"

IMPORTANCE TO AUDITORS

"Now, what could the auditors of these three entities ever say to you about how they planned and conducted their audits and decided to issue an unqualified opinion that would justify that opinion in your mind? You don't care about business failure versus audit failure, or risk assessment and reliability of audit evidence, or any of that technical mumbo jumbo. The auditors were supposed to be there for you when you needed them, and they weren't. And materiality? Anything that would have indicated a problem is material for you.

"The message is, folks, that it's a lot easier to sweat over doing a tough audit right than it is to justify your judgments and decisions after it's too late. And there's nothing that can help you if you think that a harmed investor will ever see things from your point of view."

continued >

1. What does Maxwell's story tell you about the relevance of potential business failure to the auditor?

2. Think about the responsibilities of the auditor versus the responsibility of management in strategic planning and environmental assessment. How do the requirements to consider knowledge of the external business environment deal with the issues raised by Maxwell?

AUDITORS would like to do a thorough, high-quality audit that provides value to both the users of the financial statements and their clients. At the same time, auditors need to balance the costs of conducting the audit against the risk of being sued. This chapter explains important tools for conducting a high-quality audit—assessment of risks, use of an audit risk model, and the use of materiality during the audit.

Users are indirectly informed of the importance of risks and materiality by means of the auditor's report (discussed further in Chapter 22). The scope paragraph in an auditor's report includes two important phrases that are directly related to materiality and risk. These phrases are emphasized in the following two sentences of a standard scope paragraph.

> I conducted my audit in accordance with Canadian generally accepted auditing standards. Those standards require that I plan and perform an audit *to obtain reasonable assurance* as to whether the financial statements are *free of material misstatement*.

The phrase *obtain reasonable assurance* is intended to inform users that auditors do not guarantee or ensure the fair presentation of the financial statements. The phrase communicates that there is some risk that the financial statements are not fairly stated even when the opinion is unqualified. The phrase *free of material misstatements* is intended to inform users that the auditor's responsibility is limited to material financial information. Materiality is important because it is impractical for auditors to provide assurances on immaterial amounts.

We start this chapter by looking at specific types of risks considered during the audit process, then work through the audit risk model, a framework for assessing and documenting risks during the financial statement audit process. After a detailed look at inherent risk, one of the components of the audit risk model, we work with materiality before bringing these concepts together.

Risk in Auditing and the Audit Risk Model

Risk

Risk in auditing means that the auditor accepts some level of uncertainty in performing the audit function. The auditor recognizes, for example, that there is uncertainty about the appropriateness of evidence, about the effectiveness of a client's internal control, and whether the financial statements are fairly stated when the audit is completed.

Risk—the acceptance by auditors that there is some level of uncertainty in performing the audit function.

An effective auditor recognizes that risks exist and deals with those risks in an appropriate manner. Most risks that auditors encounter are difficult to measure and require careful thought for an appropriate response. For example, assume the auditor determines that the client's industry is undergoing significant technological changes, which affect both the client and the client's customers. This change may affect the obsolescence of the client's inventory, collectability of accounts receivable, and perhaps even the ability of the client's business to continue. Responding to these risks properly is essential to achieving a quality audit.

This chapter deals with the risks that affect planning the engagement to determine the appropriate evidence to accumulate by considering risks pertaining to the client and a planning model called the audit risk model. Then, we talk about materiality, before concluding with the relationship between materiality and risk.

ILLUSTRATION CONCERNING RISKS AND EVIDENCE Before discussing the audit risk model, an illustration for a hypothetical company is provided in Table 7-1 as a frame of reference for the discussion. The illustration shows that the auditor has decided on a "medium" willingness to accept the risk that material misstatements exist after the audit is complete for all five cycles (consideration A). It is common for auditors to want an equal likelihood of misstatements for each cycle after the audit is finished to permit the issuance of an unqualified opinion. Next, the table shows that there are differences among cycles in the frequency and size of expected misstatements (B). For example, there are almost no misstatements expected in the payroll and personnel cycle but many in inventory and warehousing. The reason may be that the payroll transactions are highly routine, whereas there may be considerable complexities in recording inventory. Similarly, internal control is believed to differ in effectiveness among the five cycles (C). For example, internal controls in payroll and personnel are considered highly effective, whereas those in inventory and warehousing are considered ineffective.

The previous considerations (A, B, C) affect the auditor's decision about the appropriate extent of evidence to accumulate (D). For example, because the auditor expects few misstatements in payroll and personnel (B) and internal control is effective (C), the auditor plans for less evidence collection in the payroll and personnel cycle (D) than for inventory and warehousing. Recall that the auditor has the same (medium) level of willingness to accept material misstatements after the audit is completed for all five cycles (A), but a different extent of evidence is needed for various

Table 7-1	Illustration of Differing Evidence among Cycles				
	Sales and Collection Cycle	Acquisition and Payment Cycle	Payroll and Personnel Cycle	Inventory and Warehousing Cycle	Capital Acquisition and Repayment Cycle
A Auditor's willingness to permit material misstatements to exist after completing the audit (audit risk)	Low willingness (medium)	Low willingness (medium)	Low willingness (medium)	Low willingness (medium)	Low willingness (medium)
B Auditor's assessment of expectation of material misstatement before considering internal control (inherent risk)	Expect some misstatements (medium)	Expect many misstatements (high)	Expect few misstatements (low)	Expect many misstatements (high)	Expect few misstatements (low)
C Auditor's assessment of effectiveness of internal control to prevent or detect material misstatements (control risk)	Medium effectiveness (medium)	High effectiveness (low)	High effectiveness (low)	Low effectiveness (high)	Medium effectiveness (medium)
D Extent of evidence the auditor plans to accumulate (detection risk)	Medium level (medium)	Medium level (medium)	Low level (high)	High level (low)	Medium level (medium)

cycles. The difference is caused by differences in the auditor's expectations of mis-statements and assessment of internal control.

AUDIT APPROACH The overall audit approach designed by most firms is strategic—overview tactical plans are developed that take into account the client's objectives and strategies considering the broader business environment within which the client operates. Chapter 5 described the many steps involved in the audit process. Risk assessment helps the auditor gather the information needed to formulate conclusions for the audit risk model, which we discuss next. As part of the planning process, the auditor decides upon a strategic approach for each cycle to plan the evidence mix. Throughout this process, the audit staff meet on an as-needed basis, with full team meetings held at key decision points throughout the engagement.

Figure 7-1 shows the relationship among the components of the audit risk model (audit risk, inherent risk, control risk, and detection risk). Think of the small circles falling down the page as potential material errors. Let us use the inventory and ware-housing cycle as an example. Many types of material errors could occur, such as recording incorrect quantities, incorrect prices, theft of inventory, and double ship-ments to clients. These potential errors are errors that could occur if we do not have controls, so they are errors due to the inherent nature of the system—perhaps a com-plex system with costly inventory that is easy to steal, resulting in many potential errors (circles).

In reality, there may not be any material errors or there may be many. Since inher-ent risk for the inventory and warehousing cycle has been assessed as high, there are many potential material errors falling into the internal controls tray.

The purpose of internal controls is to prevent, detect, and correct material errors in the financial statements. If controls are good, then there are no holes (or very small ones) in the internal controls tray, and internal controls will prevent or detect these potential errors so that they can be corrected. This is called low internal control risk.

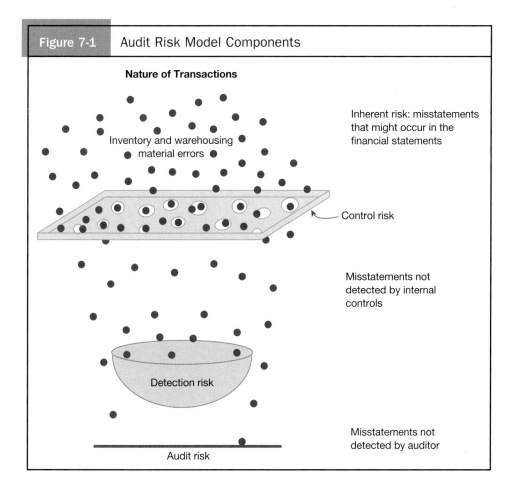

Figure 7-1 | Audit Risk Model Components

Nature of Transactions

Inventory and warehousing material errors

Inherent risk: misstatements that might occur in the financial statements

Control risk

Misstatements not detected by internal controls

Detection risk

Audit risk

Misstatements not detected by auditor

If internal controls are poor (such as in the figure), then the client will not prevent or detect the errors, and the circles (potential material errors) continue to fall (and are present in the financial statements before the auditor conducts audit testing). This means that the auditor would not rely upon internal controls, and would assess control risk as high.

An accurate control risk assessment for Figure 7-1 would result in the auditor deciding that in the inventory and warehousing cycle, there is low effectiveness in internal controls, so that there will be no reliance upon internal controls. This means that the auditor will need to conduct substantive testing to detect and quantify the errors. The detection of these errors is represented as a bowl—the auditor "catches" the errors using substantive audit procedures.

The bowl has to be large enough and the substantive procedures effective enough to detect most of the material errors. This high level of audit testing brings the auditor's detection risk (the risk of not catching an error) down to a low level. For example, if the auditor decided that medium audit risk was required, then the auditor would be prepared to accept up to 5 percent likelihood of missing a material error. If the auditor had decided upon a low audit risk, then the bowl would have to be even larger, so that perhaps only 1 percent of the errors would go undetected.

It is important that the auditor assess both inherent risk and control risk to know how much testing should be completed to achieve the desired audit risk.

Audit Risk Model for Planning

This way of dealing with risk in planning audit evidence is called the application of the **audit risk model**, a formal model reflecting the relationships among audit risk (AR), inherent risk (IR), control risk (CR), and planned detection risk (PDR). The audit risk model is discussed in the *CICA Handbook* in Section 5095, Reasonable assurance and audit risk, and in CAS 200, Overall objective of the independent auditor, and the conduct of an audit in accordance with Canadian auditing standards. A thorough understanding of the audit risk model is essential to effective auditing and to the study of the remaining chapters of this book.

The audit risk model is used primarily for planning purposes in deciding how much evidence to accumulate in each cycle. It is usually stated as follows: $AR = IR \times CR \times PDR$, where AR = audit risk, IR = inherent risk, CR = control risk, and PDR = planned detection risk (Section 5095 and CAS 200 refer to this as detection risk).

AUDIT RISK **Audit risk** is a measure of how willing the auditor is to accept that the financial statements may be materially misstated after the audit is completed and an unqualified opinion has been reached. When the auditor decides on a lower audit risk, it means the auditor wants a higher level of assurance. Auditors sometimes refer to the terms "audit assurance," "overall assurance," or "level of assurance" instead of "audit risk." **Audit assurance** or any of the equivalent terms is the complement of audit risk, that is, one minus audit risk. For example, audit risk of 2 percent is the same as audit assurance of 98 percent. In other words, audit risk of 2 percent means the auditor is willing to accept a 2-percent risk that there are material errors in the financial statements. At the same time, a 98-percent level of assurance has been obtained that the financial statements are free of material errors. Zero risk would be certainty, and a 100-percent risk would be complete uncertainty. Complete assurance (zero risk) of the accuracy of financial statements is not economically practical. It has already been established in Chapter 5 that the auditor cannot guarantee the complete absence of material misstatements.

Using the audit risk model, there is a direct relationship between audit risk and planned detection risk, and an inverse relationship between audit risk and planned evidence. Refer to Figure 7-1 to help understand this relationship. For example, as the level of audit risk decreases (i.e., the auditor wants more assurance), more evidence needs to be gathered (a bigger audit bowl), planned detection risk is reduced, and more assurance is needed from audit evidence. As we will discuss in the next chapter, auditors also often assign more experienced staff or have an additional independent review of the working papers for a client with lower audit risk.

INHERENT RISK **Inherent risk** is a measure of the auditor's assessment of the likelihood that a material misstatement might occur in the first place, that is, before considering the effectiveness of internal accounting controls. Inherent risk is the susceptibility of the financial statements to material misstatement, assuming no internal controls exist. If the auditor concludes that there is a high likelihood of misstatements, ignoring internal controls, the auditor would conclude that inherent risk is high. Internal controls are ignored in setting inherent risk because they are considered separately in the audit risk model as control risk. In Table 7-1, inherent risk (B) has been assessed high for inventory and lower for payroll and personnel and capital acquisitions and repayments. The assessment was likely based on discussions with management, knowledge of the company, and results of prior-year audits. For example, there may be thousands of inventory transactions of many different types, with prior-year files showing many errors. Payroll, personnel, and capital acquisition transactions could occur less frequently and be more frequently checked by outside parties (e.g., banks may process payroll and contracts may be reviewed externally for capital acquisitions). Factors to be examined when assessing inherent risk are discussed in the next section of this chapter. Inherent risk is normally assessed at the account balance assertion (audit objective) level.

Inherent risk—a measure of the auditor's assessment of the likelihood that there are material misstatements in a segment before considering the effectiveness of internal controls.

CONTROL RISK **Control risk** is a measure of the auditor's assessment of the likelihood that misstatements exceeding a tolerable amount in a segment will not be prevented or detected by the client's internal control. Control risk represents (1) an assessment of whether a client's internal control is effective for preventing or detecting misstatements and (2) the auditor's intention to rely on internal controls and assign a value to control risk as part of the audit plan. For example, assume the auditor concludes that internal control is completely ineffective to prevent or detect misstatements. This is the likely conclusion for inventory and warehousing in Table 7-1 (C). The auditor would therefore assign 100 percent control risk factor (the numerical maximum) to control risk, which means "no reliance." The more effective internal control, the lower the numeric risk that could be assigned to control risk.

Control risk—a measure of the auditor's assessment of the likelihood that misstatements exceeding materiality in a segment will not be prevented or detected by the client's internal controls

Before auditors can use a control risk of less than 100 percent, they must do three things: obtain an understanding of the design of the client's internal control, evaluate the design effectiveness of those controls based on the understanding, and test internal control for operational effectiveness. Understanding internal controls is required for all audits. Assessing design effectiveness and tests of controls are required when the auditor chooses to set control risk below 100 percent and to place reliance on the controls.

Understanding the corporate governance process, understanding internal control, assessing control risk, and linking their impact to evidence requirements are so important that Chapters 9 and 10 are devoted to those topics. However, it should be noted that the auditor can choose to place no reliance on internal controls after an understanding has been obtained. Then control risk must be set at 100 percent, regardless of the actual effectiveness of the underlying internal control. Use of the audit risk model in this circumstance then causes the auditor to control audit risk entirely through a low level of planned detection risk (assuming inherent risk is also high).

PLANNED DETECTION RISK **Planned detection risk** is a measure of the risk that audit evidence for a segment will fail to detect material misstatements, should such misstatements exist. There are two key points about planned detection risk. First, it is dependent on the other three factors in the model. Planned detection risk will change only if the auditor changes one of the other factors. Second, it determines the amount of evidence the auditor plans to accumulate (which grows inversely with the size of planned detection risk). Using the complement of detection risk, at 5 percent detection risk, the auditor needs to provide 95 percent assurance (a bowl in Figure 7-1 that would catch 95 percent of the potential errors) so that the evidence collected will detect material errors. If planned detection risk is reduced to 2 percent, the auditor

Planned detection risk—a measure of the risk that audit evidence for a segment will fail to detect misstatements exceeding materiality, should such misstatements exist; PDR = AR / (IR × CR).

needs to accumulate more evidence (to obtain 98 percent assurance that evidence collected will detect material errors). For example, in Table 7-1 (D), planned detection risk is low for inventory and warehousing, which causes planned evidence to be high. The opposite is true for payroll and personnel, which has high planned detection risk, requiring less evidence gathering.

A numerical example is provided to solve for detection risk, even though it is not practical to measure as precisely as these numbers imply. The numbers used are for the inventory and warehousing cycle in Table 7-1.

$$AR = 3.5\% \quad \text{(medium risk to be accepted)}$$
$$IR = 100\% \quad \text{(high risk of errors expected)}$$
$$CR = 100\% \quad \text{(low effectiveness of internal controls)}$$
$$AR = IR \times CR \times PDR \text{ or}$$
$$PDR = \frac{AR}{(IR \times CR)}$$
$$PDR = 0.035 \, / \, 1 \times 1 = 0.035 \text{ or } 3.5\%$$

(Auditor plans 3.5 percent risk of not detecting errors and seeks 96.5 percent assurance from substantive tests.)

RELATIONSHIPS AMONG AUDIT RISK MODEL COMPONENTS The audit risk desired affects the amount of evidence to be gathered. As audit risk decreases, assurance required increases and more evidence must be gathered, making the audit more costly. Think in terms of the number of audits conducted by all public accountants. What portion of these audits could include material misstatements without having an adverse effect on society? More undetected material misstatements could result in the audit being perceived as having less value.

Inherent risk and planned detection risk have an inverse relationship. Using Figure 7-1, we can see that when more material errors are likely to exist (inherent risk assessed as higher), if control risk stays the same, the detection risk bowl must be larger (more evidence to be gathered and lower detection risk).

Similarly, if inherent risk stays constant but control risk is higher (there are more holes in the control risk tray, letting more material errors through), then we again have to increase the size of our detection risk bowl (more evidence gathering needed and smaller detection risk). There is also an inverse relationship between the two types of risk.

CLIENT BUSINESS RISK AND ENGAGEMENT RISK Client business risk will be discussed in depth in the next chapter, but we explain the concept here. **Client business risk** is the risk that the client will fail to achieve its objectives, leading to business failure. Client business risk is related to the accounting concept of going concern, which addresses whether the client will be in operation for another year or longer. When the auditor assesses that client business risk will be high, then the auditor may decide to not retain or accept the client, or gather additional evidence to support potential accounts that may need to be adjusted (such as fixed assets or marketable securities).

Engagement risk, or **auditor business risk**, is the risk that the auditor or audit firm will suffer harm after the audit is finished. Engagement risk is closely related to client business risk. For example, if a client declares bankruptcy after an audit is completed, the likelihood of a lawsuit against the public accounting firm increases, even if the quality of the audit was good.

CHANGING AUDIT RISK FOR BUSINESS RISK Current standards use the term **business risk** to apply to clients (CAS 315, par. 4b; formerly *CICA Handbook* Section 5141). However, as described above, we will specifically use "client business risk" when we discuss clients. If a client decides to enter into a new product line that does poorly and does not recognize that the line needs to be disposed of, the decision could affect the entity's ability to continue as a going concern. The auditor assesses the entity's strategies as part of the development of a client risk profile. Client business risk is also considered when setting audit risk and materiality.

Client business risk—the risk that the client will fail to achieve its objectives.

Engagement risk or **auditor business risk**—the risk that the auditor or audit firm will suffer harm after the audit is finished.

Business risk—includes auditor business risk and client business risk

CAS

With respect to the audit firm, if the audit firm acquires clients that do not pay their bills, are dishonest, and result in significant litigation against the firm, then the PA firm itself will perhaps have a poor reputation and have going concern problems due to poor strategic decisions. The way firms handle auditor business risk or engagement risk is through client continuance or acceptance reviews and with techniques such as quality assurance during the audit.

Research has indicated that several factors affect business risk. Only three of those are discussed here: the degree to which external users rely on the statements, the likelihood that a client will have financial difficulties after the auditor's report is issued, and the integrity of management. These factors also affect audit risk.

The degree to which external users rely on the statements When external users place heavy reliance on the financial statements, it is appropriate that audit risk be decreased. When the statements are heavily relied on, a great social harm could result if a material misstatement were to remain undetected in the financial statements. The cost of additional evidence can be more easily justified when the loss to users from material misstatements is substantial.

Several factors are good indicators of the degree to which statements are relied on by external users:

- *Client's size.* Generally speaking, the larger a client's operations, the more widely used the statements will be. The client's size, measured by total assets or total revenues, will have an effect on audit risk.
- *Distribution of ownership.* The statements of publicly held corporations are normally relied on by many more users than those of private or closely held corporations. For these companies, the interested parties include the provincial securities administrators such as the Alberta Securities Commission, perhaps even the SEC, financial analysts, creditors, suppliers, the government, and the general public. The availability of financial statements on the internet allows for easy downloading of financial statement information for publicly traded companies. Therefore, distribution of these financial statements is potentially increasing due to technology.
- *Nature and amount of liabilities.* When statements include a large number of liabilities, they are more likely to be used extensively by actual and potential creditors than when there are few liabilities.

The likelihood that a client will have financial difficulties after the auditor's report is issued If a client is forced to file for bankruptcy or suffers a significant loss after completion of the audit, there is a greater chance of the auditor's being required to defend the quality of the audit than if the client were under no financial strain. The loss could be due to fraud, the loss of a major customer, or a computer disaster that cripples the company for a period of time. There is a natural tendency for those who lose money in a bankruptcy or because of a stock price reversal to file suit against the auditor. This can result from the honest belief that the auditor failed to conduct an adequate audit or from the users' desire to recover part of their loss regardless of the adequacy of the audit work.

In situations in which the auditor believes the chance of financial failure or loss is high, and there is a corresponding increase in business risk for the auditor, the level of audit risk should be reduced. If a subsequent challenge does occur, the auditor will then be in a better position to defend the audit results successfully. The total audit evidence and costs will increase, but this is justifiable because of the additional risk of lawsuits the auditor faces.

It is difficult for an auditor to predict financial failure before it occurs, but certain factors are good indicators of its increased probability:

- *Liquidity position.* If a client is constantly short of cash and working capital, it indicates a future problem in paying bills. The auditor must assess the likelihood and significance of a weak liquidity position getting worse.

- *Profits (losses) in previous years.* When a company has rapidly declining profits or increasing losses for several years, the auditor should recognize the future solvency problems the client is likely to encounter. It is also important to consider the changing profits relative to the balance remaining in retained earnings.
- *Method of financing growth.* The more a client relies on debt as a means of financing, the greater the risk of financial difficulty if the client's operations become less successful. It is also important to evaluate whether permanent assets are being financed with short-term or long-term loans. Large amounts of required cash outflows during a short period of time can force a company into bankruptcy.
- *Nature of the client's operations.* Certain types of businesses are inherently riskier than others. For example, other things being equal, there is a much greater likelihood of bankruptcy of a start-up technology company dependent on one product than of a diversified food manufacturer.
- *Extent of reliance upon technology and quality of support strategies.* The more a client relies upon technology, the more important it is that the company have an adequate backup and disaster recovery plan in the event of hardware or software failure. Support strategies, such as maintenance in the event of minor hardware or software problems, need to be high quality so that relatively minor problems, such as failure in a communications processor, do not cause operational shut downs. Appendix 7A, starting on page 231, describes the phases of a typical disaster recovery plan.
- *Competence of management.* Competent management is constantly alert for potential financing difficulties and modifies its operating methods to minimize the effects of short-run problems. The ability of management must be assessed as a part of the evaluation of the likelihood of bankruptcy.

audit challenge 7 - 1
Would Your Client Recover This Quickly from a Major Fire?

A major insurance company located in downtown Toronto on Bay Street occupied several floors of a high-rise building. On the tenth floor, there was a data centre housing mainframe computers, disk drives, printers, and telecommunications equipment for communicating with hundreds of insurance brokers and insurance offices. The data centre was physically separated from the offices, with an automated fire extinguishing system. On the ninth floor, immediately below the data centre, was an open area with personal computers used by the actuaries (individuals who analyze mortality rates and thus determine how much the company should charge for life insurance). On the sixth floor was a tape vault housing backup data and programs from the data centre.

On a Friday prior to a long weekend, the ninth floor open area caught fire. It was a massive fire, blackening the entire area and blowing out windows. Smoke filtered up to the tenth floor, where it seeped through holes in the data centre's walls (caused by previous movement of office partitions that had been attached to the data centre's walls). The operators (who had not been adequately trained) panicked and did not push the 15-cm-wide red button beside the exit door that would have automatically shut off the power to all systems. Instead, they rapidly left the room. Although the fire extinguishing system was activated, smoke continued to seep in, and half of the disk drives crashed.

Large volumes of water poured onto the ninth floor and below, hitting the top of the tape vault and cracking it. (The tape vault was located in the building's "water well," where the water

was supposed to flow so that it did not filter through the floors and ceilings of multiple floors.) Luckily, only about 5 cm of water settled in the bottom of the tape vault.

On Saturday morning, a human chain of 300 people transferred backup media to Bay Street, where transport trucks loaded with mainframe computing equipment and peripherals waited, hooked up to the telephone cables at the front of the building. On Tuesday morning, the mainframe systems were up and running, as if nothing had happened to the tenth floor. The ninth floor actuaries were not so lucky. All of their backup media, which were kept in their desks on the ninth floor, had been destroyed.

However, one of the actuaries had gone on holiday one week prior to the fire. Thinking that he would do some work at home, he had taken a copy of the system with him when he left. Needless to say, he was a hero when he returned a week after the fire.

CRITICAL THINKING QUESTIONS

1. What would have been the likely consequences if the company had been unable to restore operations to the main data centre until one week later? What about three weeks later?
2. This scenario indicates the importance of disaster recovery planning for central systems as well as decentralized systems. What other systems need to be backed up and why?
3. How does the quality of an organization's disaster recovery planning affect client business risk?

Table 7-2

Table 7-2	Methods Practitioners Use to Assess Audit Risk and Client Business Risk

Factors	Methods Used by Practitioners to Assess Audit Risk and Client Business Risk
External users' reliance on financial statements	• Examine the financial statements, including footnotes. • Read minutes of board of directors' meetings to determine future plans. • Examine filings with the provincial securities commission for a publicly held company. • Discuss financing plans with management.
Likelihood of financial difficulties	• Analyze the financial statements for financial difficulties using ratios and other analytical procedures. • Examine historical and projected cash flow statements for the nature of cash inflows and outflows. • Assess adequacy of disaster recovery plans.
Management integrity	• Follow the procedures discussed in Chapter 5 for client acceptance and continuance.

Management's integrity As discussed in Chapter 5, as a part of new client investigation and continuing client evaluation, if a client has questionable integrity, the auditor is likely to assess audit risk lower or not accept or even resign from the audit. Companies with low integrity often conduct their business affairs in a manner that results in conflicts with their shareholders, regulators, and customers. These conflicts, in turn, often reflect on the users' perceived quality of the audit and can result in lawsuits and other disagreements. An obvious example of a situation in which management's integrity is questionable is prior criminal conviction of a key member of management. Other examples of questionable integrity might include frequent disagreements with previous auditors, the Canada Revenue Agency, the provincial securities commission, or the stock exchange where the company is listed. Frequent turnover of key financial and internal audit personnel and ongoing conflicts with labour unions and employees may also indicate integrity problems.

To assess audit risk, the auditor must first assess each of the factors affecting audit risk. Table 7-2 illustrates the methods used by auditors to assess each of the three factors already discussed. You can see after examining Table 7-2 that the assessment of each of the factors is highly subjective, which means that the overall assessment is also highly subjective. A typical evaluation of audit risk is high, medium, or low,

concept check

C7-1 Using the audit risk model, holding all factors equal, what happens to detection risk if control risk goes down? Why?

C7-2 Why should the auditor consider client business risk when determining audit risk?

auditing in action 7 - 1
Assessing Audit Risk in Practice

Henry Rinsk, of Links, Rinsk & Rodman, Public Accountants, is the partner responsible for the audit of Hungry Food Restaurants Ltd., a chain of nine Manitoba family restaurants. The firm has audited Hungry Food for 10 years and has always found management competent, cooperative, and easy to deal with. Hungry Food is family owned with a business succession plan in place, profitable, liquid, and with little debt. Management has a reputation in the community of high integrity and good relationships with employees, customers, and suppliers.

After meeting with the other partners as part of the firm's annual client continuation meeting, Henry recommends that audit risk for Hungry Food be assessed as high. For Links, Rinsk & Rodman, this means no expansion of evidence, a "standard" review of working papers, and a "standard" assignment of personnel to the engagement.

where a low audit risk assessment means a "risky" client requiring more extensive evidence, assignment of more experienced personnel, and/or a more extensive review of working papers. As the audit progresses, additional information about the client is obtained and audit risk may be modified.

❷ Inherent Risk Assessment

Inherent Risk

The inclusion of inherent risk in the audit risk model is one of the most important concepts in auditing. It implies that auditors should attempt to predict where misstatements are most or least likely in the financial statement segments. This information affects the total amount of evidence the auditor is required to accumulate and influences how the auditor's efforts to gather the evidence are allocated among the segments of the audit. Inherent risk for the client as a whole is considered in the development of the client risk profile (discussed in the next chapter), while the audit risk model is used to consider inherent risk for each audit objective for material account balances and classes of transactions.

There is always some risk that the client has made misstatements that are individually or collectively large enough to make the financial statements misleading. The misstatements can be intentional or unintentional, and they can affect the dollar balance in accounts or disclosure. Inherent risk can be low in some instances and extremely high in others.

The audit risk model shows the common impact that inherent and control risks have on detection risk. For example, an inherent risk of 40 percent and a control risk of 60 percent affect detection risk and planned evidence the same as an inherent risk of 60 percent and a control risk of 40 percent. In both cases, the overall risk of material misstatement is the same. In both cases, multiplying IR by CR results in a denominator in the audit risk model of 24 percent. The combination of inherent risk and control risk can be thought of as the expectation of misstatements after considering the effect of internal controls on inherent risk, termed the **risk of material misstatements**. Inherent risk is the expectation of misstatements before considering the effect of internal controls.

At the start of an audit, there is not much that can be done about changing inherent risk. Instead, the auditor must assess the factors that make up the risk and modify the risk response, that is, the audit evidence collected, to take them into consideration. The auditor should consider several major factors when assessing inherent risk:

Risk of material misstatements— the expectation of misstatements after considering the effect of internal controls on inherent risk.

- Nature of the client's business, including the nature of the client's products and services.
- Nature of data processing systems and extent of use of data communications (see Chapter 10).
- Integrity of management.
- Client motivation.
- Results of previous audits.
- Initial versus repeat engagement.
- Related parties.
- Nonroutine transactions.
- Judgment required to record account balances and transactions correctly.
- Assets that are susceptible to misappropriation.
- Makeup of the population.

NATURE OF THE CLIENT'S BUSINESS Inherent risk for certain accounts is affected by the nature of the client's business. For example, there is a greater likelihood of obsolete inventory for an electronics manufacturer than for a steel fabricator. Similarly, loans receivable for a small loan company that makes unsecured loans are less likely

audit challenge 7-2
Inherent Risks, Estimating Risks of Disaster

In Canada, as in other parts of the world, many people rely on debit cards or automated banking services to pay for their purchases. Online payment systems such as PayPal are used to pay for electronic purchases. Many people carry only small amounts of cash.

On Saturday, October 27, 2001, for about 12 hours, starting at 11:00 a.m. Eastern Standard Time, there was a hardware failure at TD Canada Trust. Customers were unable to use online banking services (automated banking machines, internet banking, and telephone banking). On November 10, 2004, Scotiabank services were similarly unavailable for up to two and a half hours. In October 2004, the PayPal online payment system was sporadically unavailable for almost a whole week. These are examples of small disasters that we have gotten used to.

What about larger disasters, such as plant explosions? In Toronto, on August 10, 2008, the Sunrise Propane Industrial Gases distribution plant experienced an explosion that resulted in the death of a firefighter and an employee as well as the evacuation of five streets within a one block radius of the plant, with corporate buildings almost totally destroyed. Edmonton's AT Plastics had an explosion on October 24, 2008, that injured nine

workers. The Edmonton business was renamed Celanese EVA Performance Polymers Inc. in August 2009. A substantial investment was required to enable resumption of operations.

CRITICAL THINKING QUESTIONS

1. How would you assess the inherent risk of a bank versus a manufacturer of dangerous chemicals? What factors did you consider in your assessment?
2. Which financial statement accounts are most susceptible to risk for a bank? For an organization that produces dangerous chemicals? Why?

Sources: 1. [A TD Canada Trust advertisement], *The Globe and Mail*, October 29, 2001, p. A15. 2. Flavelle, Dana, "Scotia banking machines hit by computer glitch," November 11, 2004, www.thestar.com. 3. Freeman, Sunnay and Bill Taylor, "Residents return after blast," August 11, 2008, www.thestar.com, Accessed: November 26, 2008. 4. Kandra, Anne, "The Problem with PayPal," *PCWorld*, February 2005, www.pcworld.com. 5. Macdonald, Jim, "'It sounded like a bomb,' says resident after blast in Edmonton plastics plant," *Toronto Star*, October 25, 2008, p. A25. 6. Ochre Media, "Celanese Unveils EVA Performance Polymers Business Unit," June 26, 2009, www.plastics-technology.com/news/news_archives.asp?NewsID=256, Accessed: August 24, 2009.

to be collectable than those of a bank that makes only secured loans. Inherent risk is most likely to vary from business to business for accounts such as inventory, accounts and loans receivable, and property, plant, and equipment. The nature of the client's business should have little or no effect on inherent risk for accounts such as cash, notes, and mortgages payable. Information about the client's industry and business, as discussed in Chapter 5, is useful for assessing this factor.

NATURE OF DATA PROCESSING SYSTEMS When programs are customized by an understaffed information systems group, there is a greater likelihood of programming errors than when an organization is using standard packaged software, thus increasing the likelihood of material error, or operational error, as described in Audit Challenge 7-2. (The system acquisition or development process is discussed further in Chapter 10.)

The physical configuration of data processing systems affects the complexity of information systems. More complex systems are harder to understand and manage, increasing the likelihood of error. For example, a centralized data processing system with 15 data entry stations located on a single floor is easier to manage than a large financial institution's systems, where there are multiple central processing units, decentralized computing at minicomputers in regional centres, branches with microcomputers and automated teller machines processing transactions locally or transmitting to central locations, and electronic funds transfer transactions that are processed internationally. The scope of potential error is magnified a hundredfold in the more complex scenario. (The differences among centralized, decentralized, and distributed systems are described in Chapter 10.)

INTEGRITY OF MANAGEMENT When management is dominated by one or a few individuals who lack integrity, the likelihood of significantly misrepresented financial statements is greatly increased. For example, a lack of integrity of management has been found to exist in the great majority of significant accountants' liability cases. Management integrity affects the auditor's assessment of audit risk and, in extreme cases, may cause the auditor to reject the client (see also Chapter 5).

When management has an adequate level of integrity for the auditor to accept the engagement, but cannot be regarded as completely honest in all dealings, auditors normally reduce audit risk and also increase inherent risk. For example, management may deduct capital items as repairs and maintenance expense on tax returns. The public accounting firm should first evaluate the cycles or accounts for which management is most likely to make misstatements. A higher level of inherent risk is appropriate for those accounts or assertions where the auditor believes material misstatements may occur.

CLIENT MOTIVATION In many situations, management may believe it advantageous to misstate the financial statements. For example, if management receives a percentage of total profits as a bonus, there may be a tendency to overstate net income. Similarly, if a bond indenture requirement includes a specification that the current ratio must remain above a certain level, the client may be tempted to overstate current assets or to understate current liabilities by an amount sufficient to meet the requirement. Also, there may be considerable motivation for intentional understatement of income when management wants the company to pay less income tax. If management lacks integrity, some specific type of motivation may then lead management to misstate financial reports.

RESULTS OF PREVIOUS AUDITS Errors found in the previous year's audit have a high likelihood of occurring again in the current year's audit. This happens because many types of errors are systemic in nature, and organizations are often slow in making changes to eliminate them. Therefore, an auditor would be negligent if the results of the preceding year's examination were ignored during the development of the current year's audit program. For example, if the auditor found a significant number of errors in pricing inventory, inherent risk would likely be high, and extensive testing would have to be done in the current audit as a means of determining whether the deficiency in the client's system had been corrected. If, however, the auditor has found no errors for the past several years in conducting tests of an audit area, the auditor is justified in reducing inherent risk, provided that changes in relevant circumstances have not occurred.

INITIAL VERSUS REPEAT ENGAGEMENT Auditors gain experience and knowledge about the likelihood of misstatements after auditing a client for several years. The lack of previous years' audit results would cause most auditors to use a larger inherent risk for initial audits than for repeat engagements in which no material misstatements had been found. Most auditors set a high inherent risk in the first year of an audit and reduce it in subsequent years as they gain experience.

RELATED PARTIES Transactions between parent and subsidiary companies and those between management and the corporate entity are examples of related-party transactions. These transactions do not occur between two independent parties dealing at "arm's length." Therefore, a greater likelihood of their misstatement exists, which should cause an increase in inherent risk. Determining the existence of related parties is discussed in Chapter 8.

NONROUTINE TRANSACTIONS Transactions that are unusual for the client are more likely to be incorrectly recorded by the client than routine transactions because the client lacks experience in recording them. Examples include fire losses, major property acquisitions, and lease agreements. Knowledge of the client's business and review of minutes of meetings, as discussed in Chapter 8, are useful to learn about nonroutine transactions.

JUDGMENT REQUIRED TO RECORD ACCOUNT BALANCES AND TRANSACTIONS CORRECTLY Many account balances require estimates and a great deal of management judgment. Examples are allowance for uncollectible accounts receivable, obsolete inventory, liability for warranty payments, and bank loan loss reserves. Similarly, transactions for major repairs or partial replacement of assets are examples requiring considerable judgment to record the information correctly.

ASSETS THAT ARE SUSCEPTIBLE TO MISAPPROPRIATION The auditor should be concerned about the risk of possible defalcation in situations in which it is relatively easy to convert company assets to personal use. Such is the case when currency, marketable securities, or highly marketable inventory is not closely controlled. When the likelihood of defalcation is high, inherent risk is increased.

MAKEUP OF THE POPULATION The individual items making up the total population also frequently affect the auditor's expectation of material misstatement. For example, most auditors would use a higher inherent risk for accounts receivable when most accounts are significantly overdue than when most accounts are current. Similarly, the potential for misstatements in inventory purchased several years ago would normally be greater than for inventory purchased in the past few months. Transactions with affiliated companies, amounts due from officers, cash disbursements made payable to cash, and accounts receivable outstanding for several months are examples of situations requiring a larger inherent risk assessment and therefore greater investigation because there is usually a higher likelihood of misstatement than in more typical transactions.

ASSESSING INHERENT RISK The auditor must evaluate the preceding factors and decide on an appropriate inherent risk level for each cycle, account, and audit objective. Some factors, such as the integrity of management, will affect many or perhaps all cycles, whereas others, such as nonroutine transactions, will affect only specific accounts or audit objectives. Although the profession has not established standards or guidelines for setting inherent risk, the authors believe auditors are generally conservative in making such assessments. Most auditors would probably set inherent risk at well above 50 percent, even in the best of circumstances, and at 100 percent when there is any reasonable possibility of significant misstatements. For example, assume that in the audit of inventory, the auditor notes that (1) a large number of errors were found in the previous year and (2) inventory turnover has slowed in the current year. Many auditors would probably set inherent risk at a relatively high level (some would use 100 percent) for each audit objective for inventory in this situation.

> **concept check**
>
> C7-3 Describe the risk of material misstatement using parts of the audit risk model.
>
> C7-4 How would the complexity of information systems affect inherent risk?

3 The Importance of Materiality

Previously, paragraph 5142.04 of the *CICA Handbook* (replaced by material in CAS 320 and CAS 450, Evaluation of misstatements identified during the audit) defines **materiality** as follows:

> A misstatement . . . in financial statements is considered to be material if, in the light of surrounding circumstances, it is probable that the decision of a person who is relying on the financial statements, and who has a reasonable knowledge of business and economic activities (the user), would be changed or influenced by such misstatement . . .

It is interesting that neither CAS 320, Materiality in planning and performing an audit, nor CAS 450, Evaluation of misstatements identified during the audit, defines materiality; instead, it is spoken of in terms of three key concepts in the context of an audit (CAS 320 par. 2). The first and second concepts are included in the CICA definition above, that is, a material misstatement is considered in the context of knowledgeable users and the effect on decision making, and that material is relative to circumstances surrounding the decision and the nature of the information. A third point raised by the CAS is that the auditor considers users of financial statements as a

> **CAS**
>
> **Materiality**—the magnitude of an omission or misstatement of accounting information that, in the light of surrounding circumstances, makes it probable that the judgment of a reasonable person relying on the information would have been changed or influenced by the omission or misstatement.

group, rather than considering each user individually (such as a bank, bondholder, or shareholder). We will be using the term materiality as defined by the *CICA Handbook* section 5142 on the previous page.

The auditor's responsibility is to determine whether financial statements are materially misstated. If the auditor determines that there is a material misstatement, he or she will bring it to the client's attention so that a correction can be made. If the client refuses to correct the statements, a modified opinion must be issued (Chapter 22 explains types of opinions, such as qualified or an adverse opinion). The type of opinion issued will depend on how material and pervasive the misstatement is. Auditors must, therefore, have a thorough knowledge of the application of materiality.

A careful reading of the definition of materiality reveals the difficulty auditors have in applying materiality in practice. The definition emphasizes the decisions of users who have a reasonable knowledge of business and economic activities and who rely on the statements to make decisions. Auditors, therefore, must have knowledge of the likely users of their clients' statements and the decisions that are being made. For example, if an auditor knows financial statements will be relied on in a buy–sell agreement for the entire business, the amount that the auditor considers material may be smaller than for an otherwise similar audit. In practice, auditors often do not know who the users are or what decisions will be made. This is why the auditor obtains a knowledge of the business environment, of the client, of the purpose of the audit, and of risks before developing materiality.

There are five closely related steps in applying materiality during the planning and conduct of the audit. They are shown in Figure 7-2 and discussed in this section. The auditor starts by setting a preliminary judgment about materiality (called planning materiality) and then allocates this estimate to the segments of the audit, as shown in the first bracket of the figure. These two steps, which are part of planning, are our primary focus for the discussion of materiality in this chapter. Step 3 occurs throughout the engagement, where auditors estimate the amount of misstatements in each segment as they evaluate audit evidence. The final two steps are done near the end of the audit during the engagement completion phase and are part of evaluating the results of audit tests.

CAS 450 (containing material from the previous CICA Assurance and Related Services Guideline AuG-41, Applying the concept of materiality, suggests that an auditor be concerned with several levels of misstatement in assessing whether or not there is a material misstatement:

1. **Identified misstatements**—the actual misstatements discovered in the sample tested; they have not been corrected by management.
2. **Likely or projected misstatements**—the projection of the actual misstatements in the sample to the population; the misstatements have not been corrected by management or could be disagreements of opinion with management.
3. **Likely aggregate misstatement**—the sum of the identified misstatements and likely misstatements in the financial statements.
4. **Further possible misstatements**—the misstatements over and above the likely aggregate misstatement that result from the imprecision in the sampling process.
5. **Maximum possible misstatement**—the sum of likely aggregate misstatement plus further possible misstatements.

The auditor is sure of an identified misstatement because it was determined to be the misstatement in the sample. The projection of that error to the population plus other actual identified misstatements—the likely misstatement—is based on the assumption that the sample is representative of the population. The auditor is fairly certain about the likely aggregate misstatement when he or she is talking to the client about making an adjustment; if the likely aggregate misstatement exceeds materiality, the auditor will require an adjustment.

CAS

Identified misstatements—the actual misstatements discovered in the sample tested; the misstatements have not been corrected by management.

Likely or projected misstatements—the projection of the actual misstatements in the sample to the population; the misstatements have not been corrected by management or there is a disagreement with management; see also "Direct projection method of estimating misstatement."

Likely aggregate misstatement—the sum of the identified misstatements and likely misstatements in the financial statements.

Further possible misstatements—the misstatements over and above the likely aggregate misstatement that result from the imprecision in the sampling process.

Maximum possible misstatement—the sum of likely aggregate misstatement plus further possible misstatements.

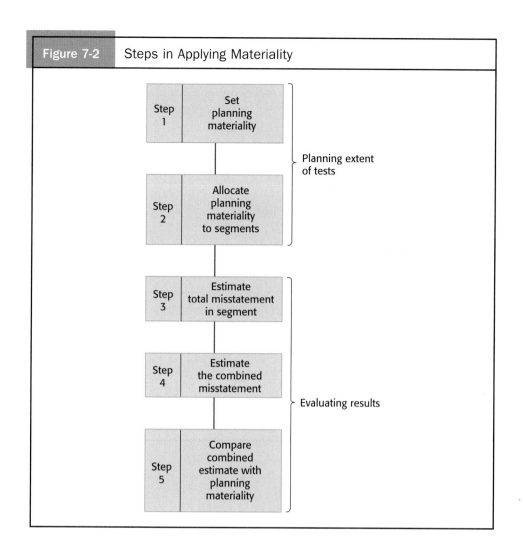

Figure 7-2   Steps in Applying Materiality

Step 1: Set planning materiality

Step 2: Allocate planning materiality to segments

} Planning extent of tests

Step 3: Estimate total misstatement in segment

Step 4: Estimate the combined misstatement

Step 5: Compare combined estimate with planning materiality

} Evaluating results

Further possible misstatement is based on the imprecision in the sampling process. There are two risks: (1) the sample may not be representative, and (2) the auditor may misinterpret evidence.[1] The auditor recognizes that further possible misstatements are possible but not probable. It would not be appropriate to ask the client to make an adjustment for further possible misstatements by virtue of their very definition. The auditor may or may not require an adjustment when the maximum possible misstatement exceeds materiality.

Set Planning Materiality

Ideally, an auditor decides early in the audit the combined amount of misstatements in the financial statements that would be considered material. CAS 320 par. 5 explains that the auditor uses materiality during the audit and when conducting the audit to determine the nature, timing, and extent of the auditing procedures; this is the planning materiality (also called performance materiality) in step 1 of Figure 7-2. It is often called a planning materiality because it may change during the engagement if circumstances change. Since materiality is defined in the context of users of financial statements, such a change would be unlikely unless additional information regarding users were obtained during the audit.

This planning materiality is the maximum amount by which the auditor believes the financial statements as a whole could be misstated and still not affect

`CAS`

---

[1] These two risks are called sampling risk and nonsampling risk, respectively. They are discussed in detail in Chapter 13.

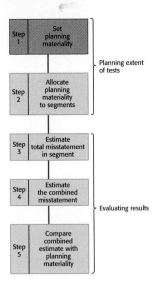

Step 1 — Set planning materiality

Planning extent of tests

Step 2 — Allocate planning materiality to segments

Step 3 — Estimate total misstatement in segment

Step 4 — Estimate the combined misstatement

Evaluating results

Step 5 — Compare combined estimate with planning materiality

the decisions of reasonable users. This judgment is one of the most important decisions the auditor makes. It requires considerable professional judgment.

The reason for setting planning materiality is to help the auditor plan the appropriate evidence to accumulate. If the auditor sets a low dollar amount, more evidence is required than for a high amount. Examine again the financial statements of Hillsburg Hardware Limited, on pages 147–162. What do you think is the combined amount of misstatements that would affect decisions of reasonable users? Do you believe a $100 misstatement would affect users' decisions? If so, the amount of evidence required for the audit is likely to be beyond that for which the management of Hillsburg Hardware can pay. Do you believe a $1 million misstatement would be material? Most experienced auditors would say that amount is far too large as a combined materiality amount for Hillsburg.

The auditor may change the planning materiality during the audit if, for example, a new user of the financial statements is identified or if many errors were encountered during the audit, and the auditor wants to widen the scope of testing. This revised figure and the reasons would need to be carefully documented, and field work completed to date reassessed in the context of the new materiality level. Reasons for using a revised judgment can include a change in one of the factors used to determine the preliminary judgment or a decision by the auditor that the preliminary judgment was too small or, more likely, too large.

FACTORS AFFECTING JUDGMENT ABOUT MATERIALITY Several factors affect setting a planning materiality for a given set of financial statements. The most important of these are discussed below.

Materiality is a relative rather than an absolute concept A misstatement of a given magnitude might be material for a small company, whereas the same dollar error could be immaterial for a large one. For example, a total error of $1 million would be extremely material for Hillsburg Hardware Limited because net income before tax is about $5.7 million. It would be immaterial for a company such as IBM, which has total assets and net income of several billion dollars. Hence, it is not possible to establish any dollar-value guidelines for a preliminary judgment about materiality applicable to all audit clients.

Bases are needed for evaluating materiality Since materiality is relative, it is necessary to have bases for establishing whether misstatements are material. Common bases include the following:

1. 5 to 10 percent of net income before taxes. This number can be fairly volatile so most auditors use normalized net income (i.e., net income adjusted for unusual and non-recurring items such as a large inventory writedown) or average net income.
2. 1/2 percent to 5 percent of gross profit.
3. 1/2 percent to 1 percent of total assets.
4. 1/2 percent to 5 percent of shareholders' equity.
5. 1/2 percent to 2 percent of revenue.
6. The weighted average of methods 1 to 5.
7. A reducing percentage of the greater of revenue and assets.
8. 1/2 percent to 2 percent of expenses or revenue as suggested by the guideline for non-profit entities.

Current practice also includes exponential models, in which materiality starts low for small bases, rises exponentially, and then levels off. Also, scaled amounts are used that are larger than the percentages shown above. Those methods that use a range of percentages generally suggest that the largest percentage be used for smaller entities and the smallest percentage be used for larger entities. For example, under method 1, 10 percent would be used if the entity were small and 5 percent if it were very large; some percentage between 5 percent and 10 percent would be used for entities between the two extremes.

Impact of qualitative factors Certain types of misstatements are likely to be more important to users than others, even if the dollar amounts are the same. The auditors cannot plan to detect smaller amounts but must react if they are discovered. For example, small amounts involving fraud and other irregularities are usually considered more important than unintentional errors of equal dollar amounts because fraud reflects on the honesty and reliability of the management or other personnel involved. To illustrate, most users would consider an intentional misstatement of inventory as being more important than clerical errors in inventory of the same dollar amount. In addition, while the amount of a fraud may be less than materiality, the impact of fraud on the entity may be much in excess of materiality. For example, assume materiality for an entity with worldwide operations was $200 million. An illegal payment in another country of $25,000 would be less than materiality but could lead, if the illegal payment were to be discovered by the authorities in the other country, to fines or seizure in that country of the entity's assets. The fines or seizures could be many times the amount of the illegal payment, resulting in loss of income or other damages that exceeded materiality.

ILLUSTRATIVE GUIDELINES The CICA currently does not provide specific materiality guidelines to practitioners. The concern is that such guidelines might be applied without considering all the complexities that should affect the auditor's final decision.

To show the application of materiality, illustrative guidelines are provided. They are intended only to help you better understand the concept of applying materiality in practice. The guidelines are stated in Figure 7-3 in the form of a policy guideline for a public accounting firm.

Figure 7-3	Illustrative Materiality Guidelines

MCCUTCHEON & WILKINSON, CHARTERED ACCOUNTANTS
Edmonton, Alberta T6G 1N4
(780) 432-6900

POLICY STATEMENT   Sally J. Wilkinson
No. 32 IC   Karen McCutcheon
Title: Materiality Guidelines

Professional judgment is to be used at all times in setting and applying materiality guidelines. In general, the following policies are to be applied:

1. The combined total of misstatements in the financial statements exceeding 10 percent is normally considered material. A combined total of less than 5 percent is presumed to be immaterial in the absence of qualitative factors. Combined misstatements between 5 percent and 10 percent require the greatest amount of professional judgment to determine their materiality.
2. The 5 to 10 percent must be measured in relation to the appropriate base. Many times there is more than one base to which errors should be compared. The following guides are recommended in selecting the appropriate base:
   a. *Income statement.* Combined misstatements in the income statement should ordinarily be measured at 5 to 10 percent of operating income before taxes. A guideline of 5 to 10 percent may be inappropriate in a year in which income is unusually large or small. When operating income in a given year is not considered representative, it is desirable to substitute as a base a more representative income measure, such as normalized net income before taxes or average operating income for a three-year period.
      In the case of clients who operate in industries where operating income before taxes is not considered to be a useful base, $\frac{1}{2}$ percent to 2 percent of revenue will be used as a guideline.
   b. *Balance sheet.* Combined misstatements in the balance sheet should originally be evaluated for total assets. For total assets, the guideline should be between $\frac{1}{2}$ and 1 percent, applied in the same way as for the income statement. An alternative is to use $\frac{1}{2}$ percent to 5 percent of shareholders' equity.
3. Qualitative factors should be carefully evaluated on all audits. In many instances they are more important than the guidelines applied to the income statement and balance sheet. The intended uses of the financial statements and the nature of the information on the statements, including footnotes, must be carefully evaluated.
4. If the guideline for the income statement is less than those selected for the balance sheet, the lesser amount should be used as a guideline for all misstatements that affect operating income before taxes. Misstatements such as misclassification errors would be evaluated using the greater amount.

Table 7-3 — Preliminary Judgment About Materiality

	Minimum		Maximum	
	Percentage	Dollar Amount (in thousands)	Percentage	Dollar Amount (in thousands)
Net income before taxes	5	248	10	496
Gross profit	1/2	199	5	1,992
Total assets	1/2	307	1	614
Shareholders' equity	1/2	112	5	1,123
Revenue (net sales)	1/2	715	2	2,862

APPLICATION TO HILLSBURG HARDWARE LIMITED Using the illustrative guidelines for McCutcheon & Wilkinson in Figure 7-3, it is now possible to decide on a preliminary judgment about materiality for Hillsburg Hardware Limited (see Table 7-3).

Assuming the auditor for Hillsburg Hardware decided that the general guidelines are reasonable, the first step would be to evaluate whether any qualitative factors significantly affect the materiality judgment. If not, considering the income statement base first, the auditor must decide that if combined misstatements on the income statement were less than $248,000, the statements would be considered fairly stated. If the combined misstatements exceeded $496,000, the statements would not be considered fairly stated. If the misstatements were between $248,000 and $496,000, a more careful consideration of all facts would be required. The auditor then applies the same process to the other three bases. Given the suggested guidelines calculated above and the fact that Hillsburg Hardware is a public company with a limited number of shareholders, the auditor would probably decide to use the larger of the net income bases, $496,000, as the planning materiality. Gross profit is also a base that fluctuates less from year to year than net income since companies may have fluctuating income levels.

The planning materiality should be adjusted for the effect of net anticipated misstatements to determine materiality available for unanticipated misstatements. The illustration in Table 7-4 is an example of adjusting for the effect of net anticipated misstatements.

The auditor, in the above example, is simply reducing the planning materiality of $496,000 for net anticipated misstatements of $55,000 to determine that $441,000 will be available for unanticipated misstatements. A useful analogy would be that of

Table 7-4 — Materiality Adjusted for Potential Misstatements

Preliminary judgment about materiality, based on net income before extraordinary items		$496,000
Less		
Anticipated misstatements from specific tests	$50,000	
Carry forward misstatements from the previous year	80,000	
Anticipated client corrections	(75,000)	55,000
Materiality available for unanticipated misstatements		$441,000

an individual going out for the evening who has $60 for dinner and a movie but needs $10 for cab fare home. The amount available for spending for the evening is $50, not $60. Similarly, the amount available for unanticipated misstatements is really $441,000, not $496,000.

Allocate Planning Materiality to Segments

Some auditors allocate materiality to segments once they have determined materiality available for unanticipated misstatements. They use the amounts allocated to determine sample sizes and the amount of testing required. However, many auditors use total materiality available for unanticipated misstatements in audit planning on the grounds that the auditor is concerned about the aggregate misstatement in the financial statements as a whole and not in the misstatement in a particular account balance.

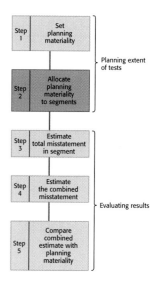

The allocation of planning materiality to segments (Step 2 in Figure 7-2) is done because auditors accumulate evidence by cycles or accounts rather than for the financial statements as a whole. If auditors have a preliminary judgment about materiality for each segment, it helps them to decide the appropriate audit evidence to accumulate. Materiality is modified by segment in response to differences in anticipated errors and risks by segment. It may also be modified because of a particular reliance on those accounts. For example, if the client is using accounts receivable and inventory as collateral on a loan, the auditor might want to collect more evidence on those accounts. For an accounts receivable balance of $1,000,000, for example, the auditor should accumulate more evidence if a misstatement of $50,000 is considered material than if $300,000 were considered material.

When allocation of materiality is used, it is allocated primarily to balance sheet rather than income statement accounts because most income statement misstatements have an equal effect on the balance sheet due to the effects of the double-entry bookkeeping system. For example, a $20,000 overstatement of accounts receivable is also a $20,000 overstatement of sales. Materiality would be allocated to either income statement or balance sheet accounts, not both, because doing so would result in double counting.

ALLOCATION ILLUSTRATED When auditors allocate the planning materiality to account balances, the materiality allocated to any given account balance is referred to as the "tolerable misstatement" for that account (see also Chapter 13). For example, if an auditor decides to allocate $100,000 of a total preliminary judgment about materiality of $200,000 to accounts receivable, tolerable misstatement for accounts receivable is $100,000. This means that the auditor is willing to consider accounts receivable fairly stated if it is misstated by $100,000 or less.

Auditors face three major difficulties in allocating materiality to balance sheet accounts:

1. Auditors expect certain accounts to have more misstatements than others.
2. Both overstatements and understatements must be considered.
3. Audit costs affect the allocation of tolerable misstatements.

Figure 7-4 on the next page illustrates the approach followed by the auditors of Hillsburg Hardware Ltd. It summarizes the balance sheet, combining certain accounts, and shows the allocation of total materiality of $441,000 (10 percent of earnings, less the effect of anticipated misstatements). Professional judgment and auditor risk assessments are used to allocate these amounts. Some of the rationale for allocation is shown at the bottom of Figure 7-4. For example, it was decided that there would be no allocation of tolerable misstatement to notes payable, even though it is as large as inventories. This happens because even if tolerable misstatement had been allocated to notes payable, confirmations would still have been necessary. It was therefore more efficient to allocate amounts to inventories. A smaller amount, $60,000, was allocated to other current assets (other accounts receivable and prepaid expenses) and to accrued payroll

	Balance Dec. 31, 2008 (in Thousands)	Tolerable Misstatement (in Thousands)
Cash	$ 828	$ 6 (a)
Trade accounts receivable (net)	18,957	265 (b)
Inventories	29,865	265 (b)
Other current assets	1,377	60 (c)
Property, plant, and equipment	10,340	48 (d)
Total assets	$61,367	
Trade accounts payable	$ 4,720	106 (e)
Notes payable—total	28,300	0 (a)
Accrued payroll and payroll tax	1,470	60 (c)
Accrued interest and dividends payable	2,050	0 (a)
Other liabilities	2,364	72 (c)
Capital stock and capital in excess of par	8,500	0 (a)
Retained earnings	13,963	NA (f)
Total liabilities and equity	$61,367	$882 (2 × $441)

NA = Not applicable

(a) Zero or small tolerable misstatement because account can be completely audited at low cost and no misstatements are expected.

(b) Large tolerable misstatement because account is large and requires extensive sampling to audit the account.

(c) Large tolerable misstatement as a percent of account because account can be verified at extremely low cost, probably with analytical procedures, if tolerable misstatement is large.

(d) Small tolerable misstatement as a percent of account balance because most of the balance is in land and buildings, which is unchanged from the prior year and need not be audited.

(e) Moderately large tolerable misstatement because a relatively large number of misstatements are expected.

(f) Not applicable—retained earnings is a residual account that is affected by the net amount of the misstatements in the other accounts.

and payroll taxes. These amounts can easily be verified within $60,000 using analytical procedures, which are low cost. If tolerable misstatement were lower, more costly audit procedures such as inspection of documents and confirmation would need to be used.

In practice, it is often difficult to predict in advance which accounts are most likely to be misstated and whether misstatements are likely to be overstatements or understatements. Similarly, the relative costs of auditing different account balances may be hard to estimate. It is a difficult professional judgment decision to allocate the planning materiality to accounts. Those firms that do so have developed rigorous guidelines and sophisticated statistical methods.

To summarize, the purpose of allocating the planning materiality to balance sheet accounts is to help the auditor decide the appropriate evidence to accumulate for each account on both the balance sheet and income statement. An aim of the allocation is to minimize audit costs without sacrificing audit quality. Regardless of how the allocation is done, when the audit is completed, the auditor must be confident that the combined misstatements in all accounts are less than or equal to the planning (or subsequently revised) materiality amount.

Estimate Misstatement and Compare

The first two steps in applying materiality involve planning, whereas the last three steps in Figure 7-2 result from performing audit tests. These steps are introduced here and discussed in greater detail in later chapters.

When the auditor performs audit procedures for each segment of the audit, a worksheet is kept of all misstatements found. For example, assume the auditor finds six client errors in a sample of 200 in testing inventory costs (identified misstatement).

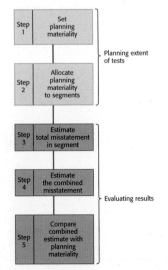

Step 1   Set planning materiality

Step 2   Allocate planning materiality to segments

Planning extent of tests

Step 3   Estimate total misstatement in segment

Step 4   Estimate the combined misstatement

Step 5   Compare combined estimate with planning materiality

Evaluating results

Reasonable Materiality Is Hard Work

What to do? OilCo has acquired a subsidiary, which has resulted in assets increasing by over $100 million to $195 million. Of the growth, $68 million is in inventory and $80 million in goodwill. Firm standards result in a calculation of materiality of only about $50,000 based on gross margin, while revenue results in only a slightly higher number of $100,000.

This means that sample sizes for inventory would approach 300 for completeness, existence, and accuracy, to obtain a reasonable level of assurance.

Can an average be taken? Since it is for only a partial year, can the whole year's materiality be used?

The firm's standards department gave the following advice: An average does not make sense when operations have changed. Using an artificially high materiality increases engagement risk for the auditor. Rather than trying to increase materiality with reasons that do not make sense, focus on the parts of the audit that are risky, that is, inventory and goodwill, spending less time on other parts of the engagement.

Source: Correspondence about materiality from an audit firm to I. Splettstoesser-Hogeterp, Fall 2008.

These misstatements are used to estimate the total misstatements in inventory (step 3). The total is referred to as an "estimate" or often a "projection" because only a sample, rather than the entire population, was audited. The projected misstatement amounts (likely misstatements) for each account are combined on the worksheet (step 4), and then the combined misstatement (likely aggregate misstatement) is compared with materiality (step 5).

Table 7-5 is used to illustrate the last three steps in applying materiality. For simplicity, only three accounts are included and the calculation of likely misstatements for accounts receivable and for inventory are shown. The planning materiality is $50,000. The likely misstatements are calculated based on actual audit tests. Assume, for example, that in auditing inventory, the auditor found $3,500 of net overstatement errors in a sample of $50,000 of the total population of $450,000. One way to calculate the estimate of the misstatements is to make a direct projection from the sample to the population and add an estimate for sampling error (further possible misstatements). The **direct projection method of estimating misstatement** (likely misstatement) is done by dividing the net misstatements in the sample by the total sampled, then multiplying the result by the total recorded population value:

> **Direct projection method of estimating misstatement**—net misstatements in the sample, divided by the total sampled, multiplied by the total recorded population value; see also "Likely misstatements."

$$\frac{\text{Net misstatements in the sample (\$3,500)}}{\text{Total sampled (\$50,000)}} \times \frac{\text{Total recorded}}{\text{population value}} = \frac{\text{Direct projection}}{\text{estimate (\$31,500)}}$$

The estimate for **sampling error** results because the auditor has sampled only a portion of the population. (This is discussed in detail in Chapters 13, 14, and 15.) It is the amount by which a projected likely misstatement amount could be different from an actual (and unknown) total as a result of the sample not being representative. In this simplified example, the estimate for sampling error is assumed to be 50 percent of the direct projection of the misstatement amounts for the accounts where sampling was used (accounts receivable and inventory).

> **Sampling error**—error that results because the auditor has sampled only a portion of the population.

In combining the misstatements in Table 7-5 on the next page, observe that the likely misstatements for the three accounts add to $43,500. The total sampling error (further possible misstatements) quite often is different from the sum of the sampling errors since varying levels of certainty must be incorporated and the total is usually calculated as a numeric range. Sampling error represents the maximum error in account details not audited.

It is unlikely that this maximum error amount would exist in all accounts subjected to sampling. Thus, sampling methodology provides for determining a combined sampling error that takes this into consideration. Again, this is discussed in detail in Chapters 13 to 15.

Table 7-5	Illustration of Comparison of Maximum Possible Misstatement to Planning Materiality		

| | Maximum Possible Misstatement | | |
Account	Likely Misstatement	Sampling Error	Total
Cash	$ 0	N/A	$ 0
Accounts receivable	$12,000	$ 6,000[1]	$18,000
Inventory	$31,500	$15,750[2]	$47,250
Total estimated misstatement amount	$43,500	$21,750	$65,250
Planning materiality			$50,000

N/A = Not applicable; cash audited 100%. (1) 12,000 × 50% (assumed) (2) 31,500 × 50% (assumed)

Table 7-5 shows that the maximum possible misstatement for the three accounts of $65,250 exceeds the planning materiality of $50,000. Furthermore, the major area of difficulty is inventory, where the maximum possible misstatement is $47,250. Because the estimated maximum possible misstatement exceeds the preliminary judgment, the financial statements are not acceptable. The auditor can either determine whether the estimated aggregate misstatement actually exceeds $50,000 by performing additional audit procedures or require the client to make an adjustment for likely misstatements. Assuming additional audit procedures are performed, they would be concentrated in the inventory area.

If the estimated maximum possible misstatement for inventory had been $24,000 ($16,000 plus $8,000 sampling error), the auditor probably would not need to expand audit tests, since the total maximum possible misstatement would be less ($18,000 + $24,000 = $42,000) than the $50,000 preliminary judgment. It is likely that the auditor would have accepted the balances in the three accounts.

concept check

C7-5 What is the difference between planned materiality and revised materiality? How does a revision to materiality affect the audit process?

C7-6 What are the advantages and disadvantages of segmenting materiality?

4 Relating Risk and Materiality to Audit Performance

Summary of Audit Risk Model Risks

Figure 7-5 summarizes the factors that affect audit risk, inherent risk, and control risk. Based on the determined audit risk, the conclusion reached with respect to inherent risk, and both the conclusion and extent of reliance determined for control risk, the auditor determines the planned detection risk and the planned audit evidence to be accumulated.

Other Materiality and Risk Considerations

AUDIT RISK FOR SEGMENTS Both control risk and inherent risk are typically estimated for each cycle, each account, and each audit objective and are likely to vary from cycle to cycle, account to account, and objective to objective on the same audit. Internal controls may be more effective for inventory-related accounts than for those related to capital assets. Control risk would therefore also be different for different accounts depending on the effectiveness of the controls. Factors affecting inherent risk, such as susceptibility to defalcation and routineness of the transactions, are also likely to differ from account to account. For that reason, it is normal to have inherent risk vary for different accounts in the same audit unless there is some strong overriding factor of concern such as management integrity.

Audit risk is ordinarily set by the auditor for the entire audit and held constant for each major cycle and account. Auditors normally use the same audit risk for each

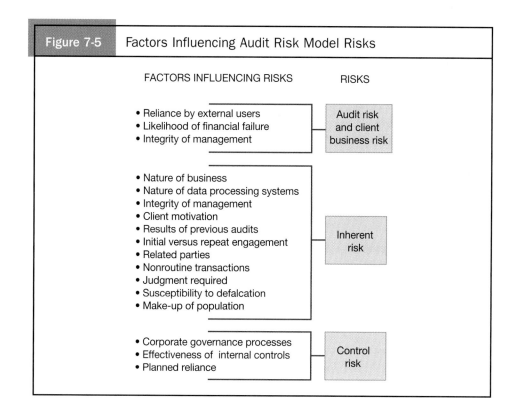

Figure 7-5 Factors Influencing Audit Risk Model Risks

FACTORS INFLUENCING RISKS   RISKS

- Reliance by external users
- Likelihood of financial failure
- Integrity of management

→ Audit risk and client business risk

- Nature of business
- Nature of data processing systems
- Integrity of management
- Client motivation
- Results of previous audits
- Initial versus repeat engagement
- Related parties
- Nonroutine transactions
- Judgment required
- Susceptibility to defalcation
- Make-up of population

→ Inherent risk

- Corporate governance processes
- Effectiveness of internal controls
- Planned reliance

→ Control risk

segment because the factors affecting audit risk are related to the entire audit, not to individual accounts. For example, the extent to which financial statements are relied on for users' decisions is usually related to the overall financial statements, not just one or two accounts. In the illustrations that follow in this and subsequent chapters, a common audit risk is used for segments and for the financial statements as a whole.

Because control risk and inherent risk may vary from cycle to cycle, account to account, or objective to objective, planned detection risk and required audit evidence will also vary. The circumstances of each engagement are different, and the extent of evidence needed will depend on the unique circumstances. For example, inventory might require extensive testing on an engagement due to weak internal controls and concern about obsolescence due to technological changes in the industry. On the same engagement, accounts receivable may require little testing because of effective internal controls, fast collection of receivables, excellent relationships between the client and customers, and good audit results in previous years. Similarly, for a given audit of inventory, an auditor may assess that there is a higher inherent risk of a valuation misstatement because of the higher potential for obsolescence but a low inherent risk of a classification misstatement because there is only purchased inventory.

RELATING RISKS TO BALANCE-RELATED AUDIT OBJECTIVES It is common in practice to assess inherent and control risks for each audit objective. Auditors are able to effectively associate most risks with different objectives. It is reasonably easy to determine the relationship between a risk and one or two objectives. For example, obsolescence in inventory would be unlikely to affect any objective other than valuation.

MEASUREMENT LIMITATIONS One major limitation in the application of the audit risk model is the difficulty of measuring the components of the model. In spite of the auditor's best efforts in planning, the assessments of audit risk, inherent risk, control risk, and, therefore, planned detection risk are highly subjective and are approximations of reality at best. Imagine, for example, attempting to assess precisely inherent risk by determining the impact of factors such as the misstatements discovered in prior years' audits and technology changes in the client's industry.

Just like other organizations, auditors use electronic tools to improve efficiency and quality. For example, digital storage of working papers and files makes their retrieval easier, and storage of working papers on a network makes their monitoring in real time easier.

The use of templates and tools to facilitate the implementation of the audit risk model help provide structured decision making. A problem arises, though, if the auditor creates a target materiality and then fills in the forms in a "backwards way" to provide support for the decision.

The methods of effective use of electronic audit tools and the risks associated with their use are some of the findings of a literature review of articles about risk monitoring and control in auditing firms.

Software tools used by auditors can be extremely complex, yet assist decision making during the audit process. Go to the internet, and do a search on "audit software." You will find out about the availability of software that will help you deal with Sarbanes-Oxley, check your program, help you detect fraud patterns, and prepare working papers.

Sources: 1. "A community of professionals helping you maximize the benefits of audit software," www.auditsoftware.net, Accessed: November 27, 2008. 2. Bedard, Jean, D. Deis, B. Curtis, and J. G. Jenkins, "Risk monitoring and control in audit firms: a research synthesis," *Auditing: A Journal of Practice & Theory*, 27(1), p. 187–218.

To offset this measurement problem, many auditors use broad and subjective measurement terms, for example, "low," "medium," and "high." Audit firms have developed automated systems that help the auditor to ensure that the appropriate questions have been answered and assist in the documentation and tabulation of conclusions reached. Table 7-6 shows how auditors can use the information to decide on the appropriate amount of evidence to accumulate for a particular transaction cycle. For example, in situation 1, the auditor has decided to accept a high audit risk. The auditor has concluded that there is a low risk of misstatement in the cycle (inherent risk) and that internal controls are effective. Therefore, a high detection risk is appropriate. As a result, a low level of evidence is needed. Situation 3 is at the opposite extreme. If both inherent and control risks are high but the auditor wants a low audit risk, considerable evidence is required. The other three situations fall between the two extremes.

It is equally difficult to measure the amount of evidence implied by a given planned detection risk. A typical audit program that is intended to reduce detection risk to the planned level is a combination of several audit procedures, each using a different type of evidence that is applied to different audit objectives. Auditors' measurement methods are too imprecise to permit an accurate quantitative measure of the combined evidence. Instead, auditors subjectively evaluate whether sufficient evidence has been planned to satisfy a planned detection risk of low, medium, or high. Presumably, measurement methods are sufficient to permit an auditor to know that

Table 7-6	Relationships of Risk to Evidence				
Situation	Audit Risk	Inherent Risk	Control Risk	Planned Detection Risk	Amount of Evidence Required
1	High	Low	Low	High	Low
2	Low	Low	Low	Medium	Medium
3	Low	High	High	Low	High
4	Medium	Medium	Medium	Medium	Medium
5	High	Low	Medium	Medium	Medium

more evidence is needed to satisfy a low planned detection risk than for medium or high. Considerable professional judgment is needed to decide how much more. Continuing research in audit firms is used to help auditors to determine the mix of evidence required and to devise more effective means of gathering evidence as the nature of business transactions change. Some firms have an emphasis on controls reliance (where possible), while others decide that analytical review and tests of details should be emphasized instead.

In applying the audit risk model, auditors are concerned about both over- and under-auditing, but most auditors are more concerned about the latter. Under-auditing exposes the public accounting firm to legal liability and loss of professional reputation.

Because of the concern to avoid under-auditing, auditors typically assess risks conservatively. For example, an auditor might not assess either control risk or inherent risk below 0.5 even when the likelihood of misstatement is low. In these audits, a low control or inherent risk might be 0.5, medium 0.8, and high 1.0 if the risks are quantified.

TESTS OF DETAILS OF BALANCES EVIDENCE-PLANNING DOCUMENTATION Practising auditors develop various types of spreadsheets, templates, or computerized links to aid in relating the considerations affecting audit evidence to the appropriate evidence to accumulate. One such spreadsheet in printed form is included in Figure 7-6 for the audit of accounts receivable for Hillsburg Hardware Limited. The eight balance-related audit objectives introduced in Chapter 5 are included in the columns at the

| Figure 7-6 | Evidence Planning Spreadsheet to Decide Tests of Details of Balances for Hillsburg Hardware Limited—Accounts Receivable |

	Existence	Rights and Obligations	Completeness	Accuracy	Valuation	Classification	Detail tie-in	Cut-off
Audit risk	high	high	high	high	high	high	high	high
Inherent risk	low	low	low	low	low	low	medium	low
Control risk – Sales								
Control risk – Cash receipts								
Control risk – Additional controls								
Analytical procedures								
Planned detection risk for tests of details of balances								
Planned audit evidence for tests of details of balances								

Materiality $496,000

top of the spreadsheet. Rows one and two are audit risk and inherent risk, which were studied in this chapter. Materiality is included at the bottom of the worksheet. The following decisions were made in the audit of Hillsburg Hardware Limited:

- *Materiality.* The preliminary judgment about materiality was set at $496,000 (10 percent of earnings before income taxes and extraordinary items of $4,961,000).
- *Audit risk.* Audit risk was assessed as high because of the good financial condition of the company, high management integrity, and the relatively few public shareholders, about 1,000.
- *Inherent risk.* Inherent risk was determined to be low for all balance-related audit objectives except valuation. In past years, there have been audit adjustments to the allowance for uncollectible accounts because it was found to be understated.

Planned detection risk would be approximately the same for each balance-related audit objective in the audit of accounts receivable for Hillsburg Hardware Limited if the only three factors the auditor needed to consider were audit risk, inherent risk, and materiality. The evidence planning spreadsheet shows that other factors must be considered before making the final evidence decisions. Control risk for the different transaction types is examined separately, as is the impact of analytical procedures. These are studied in subsequent chapters and will be integrated into the evidence planning spreadsheet at that time.

RELATIONSHIP OF MATERIALITY AND RISK AND AUDIT EVIDENCE The concepts of materiality and risk in auditing are closely related and inseparable. Materiality is a measure of magnitude or size while risk is a measure of uncertainty. Taken together they measure the uncertainty of amounts of a given magnitude. For example, the statement that the auditor plans to accumulate evidence such that there is only a 5-percent risk (audit risk) of failing to uncover misstatements exceeding materiality of $25,000 (materiality) is a precise and meaningful statement. If the statement eliminates either the risk or materiality portion, it would be meaningless. A 5-percent risk without a specific materiality measure could imply that a $100 or $1 million misstatement is acceptable. A $25,000 overstatement without a specific risk could imply that a 1-percent or an 80-percent risk is acceptable.

As a general rule, there is a fixed relationship among materiality, risk, and audit evidence. If one of those components is changed, then one or both of the remaining components must also change to achieve the same audit risk. For example, if evidence is held constant and materiality is decreased, then the risk that a material but undiscovered misstatement could exist must increase. Similarly, if materiality were held constant and risk reduced, the required evidence would increase.

Refer again to Figure 7-1, where the different components of the audit risk model interact to achieve the specified audit risk. Planned evidence (the complement of planned detection risk) is used to offset any changes in inherent or control risks for a particular transaction cycle to achieve the targeted audit risk. Note that materiality is not present in the figure—materiality does not affect any of the four risks and the risks have no effect on materiality. Yet materiality is used in addition to the risks to determine the planned evidence required.

Evaluating Results

After the auditor plans the engagement and accumulates audit evidence, results of the audit can also be stated in terms of the audit risk model. However, research has shown that using the planning model to evaluate total audit results may result in an understatement of **achieved audit risk**.[2] Achieved audit risk is the numeric value of audit

Achieved audit risk—the numeric value of audit risk using the assessed inherent risk; the value of control risk after documenting, evaluating, and testing internal controls (or the set value based on nonreliance); and the achieved detection risk.

---

[2] Research on U.S. Statement of Auditing Standards 47, which provides an evaluation form of the audit planning model, indicates that the formula can result in an understatement of achieved audit risk if the formula is used to evaluate total evidence collected.

risk using the assessed inherent risk; the value of control risk after documenting, evaluating, and testing internal controls (or the set value based on nonreliance); and the achieved detection risk.

During evaluation, the relationships can be used, but professional judgment, rather than simple reliance on the formula, is required to ensure that sufficient evidence has been collected.

The relationships show us that when insufficient evidence has been collected to achieve a specified audit risk, the following theoretical ways could be used to reduce achieved audit risk to the targeted level:

- *Reduce assessed inherent risk*. Because inherent risk is assessed by the auditor based on the client's circumstances, this assessment is done during planning and is typically not changed unless new facts are uncovered as the audit progresses. Changing inherent risk is outside of the control of the auditor.
- *Reduce assessed control risk*. Assessed control risk is affected by the client's internal controls and the auditor's tests of those controls. Auditors can reduce control risk by more extensive tests of controls if the client has effective controls.
- *Reduce achieved detection risk by increasing substantive audit tests*. Auditors reduce achieved detection risk by accumulating evidence using analytical procedures and tests of details of balances. Additional audit procedures, assuming that they are effective, and larger sample sizes both reduce achieved detection risk.

Subjectively combining these three factors to achieve an acceptably low audit risk requires considerable professional judgment. Some firms develop sophisticated approaches using computer modelling to help their auditors make those judgments, while other firms simply use automation to record the decisions made by each audit team. Audit results are studied more extensively in later chapters.

No difficulties occur when the auditor accumulates planned evidence and concludes that the assessment of each of the risks was reasonable or better than originally thought. The auditor will conclude that sufficient appropriate audit evidence has been collected for that account or cycle.

Special care must be exercised when the auditor decides, on the basis of accumulated evidence, that the original assessment of control risk or inherent risk was understated. In such a circumstance, the auditor should follow a two-step approach. First, the auditor must revise the original assessment of the appropriate risk. It would violate due care to leave the original assessment unchanged if the auditor knows it is inappropriate. Second, the auditor should consider the effect of the revision on evidence requirements, without the use of the audit risk model. Instead, the auditor should carefully evaluate the implications of the revision of the risk and modify evidence appropriately so that sufficient evidence is collected.

For example, assume that the auditor confirms accounts receivable and, on the basis of the misstatements found, concludes that the original control risk assessment as low was inappropriate due to a higher than expected number of errors in the confirmation results. The auditor should revise the estimate of control risk upward and carefully consider the effect of the revision on the additional evidence needed in the sales and collection cycles. The auditor might need to do additional tests of details on the accounts receivable balance or bad debts due to these changes.

concept check

C7-7 How does materiality affect planned evidence?

C7-8 What risks are considered before conducting tests of details?

Appendix 7A
Disaster Recovery Planning

Disaster recovery planning is also known as "business continuity planning." The purpose of such a plan is to enable a business to continue operations in the event of failure of part or all of its information systems. Something as simple as a hard drive crash (in which the reading head of the hard drive fails, destroying the head, the disk, and the data on it) can cause enormous problems if a company has not given careful thought to contingency procedures. Think of your own personal computer. What would you do if this terrible event occurred? Audit Challenge 7-1 on page 212 describes how an insurance company fared when it had a fire that destroyed some personal computers and disk drives and also caused other equipment failures.

Gary Baker's concise article in *CAmagazine*[3] several years ago breaks down the disaster recovery process into five phases. The phases are as follows:

1. MANAGEMENT COMMITMENT TO THE CONCEPT OF DISASTER RECOVERY PLANNING
Preparation of a disaster recovery plan (DRP) is time-consuming and requires the provision of funds and human resources. If management is not fully committed to this process, the resources will not be provided, and the activity will falter.

2. RANKING OF BUSINESS PROCESSES
The entity needs to ask, "What will happen if process X is not available?" Can the payroll be paid? Can goods be shipped out of the door? For organizations using paperless systems and electronic data interchange or electronic commerce, operations will likely cease if those systems are unavailable. Users need to identify what would happen if particular application processes were unavailable and the likely impact that this would have on the business. Baker suggests using one-day, three-day, and seven-day time frames when conducting this ranking.

3. IDENTIFYING MINIMUM RESOURCES REQUIRED
From step 2, the entity will have identified applications that were critical to ongoing operations. Resources required to restore these operations (and perhaps some noncritical systems as well) now need to be identified and costed. Where multiple alternatives exist, they should be similarly identified and costed.

4. PREPARE A DATA CENTRE PLAN AND A USER PLAN
The data centre plan addresses technical issues and procedures, such as obtaining hardware and software backup, and ensuring appropriate telecommunications access. The user plan identifies activities required to resume operations and can include manual alternative activities that would be completed if computing resources were unavailable.

5. TEST THE PLAN
This trial run will help both data processing personnel and users identify any shortcomings in the DRP and provide a subsequent schedule for remedying those shortcomings.

There are a variety of technical publications and articles that can be used by organizations to prepare a disaster recovery plan or to obtain more detailed guidance on the components of planning.[4] In addition to those issues mentioned by Baker, it is important that an entity have current offsite backup of its systems, carry adequate appropriate insurance coverage, and continue to maintain its disaster recovery plans once the DRP has initially been developed.

AUDIT IMPACT The existence of an effective disaster recovery plan is linked to the auditor's assessment of the viability of the entity as a going concern. If an entity using integrated Electronic Data Interchange (EDI), Electronic Funds Transfers (EFTs), and automated shipping systems were to lose these systems and not have an effective DRP, the entity would likely fail if it could not recover its systems within a short period of time. Thus, the auditor might consider either lowering the numeric value of audit risk or asking the client to disclose the lack of appropriate disaster recovery plans in a note to the financial statement.

---

[3] Baker, G., "Quick recoveries," *CAmagazine,* August 1995, p. 49–50, 53.

[4] See, for example: Doughty, K., "Business continuity: A business survival strategy," *Information Systems Control Journal*, 1, 2002, p. 28–36.

Summary

1. *What are the components of the audit risk model?* Table 7-1 describes and illustrates audit risk, inherent risk, control risk, and [planned] detection risk.

   Why does the auditor need to consider business risk, both for the client (called client business risk) and for the auditor (termed engagement risk)? Business risk is about not achieving business objectives, resulting in business failure or bankruptcy. If the client fails, then the auditor could be sued. If the auditor fails in doing the audit work correctly, the audit report could be incorrect, also resulting in the auditor being sued (and potentially going out of business).

2. *When assessing inherent risk, what does the auditor consider?* The text lists 11 major factors (page 214) that are related to the nature of the client business, the integrity of its management, the types of transactions or processes, and the susceptibility of transactions to error or manipulation, as well as whether it is an initial or repeat engagement.

3. *How is materiality used to assess the amount of work conducted during an audit engagement?* Materiality is used to assess the impact that potential errors might have on users of the financial statements. The auditor needs to conduct the audit such that the statements are free of material errors to a specified assurance level. Since materiality affects sample size, as materiality decreases, so does the need for increased audit testing.

   What quantitative and qualitative factors does an auditor consider when setting materiality? The auditor uses professional judgment to choose a base against which to calculate materiality. The numerical value decided upon is based upon factors such as the client risk profile, the extent of fluctuation of bases, and the amount of assurance required.

4. *How do the components of the audit risk model relate to the amount of evidence that should be collected during an audit?* Assessments are completed to the individual cycle, account, and audit objective level. These assessments are used, together with professional judgment, to decide upon the nature, quality, and quantity of evidence collected, resulting in a detailed audit program.

   How does materiality fit in with the audit risk model? The auditor decides upon materiality using professional judgment, with full awareness of the same information that is used to estimate the components of the audit risk model (Figure 7-1 on page 207). Then, materiality is used to help decide upon the amount of evidence that is collected on an assertion-by-assertion basis. Materiality and the components of the audit risk model do not directly affect each other, but both affect the amount of evidence collected.

   What problems arise with the use of the audit risk model if risks change once the audit fieldwork has commenced? In the end, the auditor must have sufficient evidence to state an audit opinion. If risk changes indicate that more evidence is required, the auditor needs to collect additional evidence.

   If the opposite occurs, then the auditor has collected too much evidence—however, auditors would tend to err in this direction rather than collecting too little evidence.

Visit the text's website at **www.pearsoned.ca/arens** for practice quizzes, additional case studies, and international standards information.

Review Questions

7-1 Define the "audit risk model" and explain each term in the model.

7-2 Explain the causes of an increased or decreased planned detection risk.

7-3 When does the auditor assess client business risk? Why?

7-4 How does engagement risk (auditor business risk) affect the audit process?

7-5 Explain why inherent risk is estimated for segments rather than for the overall audit. What is the effect on the amount of evidence the auditor must accumulate when inherent risk is increased from medium to high for a segment?

7-6 Explain the effect of extensive misstatements found in the prior year's audit on inherent risk, planned detection risk, and planned audit evidence.

7-7 Explain the relationship between audit risk and the legal liability of auditors.

7-8 State the categories of circumstances that affect audit risk, and list the factors that the auditor can use to indicate the degree to which each category exists.

7-9 Define the term "materiality" as it is used in accounting and auditing. What is the relationship between materiality and the phrase "obtain reasonable assurance" used in the auditor's report?

7-10 Explain why materiality is important but difficult to apply in practice.

7-11 What is meant by "planning materiality"? Identify the most important factors affecting the development of this figure.

7-12 Assume Rosanne Madden, a PA, is using 5 percent of net income before taxes as her major guideline for evaluating materiality. What qualitative factors should she also consider in deciding whether misstatements may be material?

7-13 Differentiate between identified misstatements, likely or potential misstatements, and further possible misstatements. Explain why all three are important.

7-14 How would the conduct of an audit of a medium-sized company be affected by the company's being a small part of a large conglomerate as compared with its being a separate entity?

7-15 Auditors have not been successful in measuring the components of the audit risk model. How is it possible to use the model in a meaningful way without a precise way of measuring the risk?

Discussion Questions and Problems

7-16 The existence of risk is implicit in the phrase "in my opinion" that appears in the auditor's report. The auditor is indicating that he or she is accepting some risk that the opinion rendered may be incorrect. In planning and executing an audit, the auditor strives to reduce this risk to a level that is acceptable to the client, the users, and himself or herself.

REQUIRED

Discuss the steps that the auditor takes to reduce the risk to an acceptable level. What guidance do the professional standards provide to the auditor?

7-17 Some accountants have suggested that the auditor's report should include a statement of materiality level and audit risk that the auditor used in conducting the audit.

REQUIRED

a. The proponents of such disclosure believe that the information would be useful to users of the financial statements being reported on. Explain fully why you think they have this view.

b. Some accountants oppose such disclosure. Explain why you think they are not in favour of it.

c. What is your position on the issue?

7-18 Following are six situations that involve the audit risk model as it is used for planning audit evidence requirements in the audit of inventory.

REQUIRED

a. Explain what low, medium, and high mean for each of the four risks and planned evidence.

b. Fill in the blanks for planned detection risk and planned evidence using the terms low, medium, or high.

c. Using your knowledge of the relationships among the foregoing factors, state the effect on planned evidence (increase or decrease) of changing each of the following five factors, while the other three remain constant:

1. An increase in audit risk.
2. An increase in control risk.
3. An increase in planned detection risk.
4. An increase in inherent risk.
5. An increase in inherent risk and a decrease in control risk of the same amount.

	Situation					
Risk	1	2	3	4	5	6
Acceptable audit risk	High	High	Low	Low	High	Medium
Inherent risk	Low	High	High	Low	Medium	Medium
Control risk	Low	Low	High	High	Medium	Medium
Planned detection risk	–	–	–	–	–	–
Planned evidence	–	–	–	–	–	–

7-19 Below are 10 independent risk factors:

1. The client lacks sufficient working capital to continue operations.
2. The client fails to detect employee theft of inventory from the warehouse because there are no restrictions on warehouse access and the client does not reconcile inventory on hand to recorded amounts on a timely basis.
3. The company is publicly traded.
4. The auditor has identified numerous material misstatements during prior-year audit engagements.
5. The assigned staff on the audit engagement lack the necessary skills to identify actual errors in an account balance when examining audit evidence accumulated.

6. The client is one of the industry's largest based on its size and market share.
7. The client engages in several material transactions with entities owned by family members of several of the client's senior executives.
8. The allowance for doubtful accounts is based on significant assumptions made by management.
9. The audit plan omits several necessary audit procedures.
10. The client fails to reconcile bank accounts to recorded cash balances.

REQUIRED

Identify which of the following audit risk model components relates most directly to each of the 10 risk factors:
- Audit risk
- Inherent risk
- Control risk
- Planned detection risk

7-20 You are the auditor in charge of the audit of the municipality of Sackville, New Brunswick. The municipality has a budget of about $65 million and has had a balanced budget for the last three years. There are about 10 people in the accounting office and the rest of the employees are operational, dealing with supervision of roadwork, garbage collection, and similar matters. Many services are outsourced, minimizing the need for employees. The municipality has a chief executive officer and a controller and reports to the council of elected representatives.

REQUIRED

For each of the following situations, state a preliminary conclusion for audit risk, inherent risk, control risk, and detection risk. Justify your conclusions. State any assumptions that are necessary for you to reach your conclusions.

1. This is the first year that you have been auditing Sackville. There has been extensive turnover after the recent election.

Costs are out of control, and it looks like it may be necessary to raise realty taxes by as much as 15 percent.
2. For four years now, you have been auditing Sackville. The employees are experienced, and any control recommendations that you have suggested have been discussed and, where feasible, implemented. There is a tiny budget surplus this year, and it looks as if a balanced budget is in sight again for next year.
3. Sackville is being hit by bad press. It seems that one of the purchasing agents set up a fictitious company and was billing the municipality for goods that had not been received. To make it worse, the purchasing agent's wife was the assistant accountant. The office of the provincial Auditor General has sent a letter to the controller of Sackville stating that the municipality has been selected for audit by the provincial Auditor General's Office based on a random sample and that the provincial auditors will be arriving within two weeks of the completion of your audit.

7-21 The following are different types of misstatements that can be encountered on an audit:

1. A computer programming error that resulted in the use of a method of valuing inventory that is not in accordance with generally accepted accounting principles.
2. Accidental failure to disclose a lawsuit for patent infringement when the amount of the liability is unknown.
3. The recording as capital assets expenditures that should have been recorded as repairs and maintenance.
4. The inclusion of invalid accounts in accounts receivable by preparing fictitious sales invoices to nonexisting customers.

REQUIRED

a. Assuming the amounts are equally material, rank the types of misstatements listed in terms of the difficulty of uncovering each one. (Most difficult is first.) Give reasons to support your answers.
b. Discuss whether auditors should have the same responsibility for uncovering the most difficult-to-find misstatement as for discovering the least difficult one. Consider this from the point of view of the auditors and the users of financial statements.

7-22 Statements of earnings and financial position for Prairie Stores Corporation are shown on the next page.

REQUIRED

a. Use professional judgment in determining planning materiality based on revenue, net income before taxes, total assets, and shareholders' equity. Your conclusions should be stated in terms of percentages and dollars.
b. Assume you complete the audit and conclude that your planned materiality has been exceeded. What should you do?

c. As discussed in part (b), likely net earnings from continuing operations before income taxes were used as a base for materiality when completing the audit. Discuss why most auditors use before-tax net earnings instead of after-tax net earnings when calculating materiality based on the income statement.

Statement of Earnings
Prairie Stores Corporation

	For the 53 Weeks Ended April 5, 2009	For the 52 Weeks Ended March 31, 2008	April 1, 2007
Revenue			
Net sales	$8,351,149	$6,601,255	$5,959,587
Other income	59,675	43,186	52,418
	8,410,824	6,644,441	6,012,005
Costs and expenses			
Cost of sales	5,197,375	4,005,548	3,675,369
Marketing, general, and administrative expenses	2,590,080	2,119,590	1,828,169
Provision for loss on restructured operations	64,100	–	–
Interest expense	141,662	46,737	38,546
	7,993,217	6,171,875	5,542,084
Earnings from continuing operations before income taxes	417,607	472,566	469,921
Income taxes	196,700	217,200	214,100
Earnings from continuing operations	220,907	255,366	255,821
Provision for loss on discontinued operations, net of income taxes	20,700	–	–
Net earnings	**$200,207**	**$255,366**	**$255,821**

Statement of Financial Position
Prairie Stores Corporation

Assets	April 5, 2009		March 31, 2008	
Current assets				
Cash		$39,683		$37,566
Temporary investments (at cost, which approximates market)		123,421		271,639
Receivables, less allowances of $16,808 in 2009 and $17,616 in 2008		899,752		759,001
Inventories				
Finished product	680,974		550,407	
Raw materials and supplies	443,175		353,795	
		1,124,149		904,202
Deferred income tax benefits		9,633		10,468
Prepaid expenses		57,468		35,911
Total current assets		2,254,106		2,018,787
Land, buildings, equipment at cost, less accumulated amortization		1,393,902		1,004,455
Investments in affiliated companies and sundry assets		112,938		83,455
Goodwill and other intangible assets		99,791		23,145
Total assets		**$3,860,737**		**$3,129,842**
Liabilities and Shareholders' Equity				
Current liabilities				
Notes payable		$280,238		$113,411
Current portion of long-term debt		64,594		12,336
Accounts and drafts payable		359,511		380,395
Accrued salaries, wages, and vacations		112,200		63,557
Accrued income taxes		76,479		89,151
Other accrued liabilities including goods and services tax		321,871		269,672
Current liabilities		1,214,893		928,522
Long-term debt		730,987		390,687
Other noncurrent liabilities		146,687		80,586
Accrued income tax liability		142,344		119,715
Total liabilities		2,234,911		1,519,510
Shareholders' equity				
Common stock issued, 51,017 shares in 2009 and 50,992 in 2008		200,195		199,576
Retained earnings		1,425,631		1,410,756
Total shareholders' equity		1,625,826		1,610,332
Total liabilities and shareholders' equity		**$3,860,737**		**$3,129,842**

7-23 You are evaluating audit results for current assets in the audit of Quicky Plumbing Co. You set the preliminary judgment about materiality for current assets at $12,500 for overstatements and at $20,000 for understatements. The preliminary and actual estimates are shown below.

REQUIRED

a. Justify a lower planning materiality for overstatements than understatements in this situation.

b. Explain why the totals of the tolerable misstatements exceed the planning materiality for both understatements and overstatements.

c. Explain how it is possible that three of the estimates of total misstatement have both an overstatement and an understatement.

d. Assume that you are not concerned whether the estimate of misstatement exceeds tolerable misstatement for individual accounts if the total estimate is less than the planned amount.

1. Given the audit results, should you be more concerned about the existence of material overstatements or understatements at this point in the audit of Quicky Plumbing Co.?

2. Which account or accounts will you be most concerned about in (1)? Explain.

e. Assume that the estimate of total overstatement amount for each account is less than tolerable misstatement, but that the total overstatement estimate exceeds the planned materiality.

1. Explain why this would occur.

2. Explain what the auditor should do.

Account	Tolerable Misstatement		Estimate of Total Misstatement	
	Over-statements	Under-statements	Over-statements	Under-statements
Cash	$ 2,000	$ 3,000	$ 2,000	$ 0
Accounts receivable	12,000	18,000	4,000	19,000
Inventory	8,000	14,000	3,000	10,000
Prepaid expenses	3,000	5,000	2,000	1,000
Total	$25,000	$40,000	$11,000	$30,000

Professional Judgment Problem

7-24 Joe Whitehead is planning the audit of a newly obtained client, Henderson Energy Corporation, for the year ended December 31, 2008. Henderson Energy is regulated by the provincial utility commission and because it is a publicly traded company the audited financial statements must be filed with the OSC (Ontario Securities Commission).

Henderson Energy is considerably more profitable than many of its competitors, largely due to its extensive investment in information technologies used in its energy distribution and other key business processes. Recent growth into rural markets, however, has placed some strain on 2008 operations. Additionally, Henderson Energy expanded its investments into speculative markets and is also making greater use of derivative and hedging transactions to mitigate some of its investment risks. Because of the complexities of the underlying accounting associated with these activities, Henderson Energy added several highly experienced accountants to its financial reporting team. Internal audit, which has direct reporting responsibility to the audit committee, is also actively involved in reviewing key accounting assumptions and estimates on a quarterly basis.

Whitehead's discussions with the predecessor auditor revealed that the client has experienced some difficulty in correctly tracking existing property, plant, and equipment items. This largely involves equipment located at its multiple energy production facilities. During the recent year, Henderson acquired a regional electric company, which expanded the number of energy production facilities.

Whitehead plans to staff the audit engagement with several members of the firm who have experience in auditing energy and public companies. The extent of partner review of key accounts will be extensive.

REQUIRED

Based on the above information, identify factors that affect the risk of material misstatement in the December 31, 2008, financial statements of Henderson Energy. Indicate whether the factor increases or decreases the risk of material misstatement. Also, identify which audit risk model component is affected by the factor. Use the format below:

Factor	Effect on the Risk of Material Misstatement	Audit Risk Model Component
Henderson is a new client	Increases	Inherent risk

Case

7-25 In the audit of Whirland Chemical Company, a large publicly traded company, you have been assigned the responsibility for obtaining background information for the audit. Your firm is auditing the client for the first time in the current year as a result of a dispute between Whirland and the previous auditor over the proper valuation of work-in-process inventory and the inclusion in sales of inventory that has not been delivered but has, for practical purposes, been completed and sold.

Whirland Chemical has been highly successful in its field in the past two decades, primarily because of many successful mergers negotiated by Bert Randolph, the president and chairman of the board. Even though the industry as a whole has suffered dramatic setbacks in recent years, Whirland continues to prosper, as evidenced by its constantly increasing earnings and growth. Only in the last two years have the company's profits turned downward. Randolph has a reputation for having been able to hire an aggressive group of young executives by using relatively low salaries combined with an unusually generous profit-sharing plan.

A major difficulty you face in the new audit is that Whirland lacks the highly sophisticated accounting records expected of a company of its size. Randolph believes that profits come primarily from intelligent and aggressive action based on forecasts, not by relying on historical data that come after the fact. Most of the forecast data are generated by the sales and production department rather than by the accounting department. The personnel in the accounting department do seem competent but somewhat overworked and underpaid relative to other employees. One of the recent changes that will potentially improve the record-keeping is the installation of sophisticated information systems. Not all of the accounting records are fully integrated yet, but such major areas as inventory and sales are included in the new system.

The first six months' financial statements for the current year include a profit of approximately only 10 percent less than that of the first six months of the preceding year, which is somewhat surprising, considering the reduced volume and the disposal of a segment of the business, Mercury Supply Co. The disposal of this segment was considered necessary because it had become increasingly unprofitable over the past four years. At the time of its acquisition from Roger Randolph, a brother of Bert Randolph, the company was highly profitable and was considered a highly desirable purchase. The major customer of Mercury Supply Co. was the Mercury Corporation, which is owned by Roger Randolph. Gradually, the market for its products declined as the Mercury Corporation began diversifying and phasing out its primary products in favour of more profitable business. Even though Mercury Corporation is no longer buying from Mercury Supply Co., it compensates by buying a large volume of other products from Whirland Chemical.

The only major difficulty Whirland faces right now, according to financial analysts, is underfinancing. There is a high amount of current debt and long-term debt because of the depressed capital markets. Management is reluctant to obtain equity capital at this point because the increased number of shares would decrease the earnings per share even more than 10 percent. At the present time, Randolph is negotiating with several cash-rich companies in the hope of being able to merge with them as a means of overcoming the capital problems.

REQUIRED

a. List the major concerns you would have when assessing inherent risk and audit risk for the audit of Whirland Chemical Company. Explain why they are potential problems. Provide a conclusion (high, medium, or low) for inherent risk and audit risk.

b. State the appropriate approach to investigating the significance of each item you listed in (a).

Ongoing Small Business Case: Materiality for CondoCleaners.com

7-26 CondoCleaners.com has been in business now for six months. Sales to date have been $320,000, with cost of goods sold at $275,000. There is no debt, and the company has fixed assets of $4,250 (a personal computer and some vacuum cleaners).

REQUIRED

Calculate preliminary materiality for CondoCleaners.com for the first six months of operations.

8

Client risk profile and documentation

How does an auditor decide whether a client is risky or not? This chapter identifies and talks about the many parts involved in developing a client risk profile. The auditor needs to examine not only the industry and the business environment but also many details about the client and its governance process before deciding upon client business risk, overall risks of material misstatement, and risks of fraud. After these risks have been assessed, the auditor can move on to the audit plan. Management accountants can use this information to develop actions to mitigate risks, while public accountants (PAs), internal auditors and specialists may be involved in the risk assessment process.

LEARNING OBJECTIVES

1 Explain the importance of an adequate audit planning process. Link the audit planning process to the development of a client risk profile. Explain the components of understanding the client's business and industry and assessing client business risk.

2 Describe the type of evidence that the auditor collects when developing the client risk profile and assessing client business risk. State why it is important to document related parties and transactions with them. Explain how preliminary analytical review is used during planning.

3 Determine what working papers the auditor retains to document the financial statement audit. Explain the purposes of working papers. Describe the common characteristics of high-quality working papers.

SECTIONS REFERENCED IN THIS CHAPTER

CICA Standards

CAS 230 – Audit documentation (previously Section 5145 – Documentation)

CAS 300 – Planning an audit of financial statements (previously Section 5150 – Planning)

CAS 315 – Identifying and assessing the risks of material misstatement through understanding the entity and its environment (previously Section 5141 – Understanding the entity and its environment and assessing the risks of material misstatement)

CAS 550 – Related parties (previously Section 6010 – Audit of related-party transactions)

Pssst—Would You Like to Buy a Town?

The aerial photographs of the town showed lush greenery and an ocean frontage. Other photos pictured a deserted shopping mall and deserted suburban streets, complete with mowed lawns. The American-owned mining town of Kitsault, B.C., had an asking price of $7 million according to the *Toronto Star* October 2, 2004. The town was abandoned two years after completion, in 1983, when the prices for molybdenum (used to strengthen steel) dropped, making the mine in Kitsault unprofitable.

In 2008, Avanti Mining was planning on reopening the mine, as it had resource estimates completed on the molybdenum content of the mine, believing that over 235 million pounds could be sold. It based its decision to resume mining in October 2008 on prices of US$20 per pound for molybdenum. Its website indicated that in the entire time that the Kitsault mine had previously been in operation (1967–1972 and 1981–1982), only about 30 million pounds of the metal had been mined.

Will Avanti succeed at Kitsault when other producers around the world have failed? Freeport-McMoRan Copper & Gold Inc. owns the Henderson molybdenum mine near Denver, Colorado. In November 2008, it announced that it would be reducing the labour force at that mine from 700 to 600 (a 100-employee lay-off) because of a drop in molybdenum prices down to US$12 per pound— a 60-percent price drop. At the same time, Freeport-McMoRan announced that it would place on hold the opening of another mine (the Climax mine), which was supposed to open in 2010.

IMPORTANCE TO AUDITORS

The stories of these two mining companies illustrate how many businesses are vulnerable to raw material market prices and the importance of understanding the marketplace within which a business operates. Mines are sellers of basic metals, so they are particularly vulnerable to price changes. The unfolding credit crunch in 2008 was reflected in price drops for metals. Molybdenum prices from March 2006 to September 2008 had climbed gradually from the mid-US$20 range to upward of US$30 before dropping to about US$12 in November 2008, wiping out the gains of the past few years (per **www.infomine.com**).

Some companies can increase their prices for finished goods when prices for raw materials increase; others cannot. As market prices drop, companies may be forced to shed assets or change the way they run their operations to stay profitable.

WHAT DO YOU THINK?

1. Look at the appliances in your kitchen—refrigerators, stoves, microwaves, and toasters. Many raw materials were used to make these product—aluminum, plastic, and steel. If the cost of raw materials rose, what would happen to the companies that produced these appliances?

continued >

2. Why could or couldn't they increase their prices? How does raw material price volatility affect companies that produce appliances?

3. How would raw material price volatility affect the risk profile of your client, a major refrigerator producer?

Sources: 1. Associated Press, "Henderson molybdenum production cut; Climax on hold," *Rocky Mountain News*, November 10. 2008, www.rockymountainnews.com, Accessed: November 30, 2008. 2. "Avanti Mining Finalizes Purchase of the Past Producing Kitsault Molybdenum Mine, British Columbia," October 20, 2008, News Release, www.aventi.com, Accessed: November 30, 2008. 3. Girard, Daniel, "Modern-day ghost town on the block," *Toronto Star*, October 2, 2004, p. H1, H3. 4. "Investment Mine," www.infomine.com, Accessed: November 30, 2008.

THE stories about molybdenum mines underline the importance of knowing both our client's operations and the external business environment. They also link to valuation issues in the financial statements, for if the metal goes down in price, then so will the inventory of the finished goods of that metal. Knowledge of the external environment helps detect such potential risks of misstatement in the financial statements. In this chapter, we will discuss two audit phases that comprise the remainder of the audit risk assessment process (Phase 1, preplanning, was discussed in Chapter 5). Here, we will cover Phase 2, the Client Risk Profile, in considerable detail. We will also overview Phase 3, Plan the Audit, which is continued in Chapter 12.

➊ The Importance of Audit Planning

Generally accepted auditing standards require adequate planning. This planning is done in response to risk assessment. The auditor should plan and perform the audit to reduce audit risk to an acceptably low level that is consistent with the objective of an audit. The purpose of planning is to provide for effective conduct of the audit (CAS 300, par. 03). It is important to note that the terminology of this CAS is different than in past standards (both Canadian and international) that stated that the purpose of the audit plan was to help ensure that audit risk was reduced to the planned level. For our purposes, we will assume that an effective audit is one that accomplishes the goal of reducing audit risk to the targeted level. If assistants are employed, they should be properly supervised, so the audit plan should include supervision methods for the audit team (CAS 300, par. 10).

CAS 300 (par. 8) states that the auditor must develop an audit plan that includes the following components:

- The nature, timing, and extent of audit procedures for the purpose of risk assessment.
- The nature, timing, and extent of additional audit procedures, linked to the individual audit assertions.
- Any other audit procedures that are needed for the audit to be conducted in accordance with GAAS (the exact wording is to state that the audit is conducted in compliance with the CASs).

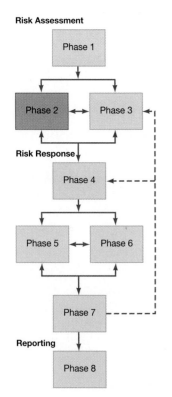

Risk Assessment

Phase 1

Phase 2 — Phase 3

Risk Response

Phase 4

Phase 5 — Phase 6

Phase 7

Reporting

Phase 8

This means that the audit plan includes a description of what the auditor will do during all phases of the audit, including preplanning and completion of the client risk profile. The audit plan is finalized when risk assessments are complete, which is why we describe Phase 3 of the audit as *Plan the Audit*. This is where the auditor determines the strategic approach for the audit.

There are three main reasons why the auditor should plan engagements properly: to enable the auditor to obtain sufficient appropriate audit evidence for the circumstances, to help keep audit costs reasonable, and to avoid misunderstandings with the client. Obtaining sufficient appropriate audit evidence is essential if the public accounting firm is to minimize legal liability and maintain a good reputation in the professional community. Keeping costs reasonable helps the firm remain competitive and thereby retain its clients, assuming the firm has a reputation for doing quality work. Avoiding misunderstandings with the client is important for good client relations and for facilitating quality work at reasonable costs. For example, suppose he or she informs the client that the audit will be completed before June 30 but is unable to finish it until August because of inadequate staff. The client is likely to be upset with the public accounting firm and may even sue for breach of contract.

Before the auditor can develop a detailed plan of action, he or she must have a clear understanding of the risks of material misstatement in the financial statements—the "what could go wrong" picture. Part of this risk assessment occurs before the client is accepted or before the decision to continue with the client takes place (during Phase 1, Preplanning, explained in Chapter 5). At that time, the auditor assesses the financial viability of the client as part of acceptance or continuance, identifies the client's reasons for an audit, conducts an independence threat analysis, obtains an engagement letter, and considers staffing for the engagement.

Develop Client Risk Profile

THE RELEVANCE OF A CLIENT RISK PROFILE In Phase 2, Client Risk Assessment, the auditor develops a thorough understanding of the client's business and industry to assess client business risk and to assess the risk of material misstatements or fraud for the financial statements overall. In Phase 3, the Audit Plan, the auditor moves to working with the audit risk model (discussed in Chapter 7). It is a knowledge of the relationships of those risks that drives the collection of data about the client. Our figure of the audit process shows the relationships between Phases 2 and 3 as cyclical— the auditor will keep working on the Client Risk Profile until sufficient information has been collected to determine Phase 3 audit risk, assess overall inherent risk, and decide upon materiality levels.

Figure 8-1 shows how understanding the client's business and industry is related to the assessment of client business risk.

UNDERSTAND CLIENT'S BUSINESS AND INDUSTRY A thorough understanding of the client's business and industry and knowledge about the company's operations are essential for doing an adequate audit. The nature of the client's business and industry affects client business risk and the risk of material misstatements in the financial statements. (Recall that client business risk is the risk that the client will fail to meet its objectives.) In recent years, several factors have increased the importance of understanding the client's business and industry:

- Information technology connects client companies with major customers and suppliers. As a result, auditors need greater knowledge about major customers and suppliers and related risks.
- Clients have expanded operations globally, often through joint ventures or strategic alliances.
- Information technology affects internal client processes, improving the quality and timeliness of accounting information.

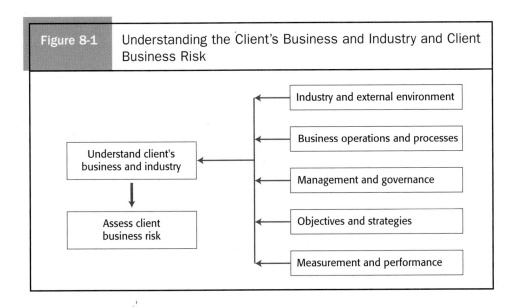

Figure 8-1 Understanding the Client's Business and Industry and Client Business Risk

- The increased importance of human capital and other intangible assets has increased accounting complexity and the importance of management judgments and estimates.
- Auditors need a better understanding of the client's business and industry to provide additional value-added services to clients. For example, audit firms often offer assurance and consulting services related to information technology and risk management services to non-public audit clients, which requires an extensive knowledge of these clients' industries.

Auditors consider these factors using a strategic systems approach to understanding the client's business. Figure 8-2 provides an overview of the approach to understanding the client's business and industry.

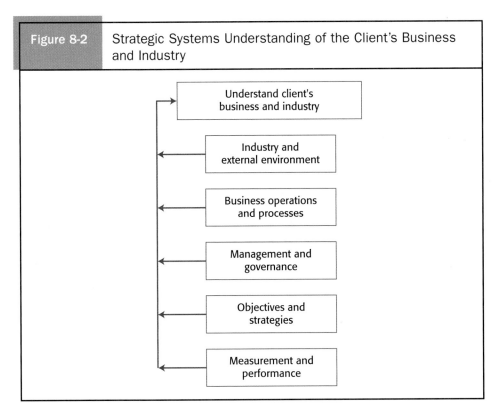

Figure 8-2 Strategic Systems Understanding of the Client's Business and Industry

Teaming Up by Industry

A high level of knowledge of a client's industry and business is so critical to conducting quality audits and providing tax and consulting services that many accounting firms provide specialized expertise by industry. Here is a sample of Canadian firms:

www.kpmg.ca/en/industries lists the following sectors: consumer and industrial businesses; energy and natural resources; financial services; information, communications, and entertainment; public sector; private companies; and private equity.

www.grantthornton.ca/sectors specializes in financial services, manufacturing and distribution, professional services, aboriginal advisory services, family enterprise, and public companies as its industry segments.

Milman & Company, Chartered Accountants, in Toronto lists corporations, professionals, individuals, scientific research and development, U.S. and international companies, and trusts and estates for the work it does.

Organizing along industry or expertise lines helps public accounting firms focus their resources to better understand their client's business and provide value-added services.

Sources: 1. Grant Thornton, www.grantthornton.ca/sectors. 2. KPMG, www.kpmg.ca/en/industries/. 3. Milman & Company, www.taxonweb.ca/pages/profile.html. All Accessed: December 1, 2008.

CAS CAS 315, Identifying and assessing the risks of material misstatement through understanding the entity and its environment (previously Section 5141, Understanding the entity and its environment and assessing the risks of material misstatement), requires the auditor to obtain knowledge of the entity's business and environment in order to assess risks and conduct the audit. The section lists factors to be understood in the external business environment, internal structures, internal controls, and risk assessment processes. This chapter and the next several chapters cover information to be documented and assessed, including internal controls, corporate governance, and fraud risks.

INDUSTRY AND EXTERNAL ENVIRONMENT There are three primary reasons for obtaining a good understanding of the client's industry:

1. Risks associated with specific industries may affect the auditor's assessment of client business risk and acceptable audit risk—and may even influence auditors against accepting engagements in riskier industries, such as high technology, biochemical, or small financial service organizations.
2. Certain inherent risks are typically common to all clients in certain industries. Familiarity with those risks aids the auditor in assessing their relevance to the client. Examples include potential inventory obsolescence in the fashion clothing industry, accounts receivable collection inherent risk in the consumer loan industry, and reserve for loss inherent risk in the casualty insurance industry.
3. Many industries have unique accounting requirements that the auditor must understand to evaluate whether the client's financial statements are in accordance with generally accepted accounting principles. For example, if the auditor is doing an audit of a city government, the auditor must understand governmental accounting and auditing requirements. Unique accounting requirements exist for construction companies, railways, not-for-profit organizations, financial institutions, and many other organizations.

Many auditor litigation cases (like those described in Chapter 4) could be the result of the auditor's failure to fully understand the nature of transactions in the client's industry. For example, several major accounting firms in the United States paid to the federal government large settlements related to audits of failed savings and loans. In some of these audits, the auditors failed to understand the nature of significant real estate transactions. Currently, some firms internationally are facing lawsuits due to the declines in the values of asset-backed paper.

The auditor must also understand the client's external environment, including such things as economic conditions, extent of competition, and regulatory requirements. For example, auditors of utility companies need more than an understanding of the industry's unique regulatory accounting requirements. They must also know how recent deregulation in this industry has increased competition and how fluctuations in energy prices impact firm operations. To develop effective audit plans, auditors of all companies must have the expertise to assess external environment risks.

Knowledge of the client's industry can be obtained in different ways. These include discussions with the auditor in the firm who was responsible for the engagement in previous years and with other auditors in the firm currently on similar engagements, as well as conferences with the client's personnel, including internal auditors. Many of the larger public accounting firms have industry specialists who can be consulted for their expertise. Smaller firms that do not have the expertise can consult the practice advisory service of their professional body. There are often industry audit guides, textbooks, and technical magazines available for the auditor to study in most major industries. Some auditors subscribe to specialized journals for those industries to which they devote a large amount of time. Considerable knowledge can also be obtained by participating actively in industry associations and training programs.

BUSINESS OPERATIONS AND PROCESSES Knowledge about the client's business that differentiates it from other companies in its industry is also needed. This knowledge will help the auditor more effectively assess audit risk and inherent risk, and will also be useful in designing analytical procedures. Table 8-1 provides examples of analytical procedures that the auditor could use.

The auditor should understand factors such as major sources of revenue, key customers and suppliers, sources of financing, and information about related parties that may indicate areas of increased client business risk. For example, many technology firms are dependent on one or a few products that may become obsolete due to new technologies or stronger competitors. Dependence on a few major customers may result in material losses from bad debts or obsolete inventory. Here we will expand on four areas: operational and reporting structure, technology infrastructure, touring the plant and offices, and identifying related parties.

Operational and reporting structure Companies filing their financial statements with a securities commission, companies whose securities are traded in a public market, and all life insurance enterprises are required to disclose segment information by industry and by geographic area and the amount of export sales. Auditors must have sufficient knowledge of a company's business to enable them to evaluate whether segment information should be disclosed and, if so, to determine whether the appropriate segment information has been disclosed by the client.

The auditor's permanent files frequently include the history of the company, a list of the major lines of business, and a record of the most important accounting policies

Table 8-1	Examples of Analytical Procedures Performed During Planning
Purpose	Analytical Procedure Performed During the Planning Phase
Understand the client's industry and business	Calculate key ratios for the client's business and compare them with industry averages.
Assess going concern	Calculate the debt-to-equity ratio and compare it with those of previous years and successful companies in the industry.
Indicate possible misstatements	Compare the gross margin with those of prior years, looking for large fluctuations.
Reduce detailed tests	Compare prepaid expenses and related expense accounts with those of prior years.

in previous years. Study of this information and discussions with the client's personnel aid in understanding the business.

Where multiple corporate structures are involved, the relationship and ownership of the organizations should be documented, as should reporting lines of key management personnel. The auditor will also determine whether the organization operates in a centralized or decentralized fashion by looking at the flow of information in an overview manner, that is, whether financial statements are managed and prepared divisionally, departmentally, or at head office, and who is responsible for development and coordination of the business. The auditor would also note the size and responsibilities of the management team.

Technology infrastructure An overview description of the type of information systems in use would cover hardware, software, maintenance processes, and level of integration. For example, does the organization use mainframe computing, local area networks, Electronic Data Interchange (EDI), or have a corporate website that is capable of processing transactions? Is packaged or customized software used to process transactions and provide reporting? An organization is likely to have advanced automated systems when its systems have one or more of the following characteristics:

- Custom-designed operational or strategic information systems.
- Use of database management systems or ERP (enterprise resource planning) systems.
- Use of data communications (including the internet).
- Use of paperless systems such as electronic data interchange or electronic funds transfer.
- A complex hardware or software processing configuration.

The existence of each of these characteristics affects the nature of information systems processing at the organization and so also affects the audit process. These characteristics and their impact on the audit are discussed further in Chapter 10.

Touring the plant and offices A tour of the client's facilities is helpful in obtaining a better understanding of the client's business and operations because it provides an opportunity to observe operations first-hand and to meet key personnel. The actual viewing of the physical facilities aids in understanding physical safeguards over assets and in interpreting accounting data by providing a frame of reference in which to visualize such assets as inventory in process, data processing equipment, and factory equipment. A knowledge of the physical layout also facilitates getting answers to questions later in the audit.

With such first-hand knowledge, the auditor is better able to identify inherent risks such as unused equipment or potentially unsaleable inventory. Discussions with non-accounting employees during the tour and throughout the audit also help the auditor learn more about the client's business to aid in assessing inherent risk.

Identifying related parties Transactions with related parties are important to auditors because they must be disclosed in the financial statements if they are material or information about them could affect decision making. Generally accepted accounting principles require disclosure of the nature of the related-party relationship; a description of transactions, including dollar amounts; and amounts due from and to related parties. Transactions with related parties are not arms-length transactions. There is, therefore, a risk that they were not valued at the same amount as they would have been if the transactions had been with an independent party. Most auditors assess inherent risk as high for related parties and related-party transactions, both because of the accounting disclosure requirements and the lack of independence between the parties involved in the transactions.

The auditor should identify all related parties and related-party transactions, as both quantitative and qualitative considerations are used to decide whether related-party transactions should be disclosed. A party is considered to be a related party if it has the ability to influence decisions, either directly or indirectly. A **related-party transaction** is any transaction between the client and a related party. Common examples include sales or purchase transactions between a parent company and its subsidiary, exchanges of equipment between two companies owned by the same person, and loans to officers. A less common example, called economic dependence, is the potential for exercise of significant influence on an audit client by, for example, its most important supplier or customer, lender, or borrower.

Because material related-party transactions must be disclosed, all related parties need to be identified and included in audit documentation early in the engagement. Having all related parties included in the audit files, as well as making sure all auditors on the team know who the related parties are, helps auditors identify undisclosed related-party transactions as they do the audit. Common ways of identifying related parties include inquiry of management, review of OSC or SEC filings, and examining shareholder listings to identify principal shareholders.

For publicly listed entities that have shares traded on the SEC, the auditor needs to be aware of regulatory restrictions. The Sarbanes–Oxley Act prohibits related-party transactions that involve personal loans to any director or executive officer of a public company. Banks and other financial institutions in the United States, as in Canada, however, are permitted to make normal loans, such as residential mortgages, to their directors and officers using market rates.

Related-party transaction—any transaction between the client and a related party.

MANAGEMENT AND GOVERNANCE Since management establishes a company's strategies and business processes, an auditor should assess management's philosophy and operating style and its ability to identify and respond to risk, as these significantly influence the risk of material misstatements in the financial statements.

A firm's governance includes its organizational structure, as well as the activities of the board of directors and the audit committee. Corporate governance will be discussed further in Chapters 9 and 10. An effective board of directors helps ensure that the company takes only appropriate risks, while the audit committee, through oversight of financial reporting, can reduce the likelihood of overly aggressive accounting.

Three closely related types of legal documents and records should be examined early in the engagement: articles of incorporation and bylaws, minutes of board of directors' and shareholders' meetings, and contracts. Some information, such as contracts, must be disclosed in the financial statements. Other information, such as authorizations in the board of directors' minutes, is useful in other parts of the audit. Early knowledge of these legal documents and records enables auditors to interpret related evidence throughout the engagement and to make sure there is proper disclosure in the financial statements.

Understand client's business and industry

Industry and external environment

Business operations and processes

Management and governance

Objectives and strategies

Measurement and performance

Articles of incorporation—a legal document granted by the federal or provincial jurisdiction in which a company is incorporated that recognizes a corporation as a separate entity. It includes the name of the corporation, the date of incorporation, capital stock the corporation is authorized to issue, and the types of business activities the corporation is authorized to conduct.

Bylaws—the rules and procedures adopted by a corporation's shareholders, including the corporation's fiscal year and the duties and powers of its officers.

Articles of incorporation and bylaws The **articles of incorporation**, granted by the federal government or by the province in which the company is incorporated, is the legal document necessary for recognizing a corporation as a separate entity. It includes the exact name of the corporation, the date of incorporation, the kinds and amounts of capital stock the corporation is authorized to issue, and the types of business activities the corporation is authorized to conduct. In specifying the kinds of capital stock, it also includes such information as the voting rights of each class of stock, preferences and conditions necessary for dividends, and prior rights in liquidation.

The **bylaws** include the rules and procedures adopted by the shareholders of the corporation. They specify such things as the fiscal year of the corporation, the frequency of shareholder meetings, the method of voting for directors, and the duties and powers of the corporate officers.

The auditor must understand the requirements of the articles of incorporation and the bylaws in order to determine whether the financial statements are properly presented. The correct disclosure of the shareholders' equity, including the proper payment of dividends, depends heavily on these requirements.

Code of ethics Companies frequently communicate the entity's values and ethical standards through policy statements and codes of conduct. For U.S. SEC filers, in response to requirements in the Sarbanes–Oxley Act, the SEC requires each public company to disclose whether it has adopted a code of ethics that applies to senior management, including the CEO, CFO, and principal accounting officer or controller. A company that has not adopted such a code must disclose this fact and explain why it has not done so. The SEC also requires companies to promptly disclose amendments and waivers to the code of ethics for any of those officers. For any organization, a code of ethics (and the processes to ensure adherence) are a powerful signal of corporate conduct. Auditors should gain knowledge of the company's code of ethics and examine any changes and waivers of the code of conduct that have implications for the governance system and related integrity and ethical values of senior management.

Corporate minutes—the official record of the meetings of a corporation's board of directors and shareholders in which corporate issues such as the declaration of dividends and the approval of contracts are documented.

Minutes of meetings and contracts The **corporate minutes** are the official record of the meetings of the board of directors and shareholders. They include summaries of the most important topics discussed at these meetings and the decisions made by the directors and shareholders. The auditor should read the minutes to obtain information that is relevant to performing the audit. There are two categories of relevant information in minutes: authorizations and discussions by the board of directors affecting inherent risk.

Common authorizations in the minutes include compensations of officers, new contracts and agreements, acquisitions of property, loans, and dividend payments. While reading the minutes, the auditor should identify relevant authorizations and include the information in the working papers by making an abstract of the minutes or by obtaining a copy and underlining significant portions. Some time before the audit is completed, there must be a follow-up of this information to ensure that management has complied with decisions made by the shareholders and the board of directors. As an illustration, the authorized compensation of officers should be traced to each individual officer's payroll record as a test of whether the correct total compensation was paid. Similarly, the auditor should compare the authorizations of loans with notes payable to make certain that these liabilities are recorded.

Information included in the minutes affecting the auditor's assessment of inherent risk are likely to involve more general discussions. To illustrate, assume that the minutes state that the board of directors discussed two topics: changes in the company's industry that affect the usefulness of existing machinery and equipment, and a possible lawsuit by Environment Canada for chemical seepage at a plant in Ontario. The first discussion is likely to affect the inherent risk of obsolete equipment and the second one the inherent risk of an illegal act; both could affect the financial statements (the valuation of fixed assets and the disclosure of a contingent liability).

Clients become involved in different types of contracts that are of interest to the auditor. These can include such diverse items as long-term notes and bonds payable, stock options, pension plans, contracts with vendors for future delivery of supplies, software usage and maintenance contracts, government contracts for completion and delivery of manufactured products, royalty agreements, union contracts, and leases.

Most contracts are of primary interest in individual parts of the audit and, in practice, receive special attention during the different phases of the detailed tests. For example, the provisions of a pension plan would receive substantial emphasis as a part of the audit of the unfunded liability for pensions. The auditor should review and abstract the documents early in the engagement to gain a better perspective of the organization and to become familiar with potential problem areas. Later these documents can be examined more carefully as a part of the tests of individual audit areas.

The existence of contracts often affects the auditor's assessed inherent risk. To illustrate, assume that the auditor determines early in the audit that the client has signed several sales contracts with severe non-performance clauses committing the company to deliver specified quantities of its product at agreed-upon prices during the current and next five years. The inherent risk for total sales, liabilities for penalties, and sales commitment disclosures are likely to be assessed as high in this situation.

Corporate governance The auditor will also consider the quality of management and governance in place at the client. Chapter 9 explains that internal controls are logically grouped into several levels or categories. The first level discussed is the control environment, the level of controls established by senior management. Since senior management, the board of directors, and the Audit Committee have a pervasive effect on the company, it is important that their policies, procedures, and key decisions be considered when developing a client risk profile. Previous material collected, such as minutes of directors' meetings and information about related parties, helps build a profile of the control environment. Discussions with the audit committee and with senior management about their decision-making processes and the ways that policies are implemented help complete the picture.

CLIENT OBJECTIVES AND STRATEGIES Strategies are approaches followed by the entity to achieve organizational objectives. Auditors should understand client objectives related to:

1. Reliability of financial reporting.
2. Effectiveness and efficiency of operations.
3. Compliance with laws and regulations.

Budgeting processes, financial targets, and press releases are sources of financial objectives. If there is undue management pressure to meet targets, these can bias management's intentions with respect to the methods used for recording transactions. The quality of transaction processing systems and information systems will affect the timeliness and accuracy of information that is recorded and summarized into the financial statements. By understanding management objectives and biases, as well as the type of accounting systems in use, the auditor knows of potential pressures on the financial statements.

Auditors need knowledge about operations to assess client business risk, inherent risk, and control risk in the financial statements. For example, product quality can have a significant impact on the financial statements through lost sales and through warranty and product liability claims. In Canada, in 2008, there were recalls of lead-painted toys, potentially listeria-infected meat, and cars and other vehicles with potential defects. Such recalls cost millions of dollars, having a major effect on the financial statements.

As part of understanding the client's objectives related to compliance with laws and regulations, the auditor should become familiar with the terms of its contracts and other legal obligations, explained in the previous section.

A clear code of ethics that indicates the organization's intentions to abide by laws and regulations, together with monitoring on the part of management to support compliance, help reduce the inherent risks associated with violations of laws and regulations.

Understand client's business and industry

Industry and external environment

Business operations and processes

Management and governance

Objectives and strategies

Measurement and performance

MEASUREMENT AND PERFORMANCE A client's performance measurement system includes key performance indicators that management uses to measure progress toward its objectives. These indicators go beyond financial statement figures, such as sales and net income, to include measures tailored to the client and its objectives. Such key performance indicators may include market share, sales per employee, unit sales growth, unique visitors to a website, same-store sales, and sales per square foot for a retailer.

Inherent risk of financial statement misstatements may be increased if the client has set unreasonable objectives or if the performance measurement system encourages aggressive accounting. For example, a company's objective may be to have the leading market share of industry sales. If management and salespeople are compensated on the basis of achieving this goal, there is increased incentive to record sales before they have been earned or record sales for non-existent transactions. In such a situation, the auditor is likely to increase assessed inherent risk and the extent of testing for the occurrence and timing transaction-related audit objectives for sales.

Performance measurement includes ratio analysis and benchmarking against key competitors. As part of understanding the client's business, the auditor should perform ratio analysis or review the client's calculations of key performance ratios.

ASSESS CLIENT BUSINESS RISK The auditor uses knowledge gained from the strategic understanding of the client's business and industry to assess client business risk, the risk that the client will fail to achieve its objectives. Client business risk can arise from any of the factors affecting the client and its environment, such as new technology eroding a client's competitive advantage or a client failing to execute its strategies as well as its competitors execute theirs.

The auditor's primary concern is the risk of material misstatements in the financial statements due to client business risk. For example, companies often make strategic acquisitions or mergers that depend on successfully combining the operations of two or more companies. If the planned synergies do not develop, the fixed assets and

audit challenge 8-1
Understanding Airship Solutions

As an auditor conducting a financial statement audit, it is important for you to understand your client and the business environment that it operates in.

But what if the business is a new niche that does not really fit as part of an existing industry grouping? Take a look at the Toronto distributor of Airship Solutions, founded in 2006. (There are also six other locations around the world, at the time of writing.) Airship Solutions is the worldwide manufacturer of the Airship blimps, manufactured to be filled with non-exploding helium.

Apparently, outside blimps are an environmentally friendly way to take high-quality aerial photographs. They also provide a highly visible form of advertising. So, we might look at aerial photography or aerial advertising. A search on the internet reveals that there are also many balloon companies that sell indoor blimps of various sizes, starting at US$400. The product that Airship provides is much more than a balloon, starting at $3,600 Canadian.

Airship is a high technology company, using CAD (computer-aided design) techniques to design its products. Its website states that the blimps are designed to earn Australian Civil Aviation Safety Authority certification; this certification allows the blimps to be flown where there are large groups of people.

CRITICAL THINKING QUESTIONS

1. How would you decide what would be a reasonable gross margin for Airship Solutions? What sources of information would you use?

2. How vulnerable would Airship be to downturns in the economy? Why?

3. What sources of information would you use to provide yourself with a thorough knowledge of this business?

Sources: 1. "Airship Solutions," www.airship.com.au, Accessed: December 1, 2008. 2. Langton, Jerry, "Blimp maker has high hopes," *Toronto Star*, October 20, 2008, p. B1, B4. 3. "Southern Balloon Works," www.southernballoonworks.com, Accessed: December 1, 2008.

goodwill recorded in the acquisition may be impaired, affecting fair presentation in the financial statements.

The auditor's assessment of client business risk considers the client's industry and other external factors as well as the client's business strategies, processes, and other internal factors. The auditor also considers management controls that may mitigate business risk, such as effective risk assessment practices and corporate governance. After evaluating client business risk, the auditor can assess the risk of material misstatement in the financial statements and then apply the audit risk model to determine the appropriate extent of audit evidence. (Use of the audit risk model was discussed in Chapter 7.)

Management is a primary source for identifying client business risks. In public companies, management should conduct thorough evaluations of relevant client business risks that affect financial reporting to be able to certify quarterly and annual financial statements and to evaluate the effectiveness of disclosure controls and procedures.

Publicly listed company management must certify that it has designed disclosure controls and procedures to ensure that material information about business risks are communicated to management. These procedures cover a broader range of information than is covered by an issuer's internal controls for financial reporting. The procedures should capture information that is relevant to assess the need to disclose developments and risks that pertain to the company's business. For example, if a subsidiary engages in significant hedging activities, controls should exist so that top management is informed of and discloses this information. Inquiries of management about identified client business risks, in advance of certifying quarterly and annual financial statements, may provide a significant source of information for auditors about client business risks affecting financial reporting.

The Sarbanes–Oxley Act requires management to certify that it has informed the auditor and audit committee of any significant deficiencies in internal control, including material weaknesses. Such information enables auditors to better evaluate how internal controls may affect the likelihood of material misstatements in financial statements.

concept check

C8-1 List each of the five components of understanding the client's business and industry, and provide an example of an audit step for the component.

C8-2 How does assessing client business risk fit into the client risk profile?

Client Risk Profile Evidence Gathering and Preliminary Analytical Review

Development of the client risk profile is the second risk assessment phase in the audit process. The first phase (pre-planning), described in Chapter 5, would have used similar evidence gathering techniques. These techniques are also used in further risk assessment techniques (such as inherent risk assessment and control risk assessment) discussed in other chapters.

Client Risk Profile Evidence Gathering

In Chapter 6 we described the types of evidence that the auditor can collect. During the risk assessment process, the auditor uses primarily four of types of evidence:

1. *Inquiries of management and others:* Thorough discussion with management will enable the auditor to target risk assessment and evidence gathering. In addition to what has already been discussed, inquiry helps the auditor determine the role and nature of organizational culture in promoting a positive ethical climate at the business, as well as determining management's style and roles. Sales, marketing, and production personnel are a valuable source of information from which to obtain an overview of business functioning.
2. *Observation:* The plant tour is an important example of observation. It can also corroborate statements that were made during inquiries.
3. *Inspection:* Examining key organizational contracts, reports, and minutes are valuable examples of inspection.

4. *Analytical procedures:* Analysis is used during many phases of the audit but is particularly relevant during risk assessment to highlight areas where inquiries of management need to be made and to target additional audit work.

In developing the client risk profile, the auditor will consider the evidence gathered in pre-planning, as well as what was present in the prior year's audit file. One of the first techniques used is analytical review, as it can provide a quick snapshot of financial results.

Preliminary Analytical Review

Auditors perform preliminary analytical procedures to better understand the client's business and to help assess client business risk. One such procedure compares client ratios with industry or competitor benchmarks to provide an indication of the company's performance. Such preliminary tests can reveal unusual changes in ratios compared with those of prior years, or to industry averages, and help the auditor identify areas with increased risk of misstatements that require further attention during the audit.

The Hillsburg Hardware Ltd. example is used to illustrate the use of preliminary analytical procedures as part of audit planning. Table 8-2 presents key financial ratios for Hillsburg Hardware Ltd., along with comparative industry information that auditors might consider during audit planning.

These ratios are based on the Hillsburg Hardware Ltd. financial statements. (See the insert on pages 147–162). Hillsburg's Annual Report to Shareholders described the company as a wholesale distributor of hardware equipment to independent, high-quality hardware stores in eastern Canada. The company is a niche provider in the overall hardware industry, which is dominated by national chains like Home Depot and Rona. Hillsburg's auditors identified potential increased competition from national chains as a specific client business risk. Hillsburg's market consists of smaller, independent hardware stores. Increased competition could affect the sales and profitability of these customers, likely affecting Hillsburg's sales and the value of

Table 8-2	Examples of Planning Analytical Procedures for Hillsburg Hardware Ltd.			
SELECTED RATIOS	HILLSBURG 12/31/08	INDUSTRY 12/31/08	HILLSBURG 12/31/07	INDUSTRY 12/31/07
Short-Term Debt-Paying Ability				
Cash ratio	0.06	0.22	0.06	0.20
Quick ratio	1.50	3.10	1.45	3.00
Current ratio	3.86	5.20	4.04	5.10
Liquidity Activity Ratios				
Accounts receivable turnover	7.59	12.15	7.61	12.25
Days to collect accounts receivable	48.11	30.04	47.96	29.80
Inventory turnover	3.36	5.20	3.02	4.90
Days to sell inventory	108.65	70.19	120.86	74.49
Ability to Meet Long-Term Obligations				
Debt to equity	1.73	2.51	1.98	2.53
Times interest earned	3.06	5.50	3.29	5.60
Profitability Ratios				
Gross profit percent	27.85	31.00	27.70	32.00
Profit margin ratio	0.05	0.07	0.05	0.08
Return on assets	0.13	0.09	0.12	0.09
Return on common equity	0.25	0.37	0.24	0.35

assets such as accounts receivable and inventory. An auditor might use ratio information to identify areas where Hillsburg faces increased risk of material misstatements.

The profitability measures indicate that Hillsburg is performing fairly well despite the increased competition from larger national chains. Although lower than the industry averages, the liquidity measures indicate that the company is in good financial condition, and the leverage ratios indicate additional borrowing capacity. Because Hillsburg's market consists of smaller, independent hardware stores, the company holds more inventory and takes longer to collect receivables than the industry average.

In identifying areas of specific risk, the auditor is likely to focus on the liquidity activity ratios. Inventory turnover has improved but is still lower than the industry average. Accounts receivable turnover has declined slightly and is lower than the industry average. The collectability of accounts receivable and inventory obsolescence are likely to be assessed as high inherent risks and will therefore likely warrant additional attention in the current year's audit. These areas likely received additional attention during the prior year's audit as well.

Analytical procedures were described in Chapter 6, which also shows the calculations for the 2008 Hillsburg figures on page 195 in Figure 6A-5. Figure 6-3 also shows common-size financial statements for Hillsburg, another form of analytical review.

Refer to Figure 8-1 (see page 243). After obtaining an understanding of the client in the context of its business environment and assessing client business risk, the auditor is ready to move on to planning using the audit risk model. As explained in Chapter 7, this involves determining audit risk, inherent risk, materiality levels, risks of material misstatement, and control risk. These are discussed further in subsequent chapters.

concept check

C8-3 What are the four types of evidence gathering used by the auditor for risk assessment?

C8-4 Provide an example of two types of analytical review that are used during the development of the client risk profile.

The Nature of Audit Working Papers

Working Papers

As explained in CAS 230, Audit documentation (previously Section 5145, Documentation), **working papers** are the written or electronic **audit documentation** kept by the auditor to support audit conclusions; these include risk assessments, procedures or tests performed, information obtained, and conclusions reached. Working papers should include all the information the auditor considers necessary to conduct the examination adequately and to provide support for the auditor's report.

PURPOSES OF WORKING PAPERS The overall objective of working papers is to aid the auditor in providing reasonable assurance that an adequate audit was conducted in accordance with GAAS. More specifically, the working papers, as they pertain to the current year's audit, provide a basis for planning and documenting all phases of the audit, a record of the evidence accumulated, the results of the tests, data for determining the proper type of auditor's report, and a basis for review by supervisors and partners. Proper controls need to be in place to ensure that the working papers are completed on time (within 60 days of the audit report date according to CAS 230 (par. A21), previously 45 days according to Section 5145) and that the file is frozen at that time. Increasingly, working papers are maintained as computerized files using specialized software, the only paper component being documentation provided by the client or external parties.

Basis for planning the audit If the auditor is to plan the current year's audit adequately, the necessary reference information must be available in the working papers. The papers include such diverse planning information as conclusions on client risk analysis, descriptive information about internal control, a time budget for individual audit areas, the audit program, and the results of the preceding year's audit.

Record of the evidence accumulated and the results of the tests The working papers are the primary means of documenting that an adequate audit was conducted in accordance with Canadian GAAS. If the need arises, the auditor must be able to

CAS

Working papers—the written or electronic audit documentation kept by the auditor to support audit conclusions; these include risk assessments, procedures or tests performed, information obtained, and conclusions reached.

Audit documentation—see "Working papers."

CAS

demonstrate to regulatory agencies, such as the British Columbia Securities Commission, and to the courts that the audit was well planned and adequately supervised; the evidence accumulated was appropriate, sufficient, and timely; and the auditor's report was proper considering the results of the examination.

Data for determining the proper type of auditor's report The working papers provide an important source of information to assist the auditor in deciding the appropriate auditor's report to issue in a given set of circumstances. The data in the papers are useful for evaluating the adequacy of audit scope and the fairness of the financial statements.

Basis for review The working papers are the primary frame of reference used by supervisory personnel to evaluate whether sufficient appropriate evidence was accumulated to justify the auditor's report.

In addition to the purposes directly related to the auditor's report, the working papers can also serve as the basis for preparing tax returns, filings with the provincial securities commissions, and other reports. They are a source of information for issuing communications to the audit committee and management concerning various matters such as internal control weaknesses or operations recommendations. Working papers also provide a frame of reference for training personnel and aid in planning and coordinating subsequent audits.

File freeze CAS 230 explains that the final version of the audit file should be assembled within 60 days after the date of the audit report. At that time, firms initiate a "file freeze." This means that if any additional information is added after that date, it needs to be separately identified and added at the front of the file, rather than throughout the working papers. Such additional information would need to be carefully assessed to ensure that it does not affect any of the audit conclusions. This method of freezing the file helps maintain the integrity of the audit conclusions.

CONTENTS AND ORGANIZATION Each public accounting firm establishes its own approach to preparing and organizing working papers, and the beginning auditor must adopt his or her firm's approach. The emphasis in this text is on the general concepts common to all working papers.

Figure 8-3 illustrates the organization of a typical set of working papers. They contain virtually everything involved in the financial statement audit. There is a definite logic to the type of working papers prepared for an audit and the way they are arranged in the files, even though different firms may follow somewhat different approaches. In the figure, the working papers start with more general information, such as corporate data in the permanent files, and end with the financial statements and auditor's report. In between are the working papers supporting the auditor's tests.

PERMANENT FILES **Permanent files** are intended to contain data of a historical or continuing nature pertinent to the current examination. These files provide a convenient source of information about the audit that is of continuing interest from year to year. Most firms, using automated working papers with scanned documents, will roll forward permanent or semi-permanent information electronically. Such information typically includes the following:

- Extracts or copies of such company documents of continuing importance as the articles of incorporation, bylaws, bond indentures, and contracts. The contracts are pension plans, leases, software usage and maintenance agreements, stock options, and so on. Each of these documents is of significance to the auditor for as many years as it is in effect.
- Analyses, from previous years, of accounts that have continuing importance to the auditor. These include accounts such as long-term debt, shareholders' equity accounts, goodwill, and capital assets. Having this information in the permanent files enables the auditor to concentrate on analyzing only the changes in the current year's balance while retaining the results of previous years' audits in a form accessible for review.

Permanent files—auditors' working papers that contain data of a historical or continuing nature pertinent to the current audit, such as copies of articles of incorporation, bylaws, bond indentures, and contracts.

| Figure 8-3 | Working Paper Contents and Organization |

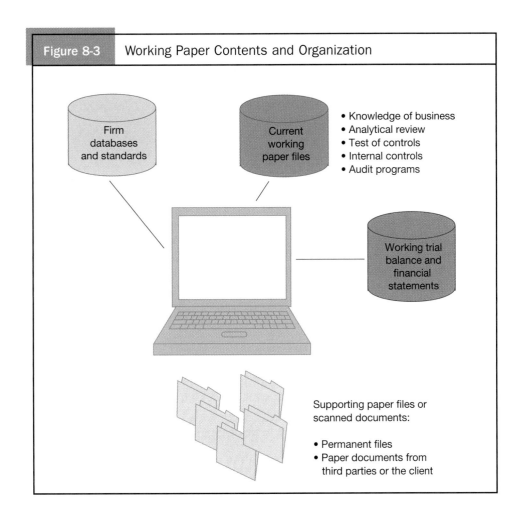

- Knowledge of business
- Analytical review
- Test of controls
- Internal controls
- Audit programs

Firm databases and standards

Current working paper files

Working trial balance and financial statements

Supporting paper files or scanned documents:

- Permanent files
- Paper documents from third parties or the client

auditing in action 8 - 2
Research on Importance of Information Technology

How many businesses do you know that do their work without information systems? Only the very smallest organizations process their transactions or do their work with paper and pencil nowadays. This applies to auditing firms as well.

Most working papers are prepared using software. There could be firm software for risk analysis and materiality decisions, databases containing industry-based audit programs, and templates for calculating information such as interest expense and prepaids. For every type of working paper that you can think of, it is likely that software or a spreadsheet template is available. Such automation can help the audit firm cope with frequent changes in audit standards.

In addition, software is used for audit time budgets, time recording, and the management of the audit firm, such as software

for billing, payroll, general ledger and financial statements. Information systems specialists use a variety of software to conduct computer-assisted audit tests geared to the risks and needs of the audit team.

Research into the perceived importance of technology use showed that use of technology was more frequent for analytical procedures, audit report preparation, sampling, searching the internet, and automated working papers. More complex risk analysis systems (such as those used to detect the potential for fraud) were less frequently used.

Sources: 1. Janvrin, Diane, James Bierstaker, and D. Jordan Lowe, "An examination of audit information technology use and perceived importance," *Accounting Horizons*, 22(1), p. 1-21. 2. Stroude, Linda, "No rest for the auditor," *CAmagazine*, August 2008, p. 33–34.

- Information related to the understanding of internal control and assessment of control risk. This includes organization charts, flowcharts, questionnaires, and other internal control information, including enumeration of controls and weaknesses in the system.
- The results of analytical procedures from previous years' audits. Among these data are ratios and percentages computed by the auditor, and the total balance or the balance by month for selected accounts. This information is useful in helping the auditor decide whether there are unusual changes in the current year's account balances that should be investigated more extensively.

Analytical procedures and the understanding of internal control and assessment of control risk are included in the current period working papers rather than in the permanent file by many public accounting firms.

Current files—all working papers applicable to the year under audit.

CURRENT FILES The **current files** include all working papers applicable to the year under audit. There is one set of permanent files for each client and a set of current files for each year's audit. The types of information included in the current file are briefly discussed in the sections that follow. As firms strive toward a paperless environment, much of this information is prepared and maintained electronically on secure systems.

Risk assessment and materiality Prior to commencing controls testing or detail testing, conclusions need to be reached on the client risk profile, materiality, audit risk, inherent risks, and control risks. Reasoning and conclusions are documented, and the resulting overall audit approach is documented. Analytical procedures for planning purposes may also be included in this section.

Audit program The audit program is kept in the relevant section with that section's working papers (e.g., accounts receivable), although some firms may also keep the audit program in a separate file. As the audit progresses, each auditor initials the program (or enters his or her password) for the audit procedures performed and records the date of completion. The inclusion in the working papers of a well-designed audit program completed in a conscientious manner is evidence of a high-quality audit.

Overall planning information Some working papers include current period information that is of an overall nature rather than information designed to support specific financial statement amounts. This includes such items as staff scheduling and budgets, abstracts or copies of minutes of the board of directors' meetings, abstracts of contracts or agreements not included in the permanent files, notes on discussions with the client, working-paper review comments, subsequent events analysis, and summary documentation indicating audit conclusions by section.

Working trial balance Since the basis for preparing the financial statements is the general ledger, the amounts included in the general ledger are the focal point of the examination. As early as possible after the balance sheet date, the auditor obtains or prepares a copy of the general ledger accounts and their year-end balances (frequently in electronic form). Once incorporated into working papers, this schedule is the **working trial balance**, a listing of the general ledger accounts and their year-end balances.

Working trial balance—a listing of the general ledger accounts and their year-end balances.

The technique used by many firms is to have the auditor's working trial balance in the same grouping format as the financial statements. Each line item on the trial balance is supported by a **lead schedule** containing the detailed accounts from the general ledger making up the line item total for a particular financial statement or working trial balance line. Each detailed account on the lead schedule is, in turn, supported by appropriate schedules evidencing the audit work performed and the conclusions reached.

Lead schedule—a working paper that contains the detailed accounts from the general ledger making up a line item total in the working trial balance.

Adjusting and reclassification entries When the auditor discovers material misstatements in the accounting records, the financial statements must be corrected.

For example, if the client failed to reduce inventory properly for obsolete raw materials, an adjusting entry can be suggested by the auditor to reflect the realizable value of the inventory. Even though adjusting entries are typically proposed by the auditor, they must be approved and made by the client because the books and records are the client's and management has primary responsibility for the fair presentation of the statements. It is therefore important to remember that when the auditor believes that an adjusting or reclassification entry is required, the auditor must ask management to make the entry. Use of automated working-paper software facilitates the necessary posting of such entries to multiple levels of working papers, from the working paper where the adjustment was described, to the lead schedule, to the working trial balance, and through to the financial statements.

Reclassification entries are frequently made in the financial statements to present accounting information properly, even when the general ledger balances are correct. A common example is the reclassification for financial statement purposes of material credit balances in accounts receivable to accounts payable. Because the balance in accounts receivable on the general ledger reflects the accounts receivable properly from the point of view of operating the company on a day-to-day basis, the reclassification entry is not included in the client's general ledger.

Only those adjusting and reclassification entries that significantly affect the fair presentation of financial statements must be made. The determination of when a misstatement should be adjusted is based on materiality. The auditor should keep in mind that several immaterial misstatements that are not adjusted could result in an overall material misstatement when the misstatements are combined. It is common for auditors to summarize on a separate working paper all adjusting and reclassification entries that have not been recorded or posted to the accounts in the books or the working papers as a means of determining their cumulative effect.

Supporting schedules The largest portion of **supporting schedule working papers** includes the detailed schedules prepared by the client or the auditors in support of specific amounts on the financial statements. Many different types of schedules are used. Use of the appropriate type for a given aspect of the audit is necessary to document the adequacy of the audit and to fulfill the other objectives of working papers. Following are the major types of supporting schedule:

- *Analysis.* An analysis is designed to show the activity in a general ledger account during the entire period under examination, tying together the beginning and ending balances. This type of schedule is normally used for accounts such as marketable securities, notes receivable, allowance for doubtful accounts, capital assets, long-term debt, and all equity accounts. The common characteristic of these accounts is the significance of the activity in the account during the year. In most cases, the **analysis working papers** have cross-references to other working papers or are automatically linked as electronic files.
- *Trial balance or list.* This type of schedule consists of the details that make up a year-end balance of a general ledger account. It differs from an analysis in that it includes only those items constituting the end-of-the-period balance. Common examples of **trial balance or list working papers** include aged trial balances or lists in support of trade accounts receivable, trade accounts payable, repairs and maintenance expenses, legal expense, and miscellaneous income. An example of a well-designed working paper is included in Figure 8-4 on the next page.
- *Reconciliation of amounts.* A **reconciliation of amounts working paper** supports a specific amount and is normally expected to tie the amount recorded in the client's records to another source of information. Examples include the reconciliation of bank balances with bank statements, the reconciliation of subsidiary accounts receivable balances with confirmations from customers, and the reconciliation of accounts payable balances with vendors' statements. An example of a working paper for a bank reconciliation is shown in Figure 16-4 on page 548.

Supporting schedule working papers—a detailed schedule prepared by the client or the auditor in support of a specific amount on the financial statements.

Analysis working paper—a supporting schedule that shows the activity in a general ledger account during the entire period under audit.

Trial balance or list working papers—a supporting schedule of the details that make up the year-end balance of a general ledger account.

Reconciliation of amounts working paper—a schedule that supports a specific amount; it normally ties the amount recorded in the client's records to another source of information, such as a bank statement or a confirmation.

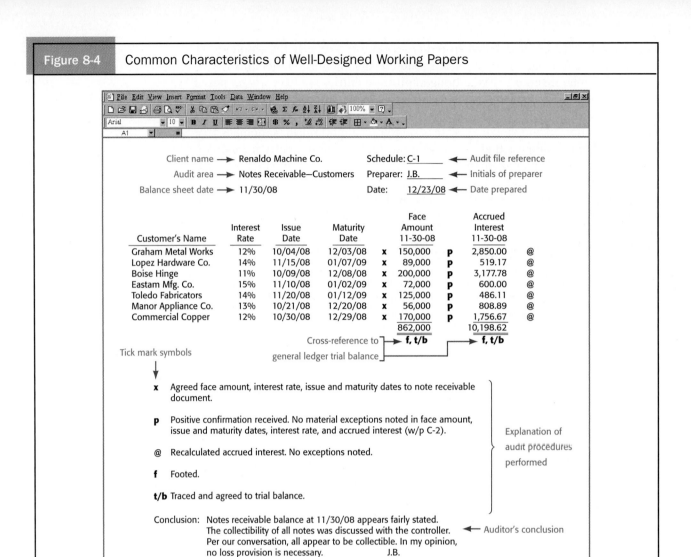

- *Tests of reasonableness.* A test of reasonableness schedule, as the name implies, contains information that enables the auditor to evaluate whether the client's balance appears to include a misstatement considering the circumstances in the engagement. Frequently, auditors test amortization expense, the provision for income taxes, and the allowance for doubtful accounts by tests of reasonableness. These tests are primarily analytical procedures.
- *Summary procedures.* This type of schedule summarizes the results of a specific audit procedure performed. Examples are the summary of the results of accounts receivable confirmation and the summary of inventory observations.
- *Examination of supporting documents.* A number of special-purpose schedules are designed to show detailed tests performed, such as examination of documents during tests of transactions or cut-offs. These schedules show no totals, and they do not tie in to the general ledger because they document only the tests performed and the results found. The schedules must, however, state a definite positive or negative conclusion about the objective of the test.
- *Informational schedule.* This type of schedule contains information as opposed to specific audit tests. These schedules include information for tax returns and data such as time budgets and the client's working hours, which are helpful in the administration of the engagement.
- *Outside documentation.* Much of the content of the working papers consists of the outside documentation gathered by auditors, such as confirmation replies and

copies of client agreements. Although not "schedules" in the real sense, these are indexed and interfiled or scanned as images. Procedures are indicated on them in the same manner as on the other schedules.

PREPARATION OF WORKING PAPERS The proper preparation of schedules to document the audit evidence accumulated, the results found, and the conclusions reached are an important part of the audit. The auditor must recognize the circumstances requiring the need for a schedule and the appropriate design of schedules to be included in the files. Although the design depends on the objectives involved, working papers should possess certain characteristics:

- Each working paper should be *properly identified* with such information as the client's name, the period covered, a description of the contents, the initials of the preparer, the date of preparation, and an index code. Where automated working-paper software is used, defaults can be set up in the software, simplifying this process.
- Working papers should be *indexed and cross-referenced* to aid in organizing and filing. One type of indexing uses alphabetic characters. The lead schedule for cash would be indexed as A-1, the individual general ledger accounts making up the total cash on the financial statements indexed as A-2 through A-4, and so on, as additional working papers are required.
- Completed working papers must clearly *indicate the audit work performed*. This is accomplished in three ways: by a written statement in the form of a memorandum, by initials on the audit procedures in the audit program, and by notations directly on the working paper schedules. Notations on working papers are accomplished by the use of tick marks, which are symbols written adjacent to the detail on the body of the schedule. These notations must be clearly explained at the bottom of the working paper.
- Each working paper should *include sufficient information* to fulfill the objectives for which it was designed. If the auditor is to prepare working papers properly, the auditor must be aware of his or her goals. For example, if a working paper is designed to list the detail and show the verification of support of a balance sheet account, such as prepaid insurance, it is essential that the detail on the working paper reconcile with the trial balance.
- The *conclusions* that were reached about the segment of the audit under consideration *should be plainly stated*.

The common characteristics of well designed working papers are indicated in Figure 8-4.

OWNERSHIP OF WORKING PAPERS The working papers prepared during the engagement, including those prepared by the client for the auditor, are the property of the auditor. The only time anyone else, including the client, has a legal right to examine the papers is when the papers are subpoenaed by a court as legal evidence or when they are required by the PA's professional organization in connection with disciplinary proceedings or practice inspection. At the completion of the engagement, working papers are retained on the public accounting firm's premises for future reference. Many firms follow the practice of microfilming or scanning the working papers after several years to reduce storage costs.

CONFIDENTIALITY OF WORKING PAPERS The need to maintain a confidential relationship with the client was discussed in Chapter 3. It was noted that the rules of conduct of the professional accounting bodies require their members not to disclose any confidential information obtained in the course of a professional engagement except with the consent of the client or, as was noted above, when required by the courts or by the professional accounting associations.

During the course of the examination, auditors obtain a considerable amount of information of a confidential nature, including officer salaries, product pricing and advertising plans, and product cost data. If auditors divulged this information to outsiders or to client employees who have been denied access, their relationship with management would be seriously strained. Furthermore, having access to the working papers would give employees an opportunity to alter information on them. For these reasons, care must be taken to protect the working papers at all times.

Ordinarily, the working papers can be provided to someone else only with the express written permission of the client; the client owns the data on the working papers. This is the case even if a PA sells his or her practice to another public accounting firm. Permission is not required from the client, however, if the working papers are subpoenaed by a court or are used in connection with disciplinary hearings or practice inspection conducted by the auditor's professional body. The auditor would normally consult with a lawyer and inform the client in these cases.

SUMMARY OF WORKING PAPERS Working papers are an essential part of every audit for effectively planning the audit, providing a record of the evidence accumulated, providing a record of the results of the tests and other information collected, deciding the proper type of auditor's report, and reviewing the work of assistants. Public accounting firms establish their own policies and approaches for working-paper preparation to make sure that these objectives are met. Public accounting firms make sure that working papers are properly prepared and are appropriate for the circumstances in the audit.

concept check

C8-5 Provide an example of a form of security that should be maintained over each of physical and electronic working papers.

C8-6 Give two examples of types of working papers that would be included in a current working paper file.

Summary

1. *Why is adequate planning essential to the audit planning process?* Planning helps ensure that the auditor gathers enough evidence of suitable quality, assists in keeping audit costs reasonable, helps avoid misunderstandings with the client, and is required by GAAS.

   How is the audit planning process linked to the development of a client risk profile? Risk assessment is a key portion of the audit plan. By assessing risks associated with the client's operations and management processes, including stating a conclusion on client business risk, the auditor helps target the audit evidence gathering process.

   How is a client risk profile developed? The client risk profile has two main parts: developing an understanding of the client's business and industry, and the assessment of client business risk. Understanding of the client's business and industry includes: the industry and external environment, business operations and processes, management and governance, objectives and strategies, and measurement and performance processes. Assessing client business risk involves looking at the results of the understanding of the client's business and industry to assess the likelihood that the organization will meet its objectives. The auditor will also consider management's risk assessment and control procedures and results of preliminary analytical review.

2. *What type of evidence does the auditor collect when compiling the client risk profile?* The auditor uses inquiries of management and others, observation, inspection, and analytical procedures.

   Why is it important to document related parties and transactions with them? Clear identification of related

parties helps the auditor ensure that this information is clearly disclosed in the financial statements. The monetary amount of related-party transactions (if material) also needs to be disclosed.

   How does analytical review aid the client risk assessment process? Analytical review can help assess the going-concern assumption and whether the company is achieving its business goals. It also provides a quick way for looking for reasonableness of financial data and for targeting further audit field work in response to assessed risks.

3. *What working papers does the auditor retain to document the planning and risk profile process?* The auditor will document observations of the client's business, relevant industry and environment characteristics, as well as information gathered about the client's business (e.g., related parties, extracts from articles of incorporation, bylaws, minutes), and conduct preliminary analytical review. Supported conclusions for each of the risk factors will be included.

   What are the purposes of working papers? They are a written record (in either paper or electronic form) providing information collected during the audit, supporting the conclusions reached, and demonstrating that the audit was conducted in accordance with Canadian GAAS.

   What are the common characteristics of high-quality working papers? The design will reflect clarity of purpose, allowing others to clearly see the work that the auditor has completed so that it can be reperformed if necessary. They will also demonstrate that adequate supervision and review were completed during the audit.

Review Questions

8-1 What benefits does the auditor derive from planning audits?

8-2 Identify the major steps in developing the client risk profile. Provide an example of audit evidence for each step.

8-3 List the types of information the auditor should obtain or review as a part of understanding the industry and external environment. Provide one specific example of how the information will be useful in conducting an audit.

8-4 When a PA has accepted an engagement from a new client that is a manufacturer, it is customary for the PA to tour the client's plant facilities. Discuss the ways in which the PA's observations made during the course of the plant tour will be of help as he or she plans and conducts the audit.

8-5 An auditor acquires background knowledge of the client's industry as an aid to his or her audit work. How does the acquisition of this knowledge aid the auditor in distinguishing between obsolete and current inventory?

8-6 Define what is meant by a "related party." What are the auditor's responsibilities for related parties and related-party transactions?

8-7 Jennifer Bailey has many clients in the manufacturing business. She has worked in this sector for many years and believes that she knows the industry well. Explain why it is important for Jennifer to develop a client risk profile every year. For each step of the client risk profile, list the benefits to the inclusion of this task as part of the client risk analysis process.

8-8 Charles Ngu is assessing the management and governance structure of Major Appliance Manufacturing Co. Describe four types of evidence that Charles would gather, and state the relevance of the evidence to the assessment of the management and governance structure of the company.

8-9 Your firm has performed the audit of Danko Inc. for several years, and you have been assigned the responsibility for the current audit. How would your review of the articles of incorporation and bylaws for this audit differ from that of the audit of a client that was audited by a different public accounting firm in the preceding year?

8-10 Identify four types of information in the client's minutes of the board of directors' meetings that are likely to be relevant to the auditor. Explain why it is important to read the minutes early in the engagement.

8-11 For the audit of Radline Manufacturing Company, the audit partner asks you to carefully read the new mortgage documents from Green Bank and extract all pertinent information. List the information in a mortgage that is likely to be relevant to the auditor.

8-12 Identify the three categories of client objectives that the auditor should understand. Indicate how each objective may affect the auditor's assessment of inherent risk and evidence accumulation.

8-13 What is the purpose of the client's performance measurement system? Give examples of key performance indicators for the following businesses: (1) a chain of retail clothing stores, (2) an internet portal, (3) a hotel chain.

8-14 Define client business risk, and describe several sources of client business risk. What is the auditor's primary concern when evaluating client business risk?

8-15 Describe top management controls and their relationship to client business risk. Give two examples of effective management and governance controls.

8-16 Explain why it is important for working papers to include each of the following: identification of the name of the client, period covered, description of the contents, initials of the preparer, date of the preparation, and an index code.

8-17 Why is it essential that the auditor not leave questions or exceptions in the working papers without an adequate explanation?

8-18 What type of working papers can be prepared by the client and used by the auditor as a part of the working-paper file? When client assistance is obtained in preparing working papers, describe the proper precautions the auditor should take.

8-19 Who owns the working papers? Under what circumstances can they be used by other people?

Discussion Questions and Problems

8-20 You have been assigned the audit of your city's largest car dealership. The car dealership has been one of your firm's audit clients for many years. It is modern and is located in a building owned by the dealership corporation. The company has recently spent almost $100,000 modernizing its vehicle repair bays, with new wiring and lift jacks.

REQUIRED

For each of the five components of understanding the client's business and industry, provide specific examples of the work that you would do to develop your understanding, and how you would document your understanding in the working paper files.

8-21 The minutes of the board of directors of Marygold Catalogue Company Ltd. for the year ended December 31, 2008, were provided to you.

Meeting of February 16, 2008

Ruth Ho, chair of the board, called the meeting to order at 4:00 p.m. The following directors were in attendance:

Margaret Aronson	Claude La Rose
Fred Brick	Lucille Renolds
Henri Chapdelaine	J. T. Schmidt
Ruth Ho	Marie Titard
Homer Jackson	Roald Asko

The minutes of the meeting of October 11, 2007, were read and approved.

Marie Titard, president, discussed the new marketing plan for wider distribution of catalogues in the western market. She made a motion for approval of increased expenditures of approximately $50,000 for distribution costs, which was seconded by Roald Asko and unanimously passed.

The unresolved dispute with the Canada Revenue Agency over the tax treatment of leased office buildings was discussed with Harold Moss, the tax partner from Marygold's public accounting firm, Moss & Lawson. In Mr. Moss's opinion, the matter would not be resolved for several months and could result in an unfavourable settlement.

J. T. Schmidt moved that the computer equipment that was no longer being used in the Kingston office, since new equipment had been acquired in 2007, be donated to the Kingston Vocational School for use in their repair and training program. Margaret Aronson seconded the motion and it was unanimously passed.

Annual cash dividends were unanimously approved as being payable April 30, 2008, for shareholders of record April 15, 2008, as follows:

Class A common—$10 per share
Class B common—$5 per share

Officers' bonuses for the year ended December 31, 2007, were approved for payment March 1, 2008, as follows:

Marie Titard—President $26,000
Lucille Renolds—Vice-President $12,000
Roald Asko—Controller $12,000
Fred Brick—Secretary-Treasurer $9,000

Meeting adjourned 6:30 p.m.

Fred Brick, Secretary

Meeting of September 15, 2008

Ruth Ho, chair of the board, called the meeting to order at 4:00 p.m. The following directors were in attendance:

Margaret Aronson	Claude La Rose
Fred Brick	Lucille Renolds
Henri Chapdelaine	J. T. Schmidt
Ruth Ho	Marie Titard
Homer Jackson	Roald Asko

The minutes of the meeting of February 16, 2008, were read and approved. Marie Titard, president, discussed the improved sales and financial condition for 2008. She was pleased with the results of the catalogue distribution and cost control for the company. No action was taken.

The nominations for officers were made as follows:
President—Marie Titard
Vice-President—Lucille Renolds
Controller—Roald Asko
Secretary-Treasurer—Fred Brick

The nominees were elected by unanimous voice vote.
Salary increases of 6 percent, exclusive of bonuses, were recommended for all officers for 2009. Marie Titard moved that such salary increases be approved; the proposal was seconded by J. T. Schmidt and unanimously approved.

Salary	2008	2009
Marie Titard, President	$90,000	$95,400
Lucille Renolds, Vice-President	$60,000	$63,600
Roald Asko, Controller	$60,000	$63,600
Fred Brick, Secretary-Treasurer	$40,000	$42,400

Roald Asko moved that the company consider adopting a pension/profit-sharing plan for all employees as a way to provide greater incentive for employees to stay with the company. Considerable discussion ensued. It was agreed without adoption that Asko should discuss the legal and tax implications with lawyer Cecil Makay and a public accounting firm reputed to be knowledgeable about pension and profit-sharing plans, Able and Bark.

Roald Asko discussed the expenditure of $58,000 for acquisition of an information system for the Kingston office to replace equipment that was purchased in 2007 and has proven ineffective. Asko moved that the transaction be approved; the move was seconded by Jackson and unanimously adopted. Fred Brick moved that a loan of $36,000 from Kingston Bank be approved. The interest is floating at 2 percent above prime. The collateral is to be the new hardware and software being installed in the Kingston office. A chequing account, with a minimum balance of $2,000 at all times until the loan is repaid, must be opened and maintained if the loan is granted. The proposal was seconded by La Rose and unanimously approved.

Lucille Renolds, chair of the audit committee, moved that the public accounting firm of Moss & Lawson be selected again for the company's annual audit and related tax work for the year ended December 31, 2009. This was seconded by Aronson and unanimously approved.

Meeting adjourned 6:40 p.m.

Fred Brick, Secretary

REQUIRED

a. How do you, as the auditor, know that all minutes have been made available to you?
b. Read the minutes of the meetings of February 16 and September 15. Use the format on the next page to list and explain information that is relevant to the 2008 audit:

c. Read the minutes of the meeting of February 16, 2008. Did any of that information pertain to the December 31, 2007, audit? Explain what the auditor should have done during the December 31, 2007, audit with respect to the 2008 minutes.

ABC Company Inc.
Notes Receivable
31/12/08

Schedule _____ Date
Prepared by _JD_ 21/1/09
Approved by _PP_ 5/2/09

Acct 110				Maker		
	Apex Co.	Ajax, Inc.	J. J. Co.	P. Smith	Martin-Peterson	Tent Co.
Date						
Made	15/6/07	21/11/07	1/11/07	26/7/08	12/5/07	3/9/08
Due	15/6/09	Demand	$200/mo	$1000/mo	Demand	$400/mo
Face amount	5000<	3591<	13180<	25000<	2100<	12000<
Value of Security	none	none	24000	50000	none	10000
Notes:						
Beg. bal.	4000^{PWP}	3591^{PWP}	12780^{PWP}	–	2100^{PWP}	–
Additions				25000		12000
Payments	>(1000)	>(3591)	>(2400)	>(5000)	>(2100)	>(1600)
End bal.						
① Current	3000 ✓	–	2400 ✓	12000	–	4800
② Long-term	–	–	7980	8000	–	5600
③ Total	3000 C	-0-	10380 C	20000 C	-0-	10400 C
	И	И	И	И	И	И
Interest						
Rate	5%	5%	5%	5%	5%	6%
Pd. to date	none	paid	31/12/08	30/9/08	paid	30/11/08
Beg. bal.	104^{PWP}	-0-^{PWP}	24^{PWP}	-0-	-0-^{PWP}	-0-
④ Earned	175 ✓	102 ✓	577 ✓	468 ✓	105 ✓	162 ✓
Received	-0-	>(102)	>(601)	>(200)	>(105)	>(108)
⑤ Accrued						
31/12/08	279	-0-	-0-	268	-0-	54
	И	И	И	И	И	И

✓ - Tested

PWP-Agrees with prior year's working papers.

① Total of $22,200 agrees with working trial balance.

② Total of $21,580 agrees with working trial balance.

③ Total of $43,780 agrees with working trial balance.

④ Total of $1,589 agrees with miscellaneous income analysis in operations W/P.

⑤ Total of $601 agrees with A/R lead schedule.

8-22 Do the following with regard to the working paper for ABC Company Inc. shown above.
  a. List the deficiencies in the working paper.
  b. For each deficiency, state how the working paper could be improved.

c. Prepare an improved working paper using electronic spreadsheet software. Include an indication of the audit work done as well as the analysis of the client data.

(Instructor's option)

8-23 Following are the auditor's calculations of several key ratios for Cragston Star Products Ltd. The primary purpose of this information is to assess the risk of financial failure, but any other relevant conclusions are also desirable.

Ratio	2008	2007	2006	2005	2004
Current ratio	2.08	2.26	2.51	2.43	2.50
Quick ratio	0.97	1.34	1.82	1.76	1.64
Earnings before taxes divided by interest expense	3.50	3.20	4.10	5.30	7.10
Accounts receivable turnover	4.20	5.50	4.10	5.40	5.60
Days to collect receivables	86.90	66.40	89.00	67.60	65.20
Inventory turnover	2.03	1.84	2.68	3.34	3.36
Days to sell inventory	179.80	198.40	136.20	109.30	108.60
Net sales divided by tangible assets	0.68	0.64	0.73	0.69	0.67
Operating income divided by net sales	0.13	0.14	0.16	0.15	0.14
Operating income divided by tangible assets	0.09	0.09	0.12	0.10	0.09
Net income divided by common equity	0.05	0.06	0.10	0.10	0.11
Earnings per share	$4.30	$4.26	$4.49	$4.26	$4.14

REQUIRED

a. What major conclusions can be drawn from this information about the company's future? How does this affect your assessment of client business risk?

b. What additional information would be helpful in your assessment of this company's business risk?

c. Based on the ratios given in the table, which particular aspects of the company do you believe should receive special emphasis in the audit?

Professional Judgment Problems

8-24 The internet has dramatically increased global e-commerce activities. Both traditional "brick and mortar" businesses and new dot-com businesses use the internet to meet business objectives. For example, eBay successfully offers online auctions as well as goods for sale in a fixed-price format.

a. Identify three specific business strategies that explain eBay's decision to offer goods for sale at fixed prices.

b. Describe three business risks related to eBay's operations. How do these risks affect your assessment of eBay's client business risk?

c. Acquisitions by eBay include PayPal, an online payment service, and Skype, an internet communications company. Discuss possible reasons why eBay made these strategic acquisitions.

d. Identify possible risks that could lead to material misstatements in the eBay financial statements if business risks related to its operations, including recent acquisitions, are not effectively managed.

8-25 You are engaged in the annual audit of the financial statements of Maulack Corp., a medium-sized wholesale company that manufactures light fixtures. The company has 25 shareholders. During your review of the minutes, you observe that the president's salary has been increased substantially over the preceding year by the action of the board of directors. His present salary is much greater than salaries paid to presidents of companies of comparable size and is clearly excessive. You determine that the method of computing the president's salary was changed for the year under audit. In previous years, the president's salary was consistently based on sales. In the latest year, however, his salary was based on net income before income taxes. Maulack Corp. is in a cyclical industry and would have had an extremely profitable year, except that the increase in the president's salary siphoned off much of the income that would have accrued to the shareholders. The president is a minority shareholder of the company.

a. What is the implication of this condition for the fair presentation of the financial statements?
b. Discuss your responsibility for disclosing this situation.
c. Discuss the effect, if any, that the situation has on:

1. The fairness of the presentation of the financial statements.
2. The consistency of the application of accounting principles.

(Adapted from AICPA)

Case

8-26 Winston Black was an audit partner at Henson, Davis, LLP. He was in the process of reviewing the audit files for the audit of a new client, McMullan Resourcing. McMullan was in the business of heavy construction. Winston was conducting his first review after the field work had been substantially completed. Normally, he would have done an initial review during the earlier planning phases as required by his firm's policies; however, he had been overwhelmed by an emergency with his largest and most important client. He rationalized not reviewing the details of the client risk analysis or other audit planning information because (1) the audit was being overseen by Sara Beale, a manager in whom he had confidence, and (2) there were a few days of field work left, where any additional audit work could be completed.

Now, Winston found that he was confronted with several problems. First, he found that his firm may have accepted McMullan without complying with its new client acceptance procedures. McMullan came to Henson, Davis on a recommendation from a friend of Winston's. Winston got "credit" for the new business, which was important to him because it would affect his compensation from the firm. Because Winston was busy, he told Sara to conduct a new client acceptance review and let him know if there were any problems. He never heard from Sara and assumed everything was in order. In reviewing Sara's preplanning documentation, he saw a check mark in the box "contact prior auditors" but found no details indicating if it was done. When he asked Sara about this, she responded:

"I called Gardner Smith (the responsible partner with McMullan's prior audit firm) and left a voicemail message for him. He never returned my call. I talked to Ted McMullan about the change of auditors, and he told me that he informed Gardner about the change and that Gardner said, 'Fine, I'll help in any way I can.' Ted said Gardner sent over copies of analyses of fixed assets and equity accounts, which Ted gave to me. I asked Ted why they replaced Gardner's firm, and he told me it was over the tax contingency issue and the size of their fee. Other than that, Ted said the relationship was fine."

The tax contingency issue that Sara referred to was a situation in which McMullan had entered into litigation with a bank from which it had received a loan. The result of the litigation was that the bank forgave McMullan several hundred thousand dollars in debt. This was a windfall to McMullan, and they recorded it as a capital gain, taking the position that it was not regular income. The prior auditors disputed this

position and insisted that a contingent tax liability be recorded. This upset McMullan, but the company agreed in order to receive an unqualified opinion. Before hiring Henson, Davis as their new auditors, McMullan requested that Henson, Davis review the situation. Henson, Davis believed the contingency was remote and agreed to the elimination of the contingent liability.

The second problem involved a long-term contract with a customer in Montreal. Under GAAP, McMullan was required to recognize income on this contract using the percentage-of-completion method. The contract was partially completed as of the year end and was material to the financial statements. When Winston went to review the copy of the contract in the audit files, he found three things. First, there was a contract summary prepared by the sales manager that set out its major features. Second, there was a copy of the contract written in French. Third, there was a signed confirmation (in English) confirming the terms and status of the contract. The space on the confirmation requesting information about any contract disputes was left blank, indicating no such problems.

Winston's concern about the contract was that to recognize income in accordance with GAAP, the contract had to be enforceable. Often, contracts contain a cancellation clause that might mitigate enforceability. Because he was not able to read French, Winston could not tell whether the contract contained such a clause. When he asked Sara about this, she responded that she had asked the company's vice-president of sales about the contract and he told her that it was their standard contract. The company's standard contract did have a cancellation clause in it, but it required mutual agreement and could not be cancelled unilaterally by the buyer.

REQUIRED

a. Evaluate whether Henson, Davis, LLP, complied with generally accepted auditing standards in their acceptance of McMullan Resources as a new client. What can they do at this point in the engagement to resolve any deficiencies if they exist?
b. Consider whether sufficient audit work has been done with regard to McMullan's Montreal contract. If not, what more should be done?
c. Evaluate and discuss whether Winston and Sara conducted themselves in accordance with generally accepted auditing standards.

ACL Problem

8-27 This problem requires the use of ACL software, which is included in the companion website at **www.pearsoned.ca/arens**. Information about installing and using ACL and solving this problem can be found in the ACL Appendix, also on the companion website. You should read all of the reference material preceding instructions about "Quick Sort" before locating the appropriate command to answer questions a-f. For this problem, open an existing ACL Project, then choose the Sample Project data files. In the "Tables" folder, open the "Payroll Analysis" subfolder, then the "Payroll" file. The suggested command or other source of information needed to solve the problem requirement is included at the end of each question.

a. Determine the number of payroll transactions in the file (read the bottom of the Payroll file screen).
b. Determine the largest and smallest payroll transaction (gross pay) for the month of September (Quick Sort).
c. Determine gross pay for September (Total).
d. Determine and print gross pay by department (Summarize).
e. Recalculate net pay for each payroll transaction for September and compare it with the amount included in the file (Computed Fields or Filter). What would be your concern if there were any differences?
f. Determine if there are any gaps or duplicates in the cheque numbers (Gaps and Duplicates). What would be your concern if there were gaps or duplicates?

Ongoing Small Business Case: Management-Prepared Working Papers at CondoCleaners.com

8-28 Since the owner, Jim, is a qualified accountant, he would like to reduce professional fees by assisting with the preparation of working papers. Jim has purchased a basic accounting software package, which he uses to record transactions. He still does all the accounting for his business.

REQUIRED
List five working papers that Jim could prepare for the audit of his business by your firm. What concerns would you have about the working papers prepared by Jim? What additional audit work would your firm need to do to be able to rely upon these working papers?

9

Internal controls and control risk

"Why bother testing internal controls? We can just look at the numbers and the supporting documents, can't we?" Well, no! In a large organization with millions of transactions, ignoring internal controls would lead to a very expensive audit. For an organization of any size, the ability to rely on the procedures performed by computer software (such as calculations) reduces the amount of audit work required. Management accountants will find this information helpful as they choose to design internal controls for their organization. Internal, external, and specialist auditors frequently are called upon to asses internal controls.

LEARNING OBJECTIVES

1 State the three primary objectives of effective internal control. Describe the differing perspectives of the client and the auditor. State the purpose of understanding controls when substantive tests are not enough for auditing a particular assertion. Identify the three basic concepts that enable an auditor's study of internal controls.

2 Explain the five components of the COSO (Committee of Sponsoring Organizations of the Treadway Commission) internal control framework.

3 Describe what the auditor does to obtain an understanding of internal controls and of their design effectiveness. State how control risk is assessed, documented, and tested. Identify key controls, and link control risk by assertion to audit strategy and further audit procedures. Explain how different types of internal control reports affect tests of controls.

4 Identify important risks and controls in small businesses.

STANDARDS REFERENCED IN THIS CHAPTER

CICA Standards

CAS 265 – Communicating deficiencies in internal control to those charged with governance and management (previously Section 5220 – Weaknesses in internal control)

CAS 315 – Identifying and assessing the risks of material misstatement through understanding the entity and its environment (previously Section 5141 – Understanding the entity and its environment and assessing the risks of material misstatement)

CAS 330 – The auditor's responses to assessed risks (previously Section 5143 – The auditor's procedures in response to assessed risks)

CAS 610 – Using the work of internal auditors (previously Section 5050 – Using the work of internal audit)

Section 5025 – Standards for assurance engagements

Section 5925 – An audit of internal control over financial reporting that is integrated with an audit of financial statements

Section 9110 – Agreed-upon procedures regarding internal control over financial reporting

Good Internal Control Prevents More Embezzlements than Good Auditors Find

Shortly after its tenth consecutive audit of the Foundation for Youth Bible Studies (FYBS), Able & Tang, LLP, were informed that FYBS's chief accountant was found to have embezzled $2 million during the past four years. FYBS wanted to know how this could have occurred without Able & Tang discovering it. The firm responded that it would have to know how the fraud was carried out to answer the question.

FYBS runs numerous small summer camps throughout the province. Although most campers pay by cheque or credit card prior to attending the camps, some campers bring payment to the camp. The local camps do not have bank accounts and are told not to accept cash or credit cards for payment. Funds collected locally by cheque were sent to the head office chief accountant for deposit. The chief accountant recorded the revenue and deposited the cheques. No record of the source or amount of these cheques was maintained at the local FYBS camps. This allowed the chief accountant to occasionally pocket some of the cheques. She did not record the revenue for the amounts that were embezzlements.

When the auditors gained an understanding of the internal control at FYBS, they regularly interviewed head office employees about how the system functioned. The audit was conducted in the fall and winter, when there were no active camps. During the course of these discussions, they were never told about the occasional funds sent from the camp. It was not clear that anyone at the head office, other than the embezzler, was aware of it. Fortunately, Able & Tang's audit report contained a qualification that they could verify only those revenues that were actually recorded. Given the qualification in the audit report and the conduct of the audit, Able & Tang were not held responsible for the loss. They helped FYBS implement new controls to prevent a similar occurrence, but, nevertheless, FYBS changed auditors.

IMPORTANCE TO AUDITORS

This case demonstrates one of the difficulties of auditing—you cannot audit what is not there. As head office personnel did not seem to be aware of the cheques sent from the camps, the auditor could not audit this process. The situation also illustrates the relevance of working with non-accounting personnel. An audit technique that this firm will likely consider for future audits is to attend operational activities even if they occur at times outside the normal audit.

WHAT DO YOU THINK?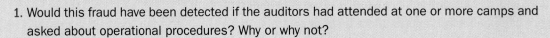

1. Would this fraud have been detected if the auditors had attended at one or more camps and asked about operational procedures? Why or why not?

2. This case illustrates how many small thefts lead to a material fraud. What are some other examples of small amounts that could rapidly accumulate to large financial statement misstatements?

3. Refer to the sample engagement letter in Chapter 5. Would the engagement letter prevent the auditors from being sued by FYBS? Why or why not?

THE opening story involving FYBS demonstrates how deficiencies in internal control can result in material misstatements in financial statements. Financial reporting problems of companies such as Enron and Nortel also exposed serious deficiencies in internal control. To address these concerns, Section 404 of the Sarbanes-Oxley Act in the United States requires auditors of public companies to assess and report on the effectiveness of internal control over financial reporting, in addition to their report on the audit of financial statements. In Canada, although public company management must attest to the quality of the company's internal controls, assessment by the auditors is not required.

Chapter 9 is the fourth chapter dealing with financial statement audit risk assessment. The study of internal control, assessment of control risk, and related evidence gathering is a major component in the audit risk model studied in Chapter 7. Control risk is "CR" in the audit risk model. It was explained in Chapter 7 that planned audit evidence can be reduced when there are effective internal controls. This chapter shows why and how this can be done.

To understand how internal control is used in the audit risk model, knowledge of key internal control concepts is needed. Accordingly, this chapter focuses on the meaning and objectives of internal control from both the client's and the auditor's point of view, the components of internal control, and the auditor's methodology for fulfilling the requirements of the second examination standard. Professional guidance in considering internal control is found in CAS 315 and 330 (formerly Sections 5141 and 5143) of the *CICA Handbook*.

❶ Differing Perspectives of Internal Control

A system of **internal control** consists of policies and procedures designed to provide management with reasonable assurance that the company achieves its objectives and goals. These policies and procedures are often called controls, and collectively, they make up the entity's internal control. There are three broad objectives in designing an effective internal control system:

> **Internal control**—the policies and procedures instituted and maintained by the management of an entity in order to provide reasonable assurance that management's objectives are met.

1. *Reliability of financial reporting.* As we discussed in Chapter 5, management is responsible for preparing statements for investors, creditors, and other users. Management has both a legal and professional responsibility to be sure that the information is fairly presented in accordance with reporting requirements such as GAAP. The objective of effective internal control over financial reporting is to fulfill these financial reporting responsibilities.

2. *Efficiency and effectiveness of operations.* Controls within a company encourage efficient and effective use of its resources to optimize the company's goals. An important objective of these controls is accurate financial and nonfinancial information about the company's operations for decision making.
3. *Compliance with laws and regulations.* In the United States, public companies are required to issue a report about the operating effectiveness of internal control over financial reporting. In Canada, management is required to report on the effectiveness of internal controls. Public, nonpublic, and not-for-profit organizations are required to follow many laws and regulations. Some relate to accounting only indirectly, such as environmental protection and human rights laws. Others are closely related to accounting, such as income tax regulations and fraud.

Client Perspectives on Internal Control

Management designs systems of internal control to accomplish all three defined objectives. The auditor's focus in both the audit of financial statements and the audit of internal controls is on controls over the reliability of financial reporting plus those controls over operations and compliance with laws and regulations that could materially affect financial reporting.

The internal control system consists of governance processes as well as many specific policies and procedures designed to provide management with reasonable assurance that the goals and objectives that it believes to be important to the entity will be met.

Control systems must be cost beneficial. The controls adopted are selected by comparing the costs to the organization relative to the benefits expected. One benefit to management, but certainly not the most important, is the reduced cost of an audit when the auditor evaluates internal control as good or excellent and assesses control risk as much below maximum (i.e., as low).

In addition to the defined purposes of internal control, management typically has the following objectives in designing effective internal control.

Maintaining reliable control systems Management must have reliable control systems so that it will have accurate information for carrying out its operations and producing financial statements. A wide variety of information is used for making critical business decisions. For example, the price to charge for products is based in part on information about the cost of making the products. Information must be reliable and timely if it is to be useful to management for decision making.

Safeguarding assets The physical assets of a company can be stolen, misused, or accidentally destroyed unless they are protected by adequate controls. The same is true of non-physical assets such as important records (e.g., confidential business proposals or research and development data) and accounting records (e.g., accounts receivable balances, financial details). Safeguarding certain assets and records has become increasingly important since the advent of computer systems. Large amounts of information stored on computer media such as disks and cartridge tapes can be destroyed or stolen if care is not taken to protect them. Management safeguards assets by controlling access and by comparisons of assets with records of those assets.

Optimizing the use of resources The controls within an organization are meant to optimize use of resources by preventing unnecessary duplication of effort and waste in all aspects of the business and by discouraging other inefficient use of resources.

Preventing and detecting error and fraud The internal controls of a company play an important role in the prevention and detection of error or fraud and other irregularities. Management must weigh cost versus benefit when considering this objective. The cost of preventing a particular misstatement should be balanced against the likelihood of the misstatement occurring and the amount of the misstatement that could occur. Risks associated with fraud are discussed further in Chapter 11.

auditing in action 9-1
Coffee, Tea, or an Internal Controls Report?

Rather than creating "Sarbanes-Oxley North," Canada has decided to go its own way. Of course, publicly listed companies that have shares traded on the SEC in the United States must follow U.S. laws and have the auditors provide an opinion on internal controls.

CICA Handbook Section 5925, An audit of internal control over financial reporting that is integrated with an audit of financial statements, provides guidance for that type of internal control report. In Canada, listed companies' managements are required to report on the effectiveness of internal control but are not required to have that report audited.

Other types of internal control reports that are not integrated with the financial statements are also possible.

Creating such internal control reports would require an assurance engagement, not addressed by the new Canadian Auditing Standards (CASs) that are aligned with International Standards on Auditing (ISAs). Accordingly, such engagements continue to be covered by *CICA Handbook* Section 5025, Standards for assurance engagements."

Depending upon the type of engagement, other standards remain relevant: Section 9110, Agreed-upon procedures regarding internal control over financial reporting, or Section 5970, Auditor's report on controls at a service organization.

These standards are geared to different levels of assurance and to different users.

AUDITOR PERSPECTIVES Evaluation of internal control and the associated control risk is part of the audit planning process. The auditor considers control risk together with inherent risk to evaluate whether there is a risk of financial statement misstatement at the level of the financial statements as a whole or for individual transactions or accounts at the assertion level (see the CAS 315 section, Risk assessment procedures and related activities). The quality of the internal controls affects the extent of tests of details conducted by the auditor.

Management's internal control objectives go beyond financial statement objectives. In other words, there are aspects of internal control that are of interest to management but not to the auditor; consequently, the auditor does not concern himself or herself with those aspects of internal control in planning the audit. An example would be internal controls that have been set up by management to ensure that accurate information about the company's market share is collected and provided to the company's marketing department.

CAS 315 paragraph 12 explains that the auditor considers internal control that is relevant to the financial statement audit. These will normally include cycles of events (transactions) that lead to information recorded in the financial statements. However, other systems, such as manufacturing quality control, could be relevant if the client has had quality control problems that have resulted in numerous product returns and the auditor is attempting to assess the value of inventory. The auditor examines whether internal controls prevent, detect, or correct material misstatements. The auditor can consider inherent risks together with control risks by assertion or can consider inherent and control risks separately. This text generally considers them separately, although practice varies. When risks of error are high, the auditor will expand tests of details, potentially abandoning tests of controls altogether.

CONTROLS RELATED TO THE RELIABILITY OF FINANCIAL REPORTING The auditor is interested primarily in controls that relate to the first of management's internal control objectives: maintaining reliable control systems. This is the area that directly impacts the reliability of the financial statements and their related assertions and therefore impacts the auditor's objective of determining that the financial statements are fairly stated. The financial statements are not likely to reflect generally accepted accounting principles correctly if the controls affecting the reliability of financial reporting are inadequate. On the other hand, the statements can be fairly stated even if the controls do not promote efficiency and effectiveness in the company's operations.

As stated in Chapter 5, auditors have significant responsibility for the discovery of management and employee fraud and, to a lesser degree, certain types of illegal acts. Auditors are therefore also concerned with a client's controls over the safeguarding of assets and compliance with applicable laws and regulations if they affect the fairness of the financial statements. Internal controls, if properly designed and implemented, can be effective in preventing and detecting fraud.

It has already been stated that auditors should emphasize controls concerned with the reliability of data for external reporting purposes, but controls affecting internal management information, such as budgets and internal performance reports, should also be examined. These types of information are often important sources for the auditor because they can be used to develop expectations for analytical procedures. If the controls over these internal reports are considered inadequate, the value of the reports as evidence diminishes.

Emphasis on controls over classes of transactions The emphasis by auditors is on controls over classes of transactions rather than on account balances. The reason is that the accuracy of the results of the accounting system (account balances) is heavily dependent upon the accuracy of the inputs and processing (transactions). For example, if products sold, units shipped, or unit selling prices are incorrectly billed to customers for sales, both sales and accounts receivable will be misstated. If controls are adequate to ensure billings, cash receipts, sales returns and allowances, and charge-offs are correct, the ending balance in accounts receivable is likely to be correct.

In the study of internal control and assessment of control risk, therefore, auditors are primarily concerned with the **transaction-related audit objectives**, discussed in Chapter 5. These objectives were discussed in detail on page 135. Table 9-1 illustrates the development of transaction-related audit objectives for sales transactions.

During the study of internal control and assessment of control risk, the auditor does consider internal controls over account balances where relevant. For example, transaction-related audit objectives typically have no effect on three balance-related audit objectives: valuation, rights and obligations, and presentation and disclosure. The auditor is likely to make a separate evaluation as to whether management has implemented internal controls for each of these three balance-related audit objectives. The auditor does not need to evaluate all controls for all assertions for all cycles— only those where there is a potential for material misstatement.

When substantive procedures are insufficient The auditor may identify some risks that cannot be effectively tested by substantive tests. For example, there may be a risk of incomplete recording of electronic commerce transactions or the risk of inaccurate

Transaction-related audit objectives—six audit objectives that must be met before the auditor can conclude that the total for any given class of transactions is fairly stated. The general transaction-related audit objectives are occurrence, completeness, accuracy, classification, timing, and posting and summarization.

Table 9-1	Sales Transaction-Related Audit Objectives
Transaction-Related Audit Objectives—General Form	**Specific Sales Transaction-Related Audit Objectives**
Occurrence	Recorded sales are for shipments made to nonfictitious customers.
Completeness	Existing sales transactions are recorded.
Accuracy	Recorded sales are for the amount of goods shipped and are correctly billed and recorded.
Classification	Sales transactions are properly classified.
Posting and Summarization	Sales transactions are properly included in the data files and are correctly summarized.
Timing	Sales are recorded on the correct dates.

calculation of invoices due to transfer of information from other subsystems. When such risks are present, the auditor is required to obtain an understanding of the controls (perhaps in information systems) that address those risks (CAS 315 par. 29).

Consider the whole picture The auditor's frame of reference is the potential risk of material misstatements at the financial statement level. So, after considering the potential for misstatements at the detailed assertion level for transactions and account balances, it is important to step back and look at the financial statements as a whole. For example, does it appear that there is a frequent risk of understatement for more than one asset account, or a frequent risk of completeness errors for multiple types of transactions? If so, consider the impact on the financial statements as a whole.

Studying Internal Control

KEY CONCEPTS There are three basic concepts underlying the study of internal control and assessment of control risk: management's responsibility, reasonable assurance, and inherent limitations.

Management's responsibility Management, not the auditor, must establish and maintain the entity's controls. This concept is consistent with the requirement that management, not the auditor, is responsible for the preparation of financial statements in accordance with Canadian GAAP. Chapter 10 describes some corporate governance strategies and how these impact control systems.

Reasonable assurance A company should develop internal controls that provide reasonable, but not absolute, assurance that the financial statements are fairly stated. Internal controls are developed by management after considering both the costs and benefits of the controls. Management is often unwilling to implement an ideal system because the costs may be too high. For example, it is unreasonable for auditors to expect the management of a small company to hire several additional accounting personnel to bring about a small improvement in the reliability of accounting data. It is often less expensive to have auditors do more extensive auditing than to incur higher internal control costs.

Inherent limitations Internal controls cannot be regarded as completely effective, regardless of the care followed in their design and implementation. Even if systems personnel could develop, design, and program an ideal system, the effectiveness of the system would also depend on the competency and dependability of the people using it. For example, assume that a procedure for counting inventory is carefully developed and requires two employees to count independently. If neither of the employees understands the instructions or if both are careless in doing the counts, the count of inventory is likely to be incorrect. Even if the count is right, management might override the procedure and instruct an employee to increase the count of quantities in order to improve reported earnings. Similarly, the employees might decide to overstate the counts intentionally to cover up a theft of inventory by one or both of them. This collaborative effort among employees to defraud is called **collusion**.

Because of these inherent limitations of controls and because auditors cannot have more than reasonable assurance of the controls' effectiveness, there is almost always some level of control risk greater than zero. Therefore, even with the most effectively designed internal controls, the auditor must obtain audit evidence beyond testing the controls for every material financial statement account.

Collusion—a cooperative effort among employees to defraud a business of cash, inventory, or other assets.

concept check

C9-1 Why does management implement internal controls?

C9-2 Does the auditor document all internal controls? Why or why not?

C9-3 Can account balances be tested with control testing only? Why or why not?

❷ COSO Components of Internal Control

COSO (the Committee of Sponsoring Organizations of the Treadway Commission, **www.coso.org**) has representatives from the American Accounting Association, the American Institute of Certified Public Accountants, Financial Executives International,

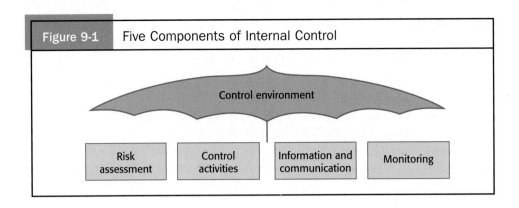

Figure 9-1	Five Components of Internal Control

Control environment

| Risk assessment | Control activities | Information and communication | Monitoring |

the Institute of Management Accountants, and the Institute of Internal Auditors. A review of the website will show that the first report issued by COSO was in 1997 with respect to fraud, while their now commonly used integrated internal control framework was released in 1992.

COSO's Internal Control—Integrated Framework describes five components of internal control that management designs and implements to provide reasonable assurance that its control objectives will be met. Each component contains many controls, but auditors concentrate on those designed to prevent or detect material misstatements in the financial statements. The COSO internal control components comprise the following:

1. Control environment.
2. Risk assessment.
3. Control activities.
4. Information and communication.
5. Monitoring.

Figure 9-1 shows that the control environment is the umbrella for the other four components. Without an effective control environment, the other four components are unlikely to result in effective internal control, regardless of their quality.

The components of internal control contain many control-related policies and procedures. The auditor is concerned primarily with those related to preventing or detecting material misstatements in the financial statements. Those aspects will be the focus of the remainder of the chapter.

The Control Environment

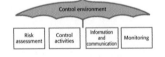

Those charged with governance—individuals responsible for overseeing the strategic direction of the entity and the accountability of the entity, including financial reporting and disclosure.

Entity-level controls—those controls that are implemented for multiple transaction cycles or for the entire organization.

Control environment—the actions, policies, and procedures that reflect the overall attitudes of top management, directors, and owners of an entity about control and its importance to the entity.

The essence of an effectively controlled organization lies in the attitude of its management. If top management believes control is important, others in the organization will sense that and respond by conscientiously observing the policies and procedures established. On the other hand, if it is clear to members of the organization that control is not an important concern to top management and is given "lip service" rather than meaningful support, it is almost certain that control objectives will not be effectively achieved. Individuals responsible for overseeing the strategic direction of the entity and the accountability of the entity, including financial reporting and disclosure, are called **those charged with governance.** As corporate governance strategies have a major impact on the control environment and the other components of internal control, these strategies, their impact upon controls, and the audit process are discussed further in Chapter 10. There we also examine the audit of **entity-level controls** (those controls that are implemented for multiple transaction cycles or for the entire organization).

The **control environment** consists of the actions, policies, and procedures that reflect the overall attitudes of top management, the directors, and the owners of an entity about control and its importance to the entity. It is the implementation of the attitudes and strategies of those charged with governance. For the purpose of understanding and assessing the control environment, the auditor should consider the most important control subcomponents.

ACTIVE INTEGRITY AND PROMOTION OF ETHICAL VALUES The methods of communicating and reinforcing integrity and ethical values are the product of the entity's ethical and behavioural standards. They include management's actions to remove or reduce incentives and temptations that might prompt personnel to engage in dishonest, illegal, or unethical acts. They also include the communication of entity values and behavioural standards to personnel through policy statements, codes of conduct, and by example.

COMMITMENT TO COMPETENCE Competence is the knowledge and skills necessary to accomplish tasks that define an individual's job. Commitment to competence includes management's consideration of the competence levels for specific jobs and how these skills translate into requisite skills and knowledge.

THE BOARD OF DIRECTORS OR AUDIT COMMITTEE PARTICIPATION The board of directors is essential for effective corporate governance because it has ultimate responsibility to make sure management implements proper internal control and financial reporting processes. An effective board of directors is independent of management, and its members stay involved in and scrutinize management's activities. Although the board delegates responsibility for internal control to management, it must regularly assess these controls. In addition, an active and objective board can often reduce the likelihood that management overrides existing controls.

To assist the board in its oversight, the board creates an audit committee that is charged with oversight responsibility for financial reporting. The audit committee is also responsible for maintaining ongoing communication with both external and internal auditors, including the approval of audit and non-audit services done by auditors for public companies. This allows the auditors and directors to discuss matters that might relate to such things as the integrity or actions of management.

The audit committee's independence from management and knowledge of financial reporting issues are important determinants of its ability to effectively evaluate internal controls and financial statements prepared by management. The major exchanges (TSX, NYSE, AMEX, and NASDAQ) require that listed companies have an audit committee composed entirely of independent directors who are financially literate. One method of assessing the quality of corporate governance is the evaluation of the effectiveness of the audit committee's oversight of the company's external financial reporting and internal control over financial reporting.

MANAGEMENT PHILOSOPHY AND OPERATING STYLE Management, through its activities, provides clear signals to employees about the importance of control. For example, does management take significant risks or is it risk-averse? Do policies exist to protect information and ensure privacy and confidentiality? Are profit plans and budget data set as "best possible" plans or "most likely" targets? Can management be described as "fat and bureaucratic," "lean and mean," "dominated by one or a few individuals," or "just right"? Does management use aggressive accounting to ensure budgets and goals are met? Understanding these and similar aspects of management's philosophy and operating style gives the auditor a sense of its attitude about control.

ORGANIZATIONAL STRUCTURE The entity's organizational structure defines the lines of responsibilities and authority that exist. By understanding the client's organizational structure, the auditor can learn the management and functional elements of the business and perceive how control-related policies and procedures can be carried out.

HUMAN RESOURCE POLICIES AND PRACTICES The most important aspect of any system of controls is personnel. If employees are competent and trustworthy, other controls can be absent, and reliable financial statements will still result. Honest, efficient people are able to perform at a high level even when there are few other controls to support them. Even if there are numerous other controls, incompetent or dishonest people can reduce the system to a shambles. Even though personnel may be competent and trustworthy, people have certain innate shortcomings. They can, for example, become bored or dissatisfied, personal problems can disrupt their performance, or their goals may change.

Because of the importance of competent, trustworthy personnel in providing effective control, the method by which persons are hired, evaluated, and compensated is an important part of internal control.

METHODS OF ASSIGNING AUTHORITY AND RESPONSIBILITY The methods of communicating assignment of authority and responsibility must take into account the reporting relationships and responsibilities existing within the entity and the entity's culture. Care must be taken that such issues as the entity's policy on ethical and social issues and organizational goals and objectives are considered. The communications might include such methods as memoranda from top management about the importance of control and control-related matters, formal organizational and operating plans, employee job descriptions and related policies, and policy documents covering employee behaviour such as conflicts of interest and formal codes of conduct, including policies forbidding software copyright violation.

MANAGEMENT CONTROL METHODS These are the methods that management uses to supervise the entity's activities. Do there exist policies indicating the status of electronic communications? Have logical access and monitoring methods (e.g., passwords and logging) been implemented to reinforce rights of usage as defined? Management methods that monitor the activities of others enhance the effectiveness of internal control in two ways. First, the implementation of such methods sends a clear message about the importance of control. Second, the methods serve to detect misstatements that may have occurred.

An example that illustrates management control methods is an effective budgeting system including subsequent periodic reports of the results of operations compared with budgets. An organization that has effective planning identifies material differences between actual results and the plan, and takes appropriate corrective action at the proper management level.

SYSTEMS DEVELOPMENT METHODOLOGY Management has the responsibility for the development and implementation of the entity's systems and procedures. The auditor should know whether management has a methodology for developing and modifying automated and manual systems and procedures or whether change occurs on an ad hoc basis.

MANAGEMENT REACTION TO EXTERNAL INFLUENCES While external influences are beyond management's control, management should be aware of these influences and be prepared to react appropriately. For example, management (and its tax advisors) should be knowledgeable about the tax laws in filing corporate tax returns so that an audit by the Canada Revenue Agency would not uncover any surprises.

Management should be aware of changes in the economy and technology in the entity's industry. For example, a retailing company should be aware of a potential downturn in the economy that could lead to reduced sales. The company should probably reduce its level of inventory in such a situation.

INTERNAL AUDIT An effective, competent, independent, and well-trained internal audit department, which reports to the audit committee of the board of directors, can greatly enhance the operations of an entity. Internal auditors are becoming more involved in planning and assessment activities, such as systems development audits, as well as monitoring the effectiveness of other control-related policies and procedures and performing operational audits (discussed further in Chapter 24).

In addition to its role in the entity's control environment, an adequate internal audit staff can contribute to reduced external audit costs by providing direct assistance to the external auditor. CAS 610 (previously Section 5050) defines the way internal auditors affect the external auditor's evidence accumulation. If the external auditor obtains evidence that supports the competence, integrity, and objectivity of internal auditors, then the external auditor can rely on the internal auditors' work in a number of ways.

After obtaining information about each of the subcomponents of the control environment, the auditor uses this understanding as a basis for assessing management's and the directors' attitudes and awareness about the importance of control. For example, the auditor might determine the nature of a client's budgeting system as a part of understanding the design of the control environment. The operation of the budgeting system might then be evaluated in part by inquiry of budgeting personnel to determine budgeting procedures and follow-up on differences between budget and actual.

Risk Assessment

Risk assessment for financial reporting is management's identification and analysis of risks relevant to the preparation of financial statements in conformity with GAAP. For example, if a company frequently sells products at a price below inventory cost because of rapid technology changes, it is essential for the company to incorporate adequate controls to overcome the risk of overstating inventory.

Risk assessment–management's identification and analysis of risks relevant to the preparation of financial statements in conformity with GAAP.

The auditor obtains knowledge about management's risk assessment process by determining how management identifies risk relevant to financial reporting, evaluates its significance and likelihood of occurrence, and decides the actions needed to address the risks. Questionnaires and discussions with management are the most common ways to obtain this understanding.

All entities, regardless of size, structure, nature, or industry, face a variety of risks from external and internal sources that must be managed. Because economic, industry, regulatory, and operating conditions constantly change, management is challenged with developing mechanisms to identify and deal with risks associated with change. Internal control under one set of conditions will not necessarily be effective under another.

Identifying and analyzing risk is an ongoing process and a critical component of effective internal control. Management must focus on risks at all levels of the organization and take actions necessary to manage them. An important first step is for management to identify factors that may increase risk. Failure to meet prior objectives, quality of personnel, geographic dispersion of company operations, significance and complexity of core business processes, introduction of new information technologies, and entrance of new competitors all represent examples of factors that may lead to increased risk. Once a risk is identified, management estimates the significance of that risk, assesses the likelihood of the risk occurring, and develops specific actions that need to be taken to reduce the risk to an acceptable level. Of course, there is no cost-beneficial way to eliminate risk. However, management must assess how much risk is prudently acceptable and strive to maintain risk within this level.

Management's risk assessment differs from, but is closely related to, the auditor's risk assessment discussed in Chapter 7. Management assesses risks as a part of designing and operating internal controls to minimize errors and fraud. Auditors assess risks to decide the evidence needed in the audit. If management effectively assesses and responds to risks, the auditor will typically accumulate less evidence than when management fails to identify or respond to significant risks.

Control activities (also known as **Application controls**) — policies and procedures that help ensure that necessary actions are taken to address risks in the achievement of the entity's objectives.

Application controls (also known as **Control activities**)–the set of manual, computer-assisted, or fully automated controls that comprise the controls for a particular transaction stream.

Control Activities

COSO describes **control activities** (also known as **application controls**) as the policies and procedures, in addition to those included in the other four components, that help ensure that necessary actions are taken to address risks in the achievement of the entity's objectives. There are potentially many such control activities in any entity, including both manual and automated controls. The control activities in individual

Table 9-2	General Controls and Their Relationship to Accounting Systems*

Manual Information System	Automated Systems
	General Control Categories • Organization and management controls • Systems acquisitions, development, and maintenance controls • Operations and information systems support
Accounting System*	Application System*
Accounting System* Control Activities • Manual controls	Application System* Control Activities • Manual controls • Computer-assisted controls • Fully automated controls

*"Accounting systems" and "application systems" are used as synonymous terms.

transaction cycles generally fall into the following five groups, which are discussed further in this section.

1. Adequate segregation of duties.
2. Proper authorization of transactions and activities.
3. Adequate documents and records.
4. Physical and logical control over assets and records.
5. Independent checks of performance and recorded data.

Before we consider the above groups, let us look at some terminology that helps us navigate the different types of controls that are present in automated information systems.

General controls—internal controls for automated information systems pertaining to more than one transaction cycle or group of accounts.

GENERAL (COMPUTER) CONTROLS When an organization uses automated information systems, general information systems controls (normally called **general controls**) are used to describe internal control activities that could affect multiple classes of transactions or multiple groups of accounts. They are described in this chapter, with a framework for auditing general controls discussed in Chapter 10. As general controls are hybrid controls that can be considered either part of the control environment or part of transaction cycle controls (depending upon how they are implemented), they are discussed in further detail in Chapter 10. Table 9-2 lists general control categories and illustrates how they pertain to automated accounting systems (also called *application systems*).

- *Organization and management controls.* Policies and procedures related to controls should be established, and segregation of incompatible functions should exist.
- *Systems acquisition, development, and maintenance controls.* Application systems could be purchased, developed, or otherwise acquired. Once acquired, changes may need to be made. Established methodologies and control systems should be in place to provide reasonable assurance that the systems are authorized and efficient and function in a manner consistent with organizational objectives.
- *Operations and information systems support.* Systems should be available when needed and used for authorized purposes. This section covers employee operational training, adequate documentation of day-to-day procedures, business continuity planning and information systems recovery, and physical and logical security.

Table 9-3 provides examples of sample objectives and the general control activities used to implement the objectives for each general control category. For the purposes of brevity, the examples are illustrative only and do not include all of the

audit challenge 9-1
Securing Employee Internet Activity

Recent Canadian statistics say that 43 percent of working adults will use the internet at work for personal reasons. Popular activities are shopping and banking.

Not only could these activities cost the employer lost productivity (if the surfing does not occur during scheduled lunch or breaks), but they could also expose the employer's information systems to security violations. Such security violations could result in data corruption or data privacy violations.

To use risk-based terminology, there is a risk of employee productivity loss, since employees could spend time surfing the Web instead of working. An appropriate control to mitigate this risk would be an internal firewall that prevents access to external websites during lunch hours (a general control).

During lunch-time surfing, the employee could connect to a pornographic website, becoming infected by an internet bot (unauthorized software routine) that attaches to the corporate website, enabling unauthorized access to the site. The risk is that a hacker could penetrate organizational security systems and either alter data (data corruption) or copy data (potential privacy violation). A general control that could mitigate this risk would be setting up virus detection systems that scan all incoming traffic (general computer control).

CRITICAL THINKING QUESTIONS

1. What other risks could arise from employee access to external websites?
2. How might these risks be mitigated?

Sources: 1. Gerstel, Judy, "Canadians love to surf while they work," *Toronto Star,* November 19, 2007, p. L1, L2. 2.Rainer, Kelly R., Efraim Turban, Ingrid Splettstoesser-Hogeterp, and Cristobal Sanchez-Rodriguez, *Introduction to Information Systems,* Canadian Edition (Mississauga: John Wiley & Sons Canada, Ltd., 2005).

---

procedures that an organization would require to achieve the specific objective. Further examples are discussed in Chapter 10.

ACCOUNTING (OR APPLICATION) CONTROL ACTIVITIES As shown in Table 9-2, an individual **accounting system** (also called an "application system") can have different types of control activities (policies and procedures). An example of an application system would be a sales system, which processes sales transactions initiated either by telephone order or by a purchase order form received in the mail. Such a sales system is part of a transaction cycle (sales, receivables, receipts). The transaction cycle could include a separate information systems process for sales, accounts receivable, and cash receipts. So, multiple application systems could be part of a transaction cycle.

> **Accounting system**—the set of manual and/or computerized procedures that collect, record, and process data and report the resulting information; also known as "application system" or "functional system."

Table 9-3	Examples of General Controls	
General Control Category	**Sample General Control Objective**	**Relevant General Control Policy or Procedure**
Organization and management controls	Individuals using the organization's systems should have access to only those systems required to do their job effectively. (Segregation of duties)*	1. Managers are to describe necessary access rights by job description. 2. Unique user identification codes and passwords are to be assigned to each employee.
Systems acquisition, development, and maintenance controls	Current authorized versions of payroll programs are in use at all times. (Authorization of transactions and activities)*	1. Management is to monitor government budgets to understand the timing of payroll table changes. 2. The software supplier is to be contacted to ensure that updated payroll software is received on a timely basis.
Operations and information systems support	Online systems should be fully operational between 8:00 a.m. and 6:00 p.m., Monday through Saturday. (Safeguards over use of assets)*	Duplicate hardware resources are to be kept functional for hardware systems.

*The phrase in parentheses shows the specific type of control activity required.

Continuing the sales system example, the sales system could have manual control activities (such as approving large sales by the sales manager), computer-assisted control activities (such as the credit manager reviewing a credit exception report prior to releasing orders for processing), or fully automated control activities (such as having the information system calculate sales taxes due on the sale). For simplicity, we will use the terms "controls" and "control activities" as synonyms.

ADEQUATE SEGREGATION OF DUTIES Six general categories of activities should be separated from one another. These are custody of assets, recording or data entry of transactions, systems development or acquisition and maintenance, computer operations, reconciliation, and authorization of transactions and activities.

Naturally, the extent of **separation of duties** depends heavily on the size of the organization. In many small companies, it is not practical to segregate the duties to the extent suggested. In these cases, audit evidence may require modification.

Separation of custody of assets from accounting The reason for not permitting the person who has temporary or permanent custody of an asset to account for that asset is to protect the firm against defalcation. Indirect access, such as access to cheque signature images, also must be separate. When one person performs both custody and accounting functions, there is an excessive risk of that person's disposing of or using the asset for personal gain and adjusting the records to relieve himself or herself of responsibility. If the cashier, for example, receives cash and is responsible for data entry of cash receipts and sales, it is possible for the cashier to take the cash received from a customer and adjust the customer's account by failing to record a sale or by recording a fictitious credit to the account.

Separation of operational responsibility from recording or data entry of transactions If each department or division in an organization were responsible for preparing its own records and reports, there would be a tendency to bias the results to improve its reported performance. In order to ensure unbiased information, record-keeping is typically included in a separate accounting department under the controller.

Separation of systems development or acquisition and maintenance from accounting Systems development or acquisition comprises activities that create (or purchase) new methods of processing transactions, thus changing the way information is entered, displayed, reported, and posted against files or databases. Maintenance activities involve changes to these processes. These functions should be monitored to ensure that only authorized programs and systems consistent with management objectives are put into place. A programmer who could enter data could enter transactions (e.g., a wage rate increase) and then suppress the logs or other reports showing the transaction. Here are two job functions in this grouping:

- *Systems analyst.* The systems analyst is responsible for the general design of the system. The analyst sets the objectives of the overall system and the specific design of particular applications.
- *Programmer.* Based on the individual objectives specified by the systems analyst, the programmer develops documentation such as flowcharts for the application, prepares computer instructions, may test the program, and documents the results.

If there is inadequate control over software systems or over individual programs, then the auditor would be unable to rely on activities handled by those systems. For example, imagine being unable to rely on interest calculations made by a bank or on the aging in the accounts receivable aged trial balance. These types of situations occur when the auditor is unable to rely on system or program changes. When the entity has systems development or maintenance functions, a quality assurance group may test the functioning of the new systems or changes, helping ensure that inadvertent errors and unauthorized functions have not been introduced.

Separation of computer operations from programming and accounting These job functions include basic procedures such as handling output reports and taking backup copies of information, and more complex functions such as set-up of functional access rights in password systems and development of information systems recovery procedures. Help-desk or computer support personnel may also be included in this area. Personnel who have physical access to media or the capability to set access rights could steal confidential information or give themselves the right to do anything on the system. Separation from authorization, entry of transactions data, and the ability to change programs makes it harder for personnel to suppress a trail of their activities.

Some organizations have a librarian to provide physical custody of the media holding the backup computer programs, transaction files, and other important computer records. The librarian provides a means of important physical control over these records and releases them only to authorized personnel.

Separation of reconciliation from data entry Reconciliation involves comparing information from two or more sources, or independently verifying the work that has been completed by others. For example, preparation of a bank reconciliation by the accounting manager independent of the accounts receivable or accounts payable personnel would detect unauthorized use or disbursements of cash.

For batch-based computer systems, a data control group handles the flow of transactions from users, passing the transactions to data entry after logging the number of them, then matching output to logged details to help ensure that all transactions have been recorded, before passing the transactions and reports back to users. An independent check by someone other than the data entry person of key information entered, such as payroll rates or customer credit limits, also serves as a form of data control function.

Proper authorization of transactions and activities If possible, it is desirable to prevent persons who authorize transactions from having control over the related assets. For example, the same person should not authorize the payment of a vendor's invoice and also sign the cheque in payment of the bill. The authorization of a transaction and the handling of the related asset by the same person increase the possibility of defalcation within the organization. A person who authorizes transactions and handles computer operations could suppress printouts documenting the transactions. Similarly, a programmer who could authorize transactions could set up a fictitious supplier, authorize payments to that supplier, then alter the accounts payable programs so that the transactions did not print on reports.

Authorization also includes authorization of new programs and changes to programs since this affects the way that transactions are processed.

Every transaction must be properly authorized if controls are to be satisfactory. If any person in an organization could acquire or expend assets at will, complete chaos would result. Authorization can be either general or specific. **General authorization** means that management establishes policies for the organization to follow. Subordinates are instructed to implement these general authorizations by approving all transactions within the limits set by the policy. Examples of general authorization are the issuance of fixed price lists for the sale of products, credit limits for customers, and fixed reorder points for making purchases. General authorization can be implemented manually or embedded within computer programs—for example, where computer systems check for and reject orders if they cause a customer's accounts receivable balance to exceed the established credit limit.

Specific authorization (or approval) has to do with individual transactions. Management is often unwilling to establish a general policy of authorization for some transactions. Instead, it prefers to make authorizations on a case-by-case basis. One example is the authorization of a sales transaction by the sales manager for a used-car company. Another example is that grocery clerks are authorized to reverse only small transactions; for larger transactions, a supervisor must insert a key or type a password before the transaction can be completed.

> **General authorization**—company-wide policies for the approval of all transactions within stated limits.

> **Specific authorization**—case-by-case approval of transactions not covered by company-wide policies.

ADEQUATE DOCUMENTS AND RECORDS Documents and records are the physical objects (paper or electronic files) on which transactions are entered and summarized. They include such diverse items as sales invoices, purchase orders, subsidiary records, sales journals, and employee time cards. Both documents of original entry and records on which transactions are entered are important, but the inadequacy of documents normally causes greater control problems.

Documents and computer files perform the function of transmitting information throughout the client's organization and among different organizations. These records must be adequate to provide reasonable assurance that all assets are properly controlled and all transactions correctly recorded. For example, if the receiving department fills out a receiving report when material is obtained, the accounts payable department can verify the quantity and description on the vendor's invoice by comparing it with the information on the receiving report. Programming errors that result in inaccurate processing can result in inaccurate records.

Certain relevant principles dictate the proper design and use of documents, electronic transactions, and input screens. These should be:

- Prenumbered or automatically numbered consecutively to facilitate control over missing records, and to aid in locating records when they are needed at a later date (significantly affects the transaction-related audit objective of completeness).
- Prepared at the time a transaction takes place, or as soon thereafter as possible. When there is a longer time interval, records are less credible and the chance for misstatement is increased (affects the transaction-related audit objective of timing).
- Sufficiently simple and described to ensure that they are clearly understood.
- Designed for multiple use whenever possible to minimize the number of different forms. For example, a properly designed and used shipping document can be the basis for releasing goods from storage to the shipping department, informing billing of the quantity of goods to bill the customer and the appropriate billing date, and updating the perpetual inventory records.
- Constructed in a manner that encourages correct preparation. This can be done by providing a degree of internal check within the form or record. For example, a document might include instructions for proper routing, blank spaces for authorizations and approvals, and designated column spaces for numerical data. Input screens would label fields that are to be entered, provide input entry edits (e.g., checking on valid date), and prevent users from proceeding until all relevant information has been completed.

Chart of accounts—a listing of all the entity's accounts, which classifies transactions into individual balance sheet and income statement accounts.

Chart of accounts A control closely related to documents and records is the **chart of accounts**, which lists and classifies transactions into individual balance sheet and income statement accounts. The chart of accounts is an important control because it provides the framework for determining the information presented to management and other financial statement users. The chart of accounts is helpful in preventing classification errors if it accurately and precisely describes which type of transactions should be in each account.

Systems documentation The procedures for proper record-keeping should be spelled out in systems documentation (in a manual or company intranet) to encourage consistent application. The documentation should provide sufficient information to facilitate adequate record-keeping and the maintenance of proper control over assets, and could include procedural manuals, software user manuals, program documentation, and computer operations procedures.

PHYSICAL AND LOGICAL CONTROL OVER ASSETS AND RECORDS It is essential to have adequate internal control to protect assets and records. If assets are left unprotected, they can be stolen. If records are not adequately protected, they can be stolen, damaged, or lost. In the event of such an occurrence, the accounting process as well as normal operations could be seriously disrupted. When a company is highly computerized, it is especially important to protect its computer equipment, programs, and data files. The equipment and programs are expensive and essential to operations. The data files are the records of the company and, if damaged, could be costly or even impossible to reconstruct.

An important type of protective measure for safeguarding physical assets and records is the use of physical precautions. An example is the use of storerooms for inventory to guard against pilferage. When the storeroom is under the control of a competent and knowledgeable employee, there is also further assurance that obsolescence is minimized. Fireproof safes and safety deposit vaults for the protection of assets such as currency and securities are other important physical safeguards.

There are three categories of controls related to safeguarding data-processing equipment, programs, and data files. As with other types of assets, physical controls are used to protect the computer facilities. Examples are locks on doors to the computer room and terminals, adequate storage space for software and data files to protect them from loss, and proper fire-extinguishing systems. Next, logical access controls deal with having software that ensures that only authorized people can use the equipment and have access to software and data files. An example is an online access password system. Finally, backup and recovery procedures are actions an organization can take in the event of a loss of equipment, programs, or data. For example, having a backup copy of programs and critical data files stored in a safe remote location together with information systems recovery procedures is important for maintaining business continuity.

INDEPENDENT CHECKS OF PERFORMANCE AND RECORDED DATA The last category of control activity is the careful and continuous review of the other controls, often referred to as **independent checks** on performance or internal verification. The need for independent checks arises because internal control tends to change over time unless there is a mechanism for frequent review. Personnel are likely to forget or intentionally fail to follow procedures or become careless unless someone observes and evaluates their performance. In addition, both fraudulent and unintentional misstatements are possible, regardless of the quality of the controls.

> **Independent checks**—internal control activities designed for the continuous internal verification of other controls.

An essential characteristic of the persons performing internal verification procedures is independence from the individuals originally responsible for preparing the data. The least expensive means of internal verification is the separation of duties in the manner previously discussed. For example, when the bank reconciliation is performed by a person independent of the accounting records and handling of cash, there is an opportunity for verification without incurring significant additional costs.

Computerized accounting systems can be designed so that many internal verification procedures can be automated as part of the system, such as separate addition of subsidiary files for agreement to general ledger totals.

Information and Communication

The purpose of an entity's **accounting information and communication systems** is to initiate, record, process, and report the entity's transactions and to maintain accountability for the related assets. An accounting information and communication system has several subcomponents, typically made up of classes of transactions such as sales, sales returns, cash receipts, acquisitions, and so on. For each class of transactions, the accounting system must satisfy all of the six transaction-related audit objectives identified earlier in Table 9-1 (see page 272). For example, the sales accounting system should be designed to ensure that all shipments of goods by a company are correctly recorded as sales (completeness and accuracy objectives) and are reflected in the financial statements in the proper period (timing objective). The system must also avoid duplicate recording of sales and recording a sale if a shipment did not occur (occurrence objective).

> **Accounting information and communication systems**—entity systems that are used to initiate, record, process, and report the entity's transactions and to maintain accountability for the related assets.

To understand the design of the accounting information system, the auditor determines (1) the major classes of transactions of the entity; (2) how those transactions are initiated and recorded; (3) what accounting records exist and their nature; (4) how the system captures other events that are significant to the financial statements, such as declines in asset values; and (5) the nature and details of the financial reporting process followed, including procedures to enter transactions and adjustments in the general ledger.

Monitoring

Monitoring—management's ongoing and periodic assessment of the quality of internal control performance to determine that controls are operating as intended and modified when needed.

Monitoring activities deal with ongoing or periodic assessment of the quality of internal control performance by management to determine that controls are operating as intended and that they are modified as appropriate for changes in conditions. Information for assessment and modification comes from a variety of sources including studies of existing internal controls, internal auditor reports, exception reporting on control activities, reports by regulators such as the Office of the Superintendent of Financial Institutions, feedback from operating personnel, and complaints from customers about billing charges.

INTERNAL AUDIT FUNCTION For many companies, especially larger ones, a competent internal audit department is essential to effective monitoring of internal controls. For an internal audit function to be effective, it is important that the internal audit staff be independent of both the operating and accounting departments, and that it report directly to a high level of authority within the organization, usually the audit committee of the board of directors.

In addition to its role in monitoring an entity's internal controls, an adequate internal audit staff can contribute to reduced external audit costs by providing direct assistance to the external auditor.

SIZE OF BUSINESS AND INTERNAL CONTROL The size of a company does have a significant effect on the nature of internal control activities and the specific monitoring controls. It is more difficult to establish adequate separation of duties in a small company. It would also be unreasonable to expect a small firm to have internal auditors. However, if the various components of internal control are examined, it becomes apparent that most are applicable to both large and small companies. Even though it may not be common to formalize policies in manuals, it is certainly possible for a small company to have competent, trustworthy personnel with clear lines of authority; proper procedures for authorization, execution, and recording of transactions; adequate documents, records, and reports; physical controls over assets and records; and, to a limited degree, checks on performance.

A major control available in a small company is the knowledge and concern of the top operating person, who is frequently an owner-manager. Knowledge about and personal interest in the organization and a close relationship with the personnel (often called "executive controls") make possible careful evaluation of the competence of the employees and the effectiveness of the overall system. For example, internal control can be significantly strengthened if the owner conscientiously performs such duties as signing all cheques after carefully reviewing supporting documents, reviewing bank reconciliations, examining accounts receivable statements sent to customers, approving credit, examining all correspondence from customers and vendors, and approving bad debts.

SUMMARY OF INTERNAL CONTROL A summary of the COSO components of internal control discussed in the preceding sections (control environment, risk assessment, control activities, information and communication, monitoring) is included in Table 9-4 with examples.

concept check

C9-4 Can a small business implement all five COSO internal control levels? Why or why not?

C9-5 Which of the five categories of COSO internal controls is most important? Justify your response.

Table 9-4	COSO Components of Internal Control

INTERNAL CONTROL

Component	Description of Component	Examples
Control environment	Actions, policies, and procedures that reflect the overall attitude of top management, directors, and owners of an entity about internal control and its importance	• Commitment to competence • Board of director and audit committee participation • Management's philosophy and operating style • Organizational structure • Human resource policies and practices
Risk assessment	Management's identification and analysis of risks relevant to the preparation of financial statements in accordance with GAAP	Risk assessment processes: • Identify factors affecting risks • Assess significance of risks and likelihood of occurrence • Determine actions necessary to manage risks Categories of management assertions that must be satisfied: • Assertions about classes of transactions and other events • Assertions about account balances • Assertions about presentation and disclosure
Control activities	Policies and procedures that management has established to meet its objectives for financial reporting	Types of specific control activities: • Adequate separation of duties • Proper authorization of transactions and activities • Adequate documents and records • Physical control over assets and records • Independent checks on performance
Information and communication	Methods used to initiate, record, process, and report an entity's transactions and to maintain accountability for related assets	Transaction-related audit objectives that must be satisfied: • Occurrence • Completeness • Accuracy • Posting and summarization • Classification • Timing
Monitoring	Management's ongoing and periodic assessment of the quality of internal control performance to determine whether controls are operating as intended and are modified when needed	• Review department exception reports • Conduct annual employee evaluations

③ Internal Controls and the Audit Process

Overview of Internal Controls and the Audit Process

This section deals with how auditors obtain information about internal control and use that information during the audit. To help understand how the auditor accomplishes this, an overview of the relevant parts of obtaining an understanding of internal

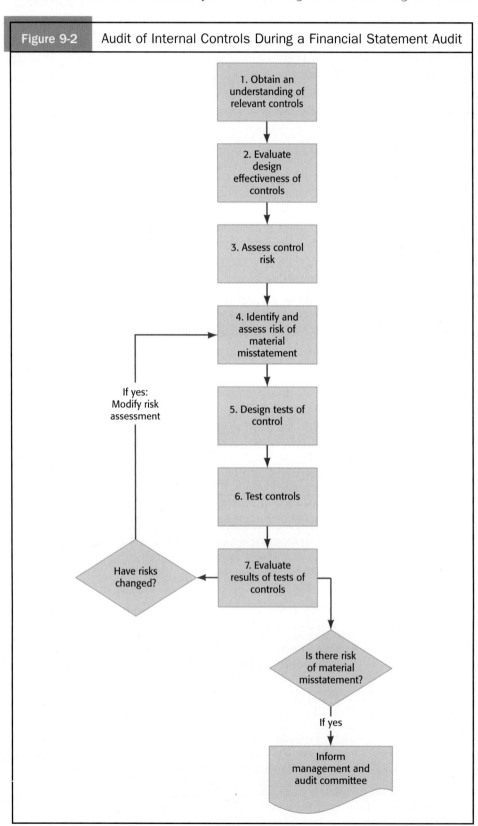

Figure 9-2   Audit of Internal Controls During a Financial Statement Audit

1. Obtain an understanding of relevant controls

2. Evaluate design effectiveness of controls

3. Assess control risk

4. Identify and assess risk of material misstatement

If yes: Modify risk assessment

5. Design tests of control

6. Test controls

7. Evaluate results of tests of controls

Have risks changed?

Is there risk of material misstatement?

If yes

Inform management and audit committee

control, assessing and evaluating risks, and relating the results to tests of financial statement balances are discussed. See Figure 9-2 for the steps involved. We also look at the impact of general controls and how controls are tested. We end with examining the impact of reporting on management's assessment of internal control.

1. OBTAIN AN UNDERSTANDING OF RELEVANT CONTROLS

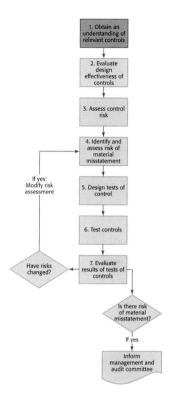

Reasons for understanding internal control sufficient to plan the examination The auditor must obtain understanding of the client's internal control sufficient to plan the examination for every audit and to assess risks. Refer to the inside front cover of this text: understanding internal control occurs during Phases 1 through 3. The extent of that understanding must, at a minimum, be sufficient to adequately plan the examination in terms of four specific planning matters.

Auditability The auditor must obtain information about the integrity of management and the nature and extent of the accounting records to be satisfied that sufficient appropriate audit evidence is available to support the financial statement balances and the auditor's report. This decision will be made during Phase 1, prior to client acceptance or continuance, and reassessed as the audit continues.

Potential material misstatements The understanding should allow the auditor to identify the types of potential errors or fraud and other irregularities that might affect the financial statements, and to assess the risk that such misstatements might occur in amounts that are material to the financial statements.

Planned detection risk Control risk in the planning form of the audit risk model directly affects detection risk for each audit objective [PDR = AR / (IR × CR)]. Information about internal control is used to assess control risk for each control objective, which, in turn, affects planned detection risk and planned audit evidence.

Design of tests The information obtained should allow the auditor to design effective tests of the financial statement balances (or transactions) for each audit assertion. Such tests include tests for monetary correctness of transactions and balances, as well as analytical procedures. These are discussed in more detail in Chapter 12.

Understanding the components of internal controls Relevant controls from each of the components of internal control must be studied, understood, and documented. As part of this process, the auditor assesses whether controls actually appear to be in place as described, for example by asking for an example of the control or by selecting a small sample and testing the control. Selected examples are given below.

Understanding the control environment Information is obtained about the control environment for each of the subcomponents discussed commencing on page 274. The auditor then uses the understanding as a basis for assessing management's and the directors' attitudes and awareness about the importance of control. For example, the auditor might determine the nature of a client's budgeting system for the company as a whole (which applies to multiple departments) as a part of understanding the design of the control environment. The description of the budgeting system might be obtained in part by (1) inquiry of budgeting personnel to determine budgeting procedures and (2) follow-up of differences between budget and actual amounts. The auditor might also examine client schedules comparing actual results to budgets and ask about the *monitoring* of variances that is done.

Understanding general controls The nature and level of complexity of automation in the information systems used at the organization will affect the amount of effort required by the auditor to understand general controls. The auditor obtains information about the organizational structure of the information systems processing department, and the hardware and software configuration of computing systems, and a general description of the types of automated systems in use. This information is used to plan the extent of work required to understand general controls. For example, if the organization has programmers on staff and many of its financial systems use customized software, then the auditor will need to spend time documenting the processes used to authorize, design, test, implement, and change such software. Refer to Chapter 10 for additional information.

Understanding the accounting system To understand the design of the accounting system, the auditor determines (1) the major classes of transactions of the entity; (2) how those transactions are initiated; (3) what accounting records and data files exist and their nature; (4) how transactions are processed from initiation to completion, including a description of processing handled by computer programs; and (5) the nature and details of the financial reporting process followed. Typically, this is accomplished and documented by a narrative description of the system or by flowcharting. (These are described later in the chapter.) The operation of the accounting system is often determined by tracing one or a few transactions through the accounting system (called a **transaction walk-through**).

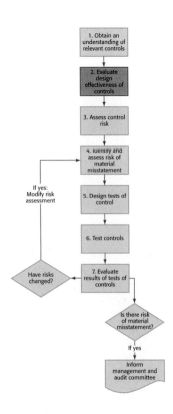

Transaction walk-through—the tracing of selected transactions through the accounting system.

Understanding the control activities Auditors obtain an understanding of the control environment, general computer controls, and accounting system in a similar manner for most audits, but obtaining an understanding of control activities varies considerably. For smaller clients, it is common to identify few or even no control activities because controls are often ineffective due to limited personnel. In that case, a high assessed level of control risk is used; that is, control risk is assessed at the maximum of 100 percent. For clients with extensive controls where the auditor believes controls are likely to be excellent, it is often appropriate to identify many controls during the controls understanding phase before deciding on the key controls to be tested. In still other audits, the auditor may identify a limited number of controls during this phase and then identify additional controls later in the process. The extent to which controls are identified is a matter of audit judgment. The key part of this process is obtaining enough understanding so that controls can be understood for each audit assertion, allowing for design of audit tests. A methodology for identifying controls is studied later in the chapter.

2. EVALUATE DESIGN EFFECTIVENESS OF CONTROLS FOR RISK ASSESSMENT Once an understanding of internal control that is sufficient for audit planning is obtained, two major assessments must be made. The preliminary assessment of auditability is undertaken as part of the client acceptance or client continuance process.

Assess whether the financial statements are auditable The first assessment is whether the entity is auditable. The factors that determine auditability are the control environment, with reference to corporate governance structures and an emphasis on the integrity of management, and the adequacy of accounting methods. Many audit procedures rely to some extent on the representations of management. For example, it is difficult for the auditor to evaluate whether inventory is obsolete without an honest assessment by management. If management lacks integrity, management may provide false representations causing the auditor to rely on unreliable evidence.

The accounting records serve as a direct source of audit evidence for most audit objectives. If the accounting records are deficient, necessary audit evidence may not be available. For example, if the client has not kept duplicate sales invoices and vendors' invoices, it would normally not be possible to do an audit. Unless the auditor can identify an alternative source of reliable evidence, or unless appropriate records can be constructed for the auditor's use, the only recourse may be to consider the entity unauditable.

When it is concluded that the entity is not auditable, the auditor discusses the circumstances with the client (usually at the highest level) and either withdraws from the engagement or issues a denial form of auditor's report (discussed further in Chapter 22).

Consider design effectiveness of controls Documentation of internal controls includes assessing controls by applying audit assertions to transaction streams. Where the auditor has identified accounts that cannot be tested only by substantive tests, the auditor will also have documented internal controls for those accounts.

During examination of design effectiveness, the auditor:

1. Considers whether controls are present for all relevant assertions.
2. Evaluates which controls are more important for the relevant assertions (these are key controls).
3. Examines potential weaknesses in internal control to determine whether there are compensating controls (alternative controls).

In the next sections of this chapter, we look at methods of documenting internal controls and how the documentation assists with considering the design effectiveness of the internal controls.

3. ASSESS CONTROL RISK The auditor assesses control risk at the assertion level and also at the financial statement level overall. The following discussion looks at the reasoning involved in assessing control risk.

Determine the level of control risk supported by the understanding obtained After obtaining an understanding of internal control, the auditor makes an initial assessment of control risk. Control risk is a measure of the auditor's expectation that internal controls will neither prevent material misstatements from occurring nor detect and correct them if they have occurred.

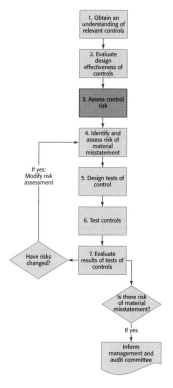

The initial assessment is made for each transaction-related audit objective for each major type of transaction. For example, the auditor makes an assessment of the existence objective for sales and a separate assessment for the completeness objective. There are different ways to express this expectation. Some auditors use a subjective expression such as high, moderate, or low. Others use numerical probabilities such as 1.0, 0.6, or 0.2.

The initial assessment usually starts with consideration of the control environment and then of general computer controls. If the attitude of management is that control is unimportant, it is doubtful that general controls or detailed control activities will be reliable. If general controls are inadequate, then the individual automated systems affecting the transaction cycles will not be reliable. The best course of action in that case is to assume that control risk for all transaction-related audit objectives is at maximum (such as high or 1.0). On the other hand, if management's attitude is positive, the auditor then considers the specific policies and procedures within the control environment, the accounting system, and control activities. Those policies and procedures are used as a basis for an assessment below maximum.

There are two important considerations about the assessment. First, the auditor does not have to make the assessment in a formal, detailed manner, as long as the flow of reasoning is documented with adequate support. In many audits, particularly of smaller companies, the auditor assumes that the control risk is at maximum whether or not it actually is. The auditor's reason for taking this approach is that he or she has concluded that it is more economical to audit the financial statement balances more extensively rather than to conduct tests of controls. Second, even though the auditor believes control risk is low, the level of control risk assessed is limited to that level supported by the evidence obtained. For example, suppose the auditor believes that control risk for unrecorded sales is low but has gathered little evidence in support of control activities for the completeness objective. The auditor's assessment of control risk for unrecorded sales must either be moderate or high. It could be low only if additional evidence were obtained in support of the pertinent controls.

Assess whether it is likely that a lower assessed control risk could be supported When the auditor believes that actual control risk may be significantly lower than the initial assessment (i.e., actual controls in place are likely significantly better), he or she may decide to support a lower assessed control risk. The most likely case where this occurs is when the auditor has identified a limited number of controls during the understanding phase. Based on the results of the initial assessment, the auditor now believes that additional controls can be identified and tested to further reduce assessed control risk.

Decide on the appropriate assessed control risk After the auditor completes the initial assessment and considers whether a lower assessed control risk is likely, he or she is in a position to decide which assessed control risk should be used: either a level already supported in the initial assessment, or an even lower level that would need to be justified by further testing. The decision as to which level to use is essentially an economic one, recognizing the trade-off between the costs of testing relevant controls and the costs of substantive tests that would be avoided by reducing assessed control risk. Assume, for example, that for the existence and accuracy transaction-related audit objectives for sales, the auditor believes that the cost of confirming accounts receivable could be reduced by $5,000 by incurring $2,000 to support a lower assessed control risk. It would be cost effective to incur the $2,000 additional cost.

Where the client uses paperless systems or advanced automated processes such as electronic data interchange, the auditor may be required to rely upon internal controls. Then, the cost-benefit decision is applied among alternative tests of controls rather than choosing between tests of controls and tests of details.

4. IDENTIFY AND ASSESS RISK OF MATERIAL MISSTATEMENT

Financial statement level All levels of internal control are considered to identify potential pervasive factors that could result in a risk of material misstatement at the financial statement level. For example, if there is a new information system being installed, and there are insufficient general controls over the conversion of information from the old system to the new system, the auditor may conduct additional tests of details to test whether material errors occurred during the implementation of the new system. An additional problem area could be potential management bias to overstate income to meet publicized earnings targets.

Assertion level The auditor will consider those assertions where there is the greatest likelihood of material misstatement if the controls are not functioning. For example, if there are many sales at each month end, then the auditor might consider that *timing* needs to be carefully considered at the year end as does completeness.

The auditor may have identified individual audit assertions for an account or risks at the financial statement level where controls do not exist or were found to be implemented in a manner that still results in the potential for misstatements. The auditor will also consider inherent risks in making this assessment. These risks will be discussed with management as well as considered during the design of both tests of controls and tests of details.

5. AND 6. DESIGN AND CONDUCT TESTS OF CONTROLS
Assessing control risk requires the auditor to consider the design of controls to evaluate whether they would be effective in meeting specific transaction-related audit objectives. In order to use specific controls as a basis for assessing control risk below maximum, specific evidence must be obtained about their effectiveness throughout all (or most) of the period under audit. The procedures to gather evidence about design and placement in operation during the understanding phase are called **procedures to obtain an understanding**. The procedures to test effectiveness of controls in support of assessing control risk below maximum are called **tests of controls**. Both are discussed in more detail later in the chapter.

7. EVALUATE RESULTS; INTEGRATE WITH PLANNED DETECTION RISK AND SUBSTANTIVE TESTS
The result of the preceding steps is the determination of the assessed level of control risk by audit objective for each of the entity's major transaction types. Where the assessed level of control risk is below maximum, it will be supported by specific tests of controls. These assessments are then related to the balance-related audit objectives for the accounts affected by the major transaction types. The appropriate level of detection risk for each balance-related audit objective is then determined using the audit risk model. The relationship of detection risk to audit objectives and the selection and design of audit procedures for substantive tests of financial statement balances are discussed and illustrated in Chapters 12 and 15.

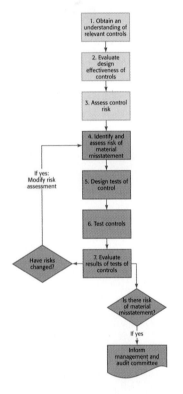

Procedures to obtain an understanding—procedures used by the auditor to gather evidence about the design and implementation of specific controls.

Tests of controls—audit procedures to test the effectiveness of controls in support of control risk assessed below maximum.

Where the results of tests of controls support the design of controls as expected, the auditor proceeds to use the same assessed control risk. If, however, the tests of controls indicate the controls did not operate effectively, the assessed level of control risk (and the potential effect on the risks of material misstatements) must be reconsidered. For example, the tests may indicate that frequent program changes occurred during the year or that the person applying the control made frequent errors. In such situations, a higher assessed level of control risk would be used unless additional controls relating to the same transaction-related audit objectives could be identified and found effective.

The reconsideration could result in different tests of controls or changes to the planned tests of details. Any potential for material misstatement must be documented and communicated to management and those charged with governance (such as the audit committee).

AUDIT PROCEDURES AND THEIR DOCUMENTATION Now that we have overviewed the process of auditing internal controls during a financial statement audit, we will look more closely at internal control audit procedures and methods of documenting internal controls. There is an enormous amount of information that is collected and organized to obtain a useful picture of how an organization handles its information and processes. There are many different ways of collecting and displaying controls to enable useful assessment.

Procedures to Obtain the Necessary Understanding

In practice, the study of a client's internal control and assessment of control risk vary considerably from client to client. For smaller clients, many auditors obtain a level of understanding sufficient only to assess whether the statements are auditable, evaluate the control environment for management's attitude, and determine the adequacy of the client's accounting system. Often, for efficiency, control activities are not tested, control risk is assumed to be maximum, and detection risk is therefore low. This approach is described as a substantive audit approach.

For many larger clients, especially for repeat engagements, the auditor plans on a low assessed level of control risk for most parts of the audit before the audit starts. This approach is a combined audit approach. The auditor has identified the risks of material misstatement and determined that internal controls can be relied on. The auditor next obtains an understanding of the control environment and the accounting system at a fairly detailed level. Then the auditor identifies specific controls that will reduce control risk, makes an assessment of control risk, and finally tests the controls for effectiveness. The auditor can conclude that control risk is low only after all three steps are completed. The three steps discussed above are now explained in more detail to illustrate further how the study of a client's internal control and assessment of control risk are done.

PROCEDURES RELATING TO UNDERSTANDING, DESIGN EFFECTIVENESS, AND IMPLEMENTATION The auditor's procedures to obtain an understanding of internal control attempt to find out about the elements of internal control, see that they have been implemented, and document the information obtained in a useful manner. The following are procedures relating to understanding, design effectiveness, and implementation.

Update and evaluate auditor's previous experience with the entity Most audits of a company are done annually by the same public accounting firm. Except for initial engagements, the auditor begins the audit with a great deal of information about the client's internal controls developed in prior years. Because systems and controls change infrequently, this information can be updated and carried forward to the current year's audit.

Make inquiries of client personnel A logical starting place for updating information carried forward from the previous audit or for obtaining information initially is with appropriate client personnel. Inquiries of client personnel at the management, supervisory, and staff level will usually be conducted as part of obtaining an understanding of the design of internal control. Care must be taken to document the information collected.

Read client's policy and systems manuals To design, implement, and maintain its internal controls, an entity must have extensive documentation of its own. This includes policy manuals and documents (e.g., a corporate code of conduct) and systems manuals and documents (e.g., an accounting manual and an organization chart). This information is studied by the auditor and discussed with company personnel to ensure that it is properly interpreted and understood.

Examine documents and records The control environment, the details of the accounting system, and the application of control activities will involve the creation of many documents and records. These will have been presented to some degree in the policy and systems manuals. By inspecting actual completed documents and records, the auditor can bring the contents of the manuals to life and better understand them. Inspection also provides evidence that the control policies and procedures have been placed in operation.

For businesses with large volumes (such as hundreds of thousands or millions of transactions) or paperless systems, the auditor is likely to use computer-assisted tests and online viewing of transactions as an alternative to viewing paper documents.

Observe the entity's activities and operations In addition to inspecting completed documents and records, the auditor can observe client personnel in the process of preparing them and carrying out their normal accounting and control activities. When the client uses paperless systems, this may require the running of test transactions through the system to verify the understanding, or specialist computer audit assistance. This further enhances understanding and verifies that control policies and procedures have been implemented.

Observation, documentation, and inquiry can be conveniently and effectively combined in the form of the transaction walk-through mentioned earlier. With that procedure, the auditor selects one or a few documents for the initiation of a transaction type and traces it (them) through the entire accounting process. At each stage of processing, the auditor makes inquiries and observes current activities, in addition to inspecting completed documentation for the transaction or transactions selected.

DOCUMENTATION OF THE UNDERSTANDING Three commonly used methods of documenting the understanding of internal control are narratives, flowcharts, and internal control questionnaires. These may be used separately or in combination, as discussed below. The auditor will use those that are most efficient in the client circumstances, that is, for a simple system a narrative will suffice, whereas for a more complex system flowcharts are more effective. The internal control questionnaire is used to document auditor conclusions and provide cross-references to supporting documentation.

Narrative—a written description of a client's internal controls, including the origin, processing, and disposition of documents and records, and the relevant control activities.

Narrative A **narrative** is a written description of a client's internal controls. A proper narrative of an accounting system and related controls includes four characteristics:

- *The origin of every document and record in the system.* For example, the description should state where customer orders come from and how sales invoices arise.
- *All processing that takes place.* For example, if sales amounts are determined by a computer program that multiplies quantities shipped by stored standard prices, that should be described.
- *The disposition of every document and record in the system.* The updating of computer files, method of storing of documents, and transferral to customers or discarding of documents should be described.
- *An indication of controls relevant to the assessment of control risk.* These typically include separation of duties (e.g., separating recording cash from handling cash), authorization and approvals (e.g., credit approvals), and internal verification (e.g., comparison of unit selling price to sales contracts).

Flowchart An internal control **flowchart** is a symbolic, diagrammatic representation of the client's documents and their sequential flow in the organization. An adequate flowchart includes the same four characteristics identified above for narratives.

Flowcharting is useful primarily because it can provide a concise overview of the client's system as an analytical tool in evaluation. A well-prepared flowchart aids in identifying inadequacies by facilitating a clear understanding of how the system operates. For most uses, it is superior to narrative descriptions as a method of communicating the characteristics of a system, especially to show adequate separation of duties. It is easier to follow a diagram than to read a description. It is also usually easier to update a flowchart, particularly one that is stored electronically, than a narrative. Most auditor flowcharting is now completed using automated working paper software. The auditor may also use the automated program or automated systems flowcharts that have been prepared by client software systems.

It would be unusual to use both a narrative and a flowchart to describe the same system, since both are intended to describe the flow of documents and records in an accounting system. Sometimes the combination of a flowchart with a supporting narrative is used. The decision to use one or the other or a combination of the two is dependent on two factors: relative ease of understanding by current- and subsequent-year auditors and relative cost of preparation.

Internal control questionnaire An **internal control questionnaire** asks a series of questions about the controls in each audit area, including the control environment, as a means of indicating to the auditor aspects of internal control that may be inadequate. In most instances, it is designed to require a "yes" or "no" response, with "no" responses indicating potential internal control deficiencies. Where automated working paper software is used, the responses can be automatically linked and cross-referenced to supporting documentation and weakness investigation working papers.

The primary advantage of the questionnaire is the ability to cover each audit area thoroughly and reasonably quickly at the beginning of the audit. The primary disadvantage is that individual parts of the client's systems are examined without providing an overall view, although recently developed internal control documentation software overcomes this weakness. In addition, a standard questionnaire is often inapplicable to some audit clients, especially smaller ones.

Figure 9-3 on the next page illustrates part of an internal control questionnaire for the sales and collection cycle of Hillsburg Hardware Limited. The questionnaire is also designed for use with the six transaction-related audit objectives. Note that each objective (A through F) is a transaction-related objective as it applies to sales transactions (see shaded portions). The same is true for all other audit areas.

We believe the use of both questionnaires and flowcharts is highly desirable for understanding the client's system. Flowcharts provide an overview of the system, and questionnaires are useful checklists to remind the auditor of many different types of controls that should exist. When properly used, a combination of these two approaches should provide the auditor with an excellent description of the system.

It is often desirable to use the client's narratives or flowcharts and have the client fill out the internal control questionnaire, as long as any subsequent reliance on controls is adequately substantiated with testing. When understandable and reliable narratives, flowcharts, and questionnaires are not available from a client, which is frequently the case, the auditor must prepare them. Many auditors rely on electronic auditing tools, including industry-specific checklists and industry-specific flowcharting templates that can be completed and viewed electronically.

Assessing Control Risk

Once the auditor has obtained descriptive information and evidence in support of the design and operation of internal control, an **assessment of control risk** by transaction-related audit objective can be made. This is normally done separately for each major type of transaction in each transaction cycle. For example, in the sales and collection

Flow chart—a diagrammatic representation of the client's documents and records, and the sequence in which they are processed.

Internal control questionnaire—a series of questions about the controls in each audit area used as a means of gaining an understanding of internal control.

Assessment of control risk—a measure of the auditor's expectation that internal controls will neither prevent material misstatements from occurring nor detect and correct them if they have occurred; control risk is assessed for each transaction-related audit objective in a cycle or class of transactions.

Figure 9-3   Partial Internal Control Questionnaire for Sales

Client _Hillsburg Hardware Limited_ _____ Audit Date _12/31/08_

Auditor _MSW_   Date Completed _9/30/08_   Reviewed by _GR_   Date Completed _10/1/08_

Objective (shaded) and Question	Yes	No	N/A	Remarks
Sales				
A. Recorded sales are for shipments actually made to existing customers.				
1. Is customers' credit approved by a responsible official, and is access to change credit limit master files restricted?	✓			_Approved By Chief Financial Officer_
2. Is the recording of sales supported by authorized shipping documents and approved customer orders?	✓			_Pam Dilley examines underlying documentation._
3. Is there adequate separation of duties between billing, recording sales, and handling cash receipts?	✓			
4. Are sales invoices prenumbered and accounted for?			✓	_Prenumbered but not accounted for. Additional substantive testing required._
B. Existing sales transactions are recorded.				
1. Is a record of shipments maintained?	✓			
2. Are shipping documents controlled from the office in a manner that helps ensure that all shipments are billed?	✓			_By Pam Dilley_
3. Are shipping documents prenumbered and accounted for?	✓			
C. Recorded sales are for the amount of goods shipped and are correctly billed and recorded.				
1. Is there independent comparison of the quantity on the shipping documents to the sales invoices?	✓			
2. Is an authorized price list used, and is access to change the price master file restricted?	✓			
3. Are monthly statements sent to customers?	✓			
D. Sales transactions are properly included in the master files and are correctly summarized.				
1. Does the computer automatically post transactions to the accounts receivable master file and general ledger?	✓			
2. Is the accounts receivable master file reconciled with the general ledger on a monthly basis?	✓			_By Erma, the chief accountant_
E. Recorded sales transactions are properly classified.				
1. Is there independent comparison of recorded sales to the chart of accounts?			✓	_All sales are on account and there is only one sales account._
F. Sales are recorded on the correct dates.				
1. Is there independent comparison of dates on shipping documents to dates recorded?		✓		_Unmatched and unrecorded shippers are reviewed weekly._

cycle, the types of transactions usually involve sales, sales returns and allowances, cash receipts, and the provision for and write-off of uncollectible accounts.

IDENTIFY TRANSACTION-RELATED AUDIT OBJECTIVES The first step in the assessment is to identify the transaction-related audit objectives to which the assessment applies. This is done by applying the transaction-related audit objectives introduced earlier, which are stated in general form, to each major type of transaction for the entity.

IDENTIFY SPECIFIC CONTROLS The next step is to identify the specific controls that contribute to accomplishing each transaction-related audit objective. The auditor identifies pertinent controls by proceeding through the descriptive information about the client's system. Those policies and procedures that, in his or her judgment, provide control over the transaction involved are identified. In doing this, it is often helpful to refer back to the types of controls that might exist and ask if they do exist. For example: Is there adequate segregation of duties, and how is it achieved? Are the documents used well designed? Are there controls over inputting to the computer system?

The auditor should identify and include those controls that are expected to have the greatest impact on meeting the transaction-related audit objectives. These are often termed **key controls**. The reason for including only key controls is that they will be sufficient to achieve the transaction-related audit objectives and should provide audit efficiency.

Key controls — those controls that are expected to have the greatest impact on meeting the transaction-related audit objectives.

IDENTIFY AND EVALUATE WEAKNESSES **Internal control weaknesses** are defined as the absence of adequate controls, which increases the risk of misstatements existing in the financial statements. If, in the judgment of the auditor, there are inadequate controls to satisfy one of the transaction-related audit objectives, expectation of such a misstatement occurring increases. For example, if no internal verification of the valuation of payroll transactions is taking place, the auditor may conclude there is a weakness in internal control.

Internal control weaknesses—the absence of adequate controls; increases the risk of misstatements in the financial statements.

A four-step approach can be used for identifying significant internal control weaknesses.

Identify existing controls Because weaknesses are the absence of adequate controls, the auditor must first know which controls exist. The methods for identifying existing controls have already been discussed.

Identify the absence of key controls Internal control questionnaires, narratives, and flowcharts are useful to identify areas in which key controls are lacking and the likelihood of misstatements is thereby increased. When control risk is assessed as moderate or high, there is usually an absence of controls.

Determine potential material misstatements that could result This step is intended to identify specific errors or fraud and other irregularities that are likely to result from the absence of controls. The importance of a weakness is proportionate to the magnitude of the errors or fraud and other irregularities that are likely to result from it.

Consider the possibility of compensating controls A **compensating control** is a control elsewhere in the system that offsets a weakness. Note that any control can be a compensating control. A common example in a smaller company is active involvement of the owner to compensate for lack of segregation of duties. When a compensating control exists, the weakness is no longer a concern because the potential for misstatement has been sufficiently reduced.

Compensating control—a control elsewhere in the system that offsets a weakness.

Figure 9-4 on the next page shows the documentation of weaknesses for the sales and collection cycle of Hillsburg Hardware Limited. The "Effect on Audit Evidence" column shows the effect of the weakness on the auditor's planned audit program.

The Control Risk Matrix

Many auditors use a control matrix to assist in the control-risk assessment process. Most controls affect more than one transaction-related audit objective, and often

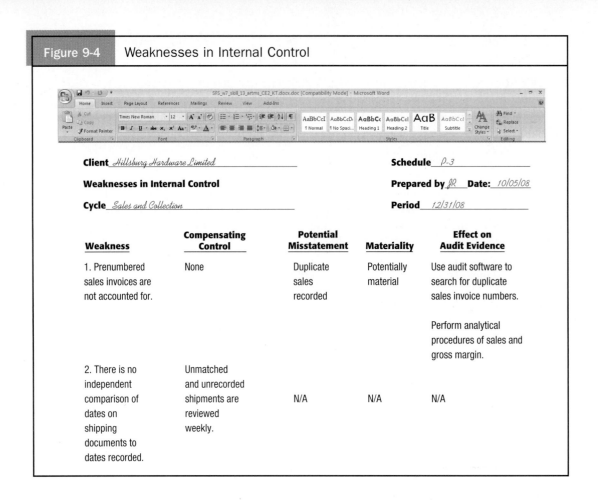

Figure 9-4 Weaknesses in Internal Control

Client _Hillsburg Hardware Limited_   **Schedule** _P-3_

Weaknesses in Internal Control   **Prepared by** _JR_   **Date:** _10/05/08_

Cycle _Sales and Collection_   **Period** _12/31/08_

Weakness	Compensating Control	Potential Misstatement	Materiality	Effect on Audit Evidence
1. Prenumbered sales invoices are not accounted for.	None	Duplicate sales recorded	Potentially material	Use audit software to search for duplicate sales invoice numbers. Perform analytical procedures of sales and gross margin.
2. There is no independent comparison of dates on shipping documents to dates recorded.	Unmatched and unrecorded shipments are reviewed weekly.	N/A	N/A	N/A

Control risk matrix—a methodology used to help the auditor assess control risk by matching key internal controls and internal control weaknesses with transaction-related audit objectives.

several different controls affect a given transaction-related audit objective. These complexities make a **control risk matrix** a useful way to summarize and assess control risk. The control risk matrix matches key internal controls and internal control weaknesses with transaction-related audit objectives as a tool for assessing control risk.

Figure 9-5 illustrates the use of a control risk matrix for sales transactions of Hillsburg Hardware Limited. In constructing the matrix, the transaction-related audit objectives for sales were listed as column headings, and pertinent controls that were identified were listed as headings for the rows. In addition, where significant weaknesses were identified, they were also entered as row headings below the listing of key controls. The body of the matrix was then used to show how the controls contribute to the accomplishment of the transaction-related audit objectives and how weaknesses impact the objectives. In this illustration, a "C" was entered in each cell where a control partially or fully satisfied an objective, and a "W" was entered to show the impact of the weaknesses.

Assess Control Risk Once controls and weaknesses have been identified and related to transaction-related audit objectives, there can be an assessment of control risk. Again, the control risk matrix is a useful tool for that purpose. Referring to Figure 9-5, the auditor assessed control risk for Hillsburg's sales by reviewing each column for pertinent controls and weaknesses, and asking, "What is the likelihood that a material misstatement of the type to be controlled would not be prevented or detected and corrected by these controls, and what is the impact of the weaknesses?" If the likelihood is high, then the control risk is high, and so forth.

Link to risk of material misstatement and substantive testing Once control risk has been assessed, the auditor documents the effect on the risk of material misstatement

	Sales Transaction-Related Audit Objectives					
internal Control	Recorded sales are for shipments actually made to nonfictitious customers (occurrence).	Existing sales transactions are recorded (completeness).	Recorded sales are for the amount of goods shipped and are correctly billed and recorded (accuracy).	Sales transactions are properly classified (classification).	Sales are recorded on the correct dates (timing).	Sales transactions are properly included in the accounts receivable master file and are correctly summarized (posting and summarization).
Credit is approved automatically by computer by comparison to authorized credit limits (C1).	C					
Recorded sales are supported by authorized shipping documents and approved customer orders (C2).	C		C			
Separation of duties for billing, recording of sales, and handling of cash receipts (C3).	C	C				C
Shipping documents are forwarded to billing daily and are billed on the subsequent day (C4).	C				C	
Shipping documents are prenumbered and accounted for weekly (C5).		C			C	
Batch totals of quantities shipped are compared with quantities billed (C6).	C	C	C			
Unit selling prices are obtained from the price list master file of approved prices (C7).			C			
Sales transactions are internally verified (C8).				C		
Statements are mailed to customers each month (C9).	C		C			C
Computer automatically posts transactions to the accounts receivable subsidiary records and to the general ledger (C10).						C
Accounts receivable master file is reconciled to the general ledger on a monthly basis (C11).						C
There is a lack of internal verification for the possibility of sales invoices being recorded more than once (W1).	W					
There is a lack of control to test for timely recording (W2).					W	
Assessed control risk	Medium	Low	Low	Low*	High	Low

*Because there are no cash sales, classification is not a problem.
C = Control; W = Weakness.
Note: This matrix was developed using an internal control questionnaire, part of which is included in Figure 9-3 (page 294), as well as flowcharts and other documentation of the auditor's understanding of internal control. Weaknesses are carried to an investigation sheet, shown in Figure 9-4 (page 296), for assessment.

by assertion and the effect on substantive testing. This is usually done by having a question either at the top or bottom of the checklist and the control risk assessment. For example, the internal control questionnaire would ask about the extent of intended reliance upon internal controls and which audit assertions had a potential for material misstatement; the control matrix would ask about the impact upon substantive testing or whether there were specific assertions that needed to be tested because substantive testing was not sufficient for that audit assertion. See Figures 9-4 and 9-5 for examples.

Figure 9-4 (page 296) shows that the auditor has considered the two weaknesses in the control matrix. The first risk could lead to a potential material misstatement, so the auditor will conduct additional audit tests to quantify the potential effect. The second apparent weakness has a compensating control, so it is then no longer a weakness—the control matrix would be updated, and the "W" changed to a "C" with the internal control that "unmatched and unrecorded shipments are reviewed weekly."

Internal Control Letter and Related Matters During the course of obtaining an understanding of the client's internal control and assessing control risk, auditors obtain information that is of interest to the audit committee in fulfilling its responsibilities. Generally, such information concerns significant deficiencies in the design or operation of internal control (weaknesses).

CAS

AUDIT COMMITTEE COMMUNICATIONS According to CAS 265 (formerly Section 5220), the auditor is required to communicate material internal control weaknesses in writing to "the audit committee or equivalent." If the client does not have an audit committee, then the communication should go to the person (or persons) in the organization who has (have) overall responsibility for internal control, such as the board of directors or the owner-manager. The communication may be oral or written. An illustrative **internal control letter** communicates these significant internal control weaknesses and is shown in Figure 9-6.

Internal control letter—a letter from the auditor to the audit committee or senior management detailing significant weaknesses in internal control.

Figure 9-6	Internal Control Letter

CHESLEY & BEDARD
Chartered Accountants
2016 Village Boulevard
Ottawa, Ontario K1S 5B6

February 12, 2009

Audit Committee
Airtight Machine Inc.
1729 Athens Street
Ottawa, Ontario K1N 6N5

In planning and performing our audit of the financial statements of Airtight Machine Inc. for the year ended December 31, 2008, we considered its internal control in order to determine our auditing procedures for the purpose of expressing our opinion on the financial statements and not to provide assurance on internal control. However, we noted certain matters involving internal control and its operation that we consider to be of such significance that we believe they should be reported to you. The matters being reported involve circumstances coming to our attention relating to significant deficiencies in the design or operation of internal control that, in our judgment, could adversely affect the organization's ability to record, process, summarize, and report financial data consistent with the assertions of management in the financial statements.

The matter noted is that there is a lack of independent verification of the data entry of the customer's name, product number, and quantity shipped on sales invoices and credit memos. As a consequence, errors in these activities could occur and remain uncorrected, adversely affecting both recorded net sales and accounts receivable. This deficiency is particularly significant because of the large size of the average sale of Airtight Machine Inc.

This report is intended solely for the information and use of the audit committee, board of directors, management, and others in Airtight Machine Inc.

Very truly yours,

Chesley & Bedard

Chesley & Bedard

MANAGEMENT LETTERS In addition to significant weaknesses in internal control, auditors often observe less significant internal control-related matters as well as opportunities for the client to make operational improvements. These types of matters should also be communicated to the client. The form of communication is often a separate letter for that purpose, called a **management letter**, which communicates less significant weaknesses or potential operational improvements to management. This letter needs to be clearly identified as a derivative report to indicate that the purpose of the engagement was not to determine weaknesses in internal control but that they were identified as a by-product of the audit. The letter would also indicate that the auditors may not have found all weaknesses.

Management letter—the auditor's written communication to management to point out less significant weaknesses in internal control and possibilities for operational improvements.

Impact of General Controls

As described earlier and shown in Table 9-2 (page 278), general (computer) controls are controls over automated information systems with respect to organization and management; systems acquisition, development, and maintenance; and operations and information systems support. Table 9-3 (page 279) provided examples of general (computer) controls.

Since general controls affect multiple transaction cycles, the quality of general controls should be assessed prior to the decision as to whether reliance will be placed on controls or procedures in automated accounting systems. A framework for assessing general controls is described in Chapter 10. The effect of general controls is discussed separately below for the three types of controls that can occur in automated accounting systems (see Table 9-2).

Manual controls **Manual controls** are performed by individuals without reliance on reports or screens prepared by automated information systems. For example, goods received from a supplier are counted and recorded on a receiving report, then compared to the bill of lading that came with the shipment on the truck. General controls would have limited impact on these controls.

Manual controls—are performed by individuals without reliance on reports or screens prepared by automated information systems.

Computer-assisted controls **Computer-assisted controls** are performed by individuals with the assistance of a computer report or computer information. For example, inventory counts are recorded in the computer system. A report is printed identifying differences between the perpetual records and the inventory count so that a different count team can verify the discrepancy. Should general controls be inadequate, the computer information used as a basis for completing this control could be unreliable.

Computer-assisted controls—controls that have a manual component and a computerized component, such as an individual using a computerized exception report to complete a task.

Fully automated controls **Fully automated controls** are performed using only automated information systems, with no manual or human intervention. For example, every morning, prior to commencing sales order processing, the accounts receivable subsystem automatically adds the accounts receivable open item file and transfers the total to a reconciliation file, where another program compares the total with the accounts receivable balance in the general ledger. If there is a difference, a warning message is sent to the accounts receivable data entry clerk. Normally, fully automated controls can best be tested with control tests. Computer-assisted audit tests that would be suitable would include test data, integrated test facilities, or reperformance (using generalized audit software). Such controls are vulnerable to general control failures, such as poor program testing.

Fully automated controls—controls that are undertaken without human intervention, such as a credit check where transactions are automatically rejected.

When identifying key controls in a system, the auditor may have identified a combination of manual, computer-assisted, and fully automated controls. For example, when considering credit approval prior to shipment, a manual control would require that each shipment be manually approved and initialled. A computer-assisted control would have the computer system print a report for the credit manager of questionable orders. The credit manager would review the report and determine which orders should be shipped. A fully automated control would have the computer system automatically reject all orders that caused customers to exceed their credit limit.

For an auditor to consider placing reliance upon either a computer-assisted or fully automated control, the auditor must have reasonable assurance that general controls over the computerized portion of the controls are effective. In particular, program change controls and access controls must be effective.

- *Program change controls.* There should be sufficient controls in place to ensure that programs throughout the year were adequately controlled. This provides reasonable assurance that there were no unauthorized program changes and that programs functioned consistently throughout the year.
- *Access controls.* Physical and logical access controls should exist to prevent unauthorized access to programs and data and to document access so that accountability can be established. If unauthorized access to programs or data can be obtained, then the auditor would not be able to place reliance on the results of those programs or data throughout the year.

Should the auditor conclude that general controls are adequate, then the auditor has the choice of relying on any of the different types of controls in the accounting system that are identified as key controls (i.e., manual, computer-assisted, or fully automated). Should general controls be poor, then the auditor may be able to rely on only manual controls. Alternatively, the auditor may decide to assess control risk at maximum and not rely on any internal controls.

Tests of Controls

The controls that the auditor has identified as reducing control risk (the key controls) must be supported by tests of controls to make sure they have been operating effectively throughout all, or most of, the audit period. For example, in Figure 9-5 (page 295), each key control must be supported by sufficient tests of controls.

PROCEDURES FOR TESTS OF CONTROLS Four types of audit procedures are used to support the operation of key internal controls. They are as follows:

Make inquiries of appropriate entity personnel Although inquiry is not generally a strong source of evidence about the effective operation of controls, it is an appropriate form of evidence. For example, the auditor may determine that unauthorized personnel are not allowed access to computer files by making inquiries of the person who controls passwords.

Inspection of documents, records, and reports Many controls leave a clear trail of documentary evidence. Suppose, for example, that when a customer order is received, it is used to update a customer accounts receivable record, which is approved for credit using the computer system. Orders that cause the customer to exceed the credit limit are printed and reviewed by the sales manager. The sales manager initials the listing for those orders that are to be accepted. (See the first and second key controls in Figure 9-5.) The auditor examines the credit exception report and ensures that required signatures or initials are present. Since this is a computer-assisted control (reliance on an automated exception report), the auditor reviews the general controls file to ensure that general controls are adequate prior to the conduct of this test. The auditor may examine a personal guarantee in a bank loan file if there is a need to increase credit, and this provides supporting evidence of the credit-granting process.

Observe control-related activities Other types of control-related activities do not leave an evidential trail. For example, separation of duties relies on specific persons performing specific tasks, and there is typically no documentation of the separate performance. (See the third key control listed in Figure 9-5.) For controls that leave no documentary evidence, the auditor generally observes them being applied. For computer-based controls, the auditor may consider the use of test data to determine whether the control is functioning. **Test data** are fictitious transactions entered in controlled circumstances and processed through the client systems. The auditor

Test data—fictitious transactions entered in controlled circumstances and processed through the client systems.

compares anticipated results with results that actually occurred from processing the transactions.

Reperform client procedures There are also control-related activities for which there are related documents and records but whose content is insufficient for the auditor's purpose of assessing whether controls are operating effectively. For example, assume prices on sales invoices are automatically retrieved from the computer master file by client personnel and not overridden. (See the seventh key control in Figure 9-5.) There is no documentation of this control, since it relies upon an automated process. In these cases, it is common for the auditor to actually reperform the control activity to see whether the proper results were obtained. For this example, the auditor can reperform the procedure by tracing the sales prices to the authorized price list in effect at the date of the transaction. Reperformance can also be automated. For example, if the company uses a complex algorithm to calculate its allowance for bad debts based on sales throughout the year, the algorithm could be duplicated and recalculated using **generalized audit software** (general purpose software capable of reading and testing client data using special-purpose modules such as extraction, sampling, and plotting). If no misstatements are found, the auditor can conclude that the procedure is operating as intended.

Generalized audit software—general purpose software capable of reading and testing client data using special-purpose modules such as extraction, sampling, and plotting.

EXTENT OF PROCEDURES The extent to which tests of controls are applied depends on the intended assessed level of control risk. The lower the assessed level of control risk, the more extensive the tests of controls must be both in terms of the number of controls tested and the extent of tests of each control. For example, if the auditor wants to use a low assessed level of control risk, a larger sample size for documentation, observation, and reperformance procedures should be applied.

Reliance on evidence from prior year's audit If evidence was obtained in the prior year's audit that indicates a key control was operating effectively, and the auditor determines that it is still in place, the extent of the tests of that control may be reduced substantially in the current year and tested as a minimum every third year. If auditors determine that a key control has been changed since it was last tested, they should test it in the current year. When there are a number of controls tested in prior audits that have not been changed, auditors should test some of those controls each year to ensure that there is a rotation of controls testing throughout the three-year period.

Testing of controls related to significant risks Significant risks are those risks that the auditor believes require special audit consideration. When the auditor's risk assessment procedures identify significant risks, the auditor is required to test the operating effectiveness of controls that mitigate these risks in the current year audit, if the auditor plans to rely on those controls to support a control risk assessment below 100 percent. The greater the risk, the more audit evidence the auditor should obtain that controls are operating effectively.

Testing less than the entire audit period Ideally, tests of controls should be applied to transactions and controls for the entire period under audit. However, it is not always possible to do so. Where less than the entire period is tested, the auditor should determine whether changes in controls occurred in the period not tested and obtain evidential matter about the nature and extent of any changes. Controls dealing with financial statement preparation occur monthly, quarterly, or at year end and should therefore be tested at those times.

RELATIONSHIP OF TESTS OF CONTROLS TO PROCEDURES TO OBTAIN AN UNDERSTAND-ING You will notice that there is a significant overlap between tests of controls and procedures to obtain an understanding. Both include inquiry, inspection, and observation. There are two primary differences in the application of these common procedures

Table 9-5	Relationship of Planned Assessed Level of Control Risk and Extent of Procedures	

	Planned Assessed Level of Control Risk	
Type of Procedure Used	High Level: Obtaining an Understanding Only	Lower Level: Tests of Controls
Inquiry	Yes—extensive	Yes—some
Inspection	Yes—with transaction walk-through	Yes—using sampling
Observation	Yes—with transaction walk-through	Yes—at multiple times
Reperformance	No	Yes—using sampling

between phases. The auditor needs to understand internal control only as it applies to the financial statements as a whole and to relevant assertions relating to significant account balances or classes of transactions. In other words, the procedures to gain an understanding are applied only to certain control policies and procedures that have been instituted by the client. The auditor will obtain knowledge about the design of the relevant policies and procedures and determine whether or not they have been implemented. Tests of controls, on the other hand, are applied only when control risk has been assessed below maximum, and then only to key controls.

The second difference is that procedures to obtain an understanding are performed only on one or a few transactions or, in the case of observations, at a single point in time. Tests of controls are performed on larger samples of transactions (perhaps 20 to 100), and often observations are made at more than one point in time.

For key controls, tests of controls other than reperformance are essentially an extension of related procedures to obtain an understanding. For that reason, when auditors plan at the outset to obtain a low assessed level of control risk, they will combine both types of procedures and perform them simultaneously.

Table 9-5 illustrates this concept in more detail, showing how audit procedures are used differently. Where only the required minimum study of internal control is planned, the auditor will conduct a transaction walk-through. In so doing, the auditor determines that the audit documentation is complete and accurate, and observes that the control-related activities described are in operation.

When the control risk is assessed below maximum, a transaction walk-through is performed and a larger and more varied sample of documents is inspected for indications of the effectiveness of the operation of controls. (The determination of appropriate sample size is discussed in Chapters 13 and 14.) Similarly, when observations are made, they will be more extensive and often at several points in time. Also, reperformance is an important test of some controls.

Two Audit Approaches

As we have explained, there are two approaches an auditor may take for a specific financial statement assertion: the substantive approach, where the auditor does not rely on internal controls; and the combined approach, where the auditor assesses control risk below maximum and does rely on internal controls.

A substantive approach is used when the auditor cannot rely on the internal controls with respect to a particular assertion or when it is not cost-effective to rely on the controls for that assertion. Control risk is set at high for that assertion; planned detection risk will therefore be low and the extent of evidence will be high. The auditor will obtain a sufficient understanding of the control environment and the accounting system to plan the audit and document the understanding and the control risk assessment; there would be no tests of controls.

A combined approach is used when the auditor can rely on the internal controls with respect to a particular assertion and control risk can be assessed at low. Even though a combined approach could be used if control risk is set at medium, it is normally not done in practice. Because control risk is set at low for that assertion, planned detection risk will be high and the extent of evidence will be low. The auditor will obtain an understanding of the control environment, the accounting system, and the control activities sufficient to plan the audit and document the understanding and the control risk assessment; controls would be tested to support the assessment of low with the extent of testing varying inversely with the assessment.

Expansion of Internal Control Testing

For some companies, the auditor reports upon management's assessment of internal control. Such a report is required by Section 404(b) of the Sarbanes-Oxley Act of 2002, affecting Canadian companies that are subsidiaries of American companies or that register securities for sale in the United States. A sample report is shown in Chapter 22 and on page 154 (Hillsburg Hardware's audit report). At the time of writing, reporting requirements for Canadian publicly listed companies have not been finalized. It appears that these companies will be reporting on the quality of their internal controls but that these reports will not need to be audited. However, it is likely that these companies will still want some form of assurance from their auditors about the quality of their internal controls. Section 9110, Agreed-upon procedures regarding internal control over financial reporting, discussed in Chapter 23, talks further about this type of reporting.

Since management's assessment of internal control covers internal control over financial reporting, the scope of the Section 404(b) internal control assessment is different from the scope of the financial statement audit. The auditor will need to assess whether additional testing is required (i.e., more testing than is needed for satisfaction of the audit assertions). Figure 9-7 describes potential differences in scope between the nature of internal control testing for an audit of internal control and an audit of financial statements. For this figure, management is concerned about additional controls that the auditor would not rely upon in the audit of the financial statements, requiring the auditor to do additional testing to be able to provide assurance upon management's assessment of internal control.

Section 5925 of the *CICA Handbook*, An audit of internal control over financial reporting performed that is integrated with an audit of financial statements, is substantially equivalent to the U.S. standard. The application and explanatory material at the end of the standard walks through the entire engagement, discussing roles, risk assessment, criteria, planning, fieldwork, and reporting in detail. As with other engagements, management

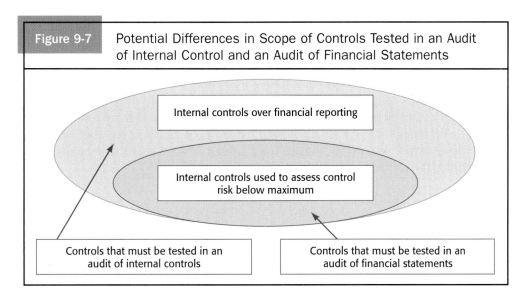

| Figure 9-7 | Potential Differences in Scope of Controls Tested in an Audit of Internal Control and an Audit of Financial Statements |

Internal controls over financial reporting

Internal controls used to assess control risk below maximum

Controls that must be tested in an audit of internal controls

Controls that must be tested in an audit of financial statements accepts responsibility for the internal control, and the same auditor who conducts the financial statement audit performs the audit of management's internal control assessment.

As part of the fieldwork, the auditor should test entity-level controls (such as the control environment and general computer controls) as well as more specific preventative and detective controls. To assist in the risk assessment process, the auditor is required to segregate transactions into one of three categories: routine, non-routine, or estimation. Only those controls that achieve a control objective are tested, and testing varies from year to year. The testing extends past the end of the fiscal year to those periods that help ensure that the financial statements are properly completed, for example, until February 15 for a December year end if that is the time when the final accrual journal entries are made for the fiscal year. Procedures are also described for the reporting and handling of weaknesses in internal control.

The sample financial statements of Hillsburg Hardware Limited at the end of Chapter 5 provide an example of a combined audit report, while Chapter 22 provides examples of reports where the auditor separately provides the opinion on the financial statements and on the effectiveness of internal control over financial reporting. The auditor could issue either a combined report or two separate reports, with the effective dates being the same as the dates for the financial statement audit.

Other special reports on internal control, such as reports on a service organization, are discussed in Chapter 23. Such special reports are normally conducted as separate engagements and are not part of the annual financial statement audit.

concept check

C9-6 How is management's risk assessment relevant to the audit?

C9-7 What is the role of monitoring to support internal controls?

C9-8 Describe the audit strategy that the auditor uses when there is reliance upon key internal controls.

 # Small Business Controls

Our discussions of internal control have indicated that small businesses frequently rely on owner/manager supervision. This is true whether a business uses manual or automated information systems. In this section, we examine the likely characteristics of a small business using the control framework of Figure 9-1 (page 274), Five Components of Internal Control.

Control Environment

The quality of the control environment depends on the attitudes of the owner/manager. If the owner/manager adequately supervises employees, hires only competent employees, and encourages practices such as the use of confidential passwords, then the organization will have a more positive control environment than a situation in which the owner is an absentee and encourages the use of illegal copies of software.

Risk Assessment

Most small business owners are very clearly aware of their risks but do not have a formal method of documenting and assessing such risks. For example, they may be aware of the volatility of raw material prices or that there is an increased risk of uncollectability of accounts receivable. The auditor might recommend to small business owners that they consider periodically meeting with outside advisors, such as an advisory committee, to help them more formally assess risks within the businesses. Small business owners frequently underestimate fraud risks because they are prone to trusting their employees. A periodic credit check on employees or spot checking employee activity on a random basis can help assure the owner that employees are executing their activities conscientiously.

Control Activities

GENERAL CONTROLS

Organization and management controls There are often fewer people in the accounting department, perhaps even only one person; thus, segregation of duties may not be possible. Controls are often informal, lacking written authorization procedures. The owner/manager can readily override controls by personally performing clerical or operating functions.

Systems acquisition, development, and maintenance controls Use of packaged software is common in the accounting systems. A variety of software packages are available; they range in quality. Where programming is undertaken, controls over changes may be poor since an informal process will likely be used rather than a structured approach.

Operations and information systems support Primarily because of the small size of the organization, the information systems are likely to be simpler systems, using a centralized form of processing. The entity is unlikely to have in-house expertise in systems and would normally place reliance on software and hardware suppliers for system support and maintenance. Passwords may be in use but are in a simple form (e.g., the accounting personnel may have a single password that allows access to all systems and all functions).

APPLICATION CONTROL ACTIVITIES When a software package is used and the entity is not capable of making changes to the software (since most software packages are provided only in machine code), certain controls in the software become important. For example, calculations in invoicing and inventory costing (mechanical accuracy), posting of transactions to subsidiary systems and to the general ledger (detail tie-in), and aging of accounts receivable (valuation) are all functions normally present in software packages; these assist the business and the auditor can rely on them.

PRACTICAL CONTROLS TO BE EXERCISED BY THE OWNER/MANAGER For controls to be practical in a small business, they need to be activities that can be performed in a short period of time; otherwise it is unlikely that an owner/manager will implement them.

Systems acquisition, development, and maintenance controls It is important that the owner/manager understand the nature of software used by the business and how business needs might change. This includes software maintenance needs. For example, if the company uses a payroll package, then the company should expect to receive an upgrade whenever tax rates change. The owner should ensure that authorized programs are implemented (i.e., only valid, copyrighted materials should be implemented). If program changes are implemented, an employee should be assigned to test and keep a record of changes. Most small businesses have a lack of expertise in the selection, design, and operation of their automated information systems and frequently call on their accountant as a business advisor to help in these areas.

Operations and information systems support Backups should be made daily, with at least two copies of recent data kept offsite. Although a formal disaster recovery plan may not be contemplated, the entity should have a current contact for hardware and software support in the event of system problems. At a minimum, documentation to provide for ongoing operations, such as a list of the procedures that are normally completed on a daily, weekly, and monthly basis, should be present.

Application control procedures These procedures include controls to prevent fraud. The most important control concept here is the separation of authorization from the recording of transactions and owner/manager controls. As in other sizes of business, the owner/manager needs to remain vigilant to prevent computer fraud and other types of fraud. Chapters 14 through 20 indicate that the owner should perform certain key activities, such as signing payroll cheques with a supporting payroll journal, signing accounts payable cheques with supporting documentation, and reviewing master file information.

concept check

C9-9 What is the key internal control risk at a small business, and how can a small business owner deal with it?

C9-10 How does a software package support a good control environment for a small business?

Summary

1. *What are the three primary objectives of internal control?* Organizations establish internal control to (i) help ensure reliable financial reporting, (ii) enable efficient and effective operations, and (iii) comply with laws and regulations.

   What are the different perspectives of the client and the auditor? The client is concerned about meeting organizational goals, which include having accurate information, safeguarding assets, optimizing the use of resources, and preventing and detecting error and fraud. The auditor needs to assess the overall risk of the engagement by considering the components of internal control, including the control environment and the controls over classes of transactions within the context of reasonable assurance.

   What does it mean that "substantive tests are not enough"? In some situations, it may be difficult to test a particular assertion using substantive tests alone. For example, in a highly automated operation, information systems may perform controls such as matching of documentation, calculations, and posting. In such cases, the auditor would find that testing of details would not provide sufficient assurance and would need to conduct control testing of the automated controls.

   What are the three basic concepts that enable an auditor's study of internal controls? (1) Management is responsible for the establishment and maintenance of the entity's controls, (2) controls help provide reasonable assurance of the fairness of the financial statements, and (3) internal controls cannot be completely effective (inherent limitations).

2. *What are the five components of internal control using the COSO framework?* They are control environment, risk assessment, control activities, information and communication, and monitoring.

3. *What does the auditor do to obtain an understanding of internal controls?* After assessing the integrity of management, the auditor uses inquiry, inspection, and observation to understand the control environment and uses inquiry, inspection, observation, and reperformance to understand general controls, accounting systems, and control and monitoring procedures.

   How is control risk assessed, documented, and tested? After obtaining an understanding of internal control, the auditor evaluates the design effectiveness of internal controls to consider whether the financial statements are auditable. Then, general controls are assessed for their impact upon control risk for the individual transaction cycles and audit objectives in the transaction cycles. Finally, each audit objective is examined for each transaction type to determine the potential risk of material misstatement based on potential reliance on internal controls for that audit objective. Normally, software is used in the documentation of this process. The auditor will then design tests of controls for those key controls where reliance will be placed, test the controls, and evaluate the results of the tests of controls. If testing corroborates the operational effectiveness of the controls, then control risk is assessed at the targeted level.

   What are key controls? Key controls are those that the auditor could rely upon and test.

   Why is it important to link control risk to audit strategy and procedures? The auditor is better able to design substantive procedures that compensate for risks during the audit engagement and thus conduct a better quality audit.

   What other types of internal control reports can an auditor issue? The auditor can issue an opinion on management's assessment of internal control and also issue special reports on internal control.

   How do such internal control reports affect audit tests? An opinion on management's assessment of internal control is conducted at the same time as the financial statement audit and may include tests of additional controls, thus expanding the amount of work that would be completed during the financial statement audit engagement.

4. *What are important risks and controls for small businesses?* Small business owners face many of the risks of other businesses, but a unique risk for them is fraud or error due to lack of segregation of duties. This is mitigated by the strong level of commitment and on-hand activities conducted by most owners (such as signing cheques) and the use of well-designed software packages.

Visit the text's website at **www.pearsoned.ca/arens** for practice quizzes, additional case studies, and international standards information.

Review Questions

9-1 Describe the three broad objectives management has when designing effective internal control.

9-2 Describe which of the three categories of broad objectives for internal controls are considered by the auditor in an audit of both the financial statements and internal control over financial reporting. Why are these categories considered?

9-3 Chapter 5 introduced the phases of the financial statement audit. Which phase is understanding internal control and assessing control risk? Which phases precede and follow understanding and assessment?

9-4 Compare management's concerns about internal control with those of the auditor.

9-5 Frequently, management is more concerned about internal controls that promote operational efficiency than about those that result in reliable financial data. How can the independent auditor persuade management to devote more attention to controls affecting the reliability of accounting information when management has this attitude?

9-6 What are the five components of internal control in the COSO internal control framework? Provide an example of a control for each component.

9-7 What is the relationship among the five components of internal control?

9-8 What is meant by the "control environment"? What are the factors the auditor must evaluate to understand it?

9-9 What is the relationship between the control environment and control systems?

9-10 The separation of operational responsibility from record keeping is meant to prevent different types of misstatements than the separation of the custody of assets from accounting. Explain the difference in the purposes of these two types of separation of duties.

9-11 Distinguish between general and specific authorization of transactions, and give one example of each type.

9-12 Explain what is meant by "independent checks on performance," and give five specific examples.

9-13 Distinguish between obtaining an understanding of internal control and assessing control risk. Also, explain the methodology the auditor uses for each.

9-14 Define what is meant by a "control" and a "weakness in internal control." Give two examples of each in the sales and collection cycle.

9-15 Frank James, a highly competent employee of Brinkwater Sales Corporation, had been responsible for accounting-related matters for two decades. His devotion to the firm and his duties had always been exceptional, and over the years he had been given increased responsibilities. Both the president of Brinkwater and the partner of an independent public accounting firm in charge of the audit were shocked and dismayed to discover that James had embezzled more than $500,000 over a 10-year period by not recording billings in the sales journal and subsequently diverting the cash receipts. What major factors permitted the defalcation to take place?

9-16 Describe the seven steps in assessing control risk during a financial statement audit.

9-17 Distinguish between the objectives of an internal control questionnaire and the objectives of a flowchart for documenting information about a client's internal control. State the advantages and disadvantages of each of these two methods.

9-18 Describe what is meant by "key control" and "control deficiency."

9-19 Explain what is meant by "significant deficiencies" as they relate to internal control. What should the auditor do when he or she has discovered significant deficiencies in internal control?

9-20 Explain what is meant by "tests of controls." Write one inspection of documents test of control and one reperformance test of control for the following internal control: hours of time cards are re-added by an independent payroll clerk and initialled to indicate performance.

9-21 Distinguish between a substantive approach and a combined approach in auditing a financial statement assertion.

Discussion Questions and Problems

9-22 The following are errors or fraud and other irregularities that have occurred in Fresh Foods Grocery Store Ltd., a wholesale and retail grocery company.

1. The incorrect price was used on sales invoices for billing shipments to customers because the incorrect price was entered into a computer file.
2. A vendor's invoice was paid twice for the same shipment. The second payment arose because the vendor sent a duplicate copy of the original two weeks after the payment was due.
3. Employees in the receiving department stole some sides of beef. When a shipment of meat was received, the receiving department filled out a receiving report and forwarded it to the accounting department for the amount of goods actually received. At that time, two sides of beef were put in an employee's pickup truck rather than in the storage freezer.
4. During the physical count of inventory of the retail grocery, one counter wrote down the wrong description of several products and miscounted the quantity.
5. A salesperson sold several hundred kilos of lamb at a price below cost because she did not know that the cost of lamb had increased in the past week.
6. On the last day of the year, a truckload of beef was set aside for shipment but was not shipped. Because it was still on hand, it was counted as inventory. The shipping document was dated the last day of the year, so it was also included as a current-year sale.

REQUIRED

a. For each error or fraud and other irregularity, identify one or more types of controls that were absent.
b. For each error or fraud and other irregularity, identify the objectives that have not been met.
c. For each error or fraud and other irregularity, suggest a control to correct the deficiency.

9-23 The division of the following duties is meant to provide the best possible controls for the Meridian Paint Company Ltd., a small wholesale store.

*1. Assemble supporting documents for general and payroll cash disbursements.

*2. Sign general disbursement cheques.

*3. Input information to prepare cheques for printing and signature so that payments are recorded in the accounts payable, payments subsidiary system.

*4. Mail cheques to suppliers and deliver cheques to employees.

5. Cancel supporting documents to prevent their reuse.

*6. Update credit limit for customers in the customer master file.

*7. Input shipping and billing information to bill customers in the order entry system.

*8. Open the mail and prepare a prelisting of cash receipts.

*9. Enter cash receipts data in the accounts receivable subsystem used to prepare the cash receipts listing, and update the accounts receivable master file.

10. Prepare daily cash deposits.

*11. Deliver daily cash deposits to the bank.

*12. Assemble the payroll time cards and input the data into the payroll system to prepare payroll cheques.

*13. Sign payroll cheques.

14. Retrieve journal entries from all subsystems (i.e., order entry, accounts receivable, accounts payable and payments, payroll) to update the general ledger at the end of each month, and review all accounts for unexpected balances.

15. Print the aged accounts receivable trial balance and review accounts outstanding more than 90 days.

*16. Print monthly statements for customers using the accounts receivable system, and then mail the statements to customers.

17. Reconcile the monthly statements from vendors with the supplier balances according to the accounts payable system.

18. Reconcile the bank account.

REQUIRED

You are to divide the accounting-related duties 1 through 18 among Robert Smith, Karen Wong, and Barbara Chiu. All of the responsibilities marked with an asterisk are assumed to take about the same amount of time and must be divided equally between Smith and Wong. Both employees are equally competent. Chiu, who is president of the company, is not willing to perform any functions designated by an asterisk but is willing to perform a maximum of two of the other functions.

(Adapted from AICPA)

9-24 Recently, you had lunch with some friends at a new restaurant in your neighbourhood. After ordering, the server entered his password into a computer and punched in your order. The server continued taking orders and you noticed the cook removing a small printout and placing it on the wall in front of him (presumably your order). When the food was ready, it was placed directly below your order. The server looked at the printout, put it in his pocket, and then brought your order to the table.

When you finished eating, the server again entered his password and printed two copies of your bill. One copy was attached to the order slip, and the second was brought to you. You decided to pay by credit card, so two copies of the credit card authorization were brought to the table for signature. You kept one and the signed copy was returned to the server.

REQUIRED

a. What internal controls (manual, computer-assisted, and automated) are present at the restaurant?

b. How could the manager of the restaurant evaluate the effectiveness of the controls?

c. What are the costs and benefits of the restaurant's controls?

9-25 Lew Pherson and Marie Violette are friends who are employed by different public accounting firms. One day, during lunch, they are discussing the importance of internal control in determining the amount of audit evidence required for an engagement. Lew expresses the view that internal control must be carefully evaluated in all companies, regardless of company size, in basically the same manner. His public accounting firm requires a standard internal control questionnaire on every audit as well as a flowchart of every major transaction area. In addition, he says the firm requires a careful evaluation of the system and a modification in the evidence accumulated based on the controls and weaknesses in the system. Marie responds that she believes internal control cannot be adequate in many of the small companies she audits, although she recognizes that the *CICA Handbook* requires her to "obtain a sufficient understanding." She disagrees with the *Handbook* Recommendations and goes on to say, "Why should I spend a lot of time obtaining an understanding of internal control and assessing control risk when I know it has all kinds of weaknesses before I start? I would rather spend the time it takes to fill out all those forms in testing whether the statements are correct."

REQUIRED

a. Express in general terms the most important difference between the nature of the potential controls available for large and small companies.

b. Criticize the positions taken by Lew and Marie, and express your own opinion about the similarities and differences that should exist in understanding internal control and assessing control risk for different-sized companies.

9-26 The following are partial descriptions of internal control for companies engaged in the manufacturing business:

1. Every day, 50 employees clock in using time cards at Generous Parts Corporation. The staff accountant collects these cards once a week and enters the data into a computer. The information entered into the computer is used in the preparation of the labour cost distribution records, the payroll journal, and the payroll cheques. The treasurer,

Webber, compares the payroll journal with the payroll cheques, signs the cheques, and gives them to Strode, the controller, who distributes them to the employees.

2. The smallest branch of Connor Cosmetics Inc. in Medicine Hat employs Mary Cooper, the branch manager, and her sales assistant, Jane Hendrix. The branch uses a bank account in Medicine Hat to pay expenses. The account is kept in the name of "Connor Cosmetics Inc.—Special Account." To pay expenses, cheques must be signed by Mary or by the treasurer of Connor Cosmetics, John Winters. Mary receives the cancelled cheques and bank statements. She reconciles the branch account herself and files cancelled cheques and bank statements in her records. She also periodically prepares reports of disbursements and sends them to the head office.

REQUIRED

a. List the weaknesses in internal control for each of the above. To identify the weaknesses, use the methodology that was discussed in the chapter.

b. For each weakness, state the type of misstatement(s) that is (are) likely to result. Be as specific as possible.

c. How would you improve internal controls for each of the two companies?

(Adapted from AICPA)

Professional Judgment Problems

9-27 Augustina Paper Supplies Ltd. is one of your favourite clients. You started work there as a junior staff, and this year you will be the senior. The company is well organized and employees are friendly. Internal controls are good and procedures are highly automated with standard industry software.

You used standard sampling methods to select a sample to count for inventory. Items were traced from the warehouse floor to the count records and from the count records to the warehouse floor. There were only one or two minor count differences, and when employees recounted the items with audit staff, records were adjusted. All inventory tags were accounted for. You thanked your audit staff for their help, completed the inventory count file, then filed it in the filing cabinet at your office.

Three weeks later, when it was time to pull everything together to conduct the year-end audit, you were horrified to discover that you could not find the inventory count file. You searched through all the files that started with G and asked clerical staff at your office to help you look, but to no avail.

REQUIRED

a. What alternatives are available to you in the completion of the audit?

b. What role does the quality of internal control play in the actions available?

c. Can an audit of inventory still be completed? Why or why not?

9-28 Gaboria Frank is the owner of Frankincents Machining Limited, a custom machining centre with 10 full-time employees and a part-time bookkeeper, Norma, who comes in two days a week. Norma convinced Gaboria to purchase a small business suite of accounting packages and a desktop computer with a laser printer. Norma has set up the records on the computer, and all accounting work is now handled using the accounting packages (i.e., order entry, accounts receivable, cash disbursements, general ledger, and payroll). It took Norma about three months, and she initially had some difficulty balancing the subsystems, but everything seems to be functioning properly now. Frank did not consult with you, his accountant, prior to implementing the systems.

REQUIRED

a. Identify the risks associated with the current method of handling accounting records at Frankincents Machining Limited.

b. Identify those activities that Frank should handle in sales, accounts receivable, cash disbursements, and payroll. Explain why.

Case

9-29 You have been asked to provide guidance to your staff with respect to which controls should be audited in the current year (versus prior years). The following internal controls were tested in prior audits. Evaluate each internal control and determine which controls must be tested in the current year's audit of the December 31, 2008, financial statements. Clearly explain why testing is or is not required in the current year.

1. The general ledger accounting software system automatically reconciles totals in each of the subsidiary master files for accounts receivable, accounts payable, and inventory accounts to the respective general ledger accounts. This control was most recently tested in the prior year. No changes to the software have been made since testing and there are strong controls over information technology (IT) security and software program changes.

2. The accounts payable clerk matches vendor invoices with related purchase orders and receiving reports and investigates any differences noted. This control was tested in the 2007 fiscal year-end audit. No changes to this control or personnel involved have occurred since testing was performed.

3. The sales system automatically determines whether a customer's purchase order and related accounts receivable balance are within the customer's credit limit. The risk of shipping goods to customers who exceed their credit limit is deemed to be a significant risk. This control was last tested in the December 31, 2006, financial statement audit.

4. The perpetual inventory system automatically extends the unit price times quantity for inventory on hand. This control was last tested in the audit of December 31, 2006, financial statements. During 2007, the client made changes to this automated information system.

5. The client's purchase accounting system was acquired from a reputable software vendor several years ago. This system contains numerous automated controls. The auditor tested those controls most recently in 2007. There have been no software updates since purchase of the software.

REQUIRED

In addition to providing guidance for each of the points above, provide guidance that could be applied to other tests of internal control to indicate which need to be tested in the current year.

Ongoing Small Business Case: COSO Controls at CondoCleaners.com

9-30 Jim's business is booming, and within six months, he has gone from his first cluster of four condominiums to 30 condominium towers within the downtown core that are serviced by his cleaning staff. Jim hired his first supervisor, Vagney, this month and has spent the past week training her. Vagney has a schedule of cleaning and drops in unannounced while cleaning is being done to do quality control checks. She has been assigned the responsibility of purchasing cleaning supplies from the local department store as well as scanning for specials to help reduce cleaning supply costs.

Jim still does the accounting, including payroll for his six full-time employees, who are paid a base pay of 20 hours per week. Jim does the scheduling to make sure that each employee receives at least 20 hours of work per week, then schedules the remaining cleaning around those 20 hours, trying to minimize the number of trips that employees need to make.

REQUIRED

Using the framework of COSO, describe each internal control category, and provide an example of controls that are present or could be present at CondoCleaners.com.

10

Corporate governance and entity-level controls

"Tone at the top" is a familiar phrase to most of us—it means that the attitudes and actions of the board, executive, and management have a pervasive impact upon the rest of the organization. The "tone at the top" has a similar effect upon the financial statement audit—if these management strategies are ineffective, it is possible that the remainder of the control systems are also floundering, and cannot be tested. Entity-level controls help to implement the "tone at the top," as such controls affect the whole organization. All types of accountants will benefit from understanding a range of entity-level controls and how they can be tested.

STANDARDS REFERENCED IN THIS CHAPTER

No standards are referenced in this chapter.

LEARNING OBJECTIVES

1 Explain the relationship between corporate governance strategies and risk management. Define the term "enterprise risk management (ERM) framework." Describe the techniques that the auditor uses to document and assess design and operating effectiveness of corporate governance.

2 Define information technology (IT) governance. Describe the attributes of good IT governance. Explain the impact of general controls on the audit process. State the effects of information systems on the eight-phase audit process.

3 State the effects of advanced information systems on the audit.

4 Provide examples of other entity-level controls. Link the impact of entity-level controls to specific audit objectives. Using a laser chequing application, provide an example of the effect of general information systems controls on the audit of transactions and balances at the audit objective level.

Healthy Corporate Governance Corrects Functional Flaws

Plato Construction Ltd. (Plato) is a newly acquired subsidiary of Largesse Construction Canada Inc. (Largesse), a public company that operates across Canada, performing construction services from design and project management through to actual construction. Largesse purchased Plato, a private company owned by Edward Platonu and five other individuals, in December 2007. Plato had been in operation for over 25 years and was a well-respected, profitable company in the Alberta construction industry, specializing in oil and gas construction. Largesse has a standard package of internal control procedures, which were provided to Plato for implementation.

During a routine audit by Largesse's auditors for compliance with internal controls for the 2008 audit, it was noted that several Largesse policies and procedures were not being followed. The auditors investigated further and found evidence that Edward had circumvented internal controls in the areas of subcontracting, construction material disposal, and payroll.

Specifically, Edward had given subcontracts to paint several buildings to his brother Ted without going to tender, as required by the new policies. Edward also had his house and cottage painted by Ted and charged it to Plato as a $20,000 subcontract cost on a large construction project.

Edward had a private bank account under the name of Plato Construction (a sole proprietorship that had been registered about 10 years ago), which he called a social fund. Demolition material that had been disposed of, like scrap steel, was used to fund this bank account. Bank records indicated that deposits into this account amounted to $250,000 for the first eight months of 2008. Edward said he used these funds to (1) give cash bonuses to employees (no tax receipts were issued for these bonuses), (2) pay for golf trips or other vacations for the executive team, and (3) have social functions with employees and their families. Edward had retained receipts and filed tax returns for Plato Construction as a social management organization.

IMPORTANCE TO AUDITORS

When fraud like this is discovered, auditors work closely with management and look to the nature of management's response to assess the quality of corporate governance and the control environment. In this situation, the auditors met with the senior management of Largesse and its audit committee immediately after the discovery of potentially fraudulent activities. The audit committee instructed the auditors to complete a full investigation by engaging the firm's forensic examiners. Largesse and its audit committee also engaged legal counsel.

Largesse's internal auditors were part of the team and were asked to provide recommendations for improvement to internal controls to prevent recurrence of control breakdowns. Reports from all the professional teams were provided to the audit committee.

As a result of these findings and after several months of investigation, Edward's employment was terminated. Plato's controller, vice-president of operations, and director of construction

continued >

services, all of whom had participated in the activities and had assisted Edward in circumventing internal controls, were also terminated.

WHAT DO YOU THINK?

1. What are some of the suspicious activities that auditors may have observed that would have led them to detecting Edward's activities?

2. What is your opinion of the "tone at the top" of Largesse? Of Plato?

3. List the different types of expertise that were required in the professional engagements described above, and state the professional qualifications that each would require. Would you be interested in doing this type of work?

Source: Contributed by a public accountant. Organizational details, individual names, and dollar amounts have been changed.

IN our opening vignette, the auditors of Largesse had continued close communication with the audit committee and senior executives of the company while dealing with a fraud that circumvented many internal controls. Management fraud, also discussed in Chapter 11, is difficult to detect because management has the ability to override controls and documentation processes. However, as the fraudulent activity becomes more pervasive, as it did at Plato, such frauds are more likely to be found out. The Largesse and Plato situation indicates two opposing qualities of corporate governance. At Plato, the corporation seemed to be a vehicle for plundering for personal gain, while at Largesse, executive management and the audit committee were concerned about corporate performance on behalf of their other stakeholders. In this chapter, we will look at how enterprise-wide risk management is implemented as part of a corporate governance strategy. Implementation of the Sarbanes-Oxley Act in the United States has been a major world-wide impetus for improved codification of risk management and internal controls in our information systems age. For further information about Sarbanes-Oxley and its integrated relationship with technology, consult *IT Control Objectives for Sarbanes-Oxley: The Role of IT in the Design and Implementation of Internal Control over Financial Reporting,* Second Edition, September 2006, published by the IT Governance Institute (**www.itgi.org**).

We also consider how corporate governance, risk management, and entitywide controls such as general information systems controls are integrated into the audit risk model, audited, and tested.

Corporate Governance Strategies and Risk Assessment Frameworks

In Chapter 9 we described those charged with governance as individuals responsible for overseeing the strategic direction of the entity and the accountability of the entity, including financial reporting and disclosure. For a public corporation, this would include the board of directors, its subcommittees (such as the audit committee), executives, and senior management. Many non-profit and public sector organizations have similar structures of governance. Smaller organizations could have an advisory committee instead of an independent board.

There has been increased scrutiny of the processes and qualifications of directors and management, with new laws and regulations imposing tasks or certifications. Before we talk about risk assessment, we briefly look at these two issues.

Role and Certification Escalation

THE ESCALATING ROLE OF BOARD MEMBERS AND THE AUDIT COMMITTEE Board members are elected by shareholders, often nominated by groups of shareholders or by management. Depending upon the type of organization, a certain percentage of the directors need to be independent (i.e., non-management, with other restrictions such as ownership or restrictions that vary by type of organization). Regulatory responses to corporate fraud, such as the Sarbanes-Oxley Act in the United States and Canadian Security Regulations in Canada, have included increased requirements for directors on the boards of public companies. Table 10-1 lists some of the tasks expected of board members and the related expertise that would need to be present in at least one board member.

As a subcommittee of the board of directors, the audit committee is composed of board members who preferably have financial expertise. There would also be other subcommittees, perhaps addressing responsibilities such as corporate strategy, risk management, IT, or privacy. There are many resources available to directors, such as training by professional organizations, experts in their own industry, auditors (external and internal), and online and text resources. As an example, Table 10-2 lists from the CICA website sample resources titled "20 Questions a Board Member (or Director) Should Ask," with the topic, effective date, and purpose. Many other professional organizations provide resources. For example, the Institute of Internal Auditors has its own publication titled "The Audit Committee: Internal Audit Oversight," which is intended to provide guidance to the audit committee in overseeing the internal audit

Table 10-1	**Board Member Sample Tasks and Expertise**
Sample Task	Expected Expertise
Approve hiring of chief executive officer	Human resources, personnel evaluation
Approve risk assessment framework and monitor risk evaluation process	Industry expertise, strategic planning, awareness of potential risks, risk assessment methodologies
Review and approve organizational and business strategies and changes thereto	Long-term planning, strategic planning, industry-specific expertise
Review and approve information systems strategy and changes thereto	Ability to link information systems strategy to business strategy; understand information systems terminology, impact, and alternatives; industry-specific expertise
Approve information systems acquisitions, business acquisitions, or contracts over specified dollar limits	Understand information systems terminology, impact, and alternatives; industry-specific expertise
Approve auditors and financial statements	Financial or accounting competence; understand complex accounting terminology and be able to ask the right questions
Oversee the work of the internal auditors	Understand risks that the organization is exposed to and alternative ways of addressing those risks

function. This is available (along with other standards and guidance documents) at **www.theiia.org/quality**.

The scope of the topics listed in Tables 10-1 and 10-2 illustrates that board members are expected to oversee all strategic and high-level functions of the organization for effective corporate governance to occur. In the next section, we will look at some of the regulatory influences that have forced this level of detail upon boards, including oversight of management certifications.

REGULATORY INFLUENCES ON THE BOARD AND MANAGEMENT Private companies and other small businesses have some of the same regulations to deal with as do larger organizations, that is, dealing with income and employee taxes, regulatory filings, and requirements of their investors and shareholders. Specific regulations for particular industries or groups (such as financial institutions, brokers, and Canadian registered charitable organizations) are beyond the scope of this text. Here, we will deal with some of the specific requirements of Canadian public companies.

An important issue that could be complex for many organizations is the coming conversion to International Financial Reporting Standards (IFRS). Canadian public companies are required to follow GAAP as codified by the *Canadian Institute of Chartered Accountants Accounting Handbook* and by current best business practices. This conversion takes place for fiscal years commencing on or after January 1, 2011. The change to IFRS may affect the way that an organization records certain transactions (such as methods of costing projects or recording foreign exchange and hedging activities). This would mean a change in the methods of recording and tracking these transactions and a resultant change to automated information systems. Associated

Table 10-2	Questions that Board Members Should Ask
Topic	Effective date of publication and purpose*
Codes of conduct	2005, Typical content for a code of conduct; help in assessing organizational culture and ethical practices
Crisis management	2008, Awareness of elements of successful crisis management
Executive compensation	2003, Balancing shareholder accountability with effective motivation and compensation of executives, including methods of remuneration
Information technology (IT)	2004, Assistance in assessing IT strategies, effectiveness, and controls
Internal audit	2007, Understanding the functions of internal audit and questions to ask of internal audit, with some internal audit best practices
International financial reporting standards (IFRS) conversions	2008, Explains issues associated with the conversion, with detail appropriate for audit committee members
Management's discussion and analysis	2008, Clarification of current legal and regulatory disclosures with methods for discussion with management
Strategy	2006, Methods to assess management's development and update of strategy; guide to active involvement in the process as well as approval
Not-for-profit strategy and planning	2008, Understanding directors' responsibilities in this area, including budgeting
Risk assessment	2006, Help in considering the effectiveness of risk assessment and working with management in this process

*Available from the CICA website Research and Guidance section, under Risk Management and Governance: www.rmgb.ca/publications/index.aspx.

internal controls would need to be adjusted and employees trained in the new processes. Resulting financial information, ratios, and bank covenants could be affected. As management and the board should approve any deviations from GAAP at the organization, as well as other major activity changes, the board could consider the implementation of a separate subcommittee to oversee this process.

CAS

In Canada, rather than an omnibus bill like Sarbanes-Oxley in the United States, regulatory filings by public companies trading on the SEC are governed by National Policy documents (previously called Multilateral Instruments) issued by the Canadian Securities Administrators (CSA—see **www.csa-acvm.ca**), an organization composed of the 13 Canadian securities regulators. These regulations are constantly changing. For example, as of December 2008, the CSA was proposing to broaden the scope of its Corporate Governance policies and practices, with new guidance for audit committees. This would affect three of the national policies (58-201, Corporate governance principles; 58-101, Disclosure of corporate governance practices; and 52-110, Audit committees). The exposure period for these documents ended in April 2009. The results of comments received could be that re-exposure will occur or that change to the policies would be made in the following year.

Table 10-3 lists some current requirements for management and board members, based upon the existing National Policy documents. A major difference between Canada and the United States is that in Canada management's evaluation of internal controls does not need to be audited by the external auditors.

The Relationship Between Corporate Governance Strategies and Risk Management

Regulations in Canada require that public companies have a board of directors and an audit committee. Most large public companies also have on their executive management team a CEO (chief executive officer), a CFO (chief financial officer), and other senior positions in functional areas such as operations, information systems, security, privacy, marketing, and human resources. The actions, policies, and procedures approved by these individuals help to develop an **organizational culture** which embodies both implicit and explicit assumptions about goals and objectives of the organization. The way that reporting lines are established create the **organizational structure**.

THE EFFECT OF ORGANIZATIONAL STRUCTURE AND CULTURE ON CORPORATE GOVERNANCE Table 10-4 on page 318 lists three organizational types, with a brief description, a likely example of such an organization, and a typical cultural norm for the organizational type. Based upon these descriptions, we can see that an **entrepreneurial structure** will not have the type of corporate governance structure that corresponds to a public company. Depending upon its size, neither would an **adhocracy**.

Most public companies would have a **bureaucratic organizational structure**. The bureaucratic structure is an enabler of clear corporate governance practices, although excessive rules and procedures can result in inefficiencies. In a bureaucracy, important internal controls are documented and codified, and there are defined employee training practices. There are distinct levels of supervision and management, including the executive management, and a board of directors, with the necessary subcommittees and mandate to document the governance process. One example would be an **information systems steering committee**, typically composed of senior executives, whose role would include oversight of IT, with the mandate to recommend technology changes to the board of directors. This committee will be described further in Section 3 of this chapter.

Organizations operate in the context of their environment, working for shareholders, and with other stakeholders such as customers, suppliers, and regulators. The organizational culture addresses the speed with which the company reacts to the environment and how it reacts and includes documented and undocumented practices.

Organizational culture—the actions, policies, and procedures performed or approved by executives and management that embody both implicit and explicit assumptions about goals and objectives of the organization.

Organizational structure—reporting lines within an organization.

Entrepreneurial structure—small, owner-operated or owner-managed, typified by informal decision making and unstructured processes.

Adhocracy—an organizational structure where teams of multidisciplinary individuals work on specific projects or assignments, and are expected to react rapidly to changing needs.

Bureaucratic organizational structure—multiple levels of management working in a slowly changing environment, providing relatively standard products or services. May be divisionalized (with many locations and a central headquarters), or professional (relying upon technical expertise with strong department heads and a weak head office).

Information systems steering committee—typically composed of senior executives, whose role would include oversight of IT, with the mandate to recommend technology changes to the board of directors.

| Table 10-3 | Canadian Public Company National Policy Requirements |

Management Certifications	Board or Audit Committee (AC) Requirements
	A majority of the directors should be independent (an absence of a direct or indirect material relationship with the company)
	The board should have a disclosed written mandate that includes responsibility for the following: a) Satisfaction with the integrity of the CEO and other executive officers and an organizational culture of integrity. b) Adopting and approving an annual strategic plan and strategic planning process that includes risk assessment. c) Identifying principal risks and systems to manage them. d) Succession planning, communication policies, internal controls, and management information systems. e) Approaches to corporate governance, including principles and guidelines. f) Ethical business conduct and the use of independent judgment.
	The audit committee should have a written charter. Specific responsibilities are in Multilateral Instrument 52–110, Audit Committees, available from www.osc.gov.on.ca.
That interim and annual filings do not contain any misrepresentations (includes financial statements, management discussion and analysis [MD&A])	AC: Review and approve MD&A; be financially literate
Interim and annual financial statements are fairly presented	AC: Review and approve financial statements; recommend to the board the external auditor and the audit fee; pre-approve any non-audit work; manage the relationship between the company and the external and internal auditors
For the above filings, that they have designed (or caused to have designed) internal controls over financial reporting and disclosures	AC: Review disclosures prior to release
Certify which internal control framework was used to design internal controls	Approve internal control framework to be used
For annual filings, that the effectiveness of the above controls have been evaluated and the conclusions disclosed in MD&A*	Understand the decision process for deciding what is or is not a material weakness
For annual and interim filings, that any material (or potentially material) changes in internal controls have been disclosed*	AC: Review filings prior to release
That material internal control weaknesses, their impact, and any plan for remediation have been disclosed in MD&A	AC: Review filings prior to release
That any fraud involving management or significant employees has been disclosed to the external auditors and the board	AC: Review filings prior to release
That any permitted exclusions are described in MD&A (e.g., proportionately consolidated entities)	AC: Review filings prior to release
	Establish policies or procedures for dealing with complaints and concerns about accounting or auditing matters

Note: Public companies that are considered to be venture capital or debt-only companies are exempted from the certifications marked with an *.

Sources: 1. National Instruments (NI) 52–109, Certification of Disclosure in Issuers' Annual and Interim Filings; 52–110, Audit Committees; 58–101, Disclosure of Corporate Governance Practices; 58–201, Effective Corporate Governance, www.osc.gov.on.ca, Accessed: August 14, 2009. 2. McCallum, Leslie, "Canada's New Rule on Internal Control Certifications Effective for December 2008 Year-Ends," *Mondaq Business Briefing*, September 7, 2008, www.mondaq.com, Accessed: December 22, 2008.

Table 10-4	Organizational Types with Possible Cultural Norms
Organizational Type with Description	**Possible Example with Cultural Norm**
Entrepreneurial structure: Small, owner-operated or owner-managed, typified by informal decision making and unstructured processes.	Example: Small manufacturing company producing specialized products. Cultural norm: Customer is king, and production schedules will be rapidly modified to meet customer needs.
Bureaucracy: Multiple levels of management working in a slowly changing environment, providing relatively standard products or services. May be divisionalized (with many locations and a central headquarters), or professional (relying upon technical expertise with strong department heads and a weak head office).	Example: Financial institution such as a bank. Cultural norm: Codified procedures must always be followed. Exceptions require approval and must be documented.
Adhocracy: Teams of multidisciplinary individuals work on specific projects or assignments and are expected to react rapidly to changing needs. Teams are broken up and reformed for specific assignments.	Example: Consulting or public accounting firm. Cultural norm: Deadlines must be met, and employees will work the necessary hours to produce high-quality work by the specified time.

For example, the CEO may regularly play golf with selected customers and suppliers, attend industry workshops, have industry data sheets provided, and review the operational reports of the organization in formal and informal settings. Such a CEO should be well placed to respond to proposals for new products or IT.

Organizational culture also includes business ethics, work ethics, and written and unwritten business practices. Senior executives, who clearly separate personal costs from business costs, encourage differences in opinion, and use business mistakes as valuable business lessons, use their own actions to encourage employees to come forward with unethical business practices. A codified set of business ethics and code of conduct help promote an honest, ethical environment where employees can participate and feel valued. If, on the other hand, management berates employees for mistakes, making them feel small and stupid, then employees will be indirectly encouraged to not ask questions and may feel that they are entitled to unauthorized benefits that come their way, such as gifts from customers or suppliers—opening the way to large-scale bribery and theft.

A codified, ethical culture where management behaves in alignment with the code supports healthy corporate governance. If the code of conduct is simply words, unsupported by management actions, then the entire organization could be prone to unethical business practices.

ENTERPRISE RISK MANAGEMENT AND RISK MANAGEMENT FRAMEWORKS Recall that a **risk** is a description of what could go wrong. In an organizational context, this means risks are events that could prevent the organization from achieving its objectives. Note that this includes a description of the event, its likelihood, timing, and what could happen—either positive or negative consequences. Risk can be managed formally or informally, for part or all of an organization. An organization that has enterprise risk management (ERM) has embodied risk management into its culture, such that every employee is aware of and addresses risk management. With ERM, each business activity has been given the mandate, training, and support to manage risks using a coordinated and integrated approach that helps to inform senior management's actions. This requires the role of a centralized risk management coordinator (perhaps even a chief risk officer) or risk management committee. Risks, like internal controls, should be "everyone's business." We define **enterprise risk management** as an organizational process that assists the organization in providing reasonable

Risk—description of what could go wrong. In an organizational context, this means risks are events that could prevent the organization from achieving its objectives. A risk description includes a description of the event, its likelihood, timing, and what could happen—either positive or negative consequences.

Enterprise risk management (ERM)—an organizational process that assists the organization in providing reasonable assurance of achieving its objectives. ERM is applied strategically and across the organization, a process designed to identify and manage potential risks that may affect the organization within the organization's risk appetite.

audit challenge 10-1
Five Risks in One Day!

Have you ever wondered how difficult it is to identify and address the risks that might affect a business? Let us look at only five of the risks that were identified in the *Toronto Star* Business section on Wednesday April 2, 2008.

First is a huge financial risk caused by a pension fund shortfall. With hundreds of employees per year deciding to retire, the organization is committed to paying pensions based upon recent salaries. It is the organization's responsibility to make sure that sufficient funds are present in the fund to meet pension obligations. If not, shortfalls must be funded within five years (unless federal regulations change). Stock market upheavals can drastically affect the value of the pension fund. The organization affected was the Ontario Teachers' Pension Plan.

Next, look at British Airways PLC, which had to cancel over 50 flights per day at the new Terminal 5 in Heathrow, London, requiring the hiring of a subcontractor (FedEx) to sort and ship stranded luggage. The cause was IT failure. Many organizations have experienced operational slowdowns or failures when software and hardware failed to perform to expectations.

Third, tightening credit is affecting sales of big-ticket items. American automobile makers, highlighted on this day in the Business section, had slower sales than they expected, resulting in increased inventories and potential layoffs. Any business in the manufacturing sector needs to keep a careful eye on sales, linking to the supply chain and reducing purchases as sales drop (or vice versa if sales increase).

An important fourth item is quality of raw materials. Toxic raw materials can result in toxic final products, as evidenced by the deaths of thousand of beloved cats and dogs in 2007. Lawsuits continued in 2008, while one of the affected companies, Menu Foods, struggled to survive.

Finally, new standards can either support or destroy product lines. In April 2008, Microsoft succeeded in having one of its document standards, Office Open XML, established as an international XML standard. This will mean that other software developers, using other document standards, may no longer be viable.

CRITICAL THINKING QUESTIONS

1. For each of the five risks identified, list an action that the organization could have taken to identify the risk prior to its actual occurrence.
2. Using the information that you have learned so far (see Chapter 9), identify five other internal risks that could occur.
3. For each of the risks that you identified in (2) above, list an action that the organization could have taken to identify the risk prior to its actual occurrence.

Sources: 1. Alloway, Tracy, "20,000 bags delayed, FedEx to the rescue," *Toronto Star*, April 9, 2008, p. B1, B8. 2. Daw, James, "Teachers' tussles with shortfall," *Toronto Star*, April 9, 2008, p. B1, B4. 3. Flavell, Dana, "Menu Foods settling pet food suits," *Toronto Star*, April 9, 2008, p. B3. 4. Reuters News Agency, "Microsoft wins fight for global standard," *Toronto Star*, April 9, 2008, p. B5. 5. Van Alphen, Tony, "Big Three's share of sales hits all-time low," *Toronto Star*, April 9, 2008, p. B1, B4.

assurance of achieving its objectives. ERM is applied strategically and across the organization: a process designed to identify and manage potential risks that may affect the organization within the organization's risk appetite.

Effective corporate governance can encourage a corporate culture that encourages risk awareness, so that a clear response to the risk can be decided, rather than waiting until a disaster such as a virus infection, defective product recall, or union strike decimates the business. Audit Challenge 10-1 illustrates examples of the many different types of risks that can be encountered in a business.

A **risk management framework** describes the tasks required for effective enterprise risk management. Such frameworks can be geared to particular industries or be applied more broadly. Corporate governance includes the approval of the risk management framework, with review of key tasks such as identification and assessment of risks and actions to be taken.

Risk management framework—describes the tasks required for effective enterprise risk management.

Sources of risk management frameworks include the following:

- Association of Insurance and Risk Managers (AIRMIC, see **www.airmic.com**).
- Alarm, the public risk management association (see **www.alarm-uk.org**).
- Canadian Institute of Chartered Accountants (see **www.cica.ca**).
- Committee of Sponsoring Organizations of the Treadway Commission (COSO, see **www.coso.org**).
- The Risk Management Association (RMA, see **www.rmahq.org/RMA**).
- Standards Australia (AS/NZ 4360:2004, Risk Management; see **www.standards.org.au/cat.asp?catid=41&contentid=197&News=1**).

Standard and Poor's (S&P's) ERM Review?

As if there were not enough specific business practices forced upon an organization, there is now the potential for an ERM review by Standard and Poor's, a rating agency. An organization's ERM capabilities in five categories (culture, controls, emerging issues, risk and capital modelling, and strategic risk management) will be summarized to provide an overall classification ranging from Excellent to Weak. It is possible that low ratings could result in an increase in an organization's borrowing costs.

What can an organization do to prepare for a review by its auditors or by S&P? It can adopt a recognized ERM framework, document its governance processes, and document how it actually conducts its enterprise risk management processes.

Sources: 1. "Criteria: Summary of Standard & Poor's Enterprise Risk Management Evaluation Process for Insurers (Criteria 11-26-2007)," www2.standardandpoors.com/portal/site/sp/en/us/page.article/2,1,6,4,1148449517749.html, Accessed: December 23, 2008. 2. Schanfield, Arnold and Dan Helming, "12 top ERM implementation challenges," *Internal Auditor*, December 2008, p. 41–44.

Prior to selecting a risk management framework, it is important that the organization decide how it will define risk, how its corporate governance team will be involved in the risk management process, and how criteria for selecting such a framework will be determined. The organization may require specialist assistance to select a suitable risk management framework, as well as training or consulting assistance for the implementation process.

Table 10-5 lists the components of the COSO Enterprise Risk Management— Integrated Framework, describes the component, and indicates how the board of directors and senior management can help to ensure effective implementation of the risk framework. The final column lists an audit technique that the auditor could use to assess the quality of corporate governance of the ERM process. The table illustrates that the board is required to have more than a simple review and approval process— it is expected to evaluate management's recommendations and analyses by using its own expertise to add to the risk management process.

Auditor Evaluation of Corporate Governance

As explained in Chapter 9, corporate governance is the crucial component of the control environment, as governance practices help to create the tone and organizational culture within an organization. Figure 10-1 on page 322 illustrates that the corporate governance structure follows from the business mission, vision, and the strategies for achieving the mission and vision. The audit of the overall effectiveness of corporate governance needs to consider the organizational structure and maturity of the organization. (For example, does the organization effectively deal with change?) Management attitudes and the ethical environment of the organization are important factors that the auditor needs to document.

An effective management and board of directors will work together to develop and evolve the strategies needed to run the business. These will include strategies in the areas of risk management (discussed in the previous section), information systems, human resources, operations, and others. Using the ERM process as a model, each strategy would have a development phase, assessment phase, and implementation phase. The implementation phase would include controls to ensure that the strategies are implemented, information and communication to promote awareness and communication, and monitoring for ongoing evaluation and adjustment. Effective governance will also look at the alignment of each of the strategies with the overall business mission and purpose, to help prevent the organization working at cross purposes (for example, a production strategy that has poor quality control or uses ineffective IT systems).

Table 10-5	Auditing Governance of Enterprise Risk Management		
COSO Enterprise Risk Management—Integrated Framework Component and Example	**Examples of Effective Corporate Governance of the Component**	**Audit Techniques to Audit the Component's Corporate Governance**
Internal environment: Risk culture, encompassing attitudes and behaviours; includes management philosophy and risk tolerance, ethical values, and integrity	• Mandatory training for board members on the concepts of enterprise risk management. • Board approval of ERM framework and code of ethics.	• Inspect board ERM training program. • Inspect board minutes and supporting documents justifying selection of ERM framework. • Inspect code of ethics.
Objective setting: Setting of risk tolerance objectives in alignment with organizational mission, vision, and strategy	• Board evaluation and approval of agreed risk terminology and • of management's recommended risk tolerances.	• Inspect board minutes and supporting documents justifying risk tolerance objectives. • Inquire of board members and management regarding the process for setting risk tolerances.
Event identification: Both internal and external events that could affect the ability to achieve the organization's objectives should be included, considering separately those that are risks and opportunities, with the latter directed toward the strategic planning process.	• Management clearly provides a strategy for identifying risks. • Board approves management's strategy and provides feedback.	• Compare the organization's identified risks to risks identified by the auditor during the client business risk assessment phase of the financial statement audit, looking for gaps. • Inspect board minutes and supporting documents where approval of risk assessment strategy is provided.
Risk assessment: Methodically consider the potential impact and likelihood of risk events.	• Board approves risk assessment methodology and • re-evaluates tolerances in light of the summarized risk evaluations.	• Inspect risk assessment documentation. • Inspect board minutes approving risk methodology and risk tolerances.
Risk response: Based upon the risk tolerance objectives, select one of four approaches for dealing with the risk: 1. Acceptance: Do nothing. 2. Avoidance: Eliminate the activity that causes the risk. 3. Mitigation: Reduce the effects of the risks by taking appropriate action. 4. Transference: Outsource, transfer, or share the risk using methods such as insurance or transfer of business processes.	• Board evaluates management's recommendations for risk responses. • Compare risk responses to recommendations of external or internal auditors or other specialized reports.	• Inspect documents recommending risk response activities. • Inspect board minutes of approval. • Inspect reports of specialists recommending specific courses of action with respect to risk responses.
Control activities: Policies and practices for ensuring that the identified risk responses are actually completed.	• Evaluate and approve management's plan for ERM control activities.	• Document the control activities, evaluate design effectiveness, and conduct tests of ERM control activities where reliance will be placed on the controls.
Information and communication: Information is gathered and communicated about the risk management process throughout all levels of the organization.	• Inquire of management and request documentation to support information and communication methods; evaluate adequacy.	• Obtain copies of and inspect regular communications.
Monitoring: ERM is monitored, feedback provided, and changes to the process made as needed.	• Evaluate management recommendations for change to ERM process.	• Inspect board minutes with respect to process and approval of change to ERM process.

Sources: 1. Committee of Sponsoring Organizations of the Treadway Commission, 2004, "Enterprise Risk Management—Integrated Framework, Executive Summary," www.coso.org/ERM-IntegratedFramework.htm, Accessed: December 23, 2008. 2. Schanfield, Arnold and Dan Helming, "12 top ERM implementation challenges," *Internal Auditor*, December 2008, p. 41–44.

The public accountant's goal in auditing corporate governance includes developing the client risk profile and effectively planning and conducting the audit. (Refer to the inside front cover of this text.) Effective corporate governance may reduce client business risk, as discussed in Chapter 5, and result in a lower assessed control risk, as explained in Chapter 9.

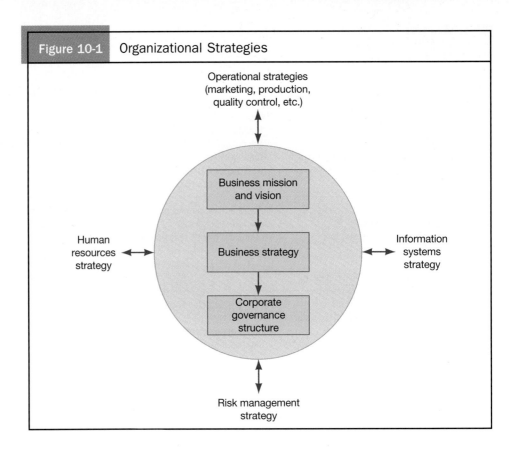

Figure 10-1   Organizational Strategies

Operational strategies (marketing, production, quality control, etc.)

Business mission and vision

Business strategy

Corporate governance structure

Human resources strategy

Information systems strategy

Risk management strategy

Using the terminology introduced in Figure 9-2, Audit of Internal Controls During a Financial Statement Audit, on page 286, the auditor will first obtain an understanding of the process of corporate governance. Techniques used (see also Table 10-5, the rightmost column) include review of board minutes, discussion with management, inspection of reports submitted to the board and to management, inspection of prior working paper files (including management letters and the organization's response thereto), inquiry of management and the board, and observation during interviews.

Checklists, flowcharts, and walk-throughs of implementation controls and reporting lines will be used to understand the components of governance.

To consider design and operating effectiveness with respect to corporate governance, the auditor will consider questions such as the following:

- Is there sufficient expertise on the board and on the management team to address weaknesses in organizational strategies? Where weaknesses exist, is external expertise engaged to assist the organization?
- Do implementations of the strategies effectively consider key components of the strategy? For example, have management and other employees been trained in risk management methods?
- Does management regularly review monitoring reports and take appropriate remedial action?
- Do the board and its committees take an active role in running the company, not simply rubber-stamp management's activities?
- Have management and the board dealt effectively with past crises?
- Do human resource policies and other resourcing policies provide sufficient resources to implement strategies?
- Does the audit committee meet with the auditors, both external and internal, and support them in their activities? Can the external or internal auditors go to the audit committee with concerns about the company's operations knowing they will be heard?

By understanding how the board and its committees (especially the audit committee) work, the auditor will be able to assess how active an oversight role should be taken with respect to the entity's accounting and financial reporting policies and practices. Answers to these questions will enable the audit team to consider whether corporate governance strategies provide a supportive backbone to the control environment at the organization. Professional judgment and involvement of the senior members of the audit team would be required to reach a general conclusion about the overall quality of corporate governance.

IT Governance and the Audit of General Information Systems Controls

As shown in Figure 10-1, IT governance needs to be considered in terms of the organization's overall mission, vision, and business strategy. After discussing IT governance, we will look at the relationship between general information systems controls and the financial statement audit planning process.

IT Governance

Just as corporate governance has received increased attention, including the development of current and more specific standards, so has IT governance. In 2007, ISACA introduced a new certification, Certified in the Governance of Enterprise information technology (CGEIT), which emphasizes the importance of this process. **IT governance** is defined as the policies, practices, and procedures that help IT resources add value while considering costs and benefits. Auditing in Action 10-1 looks at one aspect of information systems governance, security policies.

> **IT governance**—the policies, practices, and procedures that help IT resources add value while considering costs and benefits.

In this section we look both at what IT governance is and what it is not. IT governance is more than security, since it encompasses the entire organization where IT and business components work together, and involves crucial concepts such as systems development life cycle management. Accomplishing IT governance means that responsible management needs to have the authority and methodologies to accomplish the organization's IT goals. We also explore the nature of value realization and value management.

Security is only one of many policy areas that are included in information systems. Other areas include disaster recovery planning (discussed in Chapter 7), systems acquisition and maintenance policies, and organizational structure.

In addition to adding value, the goal of IT governance is to help prevent disastrous failures, such as information systems implementations that make transaction processing cumbersome or too costly. IT governance rests within a coherent information systems strategy that is developed and aligned with the organizational strategy and culture, and updated as necessary.

IT governance is a crucial subset of corporate governance. Similar to the assessment of overall corporate governance, evaluation of IT governance starts with the cultural and operating environment of the management information systems (MIS) functional areas. MIS should be viewed as a partner within the business rather than an adversary or servant. **IT dependence** should be avoided. Such dependence occurs when there is a disconnection between the business strategy and the MIS operations, exhibited when senior management, such as other executives and the board, abdicate supervision of IT. This tends to result in the reliance upon a small group of individuals within the organization for MIS needs, requirements, or operations. Instead, the CIO (chief information officer) should be a participant in executive meetings, with feedback, decision making, and information flowing among members of the executive team and other parts of the organization. There should be an absence of political games with respect to IT and other resources within the organization. For example, a history of failed, over-budget, or problematic information

> **IT dependence**—a disconnection between the business strategy and the MIS operations.

Auditing Security Policies

It seems that wherever you look, there are security breaches or attempted attacks on private data involving hundreds of thousands of individuals. In early 2007, Talvest Mutual Funds (owned by the Canadian Imperial Bank of Commerce) announced that a file with over 470,000 customer account details had been lost. In March 2008, a Trojan horse program called Sinowal was credited with tracking over more than 300,000 online bank account details over a period of three years, and in July 2008 WestJet airlines mysteriously disabled credit card check-ins at Canadian airports as a security measure. Other security measures include banning social websites, such as Facebook, from local area network access.

When considering an organization's security policy, the auditor will look at several characteristics:

(1) Is the policy comprehensive? For example, does it consider regulatory requirements (such as privacy laws), security threats that are linked to the enterprise's risk assessments and all of the different types of information systems in use at the organization?

(2) Is the policy current? In addition to new technologies and software, the organization needs to update the policy for changes in laws and regulations, consider new threats (such as new viruses), and update its software (perhaps due to updates in data encryption practices).

(3) Has the policy been communicated? Using the COSO framework, information and communication means that employees have been trained, the policy has been implemented, and this communication is part of controls and monitoring.

(4) Is it compulsory? Practices that are optional likely will not be in use. Controls and business practices should help make the policy a routine part of organizational life.

(5) Is it realistic? The security policy should have a broad set of principles that can readily be converted into controls and actions that can be implemented by the systems and people of the organization.

The internal or external auditor charged with evaluation of the security policy will look at each of the above characteristics and design tests that will help examine them.

Sources: 1. Chandra, Ishwar, "The five C's of IT policy," *Internal Auditor*, December 2008, p. 23–24. 2. Chung, Andrew, "University bans Facebook access," *Toronto Star*, September 20, 2008, p. A4. 3. Jackson, Brian, "Theories abound about data breach at Canadian airport," www.itbusiness.ca, Accessed: October 20, 2008. 3. Keiser, Gregg, "Terrible Trojan steals 500,000 bank account, credit card logins," www.itbusiness.ca, Accessed: March 11, 2008. 4. Mavin, Duncan, "Security breach at CIBC," *National Post*, www.canada.com, Accessed: July 7, 2007.

---

systems implementations could be an indication of inadequate management of issues such as data ownership and succession planning associated with IT.

Next, we look at the accountability, authority, and decision methodologies used with respect to IT. Appropriate IT governance is linked to enterprise risk management methods and a sound control environment. The use of an information systems steering committee with executive membership helps guide and oversee MIS processes. Control and audit are considered throughout the development, operations, and maintenance of systems. For example, for e-commerce systems or business functions that make extensive use of other online systems, reconciliation, audit, and testing capabilities should be built into systems, rather than added on after development is complete.

Third, a value realization and delivery framework helps the MIS department to accomplish both the demand and supply side of operations. As each system is considered and evaluated, there should be continuous assessment for alignment with the business needs and strategies. Purchasing or implementing systems simply because they are the "newest toy on the block" results in fragmented, inefficient processing. However, environmental scanning with respect to new technologies adopted or available can help the organization identify obsolescence or other factors that could require IT changes.

Finally, to enable value realization, value management methodologies should be in place. Examination and assessment of MIS throughout the systems life cycle can be facilitated by internal audit or by rotational testing by the external auditors. Operational objectives such as effectiveness, efficiency, and economy are used. The organization could develop or purchase metrics to monitor and control the value assessment process.

Impact of General Information Systems Controls on the Audit

In the previous chapter, Table 9-3 (page 279) provided sample objectives of and examples for three general control categories: (1) organization and management controls, (2) systems acquisition, development, and maintenance controls, and (3) operations and information systems support. We will now look at some common issues in each of these three control categories, before looking at the impact of information systems on the eight-phase audit process.

ORGANIZATION AND MANAGEMENT CONTROLS The method of organizing and managing the organization will vary based upon factors such as overall size, the functions that are outsourced, and whether the organization has packaged off-the-shelf programs or customized software. The nature and organization of the hardware technology supporting the organization are also a factor: for example, mainframe versus local area networks, methods of data communications, and presence of web-based purchasing or sales networks.

In this category, auditors will consider segregation of duties (discussed in Chapter 5), and the quality of documented policies and procedures affecting topics such as data ownership, data management, software ownership, privacy, and code of conduct with respect to technology. The auditor will also consider the level of technical expertise present at the organization. Specialized jobs could include database management, operating systems software support, operations job control specialists, security officers, privacy officers, business continuity coordinators, web masters, and specialized expertise in a variety of programs or programming languages.

A key question to ask is, "which personnel are super-users?" Super-users are individuals who, because of their expertise and function, have access to supervisory software or the ability to circumvent normal controls due to their expertise. For example, an operating systems software specialist works at the level of the operating system, changing security features, utility software, and the way that languages are processed by the systems. Such a person can circumvent security software. Another typical super-user is the person or team that manages security, passwords, and user access. Such individuals could set up a new user account under an assumed name that gives them access to all systems, with the potential to change their own wage rate or set up fictitious customers or suppliers. Super-users are also common in small businesses with limited segregation of duties (discussed further in Chapter 22).

Management needs to be aware of the risks associated with super-users so that effective compensating controls can be established (such as careful review of payroll wage rates and customer credit limits). The auditor aware of such risks will increase the control risks associated with affected assertions and look for and test such compensating controls (if they are to be relied upon). Take a look at Audit Challenge 10-2 on the next page, which overviews Hillsburg Hardware's general controls. Were there any super-users for either the old or current configurations?

SYSTEMS, ACQUISITION, DEVELOPMENT, AND MAINTENANCE CONTROLS Organizations employ a wide variety of software serving a broad range of purposes, such as providing the user interface, providing security, managing hardware and software, communicating information, and recording and processing transactions. Here, we focus on the process used to obtain software that serves the organization's needs.

Information Technology Control Guidelines[2] breaks down the software acquisition process into three general categories:

- In-house development (employees within the entity determine user requirements and build the software using one of many alternative development approaches)

---

[2] *Information Technology Control Guidelines*, 3rd Edition, 1998, published by the Canadian Institute of Chartered Accountants.

Hillsburg Hardware Limited in Transition

Back in 1990, when Hillsburg Hardware Limited had only 50 customers, the industry standard of a local area network with a single central server was more than adequate. All software consisted of standard packaged software. There were no onsite data processing personnel, and operating functions were shared among accounting and general staff. The receptionist was responsible for initiating backup before she left in the evening and the general manager kept a copy offsite at his home. The controller was responsible for maintaining password security profiles that controlled access rights. General controls were as follows:

- *Organization and management controls* Management had a policy of establishing segregation of duties as much as possible with the existing personnel. Functions considered incompatible with respect to financial systems were separated.
- *Systems acquisition, development, and maintenance controls* All software used was packaged software. The software was used in its original form (not modified). Software was obtained only in object code (machine language), so it could not be modified by Hillsburg Hardware personnel.
- *Operations and information systems support* Company offices were open from 8:00 a.m. to 5:00 p.m. The network was left up and running 24 hours per day. A maintenance contract was kept with a major support organization to provide onsite support in the event of equipment failure. Staff were initially trained in the software packages used and had software manuals to refer to in the event of queries. The controller prepared a set of instructions (about three pages) to be used in the event that a major disaster destroyed the building and the local area network. These instructions were intended to allow Hillsburg Hardware Limited personnel to resume operations at a local area network owned by their support organization for a fee of $500 per hour.

Two years ago, Hillsburg finally updated its aging collection of systems to an integrated database management system running on a mid-range minicomputer as the main server. Smaller servers were introduced to host email and office management products (such as word processing and spreadsheets). More sophisticated packaged accounting software was acquired, with support provided by the software supplier. Data in the databases can be exported into spreadsheet files so that staff can prepare their own reports if needed.

The company now has over 200 workstations (a combination of microcomputers and specialized cash registers) updating information and accessing the storage systems attached to the minicomputer, and three full-time information systems personnel. The information systems manager works on and supervises a range of functions, such as technical support for staff and clients and updating the website. The website was custom developed, but maintenance is handled internally. Passwords are maintained by the controller's executive assistant.

To maintain security, data from the ONHAND (Online Niche-Hardware Availability Notification Database) customer database is ported across to a group of stand-alone high-end microcomputers every night so that customers can inquire about the availability of products and the status of their orders via the internet. internet access by customers is handled via an ISP (internet Service Provider). Hillsburg decided that there would be no direct data communications access from the minicomputer and from staff computers—a small group of machines is available for staff to check email. This machine configuration is also used for electronic data interchange transactions between Hillsburg and 10 key suppliers. Transactions are copied to and from the minicomputer systems three times per day.

- *Current organization and management controls* There has been no change in policy. Duties are segregated as much as practical. Information systems support personnel do not have access to accounting data. A database administrator, who reports to the controller, is responsible for maintaining the data dictionary.
- *Current systems acquisition, development, and maintenance controls* Accounting software is still packaged software, maintained externally. Information systems personnel cannot change the accounting software. The website and the electronic data interchange software are maintained internally. Changes to these two pieces of software must be approved jointly by the chief financial officer and the vice-president, operations.
- *Current operations and information systems support* All systems have current anti-virus software, and firewalls are in place for the group of internet-accessible machines. Company offices are now open from 7:00 a.m. to 6:00 p.m. All systems are left up and running 24 hours a day. There is a more comprehensive backup and disaster recovery plan. Selected staff walk through this plan as a test every six months to ensure that systems changes have been accounted for. There are maintenance plans for all purchased hardware and software.

CRITICAL THINKING QUESTIONS

1. Describe IT governance controls that should be in place at Hillsburg Hardware Limited. State the purpose of each control that you describe.
2. List general controls present for the current systems at Hillsburg Hardware Limited for each general control category. For each control, state the risk that the control mitigates and how the auditor would test the control.
3. Identify apparent or potential control weaknesses for the current systems at Hillsburg Hardware Limited. What risks are associated with these weaknesses? What compensating controls would you look for?

- Systems acquisition (software is acquired from an outside vendor and implemented as is, or modified and implemented)
- Turnkey software development (custom software development is contracted to an outside party)

Where custom program development is routinely undertaken, formal methodologies with appropriate checkpoints should exist, as should a method of evaluating systems once they have been implemented. Policies to monitor ongoing program changes should also exist. When software systems are purchased, management should ensure that the software is consistent with organizational objectives. The type of process used will affect the nature of controls that need to be examined by the auditor.

Again, using the terminology of *Information Technology Control Guidelines*, the acquisition process is broken down into five phases:

1. *Investigation.* In this first phase, it is determined whether the proposed system should actually be obtained.
2. *Requirements analysis and initial design.* Then, it is necessary to identify and document the overall functionality and purpose of the proposed system.
3. *Development (or acquisition) and system testing.* Specific functionality of the new system is identified and developed/acquired and tested.
4. *Conversion, implementation, and post-implementation review.* Data are converted from the old to the new system, live running of the system commences, and the system is evaluated to determine whether it satisfies the entity's needs.
5. *Ongoing maintenance.* Changes to the system are made as necessary.

For the evidence-gathering process, as part of the documentation of knowledge of business, the auditor will determine what types of systems are in place, paying particular attention to those of financial or operational significance. The auditor will then make inquiries regarding the information systems change process: Are information systems developed, modified, or acquired, and have there been any changes in the current year? Where changes have taken place, the auditor may be required to conduct a conversion audit (discussed in Chapter 18), as well as assess changes to controls due to the new or modified systems.

The complexity of the software development or acquisition process needs to be determined to assess inherent risks. An overview of the process would be obtained during the preparation of the knowledge of business for the client. Controls over the acquisition or development process are part of the control environment and general information systems controls. Accordingly, such controls affect assessments of control risk and the ability to conduct tests associated with specific audit objectives at the assertion level (discussed in the final section of this chapter). Poor controls over program quality could mean that the auditor is unable to rely upon automated or combined controls for the affected transaction cycles.

Acquisition controls need to be documented and, should reliance be placed on software programs during the audit, they would need to be tested, as discussed in Chapter 9. Table 10-6 on the next page provides examples of potential controls for each phase of the acquisition process, with a suggested audit technique to test the control, should the auditor choose to rely upon it.

OPERATIONS AND INFORMATION SYSTEMS SUPPORT As with other types of general controls, the level of complexity needed to manage operations and support of systems depends upon the complexity of systems in use. Hardware configuration, types of operating systems, and whether support is handled in-house or outsourced affect the types of controls in place at the organization.

Hardware configuration As part of the knowledge of business, the auditor would determine the type of equipment in use by the entity, where it was located, how it was interconnected, and whether data communications or internet/intranet access was

Table 10-6   Sample Acquisition Controls with Suggested Audit Tests

Acquisition Process Phase	Sample Control	Suggested Audit Tests
Investigation	Formal proposals are prepared for all new systems, with cost-benefits prepared, and a structured process followed (e.g., consultation of affected users, careful consideration of alternatives).	• Review structured process used for investigation for completeness and reasonableness. • Examine cost-benefit for thoroughness and reasonableness.
Requirements analysis and initial design	Functional requirements are reviewed and approved.	• Consider appropriateness and competence of individuals assigned the task of functional requirements review. • Examine evidence of approval of functional requirements.
Development [or acquisition] and system testing	Testing plans are prepared, in alignment with functional requirements and known potential problem areas.	• Examine testing plans for reasonableness and completeness. • Examine results of testing and process used to clear problems and errors found.
Conversion, implementation, and post-implementation review	A thorough data conversion plan is prepared, considering all data types, with sufficient detail to provide for completeness, occurrence, and accuracy of data conversion.	• Review testing plans for thoroughness. • Examine and reperform reconciliations associated with data conversions of key data elements (such as general ledger account balances).
Ongoing maintenance	All program maintenance changes should be approved, documented, and tested prior to implementation.	• Examine processes used for "emergency" changes that brought systems down. • Examine evidence of approval for program changes, on a test basis.

occurring. This helps determine the complexity and scope of further controls that need to be documented and evaluated.

The simpler hardware structures are centralized (where all processing is done from a single central system, requiring that users be logged on to that system to conduct business activity) and decentralized systems (where each location of a multiple location system has stand-alone, independent processing). Such pure systems exist in smaller businesses, but are otherwise rare. For centralized systems, the auditor must document controls primarily at that one location, while for decentralized systems, multi-location issues such as commonality of software need to be considered.

Most larger systems now are distributed systems, where computing or files are shared among users and computing facilities. For example, a local area network is a distributed system, since computing can be accomplished at the individual computer level or the common file server can be used. An organization with a head office computer and branch location computing systems that transmit information to the head office is using a distributed system. Financial institutions' automated teller machines and point-of-sale terminals can also be components of distributed systems. In such systems, controls over each category of software and hardware need to be documented. Frequently, specialist assistance will be required to conduct the control documentation and evaluation process.

Type of operating system Local machines such as personal computing devices have single-user operating systems. Once a user is part of a local area network, network operating systems are used. Larger machines such as minicomputers and mainframes have complex operating systems designed to manage hundreds and even thousands of input devices, multiple programs running simultaneously, as well as data communications. Database management systems or ERP systems, discussed in the next section, add complexity. Each layer normally requires its own security system, with integration into an overall security management process. Specialist auditor assistance will normally be required to assess multi-user systems.

Table 10-7	Impact of Information Systems on Financial Statement Audit Phases

Audit Phase	Example of Impact of Automation on Audit Process
Risk Assessment	
1. Preplanning	• Identify availability of specialist expertise in the audit staff.
2. Client risk profile	• Understand information systems hardware and software infrastructure. • Document and assess IT governance processes.
3. Plan the audit	• Document and assess IT control environment including IT general controls and disaster recovery plans. • Test general controls where reliance is intended. • Document and assess key automated and combined application controls; consider each application separately to ensure adequate controls, such as segregation of duties, are in place, using passwords or other techniques.
Risk Response	
4. Design further audit procedures	• Design audit programs, considering the use of computer-assisted audit techniques and the ability to access data in client files (discussed further in Chapters 13 and 14).
5. Tests of control	• Test automated and combined application controls where reliance is intended. • Consider use of computer-assisted audit techniques for tests of controls (such as the use of test data and integrated test facilities).
6. Substantive tests	• Conduct substantive or dual-purpose tests by means of direct access to client data files (consider the use of spreadsheet software, generalized audit software, or specialized report writers).
7. Ongoing evaluation, quality control, and final evidence gathering	• Ongoing evaluation should incorporate team meetings and recommendations from IT specialists assigned to the engagement.
Reporting	
8. Complete quality control and issue auditor's report	• Consider independent information systems specialist review for high-risk engagements.

Internal versus outsourced support Most organizations using local machines or small- to medium-sized local area networks outsource their hardware and software support. As organizations get larger, they handle their own hardware and software support (by means of a help desk function or as part of the information systems support function) or adopt a hybrid model. In the hybrid model, some functions are outsourced (perhaps queries regarding packaged software), while others (such as office management software) may be handled in house. The auditor will need to consider security and access rights given to support personnel in order to determine whether or not they are super-users. If these personnel have the ability to make program changes, then the auditor would need to examine the program maintenance process and consider whether financial systems are affected.

An important issue addressed during the audit of general controls is information systems access. Organizational controls set policies and development controls address access to program changes, while operational controls include access rights given to individual users and super-users. Access controls in an automated system are used to enforce segregation of duties, a crucial aspect of both the control environment and individual functional system controls. If the auditor intends to rely upon segregation of duties in an automated environment, then access rights controls will need to be documented and tested.

This discussion is a highly summarized view of general information systems controls. You will learn more about such controls if you take a course on information systems auditing, or you could consult an information systems auditing text or a journal such as the *Information Systems Audit and Control Journal*.

IMPACT OF INFORMATION SYSTEMS ON THE EIGHT-PHASE AUDIT PROCESS Every audit that you encounter will likely have heavily automated systems, with some advanced issues, such as data communications, web-based purchasing, in-house custom development, or enterprise-wide processing (also called enterprise resource processing). Our last section in this chapter examines a selection of advanced computing issues, overviewing the impact on the audit. Here, we look at the pervasive effect that computing and information systems have upon the audit process. Table 10-7 on the previous page lists the audit phases, with examples of the impact of automation on the audit process.

The main points from Table 10-7 are the reliance on and integration of findings from information systems audit specialists for IT governance, general controls, and methods of testing for automated or combined information systems controls. Specialists could also be used to develop or run computer-assisted audit techniques.

concept check

C10-4 Provide two examples of effective IT governance practices.

C10-5 List the three categories of general controls. For each category, provide an example of an audit step that could be conducted.

C10-6 List two tasks that information systems audit specialists could complete during the financial statement audit.

Advanced Information Systems and the Audit Process

Along with the use of the internet, computing via wireless platforms and multi-user systems has become common. There is a big difference, however, between using these services as an individual user, and having basic business functions rely upon them. An organization is considered to have advanced information systems when its systems have one or more of the following characteristics:

1. Custom-designed operational or strategic information systems.
2. Use of data communications (including internet) and multiple locations.
3. Use of paperless systems such as EDI or EFT.
4. Use of database management systems.
5. Integrated computing, such as ERP systems

The existence of each of these characteristics affects the nature of information systems processing at the organization and thus also affects the audit process. Here we describe the characteristics, and the last section of the chapter describes the effects on internal controls.

Extent of Custom-Designed Operational and Strategic Information Systems

In the previous section, we listed the forms of software acquisition as being in-house development, acquisition from an outside vendor, and turnkey software development (where an outsider prepares custom software). Here, we compare custom software to standard packaged software. Figure 10-2 summarizes the advantages and disadvantages of these two types of software.

Increased use of customization can improve a business entity's ability to create a **strategic information system**—a system that provides competitive advantage or improved efficiency of operations. However, should strategic information systems fail or have errors, they increase costs and risks to the business. During the audit planning process, the auditor identifies the nature of such systems and the type of development process. In highly automated or integrated systems, auditors prefer to rely on the computer systems, since it is more efficient to test programmed controls than to conduct tests of details. Where the system development process is complex or error prone, the

Strategic information system—a system that provides competitive advantage or improved efficiency of operations.

Figure 10-2 — Advantages and Disadvantages of Custom Software and Packaged Software

	Custom Software	Packaged Software
Advantages	Tailored to meet company's exact needs.	Less costly than custom programming.
	The company conducts operations in its own often unique way.	Implementation can commence immediately after the package has been selected.
	Can more likely be used to gain strategic advantage than a software package.	Risk of system error and incorrect choice can be reduced by testing the software before purchase is made.
		Depending on the area, many packages are likely to be available.
		Annual maintenance costs are low.
		Usually comes with user and other operating documentation.
		In-house technical analysis and programming personnel are likely not needed.
DisAdvantages	Very costly to develop.	The package may not "fit" the way the company does business or may be less efficient than customized systems.
	Lengthy program development times are common, from several months to several years.	Package evaluation process is costly and time-consuming.
	Rigorous testing program required to ensure that systems are error-free.	In-house resources may be insufficient to resolve problems with system use or operations.
	Significant employee time is required for development, testing, and standard setting.	
	A methodical, iterative process that requires a high level of user and management involvement is needed to ensure greater likelihood of successful implementation.	

auditor may assess the risk of program errors occurring as high, leading to an increased assessment of inherent risk and control risk.

When systems are so strategic that their failure could affect the ability of the entity to continue as a going concern, the auditor takes a closer look at the disaster recovery planning process. The quality of recovery planning affects the going-concern assumption and potentially the assessment of client business risk, as discussed in Chapter 7. For example, if a bank's tellers and automated teller machines could not function for a lengthy period of time, banks would be unable to provide basic services. Similarly, grocery stores with point-of-sale terminals would be unable to sell goods when their systems were down.

Use of Data Communications (Including Internet) and Multiple Locations

Figure 10-3 shows a business with a head office, a branch office, and a website that is used by customers for ordering goods. Head office, at point (1), initiates data communications to connect with the branch, at point (2), using a **communications channel**—the medium used to transmit data from one location to another, for example, satellite, dedicated line, or high-speed digital line—at point (3). Customers use internet service providers to connect to the head office website, at point (4). The website is linked to the head office order-entry software. The following unauthorized activities could occur at the numbered points of Figure 10-3 on the next page:

1. A hacker could connect to the head office system, penetrating the systems and copying, altering, or removing data or programs.

Communications channel—the medium used to transmit data from one location to another, for example, satellite or dedicated line.

Figure 10-3 Potential Data Communications Risks

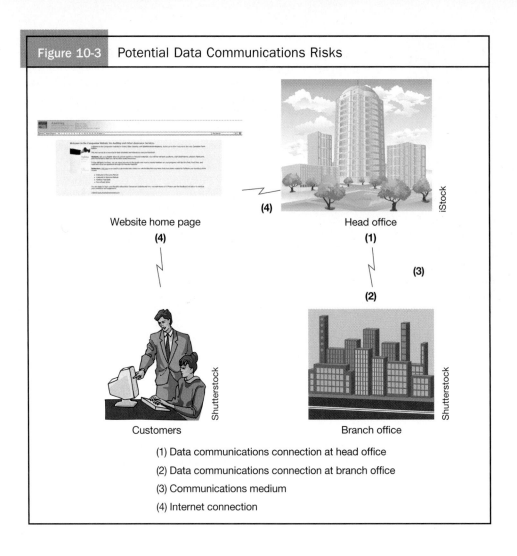

Website home page
(4)

Head office
(1)

(4)

iStock

(3)

(2)

Customers

Shutterstock

Branch office

Shutterstock

(1) Data communications connection at head office

(2) Data communications connection at branch office

(3) Communications medium

(4) Internet connection

2. A hacker could similarly penetrate the branch office system, copying, altering, or removing data or programs.
3. The line could be monitored or tapped and data copied.
4. Orders could be placed using fraudulent credit cards. A hacker could penetrate the website and alter it by placing inappropriate material on the site. A hacker could penetrate the website and gain access to the accounting systems, with the same result as 2. Viruses could be communicated and placed in the head office or branch office systems.

Table 10-8 summarizes the data communications risks and provides examples of control procedures that would be used to deal with each risk. When conducting the audit of entities that use data communications, the auditor needs to extend the assessment of general and application controls to the data communications process if reliance is to be placed upon the integrity of data that are transmitted. Table 10-8 shows that controls previously discussed, such as the use of passwords and physical segregation, can be used to effectively deal with data communications risks.

Related to data communications is the risk associated with multiple information processing locations. Table 10-9 describes examples of these risks and provides examples of control procedures that would reduce the risks.

As part of the knowledge of business, the auditor would have obtained system hardware and software configuration diagrams. These would inform the auditor about the extent of the complexity associated with data communications or multiple locations. General controls over data communications software and passwords are critical when assessing control risks associated with the accuracy and completeness of

Table 10-8   Examples of Data Communications Risks and Controls

Data Communications Risk	Examples of Control Procedures to Deal with the Risk
Inappropriate access to the accounting or other systems via data communications, with resulting loss of confidentiality or damage (see (1) and (2) on Figure 10-3).	Create multiple levels of passwords; change passwords regularly.
Data interccptcd or copied during data communications (see (3) on Figure 10-3).	Ensure that confidential data undergoes encryption (scrambling) during transmission.
Inappropriate access to the accounting or other systems via the internet, with resultant loss of confidentiality or damage (see (4) on Figure 10-3).	Physically segregate internet homepage equipment and software from other systems. Use firewalls (software or hardware that restricts access to and from internet sites).
Viruses could be placed into the head office or branch office systems, causing destruction of data or programs or disruption of service (see (4) on Figure 10-3).	Same as above. Also, acquire current anti-virus software, and keep the software current.

Table 10-9   Examples of Risks from Multiple Information Processing Locations and Control Procedures

Multiple Information Processing Locations Risk	Examples of Control Procedures to Reduce the Risk
Data processed in multiple locations could become inconsistent (e.g., inventory prices).	One location has primary responsibility for updating the information. Exception reports are printed and differences between locations followed up.
Programs could be inaccurate or unauthorized at one or more locations.	Head office controls all program changes. Branch offices are sent only the object code.
Branches could have unauthorized access to head office programs and data, or vice versa.	Clear responsibilities are assigned for data and program ownership and change rights. Adequate access control systems are used to enforce these rights (e.g., confidential passwords).
Some data sent from one location to another might not be received (i.e., incomplete or inaccurate transmissions).	Use control totals, record counts, and sequential numbering of transactions and follow up any missing or out-of-sequence data.

communicated data. The auditor must be assured that general controls are in place for the following:

- Accurate functioning of data communications software.
- Effective use of **encryption** (scrambling of data so that they cannot be read directly).
- Custody of and periodic changes to **encryption keys** (codes used to scramble and unscramble data).
- Effective functioning of **firewalls**, software or hardware that restricts access to and from internal sites.
- Effective controls over issuance, maintenance, and removal of passwords.

Once these technical general control areas have been assessed, the auditor would consider each application cycle.

Encryption—the process of scrambling data so that they cannot be read directly.

Encryption keys—codes used to scramble and unscramble data.

Firewall—software or hardware that restricts access to and from internal sites.

Use of Paperless Systems such as Electronic Data Interchange and Electronic Funds Transfer

Electronic data interchange (EDI)—an electronic method of sending documents between companies using a specified standard format.

Electronic data interchange (EDI) is an electronic method of sending documents between companies using a specified standard format. For example, a pharmaceutical manufacturer could mandate that its suppliers must accept standard purchase orders and submit invoices electronically. EDI is implemented either as a stand-alone system or integrated into the accounting systems. Stand-alone systems are used as receiving and sending stations: transactions are often printed out, reviewed, and rekeyed into the appropriate application system. In integrated systems, the EDI transaction is automatically translated into a format that can be read by the application system. EDI transactions can be sent and received directly between two organizations having direct data communications links or by means of a **value added network** (VAN) acting as an electronic mailbox and forwarding service. Thus, there are no longer paper documents that move between organizations but rather electronic documents in a standard format.

Value added network (VAN)—acts as an electronic mailbox and forwarding service.

Electronic funds transfer (EFT)—the transmission of cash equivalents using data communications.

Electronic funds transfer (EFT) (also referred to as electronic commerce or e-commerce), is the transmission of cash equivalents using data communications. Examples include the following:

- Use of a debit card by a consumer to authorize the transfer of funds from the consumer's account to a merchant's account.
- (As an extension of EDI) submission of appropriate transactions for the electronic payment of the invoice by the entity once the electronic invoice has been received and approved for payment.
- Automatic payment of employee payroll from the company's bank account to the employee's bank account.

As described in Chapter 9, both EDI and EFT systems may be difficult to test with substantive tests alone, perhaps due to the high volume of transactions or due to the absence of a paper trail. The auditor will prefer to, or may be required to, test assertions such as completeness or accuracy by relying upon the controls within the programs, using test data. These systems use software utilities or special-purpose programs to send and receive information. To rely on them, the auditor will need to understand, document, and evaluate the design effectiveness of these programs, which may require specialist assistance.

Use of Database Management Systems

A database system consists of two parts:

Database—the collection of data that is shared and used by different users for different purposes.

Database management system—the software that is used to create, maintain, and operate the database.

- The **database**: the collection of data that is shared and used by different users for different purposes.
- The **database management system**: the software that is used to create, maintain, and operate the database.

Many software packages now sold use a database as an underlying file structure, and automatically maintain the profile of the database as part of the system. The use of such a software package does not normally indicate complexity or advanced automated information systems.

Complexity is introduced where a separate database management system is acquired, and the client is required to set up a separate database administration function to maintain the data dictionary (the index of record definitions and linkages). With such systems, separate custom programs must be written to access and work with the data in the database. Thus, the database management system is separate from the application programs. Figure 10-4 illustrates how the data dictionary would be used to maintain the profile of the database contents, while access to the database through applications or a report writer is also handled by the database management system.

EFFECTS OF DATABASE MANAGEMENT SYSTEMS ON INTERNAL CONTROLS It is important for the auditor to be aware of the existence of a database management system,

Figure 10-4 Database Components

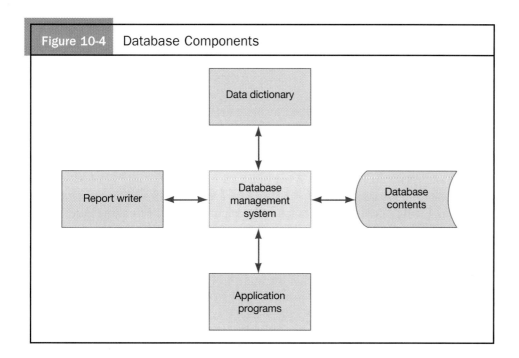

since it affects all areas of general controls. The general controls affected include the following:

Organization and management controls The database administrator requires specialized skills to establish and maintain the database. He or she should be segregated from other functions, such as data authorization. Typical responsibilities of the database administrator include creation and maintenance of the data dictionary, assistance with development of logical views of the data, allocation of physical storage for the database, provision for backup, and security and privacy of the data elements.

Systems acquisition, development, and maintenance controls The systems development life cycle necessitates added controls to ensure that (1) the database is developed in accordance with business needs and (2) programs accessing the database are accurate and authorized and control concurrent options (to ensure that several individuals do not attempt to change the same data element at the same time).

Operations and information systems support This includes the need for security over the data dictionary and over access to the database. The person in charge of this area works with the database administrator and other responsible individuals.

Each application cycle needs to be examined to ensure that the appropriate controls are in place:

- Since many departments may need to access key information, such as customer name and address, a single data "owner" should be assigned responsibility for defining access and security rules, such as who can use the data (access) and what functions they can perform (security).
- Passwords should be used to restrict access to the database based on the security rules defined above.
- There should be segregation of duties with respect to system design, database design, database administration, system operation, and authorization of data placed into the database.

Integrated Computing, such as Enterprise Resource Planning Systems

Enterprise resource planning (ERP) systems are complex, integrated computer systems based upon pre-defined relational databases. **Relational databases** are databases

Enterprise resource planning (ERP) systems—complex, integrated computer systems based upon pre-defined relational databases.

Relational databases—databases based upon linked two-dimensional tables.

based upon linked two-dimensional tables. The objective of such systems is to more closely link data so that they can be shared by all authorized organization members.

Such systems tend to require high-capacity computing, such as minicomputers or mainframes and include the complexities of database management systems, described in the previous section. Often, businesses change their methods of operations (and thus their control processes) to fit the way the software was designed. This means that when such systems are implemented, the auditor will need to document and assess such new controls.

Due to the heavy integration of data, there may be fewer checks on accuracy of data, such as reconciliations. This means that controls over the input of information have a greater importance, since the focus is to prevent errors from being entered into the system. Configurations for automatic processing (such as just-in-time ordering, or production of invoices based upon shipment data) need to be carefully managed.

Due to the heavy emphasis on access controls (which will also be important for enforcing segregation of duties), once the auditor understands the business and the ERP structure, an important focus of the audit will be access controls. General controls over multiple levels of access would be evaluated, for example, the network, functions, data elements, types of update rights, and the method of establishing new users and changing their profiles. Then, for individual applications, how users are assigned their identifications and their access rights would be assessed. The auditor will likely require specialist assistance for audit of the database management and ERP systems.

Our discussion in this section illustrates that as the nature and level of complexity of automation in the information systems used at the organization increases, so will the amount of effort required by the auditor to understand general controls. The auditor obtains information about the organizational structure of the information systems processing department, the hardware and software configuration of computing systems, and a general description of the types of automated systems in use. This is used to plan the extent of work required to understand general controls. The assessment of general controls is linked to control risk for individual functional cycles and to the assertions, discussed further in the final section of this chapter.

In the case of Hillsburg Hardware, as described in Audit Challenge 10-2, we can note that it is important that the database administration function be separated from other functions such as data authorization. Each application will need to be examined to ensure that each data element has specified "owner" groups, with appropriate access controls such as passwords. Hillsburg also uses EDI. Those applications affected by EDI, such as accounts payable, will require greater reliance on programmed controls, as there will likely be less of a paper trail. This may require greater use of computer-assisted audit techniques, and will be discussed further in the audit of the acquisition and payment cycle in Chapter 18.

concept check

C10-7 How do controls over operations affect advanced information systems?

C10-8 What are examples of risks associated with the use of EDI?

 ## Relating the Effects of Entity-Level Controls to Transactions and Balances

So far, we have talked about several categories of entity-level controls. These are corporate governance, enterprise risk management, IT governance, general information systems controls, and controls over advanced information systems. In this section, we will provide a risk associated with each of these categories, state examples of entity-level controls that would address the risk and provide the impact upon application cycles or account balances. Then, we will relate risks and controls at the entity level to specific audit objectives, concluding with an example in cash disbursements looking at an automated cheque-writing application.

Risks Addressed by Entity-Level Controls

This chapter has shown that entity-level controls cover all aspects of the organization, including financial reporting, controls over operations, and IT. To illustrate risks and

Research Reveals Sources of Wireless Risks

In December 2006, The TJX Companies, Inc. revealed that there had been a breach into its information systems over an extended period of time. It was only late in 2007 that the scope of the exposure, likely over 90 million Visa and MasterCard account details with over $65 million in fraud losses, was revealed. How did this happen?

TJX used wireless local area networks (WLAN) at its retail stores. The WLAN used an encryption standard that was outdated, making it easy to guess the encryption key when traffic was monitored. With relatively inexpensive equipment and a wireless computer, you can easily capture data transmitted using wireless technology when you are in proximity of the sending system. Two Marshall's stores in the Miami area were monitored and accessed, allowing the individuals who penetrated the system further access into TJX systems. This included data from many individuals around the world, including Canadian purchasers from Winners and Home Sense in Canada.

Other places where wireless data can easily be accessed are public wi-fi stations. Many retail providers of such wi-fi, such as coffee shops, hotels, and restaurants, do not encrypt their traffic. This means that the confidential email that you are sending from your wireless laptop in the local coffee shop could perhaps be read by the person sitting two seats away from you or by the local hacker sitting outside in his car. Surveys of 14 American and three Asian airports found that 57 percent of the wireless networks provided there were also readily accessible.

Organizations can help to prevent these kinds of breaches by ensuring that they use current security protocols and software, monitor their traffic, and have policies in place that advise employees about the risks associated with processes such as the sending of confidential data from public locations.

Sources: 1. Associated Press, "TJX breach could top 94 million cards: filing," October 24, 2007, www.theglobeandmail.com, Accessed: November 1, 2007. 2. Wildstrom, Stephen H., "Public Wi-Fi: Be very paranoid," March 12, 2008, www.businessweek.com, Accessed: December 26, 2008. 3. Wilson, Tom, "Canadian government sheds light on TJX breach," September 25, 2007, www.darkreading.com, Accessed: November 1, 2007.

controls at the entity level, we will look at the effects of wireless computing, as shown in Table 10-10 on the next page. Auditing in Action 10-2 helps explain why wireless computing is an important risk area that should be addressed by organizations.

All of the risks and controls listed in Table 10-10 are entity-level controls. This means that the risk and associated controls could affect multiple transaction cycles or account balances. Any one of the control levels being absent or not properly implemented could result in unauthorized access (e.g., copying, deletion, or changing) to the affected data in the transaction cycles. It is not simply a cascading process, where if the top control is reliable, we then go to the next, and so on. It is possible, for example, that poor enterprise risk management processes exist but that the organization still has adequate controls over the security and access to its information systems, due to recognition of the importance of these types of controls by the information systems group and individual departments.

Depending upon the missing or incomplete entity-level control, different risks could arise at the transaction or balance level, affecting different audit objectives, as discussed in our next section.

Relationship among Entity-Level Controls and Specific Audit Objectives

Entity-level controls can affect particular application cycles or balances, or they could be more pervasive, affecting the entire organization or groups of functional areas. For example, if the company is engaging in complex financial transactions, such as hedging, to try to protect foreign currency risks, an important entity control pertains to having sufficient expertise to engage in and monitor these transactions. A problem with the financial expertise will not affect other transaction cycles (such as sales, inventory, or accounts receivable) beyond the amount of the foreign currency risk. If the attempted hedging transaction is incorrectly handled, the organization could

	Table 10-10	Risks of Wireless Computing and Entity-Level Controls

Potential Risk Example	Entity-Level Control That Addresses the Risk	Impact upon Application Cycles or Account Balances
Corporate governance: Board is not familiar with the type of technology used by the organization, making it difficult to oversee risk evaluation and risk management processes.	Board receives plain-language information about the technology in use by the organization, and training in the risks associated with such technology.	It is likely that risks associated with affected cycles (for example, sales in the TJX case) will be clearly identified.
Enterprise risk management: Management may be unaware of the risks associated with the use of wireless LANs (resulting in exposure to hacking and data theft) and so fail to develop and enforce appropriate policies.	The chief information officer is involved in risk assessment processes, identifying risks associated with relevant technology, and indicating mitigation strategies that should be implemented.	Risks associated with affected cycles and balances will be identified and appropriate mitigation processes implemented and monitored.
IT governance: Acquisition processes for purchase of wireless software and hardware could be flawed, resulting in purchase of outdated software.	Acquisition processes include contacting multiple vendors, environmental scanning, and review to ensure that current technology appropriate to the application is purchased.	Current security and access controls will be acquired with the software, helping to prevent unauthorized access to data such as customer data.
General information systems controls: Operations procedures may be incomplete, resulting in needed updates to security software being delayed; this results in the software becoming ineffective, exposing data to hacking and theft.	Procedures associated with receipt of new software include following up with operations to ensure that updates are implemented on a timely basis for all affected locations.	Multiple locations processing transaction data (e.g., point-of-sale) will have current security processes and help prevent unauthorized access and manipulation.

have misstatements in the financial instruments in the financial statements or inadequate disclosure about the transactions.

If the company has acquired a new inventory management system and the implementation controls over the inventory data are poor, then the transaction cycle affected will be inventory and warehousing, perhaps resulting in inaccurate and incomplete inventory records. Inventory assertions that could be affected would be completeness, accuracy, and occurrence. Awareness of the poor controls over the inventory data could result in the auditor deciding not to rely upon the controls over inventory balances and instead to increase substantive tests, such as a greater reliance upon test counts at the year-end audit.

Poor management attitudes with respect to fraud and a view that corporate assets are also available for personal use could result in fraud risks in all application cycles, such as theft of assets, personal use of supplies and travel, and overstatement of sales. Many assertions would be affected, and such pervasive problems could result in the auditor resigning from the audit engagement.

Similarly, if processes over data security are poor (e.g., an absence of security policies, weak password maintenance processes, individuals sharing passwords), then the auditor cannot rely upon segregation of duties and may choose to use only substantive tests during the audit.

For an auditor to consider placing reliance upon either a computer-assisted or fully automated control, the auditor must have reasonable assurance that general controls over the computerized portion of the controls are effective. In particular, program change controls and access controls must be effective.

- *Program change controls.* There should be sufficient controls in place to ensure that programs throughout the year were adequately controlled. This provides reasonable assurance that there were no unauthorized program changes and that programs functioned consistently throughout the year.

- *Access controls.* Physical and logical access controls should exist to prevent unauthorized access to programs and data and to document access so that accountability can be established. If unauthorized access to programs or data can be obtained, then the auditor would not be able to place reliance on the results of those programs or data throughout the year.

Should the auditor conclude that general controls are adequate, then he or she has the choice of relying on any of the different types of controls in the accounting system that are identified as key controls (i.e., manual, computer-assisted, or fully automated). Should general controls be poor, then the auditor may be able to rely on only manual controls. Alternatively, the auditor may decide to assess control risk at maximum and not rely on any internal controls.

To illustrate the effects of entity-level controls on individual assertions and account balances, we will use the example of automated cheque printing and signing, that is, the computer system produces cheques that are automatically signed. The general ledger accounts affected are cash, expenses, and cost of goods sold. The transaction cycle is purchases and payments.

As an illustration, assume that the company had previously printed cheques using its computer systems but that cheques were signed manually. Cheques over $50,000 required two signatures, while smaller amounts required only one signature. Due to the burden of signing several hundred cheques every two weeks, management decided to implement laser chequing. Table 10-11 illustrates the categories of entity-level controls that were implemented and their effects.

Table 10-11	Controls and Effects During Laser Cheque Printing Implementation
Type of Control and Example	**Effect of Control**
IT governance: Existing policies and procedures exist for: • Software and hardware selection and implementation. • Infrastructure and computing supplies purchases.	• Finance department, in cooperation with IT, prepared and submitted a request for approval of the new application, supported by supporting documentation and a cost-benefit analysis. • The proposal indicates that the printer will be housed in a separate, locked room with limited access.
Corporate governance: • IT acquisitions require prior approval and are reviewed quarterly by the board.	• The proposal was submitted to the information systems steering Committee, and after approval, submitted to the board for approval.
General information systems controls: • Software packages must be tested prior to contract signature and acceptance. • Maintenance contracts must be acquired for all software packages purchased. • Backup and recovery plans are to be updated prior to installation of new software products. • User profile sheets are to be approved and signed by department managers prior to implementation of new software. • New software products are to be implemented on weekends and effects on existing applications tested.	• IT staff confirm that the software functions according to specifications. • Automated controls (i.e., program functioning) can be relied upon. • The company will be entitled to receive software upgrades during the duration of the maintenance contract. • In the event of major or minor disruptions (such as disk drive failure), staff will know what to do to recover programs and data. • Only authorized employees will be permitted to access the new software and the data that it produces. • Access controls can be relied upon. • In the event that the new software causes problems with existing software (perhaps due to operating systems conflicts), the implementation will be cancelled until the conflicts are resolved.

Since the application has been purchased and implemented in such a way that programmed controls and access controls can be relied upon, we can now focus upon individual assertions in the cheque printing application, as follows:

- *Occurrence:* There is physical separation (a locked room) between accounts payable personnel and the signed, printed cheques. Personnel who pick up the cheques and take them to the mail room do not have access to the software that would enable printing of cheques (an automated access control).
- *Completeness:* Computer software automatically prenumbers the cheques and accounts for the numbers (automated access control). Personnel who pick up the cheques are required to fill in a log indicating the numbers of cheques picked up; the log is reviewed and initialled by accounts payable personnel.
- *Accuracy:* There is a monthly, independent bank reconciliation, prepared by the accounting supervisor (combined control; relies upon reports from the accounts payable and cheque printing application) and reviewed by the controller (combined control; relies upon manual work completed by the accounting supervisor and an Excel spreadsheet).

The auditor would likely test the following key controls:

1. The presence of the locked room for the cheque printer, including determining who has access to the room (occurrence).
2. Review of the cheque sequence log combined with selecting a sample of cheques to determine that they are all accounted for (completeness).
3. Inspection of the printed bank reconciliations for the controller's signature (accuracy).

This example has shown how effective corporate governance, including effective IT governance, enabled the implementation of an application that was auditable. The presence of effective controls means that the auditor can design audit tests which effectively test assertions at the detailed account and transaction stream level, providing choice with respect to which key controls will be tested (if any) and whether substantive testing will be conducted.

concept check

C10-9 Provide two examples of entity-level controls. What types of entity-level controls are they?

C10-10 Why are controls over program changes important to the auditor?

Summary

1. *What is the relationship between corporate governance strategies and risk management?* Corporate governance strategies are the practices and policies followed by the board and executive management when governing the organization. Part of the corporate governance strategy would be the number and type of board committees, and their role. The board and executive management would select a risk management framework, and oversee the process of risk management.

   What is an "enterprise risk management framework"? This framework identifies the tasks that comprise effective enterprise risk management.

   List the techniques that the auditor could use to document and assess design and operating effectiveness of corporate governance. The auditor could use checklists, flowcharts, and narrative to document the results of understanding corporate governance; the understanding would be obtained using inquiry, observation, and inspection. Professional judgment would be needed to

draw conclusions about the overall quality of corporate governance.

2. *What is information technology (IT) governance?* These are the policies, practices, and procedures that help IT resources add value to the organization, while considering costs and benefits.

   What are the attributes of good IT governance? It starts by being part of the organization (i.e., MIS is viewed as partner in the business), is linked to enterprise risk management methods and a sound control environment, has a value realization and delivery framework, and has value management methodologies.

   What is the impact of general controls on the audit? Different controls have different impacts. Overall, good-quality general controls are required in order to rely upon automated or combined application controls at the assertion level.

3. *How do advanced information systems affect the eight-phase audit process?* Complexity of information systems

increases overall inherent risk and control risk. Presence of strategic information systems could result in the need for the auditor to closely assess disaster recovery plans, affecting client business risk. Such systems may result in an increased emphasis on access controls to enforce separation of duties, so the auditor may need to focus on these controls. Specialist assistance will likely be required to audit these systems.

4. *How do entity-level controls affect specific audit objectives? Provide examples.* Just like general controls (such as program change controls), all entity controls affect one or more application systems or accounts. Good-quality entity-level controls (such as high-quality systems life cycle methodologies and an effective IT steering committee) are required to be able to rely upon affected application level controls. Poor controls may result in the need for increased substantive testing.

Our laser chequing example illustrated the effect of general information systems controls on the audit of transactions and balances at the audit objective level.

Visit the text's website at **www.pearsoned.ca/arens** for practice quizzes, additional case studies, and international standards information.

Review Questions

10-1 How has the escalating role of board members and the audit committee affected corporate governance?

10-2 Describe regulatory influences on board members and management. What have been the effects of these influences?

10-3 For three organizational structure types (entrepreneurial, bureaucratic, adhocracy), briefly describe the likely characteristics of corporate governance.

10-4 What is the purpose of an information systems steering committee? How does such a committee support effective corporate governance?

10-5 List the advantages and disadvantages of enterprise risk management (ERM).

10-6 List three characteristics of good ERM.

10-7 Provide five examples of actions that board members could take to support effective ERM.

10-8 List and describe the eight phases of the COSO ERM integrated framework. Provide an example of effective corporate governance for each phase.

10-9 What is the public accountant's goal in auditing corporate governance?

10-10 How does effective corporate governance affect the audit risk model?

10-11 How does the auditor document the assessment of corporate governance?

10-12 What is the relationship between IT governance and corporate governance?

10-13 What is IT dependence and how can it be prevented?

10-14 List three categories of general controls. For each category, provide an example of an effective control.

10-15 You are auditing a manufacturing company with three different locations. For each phase of the financial statement audit, provide an example of the impact of automation on the audit process.

10-16 Why does the auditor need to assess controls over information systems acquisition, development, and maintenance?

10-17 List characteristics of advanced automated information systems. Define each characteristic and provide an example.

10-18 What is the relationship between entity-level controls and application controls?

Discussion Questions and Problems

10-19 Metro Plastics Limited is a medium-sized manufacturer of rigid plastics. It produces casings for printers, telephones, computer screens, and other types of equipment. It also produces stand-alone plastics, such as baskets and jars. Recently, Metro Plastics was purchased by a large food manufacturing conglomerate. The previous owner of Metro Plastics has agreed to stay on for three years to help provide management transition. He has also been asked to provide a presentation to the board of the conglomerate about the corporate governance and risk management practices of his company. The owner of Metro Plastics has come to you to provide some guidance about the type of information that he should provide to the board.

REQUIRED

a. What type of information should he provide to the board about corporate governance? List three corporate governance controls that might have been present at the owner-managed company.

b. What type of information should he provide about risk management practices at Metro Plastics? List three risk management practices that might have been present at the owner-managed company.

10-20 Transom Company builds trucks. It buys components from parts manufacturers and assembles them. The company has three standard models and also designs trucks to unique specifications, in consultation with customer designers and its own in-house specialists. All trucks are built to order, that is, there is no inventory of completed trucks, only of some core sub-assemblies.

REQUIRED

Using the eight phases of the COSO ERM integrated framework, identify two risks for Transom, and describe how the risks should be managed.

10-21 Friggle Corp. is a leasing and property management company located in Alberta. It provides financing to organizations wishing to purchase equipment or property and manages apartments and condominium properties. The company decided that it was time to upgrade its local area network. It decided also to purchase new accounting software but wanted to retain its old unit maintenance software, which, although 10 years old, had an easy-to-use interface that allowed maintenance personnel to track the maintenance work that they did in each unit. The controller, Joe, decided that the company should purchase the software from Midland Computers, which was owned by his brother-in-law, Tom. The prices were comparable with those of other computer networks that he priced, and Midland happened to be close by. Using materials from industry magazines, Joe decided that the best property management software to buy would be from Quebec; the software had received rave reviews about being easy to use.

The implementation was scheduled for the weekend after the June month-end close so that systems could be up and running by the following Monday. To Joe's horror, when he arrived at work on Monday, computers were still being unpacked and installed. Tom had difficulty following the installation instructions for the accounting software, which was not up and running until the end of the week. General ledger details had to be manually entered, since the software could not handle the structure of the old accounts. At the end of two weeks, Joe had the old system put back up so that Friggle could catch up on transactions and get some work out the door. It took three months of 12-hour days for all accounting staff to get the new system operational. Unfortunately, the old maintenance systems would not work with the new operating system, and a new maintenance system had to be evaluated and purchased.

REQUIRED

Assess IT governance at Friggle Corp. For weaknesses that you identify, provide recommendations for improvement.

10-22 Turner Valley Hospital plans to install a database management system, Hosp Info, that will maintain patient histories, including tests performed and their results, vital statistics, and medical diagnoses. The system also will manage personnel and payroll, medical and non-medical supplies, and patient and provincial health-care billings. The decision was taken by the board of the hospital on the advice of a consultant who was a former employee of Medical Data Services Inc., the developer of Hosp Info.

Turner Valley Hospital's chief information officer has come to your accounting firm to ask for advice on what general controls she should ask Medical Data Services Inc. to install to preserve the integrity of the information in the system and to deal with privacy issues.

The system would permit data about patients to be entered by doctors, nurses, and medical technologists.

REQUIRED

a. Describe in general terms the controls you would suggest for the system as a whole.
b. Considering the nature of Turner Valley Hospital, describe potential risks the hospital should be concerned about with respect to Hosp Info.
c. What are the advantages of such a database management system?
d. How would the quality of general controls at the hospital affect your audit?

Professional Judgment Problem

10-23 It was a typical madhouse time on the night before a payroll run. Some employees were entering time cards; other employees were checking data entry lists to time cards and calling supervisors about employee numbers that they could not read. The system started slowing down, and then staff started getting SYSTEM ERROR messages when they tried to execute menu items. Initially, technical support staff suspected a cable break or an operating system failure. Diagnostics were run, but they revealed nothing. Finally, a staff member began running the SCAN virus detection program and uncovered a new virus that seemed to have originated from the central server. The virus cost the company about 25 person-hours in technical support and about 70 hours in overtime for payroll clerks, who worked until 4 a.m.

The company has one local area network with 250 stations using linked central servers. Some stations have their own hard disks; some stations have no disk drives at all. Salespeople have laptop computers that they use to connect from remote locations to conduct customer inquiries and place customer orders.

REQUIRED

a. Identify the potential sources of the virus infection.
b. How could this virus infection have been prevented?

c. What elements of a disaster recovery plan are required for recovery from a virus infection?
d. How would the quality of access controls at the company affect your audit?

Case

10-24 Big Mall Shoe Store Limited is part of a chain of shoe stores across Canada. Each store has standard point-of-sale packaged systems that are used to update sales and inventory. The stores are linked to the head office server via the internet. This way, if a local store does not have an item in stock, local staff can check other locations for availability. Then, they telephone the other store to place a hold on the item for the customer.

At the store level, staff have several responsibilities. As part of helping customers, they select shoes and enter the sale (show code number; quantity; type of payment: cash, debit, or credit card). The information is entered into the point-of-sale cash register. If payment is by credit or debit card, staff must "swipe" the credit card into a separate credit card authorization box, wait for the authorization code, and type the authorization code into the point of sale terminal; the code is then printed on the customer invoice. All price overrides must be approved by the store manager or assistant manager by typing a separate password into the terminal.

The customer gets two pieces of paper. From the point of sale terminal the customer receives an invoice slip which shows the type of shoe purchased, cost, taxes, and total. From the credit/debit card box, the slip shows simply the amount, credit/debit card details, and authorization code. If a credit card is used, a second copy is printed which must be signed by the customer.

All employees have their own passwords which they must enter before initiating a transaction (i.e., the point-of-sale terminal is used by several employees who type in their passwords and then enter a sale, return, or adjustment transaction).

REQUIRED

Identify risks of error or fraud at the local Big Mall Shoe Store. For each risk, identify a potential control that could prevent or detect the error or fraud. For each control, state whether the control is a governance control, general control, or application control. Organize your answer in three columns, as follows:

Risk of Error or Fraud	Potential Control	Type of Control

Ongoing Small Business Case: Risk Management at CondoCleaners.com

10-25 With a thriving business doing, on average, 150 hours of cleaning per week in personal condominium units ranging in size from bachelor units to luxury three-bedroom units, Jim is feeling burned out. During the Christmas lull, he decides to take some time off and reassess the direction that he is going. He also wants to make sure that he has key risks at his business addressed.

REQUIRED

Using information that you have obtained from previous discussions of CondoCleaners.com (in particular, refer to Problem 9-30 on page 310), identify three risks that could affect CondoCleaners.com. For each risk, provide a control that could be used to mitigate the risk.

11

Fraud auditing

Why do auditors fail to catch material frauds? Fraud is difficult to identify because it is intentional and an effort is made to cover it up. Nonetheless, if auditors plan and perform their audit giving consideration to the risk and red flags of fraud, the likelihood of identification is greatly increased. Management auditors need to know about fraud to design effective internal controls, while other types of auditors need to be aware of warning signs to effectively assess the risks of fraud.

STANDARDS REFERENCED IN THIS CHAPTER

CICA Standard

CAS 240 – The auditor's responsibilities relating to fraud in an audit of financial statements (previously Section 5135 – The auditor's responsibility to consider fraud)

LEARNING OBJECTIVES

1 Define fraud, and describe the conditions where it is most likely to exist. Explain the difference between fraudulent financial reporting and misappropriation of assets.

2 Describe the features of corporate governance and of the control environment that could reduce fraud risks. Explain five principles that are part of effective fraud risk management.

3 Examine the auditor's responsibility for assessing the risk of fraud and detecting material misstatements due to fraud. Link fraud risk assessment to the financial statement audit process.

4 State the steps that an auditor should take when fraud risks are identified. Describe specific fraud risk areas, and state the auditor's responsibility once fraud is detected.

The High Cost of International Bribery

Siemens AG is an international engineering, construction, and telecommunications company with 2007 revenue of €72.5 billion. The company received unwelcome publicity commencing in November 2006 when the public became aware that Siemens seemed to have a "bribery expense account." Court proceedings later confirmed that more than €1.3 billion had been used to obtain contracts dating from 2001 through 2007 around the world, with figures as high as US$20 million for contracts to build power plants in Israel. What motivates this type of behaviour? Is it management bonuses, the drive for expansion, or simply the desire to be first? We will never know, for such data are unavailable from the more than 270 suspects focused on by the Munich, Germany, 2008, corruption trial that charged a former manager of a telecommunications division with 58 breach-of-trust charges.

Since Siemens' shares are traded on U.S. stock exchanges, the company was also fined by both the U.S. Department of Justice for bribery and falsification of corporate records and the Securities and Exchange Commission for violation of the Foreign Corrupt Practices Act. As of December 31, 2008, Siemens' costs with respect to the bribery were as follows:

1. €201 million. Fines in Munich, Germany, related to bribery (former telecommunications division).
2. €354 million. Fines in Munich, Germany, due to the failure of its supervisory committee (similar to a board of directors).
3. US$450 million. Levied by U.S. Department of Justice.
4. US$350 million. Levied by the U.S. Securities and Exchange Commission.
5. Estimated €850 million in accounting and legal fees.

This brings the total estimated cost to Siemens to about €2.5 billion. The company is also required to have a compliance monitor, reporting to the United States, who will report on the effectiveness of Siemen's organizational changes, its new internal controls, and new compliance director. The company's problems are not over, for in October 2008, Siemens' offices in Garfield Heights, United States, were raided and documents seized as part of an investigation into the awarding of contracts for the installation of lights, furnaces, and hot water heaters at 7,000 public housing units of the Cuyahoga Metropolitan Housing Authority.

IMPORTANCE TO AUDITORS

Auditors and accountants were called upon to quantify the scope of the bribes, document what had happened, and identify the weaknesses in internal controls that allowed the bribery to happen. It is unclear which levels of management were aware that the bribery was taking place.

New controls designed with the assistance of auditors will require that multiple levels of the organization be involved in controls to prevent, detect, and correct potential violations.

continued >

As discussed in the previous chapter, this will mean a top-down approach: board of director (Supervisory Board in Siemens case) and executive management approval; commitment and implementation by management, staff, and information systems; and regular monitoring, reporting, and revision.

WHAT DO YOU THINK?

1. What are the benefits that accrue to employees when they obtain contracts with bribery?

2. Identify techniques that auditors can use to detect potential changes in business practices, such as bribery.

3. What actions should auditors take with respect to Siemens subsidiaries around the world?

Sources: 1. Annan, Grace, "German court hears first suspect in corruption scandal at Siemens," *Global Insight Daily Analysis*, May 26, 2008, Retrieved from Factiva Index database, http://global.factiva.com.ezproxy.library.yorku.ca/ha/default.aspx, Accessed: January 1, 2009. 2. Garrett, Amanda, "Siemens to pay $1.6 billion to settle bribery case," *The Plain Dealer*, December 31, 2008, Retrieved from Factiva Index database, http://global.factiva.com.ezproxy.library.yorku.ca/ha/default.aspx, Accessed: January 1, 2009. 3. Gow, David, "Record U.S. fine ends Siemens bribery scandal," *The Guardian*, December 16, 2008, www.guardian.co.uk/business/2008/dec/16/regulation-siemens-scandal-bribery, Accessed: January 1, 2009. 4. Siemens Canada home page: https://www.siemens.ca/WEB/PORTAL/EN/Pages/Home.aspx, Accessed: January 1, 2009.

AS our opening case illustrates, even large, well-run companies are susceptible to fraud risks. If those risks are not effectively managed, allowing bribery or other forms of corruption to occur, the costs to the company can be high. In addition to the costs listed above, Siemens' share values declined, and it is facing investigations in many countries around the world.

Fraud risk awareness, with effective internal controls and monitoring, needs to be part of organizational culture and training and the job of every employee, from those responsible for entering transactions or enabling production through to executive management and the board of directors. In this chapter, we will look at the different types of fraud that can occur, addressing both auditor and management responsibilities.

❶ The Nature of Fraud

Types of Fraud

Fraud—an intentional misstatement of the financial statements.

Fraud is a broad legal concept, but in the context of auditing financial statements, it is defined as an intentional misrepresentation of a fact in the books of accounts and ultimately the financial statements. This misrepresentation may be directed against users of the financial statements such as shareholders or creditors or against the organization itself by covering up or disguising embezzlement, misapplication of funds, or improper use of the organization's assets by officers, employees, and third parties. The two main categories of fraud are fraudulent financial reporting and misappropriation of assets, subjects that were introduced in Chapter 5.

FRAUDULENT FINANCIAL REPORTING **Fraudulent financial reporting** is an intentional misstatement or omission of amounts or disclosures with the intent to deceive users. Most cases of fraudulent financial reporting involve the intentional misstatement of amounts. For example, WorldCom is reported to have capitalized (as fixed assets) billions of dollars that should have been expensed. The case of Siemens' convictions with respect to bribery, a form of procurement fraud, also illustrates fraudulent financial reporting: bribes hidden as other types of expenses. Omissions of amounts are less common, but a company can overstate income by omitting accounts payable and other liabilities. Fraudulent financial reporting is sometimes referred to as fraud "by the organization" as insiders perpetrate the fraud most often to boost share price or disguise losses.

Although most cases of fraudulent financial reporting involve overstatement of assets and income or omission of liabilities and expenses in an attempt to overstate income, it is important to note that companies occasionally deliberately understate income. For privately held companies, this may be done in an attempt to reduce income taxes. Companies may also intentionally understate income when earnings are high to create a reserve of earnings or "cookie jar reserves" that may be used to increase earnings in future periods. This practice is called income smoothing or earnings management. **Earnings management** involves deliberate actions taken by management to meet earnings objectives. It has been argued that many companies undertake some form of earnings management and that such activity is not necessarily fraudulent. For example, a company could choose to dispose of excess assets for a profit in a period when earnings are low to improve the reported net income. Such a management decision is not fraudulent if it is properly disclosed in the financial statements. It is the failure to disclose earnings management that makes the activity fraudulent. **Income smoothing** is a form of earnings management in which revenues and expenses are shifted between periods to reduce fluctuations in earnings. One technique to smooth income is to reduce the value of inventory and other assets of an acquired company at the time of acquisition, resulting in higher earnings when the assets are later sold. Companies may also deliberately overstate inventory obsolescence reserves and allowances for doubtful accounts in periods of higher earnings.

Another common method of fraudulent financial reporting involves inadequate disclosure in the financial statements. A central issue in the Enron case was whether the company had adequately disclosed obligations to affiliates known as special-purpose entities. Also, Hollinger International Inc. failed to disclose payments made to Conrad Black as Chairman and CEO and to other senior managers when newspaper assets were sold to third parties. Profits earned on the sale of newspapers that should have gone to the benefit of the shareholders of Hollinger were instead paid to senior management or related parties.

MISAPPROPRIATION OF ASSETS **Misappropriation of assets** is fraud that involves theft of an entity's assets. It is a fraud "against the organization" perpetrated most often by employees, customers, or suppliers. In many cases, the amounts involved are not material to the financial statements. However, the loss of company assets is an important management concern, and management's materiality threshold for fraud will likely be much lower than the materiality threshold used by the auditor for financial reporting purposes.

Misappropriation of assets is normally perpetrated at lower levels of the organization's hierarchy. In some notable cases, however, top management is involved in the theft of company assets. Because of management's greater authority and control over the organization's assets, defalcations involving top management (termed **management corruption**) can involve significant amounts. In one extreme example, the former CEO of Tyco International was charged by the SEC with stealing over US$100 million in assets.

Fraudulent financial reporting—intentional misstatement or omission of amounts or disclosure in financial statements to deceive users.

Earnings management—deliberate actions taken by management to meet earnings objectives.

Income smoothing—form of earnings management in which revenues and expenses are shifted between periods to reduce fluctuations in earnings.

Misappropriation of assets—a fraud involving the theft of an entity's assets.

Management corruption—defalcations involving top management.

Research Provides Fraud Statistics

There are numerous research statistics that tell us that fraud is costly. Thefts and misrepresentation occur in every country, in many different ways.

For example, PriceWaterhouseCoopers reported in 2007 that 52 percent of surveyed Canadian companies were victims of "economic" crime, with average losses of US$3.7 million—a staggering increase from the average Canadian losses of US$600,000 reported in 2003. PWC also reported that 14 percent of the frauds were detected by internal audit, and 37 percent were committed by management (termed middle management or higher).

The Association of Certified Fraud Examiners (ACFE) conducts an annual survey of its members. Of 959 frauds reported between January 2006 and February 2008 in the United States, the median loss was $175,000. The survey separately tracks corruption, which the ACFE defines as including conflicts of interest, bribery, illegal gratuities, and economic extortion.

The ACFE reported corruption as the most common type of fraud (27 percent of reported cases). The most costly type of fraud was financial statement manipulation, with a median loss of $2,000,000.

Although separate statistics are not kept for individual and corporate identity theft, the cost of this type of fraud is high. Phonebusters, the Canadian antifraud call centre, reported 11,381 Canadian victims of identity theft in 2008, with 7,822 from January to July 2009—a total loss over $6 million in the first seven months of 2009.

If only a small fraction of these types of losses are prevented by good internal controls, then internal controls are a good investment.

Sources: 1. Association of Certified Fraud Examiners, "2008 Report to the nation on occupational fraud and abuse,"www.acfe.com/documents/2008-rttn.pdf, Accessed: January 1, 2009. 2. PricewaterhouseCoopers, "Economic crime: people, culture & controls, The 4th biennial Global Economic Crime Survey, Canada," 2007, www.pwc.com/en_CA/ca/risk/forensic-services/publications/economic-crime-2007-en.pdf, Accessed: January 1, 2009. 3. Phonebusters, "Monthly Summary Report," 2009, www.phonebusters.com/english/documents/MonthlyStats_002.pdf, Accessed: September 1, 2009.

Examples of misappropriation of assets that could be perpetrated by an employee include theft of inventory where the records are altered to cover it up, skimming of cash, padding of expense accounts, and lapping of accounts receivable. A test to discover lapping is addressed on page 471. Examples of misappropriation of assets involving external parties include shoplifting, suppliers delivering lower-quality goods than those for which the company was charged, and complex contract fraud through bid rigging. **Procurement fraud**, which is the manipulation of the contracting process, can be very expensive for an organization. The three main forms of procurement fraud are (1) bid rigging, where the bidders for a contract collude to increase the price of the contract; (2) bid fixing, where a bidding party is provided with insider information, giving an unfair advantage; and (3) bribery and kickbacks, where the contract is awarded on the basis of a payment to a company insider involved in the contract-awarding decision. All three forms of procurement fraud are illegal and may result in the bribed employee's company paying more for the goods or services than it should.

Procurement fraud—the manipulation of the contracting process.

An organization's assets can also be stolen by means of **corporate identity theft,** where another organization represents itself as the affected company. The imposter can acquire a loan on the company's behalf, or a mortgage on corporate assets, and then disappear with the funds, leaving the organization to pay off the imposter's debt.

Corporate identity theft—another organization represents itself as the affected company.

Misappropriation of assets is much more common than fraudulent financial reporting, but we do not often see it in the news. Because such fraud is often not material to the financial statements, it is usually dealt with internally. Such actions might range from filing a complaint with the police to a quick and quiet termination of the relationship.

Conditions for Fraud

CAS

Fraud triangle—represents the three conditions of fraud: incentives/pressures, opportunities, and attitudes/rationalization.

Three conditions for fraud arising from fraudulent financial reporting and misappropriations of assets are described in paragraph A1 of the *CICA Handbook* CAS 240 (previously *CICA Handbook* Section 5135) titled "The auditor's responsibilities relating to fraud in an audit of financial statements." As shown in Figure 11-1, these three conditions are referred to as the **fraud triangle**.

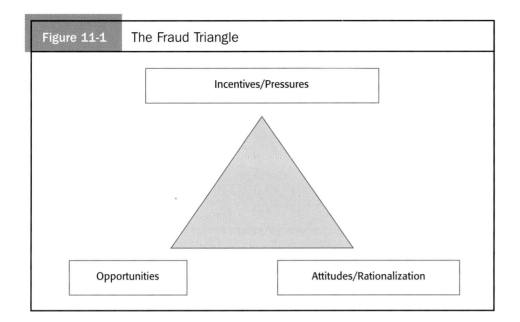

Figure 11-1 The Fraud Triangle

Incentives/Pressures

Opportunities

Attitudes/Rationalization

1. *Incentives/Pressures.* Management or other employees have incentives or pressures to commit fraud.
2. *Opportunities.* Circumstances provide opportunities for management or employees to commit fraud.
3. *Attitudes/Rationalization.* An attitude, character, or set of ethical values exists that allows management or employees to intentionally commit a dishonest act, or they are in an environment that imposes pressure sufficient to cause them to rationalize committing a dishonest act.

RISK FACTORS FOR FRAUDULENT FINANCIAL REPORTING An essential consideration by the auditor in uncovering fraud is identifying factors that increase the risk of fraud. These are referred to as **fraud risk factors** or red flags of fraud. Table 11-1 on the next page provides examples of fraud risk factors for each of the three conditions of fraud for fraudulent financial reporting. Even though the three conditions in the fraud triangle are the same for fraudulent financial reporting and misappropriation of assets, the risk factors are different. The risk factors for fraudulent financial reporting are discussed here first, followed by those for misappropriation of assets. Appendix 1 of CAS 240 of the *CICA Handbook* provides further examples of fraud risk factors for both fraudulent financial reporting and misappropriation of assets, and Appendix 3 lists examples of circumstances that could indicate the possibility of fraud. Later in the chapter, we discuss the auditor's consideration of the risk factors in uncovering fraud.

Fraud risk factors—entity factors that increase the risk of fraud.

Incentives/Pressures A common incentive for companies to manipulate financial statements is a decline in the company's financial prospects. A decline in earnings may threaten the company's ability to obtain financing and continue as a going concern. Companies may also manipulate earnings to meet analysts' forecasts of anticipated earnings for the quarter, to meet debt covenant restrictions, or to artificially maintain or inflate stock prices. In some cases, management may manipulate earnings just to preserve their reputation. Management with significant wealth tied up in stock options may have an incentive to inflate stock prices to increase the profits they earn personally when the options are exercised.

Opportunities Financial statements of all companies are potentially subject to manipulation. However, the risk of fraudulent financial reporting is greater for companies in industries where significant judgments and estimates are involved. For example, valuation of inventories is subject to greater risk of misstatement for companies with diverse inventories in many locations. The risk of misstatement of inventories is further increased if those inventories are potentially obsolete.

Table 11-1 Examples of Risk Factors for Fraudulent Financial Reporting

Three Conditions of Fraud		
Incentives/Pressures	**Opportunities**	**Attitudes/Rationalization**
Management or other employees have incentives or pressures to materially misstate financial statements.	Circumstances provide an opportunity for management or employees to misstate financial statements.	An attitude, character, or set of ethical values exists that allows management or employees to intentionally commit a dishonest act, or they are in an environment that imposes pressure sufficient to cause them to rationalize committing a dishonest act.
Examples of Risk Factors	**Examples of Risk Factors**	**Examples of Risk Factors**
Financial stability or profitability is threatened by economic, industry, or entity operating conditions. Examples include significant declines in customer demand and increasing business failures in either the industry or overall economy.	Significant accounting estimates involve subjective judgments or uncertainties that are difficult to verify.	Inappropriate or ineffective communication and support of the entity's values.
Excessive pressure for management to meet the requirements or expectations of third parties, such as the terms of debt covenant requirements.	Ineffective board of directors or audit committee oversight over financial reporting.	Known history of violations of securities laws or other laws and regulations.
Management or the board of directors' personal net worth is materially threatened by the entity's financial performance.	High turnover or ineffective accounting, internal audit, or information technology staff.	Management's practice of making overly aggressive or unrealistic forecasts to analysts, creditors, and other third parties.

Opportunities for misstatement are greater if there is turnover in accounting personnel or other weaknesses in accounting and information processes. In many cases of fraudulent financial reporting, the company had an ineffective audit committee and board of director oversight of financial reporting.

Attitudes/Rationalization The attitude of top management toward financial reporting is a critical risk factor in assessing the likelihood of fraudulent financial statements. This attitude is commonly referred to as the "tone at the top," and it is relevant to fraud risks because a poor tone at the top increases the risk of fraud and results in a poor internal control environment. If the CEO or other top managers display a significant disregard for the financial reporting process, for example, by consistently issuing overly optimistic forecasts or by being overly concerned about meeting analysts' earnings forecasts, fraudulent financial reporting is more likely. Also, management's character or set of ethical values may make it easier for it to rationalize a fraudulent act.

RISK FACTORS FOR MISAPPROPRIATION OF ASSETS The same three fraud triangle conditions apply to misappropriation of assets. However, in assessing risk factors, greater emphasis is placed on individual incentives and opportunities for theft. Table 11-2 provides examples of fraud risk factors for each of the three conditions of fraud for misappropriation of assets.

Incentives/Pressures Financial pressures are a common incentive for employees who misappropriate assets. Employees with excessive financial obligations or with drug abuse or gambling problems may steal to meet their personal financial or other needs. Managers should be alert for signs of these problems in employees with access to assets or accounting records. While a background check should be performed for all potential employees, a credit check may be included for those who will have access to assets. Dissatisfied employees may steal because of a sense of entitlement or as a form of attack against their employers. Companies can reduce fraud risk by dealing fairly with employees and monitoring employee morale.

Table 11-2 — Examples of Risk Factors for Misappropriation of Assets

Three Conditions of Fraud		
Incentives/Pressures	Opportunities	Attitudes/Rationalization
Management or other employees have incentives or pressures to misappropriate material assets.	Circumstances provide an opportunity for management or employees to misappropriate assets.	An attitude, character, or set of ethical values exists that allows management or employees to intentionally commit a dishonest act, or they are in an environment that imposes pressure sufficient to cause them to rationalize a dishonest act.
Examples of Risk Factors	Examples of Risk Factors	Examples of Risk Factors
Personal financial obligations create pressure for those with access to cash or other assets susceptible to theft to misappropriate those assets.	Presence of large amounts of cash on hand or inventory items that are small, of high value, or are in high demand.	Disregard for the need to monitor or reduce risk of misappropriating assets.
Adverse relationships between management and employees with access to assets susceptible to theft motivate employees to misappropriate those assets. Examples include the following: • Known or expected employee layoffs. • Promotions, compensation, or other rewards inconsistent with expectations.	Inadequate internal control over assets due to lack of the following: • Appropriate segregation of duties or independent checks. • Appropriate job applicant screening for employees performing key control functions. • Mandatory vacations for employees with access to assets.	Disregard for internal controls by overriding existing controls or failing to correct known internal control deficiencies.

Opportunities Opportunities for theft exist in all companies. However, opportunities are greater in companies with accessible cash or with inventory or other valuable assets, especially if the assets are small or readily portable. For example, thefts of laptop computers are fairly common and much more frequent than thefts of desktop systems. Retail establishments and other organizations that receive revenue in the form of cash are also susceptible to theft. Surveillance methods and inventory coding and tracking systems can reduce the potential for theft. For example, casinos handle extensive amounts of cash with minimal formal records of cash received. As a result, casinos make extensive use of video and human surveillance. On a more basic scale, one Canadian fast food chain has a small sign affixed to its cash registers advising patrons that if they do not receive a receipt, their meal is free. This simple control ensures that the sales are recorded in the cash register. Such a control costs the company nothing to implement, and every patron becomes a watchdog.

Weak internal controls create opportunities for theft. Inadequate separation of duties is practically a licence for employees to steal. Whenever employees have custody or even temporary access to assets and maintain the accounting records for those assets, the potential for theft exists. As an example, if inventory storeroom employees also maintain inventory records, it is relatively easy for them to take inventory items and cover the theft by adjusting the accounting records.

Fraud is more prevalent in smaller businesses and not-for-profit organizations because it is more difficult for these entities to maintain adequate separation of duties. However, even large organizations may fail to maintain adequate separation in critical areas. As an illustration, Barings Bank incurred losses in excess of $1 billion from the activities of one trader because of inadequate separation of duties.

Attitudes/Rationalization Management's attitude toward controls and ethical conduct may allow employees and managers to rationalize the theft of assets. If management cheats customers through overcharging for goods or engaging in high-pressure sales tactics, employees may feel that it is acceptable for them to behave in the same fashion by cheating on expense or time reports.

concept check

C11-1 Define fraudulent financial reporting and give two examples.

C11-2 What is the difference between earnings management and income smoothing?

C11-3 Define misappropriation of assets and give two examples.

How much would you pay for a pile of sand in a playground? Does $170,000 seem too much? This is an example of an apparent excess cost in a contract that was not tendered by the City of Toronto in 2006.

In that year alone, there were 144 contracts where a supplier is listed as the only source for the contract. Examples of the services provided were delivery of gift certificates, waste removal, restoration of a building, and installation of hot water boilers. Reasons for using these single suppliers or for not going out to tender were very brief, often single words such as "emergency."

Even when competing bids are obtained, the practice of bid rigging can occur, where multiple bidders can manipulate their bids or an insider at the organization provides information to a bidder allowing for the lowest bid to be provided.

Bid rigging is alleged to have occurred at Ontario Realty Corp. (ORC) with respect to landscaping and clean-up of properties. An employee and a contractor are alleged to have colluded in both the appointment of the contractor and in the preparation of invoices, inflating the amounts that ORC paid.

CRITICAL THINKING QUESTIONS

1. What are some ways that an organization can encourage effective bidding for provision of services or products?
2. What types of controls would the auditor look for with respect to appropriate acquisition of supply contracts?
3. How can analytical review be used to detect potential abuse of the contracting process?

Sources: 1. Maloney, Paul, "City fails to obtain tenders on $52M in goods, services," *Toronto Star*, September 18, 2007, p. A6. 2. Van Alphen, Tony, "Lawsuit defendant denies bid-rigging," *Toronto Star*, October 30, 2008, p. B8.

② Corporate Governance Oversight to Reduce Fraud Risks

The responsibility for implementing corporate governance and control procedures to minimize fraud lies with management and the board of directors or equivalent. Since the audit committee has oversight responsibility for the financial reporting process, the board often delegates responsibility for evaluating the risk of fraud to the audit committee as well. The risk of fraud can be reduced through a combination of prevention, deterrence, and detection measures. Because fraud is difficult to detect due to collusion and false documentation, a focus on fraud prevention and deterrence is often more effective and less costly. Programs and controls implemented by management to prevent fraud help reduce opportunities for it. Programs and controls implemented to deter fraud help persuade employees that they should not commit it because of the likelihood of detection and punishment.

To prevent, deter, and detect fraud the organization should first create and maintain a culture of honesty and high ethics. Secondly, the entity should effectively manage the risks of fraud. We discuss next the elements of these corporate governance and other control environment actions that help to deter fraud. Then, we will look at five principles that can help organizations develop best practices in fraud management, before considering how the audit committee can play a role in fraud risk management. Understanding these areas is helpful to auditors in assessing the extent to which clients have implemented these fraud-reducing activities.

CREATING A CULTURE OF HONESTY AND HIGH ETHICS Research indicates that the most effective way to prevent and deter fraud is to implement programs and controls that are based on core values embraced by the company. These values create an environment that reinforces acceptable behaviour and expectations of each employee, which can be used to guide their actions. These values help create a culture of honesty and ethics that provides the foundation for employees in their job responsibilities. Creating a culture of honesty and high ethics includes six elements.

Setting the tone at the top Management and the board of directors are responsible for setting the "tone at the top" for ethical behaviour in the company. Honesty and integrity by management reinforces honesty and integrity in employees throughout the organization.

Management cannot act one way and expect others in the company to behave differently. Through its actions and communications, management can show that dishonest and unethical behaviours are not tolerated, even if the results benefit the company. Statements by management about the absolute need to meet operating and financial targets create undue pressures that may lead employees to commit fraud to achieve them. In contrast, statements that indicate management's desire to aggressively pursue entity goals and targets and at the same time require honest and ethical actions to achieve those goals clearly indicate to employees that integrity is a must. Such a message demonstrates that management and the board have zero tolerance for unethical behaviour.

A tone at the top based on honesty and integrity provides the foundation upon which a more detailed code of conduct can be developed to provide more specific guidance about permitted and prohibited behaviour. Table 11-3 on the next page contains an example of the key contents of an effective code of conduct. The existence of a code of conduct is not adequate. To be effective, it must be communicated throughout the organization, employees must be educated in the code, and management and the board must lead by example. Examples of codes of ethical conduct are available at the Barrick Gold Corporation (**www.barrick.com**), BCE Inc. (**www.bce.ca**), and Royal Bank (**www.rbc.com**) websites, among others, and can be found under the corporate governance section of these websites.

Creating a positive workplace environment Research shows that wrongdoing occurs less frequently when employees have positive feelings about their employer than when they feel abused, threatened, or ignored. In a positive workplace, there is improved employee morale, which may reduce employees' likelihood of committing fraud against the company.

Management should build a positive culture and work environment by implementing programs and initiatives to increase employee morale. Employees should be encouraged to contribute to that environment and support the entity's values and code of conduct. Employees should also have the ability to obtain advice internally before making decisions that appear to have legal or ethical implications.

Part of creating a positive workplace includes providing the employees with a process to report actual or suspected wrongdoing or potential violations of the code of conduct or ethics policy. Analysis of fraud cases often shows that employees were aware of improper activities by management, but they did not communicate their concerns because they did not have a safe outlet. Organizations are now offering a complaint process in the form of a compliance or "whistle-blower" hotline that provides the employees with an opportunity to report their concerns anonymously. Some organizations outsource this service, while others have a telephone "hotline" directed to or monitored by an ethics officer or general counsel who is made responsible for investigating and reporting fraud or illegal acts. It is important that the organization have a protocol to inform the audit committee of complaints received. You can see an example of a complaint process at Barrick's website in the corporate governance section.

Hiring and promoting appropriate employees To be successful in preventing fraud, well-run companies implement effective screening policies to reduce the likelihood of hiring and promoting individuals with low levels of honesty, especially for positions of trust. Effective hiring and promotion policies may include background checks on individuals being considered for employment or for promotion to positions of trust. Background checks verify a candidate's education, employment history, and personal references, including references about character and integrity. After an employee is hired, continuous evaluation of employee compliance with the company's values and code of conduct reduces the likelihood of fraud.

Training All new employees should be trained in the company's expectations of employees' ethical conduct. Employees should be told of their duty to communicate

Table 11-3   Example Elements for a Code of Conduct

Code of Conduct Element	Description
Organizational code of conduct	The organization and its employees must at all times comply with all applicable laws and regulations, with all business conduct well above the minimum standards required by law.
General employee conduct	The organization expects its employees to conduct themselves in a businesslike manner and prohibits unprofessional activities such as drinking, gambling, fighting, and swearing on the job.
Conflicts of interest	The organization expects that employees will perform their duties conscientiously, honestly, and in accordance with the best interests of the organization and will not use their positions or knowledge gained for private or personal advantage.
Outside activities, employment, and directorships	All employees share a responsibility for the organization's good public relations. Employees should avoid activities outside the organization that create an excessive demand on their time or create a conflict of interest.
Relationships with clients and suppliers	Employees should avoid investing in or acquiring a financial interest in any business organization that has a contractual relationship with the organization.
Gifts, entertainment, and favours	Employees must not accept entertainment, gifts, or personal favours that could influence or appear to influence business decisions in favour of any person with whom the organization has business dealings.
Kickbacks and secret commissions	Employees may not receive payment or compensation of any kind, except when authorized under organizational remuneration policies.
Organization funds and other assets	Employees who have access to organization funds must follow prescribed procedures for recording, handling, and protecting money.
Organization records and communications	Employees responsible for accounting and record keeping must not make or engage in any false record or communication of any kind, whether external or internal.
Information systems	Employee usage guidelines require use of licensed software. Unauthorized software is prohibited. Emails and all electronic data are the property of the company. Offensive material may not be distributed. Policies for data usage and retention are clear.
Dealing with outside people and organizations	Employees must take care to separate their personal roles from their organizational positions when communicating on matters not involving the organization's business.
Prompt communications	All employees must make every effort to achieve complete, accurate, and timely communications in all matters relevant to customers, suppliers, government authorities, the public, and others within the organization.
Privacy and confidentiality	When handling financial and personal information about customers and others with whom the organization has dealings, employees should collect, use, and retain only the information necessary for the organization's business; internal access to information should be limited to those with a legitimate business reason for seeking that information.

Sources: 1. AICPA, *CPA's Handbook of Fraud and Commercial Crime Prevention*. 2. Laudon, Kenneth C., Jane P. Laudon and Mary Elizabeth Brabston. *Management Information Systems*, Fourth Canadian Edition, (Toronto: Prentice Hall, 2009).

actual or suspected fraud and the appropriate way to do so. Fraud awareness training should be tailored to employees' job responsibilities. For example, training for purchasing agents should be different from training for sales agents.

Confirmation Companies should require employees to confirm annually their responsibilities for complying with the code of conduct. Employees should be asked to state that they understand the company's expectations and have complied with the code and that they are unaware of any violations. These confirmations help reinforce the code of conduct policies and also help deter employees from committing fraud or other ethics violations. Most employees want to avoid making a false statement in writing and would rather disclose what they know. Follow-up by internal audit or others on disclosures and non-replies may uncover significant issues.

Discipline Employees must know that they are held accountable for failing to follow the company's code of conduct. Enforcement of violations of the code, regardless of the level of the employee committing the act, sends clear messages to all employees that compliance with the code of conduct and other ethical standards is important and expected. Thorough investigation of all violations and appropriate and consistent responses can be effective deterrents to fraud.

Other declarations Some organizations have additional declarations that they require their employees to confirm agreement with annually. Similar to a code of conduct, these declarations set the behavioural tone of the organization. Declarations that might be found in a public accounting firm include the following:

- Confidentiality policy, in which the employee and partner agree to maintain all client-related information in strict confidence.
- Independence policy, in which the employee and partner agree to be free of any influence, interest, or relationship with a client and its affairs. Independence is a requirement under the rules of professional conduct as discussed in Chapter 3, but public accounting firms often require their employees to acknowledge their adherence to the rules.
- Electronic communication policy, in which the employee and partner acknowledge that because email communications are unsecured, client matters should not be communicated over the internet and that the internet should be used for business purposes only. Email communications are the property of the employer, and the employer has the right to access these emails.
- Computer software policy in which the employee and partner agree that all software on their company-provided computer complies with the laws and licensing agreements and that they have not taken copies of company licensed software for their own use.

RESPONSIBILITY TO MANAGE RISKS OF FRAUD Fraud cannot occur without a perceived opportunity to commit and conceal the act. The primary responsibility for identifying and measuring fraud risks, taking steps to mitigate identified risks, and monitoring internal controls that prevent and detect fraud lies with management and those charged with governance for the entity. To assist management, a best practices document was prepared in 2008 jointly by the Institute of Internal Auditors, the American Institute of Public Accountants, and the Association of Certified Fraud Examiners. The guidance is titled "Managing the Business Risk of Fraud: A Practical Guide" and is available from the websites of each of these organizations. The guidance was also reviewed and endorsed by other professional associations, including the CICA.

The guide lists five basic principles, that we look at in turn, that should be part of an effective fraud risk management process:

1. As part of the corporate governance process, the board of directors and senior management should clarify their expectations regarding fraud risk in a written policy.
2. Fraud risk exposures should be assessed.
3. Controls and actions to prevent or mitigate fraud risks should be established, based upon cost-benefit, management, and board assessments.
4. In the event that prevention or mitigation fails, controls and actions should be present to help detect fraud.
5. Communication, reporting, and monitoring should be used to update the fraud management process organization-wide and on a timely basis. The process should include practices and actions that will be undertaken in the event that a potential fraud is detected.

Clarifying board expectations As explained in Chapter 10, enterprise risk management is an organization-wide process. Fraud risk management is part of enterprise risk management. The board of directors and senior management have oversight responsibility to ensure that the components of effective fraud risk management are present.

This includes approving the risk management process that will be used and the process that will be used to assess risks, including fraud risks. Senior management and the board together will decide the extent of risks that the organization is prepared to accept before moving to detailed evaluation of risk exposures. Effective fraud risk management will include establishing a culture of honesty and positive ethics, while also ensuring that the remaining four principles are documented and addressed.

Identifying and measuring fraud risks Effective fraud oversight begins with the recognition that fraud is possible and that almost any employee is capable of committing a dishonest act under the right circumstances. This recognition increases the likelihood that effective fraud prevention, deterrence, and detection programs and controls are implemented. Figure 11-2 lists factors that management could consider that may contribute to fraud in an organization. Also, if the organization conducts business in emerging economies, there is a high risk of procurement fraud in such regions.

In carrying out their responsibility, management and those charged with governance must assess fraud risks and evaluate corporate governance programs and controls to prevent, deter, and detect fraud. The assessment process should focus on the company's vulnerability to fraud. For example, the company's industry may create incentives or opportunities for employees to manipulate financial results, such as inventory reserves for a manufacturer, or to misappropriate cash for a bank. Assessing fraud risk may be part of management's overall enterprise risk management or it may be a separate process.

A fraud risk assessment, which may be conducted by internal audit, could begin by identifying the areas that are susceptible to fraud. These susceptibilities would include an assessment of areas of potential:

- Fraudulent financial reporting such as improper revenue recognition, overstatement of assets, or understatement of liabilities.
- Misappropriation of assets such as theft of cash or inventory.
- Expenditures and liabilities for an improper purpose such as bribery or kickbacks.

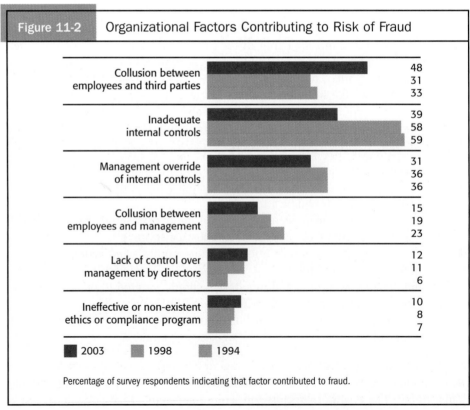

Figure 11-2 — Organizational Factors Contributing to Risk of Fraud

Factor	2003	1998	1994
Collusion between employees and third parties	48	31	33
Inadequate internal controls	39	58	59
Management override of internal controls	31	36	36
Collusion between employees and management	15	19	23
Lack of control over management by directors	12	11	6
Ineffective or non-existent ethics or compliance program	10	8	7

Percentage of survey respondents indicating that factor contributed to fraud.

- Costs or expenditures avoided by fraud such as tax evasion or fraud against employees, which could include failure to pay insurance premiums.
- Improper financial conduct by senior management or the board, such as improper expense claims, regardless of their materiality.

Mitigating fraud risks Management is responsible for designing and implementing programs and controls to mitigate fraud risks. Management can change business activities and processes prone to fraud in order to reduce incentives and opportunities for fraud. For example, management can outsource certain operations such as transferring cash collections from company personnel to a bank lockbox system. Other programs and controls may be implemented at a company-wide level, such as the training of all employees about fraud risks and strengthening employment and promotion policies.

Implementing detective controls Detective controls can be built into information systems, such as having unusual transactions delivered directly to internal audit departments. Random audits of high-risk areas (such as refunds in a retail environment) also help to detect fraud. Well-trained employees know that preventive and detective controls are present, which actually can help prevent fraud. An effective, anonymous whistle-blower program in a supportive and ethical business environment can also help the organization investigate potential fraud.

Communicating, reporting, and monitoring fraud risk management programs For areas of high fraud risk, management should periodically evaluate whether appropriate antifraud programs and controls have been implemented and are operating effectively. For example, management's review and evaluation of operating units' or subsidiaries' financial results increase the likelihood that manipulated results will be detected.

Internal audit plays a key role in monitoring activities to ensure that antifraud programs and controls are operating effectively. Internal audit activities can both detect and deter fraud. Internal auditors assist in deterring fraud by examining and evaluating internal controls that reduce fraud risk. They assist in fraud detection by performing audit procedures to search for fraudulent financial reporting and misappropriation of assets.

Management and board evaluation of internal audit findings and reports of whistle-blower programs help assess the effectiveness of results of fraud risk management.

Because management is often in a position to override internal controls, there is a strong need for corporate governance oversight for senior management actions. One of the strongest mechanisms of internal corporate governance over senior management is the audit committee of the board of directors. The audit committee's role in fraud risk oversight is discussed next.

AUDIT COMMITTEE OVERSIGHT The audit committee has primary responsibility to oversee the organization's financial reporting and internal control processes. In fulfilling this responsibility, the audit committee considers the potential for management override of internal controls and oversees management's fraud risk assessment process, as well as antifraud programs and controls. The audit committee also assists in creating an effective "tone at the top" about the importance of honesty and ethical behaviour by reinforcing the entity's zero tolerance for fraud.

Audit committee oversight also serves as a deterrent to fraud by senior management. For example, direct reporting of key findings by internal audit to the audit committee, reports by ethics officers about calls to the whistle-blower hotline, and other reports about lack of ethical behaviour or suspected fraud increase the likelihood that any attempt by senior management to involve employees in committing or concealing fraud is promptly disclosed. An open line of communication between the audit committee and members of management one or two levels below senior management

The Audit Committee Charter for many companies, such as Research in Motion, assigns the audit committee the responsibility to assist the board of directors. The committee fulfills its oversight responsibilities by reviewing financial information; systems of internal financial, business, and antifraud controls; and the audit process. The duties of the audit committee are to provide meaningful and effective oversight and counsel to the company's management. The audit committee is required to exercise constructive skepticism when relying on management and accounting professionals.

Auditors consider the ethical climate of an organization, which includes the audit committee, when assessing the risks of fraud within an organization. For example, they might consider the following factors:

- How the internal audit organization is organized, including whether the board, audit committee, and senior management respect the functions and missions of each other and of the internal audit organization.
- The importance of ethical features in the organization, such as unquestioned integrity at all levels, accountability and

responsibility taken, openness, acceptance of mistakes as a learning vehicle, commitment to improving the organization, and internal collaboration.
- The existence of formal policies that address conflicts of interest, confidentiality, compliance with laws, rules and regulations, and the reporting of any illegal or unethical behaviour.

CRITICAL THINKING QUESTIONS ❓

1. What are some of the skills that audit committee members charged with overseeing fraud risk management should have?
2. List some questions that you might ask audit committee members as part of your evaluation of the quality of their oversight of fraud risk management.

Sources: 1. Research in Motion, "Audit Committee Charter, 2009," www.rim.net/investors/governance/index.shtml, Accessed: January 2, 2009. 2. Verschoor, Curtis C., "The ethical climate barometer," *The Internal Auditor*, 61(5), 2004.

---

concept check

C11-4 Explain two ways that management can implement a positive "tone at the top."

C11-5 What is the relationship between enterprise risk management and fraud risk management?

C11-6 Describe the role of detective and preventive controls in the fraud risk management process. Provide an example of each.

can also assist the audit committee in identifying fraud by senior management. Information received from external auditors can also help the audit committee in assessing the strength of the company's internal controls and the potential for fraudulent financial reporting.

Most audit committee charters authorize and provide adequate funding for the audit committee to investigate any matters within the scope of its financial reporting oversight responsibilities. Audit committees usually have the authority to retain legal, accounting, and other professional advisers to assist in any fraud investigation. Examples of where an audit committee established a special committee to assist in the investigation of suspect financial reporting issues include Hollinger International Inc., Nortel Networks Corporation, Royal Group Technologies Limited, and Research in Motion.

③ The Auditor's Role in Assessing the Risk of Fraud

CAS

Professional skepticism—an attitude of the auditor that neither assumes management is dishonest nor assumes unquestioned honesty.

CAS 240 provides guidance to auditors in assessing the risk of fraud. Auditors must maintain a level of **professional skepticism**, which enables them to be impartial, assume that management is neither dishonest nor honest, and consider a broad set of information, including fraud risk factors, to identify and respond to fraud risk. As discussed in Chapter 5, the auditor has a responsibility to respond to fraud risk by planning and performing the audit to obtain reasonable assurance that the financial statements are free from material misstatements, whether due to errors or fraud. In this section, we look at the characteristics of professional skepticism before linking the fraud risk assessment to the financial statement audit process.

PROFESSIONAL SKEPTICISM CAS paragraphs 12 to 14 describe how the auditor documents and displays professional skepticism in the context of fraud:

1. Allowing for the potential for fraud during the current audit, even though management and those charged with governance displayed honesty and integrity in the past.
2. Unless audit procedures reveal the potential for documents that are unauthentic or have been altered, the auditor has the right to consider audit evidence and supporting documents as genuine.
3. Where evidence and the results of inquiries to client governance personnel (i.e., management and the board of directors) are inconsistent, the auditor must gather further evidence.

In practice, maintaining an attitude of professional skepticism can be difficult because despite some recent high-profile examples of fraudulent financial statements, material frauds are infrequent compared with the number of audits of financial statements conducted annually. Most auditors will never encounter a material fraud during their careers. Also, through client acceptance and continuance evaluation procedures, auditors reject most potential clients perceived as lacking honesty and integrity. CAS 240 emphasizes consideration of a client's susceptibility to fraud, regardless of the auditor's beliefs about the likelihood of fraud and management's honesty and integrity.

QUESTIONING MIND During planning for every audit, the engagement team must discuss the need to maintain throughout the audit a questioning mind in order to identify fraud risks and critically evaluate audit evidence. In maintaining a questioning mind, auditors should set aside any prior beliefs about management's integrity and honesty and should consider the potential for management override of controls, given that discovery of fraud is possible in any audit. This allows auditors to more effectively consider the potential areas of fraud risk.

CRITICAL EVALUATION OF AUDIT EVIDENCE Auditors should thoroughly probe the issues and acquire additional evidence as necessary. Auditors should be particularly careful when relying on the representations of management. Representation of management generally, in and of itself, does not represent sufficient audit evidence. Care should be taken to corroborate these representations.

Auditors should consult with other team members rather than rationalize or dismiss information or other conditions that indicate a material misstatement due to fraud may have occurred. For example, an auditor may uncover a current-year sale that should be properly reflected as a sale in the following year. Rather than conclude that the error is an isolated incident, the auditor should evaluate the reasons for the error, determine whether it was intentional or unintentional, and consider whether other such errors are likely to have occurred.

FRAUD RISK ASSESSMENT OR RESPONSE BY AUDIT PHASE Just as organizations are required to have a culture that is fraud aware, the audit team must have a culture that considers fraud risks and fraud responses throughout the audit. In this section, we will look at the overall effect of this fraud risk awareness on each audit phase, and in the next section, we will look at the auditor's responsibilities in the event that fraud or overall lack of management integrity are detected.

Table 11-4 on the next page illustrates that the auditor must consider fraud risks in every phase of the audit. Specific examples will be considered in subsequent chapters of this text as we walk through the audit planning, risk response, and reporting phases of the audit. In the remainder of this section, we consider important standards with respect to significant fraud risks, the role of analytical review, and documentation of the auditor's fraud risk assessment and evidence gathering processes.

Table 11-4 Fraud Risk Assessment or Fraud Risk Response by Audit Phase

Audit Phase	Auditor Actions
Risk Assessment	
Phase 1: Preplanning	• Consider potential for management bias during client acceptance or continuance analysis. • Include management responsibility for fraud management in the engagement letter.
Phase 2: Client risk profile	• Note pressures and business practices that could be conducive to fraud. • When assessing corporate governance, evaluate effectiveness of risk management practices. • During preliminary analytical review, include analyses that could highlight unusual transactions or trends that could be indicative of fraud.
Phase 3: Audit plan	• Document internal controls that could prevent or detect fraud. • Evaluate design effectiveness of controls in mitigating fraud risks. • Assess risks of fraud overall and for each assertion where there is potential risk of material misstatement. • Discuss risks of fraud and effects on audit plan with audit team members.
Risk Response	
Phase 4: Design further audit procedures	• Include in audit programs audit techniques that address risks of fraud.
Phase 5: Tests of controls	• If reliance is intended upon controls that mitigate risks of fraud, perform tests of control, and assess the results of tests upon risks of fraud and upon audit programs.
Phase 6: Substantive tests	• Include in audit programs substantive tests that address significant risks of fraud.
Phase 7: Ongoing evaluation, quality control, and final evidence gathering	• Assess evidence from multiple sources for inconsistencies or unusual results that could be indicators of fraud. • Modify audit programs as required to investigate inconsistencies or unusual results.
Reporting	
Phase 8: Complete quality control, and issue auditor's report	• Communicate with audit committee and management results of audit and impact upon fraud risk management processes.

SOURCES OF INFORMATION ABOUT FRAUD RISKS Information used to assess fraud risk is summarized in Figure 11-3. This information is considered in the context of the three conditions for fraud: incentives/pressures, opportunities, and attitudes/rationalization. Auditors should consider the following:

- Information obtained from communications among audit team members about their knowledge of the company and its industry, including how and where the company might be susceptible to material misstatements due to fraud.
- Responses to auditor inquiries of management about its risk management process, including views of the risks of fraud and about existing programs and controls to address specific identified fraud risks.
- Specific risk factors for fraudulent financial reporting, revenue recognition, and misappropriations of assets.
- Analytical procedures results obtained during planning that indicate possible, implausible, or unexpected analytical relationships.
- Knowledge obtained through other procedures, such as client acceptance and retention decisions, interim review of financial statements, and consideration of inherent or control risks.

Communications among the Audit Team

CAS CAS 240 requires the audit team, including the engagement partner, to conduct discussions to share insights into the susceptibility of the entity to fraud and error.

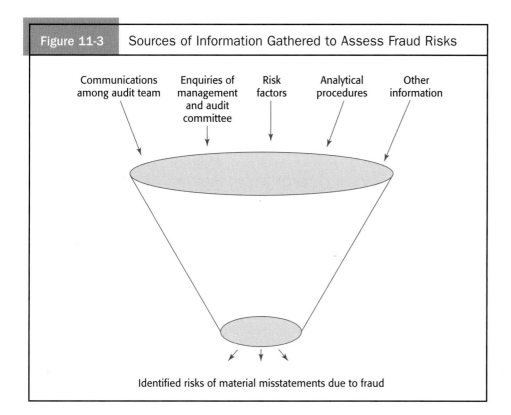

Figure 11-3   Sources of Information Gathered to Assess Fraud Risks

Communications among audit team

Enquiries of management and audit committee

Risk factors

Analytical procedures

Other information

Identified risks of material misstatements due to fraud

The results of the discussions, which should be documented, would address the following:

1. How and where the audit team believes the entity's financial statements might be susceptible to material misstatement due to fraud.
2. How management could perpetrate and conceal fraudulent financial reporting.
3. How assets of the entity could be misappropriated.
4. What circumstances exist that might be indicative of earnings management that could lead to fraudulent financial reporting.
5. What known external and internal factors affecting the entity might
   - create an incentive or pressure for management to commit fraud;
   - provide the opportunity for fraud to be perpetrated; or
   - indicate a culture or environment that enables management to rationalize fraudulent acts.
6. How the auditor might respond to the susceptibility of material misstatements due to fraud.

Discussions with the audit team should reinforce the importance of all members maintaining an independent state of mind throughout the audit and being attuned to potential new information that might change the original assessment of the risk of fraud.

INQUIRIES OF MANAGEMENT AND AUDIT COMMITTEE CAS 240 requires the auditor to make specific inquiries about fraud in every audit. Inquiries of management and others within the company are important because the likelihood of fraud is often revealed through information received in response to the auditor's questions. Inquiries provide employees an opportunity to provide the auditor with information that otherwise might not be communicated.

If the auditors had previously issued a management letter to the organization with significant internal control weaknesses that affect fraud risks, initial inquiries would address whether those weakness had been remedied and how. If they have not been remedied, then the auditor would identify the fact of non-remedy as increasing the likelihood of fraud risks.

The auditor's inquiries of management should include asking whether management has knowledge of any fraud or suspected fraud within the company. Auditor inquiries about management's process of assessing and responding to fraud risks, the nature of fraud risks identified by management, and any internal controls implemented to address those risks provide useful information. The auditor should also inquire about any information reported by management to the audit committee about fraud risks and related controls.

The audit committee or equivalent often assumes an active role in overseeing management's fraud risk assessment and response processes. CAS 240 requires the auditor to inquire of the audit committee (or others charged with governance) its views of the risks of fraud and whether the audit committee has knowledge of any fraud or suspected fraud. Part of the reason for these inquiries is to corroborate the evidence provided by management.

For entities with an internal audit function, the auditor should inquire about internal audit's views of fraud risks and whether it has any knowledge of actual or alleged fraud that was not corrected. The auditor should also ask whether internal audit performed any procedures to identify or detect fraud during the year and if management had satisfactorily responded to its findings.

The auditor should also make inquiries of others within the entity whose duties lie outside the normal financial reporting lines of responsibility. When coming into contact with company personnel throughout the audit, such as the inventory warehouse manager and purchasing agents, the auditor may inquire about the existence or suspicion of fraud. Inquiries of executives and a wide variety of other employees with different levels of authority provide opportunities for the auditor to learn about risks of fraud. When responses are inconsistent, the auditor should obtain additional audit evidence to resolve the inconsistency and to support or refute the original risk assessment.

The auditor needs to take into account the oversight structure of the entity when assessing the risk of fraud. When the entity is smaller, without an audit committee, the owner/manager may be able to exercise effective oversight thus compensating for the absence of extensive internal controls. On the other hand, the auditor needs to keep in mind that the owner/manager may be more able to override controls.

CAS

RISK FACTORS CAS 240 requires the auditor to evaluate whether fraud risk factors exist that indicate incentives or pressures to perpetrate fraud, opportunities to carry out fraud, or attitudes or rationalizations used to justify a fraudulent action. Examples of fraud risk factors considered by auditors are included in Tables 11-1 (page 350) and 11-2 (page 351) and Appendix 1 of CAS 240. Professional judgment is required when determining whether a risk factor is present and, if so, the appropriate response. Fraud risk factors do not indicate that fraud exists, only that the likelihood of fraud is higher. Auditors should consider these factors along with other information used to assess the risks of fraud.

Impact of significant fraud risks upon the audit CAS 240 states that several key areas be assumed to have significant risk of fraud or material misstatement unless there is evidence to the contrary. These are revenue recognition, financial statement journal entries, accounting estimates, and significant unusual transactions. Specific audit procedures to address these high-risk areas are discussed in the final section of this chapter.

ANALYTICAL PROCEDURES As discussed in Chapter 6, auditors should perform analytical procedures during the planning, testing, and completion phases of the audit. Analytical procedures help the auditor identify unusual or unexpected relationships that might indicate the presence of material misstatements in the financial statements.

Analytical procedures performed during planning may be helpful in identifying fraud risks. When results from analytical procedures differ from the auditor's expectations, the auditor evaluates those results along with other information to assess whether there is a heightened risk of fraud.

Because occurrences of fraudulent financial reporting often involve manipulation of revenue, CAS 240 advises the auditor to pay particular attention to analytical procedures on revenue accounts. The objective is to identify unusual or unexpected relationships involving revenue accounts that may indicate fraudulent financial reporting. For example, comparing the sales volume based on recorded revenue with actual production capacity could reveal revenues beyond the entity's production capabilities. As another example, comparing the sales revenue with accounts receivable could reveal recorded sales that lack economic substance, as bogus sales would remain unpaid and accounts receivable would grow.

OTHER INFORMATION Auditors should consider all information that they have obtained in any part of the audit as they assess the risk of fraud. Examples include information about management's integrity and honesty obtained during client acceptance and retention procedures, inquiries and analytical procedures done in connection with the auditor's review of the client's quarterly financial statements, and information considered in assessing inherent and control risks.

As shown in Figure 11-2 (page 356), the auditor considers all information, individually and in combination, that was gathered to assess fraud risks. The outcome of the assessment process is the identification of specific risks of material misstatements due to fraud. Before determining audit responses to identified fraud risks, the auditor considers management's programs and controls that may address those risks, as described later in this chapter.

DOCUMENTING FRAUD ASSESSMENT CAS 240 requires that auditors document the following matters related to their consideration of material misstatements due to fraud:

CAS

- The decisions reached during the discussion among engagement team personnel in planning the audit about the susceptibility of the entity's financial statements to material fraud.
- The assessed risk of material misstatement due to fraud, both overall and at the assertion level.
- The response to the assessed risks of material fraud that were identified, including the impact on the nature, timing, and extent of audit procedures.
- Results of the procedures performed to address the risk of management override of controls.
- The nature of communications about fraud made to management, the audit committee, or others.
- Reasons supporting a conclusion that there is not a significant risk of material improper revenue recognition.

After fraud risks are identified and documented, the auditor should evaluate factors that reduce fraud risk before developing an appropriate response to the risk of fraud. The next section discusses specific actions that the auditor can take when risks of fraud are identified, and actions that should be taken when fraud is actually discovered.

> **concept check**
>
> C11-7 Describe three ways that the auditor documents and displays professional skepticism in the context of fraud.
>
> C11-8 What actions does the auditor take to consider fraud risk during the audit plan phase of the financial statement audit?

The Auditor's Role in Responding to the Risk of Fraud

When risks of material misstatements due to fraud are identified, the auditor should first discuss these findings with management and obtain management's views of the potential fraud and existing controls designed to prevent or detect misstatements. Management may have programs designed to prevent, deter, and detect fraud as well as controls designed to mitigate specific risks of fraud. Auditors should then consider whether such programs and controls mitigate the identified risks of material misstatements due to fraud or whether control deficiencies increase the risk of fraud. Auditor responses to fraud risk include the following:

1. Change the overall conduct of the audit to respond to identified fraud risks.
2. Design and perform audit procedures to address identified risks.
3. Design and perform procedures to address the risk of management override of controls.

Change the Overall Conduct of the Audit

There are several overall responses to an increased fraud risk. If the risk of misstatement due to fraud is increased, more-experienced personnel may be assigned to the audit. Some public accounting firms assign a fraud specialist to the audit team for high-risk engagements.

Auditors should also consider management's choice of accounting principles. Careful attention should be paid to accounting principles that involve subjective measurements or complex transactions. Because there is a presumption of fraud risk in revenue recognition, auditors should also evaluate the company's revenue recognition policies.

Fraud perpetrators are often knowledgeable about audit procedures. For this reason, CAS 240 requires auditors to incorporate unpredictability in the audit plan. For example, auditors may visit inventory locations or test accounts that were not tested in prior periods. Auditors should also consider tests that address misappropriation of assets, even when the amounts are not typically material.

When the risk of fraud is increased, auditors should step outside their normal role of reviewing financial records and holding discussions with the entity's financial staff. They should gather information from as many sources as possible. For example, a review of the build-up of dust on inventory may be an indication of inventory valuation problems, or the lack of organization around the premises may be an indication of an organization in crisis. Auditors need to look beyond the audit program for what is unusual and out of the norm. Consider the doughnut as well as the hole; in other words, both what is there and what is missing.

Design and Perform Audit Procedures to Address Fraud Risks

The appropriate audit procedures used to address specific fraud risks depend on the account being audited and the type of fraud risk identified. For example, if concerns are raised about revenue recognition because of cut-off issues or channel stuffing, the auditor may review the sales journal for unusual activity near the end of the period and review the terms of sales. Specific procedures are described in the discussion of specific fraud risk areas later in this chapter. Appendix 2 of CAS 240 provides examples of audit procedures to address the risk of fraud. The auditor must exercise professional judgment when selecting the most appropriate procedure in the circumstances. The response will be unique, depending upon the auditor's assessment of the type of fraud risk factors or conditions identified and the account balance, class of transactions, and assertions affected.

Design and Perform Procedures to Address Management Override of Controls

The risk of management override of controls exists in almost all audits. Because management is in a unique position to perpetrate fraud by overriding controls that are otherwise operating effectively, auditors must perform procedures in every audit to address the risk of management override. Three procedures must be performed in every audit.

EXAMINE JOURNAL ENTRIES AND OTHER ADJUSTMENTS FOR EVIDENCE OF POSSIBLE MISSTATEMENTS DUE TO FRAUD Fraud often results from adjustments to amounts reported in the financial statements, even when there are effective internal controls in the rest of the recording processes. The auditor should first obtain an understanding of the entity's financial reporting process and internal controls over journal entries and other adjustments. Then he or she should inquire of employees involved in the financial reporting process about inappropriate or unusual activity in processing journal entries and other adjustments. CAS 240 requires testing of journal entries and other financial statement adjustments. The extent of testing is affected by the effectiveness of controls and results of the inquiries. Fraudulent journal

Auditing "beyond the call of duty" is important for every audit.

The auditors of a public company successfully discovered an intentional misstatement when they stepped away from their standard audit program.

A manufacturing company whose products were shipped around the world showed a warranty provision to be consistent with past years' allowance and actual claims experienced. Vicky, the auditor assigned to that area of the engagement, followed the audit program and confirmed with the vice-president of operations that nothing had changed since the previous year; she also reviewed the actual warranty claims experience in the prior year. Both of these procedures supported the warranty provision as reported in the draft financial statements.

As a result, Vicky was initially prepared to sign off on the section concluding that the warranty provision was adequate. But was it? One afternoon she decided to take a walk through the back shop to talk to the repairs manager. The repairs manager enjoyed talking about his job and the challenges he experienced. He explained that some of the new products in the field were experiencing problems and he was anticipating all products of a particular class would be returned for repair at a significant cost.

Because Vicky was alerted to these potential problems, she performed an additional analysis after talking to the repairs manager. The warranty provision was subsequently increased to reflect the anticipated costs of repairs. The small profit the company was showing on the financial statements was quickly changed to a loss. Had Vicky simply followed the audit program, the misstatement would not have been identified.

entries and other adjustments often occur at the end of a period; therefore, the auditor would ordinarily select entries made at the beginning and end of the reporting period. However, because fraud can occur throughout the period, professional judgment should be used when considering whether to test journal entries throughout the period.

REVIEW ACCOUNTING ESTIMATES FOR BIASES Fraudulent financial reporting is often accomplished through intentional misstatement of accounting estimates. CAS 240 requires the auditor to consider the potential for management bias when reviewing current-year estimates. The auditor is required to "look back" at significant prior-year estimates to identify any changes in the company's processes or management's judgments and assumptions that might indicate a potential bias. For example, management's estimates may have been clustered at the high end of the range of acceptable amounts in the prior year and at the low end in the current year. If a possible bias by management in making accounting estimates is identified, the auditor should consider if the cumulative effect of the bias is designed to smooth earnings or achieve a desired earnings level.

EVALUATE THE BUSINESS RATIONALE FOR SIGNIFICANT UNUSUAL TRANSACTIONS CAS 240 emphasizes understanding the underlying business rationale for significant unusual transactions that might be outside the normal course of business for the company. The auditor should gain an understanding of the purposes of significant transactions to assess whether transactions have been entered into to engage in fraudulent financial reporting. For example, the company may engage in financing transactions to avoid reporting liabilities on the balance sheet. The auditor should determine whether the accounting treatment for any unusual transaction is appropriate in the circumstances, taking into account the substance of the transaction and not the form, and whether information about the transaction is adequately disclosed in the financial statements. For significant and unusual transactions, the auditor should consider investigating the possibility of related-party transactions.

Update Risk Assessment Process

The auditor's assessment of the risks of material misstatement due to fraud should be ongoing. The auditor may identify during fieldwork conditions that change or support a judgment about the initial assessment of fraud risks. Appendix 3 of CAS 240 includes examples of circumstances that indicate the possibility of fraud. While the list is not all encompassing, it is a good reference source. For example, the auditor should be alert during fieldwork to the following:

- Discrepancies in the accounting records, including problems concerning computer processing such as extensive errors that require manual corrections, last-minute adjustments that significantly affect financial results, or employees' access rights inconsistent with their authorized duties, such as senior management preparation of journal entries.
- Conflicting or missing evidence including inconsistent, vague, or implausible responses to inquiries; unavailability of original documents; or inability to produce evidence of key systems development or program change testing in implementation activities.
- Problematic or unusual relationships between the auditor and management including unusual delays in providing requested information, undue time pressure imposed by management, unwillingness to facilitate auditor access to key electronic files for testing through computer-assisted audit techniques, or unwillingness to address identified weaknesses in internal controls on a timely basis.
- Other circumstances like accounting policies inconsistent with industry norms, changes in accounting estimates not supported by a change in circumstances, and tolerance to violation of the entity's code of conduct.

Specific Fraud Risk Areas

Depending on the client's industry, certain accounts are especially susceptible to manipulation or theft. Figure 11-4 illustrates types of fraud tracked by the Association of Certified Fraud Examiners (ACFE), using U.S. data. It is usually financial reporting fraud that receives the most notice because of the magnitude of its impact on users of the financial statements. In the 2008 ACFE survey, the median loss for financial reporting fraud was $2 million, while for other types of fraud it was $175,000. As mentioned previously, misappropriations of assets are usually immaterial to the financial statements; nonetheless, auditors should assess the risk. The following sections discuss specific high-risk accounts, including warning signs of fraud. Even with knowledge of these warning signs, fraud is extremely difficult to detect. However, awareness of these warning signs and fraud detection techniques increase the auditor's likelihood of identifying misstatements due to fraud.

REVENUE AND ACCOUNTS RECEIVABLE FRAUD RISKS Revenue and related accounts receivable and cash accounts are especially susceptible to manipulation and theft. A study sponsored by COSO found that more than half of financial statement frauds involve revenues and accounts receivable. Similarly, when sales are made for cash or are quickly converted to cash, they are also highly susceptible to theft.

FRAUDULENT FINANCIAL REPORTING—RISKS FOR REVENUE As a result of the frequency of financial reporting frauds involving revenue recognition, CAS 240 requires auditors to identify revenue recognition as a significant fraud risk in most audits. Revenue is susceptible to manipulation for several reasons. Overstatement of revenues often increases net income by an equal amount because related costs of sales are often not recorded for fictitious or prematurely recognized revenues. Also, financial analysts and other market participants place increasing emphasis on revenue growth. There are three main types of revenue manipulations: fictitious revenues, premature revenue recognition, and manipulation of adjustments to revenues.

FICTITIOUS REVENUES The most notorious forms of revenue fraud involve creating fictitious revenues. Although there have been several recent cases involving fictitious revenues, there are also many earlier examples. For example, the Ultramares case described in Chapter 4 involved fictitious revenue entries in the general ledger.

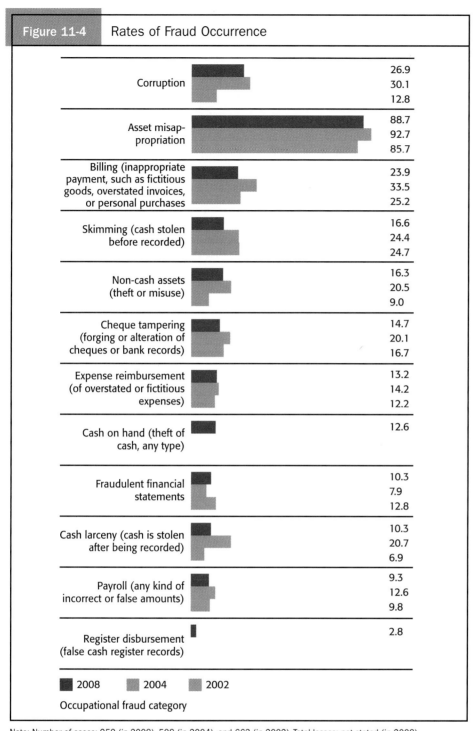

Figure 11-4   Rates of Fraud Occurrence

Occupational fraud category	2008	2004	2002
Corruption	26.9	30.1	12.8
Asset misappropriation	88.7	92.7	85.7
Billing (inappropriate payment, such as fictitious goods, overstated invoices, or personal purchases	23.9	33.5	25.2
Skimming (cash stolen before recorded)	16.6	24.4	24.7
Non-cash assets (theft or misuse)	16.3	20.5	9.0
Cheque tampering (forging or alteration of cheques or bank records)	14.7	20.1	16.7
Expense reimbursement (of overstated or fictitious expenses)	13.2	14.2	12.2
Cash on hand (theft of cash, any type)	12.6		
Fraudulent financial statements	10.3	7.9	12.8
Cash larceny (cash is stolen after being recorded)	10.3	20.7	6.9
Payroll (any kind of incorrect or false amounts)	9.3	12.6	9.8
Register disbursement (false cash register records)	2.8		

■ 2008   ▨ 2004   ▨ 2002

Note: Number of cases: 959 (in 2008), 508 (in 2004), and 663 (in 2002). Total losses: not stated (in 2008), US$761 million (in 2004), and US$7 billion (in 2002). Totals exceed 100 percent as some frauds involved multiple types. Methods of data collection changed in 2006, where comparatives and similar category totals were not provided.

Sources: Association of Certified Fraud Examiners, "Report to the Nation on Occupational Fraud and Abuse," 2008, 2004, and 2002, www.acfe.com, Accessed: January 4, 2009.

Financing arrangements are occasionally incorrectly recorded as revenue. In the Livent case, a number of transactions with third parties involved the assignment of certain intangible assets, such as the rights to stage a play, which Livent recorded as revenue. These transactions were accompanied by "side deals," which were not properly disclosed, requiring Livent to repurchase the assets in the future at amounts comparable to the consideration received by Livent on the "sale" of those assets. By failing to disclose the "side-deals," Livent improperly treated what were lending arrangements as revenue transactions.

PREMATURE REVENUE RECOGNITION Companies often accelerate the timing of revenue recognition to meet earnings or sales forecasts. **Premature revenue recognition** is the recognition of revenue before GAAP requirements for recording revenue have been met. Premature revenue recognition should be distinguished from cut-off errors, in which transactions are inadvertently recorded in the incorrect period. In the simplest form of premature revenue recognition, sales that should have been recorded in the subsequent period are recorded as current period sales.

One method of fraudulently accelerating revenue is a "bill-and-hold" sale. Sales are normally recognized at the time goods are shipped. In a bill-and-hold sale, the goods are invoiced before they are shipped. Another method involves issuing side agreements that modify the terms of the sales transaction. For example, revenue recognition is likely to be inappropriate if a major customer agrees to take a significant amount of inventory at year end, but a side agreement provides for more favourable pricing and unrestricted return of the goods if not sold by the customer. In some cases, as a result of the terms of the side agreement, the transaction does not qualify as a sale under generally accepted accounting principles.

Two notable recent examples of premature revenue recognition involve Bausch & Lomb Incorporated and Xerox Corporation. In the Bausch & Lomb case, the company shipped items that were not ordered by customers, with unrestricted right of return and promises that the goods did not have to be paid for until sold. The revenue recognition issues at Xerox were more complex. Capital equipment leases include sales, financing, and service components. Because the sales component is recognized immediately, Xerox attempted to maximize the amount allocated to this aspect of the transaction.

MANIPULATION OF ADJUSTMENTS TO REVENUES The most common adjustment to revenue involves sales returns and allowances. A company may hide sales returns from the auditor to overstate net sales and income. If the returned goods are counted as part of physical inventory, the return may actually increase reported income. In this case, an asset increase is recognized through the counting of physical inventory, but the reduction in the related accounts receivable balance is not made. The completeness of sales returns can be verified by accounting for all receiving reports. However, if management has separate procedures for receiving returned goods, or if attempts are made to circumvent normal receiving procedures, other evidence may be necessary to verify the completeness of sales returns.

Bad-debt expense is related to the revenue cycle but is normally treated as a sales expense, rather than as an adjustment to revenue. Companies may attempt to reduce bad-debt expense by understating the allowance for doubtful accounts. Because the required allowance depends on the age and quality of accounts receivable, some companies have altered the aging of accounts receivable to make them appear more current. This can usually be readily verified by testing the accuracy of the aging, which is done by comparing the date on the original invoice to the aged accounts receivable trial balance.

Warning Signs of Fraudulent Financial Reporting in Revenue

There are many potential warning signals or symptoms of revenue fraud. Two of the most important ways of detecting these are by analytical procedures and document discrepancies.

Analytical Procedures Analytical procedures, especially gross margin percentage and accounts receivable turnover, often signal revenue frauds. Fictitious revenue overstates the gross margin percentage, and premature revenue recognition also overstates gross margin if the related cost of sales is not recognized. Fictitious revenues also lower accounts receivable turnover because the fictitious revenues are not collected. Table 11-5 includes comparative sales, cost of sales, and accounts receivable data for a company in which the financial statements included fictitious revenue.

Premature revenue recognition—recognition of revenue before GAAP requirements for recording revenue have been met.

Table 11-5	Example of the Effect of Fictitious Receivables on Accounting Ratios		
	2008	2007	2006
Sales[a]	$265	$185	$105
Cost of sales	(155)	(115)	(67)
Gross profit	110	70	38
Gross profit percentage	42%	38%	36%
Year-end accounts receivable	70	38	20
Accounts receivable turnover[b]	3.8	4.9	5.3

[a]Dollar amounts in millions
[b]Accounts receivable turnover calculated as Sales/Ending accounts receivable

Note how the accounts receivable increased, as there were no cash receipts to pay for the fictitious revenues. A higher gross profit percentage, which increased from 36 percent to 42 percent, and lower accounts receivable turnover ratio, which declined from 5.3 to 3.8, helped signal fictitious revenue and accounts receivable. When performing analytical procedures, the more years available to analyze, the more informative the trend analysis will be.

In some frauds, management generated fictitious revenues to make analytical procedures results, such as gross margin, similar to the prior year's. In frauds like this, analytical procedures that compare client data with similar prior-period data are typically not useful to signal the fraud. Analytical procedures should also compare client data with industry performance data. Auditors should be aware of the risk of material misstatement related to revenue when the gross margin of the industry is declining, while the entity under audit has remained stable.

Document Discrepancies Despite the best efforts of fraud perpetrators, fictitious transactions rarely have the same level of documentary evidence as legitimate transactions.

For example, in the well-known fraud at ZZZZ Best, insurance restoration contracts worth millions of dollars were supported by one- or two-page agreements and lacked many of the supporting details and evidence, such as permits, that are normally associated with such contracts. Some of the fraudulent journal entries at WorldCom for hundreds of millions of U.S. dollars were supported by nothing more than Post-it notes.

Auditors should be aware of unusual markings and alterations on documents, and they should rely on originals rather than photocopies of documents. Because fraud perpetrators attempt to conceal fraud, even one unusual transaction in a sample should be considered a potential indicator of fraud that should be investigated.

Misappropriation of Assets—Receipts Involving Revenue

Although misappropriation of cash receipts is rarely as material as fraudulent reporting of revenues, such frauds can be costly to the organization because of the direct loss of assets. The objective of the misappropriation of assets is usually theft of cash. Many thefts of cash receipts are closely tied to the revenue cycle and are considered separately from other thefts of cash. A typical misappropriation of assets involves failure to record a sale or adjustments made to customer accounts to hide thefts of cash receipts.

Failure to Record a Sale One of the most difficult frauds to detect is when a sale is not recorded and the cash from the sale is stolen. Such frauds can be detected when goods are shipped on credit to customers. Tracing shipping documents to sales entries in the sales journal and accounting for all shipping documents can be used to verify that all sales have been recorded.

It is much more difficult to verify that all cash sales have been recorded because there are no shipping documents to verify the completeness of sales and there are no customer accounts receivable records supporting the sale. In such cases, other documentary evidence is necessary to verify that all sales are recorded. For example, a retail establishment may require that all sales be recorded on a cash register. Recorded sales can then be compared with the total amount of sales on the cash register tape.

Theft of Cash Receipts after a Sale Is Recorded It is much more difficult to hide the theft of cash receipts after a sale is recorded. If a customer's payment is stolen, regular reminder notices of unpaid accounts will quickly uncover the fraud. As a result, to hide the theft, the fraud perpetrator must reduce the customer's account in one of three ways: (1) record a sales return or allowance, (2) write off the customer's account, or (3) apply the payment from another customer to the customer's account, which is also known as "lapping."

Preventing Misappropriation of Assets—Revenues and Cash Receipts Thefts of sales and related cash receipts are normally best prevented and detected by internal controls designed to minimize the opportunity for fraud such as segregation of duties. Employees with access to cash receipts should not have access to accounting records that would allow them to manipulate customers' accounts to hide the theft. Analytical procedures and other comparisons may be useful in detecting larger frauds. Material misappropriation of cash receipts may be detected in cash flow analysis if revenues remain strong but cash shortfalls persist.

 INVENTORY FRAUD RISKS Inventory is often the largest account on many companies' balance sheets, and it is often difficult to verify the existence and valuation of inventories. As a result, inventory is susceptible to manipulation to achieve financial reporting objectives. Because inventory is also usually readily saleable, it is also susceptible to misappropriation.

FRAUDULENT FINANCIAL REPORTING—INVENTORY Fictitious inventory has been at the centre of several major cases of fraudulent financial reporting. Many large companies have varied and extensive inventory in multiple locations, making it possible for the company to add fictitious inventory to accounting records.

Auditors are required to verify the existence of physical inventories. However, audit testing is done on a sample basis, and typically not all locations with inventory are tested. In some cases involving fictitious inventories, auditors informed the client

audit challenge 11-3
Pocketing Parking Cash

Sam Ralston was in charge of a university parking lot. He was supposed to place a parking receipt on the dash of the car when he received cash from the driver, but he would often collect the cash and wave the driver in without a receipt, particularly for sporting events. The university considered it too expensive to have two employees handle parking, and it was difficult to count the paid vehicles in a lot because some cars were parked by university employees with passes.

After several years, the university rotated Sam to another lot. An astute employee in the accounting office noticed that revenues collected from the lot seemed to increase after Sam's

departure. Further investigation revealed that average revenues declined at the new lot to which Sam had been assigned. Confronted with the evidence, Sam confessed and his employment was terminated.

CRITICAL THINKING QUESTIONS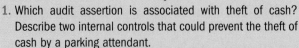

1. Which audit assertion is associated with theft of cash? Describe two internal controls that could prevent the theft of cash by a parking attendant.

2. Provide two examples of analytical review that could be conducted at a university to detect theft of cash.

in advance which inventory locations were to be tested. As a result, the client could transfer inventories to the locations being tested. In other cases, when auditors have failed to take copies of inventory count records, clients have added items to inventory after the count.

WARNING SIGNS OF FRAUDULENT FINANCIAL REPORTING—INVENTORY As for accounts receivable, there are many potential warning signals or symptoms of inventory fraud. Analytical procedures are especially important for detecting inventory fraud.

Analytical procedures Analytical procedures, especially gross margin percentage and inventory turnover, often identify inventory fraud. Fictitious inventory understates cost of goods sold and overstates the gross margin percentage. Fictitious inventory also lowers inventory turnover.

PURCHASES AND ACCOUNTS PAYABLE FRAUD RISKS Cases of fraudulent financial reporting involving accounts payable are relatively common, although less frequent than frauds involving inventory or accounts receivable. The deliberate understatement of accounts payable generally results in an understatement of purchases and cost of goods sold and an overstatement of net income. Significant misappropriations involving purchases can also occur in the form of payments to fictitious vendors, as well as kickbacks and other illegal arrangements with suppliers.

FRAUDULENT FINANCIAL REPORTING—ACCOUNTS PAYABLE Companies may engage in deliberate attempts to understate accounts payable and overstate income. This can be accomplished by not recording accounts payable until the subsequent period or by recording fictitious reductions to accounts payable.

All purchases received before the end of the year should be recorded as liabilities. This is verified by accounting for pre-numbered receiving reports. However, if the receiving reports are not pre-numbered or the company deliberately omits receiving reports from the accounting records, it may be difficult for the auditor to verify whether all liabilities have been recorded. Analytical evidence such as unusual changes in ratios may signal that accounts payable are understated.

Companies often have complex arrangements with suppliers, which results in reductions to accounts payable for advertising credits and other allowances. These arrangements may not be as well documented as acquisition transactions. Some companies have used fictitious reductions to accounts payable to overstate net income. Auditors should read agreements with suppliers when amounts are material and make sure the financial statements reflect the substance of the agreements.

MISAPPROPRIATIONS OF ASSETS—ACQUISITION AND PAYMENT CYCLE The most common fraud in the acquisitions area is for the perpetrator to issue payments to fictitious vendors and deposit the cheques in a fictitious account. These frauds can be prevented by allowing payments to be made only to approved vendors and by carefully scrutinizing documentation supporting the acquisitions by authorized personnel before payments are made. In other misappropriation cases, the accounts payable clerk or another employee steals a cheque to a legitimate vendor. The purchases information is then resubmitted for payment to the vendor. Such fraud can be prevented by cancelling supporting documents to prevent their being used to support multiple payments.

OTHER AREAS OF FRAUD RISK Almost every account is subject to manipulation. The following sections discuss other accounts with specific risks of fraudulent financial reporting or misappropriation.

Fixed Assets Fixed assets are a large balance sheet account for many companies and are often based on subjectively determined valuations. As a result, fixed assets may be a target for financial statement manipulation, especially for companies without material receivables or inventories. For example, companies may capitalize repairs or other operating expenses as fixed assets. Such frauds could be detected if the auditor examines evidence supporting fixed asset additions.

Because of their value and saleability, fixed assets are also targets for theft. This is especially true for fixed assets that are readily portable, such as laptop computers. To reduce the potential for theft, fixed assets should be physically protected whenever possible, engraved or otherwise permanently labelled, and periodically inventoried.

Payroll Expenses Payroll is rarely a significant risk area for fraudulent financial reporting. However, companies may overstate inventories and net income by recording excess labour costs in inventory.

Company employees are sometimes used to construct fixed assets. Excess labour cost may be capitalized as fixed assets in these circumstances. Material fringe benefits such as retirement benefits are also susceptible to manipulation.

Payroll fraud involving misappropriation of assets is fairly common, but the amounts involved are often immaterial. The two most common areas of fraud are the creation of fictitious employees and overstatement of individual payroll hours. The existence of fictitious employees can usually be prevented by separation of the human resource and payroll functions. Overstatement of hours is typically prevented by use of time clocks or approval of payroll hours.

Detecting Computer Fraud The use and increased complexity of computers in business make certain kinds of fraud easier to commit and harder to detect. Since data are not readily visible in paper form, computer systems can be used by management to prevent and detect fraud, by implementing adequate software controls or by having data regularly checked for unusual patterns. For example, there are computer-assisted audit techniques used by auditors to look for post office box numbers for suppliers or customers.

The outcome of a fraud committed using a computer is no different from any fraud already discussed in this chapter: Assets are misappropriated or financial statements are fraudulently reported. To prevent such a fraud, management should ensure that preventive and detective controls are present in each functional area of the business. For example, in accounts payable and purchasing, there should be access controls over the addition of new vendors and for changing addresses of existing vendors. Management should also ensure that there is segregation of duties among employees who can add new vendors and employees who can process invoices or invoice payments.

Responsibilities When Fraud Is Suspected

The 2008 ACFE fraud report found that 46.2 percent of frauds (34.2 percent in 2006) were detected by a tip or other type of information obtained by a stakeholder such as a customer or vendor. Only 19.4 percent (20.2 percent in 2006) were discovered by internal audit and only 9.1 percent (12 percent in 2006) by external audit. Yet, based upon a 2004 study, KPMG LLP reported that boards of directors look to their external auditors more than any other means of detecting financial reporting fraud.[1] However, an earlier survey, in 2003, discovered that more frauds are detected by internal controls or the internal audit function than by external auditors.[2] Internal auditors' primary focus is on controls, and it is internal controls that will prevent and detect fraud. The existence of an effective internal audit group can act as a deterrent against fraud.

One spectacular example of an internal auditor identifying a financial reporting fraud is the case of WorldCom. Cynthia Cooper, WorldCom's vice-president of internal audit, discovered that the company had been capitalizing over US$3.5 billion of expenses. She was named by *Time* magazine as one of the three "Persons of the Year" in 2002.

RESPONDING TO MISSTATEMENTS THAT MAY BE THE RESULT OF FRAUD Throughout an audit, the auditor continually evaluates whether evidence gathered and observations made indicate material misstatement due to fraud. When fraud is suspected, the auditor gathers

---

[1] KPMG 2004. Survey on the Risk of Manipulation of Financial Statements, www.kpmg.ca

[2] KPMG Forensics, Fraud Survey 2003.

additional information to determine whether fraud actually exists. Often, the auditor begins by making additional inquiries of management and others. Such discussions should be corroborated either by reference to source documents or by further analysis.

TYPES OF INQUIRY TECHNIQUES As described in Chapter 6, inquiry can be an effective audit evidence-gathering technique. Interviewing can help identify issues omitted from documentation or confirmations. The auditor can also modify questions during the interview based on the interviewee's responses.

Inquiry as an audit evidence-gathering technique should be tailored to the purpose for which it is being used. Depending on the purpose, the auditor may ask different types of questions and change the tone of the interview.

Informational inquiry An auditor uses **informational inquiry** to obtain information about facts and details that the auditor does not have. Usually the auditor wants information from the interviewee about past or current events or processes. The auditor poses open-ended questions that allow the respondent to provide details of events, processes, or circumstances. Auditors often use informational inquiry when gathering follow-up evidence about programs and controls or other evidence involving a misstatement or suspected fraud uncovered in the audit.

> **Informational inquiry**—inquiry to obtain information about facts and details the auditor does not have.

Assessment inquiry An auditor also uses inquiry to assess whether information already obtained is correct, factual, or truthful. The auditor uses **assessment inquiry** to corroborate or contradict prior information. The auditor often starts the assessment inquiry with broad, open-ended questions that allow the interviewee to provide detailed responses, which can later be followed up with more specific questions. One common use of assessment inquiry is to corroborate management responses to earlier inquiries by asking questions of other employees.

> **Assessment inquiry**—inquiry to corroborate or contradict prior information obtained.

ANALYSIS USING COMPUTERS Computer-assisted audit techniques (CAATs) can be particularly useful when the risk of fraud is assessed as high and there are large volumes of data to analyze. Common computer-assisted audit procedures that can be completed by generalized audit software include extraction (identifying transactions with certain characteristics, such as having a date outside the billing period or a high dollar amount), gap detection (looking for missing sequence numbers, such as receiving or shipping reports), duplicate detection (such as duplicate invoice numbers for the same supplier), recalculations (such as discounts or aging), stratification (grouping the transactions by a criterion such as amount or age), matching (comparing information from multiple data files, such as wage-rate master files with payroll transactions), and statistical and trend analyses (graphing or tabulating trends over a period of time). Especially when there are hundreds of thousands or millions of transactions, these techniques are essential in assisting the auditor to identify which transactions are to be examined.

OTHER RESPONSIBILITIES WHEN FRAUD IS SUSPECTED When an auditor suspects that fraud may be present, he or she is required to obtain additional evidence to determine whether material fraud has occurred. Auditors often use inquiry, as previously discussed, as part of that information-gathering process. An auditor is also required to consider the implications for other aspects of the audit. For example, fraud involving the misappropriation of cash from a small petty cash fund normally is of little significance to the auditor, unless the matter involves higher-level management. In the latter situation, the petty cash fraud may indicate a more pervasive problem involving management's integrity. This may indicate to the auditor a need to re-evaluate the fraud risk assessment and the impact on the nature, timing, and extent of audit evidence.

Sometimes, auditors identify risks of material misstatements due to fraud that have internal control implications. There may also be cases where the auditor identifies deficiencies in management's antifraud programs and controls that will result in the programs' failure to mitigate the risk of fraud. In these situations, the auditor must communicate those items to the audit committee if they are considered significant deficiencies or material weaknesses.

While all auditors need to understand what fraud is and how to respond when there is an identified fraud risk on an engagement, some accountants, called forensic accountants, specialize in fraud auditing. A fraud auditor is an accountant who, by virtue of his or her skills and experience, is an expert in detecting and documenting fraud in a company's books and records. Besides accounting and auditing knowledge, these specialists possess an investigative mentality, which is evidenced by skepticism and the ability to seek out alternative explanations and evidence.

Not all fraud auditors are forensic accountants. Forensic means "used in connection with the courts," so a forensic accountant's work would need to meet standards acceptable in court. Forensic accounting as a sub-discipline of accounting includes not only fraud auditing but also litigation support. It might involve testifying on the findings of an investigation.

Did you know that when investigating fraud, computer evidence is considered "tampered with" if a computer file had been simply opened? The forensic auditor must be aware of ways to collect paper-based and electronic evidence directly and indirectly, by such means as analysis and interviewing.

Accreditations for forensic specialists include CFE (see **www.acfe.com**) and DIFA (see **www.rotman.utoronto.ca/difa**). These programs include topics such as investigation techniques, interview techniques, and legal issues associated with forensic investigations.

CRITICAL THINKING QUESTIONS

1. Other types of specialist forensic courses are available, such as CCE (Certified Computer Examiner, www.cftco.com) and FERRT (Fingerprint Evidence Recovery and Recording Techniques, www.npia.police.uk/en/1486.htm). Why would these accreditations be relevant (or not relevant) to an investigation of financial statement manipulation?
2. What skills does an auditor bring to a forensic investigation?

RESPONSIBILITIES FOR REPORTING WHEN FRAUD IS SUSPECTED When the auditor suspects that fraud may be present, he or she should promptly discuss the matter with an appropriate level of management (even if the matter might be considered inconsequential) and should modify the audit approach for further investigation. The appropriate level of management should be at least one level above those involved. If the auditor believes that senior management may be involved in the fraud, the auditor should discuss the matter directly with the audit committee.

Reporting to the audit committee or equivalent Auditors should use professional judgment in determining which matters to report to the audit committee or equivalent. At a minimum, the auditor should communicate the following matters:

- Questions the auditor might have regarding the honesty and integrity of management.
- Any fraud involving management, no matter how trivial.
- Fraud involving employees who play a significant role in the entity's financial reporting and internal controls process.
- Matters, while not material now, that may cause the financial statements to be materially misstated in the future.

concept check

C11-9 Why is careful assessment of accounting principles part of an audit risk assessment?

C11-10 What are indicators of potentially suspicious journal entries?

C11-11 How are analytical procedures helpful in detecting potential fraud?

Reporting outside the organization The disclosure of possible fraud to parties other than the client's senior management and its audit committee is ordinarily not part of the auditor's responsibility. As described in Chapter 3, the auditor has a professional duty to maintain the confidentiality of client information. In some limited circumstances, the auditor may have a statutory duty to communicate certain matters to regulators. This would be the case for financial institutions. If in doubt, the auditor should obtain legal advice.

In exceptional circumstances, the results of the auditor's procedures may indicate such a significant risk of material misstatement due to fraud that the auditor should consider withdrawing from the audit. Such exceptional circumstances might include the entity's failure to take the appropriate actions that the auditor considers necessary, the discovery of false documentation, or significant concerns about management's or the audit committee's integrity.

Summary

1. *What is fraud and under what conditions is it most likely to exist?* Fraud in an audit context refers to the intentional misrepresentation of facts that lead to a misstatement of the financial statements. It is more likely to exist in organizations with weak internal controls, a weak internal control environment, or an unethical business culture.

   What is the difference between fraudulent financial reporting and misappropriation of assets? Fraudulent financial reporting occurs when there is an intentional misstatement of amounts or disclosures in the financial statements with the intent to deceive users of those statements. Misappropriation of assets involves the theft of assets such as cash or inventory.

2. *What features of corporate governance and of the control environment would reduce fraud risks?* The three most important things that an organization can do are (i) create and maintain a culture of honesty and high ethics; (ii) evaluate fraud risks and implement controls and programs to mitigate identified risks; and (iii) develop a fraud risk oversight process.

   What are the five principles that are part of effective fraud risk management? Those responsible for corporate governance should have a written policy with respect to their expectations of fraud risk. Fraud risk exposures should be assessed, with controls to mitigate and prevent fraud risks. Detective controls should also be present, as should communication, monitoring, and reporting to update the fraud management process.

3. *What is the auditor's responsibility for assessing the risk of fraud and detecting material misstatements due to fraud?* The auditor must consider the risk of fraud and of financial statement fraud in every audit engagement in order to obtain reasonable assurance that the statements are free from material misstatement. This is part of the audit planning process and involves the use of professional skepticism.

   How is fraud risk considered during the financial statement audit process? Each phase of the audit process is affected. The auditor needs to understand the client's processes, assess risks, design and evaluate audit procedures, as well as be aware of potential biases and the effects of unusual transactions.

4. *How should an auditor respond when there are identified fraud risks?* The auditor needs to communicate with the appropriate level of management. Then the auditor needs to appropriately modify the audit process in response to the identified risks: change the overall conduct of the audit and design and perform audit procedures to address those risks as well as the risk of potential management override.

   What are some of the specific fraud risk areas, and what is the auditor's responsibility once fraud is detected? Risks exist in every transaction cycle. Examples include theft of cash, fictitious suppliers or duplicate payments, unauthorized expenses, and overpaid or nonexistent employees. Once fraud is detected, the auditor has the responsibility to report to the appropriate level of management and the audit committee and to assess the effect on the audit and the financial statements.

Visit the text's website at www.pearsoned.ca/arens for practice quizzes, additional case studies, and international standards information.

Review Questions

11-1 What are the three conditions of fraud often referred to as "the fraud triangle"?

11-2 Give examples of risk factors for fraudulent financial reporting for each of the three fraud conditions: incentives/pressures, opportunities, and attitudes/rationalization.

11-3 Give examples of risk factors for misappropriation of assets for each of the three fraud conditions: incentives/pressures, opportunities, and attitudes/rationalization.

11-4 Describe six ways to promote a culture of honesty and high ethics.

11-5 Describe the purpose of corporate codes of conduct, and identify three examples of items addressed in a typical code of conduct.

11-6 Discuss the importance of the control environment, or "setting the tone at the top," in establishing a culture of honesty and integrity in a company.

11-7 Describe the five principles that should be addressed in an effective fraud risk management process.

11-8 Distinguish management's responsibility from the audit committee's responsibility for designing and implementing antifraud programs and controls within a company.

11-9 Explain two important characteristics of professional skepticism.

11-10 You are auditing a manufacturing company with locations in Toronto, Winnipeg, and Halifax. Using Table 11-4, list the actions that your firm would take to consider fraud risks at this company. Make your list specific to the manufacturing industry.

11-11 What sources are used by the auditor to gather information to assess fraud risks?

11-12 What should the audit team consider in its planning discussion about fraud risks?

11-13 Auditors are required to make inquiries of individuals in the company when gathering information to assess fraud risk. Identify those of whom the auditor must make inquiries.

11-14 Describe how you would document your fraud risk assessment of a real estate management company.

11-15 What are the three categories of auditor responses to fraud risks?

11-16 What three auditor actions are required to address the potential for management override of controls?

11-17 Describe the three main techniques used to manipulate revenue.

11-18 You are at the drive-through window of a fast food restaurant and notice a sign that reads "Your meal is free if we fail to give you a receipt." Why would the restaurant post this sign?

11-19 Name the two categories of inquiry and describe the purpose of each when used by an auditor to obtain additional information about a suspected fraud.

11-20 What matters related to fraud should be communicated to the audit committee?

11-21 You have identified a suspected fraud involving the company's controller. What must you do after this discovery?

Discussion Questions and Problems

11-22 During audit planning, an auditor obtained the following information:

1. Management has a strong interest in employing inappropriate means to minimize reported earnings for tax-motivated reasons.
2. Assets and revenues are based on significant estimates that involve subjective judgments and uncertainties that are hard to corroborate.
3. The company is marginally able to meet exchange listing and debt covenant requirements.
4. Significant operations are located and conducted across international borders in jurisdictions where differing business environments and cultures exist.
5. There are recurring attempts by management to justify marginal or inappropriate accounting on the basis of materiality.
6. The company's financial performance is threatened by a high degree of competition and market saturation.

REQUIRED

Classify each of the six factors into one of these fraud conditions: incentives/pressures, opportunities, or attitudes/rationalization.

11-23 Recently, there have been a significant number of highly publicized cases of management fraud involving the misstatement of financial statements. Although most client managements possess unquestioned integrity, a very small number, given sufficient incentive and opportunity, may be predisposed to fraudulently misstate reported financial conditions and operating results.

REQUIRED

a. What distinguishes management fraud from other types of fraud?
b. What are an auditor's responsibilities, under generally accepted auditing standards, to detect management fraud?

c. What are the characteristics of management fraud that an auditor should consider in order to fulfill the auditor's responsibilities for detecting management fraud under generally accepted auditing standards?
d. Three factors that heighten an auditor's concern about the existence of management fraud include (1) an intended public placement of securities in the near future, (2) management compensation dependent on operating results, and (3) a weak internal control environment evidenced by lack of concern for basic controls and disregard of the auditor's recommendations. What other factors should heighten an auditor's concern about the existence of management fraud?

(Adapted from AICPA)

11-24 The following audit procedures are included in the audit program because of heightened risks of material misstatements due to fraud:

1. Use generalized audit software to examine cash disbursements transaction files for records without cheque numbers. Do a sequence test on cheques and record any missing cheque numbers.
2. Engage an actuarial specialist to assess pension liabilities. The specialist is to examine management's assumptions about average length of employment and re-evaluate the average life expectancy of retirees used in pension accounting decisions.
3. Search the accounts receivable master file for account balances with missing or unusual customer numbers (e.g., "99999"). List customers with post office box shipping addresses. Compare customer addresses with employee addresses.
4. Send confirmations to customers for large sales transactions made in the fourth quarter of the fiscal year to obtain customer responses about terms related to the transfer of title and the ability to return merchandise.
5. Use audit software to search purchase transactions for any with non-standard vendor numbers or match to vendor names of known related parties.
6. Search sales transaction files and list any invoices without bill of lading numbers.

REQUIRED

For each of the audit procedures:
a. Describe the type of fraud risk that is likely associated with the need for this audit procedure.
b. Identify the general ledger accounts likely affected by the potential fraud misstatement.
c. Identify the audit objective(s) that this procedure addresses.

11-25 The following misstatements are included in the accounting records of Joyce Manufacturing Company:

1. A sales invoice was incorrectly added with a difference of $1,000 as a result of a data entry error.
2. A material sale was unintentionally recorded for the second time on the last day of the year. The sale had originally been recorded two days earlier.
3. Cash paid on accounts receivable was stolen by the mail clerk when the mail was opened.
4. Cash paid on accounts receivable that had been prelisted by a secretary was stolen by the bookkeeper who recorded cash receipts and accounts receivable. He failed to record the transactions.
5. A shipment to a customer was not billed because of the loss of the bill of lading.
6. Merchandise was shipped to a customer, but no bill of lading was prepared. Because billings are prepared from bills of lading, the customer was not billed.
7. A sale to a residential customer was unintentionally classified as a commercial sale.
8. Sales generated through the company's website are recorded at the point the customers submit the orders online.

REQUIRED
a. Identify whether each situation is an error or fraud.
b. For each situation, list one or more controls that should have prevented it from occurring on a continuing basis.
c. For each situation, identify evidence the auditor could use to uncover it.

(Adapted from AICPA)

11-26 Appliances Repair and Service Company bills all its customers rather than collecting in cash when services are provided. All mail is opened by Tom Gyders, the accounting manager. Gyders, a qualified accountant, is the most qualified person in the company who is in the office daily. Therefore, he can solve problems and respond to customers' needs quickly. Upon receipt of cash, he immediately prepares a listing of the cash and a duplicate deposit slip. Cash is deposited daily. Gyders uses the listing to enter the financial transactions in the computerized accounting records. He also contacts customers about uncollected accounts receivable. Because he is so knowledgeable about the business and each customer, he grants credit, authorizes all sales allowances, and charges off uncollectible accounts. The owner is extremely pleased with the efficiency of the company. He can run the business without spending much time there because of Gyders' effectiveness.

Imagine the owner's surprise when he discovers that Gyders has committed a major theft of the company's cash receipts. He did so by not recording sales, recording improper credits to recorded accounts receivable, and overstating receivables.

REQUIRED
a. Given that cash was prelisted, went only to the accounting manager, and was deposited daily, what internal control deficiency permitted the fraud?
b. What are the benefits of a prelisting of cash? Who should prepare the prelisting and what duties should that person perform?
c. Assume that an appropriate person, as discussed in part (b), prepares a prelisting of cash. What is to prevent that person from taking the cash after it is prelisted but before it is deposited?
d. Who should deposit the cash, given your answer to part (b)?

11-27 Each year near the balance sheet date, when the president of Bargon Construction, Inc. takes a three-week vacation to Mexico, she signs several cheques to pay major bills during the period she is absent. Jack Morgan, head bookkeeper for the company, uses this practice to his advantage. Morgan makes out a cheque to himself for the amount of a large vendor's invoice, and because there is no acquisitions journal, he records the amount in the cash disbursements journal as an acquisition from the supplier listed on the invoice. He holds the cheque until several weeks into the subsequent period to make sure that the auditors do not get an opportunity to examine the cancelled cheque. Shortly after the first of the year when the president returns, Morgan resubmits the invoice for payment and again records the cheque in the cash disbursements journal. At that point, he marks the invoice "paid" and files it with all other paid invoices. Morgan has been following this practice successfully for several years and feels confident that he has developed a foolproof method.

REQUIRED
a. What is the auditor's responsibility for discovering this type of embezzlement?
b. What weaknesses exist in the client's internal control?
c. What evidence could the auditor use to uncover the fraud?

(Adapted from AICPA)

11-28 The following are activities that occurred at Franklin Manufacturing, a private company.

1. Franklin's accountant did not record cheques written in the last few days of the year until the next accounting period to avoid a negative cash balance in the financial statements.
2. Franklin's controller prepared and mailed a cheque to a vendor for a carload of material that was not received. The vendor's chief accountant, who is a friend of Franklin's controller, mailed a vendor's invoice to Franklin, and the controller prepared a receiving report. The vendor's chief accountant deposited the cheque in an account he had set up with a name almost identical to the vendor's.
3. The accountant recorded cash received in the first few days of the next accounting period in the current accounting period to avoid a negative cash balance.
4. Discounts on invoices from Franklin's largest supplier were never taken, even though they were paid before the discount period expired. The president of the supplier's company provided free use of his ski lodge to the accountant who processed the cheques in exchange for the lost discounts.
5. Franklin shipped and billed goods to a customer in Winnipeg on December 23, and the sale was recorded on December 24, with the understanding that the goods would be returned on January 31 for a full refund plus a 5-percent handling fee.
6. Franklin's factory superintendent routinely took scrap metal home in his pickup and sold it to a scrap dealer to make a few extra dollars.
7. Franklin's management decided not to include a footnote about a material uninsured lawsuit against the company on the grounds that the primary users of the statements, a small local bank, would probably not understand the footnote anyway.

REQUIRED

Identify which of these activities are frauds. Justify your response.

Professional Judgment Problems

11-29 The Kowal Manufacturing Company employs 50 production workers and has the following payroll procedures:

The factory foreman interviews applicants and, on the basis of the interview, either hires or rejects them. When applicants are hired, they prepare a TD1 (Employee's Withholding Exemption Certificate) and give it to the foreman. The foreman writes the hourly rate of pay for the new employee in the corner of the TD1 form and then gives the form to a payroll clerk as notice that the worker has been employed. The foreman verbally advises the payroll department of rate adjustments.

A supply of blank time cards is kept in a box near the entrance to the factory. Each worker takes a time card on Monday morning, fills in his or her name, and punches in his or her daily arrival and departure times at a time clock. At the end of the week, the workers drop the time cards in a box near the door to the factory.

On Monday morning, the completed time cards are taken from the box by a payroll clerk. One of the payroll clerks then records the payroll transactions into a payroll software package, which posts all information to the payroll journal and automatically calculates and updates the employees' earnings records and general ledger. Employees do not receive their paycheques if they fail to turn in their time cards. The payroll clerk prints the payroll cheques using the software package and gives them to the chief accountant.

The payroll cheques are manually signed by the chief accountant and given to the foreman. The foreman distributes the cheques to the workers in the factory and arranges for the delivery of the cheques to the workers who are absent. The payroll bank account is reconciled by the chief accountant, who also prepares the various quarterly and annual payroll tax reports.

REQUIRED

a. List the fraud risks that are present at the above organization. For each risk, state the type of misstatement that could occur.
b. State whether the fraud risk could lead to misappropriation of assets or fraudulent financial reporting.
c. For each fraud risk, provide both preventive and detective controls to prevent or detect the fraud.

(Adapted from AICPA)

11-30 Froggledore Realty Limited is a brokerage firm that employs 35 real estate agents. The agents are given an office and basic telephone service (estimated at a $250 value per month) and are paid on a commission basis. The building has wireless computing so that agents can bring in their own computers. Each office has its own lock, and agents are responsible for the contents of their offices. Calls that come into the office are allocated to agents based upon their region in the city, with each agent having a clearly defined region for sales.

Potential purchasers who call in are assigned to the on-call listed agent. The office manager is responsible for accounting and for supplying the office with software and other supplies. She purchased a copy of real estate sales management software (for $750) for the office and has been burning copies, which she sells to new real estate agents for $100; she figures it pays for her time (she usually burns them on her home computer).

The owner of the business, Jim Froggledore, has told her and the accounting staff to bring in any invoices that they have for home computing so that he can use them for the business. Depending upon how well the company does, Jim gives employees a 10- to 20-percent bonus at the end of the year for the invoices.

Jenny, the receptionist, is a freelance writer and has been writing advertising copy for the business in her spare time. She charges for this as an editing contract from her small business and takes supplies from the office, which she and her husband (not employed by Jim) use for their business.

Jim recently had the offices renovated, with new carpeting and wallpaper, by his sister's business. She also painted the recently renovated basement at Jim's home and installed indoor/outdoor carpeting on his patio; all of this was included in the bill to the business. Jim prorated the invoice and charged the real estate agents for the renovations to the office.

REQUIRED

a. Assess the quality of corporate governance at Froggledore Realty Limited.
b. Is the company auditable? Why or why not?
c. If you did decide to audit the company, what audit approach would you use?
d. Are there any additional audit procedures that would be required? Why or why not? List any additional audit procedures that you would recommend, stating the fraud risk that they address and the associated audit objective.

Case

11-31 Smith is a junior on the financial statement audit of Super Computer Services Co. (SCS) for the year ended April 30, 2009. On May 6, 2009, Kent, the senior auditor assigned to the engagement, had the following conversation with Smith concerning the planning phase of the audit:*

Kent: Do you have all the audit programs updated yet for the SCS engagement?
Smith: Mostly. I still have work to do on the fraud risk assessment.
Kent: Why? Our "errors and irregularities" program from last year is still OK. It has passed peer review several times. Besides, we don't have specific duties regarding fraud. If we find it, we'll deal with it then.
Smith: I don't think so. That new CEO, Mint, has almost no salary, mostly bonuses and stock options. Doesn't that concern you?
Kent: No. Mint's employment contract was approved by the board of directors just three months ago. It was passed unanimously.
Smith: I guess so, but Mint told those stock analysts that SCS's earnings would increase 30 percent next year. Can Mint deliver numbers like that?
Kent: Who knows? We're auditing the 2009 financial statements, not 2010's. Mint will probably amend that forecast every month between now and next May.
Smith: Sure, but all this may change our other audit programs.
Kent: No, it won't. The programs are fine as is. If you find fraud in any of your tests, just let me know. Maybe we'll have to extend the tests. Or maybe we'll just report it to the audit committee.
Smith: What would they do? Green is the audit committee's chair, and remember, Green hired Mint. They've been best friends for years. Besides, Mint is calling all the shots now. Brown, the old CEO, is still on the board but Brown's never around. Brown's even been skipping the board meetings. Nobody in management or on the board would stand up to Mint.

Kent: That's nothing new. Brown was like that years ago. Brown caused frequent disputes with Jones, public accountant, the predecessor auditor. Three years ago, Jones told Brown how ineffective the internal audit department was then. Next thing you know, Jones is out and our firm is in. Why bother? I'm just as happy that those understaffed internal auditors don't get in our way. Just remember, the bottom line is . . . are the financial statements fairly presented? And they always have been. We don't provide any assurances about fraud. That's management's job.
Smith: But what about the lack of segregation of duties in the cash disbursements department? That clerk could write a cheque for anything.
Kent: Sure. That's a material weakness every year and probably will be again this year. But we're talking cost-effectiveness here, not fraud. We just have to do lots of testing on cash disbursements and report it again.
Smith: What about the big layoffs coming up next month? It's more than a rumour. Even the employees know it's going to happen, and they're real uptight about it.
Kent: I know, it's the worst kept secret at SCS, but we don't have to consider that now. Even if it happens, it will only improve next year's financial results. Brown should have let these people go years ago. Let's face it, how else can Mint even come close to the 30 percent earnings increase next year?

REQUIRED

a. Describe the fraud risk factors that are indicated in the preceding dialogue.
b. Explain how SCS's audit approach should be modified to take account of each risk factor.
c. Describe Kent's misconceptions regarding the consideration of fraud in the audit of SCS's financial statements that are contained in the preceding dialogue, and explain why each is a misconception.
d. Describe an auditor's audit documentation requirements regarding the assessment of the risk of material misstatement due to fraud.

*Copyright 1998, 2003. Adapted from the American Institute of Certified Public Accountants, Inc. Reprinted with permission.

ACL Problem

11-32 This problem requires the use of ACL software, which is included in the companion website at **www.pearsoned.ca/arens**. Information about installing and using ACL and solving this problem can be found in the ACL Appendix, also on the companion website. You should read all of the reference material preceding the instructions about "Quick Sort" before locating the appropriate command to answer question (c). For this problem, use "Metaphor_APTrans_2002 file in ACL_Demo." The suggested command or other source of information needed to solve the problem requirement is included at the end of each question.

REQUIRED

a. For each of the computer-assisted audit procedures listed in part (c), identify the audit objective(s) associated with the test. Justify your response.
b. For each of the procedures listed in part (c), state the fraud risk that is addressed by the audit procedure. Justify your response.
c. Run the following ACL tests:

   1. Total the Invoice Amount column for comparison with the general ledger balance of $276,841.33 (Total Field).
   2. Recalculate unit cost times quantity and identify any extension misstatements (Filter).
   3. Products that Metaphor purchases should not exceed $100 per unit. Print any purchase for subsequent follow-up where unit cost exceeded that amount (Filter).
   4. Identify the three vendors from which the largest total-dollar accounts payable transactions occurred during 2002 (Summarize and Quick Sort).
   5. For each of the three vendors in question 4, list any transactions that exceeded $15,000 for subsequent follow-up. Include the vendor number, invoice number, and invoice amount (Filter. Note that the Vendor Number is actually a character rather than a number, so you need to enclose it in quotes when using it in an expression.).
   6. Vendor numbers 10134 and 13440 are parties related to Metaphor. Print any accounts payable transactions with these two vendors (Filter). Also, determine the total amount of transactions with each vendor (Summarize).

d. Identify audit procedures that are required to follow up any unusual results from each ACL audit test. Explain the purpose of each audit procedure.

Ongoing Small Business Case: Theft Problems at CondoCleaners.com

11-33 Jim decided that he would no longer do the cleaning himself but would rather spend more time promoting his cleaning business at new buildings. He recently negotiated building access at a group of five top-tier condominiums, where the units sell for over $500,000 each. Happily, cleaning contracts started coming in after about two weeks, so Jim hired two new employees for these buildings.

Vagney worked with the two new employees, Jules and Char, for the first two cleanings, then each of them went in on their own for the first time to do a cleaning on Tuesday. Late in the afternoon, Jim had trouble. One unit owner complained that a $3,500 camera was missing—he had found the case behind his bookshelf. Another owner reported that she could not find her $780 iPod, which she always left in the same place on a dresser. Both had informed building management, and Jim's company was banned from all five buildings permanently.

REQUIRED

a. What are the actions that Jim should take to deal with these thefts?
b. What controls are possible to prevent thefts in the future?
c. What controls or actions should Jim have had in place to mitigate the effects of this type of risk?

12

Overall audit plan and audit program

There are so many different types of businesses—how can there be a common approach to the financial statement audit? Just like the architect of a multistorey office tower, the financial statement auditor carefully plans his or her strategy, identifying the risks involved with the client and developing an audit approach known as an audit strategy to complete the engagement. Internal auditors and specialists may participate in the financial statement audit and need to be aware of their role in the overall plan. Management accountants will be answering auditor questions and providing evidence to the auditors.

LEARNING OBJECTIVES

1 Explain what an audit strategy is. Explain the role of audit planning in the financial statement audit. Describe the purpose of an audit program. State the purpose of the five types of audit tests. Describe the role of dual-purpose tests.

2 Define evidence mix. Explain how the auditor chooses the types of audit tests to be completed.

3 Describe the methodology for designing tests of controls and tests of details in the audit program.

STANDARDS REFERENCED IN THIS CHAPTER

CICA Standards

CAS 240 – The auditor's responsibilities relating to fraud in an audit of financial statements (previously Section 5135 – The auditor's responsibility to consider fraud)

CAS 315 – Identifying and assessing the risks of material misstatement through understanding the entity and its environment (previously Section 5141 – Understanding the entity and its environment and assessing the risks of material misstatement)

CAS 330 – The auditor's responses to assessed risks (previously Section 5143 – The auditor's procedures in response to assessed risks)

CAS 520 – Analytical procedures (previously Section 5301 – Analysis)

Clients Have Changed and So Have Audits

Jared and Gabrielle were comparing notes on two of their clients. Jared's client was implementing new enterprise-wide resource software—an integrated suite of programs that have a database core. Unfortunately, the implementation did not go well. There was a programming error in the new implementation that resulted in work-in-progress work orders being set to zero at the time of the conversion. Although new orders were handled properly, there were about 3,000 jobs that were affected. These were noticed about two weeks after the conversion as billing cycles were concluded and inventory-to-job-cost reconciliations went out of whack.

Gabrielle waxed enthusiastic about her client's mass customization, with skirts and pants produced to individual orders as well as smaller production runs for retail store clients. The client had purchased software and hardware that enabled the linking of orders to the production system. The software and hardware were also able to reduce inventory of work in progress and finished goods by streamlining the link between ordering, production, and shipping. The client found that customer loyalty for customized work was very high.

IMPORTANCE TO AUDITORS

Investigation of data errors and review of account reconciliations after the software conversion at Jared's client meant that the client's year-end financial statement results were delayed by almost two months. Jared and his staff spent numerous hours reviewing data conversion plans with the client and helped compare information that was transferred from the old computer systems to the new data. The client was late filing its reports with the stock exchange, suspended trading of its shares for a month, and was threatened with delisting of its stock.

Jared was thankful that he had taken some extra information systems courses at university. He was also planning to take the Certified Information Systems Auditor Examination and move into the information systems audit group at his firm.

Gabrielle enthused about her client's new systems. "My client is finally starting to make some money on its line of custom-made skirts and pants. Lower inventory overall meant that we had to use only two staff members on the inventory count and were able to reduce the fieldwork on inventory by over 30 percent." Inventory was individually tracked, and the new information systems were found to be reliable and robust.

These two examples illustrate how the quality of the information systems and their conversion had an impact on the audit strategy and the resultant detailed testing of two different clients.

WHAT DO YOU THINK?

1. With the discovery of a major program error at Jared's client, what is the likelihood that there would be other program errors? How would this affect the time spent on gathering information about control systems?

continued >

2. Are the two systems described above strategic information systems? Why or why not? How does the nature of the system affect client business risk?

Sources: 1. Schlosser, Julie, "A handful of companies are finally perfecting made-to-order for the masses. Here's how," *Fortune*, December 13, 2004. 2. Songini, Marc L., "Bungled ERP installation whacks asyst," *Computerworld*, 39(2), 2005.

THINK about the two businesses that Jared and Gabrielle discussed. How do information systems affect the way a business is run? What impact would this have on the audit planning processes? Most businesses, even small ones, use technology in the execution of their transactions. It is important to understand how such technology is related to business processes in order to adequately plan and execute the financial statement audit.

This chapter examines the role of an audit strategy in the financial statement audit. It also looks at two phases of the financial statement audit in detail: Phase 3—Plan the Audit, which is the last risk assessment phase, and Phase 4—Design Further Audit Procedures, the first risk response phase. This critical fourth phase specifies the entire audit program, including audit procedures, sample sizes, items to select, and timing of the testing.

Audit Strategy and Audit Tests

In this section, we will use the example of Hillsburg Hardware Limited to explain the role of audit strategy in the financial statement audit. Then we will link the types of audit tests to their role in the audit strategy before considering evidence mix decisions to be made as part of the audit planning process.

Audit Strategy and Hillsburg Hardware Limited

An **audit strategy** consists of a planned approach to the conduct of audit testing, taking into account assessed risks. This means that the strategy can be developed only after the client risk profile has been developed and risks assessed. The audit strategy is the last step of Phase 3—Plan the Audit.

Audit strategy—a planned approach to the conduct of audit testing, taking into account assessed risks.

As explained in our chapters so far, Hillsburg Hardware Limited (Hillsburg) is a continuing client that has been responsive to recommendations for improvement from the auditors. There are no independence issues for the audit firm Berger, Kao, Kadous & Co., LLP (BKK), which has obtained an engagement letter and has confirmed with the client that there are no independence issues. BKK would likely assign an information systems audit specialist to the audit team to assist with the documentation and evaluation of general and application controls. Chapter 8 explained how the client risk profile would be developed, starting with an understanding of the client's business and industry. As a hardware wholesaler, Hillsburg would compete with other wholesalers and also with hardware retailers which offer discounts to commercial purchasers (such as Home Depot and Rona). This industry is suffering as consumers and

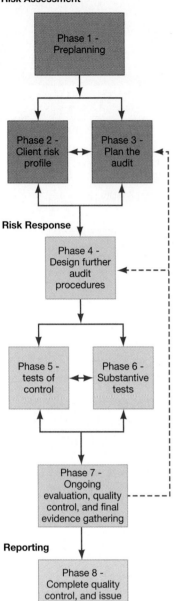

Risk Assessment

Phase 1 - Preplanning

Phase 2 - Client risk profile

Phase 3 - Plan the audit

Risk Response

Phase 4 - Design further audit procedures

Phase 5 - tests of control

Phase 6 - Substantive tests

Phase 7 - Ongoing evaluation, quality control, and final evidence gathering

Reporting

Phase 8 - Complete quality control, and issue auditor's report

businesses cut back on discretionary purchases. The Company Description (page 3 of the Hillsburg 2008 annual report) provides an overview of the business. The auditor would develop a picture of the overall business context by considering Hillsburg's local and regional competitors. Hillsburg has an active audit committee and a board that meet regularly. Although Hillsburg has not implemented an enterprise-wide risk management framework, each functional area conducts a risk assessment (including fraud risk assessment), which is evaluated by the executive management team at a semi-annual day-long retreat. Board members are invited to the retreat, and normally the chair of the board and a second board member who is also on the audit committee attend the retreat. The result of this retreat is incorporated into a risk assessment evaluation and plan that is discussed with the whole board at its quarterly meeting. Each functional area is expected to contribute to the annual strategic plan, which is similarly discussed with the board. The information systems department participates in the strategic planning exercises to ensure that computing plans address business needs and that technology capabilities are considered during the planning process.

Figure 12-1 shows the process that the audit team has followed to complete Phase 2 of the Hillsburg Audit, development of the client risk profile. The audit team members assigned to the engagement are as follows:

Partner: Joe Anthony
Manager: Leslie Ngan
Senior: Fran Moore
Assistants: Mitch Bray and one person to be assigned later

Figure 12-1 shows that work has been completed to understand the client's business and industry, assess client business risk, and complete preliminary analytical review. As part of the understanding of business, Figure 12-2 shows a partial organization chart that includes selected accounting and operating personnel. As a result of this field work and audit team consultation, client business risk (included in the risk summary in Table 12-1 on page 386) has been assessed as low.

In this Plan the Audit phase, the auditor uses the audit risk model (discussed in Chapter 7), to assist with planning. The tasks to be complete in this phase (extracted from our summary of the audit phases in Chapter 5) are as follows:

- Determine audit risk.
- Determine inherent risk.
- Set preliminary materiality levels.
- Document internal controls, including entity-level controls.
- Evaluate design effectiveness of internal controls.
- Evaluate control risk by assertion.
- Assess risk of material misstatements.
- Assess risks of fraud.
- Identify significant risks or transactions/accounts that require more than substantive tests.
- Determine risks of material misstatement at the financial statement and assertion levels.
- Discuss risks and audit plan with audit team; develop and modify staffing plans as required.
- Develop strategic audit approach overall and by cycle.

Selected conclusions reached for Hillsburg are summarized in Table 12-1 on page 386. Further conclusions are discussed in subsequent chapters where we examine individual transaction cycles and accounts. The audit risk for Hillsburg has been assessed at low, as it is a public company registered with both the OSC and the SEC, with current and long-term bank debt. This means that a high level of evidence will need to be collected.

Inherent risk has been assessed as low, primarily due to the good quality of corporate governance and monitoring processes in place at the company. This decreases

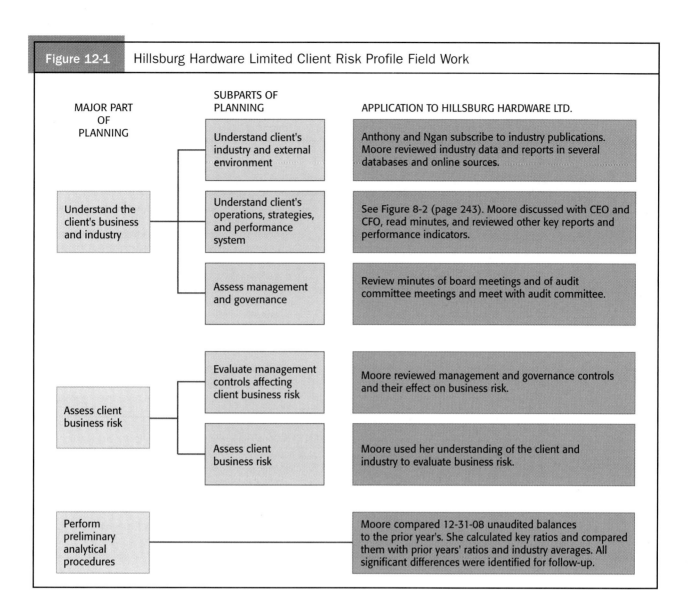

Figure 12-1 Hillsburg Hardware Limited Client Risk Profile Field Work

MAJOR PART OF PLANNING	SUBPARTS OF PLANNING	APPLICATION TO HILLSBURG HARDWARE LTD.
Understand the client's business and industry	Understand client's industry and external environment	Anthony and Ngan subscribe to industry publications. Moore reviewed industry data and reports in several databases and online sources.
	Understand client's operations, strategies, and performance system	See Figure 8-2 (page 243). Moore discussed with CEO and CFO, read minutes, and reviewed other key reports and performance indicators.
	Assess management and governance	Review minutes of board meetings and of audit committee meetings and meet with audit committee.
Assess client business risk	Evaluate management controls affecting client business risk	Moore reviewed management and governance controls and their effect on business risk.
	Assess client business risk	Moore used her understanding of the client and industry to evaluate business risk.
Perform preliminary analytical procedures		Moore compared 12-31-08 unaudited balances to the prior year's. She calculated key ratios and compared them with prior years' ratios and industry averages. All significant differences were identified for follow-up.

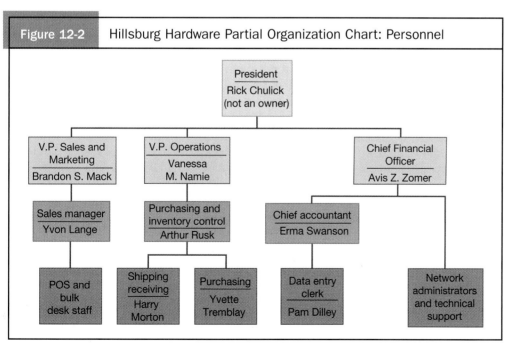

Figure 12-2 Hillsburg Hardware Partial Organization Chart: Personnel

- President
  Rick Chulick
  (not an owner)
  - V.P. Sales and Marketing
    Brandon S. Mack
    - Sales manager
      Yvon Lange
      - POS and bulk desk staff
  - V.P. Operations
    Vanessa M. Namie
    - Purchasing and inventory control
      Arthur Rusk
      - Shipping receiving
        Harry Morton
      - Purchasing
        Yvette Tremblay
  - Chief Financial Officer
    Avis Z. Zomer
    - Chief accountant
      Erma Swanson
      - Data entry clerk
        Pam Dilley
    - Network administrators and technical support

Table 12-1　Hillsburg Hardware Limited Overall Risk Summary

Type of Risk	Conclusion	Comments
Client business risk	Low	Although financial position is deteriorating, the company has plans of actions and strategies to deal with potentially plummeting revenue.
Audit risk	Low	Primary reasons include public company with long-term and current debt holder (bank).
Inherent risk	Low	Corporate governance and management integrity have been assessed as good. Results of previous audits indicate limited disagreements with the auditors and no related-party transactions. Primary judgment areas are valuation of accounts receivable and inventory, where many years of history and current data are available to assess.
Preliminary materiality	$496,000	$441,000 available for the current year after considering anticipated misstatements ($50,000), carry-forward misstatements ($80,000), and anticipated client corrections ($75,000).
Control risk	Low to medium	Varies by cycle and assertion.
		Areas where substantive testing will be insufficient: order entry assertions, assertions for electronic data interchange (EDI) transactions, assertions for automated payments.
Fraud risk	Low to moderate	Low for all transaction areas except for customer refunds (where it is moderate).
		Required significant areas of revenue recognition and journal entries to be tested.
Risk of material misstatements	Low to moderate	Revenue recognition is mandated to be a significant risk.
		Overall low risk, except for accounts receivable and inventory valuation, which are moderate.

the likelihood of material misstatements. As calculated in Chapter 7 on page 222, preliminary materiality is $496,000, but only $441,000 is available for the current year. Materiality will be used to help decide the scope of testing and to evaluate the results of testing. Control risk varies by cycle and assertion but is generally of good quality. There are three areas—order entry, EDI transactions, and automated payments—where it is considered that substantive testing will not be enough, as there is significant reliance upon automated systems in these areas.

Design effectiveness of internal controls, control risk by assertion, and risks of fraud by assertion are considered in Chapters 14 through 20. Overall risk of fraud is considered low, except for customer refunds, whose risk is considered moderate. Note that customer refunds are considered a high-risk fraud area in the retail industry and that good quality controls at Hillsburg lowered fraud risk to moderate for the company.

CAS

The audit team has concluded that the overall risk of material misstatement for the financial statements is low. The exceptions are the mandated standards in CAS 240 (previously Section 5135) that require revenue recognition to be considered a significant risk. The auditors have also raised the risk levels for accounts receivable valuation and inventory valuation due to the recession, which could result in inventory collection problems and inventory obsolescence if these accounts are not carefully managed. The related working papers, conclusions, and assessments have been discussed with the audit team.

The audit team has decided that its overall audit strategy will be a combined approach, that is, an approach that includes both tests of control and substantive tests. The reasons for this approach will be explained in the next section, Evidence Mix Decisions.

Before considering those decisions, we take a closer look at the purpose of the different types of audit tests and how those tests are used in risk assessment and in the second major component of the audit, Risk Response.

Purpose of Different Audit Tests

TYPES OF TESTS Auditors use five **types of tests** to determine whether financial statements are fairly stated: (1) risk assessment procedures, (2) procedures to obtain an understanding of internal control, (3) tests of controls, (4) analytical procedures, and (5) tests of details of balances. Note that we use the term **substantive procedures** to describe audit procedures that are used to quantify the amount of potential error in an account or transaction stream. There are two types of substantive tests: analytical procedures and tests of detail. (This means that analytical procedures are a type of test that is used for multiple purposes.) CAS 330 (previously Section 5143) requires substantive tests where the auditor has identified a significant risk at the assertion level. If the auditor is not using tests of control, then analytical procedures are not enough — tests of detail must be used. Since we have indicated earlier that the auditor must assume that revenue recognition is a significant risk (unless there is evidence to the contrary), this means that revenue recognition substantive testing will normally be conducted. The auditor is also required to conduct substantive tests related to the financial statement closing process.

We now discuss each of these five types of tests in turn.

Risk assessment procedures **Risk assessment procedures** are used to assess the likelihood of material misstatement (inherent risk plus control risk) in the financial statements. Chapter 8 described how the auditor obtains an understanding of the client's business and industry to assess client business risk and develop a client risk profile. Chapter 7 described how auditors perform procedures to assess inherent risk, and Chapter 9 discussed control risk. Collectively, procedures performed to obtain an understanding of the entity and its environment, including obtaining an understanding of internal controls, represent the auditor's risk assessment procedures.

Tests of controls, substantive tests of transactions, detailed analytical procedures, and tests of details of balances are completed in response to the auditor's assessment of the risk of material misstatements. The combination of all five types of audit procedures provides the basis for the auditor's opinion.

Procedures to obtain an understanding of internal control A major subset of the auditor's risk assessment procedures are those used to obtain an understanding of internal control. The methodology for and **procedures used to obtain an understanding**, audit procedures used to gather evidence about the design and effectiveness of implementation of internal control, were studied in Chapters 8 and 9. During the development of the client risk profile, the auditor used these techniques to understand the client's business and industry, which included controls over management and governance, strategic planning, risk assessment, and monitoring. In Phase 3, Plan the Audit, the auditor must focus attention on both the design and the operation of aspects of internal control to the extent necessary to plan the rest of the audit effectively. A critical point is that the understanding obtained must be supported with evidence. The purpose of the procedures performed, then, is to provide both understanding and evidence to support that understanding. These examples of audit procedures that relate to the auditor's understanding of internal control were identified:

- Update and evaluate the auditor's previous experience with the entity.
- Make inquiries of client personnel.
- Read client's policy and systems manuals.
- Examine documents and records.
- Walk through transactions to verify flow of transactions and controls.
- Observe entity activities and operations.

Types of tests—the five categories of audit tests auditors use to determine whether financial statements are fairly stated: risk assessment procedures, procedures to obtain an understanding of internal control, tests of controls, analytical procedures, and tests of details of balances.

Substantive procedures—audit procedures that are used to quantify the amount of potential error in an account or transaction stream.

Risk assessment procedures—used to assess the likelihood of material misstatement (inherent risk plus control risk) in the financial statements.

Procedures used to obtain an understanding—procedures used by the auditor to gather evidence about the design and implementation of specific controls.

Tests of controls A major use of the auditor's understanding of internal control is to assess control risk for each transaction-related audit objective. Examples are assessing the accuracy objective for sales transactions as low and the existence objective as moderate. Where the auditor believes control policies and procedures are effectively designed, and where it is efficient to do so, he or she will elect to assess control risk at a level that reflects that evaluation. This risk assessment is affected by the extent of automation of controls. In paperless systems or systems that rely fully upon automated controls, such as automatic reordering or EDI for document exchange, the auditor may be required to conduct tests of controls. This occurs as it may not be possible to reduce the risk of material misstatement for a specific transaction-related audit objective to an acceptably low level using only substantive tests. Audit procedures that test the effectiveness of controls in support of a reduced control risk are called **tests of controls**.

Tests of controls are performed to determine the effectiveness of both the design and the operation of specific internal controls. These tests include the following types of procedures:

- Make inquiries of appropriate client personnel.
- Examine documents, records, and reports.
- Observe control-related activities.
- Reperform client procedures.

The first two procedures are the same as those used to obtain an understanding of internal control. Thus, performing tests of controls can be thought of as a continuation of the audit procedures used to develop a client risk profile or to obtain an understanding of internal control. The main difference is that with tests of controls, the objective is more specific and the tests are more extensive and linked to the level of risk associated with the assertion being tested. For example, if the client's budgeting process is to be used as a basis for assessing a low level of risk that expenditures are misclassified, in addition to the procedures described in the example given for obtaining an understanding, the auditor might also select a recent budget report, trace its contents to source records, prove its mathematical accuracy, examine all variance reports and memos that flow from it, talk to responsible personnel about the follow-up actions they took, and examine documentation in support of those actions. In effect, when the auditor decides to assess control risk below maximum for any transaction-related audit objective, the procedures used to obtain an understanding of internal control are combined with the tests of controls. The amount of additional evidence required for tests of controls will depend on the amount and extensiveness of evidence obtained in gaining the understanding.

The purpose of tests of controls is to determine that any of the six transaction-related audit objectives which have a risk of material misstatement have been tested for the affected classes of transactions. For example, the auditor will perform tests of controls to test whether recorded sales transactions occurred and actual transactions are recorded. The auditor also performs these tests to determine if recorded sales transactions are accurately recorded, recorded in the appropriate period, correctly classified, and accurately summarized and posted to the general ledger and data files. If the auditor is confident that transactions were correctly recorded in the journals and correctly posted, he or she can be confident that general ledger totals are correct.

To illustrate typical tests of controls, it is useful to return to the control risk matrix for Hillsburg Hardware Limited in Figure 9-5, page 297. For each of the 11 controls included in Figure 9-5, Table 12-2 (on page 390) identifies a test of controls that might be performed to test its effectiveness. Note that no test of control is performed for the weaknesses in Figure 9-5. It would make no sense to determine if the absence of a control is being adequately performed.

Analytical procedures As discussed in Chapter 6, **analytical procedures** involve comparisons of recorded amounts to expectations developed by the auditor to determine

audit challenge 12-1
Testing Data Accuracy

Have you heard the term "garbage-in, garbage-out?" The term applies to quality of information—if you enter poor quality data into information systems, then the resulting reports upon which decisions are made are as poor as the data (i.e., garbage).

Think about a document that would be entered at an organization like Hillsburg Hardware Limited, such as a supplier invoice. It will have supplier name, date, invoice amount, and purchase details, such as item number, item description, quantity purchased, extended value, subtotal, taxes, and total.

To prevent data entry errors, most automated systems have features such as input edits whose role is to prevent accidental keying errors. Let us look at the date, for example, which contains a day, month, and year. The month should be between 1 and 12 and should likely be the current month. The day must be between 1 and 31 and should have a logical relationship to the month (for example, February cannot have day 31). The year should likely be the current year.

In addition to data entry controls, there are comparison, or matching, controls. Vendor names can be matched to vendor numbers, item numbers to existing numbers on file, and invoice details to previously recorded purchase order details.

CRITICAL THINKING QUESTIONS

1. Identify five different automated controls that could be applied to the invoice number of a vendor invoice.
2. What are some of the things that could go wrong if an item price is entered incorrectly? (These are risks—use audit assertions to describe the risks.)
3. For each risk you listed in (2), state a control that could prevent the risk or detect the error if it should occur. State whether the control you identified is preventive or detective.

---

whether account balances or other data seem reasonable. They often involve the calculation of ratios by the auditor for comparison with previous years' ratios and other related data. For example, the auditor could compare sales, collections, and accounts receivable in the current year to amounts in previous years and calculate the gross margin percentage for comparison with those in previous years. Analytical procedures are used in multiple audit phases, particularly for risk assessment, to understand the organization, to reduce detailed tests, and to assist with final evaluation.

There are four purposes of analytical procedures, all of which were discussed in Chapter 6: understand the client's business, assess the entity's ability to continue as a going concern, indicate the presence of possible misstatements in the financial statements, and reduce detailed audit tests. It is in the last role that analytical procedures are considered substantive tests.

All types of analytical procedures help the auditor decide the extent of other audit tests. To illustrate, if analytical procedures indicate there may be misstatements, more extensive investigation may be needed. An example is an unexpected change in the current year's gross margin percentage compared with that of the previous year. Other tests may be needed to determine if there is a misstatement in sales or cost of goods sold that caused the change. On the other hand, if no material fluctuations are found using analytical procedures and the auditor concludes that fluctuations should not have occurred, other tests may be reduced.

Analytical procedures are both substantive procedures and planning procedures to **CAS** be used in designing the nature, extent, and timing of other audit procedures. When used as substantive procedures, they would be performed at a detailed level. For example, the auditor could calculate the gross margin for each product to identify which products might be incorrectly priced or incorrectly costed. CAS 520, Analytical Procedures (previously Section 5301), explains that analytical procedures would be used when tests of details are also being conducted on the same assertion. The auditor would also need to assess the quality of the data that are being used for the analytical review. For example, as discussed in Auditing in Action 12-1 on the next page, if the auditor were to use analytical review about individual stores' gross margins, then the auditor would ensure that gross margin data were accurately recorded in the client's system.

Table 12-2	Illustration of Tests of Controls

Illustrative Key Controls	Typical Tests of Controls
Credit is approved automatically by the computer by comparison with authorized credit limits (C1).	Review exception report and ensure approval by credit manager (documentation).
Recorded sales are supported by authorized shipping documents and approved customer orders, which are attached to the duplicate sales invoice (C2).	Examine a sample of duplicate sales invoices to determine that each one is supported by an attached, authorized shipping document and approved customer order (documentation).
There is separation of duties between billing, recording sales, and handling cash receipts (C3).	Observe whether personnel responsible for handling cash have no accounting responsibilities, and inquire about their duties (observation and inquiry).
Shipping documents are forwarded to billing daily and billed the subsequent day (C4).	Observe whether shipping documents are forwarded daily to billing, and observe when they are billed (observation).
Shipping documents are issued in numerical order by the computer and are accounted for weekly (C5).	Account for a sequence of shipping documents, and trace each to the sales journal (documentation and reperformance).
Shipping documents are batched daily and compared with quantities billed (C6).	Examine a sample of daily batches, recalculate the shipping quantities, and trace totals to reconciliation with input reports (reperformance).
Unit selling prices are obtained from the price list master file of approved prices (C7).	Examine a sample of sales invoices, and match prices to authorized computer price list. Review changes to price file throughout the year for proper approval (reperformance and documentation).
Sales transactions are internally verified (C8).	Examine document package for internal verification (classification).
Statements are mailed to all customers each month (C9).	Observe whether statements are mailed for one month, and inquire about who is responsible for mailing the statements (observation and inquiry).
Once the batch of sales transactions is entered, the computer automatically posts transactions to the accounts receivable subsidiary records and to the general ledger (C10).	Trace postings from the batch of sales transactions to the subsidiary records and general ledger (reperformance).
Accounts receivable master file is reconciled to the general ledger on a monthly basis (C11).	Examine evidence of reconciliation for test month, and test accuracy of reconciliation (documentation and reperformance).

auditing in action 12-1
Using Client Analysis

Advanced Analytical Procedures Help Run Business Processes

As businesses build systems that allow for up-to-the-minute details about sales and information, they need tools for understanding such large volumes of data. Those tools are analytical procedures supported by graphical displays, known as online analytical processing (OLAP), a common feature of centralized database systems. These tools help companies track existing sales and consider sales patterns so that existing products can be upgraded and new ones developed to meet potential gaps in demand.

For example, Cascade Designs (**www.cascadedesigns.com**) is a maker of camping supplies. It uses information about inventory at its customers' stores and internal gross margin information to help with production planning. 7-Eleven (**www.7-eleven.com**)

stores use computer sales history data to manage inventory: seasonal trends are taken into account to minimize inventory while trying to avoid stock-outs of popular brands.

Rather than developing his or her own data analysis models, the auditor can use existing client analysis or data analysis software during the audit. To do so, the auditor would need to ensure that the analysis addresses risks identified during the audit.

Store information at Cascade Designs and 7-Eleven could be used to identify which stores might have problems with inventory obsolescence (i.e., slow-moving products), focusing inventory valuation testing by the auditor.

Sources: 1. Cascade Designs, www.cascadedesigns.com, Accessed: January 8, 2009. 2. Koenig, David, "7-Eleven goes wireless," *The Globe and Mail*, October 12, 2004. 3. Tedeschi, Bob, "With custom-built software, a manufacturer can take a retailer's orders in stride," *The New York Times*, October 11, 2004.

Tests of Details of Balances **Tests of details of balances** focus on the ending general ledger balances for both balance sheet and income statement accounts, but the primary emphasis in most tests of details of balances is on the balance sheet. (Terms such as "detailed tests" and "direct tests of balances" may be used interchangeably with "tests of details of balances.") Tests of details are audit procedures testing for monetary errors or fraud and other irregularities to determine whether the eight balance-related audit objectives have been satisfied for each significant account balance. Examples include direct communication in writing with customers for accounts receivable, physical examination of inventory, and examination of vendors' statements for accounts payable. These tests of ending balances are essential to the conduct of the audit because, for the most part, the evidence is obtained from a source independent of the client and, thus, is considered to be highly reliable. Examples of tests of details of balances for the financial statement closing process include tracing to underlying records, such as tracing each financial statement figure to the general ledger accounts and tracing journal entries to supporting documents. The extent of these tests depends on the results of controls and analytical procedures.

Tests of details of balances have the objective of establishing the monetary correctness of the accounts they relate to and, therefore, are substantive tests. For example, confirmations test for monetary errors or fraud and other irregularities and are therefore substantive. Similarly, counts of inventory and cash on hand are also substantive tests.

DUAL-PURPOSE TESTS A substantive test is a procedure designed to test for dollar amounts of errors or fraud and other irregularities directly affecting the correctness of financial statement balances. Such errors or fraud and other irregularities are a clear indication of misstatements of the accounts. The two main types of substantive procedures, analytical procedures and detailed tests of balances, are directed to significant account balances or classes of transactions because of the potential for a misstatement occurring (inherent risk) and because of the potential for a misstatement not being prevented or detected (control risk).

An auditor may perform auditing procedures that are both tests of controls and substantive procedures on the same sample of transactions or account balances for efficiency; such procedures are known as **dual-purpose tests**. Dual-purpose tests provide evidence of whether or not the controls being tested were operating effectively during the period and whether there are misstatements in the data produced by the accounting system. Reperformance always simultaneously provides evidence about both controls and monetary correctness.

Dual-purpose tests are often cost effective when performed with the assistance of software, for example, generalized audit software. The auditor obtains a copy of the transaction file—for example, the detailed sales transaction history file. Substantive tests the auditor would do on such a transaction file include the following:

- Adding up the transactions, providing subtotals by month, and agreeing the subtotals to the general ledger (accuracy, posting, and summarization).
- Adding up the individual lines of the invoice and comparing with the total for each invoice, printing exceptions (accuracy).

The latter test would also serve a control testing purpose. For example, differences between the auditor invoice total and the system invoice total could indicate a programming error, where invoices were not being added up correctly. Testing the accuracy of a program would be considered a control test.

SUMMARY OF TYPES OF TESTS Figure 12-3 on the next page summarizes the types of tests. Procedures to obtain an understanding of internal control and tests of controls are concerned with preparing a client risk profile and evaluating whether controls are sufficiently effective to justify reducing control risk and thereby reducing substantive audit tests. Analytical procedures emphasize the overall reasonableness of transactions and the general ledger balances, and tests of details of balances emphasize the ending balances in the general ledger. Together, the four types of audit tests enable

Tests of details of balances—audit procedures testing for monetary errors or fraud and other irregularities to determine whether the eight balance-related audit objectives have been satisfied for each significant account balance.

Dual-purpose tests—auditing procedures that are both tests of controls and substantive procedures on the same sample of transactions or account balances for efficiency.

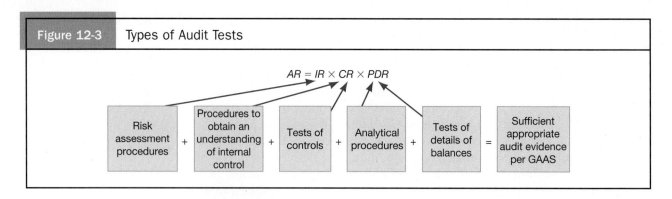

Figure 12-3 Types of Audit Tests

$$AR = IR \times CR \times PDR$$

Risk assessment procedures + Procedures to obtain an understanding of internal control + Tests of controls + Analytical procedures + Tests of details of balances = Sufficient appropriate audit evidence per GAAS

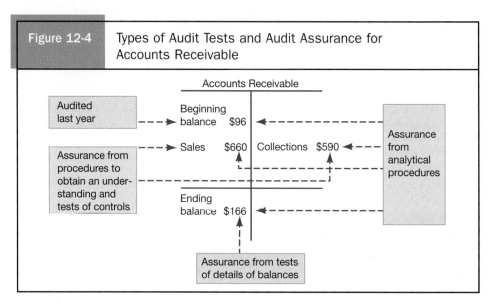

Figure 12-4 Types of Audit Tests and Audit Assurance for Accounts Receivable

concept check

C12-1 How is the audit strategy linked to the audit risk assessment processes?

C12-2 List the five types of audit tests, and provide an example of each that would be relevant to Hillsburg Hardware Limited.

the auditor to gather sufficient appropriate audit evidence to express an opinion on the financial statements.

Observe in Figure 12-3 that all five types of tests are used to satisfy sufficient appropriate audit evidence requirements. Also, observe that procedures to obtain an understanding and tests of controls reduce control risk, whereas the two substantive tests are used to satisfy planned detection risk.

Figure 12-4 shows how the four types of tests are used to obtain assurance in the audit of one account, accounts receivable. It is apparent from examining this figure that the auditor obtained a higher overall assurance for accounts receivable than the assurance obtained from any one test. The auditor can increase overall assurance by increasing the assurance obtained from any of the tests.

2   Evidence Mix Decisions

Relationship Between Tests and Evidence

Only certain types of evidence are obtained through each of the four types of tests. Table 12-3 summarizes the relationship between types of tests and types of evidence. Several observations about the table follow:

- Procedures to obtain an understanding of internal control and tests of controls involve inspection, recalculation, observation, inquiry, and reperformance.
- Confirmation is the only test that is primarily a test of details of balances.
- Inquiries of clients are made with every type of test.
- Inspection, recalculation, and reperformance are used for every type of test except analytical procedures.

Table 12-3	Relationship Between Types of Tests and Evidence							
	Type of Evidence							
Type of Test	Inspection	Observation	Inquiries of the Client	Confirmation	Recalculation	Reperformance	Analytical Procedures
Procedures to obtain an understanding of internal control	✓	✓	✓		✓	✓	
Tests of controls	✓	✓	✓		✓	✓	
Analytical procedures			✓				✓
Tests of details of balances	✓		✓	✓	✓	✓	

RELATIVE COSTS The following types of tests are listed in order of increasing cost:

- Analytical procedures.
- Procedures to obtain an understanding of internal control and tests of controls.
- Tests of details of balances.

The reason analytical procedures are least costly is the relative ease of making calculations and comparisons. Often, considerable information about potential misstatements can be obtained by simply comparing two or three numbers. Frequently, auditors calculate these ratios using computer software at minimal cost.

Tests of controls are also low in cost because the auditor is making inquiries and observations, examining such things as initials on documents and outward indications of other control procedures, and conducting reperformance, recalculations, and tracings. Frequently, tests of controls can be done on a large number of items in a few minutes, especially if computer-based work, such as the use of test data, is included. Tests of details of balances are almost always considerably more costly than any of the other types of procedures. It is costly to send confirmations and to count assets. Because of the high cost of tests of details of balances, auditors usually try to plan the audit to minimize their use, focusing these tests upon high-risk areas.

Naturally, the cost of each type of evidence varies in different situations. For example, the cost of an auditor's test counting of inventory (a substantive test of the details of the inventory balance) frequently depends on the nature and dollar value of the inventory, its location, and the number of different items.

RELATIONSHIP BETWEEN TESTS OF CONTROLS AND SUBSTANTIVE TESTS To better understand the nature of tests of controls and substantive tests, an examination of how they differ is useful. An exception in a test of controls is an indication of the likelihood of errors or fraud and other irregularities affecting the dollar value of the financial statements. An exception in a substantive test is a financial statement misstatement. Exceptions in tests of controls are often referred to as "control test deviations." Thus, control test deviations are significant only if they occur with sufficient frequency to cause the auditor to believe there may be material dollar misstatements in the statements. Substantive tests should then be performed to determine whether dollar misstatements have actually occurred.

As an illustration, assume that the client's controls require an independent clerk to verify the quantity, price, and extension of each supplier's invoice, after which the clerk must initial the original invoice to indicate performance. A test of control audit procedure would be to examine a sample of suppliers' invoices for the initials of the person who verified the quantitative data. If there is a significant number of documents without initials, the auditor should follow up with tests to determine if there are any monetary misstatements. This can be done by extending the tests of the suppliers' invoices to include verifying prices to purchase orders, extensions, and footings (reperformance) or by increasing the sample size for the confirmation of accounts payable (test of details of balances). Of course, even though the control is not operating effectively, the invoices may be correct. This will be the case if the persons originally preparing the supplier invoices did a conscientious and competent job. Similarly, even if there is an initial, there may be monetary misstatements due to initialling without performance or with careless performance of the internal control procedure.

TRADE-OFF BETWEEN TESTS OF CONTROLS AND SUBSTANTIVE TESTS As explained in Chapter 9, there is a trade-off between tests of controls and substantive tests. The auditor makes a decision while planning the control risk assessment. If control risk is assessed as high, the auditor would follow a substantive approach; if control risk is assessed lower, the auditor could follow a combined approach. Tests of controls must be performed to determine whether the lower assessed control risk is supported. If it is, planned detection risk in the audit risk model is increased and substantive procedures can therefore be reduced. Figure 12-5 shows the relationship between substantive tests and control risk assessment (including tests of controls) at differing levels of internal control effectiveness.

The shaded area in Figure 12-5 is the maximum assurance obtainable from control risk assessment and tests of controls. For example, at any point to the left of point A, assessed control risk is 1.0 because the auditor evaluates internal control as ineffective. Any point to the right of point B results in no further reduction of control risk because the public accounting firm has established the minimum assessed control risk that it will permit.

After the auditor determines the effectiveness of the client's internal controls, it is appropriate to select any point within the shaded area of Figure 12-5 consistent with the level of control risk that the auditor determines is appropriate. To illustrate, assume that the auditor contends that internal control effectiveness is at point C. Tests of controls at the C_1 level would provide the minimum control risk, given internal

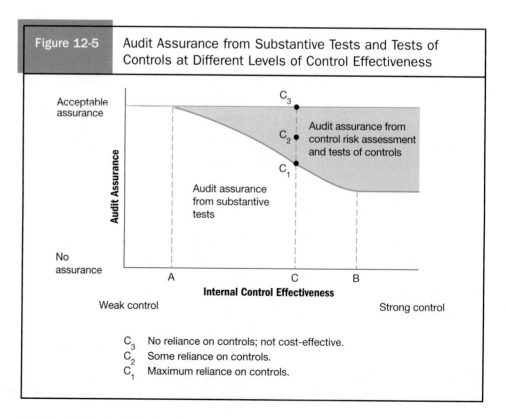

Figure 12-5 | Audit Assurance from Substantive Tests and Tests of Controls at Different Levels of Control Effectiveness

C_3 No reliance on controls; not cost-effective.
C_2 Some reliance on controls.
C_1 Maximum reliance on controls.

Research and the Audit Process

How does understanding the external environment relate to risks of financial statement misstatement? A possible source of financial statement bias is the intention of the company to influence customers and suppliers. Raman and Shahrur (2008) found that earnings management was related to the amount of research and development investments by suppliers and customers in the next period.

This means that a company that is looking for customer or supplier financial support when developing a new product could be motivated to overstate its earnings. This research article illustrates the importance of discussing non-financial issues, such as potential new product development, with clients.

Nedard and Johnstone (2004) looked at how auditors adjusted their audit process in response to increased risks,

specifically earnings manipulation risk and risk of poor corporate governance. Their results would indicate that in response to such issues as the risk of financial statement manipulation (perhaps due to new product development or high management bonuses), auditors charge more. This is reflected in both increased hours worked on the audit (that is, more testing was conducted), and the auditors actually charging a higher hourly rate, reflecting perhaps the worry associated with high-risk engagements.

Sources: 1. Bedard, Jean C. and Karla M. Johnstone, "Earnings manipulation risk, corporate governance risk, and auditors' planning and pricing decisions," *The Accounting Review,*" 79(2), 2004. 2. Kartik, Raman and Husayn Shahrur, "Relationship-specific investments and earnings management: Evidence on corporate suppliers and customers," *The Accounting Review*, 83(4), 2008, p. 1041–1081.

control. The auditor could choose to perform no tests of controls (point C_3), which would support a control risk of 1.0. Any point between the two, such as C_2, would also be appropriate. If C_2 is selected, the audit assurance from tests of controls is $C_3 - C_2$ and from substantive tests is $C - C_2$. The auditor will likely select C_1, C_2, or C_3 based upon the relative cost of tests of controls and substantive tests.

Evidence Mix

After establishing the client risk profile and the potential for material misstatements in the financial statements, there are significant variations in the extent to which the four types of tests can be used in different audits for differing levels of inherent risk and internal control effectiveness. There can also be variations from cycle to cycle within a given audit, from account balance to account balance within a particular cycle, and even between assertions for a particular account balance. This combination of the four types of tests to obtain sufficient appropriate audit evidence for a cycle or account balance is known as **audit evidence mix**.

Figure 12-6 on the next page shows the audit evidence mix for four different audits. In each case, considerable time was spent accumulating knowledge of business and in risk assessment, as well as completing analytical review for planning purposes. Assume sufficient appropriate audit evidence was accumulated for all audits. Audit 1 is of a large company, while Audits 2 through 4 are of medium-sized companies. An analysis of each audit follows.

Analysis of Audit 1—sophisticated internal controls This client is a large company with sophisticated internal controls. The auditor, therefore, performs extensive tests of controls and relies heavily on the client's internal control to reduce substantive tests. Extensive analytical procedures are also performed to reduce tests of details of balances, which are, therefore, minimized. Because of the emphasis on tests of controls and analytical procedures, this audit can be done less expensively than other types of audits.

Analysis of Audit 2—medium, some controls This company is medium-sized, with some controls and some inherent risks. The auditor has, therefore, decided to do a medium amount of testing for all types of tests except analytical procedures, which will be done extensively.

Audit evidence mix—the combination of the four types of tests to obtain sufficient appropriate audit evidence for a cycle or account balance.

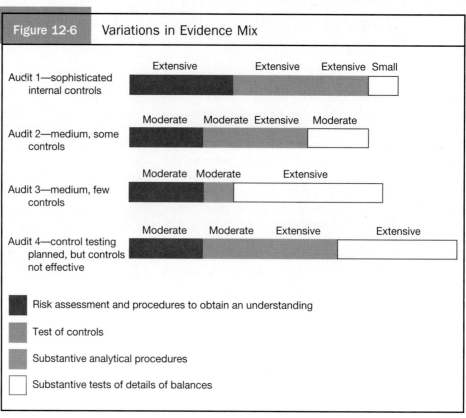

Figure 12-6 | Variations in Evidence Mix

Audit 1—sophisticated internal controls
Extensive | Extensive | Extensive | Small

Audit 2—medium, some controls
Moderate | Moderate | Extensive | Moderate

Audit 3—medium, few controls
Moderate | Moderate | Extensive

Audit 4—control testing planned, but controls not effective
Moderate | Moderate | Extensive | Extensive

■ Risk assessment and procedures to obtain an understanding

▨ Test of controls

▨ Substantive analytical procedures

□ Substantive tests of details of balances

Note: Auditors in all of the audits have completed client risk profiles, have knowledge of the business, and have completed planning analytical procedures.

Analysis of Audit 3—medium, few controls This company is medium-sized but has few effective controls and significant inherent risks. Management has decided that it is not cost-effective to implement better internal controls. No tests of controls are done because reliance on internal control is inappropriate when controls are insufficient. The emphasis is on tests of details of balances, but some analytical procedures are also done. The reason for limiting analytical procedures is the auditor's expectations of misstatements in the account balances. The cost of the audit is likely to be relatively high because of the amount of detailed substantive testing.

concept check

C12-3 Which audit test is the least costly to develop and conduct? Why?

C12-4 If an auditor conducts tests of controls but finds that controls are not functioning effectively, what is the effect upon substantive tests? Why?

Analysis of Audit 4—medium, ineffective controls The original plan on this audit was to follow the approach used in Audit 2. However, the auditor found extensive control test deviations and significant misstatements using dual-purpose tests and analytical procedures. The auditor, therefore, concluded that the internal controls were not effective. Extensive tests of details of balances are performed to offset the unacceptable results of the other tests. The costs of this audit are higher because tests of controls and dual-purpose tests were performed but could not be used to reduce tests of details of balances.

Figure 12-6 shows the relative mix of audit evidence types. It does not reflect total audit cost since the costs associated with the tests will vary, depending on the specific test selected and the extent of computerized support used for conducting the tests.

③ Creating the Audit Program

Design of the Audit Program

The audit program identifies the audit steps that are the auditor's response to the identified risks. A combined audit approach is appropriate for most audits; such an approach includes both tests of controls and substantive procedures. The audit program for most audits is designed in three parts: tests of controls, analytical procedures, and tests of details of balances. There will likely be a separate set of audit programs for each transaction cycle. An example in the sales and collection cycle might be tests of controls audit programs for sales and cash receipts; an analytical procedures audit program for the entire cycle; and tests of details of balances audit programs for cash, accounts receivable, bad-debt expense, allowance for uncollectible accounts, and miscellaneous accounts receivable.

TESTS OF CONTROLS The tests of controls audit program normally includes a descriptive section documenting the understanding obtained about internal control. It is also likely to include a description of the procedures (those necessary to obtain an understanding of internal control and to determine the design effectiveness of those internal controls) performed in order to assess control risk. After assessing control risk, the auditor will assess the significance of the risks and determine the risk of material misstatements at the assertion level. The methodology to design tests of controls is shown in Figure 12-7. The first four steps in the figure were described in Chapter 9 (refer to Figure 9-2). When controls are effective and planned control risk is low (i.e., the auditor chooses to rely on internal controls), a combined approach will be used and there will be tests of controls. Some dual-purpose tests may also be included. If control risk is assessed at maximum, the auditor will use a substantive audit approach (i.e., only substantive procedures will be used). The procedures already performed in obtaining an understanding of internal control may affect tests of controls.

Audit procedures The approach to designing tests of controls emphasizes satisfying the transaction-related audit objectives developed in Chapter 5. A three-step approach is followed when control risk is assessed below maximum:

1. Apply the transaction-related audit objectives to the class of transactions being tested, such as sales.

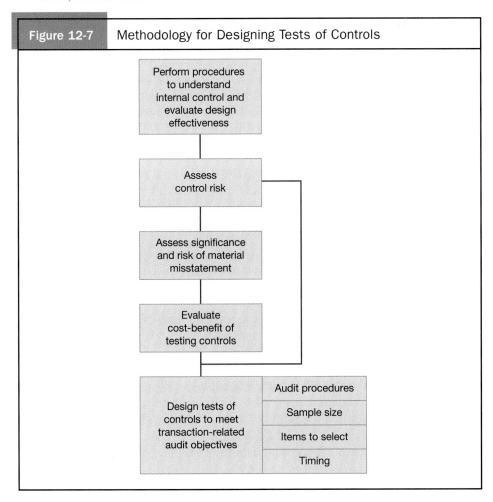

Figure 12-7	Methodology for Designing Tests of Controls

Perform procedures to understand internal control and evaluate design effectiveness

Assess control risk

Assess significance and risk of material misstatement

Evaluate cost-benefit of testing controls

Design tests of controls to meet transaction-related audit objectives

- Audit procedures
- Sample size
- Items to select
- Timing

2. Identify specific controls to be relied upon to reduce control risk or address significant risks for transaction-related audit objectives.
3. For all internal controls to which reduction in control risk is attributed (key controls), develop appropriate tests of controls. Where relevant, design appropriate dual-purpose tests (considering weakness in internal control and expected results of the tests of controls) for the potential types of errors or fraud and other irregularities related to those transaction-related audit objectives.

ANALYTICAL PROCEDURES Many auditors perform extensive analytical procedures on all audits because they are relatively inexpensive. As stated in Chapter 6, analytical procedures are performed at three different stages of the audit: in the planning stage to help the auditor decide the other evidence needed to satisfy audit risk, during the audit in conjunction with tests of details of balances as part of substantive procedures, and near the end of the audit as a final test of reasonableness.

CAS 315, Identifying and assessing the risks of material misstatement through understanding the entity and its environment (previously Section 5141), requires the use of analytical procedures during the planning phase of the audit. CAS 520 provides standards to ensure the effectiveness of analytical procedures when used as substantive procedures, although their use is optional. CAS 520 also states that analytical procedures are required as a final evaluation technique when assessing whether the financial statements are fairly stated and consistent with other evidence.

Choosing the appropriate analytical procedures requires the auditor to use professional judgment. The appropriate use of analytical procedures and illustrative ratios is discussed in Chapter 6. There are also examples in several subsequent chapters. For example, Table 15-3 on page 518 illustrates several analytical procedures for the audit of accounts receivable.

TESTS OF DETAILS OF BALANCES The methodology for designing tests of details of balances is oriented to the balance-related audit objectives developed in Chapter 5 (pages 137–139). For example, if the auditor is verifying accounts receivable, the planned tests must be sufficient to satisfy each of the objectives. In planning tests of details of balances to satisfy those objectives, many auditors follow a methodology such as the one shown in Figure 12-8 for accounts receivable. The design of these tests is normally the most difficult part of the entire planning process. Designing such procedures is subjective and requires considerable professional judgment.

A discussion of the key decisions in designing tests of details of balances as shown in Figure 12-8 follows.

Set materiality and audit risk and assess inherent risk for accounts receivable Setting the preliminary judgment about materiality for the audit as a whole is an auditor decision that was discussed in Chapter 8. A lower materiality would result in more testing of details than a higher amount. Analytical review for planning purposes, used together with a good knowledge of business and the industry, allows the auditor to identify obvious warning signals.

As discussed in Chapter 7, audit risk is normally decided for the audit as a whole, rather than by cycle. A rare exception might be when the auditor believes that a misstatement of a specific account, such as accounts receivable, would negatively affect users more than the same size misstatement of any other account. For example, if accounts receivable is pledged to a bank as security on a loan, audit risk may be set lower for sales and collections than for other cycles.

Inherent risk is assessed by identifying any aspect of the client's history, environment, or operations that indicates a high likelihood of misstatement in the current year's financial statements. This emphasizes the need for a broad-based knowledge of business that links risks to the external business environment. Once inherent risk has been assessed for the financial statements as a whole, it is assessed at the

Figure 12-8

Figure 12-8 Methodology for Designing Tests of Details of Financial Statement Balances—Accounts Receivable

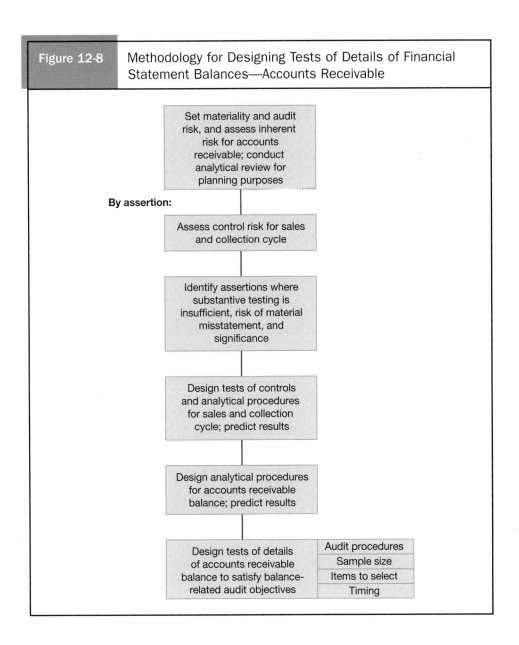

By assertion:

Set materiality and audit risk, and assess inherent risk for accounts receivable; conduct analytical review for planning purposes

Assess control risk for sales and collection cycle

Identify assertions where substantive testing is insufficient, risk of material misstatement, and significance

Design tests of controls and analytical procedures for sales and collection cycle; predict results

Design analytical procedures for accounts receivable balance; predict results

Design tests of details of accounts receivable balance to satisfy balance-related audit objectives

Audit procedures
Sample size
Items to select
Timing

assertion level. Considerations affecting overall inherent risk applied to accounts receivable include makeup of accounts receivable, nature of the client's business, and sales trends. An account balance for which inherent risk has been assessed as high would result in more evidence accumulation than for an account with low inherent risk.

Inherent risk also can be extended to individual audit objectives. For example, because of adverse economic conditions in the client's industry, the auditor may conclude that there is a high risk of uncollectible accounts receivable (realizable-value objective). Inherent risk could still be low for all other objectives.

Assess control risk Control risk is evaluated in the manner discussed in Chapter 9 and in earlier parts of this chapter. This methodology would be applied to both sales and collection in the audit of accounts receivable. Effective controls reduce control risk and therefore the evidence required for substantive procedures; inadequate controls increase the substantive evidence needed.

Identify high-risk assertions Assertions can be high risk for several reasons. The auditor may have identified the assertion as having a significant risk of fraud or material misstatement. For example, if there is an economic downturn and the client has customers with high credit limits, the auditor may want to spend additional time testing the valuation assertion, as the uncollectability of a single large account could have a significant effect. Also, there could be some assertions where substantive testing is insufficient, due to extensive reliance on automated systems, for example with automated credit checks. In the latter case, the auditor may decide that testing of internal controls could be effective, especially where general controls over program changes and information systems access are of high quality.

Design tests of controls and analytical procedures and predict results The methodology for designing tests of controls and analytical procedures was discussed earlier in this section and will be illustrated in subsequent chapters. The tests are designed with the expectation that certain results will be obtained. These predicted results affect the design of tests of details of balances as discussed below.

Design tests of details of balances to satisfy balance-related audit objectives The planned tests of details of balances include audit procedures, sample size, items to select, and timing. Procedures must be selected and designed for each account and each balance-related audit objective within each account. The balance-related audit objectives for accounts receivable are shown on page 499.

A difficulty the auditor faces in designing tests of details of balances is the need to predict the outcome of the tests of controls and analytical procedures before they are performed. This is necessary because the auditor should design tests of details of balances during the planning phase, but the appropriate design depends on the outcome of the other tests. In planning tests of details of balances, the auditor usually predicts that there will be few or no exceptions in tests of controls and analytical procedures, unless there are reasons to believe otherwise. If the results of the tests of controls and analytical procedures are not consistent with the predictions, the tests of details of balances will need to be changed as the audit progresses.

One of the most difficult parts of auditing is properly applying the factors that affect tests of details of balances. Each of the factors is subjective, requiring considerable professional judgment. The impact of each factor on tests of details of balances is equally subjective. For example, if inherent risk is reduced from medium to low, there is agreement that tests of details of balances can be reduced. Deciding the specific effect on audit procedures, sample size, timing, and items to select is a difficult decision.

TIMING OF AUDIT TESTS Audit tests can be conducted throughout the year, or, for a small audit, may be conducted in a concentrated period of time. Table 12-4 shows

Table 12-4	Timing of Selected Audit Tests		
Risk Assessment	Plan and design audit approach, update understanding of internal control, update audit program, and perform preliminary analytical procedures.	31/8/08	
Risk Response	Perform tests of controls for first nine months of the year.	30/9/08	
	Confirm accounts receivable. Observe inventory.	31/10/08	
	Count cash, perform cut-off tests, and request various other confirmations.	31/12/08	Balance sheet date
	Do analytical procedures, complete tests of controls, and do most tests of details of balances.	07/1/09	Books closed
	Summarize results, review for contingent liabilities, review for subsequent events, accumulate final evidence including analytical procedures, and finalize audit.	08/3/09	Last date of field work
Reporting	Finalize and issue auditor's report.	15/3/09	

analytical procedures being done both before and after the balance sheet date. Because of their low cost, it is common to use analytical procedures whenever they are relevant. They are frequently done early with preliminary data prior to year end as a means of planning and directing other audit tests to specific areas. The greatest benefit from calculating ratios and making comparisons occurs after the client has finished preparing its financial statements. Ideally, these analytical procedures are done before tests of details of balances so that they can then be used to determine how extensively to test balances. They are also used as a part of performing tests of balances and during the completion phase of the audit.

Table 12-4 also shows that tests of details of balances are normally done last. On some audits, all are done after the balance sheet date. When clients want to issue statements soon after the balance sheet date, however, the more time-consuming tests of details of balances will be done at interim dates prior to year end with additional work being done to **roll forward** the audited interim-date balances to year end. (A roll forward involves substantive work on journal entries and other activities during this period.) Substantive tests of balances performed before year end provide less assurance and are not normally done unless internal controls are effective.

Roll forward—substantive work on journal entries and transactions from a date prior to the balance sheet date to the year end.

ILLUSTRATIVE AUDIT PROGRAM Table 12-5 on the next page shows the tests of details of balances segment of an audit program for accounts receivable. The format used relates the audit procedures to the balance-related audit objectives. Note that most procedures satisfy more than one objective. Also, more than one audit procedure is used for each objective. Audit procedures can be added or deleted as the auditor considers necessary. Sample size, items to select, and timing can also be changed for most procedures.

The audit program in Table 12-5 was developed after consideration of all the factors affecting tests of details of balances and is based on several assumptions about inherent risk, control risk, and the results of tests of controls and analytical procedures. As indicated, if those assumptions are materially incorrect, the planned audit program will require revision. For example, analytical procedures could indicate potential errors for several balance-related audit objectives, tests of controls results could indicate weak internal controls, or new facts could cause the auditor to change inherent risk.

Most large public accounting firms develop their own standard audit programs, organized by industry, often linked by audit objective to databases including lists of expected controls and likely audit tests. Smaller firms often purchase similar audit programs from outside organizations. Standard audit programs are normally computerized and can easily be modified to meet the circumstances of individual audit engagements. One example of standard audit programs available for purchase is the CICA's *Professional Engagement Manual* (PEM). PEM is available in paper form and on CD-ROM, and contains audit programs as well as general and industry-specific checklists that auditors can use and modify for individual engagements.

Standard audit programs, whether developed internally or purchased from an outside organization, can dramatically increase audit efficiency if they are used properly. They should not be used, however, as a substitute for an auditor's professional judgment. Because each audit is different, it is usually necessary to add, modify, or delete steps within a standard audit program in order to accumulate sufficient and competent evidence.

RELATIONSHIP OF TRANSACTION-RELATED AUDIT OBJECTIVES TO BALANCE-RELATED AUDIT OBJECTIVES AND PRESENTATION AND DISCLOSURE AUDIT OBJECTIVES It has already been shown that tests of details of balances must be designed to satisfy balance-related audit objectives for each account. The extent of substantive tests can be reduced when transaction-related audit objectives have been satisfied by tests of controls. It is, therefore, important to understand how each transaction-related audit objective relates to each balance-related audit objective. Table 12-6 (on page 403)

Table 12-5 — Tests of Details of Balances Audit Program for Accounts Receivable

Sample Size	Items to Select	Timing*	Tests of Details of Balances Audit Procedures	Existence	Rights	Completeness	Accuracy	Valuation	Classification	Detail tie-in	Cut-off	Presentation and disclosure assertions
Trace 20 items; foot 2 pages and all subtotals	Random	I	1. Obtain an aged list of receivables: trace open items to supporting invoice detail, foot schedule, and trace to general ledger.							x		
All	All	Y	2. Obtain an analysis of the allowance for doubtful accounts and bad debt expense: test accuracy, examine authorization for write-offs, and trace to general ledger.	x		x	x	x		x		
100	30 largest 70 random	I	3. Obtain direct confirmation of accounts receivable and perform alternative procedures for non-responses.	x	x	x	x			x	x	
N/A	N/A	Y	4. Review accounts receivable control account for the period. Investigate the nature of, and review support for, any large or unusual entries or any entries not arising from normal journal sources. Also investigate any significant increases or decreases in sales toward year end.	x	x		x			x	x	x
All	All	Y	5. Review receivables for any that have been assigned or discounted.		x							x
N/A	N/A	Y	6. Investigate collectibility of account balances.					x				
All	All	Y	7. Review lists of balances for amounts due from related parties or employees, credit balances, and unusual items, as well as notes receivable due after one year.	x						x		x
30 transactions for sales and cash receipts; 10 for credit memos	50% before and 50% after year end	Y	8. Determine that proper cutoff procedures were applied at the balance sheet date to ensure that sales, cash receipts, and credit memos have been recorded in the correct period.								x	

*I = Interim; Y = Year end; N/A = Not applicable

shows the relationship between transaction-related and balance-related audit objectives, and how they relate to presentation and disclosure-related audit objectives used to analyze the financial statements.

This direct relationship can be illustrated by looking at sales transactions. If there are controls to ensure that all sales transactions that occur are recorded in the accounts receivable, then these controls can provide assurance with respect to the balance-related audit objective of completeness.

Table 12-6	Comparison of Audit Objectives	
Transaction-Related Audit Objective	Balance-Related Audit Objective	Presentation and Disclosure-Related Audit Objective
Occurrence	Existence and rights and obligations	Occurrence and rights and obligations
Completeness	Completeness	Completeness
Accuracy	Accuracy and valuation	Accuracy and valuation
Classification	Classification	Classification
Posting and summarization	Detail tie-in	Understandability
Timing	Cut-off	N/A

However, even when all transaction-related audit objectives are met, the auditor will still rely primarily on substantive tests of balances to meet the following balance-related audit objectives, since few internal controls are related to these audit objectives: realizable value, rights and obligations, and presentation and disclosure. Some substantive tests of balances are also likely for the other balance-related audit objectives, depending on the results of the tests of controls.

The relationship of transaction-related audit objectives to balance-related audit objectives is shown in greater detail in Figure 15-3 on page 501. This figure shows how transaction-related audit objectives for sales and cash receipts affect accounts receivable balance-related audit objectives. Note in Figure 15-3 that the existence transaction-related audit objective for sales affects the existence balance-related audit objective for accounts receivable, whereas the existence transaction-related audit objective for cash receipts affects the completeness balance-related audit objective for accounts receivable. The reason is that sales increase accounts receivable, whereas cash receipts decrease accounts receivable.

In addition to conducting tests to assess the fairness of the financial statements, the auditor is required to examine and analyze the financial statements and the related notes with respect to the audit assertions. To do so, the auditor uses presentation and disclosure-related audit objectives, as explained in Chapter 5. The first four objectives are similar to the transaction-related and balance-related audit objectives. The final audit objective, understandability, requires the auditor to examine the statements and notes from the perspective of a knowledgeable business user to assess whether information has been clearly presented.

concept check

C12-5 List the type of information that would be included in an audit program.

C12-6 Describe the type of testing required when the auditor has identified an assertion to have a significant risk of material misstatement.

Summary

1. *What is an audit strategy?* An audit strategy comprises a planned approach to the conduct of audit testing, taking into account assessed risks.

   What is the role of audit planning? Audit planning describes a structured process to document risks according to the audit risk model, to document and evaluate internal controls, and to design an audit program.

   What is the purpose of an audit program? An audit program lists the audit procedures that the auditor conducts as the risk response phase of the audit. This includes tests of control and substantive tests.

   What are the five different types of audit tests? The five types of audit tests are (1) risk assessment procedures, (2) procedures to obtain an understanding of internal control, (3) tests of controls, (4) analytical procedures, and (5) tests of details of balances. Together, detailed analytical procedures and tests of details of balances are called substantive tests.

Which type of test is a dual-purpose test? What is the purpose of such a test? A substantive test (remember that a substantive test comprises both analytical procedures and tests of details and is used to quantify errors) can be used both to quantify errors and as a test of controls.

2. *What is evidence mix?* Evidence mix is the phrase used to explain the proportion of the different types of tests used in the audit engagement.

How does the auditor choose the types of audit tests to be completed? Audit tests are selected based upon the level of assessed risks. For example, tests of control are conducted only if control risk is set below maximum and there is a potential for reliance upon internal controls.

3. *What is the methodology for selecting audit tests for the audit program?* The audit program is designed to ensure that sufficient competent evidence is gathered for each class of transaction (or account) for each relevant audit assertion. Audit tests are linked to the audit assertion in the context of assessed risks.

Visit the text's website at www.pearsoned.ca/arens for practice quizzes, additional case studies, and international standards information.

Review Questions

12-1 What are the five types of tests auditors use to determine whether financial statements are fairly stated? Identify which tests are performed to assess control risk and which tests are performed to achieve planned detection risk. Also, identify which tests will be used when auditing internal control over financial reporting.

12-2 Review the phases of the financial statement audit. List each phase that involves risk assessment. State which types of audit procedures would be used during each phase that you listed.

12-3 What is the purpose of risk assessment procedures, and how are they related to or different from the four other types of audit tests?

12-4 Distinguish between a test of controls and a substantive procedure. Give two examples of each.

12-5 Explain what is meant by "recalculation" and "reperformance." Give an example of each type of audit evidence. Why are recalculation and reperformance often dual-purpose tests?

12-6 An auditor may perform tests of controls and substantive procedures simultaneously as a matter of audit convenience. However, the substantive procedures and sample size are, in part, dependent upon the results of the tests of controls. How can the auditor resolve this apparent inconsistency?

12-7 Explain how the calculation of the gross margin percentage and the ratio of accounts receivable to sales, and their comparison to that of previous years, are related to the confirmation of accounts receivable and other tests of the accuracy of accounts receivable.

12-8 Distinguish between a combined audit approach and a substantive audit approach. Give one example of when each might be appropriate for the acquisition and payment cycle.

12-9 Assume that the client's internal controls over the recording and classifying of capital asset additions are considered weak because the individual responsible for recording new acquisitions has inadequate technical training and limited experience in accounting. How would this situation affect the evidence you should accumulate in auditing permanent assets as compared with another audit in which the controls are excellent? Be as specific as possible.

12-10 For each of the seven types of evidence discussed in Chapter 6, identify whether the evidence is applicable to procedures for risk assessment, obtaining an understanding of internal control, tests of controls, analytical procedures, or tests of details of balances.

12-11 The following are three decision factors related to the assessed level of control risk: effectiveness of internal controls, cost-effectiveness of a reduced assessed level of control risk, and results of tests of controls. Identify the combination of conditions for these three factors that is required before a reduction in substantive procedures is permitted.

12-12 State the three-step approach to designing tests of controls.

12-13 Explain the relationship between the methodology for designing tests of controls in Figure 12-7 (page 397) to the methodology for designing tests of details of balances in Figure 12-8 (page 399).

12-14 Why is it desirable to design tests of details of balances before performing tests of controls? State the assumptions the auditor must make in doing this. What does the auditor do if the assumptions prove to be incorrect?

12-15 Why do auditors frequently consider it desirable to perform audit tests throughout the year rather than wait until year end? List several examples of evidence that can be accumulated prior to year end.

Discussion Questions and Problems

12-16 The auditor of Ferguson's Inc. identified two internal controls in the sales and collection receipts cycle for testing. In the first control, the computer verifies that a planned sale on account will not exceed the customer's credit limit entered in the accounts receivable master file. In the second control, the accounts receivable clerk matches bills of lading, sales invoices, and customer orders before recording in the sales journal.

Describe how the presence of general controls over software programs and master file changes affect the extent of audit testing of each of these two internal controls.

12-17 Assume that the client's internal controls over the recording and classifying of fixed asset additions are considered deficient because the individual responsible for recording new acquisitions has inadequate technical training and limited experience in accounting.

a. What value would you assign to control risk? Why?
b. How will this situation affect the evidence you should accumulate in auditing fixed assets as compared with another audit in which the controls are excellent? Be as specific as possible.

12-18 The following are 11 audit procedures taken from an audit program:

1. Add the supplier balances in the accounts payable master file, and compare the total with the general ledger.
2. Examine vendors' invoices to verify the ending balance in accounts payable.
3. Compare the balance in employee benefits expense with previous years'. The comparison takes the increase in employee benefits rates into account.
4. Discuss the duties of the cash disbursements bookkeeper with him or her, and observe whether he or she has responsibility for handling cash or preparing the bank reconciliation.
5. Confirm accounts payable balances directly with vendors.
6. Use generalized audit software to run a gap test on the cheques issued during the year. (Print a list of cheque numbers omitted from the normal cheque number sequencing.)
7. Examine the treasurer's initials on monthly bank reconciliations as an indication of whether they have been reviewed.
8. Examine vendors' invoices and other documentation in support of recorded transactions in the acquisitions journal.
9. Multiply the commission rate by total sales, and compare the result with commission expense.
10. Examine vendors' invoices and other supporting documents to determine whether large amounts in the repair and maintenance account should be capitalized.
11. Examine the initials of vendors' invoices that indicate internal verification of pricing, extending, and footing by a clerk.

a. Indicate whether each procedure is a test of controls, an analytical procedure, or a test of details of balances.
b. Identify the type of evidence for each procedure.

12-19 Beds and Spreads, Inc. specializes in bed and bath furnishings. Its inventory system is linked through the company's website to key suppliers. The auditor identified the following internal controls in the inventory cycle:

1. The computer initiates an order only when perpetual inventory levels fall below prespecified inventory levels in the inventory master file.
2. The sales and purchasing department managers review inventory reorder points for reasonableness on a monthly basis. Approved changes to reorder points are entered into the master file by the purchasing department manager and an updated printout is generated for final review. Both managers verify that all changes were entered correctly and initial the final printout indicating final approval. These printouts are maintained in the purchasing department.
3. The computer will initiate a purchase order only for inventory product numbers maintained in the inventory master file.
4. The purchasing department manager reviews a computer-generated exception report that highlights weekly purchases that exceed $10,000 per vendor.
5. Salesclerks send damaged merchandise on the store shelves to the back storage room. The sales department manager examines the damaged merchandise each month and prepares a listing showing the estimated salvage value by product number. The accounting department uses the listing to prepare a monthly adjustment to recorded inventory values.

Consider each of the preceding controls separately.
a. What type of risk or potential error could occur if the control were absent?
b. State whether the control is manual, computer-assisted, or fully automated.
c. Describe how the extent of testing of each control would be affected in subsequent years if general controls, particularly controls over program and master file changes, are effective.
d. For each control,
   • provide an example of an audit procedure to test the control; and
   • state the transaction-related audit objective associated with the audit procedure.

12-20 The following are audit procedures from different transaction cycles:

1. Use audit software to foot and cross-foot the cash disbursements journal, and trace the balance to the general ledger.
2. Select a sample of entries in the acquisitions journal, and trace each one to a related vendor's invoice to determine whether one exists.
3. Examine documentation for acquisition transactions before and after the balance sheet date to determine whether they are recorded in the proper period.
4. Inquire of the credit manager whether each account receivable on the aged trial balance is collectable.
5. Compute inventory turnover for each major product, and compare with that of previous years.
6. Confirm with lenders a sample of notes payable balances, interest rates, and collateral.
7. Use audit software to foot the accounts payable trial balance, and compare the balance with the general ledger.

REQUIRED
a. For each audit procedure, identify the transaction cycle being audited.
b. For each audit procedure, identify the type of evidence.
c. For each audit procedure, identify whether it is a test of control or a substantive test (indicating whether it is a test of details of balances or an analytical procedure).
d. For each audit procedure, identify the related audit objective(s).
e. Specifically assess the purpose of each audit procedure, as follows:
   • For tests of control, state the risk (potential error) that is being assessed.
   • For analytical procedures, state a possible result that you would expect.
   • For tests of detail, state the type of material error that you would be quantifying.

12-21 The following internal controls for the acquisition and payment cycle were selected from a standard internal control questionnaire:

1. Vendors' invoices are recalculated prior to payment.
2. Approved price lists are used for acquisitions.
3. Prenumbered receiving reports are prepared as support for purchases and are numerically accounted for.
4. Dates on receiving reports are compared with vendors' invoices before entry into the accounts payable system.
5. The accounts payable system is updated, balanced, and reconciled to the general ledger monthly.
6. Account classifications are reviewed by someone other than the preparer.
7. All cheques are signed by the owner or the manager.
8. The cheque signer compares data on supporting documents with cheques.
9. All supporting documents are cancelled after entry.
10. After they are signed, cheques are mailed by the owner or manager, or a person under his or her supervision.

REQUIRED
a. For each control, state which transaction-related audit objective(s) is (are) applicable.
b. For each control, write an audit procedure that could be used to test the control for effectiveness.
c. For each control, identify a likely misstatement, assuming the control does not exist or is not functioning.
d. For each likely misstatement, identify a substantive audit procedure to determine if the misstatement exists.

12-22 Jennifer Schaefer, a public accountant, follows the philosophy of performing interim tests of controls on every December 31 audit as a means of keeping overtime to a minimum. Typically, the interim tests are performed some time between August and November.

REQUIRED
a. Evaluate her decision to perform interim tests of controls.
b. Under what circumstances is it acceptable for her to perform no additional tests of controls as part of the year-end audit tests?
c. If she decides to perform no additional testing, what is the effect on other tests she performs during the remainder of the engagement?

12-23 Kim Bryan, a new staff auditor, is confused by the inconsistency of the three audit partners to whom she has been assigned on her first three audit engagements. On the first engagement, she spent a considerable amount of time in the audit of cash disbursements by examining cancelled cheques and supporting documentation, but almost no time was spent on the verification of capital assets. On the second engagement, a different partner had her do less intensive tests in the cash disbursements area and take smaller sample sizes than in the first audit even though the company was much larger. On her most recent engagement under a third audit partner, there was a thorough test of cash disbursement transactions, far beyond that of the other two audits, and an extensive verification of capital assets. In fact, this partner insisted on a complete physical examination of all capital assets recorded on the books. The total audit time on the most recent audit was longer than that of either of the first two audits in spite of the smaller size of the company. Bryan's conclusion is that the amount of evidence to accumulate depends on the audit partner in charge of the engagement.

REQUIRED

a. State the differences in risk assessments that could affect the amount of evidence accumulated in each of the three audit engagements as well as the total time spent.

b. What could the audit partners have done to help Bryan understand the differences in the audit emphasis on the three audits?

c. Explain how these three audits are useful in developing Bryan's professional judgment. How could the quality of her judgment have been improved by the audits?

12-24 The following are parts of a typical audit for a company with a fiscal year end of July 31.

1. Confirm accounts payable.
2. Do tests of controls for acquisitions and payroll.
3. Do other tests of details of balances for accounts payable.
4. Do tests for review of subsequent events.
5. Preplan the audit.
6. Issue the auditor's report.
7. Understand internal control and assess control risk.
8. Do analytical procedures for accounts payable.
9. Set audit risk and decide preliminary judgment about materiality.
10. Summarize client risk profile.
11. Prepare audit programs.

REQUIRED

a. Put parts 1 through 11 of the audit in the sequential order in which you would expect them to be performed in a typical audit.

b. Identify those parts that would frequently be done before July 31.

Professional Judgment Problems

12-25 Parts for Wheels, Inc. has historically sold auto parts directly to consumers through its retail stores. Due to competitive pressure, Parts for Wheels installed an internet-based sales system that allows customers to place orders through the company's website. The company hired an outside website design consultant to create the sales system because the company's IT personnel lack the necessary experience.

Customers use the link to the inventory parts listing on the website to view product descriptions and prices. The inventory parts listing is updated weekly. To get the system online quickly, management decided not to link the order system to the sales and inventory accounting systems. Customers submit orders for products through the online system and provide credit card information for payment. Each day, accounting department clerks print submitted orders from the online system. After credit authorization is verified with the credit card agency, the accounting department enters the sale into the sales system. After that, the accounting department sends a copy of the order to warehouse personnel who process the shipment. The inventory system is updated on the basis of bills of lading information forwarded to accounting after shipment.

Customers may return parts for full refund if returned within 30 days of submitting the order online. The company agrees to refund shipping costs incurred by the customer for returned goods.

REQUIRED

a. Describe deficiencies in Parts for Wheels' online sales system that may lead to material misstatements in the financial statements. State which audit assertion is affected.

b. For each deficiency listed in part (a), identify changes in manual procedures that could be made to minimize risks, without having to reprogram the current online system.

c. Describe potential customer concerns about doing business online with Parts for Wheels. For each concern, provide one or more controls that could be implemented to address the concerns.

Case

12-26 Gale Brewer, a public accountant, had been the partner in charge of the audit of Merkle Manufacturing Company, a nonpublic company, for 13 years. Merkle had had remarkable growth and profits in the past decade, primarily as a result of the excellent leadership provided by Bill Merkle and other competent executives. Gale had always enjoyed a close relationship with the company and prided herself on having made over the years several constructive comments that had aided in the success of the firm. Several times in the past few years, Gale's firm had considered rotating a different audit team onto the engagement, but this had been strongly resisted by both Gale and Bill.

For the first few years of the audit, internal controls were inadequate and the accounting personnel had inadequate qualifications for their responsibilities. Extensive audit evidence was required during the audit, and numerous adjusting entries were necessary. However, because of Gale's constant prodding, internal controls improved gradually and competent personnel were hired. In recent years, there were normally no audit adjustments required, and the extent of the evidence accumulation was gradually reduced. During the past three years, Gale was able to devote less time to the audit because of the relative ease of conducting the audit and the cooperation obtained throughout the engagement.

In the current year's audit, Gale decided that the total time budget for the engagement should be kept approximately the same as in recent years. The senior in charge of the audit, Phil Warren, was new on the job and highly competent, and he had the reputation of being able to cut time off budgets. The fact that Bill had recently acquired a new division through merger will probably add to the time, but Phil's efficiency will probably compensate for it.

The interim tests of controls took somewhat longer than expected because of the use of several new assistants, a change in the accounting system to computerize the inventory and other accounting records, a change in accounting personnel, and the existence of a few more errors in the tests of the system. Neither Gale nor Phil was concerned about the budget deficit, however, because they could easily make up the difference at year end.

At year end, Phil assigned the responsibility for inventory to an assistant who also had not been on the audit before but was competent and extremely fast at his work. Even though the total value of inventory increased, Phil reduced the size of the sample from that of other years because there had been few errors in the preceding year. The assistant found several items in the sample that were overstated as a result of errors in pricing and obsolescence, but the combination of all of the errors in the sample was immaterial. Accordingly, Phil decided that adjustments to control risk were not warranted.

The assistant completed the tests in 25 percent less time than the preceding year's tests. The entire audit was completed on schedule and in slightly less time than the preceding year's.

There were only a few adjusting entries for the year, and only two of them were material. Gale was extremely pleased with the results and wrote a special letter to Phil and the inventory assistant complimenting them on their efficiency during the audit.

Six months later, Gale received a telephone call from Bill and was informed that the company was in serious financial trouble. Subsequent investigation revealed that the inventory had been significantly overstated. The major cause of the misstatement was the inclusion of obsolete items in inventory (especially in the new division), errors in pricing as a result of a programming error in the new computer system, and the inclusion of nonexistent inventory in the final inventory listing, which had been printed two weeks after the inventory count had actually been conducted. The new controller had been directed to intentionally overstate the inventory to compensate for the reduction in sales volume from the preceding year.

REQUIRED
a. Following the sequence of the phases in the audit process, list the major deficiencies in the audit, and state why they took place.
b. What things should have been apparent to Gale or Phil in the conduct of the audit?
c. If Gale's firm is sued by creditors, what is the likely outcome?

Ongoing Small Business Case: Auditing Revenue Recognition at CondoCleaners.com

12-27 As explained in this chapter and in previous chapters, revenue recognition is likely to have the potential for material misstatement at most audits. Recall that orders for cleaning are placed two or more days ahead of time and paid for by credit card at the time of booking. Jim records sales in his accounting records, from the internet transactions.

REQUIRED
a. What sales audit assertions are subject to misstatement at CondoCleaners.com?

b. What data would you ask Jim, the owner of CondoCleaners.com, to include in his accounting records to ensure adequate tracking of sales information is possible?
c. List the audit procedures that you would conduct to audit revenue recognition at CondoCleaners.com. For each audit procedure, list the audit assertion that it addresses, and state the risk of misstatement that it addresses.

13

Audit sampling concepts

Since the auditor uses testing of transactions, there needs to be a means of choosing which items will be examined. Then, once the items have been chosen and audited, it is important to extrapolate the results to the population. In this chapter, you will look at the different types of sampling methods that an auditor is likely to use and the role of judgment during the sampling process. All types of auditors need to decide which items to select for sampling. Management accountants may use sampling to decide which items to monitor in their role as management.

STANDARDS REFERENCED IN THIS CHAPTER

CICA Standard

CAS 500 – Audit evidence (previously Section 5300 – Audit Evidence)

CAS 530 – Audit sampling

LEARNING OBJECTIVES

1 Define sampling. State when an auditor would use statistical rather than non-statistical sampling. Describe the different types of non-probabilistic (non-statistical) sampling methods used by auditors. Provide examples of computer-assisted audit tests (CAATs) for non-statistical sampling.

2 Explain the three different ways that an auditor can select a statistical sample. List three common statistical sampling methodologies used by auditors. Provide examples of CAATs for statistical sampling.

3 Describe the 14 steps in planning and selecting a sample, performing the tests, and evaluating the sample. Describe four additional issues the auditor should consider during the sampling process. Define an anomaly. State the work that is required for an auditor to confirm that an error or misstatement is an anomaly.

What Is an Error?

Brookes & Company, LLP, uses random samples when performing audit tests whenever possible. It believes that this gives it the best chance of getting representative samples of its clients' accounting information. In the audit of Sorofu Products, a company that sells and distributes jewellery, a random sample of 60 items was selected from a population of 18,250 items in doing a test of unit and total costs. Only one of the 60 items selected was in error, but it was large. In investigating the error, Harold Brakowski, the audit staff person doing the test, was told by Sorofu's controller that the error occurred while the regular inventory clerk was on vacation and was really only an "isolated error."

When Harold extrapolated the error, he obtained a significantly material overstatement of inventory. As an alternative, he asked the human resources manager for vacation records, and determined that the inventory clerk was, indeed, on vacation for two weeks and that the error had occurred during that time. However, due to the size of the error, the audit team decided that additional substantive testing was required for that two-week period. Thirty more items were selected from that two-week period, and three additional errors were found. However, two were overstatements and one was an understatement, with the net result that the auditors could conclude that the errors in inventory at the year end were overall immaterial.

IMPORTANCE TO AUDITORS

Auditing standards require that errors be extrapolated to the entire population. However, Harold's investigation of the inventory costing error at Sorofu enabled him to split the costing transactions into two populations: a large population of transactions that were prepared while the inventory clerk was present and a smaller population that covered the clerk's two-week vacation. By obtaining an understanding of the costing process for these two populations, audit tests were designed to address them in accordance with the related risks. There was a much higher risk of error when the inventory clerk was absent, so tests of detail were required to quantify the risk of material misstatement.

WHAT DO YOU THINK?

1. How would the firm's audit response have differed if it turned out that the inventory clerk were not on vacation when the error occurred?

2. Describe three risks (or potential errors) that could occur at Sorofu with respect to inventory costing. For each risk, describe an audit step that the auditor could use to investigate the risk.

The situation at Sorofu shows us that sampling needs to be conducted in the context of the risks of error or misstatement. Samples are selected so that further testing can be conducted on the items selected. These could be tests of control or tests of detail. In this chapter, we will look at many different types of sampling. Some are more suited to control testing or to tests of detail, and certain methods are suitable for both types of testing.

The Nature of Sampling

Due to the nature of the audit, the auditor does not examine all the available evidence but rather selects evidence from the available population. Sampling is not required, but CAS 530, Audit sampling, explains in the definition section that **audit sampling** occurs when (1) less than 100 percent of the items in the population under examination are being audited, and (2) each item (described as a sampling unit) in the population could be selected as part of the sample. As sampling is part of the audit process, it must be tied to the auditor's risk assessments.

Auditing using this definition of sampling means dealing with three aspects of audit sampling: (1) planning the sample and selecting the sample, (2) performing the tests, and (3) evaluating the results. As the chapter title implies, this chapter discusses sampling concepts, as applied to tests of controls or tests of details. The sales and collection cycle and its transactions are used as a frame of reference for discussing these concepts, but the concepts apply to every cycle. Chapter 14 applies these concepts to tests of controls, and Chapter 15 applies audit sampling to tests of details of balances. Figure 13-1, which uses the same information as Figure 12-3 on page 392, shows how audit sampling is related to the types of audit tests.

Chapter 14 and Chapter 15 are directly related to Chapter 13 in that the auditor must decide the audit procedures he or she plans to perform before applying audit sampling.

Representative Samples

Whenever an auditor selects a sample from a population, the objective is to obtain one that's representative. A **representative sample** is one in which the characteristics in the sample of audit interest are approximately the same as those of the population. This means that the sampled items are similar to the items not sampled. For example, assume that a client's internal controls require a clerk to attach a shipping document to every duplicate sales invoice but that the procedure is not followed exactly 3 percent of the time. If the auditor selects a sample of 100 duplicate sales invoices and finds three missing, the sample is highly representative. If two or four such items are found in the sample, the sample is reasonably representative. If many missing items or no missing items are found, the sample is non-representative.

In practice, auditors do not know whether a sample is representative, even after all testing is completed. Auditors can, however, increase the likelihood of a sample being representative by using care in sample design, selection, and evaluation. Two things can cause a sample result to be non-representative: non-sampling error and sampling error. The risk of these occurring is termed "non-sampling risk" and "sampling risk"; both can be controlled.

CAS

Audit sampling—occurs when (1) less than 100 percent of the items in the population under examination are being audited, and (2) each item (described as a sampling unit) in the population could be selected as part of the sample.

Representative sample—a sample with the same characteristics as those of the population.

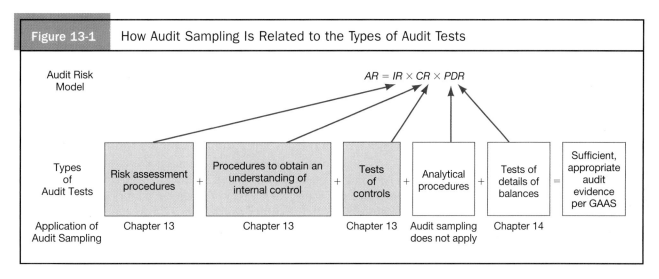

Figure 13-1 How Audit Sampling Is Related to the Types of Audit Tests

Non-sampling risk (non-sampling error) occurs when audit tests do not uncover exceptions existing in the sample. In the previous example, three shipping documents were not attached to duplicate sales invoices, and if the auditor concluded that no exceptions existed, there was a non-sampling error.

The two causes of non-sampling error are the auditor's failure to recognize exceptions and inappropriate or ineffective audit procedures. An auditor might fail to recognize an exception because of exhaustion, boredom, or lack of understanding of what constitutes an exception. Take, for example, the control of attaching a shipping document to the duplicate sales invoice. An exception would be defined as a missing document or a shipping document that does not agree to the sales invoice. An ineffective audit procedure for these exceptions would be the selection of a sample of shipping documents to determine if each is attached to a set of duplicate sales invoices. The auditor in this case would be unable to determine whether there were numerous sales invoices unsupported by shipping documents, since such sales invoices could not be selected. Careful design of audit procedures and proper supervision and instruction are ways to reduce non-sampling risk.

Sampling risk (sampling error) is an inherent part of sampling that results from testing less than the entire population. Even with zero non-sampling error, there is always a chance that a sample is not representative. For example, if a population has a 3-percent exception rate, the auditor could easily select a sample of 100 items containing no exceptions or many.

There are two ways to control sampling risk: increasing sample size and using an appropriate method of selecting sample items from the population. Increasing sample size will reduce sampling risk, and vice versa. At the extreme, testing all the items of a population will have a zero sampling risk (since this is no longer sampling). Using an appropriate sampling method will reasonably assure representativeness. This does not eliminate or even reduce sampling risk, but it does allow the auditor to measure the sample risk associated with a given sample size in a reliable manner.

Statistical versus Non-statistical Sampling

Audit sampling methods can be divided into two broad categories: statistical and non-statistical. These categories have important similarities and differences. They are similar in that they both involve the three steps identified in the introduction: (1) plan the sample and select the sample, (2) perform the tests, and (3) evaluate the results. The purpose of planning the sample is to make sure that the audit tests are performed in a manner that provides the desired sampling risk and minimizes the likelihood of non-sampling error. Selecting the sample involves deciding how to select sample items from the population. Performing the tests involves examining documents and performing other audit tests. Evaluating the results involves drawing conclusions based on the audit tests. To illustrate, assume that an auditor selects a sample of 100 duplicate sales invoices from a population, tests each to determine if a shipping document is attached, and determines that there are three exceptions. Deciding that a sample size of 100 is needed is a part of planning the sample. Deciding which 100 items to select from the population is a sample selection problem. Doing the audit procedure for each of the 100 items and determining that there were three exceptions constitutes performing the tests. Reaching conclusions about the likely exception rate in the total population when there is a sample exception rate of 3 percent is evaluating the results.

Statistical sampling differs from non-statistical sampling in that through the application of mathematical rules, it allows the quantification (measurement) of sampling risk in planning the sample (step 1) and evaluating the results (step 3). (You may remember calculating a statistical result at a 95-percent **confidence level**, which is a statement of probability, in a statistics course. The 95-percent confidence level provides a 5-percent sampling risk.) The quantification of sampling risk is appropriate only when the auditor selects the sample (step 1) using a probabilistic sample, which is discussed shortly.

In non-statistical sampling, the auditor does not quantify sampling risk. Instead, the auditor selects those sample items that he or she believes will provide the most useful information in the circumstances (i.e., non-probabilistic samples are chosen), and conclusions are reached about populations on a judgmental basis. For that reason, the selection of non-probabilistic samples is often termed **judgmental sampling**.

It is equally acceptable under professional standards for auditors to use either statistical or non-statistical sampling methods. However, it is essential that each method be applied with due care. All steps of the process must be followed carefully. When statistical sampling is used, the sample must be a probabilistic one, and appropriate statistical evaluation methods must be used with the sample results to make the sampling risk computations.

It is also acceptable to make non-statistical evaluations by using probabilistic selection, but many practitioners prefer not to do so. They believe that statistical measurement of sampling risk is inherent in those samples and should not be ignored. It is never acceptable, however, to evaluate a non-probabilistic sample as if it were a statistical sample. A summary of the relationship of probabilistic and non-probabilistic selection to statistical and non-statistical evaluation is shown in Table 13-1.

There are three types of sample selection methods commonly associated with non-statistical audit sampling and three types of sample selection methods commonly associated with statistical audit sampling. These are listed below and discussed in the following sections.

The non-probabilistic (judgmental) sample selection methods:

- Directed sample selection.
- Block sample selection.
- Haphazard sample selection.

The **probabilistic sample selection** methods:

- Simple random sample selection.
- Systematic sample selection.
- Probability proportionate-to-size sample selection.

Stratified sample selection (discussed further on page 417) can be applied to both non-probabilistic and probabilistic sample selection methods.

Non-probabilistic Sample Selection

Non-probabilistic sample selection methods are those that use professional judgment to select items from the population and do not meet the technical requirements for probabilistic sample selection. Since these methods are not based on strict mathematical probabilities, the representativeness of the sample may be difficult to determine. The information content of the sample, including its representativeness, will be based on the knowledge and skill of the auditor in applying his or her judgment in the circumstances.

DIRECTED SAMPLE SELECTION **Directed sample selection** is a non-probabilistic method of sample selection in which each item in the sample is selected on the basis

Table 13-1	Relationship of Methods of Selecting Samples to Methods of Evaluating Results	
Method of Selecting Sample	**Method of Evaluating Results**	
	Statistical	Non-statistical
Probabilistic	Preferable to use statistical	Acceptable to use non-statistical
Non-probabilistic	Not acceptable to use statistical	Mandatory to use non-statistical

of some judgmental criteria established by the auditor. The auditor does not rely on equal chances of selection, but, rather, deliberately selects items according to the criteria. Some auditors consider certain directed samples to be a form of analytical review. The important issue is ensuring that the test is clearly defined and its audit role identified. The criteria may relate to representativeness, or they may not. The following are commonly used criteria.

Items most likely to contain misstatements Frequently, auditors are able to identify which population items are most likely to be misstated. Examples are receivables outstanding for a long time, purchases from and sales to officers and affiliated companies, and unusually large or complex transactions. Computer-assisted audit tests (CAATs) could be used to list all such accounts or to provide survey summaries that enable the auditor to identify at-risk transactions. These kinds of items can be efficiently investigated by the auditor, and the results can be applied to the population only on a judgmental basis. For example, the results of examining a selection of old accounts receivable (perhaps those over 90 days old) can be applied only to the total balance of old receivables, not to the entire accounts receivable population. The reasoning underlying the evaluation of such samples is that if none of the higher-risk items selected contain misstatements, then it is less likely that a material misstatement exists in the population.

Items containing selected population characteristics The auditor may be able to describe the various types and sources of items that make up the population and design the sample to be representative by selecting one or more items of each type. For example, a sample of cash disbursements might include some from each month, each bank account or location, and each major type of acquisition. CAATs could be used to stratify the accounts by dollar amount or by location, helping the auditor decide which transactions could be susceptible to material misstatement.

Large dollar coverage A sample can often be selected to cover such a large portion of total population dollars that the risk of drawing an improper conclusion by not examining small items is not a concern. For example, all transactions that have a value in excess of 75 percent of materiality could be examined. CAATs could be used to list such transactions for further follow-up. This is a practical approach on many audits, especially smaller ones. There are also statistical methods that are intended to accomplish the same effect.

Block sample—a non-probabilistic method of sample selection in which items are selected in measured sequences.

BLOCK SAMPLE SELECTION A **block sample** is the selection of several items in sequence. Once the first item in the block is selected, the remainder of the block is chosen automatically. One example of a block sample is the selection of a sequence of 100 sales transactions from the sales journal for the third week of March. A total sample of 100 could also be selected by taking 5 blocks of 20 items each, 10 blocks of 10, or 50 blocks of 2. In Audit Challenge 13-1, reviewing all supplier comments in date order is also a block sample.

It is ordinarily acceptable to use block samples during the audit if a reasonable number of blocks are used. If few blocks are used, the probability of obtaining a non-representative sample is too great, considering the possibility of such things as employee turnover, changes in the accounting system, and the seasonal nature of many businesses. CAATs can be used to increase audit coverage by running a gap test on all transactions. A gap test will go through the whole transaction sequence (e.g., invoice numbers) and identify which numbers are missing.

A common use of block testing is testing cut-off. The auditor would select a block of invoices, receiving documents, and shipping documents spanning both sides of the year-end date to ensure that the transactions were recorded in the proper period. CAATs could be used to list the transactions that occurred during the period that the auditor is interested in. If the number of transactions is large (e.g., thousands of transactions per day), the auditor might choose a subsample of transactions from the block using one of the other sampling methods discussed in this chapter.

audit challenge 13-1
Playing with Numbers?

You found a gorgeous antique desk on eBay for an unbelievable price—only $250! The eBay statistics said that the seller had completed over 600 transactions with a 99-percent positive feedback rate, so you decided to use your credit card and buy it. You waited and waited, and four weeks later you still had not received the desk. Checking eBay again, you found that there were at least 75 negative feedback comments about customers not receiving their products, all posted within a period of three weeks. It turned out that someone had hacked into the seller's accounts and was taking the money. The positive feedback statistics were no longer valid.

Think about your auditing client, a financial organization that specializes in selling mutual funds and high-risk investments. For the last five years, the company's profits have increased steadily,

at the rate of about 20 percent per year. Now, due to the crash in worldwide stock markets and the decline in the values of funds, the company has laid off over 60 percent of its sales and administrative staff. Some sales are still occurring, but the company is having trouble meeting its payroll without dipping into its line of credit, which the bank has reduced.

CRITICAL THINKING QUESTIONS

1. What do these two examples tell us about the relationship between statistics and the environment?
2. What type of sample are the eBay data?
3. How could sampling have been used to predict potential difficulties with stock market and mutual fund values?

HAPHAZARD SAMPLE SELECTION When the auditor goes through a population and selects items for the sample without regard to their size, source, or other distinguishing characteristics, he or she is attempting to select without bias. This is called a **haphazard sample selection**. If the Audit Challenge 13-1 eBay samples were selected without regard to date order, then this would have been a haphazard sample.

The most serious shortcoming of haphazard sample selection is the difficulty of remaining completely unbiased in the selection. Because of the auditor's training and "cultural bias," certain population items are more likely than others to be included in the sample. For example, auditors may be inclined to select larger amounts or amounts from the middle of a period or to avoid round dollar amounts.

Although haphazard and block sample selection appear to be less logical than directed sample selection, they are often useful as audit tools and should not be ignored. In some situations, the cost of more complex sample selection methods outweighs the benefits obtained from using them. For example, assume that the auditor wants to trace credits from the accounts receivable transaction history files to the duplicate bank deposit slips and other authorized sources as a test for fictitious credits in the data files. A haphazard or block approach is simpler and much less costly than other selection methods in this situation and would be employed by many auditors.

> **Haphazard sample selection**—a non-probabilistic method of sample selection in which items are chosen without regard to their size, source, or other distinguishing characteristics.

> ### concept check
>
> C13-1 During the audit, a new staff member failed to record a client's 10-cent calculation error as an error. What type of error or risk does this mistake exemplify? Why?
>
> C13-2 Provide two examples of directed sample selection that could be used for the audit of inventory.

Probabilistic and Statistical Samples

Probabilistic Sample Selection

As previously indicated, to measure sampling risk, statistical sampling requires probabilistic sample selection—a method of sample selection in which it is possible to define the set of all possible samples, every possible sample item has a known probability of being selected, and the sample is selected by a random process. There are three methods commonly used by auditors to obtain probabilistic samples: simple random sample selection, systematic sample selection, and stratified sample selection. Most generalized audit software (GAS) is capable of running all of these sample selection methods. If sample sizes are high and data are accessible, it is likely more cost-effective for the auditor to use GAS rather than selecting the sample manually.

Random sample—a sample in which every possible combination of elements in the population has an equal chance of being selected.

SIMPLE RANDOM SAMPLE SELECTION A simple **random sample** is one in which every possible combination of elements in the population has an equal chance of constituting the sample. Simple random sampling is used to sample populations that are considered to have the same characteristics for audit purposes. For example, the auditor may wish to sample the client's cash disbursements for the year. A simple random sample of 60 items contained in the cash disbursements journal might be selected for that purpose. Appropriate auditing procedures would be applied to the 60 items selected, and conclusions would be drawn and applied to all cash disbursement transactions recorded for the year.

Random number selection methods When a simple random sample is obtained, a method must be used that assures that all items in the population have an equal chance of selection. Suppose that in the above example there were a total of 12,000 cash disbursement transactions for the year. A simple random sample of one transaction would be such that each of the 12,000 transactions would have an equal chance of being selected. This would be done by obtaining a random number between 1 and 12,000. If the number were 3,895, the auditor would select and test the 3,895th cash disbursement transaction recorded in the cash disbursements journal.

Random numbers are a series of digits that have equal probabilities of occurring over long runs and that have no discernible pattern. Appendix 13A on page 435 explains how you can select random numbers, using either random number tables or spreadsheet software. Some accounting firms have specialized software that they use to select random numbers.

Replacement versus non-replacement sampling Random numbers may be obtained with replacement or without replacement. In replacement sampling, an element in the population can be included in the sample more than once, whereas in non-replacement sampling, an element can be included only once. If the random number corresponding to an element is selected more than once in non-replacement sampling, it is not included in the sample a second time. Although both selection approaches are consistent with sound statistical theory, auditors normally use non-replacement sampling.

Systematic selection—a probabilistic method of sampling in which the auditor calculates an interval (the population size divided by the number of sample items desired) and selects the items for the sample based on the size of the interval and a randomly selected number between zero and the sample size.

SYSTEMATIC SAMPLE SELECTION In **systematic selection** (also known as "systematic sampling"), the auditor calculates an interval and then methodically selects the items for the sample based on the size of the interval. The interval is determined by dividing the population size by the number of sample items desired. For example, if a population of sales invoices ranges from 652 to 3,151 and the desired sample size is 125, the interval is $20 \times [(3,151 - 651) \div 125]$. The auditor must now select a random number between 0 and 19 to determine the starting point for the sample. If the randomly selected number is 9, the first item in the sample is invoice number 661 (652 + 9). The remaining 124 items are 681 (661 + 20), 701 (681 + 20), and so on through item 3,141.

The advantage of systematic sampling is its ease of use. For most populations, the systematic sample can be drawn quickly, the approach automatically puts the numbers in sequence, and the appropriate documentation is easy to develop.

A major problem with systematic selection is the possibility of bias. Because of the way systematic selection works, once the first item in the sample is selected, all other items are chosen automatically. This causes no problem if the characteristic of interest, such as a possible control deviation, is distributed randomly throughout the population; however, in some cases, characteristics of interest may not be randomly distributed. For example, if a control deviation occurred at a certain time of the month or with certain types of documents, a systematic sample could have a higher likelihood of failing to be representative than a simple random sample. It is important, therefore, when systematic selection is used, to consider possible patterns in the population data that could cause sample bias.

Probability-proportionate-to-size sampling (PPS)—see Monetary unit sampling.

A variation of systematic sample selection by unit of interest is used by the **probability-proportionate-to-size** (PPS) sampling methods described in the next section. Here, the individual dollar is considered the unit of interest. The interval is determined based upon a statistical formula, and the transactions associated with that dollar interval are selected.

STRATIFIED SAMPLE SELECTION When a sample is stratified, it is split into smaller sets where each set has a similar characteristic. For example, stratification can occur by dollar amount (sales over $50,000; sales under that amount), by location (foreign versus domestic), or by another criteria, such as whether commissions will be paid (sales from head office versus sales made by travelling sales personnel). This can improve the efficiency of the audit by focusing work on transactions that may be more readily subject to material error. After data are stratified, the sample will be selected using one of the methods previously discussed (either probabilistic or non-probabilistic).

Statistical Sampling Methodologies

Once the decision has been made to conduct statistical sampling, the auditor may choose from three broad categories of statistical sampling: attribute, probability-proportionate-to-size (PPS), and variables. (Discovery sampling is also described, but this is a subset of attribute sampling.) These methods are based upon underlying **sampling distributions**, statistical frequency distributions such as binomial or normal distributions, which are beyond the scope of this text. Review your statistics text to examine these distributions. All three categories of sampling can be used for tests of controls or tests of details, although attribute sampling is normally used for controls testing, whereas PPS and variables sampling are normally used for tests of details testing.

ATTRIBUTE SAMPLING Attribute sampling is used to estimate the proportion of items in a population containing a characteristic or **attribute** of interest. This proportion is called the **occurrence rate** or **exception rate** and is the ratio of the items containing the specific attribute to the total number of population items. The occurrence rate is usually expressed as a percentage. For example, an auditor might conclude that the exception rate, the rate where control violations occurred for the internal verification of sales invoices, is approximately 3 percent, meaning that invoices are not properly verified 3 percent of the time. This methodology is designed to answer the question, "How many items contain errors?"

Sampling distribution—a frequency distribution of the results of all possible samples of a specified size that could be obtained from a population containing some specific parameters.

Attribute sampling—a statistical, probabilistic method of sample evaluation that results in an estimate of the proportion of items in a population containing a characteristic or attribute of interest.

Attribute—the characteristic being tested for in the population.

Occurrence rate—the ratio of items in a population that contain a specific attribute to the total number of population items.

Exception rate—the percentage of items in a population that include exceptions in prescribed controls or monetary correctness.

Auditors are interested in the occurrence of the following types of exceptions in populations of accounting data:

1. Deviations from client's established controls.
2. Monetary errors or fraud and other irregularities in populations of transaction data.
3. Monetary errors or fraud and other irregularities in populations of account balance details.

Knowing the occurrence rate of such exceptions is particularly helpful for the first two types of exceptions, which relate to transactions. Therefore, auditors make extensive use of audit sampling that measures the occurrence or exception rate when performing tests of controls. With the third type of exception, the auditor usually needs to estimate the total dollar amount of the exceptions because a judgment must be made about whether the exceptions are material. When the auditor wants to know the total amount of a misstatement, he or she will use methods that measure dollars, such as PPS or variables methodologies, not the exception or occurrence rate.

The statistical sampling method most commonly used for tests of controls is attribute sampling. Whenever attribute sampling is used in this text, it refers to attribute statistical sampling for physical units. Both attribute sampling and non-statistical sampling have attributes, which are the characteristics being tested for in the population, but attribute sampling is a statistical method. Attribute sampling is used primarily for tests of controls, but auditors also use attribute sampling for substantive procedures when performing dual-purpose tests.

Attribute sampling may be based on physical units (e.g., invoices) or monetary units (e.g., dollars). In the case of the former, the occurrence or exception rate would be a percentage; in the case of the latter, the exception would be a monetary amount.

An example of attribute sampling applied to tests of controls is shown in Chapter 14.

Discovery sampling Discovery sampling, a special type of attribute sampling, is used when the auditor is looking for very few or near zero deviations. For example, if the auditor suspects that fraud or other irregularities exist in the data, the sample size needs to be designed to provide the assurance of finding at least one example of the fraud or other irregularity. This method can also be used for tests of detail in situations where few or no misstatements are expected, for example, where calculations are performed by a computer program.

PROPORTIONATE-TO-SIZE SAMPLING PPS sampling is also known as **monetary unit sampling** (MUS) or dollar unit sampling (DUS). PPS is a modified form of attribute sampling that focuses on a single unit of currency (in Canada, the dollar), rather than on a physical unit. In the balance of the text, the term "monetary unit sampling (MUS)" is used to refer to this form of sampling.

In physical unit sampling, the sampling unit is usually a document, such as a cheque, or a transaction, such as a sale. In monetary unit sampling, the sampling unit is the individual dollar. If sales for the year were made up of 15,000 transactions with a dollar value of $30 million, the sampling unit for physical unit attribute sampling would be an invoice, while the sampling unit for monetary unit sampling would be each of the thirty million dollars. In the case of the former, each of the 15,000 invoices would have an equal chance of selection; in the case of the latter, each of the $30 million would have an equal chance of selection.

Monetary unit sampling allows the result of the testing to be stated in dollar terms. This allows the auditor to specify a dollar range of potential errors for a specified confidence level. It also increases the probability that larger invoices, totalling larger dollar amounts than smaller invoices, will be selected, since an invoice including $150,000 will have a greater probability of being selected than one containing only $15. Monetary unit sampling is appropriate for tests of controls and for tests of details.

Discovery sampling—a form of attribute sampling designed to look for one or very low occurrences.

Monetary unit sampling (MUS)—a modified form of attribute sampling that focuses on a single unit of currency (in Canada, the dollar), rather than on a physical unit.

VARIABLES SAMPLING Variables sampling is used when the auditor desires a dollar or quantitative conclusion with respect to the test conducted. The general class of methods called variables sampling includes several techniques. Those described in this section are difference estimation, ratio estimation, and mean-per-unit estimation.

Difference estimation **Difference estimation** is used to measure the estimated total misstatement amount when there is both a recorded value and an audited value for each item in the sample. An example is confirming a sample of accounts receivable and determining the difference (misstatement) between the client's recorded amount and the amount the auditor considers correct for each selected account. The auditor makes an estimate of the population misstatement based on the number of misstatements, average misstatement size, and individual misstatement size in the sample. The result is stated as a point estimate plus or minus a computed precision interval at a stated confidence level.

Difference estimation frequently results in smaller sample sizes than any other method, and it is relatively easy to use. For that reason, difference estimation is used frequently by auditors.

> **Difference estimation**—a form of sampling used to estimate the difference between the recorded value and the audited value.

Ratio estimation Ratio estimation is similar to difference estimation except that the point estimate of the population misstatement is determined by multiplying the portion of sample dollars misstated by the total recorded book value. The ratio estimate results in even smaller sample sizes than difference estimation if the size of the misstatements in the population is proportionate to the recorded value of the items. If the size of the individual misstatements is independent of the recorded value, the difference estimate also results in smaller sample sizes.

Mean-per-unit estimation In mean-per-unit estimation, the auditor is concerned with the audited value rather than the error amount of each item in the sample. Except for the definition of what is being measured, the mean-per-unit estimate is calculated in exactly the same manner as the difference estimate. The point estimate of the audited value is the average audited value of items in the sample times the population size. The computed precision interval is computed on the basis of the audited value of the sample items rather than of the misstatements. When the auditor has computed the upper and lower confidence limits, a decision is made about the acceptability of the population by comparing these amounts with the recorded book value.

concept check

C13-3 List the three features of probabilistic sample selection.

C13-4 List one advantage and one disadvantage associated with systematic sample selection.

Steps in Conducting the Sampling Process

Planning, Selecting, and Evaluating a Sample

Audit sampling is applied to tests of controls and tests of details through a set of 14 well-defined steps. The steps are divided into three sections: (1) plan the sample, select the sample, (2) perform the audit procedures, and (3) evaluate the results. It is important to follow these steps carefully as a means of ensuring that both the auditing and the sampling aspects of the process are properly applied. The steps provide an outline of the discussion that follows. Table 13-14, shown at the end of the discussion on page 434, compares these steps for tests of controls (e.g., attribute sampling) and tests of details (e.g., MUS sampling).

PLAN THE SAMPLE AND SELECT THE SAMPLE

1. State the objectives of the audit test.
2. Decide if audit sampling applies.
3. Define attributes and exception or error conditions.
4. Define the population.
5. Define the sampling unit.
6. Specify tolerable exception rate or specify materiality.

7. Specify acceptable risk of assessing control risk too low or acceptable risk of incorrect acceptance.
8. Estimate the population exception rate or the misstatements in the population.
9. Determine the initial sample size.
10. Select the sample.

PERFORM THE AUDIT PROCEDURES

11. Perform the audit procedures.

EVALUATE THE RESULTS

12. Generalize from the sample to the population.
13. Analyze exceptions or misstatements.
14. Determine the acceptability of the population.

The general process of each step is described in this chapter, and related definitions are provided for new terms. Chapter 14 provides an example of tests of controls using non-statistical and physical unit attribute sampling, and Chapter 15 does the same for tests of details using non-statistical and MUS sampling.

1. STATE THE OBJECTIVES OF THE AUDIT TEST The overall objectives of the test must be stated in terms of the risks addressed and the transaction cycle being tested. Typically, the overall objective of tests of controls is to test the effectiveness of controls and to determine whether the transactions contain monetary errors or fraud and other irregularities. For tests of details, the auditor determines the maximum amount of overstatement and understatement that could exist while still providing a sample with no misstatements (or for the number of misstatements that was found). The objectives of the audit test are normally decided as a part of designing the audit program in the context of risks by assertion.

Population—the body of data about which the auditor wishes to generalize.

2. DECIDE IF AUDIT SAMPLING APPLIES The term **population** represents the body of data about which the auditor wishes to generalize.

Audit sampling applies whenever the auditor plans to reach conclusions about a population based on a sample. The auditor should examine the audit program and decide those audit procedures for which audit sampling applies. For example, in the following incomplete audit program (which is missing risks and assertions), sampling could be used for procedures 3 through 5.

1. Review sales transactions for large and unusual amounts (analytical procedure or directed sample).
2. Observe whether the duties of the accounts receivable clerk are separate from the handling of cash (test of control).
3. Examine a sample of duplicate sales invoices for the following:
   (a) Credit approval by the credit manager (test of control).
   (b) The existence of an attached shipping document (test of control).
   (c) Inclusion of a chart of accounts number (test of control).
4. Select a sample of shipping documents, and trace each to related duplicate sales invoices for existence (test of control).
5. Compare the quantity on each duplicate sales invoice with the quantity on related shipping documents (test of control).

Audit sampling is inappropriate for the first two procedures in this audit program. The first is an analytical procedure for which sampling is inappropriate. The second is an observation procedure for which no documentation exists to perform audit sampling.

For tests of details, while it is common to sample in many accounts, there are situations when sampling does not apply. For the population shown in Table 13-2, the auditor may decide to audit only items over $5,000 and ignore all others because the total of the smaller ones is immaterial. In this case, the auditor has not sampled but

Table 13-2   Sample Population

Population Item	Recorded Amount	Population Item	Recorded Amount	Population Item	Recorded Amount	Population Item	Recorded Amount
1	$1,410	11	$2,270	21	$4,865	31	$ 935
2	9,130	12	50	22	770	32	5,595
3	660	13	5,785	23	2,305	33	930
4	3,355	14	940	24	2,665	34	4,045
5	5,725	15	1,820	25	1,000	35	9,480
6	8,210	16	3,380	26	6,225	36	360
7	580	17	530	27	3,675	37	1,145
8	44,110	18	955	28	6,250	38	6,400
9	825	19	4,490	29	1,890	39	100
10	1,155	20	17,140	30	27,705	40	8,435
							$207,295

has conducted a **census**, which consists of auditing all of the transactions that satisfy a particular criteria. Similarly, if the auditor is verifying capital asset additions and there are many small additions and one extremely large purchase of a building, the auditor may decide to ignore the small items entirely. Again the auditor has not sampled but has focused on high-value items instead.

Census, conducting–consists of auditing all of the transactions that satisfy a particular criteria.

3. DEFINE ATTRIBUTES AND EXCEPTION OR ERROR CONDITIONS Whenever audit sampling is used, the auditor must carefully define the characteristics (attributes) being tested and the exception conditions. CAS 500, Considering the relevance and reliability of audit evidence (previously Section 5300), requires that items that are audited relate to the audit test. Unless a precise statement of what constitutes an attribute is made in advance, the staff person who performs the audit procedure will have no guidelines for identifying exceptions, and the audit test may not meet the desired objective.

CAS

Attributes of interest and exception conditions come directly from the audit procedures for which the auditor has decided to use audit sampling (Table 13-3). For example, based on the portion of the partial test-of-control audit program described in Step 2, the first attribute that can be tested by means of sampling is whether the duplicate sales invoice is approved for credit (Procedure 3a). A deviation condition in a manual system would be a lack of initials indicating credit approval. The absence of the defined attribute for any sample item will be an exception for that attribute.

Table 13-3   Step 3 Terms

Term Related to Planning	Test of Control (e.g., for Attribute Sample)	Test of Detail (e.g., for MUS Sample)
Define the item of interest	Identify the characteristic or *attribute* of interest	Individual dollars
Define exceptions or errors	Define the control deviation (an *exception*)	Normally any monetary difference (*an error*)

Audit sampling for tests of details of balances measures monetary misstatements in the population. Thus, the misstatement conditions are any conditions that represent a monetary misstatement in a sample item. In auditing accounts receivable, for example, any client misstatement in a sample item is a misstatement.

4. DEFINE THE POPULATION The auditor can define the population to include whatever data are desired, but he or she must sample from the entire population as it has been defined. The auditor may generalize only about that population that has been sampled. For example, in performing tests of controls of sales, the auditor generally defines the population as all recorded sales for the year. If the auditor samples from only one month's transactions, it is invalid to draw conclusions about the invoices for the entire year.

It is important that the auditor carefully define the population in advance, being consistent with the objectives of the audit tests. For different tests in the audit program of the same cycle, it may be necessary to define more than one population for a given set of audit procedures. For example, if the auditor intends to trace from sales invoices to shipping documents and from shipping documents to duplicate sales invoices, there are two populations (i.e., one population of shipping documents and another of duplicate sales invoices).

The population for tests of details using MUS or other dollar-based tests is defined as the recorded dollar population. The auditor then evaluates whether the recorded population is overstated or understated. For example, the population of accounts receivable shown above consists of 40 accounts totalling $207,295. Most accounting populations subject to audit would contain far more items totalling a much larger dollar amount.

Stratified sampling As mentioned earlier, the purpose of stratification is to permit the auditor to emphasize certain population items and de-emphasize others. In most audit sampling situations, auditors want to emphasize the larger recorded values; therefore, stratification is typically done on the basis of the size of recorded dollar values.

For example, examining the population in Table 13-2 on page 421, there are many different ways to stratify the population. One such method is shown in Table 13-4.

It is also important to test the population for completeness and detail tie-in before a sample is selected to ensure that all population items will be properly subjected to sample selection.

5. DEFINE THE SAMPLING UNIT The major consideration in defining the physical sampling unit when conducting tests of controls is making it consistent with the objectives of the audit tests. Thus, the definition of the population and the planned audit procedures usually dictate the appropriate sampling unit. For example, if the auditor wants to determine how frequently the client fails to fill a customer's order, the sampling unit must be defined as the customer's order. If, however, the objective is to determine whether the proper quantity of the goods described on the customer's order is correctly shipped and billed, it is possible to define the sampling unit as the customer's order, the shipping document, or the duplicate sales invoice.

Table 13-4	Example of Population Stratification		
Stratum	Stratum Criteria	Number Population	Dollars in Population
1	>$10,000	3	$ 88,955
2	$5,000 to $10,000	10	71,235
3	<$5,000	27	47,105
		40	$207,295

Table 13-5	Step 6 Terms	
Term Related to Planning	Test of Control (e.g., for Attribute Sample)	Test of Detail (e.g., for MUS Sample)
Specify tolerable exception rate (TER)	Specify the exception rate the auditor will permit in the population	N/A
Specify materiality	N/A	Use overall materiality available for the audit

The sampling unit for non-statistical audit sampling in tests of details of balances is almost always the item making up the account balance. For accounts receivable, it is the customer account name or number, or unpaid invoice, on the accounts receivable list. For statistical sampling, such as MUS, the definition of the sampling unit is an individual dollar.

Having the individual dollar as the sampling unit for MUS results in an automatic emphasis on physical units with larger recorded balances. Since the sample is selected on the basis of individual dollars, an account with a large balance has a greater chance of being included than an account with a small balance. For example, in accounts receivable confirmation, an account with a $5,000 balance has a 10 times greater probability of selection than one with a $500 balance, as it contains 10 times as many dollar units. As a result, there is no need to use stratified sampling with MUS. Stratification occurs automatically.

6. SPECIFY TOLERABLE EXCEPTION RATE OR SPECIFY MATERIALITY Establishing the **tolerable exception rate** (TER) requires professional judgment on the part of the auditor. TER represents the exception rate that the auditor will permit in the population and still be willing to use the assessed control risk and/or the amount of monetary errors or fraud and other irregularities in the transactions established during planning. For example, assume that the auditor decides that TER for the attribute of sales invoice credit approval is 6 percent. This means that the auditor has decided that even if 6 percent of the duplicate sales invoices are not approved for credit, the credit approval control is still effective in terms of the assessed control risk included in the audit plan.

> Tolerable exception rate (TER)— the exception rate that the auditor will permit in the population and still be willing to use the assessed control risk and/or the amount of monetary errors or fraud and other irregularities in the transactions established during planning.

TER is the result of an auditor's judgment. The suitable TER is a question of the risk associated with the audit assertion being tested, and of materiality, and is therefore affected by both the definition and the importance of the attribute in the audit plan (Table 13-5).

TER has a significant impact on sample size. A larger sample size is needed for a lower TER than for a higher TER. For example, a larger sample is required for a TER of 4 percent than for a TER of 6 percent.

For sampling for tests of details, materiality is used during the sampling process. It was stated in Chapter 7 that there were two methods for considering materiality: (1) Materiality would not be allocated to individual accounts in planning the audit (the method adopted by the text); and (2) materiality would be allocated to individual accounts at the planning stage. MUS uses method (1): The preliminary judgment about materiality is used to directly determine the tolerable misstatement amount for the audit of each account. Other sampling techniques (e.g., variables estimation) require method (2) and require the auditor to determine tolerable misstatement for each account by allocating the preliminary judgment about materiality over the accounts to be audited.

7. SPECIFY ACCEPTABLE RISK OF ASSESSING CONTROL RISK TOO LOW OR ACCEPTABLE RISK OF INCORRECT ACCEPTANCE Whenever a sample is taken, there is a risk that the quantitative conclusions about the population will be incorrect. This is always true unless 100 percent of the population is tested (called a census). As has already been stated, this is the case with both non-statistical and statistical sampling.

Table 13-6	Step 7 Terms	
Term Related to Planning	**Test of Control** (e.g., for Attribute Sample)	**Test of Detail** (e.g., for MUS Sample)
Acceptable risk of assessing control risk too low (ARACR)	The risk that the auditor is willing to take of accepting a control as effective when the true population exception rate is greater	N/A
Acceptable risk of incorrect acceptance (ARIA)	N/A	The risk that the auditor is willing to take of accepting a balance as correct when the true misstatement is greater than materiality

Acceptable risk of assessing control risk too low (ARACR)— the risk that the auditor is willing to take of accepting a control as effective or a rate of monetary errors or fraud and other irregularities as tolerable, when the true population exception rate is greater than the tolerable exception rate.

For audit sampling in tests of controls, that risk is called the **acceptable risk of assessing control risk too low** (ARACR) (Table 13-6). ARACR is the risk that the auditor is willing to take, of accepting a control as effective (or a rate of monetary errors or fraud and other irregularities as tolerable) when the true population exception rate is greater than the tolerable exception rate (TER). To illustrate, assume that TER is 6 percent, ARACR is 10 percent, and the true population exception rate is 8 percent. The control in this case is not acceptable because the true exception rate of 8 percent exceeds TER. The auditor, of course, does not know the true population exception rate. The ARACR of 10 percent means that the auditor is willing to take a 10 percent risk of concluding that the control is effective after all testing is completed, even when it is ineffective. If the auditor finds the control effective in this illustration, he or she will have over-relied on the system of internal control (used a lower assessed control risk than justified). ARACR is the auditor's measure of sampling risk.

In choosing the appropriate ARACR in a situation, the auditor must use his or her best judgment. Since ARACR is a measure of the risk that the auditor is willing to take for particular audit tests, the main consideration is the extent to which the auditor plans to reduce assessed control risk as a basis for the extent of tests of details of balances. The lower the assessed control risk, the lower will be the ARACR chosen and the planned extent of tests of details of balances. The relationship of sampling to control risk is as follows:

(1) *Control risk is set at maximum:* Tests of controls are not performed, and sampling is not used.

(2) *Control risk is set at high or medium:* Tests of controls are not performed. Tests of understanding of controls are conducted as walk-through tests. Samples are selected, but testing is limited to inquiry and transaction walk-throughs. ARACR could be set high, as the sample will be used only for understanding of controls.

(3) *Control risk is set at low:* Tests of controls are required to support this assessment. Audit sampling is required to select transactions for the tests of controls. ARACR will be set low, as reliance is intended upon the controls. The potential for material misstatement may exist, if the control is not functioning effectively.

For non-statistical sampling, it is common for auditors to use ARACR of high, medium, or low instead of a percentage. A low ARACR implies that the tests of controls are important and corresponds to a low assessed control risk and reduced substantive tests of details of balances.

The auditor can establish different TER and ARACR levels for different attributes of an audit test. For example, auditors could use higher TER and ARACR levels for tests of credit approval than for tests of the existence of duplicate sales invoices and bills of lading.

Table 13-7	Guidelines for ARACR and TER for Non-statistical Sampling: Tests of Controls	
Factor	Judgment	Guideline
Assessed control risk. Consider: Nature, extent, and timing of substantive tests (extensive planned substantive tests relate to higher assessed control risk, and vice versa). Quality of evidence available for tests of controls (a lower quality of evidence available results in a higher assessed control risk, and vice versa).	• Lowest assessed control risk • Moderate assessed control risk • Higher assessed control risk • Maximum control risk	• ARACR of low • ARACR of medium • ARACR of high • ARACR is not applicable
Significance of the transactions and related account balances that the internal controls are intended to affect.	• Highly significant balances • Significant balances • Less significant balances	• TER of 4% • TER of 5% • TER of 6%

Note: The guidelines should recognize that there may be variations in ARACRs based on audit considerations. The guidelines above are the more conservative guidelines that could be followed.

Table 13-7 presents illustrative guidelines for establishing TER and ARACR. The guidelines should not be interpreted as representing broad professional standards; however, they are typical of the types of guidelines public accounting firms issue to their staff or are embedded in software modules.

For tests of details, **acceptable risk of incorrect acceptance** (ARIA) is the risk that the auditor is willing to take of accepting a balance as correct when the true misstatement in the balance is greater than materiality. ARIA is the term equivalent to acceptable risk of assessing control risk too low (ARACR) for tests of controls.

There is an inverse relationship between ARIA and required sample size. If, for example, the auditor decides to reduce ARIA from 10 percent to 5 percent, the required sample size would increase. By reducing ARIA, we are increasing the required sampling assurance that the balance is correct from 90 percent to 95 percent, thus resulting in a larger sample size (i.e., the gathering of more evidence).

The primary factor affecting the auditor's decision about ARIA is assessed control risk in the audit risk model. When internal controls are effective, control risk can be reduced, permitting the auditor to increase ARIA. This, in turn, reduces the sample size required for the test of details of the related account balance.

A difficulty students often have is understanding how ARACR and ARIA affect evidence accumulation. In Chapter 10, it was shown that tests of details of balances for monetary errors or fraud and other irregularities can be reduced if internal controls are found to be effective through assessing control risk below maximum and performing tests of controls.

The effects of ARACR and ARIA are consistent with the reduction in tests of details of balances. If the auditor concludes that internal controls may be effective, control risk can be assessed at less than maximum. A lower control risk requires a lower ARACR in testing the controls, which in turn requires a larger sample size. If controls are found to be effective, control risk can remain low, which permits the auditor to increase ARIA (through use of the audit risk model), thereby requiring a smaller sample size in the related substantive tests of details of balances. The relationship between ARACR and ARIA is shown in Figure 13-2 on the next page.

Besides control risk, ARIA is also directly affected by audit risk and inversely by other substantive tests already performed or planned for the account balance. For example, if audit risk is reduced, ARIA should also be reduced. If analytical procedures were performed and indicate that the account balance is fairly stated, ARIA should be

Acceptable risk of incorrect acceptance (ARIA)—the risk that the auditor is willing to take of accepting a balance as correct when the true misstatement in the balance is greater than materiality.

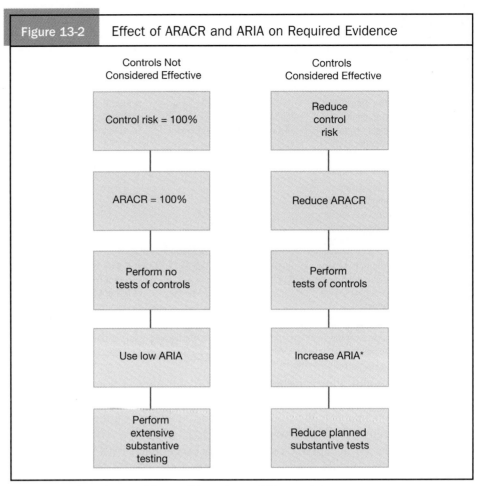

Figure 13-2 Effect of ARACR and ARIA on Required Evidence

Controls Not Considered Effective	Controls Considered Effective
Control risk = 100%	Reduce control risk
ARACR = 100%	Reduce ARACR
Perform no tests of controls	Perform tests of controls
Use low ARIA	Increase ARIA*
Perform extensive substantive testing	Reduce planned substantive tests

*Assumes tests of controls were satisfactory, which permits control risk to remain low.

Table 13-8 Step 8 Terms

Term Related to Planning	Test of Control (e.g., for Attribute Sample)	Test of Detail (e.g., for MUS Sample)
Estimated population exception rate (EPER)	The advance estimate of the percentage of exceptions in the population	N/A
Estimated misstatements in the population	N/A	The advance estimate of total dollar error in the population

increased. Stated differently, the analytical procedures are evidence in support of the account balance; therefore, less evidence from the detailed test of the balance using sampling is required to achieve audit risk. The same conclusion is appropriate for the relationship among dual-purpose tests, ARIA, and sample size for tests of details of balances. The various relationships affecting ARIA are summarized in Table 13-9.

8. ESTIMATE THE POPULATION EXCEPTION RATE OR THE MISSTATEMENTS IN THE POPULATION When conducting tests of controls, an advance **estimate of the population exception rate** (EPER) should be made to plan the appropriate sample size (Table 13-8). If the EPER is low, a relatively small sample size will satisfy the auditor's tolerable exception rate. When the expected exception rate is low, a less precise estimate of EPER can be used. To be more precise, an estimate of the population exception rate must be based on more data, that is, a larger sample.

Estimated population exception rate (EPER)—the exception rate the auditor expects to find in the population before testing begins.

Table 13-9	Relationship Among Factors Affecting ARIA, Effect on ARIA, and Required Sample Size for Audit Sampling		
Factor Affecting ARIA	**Example**	**Effect on ARIA**	**Effect on Sample Size**
Effectiveness of internal controls (control risk)	Internal controls are effective (reduced control risk)*	Increase	Decrease
Audit risk	Likelihood of bankruptcy is low (increased audit risk)	Increase	Decrease
Analytical procedures	Analytical procedures performed with no indications of likely misstatements	Increase	Decrease

*Assumes tests of controls were satisfactory, which permits control risk to remain low.

It is common to use the results of the preceding year's audit to make this estimate. If the prior year's results are not available, or if they are considered unreliable, the auditor can take a small preliminary sample of the current year's population for this purpose. It is not critical that the estimate be precise because the current year's sample exception rate is ultimately used to estimate the population characteristics.

Note that if a preliminary sample is used, it can be included in the final sample, as long as appropriate sample selection procedures are followed. For example, assume that an auditor takes a preliminary sample of 30 items to estimate the EPER that considers the entire population. Later, if the auditor decides that a total sample size of 100 is needed, only 70 additional items will need to be properly selected and tested.

Similarly, for tests of details sampling, the auditor makes this estimate based on prior experience with the client and by assessing inherent risk, considering the results of tests of controls and of analytical procedures already performed.

9. DETERMINE THE INITIAL SAMPLE SIZE Four factors determine the initial sample size for audit sampling for tests of controls: population size, TER, ARACR, and EPER. Population size is not nearly as significant a factor as the others and typically can be ignored.

auditing in action 13-2
Sampling Standards and Resources

Do you like statistics? Perhaps you could make your living being a consultant in sampling. Samples are taken by tax auditors, auditor-general auditors, and internal auditors, as well as financial statement auditors and research organizations.

One consulting firm in the United States (**www.ryanco.com**) specializes in evaluating tax audit statistics and assessing the results for appeals of tax assessments and also helps others design, conduct, and evaluate their sampling.

Many organizations provide standards with respect to sampling. For example, the federal Auditor General in Ottawa has standards that indicate when certain forms of sampling are most appropriate in value-for-money audits.

Examination of actual audit reports completed by auditor general offices in Canada as well as internal auditors of various government organizations provides insight into how sampling is important in evaluating the effectiveness of controls. For example, the internal audit report of year-end cash cut-off for the Canada Border Services Agency showed that internal auditors used the key-item approach. They selected 68 transactions of $100,000 or larger.

Their report described the errors in cut-off, with an overall conclusion that the $2 million in errors they found was immaterial to the total $1.3 billion population.

Sources: 1. Ryan, 2009, www.ryanco.com, Accessed: January 16, 2009. 2. Canada Border Services Agency, "Internal audit report of fiscal 2007-2008 year-end cash cut-off procedures," www.cbsa-asfc.gc.ca/agency-agence/reports-rapports/ae-ve/2008/iaryccp_rvipde-eng.html, Accessed: January 16, 2009. 3. Office of the Auditor General, "Conducting Surveys, Section 4: Sampling," www.oag-bvg.gc.ca/internet/English/meth_gde_e_19725.html; Accessed: January 16, 2009.

Table 13-10	Effect on Sample Size of Changing Factors
Type of Change	Effect on Initial Sample Size
Increase acceptable risk of assessing control risk too low	Decrease
Increase tolerable exception rate	Decrease
Increase estimated population exception rate	Increase
Increase population size	Increase (minor effect)

An important characteristic of non-statistical sampling as compared to statistical sampling is the need to decide the sample size using professional judgment for non-statistical methods rather than by calculation using a statistical formula. Once the three major factors affecting sample size have been determined, it is possible for the auditor to determine an initial sample size.

The **initial sample size,** determined by professional judgment, is so-called because the exceptions in the actual sample must be evaluated before it is possible to know whether the sample is sufficiently large to achieve the objectives of the tests.

Sensitivity of sample size to a change in the factors To properly understand the concepts underlying sampling in auditing, it is helpful to understand the effect of changing any of the four factors that determine sample size while the other factors are held constant. Table 13-10 illustrates the effect of increasing each of the four factors; a decrease will have the opposite effect.

A combination of two factors has the greatest effect on sample size: TER minus EPER. The difference is the precision of the planned sample estimate. For example, if TER (tolerable exception rate) is 5 percent and EPER (estimated population exception rate) is 2 percent, then precision is 3 percent. A smaller precision, which is called a more precise estimate, requires a larger sample.

Auditors using non-statistical sampling for tests of details similarly determine the initial sample size judgmentally considering the factors discussed so far. Table 13-11 summarizes the primary factors that influence sample size for non-statistical sampling of tests of details and how sample size is affected.

When the auditor uses stratified sampling, the sample size must be allocated among the strata. Typically, auditors allocate a higher portion of the sample items to larger population items. For example, using the data from Problem 15-27 on page 523, allocating a sample size of 15, the auditor might decide to select all three accounts from stratum 1, and six each from strata 2 and 3. Observe that audit sampling does not apply to stratum 1 because all population items are being audited.

For MUS sampling, sample size is determined using a statistical formula.

10. SELECT THE SAMPLE After the auditor has computed the initial sample size for the audit sampling application, he or she must choose the items in the population to be included in the sample. The sample can be chosen by using any of the probabilistic or non-probabilistic methods discussed earlier in the chapter. It is important for the auditor to use a method that will permit meaningful conclusions about the sample results.

For stratified sampling, the auditor selects samples independently from each stratum.

Monetary unit samples are samples selected with probability-proportionate-to-size (PPS). Such samples are of individual dollars in the population. Auditors cannot, however, audit individual dollars. Therefore, the auditor must determine the physical unit to perform the audit tests. For example, the auditor could select a random sample of population items and determine that dollar number 7,376 is to be selected.

Initial sample size—sample size determined by professional judgment (non-statistical sampling) or by statistical tables (attribute sampling).

Table 13-11	Factors Influencing Sample Sizes for Tests of Details of Balances	
Factor	Conditions Leading to Smaller Sample Size	Conditions Leading to Larger Sample Size
a. Control risk (ARACR). Affects acceptable risk of incorrect acceptance.	Low control risk	High control risk
b. Risk for other substantive tests related to the same assertion (including analytical procedures and other relevant substantive tests). Affects acceptable risk of incorrect acceptance.	Low risk associated with other relevant substantive tests	High risk associated with other relevant substantive tests
c. Audit risk. Affects acceptable risk of incorrect acceptance.	High audit risk	Low audit risk
d. Materiality.	Larger materiality	Smaller materiality
e. Inherent risk. Affects estimated misstatements in the population.	Low inherent risk	High inherent risk
f. Expected size and frequency of misstatements. Affects estimated misstatements in the population.	Smaller misstatements or lower frequency	Larger misstatements or higher frequency
g. Number of items in the population.	Almost no effect on sample size unless population is very small	Almost no effect on sample size unless population is very small

However, to perform the audit procedures, the auditor must identify the population item that corresponds to the 7,376th dollar, for example, the 12th invoice transaction.

11. PERFORM THE AUDIT PROCEDURES The auditor performs the test of control audit procedures by examining each item in the sample to determine whether it is consistent with the definition of the attribute and maintains a record of all the exceptions found. When audit procedures have been completed for a test of control sampling application, there will be a sample size and a number of exceptions for each attribute.

To perform the test of detail audit procedures, the auditor applies the appropriate audit procedures to each item in the sample to determine whether it is correct or contains a misstatement. For example, in the confirmation of accounts receivable, the auditor mails the sample of confirmations in the manner described in Chapter 15 and determines the amount of misstatement in each account confirmed. For nonresponses, alternative procedures are used to determine the misstatements. The auditor tracks the recorded value and the audited value so that the aggregate client misstatement can be determined.

The auditor cannot expect meaningful results from using audit sampling unless the audit procedures are applied carefully. This includes testing a transaction for each sample item selected. CAS 530 requires that if the test cannot be conducted for the item selected, then the auditor must select another transaction. For example, the auditor might select an invoice to conduct a pricing test and find that the item selected was an adjustment invoice, so the pricing test cannot be conducted. In that case, the auditor must select an additional item. The audit program should indicate in advance how such cases would be handled. For example, the audit program might say that the auditor should choose the next transaction.

CAS

Sample exception rate (SER)—
the number of exceptions in the
sample divided by the sample
size.

12. GENERALIZE FROM THE SAMPLE TO THE POPULATION For tests of controls, the **sample exception rate** (SER) can be calculated easily from the actual sample results. SER equals the actual number of exceptions divided by the actual sample size.

It is improper for the auditor to conclude that the population exception rate is exactly the same as the sample exception rate; the chance that they are exactly the same is too small. For non-statistical methods, there are two ways to generalize from the sample to the population.

1. Add an estimate of sampling error to SER to arrive at a computed upper exception rate (CUER) for a given acceptable risk of assessing control risk too low. It is extremely difficult for auditors to make sampling error estimates using non-statistical sampling because of the judgment required to do so; therefore, this approach is generally not used.

2. Subtract the sampling exception rate from the tolerable exception rate, which is called calculated sampling error (TER – SER = calculated sampling error), and evaluate whether calculated sampling error is sufficiently large to indicate that the true population exception rate is acceptable. Most auditors using non-statistical sampling follow this approach. For example, if an auditor takes a sample of 100 items for an attribute and finds no exceptions (SER = 0), and TER is 5 percent, calculated sampling error is 5 percent (TER of 5 percent – SER of 0 = 5 percent). On the other hand, if there had been four exceptions, calculated sampling error would have been 1 percent (TER of 5 percent – SER of 4 percent). It is much more likely that the true population exception rate is less than or equal to the tolerable exception rate in the first case than in the second one. Therefore, most auditors would probably find the population acceptable based on the first sample result and not acceptable based on the second.

In practice, auditors tend to test controls when they expect no exceptions. If no exceptions are found, then the control is considered to be reliable. However, when exceptions are found, it is more likely that the controls cannot be relied on, unless the situation(s) causing the control exception can be isolated (as discussed in the next section).

In addition, the auditor's consideration of whether sampling error is sufficiently large will depend on sample size. For example, if the sample size in the above example had been only 20 items, the auditor would have been much less confident that finding no exceptions was an indication that the true population exception rate did not exceed TER than finding no exceptions in a sample of 100 items. Note that under the second approach, the auditor does not make an estimate of the computed upper exception rate.

When generalizing tests of details, the auditor deals with dollar amounts rather than with exceptions. The auditor must generalize from the sample to the population by (1) projecting misstatements from the sample results to the population and (2) considering sampling error and sampling risk (ARIA). For example, assume that the auditor discovered three misstatements that netted to $389 overstatement. Can the auditor conclude that accounts receivable is overstated by $389? No, the auditor is interested in the population results (further possible misstatement is described in Chapter 7), not those for the sample (identified misstatement is defined in Chapter 7). It is therefore necessary to project from the sample to the population to estimate the population misstatement.

The first step is making a point estimate, which was defined as likely misstatement in Chapter 7. There are different ways to calculate the point estimate, but a common way is to assume that misstatements in the unaudited population are proportional to the misstatements in the sample. This calculation must be done for each stratum and then totalled, rather than for the total misstatements in the sample. Thus, the point estimate of the misstatement is determined by using a weighted-average method. For example, if the $389 total error were comprised as in Table 13-12, then the point estimate would be calculated as shown in Table 13-13.

Table 13-12 — Example of Errors Found

Stratum	Sample Size	Dollars Audited Recorded Value	Dollars Audited Audited Value	Client Misstatement
1	3	$ 88,955	$ 91,695	$(2,740)
2	6	43,995	43,024	971
3	6	13,105	10,947	2,158
	15	$146,055	$145,666	$ 389

Table 13-13 — Example of Point Estimate Calculation

Stratum	Client Misstatement + Recorded Value from Sample	X	Recorded Book Value for Stratum	=	Point Estimate of Misstatement
1	$(2,740) / $88,955		$88,955		$(2,740)
2	971 / 43,995		71,235		1,572
3	2,158 / 13,105		47,105		7,757
Total					$ 6,589

The point estimate of the error in the population is $6,589, indicating an overstatement. The point estimate, by itself, is not an adequate measure of the population misstatement, however, because of sampling error. In other words, because the estimate is based on a sample, it will be close to the true population misstatement, but it is unlikely that it is exactly the same. The auditor must consider the possibility that the true population misstatement is greater than the amount of misstatement that is tolerable in the circumstances whenever the point estimate is less than the tolerable misstatement amount. This must be done for both statistical and non-statistical samples.

13. ANALYZE EXCEPTIONS OR MISSTATEMENTS In addition to determining the SER for each attribute control tested and evaluating whether the true but unknown exception rate is likely to exceed the tolerable exception rate, it is necessary to analyze individual exceptions to determine the breakdown in the internal controls that caused them. Exceptions could be caused by carelessness of employees, misunderstood instructions, intentional failure to perform procedures, or many other factors. The nature of an exception and its cause have a significant effect on the qualitative evaluation of the system. For example, if all the exceptions in the tests of internal verification of credit authorization for sales invoices occurred while the person normally responsible for performing the tests was on vacation, this would affect the auditor's evaluation of the internal controls and the subsequent investigation. The auditor could choose to test the period substantively when the employee was on vacation and rely on internal controls for the remainder of the year. This type of exception is called an **anomaly**, because it is an exception or misstatement that is non-representative of the population as a whole. CAS 530 requires that the auditor investigate such anomalies, conducting additional audit procedures, with the goal of verifying that the anomaly really is different and not representative of the population.

Misstatements discovered during tests of details could be caused by control exceptions. For example, in confirming accounts receivable, suppose that all misstatements resulted from the client's failure to record returned goods. The auditor would

Anomaly—an exception or misstatement that is non-representative of the population as a whole.

CAS

determine why that type of misstatement occurred so often, the implications of the misstatements on other audit areas, the potential impact on the financial statements, and the effect on company operations.

An important part of misstatement analysis is deciding whether any modification of the audit risk model is needed. If the auditor concluded that the failure to record the returns discussed in the previous paragraph resulted from a breakdown of internal controls, it might be necessary to reassess control risk. That, in turn, would probably cause the auditor to reduce ARIA, which would increase planned sample size. As discussed in Chapter 7, revisions of the audit risk model must be done with extreme care because the model is intended primarily for planning, not evaluating results.

14. DETERMINE THE ACCEPTABILITY OF THE POPULATION For tests of controls, it was shown under "12. Generalize from the Sample to the Population" that most auditors subtract SER from TER when they use non-statistical sampling and evaluate whether the difference, which is calculated sampling error, is sufficiently large. If the auditor concludes that the difference is sufficiently large, the control being tested can be used to reduce assessed control risk as planned, provided a careful analysis of the cause of exceptions does not indicate the possibility of other significant problems with internal controls.

When the auditor concludes that TER − SER is too small to conclude that the population is acceptable, the auditor must take specific action. Three courses of action can be followed.

Revise TER or ARACR This alternative should be followed only when the auditor has concluded that the original specifications were too conservative. Relaxing either TER or ARACR may be difficult to defend if the auditor is ever subjected to a review by a court or to a peer review.

Expand the sample size An increase in the sample size has the effect of decreasing the sampling error if the actual sample exception rate does not increase. Of course, SER may also increase or decrease if additional items are selected.

Revise assessed control risk If the results of the tests of controls do not support the planned assessed control risk, the auditor should revise assessed control risk upward. The effect of the revision is likely to increase tests of details of balances. For example, if tests of controls of credit approval indicate that those procedures are not being followed, the auditor may not be able to rely on the control and will therefore conduct additional substantive tests at year end. This is most likely to be done through tests of the bad-debt allowance for accounts receivable and of bad-debt expense for the year.

The decision whether to increase sample size until sampling error is sufficiently small or to revise assessed control risk must be made on the basis of cost versus benefit. If the sample is not expanded, it is necessary to revise assessed control risk upward and therefore perform additional substantive tests. The cost of additional tests of controls must be compared with the cost of additional substantive tests. If an expanded sample continues to produce unacceptable results, additional substantive tests will then be necessary.

If the original test performed is testing transactions for monetary errors or fraud and other irregularities, and an exception rate higher than that assumed is indicated, the response would generally be the same as for tests of controls.

For tests of details, an auditor using non-statistical sampling cannot formally measure sampling error and therefore must subjectively consider the possibility that the true population misstatement aggregated with other misstatements exceeds materiality. This is done by considering (1) the difference between the point estimate and materiality, (2) the extent to which items in the population have been audited 100 percent, (3) whether misstatements tend to be offsetting or in only one direction, (4) the amounts of individual misstatements, and (5) sample size. To continue the example above, suppose that materiality is $40,000. In that case, the auditor may conclude that there is little chance, given the point estimate of $6,589, that the true population misstatement exceeds that amount.

Suppose that materiality is $12,000, only $5,411 greater than the point estimate. In that case, other factors would be considered. For example, if the larger items in the population were audited 100 percent (as was done here), any unidentified misstatements would be restricted to smaller items. If the misstatements tend to be offsetting and are relatively small in size, the auditor may conclude that the true population misstatement is likely to be less than materiality. Also, the larger the sample size, the more confident the auditor can be that the point estimate is close to the true population value. Therefore, the auditor would be more willing to accept that the true population misstatement is less than tolerable misstatement in this example, where the sample size is considered large, than where it is considered moderate or small. On the other hand, if one or more of these other conditions is different, the chance of a misstatement in excess of the tolerable amount may be judged to be high, and the recorded population unacceptable.

Even if the amount of likely misstatement is not considered material, the auditor must wait until the entire audit is completed before making a final evaluation. For example, the estimated total misstatement and estimated sampling error in accounts receivable must be combined with estimates of misstatements in all other parts of the audit to evaluate the effect of all misstatements on the financial statements as a whole.

For MUS and variables sampling, a formal decision rule is used for deciding the acceptability of the population. The decision rule used for MUS is similar to that used for non-statistical sampling, but it is sufficiently different to merit discussion. The decision rule will be illustrated in Chapter 15, along with the illustration of a specific sample selection.

SUMMARY OF SAMPLING STEPS Table 13-14 on the next page summarizes the steps used in sampling. It is apparent from the table that planning is an essential part of using any type of sampling. The purposes of planning are to make sure that the audit procedures are properly applied and that the sample size is appropriate for the circumstances. Sample selection is also important and must be done with care to avoid non-sampling errors. Performing the audit procedures must be done carefully to correctly determine the number of exceptions or the value of errors in the sample. It is the most time-consuming part of audit sampling.

Evaluating the results for tests of controls includes making an estimate of sampling error and comparing it with the tolerable exception rate, while for tests of details, dollar values must be extrapolated, with decision rules and methodologies varying depending upon the sampling method chosen. Exceptions or errors must be analyzed and, finally, acceptability of the population determined.

Other Considerations

For the sake of continuity, in the preceding discussion we bypassed four important aspects of using sampling that are now discussed: random selection versus statistical measurement, adequate documentation, management letters, and the need for professional judgment.

RANDOM SELECTION VERSUS STATISTICAL MEASUREMENT Students often do not understand the distinction between random (probabilistic) selection and statistical measurement. It should now be clear that random selection is a part of statistical sampling but is not, by itself, statistical measurement. To have statistical measurement, it is necessary to generalize mathematically from the sample to the population.

Table 13-14	Summary of Audit Sampling Steps	
Steps—Audit Sampling for Tests of Controls		**Steps—Audit Sampling for Tests of Details**
Plan and Select the Sample		**Plan the Sample**
1. State the objectives of the audit test.		1. State the objectives of the audit test.
2. Decide if audit sampling applies.		2. Decide if audit sampling applies.
3. Define attributes and exception conditions.		3. Define misstatement conditions.
4. Define the population.		4. Define the population.
5. Define the sampling unit.		5. Define the sampling unit.
6. Specify tolerable exception rate.		6. Specify materiality.
7. Specify acceptable risk of assessing control risk too low.		7. Specify acceptable risk of incorrect acceptance.
8. Estimate the population exception rate.		8. Estimate misstatements in the population.
9. Determine the initial sample size.		9. Determine the initial sample size.
10. Select the sample.		10. Select the sample.
Perform the Audit Procedures		**Select the Sample and Perform the Audit Procedures**
11. Perform the audit procedures.		11. Perform the audit procedures.
Evaluate the Results		**Evaluate the Results**
12. Generalize from the sample to the population.		12. Generalize from the sample to the population.
13. Analyze the exceptions.		13. Analyze the misstatements.
14. Determine the acceptability of the population.		14. Determine the acceptability of the population.

It is acceptable to use random selection procedures without drawing statistical conclusions, but this practice is questionable if a reasonably large sample size has been selected. Whenever the auditor takes a random sample, regardless of his or her basis for determining its size, there is a statistical measurement inherent in the sample. Since there is little or no cost involved in computing the upper exception rate, it should be done whenever possible. It would, of course, be inappropriate to draw a statistical conclusion unless the sample were randomly selected or selected using a formal methodology, such as interval selection with a random start.

ADEQUATE DOCUMENTATION It is important that the auditor retain adequate records of the procedures performed, the methods used to select the sample and perform the tests, the results found in the tests, and the conclusions drawn. This is necessary as a means of evaluating the combined results of all tests and as a basis for defending the audit if the need arises. Documentation is equally important for statistical and non-statistical sampling. Examples of the type of documentation commonly found in practice are included in the case illustrations for Hillsburg Hardware Limited in Chapters 14 and 15.

MANAGEMENT LETTERS Documentation, evaluation, or testing of internal controls may lead to the discovery of a variety of internal control exceptions. These should be communicated to management and the audit committee regardless of the nature of the exceptions.

NEED FOR PROFESSIONAL JUDGMENT A criticism occasionally levelled against statistical sampling is that it reduces the use of professional judgment. A review of the 14 steps discussed in this chapter for sampling shows how unwarranted this criticism is. For proper application of sampling, it is necessary to use professional judgment in most of the steps. For example, selection of the initial sample size depends primarily on the TER, ARACR, and EPER. Choosing the first two requires the exercise of high-level professional judgment; the latter requires a careful estimate. Similarly, the final evaluation of the acceptability of the population for any form of sampling must also be based on high-level professional judgment.

concept check

C13-5 An auditor is counting a sample of inventory items. Provide two examples of potential errors or misstatement that could occur.

C13-6 The auditor has decided to circularize accounts payable confirmations. What is the likely population?

Appendix 13A
Selection of Random Numbers Using Random Number Tables or Software

Random Number Tables

An example of a commonly used random number table is the Table of 105,000 Random Decimal Digits, published by the U.S. Interstate Commerce Commission. A page from that table appears in Table 13A-1 on the next page. This table has numbered rows and columns, with five digits in each column. This format is convenient for reading the table and documenting the portion of the table used. The presentation of the digits as five-digit numbers is purely arbitrary.

It is easy, but time-consuming, to select samples using a **random number table**. For example, assume that the auditor is selecting a sample of 100 sales invoices from a file of prenumbered sales invoices beginning with document number 3,272 and ending with 8,825. Since the invoices use four digits, it is necessary to use four digits in the random number table. Assuming the first four digits of each five-digit set were used, and the arbitrary starting point in the random number table in Table 13A-1 is row 1,009, column 2, then reading down, the first invoice for inclusion in the sample is 3,646. The next usable number is 6,186, since the next three numbers are all outside the population range.

Random number table—a listing of independent random digits conveniently arranged in tabular form to facilitate the selection of random numbers with multiple digits.

Software generation of random numbers It is useful to understand the use of random number tables as a means of understanding the concept of selecting simple random samples. However, most random samples obtained by auditors are obtained by using computer programs. There are three main types of these: electronic spreadsheet programs, random number generators, and generalized audit software programs.

The advantages of using computer programs in selecting random samples are time savings, reduced likelihood of auditor error in selecting the numbers, and automatic documentation. To illustrate computer generation of random numbers, Figure 13A-1 on page 437 shows a printout from a spreadsheet program. In the application illustrated, the auditor wishes to sample 30 items from a population of documents numbered from 140,672 to 283,294. The program requires only input parameters and the use of a pre-defined spreadsheet function by the auditor for a sample to be selected. The auditor can use the spreadsheet to generate random dates or ranges of sets of numbers (such as page and line numbers). It also provides output in both sorted and selected orders by means of the spreadsheet sort function.

Table 13A-1 | Random Number Table

Row	(1)	(2)	(3)	(4)	(5)	(6)	(7)	(8)
1000	37039	97547	64673	31546	99314	66854	97855	99965
1001	25145	84834	23009	51584	66754	77785	52357	25532
1002	98433	54725	18864	65866	76918	78825	58210	76835
1003	97965	68548	81545	82933	93545	85959	63282	61454
1004	78049	67830	14624	17563	25697	07734	48243	94318
1005	50203	25658	91478	08509	23308	48130	65047	77873
1006	40059	67825	18934	64998	49807	71126	77818	56893
1007	84350	67241	54031	34535	04093	35062	58163	14205
1008	30954	51637	91500	48722	60988	60029	60873	37423
1009	86723	36464	98305	08009	00666	29255	18514	49158
1010	50188	22554	86160	92250	14021	65859	16237	72296
1011	50014	00463	13906	35936	71761	95755	87002	71667
1012	66023	21428	14742	94874	23308	58533	26507	11208
1013	04458	61862	63119	09541	01715	87901	91260	03079
1014	57510	36314	30452	09712	37714	95482	30507	68475
1015	43373	58939	95848	28288	60341	52174	11879	18115
1016	61500	12763	64433	02268	57905	72347	49498	21871
1017	78938	71312	99705	71546	42274	23915	38405	18779
1018	64257	93218	35793	43671	64055	88729	11168	60260
1019	56864	21554	70445	24841	04779	56774	96129	73594
1020	35314	29631	06937	54545	04470	75463	77112	77126
1021	40704	48823	65963	39359	12717	56201	22811	24863
1022	07318	44623	02843	33299	59872	86774	06926	12672
1023	94550	23299	45557	07923	75126	00808	01312	46689
1024	34348	81191	21027	77087	10909	03676	97723	34469
1025	92277	57115	50789	68111	75305	53289	39751	45760
1026	56093	58302	52236	64756	50273	61566	61962	93280
1027	16623	17849	96701	94971	94758	08845	32260	59823
1028	50848	93982	66451	32143	05441	10399	17775	74169
1029	48006	58200	58367	66577	68583	21108	41361	20732
1030	56640	27890	28825	96509	21363	53657	60119	75385

Random Selection by Using a Computer

RANGE

Lower   140,672

Upper   283,294

RANDOM NUMBERS

SELECTION ORDER		NUMERICAL ORDER	
		Sequence	Number
1	177,611	17	142,591
2	163,763	9	144,408
3	217,029	23	147,181
4	235,986	5	150,176
5	150,176	7	153,469
6	197,030	15	156,779
7	153,469	2	163,763
8	213,150	25	167,818
9	144,408	13	176,955
10	269,030	1	177,611
11	280,501	16	188,114
12	237,619	14	189,598
13	176,955	30	191,932
14	189,598	6	197,030
15	156,779	21	197,202
16	188,114	22	204,645
17	142,591	19	208,234
18	217,753	24	209,025
19	208,234	28	210,168
20	264,071	8	213,150
21	197,202	3	217,029
22	204,645	18	217,753
23	147,181	26	227,659
24	209,025	4	235,986
25	167,818	12	237,619
26	227,659	27	242,681
27	242,681	20	264,071
28	210,168	10	269,030
29	281,047	11	280,501
30	191,932	29	281,047

Source: Random selection prepared using @RAND function of spreadsheet software.

Summary

1. *What is sampling?* Sampling occurs when someone looks at less than 100 percent of the items in a population.

   Why would an auditor use statistical rather than non-statistical sampling? With statistical sampling, the auditor can quantify sampling risk and also calculate a statistical result.

   What are the different types of non-probabilistic (non-statistical) sampling methods used by auditors? The three types are directed (items likely to contain misstatements, items containing selected population characteristics, or large dollar amounts), block, and haphazard.

   How can CAATs facilitate non-statistical sampling? When populations are large, and data are available, the auditor could select the samples using automated systems. For example, spreadsheets could be used to list high dollar value items, or GAS could be used for gap or block tests.

2. *What are the three different ways that an auditor can select a statistical sample?* The auditor could use a random number table, generate random numbers using computer software, or use systematic selection with a random start.

   List three common statistical sampling methodologies used by auditors. These are attribute sampling, probability-proportionate-to-size sampling (also known as monetary unit sampling or dollar unit sampling), and variables sampling.

   How can CAATs assist statistical sampling? Generalized audit software or other software could be used to select or evaluate the samples.

3. *Describe the 14 steps in planning and selecting a sample, performing the tests, and evaluating a sample.* These steps are listed on pages 419–420 and in Table 13-14 on page 434.

   What are four additional issues the auditor should consider during the sampling process? The auditor needs to ensure that random sampling occurs, but it is also important to generalize mathematically to provide for statistical measurement. The planning, selection, execution, and evaluation of the sampling process need to be adequately documented. Any internal control exceptions or other errors found should be properly communicated to management and the audit committee. Both judgmental and statistical sampling require extensive use of professional judgment.

   What is an anomaly and how does it affect evaluation of audit results? An anomaly is an error or misstatement that does not generalize to the entire population being audited. If it were generalized, it would result in an inaccurate projection of error. However, the auditor needs to conduct and document audit steps that confirm that the error or misstatement is indeed an anomaly.

Visit the text's website at **www.pearsoned.ca/arens** for practice quizzes, additional case studies, and international standards information.

Review Questions

13-1 State what is meant by a "representative sample," and explain its importance in sampling audit populations.

13-2 Explain the major difference between statistical and non-statistical sampling. What are the three main parts of statistical and non-statistical methods?

13-3 Explain the difference between replacement sampling and non-replacement sampling. Which method do auditors usually follow? Why?

13-4 What are the two types of simple random sample selection methods? Which of the two methods is used most often by auditors, and why?

13-5 Describe systematic sample selection, and explain how an auditor would select 35 numbers from a population of 1,750 items using this approach. What are the advantages and disadvantages of systematic sample selection?

13-6 Explain what is meant by "block sampling," and describe how an auditor could obtain five blocks of 20 sales invoices from a sales journal.

13-7 Describe what is meant by a "sampling unit." Explain why the sampling unit for verifying the existence of recorded sales differs from the sampling unit for testing for the possibility of omitted sales.

13-8 Distinguish between the TER and CUER. How is each determined?

13-9 Distinguish between a sampling error and a non-sampling error. How can each be reduced?

13-10 What major difference between tests of controls and tests of details of balances makes attribute sampling inappropriate for tests of details of balances?

13-11 Explain the difference between an attribute and an exception condition. State the exception condition for the following audit procedure: the duplicate sales invoice has been initialled, indicating the performance of internal verification.

13-12 Define "stratified sampling," and explain its importance in auditing. How could an auditor obtain a stratified sample of 30 items from each of the three strata in the confirmation of accounts receivable?

13-13 Distinguish between the point estimate of the total misstatements (likely misstatement) and the true value of the misstatements in the population. How can each be determined?

13-14 Identify the factors an auditor uses to decide the appropriate TER. Compare the sample size for a TER of 6 percent with that of 3 percent, all other factors being equal.

13-15 Identify the factors an auditor uses to decide the appropriate ARACR. Compare the sample size for an ARACR of 10 percent with that of 5 percent, all other factors being equal.

13-16 State the relationship between each of the the following:
 a. ARACR and sample size.
 b. Population size and sample size.
 c. TER and sample size.
 d. EPER and sample size.

13-17 Define what is meant by "sampling risk." Does sampling risk apply to non-statistical sampling, MUS, attribute sampling, and variables sampling? Explain.

13-18 Explain what is meant by "analysis of exceptions," and discuss its importance.

13-19 Outline a situation for which discovery sampling would be used.

13-20 Distinguish between random selection and statistical measurement. State the circumstances under which one can be used without the other.

Discussion Questions and Problems

13-21

a. For each of the following independent problems, design an unbiased random sampling plan using an electronic spreadsheet or a random number generator. The plan should include defining the sampling unit and establishing a numbering system for the population. After the plan has been designed, select the sample using the computer. Assume that the sample size is 50 for each of (1) through (4).
 1. Prenumbered sales invoices in a sales journal where the lowest invoice number is 1 and the highest is 6,211.
 2. Prenumbered bills of lading where the lowest document number is 21,926 and the highest is 28,511.
 3. Accounts receivable on 10 pages with 60 lines per page except the last page, which has only 36 full lines. Each line has a customer name and an amount receivable.
 4. Prenumbered invoices in a sales journal where each month starts over with number 1. (Invoices for each month are designated by the month and document number.) There is a maximum of 20 pages per month with a total of 185 pages for the year. All pages have 75 invoices except for the last page for each month.

b. Using systematic sampling, select the first five sample items for population (1).

13-22 For the examination of the financial statements of Scotia Inc., Rosa Schellenberg, a public accountant, has decided to apply non-statistical audit sampling in the tests of sales transactions. Based on her knowledge of Scotia's operations in the area of sales, she decides that the estimated population deviation rate is likely to be 3 percent and that she is willing to accept a 5 percent risk that the true population exception rate is not greater than 6 percent. Given this information, Rosa selects a random sample of 150 sales invoices from the 5,000 prepared during the year and examines them for exceptions. She notes the following exceptions in her working papers. There is no other documentation.

REQUIRED
 a. Which of the invoices in the table should be defined as an exception?
 b. Explain why it is inappropriate to set a single acceptable TER and EPER for the combined exceptions.
 c. State the appropriate analysis of exceptions for each of the exceptions in the sample.

Invoice No.	Comment
5028	Sales invoice had incorrect price, but a subsequent credit note was sent out as a correction.
6791	Voided sales invoice examined by auditor.
6810	Shipping document for a sale of merchandise could not be located.
7364	Sales invoice for $2,875 has not been collected and is six months past due.
7625	Client unable to locate the printed duplicate copy of the sales invoice.
8431	Invoice was dated three days later than the date of the shipping document.
8528	Customer purchase order is not attached to the duplicate sales invoice.
8566	Billing is for $100 less than it should be due to a pricing error.
8780	Client is unable to locate the printed duplicate copy of the sales invoice.
9169	Credit is not authorized, but the sale was for only $7.65.

13-23 An audit partner is developing an office training program to familiarize her professional staff with statistical decision models applicable to the audit of dollar-value balances. She wishes to demonstrate the relationship of sample sizes to population size and variability and the auditor's specifications as to tolerable misstatement and ARIA. The partner prepared the table on the next page to show comparative population characteristics and audit specifications of the two populations.

REQUIRED
In items (1) through (5) below, indicate for the specific case from the table that follows the required sample size to be selected from population 1 relative to the sample from population 2.

(1) In case 1 the required sample size from population 1 is _____.

(2) In case 2 the required sample size from population 1 is _____.

(3) In case 3 the required sample size from population 1 is _____.

(4) In case 4 the required sample size from population 1 is _____.

(5) In case 5 the required sample size from population 1 is _____.

Your answer should be selected from the following responses:

a. Larger than the required sample size from population 2.
b. Equal to the required sample size from population 2.
c. Smaller than the required sample size from population 2.
d. Indeterminate relative to the required sample size from population 2.

(Adapted from AICPA)

	Characteristics of Population 1 Relative to Population 2		Audit Specifications as to a Sample from Population 1 Relative to a Sample from Population 2	
	Size	Estimated Population Exception Rate	Tolerable Misstatement	ARIA
Case 1	Equal	Equal	Equal	Lower
Case 2	Equal	Larger	Larger	Equal
Case 3	Larger	Equal	Smaller	Higher
Case 4	Smaller	Smaller	Equal	Higher
Case 5	Larger	Equal	Equal	Lower

13-24 You have just completed the accounts receivable confirmation process in the audit of Danforth Paper Company Ltd., a paper supplier to retail shops and commercial users.

Following are the data related to this process:

Accounts receivable recorded balance $2,760,000
Number of accounts   7,320

A non-statistical sample was taken as follows:

All accounts over $10,000 (23 accounts) $465,000
77 accounts under $10,000 $81,500
Materiality $100,000
Inherent and control risk are both high.
No relevant analytical procedures were performed.

The table at right gives the results of the confirmation procedures.

REQUIRED

Evaluate the results of the non-statistical sample. Consider both the direct implications of the misstatements found and the effect of using a sample.

	Recorded Value	Audited Value
Items over $10,000	$465,000	$432,000
Items under $10,000	81,500	77,150
Individual misstatements for items under $10,000:		
Item 12	5,120	4,820
Item 19	485	385
Item 33	1,250	250
Item 35	3,975	3,875
Item 51	1,850	1,825
Item 59	4,200	3,780
Item 74	2,405	0
	19,285	14,935

Professional Judgment Problems

13-25 Diane, a computer audit technician, has been selecting payroll attribute samples for Soft Drink Distribution Systems (SDDS) Ltd. for several years. It took about a week to set up the computer-assisted audit tests, and the client gave Diane a password to have read-only access to the payroll files remotely. Every quarter, Diane spends less than half an hour selecting samples that she forwards to the audit team for their interim audit.

This year, the firm has assigned a new audit manager, Joe, to the SDDS audit. Joe has been assigned the task of trying to create a more efficient audit in order to maintain audit fees at the same level as the prior year's. Joe has informed Diane that he will no longer require her services; the staff will use systematic sampling to select a sample from the 5,000 employees. They will ask the client to provide spreadsheet files in Excel for each weekly file and then use an Excel macro to select the test. Joe believes it will take him an hour or two to set up the macro process and then another hour or two to select the sample. Since his charge-out rate is considerably less than Diane's, this will save some money on the audit.

When Diane asked Joe how he was going to evaluate the sample, he said he would use the firm's manual tables.

What should Diane do? Discuss the advantages and disadvantages of the two sample selection methods described in the case.

13-26 You have been asked to do planning for statistical testing in the control testing of the audit of cash receipts. Following is a partial audit program for the audit of cash receipts:
1. Review the cash receipts journal for large and unusual transactions.
2. Trace entries from the prelisting of cash receipts to the cash receipts journal to determine whether each is recorded.
3. Compare customer name, date, and amount on the prelisting with the cash receipts journal.
4. Examine the related remittance advice for entries selected from the prelisting to determine whether cash discounts were approved.
5. Trace entries from the prelisting to the deposit slip to determine whether each has been deposited.

REQUIRED
a. Identify which audit procedures can be tested using attributes sampling. Justify your response.
b. State the appropriate sampling unit for each of the tests in part (a).
c. Define the attributes that you would test for each of the tests in part (a). State the audit objective associated with each of the attributes.
d. Define exception conditions for each of the attributes that you described in part (c).
e. Which of the exceptions would be indicative of potential fraud? Justify your response.

Case

13-27 For the audit of Carbald Supply Company, Farda is conducting a test of sales for the first nine months of the fiscal year ended December 31, 2008. Incorrect revenue recognition has been assessed as a significant risk. Materiality is set at $750,000.

Included in the audit procedures are the following:
1. Foot and cross-foot the sales journal and trace the balance to the general ledger.
2. Review all sales transactions for reasonableness.
3. Select a sample of recorded sales from the sales journal and trace the customer name and amounts to duplicate sales invoices and the related shipping document.
4. Select a sample of shipping document numbers and perform the following tests:
   4.1 Trace the shipping document to the related duplicate sales invoice.
   4.2 Examine the duplicate sales invoice to determine whether copies of the shipping document, shipping order, and customer order are attached.
   4.3 Examine the shipping order for an authorized credit approval.
   4.4 Examine the duplicate sales invoice for an indication of internal verification of quantity, price, extensions,

and footings; trace the balance to the accounts receivable master file.
   4.5 Compare the price on the duplicate sales invoice with the sales price in the product master file and the quantity with the shipping document.
   4.6 Trace the total on the duplicate sales invoice to the sales journal and the accounts receivable master file for customer, name, amount and date.

REQUIRED
a. State the audit objective associated with each of the audit procedures.
b. Identify those audit procedures which are potential controls with respect to revenue recognition. Justify your response.
c. Identify those audit procedures where computer-assisted audit tests (CAATs) can be used for all or part of the audit procedure. State the process that the CAATs can complete.
d. What type of sampling would you use for these audit procedures? Justify your response.
e. State the appropriate sampling unit, define the attribute that you would test, and define exception conditions for each of the audit procedures.
f. Which of the audit procedures are dual-purpose tests? Justify your response.

Ongoing Small Business Case: Sampling at CondoCleaners.com

13-28 There are about 240 payroll transactions for the first nine months at CondoCleaners.com and about 1500 sales transactions. The only material asset account is fixed assets.

REQUIRED
What type of sampling might be suitable at CondoCleaners.com? Justify your response.

CHAPTER 13 | AUDIT SAMPLING CONCEPTS   441

3

Application of the audit process to the sales and collection cycle

To understand how auditing is done in practice, it is important to understand how auditing concepts are applied to specific auditing areas. The sales and collection cycle is the first area we look at for a detailed application of auditing concepts. This cycle is an important part of every audit and is reasonably straightforward. The next two chapters apply the concepts you have learned in previous chapters to the audit of sales, cash receipts, and the related income statement and balance sheet accounts in the cycle.

The objective of Chapter 14 is to help you learn the methodology for designing tests of controls for sales, cash receipts, and the other classes of transactions in the sales and collection cycle. Chapter 15 presents the methodology for designing audit procedures for the audit of account balances in the sales and collection cycle.

14

Audit of the sales and collection cycle: Tests of controls

Now that we have looked at the planning of the audit, including the risk assessment process, it is time to look at the execution phase—what are the risks associated with sales? How do we actually design and conduct the testing in response to these risks? Which tests are conducted and for what purpose? In this chapter, we look at the testing of internal controls for the sales and collection cycle. Management accountants will find this valuable when designing internal controls to mitigate risks, while auditors (financial, internal, and specialists) use their knowledge of internal controls to help assess risks and design audit tests.

STANDARDS REFERENCED IN THIS CHAPTER

No standards are referenced in this chapter.

LEARNING OBJECTIVES

1 Identify and describe typical records and transactions in the sales cycle.

2 State the relationship between overall audit planning risks and risks for sales and collections cycle assertions. Explain how the evaluation of general controls affects the audit of the sales and collection cycle. Describe the methodology for designing tests of controls for sales.

3 Describe the methodology for controls over sales returns and allowances, cash receipts transactions, uncollectible accounts, and account balances. State the effect of the results of tests of controls on the audit.

4 Illustrate the risk assessment and audit of sales and cash receipts using Hillsburg Hardware Limited to describe the typical audit process through tests of controls.

The Choice Is Simple—Rely on Internal Control or Resign

Major Financial Inc. is one of the largest clients managed out of the Montreal office of a Big Six firm. It is a financial services conglomerate with almost 200 offices in Canada and the United States, as well as branch offices overseas. The company has over 200,000 major accounts receivable, with millions of smaller accounts. It processes hundreds of millions of sales and other transactions annually.

The company's national computer centre is in a large environmentally controlled room containing mainframe computers and a great deal of ancillary equipment. There are two complete systems serving online systems, one serving as a backup for the other, as systems failure would preclude operations in all of the company's branches.

The company has an excellent system of checks and balances whereby branch office transaction totals are reconciled to head office data processing control totals daily; these, in turn, are reconciled to outside bank account records monthly. Whenever this regular reconciliation process indicates a significant out-of-balance condition, procedures are initiated to resolve the problem as quickly as possible. There is an internal audit staff that oversees any special investigative efforts that are required.

Because Major Financial Inc. is a public company, it must file its annual report with the Quebec and Ontario securities commissions within 90 days of its fiscal year end. In addition, the company likes to announce annual earnings and issue its annual report as soon after year end as feasible. Under these circumstances, there is always a great deal of pressure on the public accounting firm to complete the audit expeditiously.

IMPORTANCE TO AUDITORS

Major Financial is a high-profile audit client with numerous risks. There are many users of the financial statements and a great deal of work that needs to be completed by the internal and external auditors in a short period of time.

A standard audit planning question is, how much shall we rely on internal control? In the case of the Major Financial audit, there is only one possible answer: as much as we can. Otherwise, how could the audit possibly be completed to meet the reporting deadlines, let alone keep audit cost to a reasonable level? Accordingly, the public accounting firm conducts the audit with significant reliance on general information systems controls, specific data processing controls, reconciliation processes, and internal audit procedures. It tests these controls extensively and performs many of its audit procedures prior to year end. In all honesty, if Major Financial Inc. did not have excellent internal controls, the public accounting firm would admit that an audit of the company just could not be done.

continued >

The Typical Sales Cycle

The overall objective in the audit of the sales and collection cycle is to evaluate whether the account balances affected by the cycle are fairly presented in accordance with generally accepted accounting principles. The following are typical accounts included in the sales and collection cycle:

• Sales.
• Sales returns and allowances.
• Bad-debt expense.
• Cash discounts taken.
• Trade accounts receivable.
• Allowance for uncollectible accounts.
• Cash in bank (debits from cash receipts).

The goods and services tax is collected by an entity and remitted to the federal government. Accordingly, in Figure 5-6 on page 129, the Hillsburg Hardware trial balance shows goods and services tax payable (the net liability) as being in the acquisitions and payment cycle, which is discussed in Chapter 18.

For example, look at the adjusted trial balance for Hillsburg Hardware Limited on page 129. Accounts on the trial balance affected by the sales and collection cycle are identified by the letter S in the left margin. Each of the above accounts is included, except cash discounts taken. For other audits, the names and the nature of the accounts may vary, of course, depending on the industry and client involved. There

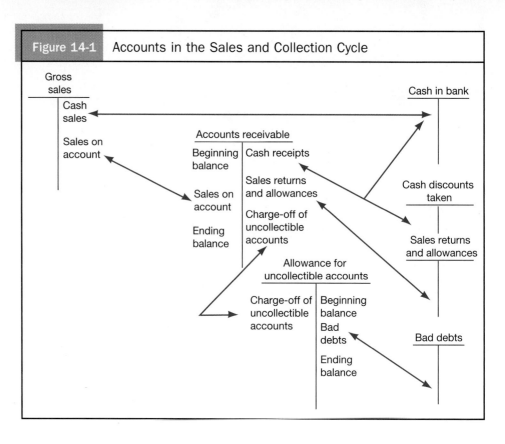

Figure 14-1 Accounts in the Sales and Collection Cycle

are differences in account titles for a service company, a retail company, and an insurance company, but the basic concepts are the same. To provide a frame of reference for understanding the material in this chapter, a retail outlet with consumers and commercial customers, such as Hillsburg Hardware, is assumed.

A brief summary of the way accounting information flows through the various accounts in the sales and collection cycle is illustrated in Figure 14-1 by the use of T-accounts. This figure shows that there are five **classes of transactions** (the categories of transactions) included **in the sales and collection cycle**:

Classes of transactions in the sales and collection cycle—the categories of transactions for the sales and collection cycle in a typical company: sales, cash receipts, sales returns and allowances, charge-off of uncollectible accounts, and bad-debt expense.

- Sales (cash and sales on account).
- Cash receipts.
- Sales returns and allowances.
- Charge-off of uncollectible accounts.
- Bad-debt expense.

Figure 14-1 also shows that with the exception of cash sales, every sales and collection cycle transaction and amount ultimately is included in one of two balance sheet accounts: accounts receivable or allowance for uncollectible accounts.

For the most part, the audit of the sales and collection cycle can be performed independently of the audit of other cycles and subjectively combined with the other parts of the audit as the evidence accumulation process proceeds. Auditors must keep in mind that the concept of materiality requires them to consider the combination of misstatements in all parts of the audit before making a final judgment on the fair presentation of the financial statements. This is done by continuously summarizing errors and integrating regular file review throughout the engagement with the many parts of the audit.

The types of audit tests discussed in Chapter 12, and shown in Figure 12-3 on page 392, are all used extensively in the audit of the sales and collection cycle. Tests of controls are used primarily to test the effectiveness of internal controls to mitigate risks over the five classes of transactions in the cycle and to test the dollar amounts of these same five classes of transactions. Analytical procedures are used to test the relationships among the account balances in the cycle, both to one another and to prior years' balances. Tests of details of balances are used to verify ending account balances, primarily accounts receivable. Tests of controls are studied in this chapter.

Nature of the Sales and Collection Cycle

The **sales and collection cycle** involves the decisions and processes necessary for the transfer of the ownership of goods and services to customers after they are made available for sale. It begins with a request by a customer and ends with the conversion of material or service into an account receivable, and ultimately into cash.

The cycle includes several classes of transactions, accounts, and business functions, as well as a number of documents, reports, and records. Information that could be included in computer data files is shown in Table 14-1. Note that this is broken down into two types: semi-permanent and transaction. **Semi-permanent (or master file) data** in the sales and collection cycle are data that are established when a customer starts purchasing and is updated as customer information changes. For example, customer name and billing address are included, and the data are generally used for the processing of multiple transactions. **Transaction information** is based upon customer activity, with normally one or more transactions for each activity, such as a sale. The classes of transactions, accounts, business functions, and documents are shown in Table 14-2 on the next page. Semi-permanent information and transaction information are updated during normal processing within the sales and collection cycle, as discussed in the remainder of this chapter.

The nature of computer processing used within a transaction cycle determines potential controls available in the system. For example, transactions can be processed using groups of transactions (also called **batch processing**), or they can be processed one at a time with immediate update against the data files (called **online processing**). Many companies use both methods. Payroll may be processed weekly in batch mode, while sales orders received over the telephone may be recorded as received. The risks of error and thus the nature of the controls available to monitor the transactions are different. Key risk differences pertain to error detection and correction and fraud. Controls in the categories of audit trails and segregation of duties help to mitigate the risks

Sales and collection cycle— involves the decisions and processes necessary for the transfer of the ownership of goods and services to customers after they are made available for sale; begins with a request by a customer and ends with the conversion of material or service into an account receivable, and ultimately into cash.

Semi-permanent (or master file) data—in the sales and collection cycle, data that are established when a customer starts purchasing and updated as customer information changes; generally used for the processing of multiple transactions.

Transaction information— information based on customer activity. There is normally one transaction for each activity. In the sales and collection cycle, examples include sale or cash payment transactions.

Batch processing—transaction processing using groups of transactions.

Online processing—the processing of transactions one at a time with an immediate update against the data files.

Table 14-1	Typical Information Included in Accounts Receivable or Sales Computer Data Files

Semi-permanent Information	Transaction Information
Semi-permanent information is often called master file data. It is established when a customer starts purchasing, and it is updated as customer information changes.	Transaction information is based on customer activity, and there is normally one transaction for each activity, such as a sale or cash payment.
Customer number or code	Customer number or code
Customer name	Customer name
Customer billing address	Transaction type (sale, credit, payment, adjustment)
Customer shipping address	Transaction date
Customer phone number	Transaction amount
Credit limit	Transaction detail (item detail)
Payment terms (includes applicable discounts)	Transaction tracking (the individual who entered the transaction)
Year-to-date sales	
Current balance outstanding	

Table 14-2	Classes of Transactions, Accounts, Business Functions, and Related Documents and Reports for the Sales and Collection Cycle		

Classes of Transactions	Accounts	Business Functions	Documents and Reports
Sales	Sales Accounts receivable	Processing customer orders Granting credit Shipping goods Billing customers and recording sales	Customer order Customer order Shipping document Sales invoice Sales journal/history report Summary sales report Accounts receivable trial balance Monthly statements
Cash receipts	Cash in bank (debits from cash receipts) Accounts receivable	Processing and recording cash receipts	Remittance advice Bank deposit detail Cash receipts journal
Sales returns and allowances	Sales returns and allowances Accounts receivable	Processing and recording sales returns and allowances	Credit memo Sales returns and allowances journal
Charge-off of uncollectible accounts	Accounts receivable Allowance for uncollectible accounts	Charging off uncollectible accounts receivable	Uncollectible account authorization form
Bad-debt expense	Bad-debt expense Allowance for uncollectible accounts	Providing for bad debts	Journal entry authorization
Master file change	Customer master file accounts	Maintaining semi-permanent data	Master file change form

Note: "Journal" and "history report" are synonymous terms.

of fraud, while audit trails and error detection and correction controls help to prevent the risks of error. A summary of the control differences is shown in Table 14-3.

Effects on other transactions or on other subsystems For both batch and online systems, a transaction could cause other automatic transactions. For example, shipment of goods to customers could result in the automatic generation of a supplier purchase order if quantities fell below a certain level. Automatic postings to the general ledger could occur based on time or based on user initiation. Auditors need to be careful when auditing using the cycle approach when automated systems are integrated. Documentation and assessment of systems should include such transactions linked from other subsystems.

For both batch and online systems, it may be possible to identify who has entered transactions by associating user identification codes (user IDs) with the data entry person. This assists with auditor evaluation of segregation of duties.

Business Functions in the Cycle and Related Documents and Records

The business functions for a cycle are the key activities that an organization must complete to execute and record business transactions. Column three of Table 14-2 identifies the nine **business functions** in a typical **sales and collection cycle**. An understanding of these business functions for the sales and collection cycle promotes

Business functions in a sales and collection cycle—the key activities that an organization must complete to execute and record business transactions for sales, cash receipts, sales returns and allowances, charge-off of uncollectible accounts, and bad debts.

Table 14-3	Control Differences Between Batch and Online Systems	
Control Category	Batch Systems	Online Systems
Audit trails	Transactions can readily be traced from source transaction through to general ledger posting. Groups of documents are totalled and entered into the system, and reports are printed showing the document details and the totals. These totals can be traced to transaction history reports or transaction journals and from there to the general ledger.	Transactions may be initiated and entered without source documents (e.g., be initiated by a telephone call and entered directly into a system). Paper will normally be produced when the goods are picked or shipped, with daily or weekly summaries printed. Controls such as document sequencing are used to ensure that all transactions are completed. A full audit trail may be available in electronic form only.
Error detection and correction	Since transactions are processed in groups, if one transaction is in error, the entire batch of transactions may be rejected from subsequent processing. Each transaction must be correct before all transactions can be processed.	The focus is on preventing incorrect transactions from being entered. For example, systems should check for invalid customer numbers and reasonableness of dates or amounts prior to processing individual transactions.
Segregation of duties	Segregation can be achieved by separating the functions of totalling and counting of source documents from data entry. A person other than the data entry person should verify that the control totals entered match the control totals prepared from source documents. This verification may be called the data control function.	Decentralization to departments can result in individual users performing traditionally incompatible functions, such as entering and verifying cash receipts and sales and accounts receivable, and updating credit limits. Passwords could be used to separate some of these functions. Alternatively, independent preparation and review of exception reports could compensate for such segregation problems.

Note: The **data control function** involves independent verification of control total and source document detail to that keyed into the system by data entry.

Data control function— independent verification of control total and source document detail to that keyed into the system by data entry.

understanding of how an audit of the cycle is conducted. The business functions for the sales and collection cycle and the most common documents and records used in each function are examined in this section.

PROCESSING CUSTOMER ORDERS The request for goods by a customer is the starting point for the entire cycle. Legally, it is an offer to buy goods under specified terms.

Customer order This is a request for merchandise by a customer. It may be received by telephone, by letter, electronically, by a printed form that has been sent to prospective and existing customers, through salespeople, or in other ways.

GRANTING CREDIT Before goods are shipped, a properly authorized person or automated control system must approve credit to the customer for sales on account. Weak practices in credit approval or in changing the credit limit in the master file frequently result in excessive bad debts and accounts receivable that may be uncollectible. For most firms, credit approval is handled by having credit limits established when the customer is set up in the customer master file. Sales are automatically

CHAPTER 14 | AUDIT OF THE SALES AND COLLECTION CYCLE: TESTS OF CONTROLS   449 authorized as long as the account receivable stays within the authorized credit limit. Once the balance approaches the credit limit, exception reports are printed for the credit manager, or other methods are used to determine whether credit limits should be extended or individual sales should continue to be approved.

SHIPPING GOODS This critical function is the first point in the cycle where company assets are given up. Most companies recognize sales when goods are shipped. A shipping document is prepared at the time of shipment; this can be done automatically based on sales order information. The shipping document, which is frequently a multicopy bill of lading, is essential to the proper billing of shipments to customers. Companies that maintain perpetual inventory records also update them on the basis of shipping information.

Shipping document This document is prepared to initiate the shipping of goods, indicating the description of the merchandise, the quantity shipped, and other relevant data. The original document is sent to the customer, and one or more copies are retained. It is also used as a signal to bill the customer. One type of shipping document is a bill of lading, which is a written contract between the carrier and the seller concerning the receipt and shipment of goods. Often bills of lading include only the number of boxes or kilograms shipped, rather than complete details of quantity and description. Throughout the text, we assume that complete details are included on bills of lading or on the internally generated shipping documents. Details of shipment are recorded so that perpetual inventory records can be updated and the billing process can commence.

BILLING CUSTOMERS AND RECORDING SALES Since the billing of customers is the means by which the customer is informed of the amount due for the goods, it must be done correctly and on a timely basis. The most important aspects of billing are making sure that all shipments made have been billed, that no shipment has been billed more than once, and that each shipment is billed for the proper amount. Billing at the proper amount is dependent on charging the customer for the quantity shipped at the authorized price. The authorized price includes consideration of freight charges, insurance, and terms of payment.

In most systems, billing of the customer includes preparation of a multicopy sales invoice and updating of the sales transactions file, customer master file, and general ledger files for sales and accounts receivable. This information is used to generate the sales journal and, along with cash receipts and miscellaneous credits, allows preparation of the accounts receivable trial balance. Point-of-sale systems, such as those seen at many retail counters, often combine data entry and update for shipment, inventory, sales systems, and cash receipts with the entry of a single transaction. The single data entry transaction results in multiple transactions in the information systems, that is, shipment records, inventory changes, sales records, and cash receipts information.

Sales invoice This is a document indicating the description and quantity of goods sold, the price including freight, insurance, terms, and other relevant data. Typically, it is printed after the customer number, quantity, and destination of goods shipped are entered. The sales invoice is the method of indicating to the customer the amount of a sale and due date of a payment. The original invoice is sent to the customer, and one or more copies are retained.

Sales journal This is a listing of the sales history transaction file on a daily, weekly, monthly, or yearly basis. A detailed sales journal includes each sales transaction. It usually indicates gross sales for different classifications, such as product lines, the entry to accounts receivable, and miscellaneous debits and credits such as goods and services tax collected. The sales journal can also include sales returns and allowances transactions.

Summary sales report This is a listing that summarizes sales for a period. The report typically includes information analyzed by key components such as customer, salesperson, product, and territory.

audit challenge 14-1
Cereal Hamburgers and Stale Cars

Cash. More cash for me, please, to support my lifestyle. This seems to be what underlies the innovative ways that employees or owners of businesses steal or engage in fraud.

Consider the case of the staff at a club-based restaurant. Staff were conspiring to provide more saleable products by adding cereal to hamburgers and watering down liquor. This enabled them to take the cash from about every fifth sale without recording it. Staff conspired to ensure that reports and supporting documents all reconciled so that the thefts could not easily be detected. Internal auditors became suspicious of the club because there was never any problem with the accounting records—they were too perfect!

This example illustrates the importance of considering past practices when examining documentation and considering documentation in the context of human behaviours.

In our second example, a car dealership was experiencing cash flow problems due to lower sales. The owner told his employees to deceive the bank about trade-ins that were received on the purchase of new cars.

As trade-ins could be used as security for the bank loan (they were part of the inventory that secured the loan), the car dealership was able to inflate its inventory by adding increasingly more fictitious used car inventory. It did this by resending old sales documents with slight alterations. The bank asked only for the front page of the documentation, which made this alteration easy. Subsequent to the detection of the fraud, the bank changed its procedures to require more rigorous documentation and periodic spot checks of client inventory.

CRITICAL THINKING QUESTIONS

1. What are the characteristics of good documentation that make it so important for record keeping?
2. Identify some common documentation errors that could easily occur. Were the internal auditors of the club right to believe that perfect documentation was a problem?

Sources: 1. Jacka, J. Mike, "Roundtable," *Internal Auditor Journal*, August 2004, p. 91–92. 2. Miles, William, "Selling cars already sold," *Fraud Magazine*, January/February 2009, 23(1), p. 14-15, 58.

Accounts receivable trial balance This is a listing of the amount owed by each customer at a point in time. It is prepared directly from the accounts receivable data files. It is most frequently an aged trial balance, showing how old the accounts receivable components of each customer's balance are as of the report date. This report can be printed showing only balances forward (i.e., the total owed by each customer) or on an open item basis (i.e., showing all sales invoices that have not been paid).

Monthly statement This is a document sent to each customer indicating the monthly beginning balance of accounts receivable, the amount and date of each sale, cash payments received, credit memos issued, and the ending balance due. It is, in essence, a copy of the customer's portion of the accounts receivable activity.

PROCESSING AND RECORDING CASH RECEIPTS The preceding four functions are necessary for getting the goods into the hands of customers, properly billing them, and reflecting the information in the accounting records. The result of these four functions is sales transactions. The remaining five functions involve the collection and recording of cash, sales returns and allowances, charge-off of uncollectible accounts, providing for bad-debt expense, and maintenance of semi-permanent information contained in customer master files.

Processing and recording cash receipts includes receiving, depositing, and recording cash. Cash includes both currency and cheques. A potential fraud risk is the possibility of theft. Theft can occur before receipts are entered in the records, as illustrated in the first example in Audit Challenge 14-1, or later. The risk of theft is reduced in the handling of cash receipts when all cash must be deposited in the bank on a timely basis and recorded in the cash receipts transaction file, which is used to prepare the cash receipts journal and update the customer master and general ledger files.

Some companies engage a bank to assist in the processing of cash receipts from customers. This could involve a lockbox system, whereby customers mail payments to a post office box address maintained by bank personnel. The bank is responsible for opening all receipts, maintaining records of all payments by customers received at the lockbox address, and depositing receipts into the company's bank account on a timely basis. In other cases, receipts are submitted electronically from customers' bank accounts to a company bank account through the use of electronic funds transfer (EFT). For consumer purchases by credit card on websites, the issuer of the credit card uses EFT to transfer funds into the company's bank account (less commission) almost immediately after the sale. For both lockbox systems and EFT, the bank provides information to the company to prepare the cash receipt entries in the company's accounting records. The use of both lockboxes and EFT allows for faster deposit of cash receipts into company bank accounts and often reduces risks associated with company personnel handling cash receipts.

Remittance advices are important when cheques are mailed to the company and accounts receivable is involved.

Remittance advice This is a document that accompanies the sales invoice mailed to the customer; it is meant to be returned to the seller with the payment. When the payment is received, the remittance advice is used to obtain the customer name, the sales invoice number, and the amount of the invoice. Often, a second copy of the sales invoice is used as a remittance advice. Alternatively, the customer may list the invoice numbers and amount paid on the cheque stub, which then serves as a remittance advice. If the customer fails to identify the invoices being paid with his or her payment, the data entry person must later allocate the payment to specific invoices. A remittance advice is used to permit the immediate deposit of cash and to improve control over the custody of assets.

Bank deposit detail This is a list prepared by an independent person (someone who has no responsibility for recording sales or accounts receivable) when cash is received. This could take the form of a listing of cheques received or a duplicate bank deposit slip. It is used to verify whether cash received was recorded and deposited at the correct amounts and on a timely basis.

Cash receipts journal This is a listing of cash receipts from collections, cash sales, and all other cash receipts. It indicates total cash received, the credit to accounts receivable at the gross amount of the original sale, trade discounts taken, and other debits and credits. The daily entries in the cash receipts journal are supported by remittance advices. The journal is generated for any period from the cash receipts transactions included in the computer files.

PROCESSING AND RECORDING SALES RETURNS AND ALLOWANCES When a customer is dissatisfied with the goods purchased, the seller frequently accepts the return of goods or grants a reduction in the charges. The company normally prepares a receiving report for the returned goods and returns them to inventory. Returns and allowances must be correctly and promptly recorded. Credit memos are normally issued for returns and allowances to aid in maintaining control and to facilitate record keeping.

Credit memo This is a document indicating a reduction in the amount due from a customer because of goods returned or an allowance granted. It often takes the same general form as a sales invoice, but it supports reductions in accounts receivable rather than increases.

Sales returns and allowances journal This is a listing of sales returns and allowances. It performs the same function as the sales journal. Many companies record these transactions using the same system as that used for the recording of sales. Transactions would thus be listed in the sales journal rather than a separate journal.

CHARGING OFF UNCOLLECTIBLE ACCOUNTS RECEIVABLE Despite the diligence of credit departments, some customers may not pay their bills. When the company concludes that an amount is no longer collectable, it must be charged off. Typically, this occurs after a customer files bankruptcy or the account is turned over to a collection agency. Proper accounting requires an adjustment for these uncollectible amounts.

Uncollectible account authorization form This is an internal document, indicating authority to write off an account receivable as uncollectible.

PROVIDING FOR BAD DEBTS The provision for bad debts must be sufficient to allow for the current period sales that the company will be unable to collect in the future. For most companies, the provision represents a residual, resulting from management's end-of-period adjustment of the allowances for uncollectible accounts. Period-end reports or journal entries are used to document this adjustment.

CUSTOMER MASTER FILE CHANGE The customer master file is a file for maintaining semi-permanent data used for processing sales, payments, and other transactions associated with customers. The master file information is provided by the customer, and reviewed and approved prior to set-up. Approval is necessary for the credit limit and payment terms in particular and for changes to these fields. It is also important that customers provide changes, such as those to shipping addresses, in writing, since an incorrect shipping address would result in goods being shipped to an incorrect (or unauthorized) location. This approval may be evidenced by a master file change form. The changes can then be authorized by an appropriate individual prior to entry.

The outstanding balance field in the customer master file is updated for sales, sales returns and allowances, and cash receipts. The total of the individual outstanding account balances in the customer master file equals the total balance of accounts receivable in the general ledger. A printout of the accounts receivable master file shows, by customer, the balance of accounts receivable at that time. It is also sometimes called "the accounts receivable subsidiary ledger" or "subledger." If the company has a database, then the master file data are directly linked to the transaction data. Other information systems have separate transaction files for unpaid transactions, sales, sales returns and allowances, and cash receipts that are used to update individual accounts receivable balances in the master file as entered, daily or weekly. Figures 5-5A, B, and C (see pages 127–128) illustrate typical transaction flows for manual, batch, and database systems.

concept check

C14-1 List the five categories of transactions. For each category, describe how the completeness audit objective would apply to the transaction.

C14-2 What is the difference between transaction data and semi-permanent data? Provide two examples of each type of data.

C14-3 Describe the difference between batch and online processing. Provide one example of applications that are best suited to each type of processing.

② Sales Cycle Audit Planning

Risk Assessment and the Sales Cycle

Our previous chapters have explained the audit planning process. Risk assessment comprises the first three phases of the audit: preplanning, client risk profile, and planning the audit. It is only then that the auditor can decide upon the risk response, which includes the design and conduct of further audit procedures, including control testing of the sales and collection cycle, discussed in this chapter. Table 14-4 on the next page lists each of the risk assessments that the auditor would have conducted during the risk assessment phase and how each affects the audit of this cycle. Control risk is not included in Table 14-4, as it is discussed separately later in this section.

Table 14-4 shows that as risks increase, the auditor is required to conduct more audit testing. The tests conducted could be tests of control or substantive tests. Let us consider the risks associated with the car dealership discussed in Audit Challenge 14-1. Client business risk for an automobile dealership may be high: such a business is at risk of failure due to decreasing automobile sales as many people lose their jobs and delay major purchases, such as automobiles. If the dealership has loans secured by inventory or accounts receivable with bank covenants, there could be an incentive to

Table 14-4	Risk Assessment and the Sales and Collection Cycle
Risk Type	**Impact upon Sales and Collection Cycle**
Client business risk	Increased client business risk could lead to greater risks of misstatement of sales.
Audit risk	As audit risk decreases, the level of assurance required increases, and the extent of testing required increases.
Inherent risk—overall	As inherent risk increases, the extent of testing required increases; inherent risks associated with the handling of cash directly affect certain audit assertions in sales (e.g., completeness).
Risk of material misstatement—overall	Management biases due to bonus incentives or stated earnings forecasts could increase the risk of misstatement of sales.
Risk of fraud—overall	Poor fraud risk management could result in increased risks of fraud, with a need to increase the extent of testing.
Identify significant risks	Revenue recognition is considered a significant risk unless the auditor has evidence to the contrary; this means that controls over revenue recognition need to be assessed and increased testing is required of assertions that affect revenue recognition.

manipulate the timing of sales or even the actual amounts of sales (the occurrence objective) to secure or maintain bank funding.

The auditor will consider client business risk and the users of the financial statements in setting audit risk. Many car dealerships have as users the bank, the automobile manufacturer, owners, employees, and regulatory agencies such as Canada Revenue Agency. As economic uncertainty increases, users may scrutinize financial statements more closely, causing the auditor to lower audit risk. The extent of audit testing would need to be increased for all sales audit assertions where there was a risk of material misstatement (e.g., completeness, accuracy, occurrence, timing).

Inherent risks at the dealership, discussed in Chapter 7, would include the auditor's assessment of corporate governance, management integrity, client motivation, and the results of previous audits. It is likely that the auditor would somewhat increase inherent risk for a car dealership in light of current economic trends. Risk of material misstatement overall would be moderate, depending upon factors such as revenue from vehicle repairs and maintenance, mix of variable and fixed costs (for example, are premises leased or owned?), and specific issues identified by the auditor. The exception could be the collectability of sales (valuation of accounts receivable), which could have increased risks, depending upon how sales of vehicles are financed.

Risk of fraud increases as the quality of the enterprise risk management process (including fraud risk) declines, and as the quality of internal controls overall declines. The auditor would pay particular attention to monitoring and supervisory controls, depending upon the size of the car dealership. The above risk assessments, including the supporting documentation of internal controls, are integrated into the auditor's control risk assessment.

Prior to examining specific controls for the sales and collection cycle, the auditor will have identified some assertions that may be prone to a risk of material misstatement. Also, prior to considering specific controls by cycle, the auditor will need to consider the results of the general controls assessment for the client.

Effect of General Controls

As described in Chapters 9 and 10, general controls can be part of the control environment and part of individual applications or transaction cycles. Prior to assessing the individual transaction cycle, the auditor documents general controls that are pervasive and that affect multiple transaction cycles. For example, access and control policies and program change control procedures affect multiple cycles. If unauthorized individuals could access and establish or change credit limits, this would cause problems with collectability of accounts. Access controls could then be tested as general controls, providing some control assurance for each application cycle that is affected. Similarly, the existence of excellent program change controls that have been tested would allow the auditor to place reliance on programs within each of the transaction cycles. Poor program change controls would suggest that the auditor could potentially rely on only manual controls in the transaction cycle. If unauthorized individuals could change how the accounts receivable aging is calculated or how invoices are calculated, the transactions would be unreliable. Thus, prior to documenting controls and assessing control risk in an individual cycle, the auditor reviews the general controls working-paper file to determine the controls in place and determines whether reliance can be placed on these controls. This assessment may be completed by a specialist within the auditor's firm and is based on the auditor's risk assessment process.

Following are the key areas that the auditor would review as part of general controls:

- Organization structure and job responsibilities within the data processing department.
- Program change controls.
- Physical access and security.
- Logical access and security.
- Documentation of programs and operations.

These categories of general controls can include complex areas, such as data communications, database management systems, internet applications, electronic data interchange, and electronic funds transfer, which were discussed in Chapter 10.

Methodology for Designing Tests of Controls for Sales

The methodology for obtaining an understanding of internal controls and designing tests of controls for sales is shown in Figure 14-2 on the next page. This methodology was studied in general terms in Chapters 9 and 12. It is applied specifically to sales in this section. The bottom box in Figure 14-2 shows the four evidence decisions the auditor must make. This section deals with deciding the appropriate audit procedures. For the timing decision, the tests are usually performed at an interim date if internal controls are effective, but they can also be done after the balance sheet date. Decisions on the appropriate sample size and the items to select are studied on page 481.

Note that the audit tests are in the context of risks of material misstatement. Risks at the individual cycle level are stated in terms of assertions. For example, there could be a material risk that sales are made to fictitious customers (occurrence), that sales are recorded in the incorrect period (timing), or that the client has not recorded revenue appropriately (accuracy). Revenue recognition would be addressed by the affected assertions; for example, sales might be classified incorrectly (classification) or deliberately overstated (accuracy).

Figure 14-2 is supported by Table 14-5 (pages 457–460), which lists the specific transaction-related audit objectives for sales along with related key controls and common tests of controls for the objectives. For those tests that the auditor chooses to conduct, such a table is a source of potential tests by audit assertion. Table 14-5 is referred to frequently throughout the section.

UNDERSTAND GENERAL CONTROLS—SALES Certain general controls, such as access controls, will vary based upon the transaction cycle. The auditor needs to determine how password changes and other forms of security have been operationalized in the cycle. For example, some systems have passwords that allow entry into all functions of a cycle, while other systems have passwords that can be tailored to individual menu items. If a company has the latter type of system, it may be able to restrict master file

Figure 14-2 | Methodology for Designing Tests of Controls for Sales

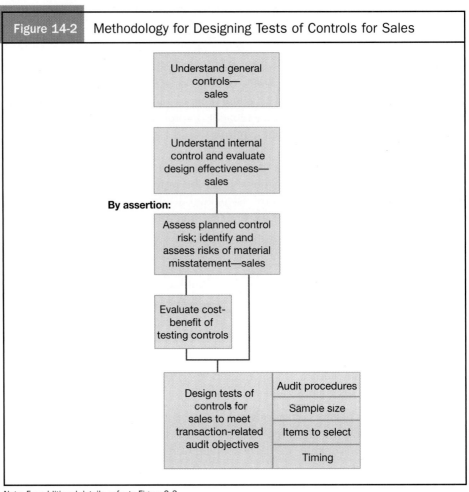

Note: For additional details, refer to Figure 9-3.

changes and credit note generation. If these restrictions were not possible, then the auditor would look for other types of controls, such as the printing and review of reports that identify master file changes that have taken place.

The nature of programs in use affects the relevance of program change controls. When a company has purchased a software package and is unable to change the package, program change controls are normally excellent, since the programs cannot be changed. If the company has custom-developed software with appropriate standards, documentation, and testing, controls over program changes are also likely to be assessed as good. When a company has informal program change procedures, poor testing, or no formal authorization of program changes, for example, program change controls are considered poor. This suggests that the auditor cannot rely on programs during the audit.

Problems with program change procedures or with access controls can have a strong impact on the auditor's assessment of control risk. The auditor may choose not to rely on any internal controls for clients with such control weaknesses.

UNDERSTAND INTERNAL CONTROL AND EVALUATE DESIGN EFFECTIVENESS—SALES

Chapter 9 discussed how auditors obtain an understanding of internal control. A typical approach for sales is to conduct interviews, review internal audit working papers, study the clients' flowcharts, prepare an internal control questionnaire, and perform walk-through tests of sales. Figure 12-2 (page 385) provided an extract of the organization chart for Hillsburg Hardware Limited. Refer to Figure 12-2 and Figure 14-5 (page 474), a flowchart for Hillsburg Hardware Limited sales and cash receipts. The auditor would develop such documentation to examine whether there are potential key controls that could be relied upon and to identify potential weaknesses in internal controls (called "evaluation of design effectiveness"), discussed further in the last section of this chapter.

Table 14-5 Summary of Transaction-Related Audit Objectives, Key Controls, and Tests of Controls for Sales

Transaction-Related Audit Objective	Key Internal Controls: Manual Systems	Key Internal Controls: Batch Systems	Key Internal Controls: Online Systems	Key Interdependent Internal Controls	Common Tests of Controls
Recorded sales are for shipments actually made to non-fictitious customers (occurrence).	• Recording of sales is supported by authorized shipping documents and approved customer purchase orders.	• Same as manual	• N/A. Likely no sales order documents.	• Review of exception reports that include unusual or large items extracted from transaction or master files.	• Examine copies of sales invoices for supporting bills of lading and customers' purchase orders. • Review the sales journal, general ledger, or trial balance for large or unusual items.*
	• Credit is approved before shipment takes place using manual review.	• Orders causing balances to exceed credit limits are printed on an exception report and are not processed for shipment.	• Orders causing balances to exceed credit limits require the entry of a supervisor password prior to shipment.†	• Orders causing balances to exceed credit limits are printed on an exception report and must be approved by a credit manager prior to shipment.	• Examine customer purchase order for credit approval. • Use test data to verify that orders causing balances to exceed credit limits are printed on exception reports. • Verify that password system has separate functionality for data entry and credit approval and that appropriate persons are assigned these functions. • Examine credit exception report for approval.
	• Sales invoices are prenumbered and properly accounted for (also satisfies completeness).	• Computer automatically generates sequential invoice numbers.	• Same as batch.	• Computer provides a report of missing invoice numbers, which are followed up by an independent person.	• Account for integrity of numerical sequence of sales invoices using block test. • Use generalized audit software to identify gaps in invoice numbers assigned.
	• N/A	• Only customer numbers existing in the customer master file are updated when they are entered.	• Sales invoices cannot be entered if the customer number is invalid.	• N/A	• Examine printouts of transactions rejected by the computer due to invalid customer numbers.†† • Observe rejection of invalid customer numbers when entered by data entry staff into online system.

Table 14-5 Summary of Transaction-Related Audit Objectives, Key Controls, and Tests of Controls for Sales (continued)

Transaction-Related Audit Objective	Key Internal Controls: Manual Systems	Key Internal Controls: Batch Systems	Key Internal Controls: Online Systems	Key Interdependent Internal Controls	Common Tests of Controls
	• Approval is required to commence selling goods to a new customer or to change semipermanent billing information.	• Approval is required to enter new customers or to change information for existing customers.	• A separate password is required to update customer master file information.	• Master file changes are printed on numerically controlled reports and reviewed by management.	• Examine master file change forms for authorization, and compare to current master file information. • Review paper customer files for credit authorization forms and approval to accept customer.
	• Monthly statements are sent to customers; complaints receive independent follow-up (also satisfies posting and summarization).	• Same as manual.	• Same as manual.	• Same as manual.	• Observe whether statements are mailed, and examine customer correspondence files.
Existing sales transactions are recorded (completeness).	• Shipping documents (i.e., bills of lading or internal shipping documents) are prenumbered and accounted for.	• Same as manual.	• Same as manual.	• Computer checks for gaps in shipping document numbers and prints a report of missing numbers for independent follow-up.	• Account for integrity of numerical sequence of shipping documents using block test. • Trace shipping documents to resultant sales invoices and entry into sales history file and accounts receivable customer master file. • Verify independent follow-up of exception reports.
Recorded sales are for the amount of goods shipped and are correctly billed and recorded (accuracy).	• Determination that prices, terms, freight, and discounts are properly authorized.	• Invoices are prepared using prices, terms, freight, and discounts established in master files.	• Same as batch.	• Exception reports are reviewed by management.	• Recompute information on sales invoices. • Examine approved computer printout of unit selling prices and compare to invoice details.†
	• Shipping documents are matched to invoices. • Invoices are prepared using prices from an approved price list.	• Same as manual. • Approved unit selling prices are entered into the master files and used for all sales.	• Shipping details are automatically used as the invoicing source. • Same as batch.		• Trace details on sales invoices to shipping documents, price lists, and customers' purchase orders. • Compare inventory selling prices in master files to approved master file change forms and invoice details.

Transaction-Related Audit Objective	Key Internal Controls: Manual Systems	Key Internal Controls: Batch Systems	Key Internal Controls: Online Systems	Key Interdependent Internal Controls	Common Tests of Controls
		• Batch totals are compared with computer summary reports.	• Invoice calculations (extensions, additions, taxes) are automatically calculated.		• Examine file of batch totals for initials of data control clerk; compare totals to summary reports.† • Prepare test data and run through invoicing program to ensure program is functioning as required.
Sales transactions are classified to the correct account (classification).	• Adequate chart of accounts is used. • Internal review and verification is completed (also satisfies timing).	• Invoices can be posted only to valid customer accounts. • Posting is done automatically to sales account based upon batch totals.	• Invoices can only be prepared for valid customer accounts. • Posting is done automatically to sales account based upon periodic totals.	• Management reviews exception reports of unusual customer data.	• Review customer master file listing for adequacy. • Examine documents supporting sales transactions for proper classification. • Examine indication of internal verification on affected documents. • Use test data to verify that transactions are posted to correct general ledger accounts or conduct manual walk-through of transactions through programs.
Sales transactions are updated correctly to the customer master file, and the posting to the general ledger summed these transactions correctly (posting and summarization).	• Transactions are summarized on a timely basis for posting to the general ledger. • Subsidiary accounts receivable records are periodically balanced to the general ledger.	• Customer master file is periodically printed for independent review. • Customer master file totals are compared with general ledger balance monthly, and differences are investigated.	• Same as batch. • Same as batch.	• Aged accounts receivable trial balances are reviewed for reasonableness. • Run-to-run totals are compared and reconciled (i.e., previous monthly accounts receivable total plus transactions reconciles to current month totals).	• Examine initials on general ledger account reconciliation indicating comparison. • Trace sales journal entries to copies of sales orders, sales invoices, and shipping documents. • Foot journals, and trace postings to general ledger and accounts receivable master files.

Table 14-5 Summary of Transaction-Related Audit Objectives, Key Controls, and Tests of Controls for Sales (continued)

Transaction-Related Audit Objective	Key Internal Controls: Manual Systems	Key Internal Controls: Batch Systems	Key Internal Controls: Online Systems	Key Interdependent Internal Controls	Common Tests of Controls
					• Use generalized audit software to add up the outstanding accounts receivable transactions and the balances in the accounts receivable master file. Compare both independent totals with the accounts receivable general ledger balance.
Sales are recorded on the correct dates (timing).	• Procedures requiring billing and recording of sales on a daily basis are performed as close to time of occurrence as possible.	• Same as manual. • System checks reasonableness of date entered.	• Same as manual. • System checks reasonableness of date entered.	• Management reviews sales and cost of sales analytical reports for reasonableness.	• Compare dates of recorded sales transactions with dates on shipping records. • Examine documents for unbilled shipments and unrecorded sales. • Verify management walk-through of analytical reports.

* This analytical procedure can also apply to other objectives, including completeness, accuracy, and timing.
† This control could also be considered an interdependent control, since both a computer-based and personal action are required.
†† This control would be tested on many audits by using the computer.

ASSESS PLANNED CONTROL RISK; IDENTIFY AND ASSESS RISKS OF MATERIAL MIS-STATEMENT—SALES The auditor uses the information obtained in understanding and evaluating design effectiveness of internal control to assess control risk. There are four essential steps to this assessment, all of which were discussed in Chapter 9.

- First, the auditor needs a framework for assessing control risk. The framework for all classes of transactions is the risks associated with the six transaction-related audit objectives. For sales, the audit objectives are shown for Hillsburg Hardware in Figure 14-6 on page 475. These six objectives are the same for every audit of sales. The auditor would include in the risk assessment process any significant risks identified earlier in the audit, or as required by auditing standards. For example, the auditor is required to consider revenue recognition as a significant risk, and document controls with respect to revenue recognition. The auditor will also consider risks over financial statement presentation and disclosure with respect to sales.
- Second, the auditor must identify the key internal controls and weaknesses for sales. These are also shown in Figure 14-6. The controls and weaknesses will be different for every audit.
- After identifying the controls and weaknesses, the auditor relates them to the objectives and cross-references them to supporting working papers. This is also shown in Figure 14-6 with Ws and Cs in appropriate columns.
- Finally, the auditor assesses control risk for each objective by evaluating the controls and weaknesses for each objective. This step is a critical one because it affects the auditor's decisions about the risks of material misstatement, and both tests of controls and substantive tests—it is a highly subjective decision. The bottom of Figure 14-6 shows the auditor's conclusions for Hillsburg Hardware Limited.

After assessing control risk, the auditor decides upon the risk of material misstatement for each identified risk. Where there is a risk of material misstatement, the auditor is required to conduct substantive tests in addition to control tests (if control tests are conducted), affecting the design of the audit program.

The section that follows discusses the key control activities for sales. A knowledge of these control activities is important for identifying the key controls and weaknesses for sales, which is the second step in assessing control risk.

Adequate separation of duties Proper separation of duties helps prevent various types of misstatements, both intentional and unintentional. To prevent fraud, it is important that anyone responsible for inputting sales and cash receipts transaction information into the computer be denied access to cash. It is also desirable to separate the credit-granting functions from the sales function, since credit checks are intended to offset the natural tendency of sales personnel to optimize volume even at the expense of high bad-debt write-offs. It is equally desirable that personnel responsible for doing internal comparisons are independent of those entering the original data. For example, comparison of batch control totals to summary reports and comparison of customer master file totals to the general ledger balance should be done by someone independent of those who input sales and cash receipt transactions.

Proper authorization The auditor is concerned about authorization at three key points: credit must be properly authorized before a sale takes place; goods should be shipped only after proper authorization; and prices, including base terms, freight, and discounts, must be authorized. The first two controls are meant to prevent the loss of company assets by shipping to fictitious customers or those who will fail to pay for the goods. Price authorization is meant to make sure the sale is billed at the price set by company policy.

Adequate documents and records Since each company has a unique system of originating, processing, and recording transactions, it may be difficult to evaluate whether its procedures are designed for maximum control; nevertheless, adequate record-keeping procedures must exist before most of the transaction-related audit objectives can be met. Some companies, for example, automatically prepare a multicopy

"Loans" and Bonuses

It is simple enough. With access to cash and accounting records, "borrow" some money from your employer until you can repay it, then pay it back. No one needs to know, least of all the customer, whose money has been borrowed to pay someone else's account (called "lapping").

This is what an internal auditor found when doing a routine audit at a retail location. The store manager was away when a customer asked a clerk about a discrepancy on her statement. Her payment had not been recorded correctly. The internal auditor stepped in to help the clerk and said he would investigate the difference. This investigation lead to the discovery of many more errors, and the manager admitted to a $20,000 theft when confronted with the discrepancies in the accounting records. The retailer provided employees the option to borrow money, so this theft was hard to consider as a "loan."

Some employees inflate sales so that they can obtain a bonus or a higher commission on their salary, hoping that the actual sales will be forthcoming. Perhaps this was the motivation for a trader at the London, U.K., location of the Toronto-Dominion Bank, who overstated the value of financial instruments that he traded by $96 million. Discovery of this overstatement resulted in the bank writing down the value of certain credit index swaps, reducing its earnings.

Auditors can play an important role in identifying potential risks of misstatement by pointing out to management where segregation of duties is absent, providing the potential for cash theft or misstatement of revenue.

Sources: 1. Jacka, J. Mike, "Roundtable," *Internal Auditor Journal*, August 2004, p. 91-92. 2. Toronto Star Wire Services, "U. K. Trader blamed for $96M hit to TD earnings," *Toronto Star*, July 5, 2008, p. B2.

prenumbered sales invoice at the time a customer order is received. Copies of this document are used to approve credit, authorize shipment, record the number of units shipped, and bill customers. Under this system, there is almost no chance of the failure to bill a customer if all invoices are accounted for periodically. Under a different system, in which the sales invoice is prepared only after a shipment has been made, the likelihood of failure to bill a customer is high unless some compensating control exists.

Prenumbered documents An important characteristic of documents for sales is the use of prenumbering, which is meant to prevent both the failure to bill or record sales and the occurrence of duplicate billings and recording thereof. Of course, it does not do much good to have prenumbered documents unless they are properly accounted for. An example of the use of this control is the filing, by a billing clerk, of a copy of all shipping documents in sequential order after each shipment is billed, with someone else periodically accounting for all numbers and investigating the reason for any missing documents. Another example is programming the computer to prepare a listing of unused numbers at month's end with follow-up by appropriate personnel.

Mailing of monthly statements The mailing of monthly statements by someone who has no responsibility for handling cash or preparing the sales and accounts receivable records is a useful control because it encourages a response from customers if the balance is improperly stated. For maximum effectiveness, all disagreements about the balance in the account should be directed to a designated person who has no responsibility for handling cash or recording sales or accounts receivable.

Internal verification procedures The use of independent persons or software for checking the processing and recording of sales transactions is essential for fulfilling each of the six transaction-related audit objectives. Examples of these procedures include accounting for the numerical sequence of prenumbered documents, checking the accuracy of document preparation, and reviewing transactions for unusual or incorrect items. Examples include review of balances exceeding credit limits, approval of master file change reports, and examination of sales statistics.

EVALUATE COST BENEFIT OF TESTING CONTROLS After the auditor has identified the key internal controls and weaknesses and assessed risks, he or she decides whether substantive tests will be reduced sufficiently to justify the cost of performing tests of controls. Auditors make this decision with the assistance of a matrix such as the one illustrated in Figure 14-6 on page 475.

Figure 14-2 and Table 14-5 are referred to during the subsequent discussion. Figure 14-2 (page 456) shows the methodology for designing tests of controls for sales. Table 14-5 (pages 457–460) provides detailed examples used throughout the chapter.

Transaction-related audit objectives (column 1) The **transaction-related audit objectives in the sales and collection cycle** included in Table 14-5 are derived from the framework developed in Chapters 5 and 9. Although certain internal controls satisfy more than one objective, it is desirable to consider each objective separately to facilitate a better assessment of control risk.

Key internal controls (columns 2 through 5) The internal controls for sales are designed to achieve the six transaction-related audit objectives discussed in Chapters 5 and 9. If the controls necessary to satisfy any one of the objectives are inadequate, the likelihood of misstatements related to that objective is increased, regardless of the controls for the other objectives. The methodology for determining existing controls was studied in Chapter 9.

The source of the controls in these columns is a list of potential key controls that would be included in a control risk matrix such as the one illustrated in Figure 14-6 (see page 475). A control may satisfy more than one audit objective if there is more than one C for that control on the control risk matrix.

Common tests of controls (column 6) For each internal control on which the auditor chooses to rely, he or she designs a **test of control in the sales and collection cycle** to verify its effectiveness. Recall that a test of control in the sales and collection cycle is an audit procedure performed to determine the effectiveness of both the design and operation of a specific internal control. Tests of controls include audit procedures testing for monetary errors or fraud and other irregularities to determine whether the six transaction-related audit objectives (or other objectives) have been satisfied for each class of transaction in the sales and collection cycle. Observe that the tests of controls in column 6 in Table 14-5 relate directly to the internal controls.

DESIGN TESTS OF CONTROLS FOR SALES

For each control on which the auditor plans to rely to reduce assessed control risk, he or she must design one or more tests of controls to verify its effectiveness. In most audits, it is relatively easy to determine the nature of the test of the control from the nature of the control. For example, if the internal control is having the sales system identify orders that cause customers to go over their credit limit and having the orders printed for subsequent approval, the test of control would include verifying that the system is functioning as designed and examining the credit exception report for approval.

The last column in Table 14-5 shows examples of tests of control for key internal controls in columns 2 through 5. For example, the first key internal control is "Recording of sales is supported by authorized shipping documents and approved customer purchase orders." The test of control is "Examine copies of sales invoices for supporting bills of lading and customers' purchase orders." For this test, it is important that the auditor start with sales invoices and examine documents in support of the sales invoices rather than go in the opposite direction. If the auditor traced from shipping documents to sales invoices, it would be a test of completeness. Direction of tests is discussed further on page 465.

A common test of control for sales is accounting for a sequence of various types of documents (such as duplicate sales invoices selected from the sales journal), watching for omitted and duplicate numbers or invoices outside the normal sequence; this is called a "block test." This test simultaneously provides evidence of both the existence and completeness objectives. Should the auditor choose to use generalized audit software, then a gap test can be conducted by scanning the entire transaction history file and identifying any gaps in the numeric sequence.

The appropriate tests of controls for separation of duties are ordinarily restricted to the auditor's observations of activities and discussions with personnel. For example, it is possible to observe whether the billing clerk has access to cash when opening incoming mail or depositing cash. It is usually also necessary to ask personnel what their responsibilities are and if there are any circumstances where their responsibilities are different from the normal policy. For example, the employee responsible for billing customers may state that he or she does not have access to cash. Future discussion may elicit that when the cashier is on vacation, that person takes over the cashier's duties. Allocation of password functionality should also be reviewed to ensure that individuals have not been assigned functions that are incompatible.

Several of the tests of controls in Table 14–5 can be performed using test data. For example, one of the key internal controls to prevent fraudulent or fictitious transactions is the inclusion of procedures to ensure that only approved information was entered into the customer master files. If a non-existent customer number is entered into the computer, it would be rejected. The auditor can test this control by attempting to enter non-existent customer numbers into the computer after making sure that the computer control is in operation.

DUAL-PURPOSE OR WEAKNESS INVESTIGATION TESTS Some of the procedures listed in Table 14-5 are performed on every audit regardless of the circumstances, whereas others are dependent on the adequacy of the controls and the results of the tests of controls. Tests that can be used to quantify the extent of potential error have two purposes. They can be used as dual-purpose tests (for assessing control risk and also as a substantive test) or as **weakness investigation tests** since they can quantify the potential dollar effect of monetary errors or fraud and other irregularities due to control weaknesses. The following sections describe potential risks or misstatements that could occur, by assertion. Then, specific audit tests to investigate or quantify the potential misstatement are discussed.

Recorded sales occurred For this objective, the auditor is concerned with the possibility of three types of misstatements: sales being included in the journals for which no shipment was made, sales recorded more than once, and shipments being made to non-existent customers and recorded as sales. The first two types of misstatements can be intentional or unintentional; the last type is always intentional. As might be imagined, the inclusion of fraudulent sales is rare. The potential consequences are significant because they lead to an overstatement of assets and income.

There is an important difference between finding intentional and unintentional overstatements of sales. An unintentional overstatement normally also results in a clear overstatement of accounts receivable, which can often be easily found through confirmation procedures. In fraud, the perpetrator will attempt to conceal the overstatement, making it more difficult for auditors to find. Substantive tests of transactions may be necessary to discover overstated sales in these circumstances.

The appropriate dual-purpose tests for testing the occurrence objective depend on where the auditor believes the misstatements are likely to take place. Many auditors do tests for the occurrence objective only if they believe that a control weakness exists so that the potential error can be quantified; therefore, the nature of the tests depends on the nature of the potential misstatement as follows.

Recorded sale for which there was no shipment The auditor can trace from selected entries in the sales journal to make sure that related copies of the shipping and other supporting documents exist. If the auditor is concerned about the possibility of a fictitious duplicate copy of a shipping document, it may be necessary to trace the amounts to the perpetual inventory records as a test of whether inventory was reduced. This would not be possible for paperless systems, which require greater reliance on programmed controls. Paperless systems are discussed further in Chapter 18.

Sale recorded more than once Duplicate sales can be determined by reviewing a numerically sorted list of recorded sales transactions for duplicate invoice or shipping

Weakness investigation tests—
tests conducted to determine whether a material error or material misstatement could occur due to a control weakness.

document numbers or by running generalized audit software tests to identify all duplicated numbers.

Shipment made to non-existent customers This type of fraud normally occurs only when the person recording sales is also in a position to authorize shipments or alter master file data. When internal controls are weak, it is difficult to detect fictitious shipments.

Another effective approach to detecting the three types of misstatements of sales transactions discussed above is to trace the credit in the accounts receivable master file to its source. If the receivable was actually collected in cash or the goods were returned, there must originally have been a sale. If the credit was for a bad-debt charge-off or a credit memo or if the account was still unpaid at the time of the audit, intensive follow-up by examining shipping and customer order documents is required, since each of these could indicate an inappropriate sales transaction.

It should be kept in mind that the ordinary audit is not primarily intended to detect fraud unless the effect on the financial statements is material. Dual-purpose tests to quantify potential errors should be necessary only if the auditor is concerned about the occurrence of fraud or material error due to inadequate controls.

Existing sales transactions are recorded In many audits, the auditor is not as concerned about the completeness objective on the grounds that overstatements of assets and income are a greater concern in the audit of sales transactions than their understatement. If there are inadequate controls, which is likely if the client does no independent internal matching between shipping documents and sales transactions to the sales journal, substantive procedures will be necessary.

An effective procedure to test for unbilled shipments is tracing selected shipping documents from a file in the shipping department to related duplicate sales invoices and the sales journal. To conduct a meaningful test using this procedure, the auditor must be confident that all shipping documents are included in the sample population. This can be done by accounting for a numerical sequence of the documents.

Direction of tests It is important that auditors understand the difference between tracing from source documents to the journals and tracing from the journals back to supporting documents. The former is a test for omitted transactions (completeness objective), whereas the latter is a test for non-existent transactions (occurrence objective).

In testing for the occurrence objective, the starting point is the journal. A sample of invoice numbers is selected from the journal and traced to duplicate sales invoices, shipping documents, and customer orders. In testing for the completeness objective, the likely starting point is the shipping document. A sample of shipping documents is selected and traced to duplicate sales invoices and the sales journal as a test of omissions.

When designing audit procedures for the occurrence and completeness objectives, the starting point for tracing the document is essential. This is referred to as the direction of tests. For example, if the auditor is concerned about the occurrence objective but traces in the wrong direction (from shipping documents to the journals), a serious audit deficiency exists. The direction of the tests is illustrated in Figure 14-3 on the next page.

When testing for the other five transaction-related audit objectives, the direction of tests is usually not relevant. For example, the accuracy of sales transactions can be tested by tracing from a duplicate sales invoice to a shipping document, or vice versa.

Recorded sales are accurately recorded The accurate recording of sales transactions concerns shipping the amount of goods ordered, accurately billing for the amount of goods shipped, and accurately recording the amount billed in the accounting records. Reperformance to ensure the accuracy of each of these aspects is ordinarily conducted in every audit.

Typical reperformance tests include recomputing information in the accounting records to verify whether it is proper. A common approach is to start with entries in the sales journal and compare the total of selected transactions with customer master

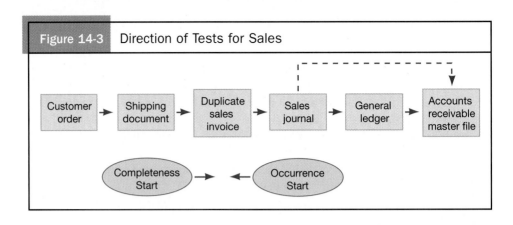

Figure 14-3 Direction of Tests for Sales

file totals and duplicate sales invoices. Prices on the duplicate sales invoices are normally compared with an approved price list, extensions and footings are recomputed, and the details listed on the invoices are compared with shipping records for description, quantity, and customer identification. Where reliance is placed on computer-based systems to perform mathematical calculations, the auditor may use test data to ensure that these calculations are properly performed. Frequently, customer purchase orders are also examined for the same information.

The comparison of tests of controls and substantive procedures for the accuracy objective is a good example of how audit time can be saved when effective internal controls exist. In manual systems, the test of controls for this objective takes minimal time because it involves examining only an initial or other evidence of internal verification. The test data approach can also be effective, since only a small number of transactions need be processed to verify that calculations are correct. As the sample size for substantive procedures can be reduced if this control is effective, a significant saving will result from performing the test of controls due to its lower cost.

Recorded sales are properly classified Charging the correct general ledger account is less of a problem in sales than in some other transaction cycles, but it is still of some concern. When there are cash and credit sales, it is important not to debit accounts receivable for a cash sale or to credit sales for collection of a receivable. It is also important not to classify sales of operating assets, such as buildings, as sales. For those companies using more than one sales classification, such as companies issuing segmented earnings statements, proper classification is essential.

It is common to test sales for proper classification as part of testing for accuracy. The auditor examines supporting documents to determine the proper classification of a given transaction and compares this with the actual account in which it is recorded. Most computer-based systems, whether batch or online, are set to post to the appropriate sales general ledger account automatically. The auditor then must determine the controls in place to ensure that unusual transactions are recorded to the correct account.

Sales transactions are properly updated in the customer master file and correctly summarized The proper inclusion of all sales transactions in the customer master file is essential because the accuracy of these records affects the client's ability to collect outstanding receivables. Similarly, the sales transactions must be correctly totalled and posted to the general ledger if the financial statements are to be correct. In every audit, it is necessary to perform some clerical accuracy tests by footing the journals and tracing the totals and details to the general ledger and the master files to check whether there are intentional or unintentional misstatements in the processing of sales transactions. For most large systems, this is accomplished using generalized audit software, whereby the auditor obtains the client data files and performs mechanical accuracy testing (such as footings or other calculations).

The extent of such tests is affected by the quality of the internal controls. Tracing individual transactions to a posting source is typically done as part of fulfilling other transaction-related audit objectives, but footing the sales journal and tracing the totals to the general ledger is done as a separate procedure.

The distinction between posting and summarization and other transaction-related audit objectives is that posting and summarization includes footing journals, transaction or open item files, master file records, and ledgers, and tracing from one to the other. Whenever footing and comparisons are restricted to these sources, the process is posting and summarization. In contrast, accuracy involves comparing documents with each other or with journals and data file records. To illustrate, comparing a duplicate sales invoice with either the sales journal or master file entry is an accuracy objective procedure. Tracing a sales transaction from a sales history file to an open item file and balancing the open item file to the customer master file are part of posting and summarization procedures.

Sales are recorded on the correct dates It is important that sales are billed and recorded as soon after shipment takes place as possible to prevent the unintentional omission of transactions from the records and to make sure sales are recorded in the proper period. At the same time that tests of controls with respect to the accuracy objective are being performed, it is common to compare the date on selected bills of lading or other shipping documents with the date on related duplicate sales invoices and the sales journal or sales history file. Significant differences indicate a potential cut-off problem. Many computer systems require that the shipping date match the invoice date or that the invoice date be within a specified time of the current date.

Revenue recognition and other significant risks The auditor will determine whether there are controls over revenue recognition, such as selection of appropriate recognition methods, and monitoring of controls over the other assertions that affect revenue recognition. Results of techniques described above, such as review of journal entries and tests of timing and accuracy, would be used to evaluate whether weaknesses exist here. The auditor would evaluate the results of the overall testing process for sales to determine whether further tests are needed.

SUMMARY OF METHODOLOGY FOR SALES It is essential to understand the relationships among the columns in Table 14-5. The first column includes the six transaction-related audit objectives. The general objectives are the same for any class of transactions, but the specific objectives vary for sales, cash receipts, and all other classes of transactions. Columns 2 through 5 list one or more illustrative internal controls for each transaction-related audit objective for different types of systems, distinguishing among manual, batch, and online. The fifth column provides examples of **interdependent controls**. These controls require both automated and manual components to satisfy the audit objective. Many of these controls are supervisory controls, whereby a manager or supervisor would review an exception report or a monthly report for unusual information, and then conduct follow-up activities.

It is essential that any given control be related to one or more risks or specific objective(s). A test of control is meaningless unless it tests a specific objective. The table contains at least one test of control in column 6 for internal controls identified in columns 2 through 5.

DESIGN- AND PERFORMANCE-FORMAT AUDIT PROCEDURES The information presented in Table 14-5 is in a "**design format**" intended to help auditors design audit programs that satisfy the transaction-related audit objectives in a given set of circumstances. If certain objectives are important in a given audit or when the controls are different for different clients, the methodology helps the auditor design an effective and efficient audit program.

After the appropriate audit procedures for a given set of circumstances have been designed, they must be performed. It is likely to be inefficient to do the audit procedures as they are stated in the design format of Table 14-5. In converting from a design to a **performance format**, procedures are combined and organized into the

Interdependent controls—
controls that require both programmed and manual components to satisfy an audit objective.

Design format audit program—
the audit procedures resulting from the auditor's decisions about the appropriate audit procedures for each audit objective; this is used to prepare a performance format audit program

Performance format audit program—the audit procedures for a class of transactions organized in the format that they will be performed; prepared from a design format audit program.

concept check

C14-4 Explain the impact of client business risk on the sales and collection cycle. Include the impact on revenue recognition.

C14-5 How do general controls over access rights affect the sales cycle?

C14-6 What are the three types of misstatements that are associated with the oc-currence objective for sales?

sequence in which they will be performed. This will allow the auditor to accomplish the following:

- Eliminate duplicate procedures.
- Make sure that when a given document is examined, all procedures to be performed on that document are done at that time.
- Do the procedures in the most effective order. For example, by footing the journal and reviewing the journal for unusual items first, the auditor gains a better perspective on doing the detailed tests.

The process of converting from a design to a performance format is illustrated for the Hillsburg Hardware Limited case application. The design format is shown in Table 14-7 on pages 477–478. The performance format is on page 480 in Figure 14-8.

③ Methodology for Control Testing in the Remainder of the Cycle

Sales Returns and Allowances

The major risk for sales returns is that material sales returns could occur after the year end. The auditor would then need to test that these returns were matched to the correct period sales. Sales allowances (also called "volume rebates") are rebates or discounts that customers receive if they achieve a particular sales volume. The risk with such amounts is that material sales allowances could be matched to the incorrect period, resulting in an overstatement of sales.

The transaction-related audit objectives and the client's methods of controlling misstatements are essentially the same for processing credit memos for sales returns and allowances as those described for sales, with two important differences. The first relates to materiality. In many instances, sales returns and allowances are so immaterial that they can be ignored in the audit altogether. The second major difference

auditing in action 14-2
Sales Can Be Returned (and Come Back to Haunt You)

Significant sales returns can occur due to product defects or because the client shipped unwanted product (known as "channel stuffing"). Evaluating the completeness of sales returns is an important part of the financial statement audit process. Bausch & Lomb experienced significant returns due to both product defects and channel stuffing.

Late in 1993, Bausch & Lomb, Inc., informed its independent distributors that they would have to purchase up to two years' inventory of contact lenses. The lenses had to be purchased before December 24, when Bausch & Lomb closed its books. The distributors claimed that their oral agreements with Bausch & Lomb meant they would not have to pay for the lenses until they were sold. If these agreements existed, the shipments of lenses should not have been recognized as sales.

Ten months after the December sales, most of the lenses had not been sold and Bausch & Lomb had collected less than 15 percent of the accounts receivable from the sales. In October 1994, Bausch & Lomb agreed to take back three-quarters of the inventory that had been shipped the previous December, resulting in an unexpected charge to quarterly earnings.

In 2006, Bausch & Lomb was forced to recall all of its ReNu with MoistureLoc contact lens solution because of a reported association with eye infections. Although the company's CEO estimated that costs associated with the recall would be in the $50 million to $70 million range, an analyst estimated that the potential liability from the recall could rise to the $500 million to $1 billion level.

Source: Adapted from: 1. Maremont, Mark, "Numbers game at Bausch & Lomb?", *Business Week*, December 19, 1994, p. 108–110. 2. Lebowitz, Jack D. and Vadim A. Mzhen, "Worldwide recall of Bausch and Lomb contact lens MoistureLoc solution," May 19, 2006, www.marylandaccidentlawblog.com/2006/05/worldwide_recall_of_bausch_and_1.html, Accessed: July 26, 2009.

relates to emphasis on objectives. For sales returns and allowances, the primary emphasis is normally on testing the existence of recorded transactions as a means of uncovering any diversion of cash from the collection of accounts receivable that has been covered up by a fictitious sales return or allowance.

Although the emphasis for the audit of sales returns and allowances is often on testing the existence of recorded transactions, the completeness objective is the most important. Unrecorded sales returns and allowances can be material and can be used by a company's management to overstate net income, as illustrated in Auditing in Action 14-2. However, because the objectives and methodology for auditing sales returns and allowances are essentially the same as for sales, we will not include a detailed study of the area.

Internal Controls and Tests of Controls for Cash Receipts

The most at-risk assertion for cash receipts is also completeness—has all cash been recorded in the accounts and not been stolen? The same methodology used for designing tests of controls over sales transactions is used for designing tests of controls over cash receipts. Cash receipts tests of controls audit procedures are developed around the same framework used for sales; that is, given the transaction-related audit objectives, key internal controls for each objective are determined so that control risk and the risks of material misstatement can be evaluated. Then, tests of controls are developed for each control to be tested to ensure the control is working and to determine monetary errors for each objective. As in all other audit areas, the tests of controls depend on the controls the auditor has identified to reduce the assessed level of control risk.

Key internal controls and common tests of controls to satisfy each of the internal control objectives for cash receipts are listed in Table 14-6 on the next page. This summary is similar to the previous one for sales. The differences are that key internal controls are shown in one column, rather then spread across four columns, and the tests of controls are split into two columns. The first column, of tests of controls, is controls that are used to detect whether controls have been followed (termed "general tests of controls"). The second column of tests of controls, used for quantification of potential errors, could serve as dual-purpose tests.

The detailed discussion of the internal controls and tests of controls that was included for the audit of sales is not included for cash receipts. Instead, the audit procedures that are most likely to be misunderstood are explained in more detail.

An essential part of the auditor's responsibility in auditing cash receipts is identification of weaknesses in internal control that increase the likelihood of fraud. In expanding on Table 14-6, the emphasis will be on those audit procedures that are designed primarily for the discovery of fraud.

DETERMINE WHETHER CASH RECEIVED WAS RECORDED The most difficult type of cash defalcation for the auditor to detect is that which occurs before the cash is recorded in the cash receipts journal or other cash listing, especially if the sale and cash receipt are recorded simultaneously. For example, if a grocery store clerk takes cash and intentionally fails to register the receipt of cash on the cash register, it is extremely difficult to discover the theft. To prevent this type of fraud, internal controls such as those included in the third objective in Table 14-6 are implemented by many companies. The type of control will, of course, depend on the type of business. For example, the controls for a retail store in which the cash is received by the same person who sells the merchandise and rings up the cash receipts (termed "point-of-sale" or "POS" systems) should be different from the controls for a company in which all receipts are received through the mail several weeks after the sales have taken place. In a point-of-sale system, the sale must be recorded for the customer to receive a receipt. This may also remove the item from inventory, but, most important, it provides a control total that must be reconciled to the total cash (including credit card or debit card amounts) that is received during the day.

Table 14-6

Table 14-6 Summary of Transaction-Related Audit Objectives, Key Controls, and Tests of Controls for Cash Receipts

Transaction-Related Audit Objective	Key Internal Control	General Tests of Controls	Quantitative/Dual-Purpose Tests of Controls
Recorded cash receipts are for funds actually received by the company (occurrence).	Separation of duties between handling cash and record keeping or data entry.	Observe separation of duties.	Review the cash receipts journal, general ledger, and accounts receivable master file or trial balance for large and unusual amounts.*
	Independent reconciliation or review of bank accounts.	Observe independent reconciliation of bank account.	Trace from cash receipts listing to duplicate deposit slip and bank statements.
Cash received is recorded in the cash receipts journal (completeness).	Separation of duties between handling cash and record keeping.	Discussion with personnel and observation.	Trace from remittances or prelisting to duplicate bank deposit slip and cash receipts journal.
	Use of remittance advices or a prelisting of cash.	As above.	Review reconciliation reports of credit card or electronic funds transfer receipts.
	Immediate endorsement of incoming cheques.	Observe immediate endorsement of incoming cheques.	
	Internal verification of the recording of cash receipts.	Examine indication of internal verification.	
	Regular monthly statements to customers.	Observe whether monthly statements are sent to customers.	
Cash receipts are deposited and recorded at the amount received (accuracy).	Approval of cash discounts.	Examine remittance advices for proper approval.	Examine remittance advices and sales invoices to determine whether discounts allowed are consistent with company policy.
	Regular reconciliation of bank accounts.	Review monthly bank reconciliations.	
	Comparison of batch totals with duplicate deposit slips and computer summary reports.	Examine file of batch totals for initials of data control clerk; compare totals with summary reports.	
Cash receipts are properly classified (classification).	Use of adequate chart of accounts or automatic posting to specified accounts.	Review chart of accounts and computer-assigned posting accounts.	Examine documents supporting cash receipts for proper classification.
Cash receipts are properly included in the customer master file and are correctly summarized (posting and summarization).	Regular monthly statements to customers.	Observe whether statements are mailed.	Foot journals, and trace postings to general ledger and accounts receivable master file.
	Use of properly approved master file change forms.	Examine master file change forms for proper authorization.	
	Comparison of customer master file or aged accounts receivable trial balance totals with general ledger balance.	Examine documentation verifying that comparison was completed.	
Cash receipts are recorded on correct dates (timing).	Procedure requiring recording of cash receipts on a daily basis.	Observe unrecorded cash at any point in time.	Compare dates of deposits with dates in the cash receipts journal.

* This analytical procedure can also apply to other objectives, including completeness, accuracy, and timing.

Proof of cash receipts—an audit procedure to test whether all recorded cash receipts have been deposited in the bank account by reconciling the total cash receipts recorded in the cash receipts journal for a given period with the actual deposits made to the bank.

It is normal practice to trace from prenumbered remittance advices, prelists of cash receipts, or the duplicate bank deposit slip to the cash receipts journal and subsidiary accounts receivable records as a test of the recording of actual cash received. This test will be effective only if the cash details were listed on a cash register tape or some other prelisting at the time the cash was received.

PREPARE PROOF OF CASH RECEIPTS A useful audit procedure to test whether all recorded cash receipts have been deposited in the bank account is a **proof of cash receipts**.

In this test, the total cash receipts recorded in the cash receipts data files for a given period, such as a month, are reconciled with the actual deposits made to the bank during the same period. There may be a difference in the two due to deposits in transit and other items, but the amounts can be reconciled and compared. The procedure cannot detect cash receipts that have not been recorded in the journals or time lags in making deposits, but it can help uncover recorded cash receipts that have not been deposited, unrecorded deposits, unrecorded loans, bank loans deposited directly into the bank account, and similar misstatements. A proof of cash receipts and cash disbursements is illustrated in Chapter 16 on page 554. This somewhat time-consuming procedure is ordinarily used only when controls are weak. In rare instances in which controls are extremely weak, the period covered by the proof of cash receipts may be the entire year.

TEST TO DISCOVER LAPPING OF ACCOUNTS RECEIVABLE **Lapping of accounts receivable**, which is a common type of defalcation, is the postponement of entries for the collection of receivables to conceal an existing cash shortage. The defalcation is perpetrated by a person who handles cash receipts and then enters them into the computer system. He or she takes the cash, defers recording the cash receipts from one customer, and covers the shortages with the receipts of another customer. These, in turn, are covered from the receipts of a third customer a few days later. The employee must continue to cover the shortage through repeated lapping, replace the stolen money, or find another way to conceal the shortage.

> **Lapping of accounts receivable**—the postponement of entries for the collection of receivables to conceal an existing cash shortage; a common type of defalcation.

This defalcation can be prevented by separation of duties. It can be detected by comparing the name, amount, and dates shown on remittance advices with cash receipts journal entries and related duplicate deposit slips. Since the procedure is relatively time-consuming, it is ordinarily performed only when there is a specific concern with potential defalcation because of a weakness in internal control.

Audit Tests for Uncollectible Accounts

The major risk with uncollectible accounts is that write-offs are used to conceal theft of cash. Occurrence of recorded write-offs is the most important transaction-related audit objective that the auditor should keep in mind in the verification of the write-off of individual uncollectible accounts. A major concern in testing accounts charged off as uncollectible is the possibility of the client covering up a defalcation by charging off accounts receivable that have already been collected. The major control for preventing this type of misstatement is proper authorization of the write-off of uncollectible accounts by a designated level of management only after a thorough investigation of the reason the customer has not paid.

Normally, verification of the accounts charged off takes relatively little time. A typical procedure is the examination of approvals by the appropriate person. For a sample of accounts charged off, it is also usually necessary for the auditor to examine correspondence in the client's files establishing the uncollectability of the accounts. In some cases, the auditor will also examine credit reports such as those provided by Dun & Bradstreet Canada Limited (see **www.dnb.ca**) or Equifax (see **www.equifax.com/home/en_ca**). After the auditor has concluded that the accounts charged off by general journal entries are proper, selected items should be traced to listings of the accounts receivable master file or to a transactions file as a test of the records.

Additional Internal Controls over Account Balances

The preceding discussion emphasized internal controls and tests of controls for the five classes of transactions that affect account balances in the sales and collection cycle. If the internal controls for these classes of transactions are determined to be effective and the related tests of controls support the conclusions, the likelihood of misstatements in the financial statements is reduced.

The auditor would use the results of these tests to assess the likelihood of material misstatement in revenue recognition and to determine whether additional testing is required with respect to financial statement disclosure of the sales and accounts receivable accounts.

In addition, there may be internal controls directly related to account balances that have not been identified or tested as a part of tests of controls. For the sales and collection cycle, these are most likely to affect three balance-related audit objectives: valuation, rights and obligations, and presentation and disclosure.

Valuation is an essential balance-related audit objective for accounts receivable because collectability of receivables is often a major financial statement item and has been an issue in a number of accountants' liability cases. It is, therefore, common for inherent risk to be high for the valuation objective.

Several controls are common for the valuation objective. One that has already been discussed is credit approval by an appropriate person. A second is the preparation of a periodic aged accounts receivable trial balance for review and follow-up by appropriate management personnel. A third control is a policy of charging off uncollectible accounts when they are no longer likely to be collected.

Rights and obligations and presentation and disclosure are rarely a significant problem for accounts receivable. Therefore, employing competent accounting personnel is usually sufficient control for these two balance-related audit objectives.

Effect of Results of Tests of Controls

The results of the tests of controls have a significant effect on the remainder of the audit, especially on the tests of details of balances part of substantive procedures. The parts of the audit most affected by the tests of controls for the sales and collection cycle are the balances in accounts receivable, cash, bad-debt expense, and allowance for doubtful accounts. Furthermore, if the results of the control tests are unsatisfactory, it is necessary to do additional substantive testing for the propriety of sales, sales returns and allowances, charge-off of uncollectible accounts, and processing of cash receipts.

At the completion of the tests of controls, it is essential to analyze each control test exception to determine its cause and the implication of the exception on assessed control risk, which may affect the supported detection risk and thereby the substantive procedures.

The most significant effect of the results of the tests of controls in the sales and collection cycle is on the confirmation of accounts receivable. The type of confirmation, the size of the sample, and the timing of the test are all affected. The effect of the tests on accounts receivable, bad-debt expense, and allowance for uncollectible accounts is considered in Chapter 15.

Figure 14-4 illustrates the major accounts in the sales and collection cycle and the types of audit tests typically used to audit these accounts. This figure also shows how the audit risk model discussed in Chapter 7 relates to the audit of the sales and collection cycle.

concept check

C14-7 What is the major risk for sales returns?

C14-8 Why is completeness a risk for cash receipts?

C14-9 How are uncollectible accounts related to fraud risks?

4 A Real-Life Example of a Sales Audit

Case Illustration—Hillsburg Hardware Limited

The concepts for testing the sales and collection cycle presented in this chapter are now illustrated for Hillsburg Hardware Limited. The company's financial statements and the general ledger trial balance were shown in Chapter 5. Additional information was included in other chapters. A study of this case is intended to illustrate a methodology for designing audit procedures and integrating different parts of the audit.

Hillsburg Hardware Limited is a retail hardware company that focuses on selling high-quality power tools to individuals and the home improvement construction

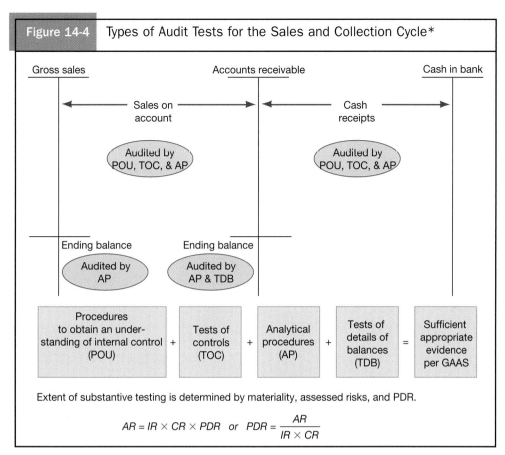

| Figure 14-4 | Types of Audit Tests for the Sales and Collection Cycle* |

Gross sales   Accounts receivable   Cash in bank

Sales on account ← →   ← Cash receipts →

Audited by POU, TOC, & AP

Audited by POU, TOC, & AP

Ending balance   Ending balance

Audited by AP

Audited by AP & TDB

| Procedures to obtain an under-standing of internal control (POU) | + | Tests of controls (TOC) | + | Analytical procedures (AP) | + | Tests of details of balances (TDB) | = | Sufficient appropriate evidence per GAAS |

Extent of substantive testing is determined by materiality, assessed risks, and PDR.

$$AR = IR \times CR \times PDR \quad or \quad PDR = \frac{AR}{IR \times CR}$$

*See Figure 14-1 on page 446 for accounts.

market. It is based in eastern Canada. A preliminary analytical review has shown continued maintenance of profit margins. This is the fourth year of the audit of this client, and there have never been any significant misstatements discovered in the tests. During the current year, a major change has occurred. The chief accountant left the firm and has been replaced by Erma Swanson. There has also been some turnover of other accounting personnel.

The overall assessment by management is that the accounting personnel are reasonably competent and highly trustworthy. The president, Rick Chulick, has been the chief operating officer for approximately 10 years. He is regarded as a highly competent, honest individual who does a conscientious job. The following information is provided from the auditor's files:

- *The organization chart and flowchart of internal control prepared for the audit.* This information is included in Figures 12-2 (page 385) and 14-5 (on the next page). Sales returns and allowances for this client are too immaterial to include in the flowchart or to verify in the audit.
- *Internal controls and weaknesses, and assessment of control risk for sales and cash receipts.* An appropriate approach to identifying and documenting internal controls and weaknesses and assessing control risk is included for sales in Figure 14-6 on page 475 and for cash receipts in Figure 14-7 on page 476. There are several things the auditor, Francine Martel, did to complete each matrix. First, she identified internal controls from flowcharts, internal control questionnaires, and discussions with client personnel. Only flowcharts are available in the Hillsburg case. Second, she identified weaknesses using the same sources. Third, she decided which transaction-related audit objectives are affected by the internal controls and weaknesses. Finally, she assessed control risk using the information obtained in the preceding three steps. The objective-by-objective matrices in Figures 14-6 and 14-7 were used primarily to help Francine effectively assess control risk.

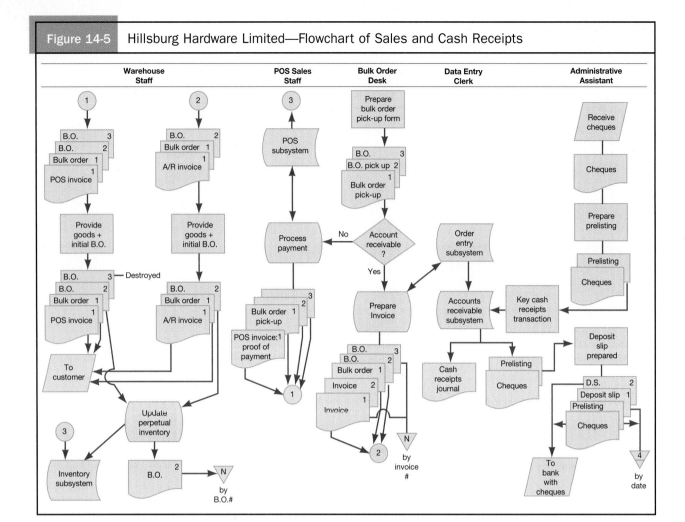

Notes

1. All correspondence is sent to the chief financial officer.
2. An exception report of missing bulk order numbers is printed weekly by the data entry clerk. The chief accountant discusses this with the warehouse staff supervisor to ensure that follow-up is undertaken.
3. All subsystems are posted to the general ledger on a daily basis after the close of business. The order-entry subsystem is also posted to the accounts receivable subsystem on a daily basis.
4. All prices in the point-of-sale (POS) system are based on prices in the master file. Should an override be necessary (e.g., due to damaged goods), the sales manager must enter his or her password to approve the price change. All such overrides will be printed on an exception report by the data entry clerk on a weekly basis. This report is reviewed by the chief accountant.
5. All prices used for accounts receivable are based on the same prices as in the POS system, with the customer discount applied. Customer discounts are negotiated at the time of customer approval, and range from 10 to 25 percent, based on the customer's projected and actual sales volume. Required on all accounts receivable invoices is an authorized customer signature that matches the signature on the in-house credit card.
6. Changes to the price master file and the customer master file for credit limits must be co-approved by the sales manager and the chief accountant on a master file change form. These changes are entered by the data entry clerk, and a sequentially numbered master file change report printed. This report is reviewed by the chief accountant for accuracy of data entry.
7. Payment at the POS desks can be made by cash, credit card, or debit card. Stand-alone credit card authorization and debit card entry machines are used to process non-cash payments. Daily totals (i.e., cash drawer, debit card totals, credit card totals) must equal the total sales recorded at each POS terminal.
8. There are two POS terminals for immediate payment and two bulk order desk terminals, where staff can inquire after inventory status and can prepare accounts receivable invoices using the order entry system for pre-authorized customers.
9. Warehouse staff compare bulk order quantities to amounts paid for or invoiced prior to providing goods, and initial the customer invoice. Customers sign copy 2 of the bulk order to indicate that goods have been taken.
10. An aged accounts receivable trial balance is printed weekly by the data entry clerk for follow-up by the chief accountant. As part of the follow-up, the trial balance total is compared to the general ledger accounts receivable balance.
11. Statements are sent to customers monthly.
12. The administrative assistant stamps incoming cheques with a restrictive endorsement immediately upon receipt.
13. Deposits are made daily by the administrative assistant. Cash from the POS terminals is counted, recorded on the duplicate deposit slip, and added to the total of cheques received for the day.
14. Daily cash receipts postings from the POS system and the accounts receivable system are reconciled to the duplicate deposit slip by the data entry clerk.
15. The bank account is reconciled by the chief accountant on a monthly basis.
16. All bad-debt expenses and write-offs of bad debts are approved by the chief financial officer after being initiated by the chief accountant.
17. Financial statements are printed monthly by the data entry clerk and reviewed by the chief financial officer and the president.
18. All management (i.e., sales, purchasing and inventory control, accounting, and the president) meet on a weekly basis to review exception reports and discuss weekly internal financial results. These meetings are not minuted.

Procedures for other locations are similar and not shown in this flow chart to simplify the discussion.

Figure 14-6	Control Risk Matrix for Hillsburg Hardware—Sales

Sales Transaction–Related Objectives

	Recorded sales are for shipments actually made to non-fictitious customers (occurrence).	Existing sales transactions are recorded (completeness).	Recorded sales are for the amount of goods shipped and are correctly billed and recorded (accuracy).	Sales transactions are properly classified (classification).	Sales transactions are updated correctly to the customer master file and the posting to the general ledger summed these transactions correctly (posting and summarization).	Sales are recorded on the correct dates (timing).
Internal Controls						
Scanned POS sales must be paid by cash, credit card, or debit card. (C1) **P**	C		C			
All external and internal credit card purchases require customer signature on the invoice. (C2)	C					
Bulk order pick-up form is matched to invoice and initialled. (C3)	C		C			
Credit is approved prior to customer account being established. (C4)	C					
Monthly statements are sent to accounts receivable customers. (C5)	C		C		C	
Bulk order forms are prenumbered, and the number is entered on the invoice. Computer system flags missing numbers on an exception report. (C6) **P**		C	C			
POS invoices and accounts receivable invoices are automatically numbered by the computer. (C7) **P**		C	C			
All invoices are prepared using prices in the inventory master file. (C8) **P**			C			
Accounts receivable terms are based on the customer master file. (C9) **P**			C			
Price overrides must be approved by sales manager password. (C10) **P**			C			
Sales manager overrides are printed on an exception report and reviewed by the chief accountant. (C11) **P**			C			
Sales control account is coded into computer system, and all POS and bulk sales are posted to that account. (C12) **P**				C		
The invoice date is automatically the computer system date. (C13) **P**						C
Posting to the data files is automatically handled by the computer system. (C14) **P**					C	
Aged accounts receivable trial balance is compared to general ledger balance monthly. (C15)					C	
Weakness						
Evidence of follow-up on exception report of missing bulk order numbers is not documented. (W1)		W				
Assessed control risk	Low	Medium	Low	Low	Low	Low

Note: **P**—These controls are either programmed controls or interdependent controls (where part of the control is programmed and part of the control is handled by a person).

C = Control

W = Weakness

	Cash Receipts Transaction–Related Audit Objectives					
	Recorded cash receipts are for funds actually received by the company (occurrence).	Cash received is recorded in the cash receipts journal (completeness).	Cash receipts are deposited at the amount received (accuracy).	Cash receipts transactions are properly classified (classification).	Cash receipts are properly included in the customer master file and are correctly summarized (posting and summarization).	Cash receipts are recorded on the correct dates (timing).
Internal Controls						
Accountant reconciles bank account. (C1)	C		C			
Cheques are stamped with a restrictive endorsement. (C2)		C				
Statements are sent to customers monthly. (C3)		C	C			
Bank deposit slip reconciled to POS and accounts receivable postings. (C4)	C	C	C			
Cash is automatically posted to cash and accounts receivable accounts. (C5)				C		
System date is used for data entry. (C6)						C
Cash receipts are deposited daily. (C7)						C
Entry of correct customer number results in automatic posting to that customer master file record. (C8)					C	
Accountant compares accounts receivable master file total with general ledger account. (C9)					C	
Weaknesses						
Prelisting of cash is not used to verify recorded cash receipts. (W1)		W				
Administrative assistant handles cheques after they are returned from cash receipts. (W2)		W				
Data entry clerk has access to cash receipts and maintains accounts receivable records. (W3)		W				
Assessed control risk	Low	High	Low	Low	Low	Low

C = Control
W = Weakness

- *The risk of material misstatement overall in sales and in revenue recognition.* These are considered low, due to the stability of the organization, and the preparation of reasonable financial statement projections that take into account the changing economic climate. Controls over the quality of financial statement disclosure are good, with both the chief financial officer and the president engaged in discussion to ensure clarity and completeness of disclosures. The auditors have been satisfied in the past with the quality and completeness of disclosures.
- *Tests of controls for each internal control.* The tests of controls for sales are included in the third and fifth columns of Table 14-7 and for cash receipts in the same columns in Table 14-8 (page 479). The source of the internal controls is Figure 14-6 for sales and Figure 14-7 for cash receipts. Francine decided the appropriate tests for each control. These were approved by the audit manager prior to conducting the tests.

Note that certain objectives in Tables 14-7 and 14-8 have only programmed controls (e.g., sales classification and timing and cash receipts classification), or existing

				Tests of Control,

Table 14-7 Internal Controls and Tests of Controls for Hillsburg Hardware Limited—Sales[*] (Design Format)

Transaction-Related Audit Objective	Existing Control[†]	Tests of Control, General	Weakness	Tests of Control, Dual-Purpose
Recorded sales are for shipments actually made to non-fictitious customers (occurrence).	Scanned POS sales must be paid by cash, credit card, or debit card. (C1) All external and internal credit card purchases require customer signature on the invoice. (C2) Bulk order pick-up form is matched to invoice and initialled. (C3) Credit is approved prior to customer account being established. (C4) Monthly statements are sent to accounts receivable customers. (C5)	Review POS procedures manual and discuss with POS staff. (6) Examine a sample of invoices for customer signature. (13.1) Examine a selection of invoices for matching bulk order form and initial. (13.3, 13.4) Examine a sample of master file change forms for evidence of approval. (14.1, 14.2) Observe whether monthly statements are mailed. (7)	Evidence of follow-up on exception report of missing bulk order numbers is not documented. (W1)	Use generalized audit software to print a list of customers exceeding their credit limit. (4.1)
Existing sales transactions are recorded (completeness).	Bulk order forms are prenumbered, and the number is entered on the invoice. Computer system flags missing numbers on an exception report. (C6) POS invoices and accounts receivable invoices are automatically numbered by the computer. (C7)	Review a sample of sales invoices for bulk order form number. (13.2) Observe system in use, and observe incremental assignment of invoice numbers. (1.2, 2.1)		Use generalized audit software to print a report of all gaps in the bulk order forms. (4.2) Use generalized audit software to print a report of all gaps in the invoice numbers. (4.3, 4.4)
Recorded sales are for the amount of goods shipped and are correctly billed and recorded (accuracy).	All invoices are prepared using prices in the inventory master file. (C8) Accounts receivable terms are based on the customer master file. (C9) Price overrides must be approved by sales manager password. (C10) Sales manager overrides are printed on an exception report and reviewed by the chief accountant. (C11)	Observe invoice preparation process. (1.3, 2.2) Request bulk order staff to enter a different term, and see if computer rejects it. (2.3) Request staff to override a price, and observe whether sales manager password is required. (1.4, 2.4) Discuss disposition of exception reports with chief accountant, and review report for evidence of review. (8)		Use generalized audit software to print a report of unusual credit terms, and trace to customer master file approval form. (4.5, 4.7)
Sales transactions are properly classified (classification).	Sales control account is coded into computer system, and all POS and bulk sales are posted to that account. (C12)	Examine a daily sales summary to verify account allocation. (5.1)		

Table 14-7

Internal Controls and Tests of Controls for Hillsburg Hardware Limited—Sales* (Design Format) (continued)

Transaction-Related Audit Objective	Existing Control[†]	Tests of Control, General	Weakness	Tests of Control, Dual-Purpose
Sales transactions are updated correctly to the customer master file, and the posting to the general ledger summed these transactions correctly (posting and summarization).	Posting to the data files is automatically handled by the computer system. (C14) Aged accounts receivable trial balance is compared with general ledger balance monthly. (C15)	Conduct walk-through testing to verify that posting process is functioning correctly for daily posting. (5.1, 5.2, 5.3)		Compare aged accounts receivable trial balance total with general ledger's. (4.6)
Sales are recorded on the correct dates (timing).	The invoice date is automatically the computer system date. (C13)	Observe invoice preparation process. (1.5, 2.5)		

* The procedures are summarized into a performance format in Figure 14-8. The number in parentheses after the procedure refers to Figure 14-8.

[†] Only the primary (key) control(s) for each objective is (are) shown. Most objectives are also affected by one or more additional controls.

controls are such that there are weaknesses (e.g., occurrence in Table 14-7; completeness in Table 14-8). The tests of controls listed in the fifth columns of Tables 14-7 and 14-8 are dual-purpose tests designed to determine if the client's accounting transactions exist, are complete, are accurate, are properly classified, are recorded on the correct dates, and are summarized in the journals and correctly posted to the appropriate ledger. Tests such as these, described in Chapter 12, are both tests of controls and substantive procedures. As was suggested earlier in this chapter, the purpose of such tests is to assist the auditor in assessing control risk and also in quantifying the potential amount of error when conducted as substantive tests.

Francine decided on the tests of controls for each transaction-related audit objective listed in the third and fifth columns of Table 14-7 (sales) and Table 14-8 (cash receipts) for the different objectives after considering assessed control risk, the tests of controls listed in the third column, and weaknesses of internal control for that objective. These tables assume that there is a potential for material misstatement in each of the objectives and that substantive tests overall can be reduced by the conduct of these tests. For illustrative purposes, we have included thorough tests, although in practice auditors might decide to conduct tests of controls only where risks of misstatement are moderate to high.

Note that the objective-by-objective format in Tables 14-7 and 14-8 is used to help Francine more effectively determine the appropriate tests. She could have chosen tests of controls just as easily by selecting tests of controls for each internal control included in Figures 14-4 (on page 473) and 14-8 (on page 480). Most audit firms use automated working-paper software that allows them to simultaneously work on audit objective assessment and the preparation of audit testing plans without the preparation of multiple lists, as shown in this text. The multiple lists are shown here to assist students in assimilation of the audit process.

TESTS OF CONTROLS AUDIT PROGRAM IN A PERFORMANCE FORMAT The tests of controls in Table 14-7 and Table 14-8 are combined into one audit program in Figure 14-8 (page 480). The cross-referencing of the numbers in parentheses shows that no procedures have been added to or deleted from Figure 14-8. The reasons Francine prepared the performance format audit program were to eliminate audit procedures that were included more than once in Tables 14-7 and 14-8 and to include them in an order that permits audit assistants to complete the procedures as efficiently as possible. Note the large number of programmed controls, walk-through tests, and general tests. These illustrate that in automated systems, where programmed controls can be

Table 14-8

**Internal Controls and Tests of Controls for Hillsburg Hardware Limited—Cash Receipts*
(Design Format)**

Transaction-Related Audit Objective	Existing Control†	Tests of Control, General	Weakness	Tests of Control, Dual-Purpose
Recorded cash receipts are for funds actually received by the company (occurrence).	Accountant reconciles bank account. (C1) Bank deposit slip reconciled to POS and accounts receivable postings. (C4)††	Observe whether Erma Swanson reconciles the bank account. (9)		Review the journals and transaction files for unusual transactions and amounts using GAS. (4.7) Summarize and prepare analysis of credits using GAS. (4.7, 4.8) Prepare a proof of cash receipts. (18) Examine a sample of daily reconciliations, verifying agreement to postings and to bank statement. (16)
Cash received is recorded in the cash receipts journal (completeness).	Cheques are stamped with a restrictive endorsement. (C2) Statements are sent to customers monthly. (C3)	Observe whether a restrictive endorsement is used on cash receipts. (10) Observe whether monthly statements are mailed. (7)	Prelisting of cash is not used to verify recorded cash receipts. (W1) Administrative assistant handles cheques after they are returned from data entry. (W2) Data entry clerk has access to cash receipts and maintains accounts receivable records. (W3)	Obtain the prelisting of cash receipts, and trace amounts to the cash receipts journal, testing for names, amounts, and dates. (19) Compare the prelisting of cash receipts with the duplicate deposit slip, testing for names, amounts, and dates. (16)
Recorded cash receipts are deposited at the amount received (accuracy).	Accountant reconciles bank account. (C1) Statements are sent to customers monthly. (C3)	Observe whether Erma reconciles the bank account. (9) Observe whether monthly statements are mailed. (7)		The procedures for the occurrence objective also fulfill this objective.
Cash receipts are properly classified (classification).	Cash is automatically posted to cash and accounts receivable accounts. (C5)	Conduct walk-through. (5.4) Observe system use. (3.1)		Examine prelisting for proper account classification. (17)
Cash receipts are properly included in the customer master file and are correctly summarized (posting and summarization).	Accountant compares aged accounts receivable trial balance total with general ledger account. (C9) Entry of correct customer number results in automatic posting to that customer master file record. (C8)	Observe whether Erma compares total with general ledger account. (12) Observe data entry and conduct walk-through test. (3)		Foot and cross-foot the cash receipts journal using GAS, and trace totals to the general ledger on a test basis. (4.8)
Cash receipts are recorded on correct dates (timing).	System date is used for data entry. (C6) Cash receipts deposited daily. (C7)	Observe whether bank deposits are made daily. (11)		Trace the total from the cash receipts journal to the bank statement, testing for a delay in deposit. (16)

GAS = generalized audit software.

* The procedures are summarized into a performance format in Figure 14-8. The number in parentheses after the procedure refers to Figure 14-8.

† Only the primary (key) control(s) for each objective is (are) shown. Most objectives are also affected by one or more additional controls.

†† This control also satisfies completeness and accuracy.

TESTS OF CONTROLS AUDIT PROCEDURES FOR SALES AND CASH RECEIPTS
(Sample Size and the Items in the Sample Are Not Included)

Tests of Programs

1. Observe use of POS system to verify that
   1.1 POS sales must be paid by cash, credit card, or debit card.
   1.2 POS invoices are automatically numbered by the computer.
   1.3 Invoices are prepared using prices automatically pulled from the inventory master file.
   1.4 Price overrides must be approved using the sales manager password. (Request an attempt to enter an override.)
   1.5 Invoice date is equal to computer system date.
2. Observe use of bulk order desk and accounts receivable sales data entry to verify that
   2.1 Accounts receivable invoices are automatically numbered by the computer.
   2.2 Invoices are prepared using prices automatically pulled from the inventory master file.
   2.3 Credit terms are pulled automatically from the customer master file. (Request an attempt to enter an incorrect credit term.)
   2.4 Price overrides must be approved using the sales manager password. (Request an attempt to enter an override.)
   2.5 Invoice date is equal to computer system date.
3. Observe cash receipts data entry process to verify that
   3.1 System date is used for data entry.

Tests of Data Using Generalized Audit Software—Included with Substantive Field Work of Accounts Receivable

4. Obtain transaction history file, open item accounts receivable file and customer master file, and conduct the following tests:
   4.1 List customers with balances exceeding their credit limit.
   4.2 List gaps in bulk order form numbers.
   4.3 List gaps in POS invoice numbers.
   4.4 List gaps in accounts receivable invoice numbers.
   4.5 List customers with discount terms exceeding 25 percent.
   4.6 Foot open item file and customer master file and agree to general ledger.
   4.7 Summarize debits and credits by customer. Prepare graphs displaying analysis of debit and credit patterns.
   4.8 Summarize cash receipts and prepare totals by day and month.

Walk-through Tests

5. Conduct walk-through tests of three transactions for each of the following activities to verify that programs are functioning as described:
   5.1 POS daily sales summary is posted to correct general ledger accounts.
   5.2 Accounts receivable daily sales are posted to correct general ledger accounts.
   5.3 Sales transactions are posted to correct customer master file accounts.
   5.4 Cash receipts are posted to correct general ledger accounts.

General Tests

6. Review system procedures and discuss with personnel to verify that procedures are being followed as described.
7. Observe whether monthly statements are mailed.
8. Discuss disposition of exception reports with appropriate member of management independently to verify consistency of treatment.
9. Observe whether the accountant reconciles the bank account.
10. Observe whether a restrictive endorsement is used on cash receipts.
11. Observe whether bank deposits are made daily.
12. Observe whether the accountant compares the accounts receivable trial balance total with the general ledger account.

Tests for Billing of Customers and Recording of Sales in the Accounts

13. Select a sample of customer invoices using a random selection process, and
    13.1 Ensure that the invoice copy has a customer signature.
    If the sale was for bulk goods:
    13.2 Verify that the bulk order form number was entered on the invoice.
    13.3 Verify that the bulk order form product description and quantity matches the invoice details.
    13.4 Locate the warehouse copy of the bulk order form and verify that the customer signature on the warehouse copy of the bulk order form matches the signature on the invoice copy.
14. Select a sample of customer master file change forms using a random selection process, and
    14.1 Verify that appropriate approvals are present.
    14.2 Trace to printout, confirming data entry of the change and verifying presence of chief accountant's initials.

Tests for Processing Cash Receipts and Recording the Amounts in the Records

15. Obtain the December prelistings of cash receipts, and trace amounts to the cash receipts journal, testing for names, amounts, and dates.
16. Compare the prelisting of cash receipts with the duplicate deposit slip, testing for names, amounts, and dates. Trace the total from the cash receipts journal to the duplicate bank deposit slip and the total per the duplicate bank deposit slip to the bank statement, testing for a delay in deposit. For these dates, also trace the totals to the POS system and accounts receivable sales system totals.
17. Examine prelisting for proper account classification.
18. Prepare a proof of cash receipts.
19. Trace selected entries from the cash receipts journal to entries in the customer master file, and test for dates and amounts.
20. Trace selected credits from the accounts receivable master file to the cash receipts journal, and test for dates and amounts.

relied on due to good general controls, the time spent on control testing can be reduced, since the effort required to conduct these tests is considerably less than the effort required to conduct sampling and tests of attributes through sampling. The generalized audit software tests are conducted at the same time as the substantive tests for accounts receivable (discussed further in Chapter 15).

Application of Attribute Sampling

To illustrate the sampling for the tests of controls concepts of Chapter 13, the sampling for the tests described in Figure 14-8 is now conducted. The only parts of the tests of the sales and collection cycle included here are the tests of payment approval by the customer, shipment verification of bulk orders, and approval of customer master file changes. It should be kept in mind that the procedures for Hillsburg Hardware Limited were developed specifically for that client and would probably not be applicable to a different audit. The audit procedures for these tests are taken from steps 13 and 14 of Figure 14-8. Although not shown on the individual working papers, each working paper would also have information showing who completed the work, when it was completed, and who reviewed the working papers.

DEFINE THE ATTRIBUTES OF INTEREST The attributes used in this application are taken directly from the audit program. The procedures that can be used as attributes for a particular application of attributes sampling depend on the definition of the sampling unit. In this case, all the procedures in the billing function can be included. The attributes used for this case are listed in Figure 14-9 on the next page.

The definition of the attribute is a critical part of attribute sampling. The decision as to which attributes to combine and which ones to keep separate is the most important aspect of the definition. If all possible types of attributes such as customer name, date, price, and quantity are separated for each procedure, the large number of attributes makes the problem unmanageable. However, if all the procedures are combined into one or two attributes, greatly dissimilar misstatements are evaluated together. Somewhere in between is a reasonable compromise.

ESTABLISH TER, ARACR, AND EPER, AND DETERMINE INITIAL SAMPLE SIZE The tolerable exception rate (TER) for each attribute is decided on the basis of the auditor's judgment of what exception rate is material. The failure to have a customer signature on an invoice (or order) would be highly significant, since this could mean an inability to collect funds from a sale that is also an account receivable or from a credit card organization. Therefore, as indicated in Figure 14-9, the lowest TER (3 percent) is chosen for attribute 1. The incorrect billing of the customer for bulk sales represents potentially significant misstatements, but no misstatement is likely to apply to the full amount of the invoice. As a result, a 4-percent TER is chosen for matching of the bulk order form details and customer signature on that form. The second attribute has a higher TER, since it is of less importance for the audit. The last item is also important, since it helps verify the authenticity of the customer.

An acceptable risk of assessing control risk too low (ARACR) of 10 percent is chosen because there are numerous other controls, such as programmed controls and management review of exception reports.

The estimated population exception rate (EPER) is based on previous years' results, modified slightly upward due to the change in personnel. Initial sample size for each attribute is determined from Table 14-9 (page 483) on the basis of the above considerations. Note that the estimated population error rates are very low, ranging from 0 to 2 percent. In practice, many auditors will only conduct tests of controls if their estimated population exception rate is 0, since encountering errors could mean that the auditor cannot rely on the controls.

Sampling information is summarized for all attributes in Figure 14-12 on page 486. Table 14-9 can be used to determine an appropriate sample size, based upon the ARACR and EPER. For convenience in selection and evaluation, the auditor decided

Figure 14-9

Figure 14-9 | Attribute Sampling Data Sheet

Client	Hillsburg Hardware Limited	Year end	31/12/08
Audit Area	Tests of Controls—Billing Function and Recording of Sales	Pop. size	145,853

Define the objective(s) Examine duplicate sales invoices and related documents to determine if the system has functioned as intended and as described in the audit program.

Define the population precisely (including stratification, if any) POS invoices and credit sales invoices for the period 1/1/08 to 31/12/08. First POS number = 140672. Last POS number = 283294. First credit sales invoice number = 3600. Last credit sales invoice number = 6831

Define the sampling unit, organization of population items, and random selection procedures Sales invoice number, POS invoice numbers, and credit recorded in the sales files sequentially; random sampling.

Description of Attributes	Planned Audit				Actual Results			
	EPER	TER	ARACR	Initial sample size	Sample size	Number of exceptions	Sample exception rate	CUER
1. Invoice copy has customer signature. (13.1)	0	3	10	76				
For Bulk Sales: 2. Bulk order form number is entered on invoice details. (13.2)	2	8	10	48				
3. Bulk order form details match invoice details. (13.3)	0	4	10	57				
4. Warehouse copy of bulk order form has customer signature. (13.4)	1	4	10	96				
5. Customer signature on warehouse copy of bulk order form matches signature on invoice. (13.4)	0	3	10	76				

Intended use of sampling results:

1. Effect on Audit Plan:

2. Recommendations to Management:

to select a sample of 75 for attribute 1, 50 for attributes 2 and 3, 100 for attribute 4, and 75 for attribute 5. On the basis of past experience, the decision was made to select 30 samples from the POS invoices and the remainder from credit sales invoices, since these have a greater proportion of bulk sales orders.

SELECT THE SAMPLE The random selection for the case is straightforward except for the need for different sample sizes for different attributes. This problem can be overcome by selecting a random sample of 50 for use on all five attributes followed by another sample of 25 for attributes 1 and 5, and an additional 25 for attribute 4. Figure 13A-1 on page 437 illustrates how the first 30 items were selected from the POS system using a spreadsheet template. The remaining items were selected in a similar manner.

PERFORM THE PROCEDURES AND GENERALIZE TO THE POPULATION The audit procedures that are included in the audit program and summarized in the attribute sampling data sheet must be carefully performed for every item in the sample. As a means of

| Table 14-9 | Determining Sample Size for Attribute Sampling |

5-Percent ARACR

Estimated Population	Tolerable Exception Rate (in percentage)										
Exception Rate (in percentage)	2	3	4	5	6	7	8	9	10	15	20
0.00	149	99	74	59	49	42	36	32	29	19	14
0.25	236	157	117	93	78	66	58	51	46	30	22
0.50	*	157	117	93	78	66	58	51	46	30	22
0.75	*	208	117	93	78	66	58	51	46	30	22
1.00	*	*	156	93	78	66	58	51	46	30	22
1.25	*	*	156	124	78	66	58	51	46	30	22
1.50	*	*	192	124	103	66	58	51	46	30	22
1.75	*	*	227	153	103	88	77	51	46	30	22
2.00	*	*	*	181	127	88	77	68	46	30	22
2.25	*	*	*	208	127	88	77	68	61	30	22
2.50	*	*	*	*	150	109	77	68	61	30	22
2.75	*	*	*	*	173	109	95	68	61	30	22
3.00	*	*	*	*	195	129	95	84	61	30	22
3.25	*	*	*	*	*	148	112	84	61	30	22
3.50	*	*	*	*	*	167	112	84	76	40	22
3.75	*	*	*	*	*	185	129	100	76	40	22
4.00	*	*	*	*	*	*	146	100	89	40	22
5.00	*	*	*	*	*	*	*	158	116	40	30
6.00	*	*	*	*	*	*	*	*	179	50	30
7.00	*	*	*	*	*	*	*	*	*	68	37

10-Percent ARACR

	2	3	4	5	6	7	8	9	10	15	20
0.00	114	76	57	45	38	32	28	25	22	15	11
0.25	194	129	96	77	64	55	48	42	38	25	18
0.50	194	129	96	77	64	55	48	42	38	25	18
0.75	265	129	96	77	64	55	48	42	38	25	18
1.00	*	176	96	77	64	55	48	42	38	25	18
1.25	*	221	132	77	64	55	48	42	38	25	18
1.50	*	*	132	105	64	55	48	42	38	25	18
1.75	*	*	166	105	88	55	48	42	38	25	18
2.00	*	*	198	132	88	75	48	42	38	25	18
2.25	*	*	*	132	88	75	65	42	38	25	18
2.50	*	*	*	158	110	75	65	58	38	25	18
2.75	*	*	*	209	132	94	65	58	52	25	18
3.00	*	*	*	*	132	94	65	58	52	25	18
3.25	*	*	*	*	153	113	82	58	52	25	18
3.50	*	*	*	*	194	113	82	73	52	25	18
3.75	*	*	*	*	*	131	98	73	52	25	18
4.00	*	*	*	*	*	149	98	73	65	25	18
4.50	*	*	*	*	*	218	130	87	65	34	18
5.00	*	*	*	*	*	*	160	115	78	34	18
5.50	*	*	*	*	*	*	*	142	103	34	18
6.00	*	*	*	*	*	*	*	182	116	45	25
7.00	*	*	*	*	*	*	*	*	199	52	25
8.00	*	*	*	*	*	*	*	*	*	60	25

*Sample is too large to be cost-effective for most audit applications.

Notes: 1. This table assumes a large population. 2. Sample sizes are the same in certain columns even when expected population exception rates differ because of the method of constructing the tables. Sample sizes are calculated for attributes sampling using the expected number of exceptions in the population, but auditors can deal more conveniently with expected population exception rates. For example, in the 15-percent column for tolerable exception rate, at an ARACR of 5 percent, initial sample size for most EPERs is 30.

Figure 14-10

Figure 14-10 — Exceptions Found During Inspection of Sample Items for Attributes

1. *Invoice copy has customer signature. (13.1)*

   Three exceptions found.

   POS invoices # 163763, 213150, and 237619 did not have customer signatures. These were all cash sales (i.e., not paid by credit card or debit card).

2. *Bulk order form number entered on invoice. (13.2)*

   Four exceptions found.

   POS invoice # 242681 missing bulk order number, although copy was attached.

   Credit sales invoice # 5802, 6137, and 8713 missing bulk order number, although copy was attached.

   No exceptions found for attributes 3, 4, and 5.

documenting the tests and providing information for review, it is common to include a worksheet of the results. Some auditors prefer to include a worksheet containing a listing of all items in the sample; others prefer to limit the documentation to identifying the exceptions. This latter approach is followed in the example (Figure 14-10). Figure 14-11 summarizes the sampling process for the testing of master file change forms.

At the completion of the testing, the exceptions are tabulated to determine the number of exceptions in the sample for each attribute. This enables the auditor to compute the sample exception rate and determine the computed upper exception rate (CUER) using Table 14-10. The exceptions for attribute 1 were considered not to be true exceptions since signatures are not required on invoices for purchases made by cash on POS invoices, although they are required for all other types of purchases. Exception information is summarized in Figure 14-12 (page 486) and Table 14-11 (page 487).

EXCEPTION ANALYSIS The final part of the application consists of analyzing the deviations to determine their cause and drawing conclusions about each attribute tested. For every attribute for which CUER exceeds TER, it is essential that some conclusion concerning follow-up action be drawn and documented. The exception analysis and conclusions reached are illustrated in Table 14-11 (page 487) and summarized at the bottom of the data sheet in Figure 14-12 (page 486).

DETERMINE THE ACCEPTABILITY OF THE POPULATION The controls tested for attributes 1 through 5 of the billing function and recording of sales can be relied on, even though the bulk order invoice number was not recorded on the sales invoice, since there were no deviations in any of the other controls. Thus, the sales population is acceptable. Master file change forms and data entry verification reports were approved using

Figure 14-11 — Testing of Master File Change Forms

Objectives: As defined in Figure 14-8 (14.1 and 14.2); authorization of master file change forms and proof of data entry verification.

Sampling: Applies to use of master file change forms throughout the year.

Population: Master file change forms used throughout the year. First form number used: 1201. Last form used: 2132.

TER: 5   **ARACR:** 10   **EPER:** 0   **Initial Sample Size:** 45

Results of Performing Procedures: Three exceptions found, on form # 1288, 1510, and 1599. In the first instance, signature of sales manager was missing. In the second and third, the signature of the chief accountant was missing. In all cases, the indicated person was on holiday. Also, for the latter two forms, the data entry report was initialled by the sales manager, since the chief accountant was absent.

	No. of Exceptions	Sample Exception Rate	CUER
Attribute 1	3	6.7	14.2
Attribute 2	2	4.4	11.4

	Table 14-10	Evaluating Sample Results Using Attribute Sampling										

	Actual Number of Deviations Found										
Sample Size	0	1	2	3	4	5	6	7	8	9	10

5-Percent ARACR

Sample Size	0	1	2	3	4	5	6	7	8	9	10
25	11.3	17.6	*	*	*	*	*	*	*	*	*
30	9.5	14.9	19.5	*	*	*	*	*	*	*	*
35	8.2	12.9	16.9	*	*	*	*	*	*	*	*
40	7.2	11.3	14.9	18.3	*	*	*	*	*	*	*
45	6.4	10.1	13.3	16.3	19.2	*	*	*	*	*	*
50	5.8	9.1	12.1	14.8	17.4	19.9	*	*	*	*	*
55	5.3	8.3	11.0	13.5	15.9	18.1	*	*	*	*	*
60	4.9	7.7	10.1	12.4	14.6	16.7	18.8	*	*	*	*
65	4.5	7.1	9.4	11.5	13.5	15.5	17.4	19.3	*	*	*
70	4.2	6.6	8.7	10.7	12.6	14.4	16.2	18.0	19.7	*	*
75	3.9	6.2	8.2	10.0	11.8	13.5	15.2	16.9	18.4	20.0	*
80	3.7	5.8	7.7	9.4	11.1	12.7	14.3	15.8	17.3	18.8	*
90	3.3	5.2	6.8	8.4	9.9	11.3	12.7	14.1	15.5	16.8	18.1
100	3.0	4.7	6.2	7.6	8.9	10.2	11.5	12.7	14.0	15.2	16.4
125	2.4	3.7	4.9	6.1	7.2	8.2	9.3	10.3	11.3	12.2	13.2
150	2.0	3.1	4.1	5.1	6.0	6.9	7.7	8.6	9.4	10.2	11.0
200	1.5	2.3	3.1	3.8	4.5	5.2	5.8	6.5	7.1	7.7	8.3

10-Percent ARACR

Sample Size	0	1	2	3	4	5	6	7	8	9	10
20	10.9	18.1	*	*	*	*	*	*	*	*	*
25	8.8	14.7	19.9	*	*	*	*	*	*	*	*
30	7.4	12.4	16.8	*	*	*	*	*	*	*	*
35	6.4	10.7	14.5	18.1	*	*	*	*	*	*	*
40	5.6	9.4	12.8	15.9	19.0	*	*	*	*	*	*
45	5.0	8.4	11.4	14.2	17.0	19.6	*	*	*	*	*
50	4.5	7.6	10.3	12.9	15.4	17.8	*	*	*	*	*
55	4.1	6.9	9.4	11.7	14.0	16.2	18.4	*	*	*	*
60	3.8	6.3	8.6	10.8	12.9	14.9	16.9	18.8	*	*	*
70	3.2	5.4	7.4	9.3	11.1	12.8	14.6	16.2	17.9	19.5	*
80	2.8	4.8	6.5	8.3	9.7	11.3	12.8	14.3	15.7	17.2	18.6
90	2.5	4.3	5.8	7.3	8.7	10.1	11.4	12.7	14.0	15.3	16.6
100	2.3	3.8	5.2	6.6	7.8	9.1	10.3	11.5	12.7	13.8	15.0
120	1.9	3.2	4.4	5.5	6.6	7.6	8.6	9.6	10.6	11.6	12.5
160	1.4	2.4	3.3	4.1	4.9	5.7	6.5	7.2	8.0	8.7	9.5
200	1.1	1.9	2.6	3.3	4.0	4.6	5.2	5.8	6.4	7.0	7.6

* Over 20 percent.

Note: This table presents computed upper deviation rates as percentages. Table assumes a large population.

existing policies, except where the designated individual was absent (see Figure 14-11 and Table 14-10). However, this enables a single individual to approve credit and customer master file changes, which could lead to manipulation. The auditor should conduct additional testing by examining master file changes during the period when one of these two individuals was absent or on holiday. We assume that once additional testing was done, no unusual transactions were discovered. The auditor can then accept the population, although additional testing of the bad-debt allowance is still advisable.

Impact of Test of Controls Results on Audit Planning

After the tests of controls have been performed, it is essential to analyze each test of control exception to determine its cause and the implication of the exception on

Figure 14-12   Attribute Sampling Data Sheet, Completed

Client	Hillsburg Hardware Limited	Year End	31/12/08
Audit Area	Tests of Controls—Billing Function and Recording of Sales	Pop. Size	145,853

Define the objective(s) Examine duplicate sales invoices and related documents to determine if the system has functioned as intended and as described in the audit program.

Define the population precisely (including stratification, if any) POS invoices and credit sales invoices for the period 1/1/08 to 31/12/08. First POS number = 140672. Last POS number = 283294. First credit sales invoice number = 3600. Last credit sales invoice number = 6831.

Define the sampling unit, organization of population items, and random selection procedures Sales invoice number, POS invoice numbers, and credit recorded in the sales files sequentially; random sampling.

Description of Attributes	Planned Audit				Actual Results			
	EPER	TER	ARACR	Initial sample size	Sample size	Number of exceptions	Sample exception rate	CUER
1. Invoice copy has customer signature. (13.1)	0	3	10	76	75	0	0	3
For Bulk Sales: 2. Bulk order form number is entered on invoice details. (13.2)	2	8	10	48	50	4	8	15.4
3. Bulk order form details match invoice details. (13.3)	0	4	10	57	50	0	0	4.5
4. Warehouse copy of bulk order form has customer signature. (13.4)	1	4	10	96	100	0	0	2.3
5. Customer signature on warehouse copy of bulk order form matches signature on invoice. (13.4)	0	3	10	76	75	0	0	3

Intended use of sampling results:

1. **Effect on Audit Plan:** Controls tested using attributes #1, 3–5 can be relied upon. Policies and procedures to remedy #2 should be discussed with management. No additional audit procedures required, since no financial impact.

2. **Recommendations to Management:** See attached weakness investigation.

assessed control risk, which may affect the supported detection risk and thereby the substantive procedures.

For Hillsburg Hardware, assume that there were no other deviations beyond those described and analyzed in Table 14-10. This means that the auditor can accept the planned control risk in all areas except valuation (due to the exceptions found with master file changes).

UPDATE THE EVIDENCE PLANNING SPREADSHEET After completing tests of controls, the auditor should complete rows 3 through 5 of the evidence planning spreadsheet. Recall from Chapter 9 that the control risk rows could have been completed before the tests of controls were done, and then modified if the test results were not satisfactory. An updated evidence planning spreadsheet is shown in Figure 14-13. The spreadsheet is used to determine the extent of substantive tests required for the cycle.

Table 14-11 Analysis of Exceptions

Attribute	Number of Exceptions	Nature of Exceptions	Effect on the Audit and Other Comments
1, sales	3	Three POS invoices paid by cash did not have customer signatures. Each invoice was for less than $50.	No effect on the audit. Hillsburg policy has been clarified that cash purchase invoices do not require customer signature.
2, sales	4	One POS invoice and three credit sales invoices did not have the bulk order number on the face of the invoice, although the invoice copy was attached.	These omissions would show on the bulk order form exception report showing missing bulk order numbers. Management indicated that, unfortunately, new employees often forget to record this number, resulting in an excessive number of items on the exception report. This usually eases off. Since this does not have a financial effect on the audit (there were no errors in goods shipped), no further audit work is required.
1, master file changes	3	Three master file change forms for new credit accounts were approved by only the sales manager or the chief accountant.	Additional work on the bad-debt allowance should be completed in the event that bad credit risks have been approved. Master file changes submitted during the period of these managers' absence should be reviewed for unusual items.
2, master file changes	2	Two data entry verification reports of master file changes were verified by the sales manager rather than by the chief accountant.	See above.

Figure 14-13 Evidence Planning Spreadsheet to Determine Tests of Details of Balances for Hillsburg Hardware Limited—Accounts Receivable

	Existence (or Occurrence)	Rights and Obligations	Completeness	Accuracy	Valuation	Classification	Detail Tie-in	Cut-off	Presentation and Disclosure
Audit risk	High	High	High	High	High	High	High	High	High
Inherent risk	Low	Low	Low	Low	Medium	Low	Low	Low	Low
Control risk – Sales	Medium	Not applicable	Low	Low	High	Low	Low	Low	Not applicable
Control risk – Cash receipts	High	Not applicable	Low	Low	Not applicable	Low	Low	Low	Not applicable
Control risk – Additional controls	None	Low	None	None	None	None	None	None	Low
Analytical procedures									
Planned detection risk for tests of details of balances									
Planned audit evidence for tests of details of balances									

Materiality $496,000

concept check

C14-10 When deciding upon which controls to test, the auditor considers cost-effectiveness. Which types of controls are likely the least costly to test? Justify your response.

C14-11 The auditor is estimating the population exception rate (EPER) in the range of 10 to 15 percent. What type of testing would the auditor conduct? Why?

The most significant effect of the results of the tests of controls in the sales and collection cycle is on the confirmation of accounts receivable. The type of confirmation, the size of the sample, and the timing of the test are all affected by the results of tests of controls. The effect of the tests on accounts receivable, bad-debt expense, and allowance for uncollectible accounts is further considered in Chapter 15.

COMMUNICATION WITH MANAGEMENT In addition to adjusting the audit procedures, the auditor should ensure that management is informed of all exceptions and that the impact of the exceptions is appropriately discussed. In some instances, the auditor will conduct such a discussion verbally, but in many instances, a management letter will be issued, in which the exception is discussed, the implications of the exception explained, and recommendations for improvement in procedures identified. For the sales and collection cycle, the auditor might communicate in writing the exceptions with respect to master file change form approval, and recommend that another individual provide a second signature on these forms in the event of the sales manager's or chief accountant's absence. The individual recommended to do this likely would be the president of the organization. The management letter should be copied to the audit committee.

Summary

1. *What are typical records and transactions in the sales cycle?* There are typically five classes of transactions included in the sales and collection cycle: sales, cash receipts, sales returns and allowances, charge-off of uncollectible accounts, and bad-debt expenses. Records include the customer master file and the transaction history file, with periodic listings such as sales journals and an aged accounts receivable trial balance.

2. *How is risk assessment linked to the sales cycle?* The auditor considers risks to evaluate the likelihood of material misstatement in sales, accounts receivable, and allowance accounts. The auditor will also assess the likelihood of revenue recognition misstatements when designing audit tests in the cycle.

   How do general controls affect the audit of the sales and collection cycle? General controls affect multiple transaction cycles, so weaknesses in general controls, such as program change controls or access controls, would mean that the auditor might not be able to rely on programmed functions or segregation of duties. Strengths in general controls may allow the auditor to rely on those controls enforced by automated systems.

   Describe the methodology for designing tests of controls for sales. The auditor needs to understand and evaluate design effectiveness of general controls that apply to sales, as well as the application controls within the sales cycle. Then, the auditor assesses planned control risk for sales and identifies and assess the risks of material misstatements in the sales cycle. The cost benefit of testing controls is examined by assertion prior to designing tests of controls for the cycle. Where desired, dual-purpose or weakness investigation tests are designed. An audit program in a performance format is used to conduct the tests.

3. *Describe the methodology for controls over sales returns and allowances, cash receipts transactions, uncollectible accounts, and account balances.* The general methodology is the same for every transaction type. It depends upon the risk for the transaction type and associated assertions as well as the materiality of the transactions.

   What is the effect of the results of tests of controls on the audit? Where controls are functioning as described, the auditor may be able to reduce tests of details. As tests of controls tend to be less expensive to conduct than tests of details, this can result in an overall lower cost high-quality audit.

4. *What is the typical audit process for tests of controls?* Hillsburg Hardware Limited is used to illustrate how the many possible controls are narrowed down to the key controls in place at an organization for the audit assertions. Then, tests are designed and a sample selected. When testing is completed, the results are evaluated and the effect on the audit identified. Then, an audit program is developed, organized by audit assertion (audit objective). To conduct the testing, the audit steps are reorganized into a performance format that facilitates efficient completion of like audit procedures.

Review Questions

14-1 Describe the nature of the following documents and records, and explain their use in the sales and collection cycle: bill of lading, sales invoice, customer master file, credit memo, remittance advice, and monthly statement to customers.

14-2 Explain the importance of proper credit approval for sales. What effect do adequate controls in the credit function have on the auditor's evidence accumulation?

14-3 Distinguish between bad-debt expense and charge-off of uncollectible accounts. Explain why they are audited in completely different ways.

14-4 List the transaction-related audit objectives for the verification of sales transactions. For each objective, state one internal control that the client can use to reduce the likelihood of misstatements.

14-5 List the most important duties that should be segregated in the sales and collection cycle. Explain why it is desirable that each duty be segregated.

14-6 Explain how prenumbered shipping documents and sales invoices can be useful controls for preventing misstatements in sales.

14-7 What three types of authorizations are commonly used as internal controls for sales? For each authorization, state a test of controls that the auditor could use to verify whether the control was effective in preventing misstatements.

14-8 Explain the purpose of footing and cross-footing the sales journal and tracing the totals to the general ledger.

14-9 What is the difference between the auditor's approach in verifying sales returns and allowances and that for sales? Explain the reasons for the difference.

14-10 Explain why auditors usually emphasize the detection of fraud in the audit of cash. Is this consistent or inconsistent with the auditor's responsibility in the audit? Explain.

14-11 List the transaction-related audit objectives for the verification of cash receipts. For each objective, state one internal control that the client can use to reduce the likelihood of misstatements.

14-12 List several audit procedures the auditor can use to determine whether all cash received was recorded.

14-13 Explain what is meant by "proof of cash receipts," and state its purpose.

14-14 Explain what is meant by "lapping," and discuss how the auditor can uncover it. Under what circumstances should the auditor make a special effort to uncover lapping?

14-15 What audit procedures are most likely to be used to verify accounts receivable charged off as uncollectible? State the purpose of each of these procedures.

14-16 Under what circumstances is it acceptable to perform tests of controls for sales and cash receipts at an interim date?

14-17 Deirdre Brandt, a public accountant, tested sales transactions for the month of March in an audit of the financial statements for the year ended December 31, 2009. Based on the excellent results of the tests of controls, she decided to significantly reduce her substantive tests of details of balances at year end. Evaluate this decision.

14-18 BestSellers.com sells fiction and non-fiction books to customers through the company's website. Customers place orders for books via the website by providing their name, address, and credit card number and expiration date. What internal controls could Best-Sellers.com implement to ensure that shipments of books occur only for customers who have the ability to pay for those books? At what point would Best-Sellers.com be able to record the sale as revenue?

14-19 ABC is a small manufacturing company that sells all of its products on credit; payment is normally due within 30 days. What are the risks associated with credit sales? What controls can ABC implement to mitigate these risks?

Discussion Questions and Problems

14-20 Items 1 through 8 are selected questions of the type generally found in internal control questionnaires used by auditors to obtain an understanding of internal control in the sales and collection cycle. In using the questionnaire for a particular client, a "yes" response to a question indicates a possible internal control, whereas a "no" indicates a potential weakness.

1. Are sales invoices independently compared with customers' orders for prices, quantities, extensions, and footings?

2. Are sales orders, invoices, and credit memoranda issued and filed in numerical sequence, and are the sequences accounted for periodically?

3. Are the selling function and cash register functions independent of the cash receipts, shipping, delivery, and billing functions?

4. Are all COD, scrap, equipment, and cash sales accounted for in the same manner as charge sales, and is the record keeping independent of the collection procedure?

5. Is the collection function independent of, and does it constitute a check on, billing and recording sales?
6. Are customer master files balanced regularly to general ledger control accounts by an employee independent of billing functions?
7. Are cash receipts entered in the accounts receivable system by persons independent of the mail-opening and receipts-listing functions?
8. Are receipts deposited intact on a timely basis?

REQUIRED

a. For each of the questions above, state the transaction-related audit objectives being fulfilled if the control is in effect.
b. For each control, list a test of control to test its effectiveness.
c. For each of the questions above, identify the nature of the potential financial misstatements.
d. For each of the potential misstatements in part (c), list an audit procedure to determine whether a material error exists.

14-21 The following errors or fraud and other irregularities are included in the accounting records of Joyce Manufacturing Ltd.:

1. The credit limit for a new customer was entered as $20,000 rather than $2,000 in the customer master file.
2. A material sale was unintentionally recorded for the second time on the last day of the year. The sale had originally been recorded two days earlier.
3. Cash paid on accounts receivable was stolen by the mail clerk when the mail was opened.
4. Cash paid on accounts receivable that had been prelisted by a secretary was stolen by the bookkeeper who enters cash receipts and accounts receivable in the accounts receivable system. He failed to enter the transactions.

5. A shipment to a customer was not billed because of the loss of the bill of lading.
6. Merchandise was shipped to a customer, but no bill of lading was prepared. Since billings are prepared from bills of lading, the customer was not billed.
7. A sale to a retail customer was unintentionally classified as a commercial sale.

REQUIRED

a. Identify whether each misstatement is an error, a fraud, or other irregularity.
b. For each misstatement, state a control that should have prevented it from occurring on a continuing basis.
c. For each misstatement, state an audit procedure that could uncover it.

14-22 YourTeam.com is an online retailer of college and professional sports team memorabilia, such as hats, shirts, pennants, and other sports logo products. Consumers select the university, college, or professional team from a pull-down menu on the company's website. For each listed team, the website provides a product description, picture, and price for all products sold online. Customers click on the product number of the items they wish to purchase. YourTeam.com has established the following internal controls for its online sales:

1. Only products shown on the website can be purchased online. Other company products not shown on the website are unavailable for online sale.
2. The online sales system is linked to the perpetual inventory system that verifies quantities on hand before processing the sale.
3. Before the sale is authorized, YourTeam.com obtains credit card authorization codes electronically from the credit card agency.
4. Online sales are rejected if the customer's shipping address does not match the credit card's billing address.

5. Before the sale is finalized, the online screen shows the product name, description, unit price, and total sales price for the online transaction. Customers must click on the Accept or Reject sales buttons to indicate approval or rejection of the online sale.
6. Once customers approve the online sale, the online sales system generates a Pending Sales file, which is an online data file that is used by warehouse personnel to process shipments. Online sales are not recorded in the sales journal until warehouse personnel enter the bill of lading number and date of shipment into the Pending Sales data file.

REQUIRED

a. For each control, identify the transaction-related audit objective(s) being fulfilled if each control is in effect.
b. For each control, describe potential financial misstatements that could occur if the control were not present.
c. For each control, identify an important general control that would affect the quality of the control.
d. For each control, list a test of control to test its effectiveness.

14-23 You were asked in February 2009 by the board of management of your church to review its accounting procedures. As part of this review, you have prepared the following comments relating to the collections made at weekly services and record-keeping for members' pledges and contributions:

1. The finance committee is responsible for preparing an annual budget based on the anticipated needs of the

various church committees and for the annual fall "pledge campaign" during which most members make a commitment to contribute a certain amount to the church over the following year.
2. The financial records are maintained by the treasurer who has authority to sign cheques drawn on the church bank account.

3. The ushers take up the collection during the services each Sunday and place it uncounted in a deposit bag in the church safe.
4. The treasurer, who is retired, comes in Monday morning, counts the collection, and deposits it into the church's bank account. Some members use predated numbered envelopes, but most do not. The treasurer enters members' contributions into a spreadsheet for numbered envelopes.
5. The treasurer issues receipts to each member every January based on the spreadsheet amounts. The contributions up to 2007 had always exceeded the amounts pledged so that the value of receipts given out was less than total contributions; the excess was recorded as "loose" or "open" collection. In 2009, the total of the receipts given out by the treasurer exceeded the total funds received by the church.
6. The church is registered as a charity under the Income Tax Act and is required to file a return each year to comply with its rules. The chairperson of the finance commit-

tee is upset because the church has received a letter from the Canada Revenue Agency in connection with the return for 2009 because the return showed receipts given exceeded the funds actually received. The letter indicated that such differences could result in removal of the church's ability to issue income tax receipts.

REQUIRED
Identify the risks of error or fraud, identify control weaknesses, and recommend improvements in procedures for the following:
a. Collections made at weekly services.
b. Record-keeping for members' pledges and contributions.
Use the methodology for identifying weaknesses that was discussed in Chapter 9. Organize your answer sheets as follows:

Risks	Weakness	Recommended Improvement

(Adapted from AICPA)

14-24 Lenter Supply Corp. is a medium-sized distributor of wholesale hardware supplies in southern Manitoba. It has been a client of yours for several years and has instituted excellent internal control for sales at your recommendation.

In providing control over shipments, the client has prenumbered "warehouse removal slips" that are used for every sale. It is company policy never to remove goods from the warehouse without an authorized warehouse removal slip. After shipment, two copies of the warehouse removal slip are sent to billing for the computerized preparation of a sales invoice. One copy is stapled to the duplicate copy of a prenumbered sales invoice, and the other copy is filed numerically. In some cases, more than one warehouse removal slip is used for billing one sales invoice. The lowest warehouse removal slip number for the year is 14682 and the highest is 37521. The lowest sales invoice number is 47821 and the highest is 68507.

In the audit of sales, one of the major concerns is the effectiveness of the controls in making sure that all shipments are billed. You have decided to use audit sampling in testing internal controls.

REQUIRED
a. State an effective audit procedure for testing whether shipments have been billed. What is the sampling unit for the audit procedure?
b. Assuming that you expect no deviations in the sample but are willing to accept a TER of 3 percent, at a 10-percent ARACR, what is the appropriate sample size for the audit test? You may complete this assignment using non-statistical sampling or attribute sampling.
c. Design a random selection plan for selecting the sample from the population using the random number table. Select the first 10 sample items using Table 13A-1 on page 436. Use a starting point of row 1013, column 3.
d. Your supervisor suggests the possibility of performing other sales tests with the same sample as a means of efficiently using your audit time. List two other audit procedures that could conveniently be performed using the same sample, and state the purpose of each of the procedures.
e. Is it desirable to test the existence of sales with the random sample you have designed in part (c)? Why or why not?

14-25 The following is a partial audit program for the audit of cash receipts:
1. Review the cash receipts journal for large and unusual transactions.
2. Trace entries from the prelisting of cash receipts to the cash receipts journal to determine if each is recorded.
3. Compare customer name, date, and amount on the prelisting with the data on the cash receipts journal.
4. Examine the related remittance advice for entries selected from the prelisting to determine if cash discounts were approved.
5. Trace entries from the prelisting to the deposit slip to determine if each has been deposited.

REQUIRED
a. Identify which audit procedures could be tested using attribute sampling.
b. What is the appropriate sampling unit for the tests in part (a)?
c. List the attributes for testing in part (a).
d. Assume an ARACR of 5 percent and a TER of 8 percent for tests of controls. The estimated population deviation rate for tests of controls is 2 percent. What is the initial sample size for each attribute?

14-26 The following questions concern the determination of the proper sample size in attributes sampling using the following table:

	1	2	3	4	5	6	7
ARACR (in percentage)	10	5	5	5	10	10	5
TER (in percentage)	6	6	5	6	20	20	2
EPER (in percentage)	2	2	2	2	8	2	0
Population size	1,000	100,000	6,000	1,000	500	500	1,000,000

REQUIRED

a. For each of the columns numbered 1 through 7, decide the initial sample size using non-statistical methods.
b. For each of the columns numbered 1 through 7, determine the initial sample size needed to satisfy the auditor's requirements using attribute sampling from the appropriate parts of Tables 14-9 and 14-10 on pages 483 and 485.
c. Using your understanding of the relationship between the following factors and sample size, state the effect on the initial sample size (increase or decrease) of changing each of the following factors while the other three are held constant:

(1) An increase in ARACR.
(2) An increase in the TER.
(3) An increase in the EPER.
(4) An increase in the population size.

d. Explain why there is such a large difference in the sample sizes for columns 3 and 6.
e. Compare your answers in part (b) with the results you determined in part (a). Which of the four factors appears to have the greatest effect on the initial sample size? Which one appears to have the least effect?
f. Why is the sample size referred to as the initial sample size?

14-27 The following are auditor judgments and audit sampling results for six populations. Assume large population sizes.

	1	2	3	4	5	6
EPER (in percentage)	2	0	3	1	1	8
TER (in percentage)	6	3	8	5	20	15
ARACR (in percentage)	5	5	10	5	10	10
Actual sample size	100	100	60	100	20	60
Actual number of exceptions in the sample	2	0	1	4	1	8

REQUIRED

a. For each population, did the auditor select a smaller sample size than is indicated by using attribute sampling tables for determining sample size? Evaluate, selecting either a larger or smaller size than those determined in the tables.
b. Calculate the SER and CUER for each population.
c. For which of the six populations should the sample results be considered unacceptable? What options are available to the auditor?
d. Why is analysis of the deviations necessary even when the populations are considered acceptable?
e. For the following terms, identify which is an audit decision, a non-statistical estimate made by the auditor, a sample result, or a statistical conclusion about the population:

(1) EPER.
(2) TER.
(3) ARACR.
(4) Actual sample size.
(5) Actual number of exceptions in the sample.
(6) SER.
(7) CUER.

Professional Judgment Problems

14-28 Marvel Distributor Company receives orders by telephone and enters them into the online sales system. Twice a day, a report is sent to the credit department listing any accounts that have exceeded their credit limit. The credit supervisor initials those orders that are to be released, and returns the report to the order staff, who release the orders. Two copies of the sales invoices are then printed, with a different numeric series than the orders.

The customer copy of the sales invoice is held in a pending file awaiting notification that the order was shipped. The shipping copy of the sales invoice is routed through the warehouse. The shipping department personnel pack the order and manually prepare a two-copy bill of lading. They enter the bill of lading number into the computer system, which triggers the release of the sale to the order staff: a sales journal is printed, and sales staff pull the listed invoices for mailing. One copy of the bill of lading is attached to the shipping copy of the invoice, and the second copy is filed numerically in the shipping area.

a. What weaknesses in internal control exist in this system? For each weakness, state the errors that could occur as a result of the weakness. For each weakness, provide a control that would prevent or detect the error.

b. What audit tests would the auditor conduct to determine whether the control weakness(es) resulted in a material error?

14-29 In performing tests of controls and substantive tests of transactions for the Oakland Hardware Company, Ben Frentz, a public accountant, is concerned with the internal verification of pricing, extensions, and footings of sales invoices and the accuracy of the calculations. In testing sales using audit sampling, a separate attribute is used for the test of control (the existence of matching shipping documents) and the substantive test of transactions (the accuracy of calculation). Because internal controls are considered good, Frentz uses a 10-percent ARACR, a zero EPER, and a 5-percent TER for both attributes. Therefore, the initial sample size is 45 items, which Ben rounds up to 50.

In conducting the tests, the auditor finds three sample items for which there were no matching shipping documents, but in all cases the invoices are for services (such as product repairs or installation). No sales invoice tested in the sample has a financial misstatement. Complete the following requirements using either a non-statistical sampling or an attributes sampling approach.

REQUIRED

a. Estimate or determine the CUER for both the attributes, assuming a population of 5,000 sales invoices.
b. Decide whether the control is acceptable.
c. Discuss the most desirable course of action that the auditor should follow in deciding the effect of the CUER exceeding the TER.
d. Explain how it is possible that the sample had three control deviations but no transactions involved monetary misstatements.
e. How would you analyze exceptions in this case?

Case

14-30 Meyer's Pharmaceutical Company, a drug manufacturer, has the following internal controls for billing and recording accounts receivable:

1. An incoming customer's purchase order is received in the order department by a clerk who enters the information into the sales management system. The system assigns an internal sequential number to the sales order. For existing customers, once the customer number has been entered, the information system automatically retrieves the customer's name and address, and credit limit. The clerk visually compares this information, writes the customer number and internal sales order number on the customer purchase order form, then enters the item number and quantity ordered. The clerk then initials the purchase order as entered, and stamps the date entered on the purchase order. The sales management system multiplies the number of items by the unit price and adds the extended amounts to produce the total amount of the invoice. The clerk visually compares the total with the purchase order. If Meyer's prices are less than the customer prices, the order is processed. If Meyer's prices are higher, the clerk sets the order status as "Pending" and takes the purchase order to the sales department for follow-up. The clerk will release the order from the "Pending" status to credit check only when one of the sales supervisors has approved the order. For large differences (greater than $500), the customer is requested to initiate a revised purchase order.

2. The sales management system compares the sum of the new order plus existing accounts receivable for the customer with the credit limit for the customer. If the amount is less than the credit limit, then the order is accepted. If the amount exceeds the credit limit, a warning is displayed on the screen, and the order is not accepted but is given the status of "Pending." All pending orders are listed on a report and printed daily for review by the credit department. Approval is granted only if credit limits are increased and authorized by the credit manager on a credit limit change form, after appropriate investigation.

3. The sales management system compares ordered amounts with inventory, and if items are in stock, prints a three-part sales order shipping document and bill of lading, which is sent to the shipping department. After the order has been shipped, two copies of the shipping document are given to the accounting department. The third copy of the sales order and bill of lading are sent with the goods to the customer.

4. An accounts receivable clerk retrieves the sales order using the sales order number, enters the quantities shipped, and generates the invoice. One copy of the shipping document goes with the invoice to the customer, and another copy is stapled to the company copy of the invoice and filed numerically. The sales order number is listed on the invoice.

5. Sales are recorded online, that is, as each invoice is prepared, it is posted against the customer master file. Each day, a daily sales journal is printed. The sales and accounts receivable posting is recorded by automatic journal entry at the end of each day, after the daily sales journal is printed. The journal entry is printed at the bottom of the daily sales journal.

REQUIRED

a. Flowchart the filling function as a means of understanding the system.

b. Identify the potential risks of misstatement (error or fraud) that could occur at Meyer's.

c. For each risk identified in part (b), identify internal controls present at Meyer's that could prevent or detect the potential misstatement. State the audit objectives associated with each internal control.

d. Have all of the transaction-related audit objectives for sales been covered in part (c)? If not, list internal controls over sales for the remaining transaction-related audit objectives.

e. For each of the internal controls in parts (c) and (d), list a useful test of control to verify the effectiveness of the control.

f. For each transaction-related audit objective for sales, list appropriate substantive tests, considering internal controls.

ACL Problem

14-31 This problem requires the use of ACL software, which is included in the companion website at **www.pearsoned.ca/arens**. Information about installing and using ACL and solving this problem can be found in the ACL Appendix, also on the companion website. You should read all of the reference material preceding the instructions for "Quick Sort" before locating the appropriate command to answer questions (a)–(e). For this problem, use the Metaphor_AR_2002 file in ACL_Demo (in the Tables folder). The suggested command or other source of information needed to solve the problem requirement is included at the end of each question.

a. Determine the total number and amount of September 2002 transactions in the file (Filter, Count, and Total Field).

b. Determine and print the total amount for each of the five types of 2002 transactions for comparison with the general ledger (Summarize). Which transaction type has the highest count?

c. For sales invoices (IN), determine the number of transactions, total amount, largest amount, and average size (Filter and Statistics).

d. Determine the difference in the number of days between the invoice date (DATE1) and the due date (DUE) for sales invoices (IN), and evaluate the impact upon internal controls (Computed Field).

e. To better decide the sales invoices to select for testing, you decide to stratify 2002 sales invoices (IN) after excluding all invoices less than $300. Print the output (Filter and Stratify). On the basis of your results, assess whether $300 is a reasonable stratification level.

Ongoing Small Business Case: Commercial Accounts at CondoCleaners.com

14-32 Many of the condominium towers that comprise CondoCleaners.com's customer base have stores or businesses located in or near the towers. Jim has decided to further expand his business by offering cleaning services to businesses. Unlike residential customers, commercial accounts generate accounts receivable, as customers would be billed monthly for their cleaning services.

REQUIRED

What controls should Jim put in place to ensure the collectability of his commercial accounts?

15

Completing the tests in the sales and collection cycle: Accounts receivable

Substantive tests are considered the "finishing touch" for the audit of an account. The controls testing provides information about the quality of the client's systems so that the auditor has enough detail to design the tests of detail. In this chapter, we will look at one specific account—trade accounts receivable—and examine how the testing is designed, selected, executed, and evaluated. All types of auditors will conduct substantive tests such as those described here to quantify potential misstatements, while management accountants will find the results of such testing useful when deciding whether adjustments should be posted to accounts.

STANDARDS REFERENCED IN THIS CHAPTER

CICA Standards

CAS 505 – External confirmations (previously Section 5303 – Confirmation)

Section 1701 – Segment disclosures

Section 3020 – Accounts and notes receivable

Section 3840 – Related-party transactions

LEARNING OBJECTIVES

1 Identify and describe the process for designing tests of details of balances for accounts receivable. Explain the relationship between transaction-related and balance-related audit objectives for the sales and collection cycle.

2 Explain when and why analytical review procedures are completed as part of the audit of sales and accounts receivable. Link substantive testing to the audit risk model.

3 Describe the accounts receivable audit tests that would be completed for each audit assertion. List reasons supporting the importance of confirmation.

4 Illustrate the risk assessment and substantive tests of accounts receivable using Hillsburg Hardware Limited. Describe the execution and evaluation of monetary unit sampling (MUS).

When More Isn't Better

On Cindy Veinot's first audit assignment, she is asked to handle the confirmation of accounts receivable. The audit client is a retailer with a large number of customer accounts. In previous years, Cindy's firm had confirmed these accounts using negative confirmations. Last year, 200 negative confirmations were sent one month prior to year end. Those that were returned showed only timing differences; none represented a misstatement in the client's books.

Before the current year's planned confirmation date, Cindy performs a review of internal controls over sales and cash receipts transactions. She discovers that a new online system for sales transactions has been implemented, but the client is having considerable problems getting it to work properly. There are a significant number of misstatements in recording sales during the past few months. Cindy's tests of controls and substantive tests of sales transactions also identify similar misstatements.

When Cindy asks her supervisor what to do, the supervisor responds, "No problem, Cindy. Just send 300 confirmation requests instead of the usual 200." Cindy recalls from her auditing class that negative confirmation requests are not considered good evidence when there are weak controls. Because customers are asked to respond only when there are differences, the auditor cannot be confident of the correct value for each misstatement in the sample. Cindy concludes that expanding the sample size is the wrong solution. When Cindy discusses her concerns with her supervisor, who responds, "You are absolutely right. I spoke too quickly. We need to sit down and think about a better strategy to find out if accounts receivable is materially misstated."

IMPORTANCE TO AUDITORS

Cindy felt comfortable talking to her supervisor about her disagreement with the audit approach that had been used in the past. A good working relationship among members of the audit team enables junior staff to question the decisions of senior staff, either to improve the audit process or to help clarify the work that needs to be done. It is also important to have the knowledge to ask questions like Cindy did. It may be that changes in internal controls or changes in sampling methods or quantities tested require new procedures to be conducted.

WHAT DO YOU THINK?

1. What other questions could Cindy have asked that would have helped her assess the audit approach for accounts receivable?

2. How do system changes affect the substantive tests conducted at an audit?

3. What information would Cindy require to select a sample for positive accounts receivable confirmations?

continued >

THE relationship between analytical procedures and tests of detail and planned detection risk are shown in Figure 15-1, using the audit risk model. We consider tests of controls for the sales and collection cycle, discussed in the previous chapter, to be part of Phase 2 of the audit process. (Recall that Phase 1 is planning.) Tests of details of balances for the sales and collection cycle, studied in this chapter, are done in Phase 3. Audit programs including both tests of controls and substantive tests are written at the same time. However, prior to conducting substantive tests, the auditor would review the results of the control tests and review whether changes are needed to assessed risks. This chapter walks you through the completion of the audit of the sales and collection cycle.

Designing Tests of Details of Balances for Accounts Receivable

Methodology for Designing Tests of Details of Balances

Figure 15-2 on the next page shows the methodology that auditors follow in determining the appropriate tests of details of balances for accounts receivable. Substantive tests (comprising analytical review and tests of details) comprise Phase 6 in the risk response portion of the eight-phase audit process model introduced in Chapter 5. The methodology for designing tests of details was introduced in Chapter 12. This methodology integrates both the audit risk model and the types of audit tests that are shown in Figure 15-1.

Recall that prior to designing audit tests the auditor will conduct preplanning (Phase 1), build a client risk profile (Phase 2) which includes preliminary analytical review, and conduct and document a variety of risk assessments that are used to develop a strategic audit approach by cycle (Phase 3). In Phase 4, the auditor will then develop the audit programs, tests of control, and substantive tests. The results of the tests of control (Phase 5), discussed in the previous chapter, are evaluated before

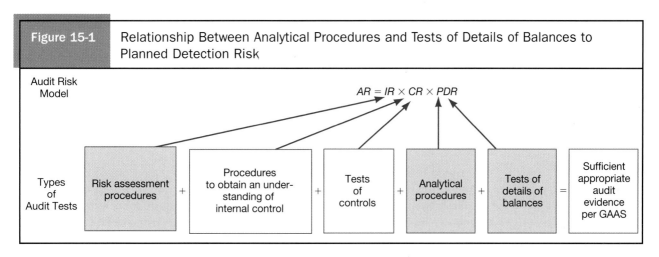

| Figure 15-1 | Relationship Between Analytical Procedures and Tests of Details of Balances to Planned Detection Risk |

Audit Risk Model

$$AR = IR \times CR \times PDR$$

| Types of Audit Tests | Risk assessment procedures | + | Procedures to obtain an understanding of internal control | + | Tests of controls | + | Analytical procedures | + | Tests of details of balances | = | Sufficient appropriate audit evidence per GAAS |

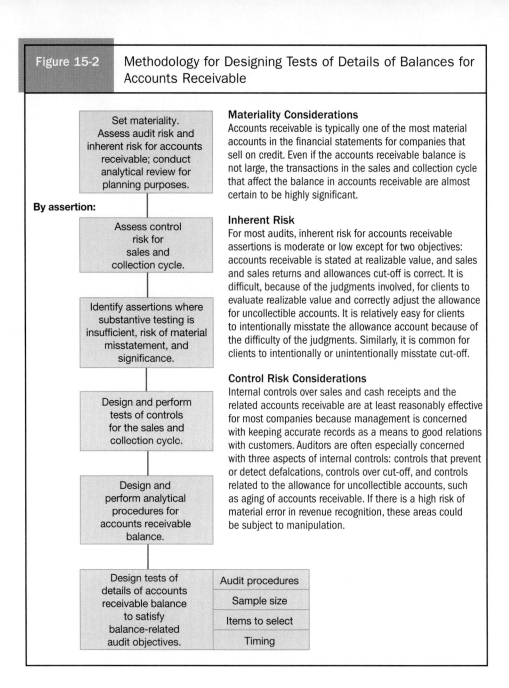

Figure 15-2 Methodology for Designing Tests of Details of Balances for Accounts Receivable

Set materiality. Assess audit risk and inherent risk for accounts receivable; conduct analytical review for planning purposes.

By assertion:

Assess control risk for sales and collection cycle.

Identify assertions where substantive testing is insufficient, risk of material misstatement, and significance.

Design and perform tests of controls for the sales and collection cycle.

Design and perform analytical procedures for accounts receivable balance.

Design tests of details of accounts receivable balance to satisfy balance-related audit objectives.

Audit procedures

Sample size

Items to select

Timing

Materiality Considerations

Accounts receivable is typically one of the most material accounts in the financial statements for companies that sell on credit. Even if the accounts receivable balance is not large, the transactions in the sales and collection cycle that affect the balance in accounts receivable are almost certain to be highly significant.

Inherent Risk

For most audits, inherent risk for accounts receivable assertions is moderate or low except for two objectives: accounts receivable is stated at realizable value, and sales and sales returns and allowances cut-off is correct. It is difficult, because of the judgments involved, for clients to evaluate realizable value and correctly adjust the allowance for uncollectible accounts. It is relatively easy for clients to intentionally misstate the allowance account because of the difficulty of the judgments. Similarly, it is common for clients to intentionally or unintentionally misstate cut-off.

Control Risk Considerations

Internal controls over sales and cash receipts and the related accounts receivable are at least reasonably effective for most companies because management is concerned with keeping accurate records as a means to good relations with customers. Auditors are often especially concerned with three aspects of internal controls: controls that prevent or detect defalcations, controls over cut-off, and controls related to the allowance for uncollectible accounts, such as aging of accounts receivable. If there is a high risk of material error in revenue recognition, these areas could be subject to manipulation.

conducting the substantive tests (Phase 6), which are the focus of this chapter. Analytical procedures, described in the next section, will be completed first, and reviewed before conducting the tests of detail.

Determining the appropriate tests of details of balances evidence is complicated because it must be decided on an objective-by-objective basis. There are several interactions that affect the evidence decision. For example, the auditor must consider inherent risk, which may differ by objective, and control risk, which also may vary by objective. The emphasis on a particular objective will vary depending upon the auditor's assessment of the likelihood of material misstatement. The amount of work conducted in sales and accounts receivable will also be affected by the auditor's assessment of the quality of controls over revenue recognition. Where the auditor believes that biases or the potential of revenue manipulation exists, there will be increased tests of details of accounts receivable and increased use of dual-purpose tests for tests of control.

To help manage the decision-making process for the appropriate tests of details of balances, auditors often use an **evidence planning spreadsheet**. This spreadsheet was first introduced in Chapter 7 (Figure 7-6, page 229) and further amplified in

Evidence planning spreadsheet— a working paper used to help the auditor decide whether planned audit evidence for tests of details of balances should be low, medium, or high for each balance-related audit objective.

Chapter 14 (Figure 14-13, page 487). The completed evidence planning spreadsheet is included as Figure 15-8 on page 518. This spreadsheet is directly related to the methodology in Figure 15-2. Both figures are discussed as we proceed.

Accounts Receivable Balance-Related Audit Objectives

The eight general **balance-related audit objectives** used to help the auditor decide the appropriate audit evidence are the same for every account balance and are applied to accounts receivable as accounts receivable balance-related audit objectives. The general objectives were first introduced in Chapter 5. These eight objectives applied to accounts receivable are:[1]

Accounts receivable balance-related audit objectives—the eight specific audit objectives used to help the auditor decide the appropriate audit evidence for accounts receivable.

- Recorded accounts receivable exist (existence).
- The client has rights to accounts receivable (rights and obligations).
- Existing accounts receivable are included (completeness).
- Accounts receivable are accurate (accuracy).
- Accounts receivable are stated at realizable value (valuation).
- Accounts receivable are properly classified (classification).
- Accounts receivable in the aged trial balance agree with related customer master file amounts, and the total is correctly added and agrees with the general ledger (detail tie-in).
- Cut-off for accounts receivable is correct (cut-off).

The first eight columns in the evidence planning spreadsheet in Figure 15-8 include the balance-related audit objectives. The auditor uses the factors in the rows to aid in assessing planned detection risk for accounts receivable, by objective. All of these factors are decided during audit planning. They were studied in Chapters 7 through 14.

Accounts Receivable Disclosure-Related Audit Objectives

The auditor also uses specific accounts receivable disclosure-related audit objectives, introduced in Chapter 5. These objectives concern fair disclosure and representation of the accounts receivable balance in the financial statements. The seven objectives that apply to accounts receivable are as follows:

- Accounts receivable balances are for transactions that actually occurred (occurrence).
- Accounts receivable includes only amounts that are collectable by the company (rights and obligations).
- Disclosures about accounts receivable are fully included (completeness).
- The accounts payable balance shown on the financial statements is materially correct (accuracy).
- Accounts receivable is shown at appropriate amounts that represent what will be collected (valuation).
- Accounts receivable is correctly grouped as current versus long-term (classification).
- Financial and non-financial information about accounts receivable is clearly shown, indicating the nature of the accounts receivable and the associated risks (understandability).

An overall conclusion for presentation and disclosure is shown in the last column of Figure 15-8.

SET MATERIALITY, ASSESS AUDIT RISK AND INHERENT RISK, AND CONDUCT PLANNING ANALYTICAL REVIEW Setting materiality starts with the auditor making the preliminary judgment about materiality for the entire financial statements. Figure 15-8 shows that

---

[1] Detail tie-in is included as the first objective here, as compared with being Objective 7 in Chapter 5, because tests for detail tie-in are normally done first.

materiality was set at $496,000 for the Hillsburg Hardware audit by including the amount on the bottom of the evidence planning spreadsheet.

Audit risk is assessed for the financial statements as a whole and is not usually allocated to various accounts or objectives. Figure 15-8 shows an audit risk of high for every objective, which will permit a higher planned detection risk for accounts receivable than if audit risk were low. Inherent risk is assessed for each objective for an account such as accounts receivable. It was assessed at low for all objectives except valuation for Hillsburg Hardware.

Planning analytical review is conducted to help target audit field work. Appendix 6A illustrated the calculation of several ratios for Hillsburg Hardware. As an example, referring to the Hillsburg Hardware balance sheet at the end of Chapter 5, the accounts receivable balance for the current year is higher, yet the allowance for bad debts is lower. The auditor would conduct additional testing to justify the lower bad-debt allowance, particularly given current economic conditions.

ASSESS CONTROL RISK FOR THE SALES AND COLLECTION CYCLE The methodology for assessing control risk was studied in general in Chapter 9 and applied to sales and cash receipts transactions in Chapter 14. The framework used to identify control activities and internal control weaknesses was a control risk matrix. Examples are included in Figures 14-6 (page 475) and 14-7 (page 476).

The internal controls studied in Chapter 14 relate specifically to transaction-related audit objectives for classes of transactions. The two primary classes of transactions in the sales and collection cycle are sales and cash receipts.

The auditor must relate control risk for transaction-related audit objectives to balance-related and presentation and disclosure audit objectives in deciding planned detection risk and planned evidence for tests of details of balances. For the most part, the relationship is straightforward. Figure 15-3 shows the relationship between transaction-related and balance-related objectives for the two primary classes of transactions in the sales and collection cycle. For example, assume that the auditor concluded that control risk for both sales and cash receipts transactions is low for the accuracy transaction-related audit objective. The auditor can, therefore, conclude that controls for the accuracy balance-related audit objective for accounts receivable are effective because the only transactions that affect accounts receivable are sales and cash receipts. Of course, if sales returns and allowances and charge-off of uncollectible accounts receivable are significant, assessed control risk must also be considered for these two classes of transactions.

Two aspects of the relationships in Figure 15-3 deserve special mention:

- For sales, the occurrence transaction-related audit objective affects the existence balance-related audit objective, but for cash receipts, the occurrence transaction-related audit objective affects the completeness balance-related audit objective.
- A similar relationship exists for the completeness transaction-related audit objective. The reason for this somewhat surprising conclusion is that an increase in sales increases accounts receivable, but an increase in cash receipts decreases accounts receivable. For example, recording a sale that did not occur violates the occurrence transaction-related audit objective and existence balance-related audit objective (both overstatements). Recording a cash receipt that did not occur violates the occurrence transaction-related audit objective, but it violates the completeness balance-related audit objective for accounts receivable because a receivable that is still outstanding is no longer included in the records.

Three accounts receivable balance-related audit objectives are not affected by assessed control risk for classes of transactions. These are valuation, rights and obligations, and presentation and disclosure. When the auditor wants to reduce assessed control risk below maximum for these three objectives, separate controls are identified and tested. This was discussed in Chapter 9.

Figure 15-8 on page 518 includes three rows for assessed control risk: one for sales, one for cash receipts, and one for additional controls related to the accounts receivable

Figure 15-3

Relationship Between Transaction-Related and Balance-Related Audit Objectives for the Sales and Collection Cycle

Class of Transactions	Transaction-Related Audit Objectives	Accounts Receivable Balance-Related Audit Objectives							
		Existence	Rights and Obligations	Completeness	Accuracy	Valuation	Classification	Detail Tie-in	Cut-off
Sales	Occurrence	X							
	Completeness			X					
	Accuracy				X				
	Classification						X		
	Posting and summarization							X	
	Timing								X
Cash receipts	Occurrence			X					
	Completeness	X							
	Accuracy				X				
	Classification						X		
	Posting and summarization							X	
	Timing								X

balance. The source of each control risk for sales and cash receipts is the control risk matrix, assuming that the tests of controls results supported the original assessment. The auditor makes a separate assessment of control risk for objectives related only to the accounts receivable balance.

IDENTIFY AT-RISK ASSERTIONS Figure 15-2 indicates three ways that the auditor assesses the assertions to identify high risks. The first is identifying those assertions where substantive testing may be insufficient. For example, if shipping documents and sales invoices are sent electronically (via electronic data interchange, EDI), and cash is received electronically, the auditor would be required to evaluate the controls over these processes. Substantive testing could be substantially reduced for the assertions of accuracy and completeness where general and automated application controls are found to be good.

Secondly, the auditor targets testing based upon risk of material misstatement. The most likely misstatements could occur with valuation (due to the judgments involved in setting the bad-debt allowance), timing (if sales are recorded in the wrong period), and occurrence (if there is a bias to misstating revenue). The auditor would then increase substantive tests for these assertions.

Finally, the auditor must increase testing where it is concluded that there are significant risks of misstatement, such as for revenue recognition. Other potential significant errors could arise with complex sales transactions or with foreign exchange exposure on accounts receivable. The auditor would increase testing for the assertions that pertain to these risks.

DESIGN AND PERFORM TESTS OF CONTROLS Chapter 14 dealt with deciding audit procedures and sample size for tests of controls and evaluating the results of those

concept check

C15-1 Why is accounts receivable often an important account to audit?

C15-2 Which balance-related audit objectives are not affected by control risk for classes of transactions? Why?

C15-3 Why is valuation a highly at-risk assertion for accounts receivable?

tests. The results of the tests of controls determine whether assessed control risk for sales and cash receipts needs to be revised. The evidence planning spreadsheet in Figure 15-8 shows three rows for control risk based on the completion and evaluation of those tests.

The next two sections focus separately on the two types of substantive tests, analytical procedures and tests of details.

❷ The Importance of Analytical Procedures

Design and Perform Analytical Procedures

As discussed in Chapter 6, analytical procedures are used throughout the audit: during planning, when performing detailed tests, and as a part of completing the audit. Those analytical procedures affecting accounts receivable or the sales cycle that are done during planning and when performing detailed tests are discussed in this chapter.

Most year-end analytical procedures are done after the balance sheet date but before tests of details of balances. It makes little sense to perform extensive analytical procedures before the client has recorded all transactions for the year and finalized the financial statements. Where auditors also provide assurance on quarterly financial results, analytical review procedures are updated periodically throughout the year.

Table 15-1 presents examples of the major types of ratios and comparisons for the sales and collection cycle and potential misstatements that may be indicated by the analytical procedures. It is important to observe in the "Possible Misstatement" column that both balance sheet and income statement accounts are affected. For example, when the auditor performs analytical procedures for sales, evidence is being obtained about both sales and accounts receivable.

Table 15-1	Analytical Procedures for Sales and Collections
Analytical Procedure	**Possible Misstatement**
Compare gross margin percentage with previous years' (by product line).	Overstatement or understatement of sales and accounts receivable.
Compare sales by month (by product line) over time.	Overstatement or understatement of sales and accounts receivable.
Examine relationship between sales and cost of sales (for example, using regression analysis).	Understatement or overstatement of sales and accounts receivable.
Compare sales returns and allowances as a percentage of gross sales with previous years' (by product line).	Understatement or overstatement of sales returns and allowances and accounts receivable.
Compare individual customer balances over a stated amount with previous years'.	Misstatements in accounts receivable and related income statement accounts.
Compare bad-debt expense as a percentage of gross sales with previous years'.	Uncollectible accounts receivable that has not been provided for.
Compare number of days that accounts receivable is outstanding with previous years'.	Overstatement or understatement of allowance for uncollectible accounts and bad-debt expense.
Compare aging categories as a percentage of accounts receivable with previous years'.	Overstatement or understatement of allowance for uncollectible accounts and bad-debt expense.
Compare allowance for uncollectible accounts as a percentage of accounts receivable with previous years'.	Overstatement or understatement of allowance for uncollectible accounts.

audit challenge 15-1
Analyzing Great Western Lumber

Lesley Stopps, a public accountant, is the auditor for Great Western Lumber Company Ltd., a wholesale wood milling company. Lesley calculates the gross margin for three product lines and obtains industry information from published data as listed at the end of this box.

In discussing the results, the controller states that Great Western has always had a higher gross margin on hardwood products than the industry because it focuses on the markets where it is able to sell at higher prices instead of emphasizing volume. The opposite is true of plywood where it has a reasonably small number of customers, each of which demands lower prices because of high volume. The controller states that competitive forces have caused reductions in plywood gross margin for both the industry and Great Western in 2007 and 2008. Great Western has traditionally had a somewhat lower gross margin for softwood than the industry until 2009, when the gross margin went up significantly due to aggressive selling.

Lesley observed that most of what the controller said was reasonable given the facts. Hardwood gross margin for the industry was stable and approximately 3.5 to 4 percent lower than Great Western's every year. Industry gross margin for plywood has declined annually but is about 10 percentage points higher than Great Western's. Industry gross margin for softwood has been stable for the three years, but Great Western's has increased by a fairly large amount.

CRITICAL THINKING QUESTIONS

1. The change in Great Western's softwood gross margin from 20.3 to 23.9 percent is a concern. What calculation helps to quantify the risk of material misstatement?
2. Identify the potential causes of the change in gross margin.
3. How would potential over- or understatements discussed in (2) affect the audit process?

Great Western and Industry Gross Margins

	2009 Gross Margin %		2008 Gross Margin %		2007 Gross Margin %	
	Great Western	Industry	Great Western	Industry	Great Western	Industry
Hardwood	36.3	32.4	36.4	32.5	36.0	32.3
Softwood	23.9	22.0	20.3	22.1	20.5	22.3
Plywood	40.3	50.1	44.2	54.3	45.4	55.6

Note: Industry figures are fictitious.

In addition to the analytical procedures in Table 15-1, there should also be a review of accounts receivable for large and unusual amounts. Individual receivables that deserve special attention are large balances; accounts that have been outstanding for a long time; receivables from affiliated companies, officers, directors, and other related parties; and credit balances. The auditor should review the listing of accounts (aged trial balance) or run exception tests against the customer master file at the balance sheet date to determine which accounts should be investigated further.

The auditor's conclusion about analytical procedures for the sales and collection cycle is incorporated into the third row from the bottom on the evidence planning spreadsheet in Figure 15-8. Analytical procedures are substantive tests and therefore reduce the extent to which the auditor needs to test details of balances, if the analytical procedures' results are favourable.

concept check

C15-4 Why does the auditor conduct analytical review as part of the substantive tests for accounts receivable?

C15-5 A company's sales have declined, while the bad-debt expense and accounts receivable have increased. What do these changes tell you?

3 The Relationship Between Assertions and Tests of Detail

DESIGN TESTS OF DETAILS OF ACCOUNTS RECEIVABLE The appropriate tests of details of balances depend upon the factors incorporated into the evidence planning spreadsheet in Figure 15-8. The second row from the bottom shows planned detection risk for

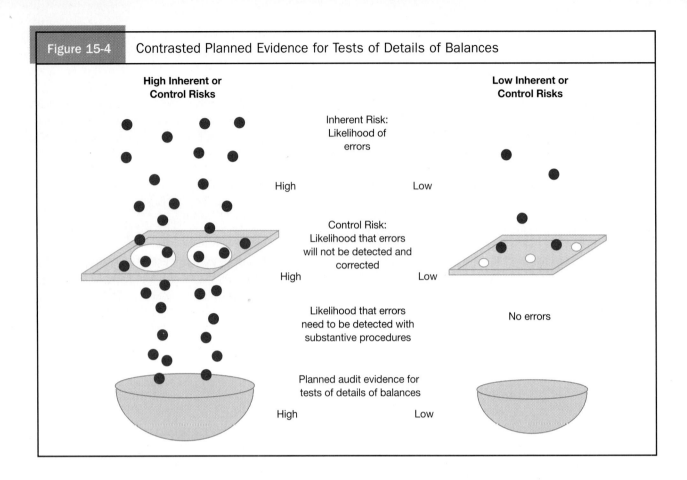

each accounts receivable balance-related audit objective. Planned detection risk for each objective is an auditor decision, decided by subjectively combining the conclusions reached about each of the factors listed above that row.

Combining the factors that determine planned detection risk is complex because the measurement for each factor is imprecise and the appropriate weight to be given each factor is highly judgmental. On the other hand, the relationship between each factor and planned detection risk is well established. Figure 7-1 on page 207 illustrated these relationships. Figure 15-4 contrasts how changes in inherent and control risks affect detection risk and thus the planned audit evidence for tests of details of balances. For example, the left side of the diagram shows high inherent risk (many errors likely) and high control risk (the control risk tray has large holes in it). The right side shows low inherent risk (few errors likely) and low control risk (the control risk tray has only a few very small holes). The auditor knows that a high inherent risk or high control risk decreases planned detection risk and increases planned substantive tests, whereas good results from dual-purpose tests can lead to increased planned detection risk and decreased planned substantive tests.

The bottom row in Figure 15-4 shows the planned audit evidence for tests of details of balances for accounts receivable, by objective. As discussed in Chapters 8 and 11, planned audit evidence is the complement of planned detection risk.

The conclusion that planned audit evidence for a given objective is high, medium, or low is determined by the auditor according to the appropriate audit procedures, sample size, items to select, and timing.

Tests of Details of Balances

Tests of details of balances for all cycles emphasize balance sheet accounts, but income statement accounts are included because they are verified more as a byproduct of the balance sheet tests. For example, if the auditor confirms account receivable balances and finds overstatements due to mistakes in billing customers, there are overstatements of both accounts receivable and sales.

Confirmation of accounts receivable is the most important test of details of accounts receivable. Confirmation is discussed briefly in studying the appropriate tests for each of the balance-related audit objectives, then separately in more detail.

The discussion of tests of details of balances for accounts receivable that follows assumes that the auditor has completed an evidence planning spreadsheet similar to the one in Figure 15-8 and has decided planned detection risk for tests of details for each balance-related audit objective. The audit procedures selected and their sample size will depend heavily on whether planned evidence for a given objective is low, medium, or high. The discussion focuses on accounts receivable balance-related audit objectives.

RECORDED ACCOUNTS RECEIVABLE EXIST The most important test of details of balances for determining the existence of recorded accounts receivable is the confirmation of customers' balances. When customers do not respond to confirmations, auditors also examine (1) supporting documents to verify the shipment of goods and (2) evidence of subsequent cash receipts to determine whether the accounts were collected. Normally, auditors do not examine shipping documents or evidence of subsequent cash receipts for any account in the sample that is confirmed, but these documents are used extensively as alternative evidence for non-responses.

THE CLIENT HAS RIGHTS TO ACCOUNTS RECEIVABLE The client's rights to accounts receivable ordinarily cause no audit problems because the receivables usually belong to the client, but in some cases a portion of the receivables may have been pledged as collateral, assigned to someone else, factored, or sold at discount. Normally, the client's customers are not aware of the existence of such matters; therefore, the confirmation of receivables will not bring it to light. A review of the minutes, discussions with the client, confirmation with banks, and the examination of correspondence files are usually sufficient to uncover instances in which the client has limited rights to receivables.

ALL VALID ACCOUNTS RECEIVABLE ARE INCLUDED It is difficult to test for account balances omitted (the completeness objective) from the aged trial balance except by comparing the customer master file with the file of outstanding transactions and with the general ledger. For example, if the client accidentally excluded an account receivable from a manually prepared trial balance, the only way it would likely be discovered is by footing the accounts receivable trial balance and reconciling the balance with the control account in the general ledger.

If all sales to a customer were omitted from the sales journal or were not entered into the order entry system, the understatement of accounts receivable would be almost impossible to uncover by tests of details of balances. For example, auditors rarely send accounts receivable confirmations with zero balances, in part because research shows that customers are unlikely to respond to requests that indicate balances are understated. The understatement of sales and accounts receivable is best uncovered by tests of controls for shipments made but not recorded (completeness objective for tests of sales transactions) and by analytical procedures.

ACCOUNTS RECEIVABLE IS ACCURATE Confirmation of accounts selected from the accounts receivable trial balance is the most common test of details of balances for the accuracy of accounts receivable. When customers do not respond to confirmation requests, auditors examine supporting documents, in the same way as described for the existence objective. Tests of the debits and credits to particular customers' balances are done by examining supporting documentation for shipments and cash receipts.

ACCOUNTS RECEIVABLE IS VALUED CORRECTLY Tests of the **valuation** objective are performed to evaluate the allowance for uncollectible accounts. Generally accepted accounting principles require that accounts receivable be stated at the amount that

Valuation (of accounts receivable)—the amount of the outstanding balances in accounts receivable that will ultimately be collected.

will ultimately be collected, which is gross accounts receivable less the allowance. The client's estimate of the total amount that is uncollectible is represented by the allowance for uncollectible accounts. The auditor evaluates whether the allowance is reasonable considering all available facts.

The starting point for the evaluation of the allowance for uncollectible accounts is to review the results of the tests of controls that are concerned with the client's credit policy. If the client's credit policy has remained unchanged and the results of the tests of credit policy and credit approval are consistent with those of the preceding year, the change in the balance in the allowance for uncollectible accounts should reflect only changes in economic conditions and sales volume. However, if the client's credit policy or the degree to which it correctly functions has significantly changed, great care must be taken to consider the effects of this change as well.

A common way to evaluate the adequacy of the allowance is to examine carefully the non-current accounts on the aged trial balance to determine which have not been paid subsequent to the balance sheet date. The size and age of unpaid balances can then be compared with similar information from previous years to evaluate whether the amount of non-current receivables is increasing or decreasing over time. The examination of credit files, discussions with the credit manager, and review of the client's correspondence file may also provide insights into the collectability of the accounts. These procedures are especially important if a few large balances are non-current and are not being paid on a regular basis.

There are two pitfalls in evaluating the allowance by reviewing individual non-current balances on the aged trial balance. First, the current accounts are ignored in establishing the adequacy of the allowance even though some of these amounts will undoubtedly become uncollectible. Second, it is difficult to compare the results of the current year with those of previous years on such an unstructured basis. If the accounts are becoming progressively uncollectible over a period of several years, this fact could be overlooked. A way to avoid these difficulties is to establish the history of bad-debt charge-offs over a period of time as a frame of reference for evaluating the current year's allowance. As an example, if historically a certain percentage of the total of each age category becomes uncollectible, it is relatively easy to compute whether the allowance is properly stated. If 2 percent of current accounts, 10 percent of 30- to 90-day accounts, and 35 percent of all balances over 90 days ultimately become uncollectible, these percentages could easily be applied to the current year's aged trial balance totals and the result compared with the balance in the allowance account. Of course, the auditor has to be careful to modify the calculations for changed conditions.

Bad-debt expense After the auditor is satisfied with the allowance for uncollectible accounts, it is easy to verify bad-debt expense. Assume that (1) the beginning balance was verified as a part of the previous audit, (2) the uncollectible accounts charged off were verified as a part of the tests of controls, and (3) the ending balance in the allowance account has been verified by various means. Then bad-debt expense is simply a residual balance that can be verified by a reperformance test.

ACCOUNTS RECEIVABLE ARE PROPERLY CLASSIFIED It is normally relatively easy to evaluate the classification of accounts receivable by reviewing the aged trial balance for material receivables from affiliates, officers, directors, or other related parties. If notes receivable or accounts that should not be classified as a current asset are included with the regular accounts, these should also be segregated. Finally, if the credit balances in accounts receivable are significant, it is appropriate to reclassify them as accounts payable.

There is a close relationship between the classification objective as discussed here and the presentation and disclosure objective. Classification concerns determining whether the client has correctly separated different classifications of accounts receivable. Presentation and disclosure concern making sure the classifications are properly presented. For example, under the classification objective, the auditor determines if

Figure 15-5   Aged Trial Balance Summary for Hillsburg Hardware Limited

Hillsburg Hardware Limited
Accounts Receivable
Aged Trial Balance
31/12/08

Schedule
Prepared by Client
Approved by

Date
5/1/09

Account Number	Customer	Balance 31/12/08	Aging, Based on Invoice Date				
			0–30 days	31–60 days	61–90 days	91–120 days	over 120 days
101011	Adams Supply Ltd.	73,290	57,966	15,324			
101044	Argonaut, Inc.	1,542	1,542				
101100	Atwater Brothers	85,518	85,518				
101191	Beekman Bearings Corp.	14,176	12,676		1,500		
101270	Brown and Phillips	13,952				13,952	
101301	Christopher Plumbing Ltd.	105,231	104,656	125	150	200	100
109733	Travellers Equipment Ltd.	29,765	29,765				
109742	Underhill Parts and Maintenance	8,963	8,963				
109810	UJW Co. Ltd.	15,832		9,832	6,000		
109907	Zephyr Plastics Corp.	74,300	60,085	14,215			
		20,196,800	10,334,169	5,598,762	2,598,746	1,589,654	75,469

receivables from related parties have been separated on the aged trial balance. Under the presentation and disclosure objective, the auditor determines if related-party transactions are correctly shown in the financial statements.

ACCOUNTS RECEIVABLE ARE CORRECTLY ADDED AND AGREE WITH THE CUSTOMER MASTER FILE AND THE GENERAL LEDGER: DETAIL TIE-IN
Most tests of accounts receivable and the allowance for uncollectible accounts are based on the **aged trial balance**. An aged trial balance is a listing of the balances in the accounts receivable customer master file at the balance sheet date. It includes the individual total balances outstanding and a breakdown of each balance by the time elapsed between the date of sale and the balance sheet date. An illustration of a typical aged trial balance summary, in this case for Hillsburg Hardware Limited, is given in Figure 15-5. Note that the total is the same as accounts receivable on the general ledger trial balance on page 129. This is an aged trial balance summary because it includes only totals for each customer. If the open item transactions were used to produce the aged trial balance, then the individual unpaid invoices would be listed to produce a detailed aged trial balance.

Testing the information on the aged trial balance for mechanical accuracy (reperformance) is a necessary audit procedure. It is ordinarily done before any other tests to assure the auditor that the population being tested agrees with the general ledger and accounts receivable master file. The total column and the columns depicting the aging must be test footed, and the total on the trial balance compared with the general ledger. In addition, a sample of individual balances should be traced to supporting documents, such as duplicate sales invoices, to verify the customer name, balance, and proper aging. The extent of the testing for detail tie-in depends on the number of accounts involved, the degree to which the customer master file data have been tested as a part of tests of controls, and the extent to which the schedule has been verified by an internal auditor or other independent person before it is given to the auditor.

For most large clients, this testing is most effectively completed using generalized audit software. The auditor obtains a copy of both the customer master file and the outstanding accounts receivable transactions. By performing the additions, aging, and subtotalling for each customer, the auditor conducts the dual purpose tests of verifying that the programs performing these functions are working correctly as well as

Aged trial balance—a listing of the balances in the accounts receivable master file at the balance sheet date, broken down according to the amount of time elapsed between the date of sale and the balance sheet date.

quantifying any error. At the same time, samples for confirmation can be selected and unusual transactions identified using the auditor's criteria. For example, balances that exceed their credit limits, or outstanding transactions over a certain size, or extremely old outstanding transactions could be listed. These would be used during tests of the relevant audit objectives.

Cut-off misstatements—
misstatements that take place
as a result of current period
transactions being recorded in a
subsequent period, or subsequent
period transactions being
recorded in the current period.

CUT-OFF FOR ACCOUNTS RECEIVABLE IS CORRECT **Cut-off misstatements** can occur for sales, sales returns and allowances, and cash receipts. They take place when current period transactions are recorded in the subsequent period or subsequent period transactions are recorded in the current period.

The objective of cut-off tests is the same regardless of the type of transaction, but the procedures vary. The objective is to verify whether transactions near the end of the accounting period are recorded in the proper period. The cut-off objective is one of the most important in the cycle because misstatements in cut-off can significantly affect current period income. For example, the intentional or unintentional inclusion of several large, subsequent-period sales in the current period or the exclusion of several current-period sales returns and allowances can materially overstate net earnings.

In determining the reasonableness of cut-off, a threefold approach is needed: first, decide on the appropriate criteria for cut-off; second, evaluate whether the client has established adequate procedures to ensure a reasonable cut-off; and third, test whether a reasonable cut-off was obtained.

Sales cut-off The criterion used by most merchandising and manufacturing clients for determining when a sale takes place is the shipment of goods, but some companies record invoices at the time title passes. The passage of title can take place before shipment (as in the case of custom-manufactured goods), at the time of shipment, or subsequent to shipment. For the correct measurement of current-period income, the method must be in accordance with generally accepted accounting principles and consistently applied.

The most important part of evaluating the client's method of obtaining a reliable cut-off is to determine the procedures in use. When a client issues prenumbered shipping documents sequentially, it is usually a simple matter to evaluate and test cut-off. Moreover, the segregation of duties between the shipping and the billing function also enhances the likelihood of recording transactions in the proper period. However, if shipments are made by company truck, the shipping records are not numbered, or shipping and billing department personnel are not independent of each other, it may be difficult, if not impossible, to be assured of an accurate cut-off.

When the client's internal controls are adequate, the cut-off can usually be verified by obtaining the shipping document number for the last shipment made at the end of the period and comparing this number with current and subsequent period recorded sales. As an illustration, assume the shipping document number for the last shipment in the current period is 1489. All recorded sales before the end of the period should bear a shipping document number preceding number 1490. There should also be no sales recorded in the subsequent period for a shipment with a shipping document numbered 1489 or lower. This can easily be tested by comparing recorded sales with the related shipping document for the last few days of the current period and the first few days of the subsequent period.

Sales returns and allowances cut-off Generally accepted accounting principles require that sales returns and allowances be matched with related sales if the amounts are material. For example, if current period shipments are returned in the subsequent period, the proper treatment of the transactions is the inclusion of the sales return in the current period. (The returned goods would be treated as current period inventory.) For most companies, however, sales returns and allowances are recorded in the accounting period in which they occur, under the assumption of approximately equal, offsetting errors at the beginning and end of each accounting period. This is acceptable as long as the amounts are not significant.

When the auditor is confident that the client records all sales returns and allowances promptly, the cut-off tests are simple and straightforward. The auditor can examine supporting documentation for a sample of sales returns and allowances recorded during several weeks subsequent to the closing date to determine the date of the original sale. If the amounts recorded in the subsequent period are significantly different from unrecorded returns and allowances at the beginning of the period under audit, an adjustment must be considered. If internal controls for recording sales returns and allowances are evaluated as ineffective, a larger sample is needed to verify cut-off.

Cash receipts cut-off For most audits, a proper cash receipt cut-off is less important than either the sales or the sales returns and allowances cut-off because the improper cut-off of cash affects only the cash and the accounts receivable balances, not earnings. Nevertheless, if the misstatement is material, it could affect the fair presentation of these accounts, particularly when cash is a small or negative balance.

The auditor tests for a cash receipts cut-off misstatement (frequently referred to as "holding the cash receipts open") by tracing recorded cash receipts to subsequent period bank deposits on the bank statement. If there is a delay of several days, this could indicate a cut-off misstatement.

The confirmation of accounts receivable may also be relied on to some degree to uncover cut-off misstatements for sales, sales returns and allowances, and cash receipts, especially when there is a long interval between the date the transaction took place and the recording date. However, when the interval is only a few days, mail delivery delays may cause confusion of cut-off misstatements with normal reconciliation differences. For example, if a customer mails and records a cheque to a client for payment of an unpaid account on December 30 and the client receives and records the amount on January 5, the records of the two organizations will be different, called a **timing difference**, on December 31. This is not a cut-off misstatement but a reconcilable difference due to the delivery time; it will be difficult for the auditor to evaluate whether a cutoff misstatement or a timing difference occurred when a confirmation reply is the source of information. This type of situation requires additional investigation such as inspection of underlying documents.

Timing difference (in an accounts receivable confirmation)—a reported difference in a confirmation from a debtor that is determined to be a timing difference between the client's and debtor's records and therefore not a misstatement.

ACCOUNTS RECEIVABLE PRESENTATION AND DISCLOSURES ARE PROPER
In addition to testing for the proper statement of the dollar amount in the general ledger, the auditor must also determine that information about the account balance resulting from the sales and collection cycle is properly presented and disclosed in the financial statements. The auditor must decide whether the client has properly combined amounts and disclosed related-party information in the statements. To evaluate the adequacy of the presentation and disclosure, the auditor must have a thorough understanding of generally accepted accounting principles and presentation and disclosure requirements.

An important part of the evaluation involves deciding whether material amounts requiring separate disclosure have actually been separated in the statements. For example, paragraph 3020.01 and Section 3840 of the *CICA Handbook* require that receivables from officers and affiliated companies be segregated from accounts receivable from customers if the amounts are material. Similarly, under Section 1701, it is necessary for companies over a certain size to disclose information about revenues, operations, and assets for different segments of the business as well as information about export sales. The proper aggregation of general ledger balances in the financial statements also requires combining account balances that individually are not relevant for external users of the statements. If all accounts included in the general ledger were disclosed separately on the statements, most statement users would be more confused than enlightened.

As a part of proper disclosure, the auditor is also required to evaluate the adequacy of the footnotes. Required footnote disclosure includes information about the pledging, discounting, factoring, assignment of accounts receivable, and amounts due from related parties. Of course, in order to evaluate the adequacy of these disclosures, it is first necessary to know of their existence and to have complete information about their nature. This is generally obtained in other parts of the audit, as discussed previously.

PRESENTATION AND DISCLOSURE AUDIT OBJECTIVES Presentation and disclosure objectives pertain to information disclosed and presented in the financial statements and notes to the financial statements. The auditor will audit both the financial and narrative information in the financial statements. The quantitative financial information has been discussed in the previous sections (such as accounts receivable actually being due to the organization), so we focus here on more qualitative aspects. For example, do the words used on the financial statement line items accurately reflect the contents of the account? Trade accounts receivable should not include related-party accounts receivable (unless the amounts are clearly insignificant), and different types of material transactions should be clearly listed as separate line items to facilitate the classification and understandability objectives.

If accounts receivable are factored, or there are long-term notes due from customers, have the terms been clearly explained in the notes to the financial statements? Have the methods of calculating allowances been explained, so that users are aware of the types of judgments used in developing these accounts? It is important that financial statements portray clearly the risks associated with the collection of assets, and allowances for bad debts or allowances for warranty expenses can be material or subject to variation if there are new, untested products.

Although the auditor does not audit management's discussion and analysis (MD&A), the auditor must read the MD&A to determine whether there are any inconsistencies with the financial statements or other information that the auditor has collected in the course of the audit.

Confirmation of Accounts Receivable

One of the most important audit procedures is the confirmation of accounts receivable. As explained in Chapter 6, confirmation can be written or oral. Auditing in Action 15-1 illustrates that electronic confirmations sent by electronic mail or other service providers are being used to provide faster response or improve response rates.

auditing in action 15-1
Better and Faster Confirmations?

It is a tight deadline, and the audit is supposed to be completed within two weeks of the year end. The auditors planned their work well and did substantial control testing prior to the year end, as well as sending confirmations as of the end of November, rather than the end of December. Yet some confirmations are best done at the end of the year, due to the risks involved.

Fortunately, the client's banks can now confirm electronically. Also, the client uses online banking, so audit staff were able to observe the client's bank balances as of December 31 by being present and asking the client to log in to all of its accounts and print off details.

Other techniques included having the client telephone customers ahead of time, letting them know that a confirmation request was coming and asking for their cooperation. Auditors obtained email addresses of major customers from the client, and emailed key confirmations as attachments ahead of time, giving the customers the option of printing off and faxing the signed confirmations. In all cases, supporting details of the outstanding invoices were provided, making it easier for the customers to respond to the confirmation request.

The client did not want one major customer confirmed, and the auditors did extensive alternative procedures for this client, as required by current standards, including running an online credit check on the customer to determine its existence and financial stability.

Key to all of these techniques is obtaining high-quality evidence that supports the information in the financial statements. Confirmation fraud does occur (where the client colludes with the customer or the confirmation is sent to a client-controlled address), so the auditor must be aware of potential management bias in overstating revenue (and accounts receivable) when using confirmation.

Sources: 1. Fox, Brian C., "Audit confirmation article falls short," *Journal of Accountancy*, June 2008, www.aicpa.org/pubs/jofa, Accessed: February 19, 2009. 2. McConnell, Donald. K. and Charles H. Schweiger, "Better Evidence Gathering," *Journal of Accountancy*, April 2008, www.aicpa.org/pubs/jofa, Accessed: February 19, 2009.

This multipurpose technique is used to satisfy the existence, accuracy, and cut-off objectives.

DEFINITION OF CONFIRMATION The most important part of the definition of a confirmation is the fact that the evidence comes from a third party. The *CICA Handbook* uses this term. A recent change is that the *CICA Handbook* previous Section 5303 used the term "direct communication," whereas CAS 505 uses "direct written response," which can be in multiple forms: paper or electronic.

Confirmations of receivables were required by Section 5303, except in cases where the auditor had assessed the combined inherent risk and control risk as low or where the auditor concludes, in planning the audit, that confirmation would be ineffective. If the auditor did not confirm receivables, he or she would gain the required assurance by other means such as review of subsequent payments or examination of documentation supporting the receivable balance. CAS 505 does not require the use of confirmations. The application and explanatory material of CAS 505 points out that confirmations may be more relevant to certain assertions (such as existence), and leaves the use of confirmations up to the auditor. Generally, the auditor will send confirmations unless the following are true:

- *Accounts receivable are immaterial.* This is common for certain companies such as retail stores with primarily cash or credit card sales.
- *The auditor considers confirmations ineffective evidence because response rates will likely be inadequate or unreliable.* In certain industries, such as hospitals, response rates to confirmations are very low.
- *The combined level of inherent risk and control risk is low, and other substantive evidence can be accumulated to provide sufficient evidence.* If a client has effective internal controls and low inherent risk for the sales and collection cycle, the auditor should be able to satisfy the evidence requirements by tests of controls, substantive tests of transactions, and analytical procedures.

Although the remaining sections in this chapter refer specifically to the confirmation of accounts receivable from customers, the concepts apply equally to other receivables such as notes receivable, amounts due from officers, and employee advances.

ASSUMPTIONS UNDERLYING CONFIRMATIONS An auditor makes two assumptions when accepting a confirmation as evidence. The first is that the person returning the confirmation is independent of the company and thus will provide an unbiased response. If this assumption is invalid, as would be the case if the confirmation of a fraudulent accounts receivable were sent to a company owned by an associate of the person committing the fraud, the value of the returned confirmation becomes zero. The second assumption is that the person returning the confirmation has knowledge of the account and the intent of the confirmation and has carefully checked the balance to his or her books and records to ensure that the confirmation is in agreement. However, this second assumption may also not always be valid. Research has shown that some people return confirmations without really checking the balance; such a confirmation would have no value.

In many cases, the auditor is able to assess the independence of the person returning the confirmation, but sometimes a relationship may exist of which the auditor is not aware. Furthermore, it is almost always impossible for an auditor to know how much care was taken in checking the balance before the confirmation was signed and returned. Thus, weaknesses may exist in the confirmation of receivables. CAS 505 requires the auditor who has any doubts about the quality of the confirmation (due to the skills of the respondent or due to his or her lack of independence) to undertake additional audit procedures.

In performing confirmation procedures, the auditor must decide the type of confirmation to use, timing of the procedures, sample size, and individual items to select. Each of these is discussed, along with the factors affecting the decision.

Confirmation Decisions

Positive confirmation—a letter, addressed to the debtor, requesting that the recipient indicate directly on the letter whether the stated account balance is correct or incorrect and, if incorrect, by what amount.

Blank confirmation form—a letter, addressed to the debtor, requesting the recipient to fill in the amount of the accounts receivable balance; considered a positive confirmation.

Type of confirmation Two common types of confirmations are used for confirming accounts receivable: positive and negative. A **positive confirmation** is a communication addressed to the debtor requesting him or her to confirm directly whether the balance as stated on the confirmation request is correct or incorrect. Figure 15-6 illustrates a positive confirmation in the audit of Island Hardware Ltd. A variation of the first type of confirmation includes a listing of outstanding invoices making up the balance or a copy of the client customer statement attached by the auditor to the confirmation request. The listing of invoices is useful when the debtor uses a voucher system for accounts payable, and attaching the statement makes it easier for the debtor to respond.

A second type of positive confirmation, often called a **blank confirmation form**, does not state the amount on the confirmation but requests the recipient to fill in the balance or furnish other information. Because blank forms require the recipient to determine the information requested before signing and returning the confirmation, they are considered more reliable than confirmations that include the information. Research shows, however, that response rates are usually lower for blank confirmation forms. These forms are preferred for accounts payable confirmations when the auditor is searching for understatement of accounts payable.

Figure 15-6	Positive Confirmation

Cockburn, Pedlar & Co.

Chartered Accountants
Cabot Bldg.
P.O. Box 123
3 King Street North
St. John's, Newfoundland
A1C 3R5

Garner Hardware
80 Main Street
Cornerbrook, Newfoundland
A2H 1C8

August 15, 2009

To Whom It May Concern:

Re: Island Hardware Ltd.
  In connection with our audit of the financial statements of the above company, we would appreciate receiving from you confirmation of your account. The company's records show an amount receivable from you of $175.00 on June 30, 2009.
  Do you agree with this amount? If you do, please sign this letter in the space below. However, if you do not, please note at the foot of this letter or on the reverse side the details of any differences.
  Please return this letter directly to us in the envelope enclosed for your convenience.

Sincerely,

Cockburn, Pedlar & Co.

Cockburn, Pedlar & Co.

Per:

Please provide Cockburn, Pedlar & Co. with this information.

J. Doe
_____

J. Doe, Accountant, Island Hardware Ltd.

The above amount was owing by me (us) at the date mentioned.

_____

Figure 15-7

Figure 15-7   Negative Confirmation

AUDITOR'S ACCOUNT CONFIRMATION

Please examine this statement carefully. If it does NOT agree with your records, please report any exceptions directly to our auditors

    Cockburn, Pedlar & Co.
    Cabot Bldg.
    P.O. Box 123
    3 King Street North
    St. John's, Newfoundland
    A1C 3R5

who are making an examination of our financial statements. A stamped, addressed envelope is enclosed for your convenience in replying.

Do not send your remittance to our auditors.

A **negative confirmation** is also addressed to the debtor but requests a response only when the debtor disagrees with the stated amount. Figure 15-7 illustrates a negative confirmation in the audit of Island Hardware Ltd. that is a gummed label and would be attached to a customer's monthly statement. Often, the client can print the auditor's negative confirmation request directly onto the customer statements.

A positive confirmation is more reliable evidence because the auditor can perform follow-up procedures if a response is not received from the debtor. With a negative confirmation, failure to reply can only be regarded as a correct response even though the debtor may have ignored the confirmation request. This explains why CAS 505 states that negative confirmation should be used only when risks of misstatement are low and when the following are true:

- The items to be confirmed are homogeneous (i.e., similar in nature) and comprise small account balances.
- No or few exceptions are likely.
- There is an expectation that the negative confirmations will be read and considered.

Offsetting the reliability disadvantage, negative confirmations are less expensive to send than positive confirmations, and thus more can be distributed for the same total cost. Negative confirmations cost less because there are no second requests and no follow-up of non-responses. The determination of which type of confirmation to use is an auditor's decision, and it should be based on the facts in the audit. Positive confirmations are more effective when the following exist:

- Individual balances of relatively large amounts.
- Few debtors or account balances.
- No suspicions or evidence of fraud or serious error.

Typically, when negative confirmations are used, the auditor puts considerable emphasis on the effectiveness of internal control as evidence of the fairness of accounts receivable and assumes the large majority of the recipients will provide a conscientious reading and response to the confirmation request. Negative confirmations are often used for audits of municipalities, retail stores, banks, and other industries in which the receivables are due from the general public. In these cases, more weight is placed on tests of controls than on confirmations.

It is also common to use a combination of positive and negative confirmations by sending positive requests to accounts with large balances and negative requests to those with small balances.

The discussion of confirmations to this point shows that there is a continuum for the type of confirmation decision, starting with using no confirmation in some circumstances, to using only negatives, to using both negatives and positives, to using only positives. The primary factors affecting the decision are the materiality of total

Negative confirmation—a letter, addressed to the debtor, requesting a response only if the recipient disagrees with the amount of the stated account balance.

CAS

accounts receivable, the number and size of individual accounts, control risk, inherent risk, the effectiveness of confirmations as audit evidence, and the availability of other audit evidence.

Timing The most reliable evidence from confirmations is obtained when they are sent as close to the balance sheet date as possible, as opposed to confirming the accounts several months before year end. This permits the auditor to test directly the accounts receivable balance on the financial statements without making any inferences about the transactions taking place between the confirmation date and the balance sheet date. However, as a means of completing the audit on a timely basis, it is frequently convenient to confirm the accounts at an interim date. This works well if internal controls are adequate and can provide reasonable assurance that sales, cash receipts, and other credits are properly recorded between the date of the confirmation and the end of the accounting period. Other factors the auditor considers in making the decision are the materiality of accounts receivable and the auditor's exposure to lawsuits because of the possibility of client bankruptcy and similar risks.

If the decision is made to confirm accounts receivable prior to year end, it may be necessary to test the transactions occurring between the confirmation date and the balance sheet date by examining such internal documents as duplicate sales invoices, shipping documents, and evidence of cash receipts, in addition to performing analytical procedures of the intervening period.

Sample size The main considerations affecting the number of confirmations to send are as follows:

- Materiality.
- Inherent risk and risk of material misstatement (relative size of total accounts receivable, number of accounts, prior-year results, and expected misstatements).
- Control risk.
- Achieved detection risk from other substantive tests (extent and results of analytical procedures and other tests of details).
- Type of confirmation (negatives normally require a larger sample size).

These factors are discussed further in the context of audit sampling for Hillsburg Hardware at the end of this chapter.

Selection of the items for testing Some type of stratification is desirable with most confirmations. A typical approach to stratification is to consider both the size of the outstanding balance and the length of time an account has been outstanding as a basis for selecting the balances for confirmation. In most audits, the emphasis should be on confirming larger and older balances, since these are most likely to include a significant misstatement. However, it is also important to sample some items from every material stratum of the population. In many cases, the auditor selects all accounts above a certain dollar amount and selects a statistical sample from the remainder.

CAS **Refusal to permit confirmation** Management may refuse the auditor permission to send certain confirmations, perhaps because there is a dispute about the account. In such cases, CAS 505 requires the auditor to corroborate management's statements and to conduct alternative audit procedures (which would be similar to procedures conducted for non-responses, discussed below). For example, if an account is under dispute, the auditor would examine correspondence with the client and consider whether the account is still collectable. The auditor needs to consider whether management's reasons for not confirming the account are reasonable and how this fits in to other assessed risks.

MAINTAINING CONTROL After the items for confirmation have been selected, the auditor must maintain control of the confirmations until they are returned from the debtor. If the client's assistance is obtained in preparing the confirmations, enclosing them in envelopes, or putting stamps on the envelopes, close supervision by the auditor is required. A return address must be included on all envelopes to make sure that undelivered mail is received by the public accounting firm. Similarly, self-addressed return envelopes accompanying the confirmations must be addressed for delivery to the public accounting firm's office. It is even important to mail the confirmations outside the client's office. All these steps are necessary to ensure independent communication between the auditor and the customer.

FOLLOW-UP ON NON-RESPONSES It is inappropriate to regard confirmations mailed but not returned by customers as significant audit evidence. For example, non-responses to positive confirmations do not provide audit evidence. Similarly, for negative confirmations, the auditor cannot conclude that the recipient received the confirmation request and verified the information requested. Negative confirmations do, however, provide some evidence of the existence assertion.

It is common when the auditor does not receive a response to a positive confirmation request to send a second and even a third request for confirmation. Even with these efforts, some debtors will not return the confirmation. The auditor can then (1) perform alternative procedures or (2) treat the non-response as an error to be projected from the sample to the population in order to assess its materiality. The objective of **alternative procedures** is to determine by a means other than confirmation whether the non-confirmed account existed and was properly stated at the confirmation date. The alternative procedures would include examining the following documentation to verify the validity and valuation of individual sales transactions making up the ending balance in accounts receivable.

Alternative procedure—the follow-up of a positive confirmation not returned by the debtor with the use of documentation evidence to determine whether the recorded receivable exists and is collectable.

Subsequent cash receipts Evidence of the receipt of cash subsequent to the confirmation date includes examining remittance advices, entries in the cash receipts records, or perhaps even subsequent credits in the supporting records. On the one hand, the examination of evidence of subsequent cash receipts is a highly useful alternative procedure because it is reasonable to assume that a customer would not make a payment unless it were for an existing receivable. On the other hand, the fact of payment does not establish whether there was an obligation on the date of the confirmation. In addition, care should be taken to specifically match each unpaid sales transaction with evidence of its payment as a test for disputes or disagreements over individual outstanding invoices.

Duplicate sales invoices These are useful in verifying the actual issuance of a sales invoice and the actual date of the billing.

Shipping documents These are important in establishing whether the shipment was actually made and as a test of cut-off.

Correspondence with the client Usually, the auditor does not need to review correspondence as a part of alternative procedures, but correspondence can be used to disclose disputed and questionable receivables not uncovered by other means.

The extent and nature of the alternative procedures depend primarily upon the materiality of the non-responses, the types of misstatements discovered in the confirmed responses, the subsequent cash receipts from the non-responses, and the auditor's conclusions about internal control. It is normally desirable to account for all unconfirmed balances with alternative procedures even if the amounts are small, as a means of properly generalizing from the sample to the population.

ANALYSIS OF DIFFERENCES When the confirmation requests are returned by the customer, it is necessary to determine the reason for any reported differences. In many cases, they are caused by timing differences between the client's and the customer's records. It is important to distinguish between these and the exceptions, which represent misstatements of the accounts receivable balance. The most commonly reported types of differences in confirmations follow.

Payment has already been made Reported differences typically arise when the customer has made a payment prior to the confirmation date, but the client has not received the payment in time for recording before the confirmation date. Such instances should be carefully investigated to determine the possibility of a cash receipts cut-off misstatement, lapping, or a theft of cash.

Goods have not been received These differences typically result because the client records the sale at the date of shipment and the customer records the purchase when the goods are received. The time the goods are in transit is frequently the cause of differences reported on confirmations. These should be investigated to determine the possibility of the customer not receiving the goods at all or the existence of a cut-off misstatement on the client's records.

The goods have been returned The client's failure to record a credit memo could result from timing differences or the improper recording of sales returns and allowances. Like other differences, these must be investigated.

Clerical errors and disputed amounts The most likely case of reported differences in a client's records occurs when the customer states that there is an error in the price charged for the goods, the goods are damaged, the proper quantity of goods was not received, and so forth. These differences must be investigated to determine whether the client is in error and what the amount of the error is.

In most instances, the auditor asks the client to reconcile the difference and, if necessary, communicates with the customer to resolve any audit disagreements. Naturally, the auditor must carefully verify the client's conclusions on each significant difference.

DRAWING CONCLUSIONS When all differences have been resolved, including those discovered in performing alternative procedures, it is important to re-evaluate internal control. Each client misstatement must be analyzed to determine whether it was consistent or inconsistent with the original assessed level of control risk. If there is a significant number of misstatements that are inconsistent with the assessment of control risk, then it is necessary to revise the assessment and consider the effect of the revision on the audit.

It is also necessary to generalize from the sample to the entire population of accounts receivable. Even though the sum of the misstatements in the sample may not significantly affect the financial statements, the auditor must consider whether the population is likely to be materially misstated. This conclusion can be reached by using statistical sampling techniques or a non-statistical basis. Projection of misstatements was discussed in Chapter 7 and is further explained in the example at the end of this chapter.

The auditor should always evaluate the qualitative nature of the misstatements found in the sample, regardless of the dollar amount of the projected misstatement. Even if the projected misstatement is less than materiality, the misstatements found in a sample can be symptomatic of a more serious problem.

The final decision about accounts receivable and sales is whether sufficient evidence has been obtained through analytical procedures, tests of controls, cut-off procedures, confirmation, and other substantive procedures to justify drawing conclusions about the correctness of the stated balance.

concept check

C15-6 How does the level of assessed control risk affect the level of planned evidence for accounts receivable?

C15-7 How does the auditor locate poor cash receipts cut-off of accounts receivable balances?

C15-8 ABC Co. has about 300 accounts receivable balances from a variety of businesses, ranging in size from about $500 to $250,000. What type of confirmations would be sent? Justify your response.

Auditing Hillsburg Hardware Accounts Receivable

Case Illustration—Hillsburg Hardware Limited

The Hillsburg Hardware Limited case illustration used in Chapter 14 continues here to include the determination of the tests of details of balances audit procedures in the sales and collection cycle. Recall that the risk of material misstatement in sales and revenue recognition were considered to be low.

Table 15-2 includes selected comparative trial balance information for the sales and collection cycle for Hillsburg Hardware Limited. Some of that information is used to illustrate several analytical procedures in Table 15-3 on the next page. None of the analytical procedures indicated potential misstatements except the ratio of the allowance of uncollectible accounts to accounts receivable. The explanation at the bottom of Table 15-3 comments on the potential error.

Table 15-2	Selected Comparative Information for Hillsburg Hardware Limited—Sales and Collection Cycle		
	Dollar Amounts (in thousands)		
	31-12-08	31-12-07	31-12-06
Gross sales	$144,328	$132,161	$123,438
Sales returns and allowances	1,242	935	753
Gross profit	39,845	36,350	33,961
Accounts receivable	20,197	17,521	13,852
Allowance for uncollectible accounts	1,240	1,311	1,283
Accounts receivable (net)	18,957	16,210	12,569
Bad-debt expense	3,323	2,496	2,796
Total current assets	51,027	49,895	49,157
Net earnings before taxes and extraordinary items	6,401	4,659	3,351
Number of accounts receivable	415	385	372
Number of accounts receivable with balances over $150,000	19	17	16

Table 15-3

Table 15-3   Analytical Procedures for Hillsburg Hardware Limited—Sales and Collection Cycle

	31-12-08	31-12-07	31-12-06
Gross profit	27.8%	27.7%	27.7%
Sales returns and allowances/gross sales	0.9%	0.7%	0.6%
Bad-debt expense/net sales	2.3%	1.9%	2.3%
Allowance for uncollectible accounts/accounts receivable	6.1%	7.5%	9.3%
Number of days receivables outstanding	48.1	43.6	39.6
Net accounts receivable/total current assets	37.2%	32.5%	25.6%

Note: Allowance as a percentage of accounts receivable has declined from 7.5 percent to 6.1 percent. Number of days receivable outstanding and economic conditions do not justify this change. Potential misstatement is approximately $282,758 ($20,197,000 × [0.075 - 0.061]).

Figure 15-8   Evidence Planning Spreadsheet to Determine Tests of Details of Balances for Hillsburg Hardware Limited—Accounts Receivable

	Existence (or Occurrence)	Rights and Obligations	Completeness	Accuracy	Valuation	Classification	Detail Tie-in	Cut-off	Presentation and Disclosure
Audit risk	High	High	High	High	High	High	High	High	High
Inherent risk	Low	Low	Low	Low	Medium	Low	Low	Low	Low
Control risk – Sales	Medium	Not applicable	Low	Low	High	Low	Low	Low	Not applicable
Control risk – Cash receipts	High	Not applicable	Low	Low	Not applicable	Low	Low	Low	Not applicable
Control risk – Additional controls	None	Low	None	None	None	None	None	None	Low
Analytical procedures	Good results	Not applicable	Good results	Good results	Unacceptable results	Good results	Good results	Good results	Not applicable
Planned detection risk for tests of details of balances	Medium	High	High	High	Low	High	High	High	High
Planned audit evidence for tests of details of balances	Medium	Low	Low	Low	High	Low	Low	Low	Low

Materiality $496,000

Fran Moore prepared the evidence planning spreadsheet in Figure 15-8 as an aid to decide the extent of planned tests of details of balances. The source of each of the rows is as follows:

- *Materiality.* The preliminary judgment about materiality was set at $496,000.

- *Assessed audit risk.* Fran assessed audit risk as high (0.05) because of the good financial condition of the company, its financial stability, and the relatively few users of the financial statements. The company has a large working capital line of credit.
- *Inherent risk.* Fran assessed inherent risk as low for all objectives except valuation. In past years, there have been audit adjustments to the allowance for uncollectible accounts because it was found to be understated. Given the decrease in credit availability overall in the financial system, there could be increased pressure on the collectability of accounts receivable this year.
- *Control risk.* Assessed control risk for sales and collections is taken from the assessment of control risk matrix for sales and cash receipts, modified by the results of the tests of controls. The control risk matrix is shown in Figures 14-6 and 14-7 on pages 475 and 476. The results of the tests of controls in Chapter 14 were consistent with the preliminary assessments of control, except for the completeness objective. The initial assessment was low, but tests of controls results changed the assessment to high.
- *Analytical procedures.* Fran chose to use analytical procedures to obtain medium levels of assurance from additional analytical procedures, as described in Table 15-3. These analytical procedures resulted in the detection of immaterial errors. All of these errors have been corrected in Hillsburg's accounts.
- *Planned detection risk and planned audit evidence.* These two rows are decided for each objective based on the conclusions in the other rows.

Table 15-4 on the next page shows the tests of details audit program for accounts receivable, by objective, and for the allowance for uncollectible accounts. The audit program reflects the conclusions for planned audit evidence on the planning spreadsheet in Figure 15-8. Table 15-5 (page 521) shows the audit program in a performance format. The audit procedures are identical to those in Table 15-4 except for procedure 2, which is an analytical procedure. The numbers in parentheses in Table 15-4 are a cross-reference between the two tables.

Using Monetary Unit Sampling to Select and Evaluate Confirmations

To illustrate the sampling for tests of details described in Chapter 13, monetary unit sampling is now conducted using accounts receivable data. Since Hillsburg Hardware has numerous accounts receivable, only portions of the population will be shown during this illustration.

The steps followed are based on the 14 steps in planning, selecting, and evaluating a sample, as shown in Chapter 13, starting on page 419.

OBJECTIVES, DECIDING IF SAMPLING APPLIES, POPULATION, AND SAMPLING UNIT When auditors sample for tests of details of balances, the objective is to determine whether the account balance being audited is fairly stated. The audit objective here is to determine the amount of monetary error associated with the existence, accuracy, and cut-off of accounts receivable. This will be accomplished by sending and evaluating confirmations of the accounts receivable balance as of December 31. Sampling can be used to select the smaller items to be confirmed, since the auditor has decided that all amounts greater than $150,000 will be confirmed. Any monetary error between the amount recorded in the customer master file or the open item invoice amount, and the confirmed amount, is considered to be an error condition.

Hillsburg Hardware has total accounts receivable outstanding of $20,196,800. Since the sampling unit is defined as an individual dollar, the population size is equal to the total outstanding accounts receivable. However, the population is being divided into two strata. High dollar amounts over $150,000 are all being confirmed. A sample will thus be selected from the remainder.

The population for each stratum consists of the total of uncollected sales invoice amounts in that dollar range.

Table 15-4

Table 15-4 Balance-Related Audit Objectives and Audit Program for Hillsburg Hardware Limited— Sales and Collection Cycle (Design Format)

Balance-Related Audit Objective	Audit Procedure
The accounts receivable on the aged trial balance exist (accuracy and existence).	Confirm accounts receivable using positive confirmations. Confirm all amounts over $150,000 and a statistical sample of the remainder. (7) Perform alternative procedures for all confirmations not returned on the first or second request. (8) Use generalized audit software (GAS) to provide reports of the following: • All customers with balances exceeding their credit limit. (1.3) • All customers with discount terms exceeding 25 percent. (1.4) • Debit and credit totals by customer. (1.5) • Customers with balances over $150,000. (1.6) • A dollar-unit sample of the remainder. (1.6)
The client has rights to the accounts receivable on the trial balance (rights and obligations).	Review the minutes of the board of directors' meetings for any indication of pledged or factored accounts receivable. (5) Inquire of management whether any receivables are pledged or factored. (5)
Existing accounts receivable are included in the aged trial balance (completeness).	Agree details of customers selected using GAS to the aged accounts receivable trial balance listing. (6)
Accounts receivable on the aged trial balance are properly classified (classification).	Review the receivables listed on the aged trial balance for notes and related-party receivables. (3) Inquire of management whether there are any related-party notes or long-term receivables included in the trial balance. (4)
Accounts receivable is stated at realizable value (valuation).	Use GAS to reperform aging for the aged accounts receivable trial balance. Agree totals by aging category to the trial balance listing. (1.7, 1.8) Discuss with the credit manager the likelihood of collecting older accounts. Examine subsequent cash receipts and the credit file on all accounts over 90 days, and evaluate whether the receivables are collectable. (9) Evaluate whether the allowance is adequate after performing other audit procedures relating to collectability of receivables. (10)
Accounts receivable in the aged trial balance agrees with related master file amounts, and the total is correctly added and agrees with the general ledger (detail tie-in).	Foot open item file and customer master file and agree to general ledger. (1.1, 1.2)
Transactions in the sales and collection cycle are recorded in the proper period (cut-off).	Select the last 40 sales transactions from the current year's sales journal and the first 40 from the subsequent year's, and trace each to the related shipping documents, checking for the date of actual shipment and the correct recording. (11) Review large sales returns and allowances after the balance sheet date to determine whether any should be included in the current period. (12)
Accounts in the sales and collection cycle and related information are properly presented and disclosed (presentation and disclosure).	Review the minutes of the board of directors' meetings for any indication of pledged or factored accounts receivable. (5) Inquire of management whether any receivables are pledged or factored. (5)

Note: The procedures are summarized in a performance format in Table 15-5. The number in parentheses after the procedure refers to Table 15-5.

SPECIFY MATERIALITY AND THE ACCEPTABLE RISK OF INCORRECT ACCEPTANCE (ARIA), PROVIDE AN ESTIMATE OF TOTAL DOLLAR ERROR IN THE POPULATION, AND DETERMINE SAMPLE SIZE

Materiality The preliminary judgment about materiality is normally the basis for the tolerable misstatement amount used. If misstatements in non–dollar-unit-sampling tests (i.e., any other tests of details) were expected, tolerable misstatement would be materiality less those amounts. Tolerable misstatement may be different for

Table 15-5	Tests of Details of Balances Audit Program for Hillsburg Hardware Limited—Sales and Collection Cycle (Performance Format)

1. Obtain a copy of the customer master file and the accounts receivable open item transaction file as of December 31, and perform the following:
   1.1 Foot both the customer master file and the accounts receivable open item file.
   1.2 Agree the totals of the two files to each other and to the general ledger account balance.
   1.3 List all customers with balances exceeding their credit limit.
   1.4 List all customers with discount terms exceeding 25 percent.
   1.5 Provide a report that shows total debits and total credits of open items by customer.
   1.6 List customer and transaction details for all customers exceeding $150,000 and a dollar-unit sample of customers with balances below $150,000.
   1.7 Reperform the aging of the open items to derive the aged accounts receivable trial balance by customer.
   1.8 Agree the totals by aging category to the client-prepared aged accounts receivable trial balance.
2. Calculate analytical procedures indicated in carry-forward working papers (not included), and follow up any significant changes from prior years.
3. Review the receivables listed on the aged trial balance for notes and related-party receivables.
4. Inquire of management whether there are any related-party notes or long-term receivables included in the trial balance.
5. Review the minutes of the board of directors' meetings, and inquire of management to determine whether any receivables are pledged or factored.
6. Agree details of customers selected using GAS to the aged accounts receivable trial balance listing.
7. Confirm accounts receivable using positive confirmations. Confirm all amounts over $150,000 and those selected in step 1.6.
8. Perform alternative procedures for all confirmations not returned on the first or second request.
9. Discuss with the credit manager the likelihood of collecting older accounts. Examine subsequent cash receipts and the credit file on all larger accounts over 90 days, and evaluate whether the receivables are collectable.
10. Evaluate whether the allowance is adequate after performing other audit procedures relating to collectability of receivables.
11. Select the last 40 sales transactions from the current year's sales journal and the first 40 from the subsequent year's, and trace each to the related shipping documents, checking for the date of actual shipment and the correct recording.
12. Review large sales returns and allowances after the balance sheet date to determine whether any should be included in the current period.

overstatements or understatements. For this example, tolerable misstatement for both overstatements and understatements is $496,000, the materiality figure for Hillsburg Hardware for total accounts receivable.

Acceptable risk of incorrect acceptance Setting ARIA is a matter of professional judgment and is often reached with the aid of the audit risk model. It is 5 percent for this example.

Estimate of the population exception rate Normally the estimate of the population exception rate for MUS is zero percent, as it is most appropriate to use MUS when no misstatements or only a few are expected. Where misstatements are expected, the total dollar amount of expected population misstatements is estimated and then expressed as a percentage of the population recorded value. In this example, some overstatement is expected. Based on past experience, a 0.5-percent expected exception rate is used.

Assumption of the average percent of misstatement for population items that contain a misstatement To determine the sample size, the auditor also needs to make assumptions about how much error there will be in items that contain a misstatement. This is termed **tainting** in *Dollar Unit Sampling: A Practical Guide for Auditors*.[2] Again, there may be a separate assumption for the upper and lower bounds. This is also a matter of professional judgment. Assumptions should be based on the auditor's knowledge of the client and past experience, and if less than 100 percent is used, the assumptions must be clearly defensible. For this example, 50 percent is used for overstatements and 100 percent for understatements.

Tainting—the average percent of misstatement for population dollars that contain a misstatement (used with MUS sampling).

---

[2] See Leslie, Donald A., Albert D. Teitlebaum, and Rodney J. Anderson, *Dollar Unit Sampling: A Practical Guide for Auditors* (Toronto: Copp Clark Pitman, 1979), p. 122–123, 390.

These assumptions are illustrated in Table 15-6:

Table 15-6	Illustration of Assumptions and Facts for Accounts Receivable Sample
Tolerable misstatement (same for upper and lower)	$496,000
Tolerable misstatement allocated to lower dollar stratum	$300,000
Average percent of misstatement assumption, overstatements	50%
Average percent of misstatement assumption, understatements	100%
ARIA	5%
Accounts receivable—recorded value	$20.2 million
Accounts receivable—amounts less than $150,000	$13.1 million
Estimated misstatement in accounts receivable	0.5%

The *sample size* for the strata of amounts less than $150,000 is calculated as shown in Table 15-7:

Table 15-7	Illustration of Sample Size Calculation		
		Upper Bound	Lower Bound
Tolerable misstatement		300,000	300,000
Average percent of error assumption (divide by):		0.50	1.00
equals		600,000	300,000
Recorded population value (divide by):		13,100,000	13,100,000
Allowable percent error bound (TER)		4.6%	2.3%
Estimated population exception rate (EPER)		0.5%	0
Required sample size from the attributes table (Table 14-9, page 483) 5% ARACR, 5% and 3% TER, and 0.5% and 0 EPER		93	157

Since only one sample is taken for both overstatements and understatements, the larger of the two computed sample sizes would be used, in this case 157 items. Normally, generalized audit software is used to determine sample size and to actually select the sample items, once the auditor has determined the ARIA, ARACR, TER, and the EPER. The sample is selected using a statistical formula. High tolerable error rates for a specific procedure such as confirmations are acceptable where the auditor also relies on other audit procedures such as tests of controls and analytical procedures.

In auditing the sample, finding any understatement amounts will cause the lower bound to exceed the tolerable limit because the sample size is based on no expected misstatements. On the other hand, several overstatement amounts might be found before the tolerable limit for the upper bound is exceeded. Where the auditor is concerned about unexpectedly finding a misstatement that would cause the population to be rejected, he or she can guard against it by arbitrarily increasing sample size above the amount determined by the tables. For example, in this illustration, the auditor might use a sample size of 190 instead of 157. Such a change would also result in a different CUER (computed upper exception rate).

SELECT THE SAMPLE AND PERFORM THE AUDIT PROCEDURES The sample of items less than $150,000 is being selected using generalized audit software with monetary unit sampling. The software will use the ARACR, TER, and EPER to calculate a dollar interval, and then choose the accounts that correspond to that dollar interval. For example, if the dollar interval is $350,000 (the interval is normally less than materiality) and the random start is 6586, then the accounts would be summed until the cumulative total reaches $6,586; this identifies the first account to be selected. When the cumulative total reaches $356,586 ($350,000 + $6,586), the second account to be selected is identified. In this way, all 157 accounts will be selected. They will then be confirmed, the results audited, and the result for each physical unit (customer account) will be applied to the selected dollar amount that it contains.

The statistical methods used to evaluate monetary unit samples permit the inclusion of a physical unit in the sample more than once. For example, an item that was $700,000 or larger would be "selected" twice, since it is twice the size of the sample interval. This is handled at Hillsburg Hardware Limited by having the data divided into two strata—the larger amounts of greater than $150,000 are all being selected.

One problem using MUS (monetary unit sampling) selection is that population items with a zero recorded balance have no chance of being selected even though they could contain misstatements. Similarly, small balances that are significantly understated have little chance of being included in the sample. This problem can be overcome by doing specific audit tests for zero- and small-balance items, assuming that they are of concern.

Another problem is the inability to include negative balances, such as credit balances in accounts receivable, in the MUS sample. It is possible to ignore negative balances for MUS selection and test those amounts by some other means. An alternative is to treat them as positive balances (which is readily done with audit software by simply using absolute values) and add them to the total number of monetary units being tested; however, this complicates the evaluation process.

Fran determined from earlier generalized audit software tests that credit amounts were insignificant and decided that no separate audit work would be done on those amounts.

Fran ensured that audit staff on the engagement properly handled the accounts receivable confirmation process. Confirmations were prepared and mailed, second requests were sent, discrepancies were reviewed, and alternative procedures were conducted for those items selected for which no replies were received.

GENERALIZE FROM THE SAMPLE TO THE POPULATION

Generalizing from the sample to the population when no misstatements are found using MUS Assume that during the audit, no misstatements were uncovered in the sample. The auditor next wants to determine the maximum amount of overstatement and understatement amounts that could exist in the population and still provide a sample with no misstatements. These are the upper misstatement bound and the lower misstatement bound, respectively. Assuming an ARIA of 5 percent, and using Table 14-10 on page 485, both the upper and lower bounds are determined by locating the intersection of the sample size (157) and the actual number of misstatements (0) in the same manner as for attribute sampling. The CUER of 2 percent on the table for 150 items represents both the upper and lower bound, expressed as a percentage.

Thus, based on the sample results and the misstatement bounds from the table, the auditor can conclude with a 5-percent sampling risk that no more than 2 percent of the dollar units in the population are misstated. To convert this percent into dollars, the auditor must make an assumption about the average percent of misstatement for population dollars that contain a misstatement. This assumption significantly affects the misstatement bounds. To illustrate this, first Fran's assumptions are shown, that is, a 50-percent misstatement assumption for overstatements and a 100-percent assumption for understatements, and a second assumption is shown with a 100-percent misstatement assumption for overstatements and a 200-percent assumption for understatements.

Assumption 1 (Fran's) Overstatement amounts equal 50 percent; understatement amounts equal 100 percent; misstatement bounds at a 5 percent ARIA are

Upper misstatement bound = $13,100,000 × 2% × 50% = $131,000
Lower misstatement bound = $13,100,000 × 2% × 100% = $262,000

The assumption is that on the average, those population items that are misstated are misstated by the full dollar amount of the recorded value. Since the misstatement bound is 2 percent, the dollar value of the misstatement is not likely to exceed $131,000 (2 percent times 50 percent of the total recorded dollar units in the population). If all the amounts are overstated, there is an overstatement of $131,000. If they are all understated, there is an understatement of $262,000.

The assumption of 100 percent or 50 percent misstatements is very conservative, especially for overstatements. Assume that the actual population exception rate is 2 percent. The following two conditions both have to exist before the $131,000 properly reflects the true overstatement amount:

1. All amounts have to be overstatements. Offsetting amounts would have reduced the amount of the overstatement.
2. All population items misstated have to be 50 percent misstated. There could not, for example, be a misstatement such as a cheque written for $226 that was recorded as $262. This would be only a 13.7 percent misstatement (262 – 226 = 36 overstatement; 36/262 = 13.7%).

In the calculation of the misstatement bounds of $131,000 overstatement and $262,000 understatement, the auditor did not calculate a point estimate and precision amount as described in the next section on judgmental sampling. This is because the tables used include both a point estimate and a precision amount to derive the upper exception rate. Even though the point estimate and precision amount are not calculated for MUS, they are implicit in the determination of misstatement bounds and can be determined from the tables. For example, in this illustration, the point estimate is zero and the statistical precision is $131,000 for overstatement and $262,000 for understatement.

Assumption 2 Overstatement amounts equal 100 percent; understatement amounts equal 200 percent; misstatement bounds at a 5 percent ARIA are

Upper misstatement bound = $13,100,000 × 2% × 100% = $262,000
Lower misstatement bound = $13,100,000 × 2% × 200% = $524,000

The justification for a larger percent for understatements is the potential for a larger misstatement in percentage terms. For example, an accounts receivable recorded at $20 that should have been recorded at $200 is understated by 900 percent [(200 – 20)/20], whereas one that is recorded at $200 that should have been recorded at $20 is overstated by 90 percent [(200 – 20)/200].

Items containing large understatement amounts may have a small recorded value, due to those misstatements. As a consequence, because of the mechanics of MUS, few of them will have a chance of being selected in the sample. Because of this, some auditors select an additional sample of small items to supplement the monetary unit sample whenever understatement amounts are an important audit concern.

Appropriate percent of misstatement assumption The appropriate assumption to make regarding the overall percent of misstatement in those population items containing a misstatement is an auditor's decision. The auditor must set these percentages based on personal judgment in the circumstances. In the absence of convincing information to the contrary, most auditors believe it is desirable to assume a 100 percent amount for both overstatements and understatements. This approach is considered highly conservative, but it is easier to justify than any other assumption. In fact, the reason upper and lower limits are referred to as misstatement bounds when MUS is used, rather than maximum likely misstatement or the commonly used statistical term "confidence limit," is due to widespread use of that conservative assumption. Unless stated otherwise, the 100 percent misstatement assumption is used in the chapter and problem materials when no misstatements are found.

Generalizing when misstatements are found This section presents the evaluation method used when there are misstatements in the sample. The same illustration is continued; the only change is the assumption about the misstatements. The sample size remains at 157 and the recorded value is still $13,100,000, but now five misstatements in the sample are assumed. The misstatements are shown in Table 15-8.

The following changes to the process of generalizing need to be incorporated:

- *Overstatement and understatement amounts are dealt with separately and then combined.* First, initial upper and lower misstatement bounds are calculated separately for overstatement and understatement amounts. Next, a point estimate of overstatements and understatements is calculated. The point estimate of understatements is used to reduce the initial upper misstatement bound, and the point estimate of overstatements is used to reduce the initial lower misstatement bound. The method and rationale for these calculations will be illustrated by using the four overstatement and one understatement amounts in Table 15-8.
- *A different misstatement assumption is made for each misstatement, including the zero misstatements.* When there were no misstatements in the sample, an assumption was required as to the average percent of misstatement for the population items misstated. The misstatement bounds were calculated showing several different assumptions. Now that misstatements have been found, sample information is available to use in determining the misstatement bounds. The misstatement assumption is still required, but it can be modified based on these actual misstatement data.

Where misstatements are found, a 100 percent assumption for all misstatements is not only exceptionally conservative, it is inconsistent with the sample results. A common assumption in practice, and the one followed in this book, is that the actual sample misstatements are representative of the population misstatements. This assumption requires the auditor to calculate the percent that each sample item is misstated (misstatement ÷ recorded balance) and apply that percent to the population. The calculation of the percent for each misstatement is shown in the last column in Table 15-8. As will be explained shortly, a misstatement assumption is still needed for the zero misstatement portion of the computed results. For this example, a 50-percent

Table 15-8	Misstatements Found			
Customer No.	Recorded Accounts Receivable Amount	Audited Accounts Receivable Amount	Misstatement	Misstatement ÷ Recorded Amount
102073	$ 6,200	$ 6,100	$ 100	0.016
105111	12,910	12,000	910	0.070
105206	4,322	4,450	(128)	(0.030)
107642	23,000	22,995	5	0.0002
109816	8,947	5,947	3,000	0.335

misstatement assumption is used for the zero misstatement portion for overstatements and 100 percent for understatement misstatement bounds.

- *The auditor must deal with layers of the computed upper exception rate (CUER) from the attribute sampling table* (see Table 14-10, page 485). The reason for doing so is that there is a different misstatement assumption for each misstatement. Layers are calculated by first determining the CUER from the table for each misstatement and then calculating each layer. Table 15-9 shows the layers in the attribute sampling table for the example at hand. The layers were determined by reading across the table for a sample size of 150 from the 0 through 4 exception columns.
- *Misstatement assumptions must be associated with each layer.* The most common method of associating misstatement assumptions with layers is to be conservative by associating the largest dollar misstatement percents with the largest layers. Table 15-10 shows the association. For example, the largest percent misstatement was 0.335 for customer 109816. This misstatement is associated with the layer factor of 0.011, the largest layer where misstatements were found. The portion of the upper precision limit related to the zero misstatement layer has a misstatement assumption of 50 percent, which is still conservative. Table 15-10 shows the calculation of misstatement bounds before consideration of offsetting amounts.

The upper misstatement bound was calculated as if there were no understatement amounts, and the lower misstatement bound was calculated as if there were no overstatement amounts.

Adjustment for offsetting amounts Most MUS users believe that the approach just discussed is overly conservative when there are offsetting amounts. If an understatement misstatement is found, it is logical and reasonable that the bound for overstatement amounts should be lower than it would be had no understatement amounts been found, and vice versa. The adjustment of bounds for offsetting amounts is made as follows: (1) a point estimate of misstatements is made for both understatement and overstatement amounts, and (2) each bound is reduced by the opposite point estimate.

The point estimate for overstatements is calculated by multiplying the average overstatement amount in the dollar units audited by the recorded value. The same approach is used for calculating the point estimate for understatements. In the example, there is one understatement amount of 3 cents per dollar unit in a sample of 150. The understatement point estimate is therefore $2,620 (0.03/150 × $13,100,000). Similarly, the overstatement point estimate is $36,785 [(0.335 + 0.07 + 0.016 + 0.0002)/150 × $13,100,000].

Table 15-11 on page 528 shows the adjustment of the bounds that follow from this procedure. The initial upper bound of $190,564 is reduced by the estimated most likely understatement error of $2,620 to an adjusted bound of $187,944. The initial lower bound of $266,323 is reduced by the estimated most likely overstatement

Table 15-9	Percent Misstatement Bounds	
Number of Misstatements	Upper Precision Limit from Table	Increase in Precision Limit Resulting from Each Misstatement (Layers)
0	0.020	0.020
1	0.031	0.011
2	0.041	0.010
3	0.051	0.010
4	0.060	0.009

Table 15-10 Illustration of Calculating Initial Upper and Lower Misstatement Bounds

Number of Misstatements (1)	Upper Precision Limit Portion* (2)	Recorded Value (3)	Misstatement Unit Error Assumption (4)	Bound Portion (Columns 2 × 3 × 4) (5)
Overstatements				
0	0.020	$13,100,000	0.50	$131,000
1	0.011	$13,100,000	0.335	48,274
2	0.010	$13,100,000	0.070	9,170
3	0.010	$13,100,000	0.016	2,096
4	0.009	$13,100,000	0.0002	24
Upper precision limit	0.06			
Initial misstatement bound				$190,564
Understatements				
0	0.020	$13,100,000	1.00	$262,000
1	0.011	$13,100,000	0.03	4,323
Lower precision limit	0.031			
Initial misstatement bound				$266,323

* ARIA of 5 percent. Sample size of 150.

amount of $36,785 to an adjusted bound of $229,538. Thus, given the methodology and assumptions followed, the auditor concludes that there is a 5-percent risk that accounts receivable is overstated by $187,944 or more, or understated by more than $229,538. It should be noted that if the misstatement assumptions were changed, the misstatement bounds would also change. The reader should be advised that the method used to adjust the bounds for offsetting amounts is but one of several in current use. The method illustrated here is taken from Leslie, Teitlebaum, and Anderson.[3] All the methods in current use are reliable and somewhat conservative.

Summary The seven steps in Table 15-12 on the next page summarize the calculation of the adjusted misstatement bounds for monetary unit sampling when there are offsetting amounts. The calculation of the adjusted upper misstatement bound for the four overstatement amounts in Table 15-8 is used to illustrate. The evaluation process for MUS is complex and is best handled using computer software.

Analyze the Misstatements and Decide the Acceptability of the Population Fran and her staff analyzed the errors described in Table 15-8. The first two overstatement errors were due to accumulated discounts taken by customers that had not been properly removed from the accounts receivable. The understatement was due to a credit note that had accidentally been issued twice, and the large $3,000 difference was due to a change in discount rate. This customer had reached such a high volume of purchases that it was moved to a higher discount level, but Hillsburg staff did not implement the discount on a timely basis. In addition to calculating misstatement bounds, Fran will discuss with Hillsburg staff their management of discounts to ensure that these errors are corrected and to determine how future errors can be prevented. Fran could also have initiated additional substantive procedures to further quantify the extent of the dollar errors associated with discount differences.

Table 15-11　Illustration of Calculating Adjusted Misstatement Bounds

Number of Misstatements	Unit Misstatement Assumption	Sample Size	Recorded Population	Point Estimate	Bounds
Initial overstatement bound					$190,564
Understatement misstatement					
1	0.030	150	$13,100,000	$ 2,620	(2,620)
Adjusted overstatement bound					$187,944
Initial understatement bound					$266,323
Overstatement misstatements					
1	0.335				
2	0.070				
3	0.016				
4	0.0002				
Sum	0.4212	150	$13,100,000	$36,785	(36,785)
Adjusted understatement bound					$229,538

Note: 150 is used as sample size for illustrative purposes.

Table 15-12　Calculation of Adjustment Misstatement Bounds for MUS with Offsetting Amounts

Steps to Calculate Adjusted Misstatement Bounds	Calculation for Misstatements in Table 15-8
1. Determine misstatement for each sample item, keeping overstatements and understatements separate.	Table 15-8 Four overstatements, one understatement
2. Calculate misstatement per dollar unit in each sample item (misstatement/recorded value).	Table 15-8 0.016, 0.07, 0.0002, 0.335
3. Layer misstatements per dollar unit from highest to lowest, including the percent misstatement assumption for sample items not misstated.	Table 15-10 0.5, 0.335, 0.07, 0.016, 0.0002
4. Determine upper precision limit using attribute sampling table, and determine the percent misstatement bound for each misstatement (layer).	Table 15-10 Total of 6 percent for four overstatements; calculate five layers. Total of 3.1 percent for one understatement; calculate two layers.
5. Calculate initial upper and lower misstatement bounds for each layer and total.	Table 15-10 Total of $190,564 and $266,323
6. Calculate point estimate for overstatements and understatements.	Table 15-11 $2,620 for overstatements $36,785 for understatements
7. Calculate adjusted upper and lower misstatement bounds.	$187,944 adjusted overstatement bound $229,538 adjusted understatement bound

Whenever a statistical method is used, a decision rule is needed to decide whether the population is acceptable. The decision rule for MUS is as follows:

If both the lower misstatement bound (LMB) and upper misstatement bound (UMB) fall between the understatement and overstatement tolerable misstatement amounts, accept the conclusion that the book value is not misstated by a material amount; otherwise, conclude that the book value is misstated by a material amount.

Action when a population is rejected When one or both of the error bounds lie outside the tolerable misstatement limits and the population is not considered acceptable, the auditor has several options. Fran could wait until tests of other audit areas were completed to see if materiality of $496,000 were exceeded for the aggregated misstatements. Alternatively, she could perform expanded tests in other areas, increase the sample size (as explained on page 432), ask that the account balance be adjusted, or request the client correct the population (which would then have to be reaudited). If the aggregated errors exceed materiality and the client will not adjust the accounts, the auditor will have to consider refusing to give an unqualified opinion.

Use of judgmental sampling Alternatively, Fran could have determined that judgmental sampling could be used to select the items to be confirmed below $150,000. She would then have followed 14 steps similar to those outlined in Chapter 13, as applied to non-statistical rather than statistical sampling.

Summary

1. *What is the process for designing tests of details of balances for accounts receivable?* Figure 15-2 provides a context: After setting materiality, assessing control risk, and designing and testing internal control, the auditor designs tests of details for each audit assertion.

   What is the relationship between transaction-related and balance-related audit objectives for the sales and collection cycle? Figure 15-3 illustrates these relationships, showing that they are generally one-to-one, except for occurrence/existence, occurrence/completeness, and completeness/existence.

2. *When and why are analytical review procedures completed as part of the audit of sales and accounts receivable?* Analytical procedures are completed during planning, as part of detailed testing and as part of completing the audit. For the detailed testing, account specific ratios are calculated. Ratios could also be calculated for customers or products to provide more assurance.

   How is the amount of substantive testing related to the audit risk model? The extent of detailed testing is related to the value of planned detection risk. As planned detection risk decreases, the amount of assurance required from tests of detail increases, resulting in the need for more substantive testing.

3. *Describe the accounts receivable audit tests that would be completed for each audit assertion.* There are many different types of tests that could be conducted, but examples by assertion are detail tie-in—adding the accounts receivable master file and agreeing to the general ledger balance; existence—confirmation; completeness—comparison of customer master file to outstanding transaction file; accuracy—confirmation; classification—review of aged trial balance; cut-off—tracing transactions near the period end date; valuation—assessing fairness of bad-debt allowance; rights—review of bank confirmation; and presentation and disclosure—examining financial statement footnotes.

   Why is confirmation one of the most important audit procedures? It is a multipurpose technique that addresses several audit assertions: existence, accuracy, and cut-off.

4. *Provide examples of risk assessments and examples of tests of detail.* Section 4 provides a risk assessment for Hillsburg Hardware, and Tables 15-4 and 15-5 list many audit procedures that could be executed as a result of that risk assessment. For example, generalized audit software is used for parallel simulation—recreation of the aged accounts receivable trial balance totals by customer.

   How is monetary unit sampling (MUS) executed and evaluated? Based upon materiality, ARACR, TER, and EPER, the software calculates a dollar interval. Then, that dollar interval is used together with a random start to select the sample. After audit tests are completed, the software can be used to calculate upper and lower precision limits, or these can be calculated manually.

Visit the text's website at **www.pearsoned.ca/arens** for practice quizzes, additional case studies, and international standards information.

Review Questions

15-1 Distinguish between tests of details of balances and tests of controls for the sales and collection cycle. Explain how the tests of controls affect the tests of details.

15-2 Cynthia Roberts, a public accountant, expresses the following viewpoint: "I do not believe in performing tests of controls for the sales and collection cycle. As an alternative, I send a lot of negative confirmations on every audit at an interim date. If I find a lot of misstatements, I analyze them to determine their cause. If internal controls are inadequate, I send positive confirmations at year end to evaluate the amount of the misstatements. If the negative confirmations result in minimal misstatements, which is often the case, I have found that internal controls are effective without bothering to perform tests of controls, and the CICA's confirmation requirement has been satisfied at the same time. In my opinion, the best test of internal controls is to go directly to third parties." Evaluate her point of view.

15-3 List five analytical procedures for the sales and collection cycle. For each test, describe a misstatement that could be identified.

15-4 Identify the eight accounts receivable balance-related audit objectives. For each objective, list one audit procedure.

15-5 Which of the eight accounts receivable balance-related audit objectives can be partially satisfied by confirmations with customers?

15-6 Distinguish between accuracy tests of gross accounts receivable and tests of the realizable value of receivables.

15-7 Explain why you agree or disagree with the following statement: "In most audits, it is more important to test carefully the cut-off for sales than for cash receipts." Describe how you perform each type of test assuming the existence of prenumbered documents.

15-8 Evaluate the following statement: "In many audits in which accounts receivable is material, the desire to confirm customer balances is a waste of time and would not be performed by competent auditors if it were not required by auditing standards. When internal controls are excellent and there is a large number of small receivables from customers who do not recognize the function of confirmation, it is a meaningless procedure. Examples include well-run utilities and department stores. In these situations, tests of controls and substantive tests of transactions are far more effective than confirmations."

15-9 Distinguish between a positive and a negative confirmation, and state the circumstances in which each should be used. Why do public accounting firms often use a combination of positive and negative confirmations on the same audit?

15-10 In what circumstances is it acceptable to confirm accounts receivable prior to the balance sheet date?

15-11 State the most important factors affecting the sample size in confirmations of accounts receivable.

15-12 In Chapter 13, one of the points brought out was the need to obtain a representative sample of the population. How can this concept be reconciled with the statement in this chapter that the emphasis should be on confirming larger and older balances, since these are most likely to contain misstatements?

15-13 An auditor is determining the appropriate sample size for testing inventory valuation using MUS. The population has 2,620 items valued at $12,625,000. The tolerable misstatement for both understatements and overstatements is $500,000 at a 10-percent ARIA. No misstatements are expected in the population. Calculate the preliminary sample size using a 100 percent average misstatement assumption.

15-14 Define what is meant by "alternative procedures," and explain their purpose. Which alternative procedures are the most reliable? Why?

15-15 Explain why the analysis of differences is important in the confirmation of accounts receivable even if the misstatements in the sample are not material.

15-16 State three types of differences that might be observed in the confirmation of accounts receivable that do not constitute misstatements. For each, state an audit procedure that would verify the difference.

15-17 Explain the relationship of each of the following to the sales and collection cycle: flowcharts, assessing control risk, tests of controls, and tests of details of balances.

15-18 Customers purchasing products through a company's website generally pay for those goods by providing their personal credit card information. Describe how a company's sale of products through its website affects the auditor's tests of accounts receivable in the financial statement audit.

Discussion Questions and Problems

15-19 The following are common tests of details of balances for the audit of accounts receivable.

1. Obtain a list of aged accounts receivable, foot the list, and trace the total to the general ledger.
2. Trace 35 accounts to the customer master file or open item transaction file for name, amount, and age categories.
3. Examine and document collections on accounts receivable for 20 days after the engagement date.
4. Request 25 positive and 65 negative confirmations of accounts receivable.
5. Perform alternative procedures on accounts not responding to second requests by examining subsequent collection documentation and shipping reports or sales invoices.

6. Test the sales cut-off by tracing entries in the sales journal for 15 days before and after the engagement date to shipping reports, if available, and/or sales invoices.
7. Determine and disclose accounts pledged, discounted, sold, assigned, or guaranteed by others.
8. Evaluate the materiality of credit balances in the aged trial balance.

REQUIRED
For each audit procedure, identify the balance-related or presentation and disclosure audit objective or objectives it partially or fully satisfies.

15-20 The following misstatements are sometimes found in the sales and collection account balances:

1. Cash received from collections of accounts receivable in the subsequent period are recorded as current period receipts.
2. The allowance for uncollectible accounts is inadequate due to the client's failure to reflect depressed economic conditions in the allowance.
3. Several accounts receivable are in dispute due to claims of defective merchandise.
4. The pledging of accounts receivable to the bank for a loan is not disclosed in the financial statements.
5. Goods shipped and included in the current period sales were returned in the subsequent period.
6. Long-term interest-bearing notes receivable from affiliated companies are included in accounts receivable.
7. The aged accounts receivable trial balance total does not equal the amount in the general ledger.
8. Several accounts receivable balances in the accounts receivable master file are not included in the aged trial balance report.
9. One accounts receivable customer included in the accounts receivable master file is included in the aged trial balance twice.

REQUIRED

a. For each misstatement, identify the balance-related or presentation and disclosure audit objective to which it pertains.
b. For each misstatement, list an internal control that should prevent it.
c. For each misstatement, list one test of details of balances audit procedure that the auditor can use to detect it.

15-21 The following are audit procedures in the sales and collection cycle:

1. Examine a sample of shipping documents to determine whether each has a sales invoice number included on it.
2. Examine a sample of non-cash credits in the accounts receivable master file to determine if the accounting supervisor has initialled each, indicating internal verification.
3. Discuss with the sales manager whether any sales allowances have been granted after the balance sheet date that may apply to the current period.
4. Add the columns on the aged trial balance, and compare the total with the general ledger.
5. Observe whether the controller makes an independent comparison of the total in the general ledger with the trial balance of accounts receivable.
6. Compare the date on a sample of shipping documents throughout the year with related duplicate sales invoices and the accounts receivable master file.
7. Examine a sample of customer orders and see if each has a credit authorization.
8. Compare the date on a sample of shipping documents a few days before and after the balance sheet date with related sales journal transactions.
9. Compute the ratio of allowance for uncollectible accounts divided by accounts receivable, and compare with those of previous years.

REQUIRED

a. For each procedure, identify the applicable type of audit evidence.
b. For each procedure, identify which of the following it is:
   (1) Test of control.
   (2) Substantive test of transactions.
   (3) Analytical procedure.
   (4) Test of details of balances.
c. For those procedures you identified as a test of control or substantive test of transactions, what transaction-related audit objective or objectives are being satisfied?
d. For those procedures you identified as a test of details of balances, what balance-related audit objective or objectives are being satisfied?

15-22 The following are audit procedures with respect to the audit of the sales, receipts, or receivables cycle:

1. Confirm accounts receivable.
2. Review sales returns after the balance sheet date to determine whether any are applicable to the current year.
3. Compare dates on shipping documents and the sales journal throughout the year.
4. Perform alternative procedures for non-responses to confirmations.
5. Examine sales transactions for related-party or employee sales recorded as regular sales.
6. Examine duplicate sales invoices for consignment sales and other shipments for which title has not passed.
7. Trace a sample of accounts from the accounts receivable master file to the aged trial balance.
8. Trace recorded sales transactions to shipping documents to determine whether a document exists.
9. Examine duplicate sales invoices for initials that indicate internal verification of extensions and footings.
10. Trace a sample of shipping documents to related sales invoice entries in the sales journal.
11. Compare amounts and dates on the aged trial balance and accounts receivable master file.
12. Trace from the sales journal to the accounts receivable master file to make sure the information is the same.
13. Inquire of management whether there are notes from related parties included with trade receivables.

REQUIRED

a. Identify which procedures are tests of details of balances, which are tests of controls and which are substantive tests of transactions.
b. State which audit assertion(s) are addressed by each audit procedure. Note that some procedures satisfy multiple assertions.

15-23 André Auto Parts Inc. sells new parts for foreign automobiles to auto dealers. Company policy requires that a prenumbered shipping document be issued for each sale. At the time of pickup or shipment, the shipping clerk writes the date on the shipping document. The last shipment made in the fiscal year ended August 31, 2009, was recorded on document 2167. Shipments are billed in the order that the billing clerk receives the shipping documents.

For late August and early September, shipping documents are billed on sales invoices as follows:

Shipping Document No.	Sales Invoice No.
2163	4332
2164	4326
2165	4327
2166	4330
2167	4331
2168	4328
2169	4329
2170	4333
2171	4335
2172	4334

The August and September sales journals include the following information:

Sales Journal—August 2009

Day of Month	Sales Invoice No.	Amount of Sale
30	4326	$ 726.11
30	4329	1,914.30
31	4327	419.83
31	4328	620.22
31	4330	47.74

Sales Journal—September 2009

Day of Month	Sales Invoice No.	Amount of Sale
1	4332	$2,641.31
1	4331	106.39
1	4333	852.06
2	4335	1,250.50
2	4334	646.58

REQUIRED

a. What are the requirements of generally accepted accounting principles for a correct sales cut-off?
b. Which sales invoices, if any, are recorded in the wrong accounting period, assuming a periodic inventory? Prepare an adjusting entry to correct the accounts for the year ended August 31, 2009.
c. Assume that the shipping clerk accidentally wrote August 31 on shipping documents 2168 through 2172. Explain how that would affect the correctness of the financial statements. How would you, as an auditor, discover that error?
d. Describe, in general terms, the audit procedures you would follow in making sure the cut-off for sales is accurate at the balance sheet date.
e. Identify internal controls that would reduce the likelihood of cut-off errors. How would you test each control?

15-24 John Gossling, a public accountant, is examining the financial statements of a manufacturing company with a significant amount of trade accounts receivable. Gossling is satisfied that the accounts are properly summarized and classified and that allocations, reclassifications, and valuations are made in accordance with generally accepted accounting principles. As part of his audit of accounts receivable, he is planning to use accounts receivable confirmations.

REQUIRED

a. Identify and describe the two forms of accounts receivable confirmation requests, and indicate the factors Gossling will consider in determining when to use each.

b. Assume that Gossling has received a satisfactory response to the confirmation requests. Describe how he could evaluate collectability of the trade accounts receivable.
c. What are the implications to a public accountant if, during his or her examination of accounts receivable, some of a client's trade customers do not respond to the request for positive confirmation of their accounts?
d. What auditing steps should a public accountant perform if there is no response to a second request for a positive confirmation?

(Adapted from AICPA)

15-25 Johnson Clock Company sells specialty clocks, watches, and other timekeeping devices. Since its inception, the company has sold items through its home office store and at industry and collector trade shows around the country. To meet the demand from collectors around the world, the company began selling items through its website. Recent financial information about Johnson's sales is summarized in the tables on the next page.

	Year Ended 12/31/09	Year Ended 12/31/08	Year Ended 12/31/07
Sales:			
Home office	$1,279,480	$1,218,552	$1,163,851
Trade show	773,265	739,259	704,391
Internet-based	147,772	122,462	52,884
Sales Returns:			
Home office	$ 25,589	$ 23,152	$ 25,605
Trade show	13,946	13,676	12,679
Internet-based	13,254	11,022	4,760

	Year Ended 12/31/09	Year Ended 12/31/08	Year Ended 12/31/07
Cost of Goods Sold:			
Home office	$831,662	$816,429	$768,142
Trade show	491,023	480,518	454,332
Internet-based	81,275	66,129	28,822
Receivables Related to Sales from:			
Home office	$126,195	$123,524	$127,545
Trade show	74,149	68,862	67,544
Internet-based	3,239	3,020	1,159
Tolerable misstatement for sales and receivables is $12,000.			

REQUIRED

Using the information given, design and perform analytical procedures for the sales and collection cycle at Johnson Clock Company. On the basis of the results of your analytical procedures, describe how the results related to the internet-based sales differ from the home office and trade show sales.

15-26 You have been assigned to the confirmation of aged accounts receivable for the audit of the Blank Paper Company Ltd. You have tested the trial balance and selected the accounts for confirmation. Before the confirmation requests are mailed, the controller asks to look at the accounts you intend to confirm in order to determine whether she will permit you to send them.

She reviews the list and informs you that she does not want you to confirm six of the accounts on your list. Two of them have credit balances, one has a zero balance, two of the other three have a fairly small balance, and the remaining balance is highly material. The reason she gives is that she feels the confirmations will upset these customers because "they are kind of hard to get along with." She does not want the credit balances confirmed because it may encourage the customers to ask for a refund.

In addition, the controller asks you to send an additional 20 confirmations to customers she has listed for you. She does this as a means of credit collection for "those who won't know the difference between a public accountant and a credit collection agency."

REQUIRED

a. Is it acceptable for the controller to review the list of accounts you intend to confirm? Discuss.
b. Discuss the appropriateness of sending the 20 additional confirmations to the customers.
c. If the auditor complies with the controller's requests, what additional audit work is required?
d. Assuming the auditor complies with all of the controller's requests, what is the effect on the auditor's opinion?

15-27 The following are the entire outstanding accounts receivable for Fran's Bookbinding Company Ltd. The population is smaller than would ordinarily be the case for statistical sampling, but an entire population is useful to show how to select samples by monetary unit sampling.

REQUIRED

a. Select a sample using systematic MUS sampling. Materiality is $50,000 and an appropriate MUS interval is $35,000. Use a starting point of 1857. Identify the physical units selected.
b. Why would an auditor use MUS?

Population Item	Recorded Amount	Population Item	Recorded Amount
1	$ 1,410	11	$ 2,270
2	9,130	12	50
3	660	13	5,785
4	3,355	14	940
5	5,725	15	1,820
6	8,210	16	3,380
7	580	17	530
8	44,110	18	955
9	825	19	4,490
10	1,155	20	17,140

Population Item	Recorded Amount	Population Item	Recorded Amount
21	$ 4,865	31	$ 935
22	770	32	5,595
23	2,305	33	930
24	2,665	34	4,045
25	1,000	35	9,480
26	6,225	36	360
27	3,675	37	1,145
28	6,250	38	6,400
29	1,890	39	100
30	27,705	40	8,435
			$207,295

15-28 You intend to use MUS as a part of the audit of several accounts for Roynpower Manufacturing Inc. You have done the audit for the past several years, and there has rarely been an adjusting entry of any kind. Your audit tests of all tests of controls for the transactions cycles were completed at an interim date, and control risk has been assessed as low. You therefore decide to use an ARIA of 10 percent for all tests of details of balances.

You intend to use MUS in the audit of the three most material asset balance sheet account balances: accounts receivable, inventory, and marketable securities. You feel justified in using the same ARIA for each audit area because of the low assessed control risk.

The recorded balances and related information for the three accounts are as follows:

	Recorded Value
Accounts receivable	$ 3,600,000
Inventory	4,800,000
Marketable securities	1,600,000
	$10,000,000

Net earnings before taxes for Roynpower are $2,000,000. You decide that materiality will be $100,000 for the client.

The audit approach will be to determine the total sample size needed for all three accounts. A sample will be selected from all $10 million, and the appropriate testing for a sample item will depend on whether the item is a receivable, inventory, or marketable security. The audit conclusions will pertain to the entire $10 million, and no conclusion will be made about the three individual accounts unless significant misstatements are found in the sample.

REQUIRED

a. Evaluate the audit approach of testing all three account balances in one sample.
b. Calculate the required sample size for each of the three accounts assuming you decide that the tolerable misstatement in each account is $100,000. (Recall that tolerable misstatement equals preliminary judgment about materiality for MUS.)
c. How would you identify which sample item in the population to audit for the number 4,627,871? What audit procedures would be performed?
d. Assume you select a sample of 100 sample items for testing and you find one misstatement in inventory. The recorded value is $987.12, and the audit value is $887.12. Calculate the misstatement bounds for the three combined accounts, and reach appropriate audit conclusions.

15-29 You have been assigned to the first examination of the accounts of North Battleford Corp. for the year ending March 31, 2009. Accounts receivable is confirmed on December 31, 2008, and at that date the receivables consisted of approximately 200 accounts with balances totalling $956,750. Seventy-five of these accounts with balances totalling $650,725 were selected for confirmation. All but 20 of the confirmation requests have been returned; 30 were signed without comments, 14 had minor differences which have been cleared satisfactorily, while 11 confirmations had the following comments:

1. We are sorry but we cannot answer your request for confirmation of our account, as Duck Lake Inc. uses an accounts payable voucher system.
2. The balance of $1,050 was paid on December 13, 2008.
3. The balance of $7,750 was paid on January 5, 2009.
4. The balance noted above has been paid.
5. We do not owe you anything as at December 31, 2008, as the goods, represented by your invoice dated December 30, 2008, number 25050, in the amount of $11,550, were received on January 5, 2009, on FOB destination terms.

6. An advance payment of $2,500 made by us in November 2008 should cover the two invoices totalling $1,350 shown on the statement attached.
7. We never received these goods.
8. We are contesting the propriety of this $12,525 charge. We think the charge is excessive.
9. Amount is okay. As the goods have been shipped to us on consignment, we will remit payment upon selling the goods.
10. The $10,000, representing a deposit under a lease, will be applied against the rent due to us during 2009, the last year of the lease.
11. Your credit memo dated December 5, 2008, in the amount of $440, cancels the balance above.

REQUIRED

What steps would you take to satisfactorily clear each of the above 11 comments?

(Adapted from AICPA)

15-30 During his interim audit visit, Charles Ai determined that one of the subsidiary companies of Mega Big Limited had experienced some very serious problems with respect to the credit management and collection of trade accounts receivable. During the first six months of the year, the accounts receivable of this subsidiary had almost doubled, the number of days' sales in accounts receivable had

increased from 39 days to 64 days, and bad-debt expense had risen sharply.

REQUIRED

Prepare an outline of the steps that should be taken to investigate the nature and causes of the credit and collection problems. (Do not consider the possibility of fraud.)

Professional Judgment Problems

15-31 You are auditing the sales and collection cycle for the Smalltown Regional Hospital, a small not-for-profit hospital. The hospital has a reputation for excellent medical services and weak record keeping. The medical people have a tradition of doing all aspects of their job correctly, but because of a shortage of accounting personnel, there is no time for internal verification or careful performance. In previous years, your firm has found quite a few misstatements in billings, cash receipts, and accounts receivable. As in all hospitals, the two largest assets are accounts receivable and property, plant, and equipment.

The hospital has several large loans payable to local banks, and the two banks have told management that they are reluctant to extend more credit, especially considering the modern hospital that is being built in a nearby city.

In previous years, your response from patients to confirmation requests has been frustrating at best. The response rate has been extremely low, and those who did respond did not know the purpose of the confirmations or their correct outstanding balance. You have had the same experience in confirming receivables at other hospitals.

You conclude that control over cash is excellent and the likelihood of fraud is extremely small. You are less confident about unintentional errors in billing, recording sales, cash receipts, accounts receivable, and bad debts.

REQUIRED

a. Identify the major factors affecting client business risk and acceptable audit risk for this audit.
b. What inherent risks are you concerned about?
c. In this audit of the sales and collection cycle, which types of tests are you likely to emphasize?
d. For each of the following, explain whether you plan to emphasize the tests and give reasons:
   (1) Tests of controls.
   (2) Substantive tests of transactions.
   (3) Analytical procedures.
   (4) Tests of details of balances.

15-32 You have audited the financial statements of the Heft Company for several years. Internal controls for accounts receivable are satisfactory. Accounting at the Heft Company is on a calendar-year basis. An interim audit, which included confirmation of the accounts receivable, was performed on August 31 and indicated that the accounting for cash, sales, sales returns and allowances, and receivables was reliable.

The company's sales are principally to manufacturing concerns. There are about 1,500 active trade accounts receivable of which about 35 percent represent 65 percent of the total dollar amount. The various accounts receivable are maintained alphabetically in a master file of accounts receivable.

Shipping document data are keyed into a computerized system that simultaneously produces a sales invoice, sales journal, and an updated accounts receivable master file.

All cash receipts are in the form of customers' cheques. Information for cash receipts is obtained from the remittance advice portions of the customers' cheques. The accounts receivable clerk compares the remittance advices with the list of cheques that was prepared by another person when the mail was received. As for sales, a cash receipts journal and updated accounts receivable master file are simultaneously prepared after the cash receipts information is entered.

Summary totals are produced monthly by the computer operations department for updating the general ledger master file accounts such as cash, sales, and accounts receivable. An aged trial balance is prepared monthly.

REQUIRED

Prepare the additional audit procedures necessary for testing the balances in the sales and collection cycle. (Ignore bad debts and allowance for uncollectible accounts.)

Case

15-33 You have accepted the engagement of auditing the financial statements of the Reis Company, a small manufacturing firm that has been your client for several years. Because you were busy working on another engagement, you sent a staff accountant to begin the audit, with the suggestion that she start with the accounts receivable.

Using the prior year's working papers as a guide, the auditor prepared a trial balance of the accounts, aged them, prepared and mailed positive confirmation requests, examined underlying support for charges and credits, and performed other work she considered necessary to obtain evidence about the validity and collectability of the receivables. At the conclusion of her work, you reviewed the working papers she prepared and found she had carefully followed the prior year's working papers.

Reis Company acquired the assets of another corporation during the year, so the nature and quality of its accounts receivable have changed. It has many more smaller accounts, as well as three larger international clients, involving foreign exchange sales transactions. Sales have gone up substantially, and the accounts receivable balance has doubled. Two of the international accounts are over six-months old and involve complex hedging transactions.

REQUIRED

a. What examination standards under generally accepted auditing standards have been violated by the personnel in the above case? Explain why you feel the standards you list have been violated.

b. How do the acquisition and the change in the nature of sales and accounts receivable affect control risk and inherent risk of accounts receivable?

c. Describe additional audit procedures that are required to effectively complete the audit of sales and accounts receivable.

ACL Problem

15-34 This problem requires the use of ACL software, which is included in the companion website at **www.pearsoned.ca/arens**. Information about installing and using ACL and solving this problem can be found in the ACL Appendix, also on the companion website. You should read all of the reference material preceding the instructions for "Quick Sort" before locating the appropriate command to answer questions (a)–(f). For this problem use the Metaphor_Trans_All file in ACL Demo, which is a file of outstanding sales invoices (each row represents an invoice transaction). The suggested command or other source of information needed to solve the problem requirement is included at the end of each question.

a. Determine the total number of invoices (read the bottom of the Metaphor_Trans_All file screen) and total unpaid invoices outstanding (NEWBAL) for comparison with the general ledger (Total Field). What audit procedures would you perform using this information?

b. How many of the invoices included a finance charge (FINCHG), and what was the total amount of the finance charges (Filter, Count Records, and Total Field)? What is the impact of locating finance charges on your assessment of the bad-debt allowance?

c. Determine and print accounts receivable outstanding from each customer and total the amount for comparison with part (a); note: remove the filter from step (b) first (Summarize and Total Field). Which customer number has the largest balance due?

d. What is the largest and smallest account balance outstanding (Quick Sort)? How would you use the information from parts (c) and (d) to assist your decision making with respect to the circularization of accounts receivable?

e. For the account with the largest balance, prepare and print an aging of the account from the transaction file using the statement date labelled "STMTTDT." Use the aging date as of 4/30/2003 and "NEWBAL" as the subtotal field (Filter and Age). What additional testing could you do with aging (using current and prior year's information) to assist with the assessment of the allowance for bad debts?

f. To better decide which customers to select for confirmation, you decide to stratify customer balances into two intervals after excluding all balances less than $5,000. How many balances are greater than $5,000? Print the output (Filter and Stratify). Assess the reasonableness of this stratification approach.

Ongoing Small Business Case: Bad Debts at CondoCleaners.com

15-35 Jim has obtained close to 50 commercial accounts for cleaning. Most customers pay well, although there are about five customers to whom he has to give reminder calls. If the account goes more than 30-days overdue, he cancels service, and no further services are provided to that customer. So far, he has done this for two accounts, which cost him about $500.

To Jim's surprise, when he walked into one of the condominium shopping malls, he found notices on three of the stores that they would be moving out. When he talked to the owners, he heard that in the current round of lease negotiations, the condominium was increasing their rents by over 30 percent, in line with current commercial rates in the neighbourhood. Those who were moving out were leasing from the condominium corporation, rather than owning their units.

REQUIRED

How will this announcement affect Jim's business? How does this affect inherent risk of the 12 commercial accounts that Jim has in this building?

Application of the audit process to other cycles

The chapters in Part 4 apply auditing concepts first presented in Chapters 5 through 12 and expanded in Chapters 13 and 14 to the other cycles in an audit. Although there are considerable similarities in auditing each cycle, there are also important differences that auditors need to understand.

Each of these chapters deals with a specific transaction cycle or part of a transaction cycle in much the same manner as Chapters 13 and 14 cover the sales and collection cycle. Each chapter in Part 4 demonstrates the relationship of risks, internal controls, tests of controls, substantive tests of transactions, and analytical procedures to the related balance sheet and income statement accounts in the cycle and to tests of details of balances.

16

Audit of cash balances

"Cash" is available in many different ways—via cheque, credit card, and debit card or transferred electronically into your bank account. It is the way that we acquire assets and discharge our debts, so it has a pivotal role in the accounting process, being one side of many different types of transactions. Here, we will look at different types of cash accounts and how they are audited. Management accountants need to understand how to control cash, while many types of auditors may be asked to design or execute audit programs pertaining to cash.

STANDARDS REFERENCED IN THIS CHAPTER

No standards are referenced in this chapter.

LEARNING OBJECTIVES

1 Identify the different types of cash accounts. Explain the relationship between cash and the other transaction cycles.

2 Link the audit of cash to corporate governance and control processes. Describe the steps in auditing the general cash account.

3 Identify the additional procedures conducted when there is suspicion of fraud. Define "kiting" and explain how is it audited.

4 Explain how an audit of the payroll cash account differs from the audit of the general cash account. Identify the special considerations that exist for EFT (electronic funds transfer) transactions. Explain how petty cash is audited.

It's *Not* Funny

Billing scam. Fake invoices. Overbilling. Funding fraud. Canadian Tire money. What do these terms have in common? All of these resulted in the theft of cash. Cash is tempting, it is often available in large amounts—and there is an expectation that when large amounts are stolen, the auditor will detect the activity. The following are examples of fraud or errors.

- The RCMP was investigating $160 million in apparently bogus software development and maintenance contracts, meaning that cash was paid for services not performed.
- The following week, an article claimed that retailers selling Canadian flags were asked to submit invoices for flags that were not shipped. The article speculated that the Canadian suppliers were paid large sums and inexpensive flags from China were purchased by the government offices instead—so a purchasing agent somewhere made a tidy profit.
- The president of a pizza franchise was charged for taking money from potential franchisees, promising a complete business with support and training, but services were not delivered.
- A Burlington, Ontario, man was charged and pleaded guilty to defrauding the Dufferin-Peel Catholic School Board of over $800,000. Rather than providing legitimate services to the board, invoices were submitted for services that were never provided.
- A CIBC (Canadian Imperial Bank of Commerce) automated teller machine in Moncton, New Brunswick, disbursed Canadian Tire money instead of real cash. CIBC stated that the money must have come in from customers, but who stocked the cash machine?

IMPORTANCE TO AUDITORS

Cash affects every transaction cycle—customers pay cash for goods or services, and organizations themselves pay cash for their own raw materials and to their employees. Auditors are responsible for auditing both the final balance of cash (if it is material) and the authenticity of the transactions that were recorded. If the organization's control of cash is poor, then the transactions may be incorrect or fictitious.

It would certainly be a most unhappy business that paid for poor-quality raw materials, or one that received counterfeit cash in payment, or one that found that fraudulent credit card transactions had been rejected after goods had been shipped.

WHAT DO YOU THINK?

1. What are some of the controls that would prevent Canadian Tire money from being loaded into an ATM?

continued >

2. How could an automated cash register prevent fraudulent credit cards from being accepted to pay for purchases?

3. What are some of the ways that a business could hide the fact that its sole purpose was money laundering?

Sources: 1. Brennan, Richard, "Defence billing scam 'very sophisticated,'" *Toronto Star*, March 12, 2004, p. A12. 2. Canadian Press, "Flag retailers claim government paid for fake invoices," *Toronto Star*, March 19, 2004, p. A17. 3. CBC News, "ATM gives customers Canadian Tire Money," December 2, 2004, www.cbc.ca, Accessed: May 20, 2008. 3. Daw, James, "Pizza franchise chain founder charged," *Toronto Star*, March 19, 2004, p. F1, F4. 4. Mitchell, Bob, "Educator guilty in school funding fraud," *Toronto Star*, March 19, 2004, p. E5.

AS an auditing student, you can understand the importance of paying for only those goods and services that a company receives. Yet, we need to remember that not all internal controls are perfect and that harried employees may not carefully check all the documents pertaining to disbursements of cash. What kinds of questions would you ask about the processing of cash payments? To what extent would you examine detailed records? What would be the inherent risk associated with cash in most organizations?

Evidence accumulated for cash balances depends heavily on the results of the tests in the transaction cycles. Understanding the cash account is important because it links to all of those cycles. The auditor needs to consider the assessed risks from each cycle when auditing cash.

We start by looking at how cash is processed in an organization, before examining corporate governance and control issues. Then, we look at audit procedures conducted for different types of cash accounts.

Cash and the Transaction Cycles

Types of Cash Accounts

It is important to understand the different types of cash accounts because the auditing approach to each varies. The following are the major types of cash accounts.

General cash account—the primary bank account for most organizations; virtually all cash receipts and disbursements flow through this account at some time.

GENERAL CASH ACCOUNT The **general cash account** is the primary bank account, a focal point of cash for most organizations because virtually all cash receipts and disbursements flow through this account at some time. The disbursements for the acquisition and payment cycle are normally paid from this account, and the receipts of cash in the sales and collection cycle are deposited into the account. In addition, the deposits and disbursements for all other cash accounts are normally made through the general account. Most small companies have only one bank account—the general cash account.

Imprest payroll account—a bank account to which the exact amount of payroll for the pay period is transferred by cheque from the employer's general cash account.

IMPREST PAYROLL ACCOUNT Some companies, as a means of improving internal control, establish a separate imprest bank account for making payroll payments to employees. In an **imprest payroll account**, a fixed balance, such as $1,000, is maintained in a separate bank account. Then, only the exact amount of the payroll is placed in this account. Immediately before each pay period, one cheque is drawn on the general cash account to deposit the total amount of the net payroll in the payroll account. After all payroll cheques have cleared the imprest payroll account, the bank account should have a $1,000 balance. The only deposits into the account are of the periodic weekly (or semi-monthly) payroll, and the only disbursements are payments to employees. For companies with many employees, the use of an imprest payroll account can improve internal control and reduce the time needed to reconcile bank accounts.

BRANCH BANK ACCOUNT For a company operating in multiple locations, it is frequently desirable to have a separate bank balance at each location. **Branch bank accounts** are useful for building public relations in local communities and permitting the decentralization of operations to the branch level.

The branch bank account could be used as a general account, or there could be one bank account for receipts and a separate one for disbursements. All receipts are deposited in the branch bank, and the total is transferred to the general account. The disbursement account is set up on an imprest basis but in a different manner from an imprest payroll account. A fixed balance is maintained in the imprest account, and the authorized branch personnel use these funds for disbursements at their own discretion as long as the payments are consistent with company policy. When the cash balance has been depleted, an accounting is made to the home office and a reimbursement is made to the branch account from the general account after the expenditures have been approved. The use of an imprest branch bank account improves controls over receipts and disbursements.

IMPREST PETTY CASH FUND An **imprest petty cash fund** is actually not a bank account, but is a fund of cash used for small cash purchases that can be paid more conveniently and quickly by cash than by cheque. An imprest petty cash fund is set up on the same basis as an imprest branch bank account, but the expenditures are normally for a much smaller amount. Typical expenses include minor office supplies, stamps, and small contributions to local charities. Usually a petty cash account does not exceed a few hundred dollars and may not be replenished more than once or twice each month.

CASH EQUIVALENTS Excess cash, accumulated during certain parts of the operating cycle, that will be needed in the reasonably near future is often invested in short-term, highly liquid cash equivalents. Examples include term deposits, certificates of deposit, and money market funds. **Cash equivalents**, which can be highly material, are included in the financial statements as part of the cash account only if they are short-term investments that are readily convertible to known amounts of cash within a short time and there is little risk of a change in value from interest rate changes. Marketable securities and longer-term interest-bearing investments are not cash equivalents.

SUMMARY Figure 16-1 on the next page shows the relationship of general cash to the other cash accounts. All cash either originates from or is deposited into general cash. This chapter focuses on three types of accounts: the general cash account, the imprest payroll bank account, and the imprest petty cash fund. The others are similar to these.

Cash in the Bank and Transaction Cycles

A brief discussion of the relationship between cash in the bank and the other transaction cycles serves a dual function: it highlights the importance of the tests of various transaction cycles to the audit of cash, and it aids in further understanding the integration of the different transaction cycles. Figure 16-2 on page 543 illustrates the relationships of the various transaction cycles, the focal point being the general cash account.

An examination of Figure 16-2 indicates why the general cash account is considered significant in almost all audits, even when the ending balance is immaterial. The amount of cash flowing into and out of the cash account is frequently larger than for any other account in the financial statements. Furthermore, the susceptibility of cash to defalcation is greater than for other types of assets because most other assets must be converted to cash to make them usable.

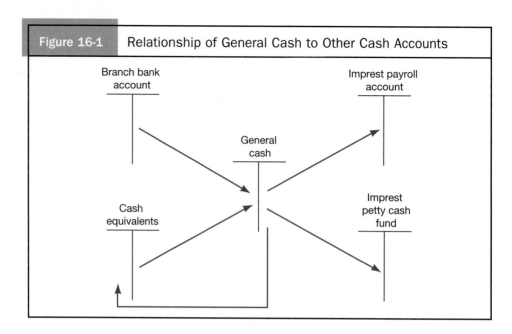

Figure 16-1   Relationship of General Cash to Other Cash Accounts

In the audit of cash, an important distinction should be made between verifying the client's reconciliation of the balance on the bank statement to the balance in the general ledger and verifying whether recorded cash in the general ledger correctly reflects all cash transactions that took place during the year. It is relatively easy to verify the client's reconciliation of the balance in the bank account to the general ledger, which is the primary subject of this chapter, but a significant part of the total audit of a company involves verifying whether cash transactions are properly recorded. For example, each of the following misstatements ultimately results in the improper payment of, or the failure to receive, cash, but none will normally be discovered as a part of the audit of the bank reconciliation:

Sales and accounts receivable transaction cycle

- Failure to bill a customer.
- Billing a customer at a lower price than called for by company policy.
- A defalcation of cash by interception of collections from customers before they are recorded. The account receivable is charged off as a bad debt.

Acquisition and payment cycle

- Duplicate payment of a vendor's invoice.
- Improper payments of officers' personal expenditures.
- Payment for raw materials that were not received.

Payroll and personnel cycle

- Payment to an employee for more hours than he or she worked.

Capital acquisition and repayment cycle

- Payment of interest to a related party for an amount in excess of the going rate.

If these misstatements are to be uncovered in the audit, their discovery must come about through tests of controls. The first three misstatements could be discovered as part of the audit of the sales and collection cycle, the next three in the audit of the acquisitions and payment cycle, and the last two in the tests of the payroll and personnel cycle and the capital acquisition and repayment cycle, respectively.

Entirely different types of misstatements are normally discovered as part of the tests of a bank reconciliation. For example:

- Failure to include on the outstanding cheque list a cheque that has not cleared the bank, even though it has been recorded in the cash disbursements journal.

concept check

C16-1 Describe the difference between a general cash account and an imprest bank account.

C16-2 For each of the following transaction cycles, provide an example of an error in cash that would affect the cycle: sales and accounts receivable, acquisition and payment, payroll and personnel.

Figure 16-2

Relationships of Cash in the Bank and Transaction Cycles

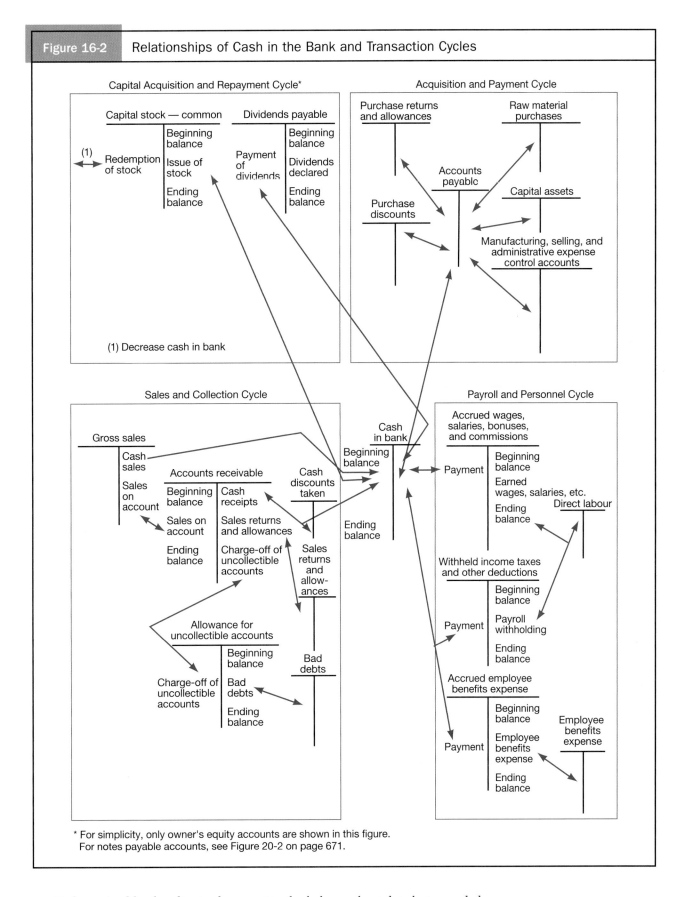

* For simplicity, only owner's equity accounts are shown in this figure.
  For notes payable accounts, see Figure 20-2 on page 671.

- Cash received by the client subsequent to the balance sheet date but recorded as cash receipts in the current year.
- Deposits recorded as cash receipts near the end of the year, deposited in the bank, and included in the bank reconciliation as a deposit in transit.

- Payments on notes payable that were debited directly to the bank balance by the bank but were not entered in the client's records.

The appropriate methods for discovering the preceding misstatements by testing the client's bank reconciliation will become apparent as we proceed. At this point, it is important that you distinguish between tests of controls that are related to the cash account and tests that determine whether the book balance reconciles to the bank balance.

❷ Audit of the General Cash Account

Controls over cash are identified in every transaction cycle. For example, cash received at point-of-sale terminals is reconciled to sales, bank reconciliations are independently prepared, accounts receivable write-offs need to be independently authorized, and payments for products are made only with authorized purchase orders with supporting receiving documents. Thus, the auditor will consider the results of control risk for every transaction cycle when coming to a conclusion about controls over cash.

In addition, management attitudes toward cash and the nature of the treasury management function are important factors. In Chapter 4, we talked about money laundering. If a business has plenty of cash, but there never seem to be any customers about (such as at a restaurant), then the business could be engaging in money laundering. If a company has invested in questionable marketable securities that are no longer liquid (such as occurred with the asset-backed-paper fiasco in 2008 and the $50 billion mutual fund Madoff fraud in the United States), then the company will be in a cash squeeze, as it can no longer liquidate its investments.

Cycle-based indicators that could lead to cash liquidity problems could be gradually aging accounts receivable, obsolete inventory or poorly managed inventory, inability to take advantage of cash discounts in accounts payable, and difficulty meeting payroll or income tax obligations. By asking management about its policies with respect to cash management and cash investment, as well as gathering information from the different cycles, the auditor will obtain information about the likelihood of cash misstatements.

Turning to Hillsburg Hardware Limited, note that on the trial balance, on page 129, there is only one cash account. All cycles, except inventory and warehousing, directly affect cash in the bank.

In testing the year-end balance in the general cash account, the auditor must accumulate sufficient evidence to evaluate whether cash, as stated on the balance sheet, is fairly stated and properly disclosed in accordance with the balance-related audit objectives. Rights to general cash, its classification on the balance sheet, and the valuation of cash are usually not a problem due to the inherent nature of cash.

The methodology for auditing year-end cash is essentially the same as for all other balance sheet accounts. This methodology is shown in Figure 16-3.

INTERNAL CONTROLS Internal controls over the year-end cash balances in the general account can be divided into two categories: (1) controls over the transaction cycles affecting the recording of cash receipts and disbursements and (2) independent bank reconciliations.

Controls affecting the recording of cash transactions are discussed in chapters pertaining to those cycles. For example, in the acquisition and payment cycle, major controls include the adequate segregation of duties between the cheque signing and the accounts payable functions, the signing of cheques by only a properly authorized person, the use of prenumbered cheques that are printed on special paper, adequate control of blank and voided cheques, careful review of supporting documentation by the cheque signer before cheques are signed, and adequate internal verification. If the controls affecting cash-related transactions are adequate, it is possible to reduce the audit tests of the year-end bank reconciliation.

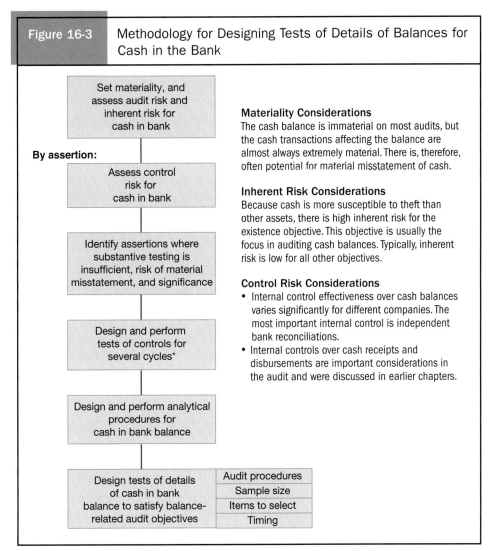

Figure 16-3 Methodology for Designing Tests of Details of Balances for Cash in the Bank

Set materiality, and assess audit risk and inherent risk for cash in bank

By assertion:

Assess control risk for cash in bank

Identify assertions where substantive testing is insufficient, risk of material misstatement, and significance

Design and perform tests of controls for several cycles*

Design and perform analytical procedures for cash in bank balance

Design tests of details of cash in bank balance to satisfy balance-related audit objectives

| Audit procedures |
| Sample size |
| Items to select |
| Timing |

Materiality Considerations
The cash balance is immaterial on most audits, but the cash transactions affecting the balance are almost always extremely material. There is, therefore, often potential for material misstatement of cash.

Inherent Risk Considerations
Because cash is more susceptible to theft than other assets, there is high inherent risk for the existence objective. This objective is usually the focus in auditing cash balances. Typically, inherent risk is low for all other objectives.

Control Risk Considerations
• Internal control effectiveness over cash balances varies significantly for different companies. The most important internal control is independent bank reconciliations.
• Internal controls over cash receipts and disbursements are important considerations in the audit and were discussed in earlier chapters.

*Cycles affected include sales and collection, acquisition and payment, payroll and personnel, and capital acquisition and repayment.

A monthly **bank reconciliation** of the differences between the cash balance recorded in the general ledger and in the general bank account on a timely basis by someone independent of the handling or recording of cash receipts and disbursements is an essential control over the cash balance. The reconciliation is important to ensure that the books reflect the same cash balance as the actual amount of cash in the bank after consideration of reconciling items, but even more important, the independent reconciliation provides a unique opportunity for an internal verification of cash receipts and disbursements transactions. If the bank statements are received unopened by the reconciler and physical control is maintained over the statements until the reconciliations are complete, the cancelled cheques, duplicate deposit slips, and other documents included in the statement can be examined without concern for the possibility of alteration, deletions, or additions. A careful bank reconciliation by competent client personnel includes the following:

Bank reconciliation—the monthly reconciliation, usually prepared by client personnel, of the differences between the cash balance recorded in the general ledger and the amount in the bank account.

• Compare cancelled cheques with the cash disbursements journal for date, payee, and amount.
• Examine cancelled cheques for signature, endorsements, and cancellation.
• Compare deposits in the bank with recorded cash receipts for date, customer, and amount.
• Account for the numerical sequence of cheques, and investigate missing ones.

- Reconcile all items causing a difference between the book and the bank balance, and verify their propriety.
- Reconcile total debits on the bank statement with the totals in the cash disbursements journal.
- Reconcile total credits on the bank statement with the totals in the cash receipts journal.
- Review month-end interbank transfers for propriety and proper recording.
- Follow up on outstanding cheques and stop-payment notices.

The first four of these internal procedures are directly related to the tests of controls of transaction cycles. The last five are directly related to the reconciliation of the book and bank balance and are discussed in greater detail later.

Because of the importance of the monthly reconciliation of bank accounts, another common control for many companies is having a responsible employee review the monthly reconciliation as soon as possible after its completion.

ANALYTICAL PROCEDURES In many audits, the year-end bank reconciliation is verified on a 100-percent basis. Testing the reasonableness of the cash balance is therefore less important than for most other audit areas.

It is common for auditors to compare the ending balance on the bank reconciliation, deposits in transit, outstanding cheques, and other reconciling items with the prior-year reconciliation. Similarly, auditors normally compare the ending balance in cash with previous months' balances. These analytical procedures may uncover misstatements in cash.

AUDIT PROCEDURES FOR YEAR-END CASH A major consideration in the audit of the general cash balance is the possibility of fraud. The auditor must extend his or her procedures in the audit of year-end cash to determine the possibility of a material fraud when there are inadequate internal controls, especially the improper segregation of duties between the handling of cash and the recording of cash transactions in the journals. The study of cash in the following section assumes the existence of adequate controls over cash; therefore, fraud detection is not emphasized. At the completion of the study of typical audit procedures for the verification of year-end cash, procedures designed primarily for the detection of fraud are discussed.

audit challenge 16-1
Testing for Greed, Using Generalized Audit Software (GAS) as an Analytical Tool

Does something seem unusual at your client but you cannot quite put your finger on it? Perhaps there seems to be less cash than usual, and purchases are slightly up, reducing costs of goods sold, but sales have not increased.

Consider asking the client for a copy of its entire transaction file for purchasing and payments, and running a series of investigative analytical review procedures.

You could run totals of purchases by supplier and by month, and look for round amounts, duplicate payments, or suppliers with addresses that are the same as employee addresses. You could also ask for the payroll data file and match last names of employees with names of supplier contacts.

In any event, you will get more information about the nature of transactions and have more confidence about where to focus your audit work.

You could also identify actions that would help the company improve its purchases: for example, by testing purchases for raw materials, you could look for discrepancies in purchase cost from one supplier to the next and ask about the supplier selection process to ensure that all purchases are approved.

CRITICAL THINKING QUESTIONS ❓

1. If you had a copy of the sales returns for a particular store, what types of data analysis would you do on the returns to look for potential fictitious returns (i.e., theft of cash)?
2. What types of transaction inquiries would you run on cash receipts in the accounts receivable file to test for lapping (i.e., theft of cash by crediting accounts receivable to the incorrect account)?

The starting point for the verification of the balance in the general bank account is obtaining a bank reconciliation from the client for inclusion in the auditor's working papers. Figure 16-4 on the next page shows a bank reconciliation after adjustments. Note that the bottom figure in the working paper is the adjusted balance in the general ledger. Although the bank reconciliation is normally prepared manually or using a spreadsheet, many accounting systems allow the client to use computerized systems to prepare the list of outstanding cheques.

The frame of reference for the audit tests is the bank reconciliation. The balance-related audit objectives and common tests of details of balances are shown in Table 16-1 on page 549. As in all other audit areas, the actual audit procedures depend on the risks and controls in the transaction cycles. Also, because of their close relationship in the audit of year-end cash, the existence of recorded cash in the bank, accuracy, and inclusion of existing cash (completeness) are combined. These three objectives are the most important ones for cash and therefore receive the greatest attention.

The following three procedures are discussed thoroughly because of their importance and complexity.

Receipt of a bank confirmation The direct receipt of a confirmation from every bank or other financial institution with which the client does business is necessary for every audit, except when there are an unusually large number of inactive accounts. If the bank does not respond to a confirmation request, the auditor must send a second request or ask the client to telephone the bank. As a convenience to CAs as well as to bankers who are requested to fill out bank confirmations, the CICA has approved the use of a **standard bank confirmation form,** through which the bank responds to the auditor's requires for information about the client's bank balances, loan information, and contingent liabilities. Figure 16-5 on page 550 is an illustration of such a completed standard bank confirmation. This standard form has been agreed upon by the CICA and the Canadian Bankers Association. CGAAC and the Canadian Bankers Association have approved a similar bank confirmation form for use by CGAs.

Standard bank confirmation form—a form approved by the CICA and Canadian Bankers Association through which the bank responds to the auditor's request for information about the client's bank balances, loan information, and contingent liabilities.

The importance of bank confirmations in the audit extends beyond the verification of the actual cash balance. It is typical for the bank to confirm loan information and bank balances on the same form. The confirmation in Figure 16-5 includes three outstanding loans and a contingent liability. Information on liabilities to the bank for notes, mortgages, or other debt typically includes the amount of the loan, the date of the loan, its due date, interest rate, and the existence of collateral.

The auditor completes the sections labelled "client," "chartered accountant," "financial institution," and "confirmation date"; a signing officer from the client signs in the "client" box authorizing the bank to provide the information; and the auditor sends the confirmation to the bank. While the bank should exercise due care in completing the confirmation, errors can occur. The auditor may wish to communicate with the bank if there is any information on the returned confirmation about which he or she is doubtful or if any information that was expected is not reported.

After the bank confirmation has been received, the balance in the bank account confirmed by the bank should be traced to the amount stated on the bank reconciliation. Similarly, all other information on the reconciliation should be traced to the relevant audit working papers. In any case, if the information is not in agreement, an investigation must be made of the difference.

Receipt of a cut-off bank statement A **cut-off bank statement** includes a partial-period bank statement and the related cancelled cheques, duplicate deposit slips, and other documents included with bank statements, mailed by the bank directly to the public accounting firm's office. The purpose of the cut-off bank statement is to verify the reconciling items on the client's year-end bank reconciliation with evidence that is inaccessible to the client. To fulfill this purpose, the auditor requests that the client have the bank send directly to the auditor the statement for 7 to 10 days subsequent to the balance sheet date.

Cut-off bank statement—a partial-period bank statement and the related cancelled cheques, duplicate deposit slips, and other documents included in bank statements, mailed by the bank directly to the auditor. The auditor uses it to verify reconciling items in the client's year-end bank reconciliation.

Figure 16-4   Working Paper for a Bank Reconciliation

Microsoft Excel - Book2

File   Edit   View   Insert   Format   Tools   Data   Window   Help   Acrobat

Arial   10   **B** *I* U

A1

Clawson Industries
Bank Reconciliation
12/31/08

Schedule	A-2	Date
Prepared by	Client / DED	1/10/09
Approved by	SW	1/18/09

Acct. 101 – General account, First Canadian Bank

Balance per Bank			109713	X A-2/1
Add:				
Deposits in transit				
12/30		10017 ✓		
12/31		11100 ✓	21117	
Deduct				
Outstanding cheques				
# 7993	12/16	3068 X		
8007	12/16	9763 X		
8012	12/23	11916 X		
8013	12/23	14717 X		
8029	12/28	A-7 37998 X		
8038	12/30	A-7 10000 X	<87462>	
Other reconciling items: Bank error				
Deposit for another bank customer credited to general account by bank, in error			<15200>	A-3
Balance per bank, adjusted			28168	T/B
			Ⅴ	
Balance per books before adjustments			32584	A-1
Adjustments:				
Unrecorded bank service charge		216		A-3
Non-sufficient funds cheque returned by bank, not collectable from customer		4200	<4416>	C-3/1
Balance per books, adjusted			28168	A-1
			Ⅴ	

X *Traced and agreed to bank confirmation.*

✓ *Traced deposit to the December 2008 cash receipts records and to the January 2009 bank cut-off statement, noting its proper classification as a deposit in transit at 12/31/08*

X *Traced cheque to December 2008 cash disbursements records and to the January 2009 bank cut-off statement, noting its proper classification as an outstanding cheque at 12/31/08*

T/B *Traced to 12/31/08 adjusted trial balance*

Ⅴ *Footed*

Table 16-1 — Balance-Related Audit Objectives and Tests of Details of Balances for General Cash in the Bank

Balance-Related Audit Objective	Common Tests of Details of Balances Procedures	Comments
Cash in the bank as stated on the bank reconciliation foots correctly and agrees with the general ledger (detail tie-in).	Foot the outstanding cheque list and deposits in transit. Prove the bank reconciliation as to additions and subtractions, including all reconciling items. Trace the book balance on the reconciliation to the general ledger.	These tests are done entirely on the bank reconciliation, with no reference to documents or other records except the general ledger.
Cash in the bank as stated on the reconciliation exists (existence). Existing cash in the bank is included (completeness). Cash in the bank as stated on the reconciliation is accurate (accuracy).	(See extended discussion for each of these.) Obtain and test a bank confirmation. Obtain and test a cut-off bank statement. Test the bank reconciliation. Perform extended tests of the bank reconciliation. Prepare proof of cash. Test for kiting.	The first three procedures are the most important objectives for cash in the bank. The procedures are combined because of their close interdependence. The last three procedures should be done only when there are internal control weaknesses.
Cash receipts and cash disbursements transactions are recorded in the proper period (cut-off).	Cash receipts Count the cash on hand on the first day of the year and subsequently trace to deposits in transit and the cash receipts journal. Trace deposits in transit to subsequent period bank statement (cut-off bank statement). Cash disbursements Record the last cheque number used on the last day of the year, and subsequently trace to the outstanding cheques and the cash disbursements journal. Trace outstanding cheques to subsequent period bank statement.	When cash receipts received after year end are included in the journal, a better cash position than actually exists is shown. It is called the "holding open the cash receipts" journal. The "holding open the cash disbursements" journal reduces accounts payable and usually overstates the current ratio. The first procedure listed for receipts and disbursement cut-off tests requires the auditor's presence on the client's premises at the end of the last day of the year.
Cash in the bank is properly presented and disclosed (presentation and disclosure).	Examine minutes, loan agreements, and obtain confirmation for restrictions on the use of cash and compensating balances. Review financial statements to make sure (a) material savings accounts and guaranteed investment certificates, if access is restricted, are disclosed separately from cash in the bank; (b) cash restricted to certain uses and compensating balances are adequately disclosed; and (c) bank overdrafts are included as current liabilities.	An example of a restriction on the use of cash is cash deposited with a trustee for the payment of mortgage interest and taxes on the proceeds of a construction mortgage. A compensating balance is the client's agreement with a bank to maintain a specified minimum in its chequing account.

Many auditors prove the subsequent-period bank statement if a cut-off statement is not received directly from the bank. The purpose of this proof is to test whether the client's employees have omitted, added, or altered any of the documents accompanying the statement. It is a test for intentional misstatements. The auditor performs the proof in the month subsequent to the balance sheet date by (1) footing all the cancelled cheques, debit memos, deposits, and credit memos; (2) checking to see that the bank statement balances when the footed totals are used; and (3) reviewing the items included in the footings to make sure they were cancelled by the bank in the proper period and do not include any erasures or alterations.

BANK CONFIRMATION

(Areas to be completed by client are marked §, while those to be completed by the financial institutions are marked †)

FINANCIAL INSTITUTION	CLIENT (Legal Name) §
(Name, branch, and full mailing address) §	Koa Foods Inc.
Bank of Columbia	St. Jacobs, Ontario
Westmount & Old Post Road	N0L 1K0
Waterloo, Ontario	The financial institution is authorized to provide the details
N2L 5M1	requested herein to the below-noted firm of accountants
	§ *J Koa*
CONFIRMATION DATE § December 31, 2008	Client's authorized signature
(All information to be provided as of this date)	Please supply copy of the most recent credit facility agreement
(See Bank Confirmation Completion Instructions)	(initial if required) § _____

1. LOANS AND OTHER DIRECT AND CONTINGENT LIABILITIES (If balances are nil, please state.)

NATURE OF LIABILITY/ CONTINGENT LIABILITY †	INTEREST (Note rate per contract) RATE † DATE PAID TO †		DUE DATE †	DATE OF CREDIT FACILITY AGREEMENT †	AMOUNT AND CURRENCY OUTSTANDING †
Loan	8%	31/12/08	Demand	5/5/03	$90,000
Loan	9%	30/11/08	30/5/10	1/4/02	$120,000
Loan	10%	31/12/08	Demand	1/6/04	$20,000
Guarantee	N/A		N/A	1/1/97	$8,000

ADDITIONAL CREDIT FACILITY AGREEMENT(S)

Note the date(s) of any credit facility agreement(s) not drawn upon and not referenced above †

2. DEPOSITS/OVERDRAFTS

TYPE OF ACCOUNT §	ACCOUNT NUMBER §	INTEREST RATE §	ISSUE DATE (if applicable) §	MATURITY DATE (if applicable) §	AMOUNT AND CURRENCY (Bracket if Overdraft) †
General	65422	—	—	—	$109,713
Payroll	65432	—	—	—	$4,000

EXCEPTIONS AND COMMENTS
(See Bank Confirmation Completion Instructions) †

STATEMENT OF PROCEDURES PERFORMED BY FINANCIAL INSTITUTION †
The above information was completed in accordance with the Bank Confirmation Completion Instructions.

Bill Brown _____   Branch Contact W. Brown   (519) 884-1921
Authorized signature of financial institution   Name and telephone number

Please mail this form directly to our chartered accountant in the enclosed addressed envelope.

Name:	Kadous & Co.
Address:	P.O. Box 1939
	Waterloo, Ontario N2L 1G1
Telephone:	(519) 999-1234
Fax:	(519) 999-1235

Developed by the Canadian Bankers Association and the Canadian Institute of Chartered Accountants

Tests of the bank reconciliation The reason for testing the bank reconciliation is to verify whether the client's recorded bank balance is the same amount as the actual cash in the bank except for deposits in transit, outstanding cheques, and other reconciling items. In testing the reconciliation, the cut-off bank statement provides the information for conducting the tests. Several major procedures are involved:

- Verify that the client's bank reconciliation is mathematically accurate.
- Trace the balance on the cut-off statement to the balance per bank on the bank reconciliation. A reconciliation is incomplete until these two are the same.
- Trace cheques included with the cut-off bank statement to the list of outstanding cheques on the bank reconciliation and to the cash disbursements journal. All cheques that cleared the bank after the balance sheet date and were included in the cash disbursements journal should also be included on the outstanding cheque list. If a cheque was included in the cash disbursements journal, it should be included as an outstanding cheque if it did not clear before the balance sheet date. Similarly, if a cheque cleared the bank prior to the balance sheet date, it should not be on the bank reconciliation.
- Investigate all significant cheques included on the outstanding cheque list that have not cleared the bank on the cut-off statement. The first step in the investigation should be tracing the amount of any items not clearing to the cash disbursements journal. The reason for the cheque not being cashed should be discussed with the client, and if the auditor is concerned about the possibility of fraud, the vendor's accounts payable balance should be confirmed to determine whether the vendor has recognized the receipt of the cash in its records. In addition, the cancelled cheque should be examined prior to the last day of the audit if it becomes available.
- Trace deposits in transit to the subsequent bank statement. All cash receipts not deposited in the bank at the end of the year should be traced to the cut-off bank statement to ensure they were deposited shortly after the beginning of the new year.
- Account for other reconciling items on the bank statement and bank reconciliation. These include such items as bank service charges, bank errors and corrections, and unrecorded note transactions debited or credited directly to the bank account by the bank. These reconciling items should be carefully investigated to ensure they have been treated properly by the client.

SUMMARY OF AUDIT TESTS FOR THE GENERAL CASH ACCOUNT Figure 16-6 on the next page illustrates the types of audit tests (excluding risk assessment) used to audit the general cash account. This figure also shows how the audit risk model discussed in Chapter 7 relates to the audit of the general cash account.

concept check

C16-3 Why do the risks of every transaction cycle affect cash?

C16-4 What is the purpose of a bank reconciliation?

Fraud-Oriented Procedures

It is frequently necessary for auditors to extend their year-end audit procedures to test more extensively for the possibility of material fraud when there are material internal control weaknesses. Many fraudulent activities are difficult, if not impossible, to uncover; nevertheless, auditors are responsible for making a reasonable effort to detect fraud when they have reason to believe it may exist. The following procedures for uncovering fraud are discussed in this section: extended tests of the bank reconciliation, proofs of cash, and tests for kiting.

Extended tests of the bank reconciliation When the auditor believes that the year-end bank reconciliation may be intentionally misstated, it is appropriate to perform extended tests of the year-end bank reconciliation. The purpose of the extended procedures is to verify whether all transactions included in the journals for the last

Figure 16-6   Types of Audit Tests Used for General Cash

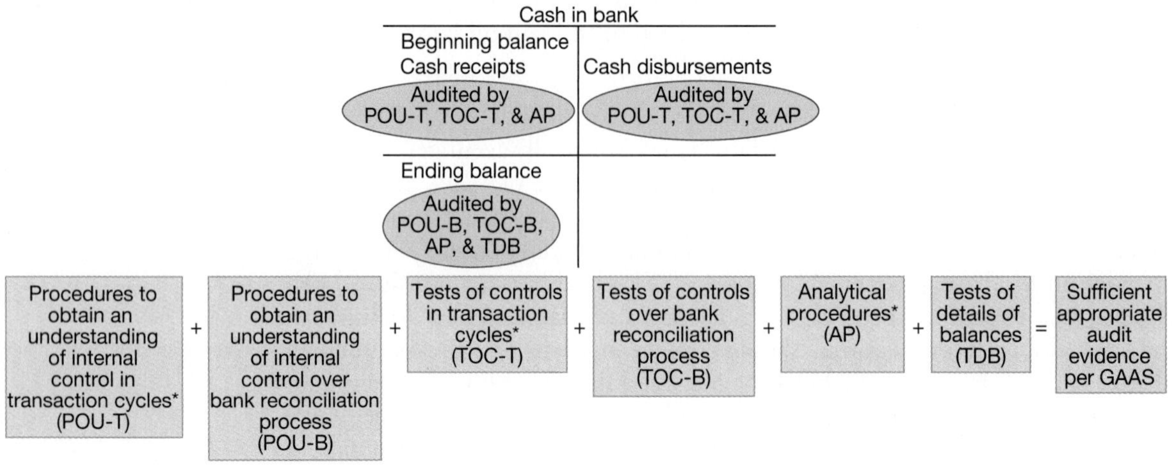

Extent of substantive testing is determined by assessed risks, materiality, and *PDR*. *PDR* is affected by factors in the audit risk model:

$$AR = IR \times CR \times PDR \quad or \quad PDR = \frac{AR}{IR \times CR}$$

* Procedures to obtain an understanding of internal control, tests of controls in transaction cycles, and analytical procedures are done for the four transaction cycles included in Figure 16-2. The primary tests of the ending cash balance are tests of details of balances.

month of the year were correctly included in or excluded from the bank reconciliation and to verify whether all items in the bank reconciliation were correctly included. Let us assume that there are material internal control weaknesses and that the client's year end is December 31. A common approach is to start with the bank reconciliation for November and compare all reconciling items with cancelled cheques and other documents in the December bank statement. In addition, all remaining cancelled cheques and deposit slips in the December bank statement should be compared with the December cash disbursements and receipts journals. All uncleared items in the November bank reconciliation and the December cash disbursements and receipts journals should be included in the client's December 31 bank reconciliation. Similarly, all reconciling items in the December 31 bank reconciliation should be items from the November bank reconciliation and December's journals that have not yet cleared the bank.

In addition to the tests just described, the auditor must also carry out procedures subsequent to the end of the year using the bank cut-off statement. These tests would be performed in the same manner as previously discussed.

Proof of cash Auditors sometimes prepare a proof of cash when the client has material internal control weaknesses in cash. A **proof of cash** is a four column working paper used to reconcile the bank's records of the client's beginning balance, cash deposits, cleared cheques, and ending balance for the period with the client's records. It includes the following:

- A reconciliation of the balance on the bank statement with the general ledger balance at the beginning of the proof-of-cash period.
- A reconciliation of cash receipts deposited with the cash receipts journal for a given period.
- A reconciliation of cancelled cheques clearing the bank with the cash disbursements journal for a given period.
- A reconciliation of the balance on the bank statement with the general ledger balance at the end of the proof-of-cash period.

Proof of cash—a four-column working paper prepared by the auditor to reconcile the bank's records of the client's beginning balance, cash deposits, cleared cheques, and ending balance for the period with the client's records.

When Cash That You Thought You Received Must Be Returned . . .

Retailers commonly receive payment for their products by debit card, credit card, and cash. If retailer systems do not check current published lists for fraudulent debit cards or credit cards, then the retailer is liable for the funds and must return the cash. There may also be other circumstances. For example, if computer systems were down and the retailer did not take an imprint of the fictitious card, that money would need to be returned by the retailer.

Is this a big problem? Definitely! The Interac Association stated that in 2007 about 159,300 Canadian debit card holders had their cash used (and then returned) for close to $107 million.

Methods of fraud include placing a skimmer on an ATM (so that your card can be copied) together with a hidden camera (to capture your password) and hacking debit card information from the internet.

As an auditor, you can help by reviewing your retail client's controls over checks for fraudulent debit and credit cards and making sure that these procedures are up to date.

Sources: 1. Appleby, Timothy, "Soaring rates of debit fraud prompt switch to smart cards," March 14, 2008, globeandmail.com, Accessed: March 12, 2009. 2. "Couple charged in ATM scam," *Toronto Star*, October 2, 2008, p. A13.

A proof of cash of this nature is commonly referred to as a four-column proof of cash—one column is used for each type of information listed above. A proof of cash can be performed for one or more interim months, the entire year, or the last month of the year. Figure 16-7 on the next page shows a four-column proof of cash for an interim month.

The auditor uses a proof of cash to determine whether the following occurred:

- All recorded cash receipts were deposited.
- All deposits in the bank were recorded in the accounting records.
- All recorded cash disbursements were paid by the bank.
- All amounts that were paid by the bank were recorded.

The concern in an interim-month proof of cash is not with adjusting account balances but, rather, with reconciling the amounts per books and bank.

When the auditor does a proof of cash, he or she is combining tests of controls and tests of details of balances. For example, the proof of the cash receipts is a test of recorded transactions, whereas the bank reconciliation is a test of the balance in cash at a particular time. The proof of cash is an excellent method of comparing recorded cash receipts and disbursements with the bank account and with the bank reconciliation. However, the auditor must recognize that the proof of cash disbursements is not for discovering cheques written for an improper amount, fraudulent cheques, or other misstatements in which the dollar amount appearing on the cash disbursements records is incorrect. Similarly, the proof of cash receipts is not useful for uncovering the theft of cash receipts or the recording and deposit of an improper amount of cash.

Tests for kiting Embezzlers occasionally cover a defalcation of cash by a practice known as **kiting**: transferring money from one bank to another and improperly recording the transaction, which overstates cash. Near the balance sheet date, a cheque is drawn on one bank account and immediately deposited in a second account for credit before the end of the accounting period. In making this transfer, the embezzler is careful to make sure that the cheque is deposited at a late enough date that it does not clear the first bank until after the end of the period. Assuming that the bank transfer is not recorded until after the balance sheet date, the amount of the transfer is recorded as an asset in both banks. Although there are other ways of perpetrating this fraud, each involves the basic device of increasing the bank balance to cover a shortage by the use of bank transfers.

A useful approach to test for kiting, as well as for unintentional errors in recording bank transfers, is listing all bank transfers made a few days before and after the balance sheet date and tracing each to the accounting records for proper recording. An example of a bank transfer schedule is included in Figure 16-8 on page 555. The

Kiting—the transfer of money from one bank account to another and improperly recording the transfer so that the amount is recorded as an asset in both accounts; used by embezzlers to cover a defalcation of cash.

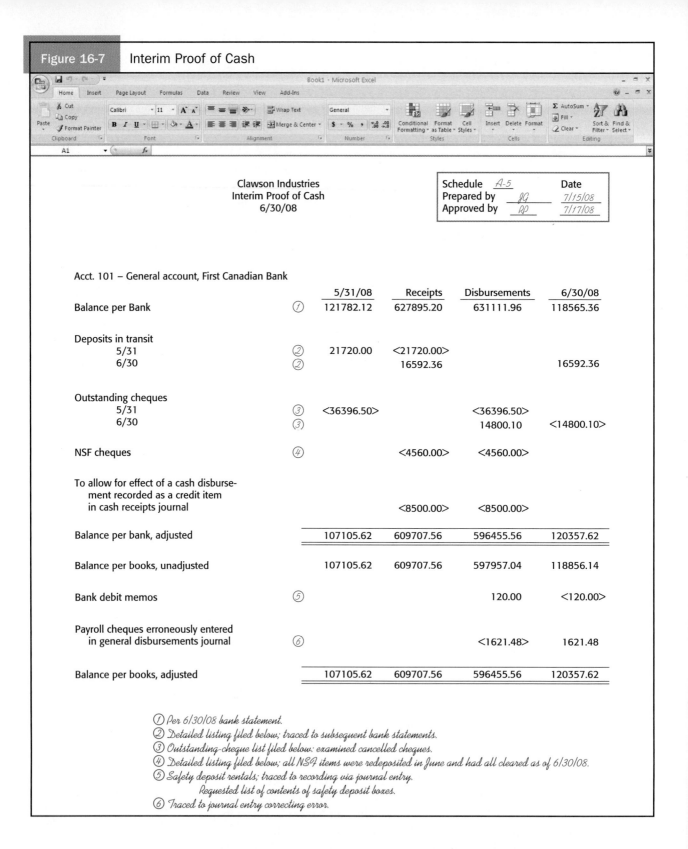

Figure 16-7   Interim Proof of Cash

Clawson Industries
Interim Proof of Cash
6/30/08

	Schedule	A-5	Date
	Prepared by	JG	7/15/08
	Approved by	RP	7/17/08

Acct. 101 – General account, First Canadian Bank

		5/31/08	Receipts	Disbursements	6/30/08
Balance per Bank	①	121782.12	627895.20	631111.96	118565.36
Deposits in transit					
5/31	②	21720.00	<21720.00>		
6/30	②		16592.36		16592.36
Outstanding cheques					
5/31	③	<36396.50>		<36396.50>	
6/30	③			14800.10	<14800.10>
NSF cheques	④		<4560.00>	<4560.00>	
To allow for effect of a cash disbursement recorded as a credit item in cash receipts journal			<8500.00>	<8500.00>	
Balance per bank, adjusted		107105.62	609707.56	596455.56	120357.62
Balance per books, unadjusted		107105.62	609707.56	597957.04	118856.14
Bank debit memos	⑤			120.00	<120.00>
Payroll cheques erroneously entered in general disbursements journal	⑥			<1621.48>	1621.48
Balance per books, adjusted		107105.62	609707.56	596455.56	120357.62

① Per 6/30/08 bank statement.
② Detailed listing filed below; traced to subsequent bank statements.
③ Outstanding-cheque list filed below; examined cancelled cheques.
④ Detailed listing filed below; all NSF items were redeposited in June and had all cleared as of 6/30/08.
⑤ Safety deposit rentals; traced to recording via journal entry.
   Requested list of contents of safety deposit boxes.
⑥ Traced to journal entry correcting error.

working paper shows that there were four bank transfers shortly before and after the balance sheet date.

There are several things that should be audited on the bank transfer schedule:

- The accuracy of the information on the bank transfer schedule should be verified. The auditor should compare the disbursement and receipt information on the schedule with the cash disbursements and cash receipts journals to make sure that

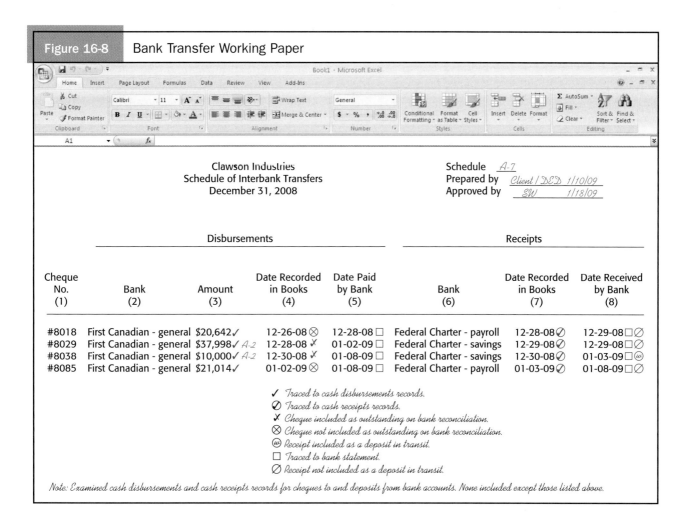

Figure 16-8 Bank Transfer Working Paper

Clawson Industries
Schedule of Interbank Transfers
December 31, 2008

Schedule _A-7_
Prepared by _Client / DED 1/10/09_
Approved by _SW   1/18/09_

		Disbursements					Receipts	
Cheque No. (1)	Bank (2)	Amount (3)	Date Recorded in Books (4)	Date Paid by Bank (5)	Bank (6)	Date Recorded in Books (7)	Date Received by Bank (8)	
#8018	First Canadian - general	$20,642✓	12-26-08⊗	12-28-08☐	Federal Charter - payroll	12-28-08⊘	12-29-08☐⊘	
#8029	First Canadian - general	$37,998✓ A-2	12-28-08✗	01-02-09☐	Federal Charter - savings	12-29-08⊘	12-29-08☐⊘	
#8038	First Canadian - general	$10,000✓ A-2	12-30-08✗	01-08-09☐	Federal Charter - savings	12-30-08⊘	01-03-09☐ⓦ	
#8085	First Canadian - general	$21,014✓	01-02-09⊗	01-08-09☐	Federal Charter - payroll	01-03-09⊘	01-08-09☐⊘	

✓ Traced to cash disbursements records.
⊘ Traced to cash receipts records.
✗ Cheque included as outstanding on bank reconciliation.
⊗ Cheque not included as outstanding on bank reconciliation.
ⓦ Receipt included as a deposit in transit.
☐ Traced to bank statement.
⊘ Receipt not included as a deposit in transit.

Note: Examined cash disbursements and cash receipts records for cheques to and deposits from bank accounts. None included except those listed above.

it is accurate. Similarly, the dates on the schedule for transfers that were received and disbursed should be compared with the bank statement. Finally, cash disbursements and receipts journals should be examined to ensure that all transfers a few days before and after the balance sheet date have been included on the schedule. The symbol explanations on the working paper in Figure 16-8 indicate that these steps have been taken.

- The bank transfers must be recorded in both the receiving and disbursing banks. If, for example, there was a $10,000 transfer from Bank A to Bank B but only the disbursement was recorded, this would be evidence of an attempt to conceal a cash theft.

- The date of the recording of the disbursements and receipts for each transfer must be in the same fiscal year. In Figure 16-8, the dates in the two "date recorded in books" columns [columns (4) and (7)] are in the same period for each transfer; therefore, they are correct. If a cash disbursement was recorded in the current fiscal year and the receipt in the subsequent fiscal year, it might be an attempt to cover a cash shortage.

- Disbursements on the bank transfer schedule should be correctly included in or excluded from year-end bank reconciliations as outstanding cheques. In Figure 16-8, the 12-31-08 bank reconciliation should include outstanding cheques for the second and third transfers but not the other two. [Compare the dates in columns (4) and (5).] Understating outstanding cheques on the bank reconciliation indicates the possibility of kiting.

• Receipts on the bank transfer schedule should be correctly included in or excluded from year-end bank reconciliations as deposits in transit. In Figure 16-8, the 12-31-08 bank reconciliation should indicate a deposit in transit for the third transfer but not for the other three. (Compare the dates for each transfer in the last two columns.) Overstating deposits in transit on the bank reconciliation indicates the possibility of kiting.

Even though audit tests of bank transfers are usually fraud-oriented, they are often performed on audits in which there are numerous bank transfers, regardless of the internal controls. When there are numerous intercompany transfers, it is difficult to be sure that each is correctly handled unless a schedule of transfers near the end of the year is prepared and each transfer is traced to the accounting records and bank statements. In addition to the possibility of kiting, inaccurate handling of transfers could result in a misclassification between cash and accounts payable. Due to the materiality of transfers and the relative ease of performing the tests, many auditors believe that the tests should always be performed.

Summary of fraud-oriented procedures In designing audit procedures for uncovering fraud, careful consideration should be given to the nature of the weaknesses in internal control, the type of fraud that is likely to result from the weaknesses, the potential materiality of the fraud, and the audit procedures that are most effective in uncovering the misstatement. When auditors are specifically testing for fraud, they should keep in mind that audit procedures other than tests of details of cash balances may also be useful. Examples of procedures that may uncover fraud in the cash receipts area include the confirmation of accounts receivable, tests for lapping, reviewing the general ledger entries in the cash account for unusual items, tracing from customer orders to sales and subsequent cash receipts, and examining approvals and supporting documentation for bad debts and sales returns and allowances. Similar tests can be used for testing for the possibility of fraudulent cash disbursements.

concept check

C16-5 When could kiting occur and what does it do? How?

C16-6 How can the auditor test for kiting?

❹ Additional Examples of Cash Auditing

Audit of the Payroll Bank Account

Tests of the payroll bank reconciliation should take only a few minutes if there is an imprest payroll account and an independent reconciliation of the bank account such as that described for the general account. Typically, the only reconciling items are outstanding cheques, and, for most audits, the great majority clear shortly after the cheques are issued. In testing the payroll bank account balances, it is necessary to obtain a bank reconciliation, a bank confirmation, and a cut-off bank statement. The reconciliation procedures are performed in the same manner as those described for general cash. Naturally, extended procedures are necessary if the controls are inadequate or if the bank account does not reconcile with the general ledger imprest cash balance.

The discussion in the preceding paragraph should not be interpreted as implying that the audit of payroll is unimportant. Chapter 17 will show the reader that the most important audit procedures for verifying payroll are tests of controls. Most common payroll misstatements will be discovered by those procedures rather than by checking the imprest bank account balance.

Audit of Electronic Cash Transactions

As described in Audit Challenge 16-2, many organizations receive cash or make cash payments electronically. For a typical small to medium-sized business, electronic cash receipts are used if the business sells to customers over the counter and accepts debit card payments from those customers. Electronic cash payments include automatic payments for loans, insurance, and payroll to employees. More sophisticated or

Many organizations use electronic funds transfers (EFTs) when they are transferring cash among banks, collecting from customers, paying employees, and paying vendors. Under these systems, cash is transferred instantly. For example, when Hillsburg Hardware Limited receives a debit card payment from ABC Hardware Ltd., the cash is transferred immediately from ABC's bank account to Hillsburg's bank account. No cheque is issued.

EFTs such as those via debit card and electronic data interchange (EDI) have the potential to improve internal controls, since there is no cash handling by employees. However, the risk of incorrect transfers or theft by unauthorized transfers still exists.

When assessing internal controls, the auditor needs to evaluate and document controls in all software involved (data communications, data transfer, specialized EDI programs, and access). With electronic payments, year-end balances of accounts receivable, accounts payable, or inventory may be reduced. Where funds are transferred electronically, there is an increased need for the enhanced security features of encryption, access control, and authentication (verifying the identity of the parties to a transaction). Auditors may also choose to use computer-assisted audit techniques (CAATs).

CRITICAL THINKING QUESTIONS

1. When accounts receivable and inventory are small (i.e., immaterial), what type of audit testing is used for the sales and accounts receivable transactions? Why?
2. What is the role of password protection in the use of EDI and EFT? How does the auditor test such controls?

---

larger businesses could use **electronic data interchange** (EDI—the electronic transfer of business documents, such as invoices or purchase orders) with their **electronic funds transfers** (EFTs—the electronic transfer of funds, either as payment or receipt, e.g., using a debit card).

Electronic data interchange (EDI)—the electronic transfer of business documents, such as invoices and purchase orders.

Electronic funds transfer (EFT)—the electronic transfer of funds, either as payment or receipt (e.g., using a debit card).

CONTROL OVER DEBIT CARD CASH RECEIPTS When a business accepts debit card payments from its customers, the customer swipes his or her debit card and enters a personal identification number (PIN) to authorize the transfer of funds from the customer's bank account to the organization's bank account. At the same time, a two-part receipt is provided, with one copy going to the customer and the other to the organization.

Although most debit card transactions are processed accurately, a very small percentage are not. The organization should therefore continue its cash reconciliation functions as part of the bank reconciliation for these electronic transactions. Most organizations keep track of payment methods automatically using their point-of-sale (POS) systems. Thus, the daily sales are broken down by cash, debit card, credit card, cheque, and accounts receivable. When performing the bank reconciliation, the debit card total should agree with the amounts automatically deposited into the bank. This reconciliation should be handled by a person independent of the POS function. These receipts should be tested as part of the sales and receivables transaction cycle.

Control over Electronic Payments

AUTOMATIC PRE-AUTHORIZED MONTHLY PAYMENTS Loan payments, interest payments, and insurance payments made on monthly or other regular intervals are based on a loan agreement or regular invoice. When the bank statement is sent to an organization, the only evidence of this payment will likely be a line on the bank statement showing the amount, a reference number, and possibly the name of the company that was paid.

The organization under audit should have controls to ensure that only authorized amounts are set up for payment and that all automatic withdrawals are recorded in the accounts in the period made. These payments should be tested as part of the purchases and payments cycle.

PAYROLL PAYMENTS As with a payroll paid by cheque, payroll payments made electronically should be made using an imprest bank account.

Payment is usually initiated by the organization sending to the bank or other financial institution a set of forms or electronic data files specifying how much employees should be paid, what deductions should be made, the appropriate tax withholdings, and the bank accounts to which the funds should be transferred. The bank may (or may not) do the actual calculations, process payments, and send either a listing or a data file to the organization of payments made.

Again, there is a two-step authorization phase here. The first step covers master file information (e.g., wage rate, withholdings rate, bank account number), and the second covers the actual wages paid in a specific pay period. These controls should be documented, evaluated, and tested as part of the personnel and payroll cycle. As part of control over cash, a person independent of payroll should verify bank account numbers used for payments and should verify that payments from the imprest bank account match the payroll journal.

AUDIT OF ELECTRONIC RECEIPTS AND PAYMENTS The extent of audit work conducted on the bank reconciliation depends on the assessed quality of internal controls. There are usually fewer outstanding bank transactions for electronic transactions than for paper transactions sent via mail, since the timing difference between invoice and receipt is minimal.

When client personnel prepare the bank reconciliation, electronic payments should be agreed to an authorized schedule of such payments by date, payee account number, and amount. The auditor would review the authorized schedule of payments and controls over its preparation. Similarly, deposits would be traced to the client's POS system records.

For the imprest payroll account reconciliation, the auditor would review the documentation received from the bank and agree details to the reconciliation.

SUMMARY For electronic receipts and payments, the discussion shows that there are changes in the types of controls required and the type of evidence available to the auditor. However, standard audit procedures are still used to verify existence, completeness, and accuracy.

Audit of Petty Cash

Petty cash is a unique account because it is frequently immaterial in amount, and yet it is verified on most audits. The account is verified primarily because of the potential for defalcation and the client's expectation of an audit review even when the amount is immaterial.

INTERNAL CONTROLS OVER PETTY CASH The most important internal control for petty cash is the use of an imprest fund that is the responsibility of one individual. In addition, petty cash funds should not be mingled with other receipts, and the fund should be kept separate from all other activities. There should also be limits on the amount of any expenditure from petty cash, as well as on the total amount of the fund. The type of expenditure that can be made from petty cash transactions should be well defined by company policy.

Whenever a disbursement is made from petty cash, adequate internal controls require a responsible official's approval on a prenumbered petty cash form. The total of the actual cash and cheques in the fund plus the total unreimbursed petty cash forms that represent actual expenditures should equal the total amount of the petty cash fund stated in the general ledger. Periodically, surprise counts and a reconciliation of the petty cash fund should be made by the internal auditor or another responsible official.

When the petty cash balance runs low, a cheque payable to the petty cash custodian should be written on the general cash account for the replenishment of petty cash. The cheque should be for the exact amount of the prenumbered vouchers that are submitted as evidence of actual expenditures. These vouchers should be verified by the accounts payable clerk and cancelled to prevent their reuse.

AUDIT TESTS FOR PETTY CASH The emphasis in verifying petty cash should be on testing petty cash transactions rather than the ending balance in the account. Even if the amount of the petty cash fund is small, there is potential for numerous improper transactions if the fund is frequently reimbursed.

An important part of testing petty cash is first determining the client's procedures for handling the fund by discussing internal control with the custodian and examining the documentation of a few transactions. As a part of obtaining an understanding of internal control, it is necessary to identify internal controls and weaknesses. Even though most petty cash systems are not complex, it is often desirable to use a flowchart and an internal control questionnaire, primarily for documentation in subsequent audits. The tests of controls depend on the number and size of the petty cash reimbursements and the auditor's assessed level of control risk. When control risk is assessed at a low level and there are few reimbursement payments during the year, it is common for auditors not to test any further for reasons of immateriality. When the auditor decides to test petty cash, the two most common procedures are counting the petty cash balance and carrying out detailed tests of one or two reimbursement transactions. In such a case, the primary procedures should include footing the petty cash vouchers supporting the amount of the reimbursement, accounting for a sequence of petty cash vouchers, examining the petty cash vouchers for authorization and cancellation, and examining the attached documentation for reasonableness. Typical supporting documentation includes cash register tapes, invoices, and receipts.

Petty cash tests can ordinarily be performed at any time during the year, but as a matter of convenience, they are typically done on an interim date. If the balance in the petty cash fund is considered material, which is rarely the case, it should be counted at the end of the year. Unreimbursed expenditures should be examined as part of the count to determine whether the amount of unrecorded expenses is material.

concept check

C16-7 How do EDI and EFTs affect the audit trail at a business?

C16-8 How do EDI and EFTs affect the audit process?

Summary

1. *What are the different types of cash accounts?* They are the general cash account, the imprest payroll account, branch bank accounts, an imprest petty cash fund, and cash equivalents.

   Explain the relationship between cash and the other transaction cycles. Cash flows in and out of the cash account, with the other side of the accounting entry normally being in a different transaction cycle. For example, payroll payments, accounts payable payments, and receipts from sales all are recorded via the cash account.

2. *How does the auditor consider corporate governance and internal controls when conducting the audit of cash?* The auditor evaluates and assesses controls in the other cycles and their impact upon cash. During the risk assessment process, the auditor will examine the control environment with respect to cash management and consider the impact upon all of the transaction cycles.

   Describe the steps in auditing the general cash account. Figure 16-3 described the risk-based audit approach as it applies to cash. After assessing control risk on an assertion basis, tests of controls are designed and performed, followed by the design and completion of

tests of details. Year-end procedures include obtaining a bank confirmation and a bank cut-off statement, as well as tests of the bank reconciliation.

3. *What additional procedures are conducted when there is suspicion of fraud?* Extended tests of the bank reconciliation or a proof of cash could be completed.

   What is "kiting" and how is it audited? If kiting (taking advantage of timing differences between banks to inflate cash) is suspected, then the auditor would prepare a bank transfer working paper.

4. *How is an audit of the payroll cash account different from the audit of the general cash account?* The payroll account may be an imprest account, containing only payroll cheques issued to employees. Having only a single transaction type means that it is easier to audit the account.

   What special considerations exist for EFT transactions? Such transactions could involve complex software and access controls, requiring an increased reliance on automated computer controls.

   How is petty cash audited? The auditor would likely examine controls over petty cash and conduct a petty cash count.

Review Questions

16-1 Explain the relationship among the initial assessed level of control risk, tests of controls for cash receipts, and tests of details of cash balances.

16-2 Explain the relationships among the initial assessed level of control risk, tests of controls for cash disbursements, and tests of details of cash balances. Give one example in which the conclusions reached about internal controls in cash disbursements would affect the tests of cash balances.

16-3 Why is the monthly reconciliation of bank accounts by an independent person an important internal control over cash balances? Which individuals would generally not be considered independent for this responsibility?

16-4 Evaluate the effectiveness and state the shortcomings of the preparation of a bank reconciliation by the accountant in the manner described in the following statement: "When I reconcile the bank account, the first thing I do is to sort the cheques in numerical order and find which numbers are missing. Next I determine the amount of the uncleared cheques by referring to the cash disbursements journal. If the bank account reconciles at that point, I am all finished with the reconciliation. If it does not, I search for deposits in transit, cheques from the beginning of the outstanding cheque list that still have not cleared, other reconciling items, and bank errors until it reconciles. In most instances, I can do the reconciliation in 20 minutes."

16-5 How do bank confirmations differ from positive confirmations of accounts receivable? Distinguish between them in terms of the nature of the information confirmed, the sample size, and the appropriate action when the confirmation is not returned after the second request. Explain the rationale for the differences between these two types of confirmations.

16-6 Evaluate the necessity for following the practice described by an auditor: "In confirming bank accounts, I insist upon a response from every bank the client has done business with in the past two years, even though the account may be closed at the balance sheet date."

16-7 Describe what is meant by a cut-off bank statement and state its purpose.

16-8 Why are auditors usually less concerned about the client's cash receipts cut-off than the cut-off for sales? Explain the procedure involved in testing for the cut-off for cash receipts.

16-9 What is meant by an "imprest bank account" for a branch operation? Explain the purpose of using this type of bank account.

16-10 When the auditor fails to obtain a cut-off bank statement, it is common to "prove" the entire statement for the month subsequent to the balance sheet date. How is this done and what is its purpose?

16-11 Distinguish between "lapping" and "kiting." Describe audit procedures that can be used to uncover each.

16-12 Assume that a client with excellent internal controls uses an imprest payroll bank account. Explain why the verification of the payroll bank reconciliation ordinarily takes less time than the tests of the general bank account, even if the number of cheques exceeds those written on the general account.

16-13 Distinguish between the verification of petty cash reimbursements and the verification of the balance in the fund. Explain how each is done. Which is more important?

16-14 Why is there a greater emphasis on the detection of fraud in tests of details of cash balances than for other balance sheet accounts? Give two specific examples that demonstrate how this emphasis affects the auditor's evidence accumulation in auditing year-end cash.

16-15 Explain why, in verifying bank reconciliations, most auditors emphasize the possibility of a non-existent deposit in transit being included in the reconciliation and an outstanding cheque being omitted rather than the omission of a deposit in transit and the inclusion of a non-existent outstanding cheque.

16-16 How would a company's bank reconciliation reflect an electronic deposit of cash received by the bank—from credit card agencies that make payments on behalf of customers purchasing products from the company's website—but not recorded in the company's records?

Discussion Questions and Problems

16-17 The following are fraud and other irregularities that might be found in the client's year-end cash balance. (Assume the balance sheet date is June 30.)

1. A cheque was omitted from the outstanding cheque list on the June 30 bank reconciliation. It cleared the bank July 7.

2. A cheque was omitted from the outstanding cheque list on the bank reconciliation. It cleared the bank September 6.

3. Cash receipts collected on accounts receivable from July 2 to July 5 were included as June 29 and 30 cash receipts.

4. A loan from the bank on June 26 was credited directly to the client's bank account. The loan was not entered in the books as of June 30.
5. A cheque that was dated June 26 and disbursed in June was not recorded in the cash disbursements journal, but it was included as an outstanding cheque on June 30.
6. A bank transfer recorded in the accounting records on July 2 was included as a deposit in transit on June 30.
7. The outstanding cheques on the June 30 bank reconciliation were underfooted by $2,000.

REQUIRED
a. Assuming that each of these misstatements was intentional, state the most likely motivation of the person responsible.
b. What control could be instituted for each intentional misstatement to reduce the likelihood of occurrence?
c. List an audit procedure that could be used to discover each misstatement.

16-18 The following audit procedures are concerned with tests of details of general cash balances:
1. Obtain a standard bank confirmation from each bank with which the client does business.
2. Compare the balance on the bank reconciliation obtained from the client with the bank confirmation.
3. Compare the cheques returned along with the cut-off bank statement with the list of outstanding cheques on the bank reconciliation.
4. List the cheque number, payee, and amount of all material cheques not returned with the cut-off bank statement.
5. Review minutes of the board of directors' meetings, loan agreements, bank confirmation for interest-bearing deposits, restrictions on the withdrawal of cash, and compensating balance agreements.
6. Prepare a four-column proof of cash.
7. Compare the bank cancellation dates with the dates on the cancelled cheques for cheques dated on or shortly before the balance sheet date.
8. Trace deposits in transit on the bank reconciliation to the cut-off bank statement and the current-year cash receipts journal.

REQUIRED
Explain the objective of each.

16-19 You are auditing general cash for Trail SupplyCorp. for the fiscal year ended July 31. The client has not prepared the July 31 bank reconciliation. After a brief discussion with the owner, you agree to prepare the reconciliation with assistance from one of Trail Supply's clerks. You obtain the following information:

	General Ledger	Bank Statement
Beginning balance	$ 4,611	$ 5,753
Deposits		25,056
Cash receipts journal	25,456	
Cheques cleared		(23,615)
Cash disbursements journal	(21,811)	
July bank service charge		(87)
Note paid directly		(6,100)
NSF cheque		(311)
Ending balance	$ 8,256	$ 696

June 30 Bank Reconciliation

Information in General Ledger and Bank Statement	
Balance per bank	$5,753
Deposits in transit	600
Outstanding cheques	1,742
Balance per books	4,611

In addition, the following information is obtained:
1. The total of outstanding cheques on June 30 was $1,692.
2. The total for cheques that were recorded in the July disbursements journal was $20,467.
3. A cheque for $1,060 cleared the bank but had not been recorded in the cash disbursements journal. It was for an acquisition of inventory. Trail Supply uses the periodic inventory method.
4. A cheque for $396 was charged to Trail Supply but had been written on an associated company's bank account.
5. Deposits included $600 from June and $24,456 for July.
6. The bank withdrew from Trail Supply's account a non-sufficient funds (NSF) customer cheque totalling $311. The credit manager concluded that the customer intentionally closed its account and that the owner had left the city. The account was turned over to a collection agency.
7. The bank deducted $5,800 plus interest from Trail Supply's account for a loan made by the bank under an agreement signed four months ago. The note payable was recorded at $5,800 on Trail Supply's books.

REQUIRED
a. Prepare a bank reconciliation that shows both the unadjusted and adjusted balances per the books.
b. Identify the nature of adjustments required.
c. What audit procedures would you use to verify each item in the bank reconciliation?

16-20 Regional Transport Company is a large branch of a national company. Regional maintains its own bank account. Cash is periodically transferred to the central head office account in Montreal. On the branch account's records, bank transfers are recorded as a debit to the home office clearing account and a credit to the branch bank account. Similarly, the home office account is recorded as a debit to the central bank account and a credit to the branch office clearing account. Gordon Light is the head bookkeeper for both the home office and the branch bank accounts. Because he also reconciles the bank account, the senior auditor, Cindy Marintette, is concerned about this internal control weakness.

As a part of the year-end audit of bank transfers, Cindy asks you to schedule the transfers for the last few days in 2008 and the first few days of 2009. You prepare the following list:

Amount of Transfer	Date Recorded in the Home Office Cash Receipts Journal	Date Recorded in the Branch Office Cash Disbursements Journal	Date Deposited in the Home Office Bank Account	Date Cleared the Branch Bank Account
$12,000	12-27-08	12-29-08	12-26-08	12-27-08
26,000	12-28-08	01-02-09	12-28-08	12-29-08
14,000	01-02-09	12-30-08	12-28-08	12-29-08
11,000	12-26-08	12-26-08	12-28-08	01-03-09
15,000	01-02-09	01-02-09	12-28-08	12-31-08
28,000	01-07-09	01-05-09	12-28-08	01-03-09
37,000	01-04-09	01-06-09	01-03-09	01-05-09

REQUIRED

a. State the appropriate audit procedures you should perform in verifying each bank transfer.

b. Prepare any adjusting entries required in the home office records.

c. Prepare any adjusting entries required in the branch bank records.

d. State how each bank transfer should be included in the December 31, 2008, bank reconciliation for the home office account after your adjustments in part (b).

e. State how each bank transfer should be included in the December 31, 2008, bank reconciliation of the branch bank account after your adjustments in part (c)

16-21 In connection with an audit you are given the following worksheet:

Bank Reconciliation, December 31, 2008

Balance per ledger December 31, 2008		$17,174.86
Add:		
Cash receipts received on the last day of December and charged to "cash in bank" on books but not deposited		2,662.25
Debit memo for customer's cheque returned unpaid (cheque is on hand but no entry has been made on the books)		200.00
Debit memo for bank service charge for December		5.50
		$20,142.61
Deduct:		
Cheques drawn but not paid by bank (see detailed list below)	$2,267.75	
Credit memo for proceeds of a note receivable that had been left at the bank for collection but which has not been recorded as collected	400.00	
Cheques for an account payable entered on books as $240.90 but drawn and paid by bank as $419.00	178.10	(2,945.85)
Computed balance		17,196.76
Unlocated difference		(200.00)
Balance per bank (checked to confirmation)		$16,996.76

Cheques Drawn But Not Paid by Bank

No.	Amount
573	$ 67.27
724	9.90
903	456.67
907	305.50
911	482.75
913	550.00
914	366.76
916	10.00
917	218.90
	$2,267.75

REQUIRED

a. Prepare a corrected reconciliation.

b. Prepare journal entries for items that should be adjusted prior to closing the books.

(Adapted from AICPA)

16-22 You are doing the first-year audit of Sherman School District and have been assigned responsibility for doing a four-column proof of cash for the month of October 2009. You obtain the following information:

1. Balance per books	September 30	$ 8,106
	October 31	3,850
2. Balance per bank	September 30	5,411
	October 31	6,730
3. Outstanding cheques	September 30	$ 916
	October 31	1,278
4. Cash receipts for October	per bank	26,536
	per books	19,711
5. Deposits in transit	September 30	3,611
	October 31	693

6. Interest on a bank loan for the month of October, charged by the bank but not recorded, was $596.
7. Proceeds on a note of the Jones Company were collected by the bank on October 28 but were not entered on the books:

Principal	$3,300
Interest	307
	$3,607

8. On October 26, a $407 cheque of the Billings Company was charged to Sherman School District's account by the bank in error.
9. Dishonoured cheques are not recorded on the books unless they permanently fail to clear the bank. The bank treats them as disbursements when they are dishonoured and as deposits when they are redeposited. Cheques totalling $609 were dishonoured in October; $300 was redeposited in October and $309 in November.

REQUIRED

a. Prepare a four-column proof of cash for the month ended October 31. It should show both adjusted and unadjusted cash.
b. Prepare all adjusting entries.

Professional Judgment Problems

16-23 Yip-Chuk Inc. had weak internal control over its cash transactions. Facts about its cash position at November 30 were as follows:

The cashbooks showed a balance of $18,901.62, which included undeposited receipts. A credit of $100 on the bank's records did not appear on the books of the company. The balance per bank statement was $15,550. Outstanding cheques were no. 62 for $116.25, no. 183 for $150.00, no. 284 for $253.25, no. 8621 for $190.71, no. 8623 for $206.80, and no. 8632 for $145.28.

The cashier, Khalid Nasser, embezzled all undeposited receipts in excess of $3,794.41 and prepared the reconciliations shown in the table on the right.

REQUIRED

a. Prepare a supporting schedule showing how much Khalid embezzled.

Balance, per books, November 30		$18,901.62
Add: Outstanding cheques		
8621	$190.71	
8623	206.80	
8632	145.28	
		442.79
		19,344.41
Less: Undeposited receipts		3,794.41
Balance per bank, November 30		15,550.00
Deduct: Unrecorded credit		100.00
True cash, November 30		$15,450.00

b. How did he attempt to conceal his theft?
c. Using only the information given, name two specific features of internal control that were apparently missing.

(Adapted from AICPA)

16-24 Santasgiftworld.com is an online retailer of children's toys. The chief executive officer has noticed that margins have been deteriorating over those of previous years due to an increase in cost of goods sold coupled with a much faster increase in freight out and bad-debt expenses. He has also heard through the grapevine that some customers have complained of unauthorized charges on their credit cards. Other customers have complained of placing orders and never having received them, necessitating replacement shipments. Still more complaints of unauthorized charges have been received from individuals claiming never to have ordered products at all. You have been contacted to help Santasgiftworld.com improve its operations and to prevent possible litigation arising from continuing problems of this type.

Santasgiftworld.com employs 100 individuals. Its customer base consists mainly of individuals but also smaller toy stores, day-care centres, and schools, all of which order through the company website. The website has pages where customers can view all of the products and prices. There is a virtual shopping cart available for each customer once he or she has set up an account. A customer choosing to make a purchase simply clicks on the direct link to the shopping cart from the desired product and proceeds to checkout. There the customer is prompted to choose a major credit card payment method and enter the shipping address. Once this information has been entered, the customer chooses a shipping method: Canada Post, UPS, or Federal Express. The customer is then informed of the total price and the date to expect shipment.

Every two hours, the orders placed on the website are reviewed, then entered into the company's main database for fulfillment. Once an order is shipped, credit card information is extracted and transmitted for settlement in Santasgiftworld.com's favour.

Orders have been placed with the company, but the customers in question honestly deny ever submitting those orders. It turns out that many of those orders had been placed by the children of the customers, without the customers' knowledge. The children were able to gain access to their parents' accounts after the web ordering system recognized cookies on the hard drives. When the children went to the website, the page recognized them as the users of the account and gave them authorized access to make purchases.

REQUIRED

Identify application control weaknesses at Santasgiftworld.com. For each control weakness,
a. state the exposure created;
b. provide a recommendation to prevent or detect the exposure;
c. provide an audit test of detail that could be used in assessing the impact on the financial statements; and
d. identify the audit objective(s) addressed by the audit tests.

Case

16-25 The following information was obtained in an audit of the cash account of Tuck Company as of December 31, 2009. Assume that the auditor has satisfied himself as to the propriety of the cash data files, the bank statements, and the returned cheques, except as noted.

1. The bookkeeper's bank reconciliation at November 30, 2009.

Balance per bank statement		$19,400
Add: Deposit in transit		1,100
Total		$20,500
Less: Outstanding cheques		
#2540	$140	
#1501	750	
#1503	580	
#1504	800	
#1505	30	(2,300)
Balance per books		$18,200

2. A summary of the bank statement for December 2009.

Balance brought forward	$ 19,400
Deposits	148,700
	168,100
Charges	(132,500)
Balance, December 31, 2009	$ 35,600

3. A summary of the cash records for December 2009 before adjustments.

Balance brought forward	$ 18,200
Receipts	149,690
	167,890
Disbursements	(124,885)
Balance, December 31, 2009	$ 43,005

4. Included with cancelled cheques returned with the December bank statement were the cheques listed on the next page.
5. The Tuck Company discounted its own 60-day note for $9,000 with the bank on December 1, 2009. The discount rate was 6 percent. The accountant recorded the proceeds as a cash receipt at the face value of the note.
6. The accountant records customers' dishonored cheques as a reduction of cash receipts. When the dishonored cheques are redeposited, they are recorded as a regular cash receipt. Two NSF cheques for $180 and $220 were returned by the bank during December. Both cheques were redeposited and were recorded by the accountant.
7. Cancellations of Tuck Company cheques are recorded by a reduction of cash disbursements.
8. December bank charges were $20. In addition, a $10 service charge was made in December for the collection of a foreign draft in November. These charges were not recorded on the books.
9. Cheque 2540 listed in the November outstanding cheques was drawn in 2010. Because the payee cannot be located, the president of Tuck Company agreed to the auditor's suggestion that the cheque be written back into the accounts by a journal entry.
10. Outstanding cheques at December 31, 2009, totalled $4,000, excluding cheques 2540 and 1504.
11. The cut-off bank statement disclosed that the bank had recorded a deposit of $2,400 on January 2, 2010. The accountant had recorded this deposit on the books on December 31, 2009, and then mailed the deposit to the bank.

Number	Date of Cheque	Amount of Cheque	Comment
1501	November 28, 2009	$ 75	This cheque was in payment of an invoice for $750 and was recorded in the records as $750.
1503	November 28, 2009	$ 580	This cheque was in payment of an invoice for $580 and was recorded in the records as $580.
1523	December 5, 2009	$ 150	Examination of this cheque revealed that it was unsigned. A discussion with the client disclosed that it had been mailed inadvertently before it was signed. The cheque was endorsed and deposited by the payee and processed by the bank, even though it was a legal nullity. The cheque was recorded in the cash disbursements journal.
1528	December 12, 2009	$ 800	This cheque replaced 1504, which was returned by the payee because it was damaged. Cheque 1504 was not cancelled on the books.
–	December 19, 2009	$ 200	This was a counter cheque drawn at the bank by the president of the company as a cash advance for travel expense. The president forgot to inform the bookkeeper about the cheque.
–	December 20, 2009	$ 300	The drawer of this cheque was the Tucker Company.
1535	December 20, 2009	$ 350	This cheque had been labeled NSF and returned to the payee because the bank had erroneously believed that the cheque was drawn by Luck Company. Subsequently, the payee was advised to redeposit the cheque.
1575	January 5, 2010	$10,000	This cheque was given to the payee on December 30, 2009, as a postdated cheque with the understanding that it would not be deposited until January 5. The cheque was not recorded on the books in December.

REQUIRED

Prepare a four-column proof of cash reconciling the cash receipts and cash disbursements recorded on the bank statement with the company's books for the month of December 2009. The reconciliation should agree with the cash figure that will appear in the company's financial statements.

(Adapted from AICPA)

Ongoing Small Business Case: PayPal.com Problems at CondoCleaners.com

16-26 To increase his reach with customers in condominium towers, Jim has decided to accept payment from users of PayPal.com in addition to the credit card payments that he was accepting via his secure website. Jim had been using PayPal.com for about three months. One morning he received upset emails from several of his customers complaining that they had been billed several times for the same service. Yet when Jim looked at his PayPal records, he found that only one payment had been processed in his favour.

Upon contacting the affected customers, Jim found that the customers had responded to a phishing email and had given their payment information to unauthorized individuals who had copied the transaction information and collected additional money.

REQUIRED

What are Jim's responsibilities in this case? What actions would you suggest that he take?

17

Audit of the payroll and personnel cycle

A payroll payment helps us buy groceries, pay rent or a mortgage, and pay for tuition. For many workers, it may be the crucial reason to show up for work every day. For a business, it can be the largest expense—if payroll is too high, gross margins are too low and the company could go into receivership. Good human resource policies help a business hire competent, honest employees who help provide for an effective and honest control environment. Management accountants implement controls over payroll and human resources, while various types of auditors examine payroll to evaluate those controls and to consider the risks of payroll fraud.

LEARNING OBJECTIVES

1 Explain the importance of the payroll and personnel cycle. Differentiate this cycle from other cycles. Describe the functions and records in this cycle.

2 List typical audit tests of controls by assertion.

3 Consider the impact of outsourcing on the controls over, and the audit of, payroll. Apply these principles to other application cycles.

4 Highlight the misstatements that could be detected by an analytical review of payroll. Describe the liability and expense accounts in the payroll cycle that are tested using tests of details.

STANDARDS REFERENCED IN THIS CHAPTER

CICA Standards

CAS 402 – Auditor considerations relating to an entity using a service organization (previously Section 5310 – Audit evidence considerations when an entity uses a service organization)

Section 5970 – Auditor's report on controls at a service organization

International Standard

ISAE (International Standard on Assurance Engagements) 3402 – Assurance reports on controls at a third-party service organization

Viral Can Be a Good Word or a Nasty Surprise

Viral networking is an advertising or connection phrase of the present—it is the way that you communicate by word of mouth, electronically. The method is being used to promote organization-wide social networks intended to keep employees happy, connected, and well-informed. Such systems are being adopted by a broad range of organizations, including accounting firms.

One large example is IBM, which started with an internal directory of 450,000 employees in 2000. The directory was so heavily used that IBM developed an experimental social network called Beehive that was behind the company's firewall. After nine months of experimental use, it was up to 38,000 users. IBM claims that the site fosters innovation, as employees talk electronically, rather than around the water cooler or coffee machine.

Such social networking can encourage employees to make effective use of their existing tools for communication. In this way, the viral approach can be positive. However, an unhappy employee can also destroy a company by planting a virus.

A contract employee of Fannie Mae (in the United States) was charged with planting Trojan horse (delayed) computer malware at the company in January 2009. Employed there for three years, he had access to hardware (servers) and operating system–level software. The Trojan horse was set to delete company employees' access to all 4,000 servers and then destroy all of the corporate data by overwriting them with zeros. Thankfully, the malware was detected by a senior computer engineer. Had the malware been executed, the effects on the company could have been minor or disastrous, depending upon the quality of its disaster recovery and quality assurance processes.

IMPORTANCE TO AUDITORS

Auditors examine risks and controls in the payroll and personnel cycle for several reasons, including evaluating the quality of segregation of duties (which affects every financial cycle) and the quality of controls over payment of payroll. Internal auditors may be concerned about what is posted on a social networking site if confidential strategic planning information can be readily posted. Employee termination procedures should include disabling employee access to both transaction processing systems and internal social network sites. This is an added administrative process that developers of social network sites may not have considered. Auditors can contribute by pointing out the need for such procedures.

All types of auditors would have nightmares about the potential for employees planting a virus if the organization's controls over preventing and detecting these were poor. Times of economic transition, when employees are concerned about their jobs, or when a corporation is engaged in contentious activities, could increase the risks of internal sabotage. Auditors can help to point out these risks and provide recommendations to improve controls.

continued >

1. What risks might be present in the payroll cycle with respect to the use of an organization's internal information systems, including social networking sites?

2. How does employee motivation affect the quality of internal controls?

3. During what phases of the audit does the auditor assess employee motivation? Provide examples of audit techniques that the auditor would use to assess employee motivation to correctly execute internal control procedures.

Sources: 1. Brandel, Mary, "The new employee connection: social networking behind the firewall," *Computerworld*, August 11, 2008, www.computerworld.com, Accessed: September 2, 2008. 2. Kloppott, Freeman, "Ex-Fannie Mae worker charged with planting computer virus," *The Examiner*, January 29, 2009, www.dcexaminer.com, Accessed: January 29, 2009.

ALTHOUGH this chapter focuses on the audit of the payroll and personnel cycle, our opening vignette illustrates the importance of motivated employees in implementing effective internal controls. If the senior computer engineer at Fannie Mae had not been browsing through computer files, then the Trojan horse malware would not have been detected. In this chapter we will talk about termination controls (such as removing passwords when employees leave or are terminated), as well as controls over payment and processing of payroll.

---

①   The Nature and Importance of the Payroll and Personnel Cycle

Payroll and personnel cycle—the transaction cycle that begins with the hiring of personnel, includes obtaining and accounting for services from the employees, and ends with payment to the employees for the services performed and to the government and other institutions for withheld and accrued employee benefits.

The **payroll and personnel cycle** is the transaction cycle that begins with the hiring of personnel. It includes obtaining and accounting for services from the employees. It ends with payment to the employees for the services performed and to the government and other institutions for withheld and accrued employee benefits. It involves the employment and payment of all employees, regardless of classification or method of determining compensation. The employees include executives on straight salary plus bonus, office workers on monthly salary with or without overtime, salespeople on a commission basis, and factory and unionized personnel paid on an hourly basis.

The cycle is important for several reasons. First, the salaries, wages, employee benefits (e.g., Canada Pension, employment insurance, health and dental care), and other employer costs (e.g., workplace safety insurance) are a major expense in all companies. Second, labour is such an important consideration in the valuation of inventory in manufacturing and construction companies that the improper classification and allocation of labour can result in a material misstatement of net income. Finally, payroll is an area in which large amounts of company resources can be wasted through inefficiency or stolen through fraud.

The Hillsburg Hardware Limited trial balance on page 129 in Chapter 5 includes typical general ledger accounts affected by the payroll and personnel cycle. They are identified as payroll and personnel accounts by the letter P in the left column. In larger companies, many general ledger accounts are affected by payroll. It is common, for example, for large companies to have 50 or more payroll expense accounts. Payroll also affects work-in-process and finished goods inventory accounts for manufacturing companies.

As with the sales and collection cycle, the audit of the payroll and personnel cycle includes obtaining an understanding of internal control, assessment of control risk, tests of controls, analytical procedures, and tests of details of balances.

There are several important differences between the payroll and personnel cycle and other cycles in a typical audit:

- There is only one class of transactions for payroll. Most cycles include at least two classes of transactions. For example, the sales and collection cycle includes both sales and cash receipts transactions and often sales returns and charge-off of uncollectibles. Payroll has only one class because the receipt of services from employees and the payment for those services through payroll occur within a short period.
- Transactions are far more significant than related balance sheet accounts. Payroll-related accounts such as accrued payroll and withheld taxes are usually small compared with the total amount of transactions for the year.
- Internal controls over payroll are effective for almost all companies, even small ones. The reasons for effective controls are harsh federal and provincial penalties for errors in withholding and paying payroll taxes, and employee morale problems if employees are not paid or are underpaid.

Because of these three characteristics, auditors typically emphasize tests of controls and analytical procedures in the audit of payroll.

The way in which accounting information flows through the various accounts in the payroll and personnel cycle is illustrated by T-accounts in Figure 17-1 on the next page. In most systems, the accrued wages and salaries account is used only at the end of an accounting period. Throughout the period, expenses are charged when the employees are actually paid rather than when the labour costs are incurred. The accruals for labour are recorded by adjusting entries at the end of the period for any earned but unpaid labour costs.

Functions in the Cycle, Related Documents and Records, and Internal Controls

The payroll and personnel cycle begins with the hiring of personnel and ends with payment to the employees for the services performed and to the government and other institutions for employee withholdings (i.e., income tax, Canada [or Quebec] Pension Plan, employment insurance), and employee benefits (i.e., required contributions by the employer for the Canada [or Quebec] Pension Plan, employment insurance, workplace safety insurance, hospital insurance plans, provincial health and education taxes; and voluntary or negotiated employer contributions to company pension, medical, or dental plans). In between, the cycle involves obtaining services from the employees consistent with the objectives of the company and accounting for the services in a proper manner.

Column 3 of Table 17-1 (see page 571) identifies the six business functions in a typical payroll and personnel cycle. The table also shows the relationships among the business functions, classes of transactions, accounts, and documents and records. The business functions and related documents are discussed in this section. In addition, there is a discussion of key internal controls to prevent errors or fraud and irregularities in providing data and to ensure the safety of assets.

PERSONNEL AND EMPLOYMENT The personnel (or human resources) department provides an independent source for interviewing and hiring qualified personnel. The

Figure 17-1 | Accounts in the Payroll and Personnel Cycle

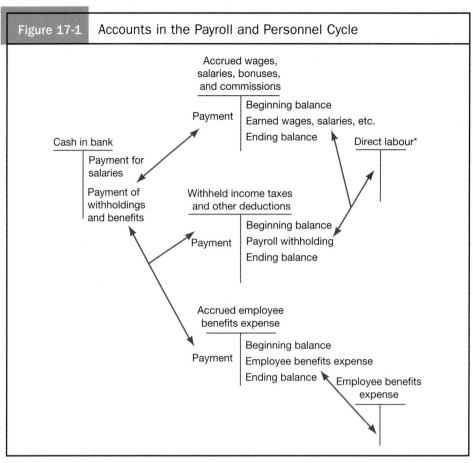

*Separate operating accounts for payroll also normally include officers' salaries and bonuses, office salaries, sales salaries and commissions, and indirect manufacturing labour. These accounts have the same relationship to accrued wages and withheld taxes and other deductions that is shown for direct labour. Some companies use a payroll service that performs all of the above functions.

department is also an independent source of records for the internal verification of wage information, and for confirming segregation of duties by means of access rights.

Personnel records Personnel records include such data as the date of employment, personnel investigations, approval of rates of pay, authorized deductions, performance evaluations, and termination of employment.

Personnel records—records that include such data as the date of employment, personnel investigations, rates of pay, authorized deductions, performance evaluations, and termination of employment.

Deduction authorization forms These are forms authorizing payroll deductions, including the number of exemptions for withholding of income taxes (TD-1), Canada Savings Bonds, charitable contributions, union dues, government or private insurance, and pension, medical, or dental plans.

Rate authorization form This is a form authorizing the rate of pay. The source of the information is a labour contract, authorization by management, or, in the case of officers, authorization from the board of directors.

Internal controls From an audit point of view, the most important internal controls in personnel involve formal methods of informing the timekeeping and payroll preparation personnel about new employees, the authorization of initial and periodic changes in pay rates, and the termination date of employees no longer working for the company. As a part of these controls, segregation of duties is extremely important. No individual with access to time cards, payroll records, or cheques should also be permitted access to personnel records. A second important control is the adequate investigation of the competence and trustworthiness of new employees.

ACCESS RIGHTS MANAGEMENT This process includes identifying which information systems and which functions within a particular information system the employee is

Table 17-1

Table 17-1   Classes of Transactions, Accounts, Business Functions, and Related Documents and Records for the Payroll and Personnel Cycle

Class of Transactions	Accounts	Business Functions	Documents and Records
Payroll	Payroll cash	Personnel and employment	Personnel records
	Payroll expense accounts		Deduction authorization form
	Payroll withholding accounts	Master file change	Rate authorization form
	Payroll accrual accounts		
		Access rights management	Access rights approval form
			Access rights change form
			Code of conduct statement
		Timekeeping and payroll preparation	Time card
			Job time ticket
			Summary payroll report
			Payroll journal
			Payroll master file
			Payroll transaction and history files
		Payment of payroll	Payroll cheque
		Preparation of employee withholdings and benefit remittance forms and payment of taxes	Form T4
			Employee withholdings and benefit remittance forms

to have access to. When employees change jobs within the company (perhaps due to promotion), or leave the company, these access rights need to be updated. It is important because it is the organization's method of enforcing segregation of duties of its information systems.

Employee access rights approval form This form should be completed by the employee's supervisor, limiting the person's access to information based upon the work that the employee is expected to perform. It should be approved by the supervisor and another senior employee, validated after the employee has been set up on the system, and filed in the employee's personnel file.

Access rights change form Information systems personnel need to be formally notified when employees change jobs or when they leave the company so that their access rights are changed or removed. This form would be approved by relevant management and stored in the employee file.

Code of conduct statement Many organizations have a code of conduct statement for various purposes: information technology usage, privacy of information, and corporate code of conduct. Having employees read and sign these documents informs them of corporate policies and results in a signed commitment to implement the stated policies. The signed document would be filed in the employee's personnel file. Some organizations require annual updating of these documents, and handle the administration of codes of conduct electronically.

Internal controls Management of access rights is an important function of the payroll and personnel cycle that affects all areas of the organization. It reflects the organization's attitudes toward segregation of duties. Clear policies and practices for employee set up and change of access rights include designation of the individuals who are authorized to approve access rights, and processes to check that they have been set up properly, with periodic review.

TIMEKEEPING AND PAYROLL PREPARATION This function is of major importance in the audit of payroll because it directly affects payroll expense for the period. It includes the preparation of time cards or time records by employees; the summarization and calculation of gross pay, deductions, and net pay; the preparation of payroll cheques; and the preparation of payroll records. There must be adequate controls to prevent misstatement in each of these activities.

Time card or time record A **time card** is a document indicating the time an employee started and stopped working each day and the number of hours the employee worked. For many employees, the time record is prepared automatically by time clocks. Time cards are usually submitted weekly. Alternatively, many companies assign each employee a magnetic-stripe card. Each employee "swipes" the card through a time clock, and a computer system tracks the employee's time, producing electronic records and printed reports of the time worked.

Job time ticket This document indicates particular jobs on which a factory employee worked during a given period. This form is used only when an employee works on different jobs or in different departments. Use of electronic systems and magnetic-stripe cards allows companies to track time spent on specific jobs using computer systems rather than by handling job tickets for each job.

Summary payroll report This computer-generated document summarizes payroll for a period in various forms. One summary lists the totals debited to each general ledger account for payroll charges. These will equal gross payroll for the period. Another common summary for a manufacturing company lists the totals charged to various jobs in a job-cost accounting system. Similarly, commissions earned by each salesperson may be summarized.

Payroll journal This is a journal for recording payroll payments (cheque or direct deposit). It typically indicates gross pay, withholdings, and net pay. The payroll journal is generated for any time period from the payroll transactions included in the computer files. The totals from the journal are also included in the payroll master file, by employee. Journal totals are posted to the general ledger by the computer.

Payroll master file This file summarizes each payroll transaction, by employee, and maintains total employee wages paid for the year to date. The **payroll master file** is updated from payroll computer transaction files. The total of the individual employee earnings in the master file equals the total balance of gross payroll in various general ledger accounts.

Payroll transaction and history files The transaction record for each employee includes gross pay for each payroll period, deductions from gross pay, net pay, cheque number (or direct deposit transaction number), and date. This information is used to update the payroll master file.

Internal controls Adequate control over the time in the time records includes the use of a time clock or other method of making certain that employees are paid for the number of hours they worked. There should also be controls to prevent anyone from checking in for several employees or submitting a fraudulent time record.

The summarization and calculation of the payroll can be controlled by well-defined policies for the payroll department, separation of duties to provide automatic cross-checks, reconciliation of payroll hours with independent production records, and independent internal verification of all important data. For example, payroll policies should require a competent, independent person to recalculate actual hours worked, review for the proper approval of all overtime, and examine time records for deletions and alterations or for unusually long hours. Similarly, batch control totals over hours worked can be calculated when payroll time cards are used and compared with the actual hours entered by the computer. Finally, a printout of wage and withholding rates included in the computer files can be obtained and compared with authorized rates in the personnel files.

Controls over the preparation of payroll cheques include preventing those responsible for preparing the cheques from having access to time records, signing or distributing cheques, or independently verifying payroll output. In addition, the cheques should be prenumbered and verified through independent bank reconciliation procedures.

When manufacturing labour affects inventory valuation, special emphasis should be put on controls to make sure labour is distributed to proper account classifications. There must also be adequate internal controls for recording job time records and other relevant payroll information in the cost accounting records. Independent internal verification of this information is an essential control.

PAYMENT OF PAYROLL The actual signing and distribution of the cheques must be properly handled to prevent their theft.

Payroll cheque This is a cheque written to the employee for services performed. The cheque is prepared as a part of the payroll preparation function, but the authorized signature makes the cheque an asset. The amount of the cheque is the gross pay less taxes and other deductions withheld. After the cheque is cashed and returned to the company from the bank, it is referred to as a cancelled cheque. It is now common for net pay to be directly deposited into employees' bank accounts. The equivalent record would then be an authorization list for the direct deposits.

Internal controls Controls over cheques or direct deposit authorization should include limiting the authorization to a responsible employee who does not have access to timekeeping or the preparation of the payroll. Where physical cheques are used, the distribution of payroll should be by someone who is not involved in the other payroll functions. Any unclaimed cheques should be immediately returned for redeposit. If a cheque-signing machine is used to replace a manual signature, the same controls are required; in addition, the cheque-signing machine must be carefully controlled.

auditing in action 17-1
Wage Inflation or Deflation?

Throughout the audit risk assessment process, the auditor looks for management bias, perhaps management's misstating revenue or recording information in the incorrect period so that management can receive a larger bonus. The dollar effects of these deliberate errors can be large.

Throughout the financial trading community, traders and management are rewarded based upon organizational profits. For example, in 2006, Merrill Lynch paid out over $5 billion in bonuses, retaining $7.5 billion in earnings. However, these profits disappeared as mortgage-backed papers declined in value in the following years. Inadequate risk assessment and risk management resulted in huge bonuses being paid.

Another potential abuse is the back-dating of stock options. The incentive exists for stock options to be dated for a date when stock prices are low—then the recipient of the option can purchase the stock at a low price and resell to obtain an immediate profit. The options are to be disclosed, with tax consequences for the recipient and income effects upon the organization.

Research In Motion Ltd. of Waterloo, Ontario, one of over 200 companies investigated for back-dating of stock options in 2007, was the subject of a cease-trading order in 2007 for not releasing its financial statements on time. The delay occurred because restatements were required for the years 2005, 2006, and 2007 to correct information with respect to back-dating of stock options.

Sources: 1. Canadian Press, "RIM files restated results," *Toronto Star*, May 18, 2007, www.thestar.com, Accessed: May 21, 2007. 2. Story, Louise, "On Wall Street, bonuses, not profits, were real," *The New York Times*, December 18, 2008, www.nytimes.com, Accessed: December 18, 2008.

Imprest payroll account—a bank account to which the exact amount of payroll for the pay period is transferred by cheque from the employer's general cash account.

Most companies use an **imprest payroll account** to prevent the payment of unauthorized payroll transactions. An imprest payroll account is a separate payroll account in which a small balance is maintained. A cheque for the exact amount of each net payroll is transferred from the general account to the imprest account immediately before the distribution of the payroll. The advantages of an imprest account are that it limits the client's exposure to payroll fraud, allows the delegation of payroll cheque-signing duties, separates routine payroll expenditures from irregular expenditures, and facilitates cash management. It also simplifies the reconciliation of the payroll bank account if it is done at the low point in the payment cycle.

Where employee payments are made directly into their bank account, independent verification of the reports produced by the bank or payroll service provider should occur in lieu of the independent cheque-signing process.

PREPARATION OF T4 FORM AND EMPLOYEE WITHHOLDINGS AND BENEFITS REMITTANCE FORMS The timely preparation and mailing of T4 form and employee withholdings and benefits remittance forms is required by federal and provincial laws.

T4 form—a form issued to each employee summarizing the earnings record for the calendar year.

Employee withholdings and benefits remittance forms—forms that the employer submits to federal and provincial authorities for the payment of withholdings and employee benefits.

T4 form The **T4 form** is issued for each employee summarizing the earnings record for the calendar year. The information includes gross pay, income taxes withheld, other withholdings, and taxable benefits such as employer contributions to government or privately sponsored medical plans. The same information is also submitted to the Canada Revenue Agency and, if appropriate, to provincial tax authorities. This information is prepared from the payroll master file.

Employee withholdings and benefits remittance forms The **employee withholdings and benefits remittance forms** are submitted to the federal government and to other organizations for the payment of withholdings and employee benefits. The nature and due date of the forms vary depending on the type of withholding or benefit and the size of the organization (e.g., weekly, monthly, or quarterly). These forms are prepared from information in the payroll master file or payroll history file. As dollar volume increases, more frequent remittances are required.

Internal controls The most important control in the preparation of these returns is a well-defined set of policies that carefully indicate when each form must be filed. Most automated payroll systems include the preparation of payroll tax returns using the information in the payroll transaction and master files. The independent verification of the output by a competent individual is an important control to prevent misstatements and potential liability for taxes and penalties.

concept check

C17-1 Why is it important for the auditor to audit the payroll cycle?

C17-2 Why is it likely that the auditor will focus on the audit of payroll transactions rather than payroll balances?

C17-3 How does the audit of access rights management in the payroll cycle affect the audit of other transaction cycles?

② Internal Control Testing

Figure 17-2 shows the methodology for designing tests of controls for the payroll and personnel cycle. It is the same methodology used in Chapter 14 for the sales and collection cycle.

Internal control for payment of payroll is normally highly structured and well controlled in order to control cash disbursed and to minimize employee complaints and dissatisfaction. It is common to use electronic data-processing techniques to prepare all journals and payroll payments. In-house systems are often used, as are outside service-centre systems such as those of banks and financial institutions. Thus, general controls such as control over program changes and program updates and over access to data files must be evaluated. It is usually easy to establish good control over payments in the payroll and personnel cycle. For factory and office employees, there is usually a large number of relatively homogeneous, small-amount transactions. There are fewer executive payroll transactions, but they are ordinarily consistent in timing, content, and amount. Because of relatively consistent payroll concerns from company to company, high-quality computer software packages are available, resulting in good controls over program changes. Consequently, auditors seldom expect to find

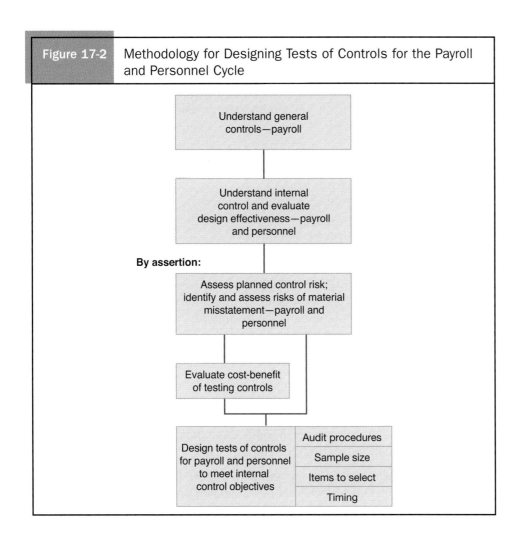

Figure 17-2 Methodology for Designing Tests of Controls for the Payroll and Personnel Cycle

Understand general controls—payroll

Understand internal control and evaluate design effectiveness—payroll and personnel

By assertion:

Assess planned control risk; identify and assess risks of material misstatement—payroll and personnel

Evaluate cost-benefit of testing controls

Design tests of controls for payroll and personnel to meet internal control objectives

| Audit procedures |
| Sample size |
| Items to select |
| Timing |

exceptions in testing payroll transactions. Occasionally control test deviations occur, but most monetary errors or fraud and other irregularities are corrected by internal verification controls or in response to employee complaints.

Where auditors tend to find problems is with management of access controls. Small- to medium-sized businesses may have inadequate controls over access to information systems, resulting in the need to rely solely on substantive tests. Larger organizations with more formal systems tend to have better controls over the initial set-up of employees but may have weaknesses in access-control change management.

Internal Controls and Tests of Controls

Tests of control procedures are the most important means of verifying account balances in the payroll and personnel cycle. The emphasis on tests of controls is due to the lack of independent third-party evidence, such as confirmation for verifying accrued wages, withholdings, accrued benefits payable, and other balance sheet accounts. Furthermore, in most audits, the amounts in the balance sheet accounts are small and can be verified with relative ease if the auditor is confident that payroll transactions are correctly recorded and that withholding and benefit remittance forms are properly prepared.

Even though the tests of controls are the most important part of testing payroll, many auditors spend little time in this area. In many audits, there is a minimal risk of material misstatements, even though payroll is frequently a significant part of total expenses. There are three reasons for this: (1) employees are likely to complain to management if they are underpaid, (2) all payroll transactions are typically uniform and uncomplicated, and (3) payroll transactions are extensively audited by federal and provincial governments for income tax withholding and for pension, employment insurance, and health care payments.

Following the same approach used in Chapter 14 for tests of sales and cash receipts transactions, the internal controls and tests of controls for each objective and related monetary misstatements are summarized in Table 17-2. Again, the reader should recognize the following:

- The internal controls will vary from company to company; therefore, the auditor must identify the controls and weaknesses for each organization.
- Controls the auditor intends to use for reducing assessed control risk must be tested with tests of controls.
- The tests of controls will vary depending on the assessed control risk and the other considerations of the audit, such as the effect of payroll on inventory. Where an outside service organization is used to process payroll, the auditor must consider whether controls at the client are sufficient to ensure that the transaction-related audit objectives are satisfied. If not, the auditor may need to request evidence regarding controls at the service organization, including the existence of a service auditor's report on controls, discussed in the next section.
- The tests of controls are not actually performed in the order given in Table 17-2. The tests of controls are performed in as convenient a manner as possible, using a performance format audit program.

PAYROLL WITHHOLDINGS AND BENEFITS REMITTANCE FORMS AND PAYMENTS Payroll withholdings and benefits are an important consideration in many companies, both because the amounts are often material and because the potential liability for failure to file forms in a timely manner can be severe.

Preparation of payroll withholdings and benefits remittance forms As a part of understanding the internal control structure, the auditor should review the preparation of at least one of each type of employee withholding and benefits remittance form that the client is responsible for filing. There is a potential liability for unpaid balances, as well as penalty and interest if the client fails to prepare the forms properly.

A detailed reconciliation of the information on the remittance forms and the payroll records may be necessary when the auditor believes that there is a reasonable chance the remittance forms may be improperly prepared. Indications of potential errors in the forms include the past payment of penalties and interest for improper payments, new personnel in the payroll department who are responsible for the preparation of the remittance forms, the lack of internal verification of the information, and the existence of serious liquidity problems for the client.

Payment of the taxes withheld and other withholdings and benefits in a timely manner It is desirable to test whether the client has fulfilled its legal obligations in submitting payments for all payroll withholdings and benefits as a part of the payroll tests even though the payments are usually made from general cash disbursements. The withholdings of concern in these tests are such items as those for income taxes, Canada (or Quebec) Pension Plan, employment insurance, union dues, insurance, and Canada Savings Bonds. The auditor must first determine the client's requirements for submitting the payments. The requirements are determined by reference to such sources as tax laws, Canada Pension Plan rules, employment insurance rules, union contracts, and agreements with employees. After the auditor knows the requirements, it is easy to determine whether the client has paid the proper amount in a timely manner by comparing the subsequent payment with the payroll records.

INVENTORY AND FRAUDULENT PAYROLL CONSIDERATIONS Auditors often extend their audit-of-payroll procedures considerably (1) when payroll significantly affects the valuation of inventory and (2) when the auditor is concerned about the possibility of material fraudulent payroll transactions.

Table 17-2		Summary of Transaction-Related Audit Objectives, Key Controls, and Tests of Controls for Payroll	

Transaction-Related Audit Objectives	Key Internal Controls	Common Tests of Controls	
Recorded payroll payments are for work actually performed by existing employees (occurrence).	Time records are approved by supervisors. Time clock is used to record time. Adequate personnel files. Separation of duties between personnel, timekeeping, and payroll disbursements supported by authorized access rights forms. Only employees existing in the computer data files are accepted when they are entered. Authorization to issue cheques.	Examine the cards or listings for indication of approvals. Examine time records. Review personnel policies. Review organization chart, discuss with employees, and observe duties being performed. Compare authorized duties with duties permitted on access rights forms. Examine printouts of transactions rejected by the computer as having non-existent employee numbers, or determine whether invalid entries are accepted at point of entry.[†]	Examine payroll records for evidence of approval. Review the payroll journal, general ledger, and payroll earnings records for large or unusual amounts.[*†] Compare cancelled cheques with payroll journal for name, amount, and date. Examine cancelled cheques for proper endorsement. Compare cancelled cheques with personnel records.
Existing payroll transactions are recorded (completeness).	Payroll cheques are prenumbered and accounted for. Independent preparation of bank reconciliation.	Account for a sequence of payroll cheques, or conduct gap testing.[†] Discuss with employees and observe reconciliation.	Reconcile the disbursements in the payroll journal with the disbursements on the payroll bank statement. Prove the bank reconciliation.
Recorded payroll transactions are for the amount of time actually worked and at the proper pay rate; withholdings are properly calculated (accuracy).	Internal verification of calculations and amounts. Batch totals are compared with computer summary reports. Authorization of wage rate, salary, or commission rate. Authorization of withholdings, including amounts for insurance and Canada Savings Bonds.	Examine indication of internal verification. Examine file of batch totals for initials of data control clerk; compare totals with summary reports.[†] Examine payroll records for indication of internal verification. Examine authorizations in personnel file.	Recompute hours worked from time records. Compare pay rates with union contract, approval by board of directors, or other source. Recompute gross pay.[†] Check withholdings by reference to appropriate tables[†] and authorization forms in personnel file. Recompute net pay.[†] Compare cancelled cheque with payroll journal for amount.
Payroll transactions are properly classified (classification).	Adequate chart of accounts. Internal verification of classification.	Review chart of accounts. Examine indication of internal verification; determine that software posts to correct accounts.[†]	Compare classification with chart of accounts or procedures manual. Review time records for employee department and job records for job assignment, and trace through to labour distribution.
Payroll transactions are recorded on the correct dates (timing).	Procedures requiring recording transactions as soon as possible after the payroll is paid. Internal verification.	Examine the procedures manual and observe when recording takes place. Examine indication of internal verification.	Compare date of recorded cheque in the payroll journal with date on cancelled cheques and time records. Compare date on cheque with date the cheque cleared the bank.
Payroll transactions are properly included in the payroll master file and transaction files; they are properly summarized (posting and summarization).	Internal verification of payroll file contents. Comparison of payroll master file with payroll general ledger totals.	Examine indication of internal verification. Examine initialled summary total reports indicating comparisons have been made.	Test clerical accuracy by footing the payroll journal and tracing postings to general ledger and the payroll master file.[†]

* This analytical procedure can also apply to other objectives, including completeness, valuation, and timeliness.
† This control would be tested on many audits by using the computer, possibly with generalized audit software.

Relationship between payroll and inventory valuation For audits where payroll is a significant portion of inventory (a frequent occurrence for manufacturing and construction companies), the improper account classification of payroll can significantly affect asset valuation for accounts such as work in process, finished goods, or construction in process.

For example, the overhead charged to inventory at the balance sheet date can be overstated if the salaries of administrative personnel are inadvertently or intentionally charged to indirect manufacturing overhead. Similarly, the valuation of inventory is affected if the direct labour cost of individual employees is improperly charged to the wrong job or process. When some jobs are billed on a cost-plus basis, revenue and the valuation of inventory are both affected by charging labour to incorrect jobs.

When labour is a material factor in inventory valuation, there should be special emphasis on testing the internal controls over proper classification of payroll transactions. Consistency from period to period, which is essential for classification, can be tested by reviewing the chart of accounts and procedures manuals. It is also desirable to trace job records or other evidence that an employee has worked on a particular job or process to the accounting records that affect inventory valuation. For example, if each employee must account for all of his or her time on a weekly basis by allocating individual job numbers, a useful test is to trace the recorded hours of several employees for a week to the related job-cost records to make sure each has been properly recorded. It may also be desirable to trace from the job-cost records to employee summaries as a test for non-existent payroll charges being included in inventory.

TESTS FOR NON-EXISTENT PAYROLL Although auditors are not primarily responsible for the detection of fraud, they must extend audit procedures when internal controls over payroll are inadequate. There are several ways employees can significantly defraud a company in the payroll area. This discussion is limited to tests for the two most common types—non-existent employees and fraudulent hours.

The issuance of payroll payments to individuals who do not work for the company (non-existent employees) frequently results from the continuance of an employee's remuneration after his or her employment has been terminated. Usually, the person committing this type of defalcation is a payroll clerk, supervisor, fellow employee, or perhaps former employee. For example, under some systems, a supervisor could clock in daily for an employee and approve the time record at the end of the period. If the supervisor also distributes paycheques, considerable opportunity for defalcation exists.

Certain procedures can be performed on cancelled cheques as a means of detecting defalcation. A procedure used on payroll audits is comparing the names on cancelled cheques with time cards and other records for authorized signatures and reasonableness of the endorsements. It is also common to scan endorsements on cancelled cheques for unusual or recurring second endorsements as an indication of a possible fraudulent cheque. The examination of cheques that are recorded as voided is also desirable to make sure they have not been fraudulently used. Where employees are paid automatically by bank deposits to the employees' accounts, the auditor can look for duplicated bank account numbers, post office boxes, or for common employee addresses.

A test for non-existent employees is tracing selected transactions recorded in the payroll journal to the personnel department to determine whether the employees were actually employed during the payroll period. The endorsement on the cancelled cheque written out to an employee can be compared with the authorized signature on the employee's withholding authorization forms.

A procedure that tests for proper handling of terminated employees is selecting several files from the personnel records for employees who were terminated in the current year to determine whether each received his or her termination pay and severance documents in accordance with company policy. Continuing payments to terminated employees are tested by examining the payroll records in the subsequent period to verify that the employee is no longer being paid. This procedure is effective only if the personnel department is informed of terminations.

In some cases, where employees are paid by cheque, the auditor may request a surprise payroll pay-off. This is a procedure whereby each employee must pick up and sign for his or her cheque in the presence of a supervisor and the auditor. Any cheques that have not been claimed must be subject to an extensive investigation to determine whether an unclaimed cheque is fraudulent. Surprise pay-off is frequently expensive and in some cases may even cause problems with a labour union, but it may be the only means of detecting a defalcation.

Fraudulent hours exist when an employee reports more time than was actually worked. Refer to Audit Challenge 17-1. Can you see how there are at least four people who can manipulate payroll information? Because of the lack of available evidence, it is usually difficult for an auditor to determine whether an employee records more time on his or her time card or time record than was actually worked. One procedure is reconciling the total hours paid according to the payroll records with an independent record of the hours worked, such as those often maintained by production control. Alternatively, it may be possible to observe an employee clocking in more than one time card due to a buddy arrangement. However, it is ordinarily easier for the client to prevent this type of defalcation by adequate controls than for the auditor to detect it.

ANALYSIS OF EXCEPTIONS AND CONCLUSIONS As mentioned previously, because of the use of automation, which provides consistent processing, and the normally high level of controls in place over payroll, the auditor expects to find few, if any, errors. There are, however, specific types of errors that give the auditor particular concern in auditing payroll transactions:

- Classification errors in charging labour to inventory and job-cost accounts. As previously indicated, these can result in misstated earnings.
- Computational errors when a computerized system is used. Recall that one of the primary characteristics of the computer is processing consistency. If a calculation error is made for one item, it is probably made on every other similar item. As indicated, these errors are rare due to the high-quality of most software packages.
- Any errors that indicate possible fraud, particularly relating to the executive payroll.

audit challenge 17-1
Improving Access Control Management

Jebrah Manufacturing Limited (JML) is a medium-sized company with about 50 employees. It has a local area network, production systems software, timekeeping software, and accounting systems. These are all locally purchased and locally maintained software systems. There are no in-house information systems personnel.

The controller is responsible for setting up new users and changing user capabilities based upon scripts (standard instructions) provided by the network supplier. If she has any problems, she telephones the network supplier, which logs on to the system and makes the changes for her online.

All three accounting personnel and the owner of the company have access to all accounting systems. Manufacturing employees have access to timekeeping and production systems.

The controller prepares the bank reconciliation, but the owner signs payroll cheques and accounts payable cheques (with supporting documentation attached). The controller is responsible for recording all changes in wage rates in the accounting systems and writing off accounts receivable. The receptionist is responsible for printing reports, while there are two staff members who handle both accounts payable and accounts receivable transactions.

CRITICAL THINKING QUESTIONS

1. Describe the problems in segregation of duties for each application cycle: payroll, accounts receivable, and accounts payable. For each problem, state what could go wrong (the risk).
2. What are some of the practical changes that can be made at this company to improve internal controls? Justify your response.

C17-4 Why might auditors limit the number of transactions tested in the payroll cycle?

C17-5 Provide two examples of payroll tests that could be used to verify the accuracy of payroll costs included in inventory.

Generally, the tests of controls performed in the payroll cycle will use attribute sampling under a plan that assumes a zero deviation rate. Sampling size should be large enough to give the auditor a reasonable chance of finding at least one deviation if an intolerable number of deviations exist.

If a computational error or an error indicating possible fraud is found, specific investigation will be required to determine what allowed such an error to occur. Generally, further sampling and estimation are not done; rather, a non-statistical approach based on the circumstances is taken.

If no exceptions are found, or if those found are not alarming or unexpected, the auditor will conclude that assessed control risk can be reduced as planned, and he or she will proceed with the tests of details of balances of the affected accounts without modification.

3 Payroll Outsourcing and Third-Party Audits

The Nature of Outsourcing

Organizations face resource constraints, usually on time and expertise. In a small-to medium-sized business, the owner or senior manager may need to be conversant with every aspect of the business, including payroll, investments, raw material pricing, and collection of accounts receivable. As management time becomes scarce, the owner can either hire new employees or use external assistance (contract assistance, consulting, or outsourcing). Outsourcing of some kind has existed for many years—think about factoring of accounts receivable, where the receivables are sold and someone else does the collection. Outsourcing has simply become more common. With the large disparity of wages in different places around the world, paying someone else to do the work is less costly than doing it yourself. This is supported by the facility, provided by the internet, to communicate large volumes of information at low cost. A secondary driver for outsourcing is cost—reducing the cost of a function by outsourcing to an organization that specializes in that function helps the client organization.

Examples of functions that can be outsourced include call-centre functions, accounting functions, human resource functions, pension fund management, and recording or posting of transactions such as payroll.

We discuss outsourcing in this chapter because payroll is a commonly outsourced function, handled with a variety of technologies perhaps by the bank using batch processing on paper forms or online data entry, by another service bureau that specializes in payroll, or by an internet-based application service provider so that payroll transactions can be entered anywhere.

From the perspective of an assurance engagement, the outsourcing organization that provides services to a client is called the **service organization**. The client which uses the service organization is a **user entity**.

The remainder of this section focuses on the responsibilities of the **user auditor**, who is reporting on the financial statements of the user entity. In that role, the auditor needs to consider the types of controls available at both the user entity and the service organization and may rely upon third-party service organization reports as a source of information when conducting the audit.

Service organization—an outsourcing organization that provides services to the client.

User entity—a client who uses a service organization.

User auditor—the person reporting on the financial statements of the user entity.

ROLE OF RISK ASSESSMENT During the risk assessment phase of the financial statement audit, the financial statement auditor of the client will find out how the business of the client is managed. This includes finding out about service organizations (outsourcers) and what they do. If the client uses a service organization for the processing of payroll, the auditor will likely consider this to be significant, as payroll tends to be material. Payroll is normally a large part of the cost of goods sold, whether for service or manufacturing organizations.

Mini-outsourcing

Payroll is picky. The amounts have to be exact, many deductions have to be taken, and several remittances and forms must be submitted to regulatory agencies. Fines are heavy if you remit too little or if you remit late.

A small business owner could spend several hours per week doing payroll or checking the work of an employee who prepares the payroll, thus losing productive time.

NEBS Payweb.ca is an example of a payroll system that works for small and large businesses. Hours and wage rates are entered using the internet, from any location that has internet access. Then payroll payment is deposited directly to the employee bank account or to a debit card activated by the employer.

NEBS Payweb.ca also takes care of providing remittances (such as federal taxes), by withdrawing the funds from the company bank account and remitting to the regulatory agency with the appropriate reports. Transaction reports can be viewed online or printed.

CRITICAL THINKING QUESTIONS

1. What are the risks associated with using NEBS Payweb.ca or other internet-based service providers for payroll processing?
2. How would you mitigate the risks that you identified in (1)?
3. NEBS Payweb.ca has thousands of clients. What would be the advantages and disadvantages of a service auditor's report for NEBS Payweb.ca?

Sources: 1. Bradbury, Danny, "Payroll work makes for a heavy load," *National Post*, February 11, 2008, p. FP4. 2. NEBS Payweb.ca, www.payweb.ca, Accessed: March 27, 2009.

The purpose of risk assessment includes determining the likelihood of material error in the account. The auditor may need to consider controls at both the user entity and at the service organization to assess control risk.

CONTROLS AT THE USER ENTITY Controls at the user entity will normally focus around input (submitting information to the service organization, such as wage rates and hours worked) and output (reviewing reports received, such as the payroll journal). If the client has sufficient controls to prevent or detect errors, then the auditor can spend less time considering the controls at the service organization.

For example, a form is used at the client to record new employees and their wage rates, approved by a manager. This form is provided as a data entry source to an online payroll service provider. All new employee data (or changes) are entered. Then the changed information is printed at the client location and checked independently (compared with the original wage-rate change form). Evidence of this checking is documented with an initial. This sequence of controls satisfies occurrence and accuracy.

For each pay, employees use a magnetic-stripe card to clock in and clock out. The data from the pay recording system are printed and approved by a manager before being transferred to the online payroll service provider. Then, the service provider creates the payroll records and transmits the payroll journal to the client before distributing pay. The controller reviews the payroll journal and compares the total hours worked with the payroll time records before entering a password that releases the pay for processing. He or she also prepares a requisition form, approved by the executive management, for transfer of funds from the general bank account to the payroll service provider for payment of net pay and government tax remittances. These controls deal with accuracy and completeness.

Finally, the payroll journal is used to prepare a journal entry, posted by the controller to the general ledger (classification, timing, and posting and summarization).

The major control not performed by the client is the actual recalculation of the payroll and its remittances. However, it is likely that material errors would be detected by the client review process listed above. Assuming that the activities at the client are conscientiously performed, the auditor would likely assess control risk as low, relying upon the client's controls and adding some substantive tests of the actual payroll calculations. There would be no need to test the controls at the service organization.

CONTROLS AT THE SERVICE ORGANIZATION Payroll could be complex, involving distributions to many cost centres. Perhaps there are 5,000 employees, who are entering time from remote locations, using multiple labour codes. Store managers enter passwords to approve wages but are not involved in calculating pay or in remittances. Head office simply takes the totals from the reports and posts them for monthly remittances. In this situation, reliance is placed heavily upon the service organization for calculation of pay and distribution of remittances. There could also be poor controls over checking for authorized employees, so the auditor might be concerned that someone at the service organization could enter an unauthorized employee and create a fictitious pay.

The auditor could go to the service organization and determine the controls directly or obtain a service auditor's report. CAS 402, Auditor considerations relating to an entity using a service organization (previously Section 5310), documents the standards an auditor needs to follow when a client uses a service organization. ISAE (International Standard on Assurance Engagements) 3402, Assurance reports on controls at a third-party service organization (forthcoming as a Canadian standard, presently Section 5970), describes the types of reports that an auditor can use to assist in that audit process.

CAS 402 applies where the service organization's services are part of the client's information systems and the transactions are material. It does not apply where the user specifically authorizes all transactions, such as the use of a chequing account at a bank.

OTHER CYCLES AND SERVICE AUDITOR REPORTS Any cycle or function can be outsourced. This includes the whole accounting function, internal audit, investment management, and human resources management. It becomes crucial for the auditor to work with the service organization (or a service auditor report) when the client has given up control over functions or transactions and the auditor determines that there is potential for material error when considering only the client controls.

In such a case, the auditor will need either to contact the service organization directly to provide an unqualified report on the financial statements, or to obtain a service auditor report (described in ISAE 3402) that provides evidence that controls at the service organization are operating effectively.

4   Analytical Review and Tests of Detail

Analytical Procedures

The use of analytical procedures is as important in the payroll and personnel cycle as it is in every other cycle. Table 17-3 illustrates analytical procedures for the balance sheet and income statement accounts in the payroll and personnel cycle. Most of the relationships included in Table 17-3 are highly predictable and are therefore useful for uncovering areas in which additional investigation is desirable. The auditor should consider any changes in business policies or business practices when conducting the analytical procedures.

Tests of Details of Balances for Liability and Expense Accounts

Figure 17-3 on page 584 summarizes the methodology for deciding the appropriate tests of details of balances for payroll liability accounts. The methodology is the same as that followed in Chapter 15 for accounts receivable. Normally, however, payroll-related liabilities are less material than accounts receivable; therefore, there is less inherent risk.

The verification of the liability accounts associated with payroll, often termed **accrued payroll expenses**, ordinarily is straightforward if internal controls are operating

CAS

concept check

C17-6 Provide two examples of outsourcing at an organization.

C17-7 When will the auditor need to consider controls at the outsourcing organization?

Accrued payroll expenses—the liability accounts associated with payroll including accounts for accrued salaries and wages, accrued commissions, accrued bonuses, and accrued employee benefits.

Table 17-3	Analytical Procedures for the Payroll and Personnel Cycle
Analytical Procedure	**Possible Misstatement Detected in**
Compare payroll expense account balance with previous years' (adjusted for pay rate increases and increases in volume).	Payroll expense accounts
Compare direct labour as a percentage of sales with previous years'.	Direct labour
Compare commission expense as a percentage of sales with previous years'.	Commission expense
Compare payroll benefits expense as a percentage of salaries and wages with previous years' (adjusted for changes in the benefits rates)	Payroll benefits expense and payroll benefits liability
Compare accrued payroll benefits accounts with previous years'.	Accrued payroll benefits and payroll benefits expense

effectively. When the auditor is satisfied that payroll transactions are being properly recorded in the payroll journal and the related employee withholding and benefits remittance forms are being accurately prepared and promptly paid, the tests of details of balances can be completed rapidly.

The objectives in testing payroll-related liabilities are to determine whether accruals in the trial balance are stated at correct amounts (accuracy) for all payroll accounts (completeness), and transactions in the payroll and personnel cycle are recorded in the proper period (cut-off). The primary concern in both objectives is to make sure there are no understated or omitted accruals. The major liability accounts in the payroll and personnel cycle are discussed next.

AMOUNTS WITHHELD FROM EMPLOYEES' PAY Income taxes withheld but not yet disbursed can be tested by comparing the balance with the payroll journal, the withholding remittance form prepared in the subsequent period, and the subsequent period cash disbursements. Other withheld items such as the Canada (or Quebec) Pension Plan, employment insurance, union dues, Canada Savings Bonds, and insurance can be verified in the same manner. If internal controls are operating effectively, cut-off and accuracy can easily be tested at the same time by these procedures.

ACCRUED SALARIES AND WAGES The accrual for salaries and wages arises whenever employees are not paid for the last few days or hours of earned wages until the subsequent period. Salaried personnel may receive all of their pay, except overtime, on the last day of the month, but frequently several days of wages for hourly employees are unpaid at the end of the year.

The correct cut-off and valuation of accrued salaries and wages depend on company policy, which should be followed consistently from year to year. Some companies calculate the exact hours of pay that were earned in the current period and paid in the subsequent period, whereas others compute an approximate proportion; if the subsequent payroll results from three days' employment during the current year and two days' employment during the subsequent year, the use of 60 percent of the subsequent period's gross pay as the accrual is an example of an approximation.

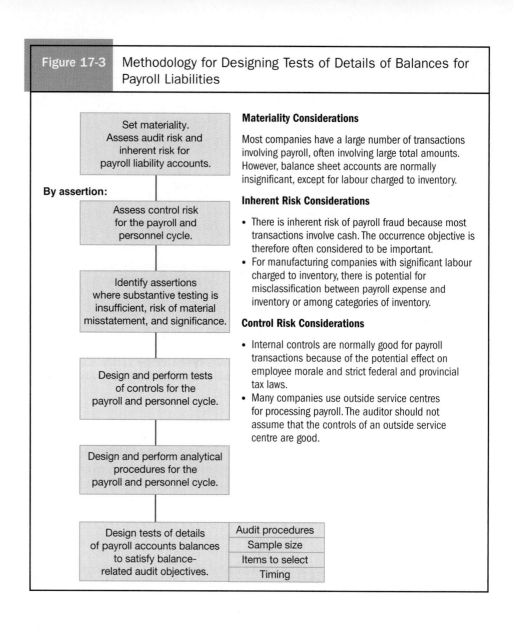

Figure 17-3 Methodology for Designing Tests of Details of Balances for Payroll Liabilities

Set materiality.
Assess audit risk and inherent risk for payroll liability accounts.

By assertion:

Assess control risk for the payroll and personnel cycle.

Identify assertions where substantive testing is insufficient, risk of material misstatement, and significance.

Design and perform tests of controls for the payroll and personnel cycle.

Design and perform analytical procedures for the payroll and personnel cycle.

Design tests of details of payroll accounts balances to satisfy balance-related audit objectives.

Audit procedures
Sample size
Items to select
Timing

Materiality Considerations

Most companies have a large number of transactions involving payroll, often involving large total amounts. However, balance sheet accounts are normally insignificant, except for labour charged to inventory.

Inherent Risk Considerations

- There is inherent risk of payroll fraud because most transactions involve cash. The occurrence objective is therefore often considered to be important.
- For manufacturing companies with significant labour charged to inventory, there is potential for misclassification between payroll expense and inventory or among categories of inventory.

Control Risk Considerations

- Internal controls are normally good for payroll transactions because of the potential effect on employee morale and strict federal and provincial tax laws.
- Many companies use outside service centres for processing payroll. The auditor should not assume that the controls of an outside service centre are good.

Once the auditor has determined the company's policy for accruing wages and ensures it is consistent with that of previous years, the appropriate audit procedure to test for cut-off and valuation is evaluating the reasonableness of the method and then recalculating the client's accrual. The most likely error of any significance in the balance is the failure to include the proper number of days of earned but unpaid wages.

ACCRUED COMMISSIONS The same concepts used in verifying accrued salaries and wages are applicable to accrued commissions, but the accrual is often more difficult to verify because companies frequently have several different types of agreements with salespeople and other commissioned employees. For example, some salespeople may be paid a commission every month and earn no salary, while others get a monthly salary plus a commission paid quarterly. In some cases, the commission varies for different products and may not be paid until several months after the end of the year. In verifying accrued commissions, it is necessary to first determine the nature of the commission agreement and then to test the calculations based on the agreement. It is important to compare the method of accruing commissions with that of previous years for purposes of consistency. If the amounts are material, it is also common to confirm the amount that is due directly with the employees.

ACCRUED BONUSES In many companies, the year-end unpaid bonuses to officers and employees are such a major item that the failure to record them would result in a material misstatement. The verification of the recorded accrual can usually be accomplished by comparing it with the amount authorized in the minutes of the board of directors' meetings.

ACCRUED VACATION PAY, SICK PAY, AND OTHER BENEFITS The consistent accrual of these liabilities relative to those of the preceding year is the most important consideration in evaluating the fairness of the amounts. The company policy for recording the liability must first be determined, followed by the recalculation of the recorded amounts.

ACCRUED EMPLOYEE BENEFITS This account will include the employer's share of Canada (or Quebec) Pension Plan payments and employment insurance payments as well as workplace safety insurance. The employer's share can be verified by examining remittance forms prepared in the subsequent period to determine the amount that should have been recorded as a liability at the balance sheet date.

TESTS OF DETAILS OF BALANCES FOR PAYROLL EXPENSE ACCOUNTS Several accounts in the income statement are affected by payroll transactions. The most important are officers' salaries and bonuses, office salaries, sales salaries and commissions, and direct manufacturing labour. There is frequently a further breakdown of costs by division, product, or branch. Fringe benefits such as dental insurance may also be included in the expenses.

There should be relatively little additional testing of the income statement accounts in most audits beyond the analytical procedures, tests of controls, and related tests of liability accounts, which have already been discussed. Extensive additional testing should be necessary only when weaknesses are found in internal control, significant errors are discovered in the liability tests, or major unexplained variances are found in the analytical procedures. Nevertheless, some income statement accounts are often tested in the personnel and payroll cycle. These include officers' compensation, commissions, and total payroll.

Officers' compensation It is common to verify whether the total compensation of officers is the amount authorized by the board of directors because disclosure of the salaries and other compensation of the top five officers is required by certain provincial securities commissions. Verification of the officers' compensation is also warranted because some individuals may be in a position to pay themselves more than the authorized amount. The usual audit test is to obtain the authorized salary of each officer from the minutes of the board of directors' meetings and compare it with the related earnings record.

Commissions Commission expense can be verified with relative ease if the commission rate is the same for each type of sale and the necessary sales information is available in the accounting records. The total commission expense can be verified by multiplying the commission rate for each type of sale by the amount of sales in that category. If the calculations are complex, the auditor may decide that these calculations should be tested using generalized audit software or automated audit techniques. If the desired information is not available, it may be necessary to test the annual or monthly commission payments for selected salespeople and trace those to the total commission payments. When the auditor believes it is necessary to perform these tests, they are normally done in conjunction with tests of accrued liabilities.

Employee benefits expense Employee benefits expense for the year can be tested by first reconciling the total payroll on each employee benefits remittance form with the total payroll for the entire year. Total employee benefits expense can then be recomputed by multiplying the appropriate rate by the payroll.

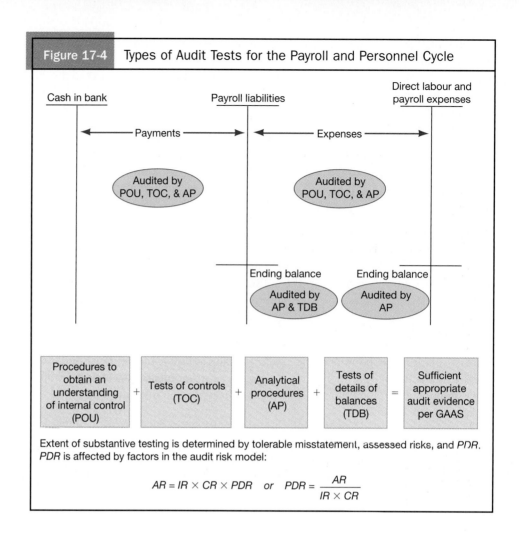

Figure 17-4 Types of Audit Tests for the Payroll and Personnel Cycle

Cash in bank

Payroll liabilities

Direct labour and payroll expenses

◄——— Payments ———► ◄——— Expenses ———►

Audited by POU, TOC, & AP

Audited by POU, TOC, & AP

Ending balance

Ending balance

Audited by AP & TDB

Audited by AP

| Procedures to obtain an understanding of internal control (POU) | + | Tests of controls (TOC) | + | Analytical procedures (AP) | + | Tests of details of balances (TDB) | = | Sufficient appropriate audit evidence per GAAS |

Extent of substantive testing is determined by tolerable misstatement, assessed risks, and *PDR*. *PDR* is affected by factors in the audit risk model:

$$AR = IR \times CR \times PDR \quad or \quad PDR = \frac{AR}{IR \times CR}$$

The calculation is frequently time-consuming or complex because the benefits are usually applicable on only a portion of the payroll and the rate may change part way through the year if the taxpayer's financial statements are not on a calendar-year basis. On most audits, the calculation is costly and is unnecessary unless analytical procedures indicate a problem that cannot be resolved through other procedures. When the auditor believes that the test is necessary, it is ordinarily done using generalized audit software in conjunction with tests of employee benefits accruals.

Total payroll A test closely related to the one for employee benefits is the reconciliation of total payroll expense in the general ledger with the T4 Summary that the company must send to the Canada Revenue Agency by the end of February each year. The objectives of the test are to determine whether payroll transactions were charged to a non-payroll account or not recorded in the payroll journal at all. The audit objectives are certainly relevant, but it is questionable whether the procedure is useful in uncovering the type of error as intended. Since both the T4 Summary and the payroll are usually prepared directly from the payroll master file, the errors, if any, are likely to be present in both records. The procedure may be worthwhile in rare situations, but it is usually unnecessary. Tests of controls are a better means of uncovering these two types of errors in most audits.

SUMMARY Figure 17-4 illustrates the major accounts in the payroll and personnel cycle and the types of audit tests used to audit these accounts. This figure also shows how the audit risk model discussed in Chapter 7 relates to the audit of the payroll and personnel cycle.

concept check

C17-8 Describe the three assertions that are important when testing payroll-related liabilities.

C17-9 When would the auditor conduct tests of details of balances for payroll expense accounts?

Summary

1. *Why is the payroll and personnel cycle important?* This cycle involves the employment and payment of all employees. Salaries, wages, and associated benefits are a major expense; labour is an important cost component for manufacturing and construction companies and, if improperly managed, could result in wasted resources.

 What differentiates this cycle from other cycles? There is only one class of transaction. The total transaction value can be far more significant than balance sheet accounts. Internal control over payroll tends to be effective for most companies due to harsh federal and provincial penalties for errors in withholdings and taxes.

 Describe the functions and records in this cycle. Table 17-1 lists each of the business functions (personnel and employment, master file change, access rights management, timekeeping and payroll preparation, payment, preparation of withholding and tax remittances) with the associated documents and records.

2. *List typical audit tests of controls by assertion.* Table 17-2 lists transaction-related audit objectives, key internal controls, and common tests of controls for payroll. For example, a test of occurrence is examining payroll records for evidence of approval.

3. *How does outsourcing affect the controls and audit of payroll?* If payroll is outsourced, then the outsourcing organization could conduct some controls that affect the reliability and auditability of the accounts of transactions. The auditor may need to assess or audit the controls at the service organization.

 How do these principles apply to other application cycles? Other cycles are audited in a manner similar to that of payroll: the auditor considers controls at both the client and the service organization and may use a service auditor's report as part of the audit process.

4. *What misstatements could a payroll analytical review process detect?* Table 17-3 lists several analytical procedures that could detect potential errors in the following accounts: payroll expense, direct labour, commission expense, payroll benefits expenses, and liabilities.

 Which liability and expense accounts in the payroll cycle are tested using tests of details? The auditor would test the following accounts: withholding benefits and taxes, accrued salaries and wages, accrued commissions, accrued vacation pay, accrued sick benefits, officers' compensation, commissions, employee benefits, and payroll costs.

Visit the text's website at www.pearsoned.ca/arens for practice quizzes, additional case studies, and international standards information.

Review Questions

17-1 Identify five general ledger accounts that are likely to be affected by the payroll and personnel cycle in most audits.

17-2 Explain the relationship between the payroll and personnel cycle and inventory valuation.

17-3 List five tests of controls that can be performed for the payroll cycle, and state the purpose of each control being tested.

17-4 Explain why the percentage of total audit time in the cycle devoted to performing tests of controls may be less for the payroll and personnel cycle than for the sales and collection cycle.

17-5 Evaluate the following comment by an auditor: "My job is to determine whether the payroll records are fairly stated in accordance with generally accepted accounting principles, not to find out whether the client is following proper hiring and termination procedures. When I conduct an audit of payroll, I keep out of the personnel department and stick to the time cards, journals, and payroll cheques. I don't care whom the client hires and whom it fires, as long as it properly pays the employees it has."

17-6 What is the purpose of testing both employee access rights set-up and employee access rights changes? What would be the impact upon the audit if either or both of these processes had control weaknesses?

17-7 The company you are auditing has a local area network with office automation software, accounting software, and point of sale equipment. Provide examples of five different categories of access rights, and state the control purpose of each access right category.

17-8 Distinguish between the following payroll audit procedures, and state the purpose of each: (1) Trace a random sample of prenumbered time cards to the related payroll cheques in the payroll register, and compare the hours worked with the hours paid, and (2) trace a random sample of payroll cheques from the payroll register to the related time cards, and compare the hours worked with the hours paid. Which of these two procedures is typically more important in the audit of payroll? Why?

17-9 In auditing payroll withholding and payroll benefits expense, explain why emphasis should normally be on evaluating the adequacy of the preparation procedures for employee withholding and benefits remittance forms rather than on the employee withholding and benefits liability. Explain the effect that inadequate preparation procedures will have on the remainder of the audit.

17-10 List several analytical procedures for the payroll and personnel cycle, and explain the type of error that might be indicated when there is a significant difference in the comparison of the current year's and previous years' results for each of the tests.

17-11 Explain the circumstances under which an auditor should perform audit tests designed primarily to uncover fraud in the payroll and personnel cycle. List three audit procedures that are primarily for the detection of fraud, and state the type of fraud that the procedure is meant to uncover.

17-12 Distinguish among a payroll mater file, a TD-1 form, and a T4 payroll summary return. Explain the purpose of each.

17-13 List the supporting documents and records the auditor will examine in a typical payroll audit where there is a high risk of fraud.

17-14 List the types of authorizations in the payroll and personnel cycle, and state the type of misstatement that is enhanced when each authorization is lacking.

17-15 Explain why it is common to verify total officers' compensation even when the tests of controls results in payroll are excellent. What audit procedures can be used to verify officers' compensation?

17-16 Explain what is meant by an "imprest payroll account." What is its purpose as a control over payroll?

17-17 List several audit procedures that the auditor can use to determine whether payroll transactions are recorded at the proper amount.

Discussion Questions and Problems

17-18 Items 1 through 9 are selected questions typically found in questionnaires used by auditors to obtain an understanding of internal control in the payroll and personnel cycle. In using the questionnaire for a client, a "yes" response to a question indicates a possible internal control, whereas a "no" indicates a potential deficiency.

1. Does an appropriate official authorize initial rates of pay and any subsequent changes in rates?
2. Are written notices documenting reasons for termination required?
3. Are formal records such as time cards used for keeping time?
4. Is approval by a department head or foreperson required for all time cards before they are submitted for payment?
5. Does anyone verify pay rates, overtime hours, and computations of gross payroll before payroll cheques are prepared?
6. Does adequate means exist for identifying jobs or products, such as work orders, job numbers, or some similar identification provided to employees to ensure proper coding of time records?

7. Are employees paid by cheques prepared by persons independent of timekeeping?
8. Are employees required to show identification to receive paycheques?
9. Is a continuing record maintained of all unclaimed wages?

REQUIRED

a. For each of the questions, state the transaction-related audit objective(s) being fulfilled if the control is in effect.
b. For each control, list a test of control to test its effectiveness.
c. For each of the questions, identify the nature of the potential financial misstatement(s) if the control is not in effect.
d. For each of the potential misstatements in part (c), list a substantive audit procedure for determining whether a material misstatement exists.

17-19 Following are some of the tests of controls and substantive tests of transactions procedures often performed in the payroll and personnel cycle. (Each procedure is to be done on a sample basis.)

1. Reconcile the monthly payroll total for direct manufacturing labour with the labour-cost distribution.
2. Examine the time card for the approval of a foreperson.
3. Recompute hours on the time card, and compare the total with the total hours for which the employee has been paid.
4. Compare the employee name, date, cheque number, and amounts on cancelled cheques with the payroll journal.
5. Trace the hours from the employee time cards to job tickets to make sure that the total reconciles, and trace each job ticket to the job-cost record.

6. Account for a sequence of payroll cheques in the payroll journal.
7. Select employees who have been terminated from the personnel file, and determine whether their termination pay was in accordance with the union contract. As part of this procedure, examine two subsequent periods to determine whether the terminated employee is still being paid.

REQUIRED

a. Identify whether each of the procedures is primarily a test of control or a substantive test of transactions.
b. Identify the transaction-related audit objective(s) of each of the procedures.

17-20 The following misstatements are included in the accounting records of Lathen Manufacturing Ltd.:

1. Direct labour was unintentionally charged to job 620 instead of job 602 by the payroll clerk when he entered the job tickets. Job 602 was completed, and the costs were expensed in the current year, whereas job 620 was included in work in process.

2. Jane Block and Frank Demery take turns "punching in" for each other every few days. The absent employee comes in at noon and tells the supervisor that he or she had car trouble or some other problem. The supervisor does not know the employee is getting paid for the time.

3. The supervisor submits a fraudulent time card for a former employee each week and delivers the related payroll cheque to the employee's house on the way home from work. They split the amount of the paycheque.

4. Employees frequently overlook recording their hours worked on job-cost tickets as required by the system. Many of the client's contracts are on a cost-plus basis.

5. The payroll clerk prepares a cheque to the same nonexistent person every week when entering payroll transactions in the microcomputer system, which also records the amount in the payroll journal. The clerk submits it along with all other payroll cheques for signature. When the cheques are returned to the clerk for distribution, the clerk takes the cheque and deposits it in a special bank account bearing that person's name.

6. In withholding income taxes from employees, the computer operator overrides the standard tax calculation, taking $2 extra from dozens of employees each week and crediting the amount to the operator's own employee earnings record.

REQUIRED
a. For each misstatement, state a control that should have prevented it from occurring on a continuing basis.
b. For each misstatement, state a test of control audit procedure that could uncover it.

17-21 In comparing total employee benefits expense with that of the preceding year, Marilyn Brendin, public accountant, observed a significant increase, even though the total number of employees had increased only from 175 to 195. To investigate the difference, she selected a large sample of payroll disbursement transactions and carefully tested the withholdings for each employee in the sample by referring to Canada Pension Plan, employment insurance, and other benefits withholding tables. In her test, she found no exceptions; therefore, she concluded that employee benefits expense was fairly stated.

REQUIRED
a. Evaluate Brendin's approach to testing employee benefits expense.
b. Discuss a more suitable approach for determining whether employee benefits expense was properly stated in the current year.

17-22 As part of the audit of McGree Plumbing and Heating Ltd., you have responsibility for testing the payroll and personnel cycle. Payroll is the largest single expense in the client's trial balance, and hourly wages make up most of the payroll total. Employees are paid every two weeks. A unique aspect of the business is the extensive overtime incurred by employees on some days. It is common for employees to work only three or four days during the week but to work long hours while they are on the job. McGree's management has found that this actually saves money, in spite of the large amount of overtime, because the union contract requires payment for all travel time. Since many of the employees' jobs require long travel times and extensive start-up costs, this policy is supported by both McGree and the employees.

You have already carefully evaluated and tested the payroll and personnel cycle's internal control and concluded that it contains no significant weaknesses. Your tests included tests of the time records, withholdings, pay rates, the filing of all required employee withholding and benefits remittance forms, payroll cheques, and all other aspects of payroll.

As part of the year-end tests of payroll, you are responsible for verifying all accrued payroll as well as the company's liability for withholdings and accrued benefits. The accrued factory payroll includes the last six working days of the current year. The client has calculated accrued wages by taking 60 percent of the subsequent period's gross payroll and has recorded it as an adjusting entry to be reversed in the subsequent period.

REQUIRED
List all audit procedures, organized by assertion, you would follow in verifying accrued payroll and the liability for withholdings and accrued employee benefits.

17-23 In the audit of Larnet Manufacturing Corp., the auditor concluded that internal controls were inadequate because of the lack of segregation of duties. As a result, the decision was made to have a surprise payroll pay-off one month before the client's balance sheet date. Since the auditor had never been involved in a payroll pay-off, she did not know how to proceed.

REQUIRED
a. What is the purpose of a surprise payroll pay-off?
b. What other audit procedures can the auditor perform that may fulfill the same objectives?

c. Discuss the procedures that the auditor should require the client to observe when the surprise payroll pay-off is taking place.

d. At the completion of a payroll pay-off, there are frequently several unclaimed cheques. What procedures should be followed for these?

17-24 During the first-year audit of Omato Wholesale Stationery Ltd., you observe that commissions amount to almost 25 percent of total sales, which is somewhat higher than in previous years. Further investigation reveals that the industry typically has larger sales commissions than Omato and that there is significant variation in rates depending on the product sold.

At the time a sale is made, the salesperson records his or her commission rate and the total amount of the commissions on the office copy of the sales invoice. When sales are entered into the information system for the recording of sales, the debit to sales commission expense and credit to accrued sales commission are also recorded. As part of recording the sales and sales commission expense, the accounts receivable clerk verifies the prices, quantities, commission rates, and all calculations on the sales invoices. Both the customer master file and the salespersons' commission master files are updated when the sale and sales commission are recorded. On the fifteenth day after the end of the month, the salesperson is paid for the preceding month's sales commissions.

REQUIRED

a. Develop an audit program, by assertion, to verify sales commission expense assuming that no audit tests have been conducted in any audit area to this point.

b. Develop an audit program, by assertion, to verify accrued sales commissions at the end of the year assuming that the tests you designed in part (a) resulted in no significant misstatements.

17-25 In many companies, labour costs represent a substantial percentage of total dollars expended in any one accounting period. One of the auditor's primary means of verifying payroll transactions is a detailed payroll test.

You are making an annual examination of Lethbridge Inc., a medium-sized manufacturing company. You have selected a number of hourly employees for a detailed payroll test. The worksheet outline at right has been prepared.

REQUIRED

a. What factors should the auditor consider in selecting his or her sample of employees to be included in any payroll test?

b. Using the column numbers as a reference, state the principal way(s) that the information for each heading would be verified.

c. In addition to the payroll test, the auditor employs a number of other audit procedures in the verification of payroll transactions. List five additional procedures that may be employed and the corresponding audit objective.

Column Number	Heading
1	Employee number
2	Employee name
3	Job classification
	Hours worked:
4	Straight time
5	Premium time
6	Hourly rate
7	Gross earnings
	Deductions:
8	Income tax withheld
9	Canada Pension Plan withheld
10	Employment insurance withheld
11	Union dues
12	Amount of cheque
13	Cheque number
14	Account number charged
15	Description of account

(Adapted from AICPA)

Professional Judgment Problems

17-26 Archer Uniforms, Inc. is a distributor of professional uniforms to retail stores that sell work clothing to professionals such as doctors, nurses, and security guards. Traditionally, most of the sales are to retail stores throughout Canada and the United States. Most shipments are processed in bulk for direct delivery to retail stores or to the corporate warehouse distribution facilities for retail store chains. In early 2009, Archer Uniforms began offering the sale of uniforms directly to professionals through its company website. Professionals can access information about uniform styles, sizes, and prices. Purchases are charged to the customer's personal credit card. Management made this decision based on its conclusion that the online sales would tap a new market of professionals who do not have easy access to retail stores. Thus, the volume of shipments to retail stores is expected to remain consistent.

Given that Archer's IT staff lacked the experience necessary to create and support the online sales system, management engaged an IT consulting firm to design and maintain the online sales system.

REQUIRED

a. Before performing analytical procedures related to the payroll and personnel cycle accounts, develop expectations of how these recent events at Archer Uniforms, Inc. will affect payroll expense for the following departments during 2009 compared with prior years'. Indicate the degree (extensive, moderate, little) to which you expect the payroll expense account balance to increase or decrease during 2009, with reasons supported by the facts of the case.

1. Warehouse and Shipping Department.
2. IT Department.
3. Accounts Receivable Department.
4. Accounts Payable Department.
5. Receiving Department.
6. Executive Management.
7. Marketing.

b. Provide additional audit procedures (by assertion) that might be required.

17-27 Cilly Stress, a fourth-year honours computer science student at a highly regarded university, was working as part-time cleaning staff at the Classy Manufacturing Company (CMC) when she was expelled from school for misuse of the university's computer resources.

Cilly was able to improve her employment status to full-time cleaning staff. She enjoyed working the night shift, where she found lots of time and opportunity to snoop around the company's office and computing centre. She learned from documentation in the recycling bins that CMC was in the process of updating its extensive policy and procedures documentation and placing it online.

Through continued efforts in searching waste bins and documents left on desktops and unlocked cabinets, as well as some careful observation of password entry by people who were working late, Cilly soon learned enough to log in to the company's information systems and ultimately to print out lists of user identification codes and passwords using a Trojan horse program. She was able to obtain all the passwords she needed to set herself up as a supplier, customer, and systems operator.

As a customer, she was able to order enough goods so that the inventory procurement system would automatically trigger a need for purchase of raw materials. Then, as a supplier, she was ready to deliver the goods at the specified price (by returning the goods that she had "purchased"). As a supervisor, she was able to write off the uncollected accounts receivable from her customer accounts while being paid as a supplier. On average, she was able to embezzle about $125,000 per month.

Cilly's fraud was detected by a suspicious delivery person, who wondered why he was delivering goods to an empty building lot.

REQUIRED

a. Describe weaknesses in human resources and access policies at CMC. For each weakness, indicate the impact and provide a recommendation for improvement.

b. Identify routine audit procedures that might have produced evidence that, with further investigation, could have revealed the fraud. Describe the evidence in the test results that would have triggered the investigation.

Case

17-28 Roost and Briley, public accountants, are doing the audit of Leggert Lumber Co., an international wholesale lumber broker. Because of the nature of their business, payroll and telephone expense are the two largest expenses.

You are the auditor in-charge on the engagement responsible for preparing the audit program for the payroll and personnel cycle. Leggert Lumber uses a computer service company to prepare weekly payroll payments, update earnings records, and prepare the weekly payroll journal for its 30 employees. The president maintains all personnel files, knows every employee extremely well, and is a full-time participant in the business.

All employees, except the president, check into the company building daily, swiping their magnetic-stripe cards in a time clock. The president's secretary, Mary Clark, observes employees clocking in and out.

At the end of each week Mary prints a listing of hours worked from the timekeeping system, and the president approves all hours worked. Each Tuesday, Mary transcribes the hours worked onto an electronic payroll input form for email to the computer service centre. She prints and files a

copy of the form. The form has the following information for each employee:

Information	Source
Employee name	Hours worked listing
Social Insurance Number	Employee list
Hourly wage rate*	Wage rate list (approved by president)
Regular hours	Hours worked listing
Overtime hours	Hours worked listing
Special deductions*	Special form (prepared by employee)
TD-1 information*	TD-1 form
Termination of employment*	President

*Included on input form only for new employees, terminations

The service centre uses an automated routine to transfer the information from the electronic payroll input form to its payroll processing system, then updates master files, and prepares payroll payment remittance advices, direct deposit payroll information, and a payroll register. The payroll register has the following headings:

Employee Name	Income Taxes Withheld
Social Insurance Number	Employment insurance withheld
Regular hours	Canada pension payments withheld
Overtime hours	Deduction codes for other deductions
Regular payroll dollars	Other deductions amounts
Overtime payroll dollars	Net pay
Gross payroll	Remittance advice number

The payroll journal has a line for each employee and a total for each dollar value column.

The payroll remittances and the journal are emailed to Mary, who compares the information on the journal with her payroll input form and initials the journal. She then emails the service centre that she is in agreement with the journal, which initiates the direct deposit of the payroll to the employee bank accounts. She gives the remittance advices to the president, who personally delivers them to the employees.

Mary posts the totals from the payroll journal to the general ledger. Bank statements are mailed to the president, and he prepares a monthly bank reconciliation.

REQUIRED
a. Is there any loss of documentation because of the computer service centre? Explain.
b. For each transaction-related audit objective for the payroll and personnel cycle, write appropriate tests of controls and substantive tests of transactions audit procedures. Consider both controls and deficiencies in writing your program. Label each procedure as either a test of control or a substantive test of transactions.
c. Are there any weaknesses in internal control at Leggert? If so, describe the weaknesses, state the impact of each weakness, and provide recommendations for improvement for each weakness.

Ongoing Small Business Case: Payroll at CondoCleaners.com

17-29 Jim is handling the payroll of his 15 full-time employees. As Jim allocates the work, he knows the hours that his employees have worked, and he daily records the data in a spreadsheet. At the end of the week, he uses the online calculator at Canada Revenue Agency's (CRA) website to calculate the gross pay and deductions. He then records this information in his spreadsheet. He uses a second spreadsheet to calculate the required remittances which he sends to the CRA every month.

REQUIRED
What are the advantages and disadvantages of the methods that Jim uses to calculate payroll? What other low-cost alternatives are available to him?

18

Audit of the acquisition and payment cycle

How do you pay your bills? Do you have a credit card statement that is paid monthly? Do you have any payments that you pay by cheque or via electronic banking? Profit-oriented and other businesses have many different ways that they pay their bills. As auditors, we need to be concerned, first of all, that only appropriate bills are recorded in the financial statements, and also that none is omitted. Then, we also audit the payment process. Management accountants can design and monitor controls to help deter payment fraud, while auditors may focus on validity of payments.

STANDARDS REFERENCED IN THIS CHAPTER

CICA Standard

CAS 550 – Related parties (previously Section 6010 – Audit of related-party transactions)

LEARNING OBJECTIVES

1 Describe the major business functions, documents, and records in the acquisition and payment cycle. List which accounts give rise to accrued liabilities.

2 Explain the design of controls for the acquisition and payment cycle. Describe the impact of information systems conversions on the audit process.

3 Design substantive tests (analytical review and tests of details) for accounts payable. Explain the relevance of understatement of accounts payable versus overstatement.

4 Analyze the risks and audit processes for selected accounts.

Who Audits the RCMP?

The allegations were that senior management at the RCMP (Royal Canadian Mounted Police) used funds from the RCMP pension fund for personal use (such as golf games) during the period 2003 through 2007 and issued contracts to associates that did not provide value to the pension fund. These expenses ran into the millions of dollars: in March 2007, $3.4 million was reported as being "returned" to the assets of the pension plan, with another $1.3 million of questionable contracts being reviewed for their value to the organization.

Also alleged was that employee harassment and punitive employee transfers were used as a means of preventing disclosure of misuse of the pension funds. These actions were attributed to senior management of the RCMP, and reflected a poor ethical tone throughout the organization.

IMPORTANCE TO AUDITORS

Is it greed that makes cash so sticky? There are many different types of accounts payable fraud; such fraud is often difficult to detect. The auditor needs to be particularly careful, when examining the methods used to audit issuance of contracts (for materials, maintenance, or other outsourcing), to identify factors that indicate risks of fraud. Similarly, travel expenses and general expense accounts may need to be carefully examined when there is a lack of segregation of duties, or where such expenses seem to be unusually high.

WHAT DO YOU THINK?

1. What are examples of controls that could prevent or detcct duplicate payment of expenses in a travel expense account?

2. How can senior management prevent the issuance of fictitious or inflated contracts for the purchase of goods or services?

3. List five factors that would indicate increased risk of accounts payable fraud at an organization.

Sources: 1. Maccharles, Tonda, "Officers' testimony shocks MPs," *Toronto Star*, March 29, 2007, p. A6. 2. Maccharles, Tonda, "RCMP chiefs got ethics warnings, MPs told," *Toronto Star*, May 15, 2007, p. A1, A6. 3. Maccharles, Tonda, "RCMP internal culture ripped," *Toronto Star*, December 11, 2007, p. A4.

WHAT types of audit tests would detect fictitious purchases? Or fictitious customers? This case illustrates how management's overriding of controls led to the misuse of millions of dollars. Did management hide these transactions so that they were not detected or reported by the external auditors? Auditors need to be aware of risks and associated audit tests for the purchase cycle.

The Nature of the Acquisition and Payment Cycle

The acquisition of goods and services includes such items as the purchase of raw materials, equipment, supplies, utilities, repairs and maintenance, and research and development. The cycle does not include the acquisition and payment of employees' services or the internal transfers and allocations of costs within the organization. The former are a part of the payroll and personnel function, and the latter are audited as part of the verification of individual assets or liabilities. The acquisition and payment cycle also excludes the acquisition and repayment of capital (interest-bearing debt and owners' equity), which are considered separately in Chapter 20.

In this chapter, the format for discussing internal control introduced in earlier chapters is repeated. Several important balance sheet accounts that are a part of the acquisition and payment cycle are included. These are manufacturing equipment, prepaid insurance, and accrued liabilities. The chapter also discusses tests of details of income statement accounts included in the acquisition and payment cycle.

The **acquisition and payment cycle** includes two distinct classes of transactions—acquisitions of goods and services and cash disbursements for those acquisitions. Purchase returns and allowances is also a class of transactions, but for most companies the amounts are immaterial.

Acquisition and payment cycle—the transaction cycle that includes the acquisition of and payment for goods and services from suppliers outside the organization.

There are a larger number and variety of accounts in the acquisition and payment cycle in a typical company than for any other cycle. Examine the trial balance for Hillsburg Hardware Limited on page 129. Accounts affected by the acquisition and payment cycle are identified by the letter "A" in the left column. Note first that accounts affected by the cycle include asset, liability, expense, and miscellaneous income accounts, and second, the large number of accounts affected. It is not surprising, therefore, that it often takes more time to audit the acquisition and payment cycle than any other cycle.

The way the accounting information flows through the various accounts in the acquisition and payment cycle is illustrated by T-accounts in Figure 18-1 on the next page. To keep the illustration manageable, only a control account is shown for the three major categories of expenses used by most companies. For each control account, examples of the subsidiary expense accounts are also given.

Figure 18-1 shows that every transaction is either debited or credited to accounts payable. Because many companies make some purchases directly by cheque or through petty cash, the figure is an oversimplification. We assume that cash transactions are processed in the same manner as transactions flowing through accounts payable.

The acquisition and payment cycle involves the decisions and processes necessary for obtaining the goods and services for operating a business. The cycle typically begins with the initiation of a purchase requisition by an authorized employee who needs the goods or services and ends with payment for the benefits received. Although the discussion that follows deals with a small manufacturing company that makes tangible products for sale to third parties, the same principles apply to a service company, a government unit, or any other type of organization.

Column 3 of Table 18-1 on page 597 identifies the five business functions in a typical acquisition and payment cycle. The table shows the relationships among the classes of transactions, accounts, business functions, and documents and records. In the first three sections of this chapter, we focus on goods and services related to the cost of goods sold to the business. In the final section of this chapter, we consider asset acquisition and other selected accounts.

PROCESSING PURCHASE ORDERS The request for goods or services by the client's personnel is the starting point for the cycle. The exact form of the request and the required approval depend on the nature of the goods and services and company policy.

Purchase requisition A **purchase requisition** is a written request for goods and services by an authorized employee. It may take the form of a request for such acquisitions as materials by a shop supervisor or the storeroom supervisor, outside repairs by office

Purchase requisition—request by an authorized employee to the purchasing department to place an order for inventory and other items used by an entity.

| Figure 18-1 | Accounts in the Acquisition and Payment Cycle |

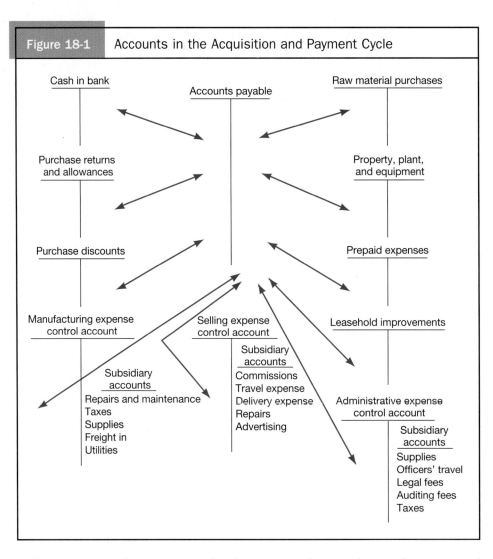

or factory personnel, or insurance by the vice-president in charge of property and equipment.

Purchase order — a document prepared by the purchasing department indicating the description, quantity, and related information for goods and services that the company intends to purchase.

Purchase order A **purchase order** records the description, quantity, and related information for goods and services that the company intends to purchase. This document is frequently used to indicate authorization to procure goods and services. Purchase order details are retained in a purchase order transaction file.

Vendor master file This file sums individual acquisitions, cash disbursements, and acquisition returns and allowances for each vendor. Those companies that have automated purchasing systems ensure that authorized vendor information, such as credit terms, contact name, and shipping terms, is established and recorded in the vendor master file. The file also keeps track of total purchase commitments and total liabilities (unpaid invoices) by vendor.

Purchase order transaction file As purchase commitments are made, transaction details are recorded in the purchase order file. Automated systems automatically number the purchase orders sequentially and assist in tracking purchase commitments, expected delivery dates, and items that have been back-ordered (i.e., when the vendor currently does not have stock but shipments are expected later).

Internal controls Proper authorization for acquisitions and changes to the vendor master file is an essential part of this function because it ensures that the goods and services acquired are for authorized company purposes, and it avoids the acquisition of excessive and unnecessary items. Most companies permit general authorization for the acquisition of regular operating needs, such as inventory at one level and

Table 18-1   Classes of Transactions, Accounts, Business Functions, and Related Documents and Records for the Acquisition and Payment Cycle

Classes of Transactions	Accounts	Business Functions	Documents and Records
Acquisitions	Inventory	Processing purchase orders	Purchase requisition
	Property, plant, and equipment		Purchase order
	Prepaid expenses		Vendor master file
	Leasehold improvements		Purchase transaction file
	Accounts payable		
	Manufacturing expenses		
	Selling expenses		
	Administrative expenses		
		Receiving goods and services	Receiving report
		Recognizing the liability	Acquisitions journal
		Vendor master file changes	Summary acquisitions report
			Vendor's invoice
			Debit memo
			Vendor transaction file
			Voucher
			Vendor master file
			Accounts payable trial balance
			Vendor's statement
Cash disbursements	Cash in bank (from cash disbursements)	Processing and recording cash disbursements	Cheque or payment
	Accounts payable		Payment transaction file
	Purchase discounts		Cash disbursements journal

acquisitions of capital assets or similar items at another. For example, acquisitions of capital assets in excess of a specified dollar limit may require board of directors' action; items acquired relatively infrequently, such as insurance policies and long-term service contracts, are approved by certain officers; supplies and services costing less than a designated amount are approved by supervisors and department heads; and some types of raw materials and supplies are re-ordered automatically whenever they fall to a predetermined level, often by direct communication with vendors' computers. Where automatic purchase orders are generated, care must be taken to ensure that re-order points are monitored so that only those goods still required by the company are purchased.

After an acquisition has been approved, a purchase order to acquire the goods and services must be initiated. A purchase order is issued to a vendor for a specified item at a certain price to be delivered at or by a designated time. The purchase order is usually in writing and is a legal document that is an offer to buy.

It is common for companies to establish purchasing departments to ensure an adequate quality of goods and services at a minimum price. For good internal control, the purchasing department should not be responsible for authorizing the acquisition or receiving the goods.

RECEIVING GOODS AND SERVICES The receipt by the company of goods and services from the vendor is a critical point in the cycle because it is the point at which most companies first recognize the acquisition and related liability on their records. When goods are received, adequate control requires examination for description, quantity, timely arrival, and condition.

Receiving report A **receiving report** document is prepared at the time tangible goods are received and indicates the description of the goods, the quantity received, the date received, and other relevant data. The receipt of goods and services in the

Receiving report—a document prepared by the receiving department at the time tangible goods are received, indicating the description of the goods, the quantity received, the date received, and other relevant data; part of the documentation necessary for payment to be made.

normal course of business represents the date that clients normally recognize the liability for an acquisition. Where an organization has automated purchase order systems, the receipt needs to be entered into the computer system to signal that the goods have been received. This information would also be used to update perpetual inventory systems.

Internal controls Most companies have the receiving department initiate a receiving report as evidence of the receipt and examination of goods. One copy is normally sent to the storeroom, where it is used to update the quantity fields of the computer records, and another to the accounts payable department for its information needs. To prevent theft and misuse, it is important that the goods be physically controlled from the time of their receipt until their disposal. The personnel in the receiving department should be independent of the storeroom personnel and the accounting department. Finally, the accounting records should transfer responsibility for the goods as they are transferred from receiving to storage and from storage to manufacturing.

RECOGNIZING THE LIABILITY The proper recognition of the liability for the receipt of goods and services requires prompt and accurate recording. The initial recording has a significant effect on the recorded financial statements and the actual cash disbursement; therefore, great care must be taken to include only existing company acquisitions at the correct amounts.

Acquisitions journal This journal lists acquisition transactions. A detailed acquisitions journal includes each acquisition transaction. It usually includes several classifications for the most significant types of acquisitions, such as the purchase of inventory, repairs and maintenance, supplies, the entry to accounts payable, and miscellaneous debits and credits. The acquisitions journal can also include acquisition returns and allowances transactions if a separate journal is not used. The acquisitions journal is generated for any period from the acquisition transactions included in the computer files. Individual transaction amounts are posted to the vendor master file and journal totals are posted to the general ledger.

Summary acquisitions report This report summarizes acquisitions for a period. The report typically includes information analyzed by key components such as account classification, type of inventory, and division.

Vendor's invoice The **vendor's invoice** indicates details, such as the description and quantity of goods and services provided, price including freight, cash discount terms, and date of the billing. It is an essential document because it specifies the amount of money owed to the vendor for an acquisition.

Debit memo The **debit memo** indicates a reduction in the amount owed to a vendor because of returned goods or an allowance granted. It often takes the same general form as a vendor's invoice, but it supports reductions in accounts payable rather than increases.

Vendor transaction file This file, detailing transactions of individual vendors, indicates both the details of the vendor's invoice and the debit memo details from accounts payable. Payments to vendors are deducted from outstanding transactions and recorded in a payment transaction file. Unpaid transactions are used to prepare the accounts payable trial balance. The sum of the unpaid transactions should always agree with the sum of liabilities in the vendor master file and with the general ledger accounts payable total.

Voucher This document may be used by organizations to establish a formal means of recording and controlling acquisitions. Vouchers include a cover sheet or folder for containing documents and a package of relevant documents such as the purchase order, copy of the packing slip, receiving report, and vendor's invoice. After payment, a copy of the cheque or other payment advice is added to the voucher package.

Vendor master file As described earlier, the **vendor master file** has sums of individual acquisitions, cash disbursements, and acquisition returns and allowances for each vendor. The master file is updated from the purchase order, receiving report, invoice, returns and allowances, and cash disbursements transaction files. The total of the individual account balances in the master file equals the total balance of accounts payable in the general ledger.

Accounts payable trial balance The **accounts payable trial balance** is a listing by each vendor of the amount owed at a point in time. It is prepared directly from the accounts payable master file and open item transaction files. It can be prepared in summary form (showing totals only by vendor) or in detail (showing the current month's transactions plus any unpaid transactions making up the opening balance).

Vendor's statement The **vendor's statement**, prepared monthly by the vendor, indicates a customer's beginning balance, acquisitions, returns and allowances, payments, and ending balance. These balances and activities are the vendor's representations of the transactions for the period and not the client's. Except for disputed amounts and timing differences, the client's accounts payable transaction file details and vendor master file totals should be the same as the vendor's statement.

Internal controls In some companies, the recording of the liability for acquisitions is made on the basis of the receipt of goods and services, and in other companies, it is deferred until the vendor's invoice is received. In either case, the accounts payable department typically has responsibility for verifying the propriety of acquisitions. This is done by comparing the details on the purchase order, the receiving report, and the vendor's invoice to determine that the descriptions, prices, quantities, terms, and freight on the vendor's invoice are correct. Typically, extensions, footings, and account distribution are also verified.

The level of automation of the accounts payable system varies. Some organizations simply record the total amount of the vendor invoice into the accounts payable system. In that case, it is important that all of the above steps, including recalculation of the vendor invoice, are completed before the invoice is entered into the system. For highly integrated computer systems, the vendor invoice details entered manually or received electronically include each line of the invoice (i.e., the item number, description, quantity, price, and terms). The computer systems can then make the comparison with the purchase order details and recalculate the vendor invoice. Accurate and

Vendor's invoice—a document that specifies the details of an acquisition transaction and amount of money owed to the vendor for an acquisition.

Debit memo—a document indicating a reduction in the amount owed to a vendor because of returned goods or an allowance granted.

Vendor master file—a computer file for maintaining a record for each vendor of individual acquisitions, cash disbursements, and acquisition returns and allowances, and vendor balances.

Accounts payable trial balance—a listing by each vendor of the amount owed at a point in time; prepared directly from the accounts payable master file.

Vendor's statement—a statement prepared monthly by the vendor, which indicates the customer's beginning balance, acquisitions, payments, and ending balance.

authorized entry of receiving order details by the organization's personnel is important so that the system can confirm that the quantity received is equal to the quantity ordered and the quantity billed by the vendor.

An important control in the accounts payable and information processing departments is requiring that those personnel who record acquisitions do not have access to cash, marketable securities, and other assets. Adequate documents and records, proper procedures for record keeping, and independent checks on performance are also necessary controls in the accounts payable function.

PROCESSING AND RECORDING CASH DISBURSEMENTS For most companies, payment is made by computer-prepared cheques from information included in the acquisition transactions file at the time goods and services are received. Regular suppliers may be set up for direct deposit to their bank accounts using electronic data interchange (EDI) or other methods of electronic funds transfer (EFT). Printed cheques are typically prepared in a multi-copy format, with the original going to the payee, one copy being filed with the vendor's invoice and other supporting documents, and another copy being filed numerically. If laser-printed cheques are used, then normally only one copy is printed, as the documents are available electronically. Individual payments are recorded as cash disbursement transactions.

Cheque for payment This is the means of paying for the acquisition when payment is due. After the cheque is signed by an authorized person, it is an asset. Therefore, signed cheques should be mailed by the signer or a person under his or her control. When cashed by the vendor and cleared by the client's bank, it is referred to as a "cancelled cheque." Electronic payments should require release using a password before being submitted to the bank or payment clearing centre. Rather than having a cheque number, such payments will have a remittance number.

Cash disbursements journal The cash disbursements journal is generated for any period from the cash disbursement (payment) transactions included in the computer files. Details from the transaction files are posted to the vendor transaction file and vendor master file. Transaction totals are posted to the general ledger.

Internal controls The most important controls in the cash disbursements function include the following:

- The signing of cheques (or authorization of payment release) by an individual with proper authority.
- Separation of responsibilities for approving the payments and performing the accounts payable function.
- Careful examination of the supporting documents by the cheque signer at the time the cheque is signed.

The cheques should be prenumbered and printed on special paper that makes it difficult to alter the payee or amount. Care should be taken to provide physical control over blank, voided, and signed cheques. It is also important to have a method of cancelling the supporting documents to prevent their reuse as support for another cheque at a later time. A common method is to mark the documents as "entered" when recorded in the computer system and to write the cheque number on the supporting documents when cheques are issued or documents are paid (e.g., by electronic bank transfer).

concept check

C18-1 Why is it important for an organization to use purchase orders?

C18-2 What is the purpose of matching receiving report and invoice details to purchase orders?

② Tests of Controls

In a typical audit, the most time-consuming accounts to verify by tests of details of balances are accounts receivable, inventory, capital assets, accounts payable, and expense accounts. Of these five, four are directly related to the acquisition and payment cycle. The net time saved can be dramatic if the auditor can reduce the tests of details of the accounts by using tests of controls to verify the effectiveness of internal controls for acquisitions and cash disbursements.

Prior to considering tests in this cycle, the auditor will have assessed the quality of corporate governance, the risks of management override in the payment cycle, and the level of fraud risk associated with the cycle. Tests of controls for the acquisition and payment cycle are divided into two broad areas: tests of acquisitions and tests of payments. Acquisition tests concern four of the five functions discussed earlier in the chapter: processing purchase orders, vendor master file changes, receiving goods and services, and recognizing the liability. Tests of payments concern the fifth function, processing and recording cash disbursements.

The six transaction-related audit objectives developed in Chapters 5 and 9 are again used as the frame of reference for designing tests of controls for acquisition and cash disbursement transactions. For each objective, the auditor must go through the same logical process that has been discussed in previous chapters. First, the auditor must understand the general controls applicable to the cycle and the cycle's internal controls to determine which controls exist and assess their design effectiveness. Then, an initial assessment of control risk and risk of material misstatement can be made for each objective. The auditor must decide which controls he or she plans to test to satisfy the initial assessment of control risk. After the auditor has developed the audit procedures for each objective, the procedures can be combined into an audit program that can be efficiently performed. Figure 18-2 summarizes that methodology. It is the same one used in Chapter 14 for sales and cash receipts. Again, the emphasis in the methodology is on determining the appropriate audit procedures, sample size, items to select, and timing.

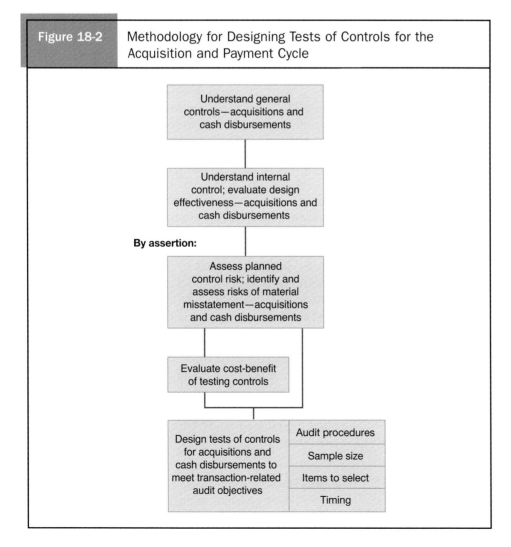

Figure 18-2 Methodology for Designing Tests of Controls for the Acquisition and Payment Cycle

Understand general controls—acquisitions and cash disbursements

Understand internal control; evaluate design effectiveness—acquisitions and cash disbursements

By assertion:

Assess planned control risk; identify and assess risks of material misstatement—acquisitions and cash disbursements

Evaluate cost-benefit of testing controls

Design tests of controls for acquisitions and cash disbursements to meet transaction-related audit objectives | Audit procedures / Sample size / Items to select / Timing

VERIFYING ACQUISITIONS Key internal controls and common tests of controls for each transaction-related audit objective are summarized in Table 18-2. An assumption underlying the internal controls and audit procedures is the existence of a separate acquisitions process for recording all acquisitions.

In studying Table 18-2, it is important to relate internal controls to objectives and to relate tests of controls to both internal controls and monetary misstatements that would be absent or present due to controls and weaknesses in the system. It should be kept in mind that a set of audit procedures for a particular audit engagement will vary with the internal controls and other circumstances.

Four of the objectives for acquisitions deserve special attention. A discussion of each of these objectives follows.

Recorded acquisitions are for goods and services received, consistent with the best interests of the client (occurrence) If the auditor is satisfied that the controls are adequate for this objective, tests for improper and non-existent transactions can be greatly reduced. Adequate controls are likely to prevent the client from including as a business expense or asset those transactions that primarily benefit management or other employees rather than the entity being audited. In some instances, improper transactions are obvious, such as the acquisition of unauthorized personal items by employees or the actual embezzlement of cash by recording a fraudulent purchase in the purchases journal. In other instances, the propriety of a transaction is more difficult to evaluate, such as the payment of officers' memberships in country clubs, expense-paid vacations to foreign countries for members of management and their families, and management-approved illegal payments to officials of foreign countries. If the controls over improper and non-existent transactions are inadequate, extensive examination of supporting documentation is necessary.

Existing acquisitions are recorded (completeness) Failure to record the acquisition of goods and services received directly affects the balance in accounts payable and may result in an overstatement of net income and owners' equity. Because of this, auditors are usually very concerned about the completeness objective. In some instances, it may be difficult to perform tests of details to determine whether there are unrecorded transactions, and the auditor must rely on controls for this purpose. Effective internal control, properly tested, can significantly reduce audit costs.

Acquisitions are accurately recorded (accuracy) When a client uses perpetual inventory records, the tests of details of inventory can be significantly reduced if the auditor believes the perpetual records are accurate. The controls over the acquisitions included in the perpetual records are normally tested as part of the tests of controls for acquisitions, and the controls over this objective play a key role in the audit. The inclusion of both quantity and unit costs in the inventory perpetual records permits a reduction in the tests of the physical count and the unit costs of inventory if the controls are operating effectively. As another example, if the auditor has found that controls over the accuracy of capital assets are good, it is acceptable to test fewer current period acquisitions.

Acquisitions are correctly classified (classification) Although all accounts are affected to some degree by effective controls over classification, the two areas most affected are current-period acquisitions of capital assets and all expense accounts, such as repairs and maintenance, utilities, and advertising. Since performing documentation tests of current-period capital asset acquisitions and expense accounts for accuracy are relatively time-consuming audit procedures, the saving in audit time can be significant.

VERIFYING CASH DISBURSEMENTS The same format used in Table 18-2 for acquisitions is also used in Table 18-3 (see page 604) for cash disbursements. The assumption underlying these controls and audit procedures is the existence of separate cash disbursements

Table 18-2

Table 18-2 Summary of Transaction-Related Audit Objectives, Key Controls, and Tests of Controls for Acquisitions

Transaction-Related Audit Objective	Key Internal Control	Common Tests of Controls	
Recorded acquisitions are for goods and services received, consistent with the best interests of the client (occurrence).	Existence of purchase requisition, purchase order, receiving report, and vendor's invoice attached to the voucher.[†]	Examine documents in voucher for existence.	Review the acquisitions journal, general ledger, and transaction files for large or unusual amounts.[*]
	Approval of acquisitions at the proper level.	Examine indication of approval.	Examine underlying documents for reasonableness and authenticity (vendors' invoices, receiving reports, purchase orders, and requisitions).
	Cancellation of documents to prevent their reuse.	Examine indication of cancellation.	
	Internal verification of vendors' invoices, receiving reports, purchase orders, and purchase requisitions.[†]	Examine indication of internal verification.[‡]	Trace inventory purchases to inventory files. Examine capital assets acquired.
	New vendors and changes to vendor file approved.	Examine master file change forms; trace details to vendor master file.	Review vendor master file for unusual credit terms, prices, or P.O. box addresses.[‡]
	Vendor master file independently examined periodically.	Discuss review process with management.	
Existing acquisition transactions are recorded (completeness).	Purchase orders are prenumbered and accounted for.	Account for a sequence of purchase orders.[‡]	Trace from a file of receiving reports to the acquisitions journal.[†]
	Receiving reports are prenumbered and accounted for.[†]	Account for a sequence of receiving reports.[‡]	Trace from a file of vendors' invoices to the acquisitions journal.
	Vouchers are prenumbered and accounted for.	Account for a sequence of vouchers.[‡]	
	Internal verification of calculations and amounts.		
Recorded acquisition transactions are accurate (accuracy).	Batch totals are compared with computer summary reports.	Examine indication of internal verification.[‡]	Compare recorded transactions in the acquisitions journal with the vendor's invoice, receiving report, and other supporting documentation.[†‡]
	Approval of acquisitions for prices and discounts.	Examine file of batch totals for initials of data control clerk; compare totals to summary reports.[‡]	Recompute the clerical accuracy on the vendors' invoices, including discounts and freight.[‡]
		Examine indication of approval.	
Acquisition transactions are properly classified (classification).	Adequate chart of accounts.	Examine procedures manual and chart of accounts.	Compare classification with chart of accounts by reference to vendors' invoices.
	Automatic updates and posting.	Enter test transactions or observe entry; trace to correct file.	
Acquisition transactions are properly included in the vendor and inventory master files, and are properly summarized (posting and summarization).	Comparison of accounts payable master file or trial balance totals with general ledger balance.	Examine initials on general ledger accounts indicating comparison.	Test clerical accuracy by footing the journals and tracing postings to general ledger and accounts payable and inventory master files.
Acquisition transactions are recorded on the correct dates (timing).	Procedures require recording transactions as soon as possible after the goods and services have been received.	Examine procedures manual; observe whether unrecorded vendors' invoices exist. Observe data entry process.	Compare dates of receiving reports and vendors' invoices with dates in the acquisitions journal.[†]
	Transaction date must be system date (today's date) or a reasonable date.		

[*] This analytical procedure can also apply to other objectives, including completeness, valuation, and timing.

[†] Receiving reports are used only for tangible goods and are therefore not available for services, such as utilities and repairs and maintenance. Frequently, vendors' invoices are the only documentation available.

[‡] This control would be tested on many audits by using the computer.

Table 18-3

Summary of Transaction-Related Audit Objectives, Key Controls, and Tests of Controls for Cash Disbursements

Transaction-Related Audit Objective	Key Internal Control	Common Tests of Controls	
Recorded cash disbursements are for goods and services actually received (occurrence).	Adequate segregation of duties between accounts payable and custody of signed cheques.	Discuss with personnel and observe activities.	Review the cash disbursements journal, general ledger, and vendor master file for large or unusual amounts.[*]
	Examination of supporting documentation before signing of cheques by an authorized person.	Discuss with personnel and observe activities.	Trace the cancelled cheque to the related acquisitions journal entry; examine for payee name and amount.
	Approval of payment on supporting documents at the time cheques are signed or prior to release of payments for direct deposit.	Examine indication of approval. Review and test controls over access rights for payment approval.	Examine cancelled cheque for authorized signature, proper endorsement, and cancellation by the bank. Examine supporting documents as a part of the tests of acquisitions.
Existing cash disbursement transactions are recorded (completeness).	Cheques and payment records are prenumbered and accounted for. A bank reconciliation is prepared monthly by an employee independent of recording cash disbursements or custody of assets.	Account for a sequence of cheques or payment records.[†] Examine bank reconciliations and observe their preparation.	Reconcile recorded cash disbursements with the cash disbursements on the bank statement (proof of cash disbursements).
Recorded cash disbursement transactions are accurate (accuracy).	Internal verification of calculations and amounts. Monthly preparation of a bank reconciliation by an independent person.	Examine indication of internal verification.[†] Examine bank reconciliations; observe their preparation.	Compare cancelled cheques with the related acquisitions journal and cash disbursements journal entries.[†] Recompute cash discounts.[†] Prepare a proof of cash disbursements.
Cash disbursement transactions are properly classified (classification).	Adequate chart of accounts. Internal verification of classification.	Examine procedures manual and chart of accounts. Examine indication of internal verification.	Compare classification with chart of accounts by reference to vendors' invoices and acquisitions journal.
Cash disbursement transactions are properly included in the vendor master file and properly summarized (posting and summarization).	Internal verification of vendor master file contents. Comparison of vendor master file or trial balance totals with general ledger balance.	Examine indication of internal verification.[†] Examine initials on general ledger accounts indicating comparison.	Test clerical accuracy by footing journals and tracing postings to general ledger and vendor master file.[†]
Cash disbursement transactions are recorded on the correct dates (timing).	Procedures requiring recording of transactions as soon as possible after the cheque has been signed. Transaction date must be system date.	Examine procedures manual; observe whether unrecorded cheques exist. Observe data entry process.	Compare dates on cancelled cheques with the cash disbursements journal. Compare dates on cancelled cheques with the bank cancellation date.

[*] This analytical procedure can also apply to other objectives, including completeness, accuracy, and timing.
[†] This control would be tested on many audits by using the computer.

and acquisitions processes. The comments made about the methodology and process for developing audit procedures for acquisitions apply equally to cash disbursements.

Once the auditor has decided on procedures, the acquisitions and cash disbursements tests are typically performed concurrently. For example, for a transaction

Conversion to New System Hides $5 Million Error

A large pharmaceutical distribution company had been using complex data processing methods for many years. It had custom-programmed accounting systems and used data communications to send and receive orders and other business documents. The accounts payable system was falling behind—it was based on batch processing and not integrated with the purchasing system.

Accordingly, the information systems personnel designed and tested many new programs for updating the accounts payable and purchasing systems. These systems were put in place at the company's year-end date, January 31. Systems were run in parallel (i.e., both the old and new systems were used) for the month of January, with the new system used exclusively effective February 1. The auditors relied on the equivalency of the two systems and on the fact that the company normally had excellent controls in accounts payable and cash disbursements.

However, due to excessive workload, goods received on January 31 were not recorded until February 1 and, therefore, were recorded only in the new system. Thus, accounts payable and purchases were understated by $5 million, resulting in an overstatement of income—a highly significant cut-off error.

This error was detected by the auditors in the following year's audit, resulting in a restatement of the prior financial statements. The client was very understanding but commented, "We knew the financial results last year were too good to be true!"

CRITICAL THINKING QUESTIONS

1. What analytical review procedures could have pointed to the cut-off error?
2. What audit procedures should the auditors have used to identify the error?

---

selected for examination from the acquisitions journal, the vendor's invoice and the receiving report are examined at the same time as the related cancelled cheque or direct deposit payment record.

ATTRIBUTE SAMPLING FOR TESTS OF CONTROLS Because of the importance of tests of controls for acquisitions and cash disbursements, the use of attribute sampling is common in this audit area. The approach is basically the same as for the tests of controls of sales discussed in Chapter 14. It should be noted, however, with particular reference to the most essential transaction-related audit objectives presented earlier, that most of the important attributes in the acquisition and payment cycle have a direct monetary effect on the accounts. Furthermore, many of the types of errors or fraud and other irregularities that may be found represent a misstatement of earnings and are of significant concern to the auditor. For example, there may be inventory cut-off misstatements or an incorrect recording of an expense amount. Because of this, the tolerable exception rate selected by the auditor in tests of many of the attributes in this cycle is relatively low. Since the dollar amounts of individual transactions in the cycle cover a wide range, it is also common to segregate very large and unusual items and to test them on a 100-percent basis.

Audit of System Conversions

Organizations are not static. With time, as an organization grows or shrinks or changes its business objectives, the procedures within an organization also change. Often, when the auditor returns to conduct the audit, he or she identifies minor changes in procedures, causing minor changes in risk assessments, internal control testing, and tests of details.

At other times, the organization has undertaken a major change in its systems by implementing a new computer system or has made major changes to a particular system. For example, a client that previously processed its accounts payable and cash disbursements manually could use a standard accounting software package. A large client could change a batch-processing accounts payable and cash disbursements system to an online processing system, as described in Audit Challenge 18-1.

When an organization changes an entire system or set of systems, there are three issues that the auditor needs to address:

- A new system of internal controls will need to be documented and evaluated.
- The auditor will need to audit the actual data conversion process.
- The auditor will need to determine whether accounting policies have been changed.

NEW SYSTEM OF INTERNAL CONTROLS When new computer programs are put in place, the controls that are part of those programs will change. For example, if the system changes from batch to online, then controls to ensure data-entry accuracy will likely occur as information is entered rather than for a group of transactions. If a system changes from manual to automated, then new controls (such as automatic calculation of invoice extensions) will be present in the programs instead of being completed manually, as done previously. Also, activities done by persons handling these systems may change.

The auditor needs to document the new procedures, evaluate them, and determine their effect on control risk. Should reliance on the programmed controls be tested, the auditor may have the option of using the same audit procedures as in prior years or may need to design new audit procedures, such as the creation of test transactions to determine that programs are functioning as intended. If the client has run its systems in parallel (i.e., run both the old and the new systems for a certain period), then the auditor can evaluate the new system by examining the records kept during this parallel process.

AUDITING THE DATA CONVERSION PROCESS The mere occurrence of an information systems conversion raises the potential for material error, as illustrated by Audit Challenge 18-1. When computer systems are established for the first time, a major task is the creation of master files. For example, purchase orders cannot be processed or accounts payable vendor invoices entered if the vendor information such as name, address, and terms are not established in the vendor master file. Quantities ordered or received cannot be entered if the inventory item, description, and price do not exist in the inventory master file. The number of vendors could be in the hundreds, while the number of inventory items could number in the thousands.

Determining the audit procedures required involves a risk assessment process. Inherent risk may increase because these are new systems in place and employees may not be aware of the actions required. By determining the extent of employee training and the rigour of the implementation process, the auditor can assess whether inherent risk is affected. The rigour of the implementation process also affects control risk. If the implementation process is properly planned, conducted, and supervised, the auditor can rely on these controls. Conversely, if controls over the conversion process are poor or are not documented, the auditor must conduct tests of details. Table 18-4 combines the features of Tables 18-2 and 18-5 (see page 609) to describe audit objectives for the conversion of a batch system to an online system. Table 18-4 shows possible key controls, tests of controls, and tests of details that would be required should controls be absent or not relied upon.

Note that two audit objectives are not included. Classification is not included, since accuracy and agreement between the two systems ensures that classification is satisfied. The same is true for posting and summarization: if individual and total vendor amounts are correct and details from the old system agree with those of the new system, then posting and summarization are also satisfied.

A careful review of Table 18-4 shows that the tests can be simplified to the following three types:

- Tests comparing details from the new system with those of the old system to verify that only accurate, authorized information has been established.
- Tests comparing details from the old system with those of the new system to ensure accuracy and that no transactions have been omitted.

concept check

C18-3 How do high-quality perpetual records affect the auditor's tests of controls of inventory acquisitions?

C18-4 Provide examples of two controls that improve completeness over recording of acquisitions transactions.

C18-5 When conducting a systems conversion audit, why does the auditor need to test the data details between the old and the new master files in both directions, that is, from old to new and from new to old?

Table 18-4	Audit Objectives, Key Controls, Tests of Controls, and Tests of Details for System Conversion of Accounts Payable		
Audit Objective	**Key Internal Control**	**Common Tests of Controls**	**Common Tests of Details**
Only authorized vendors are established with balances for goods and services actually received (existence).	Agree vendor file details for each vendor from the new (online) system with those of the old (batch) system.	Review vendor file listings for evidence of agreement.	On a test basis, agree vendor file details for each vendor from the new (online) system to the old (batch) system.
All vendor balances as of the date of conversion are included (completeness).	Agree aged accounts payable trial balance details from the old (batch) system with those of the new (online) system for each vendor and in total. Agree the total with that of the general ledger.	Review aged accounts payable trial balance listings for evidence of comparison.	On a test basis, agree aged accounts payable trial balance details from the old (batch) system with those of the new (online) system for each vendor and in total. Agree total with that of general ledger.
Details in the new system agree to details from the old system. New information is accurate (accuracy).	Same as for completeness.	Same as for completeness.	Same as for completeness.
Information is recorded in the appropriate system and is not omitted (cut-off).	Procedures exist to ensure appropriate cut-off of transactions (i.e., transactions are recorded only once in the proper system and are not omitted).	Conduct cut-off tests, as described on page 611, for receiving reports and vendor invoices.	Same as for tests of controls.

- Cut-off testing to ensure that transactions are included in only the proper system and have not been omitted.

Thus, a **conversion audit** comprises the audit procedures required when an organization changes its system to a different information system. The emphasis is on the accurate and authorized establishment of new master files and on the cut-off of transactions in the appropriate system.

Conversion audit—the audit procedures required when an organization changes its system to a different information system.

DETERMINING WHETHER ACCOUNTING POLICIES HAVE CHANGED This could be done concurrently with inventory costing. For example, if inventory is counted only at year end (a periodic system), it would be costed on a FIFO (first-in, first-out) basis, whereas most computer systems use average costing or weighted average costing. Should the method of inventory costing change, the auditor would need to gather and include sufficient evidence that there is adequate disclosure in the financial statements for this change in accounting policy.

Substantive Testing of Accounts Payable

Accounts payable are unpaid obligations for goods and services received in the ordinary course of business. It is sometimes difficult to distinguish between accounts payable and accrued liabilities, but it is useful to define a liability as an account payable if the total amount of the obligation is known and owed at the balance sheet date. The accounts payable account then includes obligations for the acquisition of raw materials, equipment, utilities, repairs, and many other types of goods and services that were received before the end of the year. The great majority of accounts payable can also be recognized by the existence of vendors' invoices for the obligation. Accounts payable should also be distinguished from interest-bearing obligations. If an obligation includes the payment of interest, it should be recorded properly as a note payable, contract payable, mortgage payable, or bond payable.

The methodology for designing tests of details for accounts payable is summarized in Figure 18-3. This methodology is the same as that used for accounts receivable in Chapter 15. It is common for accounts payable to be significant, with the potential for material error. Internal controls are often ineffective for accounts payable because many companies depend on the vendors to bill them and remind them of unpaid bills. Tests of details for accounts payable, therefore, often need to be extensive.

INTERNAL CONTROLS The effects of the client's internal controls on accounts payable tests can be illustrated by two examples. In the first, assume that the client has highly effective internal controls over recording and paying for acquisitions. The receipt of goods is promptly documented by prenumbered receiving reports; prenumbered vouchers are promptly and efficiently prepared and recorded in the acquisition transactions file and vendor master file. Cash disbursements are also made promptly when due, and the disbursements are immediately recorded in the cash disbursements transactions file and the vendor master file. On a monthly basis, individual accounts payable balances in the vendor master file are reconciled with vendors' statements, and the total is compared with that in the general ledger by an independent person. Under these circumstances, the verification of accounts payable should require little audit effort once the auditor tests and concludes that internal controls are operating effectively.

In the second example, assume that receiving reports are not used, the client defers recording acquisitions until cash disbursements are made, and because of a

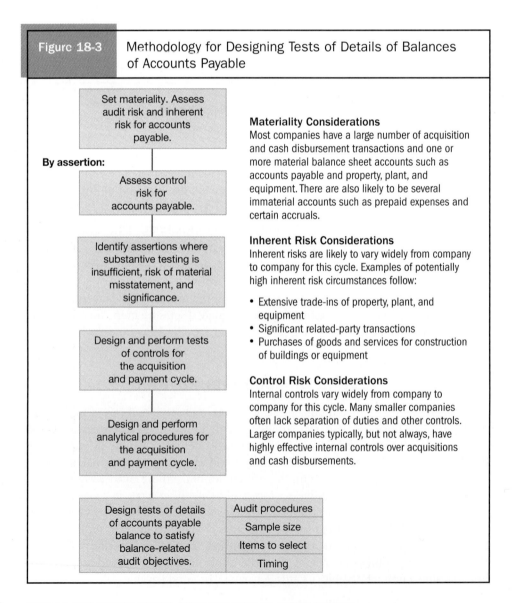

| Figure 18-3 | Methodology for Designing Tests of Details of Balances of Accounts Payable |

By assertion:

Set materiality. Assess audit risk and inherent risk for accounts payable.

Assess control risk for accounts payable.

Identify assertions where substantive testing is insufficient, risk of material misstatement, and significance.

Design and perform tests of controls for the acquisition and payment cycle.

Design and perform analytical procedures for the acquisition and payment cycle.

Design tests of details of accounts payable balance to satisfy balance-related audit objectives.

Audit procedures
Sample size
Items to select
Timing

Materiality Considerations
Most companies have a large number of acquisition and cash disbursement transactions and one or more material balance sheet accounts such as accounts payable and property, plant, and equipment. There are also likely to be several immaterial accounts such as prepaid expenses and certain accruals.

Inherent Risk Considerations
Inherent risks are likely to vary widely from company to company for this cycle. Examples of potentially high inherent risk circumstances follow:

• Extensive trade-ins of property, plant, and equipment
• Significant related-party transactions
• Purchases of goods and services for construction of buildings or equipment

Control Risk Considerations
Internal controls vary widely from company to company for this cycle. Many smaller companies often lack separation of duties and other controls. Larger companies typically, but not always, have highly effective internal controls over acquisitions and cash disbursements.

weak cash position bills are frequently paid several months after their due date. When an auditor faces such a situation, there is a high likelihood of an understatement of accounts payable. Extensive tests of details of accounts payable are necessary to determine whether accounts payable are properly stated at the balance sheet date.

The most important controls over accounts payable have already been discussed as part of the control and recording of acquisitions and cash disbursements. In addition to these controls, it is important to have a monthly reconciliation of vendors' statements with recorded liabilities and of the outstanding transaction file with the vendor master file and the general ledger. This should be done by an independent person or using computer software.

ANALYTICAL PROCEDURES The use of analytical procedures is as important in the acquisition and payment cycle as it is in every other cycle. Table 18-5 illustrates analytical procedures for the balance sheet and income statement accounts in the acquisition and payment cycle that are useful for uncovering areas in which additional investigation is desirable.

One of the most important analytical procedures for uncovering misstatements of accounts payable is comparing current-year expense totals with those of prior years. For example, by comparing current utilities expense with the prior year's, the auditor may determine that the last utilities bill for the year was not recorded. Comparing expenses with prior years' is an effective analytical procedure for accounts payable because expenses from year to year are relatively stable if income is stable. Examples include rent, utilities, and other expenses billed on a regular basis.

BALANCE-RELATED AUDIT OBJECTIVES FOR TESTS OF DETAILS The overall objective in the audit of accounts payable is to determine whether accounts payable are fairly stated and properly disclosed. Seven of the eight balance-related audit objectives discussed in Chapter 5 are applicable to accounts payable. Valuation is not applicable to liabilities.

The difference in emphasis in auditing assets and liabilities results directly from the legal liability of public accountants. If, subsequent to the issuance of the audited financial statements, equity investors, creditors, and other users determine that owners' equity was materially overstated, a lawsuit against the public accounting firm is fairly likely. Since an overstatement of owners' equity can arise either from an overstatement of assets or from an understatement of liabilities, it is natural for public accountants to emphasize those two types of misstatements. This means that when auditing liabilities, the auditor looks primarily for understatements, which usually have the effect of understating liabilities and overstating income.

TESTS OF DETAILS OF ACCOUNTS PAYABLE The same balance-related audit objectives that were used as a frame of reference for verifying accounts receivable in Chapter 15

Table 18-5	Analytical Procedures for Acquisition and Payment Cycle
Analytical Procedure	**Possible Misstatement**
Compare acquisition-related expense account balances with prior years'.	Misstatement of accounts payable and expenses.
Review list of accounts payable for unusual, non-vendor, and interest-bearing payables.	Classification misstatement for non-trade liabilities.
Compare individual accounts payable with previous years'.	Unrecorded or non-existent accounts, or misstatements.
Calculate ratios such as purchases divided by accounts payable, and accounts payable divided by current liabilities.	Unrecorded or non-existent accounts, or misstatements.

are also applicable to liabilities with three minor modifications. The first difference is that the ownership objective does not apply to accounts payable. The second difference relates to the rights and obligations objective. For assets, the auditor is concerned with the client's rights to the use and disposal of assets. For liabilities, the auditor is concerned with the client's obligations for the payment of the liability. If the client has no obligation to pay a liability, it should not be included as a liability. The third difference was discussed above: in auditing liabilities, the emphasis is on the search for understatements rather than for overstatements.

Table 18-6 includes the balance-related audit objectives and common tests of details of balances procedures for accounts payable. The actual audit procedures will vary considerably depending on the nature of the entity, the materiality of accounts payable, the nature and effectiveness of internal controls, and inherent risk.

OUT-OF-PERIOD LIABILITY TESTS Because of the emphasis on understatements in liability accounts, out-of-period liability tests are important for accounts payable. The extent of tests to uncover unrecorded accounts payable, frequently referred to as "the search for unrecorded accounts payable," depends heavily on assessed control risk and the materiality of the potential balance in the account. The same audit procedures used to uncover unrecorded payables are applicable to the accuracy objective. The audit procedures that follow are typical tests.

Table 18-6	Balance-Related Audit Objectives and Tests of Details of Balances for Accounts Payable
Balance-Related Audit Objective	**Common Tests of Details of Balances Procedures**
Accounts payable in the accounts payable list agree with related master file, and the total is correctly added and agrees with that of the general ledger (detail tie-in).	Foot the accounts payable list.* Trace the total to the general ledger. Trace individual vendor's invoices to transaction file for names and amounts.
Accounts payable in the accounts payable list exist (existence).	Trace from accounts payable list to vendors' invoices and statements. Confirm accounts payable, emphasizing large and unusual amounts.
Existing accounts payable are in the accounts payable list (completeness).	Perform out-of-period liability tests (see discussion).
Accounts payable in the accounts payable list are accurate (accuracy).	Perform same procedures as those used for existence objective and out-of-period liability tests.
Accounts payable in the accounts payable list are properly classified (classification).	Review the list and master file for related parties, notes, or other interest-bearing liabilities, long-term payables, and debit balances.
Transactions in the acquisition and payment cycle are recorded in the proper period (cut-off).	Perform out-of-period liability tests (see discussion). Perform detailed tests as a part of physical observation of inventory (see discussion). Test for inventory in transit (see discussion).
The company has an obligation to pay the liabilities included in accounts payable (obligations).	Examine vendors' statements, and confirm accounts payable.
Accounts in the acquisition and payment cycle are properly presented and disclosed (disclosure).	Review financial statements to make sure material related-party, long-term, and interest-bearing liabilities are segregated.

*This test of details would be conducted on many audits by using the computer.

Examine underlying documentation for subsequent cash disbursements The purpose of this audit procedure is to uncover payments made in the subsequent accounting period that represent liabilities at the balance sheet date. The supporting documentation is examined to determine whether a payment was for a current-period obligation. For example, if inventory was received prior to the balance sheet date, it will be so indicated on the receiving report. Frequently, documentation for payments made in the subsequent period are examined for several weeks, especially when the client does not pay its bills on a timely basis. Any payment that is for a current-period obligation should be traced to the accounts payable trial balance to make sure it has been included as a liability.

Examine underlying documentation for bills not paid several weeks after the year end This procedure is carried out in the same manner as the preceding one and serves the same purpose. The only difference is that it is done for unpaid obligations near the end of the examination rather than for obligations that have already been paid. For example, in an audit with a March 31 year end, if the auditor examines the supporting documentation for cheques paid until June 28, bills that are still unpaid at that date should be examined to determine whether they are obligations of the year ended March 31. For large audit engagements or for organizations with good internal controls, the auditor would limit these tests to a sample of transactions or reduce the period of investigation to a shorter period (perhaps two or three weeks).

Trace receiving reports issued before year end to related vendors' invoices All merchandise received before the year end of the accounting period, indicated by the issuance of a receiving report, should be included as accounts payable. By tracing receiving reports issued at and before year end to vendors' invoices and making sure they are included in accounts payable, the auditor is testing for unrecorded obligations.

Trace vendors' statements that show a balance due to the accounts payable trial balance If the client maintains a file of vendors' statements, any statement indicating a balance due can be traced to the listing to make sure it is included as an account payable.

Send confirmations to client's vendors Although the use of confirmations for accounts payable is less common than for accounts receivable, it is common testing for vendors omitted from the accounts payable list, omitted transactions, and misstated account balances. Sending confirmations to active vendors for which a balance has not been included in the accounts payable list is a useful means of searching for omitted amounts. This type of confirmation is commonly referred to as "zero balance confirmation." See Figure 18-4 (page 613) for an example.

CUT-OFF TESTS Cut-off tests for accounts payable are intended to determine whether transactions recorded a few days before and after the balance sheet date are included in the correct period. The five audit procedures discussed in the preceding section are directly related to cut-off for acquisitions, but they emphasize understatements. To test for overstatement cut-off amounts, the auditor should trace receiving reports issued after year end to related invoices to make sure they are not recorded as accounts payable (unless they are inventory in transit, which will be discussed shortly).

Two aspects are enlarged upon here: the examination of receiving reports and the determination of the amount of inventory in transit.

Relationship of cut-off to physical observation of inventory In determining that the accounts payable cut-off is correct, it is essential that the cut-off tests be coordinated with the physical observation of inventory. For example, assume that an inventory acquisition for $40,000 is received late in the afternoon of December 31, after the physical inventory is completed. If the acquisition is included in accounts payable and purchases but excluded from inventory, the result is an understatement of net earnings of $40,000. Conversely, if the acquisition is excluded from both inventory and accounts payable, there is a misstatement in the balance sheet, but the income statement is correct. The only way the auditor will know which type of misstatement has occurred is to coordinate cut-off tests with the observation of inventory.

The cut-off information for purchases should be obtained during the physical observation of the inventory. At this time, the auditor should review the procedures in the receiving department to determine that all inventory received was counted, and the auditor should record in his or her working papers the last inventory receiving report number. During the year-end fieldwork, the auditor should then test the accounting records for cut-off. The auditor should trace receiving report numbers to the accounts payable records to verify that they are correctly included or excluded.

For example, assume that the number of the last receiving report representing inventory included in the physical count was 3167. The auditor should record this document number and subsequently trace it and several preceding numbers to their related vendor's invoice and to the accounts payable list or the accounts payable transaction file to determine that they are all included. Similarly, accounts payable for purchases recorded on receiving reports with numbers larger than 3167 should be excluded from accounts payable.

When the client's physical inventory takes place before the last day of the year, it is still necessary to perform an accounts payable cut-off at the time of the physical count in the manner described in the preceding paragraph. In addition, the auditor must verify whether all acquisitions taking place between the physical count and the end of the year were added to the physical inventory and accounts payable. For example, if the client takes the physical count on December 27 for a December 31 year end, the cut-off information is taken as of December 27. During the year-end examination, the auditor must first test to determine whether the cut-off was accurate as of December 27. After determining that the December 27 cut-off is accurate, the auditor must test whether all inventory received subsequent to the physical count, but before the balance sheet date, was added to inventory and accounts payable by the client.

Inventory in transit The method of shipping can affect the recording of accounts payable. With **FOB** (freight on board) **destination** shipping, title passes to the buyer when it is received for inventory. Therefore, only inventory received prior to the balance sheet date should be included in inventory and accounts payable at year end. When an acquisition is on an **FOB origin** basis, title passes to the buyer when goods are shipped, so the inventory and related accounts payable must be recorded in the current period if shipment occurred before the balance sheet date.

Determining whether inventory has been purchased on an FOB destination or origin basis is done by examining vendors' invoices. The auditor should examine invoices for merchandise received shortly after year end to determine if they were on an FOB origin basis. For those that were and when the shipment dates were prior to the balance sheet date, the inventory and related accounts payable must be recorded in the current period if the amounts are material.

RELIABILITY OF EVIDENCE In determining the appropriate evidence to accumulate for verifying accounts payable, it is essential that the auditor understand the relative reliability of the three primary types of evidence ordinarily used: vendors' invoices, vendors' statements, and confirmations.

Distinction between vendors' invoices and vendors' statements In verifying the amount due to a vendor, the auditor should make a major distinction between vendors' invoices and vendors' statements. In examining vendors' invoices and related supporting documents, such as receiving reports and purchase orders, the auditor gets highly reliable evidence about individual transactions. A vendor's statement is not as desirable as invoices for verifying individual transactions because a statement includes only the total amount of the transaction. The units acquired, price, freight, and other data are not included. However, a statement has the advantage of including the ending balance according to the vendor's records.

FOB destination—shipping contract in which title to the goods passes to the buyer when the goods are received.

FOB origin—shipping contract in which title to the goods passes to the buyer at the time that the goods are shipped.

Which of these two documents is better for verifying the correct balance in accounts payable? The vendor's statement is superior for verifying accounts payable because it includes the ending balance. The auditor could compare existing vendors' invoices with the client's list and still not uncover missing ones, which is the primary concern in accounts payable. Which of these two documents is better for testing acquisitions in tests of control? The vendor's invoice is superior for verifying transactions because the auditor is verifying individual transactions and the invoice shows the details of the acquisitions.

Difference between vendors' statements and confirmations The most important distinction between a vendor's statement and a confirmation of accounts payable is the source of the information. A vendor's statement has been prepared by an independent third party, but it is in the hands of the client at the time the auditor examines it. This provides the client with an opportunity to alter a vendor's statement or to make particular statements unavailable to the auditor. A confirmation of accounts payable, which normally is a request for an itemized statement sent directly to the public accountant's office, provides the same information but can be regarded as more reliable. In addition, confirmations of accounts payable frequently include a request for information about notes and acceptances payable, as well as consigned inventory that is owned by the vendor but stored on the client's premises. An illustration of a typical accounts payable confirmation request is given in Figure 18-4.

The confirmation of accounts payable is less common than confirmation of accounts receivable. If the client has adequate internal controls and vendors' statements are available for examination, then confirmations are normally not sent. However, when the client's internal controls are weak, when statements are not available or when the auditor questions the client's integrity, then it is desirable to send confirmation

Figure 18-4	Accounts Payable Confirmation Request

Roger Mead Ltd.
1600 Westmount Ave. N.
Kenora, Ontario
P9N 1X7

January 15, 2010

Szabo Sales Co. Ltd.
2116 King Street
Kenora, Ontario
P9N 1G3

To Whom It May Concern:

Our auditors, Adams and Lelik, LLP, are conducting an audit of our financial statements. For this purpose, please furnish directly to them, at their address noted below, the following information as of December 31, 2009.

(1) Itemized statements of our accounts payable to you showing all unpaid items
(2) A complete list of any notes and acceptances payable to you (including any which have been discounted) showing the original date, dates due, original amount, unpaid balance, collateral and endorsers
(3) An itemized list of your merchandise consigned to us

Your prompt attention to this request will be appreciated. A stamped, addressed envelope is enclosed for your reply.

Yours truly,

Adams and Lelik, LLP
215 Tecumseh Crescent
Kenora, Ontario
P9N 2K5

Roger Mead Ltd.
per Sally Palm

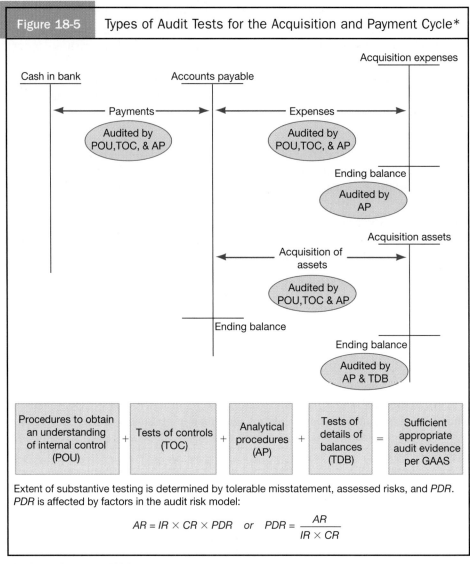

Figure 18-5 Types of Audit Tests for the Acquisition and Payment Cycle*

Extent of substantive testing is determined by tolerable misstatement, assessed risks, and *PDR*. *PDR* is affected by factors in the audit risk model:

$$AR = IR \times CR \times PDR \quad or \quad PDR = \frac{AR}{IR \times CR}$$

*See Figure 18-1 on page 596 for accounts.

requests to vendors. Because of the emphasis on understatements of liability accounts, the accounts confirmed should include large accounts, active accounts, accounts with a zero balance, and a representative sample of all others.

When vendors' statements are examined or confirmations are received, there must be a reconciliation of the statement or confirmation with the accounts payable list. Frequently, differences are caused by inventory in transit, cheques mailed by the client but not received by the vendor at the statement date, and delays in processing the accounting records. The reconciliation is of the same general nature as that discussed in Chapter 15 for accounts receivable. The documents typically used to reconcile the balances on the accounts payable list with the confirmation or vendor's statement include receiving reports, vendors' invoices, and cancelled cheques.

SAMPLE SIZE Sample sizes for accounts payable tests vary considerably depending on such factors as the materiality of accounts payable, number of accounts outstanding, assessed control risk, and results of the prior year. When a client's internal controls are weak, which is not uncommon for accounts payable, almost all population items must be verified. In other situations, minimal testing is needed.

Statistical sampling is less commonly used for the audit of accounts payable than for accounts receivable. It is more difficult to define the population and determine the population size in accounts payable. Since the emphasis is on omitted accounts payable, it is essential that the population include all potential payables.

concept check

C18-6 Why is an organization more likely to have poor internal controls over accounts payable than over accounts receivable?

C18-7 Provide two examples of analytical procedures that could indicate a possible misstatement in accounts payable.

Figure 18-5 illustrates the major accounts in the acquisition and payment cycle and the types of audit tests used to audit these accounts. This figure also shows how the audit risk model discussed in Chapter 7 relates to the audit of the acquisition and payment cycle.

Completing the Tests in the Acquisition and Payment Cycle: Verification of Selected Accounts

Examining Other Accounts: Auditing Manufacturing Asset Acquisitions

An important characteristic of the acquisition and payment cycle is the large number of accounts involved. These include the following:

- Accounts payable
- Accrued professional fees
- Accrued property taxes
- Buildings
- Cash in the bank
- Commercial franchises
- Cost of goods sold
- Goods and Services Tax payable
- Income tax expense
- Income taxes payable
- Insurance expense
- Inventory
- Land
- Leases and leasehold improvements
- Manufacturing equipment
- Organization costs
- Patents, trademarks, and copyrights
- Prepaid insurance
- Prepaid rent
- Prepaid taxes
- Professional fees
- Property taxes
- Rent expense
- Supplies
- Travel expense
- Utilities

The methodology for designing tests of details of balances for the above accounts is the same as that shown in Figure 18-3 for accounts payable. Each account is a part of the acquisition and payment cycle. Therefore, the only change required in the figure is the replacement of accounts payable with the account being audited. For example, if the account being discussed is accrued property taxes, simply substitute accrued property taxes for accounts payable in the first, second, and last boxes in the figure.

The types of audit tests used to audit the above accounts are the same as those shown in Figure 18-5, which also illustrates how the audit risk model discussed in Chapter 7 relates to the audit of these accounts.

Capital assets are assets that have expected lives of more than one year, are used in the business, and are not acquired for resale. The intention to use the assets as a part of the operation of the client's business and their expected life of more than one year are the significant characteristics that distinguish these assets from inventory, prepaid expenses, and investments.

Capital assets can be classified as follows:

- Land and land improvements.
- Buildings and building improvements.
- Manufacturing equipment.
- Furniture and fixtures.
- Autos and trucks.
- Leasehold improvements.
- Construction of property, plant, and equipment in process.

Audit of Manufacturing Equipment

In this section, the audit of manufacturing equipment is discussed as an illustration of an appropriate approach to the audit of all capital asset accounts. When there are significant differences in the verification of other types of capital assets, they are briefly examined.

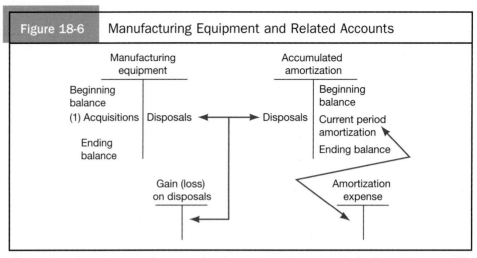

| Figure 18-6 | Manufacturing Equipment and Related Accounts |

(1) Acquisitions of manufacturing equipment arise from the acquisition and payment cycle. See Figure 18-1 on page 596.

OVERVIEW OF THE ACCOUNTS The accounts commonly used for manufacturing equipment are illustrated in Figure 18-6. The relationship of manufacturing equipment to the acquisition and payment cycle is apparent when examining the debits to the asset account. Since the source of debits in the asset account is the acquisitions journal, the accounting system has already been tested for recording the current period's additions to manufacturing equipment as part of the test of the acquisition and payment cycle.

Capital asset master file—a computer file containing records for each piece of equipment and other types of property owned; the primary accounting record for manufacturing equipment and other capital asset accounts.

The primary accounting record for manufacturing equipment and other capital asset accounts is generally a property or **capital asset master file** with supporting purchase, disposal, and amortization[1] transactions. The contents of the data files must be understood for a meaningful study of the audit of manufacturing equipment. The files will be composed of a set of records, one for each piece of equipment and other types of property owned. In turn, each record will include descriptive information, date of acquisition, original cost, current-year amortization, and accumulated amortization for the property. The totals of detailed transactions for each property item will equal the total in the master file for that piece of property, and the total of the master file for all items of property will equal the general ledger balances for the related accounts.

The files will also contain information about property acquired and disposed of during the year. Proceeds, gains, and losses will be included for disposals.

AUDITING MANUFACTURING EQUIPMENT Manufacturing equipment is normally audited differently from current asset accounts for three reasons: (1) there are usually fewer current-period acquisitions of manufacturing equipment, (2) the amount of any given acquisition is often material, and (3) the equipment is likely to be kept and maintained in the accounting records for several years. Because of these differences, the emphasis in auditing manufacturing equipment is on the verification of current-period acquisitions rather than on the balance in the account carried forward from the preceding year. In addition, the expected life of assets over one year requires amortization and accumulated amortization accounts, which are verified as part of the audit of the assets. Additions should be traced to the capital cost allowance section of the tax working papers.

---

[1] The term "amortization" is used in *CICA Handbook* Section 3061, Property, Plant and Equipment, to describe the process of charging the cost of a capital asset to expense over its useful life. However, many organizations and accountants refer to the process as "depreciation," especially when using the term in connection with property, plant, and equipment. This text will use the term "amortization."

Table 18-7	Analytical Procedures for Manufacturing Equipment
Analytical Procedure	**Possible Misstatement**
Compare amortization expense divided by gross manufacturing equipment cost with previous years'.	Misstatement in amortization expense and accumulated amortization.
Compare accumulated amortization divided by gross manufacturing equipment cost with previous years'.	Misstatement in accumulated amortization.
Compare monthly or annual repairs and maintenance, supplies expense, small tools expense, and similar accounts with previous years'.	Expensing amounts that should be capital items.
Compare gross manufacturing cost divided by some measure of production with previous years'.	Idle equipment or equipment that has been disposed of but not written off.

Although the approach to verifying manufacturing equipment is different from that used for current assets, several other accounts are verified in a similar way. These include patents, copyrights, catalogue costs, and all capital asset accounts.

In the audit of manufacturing equipment, it is helpful to separate the tests into the following categories:

- Analytical procedures.
- Verification of current-year acquisitions.
- Verification of current-year disposals.
- Verification of the ending balance in the asset account.
- Verification of amortization expense.
- Verification of the ending balance in accumulated amortization.

ANALYTICAL PROCEDURES As in all audit areas, the nature of the analytical procedures depends on the nature of the client's operations. Table 18-7 illustrates the type of ratio and trend analysis frequently performed for manufacturing equipment.

VERIFICATION OF CURRENT-YEAR ACQUISITIONS The proper recording of current-year additions is important because of the long-term effect the assets have on the financial statements. The failure to capitalize a capital asset or the recording of an acquisition at the improper amount, affects the balance sheet until the firm disposes of the asset. The income statement is affected until the asset is fully amortized.

The balance-related audit objectives and common audit tests are shown in Table 18-8 on the next page. As in all other audit areas, the actual audit tests and sample size depend heavily on materiality, assessed risks, and the results of prior-year tests. Materiality is of special importance for verifying current-year additions. They vary from immaterial amounts in some years to a large number of significant acquisitions in others. Accuracy and classification are usually the major objectives for this part of the audit.

The starting point for the verification of current-year acquisitions is normally a schedule obtained from the client of all acquisitions recorded in the general ledger during the year. A typical schedule lists each addition separately and includes the date of the acquisition, vendor, description, notation whether new or used, life of the asset for amortization purposes, amortization method, cost, and any relevant income tax information such as capital cost allowance rates and the investment tax credit if applicable. The client obtains this information from the capital asset master file.

In studying Table 18-8, one should recognize the importance of examining vendors' invoices and related documents in verifying acquisitions of manufacturing equipment. This subject is discussed in the next section.

EXAMINATION OF SUPPORTING DOCUMENTATION The most common audit test to verify additions is examination of vendors' invoices and receiving reports. Additional

Table 18-8   Balance-Related Audit Objectives and Tests of Details of Balances for Manufacturing Equipment Additions

Balance-Related Audit Objective	Common Tests of Details of Balances Procedures	Comments
Current-year acquisitions in the acquisitions schedule agree with related data file amounts, and the total agrees with that of the the general ledger (detail tie-in).	Foot the acquisitions schedule. Trace the total to the general ledger. Trace the individual acquisitions to the data files for amounts and descriptions.	These tests should be limited unless controls are weak. All increases in the general ledger balance for the year should reconcile to the schedule.
Current-year acquisitions as listed exist (existence).	Examine vendors' invoices and receiving reports. Physically examine assets.	It is uncommon to physically examine additions unless controls are weak or amounts are material.
Existing acquisitions are recorded (completeness).	Examine vendors' invoices of closely related accounts such as repairs and maintenance to uncover items that should be manufacturing equipment. Review lease and rental agreements.	This objective is one of the most important ones for manufacturing equipment.
Current-year acquisitions as listed are owned (ownership).	Examine vendors' invoices.	Ordinarily no problem exists for equipment. Property deeds, abstracts, and tax bills are frequently examined for land or major buildings.
Current-year acquisitions as listed are accurate (accuracy).	Examine vendors' invoices.	Extent depends on inherent risk and effectiveness of internal controls.
Current-year acquisitions as listed are properly classified (classification).	Examine vendors' invoices in manufacturing equipment account to uncover items that should be classified as office equipment, part of the buildings, or repairs. Examine vendors' invoices of closely related accounts such as repairs to uncover items that should be manufacturing equipment. Examine rent and lease expense for capitalizable leases.	The objective is closely related to tests for completeness. It is done in conjunction with that objective and tests for accuracy.
Current-year acquisitions are recorded in the proper period (cut-off).	Review transactions near the balance sheet date for proper period.	Usually done as a part of accounts payable cut-off tests.
The client has rights to current-year acquisitions (rights).	Examine vendors' invoices.	Ordinarily no problem exists for equipment. Property deeds and tax bills are frequently examined for land or major buildings.

testing besides that which is done as a part of the tests of controls is frequently considered necessary to verify the current-period additions because of the complexity of many equipment transactions and the materiality of the amounts. It is ordinarily unnecessary to examine supporting documentation for each addition, but it is normal to verify large and unusual transactions for the entire year as well as a representative sample of typical additions. The extent of the verification depends on the auditor's assessed control risk for acquisitions and the materiality of the additions.

Tests for acquisitions are accomplished by comparing the charges on vendors' invoices with recorded amounts. The auditor must be aware of the client's capitalization policies to determine whether acquisitions are valued in accordance with generally accepted accounting principles and are treated consistently with those of the preceding year. For example, many clients automatically expense items that are less than a certain amount, such as $100. The auditor should be alert for the possibility of material transportation and installation costs, as well as the trade-in of existing equipment.

The auditor should ensure that government grants for fixed assets are properly accounted for. Also, recording of fixed asset costs should be accurate, including exchange, installation costs, and shipping.

In conjunction with testing current-period additions for existence and valuation, the auditor should review recorded transactions for proper classification. In some cases, amounts recorded as manufacturing equipment should be classified as office equipment or as a part of the building. There is also the possibility that the client has improperly capitalized repairs, rents, or similar expenses.

The inclusion of transactions that should properly be recorded as assets in repairs and maintenance expense, lease expense, supplies, small tools, and similar accounts is a common client error. The error results from lack of understanding of generally accepted accounting principles and some clients' desire to avoid income taxes. The likelihood of these types of misclassifications should be evaluated as part of the auditor's risk assessment and when obtaining an understanding of internal controls in the acquisition and payment cycle. If the auditor concludes that material misstatements are likely, it may be necessary to vouch the larger amounts debited to the expense accounts. It is a common practice to do this as a regular part of the audit of the capital asset accounts.

VERIFICATION OF CURRENT-YEAR DISPOSALS

Internal controls The most important internal control over the disposal of manufacturing equipment is the existence of a formal method to inform management of the sale, trade-in, abandonment, or theft of recorded machinery and equipment. If the client fails to record disposals, the original cost of the manufacturing equipment account will be overstated indefinitely, and the net book value will be overstated until the asset is fully amortized. Another important control to protect assets from unauthorized disposal is the requirement of authorization for the sale or other disposal of manufacturing equipment. Finally, there should be adequate internal verification of recorded disposals to make sure assets are correctly removed from the accounting records.

Audit tests The two major objectives in the verification of the sale, trade-in, or abandonment of manufacturing equipment are that existing disposals are recorded and that recorded disposals are accurately valued.

The starting point for verifying disposals is the client's schedule of recorded disposals or an extract of disposals from the fixed asset data files. The schedule typically includes the date at which the asset was disposed of, the name of the person or firm acquiring the asset, the selling price, the original cost of the asset, the acquisition date, the accumulated amortization of the asset, and the capital cost allowance recapture, if any. Mechanical accuracy tests of the schedule are necessary, including footing the schedule, tracing the totals on the schedule to the recorded disposals, and tracing the cost and accumulated amortization of the disposals to the fixed asset master file. The proceeds from disposal should be traced to the capital cost section of the tax working papers.

Because the failure to record disposals of manufacturing equipment no longer used in the business can significantly affect the financial statements, the search for unrecorded disposals is essential. The nature and adequacy of the controls over disposals affect the extent of the search. The following procedures are frequently used for verifying disposals:

- Review whether newly acquired assets replace existing assets.
- Analyze gains on the disposal of assets and miscellaneous income for receipts from the disposal of assets.
- Review plant modifications and changes in product line, taxes, or insurance coverage for indications of deletions of equipment.
- Make inquiries of management and production personnel about the possibility of the disposal of assets.

When an asset is sold or disposed of without having been traded in for a replacement asset, the valuation of the transaction can be verified by examining the related sales invoice and fixed asset master file. The auditor should compare the cost and accumulated amortization in the master file with the recorded entry in the general journal and recompute the gain or loss on the disposal of the asset for comparison with the accounting records.

Two areas deserve special attention in the valuation objective. The first is the trade-in of an asset for a replacement. When trade-ins occur, the auditor should ensure that the new asset is properly capitalized and that the replaced asset is properly eliminated from the records, considering the book value of the asset traded in and the additional cost of the new asset. The second area of special concern is the disposal of assets affected by capital cost allowance recapture. Since the recapture affects the current year's income tax expense and liability, the auditor must evaluate its significance. While discussion of the tax implications is beyond the scope of this text, the auditor should ensure that the proceeds on disposal are properly recorded in the tax working papers.

VERIFICATION OF ASSET BALANCE

Internal controls The nature of the internal controls over existing assets determines whether it is necessary to verify manufacturing equipment acquired in prior years. Important controls include the use of a master file for individual capital assets, adequate physical controls over assets that are easily movable (e.g., tools, vehicles), assignment of identification numbers to each plant asset, and periodic physical count of capital assets and their reconciliation by accounting personnel. A formal method of informing the accounting department of all disposals of permanent assets is also an important control over the balance of assets carried forward into the current year.

Audit tests Usually, the auditor does not obtain a list from the client of all assets included in the ending balance of manufacturing equipment. Instead, audit tests are determined on the basis of the master file.

Typically, the first audit step concerns the detail tie-in objective: Manufacturing equipment as listed in the master file agrees with the general ledger. Examining a printout of the master file that totals to the general ledger balance is ordinarily sufficient. The auditor may choose to test foot a few pages or use generalized audit software to reconcile balances in the data files.

After assessing control risk for the existence objective, the auditor must decide whether it is necessary to verify the existence of individual items of manufacturing equipment included in the master file. If the auditor believes there is a high risk of significant disposed capital assets that are still recorded in the accounting records, an appropriate procedure is selecting a sample from the master file and examining the actual assets. In rare cases, the auditor may believe that it is necessary that the client take a complete physical inventory of capital assets to make sure they actually exist. If a physical inventory is taken, the auditor normally observes the count.

Ordinarily, it is unnecessary to test the valuation of capital assets recorded in prior periods because presumably they were verified in previous audits at the time they were acquired. However, the auditor should be aware that companies might occasionally have on hand manufacturing equipment that is no longer used in operations. If the amounts are material, the auditor should evaluate whether they should be written down to net realizable value or at least be disclosed separately as "non-operating equipment."

A major consideration in verifying the ending balance in capital assets is the possibility of existing legal encumbrances (presentation and disclosure objectives). A number of methods are available to determine if manufacturing equipment is encumbered. These include reading the terms of loan and credit agreements and mailing loan confirmation requests to banks and other lending institutions. Information with respect to encumbered assets may also be obtained through discussions with the client or confirmations with company lawyers. In Ontario, the auditor may obtain information from the Department of Corporate and Consumer Affairs, for a small fee, about the existence of encumbrances under the Personal Property Security Act. Other provinces have similar procedures for checking on liens and encumbrances.

The proper presentation and disclosure of manufacturing equipment in the financial statements must be carefully evaluated to ensure that generally accepted accounting principles are followed. Manufacturing equipment should include the gross cost and should ordinarily be separated from other permanent assets. Leased property should also be disclosed separately, and all liens on property must be included in the footnotes.

VERIFICATION OF AMORTIZATION EXPENSE Amortization expense is one of the few expense accounts that is not verified as a part of tests of controls. The recorded amounts are determined by internal **allocations** to particular expense accounts rather than by exchange transactions with outside parties. When amortization expense is material, more tests of details of amortization expense are required than for an account that has already been verified through tests of controls.

Allocation—the division of certain expenses, such as amortization and manufacturing overhead, among several expense accounts.

The most important objectives for amortization expense are proper valuation and accuracy. These involve determining whether the client is following a consistent amortization policy from period to period and whether the client's calculations are accurate. In determining the former, there are four considerations: the useful life of current-period acquisitions, the method of amortization, the estimated salvage value, and the policy of amortizing assets in the year of acquisition and disposition. The client's policies can be determined by having discussions with the client and comparing the responses with the information in the auditor's permanent files.

In deciding on the reasonableness of the useful lives assigned to newly acquired assets, the auditor must consider a number of factors: the actual physical life of the asset, the expected useful life (taking into account obsolescence and the company's normal policy of upgrading equipment), and established company policies on trading-in equipment. Occasionally, changing circumstances may necessitate a re-evaluation of the useful life of an asset. When this occurs, a change in accounting estimate rather than a change in accounting principle is involved. The effect of this on amortization must be carefully evaluated. The auditor needs to consider management bias toward higher or lower income and the overall risk of material misstatement when examining such accounting policies.

A useful method of testing amortization is to make a calculation of its overall reasonableness. The calculation is made by multiplying the unamortized capital assets by the amortization rate for the year. In making these calculations, the auditor must make adjustments for current-year additions and disposals, assets with different lengths of life, and assets with different methods of amortization. The calculations can be made fairly easily if the public accounting firm includes in the permanent file a breakdown of the capital assets by method of amortization and length of life. If the overall calculations are reasonably close to the client's totals and if assessed control risk for amortization expense is low, tests of details for amortization can be minimized.

In many audits, it is also desirable to check the mechanical accuracy of amortization calculations. This is done by recomputing amortization expense for selected assets to determine whether the client is following a proper and consistent amortization policy. To be relevant, the detailed calculations should be tied into the total amortization calculations by footing the amortization expense on the property master file and reconciling the total with the general ledger.

VERIFICATION OF ACCUMULATED AMORTIZATION The debits to accumulated amortization are normally tested as a part of the audit of disposals of assets, whereas the credits are verified as a part of amortization expense. If the auditor traces selected transactions to the accumulated amortization records in the property master file as a part of these tests, little additional testing should be required.

Two objectives are usually emphasized in the audit of accumulated amortization:

- Accumulated amortization as stated in the asset master file agrees with the general ledger. This objective can be satisfied by test footing the accumulated amortization on the asset master file and tracing the total to the general ledger.
- Accumulated amortization in the master file is properly valued.

In some cases, the life of manufacturing equipment may be significantly reduced because of such changes as reductions in customer demands for products, unexpected physical deterioration, or a modification in operations. Because of these possibilities and if the decline in asset value is permanent, it may be appropriate to write the asset down to net realizable value.

Prepaid Assets and Intangibles

AUDIT OF PREPAID EXPENSES, DEFERRED CHARGES, AND INTANGIBLES Prepaid expenses, deferred charges, and intangibles are assets that vary in life from several months to several years. Their inclusion as assets results more from the concept of matching expenses with revenues than from their resale or liquidation value. The following are examples:

- Prepaid rent
- Organization costs
- Prepaid taxes
- Patents

- Prepaid insurance
- Trademarks
- Deferred charges
- Copyrights

There is a major difference in audit approach between tangible assets and intangible assets. Intangible assets include goodwill, copyrights and trademarks, deferred expenses (such as research and development) and may even include capitalized charges for brand names that have a good reputation in the market. Such assets can be extremely difficult to value, as they do not have a ready market, and could plummet in value overnight. For example, the value of a trade name could drop if there are production problems with the brand, or if the brand is targeted in a terrorist activity. The auditor needs to ensure that there is an audit staff member on the team who is expert in dealing with such intangible assets so that management's assessment of the value of the asset and of any amortization can be fairly judged. Independent expert valuation may also be required.

In this section, the audit of prepaid insurance is discussed as an account representative of this group because (1) it is found in most audits—virtually every company has some type of insurance; (2) it is typical of the problems frequently encountered in the audit of this class of accounts; and (3) the auditor's responsibility for the review of insurance coverage is an additional consideration not encountered in the other accounts in this category.

Overview of prepaid insurance The accounts typically used for prepaid insurance are illustrated in Figure 18-7. The relationship between prepaid insurance and the acquisition and payment cycle is apparent in examining the debits to the asset account. Since the source of the debits in the asset account is the purchase journal, the payments of insurance premiums have already been partially tested by means of the acquisition and cash disbursement transactions.

Internal controls The internal controls for prepaid insurance and insurance expense can be divided into three categories: controls over the acquisition and recording of insurance, controls over insurance coverage, and controls over the charge-off of insurance expense.

Controls over the acquisition and recording of insurance are a part of the acquisition and payment cycle. These should include proper authorization for new insurance policies and payment of insurance premiums consistent with the procedures discussed in that cycle.

A record of insurance policies in force and the due date of each policy (**insurance register** or spreadsheet) is an essential control to make sure the company has adequate insurance at all times. The control should include a provision for periodic review of the adequacy of the insurance coverage by an independent qualified person.

Insurance register—a record of insurance policies in force and the due date of each policy.

The detailed records of the information in the prepaid insurance register should be verified by someone independent of the person preparing them. A closely related control is the use of monthly "standard journal entries" for insurance expense. If a significant entry is required to adjust the balance in prepaid insurance at the end of the year, it indicates a potential misstatement in the recording of insurance expense throughout the year or in the calculation of the year-end balance in prepaid insurance.

Audit tests Throughout the audit of prepaid insurance and insurance expense, the auditor should keep in mind that the amount in insurance expense is a residual based on the beginning balance in prepaid insurance, the payment of premiums during the year, and the ending balance. The only verifications of the balance in the expense account that are ordinarily necessary are analytical procedures and a brief test to be sure that the charges to insurance expense arose from credits to prepaid insurance.

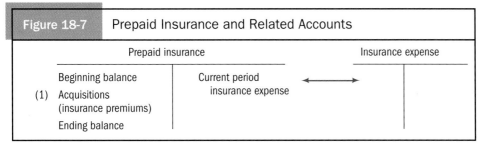

Figure 18-7	Prepaid Insurance and Related Accounts

Prepaid insurance		Insurance expense	
Beginning balance	Current period insurance expense		
(1) Acquisitions (insurance premiums)			
Ending balance			

(1) Acquisitions of insurance premiums arise from the acquisition and payment cycle. This can be observed by examining Figure 18-1 on page 596.

Since the payments of premiums are tested as part of the tests of controls and analytical procedures, the emphasis in the tests of details of balances is on prepaid insurance and on examining the adequacy of insurance coverage.

In the audit of prepaid insurance, a schedule is obtained from the client or prepared by the auditor that includes each insurance policy in force, policy number, insurance coverage for each policy, premium amount, premium period, insurance expense for the year, and prepaid insurance at the end of the year. An example of a schedule obtained from the client for the auditor's working papers is given in Figure 18-8. The auditor's tests of prepaid insurance are normally indicated on the schedule.

ANALYTICAL PROCEDURES A major consideration in the audit of prepaid insurance is the frequent immateriality of the beginning and ending balances. Furthermore, few transactions are debited and credited to the balance during the year, most of which are small and simple to understand. Therefore, the auditor may not conduct detailed audit steps but simply rely upon analytical review. Analytical procedures are important as a means of identifying potentially significant misstatements.

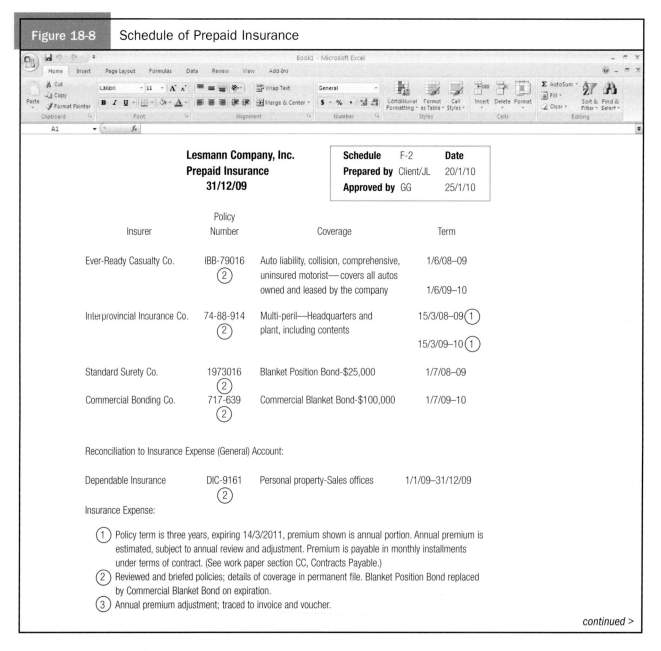

Figure 18-8   Schedule of Prepaid Insurance

continued >

The following are commonly performed analytical procedures of prepaid insurance and insurance expense:

- Compare total prepaid insurance and insurance expense with those of previous years as a test of reasonableness.
- Compute the ratio of prepaid insurance to insurance expense, and compare it with those of previous years.
- Compare the individual insurance policy coverage on the schedule obtained from the client with the preceding year's schedule as a test of the elimination of certain policies or a change in insurance coverage.
- Compare the computed prepaid insurance balance for the current year on a policy-by-policy basis with that of the preceding year as a test of an error in calculation.
- Review the insurance coverage listed on the prepaid insurance schedule with an appropriate client official or insurance broker for adequacy of coverage. The auditor cannot be an expert on insurance matters, but his or her understanding of accounting and the valuation of assets is important in making certain a company is not underinsured.

Figure 18-8   Schedule of Prepaid Insurance (*Continued*)

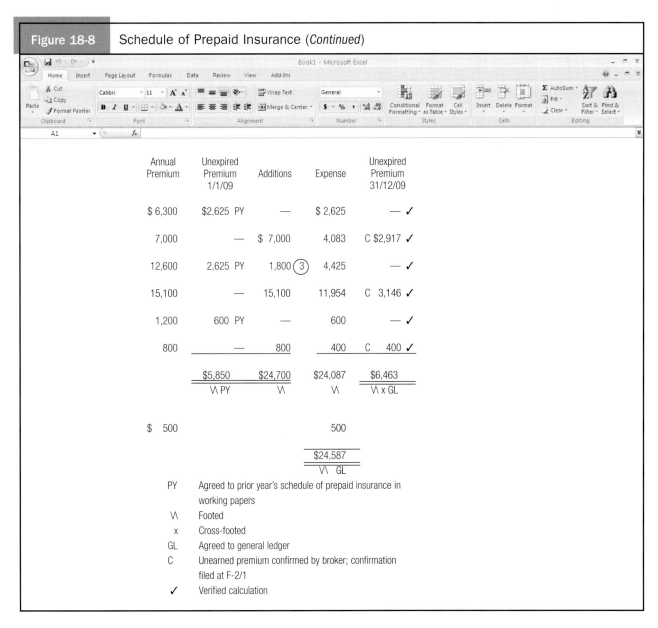

Annual Premium	Unexpired Premium 1/1/09	Additions	Expense	Unexpired Premium 31/12/09
$ 6,300	$2,625 PY	—	$ 2,625	— ✓
7,000	—	$ 7,000	4,083	C $2,917 ✓
12,600	2,625 PY	1,800 ③	4,425	— ✓
15,100	—	15,100	11,954	C 3,146 ✓
1,200	600 PY	—	600	— ✓
800	—	800	400	C 400 ✓
	$5,850	$24,700	$24,087	$6,463
	Ⅵ PY	Ⅵ	Ⅵ	Ⅵ x GL
$ 500			500	
			$24,587	
			Ⅵ GL	

PY   Agreed to prior year's schedule of prepaid insurance in working papers

Ⅵ   Footed

x   Cross-footed

GL   Agreed to general ledger

C   Unearned premium confirmed by broker; confirmation filed at F-2/1

✓   Verified calculation

For many audits, no additional tests need be performed beyond the review for overall reasonableness unless the tests indicate a high likelihood of a significant misstatement or assessed control risk is high. The discussion of these high-risk tests is organized around the balance-related audit objectives for performing tests of details of asset balances. Valuation is not applicable.

INSURANCE POLICIES IN THE PREPAID SCHEDULE ARE VALID, AND ALL EXISTING POLICIES ARE LISTED (EXISTENCE AND COMPLETENESS) The verification of existence and tests for omissions of the insurance policies in force can be tested in one of two ways: by referring to supporting documentation or by obtaining a confirmation of insurance information from the company's insurance agent. The first approach entails examining insurance invoices and policies in force. If these tests are performed, they should be done on a limited test basis. Sending a confirmation to the client's insurance agent is preferable because it is usually less time-consuming than vouching tests, and it provides 100-percent verification.

THE CLIENT HAS RIGHTS TO ALL INSURANCE POLICIES IN THE PREPAID SCHEDULE (RIGHTS) The party who will receive the benefit if an insurance claim is filed has the rights. Ordinarily, the recipient named in the policy is the client, but when there are mortgages or other liens, the insurance claim may be payable to a creditor. The review of insurance policies for claimants other than the client is an excellent test of unrecorded liabilities and pledged assets.

PREPAID AMOUNTS ON THE SCHEDULE ARE ACCURATE, AND THE TOTAL IS CORRECTLY ADDED AND AGREES WITH THE GENERAL LEDGER (ACCURACY AND DETAIL TIE-IN) The accuracy of prepaid insurance involves verifying the total amount of the insurance premium, the length of the policy period, and the allocation of the premium to unexpired insurance. The amount of the premium for a given policy and its period can be verified simultaneously by examining the premium invoice or the confirmation from an insurance agent. Once these two have been verified, the client's calculations of unexpired insurance can be tested by recalculation. The schedule of prepaid insurance can then be footed and the totals traced to the general ledger to complete the detail tie-in tests.

THE INSURANCE EXPENSE RELATED TO PREPAID INSURANCE IS PROPERLY CLASSIFIED (CLASSIFICATION) The proper classification of debits to different insurance expense accounts should be reviewed as a test of the income statement. In some cases, the appropriate expense account is obvious because of the type of insurance (e.g., insurance on a piece of equipment), but in other cases, allocations are necessary. For example, fire insurance on the building may require allocation to several accounts, including manufacturing overhead. Consistency with previous years is the major consideration in evaluating classification.

INSURANCE TRANSACTIONS ARE RECORDED IN THE PROPER PERIOD (CUT-OFF) Cut-off for insurance expense is normally not a significant problem because of the small number of policies and the immateriality of the amount. If the cut-off is checked, it is reviewed as part of accounts payable cut-off tests.

PREPAID INSURANCE IS PROPERLY DISCLOSED (PRESENTATION AND DISCLOSURE) In most audits, prepaid insurance is combined with other prepaid expenses and included as a current asset. The amount is usually small and not a significant consideration to statement users.

Audit of Accrued Liabilities

Accrued liabilities are estimated unpaid obligations for services or benefits that have been received prior to the balance sheet date. Many accrued liabilities represent future obligations for unpaid services resulting from the passage of time but are not payable at the balance sheet date. For example, the benefits of property rental accrue

Accrued liabilities—estimated unpaid obligations for services or benefits that have been received prior to the balance sheet date; include accrued commissions, accrued income taxes, accrued payroll, and accrued rent.

throughout the year; therefore, at the balance sheet date, a certain portion of the total rent cost that has not been paid should be accrued. If the balance sheet date and the date of the termination of the rent agreement are the same, any unpaid rent is more appropriately called "rent payable" than an "accrued liability."

A second type of accrual is one in which the amount of the obligation must be estimated due to the uncertainty of the amount due. An illustration is accrued warranty costs with respect to a new or modified product: the company would have difficulty estimating the warranty expense, since experience with established products would be of only very limited assistance. The following are common accrued liabilities, including payroll-related accruals, discussed as a part of Chapter 17:

- Accrued officers' bonuses
- Accrued commissions
- Accrued income taxes
- Accrued interest
- Accrued payroll

- Accrued payroll taxes
- Accrued pension costs
- Accrued professional fees
- Accrued rent
- Accrued warranty costs

The verification of accrued expenses varies depending on the nature of the accrual and the circumstances of the client. For most audits, accruals take little audit time, but in some instances accounts such as accrued income taxes, warranty costs, and pension costs are material and require considerable audit effort. To illustrate, we discuss the audit of accrued property taxes.

Auditing Accrued Property Taxes The accounts typically used by companies for accrued property taxes are illustrated in Figure 18-9. The relationship between accrued property taxes and the acquisition and payment cycle is the same as for prepaid insurance and is apparent from examining the debits (payments) to the liability account. Since the source of the payments is the cash disbursement journal, the payments of property taxes have already been partially tested by means of the tests of the acquisition and payment cycle.

The balance in property tax expense is a residual amount that results from the beginning and ending balances in accrued property taxes and the payments of property taxes. Therefore, the emphasis in the tests should be on the ending property tax liability and payments. In verifying accrued property taxes, all eight balance-related audit objectives except realizable value are relevant, but two are of special significance:

1. Existing properties for which accrual of taxes is appropriate are on the accrual schedule. The failure to include properties for which taxes should be accrued would understate the liability (completeness). A material misstatement could occur, for example, if taxes on property were not paid before the balance sheet date and were not included as accrued property taxes.
2. Accrued property taxes are accurately recorded. The greatest concern in accuracy is the consistent treatment of the accrual from year to year (accuracy).

The primary methods of testing for the inclusion of all accruals are (1) to perform the accrual tests in conjunction with the audit of current-year property tax payments

Figure 18-9   Accrued Property Taxes and Related Accounts

Accrued Property Taxes		Property Tax Expense
(1) Payments (property taxes)	Beginning balance	
	Current period property tax expense	
	Ending balance	

(1) Payments of property taxes arise from the acquisition and payment cycle. This can be observed by examining Figure 18-1 on page 596.

and (2) to compare the accruals with those of previous years. In most audits, there are few property tax payments, but each payment is often material, and therefore it is common to verify each one.

First, the auditor should obtain a schedule of property tax payments from the client and compare each payment with the preceding year's schedule to determine whether all payments have been included in the client-prepared schedule. It is also necessary to examine the permanent asset working papers for major additions and disposals of assets that may affect the property taxes accrual. If the client is expanding its operations, all property affected by local property tax regulations should be included in the schedule even if the first tax payment has not yet been made.

After the auditor is satisfied that all taxable property has been included in the client-prepared schedule, it is necessary to evaluate the reasonableness of the total amount of property taxes on each property being used as a basis to estimate the accrual. In some instances, the total amount has already been set by the taxing authority, and it is possible to verify the total by comparing the amount on the schedule with the tax bill in the client's possession. In other instances, the preceding year's total payments must be adjusted for the expected increase in property tax rates.

The auditor can verify the accrued property tax by recomputing the portion of the total tax applicable to the current year for each piece of property. In making this calculation, it is essential to use the same portion of each tax payment as the accrual that was used in the preceding year unless justifiable conditions exist for a change. After the accrual and property tax expense for each piece of property have been recomputed, the totals should be added and compared with the general ledger. In many cases, property taxes are charged to more than one expense account. When this happens, the auditor should test for proper classification by evaluating whether the proper amount was charged to each account.

Audit of Operations

The audit of operations is meant to determine whether the income and expense accounts in the financial statements are fairly presented in accordance with generally accepted accounting principles. The auditor must be satisfied that each of the income and expense totals included in the income statement as well as net earnings are not materially misstated.

In conducting audit tests of the financial statements, the auditor must always be aware of the importance of the income statement to users of the statements. Many users rely more heavily on the income statement than on the balance sheet for making decisions. Equity investors, long-term creditors, union representatives, and frequently even short-term creditors are more interested in the ability of a firm to generate profit than in the liquidity value or book value of the individual assets.

Considering the purposes of the statement of earnings, the following two concepts are essential in the audit of operations:

1. The matching of periodic expense to periodic income is necessary for a proper determination of operating results.
2. The consistent application of accounting principles for different periods is necessary for comparability.

These concepts must be applied to the recording of individual transactions and to the combining of accounts in the general ledger for statement presentation.

APPROACH TO AUDITING OPERATIONS The audit of operations is an integrated part of the total audit process. Initial risk assessment by cycle will help the auditor target those accounts that have a high risk of material misstatement. A misstatement of an income statement account will most often equally affect a balance sheet account, and vice versa. The audit of operations is so intertwined with the other parts of the audit that it is necessary to interrelate different aspects of testing operations with the different types of tests previously discussed. A brief description of these tests serves as a review of material covered in other chapters; but, more important, it shows the interrelationship of different parts of the audit with operations testing. The parts of the audit directly affecting the audit of operations are as follows:

- Analytical procedures.
- Tests of controls.
- Analysis of account balances.
- Tests of details of balance sheet accounts.
- Tests of allocations.

This section emphasizes the operations accounts directly related to the acquisition and payment cycle, but the same basic concepts apply to the operations accounts in all other cycles.

ANALYTICAL PROCEDURES Analytical procedures were first discussed in Chapter 6 as a general concept and have been referred to in subsequent chapters as part of particular audit areas.

Analytical procedures should be considered part of the test of the fairness of the presentation of both balance sheet and income statement accounts. A few analytical procedures and their effect on audit of operations in the acquisition and payment cycle are shown in Table 18-9.

TESTS OF CONTROLS Tests of controls have the effect of simultaneously verifying balance sheet and operations accounts. For example, when an auditor concludes that internal controls provide reasonable assurance that transactions in the acquisitions journal exist and are accurately recorded, correctly classified, and recorded in a timely manner, then evidence exists as to the correctness of individual balance sheet accounts (e.g., accounts payable and capital assets) and income statement accounts (e.g., advertising and repairs). Conversely, inadequate controls and misstatements discovered through tests of controls are an indication of the likelihood of misstatements in both the income statement and the balance sheet.

Understanding internal control and the related tests of controls to determine the appropriate assessed control risk is the most important means of verifying many of the operations accounts in each of the transaction cycles. For example, if the auditor concludes after adequate tests that assessed control risk can be reduced to low, the only

Table 18-9	Typical Analytical Procedures for Operations
Analytical Procedure	**Possible Misstatement**
Compare individual expenses with previous years'.	Overstatement or understatement of a balance in an expense account.
Compare individual asset and liability balances with previous years'.	Overstatement or understatement of a balance sheet account that would also affect an income statement account (i.e., a misstatement of inventory affects cost of goods sold).
Compare individual expenses with budgets.	Misstatement of expenses and related balance sheet accounts.
Compare gross margin percentage with previous years'.	Misstatement of cost of goods sold and inventory.
Compare inventory turnover ratio with previous years'.	Misstatement of cost of goods sold and inventory.
Compare prepaid insurance and insurance expense with previous years'.	Misstatement of insurance expense and prepaid insurance.
Compare commission expense divided by sales with previous years'.	Misstatement of commission expense and accrued commissions.
Compare individual manufacturing expenses divided by total manufacturing expenses with previous years'.	Misstatement of individual manufacturing expenses and related balance sheet accounts.

additional verification of operating accounts such as utilities, advertising, and purchases should be analytical procedures and cut-off tests. However, certain income and expense accounts are more effectively audited using tests of details.

ANALYSIS OF ACCOUNT BALANCES For some accounts, the risk of material misstatement or lack of disclosure is high (e.g., related-party transactions and legal expense). The amounts included in the such accounts must be analyzed even though analytical review and tests of controls have been completed.

Expense account analysis—the examination of underlying documentation of individual transactions and amounts making up the total of an expense account.

Expense account analysis is the examination of underlying documentation of the individual transactions and amounts making up the total particular expense account. The underlying documents are similar in nature to those used for examining transactions as part of tests of acquisitions transactions and include invoices, receiving reports, purchase orders, and contracts. Figure 18-10 illustrates a typical working paper showing expense analysis for legal expenses.

The major difference between expense account analysis and internal control testing is the degree of concentration on an individual account. Since the tests of controls are meant to assess the appropriate level of control risk, they constitute a general review that usually includes the verification of many different accounts. The analysis of expense and other operations accounts consists of the examination of the transactions in specific accounts to determine the propriety, classification, valuation, and other specific information about each account analyzed.

Assuming satisfactory classification results are found in tests of controls and substantive tests of transactions, auditors normally restrict expense analysis to those accounts with a relatively high likelihood of material misstatement. For example, auditors often analyze repairs and maintenance expense accounts to determine if they erroneously include property, plant, and equipment transactions; rent and lease expense are analyzed to determine the need to capitalize leases; and legal expense is analyzed to determine whether there are potential contingent liabilities, disputes, illegal acts, or other legal issues that may affect the financial statements. Accounts such as utilities, travel expense, and advertising are rarely analyzed unless analytical procedures indicate high potential for material misstatement.

Frequently, the expense account analysis is done as a part of the verification of the related asset. For example, it is common to analyze repairs and maintenance as part of verifying capital assets, rent expense as part of verifying prepaid or accrued rent, and insurance expense as part of testing prepaid insurance.

TESTS OF ALLOCATIONS Several expense accounts that have not yet been discussed arise from the internal allocation of accounting data. These include expenses such as the amortization of capital assets and the amortization of copyrights and catalogue costs. The allocation of manufacturing overhead between inventory and cost of goods sold is an example of a different type of allocation that affects the expenses.

Allocations are important because they determine whether a particular expenditure is an asset or a current-period expense. If the client fails to follow generally accepted accounting principles or fails to calculate the allocation properly, the financial statements can be materially misstated. The allocation of many expenses such as the amortization of capital assets and the amortization of copyrights is required because the life of the asset is greater than one year. The original cost of the asset is verified at the time of acquisition, but the charge-off takes place over several years. Other types of allocations directly affecting the financial statements arise because the life of a short-lived asset does not expire on the balance sheet date. Examples include prepaid rent and insurance. Finally, the allocation of costs between current-period manufacturing expenses and inventory is required by generally accepted accounting principles as a means of reflecting all the costs of making a product. Intangible assets with an indefinite life are not written off. The auditor needs to assess whether the life of the asset is still indefinite and whether there has been an impairment of value of any of the intangibles.

Figure 18-10 | Expense Analysis for Legal Expenses

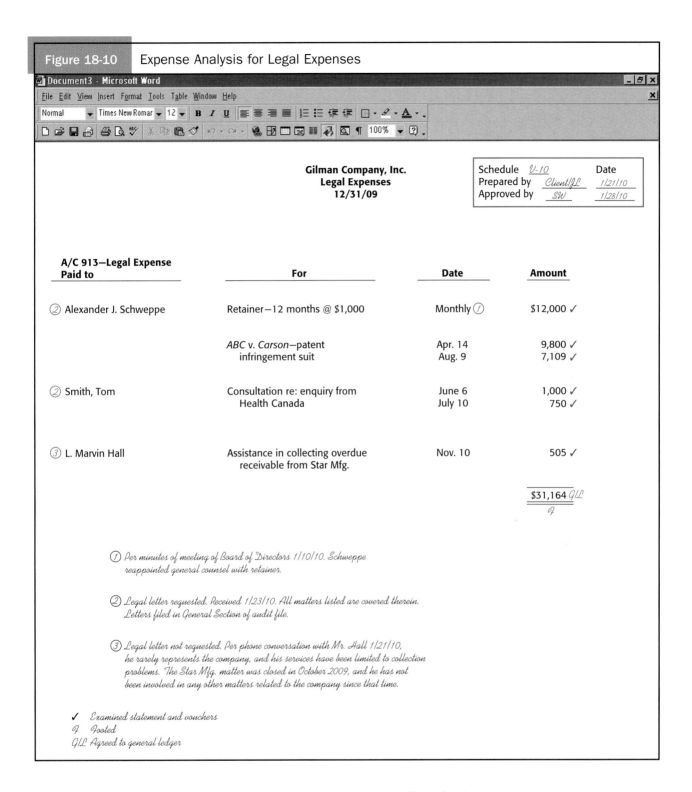

Income statement accounts resulting from allocations are typically audited using analytical procedures. However, additional detailed testing (primarily recalculation) is frequently needed.

In testing the allocation of expenditures such as prepaid insurance and manufacturing overhead, the two most important considerations are adherence to generally accepted accounting principles and consistency with the preceding period. The two most important audit procedures for allocations are tests for overall reasonableness and recalculation of the client's results. It is common to perform these tests as part of the audit of the related asset or liability accounts. For example, amortization expense is usually verified as part of the audit of capital assets; the amortization of patents is tested as part of verifying new patents or the disposal of existing ones; and the allocations between inventory and cost of goods sold are verified as part of the audit of inventory.

Review of Related-Party Transactions

CAS

During the risk assessment process, CAS 550, Related parties (formerly Section 6010), requires the auditor to consider risks of material misstatement or fraud that could be associated with related-party transactions. The auditor will also consider the controls and procedures that management has in place for the identification and disclosure of such transactions. In particular, if the client does not disclose related-party transactions to the auditor and the auditor discovers these, the auditor would need to carefully reassess why such transactions were not detected by the client's regular processes.

While the examination of underlying documents in the tests of controls is designed primarily to verify transactions with third parties, related transactions with affiliates and subdivisions within the client's organization are also included in the examination. The possibility of improper recording and disclosure of transactions between independent entities was discussed in Chapter 8 in the section dealing with related-party transactions.

CAS 550 adopts a risk-based approach and provides guidance to the auditor for assessing inherent and control risks and ultimately determining the extent of substantive testing for related-party transactions. The Application section of CAS 550 provides examples of audit procedures and of how related-party transactions could be measured.

When a client deals with related parties, the *CICA Handbook* requires that the nature of the relationship, the nature and extent of transactions, and amounts due to and from the related parties, including contractual obligations and contingencies, be properly disclosed for the financial statements to be in conformity with GAAP. Services and inventory acquired from related parties must be properly valued, and other exchange transactions must be carefully evaluated for propriety and reasonableness. Related-party transactions must be audited more extensively than those with third parties.

concept check

C18-8 What possible misstatements could occur with manufacturing equipment?

C18-9 How is the audit of prepaid insurance related to the going concern assumption?

Summary

1. *What are the major business functions, documents, and records in the acquisition and payment cycle?* Table 18-1 states that the business functions for acquisitions are processing purchase orders, receiving goods and services, recognizing liabilities, and vendor master file changes, while the business function for cash disbursements (payments) is the processing and recording of cash disbursements. The table also lists documents, records, and accounts.

   Which accounts give rise to accrued liabilities? Typical accounts include payroll remittances (such as employment insurance and Canada Pension) and unpaid wages.

2. *How are tests of controls designed for the acquisition and payment cycle?* We follow the same methodology for the acquisition and payment cycle as for other cycles—after assessing risks at the organization level, we move to

understanding controls at the cycle level so that risks can be assessed and tested by assertion. Then, tests of controls are designed for those assertions where the auditor chooses to place reliance upon the control.

   What is a system conversion? A system conversion occurs when an organization replaces or makes major changes to its existing systems (whether manual or automated).

   What issues does the auditor need to address during a conversion audit? The auditor needs to consider that there is likely a new system of internal controls that will need to be documented and evaluated. The auditor will also need to audit the actual data conversion process and determine whether there have been any changes in accounting policies.

3. *Why is accounts payable considered separately from acquisitions or payments?* Accounts payable is the ending balance sheet obligation, whereas acquisitions and payments are the transactions that occur throughout the year.

How does the auditor design substantive tests for accounts payable? As for other cycles, the auditor considers risks, such as risks of understatement. Typical substantive tests include scrutinizing subsequent payments and reconciling supplier statements.

Why is the auditor more concerned about understatement of accounts payable than overstatement? Should accounts payable be understated, income would be overstated. There is likely to be a greater legal liability to an auditor if a potential investor relies on overstated income than understated income.

4. *In our final section, we considered risks and audit processes for several accounts. In addition to inventory, what are the other expense accounts that need to be audited?* Any expense accounts that have the potential to be misstated by a material amount should be audited. The auditor could use analytical review to target those accounts that need further testing.

What process should be followed in the audit of manufacturing equipment, an asset? The auditor needs to consider the risk of misstatement by audit objective in order to target testing. Analytical procedures (Table 18-7) can be helpful. Then, a sample of transactions would be selected for verification to supporting acquisitions documentation (e.g., invoices or purchase contracts) and tests of details conducted for relevant audit objectives (Table 18-8).

Why is the audit of prepaid expenses important? Prepaid expenses are important in the process of matching expenses with revenues. Misstatements in prepaid expenses would also result in misstatements in revenue.

How are prepaid expenses audited? Risks and internal controls are assessed before designing audit tests that include determination of the period covered by the prepaid assets and calculation of the portion that is to be expensed.

Why are intangible assets difficult to audit? Intangible assets not acquired at arms length are difficult to value. There may be limited evidence establishing useful life, making it difficult to assess management's valuation or the amount of amortization for the year.

What are some examples of typical accrued liabilities? Accruals include management bonuses, interest, payroll costs, property taxes, and insurance.

How are accrued property taxes audited? Assuming amounts are material, the auditor will normally look at current-year payments, recalculate the amount to be recorded in the current year, and compare treatment with that of prior years.

What is the process for auditing income and expense accounts? Based upon risk assessment and the quality of internal controls, the primary techniques include analytical review and tracing to source documents for selected accounts or sampled items.

Why is analytical review an important technique in the audit of operations? Analytical review allows the auditor to test the fairness of presentation of both the balance sheet and income statement amounts.

Visit the text's website at **www.pearsoned.ca/arens** for practice quizzes, additional case studies, and international standards information.

Review Questions

18-1 List one possible internal control for each of the six transaction-related audit objectives for cash disbursements. For each control, list a test of controls to test its effectiveness.

18-2 List one possible control for each of the six transaction-related audit objectives for acquisitions. For each control, list a test of controls to test its effectiveness.

18-3 What is the importance of cash discounts to the client, and how can the auditor verify whether they are being used in accordance with company policy?

18-4 What are the similarities and differences in the objectives of the following two procedures?
1. Select a random sample of receiving reports, and trace them to related vendors' invoices and acquisitions journal entries, comparing the vendor's name, type of material and quantity acquired, and total amount of the acquisition.
2. Select a random sample of acquisitions journal entries, and trace them to related vendors' invoices and receiving reports, comparing the vendor's name, type of material and quantity acquired, and total amount of the acquisition.

18-5 Explain why most auditors consider the receipt of goods and services the most important point in the acquisition and payment cycle.

18-6 Explain the relationship between tests of the acquisition and payment cycle and tests of inventory. Give specific examples of how these two types of tests affect each other.

18-7 Explain the relationship between tests of the acquisition and payment cycle and tests of accounts payable. Give specific examples of how these two types of tests affect each other.

18-8 Explain why it is common for auditors to send confirmation requests to vendors with "zero balances" on the client's accounts payable listing but uncommon to follow the same approach in verifying accounts receivable.

18-9 Distinguish between a vendor's invoice and a vendor's statement. Which document should ideally be used as evidence in auditing acquisition transactions and which for directly verifying accounts payable balances? Why?

18-10 In testing the cut-off of accounts payable at the balance sheet date, explain why it is important that auditors coordinate their tests with the physical observation of inventory. What can the auditor do during the physical inventory to enhance the likelihood of an accurate cut-off?

18-11 John has discovered that his client converted to an integrated set of software packages one month prior to the year end. During the last month of the fiscal year, the client ran systems in parallel. John decides that he can do the audit as usual because the old system is still in operation. Next year, he will have to audit only the new system because the old system will no longer be in use. Evaluate John's decision regarding the conduct of the audit.

18-12 Explain the relationship between tests of controls for the acquisition and payment cycle and tests of details of balances for the verification of capital assets. Which aspects of capital assets are directly affected by the tests of controls, and which are not?

18-13 Explain why the emphasis in auditing capital assets is on the current-period acquisitions and disposals rather than on the balances in the account carried forward from the preceding year. Under what circumstances would the emphasis be on the balances carried forward?

18-14 What is the relationship between the audit of property accounts and the audit of repair and maintenance accounts? Explain how the auditor organizes the audit to take this relationship into consideration.

18-15 List and briefly state the purpose of all audit procedures that might reasonably be applied by an auditor to determine that all capital asset retirements have been recorded on the books.

18-16 In auditing amortization expense, what major considerations should the auditor keep in mind? Explain how each can be verified.

18-17 List the factors that should affect the auditor's decision whether or not to analyze a particular account balance. Considering these factors, list four expense accounts that are commonly analyzed in audit engagements.

18-18 Why does the auditor examine transaction detail for subsidiaries, affiliates, officers, and directors?

Discussion Questions and Problems

18-19 The following auditing procedures were performed in the audit of accounts payable:

1. Examine supporting documents for cash disbursements several days before and after year end.
2. Examine the acquisition and payment journals for the last few days of the current period and first few days of the succeeding period, looking for large or unusual transactions.
3. Trace from the general ledger trial balance and supporting working papers to determine if accounts payable, related parties, and other related assets and liabilities are properly included on the financial statements.
4. For liabilities that are payable in a foreign currency, determine the exchange rate and check calculations.
5. Discuss with the controller whether any amounts included on the accounts payable list are due to related parties, debit balances, or notes payable.
6. Obtain vendors' statements from the controller, and reconcile to a listing of accounts payable.
7. Obtain vendors' statements directly from vendors, and reconcile to the listing of accounts payable.
8. Obtain the accounts payable aged trial balance listing and the accounts payable open transaction file. Add the data file again, and agree totals with the listing and to the general ledger.

REQUIRED

a. For each procedure, identify the type of audit evidence used.

Audit Procedure	Balance-Related Audit Objective							
	Existence	Completeness	Accuracy	Classification	Detail Tie-in	Cut-off	Obligations	Presentation and Disclosure
1		X				X		
2								
3								
4								
5								
6								
7								
8								

b. For each procedure, use the matrix above to identify which balance-related audit objective(s) was (were) satisfied. (Procedure 1 is completed as an illustration.)

c. Evaluate the need to have certain objectives satisfied by more than one audit procedure.

18-20 You are the staff auditor testing the combined purchase and cash disbursements journal for a small audit client.

Internal control is regarded as reasonably effective, considering the number of personnel.

The auditor in charge has decided that a sample of 80 items should be sufficient for this audit because of the excellent controls and gives you the following instructions:

1. All transactions selected must exceed $100.
2. At least 50 of the transactions must be for purchases of raw materials because these transactions are typically material.
3. It is not acceptable to include the same vendor in the sample more than once.
4. All vendors' invoices that cannot be located must be replaced with a new sample item.
5. Both cheques and supporting documents are to be examined for the same transactions.
6. The sample must be random, after modifications for instructions 1 through 5.

REQUIRED

a. Evaluate each of these instructions for testing acquisition and cash disbursement transactions.
b. Explain the difficulties of applying each of these instructions to attributes sampling.

18-21 You were in the final stages of your examination of the financial statements of Ozine Corporation for the year ended December 31, 2009, when you were consulted by the corporation's president. He believed that there was no point to your examining the 2010 acquisitions data files and testing data in support of 2010 entries. He stated that (1) bills pertaining to 2009 that were received too late to be included in the December acquisitions data files were recorded by the corporation as of the year end by journal entry, (2) the internal auditor made tests after the year end, and (3) he would furnish you with a letter confirming that there were no unrecorded liabilities.

REQUIRED

a. Should a public accountant's test for unrecorded liabilities be affected by the fact that the client made a journal entry to record 2009 bills that were received late? Explain.
b. Should a public accountant's test for unrecorded liabilities be affected by the fact that a letter is obtained in which a responsible management official confirms that, to the best of his or her knowledge, all liabilities have been recorded? Explain.
c. Should a public accountant's test for unrecorded liabilities be eliminated or reduced because of the internal audit tests? Explain.
d. Assume that the corporation, which handled some government contracts, had no internal auditor but that an auditor from the Auditor General's office spent three weeks auditing the records and was just completing her work at this time. How would the public accountant's unrecorded liability test be affected by the work of the auditor from the Auditor General's office?
e. What sources in addition to the 2009 acquisitions data files should the public accountant consider to locate possible unrecorded liabilities?

(Adapted from AICPA)

18-22 Because of the small size of the company and the limited number of accounting personnel, Dry Goods Wholesale Company Ltd. initially records all acquisitions of goods and services at the time that cash disbursements are made. At the end of each quarter when financial statements for internal purposes are prepared, accounts payable are recorded by adjusting journal entries. The entries are reversed at the beginning of the subsequent period. Except for the lack of a purchasing system, the controls over acquisitions are excellent for a small company. (There are adequate prenumbered documents for all receipt of goods, proper approvals, and adequate internal verification wherever possible.)

Before the auditor arrives for the year-end audit, the bookkeeper prepares adjusting entries to record the accounts payable as of the balance sheet date. The aged trial balance is listed as of the year end, and a manual schedule is prepared adding the amounts that were entered in the following month. Thus, the accounts payable balance equals the aged trial balance plus the following month's journal entry for invoices received after the year end. All vendors' invoices supporting the journal entry are retained in a separate file for the auditor's use.

In the current year, the accounts payable balance has increased dramatically because of a severe cash shortage. (The cash shortage apparently arose from expansion of inventory and facilities rather than lack of sales.) Many accounts have remained unpaid for several months, and the client is getting pressure from several vendors to pay the bills. Since the company had a relatively profitable year, management is anxious to complete the audit as early as possible so that the audited statements can be used to obtain a larger bank loan.

REQUIRED

a. Explain how the lack of a complete aged accounts payable trial balance will affect the auditor's tests of controls for acquisitions and cash disbursements.
b. What should the auditor use as a sampling unit in performing tests of acquisitions?
c. Assume that no misstatements are discovered in the auditor's tests of controls for acquisitions and cash disbursements. How will that assumption affect the verification of accounts payable?
d. Discuss the reasonableness of the client's request for an early completion of the audit and the implications of the request from the auditor's point of view.
e. List the audit procedures that should be performed in the year-end audit of accounts payable to meet the cut-off objective.
f. State your opinion as to whether it is possible to conduct an adequate audit in these circumstances.

18-23 Donnen Designs Inc. is a small manufacturer of women's casual-wear jewellery, including bracelets, necklaces, earrings, and other moderately priced accessory items. Most of its products are made of silver, various low-cost stones, beads, and other decorative jewellery pieces. Donnen Designs is not involved in the manufacturing of high-end jewellery items such as those made of gold and semiprecious or precious stones.

Personnel responsible for purchasing raw material jewellery pieces for Donnen Designs would like to place orders directly with suppliers who offer their products for sale through websites. Most suppliers provide pictures of all jewellery components on their websites, along with pricing and other sales-term information. Customers which have valid business licenses are able to purchase the products at wholesale, rather than retail, prices. Customers can place orders online and pay for those goods immediately by using a valid credit card. Purchases made by credit card are shipped by the suppliers once the credit approval is received from the credit card agency, which usually occurs the same day. Customers can also place orders online with payment being made later by cheque. However, in that event, purchases are not shipped until the cheque is received and cashed by the supplier. Some of the suppliers have a 30-day full-payment refund policy, whereas other suppliers accept returns but only grant credit toward future purchases from that supplier.

REQUIRED

a. Identify advantages for Donnen Designs if management allows purchasing personnel to order goods online through supplier websites.

b. Identify potential risks associated with Donnen Designs' purchase of jewellery pieces through supplier websites.

c. Describe advantages of allowing purchasing agents to purchase products online using a Donnen Designs credit card.

d. Describe advantages of allowing purchasing agents to purchase products online with payment made only by cheque.

e. What internal controls could be implemented to ensure the following?

(1) Donnen allows purchasing agents to purchase jewellery items using Donnen credit cards, and purchasing agents do not use those credit cards to purchase non-jewellery items for their own purposes.

(2) Purchasing agents do not order jewellery items from the suppliers and ship those items to addresses other than Donnen addresses.

(3) Donnen does not end up with unused credits with jewellery suppliers as a result of returning unacceptable jewellery items to suppliers which only grant credit toward future purchases.

18-24 Hardware Manufacturing Company Limited, a closely held corporation, has operated since 1994 but has not had its financial statements audited. The company now plans to issue additional capital stock to be sold to outsiders and wishes to engage you to examine its 2009 transactions and render an opinion on the financial statements for the year ended December 31, 2009.

The company has expanded from one plant to three and has frequently acquired, modified, and disposed of all types of equipment. Capital assets have a net book value of 70 percent of total assets and consist of land and buildings, diversified machinery and equipment, and furniture and fixtures. Some property was acquired by donation from shareholders.

Amortization was recorded by several methods using various estimated lives.

REQUIRED

a. Should you confine your examination solely to 2009 transactions as requested by this prospective client whose financial statements have not previously been examined? Why or why not?

b. Prepare an audit program for the January 1, 2009, opening balances of the land, building, and equipment asset and accumulated amortization accounts of Hardware Manufacturing Company Limited, organized by audit objective.

(Adapted from AICPA)

18-25 As part of the audit of different audit areas, it is important to be alert to the possibility of unrecorded liabilities. For each of the following audit areas or accounts, describe a liability that could be uncovered and the audit procedures that could uncover it.

a. Minutes of the board of directors' meetings.

b. Land and buildings.

c. Rent expense.

d. Interest expense.

e. Cash surrender value of life insurance.

f. Cash in the bank.

g. Officers' travel and entertainment expense.

18-26 In performing tests of the acquisition and payment cycle for Oakville Manufacturing, Inc., the staff assistant did a careful and complete job. Since internal controls were evaluated as excellent before tests of controls were performed and were determined to be operating effectively on the basis of the lack of exceptions in the tests of controls, the decision was made to reduce significantly the tests of expense account analysis. The auditor in charge decided to reduce, but not eliminate, the acquisition-related expense account analysis for repair expense, legal and other professional expense, miscellaneous expense, and utilities expense on the grounds that they should always be verified more extensively than normal accounts. The decision was also made to eliminate all account analysis for the purchase of raw materials, amortization expense, supplies expense, insurance expense, and the current-period additions to capital assets.

REQUIRED

a. List considerations in the audit other than the quality of internal controls that should affect the auditor's selection of accounts to be analyzed.

b. Assuming no significant problems were identified on the basis of the other considerations in part (a), evaluate the auditor's decision to reduce but not eliminate expense account analysis for each account involved. Justify your conclusions.

c. Assuming no significant problems were identified on the basis of the other considerations in part (a), evaluate the auditor's decision to eliminate expense account analysis for each account involved. Justify your conclusions.

Professional Judgment Problems

18-27 In testing cash disbursements for Immanuel Klein Ltd., you perform minimum tests of 15 transactions as a means of assessing control risk. In your tests, you discover the following exceptions:

1. Two items in the acquisitions journal have been misclassified.
2. Three invoices had not been initialled by the controller, but there were no dollar misstatements evident in the transactions.
3. Five receiving reports were recorded in the acquisitions journal at least two weeks later than their date on the receiving report.
4. One invoice had been paid twice. The second payment was supported by a duplicate copy of the invoice. Both copies of the invoice had been marked "paid."
5. One cheque amount in the cash disbursements journal was for $100 less than the amount stated on the vendor's invoice.
6. One voided cheque was missing.

7. Two receiving reports for vendors' invoices were missing from the transaction packet. One vendor's invoice had an extension error, and the invoice had been initialled to verify that the amount had been checked.

REQUIRED

a. Identify whether each of exceptions 1 through 7 was a control test deviation, a monetary error or fraud and other irregularity, or both.

b. For each exception, identify which transaction-related audit objective was not met.

c. What is the audit importance of each of these exceptions?

d. What follow-up procedures would you use to determine more about the nature of each exception?

e. How would each of these exceptions affect the balance of your audit? Be specific.

f. Identify internal controls that should have prevented each misstatement.

18-28 Eugene Fikursky, a staff assistant, was asked to analyze interest and legal expense as a part of the first-year audit of Chinook Manufacturing Corp. In searching for a model to follow, Fikursky looked at other completed working papers in the current audit file and concluded that the closest thing to what he was looking for was a working paper for repair and maintenance expense account analysis. Following the approach used in analyzing repairs and maintenance, he made a schedule of all interest and legal expenses in excess of $500 and verified them by examining supporting documentation.

REQUIRED

a. Evaluate Fikursky's approach to verifying interest and legal expense.

b. Suggest a better approach to verifying these two account balances.

Case

18-29 As the manager of the audit of Vernal Manufacturing Inc., you are investigating the operations accounts. The auditor in charge assessed control risk for all cycles as low, supported by tests of controls. There are no major inherent risks affecting operations. Accordingly, in auditing the operations accounts, you decide to emphasize analytical procedures. The auditor in charge prepared a schedule of the key income statement accounts that compares the prior year totals to the current year's and includes explanations of variances obtained from discussions with client personnel. This schedule is included in Exhibit I on page 638.

REQUIRED

a. Evaluate the explanations for variances provided by client personnel. List any explanations alternative to those given.

b. Indicate which variances are of special significance to the audit and how they should affect additional audit procedures.

EXHIBIT I   Vernal Manufacturing Inc. Operations Accounts 31/12/09

ACCOUNT	PER G/L 31/12/08	PER G/L 31/12/09	CHANGE AMOUNT	CHANGE PERCENT	EXPLANATIONS BY CLIENT
Sales*	$8,467,312	$9,845,231	$1,377,919	16.3	Sales increase due to two new customers who account for 20% of volume. Larger
Sales returns and allowances	(64,895)	(243,561)	(178,666)	275.3	returns due to need to cement relations with these customers.
Gain (loss) on sale of assets	43,222	(143,200)	(186,422)	-431.3	
Interest income	243	223	(20)	-8.2	Trade-in of several sales cars that needed replacement.
Miscellaneous income	6,365	25,478	19,113	300.3	
	8,452,247	9,484,171	1,031,924	12.2	
Cost of goods sold:					
Beginning inventory	1,487,666	1,389,034	(98,632)	-6.6	Increase in these accounts due to increased volume with new customers as indi-cated above.
Purchases	2,564,451	3,430,865	866,414	33.8	
Freight in	45,332	65,782	20,450	45.1	
Purchase returns	(76,310)	(57,643)	18,667	-24.5	
Factory wages	986,755	1,145,467	158,712	16.1	
Factory benefits	197,652	201,343	3,691	1.9	
Factory overhead	478,659	490,765	12,106	2.5	
Factory amortization	344,112	314,553	(29,559)	-8.6	
Ending inventory	(1,389,034)	(2,156,003)	(766,969)	55.2	Inventory being held for new customers.
	4,639,283	4,824,163	184,880	4.0	
Selling, general and administrative:					
Executive salaries	167,459	174,562	7,103	4.2	Normal salary increases.
Executive benefits	32,321	34,488	2,167	6.7	
Office salaries	95,675	98,540	2,865	3.0	
Office benefits	19,888	21,778	1,890	9.5	
Travel and entertainment	56,845	75,583	18,738	33.0	Sales and promotional expenses increased in an attempt to obtain new major
Advertising	130,878	156,680	25,802	19.7	customers. Two obtained and program will continue.
Other sales expense	34,880	42,334	7,454	21.4	
Stationery and supplies	38,221	21,554	(16,667)	-43.6	Probably a misclassification; will investigate.
Postage	14,657	18,756	4,099	28.0	Normal increase.
Telephone	36,551	67,822	31,271	85.6	Normal increase.
Dues and memberships	3,644	4,522	878	24.1	Normal increase.
Rent	15,607	15,607	0	0.0	
Legal fees	14,154	35,460	21,306	150.5	Timing of billing for fees.
Accounting fees	16,700	18,650	1,950	11.7	Normal increase.
Amortization	73,450	69,500	(3,950)	-5.4	Normal change.
Bad-debt expense	166,454	143,871	(22,583)	-13.6	Haven't reviewed yet for the current year.
Insurance	44,321	45,702	1,381	3.1	Normal change.
Interest expense	120,432	137,922	17,490	14.5	Normal change.
Other expense	5,455	28,762	23,307	427.3	Amount not material.
	1,087,592	1,212,093	124,501	11.4	
	5,726,875	6,036,256	309,381	5.4	
Income before taxes	2,725,372	3,447,915	722,543	26.5	Increase due to increased income before tax.
Income taxes	926,626	1,020,600	93,974	10.1	
Net income	$1,798,746	$2,427,315	$ 628,569	34.9	

Ongoing Small Business Case: E-Payments at CondoCleaners.com

18-30 In addition to payroll, the costs of running Condo-Cleaners.com are web services, telecommunications, cleaning supplies, and vehicle costs. Jim pays most of these costs using his personal credit card. He then separates the receipts, recording business expenses in a spreadsheet, marking any personal costs as "personal" on the credit card statement. He keeps the credit card statement and receipts in support of his expenses.

REQUIRED

Identify audit issues associated with the audit of expenses at CondoCleaners.com.

19

Audit of the inventory and warehousing cycle

Look around your room. What is in it—bookshelves, a desk, carpeting, books, pens, pencils, paper supplies? All of these items are produced by companies, stored, and then sold to businesses that distribute or sell these products to consumers. The diversity of organizations involved in the manufacture, distribution, and sales of products is reflected in the many different types of accounting systems to track the costs and routing of inventory. Management accountants can help to develop and monitor controls and costs in such a supply chain, while auditors are interested in examining the effectiveness of such controls.

STANDARDS REFERENCED IN THIS CHAPTER

CICA Standard

CAS 501 – Audit evidence: specific considerations for selected items (previously Section 6030 – Inventories; Section 6560 – Communications with law firms regarding claims and possible claims [including the joint policy statement])

LEARNING OBJECTIVES

1 Identify the components of the inventory and warehousing cycle.

2 Describe the five different parts of the inventory and warehousing cycle that are audited. Provide an overview of the process used to audit the inventory and warehousing cycle.

3 Explain the role of each of the following types of tests in the audit of inventory: (i) analytical review, (ii) physical observation of inventory, and (iii) pricing and compilation tests.

4 Describe how the relationships among the tests of different cycles affect the audit of inventory.

Listeria Hysteria Caused by Meat Slicers

Ingestion of Listeria bacteria *(Listeria monocytogenes)* can result in an illness called listeriosis. Listeriosis can result in mild flu-like symptoms, serious problems similar to food poisoning, or even death, as the lining of the brain can become inflamed. The bacteria are common in the environment but are readily destroyed with proper cooking procedures. They can build up in most raw meats and fish as well as in soft or semisoft cheeses made from unpasteurized milk. In August 2008, listeriosis cases suddenly increased across Canada, linked to over 20 deaths, a total of 38 confirmed cases of the disease, and many more suspected cases.

It appeared that the common element among those affected by the illness was ingestion of Maple Leaf deli meats such as ham, corned beef, roast beef, turkey, and salami. Independent tests conducted in mid-August 2008 on such Maple Leaf meats led to a massive recall of all Maple Leaf meat products and a shut down of a meat-processing facility in Toronto. The cost of the recall, clean-up, and additional marketing costs ultimately resulted in Maple Leaf Foods posting a loss for the quarter ended September 30, 2008, with sales reductions in the range of 30 to 50 percent. As part of the public relations process, the company had nationwide public relations campaigns, renovated the affected meat production plant, and revised its food safety protocols.

IMPORTANCE TO AUDITORS

Increased amounts of bacteria in food products can come from many sources. The bacteria could build up in equipment, as suspected at Maple Leaf Foods, or other causes may be poor handling or storage of food products by the supplier, producer, retailer, or ultimate consumer. In the hands of the producer, such a build up of bacteria would be attributed to poor quality control during the manufacturing and storage process. Auditors would be concerned about quality control at food processing and storage facilities to help prevent illness and public relations nightmares as occurred at Maple Leaf Foods. For all types of producers, quality control is important because poor quality can result in returned and unsaleable products or in rework costs. Then inventory costs are overstated and allowances understated.

WHAT DO YOU THINK?

1. What types of questions would auditors ask about production quality control at a company such as Maple Leaf Foods?

2. Identify other sources of information that the auditor would examine when considering the valuation of processed-meat inventories.

3. What is the role of corporate governance in the management of product quality control?

continued >

Sources: 1. Cribb, Robert, "Tests stun listeria experts," *Toronto Star*, October 9, 2008, p. A1, A8. 2. Lu, Vanessa, "Maple Leaf suspects slicers," *Toronto Star*, September 6, 2008, p. A4. 3. Flavelle, Dana, "Maple Leaf Foods profits sliced by listeria outbreak," *Toronto Star*, October 30, 2008, p. B1, B3. 4. Ministry of Health and Long-Term Care, "Diseases: Listeria," www.health.gov.on.ca/english/public/pub/disease/listeria.html, Accessed: April 9, 2009. 5. Torstar News Service, "Maple Leaf aims to clean brand's image," *Metronews*, December 16, 2008, p. 8.

IMPLEMENTATION of effective quality control procedures over the management of the inventory supply chain includes effective management of the associated information as well as of the raw materials, work in progress, and finished goods. Organizations may use automated inventory management, as it enables them to provide expanded descriptions of their inventory products on a real-time basis to key business partners such as suppliers and customers, perhaps via the internet. Information about quantities on hand, the quality and location of products, and other key inventory data help inventory suppliers work with management to monitor the flow of goods. Think about our control framework: the control environment, general controls, and application controls. What are some examples of controls that Maple Leaf Foods would need to implement to provide effective quality management of its supply chain?

 ## The Nature of the Inventory and Warehousing Cycle

Inventory takes many different forms, depending on the nature of the business. For retail or wholesale businesses, the most important inventory is merchandise on hand that is available for sale. For hospitals, it includes food, drugs, and medical supplies. A manufacturing company has raw materials, purchased parts, and supplies for use in production; goods in the process of being manufactured; and finished goods available for sale. For an organization to have the optimum quantity and quality of inventory, it needs to have a well-organized supply chain—a flow of materials, information, services, and funds. This is why the audit of accounts payable and purchasing (discussed in the previous chapter) needs to be linked with the audit of inventory.

We have selected manufacturing company inventories for presentation in this text. However, most of the principles discussed apply to other types of businesses as well.

For the reasons given below, the audit of inventories is often the most complex and time-consuming part of the audit:

- Inventory is generally a major item on the balance sheet, and it is often the largest item making up the accounts included in working capital.
- The inventory items are often in different locations, which makes physical control and counting difficult. Companies must have their inventory accessible for the efficient manufacture and sale of the product, but this dispersal creates significant audit problems.
- The diversity of the items in inventories creates difficulties for the auditor. Such items as jewels, chemicals, and electronic parts present problems with observation and valuation.

Figure 19-1　Flow of Inventory and Costs

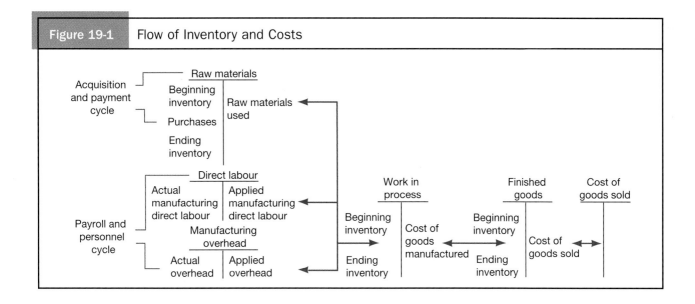

- The valuation of inventory is difficult due to such factors as obsolescence and the need to allocate manufacturing costs to inventory.
- There are several acceptable inventory valuation methods, but any given client must apply a method consistently from year to year. Moreover, an organization may prefer to use different valuation methods for different parts of the inventory, which is acceptable under GAAP.

The trial balance for Hillsburg Hardware Limited on page 129 shows that only two accounts are affected by inventories and warehousing: inventory and cost of goods sold. However, both accounts are highly material. For a manufacturing company, a great many accounts are affected because labour, acquisitions of raw materials, and all indirect manufacturing costs affect inventory.

The physical flow of goods and the flow of costs in the **inventory and warehousing cycle** for a manufacturing company are shown in Figure 19-1 above. The direct tie-in of the inventory and warehousing cycle to the acquisition and payment cycle and to the payroll and personnel cycle can be seen by examining the debits to the raw materials, direct labour, and manufacturing overhead T-accounts. The direct tie-in to the sales and collection cycle occurs at the point where finished goods are relieved (credited) and a charge is made to cost of goods sold. This close relationship to other transaction cycles in the organization is a basic characteristic of the audit of the inventory and warehousing cycle.

Inventory and warehousing cycle—the transaction cycle that involves the physical flow of goods through the organization, as well as related costs.

Functions in the Cycle and Internal Controls

The inventory and warehousing cycle can be thought of as comprising two separate but closely related systems: one involving the actual physical flow of goods and the other the related costs. As inventories move through the company, there must be adequate controls over both their physical movement and their related costs. A brief examination of the six functions making up the inventory and warehousing cycle will help you understand these controls and the audit evidence needed to test their effectiveness.

PROCESS PURCHASE ORDERS Purchase requisitions are used to tell the purchasing department for which inventory items it should place orders. Requisitions may be initiated by stockroom personnel when inventory reaches a predetermined level, orders may be placed for the materials required to produce a particular customer order, or orders may be initiated on the basis of a periodic inventory count by a responsible person. Regardless of the method followed, the controls over purchase requisitions and the related purchase orders are evaluated and tested as part of the acquisition and payment cycle. Many organizations use only purchase orders, relying on automated systems to identify the need to obtain materials or products.

RECEIVE NEW MATERIALS Receipt of the ordered materials is also part of the acquisition and payment cycle. Materials received should be inspected for quantity and quality. The receiving department produces a receiving report that becomes a part of the documentation necessary before payment is made. After inspection, the materials are sent to the storeroom, and the receiving documents are typically sent to purchasing, the storeroom, and accounts payable. Control and accountability are necessary for all transfers.

STORE RAW MATERIALS When materials are received, they are stored in the stockroom until needed for production. Materials are issued out of stock to production upon presentation of a properly approved materials requisition, work order, or similar document that indicates the type and quantity of materials needed. This requisition document is used to update the perpetual inventory master files and to make book transfers from the raw materials to work-in-process accounts.

PROCESS GOODS The processing portion of the inventory and warehousing cycle varies greatly from company to company. The determination of the items and quantities to be produced is generally based on specific orders from customers, sales forecasts, predetermined finished goods inventory levels, or economic production runs. Frequently, a separate production control department is responsible for the determination of the type and quantity of items to be produced. Within the various production departments, provision must be made to account for the quantities produced, control scrap, have quality controls, and physically protect the material in process. The production department must generate production and scrap reports so that the accounting department can reflect the movement of materials in the books and determine accurate costs of production.

In any company involved in manufacturing, an adequate cost accounting system is an important part of the processing-of-goods function. The system is necessary to indicate the relative profitability of the various products for management planning and control and to value inventories for financial statement purposes. There are two types of cost systems used by manufacturers (although many variations and combinations of these systems are employed): job cost and process cost. The main difference is whether costs are accumulated by individual jobs when material is issued and labour costs incurred (**job cost system**), or whether they are accumulated by particular processes, with unit costs for each process assigned to the products passing through the process (**process cost system**).

Cost accounting records consist of master files, worksheets, and reports that accumulate material, labour, and overhead costs by job or process as the costs are incurred. When jobs or products are completed, the related costs are transferred from work in process to finished goods on the basis of production-department reports.

STORE FINISHED GOODS As finished goods are completed by the production department, they are placed in the stockroom awaiting shipment. In companies with good internal controls, finished goods are kept under physical control in a separate limited-access area. The control of finished goods is often considered part of the sales and collection cycle.

SHIP FINISHED GOODS Shipping of completed goods is an integral part of the sales and collection cycle. Any shipment or transfer of finished goods must be authorized by a properly approved shipping document. The controls for shipment have been studied in previous chapters.

PERPETUAL INVENTORY FILES One of the records for inventory that has not been previously discussed is **perpetual inventory data files,** containing records of inventory items purchased, used, sold, and on hand for merchandise, raw materials, and

Job cost system—the system of cost accounting in which costs are accumulated by individual jobs when material is used and labour costs are incurred.

Process cost system—the system of cost accounting in which costs are accumulated for a process, with unit costs for each process assigned to the products passing through the process.

Perpetual inventory data files—continuously updated computerized records of inventory items purchased, used, sold, and on hand for merchandise, raw materials, and finished goods. The master file normally contains the balance of quantity on hand, as well as prices and description of items. The transaction files contain activity details, such as shipments (items sold) and receipts (goods purchased).

finished goods. Separate perpetual records are normally kept for raw materials and finished goods. Most companies do not use perpetuals for work in process.

The perpetual inventory master file normally includes only information such as item number, description, unit cost, quantity on hand, and quantity on order. The supporting transaction files contain supporting records of the units of inventory purchased and sold. Sales price information and vendor information could also be included in data files.

For acquisitions of raw materials, the perpetual inventory master file is updated automatically when acquisitions of inventory are processed as part of recording acquisitions. For example, when the computer system enters the number of units and unit cost for each raw material purchase, this information is used to update perpetual inventory master files along with the acquisitions journal and accounts payable master file. Chapter 18 described the recording of acquisition transactions.

Transfers of raw materials from the storeroom must be separately entered into the computer to update the perpetual records. Typically, only the units transferred need to be entered because the computer can determine the unit costs from the master file. Raw materials perpetual inventory data files that have unit costs include, for each raw material, beginning and ending units on hand, units and unit cost of each purchase, and units and unit cost of each transfer into production.

Finished goods perpetual inventory data files include the same type of information as raw materials perpetuals but are considerably more complex if costs are included along with units. Finished goods costs include raw materials, direct labour, and allocations of manufacturing overhead, which requires detailed record keeping. When finished goods perpetuals include unit costs, the cost accounting records must be integrated into the computer system.

SUMMARY OF INVENTORY DOCUMENTATION The physical movement and related documentation in a basic inventory and warehousing cycle are shown in Figure 19-2. The figure re-emphasizes the important point that the recording of costs and movement of inventory as shown in the books must correspond to the physical movements and processes.

concept check

C19-1 Provide two reasons why there could be a material error in inventory.

C19-2 Describe the two separate subsystems used to assess controls in the inventory and warehousing cycle.

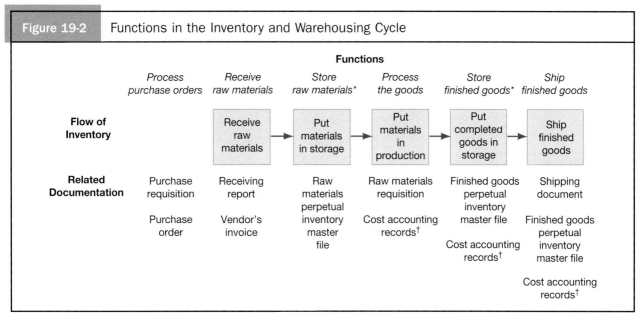

Figure 19-2	Functions in the Inventory and Warehousing Cycle

Functions

	Process purchase orders	Receive raw materials	Store raw materials*	Process the goods	Store finished goods*	Ship finished goods
Flow of Inventory		Receive raw materials	Put materials in storage	Put materials in production	Put completed goods in storage	Ship finished goods
Related Documentation	Purchase requisition	Receiving report	Raw materials perpetual inventory master file	Raw materials requisition	Finished goods perpetual inventory master file	Shipping document
	Purchase order	Vendor's invoice		Cost accounting records†	Cost accounting records†	Finished goods perpetual inventory master file
						Cost accounting records†

* Inventory counts are taken and compared with perpetual inventory master files at any stage of the cycle. The auditor must determine that cut-off for recording documents corresponds to the physical location of the items in the process. A count must ordinarily be taken at least once a year. If the perpetual system is operating well, this can be done on a cyclical basis throughout the year.

† Includes cost information for materials, direct labour, and overhead.

② The Audit of Inventory

The overall objective in the audit of the inventory and warehousing cycle is to determine that raw materials, work in process, finished goods inventory, and cost of goods sold are fairly stated on the financial statements. The bias in recording inventory would be toward overstatement, accomplished by valuing inventory too high (the accuracy and valuation assertions), or toward including inventory that does not exist (occurrence). The auditor would keep in mind these risks of overstatement while auditing inventory. If other risks were identified during audit planning (for example, the potential for accuracy errors due to a complex information system), then the auditor would also consider those risks.

The audit of the inventory and warehousing cycle can be divided into an examination of five distinct parts of the cycle (Figure 19-3).

ACQUIRE AND RECORD RAW MATERIALS, LABOUR, AND OVERHEAD This part of the inventory and warehousing cycle includes the first three functions in Figure 19-2: processing of purchase orders, receipt of raw materials, and storage of raw materials. The internal controls over these three functions are first studied, then tested, as part of performing tests of controls in the acquisition and payment cycle and the payroll and personnel cycle. At the completion of the acquisition and payment cycle, the auditor is likely to be satisfied that acquisitions of raw materials and manufacturing costs are correctly stated. Samples should be designed to ensure that these systems are adequately tested. Similarly, when labour is a significant part of inventory, the payroll and personnel cycle tests should verify the proper accounting for these costs.

TRANSFER ASSETS AND COSTS Internal transfers include the fourth and fifth functions in Figure 19-2: processing the goods and storing finished goods. These two activities are not related to any other transaction cycles and therefore must be studied and tested as part of the inventory and warehousing cycle. The accounting records concerned with these functions of manufacture, processing, and storage are referred to as the **cost accounting records**.

Cost accounting records—the accounting records concerned with the manufacture and processing of the goods and storing finished goods.

SHIP GOODS AND RECORD REVENUE AND COSTS The recording of shipments and related costs, the last function in Figure 19-2, is part of the sales and collection cycle. The internal controls over this function are studied and tested as part of auditing the

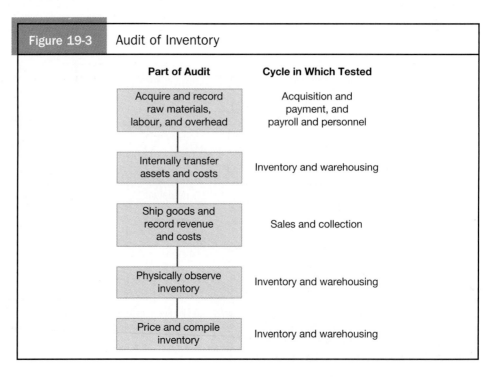

Figure 19-3	Audit of Inventory

Part of Audit	Cycle in Which Tested
Acquire and record raw materials, labour, and overhead	Acquisition and payment, and payroll and personnel
Internally transfer assets and costs	Inventory and warehousing
Ship goods and record revenue and costs	Sales and collection
Physically observe inventory	Inventory and warehousing
Price and compile inventory	Inventory and warehousing

sales and collection cycle. The tests of controls should include procedures to verify the accuracy of the perpetual inventory master files.

PHYSICALLY OBSERVE INVENTORY Observing the client taking a physical inventory count is necessary to determine whether recorded inventory actually exists at the balance sheet date and is properly counted by the client. Inventory is the first audit area for which physical examination is an essential type of evidence used to verify the balance in an account. Physical observation is discussed further in this chapter.

PRICE AND COMPILE INVENTORY Costs used to value the physical inventory must be tested to determine whether the client has correctly followed an inventory method that is in accordance with generally accepted accounting principles and is consistent with the method of previous years. Audit procedures used to verify these inventory costs are referred to as **inventory price tests**. In addition, the auditor must verify whether the physical counts were correctly summarized, the inventory quantities and prices were correctly extended, and the extended inventory was correctly footed. These tests are called **inventory compilation tests**.

Inventory price tests—audit procedures used to verify the costs used to value physical inventory.

Inventory compilation tests—audit procedures used to verify whether physical counts of inventory were correctly summarized, inventory quantities and prices were correctly extended, and extended inventory was correctly footed.

Figure 19-3 summarizes the five parts of the audit of the inventory and warehousing cycle and shows the cycle in which each is audited. The first and third parts of the audit of the inventory and warehousing cycle have already been discussed in connection with the other cycles. The importance of the tests of these other cycles should be kept in mind throughout the remaining sections of this chapter.

Audit of Cost Accounting

The cost accounting systems and controls of different companies vary more than most other areas because of the wide variety of items of inventory and the level of sophistication desired by management. For example, a company that manufactures an entire line of farm machines would have completely different kinds of cost records and internal controls than a steel fabricating shop that makes and installs custom-made metal cabinets. Not surprisingly, small companies with owners who are actively involved in the manufacturing process need less sophisticated records than do large multi-product companies.

COST ACCOUNTING CONTROLS **Cost accounting controls** are controls related to the physical inventory and the consequent costs, from raw materials requisitioning through to completed manufacturing and storage. It is convenient to divide these controls into two broad categories: (1) physical controls over raw materials, work in process, and finished goods inventory; and (2) controls over the related costs.

Cost accounting controls—controls over physical inventory and the related costs from the point at which raw materials are requisitioned to the point at which the manufactured product is completed and transferred to storage.

Almost all companies need physical controls over their assets to prevent loss from misuse and theft. The use of physically segregated, limited-access storage areas for raw materials, work in process, and finished goods is one major control to protect assets. In some instances, the assignment of custody of inventory to specific responsible individuals may be necessary to protect the assets. Approved prenumbered documents for authorizing movement of inventory also protect the assets from improper use. Copies of these documents should be sent directly to accounting by the persons issuing them, bypassing people with custodial responsibilities. An example of an effective document of this type is an approved materials requisition for obtaining raw materials from the storeroom.

Perpetual inventory data files maintained by persons who do not have custody of or access to assets are another useful cost accounting control. Perpetual inventory data files are important for a number of reasons: they provide a record of items on hand, which is used to initiate production or purchase of additional materials or goods; they provide a record of the use of raw materials and the sale of finished goods, which can be reviewed for obsolete or slow-moving items; and they provide a record that can be used to pinpoint responsibility for custody as part of the investigation of differences between physical counts and the amounts shown on the records.

Inventory needs to be saleable or usable. This means producing high-quality inventory, shipping it, and tracking it.

Some purchases can cause damages beyond the original product purchased. For example, a part replaced in a machine could damage the machine if the part is defective. A digital picture frame or geographic positioning system connected to your personal computer (PC) could create a vulnerability on your PC by coming with a preloaded virus. A digital picture frame made in China and sold by Target (a U.S. department-store chain) was found to contain four different viruses, including malware that traps passwords. Such programs, known as Trojan horses, can be used to infect thousands of computers.

Retailers that sell such products could be subject to lawsuits (or at a minimum bad press and returned products) for selling such products. Manufacturers should have quality control procedures in place that prevent having unauthorized software (such as viruses) loaded on their products.

Best Buy also had problems with some of its digital picture frames. In particular, Insignia 10-inch digital frames were found to have a virus. The retailer removed the item from the shelves when it found out, and no longer sells the product.

CRITICAL THINKING QUESTIONS

1. What are some examples of quality control procedures that a digital product manufacturer could use to prevent or detect unauthorized viruses on its products?
2. How would an auditor test such quality control procedures?
3. Why are quality control procedures relevant to the financial statement process and to the costs of inventory?

Sources: 1. McMillan, Robert, "Trojan lurks, waiting to steal admin info," *Network World Canada*, 14(14), July 18, 2008. 2. Sullivan, Bob, "Digital picture frames infected with virus," January 2, 2008, http://redtape.msnbc.com, Accessed: April 9, 2009.

Another important consideration in cost accounting is the existence of adequate internal controls that integrate production and accounting records for the purpose of obtaining accurate costs for all products. The existence of adequate cost records aids management in pricing, controlling costs, and costing inventory.

TESTS OF COST ACCOUNTING The concepts in auditing cost accounting are no different from those discussed for any other transaction cycle. Figure 19-4 shows the methodology that the auditor should follow in determining which tests to perform. In auditing cost accounting, the auditor is concerned with four aspects: physical controls over inventory, documents and records for transferring inventory, perpetual inventory master files and transaction files, and unit cost records.

Physical controls The auditor's tests of the adequacy of the physical controls over raw materials, work in process, and finished goods must be restricted to observation and inquiry. For example, the auditor can examine the raw materials storage area to determine whether the inventory is protected from theft and misuse by the existence of a locked storeroom. The existence of an adequate storeroom with a competent custodian in charge also ordinarily results in the orderly storage of inventory. If the auditor concludes that the physical controls are so inadequate that the inventory will be difficult to count, the auditor should expand his or her observation of physical inventory tests to ensure that an adequate count is carried out.

Documents and records for transferring inventory The auditor's primary concerns in verifying the transfer of inventory from one location to another are that the recorded transfers are valid (the inventory exists), the transfers that have actually taken place are recorded, and the quantity, description, and date of all recorded transfers are accurate. First, it is necessary to understand the client's internal controls for recording transfers before relevant tests can be performed. Once the internal controls are understood, the tests can easily be performed by examining documents and records. For example, a procedure to test the existence and accuracy of the transfer of goods from the raw materials storeroom to the manufacturing assembly line is accounting for a sequence of raw material requisitions, examining the requisitions for

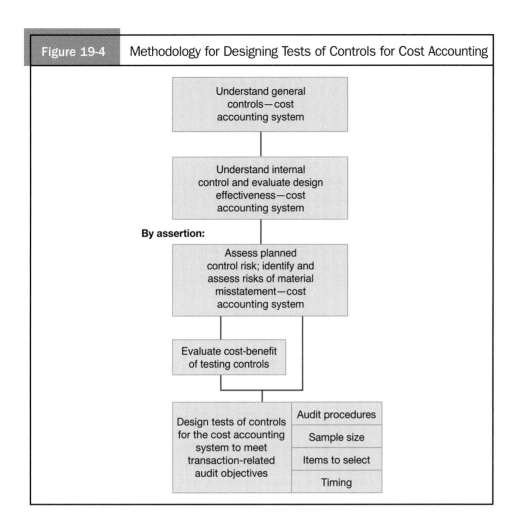

proper approval, and comparing the quantity, description, and date with the information on the raw material perpetual inventory transaction files. Similarly, completed production records can be compared with perpetual inventory files to be sure all manufactured goods were physically delivered to the finished goods storeroom.

Technology has improved the ability to track the movement of goods throughout production. For example, products are labelled with standardized bar codes that can be scanned by laser to track the movement of inventory items.

Perpetual inventory master and transaction files The existence of adequate perpetual inventory master files has a major effect on the timing and extent of the auditor's physical examination of inventory. For one thing, when there are accurate perpetual inventory master files, it is frequently possible to test the physical inventory prior to the balance sheet date. An interim physical inventory can result in significant cost savings for both the client and the auditor and enables the client to receive the audited statements earlier. Perpetual inventory master files also enable the auditor to reduce the extent of the tests of physical inventory when the assessed level of control risk related to physical observation of inventory is low.

Tests of the perpetual inventory master files and supporting detail transaction files for the purpose of reducing the tests of physical inventory or changing their timing are done through the use of documentation. Documents to verify the purchase of raw materials can be examined when the auditor is verifying acquisitions as part of the tests of the acquisition and payment cycle. Documents supporting the reduction of raw materials inventory for use in production and the increase in the quantity of finished goods inventory when goods have been manufactured are examined as part of the tests of the cost accounting documents and records in the manner discussed in the preceding section. Support for the reduction in the finished goods inventory through the sale of goods to customers is ordinarily tested as part of the sales and collection cycle. Usually, it is relatively easy to test the accuracy of the perpetuals after the auditor determines how internal controls are designed and decides to what degree assessed control risk should be reduced.

Unit cost records Obtaining accurate cost data for raw materials, direct labour, and manufacturing overhead is an essential part of cost accounting. Adequate cost accounting records must be integrated with production and other accounting records in order to produce accurate costs of all products. Cost accounting records are pertinent to the auditor in that the valuation of ending inventory depends on the proper design and use of these records.

In testing the inventory cost records, the auditor must first develop an understanding of general controls applicable to this cycle and of internal control. This is frequently somewhat time-consuming because the flow of costs is usually integrated with other accounting records, and it may not be obvious how internal control provides for the internal transfers of raw materials and for direct labour and manufacturing overhead as production is carried out.

Once the auditor understands internal control, the approach to internal verification involves the same concepts that were discussed in the verification of sales and acquisition transactions. Whenever possible, it is desirable to test the cost accounting records as part of the acquisition, payroll, and sales tests to avoid testing the records more than once. For example, when the auditor is testing acquisition transactions as part of the acquisition and payment cycle, it is desirable to trace the units and unit costs of raw materials to the perpetual inventory data files and the total cost to the cost accounting records. Similarly, when payroll cost data are maintained for different jobs, it is desirable to trace data from the payroll summary directly to the job cost record as a part of testing the payroll and personnel cycle.

A major difficulty in the verification of inventory cost records is determining the reasonableness of cost allocations. For example, the assignment of manufacturing overhead costs to individual products entails certain assumptions that can significantly affect the unit costs of inventory and therefore the fairness of the inventory valuation. In evaluating these allocations, the auditor must consider the reasonableness of both the numerator and the denominator that result in the unit costs. For example, in testing overhead applied to inventory on the basis of direct labour dollars, the overhead rate should approximate total actual direct labour dollars. Since total manufacturing overhead is tested as part of the tests of the acquisition and payment cycle and direct labour is tested as part of the payroll and personnel cycle, determining the reasonableness of the rate is not difficult. However, if manufacturing overhead is applied on the basis of machine hours, the auditor must verify the reasonableness of the machine hours by separate tests of the client's machine records. The major consideration in evaluating the reasonableness of all cost allocations, including manufacturing overhead, is consistency with those of previous years.

concept check

C19-3 The audit of inventory is broken down into five distinct parts (refer to Figure 19-3). List and describe the three parts that are audited in the inventory cycle.

C19-4 Provide three examples of cost accounting controls. State the purpose of each control.

③ **Conducting the Audit Tests**

Analytical Procedures

Analytical procedures are as important in auditing inventory and warehousing as in any other cycle. Table 19-1 includes several common analytical procedures and possible misstatements that may be indicated when fluctuations exist. Several of those analytical procedures have also been included in other cycles. An example is the gross margin percent.

Tests of Details for Inventory

The methodology for deciding which tests of details of balances to do for inventory and warehousing is essentially the same as that discussed for accounts receivable,

Table 19-1	Analytical Procedures for the Inventory and Warehousing Cycle

Analytical Procedure	Possible Misstatement
Compare gross margin percentage with previous years'.	Overstatement or understatement of inventory and cost of goods sold.
Compare inventory turnover (costs of goods sold divided by average inventory) with previous years'.	Obsolete inventory, which affects inventory and cost of goods sold.
Compare unit costs of inventory with previous years'.	Overstatement or understatement of inventory. Overstatement or understatement of unit costs.
Compare extended inventory value with previous years'.	Misstatements in compilation, unit costs, or extensions that affect inventory and cost of goods sold.
Compare current-year manufacturing costs with previous years' (variable costs should be adjusted for changes in volume).	Misstatements of unit costs of inventory, especially direct labour and manufacturing overhead, which affect inventory and cost of goods sold.

accounts payable, and all other balance sheet accounts. It is shown in Figure 19-5 on the next page. Note that test results of several other cycles besides inventory and warehousing affect tests of details of balances for inventory.

Because of the complexity of auditing inventory, two aspects of tests of details of balances are discussed separately: (1) physical observation and (2) pricing and compilation. These topics are studied in the next two sections.

Physical Observation of Inventory

Prior to the late 1930s, auditors generally avoided responsibility for determining either the physical existence of inventory or the accuracy of the count of inventory. Audit evidence for inventory quantities was usually restricted to obtaining a certificate from management as to the correctness of the stated amount. In 1938, the discovery of major fraud in the McKesson & Robbins Company in the United States caused a re-appraisal by the accounting profession of its responsibilities relating to inventory. In brief, the financial statements for McKesson & Robbins at December 31, 1937, which were "certified" by a major accounting firm, reported total consolidated assets of $87 million. Of this amount, approximately $19 million was subsequently determined to be fictitious ($10 million in inventory and $9 million in receivables). Due primarily to its adherence to the generally accepted auditing practices of that period, the auditing firm was not held directly at fault in the inventory area. However, it was noted that if certain procedures, such as observation of the physical inventory, had been carried out, the fraud would probably have been detected.

With the advent of highly automated perpetual inventory systems, integrated with point-of-sale systems, and warehouses run with the use of automated conveyer systems integrated to identification codes, the auditor will be more likely to rely upon some of the controls present in such automated systems.

Standards for the audit of inventory are provided by CAS 501, Audit evidence: specific considerations for selected items (previously Sections 6030, 6560, and AuG-26). When inventory is material, the auditor should attend the client's physical inventory count unless it is impractical to do so. The purpose of attendance is to observe that the inventory actually exists and its condition (to assist with the valuation objective). The CAS provides specific instructions for audit procedures that the auditor should perform (evaluation of the processes used during the count, including

CAS

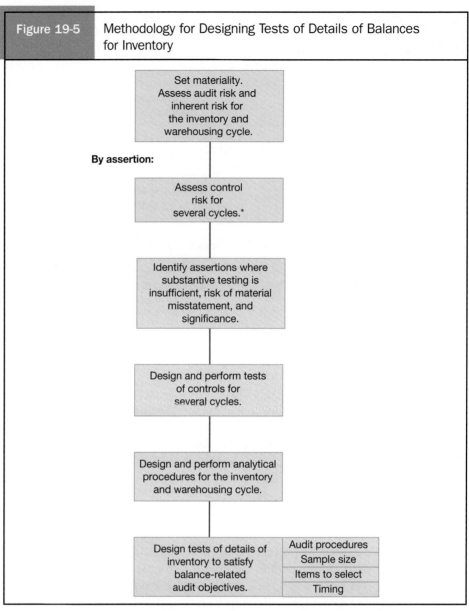

Figure 19-5 Methodology for Designing Tests of Details of Balances for Inventory

Set materiality. Assess audit risk and inherent risk for the inventory and warehousing cycle.

By assertion:

Assess control risk for several cycles.*

Identify assertions where substantive testing is insufficient, risk of material misstatement, and significance.

Design and perform tests of controls for several cycles.

Design and perform analytical procedures for the inventory and warehousing cycle.

Design tests of details of inventory to satisfy balance-related audit objectives.

| Audit procedures |
| Sample size |
| Items to select |
| Timing |

*Cycles affecting tests of balances for inventory include inventory and warehousing cycle (cost accounting system), sales and collection cycle (sales only), acquisition and payment cycle (acquisitions only), and payroll and personnel cycle.

methods to record count results and tracking count results to their final recording into financial records).

If for some reason the auditor cannot attend the physical count, standards permit the auditor to apply other procedures. Absence at the inventory count must be justified. For example, an auditor who was appointed after a company's year end would not find it practical to count inventory; driving 100 km to attend an inventory count at a remote location may be neither practical nor convenient but would be required. Alternative procedures would need to be of high quality and considered in the context of management biases and assessed risks of material misstatement. For example, if appointed after the year end, the auditor could attend a current perpetual inventory count and roll backward with the records.

An essential point of the standards is the distinction between the observation of the physical count and the responsibility for taking the count. The client has the responsibility for setting up the procedures for taking an accurate physical inventory and actually making and recording the counts. The auditor's responsibility is to evaluate and observe the client's physical procedures and draw conclusions about the adequacy of those procedures and about the quantity and condition of the physical inventory.

CONTROLS Regardless of the client's inventory record-keeping method, there must be a periodic physical count of the inventory items on hand, unless inventory is clearly immaterial. This can happen with just-in-time inventory practices, where the client is integrated heavily with supplier information systems and suppliers are required to provide inventory as needed for production. If a count is needed, it can be taken at or near the balance sheet date, at a preliminary date, or on a cycle basis throughout the year. The last two approaches are appropriate only if there are adequately controlled perpetual inventory master files and transaction files.

In connection with the client's physical count of inventory, adequate controls include proper instructions for the physical count, supervision by responsible personnel, independent internal verification of the counts, independent reconciliations of the physical counts with perpetual inventory master files, and adequate control over count tags, sheets, or computerized records.

An important aspect of the auditor's understanding of the client's physical inventory controls is complete familiarity with them before the inventory-taking begins. This is necessary to evaluate the effectiveness of the client's procedures, but it also enables the auditor to make constructive suggestions beforehand. If the inventory instructions do not provide adequate controls, the auditor must spend more time ensuring that the physical count is accurate.

Where procedures for managing inventory are highly automated, with a limited paper trail, the auditor will need to pay particular attention to controls, as tests of details may not be sufficient to provide adequate assurance with respect to the final inventory value.

AUDIT DECISIONS The auditor's decisions in the physical observation of inventory are of the same general nature as in any other audit area: selection of audit procedures, timing, determination of sample size, and selection of the items for testing. The selection of the audit procedures is discussed throughout this section; the other three decisions are discussed briefly at this time.

Timing The auditor decides whether the physical count can be taken prior to year end primarily on the basis of the accuracy of the perpetual inventory files. When an interim physical count is permitted, the auditor observes it at that time and also tests the perpetuals for transactions from the date of the count to year end. When the perpetuals are accurate, it may be unnecessary for the client to count the inventory every year. Instead, the auditor can compare the perpetuals with the actual inventory on a sample basis at a convenient time. When there are no perpetuals and the inventory is material, a complete physical inventory must be taken by the client near the end of the accounting period and tested by the auditor at the same time.

Sample size Sample size in physical observation is usually difficult to specify in terms of the number of items because the emphasis during the tests is on observing the client's procedures rather than on selecting particular items for testing. A convenient way to think of sample size in physical observation is in terms of the total number of hours spent rather than the number of inventory items counted. The most important determinants of the amount of time needed to test the inventory are the adequacy of the internal controls over the physical counts, the accuracy of the perpetual inventory files, the total dollar amount and the type of inventory, the number of different significant inventory locations, and the nature and extent of misstatements discovered in previous years and other inherent risks. In some situations, inventory is such a significant item that dozens of auditors are necessary to observe the physical count, whereas in other situations, one person can complete the observation in a short time. Special care is warranted in the observation of inventory because of the difficulty of expanding sample size or reperforming tests after the physical inventory has been taken.

Selection of items The selection of the particular items for testing is an important part of the audit decision in inventory observation. Care should be taken to observe the counting of the most significant items and a representative sample of typical inventory items, to inquire about items that are likely to be obsolete or damaged, and to discuss with management the reasons for excluding any material items.

PHYSICAL OBSERVATION TESTS The same balance-related audit objectives that have been used in previous sections for tests of details of balances provide the frame of reference for discussing the physical observation tests. However, before the specific objectives are discussed, some comments that apply to all the objectives are appropriate.

The most important part of the observation of inventory is determining whether the physical count is being taken in accordance with the client's instructions. To do this effectively, it is essential that the auditor be present while the physical count is taking place. When the client's employees are not following the inventory instructions, the auditor must either contact the supervisor to correct the problem or modify the physical observation procedures. For example, if the procedures require one team to count the inventory and a second team to recount it as a test of accuracy, the auditor should inform management if he or she observes both teams counting together.

Obtaining an adequate understanding of the client's business is even more important in physical observation of inventory than for most aspects of the audit because inventory varies so significantly for different companies. A proper understanding of the client's business and its industry enables the auditor to ask about and discuss such problems as inventory valuation, potential obsolescence, and existence of consignment inventory intermingled with owned inventory. A useful starting point for the auditor to become familiar with the client's inventory is a tour of the client's facilities, including receiving, storage, production, planning, and record-keeping areas. The tour should be led by a supervisor who can answer questions about production, especially about any changes in the past year.

Common tests of details audit procedures for physical inventory observation are shown in Table 19-2. Detail tie-in and presentation and disclosure are the only balance-related audit objectives not included in the table. These objectives are discussed under compilation of inventory. The assumption throughout is that the client records inventory on prenumbered tags on the balance sheet date. In reality, smaller businesses may use inventory sheets rather than inventory tags. Larger businesses with heavily automated systems will not use tags at all. Rather, individuals will use hand-held scanners to scan each inventory location and item code, then manually enter the amount counted.

In addition to the detailed procedures included in Table 19-2, the auditor should walk through all areas where inventory is warehoused to make sure that all inventory has been counted and properly tagged. When inventory is in boxes or other containers, these should be opened during test counts. It is desirable to compare high dollar value inventory with counts in the previous year and inventory master files as a test of reasonableness. These two procedures should not be done until the client has completed the physical counts.

Audit of Pricing and Compilation

An important part of the audit of inventory is performing all the procedures necessary to make certain the physical counts were properly priced and compiled. Pricing includes all the tests of the client's unit prices to determine whether they are correct. Compilation includes all the tests of the summarization of the physical counts, the extension of price times quantity, footing the inventory summary, and tracing the totals to the general ledger.

PRICING AND COMPILATION CONTROLS The existence of adequate internal control for unit costs that is integrated with production and other accounting records is important to ensure that reasonable costs are used for valuing ending inventory. One important internal control is the use of **standard cost records** that indicate variances in material, labour, and overhead costs and can be used to evaluate production. When

Standard cost records—records that indicate variances between projected material, labour, and overhead costs, and the actual costs.

Balance-Related Audit Objective	Common Inventory Observation Procedures	Comments
Inventory as recorded on tags exists (existence).	Select a random sample of tag numbers, and identify the tag with that number attached to the actual inventory.	The purpose is to uncover the inclusion of non-existent items as inventory.
	Observe whether movement of inventory takes place during the count.	
Existing inventory is counted and tagged, and tags are accounted for to make sure none is missing (completeness).	Examine inventory to make sure it is tagged.	Special concern should be directed to omission of large sections of inventory.
	Observe whether movement of inventory takes place during the count.	
	Inquire as to inventory in other locations.	
	Account for all used and unused tags to make sure none is lost or intentionally omitted.	This test should be done at the completion of the physical count.
	Record the tag numbers for those used and unused for subsequent follow-up.	This test should be done at the completion of the physical count.
Inventory is counted accurately (accuracy).	Recount client's counts to make sure the recorded counts are accurate on the tags (also check descriptions and unit of count, such as dozen or gross).	Recording client counts in the working papers on *inventory count sheets* is done for two reasons: to obtain documentation that an adequate physical examination was made and to test for the possibility that the client might change the recorded counts after the auditor leaves the premises.
	Compare physical counts with perpetual inventory master file.	
	Record client's counts for subsequent testing.	
Inventory is classified correctly on the tags (classification).	Examine inventory descriptions on the tags and compare with the actual inventory for raw material, work in process, and finished goods.	These tests would be done as a part of the first procedure in the valuation objective.
	Evaluate whether the percent of completion recorded on the tags for work in process is reasonable.	
Information is obtained to make sure sales and inventory purchases are recorded in the proper period (cut-off).	Record in the working papers for subsequent follow-up the last shipping document number used at year end.	Obtaining proper cut-off information for sales and purchases is an essential part of inventory observation. The appropriate tests during the fieldwork were discussed for sales in Chapter 14 and for purchases in Chapter 18.
	Make sure the inventory for that item was excluded from the physical count.	
	Review shipping area for inventory set aside for shipment but not counted.	
	Record in the working papers for subsequent follow-up the last receiving report number used at year end.	
	Make sure the inventory for that item was included in the physical count.	
	Review receiving area for inventory that should be included in the physical count.	
Obsolete and unusable inventory items are excluded or noted (valuation).	Test for obsolete inventory by inquiry of factory employees and management, and be alert for items that are damaged, rust- or dust-covered, or located in inappropriate places.	
The client has right to inventory recorded on tags (rights and obligations).	Inquire as to consignment or customer inventory included on client's premises.	
	Be alert for inventory that is set aside or specially marked as indications of non-ownership.	

standard costs are used, procedures must be designed to keep the standards updated for changes in production processes and costs. The review of unit costs for reasonableness by someone independent of the department responsible for developing the costs is also a useful control over valuation.

An internal control designed to prevent the overstatement of inventory through the inclusion of obsolete inventory is a formal review and reporting of obsolete, slow-moving, damaged, and overstated inventory items. The review, which should be done by a competent employee, includes reviewing perpetual inventory master files for inventory turnover, possibly using generalized audit software, and holding discussions with engineering or production personnel.

Compilation internal controls are needed to provide a means of ensuring that the physical counts are properly summarized, priced at the same amount as the unit perpetual records, correctly extended and totalled, and included in the general ledger at the proper amount. Important compilation internal controls are adequate documents and records for taking the physical count, adequate controls over program changes, and proper internal verification. If the physical inventory is taken on prenumbered tags and carefully reviewed before the personnel are released from the physical examination of inventory, there should be little risk of misstatement in summarizing the tags. The most important internal control over accurate determination of prices, extensions, and footings is adequate controls over the programs that perform these calculations, with internal verification or review of output reports by a competent, independent person.

PRICING AND COMPILATION PROCEDURES Balance related audit objectives for tests of details of balances are also useful in discussing pricing and compilation procedures. The objectives and related tests are shown in Table 19-3, except for the cut-off objective. Physical observation, which was previously discussed, is a major source of cut-off information for sales and purchases. The tests of the accounting records for cut-off are done as part of sales (sales and collection cycle) and purchases (acquisition and payment cycle).

The frame of reference for applying the objectives is a listing of inventory obtained from the client that includes each inventory item's description, quantity, unit price, and extended value. The inventory listing is in inventory item description order with raw material, work in process, and finished goods separated. The total equals the general ledger balance.

The proper valuation (pricing) of inventory is often one of the most important and time-consuming parts of the audit. In performing pricing tests, three things about the client's method of pricing are extremely important: the method must be in accordance with generally accepted accounting principles, the application of the method must be consistent from year to year, and cost versus market value (replacement cost or net realizable value) must be considered. Because the method of verifying the pricing of inventory depends on whether items are purchased or manufactured, these two categories are discussed separately.

Pricing purchased inventory The primary types of inventory included in this category are raw materials, purchased parts, and supplies. As a first step in verifying the valuation of purchased inventory, it is necessary to establish clearly whether FIFO (first in, first out), LIFO (last in, first out), weighted average, or some other valuation method is being used. It is also necessary to determine which costs should be included in the valuation of a particular item of inventory. For example, the auditor must find out whether freight, storage, discounts, and other costs are included and compare the findings with the preceding year's audit working papers to ensure that the methods are consistent.

In selecting specific inventory items for pricing, emphasis should be put on the larger dollar amounts and on products that are known to have wide fluctuations in price, but a representative sample of all types of inventory and departments should be included as well. Stratified variable or monetary unit sampling is commonly used in these tests.

Table 19-3	**Balance-Related Audit Objectives and Tests of Details of Balances for Inventory Pricing and Compilation**

Balance-Related Audit Objective	Common Tests of Details of Balances Procedures
Inventory in the inventory listing schedule agrees with the physical inventory counts, the extensions are correct, and the total is correctly added and agrees with the general ledger (detail tie-in).	Perform compilation tests (see existence, completeness, and accuracy objectives). Extend the quantity times the price on selected items. Foot the inventory listing schedules for raw materials, work in process, and finished goods. Trace the totals to the general ledger.
Inventory items in the inventory listing schedule exist (existence).	Trace inventory listed in the schedule to inventory tags and auditor's recorded counts for existence and description.
Existing inventory items are included in the inventory listing schedule (completeness).	Account for unused tag numbers shown in the auditor's working papers to make sure no tags have been added. Trace from inventory tags to the inventory listing schedules, and make sure inventory on tags is included. Account for tag numbers to make sure none has been deleted.
Inventory items in the inventory listing schedule are accurate (accuracy).	Trace inventory listed in the schedule to inventory tags and auditor's recorded counts for quantity and description. Perform price tests of inventory. For a discussion of price tests, see text material on pages 654–658.
Inventory items in the inventory listing schedule are properly classified (classification).	Compare the classification into raw materials, work in process, and finished goods by comparing the descriptions on inventory tags and auditor's recorded test counts with the inventory listing schedule.
Inventory items in the inventory listing are stated at realizable value (valuation).	Perform test of lower of cost or market, selling price, and obsolescence.
The client has rights to inventory items in the inventory listing schedule (rights and obligations).	Trace inventory tags identified as non-owned during the physical observation to the inventory listing schedule to make sure these have not been included. Review contracts with suppliers and customers, and inquire of management about the possibility of the inclusion of consigned or other non-owned inventory or the exclusion of owned inventory.
Inventory and related accounts in the inventory and warehousing cycle are properly disclosed (presentation and disclosure).	Examine financial statements for proper presentation and disclosure, including: • Separate disclosure of raw materials, work in process, and finished goods. • Proper description of the inventory costing method. • Description of pledged inventory. • Inclusion of significant sales and purchase commitments.

The auditor should list the inventory items he or she intends to verify for pricing and request that the client locate the appropriate vendors' invoices. It is important that a sufficient number of invoices be examined to account for the entire quantity of inventory for the particular item being tested, especially for the FIFO valuation method. Examining a sufficient number of invoices is useful in uncovering situations in which clients value their inventory on the basis of the most recent invoice only and, in some cases, in discovering obsolete inventory. As an illustration, assume that the client's valuation of a particular inventory item is $12 per unit for 1,000 units, using FIFO. The auditor should examine the most recent invoices for acquisitions of that inventory item made in the year under audit until the valuation of all of the 1,000 units is accounted for. If the most recent acquisition of the inventory item was for 700 units at $12 per unit and the immediately preceding acquisition was for 600 units at $11.30 per unit, then the inventory item in question was overstated by $210 (300 × $0.70).

When the client has perpetual inventory master files that include unit costs of acquisitions, it is usually desirable to test the pricing by tracing the unit costs to the perpetuals rather than to vendors' invoices. In most cases, the effect is to reduce the cost of verifying inventory valuation significantly. Naturally, when the perpetuals are used to verify unit costs, it is essential to test the unit costs on the perpetuals to vendors' invoices as a part of the tests of the acquisition and payment cycle.

Pricing manufactured inventory The auditor must consider the cost of raw materials, direct labour, and manufacturing overhead in pricing work in process and finished goods. The need to verify each of these has the effect of making the audit of work-in-process and finished goods inventory more complex than the audit of purchased inventory. Nevertheless, such considerations as selecting the items to be tested, testing for whether cost or market value is lower, and evaluating the possibility of obsolescence also apply.

In pricing raw materials in manufactured products, it is necessary to consider both the unit cost of the raw materials and the number of units required to manufacture a unit of output. The unit cost can be verified in the same manner as that used for other purchased inventory—by examining vendors' invoices or perpetual inventory master files. Then it is necessary to examine engineering specifications, inspect the finished product, or find a similar method to determine the number of units it takes to manufacture a particular product.

Similarly, the hourly costs of direct labour and the number of hours it takes to manufacture a unit of output must be verified while testing direct labour. Hourly labour costs can be verified by comparison with labour payroll or union contracts. The number of hours needed to manufacture the product can be determined from engineering specifications or similar sources.

The proper manufacturing overhead in work in process and finished goods is dependent on the approach being used by the client. It is necessary to evaluate the method being used for consistency and reasonableness and to recompute the costs to determine whether the overhead is correct. For example, if the rate is based on direct labour dollars, the auditor can divide the total manufacturing overhead by the total direct labour dollars to determine the actual overhead rate. This rate can then be compared with the overhead rate used by the client to determine unit costs.

When the client has standard cost records, an efficient and useful method of determining valuation is the review and analysis of variances. If the variances in material, labour, and manufacturing overhead are small, they are evidence of reliable cost records.

Cost or market In pricing inventory, it is necessary to consider whether replacement cost or net realizable value is lower than historical cost. For purchased finished goods and raw materials, the most recent cost of an inventory item as indicated on a vendor's invoice of the subsequent period is a useful way to test for replacement cost. All manufacturing costs must be considered for work in process and finished goods for manufactured inventory. It is also necessary to consider the sales value of inventory items and the possible effect of rapid fluctuation of prices to determine net realizable value. Finally, in the evaluation process, it is necessary to consider the possibility of obsolescence.

concept check

C19-5 The inventory balance is highly material. Does the auditor have a choice with respect to observation of inventory? Why or why not?

C19-6 Why is the audit technique of observation important during the physical inventory count?

Integration of the Tests

The most difficult part of understanding the audit of the inventory and warehousing cycle is grasping the interrelationship of the many different tests the auditor makes to evaluate whether inventory and cost of goods sold are fairly stated. Figure 19-6 and the discussion that follows are designed to aid the reader in perceiving the audit of the inventory and warehousing cycle as a series of integrated tests.

TESTS OF THE ACQUISITION AND PAYMENT CYCLE Whenever the auditor verifies acquisitions as part of the tests of the acquisition and payment cycle, evidence is being obtained about the accuracy of raw materials purchased and all manufacturing overhead costs except labour. These acquisition costs either flow directly into cost of goods sold or become the most significant part of the ending inventory of raw material, work in process, and finished goods. In audits involving perpetual inventory master files, it is common to test these as a part of tests of controls procedures in the acquisition and payment cycle. Similarly, if manufacturing costs are assigned to individual jobs or processes, they are usually tested as part of the same cycle.

TESTS OF THE PAYROLL AND PERSONNEL CYCLE When the auditor verifies labour costs, the same comments apply as for acquisitions. In most cases, the cost accounting records for direct and indirect labour costs can be tested as part of the audit of the payroll and personnel cycle if there is adequate advance planning.

Figure 19-6	Interrelationship of Various Audit Tests

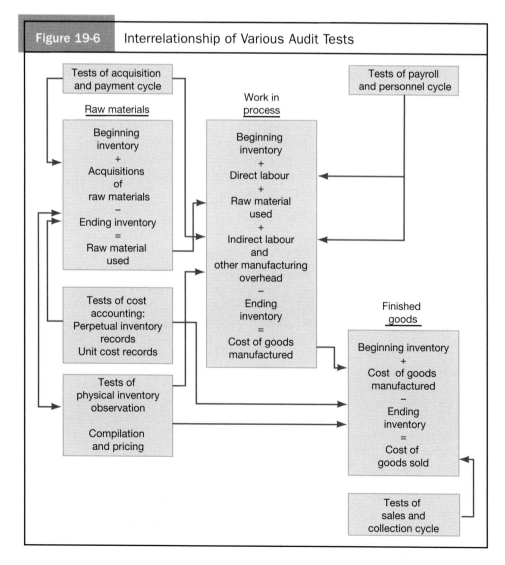

TESTS OF THE SALES AND COLLECTION CYCLE Although the relationship is less close between the sales and collection cycle and the inventory and warehousing cycle than between the two cycles previously discussed, it is still important. Most of the audit testing in the storage of finished goods as well as the shipment and recording of sales takes place when the sales and collection cycle is tested. In addition, if standard cost records are used, it may be possible to test the standard cost of goods sold at the same time that sales tests are performed.

TESTS OF COST ACCOUNTING Tests of cost accounting are meant to verify the controls affecting inventory that were not verified as part of the three previously discussed cycles. Tests are made of the physical controls, transfers of raw material costs to work in process, transfers of costs of completed goods to finished goods, perpetual inventory master files, and unit cost records.

PHYSICAL INVENTORY, COMPILATION, AND PRICING In most audits, the underlying assumption in testing the inventory and warehousing cycle is that cost of goods sold is a residual of (1) beginning inventory (2) plus acquisitions of raw materials, direct labour, and other manufacturing costs (3) minus ending inventory. When the audit of inventory and cost of goods sold is approached with this idea in mind, the importance of ending inventory can be seen. Physical inventory, compilation, and pricing are each equally important in the audit because a misstatement in any one results in misstated inventory and cost of goods sold.

In testing the physical inventory, it is possible to rely heavily on the perpetual inventory master files if they have been tested as part of one or more of the previously discussed tests. In fact, if the perpetual inventory master files are considered reliable, the auditor can observe and test the physical count at some time during the year and rely on the perpetuals to keep adequate records of the quantities.

When testing the unit costs, it is also possible to rely, to some degree, on the tests of the cost records made during the tests of transaction cycles. The existence of standard cost records is also useful for the purpose of comparison with the actual unit costs. If the standard costs are used to represent historical costs, they must be tested for reliability.

Throughout the audit, the auditor must also be aware of events that can affect the value of the inventory. Audit Challenge 19-2 illustrates two examples of instant changes in inventory value. Some products that contain precious or semi-precious raw materials, such as jewellery, could also have rapid changes in value.

concept check

C19-7 How do tests of the acquisition and payment cycle support the audit of inventory?

C19-8 How do tests of labour costs fit into the audit of inventory?

audit challenge 19-2
What's It Worth?

Everybody loves toys, right? Wrong, when they have been painted with lead-based paint or contain raw materials with lead. Then, the value plummets, media get involved, and toys are pulled off retailer shelves and recalled by manufacturers. This happened in fall 2008, worldwide, as many toys made in China were found to have lead-based paint or other lead-based components. Apparently, the largest recall on record was for themed RCMP products.

Toys found with lead included stuffed toys, kits to build jewellery, baby pacifiers, and costume jewellery. These toys were pulled from the retailers' shelves. If a retailer cannot get back its money for such toys, then it has lost the cost of the toys. Other costs might include returning products, as well as legal action, if large dollar amounts are involved.

Instant value of plastic 500-ml bottles was created in January 1, 2009, when the bottles started attracting a 25-cent deposit. But what about the costs? Companies will now need a distribution system to collect and recycle the bottles.

CRITICAL THINKING QUESTIONS

1. Provide three different reasons why manufactured inventory could go down in value.
2. How would the auditor test to ensure that inventory has not gone down in value for the reasons that you described in part (1).

Sources: 1. Bruser, David, "Tests find toxic toys in stores across GTA," *Toronto Star*, October 4, 2008, p. A1, A16–A17. 2. Flavelle, Dana, "Bottled water company to launch refund program," *Toronto Star*, October 2, 2008, p. B1, B4. 3. Torstar News Service, "RCMP toys recalled," *Metro*, November 19, 2008, p. 12.

Summary

1. *What are the components of the inventory and warehousing cycle?* The inventory and warehousing cycle normally has the following functions: processing of purchase orders, receiving of material, storage of raw materials, processing of products, storage of work in process and finished goods, shipment of finished goods, and update of inventory records.

2. *What are the five different parts of the inventory and warehousing cycle that are audited?* For the purposes of auditing the cycle, it is divided into the following parts: (i) acquisition and recording of raw materials, labour, and overhead; (ii) transferring assets and costs among inventory types (to work in process and to finished goods); (iii) shipment of goods and recording of associated revenue and costs; (iv) physically observing the inventory count process; and (v) conducting pricing and compilation tests of inventory.

   Provide an overview of the process used to audit the inventory and warehousing cycle. In the context of the overall risk of the engagement and the cycle, the auditor documents general and application level controls, assesses control risks, and tests those controls, by assertion, where there is intended reliance. After assessing the results of the tests of controls, analytical procedures and tests of detail are conducted.

3. *What role does each of the following types of tests play in the audit of inventory?* (i) *Analytical review*—This review assesses the likelihood of potential misstatements and targets tests of detail. (ii) *Physical observation of inventory*—This is a set of procedures that provides assurance for the following assertions: existence, completeness, accuracy, classification, cut-off, valuation, and rights and obligations; see Table 19-2. (iii) *Pricing and compilation tests*—Using Table 19-3, we can see that these tests provide assurance with respect to detail tie-in, existence, completeness, accuracy, classification, valuation, rights and obligations, and presentation and disclosure.

4. *How does the relationship among the tests of different cycles affects the audit of inventory?* Tests of the acquisition and payment cycle provide evidence about the accuracy of raw materials purchases and all manufacturing overhead costs except labour. Tests of the payroll and personnel cycle provide assurance with respect to the labour cost components of inventory. Tests of both of these cycles, as well as of the sales and collection cycle, provide assurance with respect to the cut-off assertion for all of these cycles, as well as the inventory and warehousing cycle.

Review Questions

19-1 Give the reasons why inventory is often the most difficult and time-consuming part of many audit engagements.

19-2 Explain the relationship between the acquisition and payment cycle and the inventory and warehousing cycle in the audit of a manufacturing company. List several audit procedures in the acquisition and payment cycle that support your explanation.

19-3 What is meant by "cost accounting records," and what is their importance in the conduct of an audit?

19-4 Many auditors assert that certain audit tests can be significantly reduced for clients with adequate perpetual records that include both unit and cost data. What are the most important tests of the perpetual records that the auditor must make before he or she can reduce the assessed level of control risk? Assuming the perpetuals are determined to be accurate, which tests can be reduced?

19-5 Before the physical examination, the auditor obtains a copy of the client's inventory instructions and reviews them with the controller. In obtaining an understanding of inventory procedures for a small manufacturing company, these deficiencies are identified: shipping operations will not be completely halted during the physical examination, and there will be no independent verification of the original inventory count by a second counting team. Evaluate the importance of each of these deficiencies, and state its effect on the auditor's observation of inventory.

19-6 At the completion of an inventory observation, the controller requested a copy of all recorded test counts from the auditor to facilitate the correction of all discrepancies between the client's and the auditor's counts. Should the auditor comply with the request? Why or why not?

19-7 What major audit procedures are involved in testing for the ownership of inventory during the observation of the physical counts and as part of subsequent valuation tests?

19-8 In the verification of the amount of the inventory, the auditor should identify slow-moving and obsolete items. List the auditing procedures that could be employed to determine whether slow-moving or obsolete items have been included in inventory.

19-9 During the taking of physical inventory, the controller intentionally withheld several inventory tags from the employees responsible for the physical count. After the auditor left the client's premises at the completion of the inventory observation, the controller recorded non-existent inventory on the tags and thereby significantly overstated earnings. How could the auditor have uncovered the misstatement, assuming there are no perpetual records?

19-10 Explain why a proper cut-off of purchases and sales is heavily dependent on the physical inventory observation. What information should be obtained during the physical count to make sure cut-off is accurate?

19-11 Define what is meant by "compilation tests." List several examples of audit procedures to verify compilation.

19-12 Included in the December 31, 2009, inventory of Kupitz Supply Ltd. are 2,600 deluxe ring binders in the amount of $5,902. An examination of the most recent purchases of binders showed the following costs: January 26, 2010, 2,300 at $2.42 each; December 6, 2009, 1,900 at $2.28 each; and November 26, 2009, 2,400 at $2.07 each. What is the misstatement in valuation of the December 31, 2009, inventory for deluxe ring binders assuming FIFO inventory valuation? What would your answer be if the January 26, 2010, purchase were for 2,300 binders at $2.12 each?

19-13 Ruswell Manufacturing Ltd. applied manufacturing overhead to inventory at December 31, 2009, on the basis of $3.47 per direct labour hour. Explain how you would evaluate the reasonableness of total direct labour hours and manufacturing overhead in the ending inventory of finished goods.

19-14 Each employee of Gedding Manufacturing Corp., a firm using a job-cost inventory costing method, must reconcile his or her total hours worked to the hours worked on individual jobs using a job time sheet at the time weekly payroll time cards are prepared. The job time sheet is then stapled to the time card. Explain how you could test the direct labour dollars included in inventory as part of the payroll and personnel tests.

19-15 Assuming that the auditor properly documents receiving report numbers as part of the physical inventory observation procedures, explain how he or she should verify the proper cut-off of purchases, including tests for the possibility of raw materials in transit, later in the audit.

Discussion Questions and Problems

19-16 Items 1 through 8 are selected questions typically found in questionnaires used by auditors to obtain an understanding of internal controls in the inventory and warehousing cycle. In using the questionnaire for a particular client, a "yes" response to a question indicates a possible internal control, whereas a "no" indicates a potential weakness.

1. Does the receiving department prepare prenumbered receiving reports and account for the numbers periodically for all inventory received, showing the description and quantity of materials?
2. Is all inventory stored under the control of a custodian in areas where access is limited?
3. Are all shipments to customers authorized by prenumbered shipping documents?
4. Is a detailed perpetual inventory master file maintained for raw materials inventory?
5. Are physical inventory counts made by someone other than storekeepers and those responsible for maintaining the perpetual inventory master file?

6. Are standard cost records used for raw materials, direct labour, and manufacturing overhead?
7. Is there a stated policy with specific criteria for writing off obsolete or slow-moving goods?
8. Is the clerical accuracy of the final inventory compilation checked by a person independent of those responsible for preparing it?

REQUIRED

a. For each of the preceding questions, state the purpose of the internal control.
b. For each internal control, list a test of controls to test its effectiveness.
c. For each of the preceding questions, identify the nature of the potential financial misstatement(s) if the control is not in effect.
d. For each of the potential misstatements in part (c), list a substantive audit procedure to determine whether a material misstatement exists.

19-17 The following errors or omissions are included in the inventory and related records of Westbox Manufacturing Company Ltd.:

1. An inventory item was priced at $12 each instead of at the correct cost of $12 per dozen.
2. During the physical inventory-taking, the last shipments for the day were excluded from inventory and were not included as a sale until the subsequent year.
3. The clerk in charge of the perpetual inventory master file altered the quantity on an inventory tag to cover up the shortage of inventory caused by his theft during the year.

4. After the auditor left the premises, several inventory tags were lost and were not included in the final inventory summary.
5. In recording raw materials purchases, the improper unit price was included in the perpetual inventory transaction file and master file. Therefore, the inventory valuation was misstated because the physical inventory was priced by referring to the perpetual records.
6. During the physical count, several obsolete inventory items were included.

7. Because of a significant increase in volume during the current year and excellent control over manufacturing overhead costs, the manufacturing overhead rate applied to inventory was far greater than actual cost.

REQUIRED

a. For each misstatement, state an internal control that should have prevented it from occurring.

b. For each misstatement, state a substantive audit procedure that could be used to uncover it.

19-18 You encountered the following situations during the December 31, 2009, physical inventory of Latner Shoe Distributing Corp.

a. Latner maintains a large portion of the shoe merchandise in 10 warehouses throughout eastern and central Canada. This ensures swift delivery service for its chain of stores. You are assigned alone to the Halifax warehouse to observe the physical inventory process. During the inventory count, several express trucks pulled in for loading. Although infrequent, express shipments must be attended to immediately. As a result, the employees who were counting the inventory stopped to assist in loading the express trucks. What should you do?

b. (1) In one storeroom of 10,000 items, you have test counted about 200 items of high value and a few items of low value. You found no misstatements. You also note that the employees are diligently following the inventory instructions. Do you think you have tested enough items? Explain.

(2) What would you do if you counted 150 items and found a substantial number of counting errors?

c. In observing an inventory of liquid shoe polish, you note that a particular lot is five years old. From inspection of some bottles in an open box, you find that the material has solidified in most of the bottles. What action should you take?

d. During your observation of the inventory count in the main warehouse, you found that most of the prenumbered tags that had been incorrectly filled out are being destroyed and thrown away. What is the significance of this procedure, and what action should you take?

19-19 In connection with her examination of the financial statements of Knutson Products Co. Ltd., an assembler of home appliances, for the year ended May 31, 2010, Raymonde Mathieu, public accountant, is reviewing with Knutson's controller the plans for a physical inventory at the company warehouse on May 31, 2010.

Finished appliances, unassembled parts, and supplies are stored in the warehouse, which is attached to Knutson's assembly plant. The plant will operate during the count. On May 30, the warehouse will deliver to the plant the estimated quantities of unassembled parts and supplies required for May 31 production, but there may be emergency requisitions on May 31. During the count, the warehouse will continue to receive parts and supplies and to ship finished appliances. However, appliances completed on May 31 will be held in the plant until after the physical inventory.

REQUIRED

What procedures should the company establish to ensure that the inventory count includes all items that should be included and that nothing is counted twice?

(Adapted from AICPA)

19-20 The table below shows sales, cost of sales, and inventory data for Aladdin Products Supply Inc., a wholesale distributor of cleaning supplies. All amounts are in thousands.

	2010	2009	2008	2007
Sales	$23.2	$21.7	$19.6	$17.4
Cost of sales	17.1	16.8	15.2	13.5
Beginning inventory	2.3	2.1	1.9	1.5
Ending inventory	2.9	2.3	2.1	1.9

REQUIRED

a. Calculate the following ratios:
   (1) Gross margin as a percentage of sales.
   (2) Inventory turnover.

b. List several logical causes of the changes in the two ratios.

c. Assume that $500,000 is considered material for audit planning purposes for 2010. Could any of the fluctuations in the computed ratios indicate a possible material misstatement? Demonstrate this by performing a sensitivity analysis.

d. What should the auditor do to determine the actual cause of the changes?

19-21 Often, an important aspect of a public accountant's audit of financial statements is observation of the taking of physical inventory.

REQUIRED

a. What are the general objectives or purposes of the public accountant's observation of the taking of the physical inventory? (Do not discuss the procedures or techniques involved in making the observation.)

b. For what purposes does the public accountant make and record test counts of inventory quantities during observation of the taking of the physical inventory? Discuss.

c. A number of companies employ outside service companies that specialize in counting, pricing, extending, and footing inventories. These service companies usually furnish a certificate attesting to the value of the inventory.

Assume that a service company took the inventory on the balance sheet date.

(1) How much reliance, if any, can the public accountant place on the inventory certificate of outside specialists? Discuss.

(2) What effect, if any, would the inventory certificate of outside specialists have upon the type of report the public accountant would render? Discuss.

(3) What reference, if any, would the public accountant make to the certificate of outside specialists in the standard audit report?

19-22 You are testing the summarization and cost of raw materials and purchased part inventories as part of the audit of Rubber Products and Supply Corp. There are 2,000 inventory items with a total recorded value of $648,500.

Your audit tests will compare recorded descriptions and counts with the final inventory listing, compare unit costs with vendors' invoices, and extend unit costs times quantity. A misstatement in any of those is defined as a difference. You plan to use monetary unit sampling.

You make the following decisions about the audit of inventory:

Tolerable misstatement (same for upper as for lower)	$24,000
Average percent of error assumption—overstatements	50%
Average percent of error assumption—understatements	100%
Acceptable risk of incorrect acceptance	5%
Estimated error rate in the population	5%

REQUIRED

a. What are the advantages of using monetary unit sampling in this situation?

b. What is the sample size necessary to achieve your audit objectives using monetary unit sampling?

c. Disregarding your answer to part (b), assume that a sample of 125 items is selected and that the following differences between book and audited values are identified (understatements are in parentheses). The book or recorded amounts are also shown.

Item No.	Difference	Book Amount
1	$19	$ 700
2	11	136
3	(19)	820
4	40	250
5	90	300
6	38	210
7	(90)	2,150
8	70	300
9	(85)	950
Total	$74	

For each of the other 116 items in the sample, there was no difference between book and audited values.

Based on this sample, calculate the adjusted overstatement and understatement error bounds.

d. Are the book values misstated?

Professional Judgment Problems

19-23 Technology Parts Inc. is a wholesaler of computer hardware components. The company purchases inventory items in bulk directly from parts manufacturers and sells the parts to computer and other technology equipment manufacturers that use them as components in their products. Technology Parts Inc. grants suppliers access to its inventory management system through its website. Suppliers have real-time access to information about the parts inventory, including information about quantities held, storage locations, and forecast of product demand. In addition, customers have access through the website to information containing product descriptions, price, delivery estimates, availability status, and quality and reliability ratings. Customers can also access information to assess the compatibility of selected parts with other components used in their production processes.

REQUIRED

a. Identify business objectives that Technology Parts' management may be able to achieve by providing this information online to key suppliers and customers.

b. How might the availability of the information to suppliers and customers increase Technology Parts' business risk?

c. What processes should Technology Parts' management implement to minimize business risks?

d. How might the availability of the information increase the risk of material misstatements in the financial statements?

e. How are the components of the audit risk model affected by the internet access?

19-24 As a part of your clerical tests of inventory for Martin Manufacturing, you have tested about 20 percent of the dollar items and have found the following exceptions:

1. Extension errors:

Description	Quantity	Price	Extension as Recorded
Wood	465 board feet	$ 0.12/board foot	$ 5.58
Metal-cutting tools	29 units	30.00 each	670.00
Cutting fluid	16 barrels	40.00/barrel	529.00
Sandpaper	300 sheets	0.95/hundred	258.00

2. Differences located in comparing last year's costs with the current year's costs on the client's inventory lists:

Description	Quantity	This Year's Cost	Preceding Year's Cost
TA-114 precision-cutting torches	12 units	$500.00 each	Unable to locate
Aluminum scrap	4,500 pounds	5.00/ton	$65.00/ton
Lubricating oil	400 gallons	6.00/gallon	4.50/barrel

3. Test counts that you were unable to find when tracing from the test counts to the final inventory compilation:

Tag No.	Quantity	Current Year Cost	Description
2958	15 tons	$75.00/ton	Cold-rolled bars
0026	2,000 feet	2.25/foot	4-inch aluminum stripping

4. Page total, footing errors:

Page No.	Client Total	Correct Total
14	$1,375.12	$1,375.08
82	8,721.18	8,521.18

REQUIRED

a. State the amount of the actual misstatement in each of the four tests. For any item for which the amount of the misstatement cannot be determined from the information given, state the considerations that will affect your estimate of the misstatement.

b. As a result of your findings, what will you do about clerical accuracy tests of the inventory in the current year?

c. What changes, if any, would you suggest in internal controls and procedures for Martin Manufacturing during the compilation of next year's inventory to prevent each type of misstatement?

Case

19-25 Comfy Casuals (CC), a chain of retail stores, is facing a decision about its supplier portal. Should it be upgraded? Supplier management is important at CC, as happy suppliers provide high-quality products on a timely basis.

"Essentially, we process payments, lots of payments, about 61,000 per year. Of course, to process payments correctly, we maintain vendor information, answer questions from vendors, and both send and receive information," said Chuang, the Manager of Accounts Payable and Vendor Services at CC. Chuang was providing an overview of the accounts payable process to the new internal auditor, Marissa. Marissa's job was to be part of the assessment team for a potential upgrade to one of the software tools used by the accounts payable group, called iSupplier. iSupplier was implemented in mid-June 2007 at a cost of about $200,000. It is used by CC's suppliers to find out about the status of their accounts with CC.

To prepare herself for this first meeting, Marissa had examined the supplier section of CC's website. There, under the FAQ (frequently asked questions) section, she found a PowerPoint presentation about iSupplier for vendors. It explained that vendors could quickly access their transaction information and find out the status of their payments. The presentation and forms for suppliers were in an open website, accessible to the general public.

The accounts payable team uses Oracle software: general ledger, accounts payable, iSupplier, and iExpense. These systems are interfaced to functional systems that provide sales invoicing information, purchase order information, inventory management information, freight carrier information, and domestic and foreign payments (banking information).

Marissa was initially puzzled by the vendor services functions. Chuang explained that most of the suppliers had incentive transactions or variable pricing that had to be carefully monitored. New suppliers might choose to participate in special sales promotions, reducing their prices for a set volume of items. Many suppliers also received volume bonuses if CC sales exceeded particular thresholds or shipment bonus pricing if their products arrived on time. These arrangements are negotiated by buyers and approved by purchasing management.

Marissa cleared the cobwebs out of her mind by sorting out the terminology. Out loud, she wondered, "How is it possible that four people handle over 61,000 invoices per year?"

"First, you need to remember that we have three different classes of payments. Employees who are reimbursed for expenses are considered vendors. Their payments are approved by their immediate supervisors. Second, there are store suppliers, paid based upon approved purchase orders, and third, internal sundry suppliers, such as store costs, courier charges, or utility bills. All sundries have to be approved by the manager of the area. For the store suppliers, we do not pay by invoice; we pay by purchase order and bill of lading."

Chuang went on to explain that 10 years ago there were eight more people in the accounts payable department, who laboriously entered invoices and tried in vain to match invoices with purchase orders and receiving information. CC made the decision then to get rid of accounts payable retail supplier invoices. Payment is now made based upon terms from the purchase orders, which are electronically initiated by the buyers. The computer system logs all transactions so that it is possible to see who initiated and modified any electronic documents.

Received quantities from the bill of lading are entered into the system when goods are received at one of three regional distribution centres. When goods are unpacked and counted, any differences between the bill of lading and the count are recorded into the computer systems and processed as debits or credits associated with the bill of lading and the purchase order. Payment is made based upon the payment terms and currency set up in the vendor file. The most common payment term is net 30 days. Each vendor has one currency set up for payment. Many vendors are set up as receiving electronic payments rather than cheque or international money order. Payment is then made electronically, and an automatic email message is sent to the supplier, listing the payment amount and the payment details. The supplier must contact the accounts payable group at CC to set up the email account that will receive this banking information.

There is constant change in the vendor profiles. Four years ago, there were about 5,000 active suppliers to the retail stores, and now there are about 10,000. This increase of 5,000 suppliers means an average increase of about 1,250 suppliers per year, a large number of new vendors that are processed! It is actually more time-consuming to process the approximately 20,000 sundry invoices than the product vendor payments, as the sundry payment invoices must be manually entered. Also, due to frequent address changes, addresses are checked carefully for each sundry invoice.

Chuang pulled out a copy of the RFP (request for proposal) that had been used in 2005 for several subsystems, including one for the web-based iSupplier system, and handed it to Marissa, for her reference. "Take a look at the activity volumes. You'll see that the accounts payable help desk received about 7,250 telephone calls and emails in the most recent fiscal year prior to this RFP. We had one full-time person recording and tracking all of these queries. Then many people had to answer the queries and give their answers back to the person doing the tracking. Now we are down to one part-time person doing the tracking, and she can answer many of the queries herself. I suspect that without iSupplier, we would have needed more than one person for answering queries from all these new suppliers."

Chuang was hoping to encourage greater vendor use of iSupplier by having actual documents (such as special pricing or volume bonus agreements) available on the iSupplier secure website.

"So how many suppliers are using iSupplier now?" Chuang was not sure and had to call in Stephanie, the accounts payable supervisor. It turned out that there were 800 vendors registered, or about 1,200 users. Most were retail store suppliers, although some of the major landlords had registered as well. This was not a very large take-up, even considering only the 2,500 retail product suppliers. Vendors seemed to like the one-to-one service and to deal with a person directly when they had questions.

REQUIRED

a. What controls should be present over supplier master file changes at CC?

b. What risks are present for inventory misstatements at CC? For each risk, provide an example of an internal control that would prevent or detect the risk.

c. Prepare a qualitative and quantitative analysis that evaluates the success of the iSupplier implementation over a period of three years. Has the implementation been successful? Why or why not?

20

Audit of the capital acquisition and repayment cycle

Owners' equity may be considered a residual account for corporations—this is where the result of current operations is posted. However, other large transactions, such as dividend payments and the equity portion of financial instruments, also flow through this account. The auditor needs to carefully examine each of these potentially large transactions. Management accountants need to understand the impact of capitalization choices, while auditors need to assess realizable value as well as the cost of potentially complex financial instruments.

STANDARDS REFERENCED IN THIS CHAPTER

No standards are referenced in this chapter.

LEARNING OBJECTIVES

1 Describe the four key characteristics of the capital acquisition and repayment cycle. State the methodology for designing tests of balances for notes payable. Itemize the purpose of conducting analytical procedures for notes payable.

2 Describe the difference in equity between public and closely held corporations. Provide examples of common internal controls over owners' equity transactions. List the main concerns when auditing capital stock.

Audit Continuity Supports Client Discontinuity

Flanagan Holdings was a growing consolidator of companies in the Canadian real estate industry. During the four years since its initial public offering, Flanagan had had significant staff turnover, including at senior executive levels. Geoff, the new CFO (chief financial officer) of Flanagan, was responsible for completing the unaudited interim financial statements for the quarter ended June 30, 2010. He had reviewed the company's working papers and loan agreements and had come to the conclusion that Flanagan was in breach of a bank loan with Big Blue Bank due to the devaluation of some of Flanagan's investment papers.

Geoff contacted the loan manager at his Big Blue branch (who is also new, having been assigned to his company's account for only six months), and they both agreed that it seemed that Flanagan had been in violation of the loan agreement since the inception of the loan two years ago. Feeling concerned, Geoff contacted the partner assigned to Flanagan's audit to find out what the financial statement disclosure issues were. The partner stated that if Flanagan were in breach of the loan agreement, the debt would be classified as a current liability and additional note disclosures explaining the breach would be required, unless the bank issued a waiver for the offending clause. However, the partner referred Geoff to Lana, the audit manager who had been working with Flanagan since its inception four years ago.

Lana reviewed the 2008 audit files—the year the lending agreement was executed. She remembered having analyzed the loan agreements carefully due to their magnitude. Lana found in the firm's permanent file her analysis of the loans and also a reference to a legal interpretation that the audit firm had obtained. The legal interpretation clarified the terms of the loan agreement and confirmed that Flanagan was not in violation of the loan. Lana provided a copy of the legal agreement to Geoff and to Big Blue's loan manager.

IMPORTANCE TO AUDITORS

Flanagan's story illustrates the importance of maintaining well-documented and organized audit files in respect of client issues. The audit firm was able to support both the auditor's report and a client on an important issue. By understanding the impact to the financial statements and having legal support for a highly technical issue, the firm was able to provide continuity where both the client and the bank had employee turnover.

WHAT DO YOU THINK?

1. What are some other examples of ways specialists can assist auditors in the audit of the capital acquisition and repayment cycle?
2. Describe additional documentation that should have been present at both Flanagan and Big Blue.

Sources: Contributed by a qualified accountant in public practice.

LOAN agreements and methods of borrowing and investing funds are not stable—new types of instruments are regularly created. Some are stable, while others turn out to be problematic, such as the mortgage-backed papers that crashed in 2008 and 2009. Specialists on the audit team help the firm assess risks and provide audit support for short-term and long-term financial instruments during the engagement. In this chapter, we focus on notes payable and certain owners' equity transactions to illustrate the audit of the capital acquisition cycle.

❶ The Nature of the Capital Acquisition and Repayment Cycle

The final transaction cycle, capital acquisition and repayment, relates to the acquisition of capital resources such as interest-bearing debt and owners' equity as well as the repayment of capital. The **capital acquisition and repayment cycle** also includes the payment of interest and dividends. The following are the major accounts in the cycle:

- Notes payable
- Contracts payable
- Mortgages payable
- Capital stock—preferred
- Capital stock—common
- Retained earnings
- Bonds payable
- Interest expense and accruals
- Dividends declared
- Dividends payable
- Proprietorship—capital account
- Partnership—capital accounts
- Options and foreign exchange contracts
- Other financial instruments

> **Capital acquisition and repayment cycle**—the transaction cycle involving the acquisition of capital resources, in the form of interest-bearing debt and owners' equity, and the repayment of the capital.

Four characteristics of the capital acquisition and repayment cycle significantly influence the audit of these accounts:

1. Relatively few transactions affect the account balances, but each transaction is often highly material in amount. For example, bonds are infrequently issued by most companies, but the amount of a bond issue is normally large. Due to the large size of most bond issues, it is common to verify each transaction taking place in the cycle for the entire year as part of verifying the balance sheet accounts. Audit working papers include the beginning balance of every account in the capital acquisition and repayment cycle and document every transaction that occurred during the year.

2. The exclusion of a single transaction could be material in itself. Considering the effect of understatements of liabilities and owners' equity, which was discussed in Chapter 18, omission is a major audit concern.

3. There is a legal relationship between the client entity and the holder of the stock, bond, or similar ownership document. In the audit of the transactions and amounts in the cycle, the auditor must ensure that the significant legal requirements affecting the financial statements have been properly fulfilled and adequately disclosed in the statements.

4. There is a direct relationship between the interest and dividend accounts and debt and equity. In the audit of interest-bearing debt, it is desirable to simultaneously verify the related interest expense and interest payable. This holds true for owners' equity, dividends declared, and dividends payable.

The audit procedures for many of the accounts in the capital acquisition and repayment cycle can best be understood by selecting representative accounts for study. Therefore, this chapter discusses (1) the audit of notes payable and the related interest expense and interest payable, to illustrate interest-bearing capital, and (2) common stock, retained earnings, and dividends.

The methodology for determining tests of details of balances for capital acquisition accounts is the same as that followed for all other accounts. For example, the methodology for notes payable is shown in Figure 20-1.

Notes Payable

Note payable—a legal obligation to a creditor, which may be unsecured or secured by assets.

A **note payable** is a legal obligation to a creditor, which may be unsecured or secured by assets. Typically, a note is issued for a period somewhere between one month and one year, but there are also long-term notes of over a year. Notes are issued for many different purposes, and the pledged property includes a wide variety of assets such as securities, inventory, and capital assets. The principal and interest payments on the notes must be made in accordance with the terms of the loan agreement. For short-term loans, a principal and interest payment is usually required only when the loan

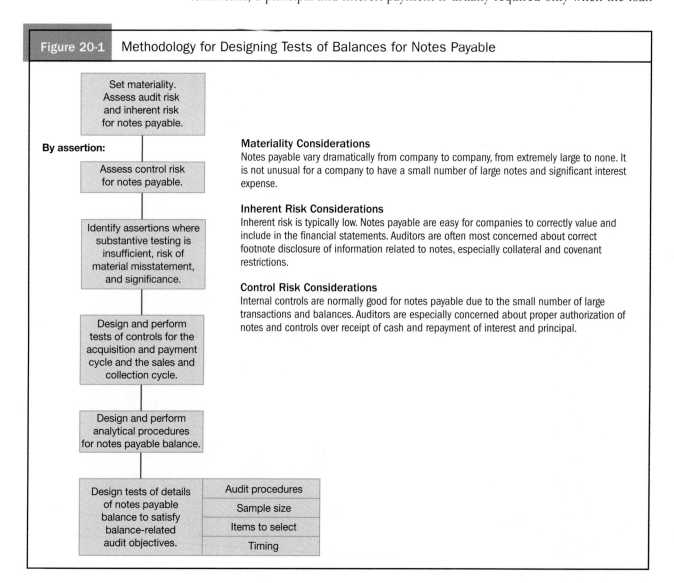

| Figure 20-1 | Methodology for Designing Tests of Balances for Notes Payable |

Materiality Considerations
Notes payable vary dramatically from company to company, from extremely large to none. It is not unusual for a company to have a small number of large notes and significant interest expense.

Inherent Risk Considerations
Inherent risk is typically low. Notes payable are easy for companies to correctly value and include in the financial statements. Auditors are often most concerned about correct footnote disclosure of information related to notes, especially collateral and covenant restrictions.

Control Risk Considerations
Internal controls are normally good for notes payable due to the small number of large transactions and balances. Auditors are especially concerned about proper authorization of notes and controls over receipt of cash and repayment of interest and principal.

becomes due; but for loans over 90 days, the note usually calls for monthly or quarterly interest payments.

OVERVIEW OF ACCOUNTS The accounts used for notes payable and related interest are shown in Figure 20-2. It is common to include tests of principal and interest payments as a part of the audit of the acquisition and payment cycle because the payments are recorded in the cash disbursement journal. However, due to their relative infrequency, in many cases no capital transactions are included in the tests of controls sample. Therefore, it is also normal to test these transactions as part of the capital acquisition and repayment cycle.

OBJECTIVES The auditor considers risks of management bias when setting the objectives for auditing notes. For example, the auditor will consider the extent of related parties and the clarity of disclosure with respect to the notes. Assuming that disclosure is adequate and the auditor believes that management has fairly disclosed notes, the objectives of the auditor's examination of notes payable is to determine whether the following are true:

- The internal controls over notes payable are adequate.
- Transactions for principal and interest involving notes are properly authorized and recorded as defined by the six transaction-related audit objectives.
- The liability for notes payable and the related interest expense and accrued liability are properly stated as defined by seven of the eight balance-related audit objectives. (Realizable value is not applicable to liability accounts.)

Figure 20-2	Notes Payable and the Related Interest Accounts

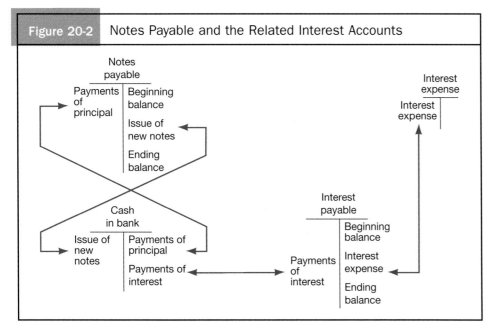

INTERNAL CONTROLS There are four important controls over notes payable.

Proper authorization for the issue of new notes Responsibility for the issuance of new notes should be vested in the board of directors or high-level management personnel. Generally, two signatures of properly authorized officials are required for all loan agreements. The amount of the loan, the interest rate, the repayment terms, and the particular assets pledged are all part of the approved agreement. Whenever notes are renewed, it is important that they be subject to the same authorization procedures as those for the issuance of new notes.

Adequate controls over the repayment of principal and interest The periodic payments of interest and principal should be controlled as part of the acquisition and payment cycle. At the time the note was issued, the accounting department should have received a copy in the same manner in which it receives vendors' invoices and receiving reports. The accounts payable department should automatically issue cheques for the notes when they fall due, again in the same manner in which it prepares cheques for acquisitions of goods and services. The copy of the note is the supporting documentation for payment.

Proper documents and records These include the maintenance of subsidiary records and control over blank and paid notes by a responsible person. Paid notes should be cancelled and retained under the custody of an authorized official.

Periodic, independent verification Periodically, the detailed note records should be reconciled with the general ledger and compared with the note holders' records by an employee who is not responsible for maintaining the detailed records. At the same time, an independent person should recompute the interest expense on notes to test the accuracy and propriety of the record keeping.

TESTS OF CONTROLS Tests of notes payable transactions involve the issue of notes and the repayment of principal and interest. The audit tests are part of tests of controls for cash receipts (Chapter 14) and cash disbursements (Chapter 18). Additional tests of controls are often performed as part of tests of details of balances due to the materiality of individual transactions.

Tests of controls for notes payable and related interest should emphasize testing the four important internal controls discussed in the previous section. In addition, the accurate recording of receipts from note proceeds and payments of principal and interest is emphasized.

ANALYTICAL PROCEDURES Analytical procedures are essential for notes payable because tests of details for interest expense and accrued interest can frequently be eliminated when results are favourable. Table 20-1 illustrates typical analytical procedures for notes payable and related interest accounts.

The auditor's independent estimate of interest expense, using average notes payable outstanding and average interest rates, tests the reasonableness of interest

Table 20-1	Analytical Procedures for Notes Payable
Analytical Procedure	**Possible Misstatement**
Recalculate approximate interest expense on the basis of average interest rates and overall monthly notes payable.	Misstatement of interest expense or accrued interest, or omission of an outstanding note payable.
Compare individual notes outstanding with the prior year's.	Omission or misstatement of a note payable.
Compare total balance in notes payable, interest expense, and accrued interest with prior year's.	Misstatement of notes payable, interest expense, or accrued interest.

expense but also tests for omitted notes payable. If actual interest expense is materially larger than the auditor's estimate, one possible cause could be interest payments on unrecorded notes payable.

TESTS OF DETAILS OF BALANCES The normal starting point for the audit of notes payable is a schedule of notes payable and accrued interest obtained from the client. A typical schedule is shown in Figure 20-3 on the next page. The usual schedule includes detailed information for all transactions that took place during the entire year for principal and interest, the beginning and ending balances for notes and interest payable, and descriptive information about the notes, such as the due date, the interest rate, and the assets pledged as collateral. Such a schedule is also used to ensure adequate disclosure in the financial statements. Tests for presentation and disclosure are included in the last row of Table 20-2.

When there are numerous transactions involving notes during the year, it may not be practical to obtain a schedule of the type shown in Figure 20-3. In that situation, the auditor is likely to request that the client prepare a schedule or computer spreadsheet of only those notes with unpaid balances at the end of the year. This would

Table 20-2	Objectives and Tests of Details for Notes Payable and Interest	
Balance-Related Audit Objectives	**Common Tests of Details of Balances Procedures**	**Comments**
Notes payable in the notes payable schedule agree with the client's notes payable register or master file (detail tie-in).	Foot the notes payable list for notes payable and accrued interest.* Trace the totals to the general ledger. Trace the individual notes payable to the master file.	Frequently, these are done on a 100-percent basis because of the small population size.
Notes payable in the schedule exist (existence).	Confirm notes payable. Examine duplicate copy of notes for authorization. Examine corporate minutes for loan approval.	
Existing notes payable are included in the notes payable schedule (completeness).	Examine notes paid after year end to determine whether they were liabilities at the balance sheet date. Obtain a standard bank confirmation that includes specific reference to the existence of notes payable from all financial institutions with which the client does business. (Bank confirmations are discussed more fully in Chapter 16.) Review the bank reconciliation for new notes credited directly to the bank account by the bank. (Bank reconciliations are also discussed more fully in Chapter 16.) Obtain confirmations from creditors who have held notes from the client in the past and are not currently included in the notes payable schedule. This is the same concept as a "zero balance" confirmation in accounts payable. Analyze interest expense to uncover a payment to a creditor who is not included in the notes payable schedule. This procedure is automatically done if the schedule is similar to the one in Figure 20-3 because all interest payments are reconciled with the general ledger. Examine paid notes for cancellation to make sure they are not still outstanding. They should be maintained in the client's files. Review the minutes of the board of directors for authorized but unrecorded notes.	This objective is important for uncovering both errors and fraud and other irregularities. The first three of these procedures are done on most audits. The others are frequently done only when internal controls are weak.
Notes payable and accrued interest on the schedule are accurate (accuracy).	Examine duplicate copies of notes for principal and interest rates. Confirm notes payable, interest rates, and last date for which interest has been paid with holders of notes. Recalculate accrued interest.*	In some cases, it may be necessary to calculate, using present-value techniques, the imputed interest rates, or the principal amount of the note. An example is when equipment is acquired for a note.*

continued >

Table 20-2   Objectives and Tests of Details for Notes Payable and Interest (*Continued*)

Balance-Related Audit Objectives	Common Tests of Details of Balances Procedures	Comments
Notes payable in the schedule are properly classified (classification).	Examine due dates on duplicate copies of notes to determine whether all or part of the notes are a non-current liability. Review notes to determine whether any are related-party notes or accounts payable.	
Notes payable are included in the proper period (cut-off).	Examine duplicate copies of notes to determine whether notes were dated on or before the balance sheet date.	Notes should be included as current-period liabilities when dated on or before the balance sheet date.
The company has an obligation to pay the notes payable (rights and obligations).	Examine notes to determine whether the company has obligations for payment.	
Notes payable, interest expense, and accrued interest are properly presented and disclosed (presentation and disclosure).	Examine duplicate copies of notes. Confirm notes payable. Examine notes, minutes, and bank confirmations for restrictions. Examine balance sheet for proper disclosure of non-current portions, related parties, assets pledged as security for notes, and restrictions resulting from notes payable.	Proper financial statement presentation, including footnote disclosure, is an important consideration for notes payable.

*This test could be completed using spreadsheet software or other computerized methods in audits where volume is high.

Figure 20-3   Schedule of Notes Payable and Accrued Interest

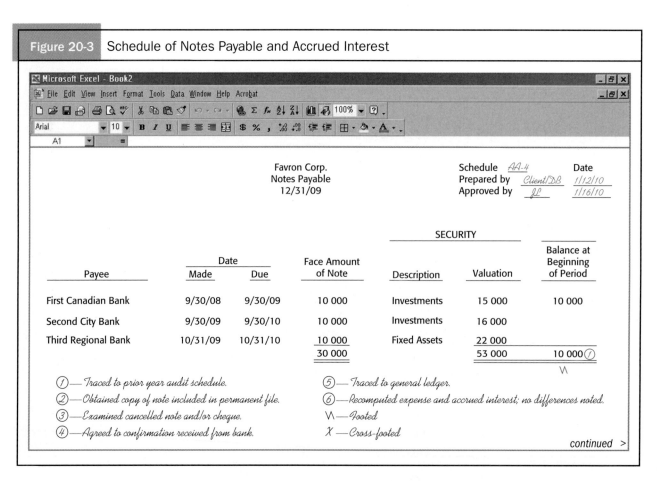

show a description of each note, its ending balance, and the interest payable at the end of the year, including the collateral and interest rate.

The objectives and common audit procedures are summarized in Table 20-2. Realizable value is not included in the table because it is not applicable to notes payable. The schedule of notes payable is the frame of reference for the procedures. The amount of testing depends heavily on materiality of notes payable and the effectiveness of internal controls.

The three most important balance-related audit objectives in notes payable are as follows:

- Existing notes payable are included (completeness).
- Notes payable in the schedule are accurately recorded (accuracy).
- Notes payable are properly presented and disclosed (presentation and disclosure).

The first two objectives are important because a misstatement could be material if even one note is omitted or incorrect. Presentation and disclosure are important because generally accepted accounting principles require that the footnotes adequately describe the terms of notes payable outstanding and the assets pledged as collateral for the loans. If there are significant restrictions on the activities of the company required by the loans, such as compensating balance provisions or restrictions on the payment of dividends, these must also be disclosed in the footnotes.

concept check

C20-1 What audit assertion is at most risk for the audit of capital?

C20-2 Who should be responsible for the approval of new debt such as notes payable? Why?

Closely held corporation—a corporation whose stock is not publicly traded; typically, there are only a few shareholders and few, if any, capital stock account transactions during the year; also known as a private corporation.

❷ Owners' Equity

A major distinction must be made in the audit of owners' equity between publicly held and **closely held corporations** (also known as private corporations). Public companies are permitted by their articles of incorporation to issue shares to the public;

Figure 20-3 Schedule of Notes Payable and Accrued Interest (*Continued*)

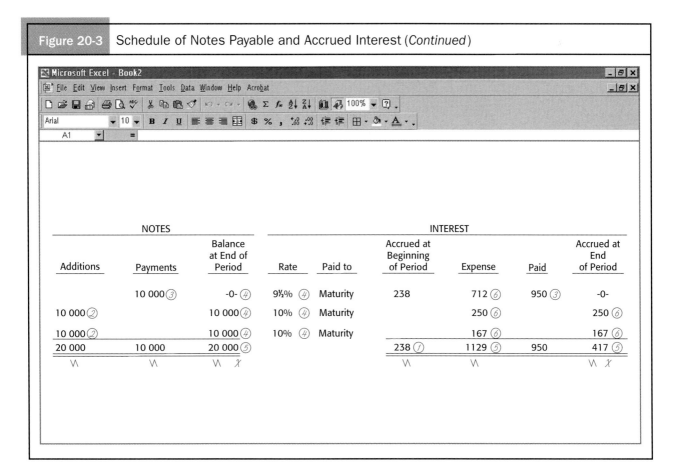

NOTES			INTEREST					
Additions	Payments	Balance at End of Period	Rate	Paid to	Accrued at Beginning of Period	Expense	Paid	Accrued at End of Period
	10 000③	-0-④	9½%④	Maturity	238	712⑥	950③	-0-
10 000②		10 000④	10%④	Maturity		250⑥		250⑥
10 000②		10 000④	10%④	Maturity		167⑥		167⑥
20 000	10 000	20 000⑤			238⑦	1129⑤	950	417⑤
⋀	⋀	⋀ 𝒳			⋀	⋀		⋀ 𝒳

---

closely held companies tend to be private companies with restricted share ownership. In most closely held corporations, there are few, if any, transactions during the year for capital stock accounts, and there are typically only a few shareholders. The only transactions entered in the owners' equity section are likely to be the change in owners' equity for the annual earnings or loss and the declaration of dividends, if any. The amount of time spent verifying owners' equity is frequently minimal for closely held corporations even though the auditor must test the existing corporate records.

Publicly held corporation—a corporation whose stock is publicly traded; typically, there are many shareholders and frequent changes in the ownership of the stock.

For **publicly held corporations**, the verification of owners' equity is more complex due to the larger numbers of shareholders and frequent changes in the individuals holding the stock. In this section, the appropriate tests for verifying the major accounts—capital stock, retained earnings, and the related dividends—in a publicly held corporation are discussed. The other accounts in owners' equity are verified in much the same way as these.

OVERVIEW OF ACCOUNTS An overview of the specific owners' equity accounts discussed in this section is given in Figure 20-4.

OBJECTIVES The objectives of the auditor's examination of owners' equity is to determine whether the following are true:

- The internal controls over capital stock and related dividends are adequate.
- Owners' equity transactions are recorded properly as defined by the six transaction-related audit objectives.
- Owners' equity balances are properly presented and disclosed as defined by the balance-related audit objectives for owners' equity accounts. (Rights/obligations and realizable value are not applicable.) Audit Challenge 20-1 illustrates problems that can occur with credit.

INTERNAL CONTROLS Several important internal controls are of concern to the independent auditor in owners' equity: proper authorization of transactions, proper record keeping, adequate segregation of duties between maintaining owners' equity records and handling cash and stock certificates, and the use of an independent registrar and stock transfer agent.

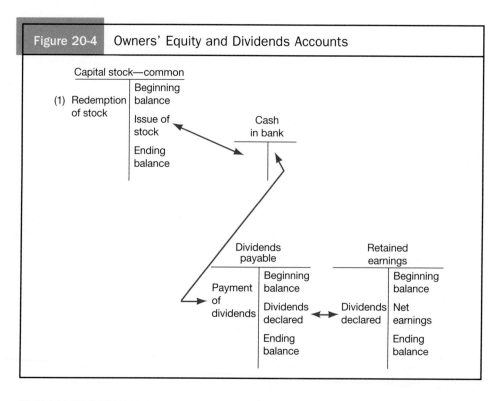

| Figure 20-4 | Owners' Equity and Dividends Accounts |

Proper authorization of transactions Since each owners' equity transaction is typically material, many of these transactions must be approved by the board of directors. The following types of owners' equity transactions usually require specific authorization:

- *Issuance of capital stock* The authorization includes the type of the equity to issue (e.g., preferred or common stock), number of shares to issue, issue price (also known as the stated value), privileges or conditions that attach to the stock, and date of the issue.
- *Repurchase or redemption of capital stock* The repurchase or redemption of common or preferred shares, the timing of repurchase (redemption), and the amount to pay for the shares should all be approved by the board of directors.
- *Declaration of dividends* The board of directors should authorize the form of dividends (e.g., cash or stock), the amount of the dividend per share, and the record and payment dates of the dividends.

Proper record keeping and segregation of duties When a company maintains its own records of stock transactions and outstanding stock, internal controls must be adequate to ensure that the actual owners of the stock are recognized in the corporate records, the correct amount of dividends is paid to the shareholders owning the stock as of the dividend record date, and the potential for employee fraud is minimized. The proper assignment of personnel and adequate record-keeping procedures are useful controls for these purposes.

The most important procedures for preventing misstatements in owners' equity are (1) well-defined policies for preparing stock certificates and recording capital stock transactions and (2) independent internal verification of information in the records. The client must be certain when issuing and recording capital stock that there is compliance with the relevant federal (for federally incorporated companies) or provincial (for provincially incorporated companies) laws governing corporations and the requirements in the articles of incorporation. For example, the classes of shares and the number of shares that the company is authorized to issue affect issuance and recording.

audit challenge 20-1
Credit Troubles

Recording long-term credit transactions sounds simple enough—record the debt, and expense the interest. Yet this is not always the case. Consider the ICAO (Institute of Chartered Accountants of Ontario). In July 2008, the ICAO announced that it was restating its financial statements due to an error of close to $1 million, which reduced members' equity. Costs associated with debt were capitalized rather than expensed when a complex swap took place with two different lenders.

The good thing is that the ICAO can readily obtain the credit that it needs. Consider another organization, such as Air Canada. The airline has been in and out of the news for many years, close to financial ruin. Air Canada's share price increased when it announced that it had signed a deal with CIBC (Canadian Imperial Bank of Commerce) for a loan of $100 million.

Other loans listed for Air Canada were with foreign organizations, such as one loan of US$195 million from General Electric Capital Corp. This might be a problem—with a changing U.S. dollar, the actual loan repayment and interest amounts will vary in terms of Canadian dollars unless the loan was hedged.

CRITICAL THINKING QUESTIONS

1. What are the risks associated with foreign currency loans? How would these risks be disclosed in the financial statements?
2. How does the financial stability of an organization affect its interest rates? How can the auditor use loan interest rate information during the conduct of the audit?

Sources: 1. Buckstein, Jeff, "ICAO 'embarrassed' by accounting glitch," *The Bottom Line*, 24(8), July, 2008, p. 1, 3; 2. The Canadian Press. "Air Canada lands credit," *Toronto Star*, January 1, 2009, p. B2.

A control over capital stock used by most companies is the maintenance of stock certificate books and shareholders' capital stock master and transaction files. A **capital stock certificate book** is a record of the issuance and repurchase of capital stock for the life of the corporation. For large public corporations, these records would be automated rather than kept manually. There would normally be a book or file for each type (preferred or common) and each class (common, class A; common, class B; etc.). The record for a particular capital stock transaction includes such information as the certificate number, the number of shares issued, the name of the person to whom it was issued, and the issue date. When shares are repurchased, the capital stock certificate book should include the cancelled certificates and the date of their cancellation. A shareholders' capital stock master file is the record of the outstanding shares at any given time. The master file acts as a check on the accuracy of the capital stock certificate book or transaction details and the preferred and common stock balances in the general ledger. It is also used as the basis for the payment of dividends.

The disbursement of cash for the payment of dividends should be controlled in much the same manner as was described in Chapter 17 for the preparation and payment of payroll. Dividend cheques should be prepared from the capital stock certificate book by someone who is not responsible for maintaining the capital stock records. After the cheques are prepared, it is desirable to have an independent verification of the shareholders' names and the amount of the cheques and a reconciliation of the total amount of the dividend cheques with the total dividends authorized in the minutes. The use of a separate imprest dividend account is desirable to prevent the payment of a larger amount of dividends than was authorized.

Independent registrar and stock transfer agent Some companies engage an independent registrar and stock transfer agent (usually one organization such as a trust company performs both tasks, but the job may be split between two such organizations) as a control to prevent the improper issuance of share certificates and to maintain shareholder records. The function of an independent registrar is to ensure that stock is issued by a corporation in accordance with the capital stock provisions in the articles of incorporation and the authorization of the board of directors. The **independent registrar** is responsible for signing all newly issued share certificates and making sure old certificates are received and cancelled before a replacement certificate is issued when there is a change in the ownership of the stock.

Most large corporations also employ the services of a **stock transfer agent** for the purpose of maintaining the shareholder records, including those documenting transfers of share ownership. The employment of a transfer agent not only serves as a control over the share records by putting them in the hands of an independent organization but reduces the cost of record keeping. Many companies also have the transfer agent disburse cash dividends to shareholders, thereby further transferring internal control. Corporations should have adequate procedures to verify on a periodic basis that transfer agents perform only authorized transactions.

AUDIT OF CAPITAL STOCK There are four main concerns in auditing capital stock:

- Existing capital stock transactions are recorded (completeness).
- Recorded capital stock transactions exist and are accurately recorded (occurrence and accuracy).
- Capital stock is accurately recorded (accuracy).
- Capital stock is properly presented and disclosed (presentation and disclosure).

The first two concerns involve tests of controls, and the last two involve tests of details of balances.

Existing capital stock transactions are recorded This objective is easily satisfied when a registrar or transfer agent is used. The auditor can confirm with him or her whether any capital stock transactions occurred and the valuation of existing transactions. Review of the minutes of the board of directors' meetings, especially near the balance sheet date, and examination of client-held stock records are also useful to uncover issuances and repurchases of capital stock.

Recorded capital stock transactions exist and are accurately recorded The issuance of new capital stock for cash, the merger with another company through an exchange of stock, the donation of shares, and the repurchase of shares each requires extensive auditing. Regardless of the controls in existence, it is normal practice to verify all capital stock transactions because of their materiality and permanence in the records. Existence can ordinarily be tested by examining the minutes of the board of directors' meetings for proper authorization.

Accurate recording of capital stock transactions for cash can be readily verified by confirming the amount with the transfer agent and tracing the amount of the recorded capital stock transactions to cash receipts. (In the case of repurchased shares, the amounts are traced to the cash disbursements journal.) In addition, the auditor must verify whether the correct amounts were credited to capital stock by referring to the articles of incorporation to determine the stated value of the capital stock.

When capital stock transactions involve stock dividends, acquisition of property for stock, mergers, or similar non-cash transfers, the verification of valuation may be considerably more difficult. For these types of transactions, the auditor must be certain that the client has correctly computed the amount of the capital stock issue in accordance with generally accepted accounting principles. For example, in the audit of a major merger transaction, the auditor has to evaluate whether the transaction is a purchase or, in very rare instances, a pooling of interests. Frequently, considerable research is necessary to determine which accounting treatment is correct for the existing circumstances. After the auditor reaches a conclusion as to the appropriate method, it is necessary to verify that the amounts were correctly computed.

Capital stock is accurately recorded The ending balance in the capital stock account is verified by first determining the number of shares outstanding at the balance sheet date. A confirmation from the transfer agent is the simplest way to obtain this information. When no transfer agent exists, the auditor must rely on examining the stock records and accounting for all shares outstanding in the stock certificate records, examining all cancelled certificates, and accounting for blank certificates. After the auditor is satisfied that the number of shares outstanding is correct, the recorded value in the capital account can be verified by multiplying the number of shares by the stated value of the stock. It is audited by verifying the share amounts of recorded transactions during the year and adding them to or subtracting them from the beginning balance in the account.

A major consideration in the accuracy of capital stock is verifying whether the number of shares used in the calculation of earnings per share is accurate. It is easy to determine the correct number of shares to use in the calculation when there is only one class of stock and a small number of capital stock transactions. The problem becomes much more complex when there are convertible securities, stock options, or stock warrants outstanding.

Capital stock is properly presented and disclosed The most important sources of information for determining proper presentation and disclosure are the articles of incorporation, the minutes of board of directors' meetings, and the auditor's analysis of capital stock transactions. The auditor should determine that there is a proper description of each class of stock, including such information as the number of shares issued and outstanding and any special rights of an individual class. The proper disclosure of stock options, stock warrants, and convertible securities should also be verified by examining legal documents or other evidence of the provision of these agreements.

AUDIT OF DIVIDENDS The emphasis in the audit of dividends is on the transactions rather than the ending balance. The exception is when there are dividends payable.

The six transaction-related audit objectives for transactions are relevant for dividends. Dividends are usually audited or confirmed with outside agents on a 100-percent basis and cause few problems. The following are the most important objectives, including those concerning dividends payable:

- Recorded dividends occurred (occurrence).
- Existing dividends are recorded (completeness).
- Dividends are accurately recorded (accuracy).
- Dividends that exist are paid to shareholders (existence).
- Dividends payable are recorded (completeness).
- Dividends payable are accurately recorded (accuracy).

Existence of recorded dividends can be checked by examining the minutes of board of directors' meetings for the amount of the dividend per share and the dividend date. When the auditor examines the board of directors' minutes for dividends declared, the auditor should be alert to the possibility of unrecorded dividends declared, particularly shortly before the balance sheet date. A closely related audit procedure is reviewing the permanent audit working-paper file to determine if there are restrictions on the payment of dividends in bond indenture agreements or preferred stock provisions.

The accuracy of a dividend declaration can be audited by recomputing the amount on the basis of the dividend per share and the number of shares outstanding. If the client uses a transfer agent to disburse dividends, the total can be traced to a cash disbursement entry to the agent and also confirmed.

When a client keeps its own dividend records and pays the dividend itself, the auditor can verify the total amount of the dividend by recalculation and reference to cash disbursed. In addition, it is necessary to verify whether the payment was made to the shareholders who owned the stock at the dividend record date. The auditor can test this by selecting a sample of recorded dividend payments and tracing the payee's name on the cancelled cheque to the dividend records to ensure the payee was entitled to the dividend. At the same time, the amount and the authenticity of the dividend cheque can be verified.

Tests of dividends payable should be done in conjunction with declared dividends. Any unpaid dividend should be included as a liability.

AUDIT OF RETAINED EARNINGS For most companies, the only transactions involving retained earnings are net earnings for the year and dividends declared. But there may also be corrections of prior-period earnings, prior-period adjustments charged or credited directly to retained earnings, and the setting up or elimination of appropriations of retained earnings.

The starting point for the audit of retained earnings is an analysis of retained earnings for the entire year. The audit schedule showing the analysis, which is usually part of the permanent file, includes a description of every transaction affecting the account.

The audit of the credit to retained earnings for net income for the year (or the debit for a loss) is accomplished by simply tracing the entry in retained earnings to the net earnings figure on the income statement. The performance of this procedure must, of course, take place fairly late in the audit after all adjusting entries affecting net earnings have been completed.

An important consideration in auditing debits and credits to retained earnings other than net earnings and dividends is determining whether the transactions should have been included. For example, prior-period adjustments can be included in retained earnings only if they result from a change in accounting policy or are intended to correct an error in prior-period financial statements. Once the auditor is satisfied that the recorded transactions are appropriately classified as retained earnings transactions, the next step is to decide whether they are accurately recorded. The audit evidence necessary to determine accuracy depends on the nature of the transactions.

If there is a requirement for an appropriation of retained earnings for a bond sinking fund, the correct amount of the appropriation can be determined by examining the bond indenture agreement.

Another important consideration in the audit of retained earnings is evaluating whether there are any transactions that should have been included but were not. If a stock dividend was declared, for instance, the market value of the securities issued should be capitalized by a debit to retained earnings and a credit to capital stock. Similarly, if the financial statements include appropriations of retained earnings, the auditor should evaluate whether it is still necessary to have the appropriation as of the balance sheet date. As an example, an appropriation of retained earnings for a bond sinking fund should be eliminated by crediting retained earnings after the bond has been paid off.

Of primary concern in determining whether retained earnings are correctly disclosed on the balance sheet is the existence of any restrictions on the payment of dividends. Frequently, agreements with bankers, shareholders, and other creditors prohibit or limit the amount of dividends the client can pay. These restrictions must be disclosed in the footnotes to the financial statements.

concept check

C20-3 Provide examples of outsourcing as applied to management of share records.

C20-4 List examples of complex transactions that could affect retained earnings.

Summary

1. *What are the four key characteristics of the capital acquisition and repayment cycle?* (i) There are relatively few transactions, but these are often highly material. (ii) The exclusion of a single transaction could result in a material misstatement. (iii) A legal relationship exists between the client and the holder of the capital instrument. (iv) There is a direct relationship between interest or dividends paid and the corresponding debt or equity amount.

   What is the methodology for designing tests of balances for notes payable? After assessing risks and allocating materiality, tests of controls (if appropriate) are designed, tested, and evaluated. Then, analytical procedures are performed, followed by the design and execution of tests of details of balances.

   What is the purpose of conducting analytical procedures for notes payable? These calculations are designed to detect potential misstatements in interest expense, accrued interest, or notes payable, including the potential omission of a note.

2. *What is the difference in equity between publicly held and closely held corporations?* Publicly held companies tend to have a more complex share structure than closely held corporations, resulting in a greater variety of transactions. Also, as there are more shareholders, there tend to be more changes in ownership of share capital.

   Provide examples of common internal controls over owners' equity transactions. To ensure proper authorization, transactions such as declaration of dividends, purchase, redemption, and issuance of capital stock should be approved by the board of directors. Adequate records should be kept of changes in share ownership to ensure payment of dividends to owners of shares. An independent registrar and stock transfer agent may be used to help ensure adequate segregation of duties.

   What are the main concerns when auditing capital stock? The auditor is concerned about the following assertions: completeness of all capital stock transactions, accurate recording of capital stock transactions, accurate recording of issued capital, and proper presentation and disclosure of capital stock.

Review Questions

20-1 List four examples of interest-bearing liability accounts commonly found in balance sheets. What characteristics do these liabilities have in common? How do they differ?

20-2 Why are liability accounts that are included in the capital acquisition and repayment cycle audited differently from accounts payable?

20-3 It is common practice to audit the balance in notes payable in conjunction with the audit of interest expense and interest payable. Explain the advantages of this approach.

20-4 With which internal controls should the auditor be most concerned in the audit of notes payable? Explain the importance of each.

20-5 Which analytical procedures are most important in verifying notes payable? Which types of misstatements can the auditor uncover by the use of these tests?

20-6 Why is it more important to search for unrecorded notes payable than for unrecorded notes receivable? List several audit procedures the auditor can use to uncover unrecorded notes payable.

20-7 What is the primary purpose of analyzing interest expense? Given this purpose, what primary considerations should the auditor keep in mind when doing the analysis?

20-8 Distinguish between the tests of controls and tests of details of balances for liability accounts in the capital acquisition and repayment cycle.

20-9 List four types of restrictions that long-term creditors often put on companies when granting them a loan. How can the auditor find out about each of these restrictions?

20-10 What are the primary objectives in the audit of owners' equity accounts?

20-11 Evaluate the following statement: "The corporate charter and the bylaws of a company are legal documents; therefore, they should not be examined by the auditors. If the auditor wants information about these documents, a lawyer should be consulted."

20-12 What are the major internal controls over owners' equity?

20-13 How does the audit of owners' equity for a closely held corporation differ from that for a publicly held corporation? In what respects are there no significant differences?

20-14 Describe the duties of a stock registrar and a transfer agent. How does the use of their services affect the client's internal controls?

20-15 What kinds of information can be confirmed with a transfer agent?

20-16 Evaluate the following statement: "The most important audit procedure to verify dividends for the year is a comparison of a random sample of cancelled dividend cheques with a dividend list that has been prepared by management as of the dividend record date."

20-17 Explain how the audit of dividends declared and paid is affected if a transfer agent disburses dividends for a client. What audit procedures are necessary to verify dividends paid when a transfer agent is used?

20-18 What should be the major emphasis in auditing the retained earnings account? Explain your answer.

20-19 Explain the relationship between the audit of owners' equity and the calculations of earnings per share. What are the main auditing considerations in verifying the earnings-per-share figure?

Discussion Questions and Problems

20-20 Items 1 through 6 are questions typically found in a standard internal control questionnaire used by auditors to obtain an understanding of internal control for notes payable. In using the questionnaire for a particular client, a "yes" response indicates a possible internal control, whereas a "no" indicates a potential weakness.

1. Are liabilities for notes payable incurred only after written authorization by a proper company official?
2. Is a notes payable master file maintained?
3. Is the individual who maintains the notes payable master file someone other than the person who approves the issuance of new notes or handles cash?
4. Are paid notes cancelled and retained in the company files?
5. Is a periodic reconciliation made of the notes payable master file with the actual notes outstanding by an individual who does not maintain the master file?

6. Are interest expense and accrued interest recomputed periodically by an individual who does not record interest transactions?

REQUIRED

a. For each of the preceding questions, state the purpose of the control.
b. For each of the preceding questions, identify the type of financial statement misstatement that could occur if the control were not in effect.
c. For each of the potential misstatements in part (b), list an audit procedure that could be used to determine whether a material misstatement existed.

20-21 The following are frequently performed audit procedures for the verification of bonds payable issued in previous years:

1. Obtain a copy of the bond indenture agreement, and review its important provisions.
2. Determine that each of the bond indenture provisions has been met.
3. Analyze the general ledger account for bonds payable, interest expense, and unamortized bond discount or premium.
4. Test the client's calculations of interest expense, unamortized bond discount or premium, accrued interest, and bonds payable.
5. Obtain a confirmation from the bondholder.

REQUIRED
a. State the purpose of each of the five audit procedures listed.
b. List the provisions for which the auditor should be alert in examining the bond indenture agreement.
c. For each provision listed in part (b), explain how the auditor can determine whether its terms have been met.
d. Explain how the auditor should verify the unamortized bond discount or premium.
e. List the information that should be requested in the confirmation of bonds payable with the bondholder.

20-22 The following covenants are extracted from the indenture of a bond issue outstanding from McMullen Corp. The indenture provides that failure to comply with its terms in any respect automatically advances the due date of the loan to the date of non-compliance (the regular date is 20 years from now).

REQUIRED

List any audit steps or reporting requirements that you feel should be taken or recognized in connection with each one of the following with respect to your audit of McMullen Corp.:

a. The debtor company shall endeavour to maintain a working capital ratio of 2:1 at all times, and, in any fiscal year following a failure to maintain said ratio, the company shall restrict compensation of officers to a total of $750,000. Officers for this purpose shall include a chair of the board of directors, a president, all vice-presidents, a secretary, and a treasurer.

b. The debtor company shall keep all property that is security for this debt insured against loss by fire to the extent of 100 percent of its actual value. Policies of insurance comprising this protection shall be filed with the trustee.
c. The debtor company shall pay all taxes legally assessed against the property that is security for this debt within the time provided by law for payment without penalty, and shall deposit receipted tax bills or equally acceptable evidence of payment of same with the trustee.
d. A sinking fund shall be deposited with the trustee using semi-annual payments of $300,000, from which the trustee shall, in his or her discretion, purchase bonds of this issue.

(Adapted from AICPA)

20-23 Evangeline Ltd. took out a 20-year mortgage for $2,600,000 on June 15, 2009, and pledged its only manufacturing building and the land on which the building stands as collateral. Each month subsequent to the issue of the mortgagee, a monthly payment of $20,000 is paid to the mortgagor. You are in charge of the current-year audit for Evangeline, which has a balance sheet date of December 31, 2009. The client has been audited previously by your public accounting firm, but this is the first time Evangeline Ltd. has had a mortgage.

REQUIRED

a. Explain why it is desirable to prepare a working paper for the permanent file for the mortgage. What type of information should be included in the working paper?
b. Explain why the audits of mortgage payable, interest expense, and interest payable should all be done together.
c. List the audit procedures that should ordinarily be performed to verify the issue of the mortgage, the balance in the mortgage and interest payable accounts at December 31, 2009, and the balance in interest expense for the year 2009.

20-24 The following audit procedures are commonly performed by auditors in the verification of owners' equity:

1. Review the articles of incorporation and bylaws for provisions about owners' equity.
2. Review the minutes of the board of directors' meetings for the year for approvals related to owners' equity.
3. Analyze all owners' equity accounts for the year and document the nature of any recorded change in each account.

4. Account for all certificate numbers in the capital stock book for all shares outstanding.
5. Examine the stock certificate book for any stock that was cancelled.
6. Recompute earnings per share.
7. Review debt provisions and senior securities with respect to liquidation preferences, dividends in arrears, and restrictions on the payment of dividends or the issue of stock.

a. State the purpose of each of these seven audit procedures, including the audit assertion(s).

b. List the type of misstatements the auditors could uncover by the use of each audit procedure.

20-25 The Bergonzi Corporation is a medium-sized wholesaler of grocery products with 4,000 shares of stock outstanding to approximately 25 shareholders. Because of the age of several retired shareholders and the success of the company, management has decided to pay dividends six times a year. The amount of the bimonthly dividend per share varies depends on the profits, but it is ordinarily between $5 and $7 per share. The chief accountant, who is also a shareholder, prepares the dividend cheques, records the cheques in the dividend journal, and reconciles the bank account. Important controls include manual cheque signing by the president and the use of an imprest dividend bank account.

The auditor verifies the dividends by maintaining a schedule of the total shares of stock issued and outstanding in the permanent working papers. The total amount of stock outstanding is multiplied by the dividends per share authorized in the minutes to arrive at the current total dividend. This total is compared with the deposit that has been made to the imprest dividend account. Since the transfer of stock is infrequent, it is possible to verify dividends paid for the entire year in a comparatively short time.

REQUIRED

a. Evaluate the usefulness of the approach followed by the auditor in verifying dividends in this situation. Include both the strengths and the weaknesses of the approach.

b. List other audit procedures that should be performed in verifying dividends in this situation. Explain the purpose of each procedure.

20-26 The Fox Company is a medium-sized industrial client that has been audited by your public accounting firm for several years. The only interest-bearing debt owed by Fox Company is $200,000 in long-term notes payable held by the bank. The notes were issued three years previously and will mature in six more years. Fox Company is highly profitable, has no pressing needs for additional financing, and has excellent internal controls over the recording of loan transactions and related interest costs.

REQUIRED

a. Describe the auditing procedures that you think will be necessary for notes payable and related interest accounts in these circumstances.

b. How would your answer differ if Fox Company were unprofitable, had a need for additional financing, and had weak internal controls?

Professional Judgment Problems

20-27 E-Antiques Inc. is an internet-based market maker for buyers and sellers of antique furniture and jewellery. The company allows sellers of antique items to list descriptions of those items on the E-Antiques website. Interested buyers review the website for antique items and then enter into negotiations directly with the seller for purchase. E-Antiques receives a commission for each transaction.

The company, founded in 2000, initially obtained capital through equity funding provided by the founders and through loan proceeds from financial institutions. In early 2009, E-Antiques became a publicly held company when it began selling shares on a national stock exchange. Although the company had never generated profits, the stock offering generated huge proceeds based on favourable expectations for the company, and the stock quickly increased to above $100 per share.

Management used the proceeds to pay off loans to financial institutions and to reacquire shares issued to the company founders. Proceeds were also used to fund purchases of hardware and software to support the online market. The balance of unused proceeds is currently held in the company's bank accounts.

REQUIRED

a. Before performing analytical procedures related to the capital acquisition and repayment cycle accounts, consider how the process of becoming publicly held would affect accounts at E-Antiques Inc. Describe whether each of the following balances would increase, decrease, or experience no change between 2008 and 2009 because of the public offering.
(1) Cash.
(2) Accounts receivable.
(3) Property, plant, and equipment.
(4) Accounts payable.
(5) Long-term debt.
(6) Common stock.
(7) Retained earnings.

(8) Dividends.

(9) Revenues.

b. During 2010, the stock price for E-Antiques plummeted to around $19 per share. No new shares were issued during 2010. Describe the impact of this drop in stock price on the following accounts for the year ended December 31, 2010:

(1) Common stock.

(2) Retained earnings.

c. How does the decline in stock price affect your assessment of client business risk and acceptable audit risk?

20-28 You are a public accountant engaged in an audit of the financial statements of Pate Corporation for the year ended December 31, 2009. The financial statements and records of Pate Corporation have not been audited by a public accountant in prior years.

The stockholders' equity section of Pate Corporation's balance sheet at December 31, 2009, follows:

Stockholders' Equity	
Capital stock 10,000 shares of $10 par value authorized; 5,000 shares issued and outstanding	$ 50,000
Capital contributed in excess of par value of capital stock	32,580
Retained earnings	47,320
Total stockholders' equity	$129,900

Pate Corporation was founded in 2000. The corporation has 10 stockholders and serves as its own registrar and transfer agent. There are no capital stock subscription contracts in effect.

REQUIRED

a. Prepare the detailed audit program for the audit of the three accounts comprising the stockholders' equity section of Pate Corporation's balance sheet. (Do not include in the audit program the verification of the results of the current year's operations.)

b. After every other figure on the balance sheet has been audited, it might appear that the retained earnings figure is a balancing figure and requires no further verification. Why does the public accountant verify retained earnings as is done with the other figures on the balance sheet? Discuss.

(Adapted from AICPA)

Case

20-29 The ending general ledger balance of $186,000 in notes payable for Sisam Manufacturing Inc. is made up of 20 notes to eight different payees. The notes vary in duration anywhere from 30 days to two years and in amount from $1,000 to $10,000. In some cases, the notes were issued for cash loans; in other cases, the notes were issued directly to vendors for the purchase of inventory or equipment. The use of relatively short-term financing is necessary because all existing properties are pledged for mortgages. Nevertheless, there is still a serious cash shortage.

Record-keeping procedures for notes payable are not good, considering the large number of loan transactions. There is neither a notes payable master file nor an independent verification of ending balances; however, the notes payable records are maintained by a secretary who does not have access to cash.

The audit has been done by the same public accounting firm for several years. In the current year, the following procedures were performed to verify notes payable:

1. Obtain a list of notes payable from the client, foot the notes payable balances on the list, and trace the total to the general ledger.

2. Examine duplicate copies of notes for all outstanding notes included on the listing. Compare the name of the lender, amount, and due date on the duplicate copy with the list.

3. Obtain a confirmation from lenders for all listed notes payable. The confirmation should include the due date of the loan, the amount, and interest payable at the balance sheet date.

4. Recompute accrued interest on the list for all notes. The information for determining the correct accrued interest is to be obtained from the duplicate copy of the note. Foot the accrued interest amounts, and trace the balance to the general ledger.

REQUIRED

a. What should be the emphasis in the audit of notes payable in this situation? Explain.

b. State the purpose of each of the four audit procedures listed.

c. Evaluate whether each of the four audit procedures was necessary. Evaluate the sample size for each procedure.

d. List other audit procedures that should be performed in the audit of notes payable in these circumstances.

5

Completing the audit and offering other services

Chapter 1 introduced the many different types of accountants and the types of services they provide. The chapters in this part expand on this discussion. The provision of special skills during audit engagements, assurance services other than audits, and non-assurance services constitutes an important contribution by accountants to the business community, as long as the audit engagements are performed in conformity with the professional rules of conduct and while maintaining objectivity and independence.

The last of Phase 7 of a financial statement audit is "Ongoing evaluation, quality control, and final evidence gathering," which is covered in Chapter 21. Even when the other phases of the audit are done well, if this final evidence gathering phase is done poorly, the quality of the audit will be low. If the planning phases and the other risk response phases are done well, the completion phase is typically relatively easy.

Chapter 22 addresses the final phase of the financial statement audit, reporting. We look at the standard audit report in detail, as well as alternatives to the standard audit report.

Chapter 23 focuses on small business: both non-profit and for-profit enterprises. Review and compilation engagements are the primary focus of this chapter. Chapter 23 also discusses the standards for assurance engagements, including compilation and review engagements, and provides a framework for the conduct of such engagements. Included is a discussion of interim financial information and future-oriented information, useful for businesses acquiring debt or share capital.

Chapter 24 covers services performed most often by governmental and internal auditors, including risk assessment and systems control design, training and education on risk management and internal controls, specialized audits such as operational audits, and financial statement audits.

21

Completing the audit

As the audit progresses, the auditor continues to evaluate results to determine whether planned risks match actual risks. When all cycle, account, and assertion tests have been completed, the evidence as a whole needs to be examined, together with some additional tests that are non–cycle-specific. Then, the auditor can decide whether sufficient evidence has been collected to provide an audit opinion. Management accountants and internal auditors can use awareness of this phase to learn about the type of information that they would need to provide to the external auditors, while all auditors will benefit from understanding the type of evidence gathered in this final phase.

LEARNING OBJECTIVES

1 Describe how the auditor searches for contingent liabilities. State the purpose of obtaining a confirmation from the client's law firms. Explain why these "legal letters" must be in a specified format. Describe examples of procedures conducted during a review for subsequent events.

2 Provide examples of work completed as part of the final evidence-gathering process.

3 Describe the actions that the auditor takes to evaluate the adequacy of accumulated evidence. State how quality control procedures are incorporated into this final risk response phase of the audit.

4 Describe the communications the auditor is required to send after the completion of the audit.

STANDARDS REFERENCED IN THIS CHAPTER

CICA Standards

CAS 240 – The auditor's responsibilities relating to fraud in an audit of financial statements (previously Section 5135 – The auditor's responsibility to consider fraud)

CAS 250 – Consideration of laws and regulations in an audit of financial statements (previously Section 5136 – Misstatements: illegal acts)

CAS 260 – Communications with those charged with governance (previously Section 5751 – Communications with those having oversight responsibility of the financial reporting process)

CAS 450 – Evaluation of misstatements identified during the audit (previously Section 5142 – Materiality)

CAS 501 – Audit evidence: specific considerations for selected items (previously Section 6030 – Inventories; Section 6560 – Communications with law firms regarding claims and possible claims [including the joint policy statement])

CAS 520 – Analytical procedures (previously Section 5301 – Analysis)

CAS 550 – Related parties (previously Section 6010 – Audit of related-party transactions)

CAS 560 – Subsequent events (previously Section 5405 – Date of the auditor's report; Section 6550 – Subsequent events)

CAS 570 – Going concern

CAS 580 – Written representations (previously Section 5370 – Management representations)

CAS 720 – The auditor's responsibility relating to other information in documents containing audited financial statements (previously Section 7500 – Annual reports, interim reports, and other public documents)

Good Review Requires More Than Looking at Working Papers

Larry Bedard, an audit senior of Messier, Nixon & Royce, assigned to staff assistant Clawson Lum the audit of accounts payable of Westside Industries Ltd., a large equipment manufacturer. Accounts payable is a major liability account for a manufacturing company, and testing accounts payable cut-off is an important audit area. Testing primarily involves reviewing the liability recorded by the client by examining subsequent payments to suppliers and other creditors to assure that they were properly recorded.

Larry observed that Clawson was spending a lot of time on the phone, apparently on personal matters. Shortly before the audit was completed, Clawson announced that he was leaving the firm. In spite of Clawson's distractions due to his personal affairs, he completed the audit work he was assigned within the budgeted time.

Because of Larry's concern about Clawson's work habits, he decided to review the working papers with extreme care. Every schedule he reviewed was properly prepared, with tick marks entered and explained by Clawson, indicating that he had made an extensive examination of underlying data and documents and had found the client's balance to be adequate as stated. Specifically, there were no payments subsequent to year end for inventory purchases received during the audit period that had not been accrued by Westside.

When Larry finished the audit, he turned the working papers over to Kelsey Mayburn, an audit manager on the engagement, for review. She had considerable knowledge about equipment manufacturers and about Westside Industries. Kelsey reviewed all the working papers, including the analytical procedures performed during the audit. After performing additional analytical procedures during her review, she contacted Larry to inform him that accounts payable did not seem reasonable to her. She asked him to do some additional checking. Larry went back and looked at all the documents that Clawson had indicated in the working papers that he had inspected. It was quickly apparent that Clawson either had not looked at the documents or did not know what he was doing when he inspected them. Almost $1 million of documents applicable to the December 31, 2009, audit period had not been included as liabilities. Kelsey's review likely saved Messier, Nixon & Royce significant embarrassment or worse consequences.

IMPORTANCE TO AUDITORS

This case illustrates the unfortunate fact that Clawson apparently violated the rules of conduct during his time at the Westside audit by preparing working papers that were incorrect. However, the positive side is that Kelsey discovered this through her experience in other audit engagements and by performing additional analytical review. This explains why audit firms will have a "cold review" on high-risk engagements (i.e., having someone who has not been involved in the engagement review the audit file) so that additional eyes can look for potential anomalies.

continued >

① Phase 7 and Selected Final Audit Procedures

The final risk response phase of the financial statement audit process includes final evidence gathering and the completion of checklists and review that wrap up the integration of the audit working paper file. The process is primarily hierarchical— that is, individual working papers are integrated into sections, sections are reviewed for completion, and then the file is viewed in its entirety to determine the appropriate audit report. In this section, we discuss two specific types of audit procedures: review for contingent liabilities and review for subsequent events.

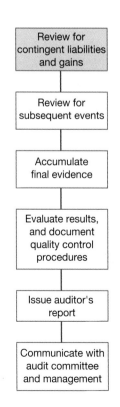

Review for Contingent Liabilities

A **contingent liability** (or asset) arises due to an existing condition or situation involving uncertainty as to possible gain or loss to an enterprise that will ultimately be resolved when one or more future events occur or fail to occur.

The auditor is concerned both with the nature of the future event and with the amount involved. Just as he or she is concerned with recognizing a contingent liability, the auditor must also be able to recognize a recorded asset that is really a contingent asset and that has the effect of overstating the net worth of the business.

Three conditions indicate the existence of a contingent liability: (1) there is a potential future payment to an outside party that results from an existing condition, (2) there is uncertainty about the amount of the future payment, and (3) the outcome will be resolved by some future event or events. For example, contingencies include lawsuits that have been filed but not yet resolved.

This uncertainty of the future payment can vary from extremely likely to highly unlikely or it may not be determinable. Contingencies are assessed using three levels of likelihood of occurrence and the appropriate financial statement treatment for each likelihood; the three levels are *likely*, *unlikely*, and *not determinable*. The ability to estimate the amount of the loss is also a factor that must be considered. Table 21-1 describes the various alternatives. Although the *CICA Handbook* does not require disclosure of "unlikely" events, if such a potential event could have a significant adverse effect, disclosure should be considered. International accounting standards require that if the liability is determinable and the amount is owed (i.e., it is a liability), then it should be recorded. The decision as to the appropriate treatment requires considerable professional judgment. (A contingent gain should never be accrued, but rather, if its future confirmation is very likely, it should be disclosed in the notes.)

When the proper disclosure in the financial statements of material contingencies is through footnotes, the footnote should describe the nature of the contingency to the extent it is known, an estimate of the amount, or a statement that the amount cannot be estimated. The following is an illustration of a footnote related to pending litigation:

> The Company is a defendant in a legal action instituted in the Alberta Court of the Queen's Bench by Mountain Supply Ltd. for alleged product defect. The amount claimed is $792,000 and the Company is vigorously contesting the claim. The Company's legal counsel is unable, at the present time, to give any opinion with respect to the merits of this action. Settlement, if any, that may be made with respect to these actions is expected to be accounted for as a charge against income for the period in which settlement is made.

Certain contingent liabilities are of considerable concern to the auditor:

- Pending litigation for patent infringement, product liability, or other actions.
- Income tax disputes.
- Product warranties.
- Notes receivable discounted.
- Guarantees of obligations of others.
- Unused balances in outstanding letters of credit.

Auditing standards make it clear that management, not the auditor, is responsible for identifying and deciding the appropriate accounting treatment for contingent liabilities. In many audits, it is impractical for auditors to uncover contingencies without management's cooperation.

The auditor's objectives in verifying contingent liabilities are to evaluate the accounting treatment of known contingent liabilities and to identify, to the extent practical, any contingencies not already identified by management.

AUDIT PROCEDURES Many of these potential obligations are ordinarily verified as an integral part of various segments of the engagement rather than as a separate activity near the end of the audit. For example, guarantees of obligations of others may be tested as part of confirming bank balances and loans from banks. Similarly, income tax disputes can be checked as part of analyzing income tax expense,

Table 21-1	Likelihood of Occurrence of Contingencies and Financial Statement Treatment
Likelihood of Occurrence of Event	**Financial Statement Treatment**
Unlikely to occur	No disclosure is necessary.
Not determinable	Footnote disclosure is necessary.
Likely to occur and the amount can be estimated	Financial statement accounts are adjusted.
Likely to occur and the amount cannot be estimated	Footnote disclosure is necessary.

reviewing the general correspondence file, and examining Canada Revenue Agency reports and statements. Even if the contingencies are verified separately, it is common to perform the tests well before the last few days of completing the engagement to ensure their proper verification. The tests of contingent liabilities near the end of the engagement are more a review than an initial search.

The appropriate audit procedures for testing contingencies are less well defined than those already discussed in other audit areas because the primary objective at the initial stage of the tests is to determine the existence of contingencies. As the reader knows from the study of other audit areas, it is more difficult to discover unrecorded transactions or events than to verify recorded information. Once the auditor is aware that contingencies exist, the evaluation of their materiality and the disclosure required can ordinarily be satisfactorily resolved.

The following are some audit procedures commonly used to search for contingent liabilities. The list is not all-inclusive, and each procedure is not necessarily performed on every audit.

- Inquire of management (orally and in writing) regarding the possibility of unrecorded contingencies. In these inquiries, the auditor must be specific in describing the different kinds of contingencies that may require disclosure. Naturally, inquiries of management are not useful in uncovering the intentional failure to disclose existing contingencies, but if management has overlooked a particular type of contingency or does not fully comprehend accounting disclosure requirements, the inquiry can be fruitful. At the completion of the audit, management is typically asked to make a written statement as part of the letter of representation that it is unaware of any undisclosed contingent liabilities.
- Review current and previous years' Canada Revenue Agency notices of assessment. The reports may indicate areas in which disagreement over unsettled years is likely to arise. If an audit by the Canada Revenue Agency has been in progress for a long time, there is an increased likelihood of an existing tax dispute.
- Review the minutes of directors' and shareholders' meetings for indications of lawsuits or other contingencies.
- Analyze legal expense for the period under audit, and review invoices and statements from the client's law firms for indications of contingent liabilities, especially lawsuits and pending tax assessments.
- Obtain a confirmation from all major law firms performing legal services for the client as to the status of pending litigation or other contingent liabilities. This procedure is discussed in more depth shortly.
- Review existing working papers for any information that may indicate a potential contingency. For example, bank confirmations may indicate notes receivable discounted or guarantees of loans.
- Obtain letters of credit in force as of the balance sheet date, and obtain a confirmation of the used and unused balances.
- Read contracts, agreements, and related correspondence and documents.

EVALUATION OF KNOWN CONTINGENT LIABILITIES If the auditor concludes that there are contingent liabilities, he or she must evaluate the significance of the potential liability and the nature of the disclosure that is necessary in the financial statements. The potential liability is sufficiently well known in some instances to be included in the statements as an actual liability. In other instances, disclosure may be unnecessary if the contingency is highly remote or immaterial. The public accounting firm may obtain a separate evaluation of the potential liability from its own law firm rather than relying on management or management's lawyers. The client's law firm is an advocate for the client and frequently loses perspective in evaluating the likelihood of losing the case and the amount of the potential judgment.

COMMITMENTS Closely related to contingent liabilities are **commitments** (agreements that the entity will hold to a fixed set of conditions), such as to purchase raw

Commitments—agreements that the entity will hold to a fixed set of conditions, such as the purchase or sale of merchandise at a stated price, at a future date, regardless of what happens to profits or to the economy as a whole.

materials or to lease facilities at a certain price, agreements to sell merchandise at a fixed price, bonus plans, profit-sharing and pension plans, royalty agreements, and similar items. For a commitment, the most important characteristic is the agreement to commit the firm to a set of fixed conditions in the future, regardless of what happens to profits or the economy as a whole. In a free economy, presumably the entity agrees to commitments as a means of bettering its own interests, but these commitments may turn out to be less or more advantageous than originally anticipated.

The *CICA Handbook* requires disclosure of the details of any contractual obligation that is significant to a client's current financial position or future operations. All commitments are ordinarily either described together in a separate footnote or combined in a footnote related to contingencies.

The search for unknown commitments is usually performed as part of the audit of each audit area. For example, in verifying sales transactions, the auditor should be alert to sales commitments. Similarly, commitments for the purchase of raw materials or equipment can be identified as part of the audit of each of these accounts. The auditor should also be aware of the possibility of commitments as he or she is reading contracts and correspondence files and should therefore query management.

Obtain Confirmation from Client's Law Firms

Inquiry of the client's law firms—a confirmation letter in a specific format from the client's legal counsel informing the auditor of pending litigation or any other information involving legal counsel that is relevant to financial statement disclosure.

Outstanding claim—a lawsuit that has been brought against a client; also known as an "Asserted claim."

Unasserted claim—a potential legal claim against a client where the condition for a claim exists but no claim has been filed; also known as "Possible claim."

A major procedure on which auditors rely for evaluating known litigation or other claims against the client and identifying additional ones is sending a letter of **inquiry of the client's law firms** (a confirmation letter in a specific format that requests information about pending litigation or other relevant information with respect to legal claims). There are two categories of lawsuits: an **outstanding** (or **asserted**) **claim** exists when a suit has been brought or when the client has been notified that a suit will be brought; a **possible** or **unasserted claim** exists when no suit has been filed but is possible. An example of the latter is a situation in which the lawyer is aware of a violation of a patent agreement that could be damaging to the client.

auditing in action 21-1
Will It Take Death or Disaster for the Client to Act?

As an auditor, assessing corporate governance includes assessing the organization's responsibility for the health and well-being of employees and other individuals. For example, the Basel Convention prohibits the exporting of electronic waste (e.g., computers, monitors, etc.), yet it seems that many organizations violate this convention.

In a more vivid example, employees of a Canadian waste management company complained about the speed and reckless manner in which a driver was operating a front-end loader in the plant. Subsequently, an employee who was acting as a "spotter" for a backward-driving task was killed by this same driver. The company was fined $300,000 for health and safety violations for failing to ensure that the front-end loader was driven by a competent person. The U.S. parent company refused to book correcting journal entries advised by its auditors. The auditors made a "deal" for the parent company to book these entries over a

period of 10 years, which the company did not do. The auditors were fined US$7 million by the SEC for participating in this side deal.

It is important that auditors consider the behaviour of management with respect to known laws, regulations, and the health and safety of its employees, as this may be an indicator of management's attitude toward the integrity of the financial statements. Such behaviour could also lead to contingent liabilities such as fines as consequences of violations or to costs such as clean-up of environmentally polluted areas.

Sources: 1. Beasley, Mark S., Frank A. Buckless, Steven M. Glover, and Douglas F. Prawitt, *Auditing Cases, an Interactive Learning Approach*, Second Edition (Toronto: Prentice Hall, 2003). 2. Ontario Ministry of Labour, "Canadian Waste Services Inc. fined $300,000 for health and safety violation," 2004, www.labour.gov.on.ca/english/news/pdf/2004/04-55.pdf, Accessed: July 30, 2009. 3. Ross, Rachel, "Toxic exportation," *Toronto Star*, January 3, 2005, p. D1, D3.

The auditor relies on the lawyer's expertise and knowledge of the client's legal affairs to provide a professional opinion about the expected outcome of existing lawsuits and the likely amount of the liability, including court costs. The lawyer is also likely to know of pending litigation and claims that management may have overlooked.

Many public accounting firms analyze legal expense for the entire year and have the client send a standard lawyer's letter to every law firm with which it has been involved in the current or preceding year, plus any law firm that it occasionally engages. In some cases, this involves a large number of law firms, including some dealing in aspects of law that are far removed from potential lawsuits.

The standard letter of confirmation to the client's law firm, which should be prepared on the client's letterhead and signed by one of the company's officials, should include the following:

- A list, prepared by management, of outstanding and possible claims with which the lawyer has had significant involvement.
- A description of the nature and the current status of each claim and possible claim.
- An indication of management's evaluation of the amount and likelihood of loss or gain for each listed claim and possible claim.
- A request that the lawyer reply to the client, with a signed copy going to the public accounting firm, advising whether management's descriptions and evaluations of the outstanding and possible claims are reasonable.

Lawyers are not required to mention any omission of possible claims in their response to the inquiry letter and, thus, do not directly notify the auditor of them. Instead, lawyers discuss these possible claims with the client separately and inform management of its responsibility to inform the auditor. Whether management does so or not is its decision; CAS 501 par. 10 (previously Section 6560.19) requires the auditor to obtain a letter of representation from management that it has disclosed all known outstanding and possible claims. In short, unless management discloses the existence of possible claims to the auditor, the auditor has no means of discovering whether or not any such claims exist.

CAS

Any differences between management's identification and assessment of outstanding and possible claims and the law firm's would be resolved, if possible, in a meeting of the law firm, the auditor, and management. Failure to resolve the differences would force the auditor to consider a reservation of opinion on the auditor's report.

An example of a standard inquiry letter sent to a lawyer's office is shown in Figure 21-1 on the next page. The letter should be sent toward the end of the audit so that the lawyer is communicating about contingencies up to approximately the date of the auditor's report.

LIMITED OR NON-RESPONSES FROM LAW FIRMS Law firms in recent years have become reluctant to provide certain information to auditors because of their own exposure to legal liability for providing incorrect or confidential information. The nature of the refusal of law firms to provide auditors with complete information about contingent liabilities falls into two categories: the refusal to respond due to a lack of knowledge about matters involving contingent liabilities, and the refusal to disclose information that the lawyer regards as confidential. As an example of the latter, the lawyer might be aware of a violation of a patent agreement that could result in a significant loss to the client if the violation were public knowledge (possible claim). The inclusion of the information in a footnote could actually cause the lawsuit and, therefore, be damaging to the client.

When the nature of the lawyer's legal practice does not involve contingent liabilities, the lawyer's refusal to respond causes no audit problems. It is certainly reasonable for lawyers to refuse to make statements about contingent liabilities when they are not involved with lawsuits or with similar aspects of the practice of law that directly affect financial statements.

	Figure 21-1 Typical Inquiry of Lawyer

Peppertree Produce Inc.
293 rue Crécy
Montréal, Québec

January 26, 2010

Rowan and Gunz
Barristers and Solicitors,
412 Côte des Neiges,
Montréal, Québec
H3C 1J7

To Whom It May Concern:

In connection with the preparation and audit of our financial statements for the fiscal period ended December 31, 2009, we have made the following evaluations of claims and possible claims with respect to which your firm's advice or representation has been sought:

Description	Evaluation
Calvert Growers vs. Peppertree Produce Inc., non-payment of debt in the amount of $16,000, trial date not set.	Peppertree Produce Inc. disputes this billing on the grounds that the produce was spoiled and expects to successfully defend this action.
Desjardins, Inc. vs. Peppertree Produce Inc., damages for breach of contract in the amount of $40,000, trial date not set.	It is probable that this action will be successfully defended.
Foodex Ltd. has a possible claim in connection with apples sold to them by Peppertree Produce Inc. The apples apparently had not been properly washed by the growers to remove insect spray, and a number of Foodex Ltd.'s customers became ill after eating said apples.	No claim has yet been made, and we are unable to estimate possible ultimate loss.

Would you please advise us, as of February 28, 2010, on the following points:
a. Are the claims and possible claims properly described?
b. Do you consider that our evaluations are reasonable?
c. Are you aware of any claims not listed above that are outstanding? If so, please include in your response letter the names of the parties and the amount claimed.

   This inquiry is made in accordance with the Joint Policy Statement of January, 1978, approved by the Canadian Bar Association and the Auditing Standards Committee of the Canadian Institute of Chartered Accountants.

   Please address your reply, marked "Privileged and Confidential," to this company, and send a signed copy of the reply directly to our auditors, Jeannerette & Cie, Comptables Agrées, 1133 rue Sherbrooke, Montréal, Québec, H3C 1M8.

Yours truly,

Charles D. Peppertree

Charles D. Peppertree, President

c.c. Jeannerette & Cie

A serious audit problem does arise, however, when a lawyer refuses to provide information that is within the lawyer's jurisdiction and may directly affect the fair presentation of financial statements. If a lawyer refuses to provide the auditor with information about material existing lawsuits (outstanding claims) or possible claims, the auditor's report would have to be modified to reflect the lack of available evidence. The "Joint Policy Statement concerning communications with law firms regarding claims and possible claims in connection with the preparation and audit of financial statements," an appendix to CAS 501 (previously Section 6560) of the *CICA Handbook*, has the effect of encouraging lawyers to cooperate with auditors in obtaining information about contingencies, as the law firm's confidential relationship with its clients will not be violated. The Joint Policy Statement was approved by the Canadian Bar Association, the Council of the Bermuda Bar Association, and the Auditing Standards Committee (now the Auditing and Assurance Standards Board) of the CICA.

Review for Subsequent Events

The auditor must review **subsequent events** (i.e., transactions and events occurring after the balance sheet date) to determine whether anything occurred that might affect the fair presentation or disclosure of the statements being audited. The auditing procedures required by forthcoming CAS 560, Subsequent events (previously Section 6550), to verify these transactions and events are often referred to as the **review for subsequent events** or post-balance sheet review.

The auditor's responsibility for reviewing for subsequent events is normally limited to the period beginning with the balance sheet date and ending with the date of the auditor's report. Since the date of the auditor's report usually corresponds with the completion of the important auditing procedures in the client's office, the subsequent events review should be completed near the end of the engagement. Figure 21-2 shows the period covered by a subsequent events review and the timing of that review.

TYPES OF SUBSEQUENT EVENTS Two types of subsequent events require consideration by management and evaluation by the auditor: (1) those that have a direct effect on the financial statements and require adjustment and (2) those that have no direct effect on the financial statements but for which disclosure is advisable.

Those that have a direct effect on the financial statements and require adjustment These events or transactions provide additional information to management in determining the valuation of account balances as of the balance sheet date and to auditors in verifying the balances. For example, if the auditor is having difficulty determining the correct valuation of inventory because of obsolescence, the sale of raw material inventory as scrap in the subsequent period should be used as a means of determining the correct valuation of the inventory as of the balance sheet date.

Such subsequent-period events as the following require an adjustment of account balances in the current year's financial statements if the amounts are material:

- The declaration of bankruptcy due to the deteriorating financial condition of a customer with an outstanding accounts receivable balance.
- The settlement of litigation at an amount different from the amount recorded on the books.

Subsequent events—transactions and other pertinent events that occurred after the balance sheet date and that affect the fair presentation or disclosure of the statements being audited.

Review for subsequent events—the auditing procedures performed by auditors to identify and evaluate subsequent events.

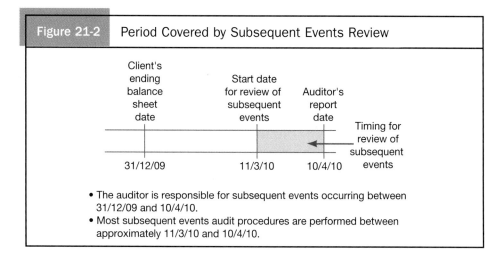

| Figure 21-2 | Period Covered by Subsequent Events Review |

- The auditor is responsible for subsequent events occurring between 31/12/09 and 10/4/10.
- Most subsequent events audit procedures are performed between approximately 11/3/10 and 10/4/10.

- The disposal of equipment not being used in operations at a price below the current book value.
- The sale of investments at a price below recorded cost.

Whenever subsequent events are used to evaluate the amounts included in the statements, care must be taken to distinguish between conditions that existed at the balance sheet date and those that came into being after the end of the year. The subsequent information should not be incorporated directly into the statements if the conditions causing the change in valuation did not take place until after year end. For example, the sale of scrap in the subsequent period would not be relevant in the valuation of inventory for obsolescence if the obsolescence took place after the end of the year. Also, an amount outstanding from a customer who declared bankruptcy after year end, due to uninsured fire damage to its premises, should not be removed from the accounts receivable balance until the year the damage took place.

Those that have no direct effect on the financial statements but for which disclosure is advisable Subsequent events of this type provide evidence of conditions that did not exist at the date of the balance sheet being reported on but are so significant that they require disclosure even though they do not require adjustment. Ordinarily, these events can be adequately disclosed by the use of footnotes, but occasionally one event may be so significant as to require supplementing the historical statements with statements that include the effect of the event as if it had occurred on the balance sheet date (i.e., pro forma statements).

Following are examples of events or transactions occurring in the subsequent period that may require disclosure rather than an adjustment in the financial statements:

- Decline in market value of investments.
- Issuance of bonds or shares.
- Decline in market value of inventory as a consequence of government action barring further sale of a product.
- Uninsured loss of inventories as a result of fire or other disaster.
- Purchase of a business or trademark.

AUDIT TESTS Audit procedures for the subsequent events review can be conveniently divided into two categories: (1) procedures normally integrated as part of the verification of year-end account balances and (2) those performed specifically for the purpose of discovering events or transactions that must be recognized as subsequent events.

The first category includes cut-off and valuation tests that are done as part of the tests of details of balances. For example, subsequent-period sales and acquisition transactions are examined to determine whether the cut-off is accurate. Similarly, many valuation tests involving subsequent events are also performed as part of the verification of account balances. As an example, it is common to test the collectability of accounts receivable by reviewing subsequent-period cash receipts. It is also a normal audit procedure to compare the subsequent-period purchase price of inventory with the recorded cost as a test of lower of cost or market valuation. The procedures for cut-off and valuation have been discussed sufficiently in preceding chapters and are not repeated here.

The second category of tests is performed specifically for the purpose of obtaining information that must be incorporated into the current year's account balances or footnotes. These tests include the following:

Inquire of management Inquiries vary from client to client but normally are about the existence of potential contingent liabilities or commitments, significant changes in the assets or capital structure of the company, the current status of items that were not completely resolved at the balance sheet date, and the existence of unusual adjustments made subsequent to the balance sheet date.

Inquiries of management about subsequent events must be held with the proper client personnel to obtain meaningful answers. For example, discussing tax or union matters with the accounts receivable supervisor would not be appropriate. Most inquiries should be made of the controller, the vice-presidents, or the president, depending on the information desired.

Correspond with law firms Correspondence with law firms, which was previously discussed, takes place as part of the search for contingent liabilities. In obtaining confirmation letters from law firms, the auditor must remember his or her responsibility for testing for subsequent events up to the date of approval of the financial statements. A common approach is to request that the law firm date and mail the letter as of the expected approval date for the financial statements.

Review internal financial statements prepared subsequent to the balance sheet date The emphasis in the review should be on (1) changes in the business relative to results for the same period in the year under audit and (2) changes after year end. The auditor should pay particular attention to major changes in the business or environment in which the client is operating. The statements should be discussed with management to determine whether they are prepared on the same basis as the current-period statements, and there should be inquiries about significant changes in operating results.

Review records prepared subsequent to the balance sheet date Journals, data files, and ledgers should be reviewed to determine the existence and nature of any transaction related to the current year. If the journals are not kept up to date, the documents relating to the journals should be reviewed.

Examine minutes prepared subsequent to the balance sheet date The minutes of shareholders' and directors' meetings subsequent to the balance sheet date must be examined for important subsequent events affecting the current-period financial statements.

Obtain a letter of representation The letter of representation written by the client to the auditor formalizes statements the client has made about different matters throughout the audit, including discussions about subsequent events.

concept check

C21-1 Why are contingent liabilities difficult to identify?

C21-2 When reviewing legal expenses, which transactions should the auditor examine, and why?

C21-3 List three audit techniques that could be used to identify relevant subsequent events.

Accumulate Final Evidence

The auditor has a few final accumulation responsibilities that apply to all cycles besides the search for contingent liabilities and the review for subsequent events. The four most important ones (final analytical review procedures, evaluation of going concern assumption, client representation letter, and other information in annual reports), as well as management discussion and analysis, are discussed in this section. All are done late in the engagement.

FINAL ANALYTICAL PROCEDURES Analytical procedures were introduced in Chapter 6 and applied to specific cycles in several chapters. Analytical procedures are normally used as part of planning the audit, during the performance of detailed tests in each cycle as part of substantive procedures, and at the completion of the audit.

Analytical procedures done during the completion of the audit are useful as a final review for material misstatements or financial problems not noted during other testing, and to help the auditor take a final objective look at the financial statements. It is common for a partner to closely review the analytical procedures during the final review of working papers and financial statements. Typically, a partner has a good understanding of the client and its business because of ongoing relationships. Knowledge of the client's business and its business environment combined with effective analytical procedures help identify possible oversights in an audit. CAS 520 (previously Section 5301) requires the auditor to use analytical procedures as part of the completion phase of the audit.

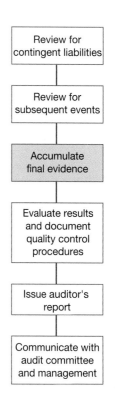

Review for
contingent liabilities

Review for
subsequent events

Accumulate
final evidence

Evaluate results
and document
quality control
procedures

Issue auditor's
report

Communicate with
audit committee
and management

auditing in action 21-2
Tumbling Revenue Troubles

Arpad Takacs had been the owner of Cam Tool & Die Ltd. for about 30 years. His sales dropped from $45 million in 2007 to $28 million in 2008, as a result of the difficulties in the automotive industry, the primary sector that Cam Tool served. The number of employees had gone from a high of 340 to only 90 just prior to closure.

Apparently, losses escalated rapidly after the barely profitable 2008 fiscal year, and the bank was distressed that Takacs had not kept it informed and had not considered other sources of capital. The 2008 financial results were delayed several months, and prospective business plans were not provided to the bank by the deadline it requested. Accordingly, the bank pushed the company into receivership.

Consider another company affected by the recession, Mattamy Homes, that laid off 50 employees in November 2008.

The company's sales dropped from $1.5 billion in 2007 to below $1.4 billion in 2008, and Mattamy Homes is facing a real estate market where home sales are continuing to drop drastically. (For example, prices were down 35 percent for the first 11 months of 2008 in the Toronto area, which explains Mattamy's layoffs.)

Mattamy has responded by closing one of its offices and is pursuing partnerships with other builders to reduce its own investment costs. It continues to innovate and look for ways to reduce costs while maintaining quality.

Auditors of such companies as Mattamy would need to stay vigilant against the possibility that revenues may tumble so far that costs cannot be covered, as happened at Cam Tool.

Sources: 1. Hamilton, Tyler, "Tooling firm's demise 'big loss,'" *Toronto Star*, April 15, 2009, p. B1, B6. 2. Wong, Tony, "Between bricks and a hard place," *Toronto Star*, January 17, 2009, p. B1, B6.

CAS **EVALUATION OF GOING-CONCERN ASSUMPTION** The Commission to Study the Public's Expectation of Audits (Macdonald Commission) suggested in its Recommendation 10 that management should disclose in the financial statements if "there is significant danger that [the company] may not be able to continue as [a going concern] throughout the foreseeable future."[1] The implication of this and other recommendations is that the auditor should pay particular attention to the going-concern assumption during the audit, especially when performing the final review of the disclosures in the financial statements. Forthcoming CAS 570, Going concern, requires that the auditor evaluate management's assessment of the ability of the entity to continue as a going concern based upon evidence collected throughout the audit. This includes taking into account information obtained after the year end, as described in the subsequent events section of this chapter.

CAS 570 further requires that if the auditor concludes that there is substantial doubt of a going concern, that the auditor inquire of management and consider actions that management is taking, such as having specific plans for refinancing, that would enable the entity to continue in operations. If there is significant uncertainty, then the auditor's report should include an explanatory paragraph following the opinion paragraph to describe that conclusion, and the auditor may be required to further modify the auditor's report, as described in Chapter 22.

Auditing in Action 21-2 describes two businesses which dealt with going-concern issues in significantly different ways—resulting in ongoing business for one, and bankruptcy for the other.

CLIENT REPRESENTATION LETTER *CICA Handbook* CAS 580, Written representations (previously Section 5370, Management representations), requires that the auditor obtain a written management representation letter from management to confirm information that has been provided to the auditor during the audit engagement. The auditor may obtain written representations for any audit area. However, there are four

---

[1] "50 ways to change our ways," *CAmagazine*, July 1988, p. 42. The July 1988 issue of *CAmagazine* includes several articles dealing with the report of the Commission to Study the Public's Expectations of Audits (Macdonald Commission).

other situations where written client representations play an important role during most audit engagements:

1. CAS 250 (formerly Section 5136) requires written representation from management regarding awareness of non-compliance with laws and regulations.
2. CAS 550 (previously Section 6010) indicates the auditor should have written representation with respect to related-party transactions and their disclosure.
3. CAS 560 (previously Section 6550) states that the auditor would normally include, as part of a subsequent events review, written confirmation from management of any verbal representations and a statement that subsequent events have been adjusted or disclosed.
4. CAS 501 (previously Section 6560) requires written representation from the client that outstanding and possible legal claims have been disclosed.

CAS

CAS 580 explains that a **written representation** is a written statement by management that documents management's representations or other audit evidence (normally oral information) that has been provided during the audit. The client representation letter is prepared on the client's letterhead, addressed to the public accounting firm, and signed by high-level corporate officials, usually the president and chief financial officer.

Written representation—a written statement by management that documents management's representations or other audit evidence (normally oral information) that has been provided during the audit.

There are two purposes of the written representation (also called a management or client representation letter):

- *To impress upon management its responsibility for the assertions in the financial statements.* For example, if the letter of representation includes a reference to pledged assets and contingent liabilities, honest management may be reminded of its unintentional failure to disclose the information adequately. To fulfill this objective, the written representation should be sufficiently detailed to act as a reminder to management.
- *To document the responses from management to inquiries about various aspects of the audit.* This provides written documentation of client representations in the event of disagreement or a lawsuit between the auditor and the client.

The letter should be dated subsequent to the date of completion of field work. It may be necessary to have a second written representation if the date of the auditor's report date is substantially later to make sure there are representations related to the subsequent events review. To prevent surprises, the auditor should discuss the type of representations with the client during the planning of the audit and as needed throughout the engagement. The representation letter implies that it has originated with the client, but it is common practice for the auditor to prepare the letter and request the client to type it on the company's letterhead and sign it if management is in agreement. Refusal by a client to prepare and sign the letter should probably cause the auditor to consider a qualified opinion or denial of opinion of the auditor's report, as described further in the next chapter.

Many specific matters should be included, when applicable, in a client representation letter. A few of these follow:

- Management's acknowledgment of its responsibility for the fair presentation of the financial statements in conformity with Canadian generally accepted accounting principles or [an appropriate disclosed] basis of accounting.
- Availability of all financial records and related data.
- Completeness and availability of all minutes of meetings of shareholders, directors, and committees of directors.
- Information concerning related-party transactions and related amounts receivable or payable.
- Plans or intentions that may affect the carrying value or classification of assets or liabilities.
- Disclosure of compensating balances or other arrangements involving restrictions on cash balances and disclosure of lines of credit or similar arrangements.

CHAPTER 21 I COMPLETING THE AUDIT   699

A client written representation is a written statement from a non-independent source and therefore cannot be regarded as reliable evidence. Accordingly, where possible, the auditor should seek evidence to substantiate management's assertions. The letter does provide minimal evidence that management has been asked certain questions, but its primary purpose is psychological and to protect the auditor from potential claims by management that it was unaware of its responsibilities. There are occasions, though, when written representations may be the only source of audit evidence (for example, management intends to launch a new product line).

Other information in the annual report—information that is not a part of published financial statements but is published with them; must be read by auditors for inconsistencies with the financial statements and misleading information.

OTHER INFORMATION IN ANNUAL REPORTS CAS 720 (formerly Section 7500) of the *CICA Handbook* details the auditor's responsibility for **other information in the annual report** of a company, which is published with the financial statements. The primary responsibility is to ensure that the financial statements and auditor's report are accurately reproduced in the annual report. If the company's annual report has not been issued, correcting any misstatement is relatively easy; the auditor can simply ask management to correct the misstatement in the report. On the other hand, if the financial statements and annual report have already been issued when the misstatement is discovered, the auditor must be satisfied that management will take "reasonable steps" to notify users about the misstatement. If the auditor is not so satisfied, notice should be given to the board of directors, and consideration should be given to what further action should be taken.

Misstatement of fact—an inconsistency between the financial statements and additional information, such as the annual report.

CAS 720 also requires the auditor to review the additional information to determine if there is an inconsistency between the financial statements and the additional information, termed a **misstatement of fact**. For example, assume that the president's letter in the annual report refers to an increase in earnings per share from $2.60 to $2.93. The auditor is required to compare that information with that in the financial statements to make sure that it corresponds. If an error exists in the financial statements and the statements have not been issued yet, the auditor should have the error corrected or issue a reservation of opinion; if the statements have been issued, the auditor should treat the error as a subsequent discovery of a misstatement (CAS 560) and notify management. If it is the annual report that requires revision, the auditor should notify management. If the auditor cannot gain satisfaction from management, including the audit committee and the board of directors, the auditor should consider what further action is warranted.

The auditor has responsibilities beyond searching for misstatements in the financial statements in the annual report and for inconsistencies between the financial statements and other material in the annual report; CAS 720 requires the auditor to advise management of any material misstatements of fact that are contained in the annual report (or as posted on the company website or on **sedar.com**). The annual report may include, for instance, information about a fictitious lucrative contract with the company, which would affect the following years' business and profits significantly. If management refuses to correct the misstatements, the auditor should advise the audit committee and the board of directors. If satisfaction is still not obtained by the auditor, further action should be considered.

MANAGEMENT DISCUSSION AND ANALYSIS The academic and professional literature include descriptions of research and articles that indicate that users of financial statements and annual reports are interested in an entity's future as well as its past and present. While an entity's financial statements, including the notes to those statements, present information about the entity's financial position and financial history, until recently, there was little information to inform users of expectations of the entity's management for the foreseeable future. In addition, there was a belief that it would be helpful to users if management were to provide a narrative expressing its interpretation of the entity's financial position and operations.

In Canada and the United States, securities regulators, recognizing that there is a limit to the amount of information that can be communicated by the financial statements, including the notes, are requiring companies that borrow money from or sell stock to the public to provide a comment from management in the annual report; the comment would be supplementary to the financial statements and provide information about management's expectations. Such a report by management supplementary to the financial statements has come to be known as **management discussion and analysis** (MD&A).

MD&A is generally required by securities administrators in Canada. For example, the Ontario Securities Commission (OSC) requires most of its larger registrants to provide MD&A in their annual reports and with interim financial statements. There is also a series of prescribed questions that must be answered by management in the MD&A filed with the securities commissions. The general purpose of MD&A is to describe the performance of the company and the risks within which it operates. To assist boards of directors and senior management, the CICA established the Canadian Performance Reporting Board, which authorizes the CICA to publish guidance documents, issue papers, and research reports. An important guidance document is titled "Management's Discussion and Analysis: Guidance on Preparation and Disclosure." The guidance provides general disclosure principles, a disclosure framework, and a framework for overseeing the reliability and timeliness of disclosure. The intention is that the guidance be used by management, the board of directors, and the audit committee throughout the financial oversight process.

The auditor's role with respect to MD&A arises from the fact that MD&A is included in the annual report and thus falls under the auditor's review pursuant to CAS 720.

<aside>
Management discussion and analysis (MD&A)—supplemental analysis and explanation by management that accompanies but does not form part of the financial statements.

concept check

C21-4 Why is partner examination of final analytical review important?

C21-5 Describe management's and the auditor's responsibilities with respect to the going-concern assumption.
</aside>

③ Evaluate Results and Document Quality Control Procedures

After performing all audit procedures in each audit area, the auditor must integrate the results into one overall conclusion. The audit procedures, their ongoing evaluation and supervision, and the quality control procedures executed over those audit procedures form an integral part of the audit. Ultimately, the auditor must decide whether sufficient appropriate audit evidence has been accumulated to warrant the conclusion that the financial statements are stated in accordance with generally accepted accounting principles.

Refer to the figure on the inside cover of this text. Phases 1 through 7 comprise the parts of the audit that must be reviewed in the evaluation of results. The emphasis is satisfactory mitigation of risks identified in the planning stage of the audit. The reviewer will also review the conclusions reached through tests of controls, analytical procedures, and tests of details of balances for each of the functional transaction cycles audited. Major activities in supporting decisions and the quality of the working paper file follow.

SUFFICIENCY OF EVIDENCE The final summarization of the adequacy of the evidence is a review by the auditor of the entire audit to determine whether all important aspects have been adequately tested considering the risks of the engagement. A major step in this process is reviewing the audit programs to make sure that all parts have been accurately completed and documented and that risks by audit objectives have been addressed. An important part of the review is deciding whether the audit program is adequate considering the problem areas that were discovered as the audit progressed. For example, if misstatements were discovered as part of the tests of sales, the initial plans for the tests of details of accounts receivable balances may have been insufficient. The final review should evaluate whether the revised audit program is adequate.

As an aid in drawing final conclusions about the adequacy of the audit evidence, auditors frequently use **completing the engagement checklists**. These are reminders of aspects of the audit that must not be overlooked. An illustration of part of a completing-the-engagement checklist is given in Figure 21-3 on the next page.

If the auditor concludes that he or she has not obtained sufficient evidence to draw a conclusion about the fairness of the client's representations, there are two

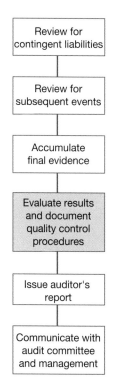

<aside>
Completing the engagement checklist—a reminder to the auditor of aspects of the audit that may have been overlooked.
</aside>

Figure 21-3 | Partial "Completing the Engagement" Checklist

	Yes	No	W/P Ref.

1. Examination of prior year's working papers
  a. Were last year's working papers and review notes examined for areas of emphasis in the current-year audit? _____ _____ _____
  b. Was the permanent file reviewed for items that affect the current year? _____ _____ _____

2. Internal control
  a. Has internal control been adequately understood and reviewed? _____ _____ _____
  b. Is the scope of the audit adequate in light of the assessed level of control risk? _____ _____ _____
  c. Have all major weaknesses been included in a management letter and material weaknesses in a letter to the audit committee or senior management? _____ _____ _____

3. General documents
  a. Were all current-year minutes and resolutions reviewed, abstracted, and followed up? _____ _____ _____
  b. Has the permanent file been updated? _____ _____ _____
  c. Have all major contracts and agreements been reviewed and abstracted or copied to ascertain that the client complies with all existing legal requirements? _____ _____ _____

choices: (1) additional evidence must be obtained, or (2) a qualified opinion or a denial of opinion must be issued, as explained further in the next chapter.

EVIDENCE SUPPORTING AUDITOR'S OPINION An important part of evaluating whether the financial statements are fairly stated is summarizing the misstatements uncovered in the audit. Whenever the auditor uncovers misstatements that are in themselves material, entries should be proposed to the client to correct the statements. It may be difficult to determine the appropriate amount of adjustment because the true value of the misstatement is unknown; nevertheless, it is the auditor's responsibility to determine the required adjustment. In addition to material misstatements, often there is discovered a large number of immaterial misstatements that are not adjusted at the time they are found. It is necessary to combine individually immaterial misstatements to evaluate whether the combined amount is material. The auditor can keep track of the misstatements and combine them in several different ways, but many auditors use a convenient method known as an **unadjusted misstatement worksheet** or summary of possible adjustments to track known and potential misstatements. It is relatively easy to evaluate the overall significance of several immaterial misstatements with this type of working paper, an example of which appears in Figure 21-4.

The auditor should consider carry-forward misstatements from the previous year in analyzing misstatements and the need for adjustment. For example, if closing inventory was understated by $15,000 in 2008 and overstated by $10,000 in 2009, the effect on income in 2009 would be $25,000. Although the individual misstatements may be immaterial, the combined effect might well be material and require adjustment.

If the auditor believes that he or she has sufficient evidence but that it does not warrant a conclusion of fairly presented financial statements, the auditor again has two choices: the statements must be revised to the auditor's satisfaction, or a modified audit opinion must be issued.

Unadjusted misstatement worksheet—a summary of misstatements used to help the auditor assess whether the combined amount is material; also known as a summary of possible adjustments.

Figure 21-4   Unadjusted Misstatement Audit Schedule

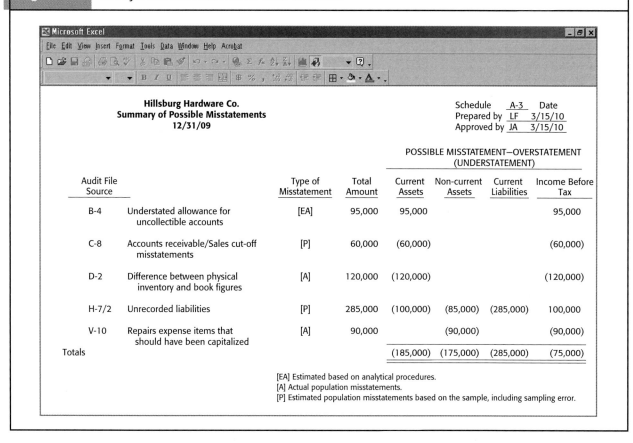

Microsoft Excel

File Edit View Insert Format Tools Data Window Help Acrobat

Hillsburg Hardware Co.
Summary of Possible Misstatements
12/31/09

Schedule A-3 Date
Prepared by LF 3/15/10
Approved by JA 3/15/10

Audit File Source		Type of Misstatement	Total Amount	POSSIBLE MISSTATEMENT—OVERSTATEMENT (UNDERSTATEMENT)			
				Current Assets	Non-current Assets	Current Liabilities	Income Before Tax
B-4	Understated allowance for uncollectible accounts	[EA]	95,000	95,000			95,000
C-8	Accounts receivable/Sales cut-off misstatements	[P]	60,000	(60,000)			(60,000)
D-2	Difference between physical inventory and book figures	[A]	120,000	(120,000)			(120,000)
H-7/2	Unrecorded liabilities	[P]	285,000	(100,000)	(85,000)	(285,000)	100,000
V-10	Repairs expense items that should have been capitalized	[A]	90,000		(90,000)		(90,000)
Totals				(185,000)	(175,000)	(285,000)	(75,000)

[EA] Estimated based on analytical procedures.
[A] Actual population misstatements.
[P] Estimated population misstatements based on the sample, including sampling error.

FINANCIAL STATEMENT DISCLOSURES A major consideration in completing the audit is determining whether the disclosures in the financial statements are adequate. Throughout the audit, the emphasis in most examinations is on verifying the accuracy of the balances in the general ledger by testing the most important. Another important task is to ensure that the account balances from the general ledger balances are correctly aggregated and disclosed on the financial statements. Adequate disclosure includes consideration of all of the statements including related footnotes.

Review for adequate disclosure in the financial statements at the completion of the audit is not the only time the auditor is interested in proper disclosure. Unless the auditor is constantly alert to disclosure problems, it is impossible to perform the final disclosure review adequately. For example, as part of the examination of accounts receivable, the auditor must be aware of that accounts receivable, notes receivable, and other amounts due must be shown with clear distinctions between amounts due from affiliates (or other related parties) and those due from customers. Similarly, there must be a segregation of current from non-current receivables and a disclosure of the factoring or discounting of notes receivable if such is the case. An important part of verifying all account balances is determining whether generally accepted accounting principles were properly applied on a basis consistent with that of the preceding year. The auditor must carefully document this information in the working papers to facilitate the final review.

As part of the final review for financial statement disclosure, many public accounting firms require the completion of a **financial statement disclosure checklist** for every engagement. This questionnaire is designed to remind the auditor of common disclosure problems encountered on audits and to facilitate the final review of the entire audit by an independent partner. An illustration of a partial financial statement disclosure checklist is given in Figure 21-5 on the next page.

Financial statement disclosure checklist—a questionnaire that reminds the auditor of disclosure problems commonly encountered in audits and that facilitates the final review of the entire audit by an independent partner.

	Yes	No	W/P Ref.
1. Are the following disclosures in the financial statements or notes:			
a. Cost for each major category of capital assets?	_____	_____	_____
b. The amount of amortization for the period?	_____	_____	_____
c. Accumulated amortization, including the amount of any write-downs, for each major category of capital assets at the balance sheet date?	_____	_____	_____
d. The amount of any write-downs during the period?	_____	_____	_____
e. The amortization method used, including the amortization period or rate, for each major category of capital assets including leased assets?	_____	_____	_____
f. The net carrying amount of a capital asset not being amortized because it is under construction or development or has been removed from service for an extended period?	_____	_____	_____
2. Are the nature, basis of measurement, amount, and related gains and losses of non-monetary transactions disclosed?	_____	_____	_____
3. Has consideration been given to disclosure of fully amortized capital assets still in use?	_____	_____	_____
4. Are carrying amounts of property mortgaged and encumbered by indebtedness disclosed?	_____	_____	_____
5. Is the carrying amount of property that is not a part of operations and is idle or held for investment or sale segregated?	_____	_____	_____

WORKING PAPER REVIEW AND DOCUMENTATION OF SUPERVISION Regular planning meetings, consultation, and the use of specialists are part of the audit process for most large audit engagements. Records of these planning meetings and their results would be included in the working paper file. Ongoing **working paper review** consists primarily of documenting ongoing supervision that has taken place during the conduct of the engagement by means of independent examination of the working papers by another member of the audit firm. There are three main reasons why it is essential that the working papers be thoroughly reviewed by another member of the audit firm at the completion of the audit:

Working paper review—a review of the completed audit working papers by another member of the audit firm to ensure quality and counteract bias.

- *To evaluate the performance of inexperienced personnel.* A considerable portion of most audits is performed by audit personnel with less than four or five years of experience. These people may have sufficient technical training to conduct an adequate audit, but their lack of experience affects their ability to make sound professional judgments in complex situations.
- *To make sure that the audit meets the public accounting firm's standard of performance.* Within any organization, the performance quality of individuals varies considerably, but careful review by top-level personnel in the firm assists in maintaining a uniform quality of auditing.
- *To counteract the bias that frequently enters into the auditor's judgment.* Auditors may attempt to remain objective throughout the audit, but it is easy to lose proper perspective on a long audit when there are complex problems to solve.

Except for a final independent review, which is discussed shortly, the review of the working papers should be conducted by someone who is knowledgeable about the client and the unique circumstances in the audit. Therefore, the initial review of the working papers prepared by any given auditor is normally done by the auditor's immediate supervisor. For example, the least experienced auditor's work is ordinarily reviewed by the audit senior; the senior's immediate supervisor, who is normally a supervisor or manager, reviews the senior's work and also reviews less thoroughly the papers of the inexperienced auditor.

When several staff are working together at an engagement, team review by means of interview is used. The senior meets with staff on a daily basis, discusses the nature of findings, and ensures that these are appropriately recorded in the electronic working papers before the actual client documents are returned to the client. Finally, the partner assigned to the audit must review all working papers, but the partner reviews those prepared by the supervisor or manager more thoroughly than the others. Except for the final independent review, most of the working paper review is done as each segment of the audit is completed.

INDEPENDENT REVIEW At the completion of larger audits, the financial statements and the entire set of working papers are often reviewed by a completely **independent reviewer** who has not participated in the engagement. This reviewer, usually a partner, frequently takes an adversarial position to ensure the adequacy of the conduct of the audit. The audit team must be able to justify the evidence they have accumulated and the conclusions they have reached on the basis of the unique circumstances of the engagement. This type of review may also include a second independent review if the engagement is considered high risk by the audit firm.

concept check

C21-6 What method does the auditor use to determine whether sufficient appropriate audit evidence has been collected?

C21-7 What is the purpose of independent review of the working papers?

Independent review—a review of the financial statements and the entire set of working papers by a completely independent reviewer to whom the audit team must justify the evidence accumulated and the conclusions reached.

4 Auditor Communications and Subsequent Facts

Communicate with the Audit Committee and Management

As part of the planning process, the auditor would have communicated the planned scope and timing of the audit with those charged with the governance of the entity. CAS 260 (previously not covered in the relatively equivalent prior Section 5751) requires that the auditor examine the organizational structure of the entity to determine that reporting is being done to the appropriate person or group. In most large organizations, this will be the audit committee but will also include one or more individuals in executive management.

After the audit is completed, there are several potential communications from the auditor to client personnel. These would include significant findings from the audit, which could include misstatements, potential fraud, or difficulties encountered during the audit.

COMMUNICATE MISSTATEMENTS AND ILLEGAL ACTS CAS 260 par. 12 (previously Section 5751) of the *CICA Handbook* requires that the auditor ensure that the appropriate level of management is informed of material weaknesses in the design, implementation, or operating effectiveness of internal control. Forthcoming CAS 450 requires that the auditor communicate all except clearly trivial misstatements and ask management to correct them. In addition, the auditor must ensure that the audit committee or similarly designated group (e.g., board of directors or board of trustees) is informed of all significant misstatements, whether or not they are adjusted. Misstatements include intentional (fraud or other irregularities) and unintentional (errors) misstatements. The audit committee can be informed by either the auditor or management, and this should be done on a timely basis. This requirement indicates the increased concern over the auditor's responsibility for the detection and prevention of misstatements.

Illegal acts are violations of laws or government regulations. Forthcoming CAS 250 (formerly Section 5136) requires the auditor to understand the regulatory environment in which the entity operates so that any observed illegal or possibly

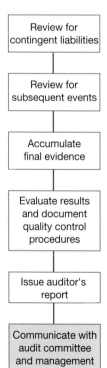

Review for contingent liabilities

Review for subsequent events

Accumulate final evidence

Evaluate results and document quality control procedures

Issue auditor's report

Communicate with audit committee and management

illegal acts, such as non-compliance with waste disposal regulations, can be communicated to the audit committee or equivalent group on a timely basis. The audit committee may also expect the auditor to communicate such matters as unusual actions that increase the risk of loss to the company; actions that could cause serious embarrassment to the entity, such as breaches of the company's code of conduct; significant transactions that appear to be inconsistent with the ordinary course of business; and other matters. The audit committee's wishes should be discussed and clarified with the audit committee prior to the auditor's undertaking of the audit fieldwork.

COMMUNICATE REPORTABLE INTERNAL CONTROL CONDITIONS As discussed in Chapter 5, CAS 240 (previously Section 5135) includes misstatements that indicate significant deficiencies in the design or operation of internal control in its definition of significant misstatements that must be reported to the audit committee. Although the auditor has no duty to report less significant internal control weaknesses identified during the audit to the client, he or she commonly does so as a client service. In addition, some auditors provide suggestions for improvements in internal control. In larger companies, this communication is made to the audit committee, and in smaller companies, to the owners or senior management. The nature and form of this communication were discussed in Chapter 9. The auditor is required to report to both management and the audit committee any weakness in internal control that could lead to material errors.

OTHER COMMUNICATION WITH AUDIT COMMITTEE For audits where there is an audit committee or similarly designated body, the auditor should communicate certain additional information obtained during the audit. Like all communications with the audit committee (or alternative individuals responsible for the governance of the entity), the purpose is to keep the committee informed of auditing issues and findings that will assist it in performing its supervisory role for financial statements.

Audit committees were introduced in Chapter 3. The audit committee has an important oversight role for many companies. The following are issues that should be discussed or communicated with the audit committee, or a similarly designated body, by the auditor with the intent of keeping the audit committee informed:

- The auditor's responsibilities under generally accepted auditing standards, including responsibility for understanding and evaluating internal control and the concept of reasonable rather than absolute assurance.
- Confirmation of the auditor's independence, including a breakdown (billed between audit and other services) of the fees, and a disclosure of any relationships between the auditor and the client (or its related entities or directors, officers, or employees).
- Planning of the current audit, including such matters as the general approach, areas of perceived high risk, materiality and risk levels selected, planned reliance on other auditors (including the internal audit department), and timing of the audit.
- The significant accounting principles and policies selected and applied to the financial statements, the existence of acceptable alternatives, and the acceptability of those selected by management.
- Management's judgments and estimates of sensitive accounting-related issues and the auditor's conclusions about the reasonableness of them.
- Disagreements with management about the scope of the audit, applicability of accounting principles, and wording of the auditor's report, whether or not satisfactorily resolved.
- Difficulties encountered in performing the audit, such as lack of availability of client personnel, failure to obtain necessary information, and an unreasonable timetable in which to complete the audit.

- Any unresolved matters arising from review of the entire annual report and identification of misstatements in reproducing the financial statements or the auditor's report or of inconsistencies between the statements and other information in the report.
- The auditor's opinions about the subjects of any consultations with other accountants about accounting or auditing matters, if the auditor becomes aware of these consultations.
- Any major issues discussed with management in connection with the appointment of the auditor, including those related to the application of accounting principles, auditing standards, and fees.

Communication with the audit committee normally takes place more than once during each audit and can be oral, written, or both, although certain communications, such as the independence letter and possible material misstatements, must be in writing. For example, issues dealing with the auditor's responsibilities and significant accounting policies are usually discussed early in the audit, preferably during the planning phase. Disagreements with management and difficulties encountered in performing the audit would be communicated after the audit is completed or earlier if the problems hinder the auditor's ability to complete the audit. The most important matters are communicated in writing to minimize misunderstanding and to provide documentation in the event of subsequent disagreement.

MANAGEMENT LETTERS The purpose of a management letter (letter of recommendation) is to inform the client of the public accountant's recommendations for improving the client's business. The recommendations focus on suggestions for more efficient operations. The combination of the auditor's experience in various businesses and a thorough understanding gained in conducting the audit place the auditor in a unique position to provide management with assistance.

A management letter is different from the required communication of material weaknesses in internal control of CAS 260. The latter is required whenever there are significant internal control weaknesses. A management letter is optional and is intended to help the client operate its business more effectively. Auditors write management letters for two reasons: (1) to encourage a better relationship between the public accounting firm and management and (2) to suggest additional tax and management advisory services that the public accounting firm can provide.

There is no standard format or approach for writing management letters. Each letter should be developed to meet the style of the auditor and the needs of the client, consistent with the public accounting firm's concept of management letters. It should be noted that many auditors combine the management letter with the required communication on internal control-related matters.

concept check

C21-8 List two examples of information that must be communicated by the auditor to the audit committee.

C21-9 Why would an auditor submit a management letter to the client?

Summary

1. *How does the auditor search for contingent liabilities?* Toward the end of the engagement, it is called a "review" for contingent liabilities, since each cycle has procedures that are intended to search for contingent liabilities (e.g., review of bank confirmations). At this stage, the auditor conducts final inquiries with management, reviews the working papers for comments about tax assessments, directors' and shareholders' meetings, and legal expenses, and ensures that legal documents such as contracts have been examined. Legal letters are reviewed for the responses received.

What is the purpose of obtaining a confirmation from the client's law firms? These confirmations are used to evaluate known litigation or other claims against clients for potential contingent liabilities.

Why must these "legal letters" be in a specified format? In order to protect their client's confidentiality, lawyers indicate whether they agree or disagree with the information that is provided by the client, in a format that has been approved by Bar Associations and the CICA.

Describe examples of procedures conducted during a review for subsequent events. Testing is done in each transaction cycle (e.g., during cut-off testing of documents). Other procedures include procedures listed with contingent liabilities above. In addition, the auditor reviews internal financial statements or budgets completed after the year end and reviews minutes and records prepared after the balance sheet date.

2. *Provide examples of work completed as part of the final evidence gathering process.* The auditor will calculate final analytical procedures and again evaluate the going-concern assumption. The client will be asked to prepare and sign a representation letter. The auditor will review information that management plans to include in the annual report and the management discussion and analysis.

3. *What does the auditor do to evaluate the adequacy of accumulated evidence?* The partner and the engagement review team, in consultation with the audit team, will review the quality and sufficiency of evidence for all cycles, assertions, and end-of-engagement processes in the context of audit risk and the client risk profile.

How are quality control procedures incorporated into this final risk response phase of the audit? In addition to the above review, an independent review or a standards department review helps to ensure that the audit is conducted to high standards.

4. *What communications is the auditor required to send after the completion of the audit?* The following communications are sent throughout the engagement (or on a timely basis after the engagement is completed): any reportable internal controls that could lead to material weaknesses, material misstatements, management letter, and independence letter. In addition, any other matters that need to be communicated, such as suspicion of fraud or illegal acts, would also be sent.

Visit the text's website at **www.pearsoned.ca/arens** for practice quizzes, additional case studies, and international standards information.

Review Questions

21-1 Distinguish between a contingent liability and an actual liability, and give three examples of each

21-2 In the audit of James Mobley Ltd., you are concerned about the possibility of contingent liabilities resulting from income tax disputes. Discuss the procedures you could use for an extensive investigation in this area.

21-3 Explain why the analysis of legal expense is an essential part of every audit engagement.

21-4 During the audit of Merrill Manufacturing Corp., Ralph Pyson, a public accountant, has become aware of four lawsuits against the client through discussions with the client, reading corporate minutes, and reviewing correspondence files. How should Ralph determine the materiality of the lawsuits and the proper disclosure in the financial statements?

21-5 Describe the action that an auditor should take if a law firm refuses to provide information that is within its jurisdiction and may directly affect the fair presentation of the financial statements.

21-6 Distinguish between subsequent events requiring adjustment and those requiring disclosure. Give two examples of each type.

21-7 In obtaining confirmations from law firms, Betty Chui's aim is to receive the confirmation letters as early as possible after the balance sheet date. This provides her with a signed letter from every law firm in time to investigate properly any exceptions. It also eliminates the problem of a lot of unresolved issues near the end of the audit. Evaluate Betty's approach.

21-8 Explain why an auditor would be interested in a client's future commitments to purchase raw materials at a fixed price.

21-9 What major considerations should the auditor take into account in determining how extensive the review of subsequent events should be?

21-10 Compare and contrast the accumulation of audit evidence and the evaluation of the adequacy of the disclosures in the financial statements. Give two examples in which adequate disclosure could depend heavily on the accumulation of evidence and two others in which audit evidence does not normally affect the adequacy of the disclosure significantly.

21-11 Explain the meaning of the following: The auditor should actively evaluate whether there is substantial doubt about the client's ability to continue as a going concern.

21-12 Distinguish between a management representation letter and a management letter, and state the primary purpose of each. List some items that might be included in each letter.

21-13 What is meant by "reading other financial information" in annual reports? Give an example of the type of information that the auditor would be examining.

21-14 Explain why you think securities regulators in certain jurisdictions require public companies to provide MD&A in their annual reports.

21-15 Distinguish between regular working-paper review and independent review, and state the purpose of each. Give two examples of important potential findings in each of these two types of review.

Discussion Questions and Problems

21-16 Kathy Choi, a public accountant, has completed the audit of notes payable and other liabilities for Valley River Electrical Services Ltd. and now plans to audit contingent liabilities and commitments.

REQUIRED

a. Distinguish between contingent liabilities and commitments, and explain why both are important in an audit.

b. Identify three useful audit procedures for uncovering contingent liabilities that Kathy would likely perform in the normal conduct of the audit, even if she had no responsibility for uncovering contingencies.

c. Identify three other procedures Kathy would likely perform specifically for the purpose of identifying undisclosed contingencies.

21-17 In an examination of Marco Corporation as of December 31, 2009, the following situations exist. No related entries have been made in the accounting records.

1. Marco Corporation has guaranteed the payment of interest on the 10-year, first-mortgage bonds of Chen Corp., an affiliate. Outstanding bonds of Chen Corp. amount to $150,000 with interest payable at 8 percent per annum, due June 1 and December 1 each year. The bonds were issued by Chen on December 31, 2007, and all interest payments have been met by that company with the exception of the payment due December 1, 2009. Marco Corporation states that it will pay the defaulted interest to the bondholders on January 15, 2010.

2. During the year 2009, Marco Corporation was named as a defendant in a suit by Dalton Inc. for damages for breach of contract. A decision adverse to Marco Corporation was rendered, and Dalton Inc. was awarded $40,000 in damages. At the time of the audit, the case was under appeal to a higher court.

3. On December 23, 2009, Marco Corporation declared a common share dividend of 1,000 shares with a stated value of $100,000, payable February 2, 2010, to the common shareholders of record on December 30, 2009.

REQUIRED

a. Describe the audit procedures that you would use to learn about each of the above situations.

b. Describe the nature of the adjusting entries or disclosure, if any, that you would require for each of these situations.

(Adapted from AICPA)

21-18 Melanie Adams is a public accountant in a medium-sized public accounting firm and takes an active part in the conduct of every audit she supervises. She follows the practice of reviewing all working papers of subordinates as soon as it is convenient, rather than waiting until the end of the audit.

When the audit is nearly finished, Melanie reviews the working papers again to make sure she has not missed anything significant. Since she makes most of the major decisions on the audit, there is rarely anything that requires further investigation. When she completes the review, she prepares a draft of the financial statements, gets them approved by management, and has them assembled in her firm's office. No other public accountant reviews the working papers because Melanie is responsible for signing the auditor's reports.

REQUIRED

a. Evaluate the practice of reviewing the working papers of subordinates on a continuing basis rather than when the audit is completed.

b. Is it acceptable for Melanie to prepare the financial statements rather than have the client assume that responsibility?

c. Evaluate the practice of not having a review of the working papers by another public accountant in the firm.

21-19 Ruben Chavez, a public accountant, has prepared a management representation letter for the president and controller to sign. It contains references to the following items:

1. Inventory is fairly stated at the lower of cost or market and includes no obsolete items.

2. All actual and contingent liabilities are properly included in the statements.

3. All subsequent events of relevance to the financial statements have been disclosed.

REQUIRED

a. Why is it desirable to have a letter of representation from the client concerning the above matters when the audit evidence accumulated during the course of the engagement is meant to verify the same information?

b. To what extent is the letter of representation useful as audit evidence? Explain.

c. List several other types of information commonly included in a letter of representation.

21-20 In connection with your examination of the financial statements of Olars Mfg. Corporation for the year ended December 31, 2009, your review of subsequent events disclosed the following items:

1. January 3, 2010: The provincial government approved a plan for the construction of an express highway. The plan will result in the expropriation of a portion of land owned by Olars Mfg. Corporation. Construction will begin in late 2010. No estimate of the condemnation (expropriation) award is available.

2. January 4, 2010: The funds for a $25,000 loan to the corporation made by Mr. Olars, the president, on July 15, 2009, were obtained by him by a loan on his personal life insurance policy. The loan was recorded in the account "loan from officers." Mr. Olars' source of the funds was not disclosed in the company records. The corporation pays the premiums on the life insurance policy, and Mrs. Olars, wife of the president, is the beneficiary.

3. January 7, 2010: The mineral content of a shipment of ore, which was en route on December 31, 2009, was determined to be 72 percent. The shipment was recorded at year end at an estimated content of 50 percent by a debit to raw material inventory and a credit to accounts payable in the amount of $20,600. The final liability to the vendor is based on the actual mineral content of the shipment.

4. January 15, 2010: As a result of a series of personal disagreements between Mr. Olars and his brother-in-law, the treasurer, the latter resigned, effective immediately, under an agreement whereby the corporation would purchase his 10-percent stock ownership at book value as of December 31, 2009. Payment is to be made in two equal amounts in cash on April 1, 2010, and October 1, 2010. In December 2009, the treasurer obtained a divorce from his wife, who is Mr. Olars' sister.

5. January 31, 2010: As a result of reduced sales, production was curtailed in mid-January and some workers were laid off. On February 5, 2010, all the remaining workers went on strike. To date, the strike is unsettled.

6. February 10, 2010: A contract was signed whereby Mammoth Enterprises purchases from Olars Mfg. Corporation all of the latter's capital assets (including rights to receive the proceeds of any property condemnation), inventories, and the right to conduct business under the name "Olars Mfg. Division." The effective date of the transfer will be March 1, 2010. The sale price was $500,000, subject to adjustment following the taking of a physical inventory. Important factors contributing to the decision to enter into the contract were the policy of the board of directors of Mammoth Enterprises to diversify the firm's activities and the report of a survey conducted by an independent market appraisal firm that revealed a declining market for Olars products.

REQUIRED
Assume that the items described came to your attention prior to completion of your audit work on February 15, 2010. For each item:
a. Give the audit procedures, if any, that would have brought the item to your attention. Indicate other sources of information that may have revealed the item.
b. Discuss the disclosure that you would recommend for the item, listing all details that you would suggest should be disclosed. Indicate those items or details, if any, that should not be disclosed. Give your reasons for recommending or not recommending disclosure of the items or details.

(Adapted from AICPA)

21-21 In a letter to the audit committee of Cline Wholesale Company, Jerry Schwartz, a public accountant, informed it of weaknesses in the control of inventory. In a separate letter to senior management, he elaborated on how the weaknesses could result in a significant misstatement of inventory caused by the failure to recognize the existence of obsolete items. In addition, Jerry made specific recommendations in the management letter on how to improve internal control and save clerical time by installing a computer system for the company's perpetual records. Management accepted the recommendations and installed the system under Jerry's direction. For several months, the system worked beautifully, but unforeseen problems developed when a master file was erased. The cost of reproducing and processing the inventory records to correct the error was significant, and management decided to scrap the entire project. The company sued Jerry for failure to use adequate professional judgment in making the recommendations.

REQUIRED
a. What is Jerry's legal and professional responsibility in the issuance of management letters?
b. Discuss the major considerations that will determine whether he is liable in this situation.
c. Did Jerry abide by the Professional Rules of Conduct? Explain your reasoning.

21-22 In analyzing legal expense for Boastman Bottle Company, Bart Little, a public accountant, observes that the company has paid legal fees to three different law firms during the current year. In accordance with his accounting firm's normal operating practice, Bart requests standard confirmation letters as of the balance sheet date from each of the three law firms.

On the last day of fieldwork, Bart notes that one of the confirmations has not yet been received. The confirmation from the second law firm contains a statement to the effect that the law firm deals exclusively in registering patents and refuses to comment on any lawsuits or other legal affairs of the client. The confirmation letter from the third law firm states that there is an outstanding unpaid bill due from the client and recognizes the existence of a potentially material lawsuit against the client but refuses to comment further to protect the legal rights of the client.

REQUIRED

a. Evaluate Bart's approach to requesting the confirmations and his follow-up on the responses.
b. What should Bart do about each of the confirmations?

21-23 Betty Ann Jarrett, a public accountant, was reading the annual report of Watgold Ltd. and noticed that the president's report contradicted several items in the audited financial statements included in the report.

REQUIRED

What are Betty Ann's responsibilities in this instance?

Professional Judgment Problem

21-24 You are a public accountant in the public accounting firm of Lind and Hemming. One of your larger clients is Yukon Corp., a company incorporated under the Canada Business Corporations Act, which has a December 31 year end. Yukon's 2009 audit was completed in January 2010; the auditor's report was dated January 28, 2010.

It is now August 2010 and professional staff from your office are working at Yukon doing interim work on the December 31, 2010, audit. Yesterday, the senior in charge of the audit gave you a memo dated August 4, 2010, revealing that

the staff have discovered that several large blocks of inventory were materially overpriced at December 31, 2009, and have since been written down to reflect their true value.

You have just finished reviewing again the 2009 working papers and have determined that the error was a sampling error; your firm does not appear to have been negligent.

REQUIRED

What action would you take and why? Support your answer.

Case

21-25 In your audit of Aviary Industries for the calendar year 2009, you found a number of matters that you believe represent possible adjustments to the company's books. These matters are described below. Management's attitude is that "once the books are closed, they're closed," and management does not want to make any adjustments. Planning materiality for the engagement was $100,000, determined by computing 5 percent of expected income before taxes. Actual income before taxes on the financial statements prior to any adjustments is $1,652,867.

Possible adjustments:

1. Several credit memos that were processed and recorded after year end relate to sales and accounts receivable for 2009. These total $23,529.
2. Inventory cut-off tests indicate that $22,357 of inventory received on December 30, 2009, was recorded as purchases and accounts payable in 2010. These items were included in the inventory count at year end and therefore were included in ending inventory.
3. Inventory cut-off tests also indicate several sales invoices recorded in 2009 for goods that were shipped in early 2010. The goods were not included in inventory but were set aside in a separate shipping area. The total amount of these shipments was $36,022. (Ignore cost of sales for this item.)

4. At the end of 2009, the company wrote several cheques for accounts payable that were held and not mailed until January 15, 2010. These totalled $48,336. Recorded cash and accounts payable at December 31, 2009, are $2,356,553 and $2,666,290, respectively.
5. The company has not established a reserve for obsolescence of inventories. Your tests indicate that such a reserve is appropriate in an amount somewhere between $20,000 and $40,000.
6. Your review of the allowance for uncollectible accounts indicates that it may be understated by between $25,000 and $50,000.

REQUIRED

a. Determine the adjustments that you believe must be made for Aviary's financial statements to be fairly presented. Include the amounts and accounts affected by each adjustment.
b. Why might Aviary Industries' management resist making these adjustments?
c. Explain what you consider the most positive way of approaching management personnel to convince them to make your proposed changes.
d. Describe your responsibilities related to unadjusted misstatements that management has determined are immaterial individually and in the aggregate.

22

Auditor reporting

Reports are essential to the audit and other attestation processes because they provide information about what is being attested to, what the public accountant did, and the conclusions reached based upon sufficient and appropriate evidence. Standard wording and rules about the types of reports guide their preparation. Accountants as users of these reports need to understand their meaning, while public accountants consider what type of report is available when.

LEARNING OBJECTIVES

1 State the requirements for a standard unqualified audit report. Describe the component parts and their significance. State the relevance of the audit report date and when dual dating might occur.

2 Describe the categories of auditor's report, providing examples of the variations in wording and additional paragraphs that are used.

3 Describe the difference between an adverse opinion and a disclaimer of opinion. Explain how materiality is related to the wording changes used for these types of opinions. Provide examples of other changes to the independent auditor's report.

STANDARDS REFERENCED IN THIS CHAPTER

CICA Standards

CAS 560 – Subsequent events (previously Section 5405 – Date of the auditor's report; Section 6550 – Subsequent events)

CAS 600 – Special considerations: audits of group financial statements (including the work of component auditors) (previously Section 6930 – Reliance on another auditor)

CAS 620 – Using the work of an auditor's expert (previously Section 5049 – Use of specialists in assurance engagements)

CAS 700 – Forming an opinion and reporting on financial statements (previously Section 5400 – The auditor's standard report)

CAS 705 – Modifications to the opinion in the independent auditor's report (previously Section 5510 – Reservations in the auditor's report)

CAS 706 – Emphasis of matter paragraphs and other matter(s) paragraphs in the independent auditor's report (previously Section 5600 – Auditor's report on financial statements prepared using a basis of accounting other than generally accepted accounting principles)

CAS 710 – Comparative information: corresponding figures and comparative financial statements (previously Section 5701 – Other reporting matters; AuG-8 – Auditor's report on comparative financial statements)

Section 7110 – Auditor involvement with offering documents of public and private entities

Section 7115 – Auditor involvement with offering documents of public and private entities: current legislative and regulatory requirements

AuG-10 – Legislative requirements to report on the consistent application of generally accepted accounting principles

AuG-21 – Canada–US reporting differences

AuG-40 – Auditor's report on the financial statements of federally regulated financial institutions

A Qualified Audit Report—Problems with Management Integrity

Halvorson & Co., public accountants, had been the auditors of Fine Furniture Inc. (FFI) for many years. Halvorson was a top-tier accounting firm with national offices across the country. It was proud of the quality of its staff and the type of service it provided to its clients. FFI was a medium-sized client that had been with the firm for over 20 years, a great accomplishment given the volatility of the furniture industry, and the local partners knew the owners well. Recently, Al Trent, one of the firm's senior qualified accountants, had joined Fine Furniture Inc. as the chief financial officer. Al was well liked and had been with Halvorson since he left university.

Bruce Marks, the partner in charge of the FFI audit, was livid as Steve Smith, a newly hired qualified accountant, left the partner's office with a dejected look on his face. Samantha, one of the audit seniors in the office, spoke to Bruce later in the day after he had calmed down. Bruce was steaming about a situation that had arisen the previous day. This year, Fine Furniture Inc. was going to receive a qualified independent auditor's report with respect to inventory. Bruce used phrases like "unable to determine the quantity of inventory on hand at year end" and "potential overstatement of expenses" as he explained what was going to happen to the audit report. Bruce was particularly angry because he was now faced with having to report Al Trent to the provincial institute of chartered accountants for unethical behaviour and having to discipline Steve Smith due to the events at FFI. He exclaimed that both of these highly qualified and competent men should have known better.

Steve had gone first to the east-end location of FFI to count inventory. The furniture inventory was well organized and labelled, and it had taken him only an hour to complete his test counts and gather necessary documentation. The inventory count had gone well. Al had shown him around and then offered to take Steve to lunch and for a round of golf. Steve knew Al only by reputation and had felt this was a good way to get to know the senior financial officer at the company while also getting in a round of golf.

About five hours later, Steve finally made it to the west-end location of FFI. Unfortunately, here, inventory was not that well organized. It was simply a storage location operated by part-time staff, who looked particularly harried. The location was very busy, with shipments constantly leaving and arriving. It was almost as if the staff were not aware there was an inventory count that afternoon. Even though Steve was tired, he managed to jot down very specific details of inventory, including serial numbers. At that point he realized several of the items had the same serial numbers as those he had seen in the east-end location. It was like being hit with a tonne of bricks.

Without communicating his concerns to the FFI staff, Steve methodically went through the contents of the warehouse, staying late into the evening. Fully two-thirds of the items he had counted at the east-end location were also here at the west end. Steve grimaced as he realized

continued >

what Al had done while filling up his car with gasoline that afternoon. Al had purchased several food items at the gas bar and had asked the attendant to just "include it with the gas" as he paid for the bill with what looked like a company credit card. It must be routine if he did it even in Steve's presence—not material transactions, but clearly an indication of Al's ethics with respect to business practices.

Steve went home and wrote up what had happened that day, knowing that it was partially his own behaviour that had given FFI the opportunity to ship inventory from the east end to the west end. If he had not noted down serial numbers, the attempt to inflate inventory values would not have been detected.

IMPORTANCE TO AUDITORS

Users of financial statements rely on the auditor's report to provide assurance on the company's financial statements. Auditors assume that management is honest and that unethical behaviour (such as moving inventory from one location to another) will not be pursued, When such actions are detected, then the auditor must rethink the risks associated with the engagement.

WHAT DO YOU THINK?

1. What if Steve had not detected FFI's attempt to inflate inventory? Which users would have been affected and how?

2. Based upon the case facts above, what other accounts should the auditor further investigate before finalizing the audit report?

ISSUANCE of the auditor's report is part of the final phase in the risk-based audit process. Careful review of the working papers (including accumulated evidence) provides the auditor with the basis for the audit opinion. In most cases, the auditor is able to provide sufficient evidence to state that the financial statements present fairly the financial position of the company. In some cases, the evidence is unavailable, or the auditor disagrees with management about what has been presented in the financial statements. This chapter presents ways that the auditor explains disagreements and provides a standard audit opinion. We begin by describing the content of that standard auditor's report.

 ## The Standard Independent Auditor's Report

Standard Unqualified Independent Auditor's Report

The most common type of audit report is the **standard unqualified independent auditor's report**. It is also often referred to as the auditor's standard report. It is used when all auditing conditions have been met, no significant misstatements have been discovered and left uncorrected, and the auditor believes that the financial statements are fairly stated in accordance with generally accepted accounting principles (GAAP). The specific conditions required to issue this report are as follows:

1. An audit engagement has been undertaken to express an opinion on financial statements.
2. Generally accepted auditing standards (GAAS) have been followed by the auditor in all respects on the engagement.
3. Sufficient appropriate audit evidence has been accumulated, and the auditor has conducted the engagement in a manner that concludes that the examination standards have been met.
4. The financial statements, which include the balance sheet, the income statement, the statement of retained earnings, the cash flow statement, and the notes to the financial statements, are fairly presented in accordance with an appropriate disclosed basis of accounting, usually Canadian generally accepted accounting principles.
5. There are no circumstances which, in the opinion of the auditor, would require modifying the wording of the report or adding an additional explanatory paragraph.

When these conditions are met, the standard unqualified auditor's report on the financial statements, as shown in Figure 22-1 on pages 716–717, is issued. Different auditors may vary the wording of the standard report slightly, but the meaning will be the same. As Canada is adopting international auditing standards, the format of the audit report will depend upon when it is issued. The prior Canadian standard, shown on the left hand side of Figure 22-1, can be issued for those clients with a fiscal year ending on or by December 14, 2010. After that date, the report shown on the right hand side would be issued. Note that after the introductory statement, the new standards require that paragraphs be labelled, for improved communication with the reader.

PARTS OF STANDARD UNQUALIFIED AUDITOR'S REPORT Each standard unqualified auditor's report includes several distinct parts. These parts are labelled in bold letters in Figure 22-1. The following discussion focuses on the international standards, adopted by Canada as part of Canadian Auditing Standards (CASs).

`CAS`

1. *Report title.* CAS 700 par. 21 (previously Section 5400.07) states that the auditor's report should have a title that clearly explains its purpose. The convention prior to the adoption of the CASs was to simply use the term "Auditor's report." However, CAS 700 emphasizes that the auditor is independent, so the title now requires reference to the auditor's independence.
2. *Addressee.* CAS 700 par. 22 and A16 (previously 5400.35) require that the addressee be the parties who have hired the auditors, or as required by law in the local jurisdiction. Normally, the addressees are the shareholders, since it is usually they who appoint the auditor.
3. *Introductory statement.* The first part of the auditor's report does three things. First, it makes the simple statement that the public accounting firm has done an audit. (Later sections clarify what is meant by an audit.)

    Second, it lists the financial statements that were audited, including the balance sheet date and the period for the income statement, the statement of retained earnings, and the cash flow statement. Note that there is a terminology difference—the CAS uses "statement of changes in equity" rather than "statement of retained earnings." While the older Canadian standards do not mention the notes to the financial statements, the new standards require reference to the disclosure of accounting policies used and the other notes to the financial statements.

    Third, the prior standard introductory paragraph states that the financial statements are the responsibility of management and that the auditor's responsibility is to express an opinion on the financial statements; this paragraph (a) communicates that management is responsible for selecting the appropriate generally accepted accounting principles and for making the measurement decisions and

Canadian Predecessor Standards: Year Ends Prior to December 14, 2010		International Standards: Year Ends on or After December 14, 2010	
Report Section Title	**Report Example**	**Report Example**	**Report Section Title**
Report Title	AUDITOR'S REPORT	INDEPENDENT AUDITOR'S REPORT	Report Title
Addressee	To the Shareholders of Hillsburg Hardware Ltd.	To the Shareholders of Hillsburg Hardware Ltd.	Addressee
Introductory paragraph	We have audited the balance sheet of Hillsburg Hardware Ltd. as at December 31, 2009, and the statements of income, retained earnings, and cash flows for the year then ended.	We have audited the accompanying financial statements of Hillsburg Hardware Ltd., which comprise the balance sheet as at December 31, 2010, income statement, statement of changes in equity, cash flow statement for the year then ended, and a summary of significant accounting policies and other explanatory notes.	Introductory statement
		Management's Responsibility for the Financial Statements	Management responsibility
	These financial statements are the responsibility of the company's management.	Management is responsible for the preparation and fair presentation of these financial statements in accordance with Canadian generally accepted accounting principles. This responsibility includes designing, implementing, and maintaining internal control relevant to the preparation and fair presentation of financial statements that are free from material misstatement, whether due to fraud or error; selecting and applying appropriate accounting policies; and making accounting estimates that are reasonable in the circumstances.	
		Auditor's Responsibility	Auditor Responsibility
	Our responsibility is to express an opinion on these financial statements based on our audit.	Our responsibility is to express an opinion on these financial statements based on our audit.	
Scope paragraph	We conducted our audit in accordance with Canadian generally accepted auditing standards. Those standards require that we plan and perform an audit to obtain reasonable assurance whether the financial statements are free of material misstatement.	We conducted our audit in accordance with Canadian generally accepted auditing standards. Those standards require that we comply with ethical requirements and plan and perform the audit to obtain reasonable assurance whether the financial statements are free from material misstatement.	

Canadian Predecessor Standards: Year Ends Prior to December 14, 2010		International Standards: Year Ends on or After December 14, 2010	
	An audit includes examining, on a test basis, evidence supporting the amounts and disclosures in the financial statements. An audit also includes assessing the accounting principles used and significant estimates made by management, as well as evaluating the overall financial statement presentation.	An audit involves performing procedures to obtain audit evidence about the amounts and disclosures in the financial statements. The procedures selected depend on the auditor's judgment, including the assessment of the risks of material misstatement of the financial statements, whether due to fraud or error. In making those risk assessments, the auditor considers internal control relevant to the entity's preparation and fair presentation of the financial statements in order to design audit procedures that are appropriate in the circumstances, but not for the purpose of expressing an opinion on the effectiveness of the entity's internal control. An audit also includes evaluating the appropriateness of accounting policies used and the reasonableness of accounting estimates made by management, as well as evaluating the overall presentation of the financial statements.	
		We believe that the audit evidence we have obtained is sufficient and appropriate to provide a basis for our audit opinion.	
Opinion paragraph		Opinion	Opinion paragraph
	In our opinion, these financial statements present fairly, in all material respects, the financial position of the company as at December 31, 2009, and the results of its operations and cash flows for the year then ended in accordance with Canadian generally accepted accounting principles.	In our opinion, the financial statements present fairly, in all material respects, the financial position of Hillsburg Hardware Ltd. as of December 31, 2010, and of its financial performance and its cash flows for the year then ended in accordance with Canadian generally accepted accounting principles.	
Name and designation of public accounting firm	*Boritz, Kao, Kadous & Co.* Boritz, Kao, Kadous & Co., LLP	*Boritz, Kao, Kadous & Co.* Boritz, Kao, Kadous & Co., LLP	Auditor's signature
Auditor's report date	February 15, 2010	March 1, 2011	Date of the auditor's report
Place of issue	Halifax, Nova Scotia	444 Transom Street, Halifax, Nova Scotia B3M 3JP	Auditor's address

disclosures in applying those principles, and (b) clarifies the respective roles of management and the auditor. In the new version, these responsibilities are more detailed and provided in separate paragraphs.

4. *Management responsibility.* The old standard audit opinion states simply that the financial statements are the responsibility of management. The new standards require much more detail, describing the criteria used for preparing those financial statements (normally Canadian GAAP, although other frameworks will be acceptable). Then, the paragraph explains that management is also responsible for the decisions underlying the financial statements, including development and monitoring of internal controls and the application of reasonable estimates so that the statements are free of material misstatement. Review this paragraph carefully—you will see that it corresponds clearly to what we have discussed as the responsibility of management in previous chapters of this text.

5. *Auditor responsibility.* Previously part of both the introductory and scope paragraphs, the new auditor responsibility paragraph starts with a summary statement that explains the purpose of the audit—the expression of an opinion on the financial statements described in the first sentence. Then, further detail is provided, stating that the auditor followed generally accepted auditing standards during the performance of the audit. It tells the reader what those standards comprise: The audit is designed to obtain reasonable assurance whether the statements are free of material misstatement. The inclusion of the word "material" conveys the meaning that auditors search for significant misstatements, not minor errors that do not affect users' decisions. The use of the term "reasonable assurance" is intended to indicate that an audit cannot be expected to completely eliminate the possibility that a material error or fraud or other irregularity will exist in the financial statements. In other words, an audit provides a high level of assurance, but not a guarantee.

The remainder briefly describes important aspects of what an audit does and does not include. It starts with the basis of the audit—that is, the auditor's use of professional judgment in the context of a risk assessment (considering risks of error or fraud) to select audit procedures for the conduct of the audit. It includes assessing internal controls over financial systems that affect the financial statements but does not provide an opinion over those controls (as internal controls can and do change over time).

In the older standard, the words "test basis" indicate that sampling was used, rather than an audit of every transaction and amount on the statements. The newer standard focuses on risk assessment rather than audit testing.

While the management responsibility paragraph of the report states that management is responsible for the preparation and content of the financial statements, this paragraph states that the auditor has the responsibility to evaluate the appropriateness of those accounting principles, estimates, financial statement disclosures, and presentations given. The auditor cannot simply accept management's representations about appropriateness. The final sentence in the new standard report explicitly refers to the quality of the evidence collected: sufficient and appropriate—that is, enough high-quality evidence has been obtained to allow the auditor to provide an opinion on the financial statements.

6. *Opinion paragraph.* The final paragraph in the standard auditor's report states the auditor's conclusions based on the results of the audit. This part of the auditor's report is so important that often the entire report is referred to as simply the auditor's opinion. The opinion paragraph is stated as an opinion, rather than as a statement of absolute fact or as a guarantee. The intent is to indicate that the conclusions are based on professional judgment. The phrase "in our opinion" indicates that there may be some information risk associated with the financial statements, even though the statements have been audited. Note that the new format uses the terms "financial performance" rather than "results of operations" when describing the activity of the entity for the period under audit.

The opinion paragraph is directly related to the generally accepted auditing reporting standards described in Figure 2-4 on page 35. The auditor is required to state an opinion about the financial statements taken as a whole, including a conclusion about whether the company followed an appropriate disclosed basis of accounting, usually Canadian generally accepted accounting principles.

One of the most controversial parts of the auditor's report is the meaning of the term "presents fairly." The auditor means that the financial statements are fairly presented in accordance with the accounting principles described in the opinion paragraph. A layperson may mistake "presents fairly" to mean that the values in the financial statements represent the realizable values of the assets. It is important that lay people understand the auditor's message. The auditor cannot and does not check every transaction.

7. *[Signature] Name of public accounting firm.* The name identifies the public accounting firm or practitioner who has performed the audit. Typically, the firm's name is used since the entire firm has the legal and professional responsibility to make certain the quality of the audit meets professional standards as illustrated in Figure 22-1.

auditing in action 22-1
What's in a Date?

Several audit firms have stated that the CASs and forthcoming auditing changes will not really affect them, as there are few substantive changes and they are already performing their work substantially in accordance with the new standards (Buckstein, 2009). Yet there is at least one change that will have a significant effect on the conduct of the audit—the change in the way the independent auditor's report is dated.

Prior to the implementation of CAS 700, Forming an opinion and reporting on financial statements, the audit report date was set at the date of substantial completion of field work for the financial statement audit. This meant that the auditors were on the client premises, doing their work, with full access to client records and discussions with management. Then they would pick up their laptops and files and leave and perhaps wait for one or two more confirmations to be received or phone calls to be made, and the audit would be considered done. So the last day on the client's premises was equal to the date of the audit report.

CAS 700 states in paragraph 41 that the report date must be equal to or later than the date both when the financial statements have been prepared and when someone with authority at the client has accepted responsibility for those financial statements. Interpretations of this requirement conclude that for larger companies this means that the board of directors must approve the financial statements, and for smaller companies the owner/manager must approve the financial statements.

In our example, the financial statements were approved, as audited, six weeks after the auditors left the premises of the client. But now the auditor is subject to paragraph 6 of CAS 560, Subsequent events, which requires that the auditor assess client transactions and events after the fiscal year end (financial statement date) up to the date of the audit report. So the auditor goes back out to the client, examines any legal invoices that have been received, reviews bank statements, talks to management, and, if all goes well, there will be no further adjustments to the financial statements. However, if there is a new lawsuit that should be disclosed in the financial statements, then the financial statements need to be adjusted and approved by the board again—an unfortunate worst-case scenario.

For a small company, the auditors can submit suggested journal entries, discuss them with the owner/manager, have the entries posted, and get the financial statements approved before leaving the client premises. In this situation, substantial completion of field work will still equal the audit report date and also the date that responsibility has been taken for the statements. However, for a larger client it could mean that the auditors would leave the client, it would take three weeks for potential adjustments to be approved, and that the next board meeting would be scheduled another three weeks later, resulting in a six-week delay.

The impact on auditors is that careful planning needs to take place to ensure that the audit is completed on time, that meetings of board members are scheduled on time, and that the client keeps track of any potential events that could affect the financial statements, expediting the subsequent events review that will need to occur between the date of substantial completion of field work and the date of the independent auditor's report.

Sources: 1. Buckstein, Jeff, "Are you ready for ISA?", *CAMagazine*, April, 2009, p. 18–23, 25. 2. Canadian Institute of Chartered Accountants, *Canadian Auditing Standard 560, Subsequent Events*, 2008. 3. International Federation of Accountants, *International Standard on Auditing ISA 700, The Independent Auditor's Report on General Purpose Financial Statements, Exposure Draft*, July 2007.

CAS

8. *Date of the auditor's report.* Prior to adoption of international standards, the appropriate date for the report as illustrated on the left hand side of Figure 22-1 was the one on which the auditor had completed the most important auditing procedures in the field. Section 5405.06 referred to ". . . substantial completion of examination. . . ." This date was considered to be the date when the auditor had enough evidence to support an opinion on the financial statements. However, CAS 700 par. 41(b) states that the audit report can be dated only after those with sufficient responsibility at the entity have taken responsibility for the financial statements. For most organizations this means that the board of directors must approve the financial statements. For smaller organizations it may be a primary shareholder, such as an owner/operator, who approves the financial statements.

This date is important to users because it indicates the last day of the auditor's responsibility for the review of significant events that occurred after the date of the financial statements. For example, if the balance sheet is dated December 31, 2009, and the audit report is dated March 1, 2010, the implication is that the auditor has searched for material, unrecorded transactions, and events that occurred up to March 1, 2010, that may have had an effect on the 2009 statements.

CAS

Dual Dating CAS 560, Subsequent events (previously Section 5405, Date of the auditor's report), discusses, among other things, double dating of the auditor's report. Double dating is done when a material event occurs after the date of the auditor's report and before the date the report is issued. The preference is for the auditor to do additional field work based upon the revised, reapproved financial statements so that the audit report applies to the whole set of financial statements (CAS 560, par. 11). However, if it is possible for the auditor to conduct work separately for the material event, the auditor may double date the report as follows:

> March 1, 2010
> except for Note 17 which is
> as of April 2, 2010

If the effect of the event were so material as to change the 2009 financial statements significantly, the auditor would probably extend the audit for the financial statements as a whole and date the report with the revised date as approved by the board. In the example provided, the new date of the auditor's report would be April 2, 2010.

9. *Auditor's address.* CAS 700, par. 42, requires that the place of issue be identified. This could be in the letterhead on which the auditor's report is printed or at the foot of the report as is illustrated in Figure 22-1.

concept check

C22-1 What criterion does the auditor use to assess the client's financial statements?

C22-2 Provide four facets of the auditor's responsibility that are included in the Auditor Responsibility section of the independent auditor's report.

② How the Auditor Provides Additional Information

Categories of Auditor's Reports

Most users of financial statements read the independent auditor's report. When the report consists of three standard paragraphs, they conclude that the five conditions listed on page 715 have been met.

A deviation from the standard unqualified report will cause knowledgeable users of financial statements to recognize that the auditor intends to communicate additional or limiting information. In extreme cases, the auditor may conclude that the financial statements are materially misstated, but usually the cause of the deviation is less significant.

The categorization of audit reports in Figure 22-2 is used throughout the remainder of this chapter. The departures from a standard unqualified report are considered increasingly severe as one follows down the figure. A disclaimer or adverse opinion is normally far more important to users than an unqualified report with an explanatory paragraph or modified wording.

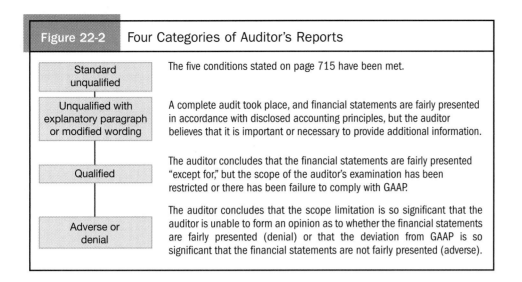

Figure 22-2 Four Categories of Auditor's Reports

Standard unqualified	The five conditions stated on page 715 have been met.
Unqualified with explanatory paragraph or modified wording	A complete audit took place, and financial statements are fairly presented in accordance with disclosed accounting principles, but the auditor believes that it is important or necessary to provide additional information.
Qualified	The auditor concludes that the financial statements are fairly presented "except for," but the scope of the auditor's examination has been restricted or there has been failure to comply with GAAP.
Adverse or denial	The auditor concludes that the scope limitation is so significant that the auditor is unable to form an opinion as to whether the financial statements are fairly presented (denial) or that the deviation from GAAP is so significant that the financial statements are not fairly presented (adverse).

Unqualified Auditor's Report with Explanatory Paragraph or Modified Wording

In certain situations, an unqualified auditor's report is issued, but the wording deviates from the standard unqualified report. The unqualified report with explanatory paragraph or modified wording meets the criteria of a complete audit with satisfactory results and financial statements that are fairly presented, but the auditor believes it is necessary to provide additional information. In a qualified, adverse, or disclaimer report, the auditor either has not performed a complete audit or is not satisfied that the financial statements are fairly presented. CAS 706 (previously covered in Sections 5600 and 5701) provides examples.

UNQUALIFIED AUDITOR'S REPORT WHEN THE APPROPRIATE DISCLOSED BASIS OF ACCOUNTING IS NOT GAAP In certain situations, an unqualified auditor's report is issued when the disclosed basis of accounting is not generally accepted accounting principles.

The auditor's report is required to state which accounting framework is used by the entity. CAS 706 (formerly Section 5600) covers non-GAAP statements, which might include financial statements prepared in accordance with regulatory legislation or with contractual requirements. In such circumstances, the auditor would express the opinion that the financial statements presented fairly the financial position, financial performance, and cash flows in accordance with the disclosed basis of accounting.

MODIFICATIONS IN THE STANDARD UNQUALIFIED AUDITOR'S REPORT The auditor may be reporting under a statute that requires the inclusion of information in addition to that provided in the auditor's report. Normally, such explanatory information should be included after the opinion paragraph. For example, Assurance and Related Services Guideline 40 (AuG-40), Auditor's report on the financial statements of federally regulated financial institutions, provides guidance on the wording of the auditor's report of a financial institution governed by a federal statute such as the Bank Act or the Insurance Companies Act. Similarly, AuG-10, Legislative requirements to report on the consistent application of GAAP, allows the auditor to state that accounting principles have been applied on a basis consistent with that of the preceding year.

CAS 706 (previously Section 5701.05) also suggests that if the auditor wishes to expand his or her report to include other information and explanations, such information should be included in a paragraph following the opinion paragraph. For example, when comparative financial statements are presented that were not audited or were audited by another auditor, that information would be disclosed in a paragraph following the opinion paragraph, where permitted by law.

REPORTING ON COMPARATIVE FINANCIAL STATEMENTS CAS 710, Comparative information—corresponding figures and comparative financial statements (previously partially covered in AuG-8, Auditor's report on comparative financial statements) affects those companies filing financial statements with the Ontario Securities Commission (OSC). The *CICA Handbook* normally requires the auditor to report only on the current year's financial statements, called the **corresponding figures approach**. Publicly listed organizations must refer to both periods under audit, called the **comparative financial statements approach**. CAS 710 is expected to provide examples of wording that would be used for the standard unqualified report, and examples of opinions with reservations for both the corresponding figures and comparative financial statements approaches.

CANADA–UNITED STATES REPORTING DIFFERENCES Cross-listed organizations are those companies that are listed on multiple stock exchanges. AuG-21, Canada–United States reporting differences, provides guidance to the auditor on report preparation for Canadian companies where the audit report would differ under Canadian and U.S. GAAP due to treatment differences for disclosures of going-concern problems and of changes in generally accepted accounting principles between periods.

The guideline requires that the report be prepared in accordance with Canadian GAAS and that any additional comments required be attached but be distinct from the auditor's report.

CHANGES IN GAAP OR THE APPLICATION THEREOF CAS 700, par. 13 (previously Section 5400.17), requires the auditor to evaluate a change in accounting principle or in the application of an accounting principle in the financial statements being reported on and to assess whether or not the new principle, or the application, is in accordance with generally accepted accounting principles. In addition, the auditor must assess whether the method of accounting for the change, which may be retroactive or prospective, and the disclosure of the change, are also in accordance with GAAP.

If the change, its application, and its disclosure are in accordance with GAAP, the auditor should express an unqualified opinion. On the other hand, if the change or its application or its disclosure in the financial statements is not in accordance with GAAP, the auditor should issue a qualified or adverse opinion.

Certain changes in the financial statements may not be changes in a principle or in its application. Examples of such changes include the following:

1. Changes in an estimate, such as a decrease in the life of an asset for amortization purposes.
2. Error corrections not involving principles, such as a previous year's mathematical error.
3. Variations in format and presentation of financial information.
4. Changes because of substantially different transactions or events, such as new endeavours in research and development or the sale of a subsidiary.

A change in estimate need not be disclosed in the notes although disclosure may be desirable. A material error correction, on the other hand, must be fully disclosed.

Unusual Uncertainties Affecting the Financial Statements

Management customarily makes a number of estimates in the preparation of financial statements, including the useful lives of amortizable assets, the collectability of receivables, and the realizability of inventory and other assets. There is usually enough evidence to permit reasonable estimation of these items. Sometimes, the auditor encounters a situation in which the outcome of a matter cannot be reasonably estimated at the time the statements are being issued. These matters are defined as contingencies. Examples include threats of the expropriation of assets, income tax or litigation contingencies (collectable or payable), and guarantees of the indebtedness of others.

Corresponding figures approach—the auditor reports only on the current year's financial statements.

Comparative financial statements approach—both periods under audit (current and prior) are reported on.

There are also less specific situations in which the ability of the company to continue as a going concern is open to question. CAS 570, Going concern (previously covered in Section 5510.51–53), addresses this problem. The going-concern assumption and potential liquidity issues are discussed further in the audit planning and evidence chapters.

CAS

The appropriate type of opinion to issue when either specific or general uncertainties exist depends on the materiality of the items in question and on the disclosure of the items by management in the notes. An unqualified opinion is appropriate if the uncertainty is not disclosed but is immaterial. If the amount involved is material but the accounting treatment, disclosure, and presentation of either a contingency or going concern problem are in accordance with GAAP, the auditor would refer to the uncertainty in the auditor's report by adding an emphasis-of-matter paragraph after the opinion paragraph. The auditor must be very sure that the disclosure is such that it draws attention to the uncertainty.

concept check

C22-3 How is the audit report modified if the entity has a basis of accounting other than GAAP?

C22-4 Describe the difference between the corresponding figures and the comparative financial statements approach.

③ Changes to the Audit Opinion

Conditions Requiring a Departure from an Unqualified Auditor's Report

It is essential that auditors and readers of auditor's reports understand the circumstances when a standard unqualified report is not appropriate (called a reservation of opinion) and the type of auditor's report issued in each circumstance. In the study of auditor's reports that depart from an unqualified report, there are three closely related topics: (1) the conditions requiring a departure from an unqualified opinion, (2) the types of opinions other than unqualified, and (3) materiality.

First, the two conditions requiring a departure are briefly summarized. Each is discussed in greater depth later in the chapter.

1. THE SCOPE OF THE AUDITOR'S EXAMINATION HAS BEEN RESTRICTED When the auditor has not accumulated sufficient evidence to determine if financial statements are stated in accordance with GAAP, a scope restriction exists. There are two major causes of scope restrictions: (1) restrictions imposed by the client and (2) those caused by circumstances beyond either the client's or auditor's control. An example of a client restriction is management's refusal to permit the auditor to confirm material receivables or to physically examine material inventory. An example of a restriction caused by circumstances is when the engagement is not agreed upon until after the client's year end. It may not be possible to physically observe inventories, do certain cut-off tests, or perform other important procedures after the balance sheet date.

2. THE FINANCIAL STATEMENTS HAVE NOT BEEN PREPARED IN ACCORDANCE WITH GAAP CAS CAS 705, Application and other explanatory material (previously in Section 5510.06), describes examples of departures from generally accepted accounting principles that could result in material misstatement. These can generally be grouped into three categories:

1. An inappropriate accounting treatment, for example, failure to capitalize a capital lease.
2. An inappropriate valuation of an item in the financial statements, for example, failure to provide an adequate allowance for doubtful accounts.
3. A failure to disclose essential information in an informative manner, for example, failure to adequately disclose a going concern problem or a material contingency.

Auditor's Reports Other Than Unqualified

Whenever either of the two conditions requiring a departure from an unqualified report exists and is material, a report other than an unqualified report must be issued.

Three main types of auditor's reports are issued under these conditions: (1) qualified opinion, (2) adverse opinion, and (3) disclaimer (previously called a denial) of opinion.

QUALIFIED OPINION

A **qualified opinion** or reservation of opinion can result from a limitation on the scope of the audit or failure to follow generally accepted accounting principles. A qualified report is issued when the auditor believes that financial statements are fairly stated but that either there was a material, but not pervasive, limitation in the scope of the audit, or there was a failure to follow GAAP that resulted in a material, but not pervasive, misstatement in the financial statements.

A qualified opinion can be used only as follows:

1. *For a scope limitation*: The auditor's fieldwork has been restricted, but the restriction is confined to a specific area such as opening inventory.
2. *For a departure from GAAP or other known material misstatement*: The financial statements are fairly presented except for failure to comply with one or more GAAP or there is another known misstatement, and the effect can be quantified or isolated.

An **adverse opinion** or a disclaimer must be used if the auditor believes the condition being reported upon is extremely material or pervasive. For this reason, the qualified opinion is considered a less severe type of report for disclosing departures than an adverse opinion or a disclaimer.

Whenever an auditor issues a qualified opinion, he or she must use the term *except for* or, less frequently, *except that* or *except as* in the opinion paragraph. The implication is that the auditor is satisfied that the overall financial statements are correctly stated "except for" a particular part. Details of the exception are provided in a separate paragraph titled "Basis for exception" placed prior to the opinion paragraph. Examples of qualifications are given later in the chapter. It is unacceptable to use these phrases with any type of audit opinion other than a qualified one.

Qualified opinions are fairly rare in practice. The provincial securities commissions will accept qualified statements from a public company only in rare circumstances. Lenders or creditors may not accept qualified statements from private companies. Consequently the conditions giving rise to the qualifications are often corrected.

ADVERSE OPINION

An adverse opinion is used only when the auditor concludes that the overall financial statements are materially misstated or misleading such that they do not present fairly the financial position or results of operations and changes in cash flows in conformity with generally accepted accounting principles because of a departure from GAAP or other known material error.

DISCLAIMER OF OPINION

A **disclaimer of opinion** is issued whenever the auditor has been unable to satisfy himself or herself that the overall financial statements are fairly presented. The necessity for denying an opinion may arise because of a severe limitation on the scope of the audit examination, which would prevent the auditor from expressing an opinion on the financial statements as a whole.

The disclaimer is distinguished from an adverse opinion in that it can arise only from a lack of knowledge by the auditor, whereas to express an adverse opinion the auditor must have knowledge that the financial statements are not fairly stated. Both disclaimers and adverse opinions are used only when the extent of the scope limitation or the effects of material misstatements are material and pervasive.

Materiality

Materiality is an essential consideration in determining the appropriate type of report for a given set of circumstances. For example, if a misstatement is immaterial relative to the financial statements of the entity for the current period and is not expected to have a material effect in future periods, it is appropriate to issue an unqualified report.

Another consideration is the pervasiveness of the scope limitation or of the material misstatement. If the scope limitation is pervasive, a disclaimer is appropriate; if a

Qualified opinion—a report issued when the auditor believes that financial statements are fairly stated but that either there was a material, but not pervasive, limitation in the scope of the audit, or there was a failure to follow GAAP that resulted in a material, but not pervasive, misstatement in the financial statements.

Adverse opinion—a report issued when the auditor believes the financial statements are materially misstated or misleading as a whole such that they do not present fairly the entity's financial position or the results of its operations and cash flows in conformity with generally accepted accounting principles or other known material error.

Disclaimer of opinion—a report issued when the auditor has not been satisfied that the overall financial statements are fairly presented.

departure from GAAP is pervasive, an adverse opinion is appropriate. If the limitation or non-GAAP/material misstatement conditions are material but not pervasive, a qualified opinion is appropriate.

Recall that **material misstatements** are misstatements in the financial statements, knowledge of which would affect or change the decision of a reasonable user of the statements.

Material misstatement—a misstatement in the financial statements, knowledge of which would affect a decision of a reasonable user of the statements.

In applying this definition, three levels are used for determining the type of opinion to issue. The relationship of level to type of opinion is presented in Table 22-1.

AMOUNTS ARE IMMATERIAL When a misstatement in the financial statements exists but is unlikely to affect the decisions of a reasonable user, it is considered to be immaterial. An unqualified opinion is therefore appropriate. For example, assume management recorded unexpired insurance as an asset in the previous year and decided to expense it in the current year to reduce record-keeping costs. Management failed to follow GAAP, but if the amounts are small, the misstatement would be immaterial, and a standard unqualified auditor's report would be appropriate.

AMOUNTS ARE MATERIAL BUT NOT PERVASIVE The second level of materiality exists when a misstatement in the financial statements would affect a user's decision but the overall statements are still useful. For example, knowledge of a large misstatement in capital assets might affect a user's willingness to loan money to a company if the assets were the collateral. A misstatement of inventory does not mean that cash, accounts receivable, and other elements of the financial statements, or the financial statements as a whole, are materially incorrect.

To make materiality decisions when a condition requiring a departure from an unqualified report exists, the auditor must evaluate all effects on the financial statements. Assume the auditor is unable to satisfy himself or herself as to whether inventory is fairly stated (scope limitation) in deciding on the appropriate type of opinion. Because of the effect of a misstatement in inventory on other accounts and on totals in the statements, the auditor needs to consider the materiality of the combined effect on inventory, total current assets, total working capital, total assets, income taxes, income taxes payable, total current liabilities, cost of goods sold, net income before taxes, and net income after taxes.

Table 22-1	Relationship of Materiality to Type of Opinion and Significance in Terms of Reasonable User's Decision		
		Type of Audit Report	
		Auditing Related	Accounting Related
Materiality Level	Significance in Terms of Reasonable User's Decisions	Scope Restricted by Client or Conditions	Financial Statements Not Prepared in Accordance with GAAP* or Have Other Misstatements
Immaterial	Decisions are unlikely to be affected.	Unqualified: Standard report	Unqualified: Standard report
Material but not pervasive	Decisions are likely to be affected, only if the information in question is important to the specific decisions being made. The overall financial statements are considered fairly stated. Thus, there is a material error, but it does not overshadow the financial statements as a whole.	Qualified: Additional paragraph and qualified opinion (*except for*)	Qualified: Qualified scope, additional paragraph, and qualified opinion (*except for*)
Material and pervasive	Most or all decisions based on the financial statements are likely to be significantly affected. The overall fairness of the financial statements is in question.	Disclaimer of opinion	Adverse opinion

*or an appropriate disclosed basis of accounting

When the auditor concludes that a misstatement is material but does not overshadow the financial statements as a whole (i.e., is not pervasive), a qualified opinion (using "except for") is appropriate.

AMOUNTS ARE MATERIAL AND PERVASIVE SUCH THAT OVERALL FAIRNESS OF STATEMENTS IS IN QUESTION The highest level of misstatement exists when users are likely to make incorrect decisions if they rely on the overall financial statements. Using the previous example of inventory, a large misstatement could be so material to the financial statements as a whole that the auditor's report should indicate the financial statements taken as a whole cannot be considered fairly stated. When the highest level of misstatement exists, the auditor must issue either a disclaimer of opinion or an adverse opinion.

When determining whether an exception is material and pervasive, the extent to which the exception affects different parts of the financial statements must be considered. This is referred to as pervasiveness. A misclassification between cash and accounts receivable affects only those two accounts and is therefore not pervasive. On the other hand, many accounts are affected by a failure to record a material sale. This type of error could be pervasive because it affects sales, accounts receivable, income tax expense, accrued income taxes, and retained earnings, which, in turn, affect current assets, total assets, current liabilities, total liabilities, owners' equity, gross margin, and operating income.

As misstatements become more pervasive, the likelihood of issuing an adverse opinion rather than a qualified opinion is increased. For example, if the auditor decides a misclassification between cash and accounts receivable is material, it should result in a qualified opinion; and if the failure to record a sale of the same dollar amount is pervasive, it should result in an adverse opinion.

MATERIALITY DECISIONS In theory, the effect of materiality on the type of opinion to issue is straightforward. In application, deciding upon actual materiality in a given situation can be a difficult judgment. There are no simple, well-defined guidelines that enable auditors to decide when something is immaterial, material, or material and pervasive.

There are differences in applying materiality for deciding whether failure to follow GAAP is material and in deciding whether a scope limitation is material.

MATERIALITY DECISIONS—GAAP DEPARTURE OR OTHER MATERIAL MISSTATEMENT When a client has failed to follow GAAP or there is another known material misstatement, the audit report will be unqualified, qualified opinion only, or adverse, depending on the materiality and pervasiveness of the departure. Several aspects of materiality must be considered.

Dollar amounts compared with a base The primary concern in measuring materiality when a client has failed to follow GAAP is usually the total dollar misstatement in the accounts involved, compared to some base. A $10,000 misstatement might be material for a small company but not for a larger one. Misstatements must, therefore, be compared with some measurement base before a decision can be made about the materiality of the failure to follow GAAP. Common bases include net income before taxes, total assets, revenue, gross profit, and shareholders' equity.

To evaluate overall materiality, the auditor must combine all unadjusted errors and judge whether there may be individually immaterial errors that, when combined, significantly affect the statements. When comparing potential misstatements with a base, the auditor must carefully consider all accounts affected by a misstatement (pervasiveness). It is, for example, important to consider the effect of an understatement of ending inventory on cost of goods sold, income before taxes, income tax expense, and accrued income taxes payable.

Measurability The dollar error of some misstatements cannot be accurately measured. For example, a client's unwillingness to disclose an existing lawsuit or the acquisition of a new company subsequent to the balance sheet date is difficult, if not impossible, to measure in terms of dollar amounts. The materiality question the auditor must evaluate in such a situation is the effect on statement users of the failure to make the disclosure.

Nature of the item The decision of a user may also be affected by the kind of misstatement in the financial statements. The following may affect the user's decision and, therefore, the auditor's opinion, in a different way than most misstatements.

1. Transactions are illegal or fraudulent.
2. An item may materially affect some future period even though it is immaterial when only the current period is considered.
3. An item has a "psychological" effect (e.g., small profit versus small loss or cash balance versus overdraft).
4. An item may be important in terms of possible consequences arising from contractual obligations (e.g., the effect of failure to comply with a debt restriction may result in a material loan being called).

MATERIALITY DECISIONS—SCOPE LIMITATIONS When there is a scope limitation in an audit, the audit report will be unqualified, qualified scope and opinion, or disclaimer, depending on the materiality and pervasiveness of the scope limitation. The auditor will consider the same three factors included in the previous discussion, but they will be considered differently. The size of potential misstatements, where there are scope limitations, is important in determining whether an unqualified report, a qualified report, or a disclaimer of opinion is appropriate. For example, if recorded accounts payable of $400,000 was not audited, the auditor must evaluate the potential misstatement in accounts payable and decide how materially the financial statements could be affected. The pervasiveness of these potential misstatements must also be considered.

It is typically more difficult to evaluate the materiality of potential misstatements resulting from scope limitations than for failure to follow GAAP. Misstatements resulting from failure to follow GAAP or due to other errors are known. Those resulting from scope limitations must usually be subjectively measured in terms of potential or likely misstatements. For example, the recorded accounts payable of $400,000 might be understated by more than a million dollars, which may affect several totals including gross margin, net earnings, and total liabilities.

Discussion of Conditions Requiring a Departure

This part of the chapter examines the conditions requiring a departure from an unqualified report in greater detail and shows examples of reports. All of the examples use international standards (forthcoming as Canadian standards) as their basis.

AUDITOR'S SCOPE HAS BEEN RESTRICTED There are two major categories of scope restrictions: (1) those caused by a client and (2) those caused by conditions beyond the control of either the client or the auditor. The effect on the auditor's report is the same for both, but the interpretation of materiality is likely to be different. Whenever there is a scope restriction, the appropriate response is to issue an unqualified report, a qualification of scope and opinion, or a disclaimer of opinion, depending on materiality and pervasiveness.

For client-imposed restrictions, the auditor should be concerned about the possibility that management is trying to prevent discovery of misstated information. In such cases, it would be appropriate to issue a disclaimer of opinion whenever materiality and pervasiveness are in question. When restrictions are due to conditions beyond the client's control, a qualification of scope and opinion is more likely.

CAS 705, par. 11-13, emphasizes the severity of a scope restriction by providing an escalating set of actions that the auditor should take when a scope restriction is imposed by the client. First, the auditor should request that the scope restriction be removed. If that is not done, then the auditor is required to communicate with those charged with governance (such as the board of directors) to ensure that they are aware of the scope restriction and to describe the impact on the audit. If the scope limitation is both material and pervasive, the first choice is for the auditor to resign from the engagement—if the auditor cannot resign or this is considered impractical, only then would the auditor issue a disclaimer in the audit report.

Two restrictions occasionally imposed by clients on the auditor's scope relate to the observation of physical inventory and the confirmation of accounts receivable, but other restrictions may also occur. Reasons for client-imposed scope restrictions may be a desire to save audit fees and, in the case of confirming receivables, to prevent possible conflicts between the client and customer when amounts differ. Unfortunately, scope restrictions have also been used to hide fraud, so a scope restriction can be a huge warning sign with respect to potential fraud or financial statement manipulation.

A qualified report or disclaimer of opinion resulting from a client restriction requires a reservation paragraph to describe the restriction (called "basis for disclaimer of opinion"); the reservation paragraph is located between the auditor's responsibility and opinion paragraph. In addition, the opinion paragraph must be modified. For a disclaimer, it is renamed "disclaimer of opinion."

The most common case in which conditions beyond the client's and auditor's control cause a scope restriction is an engagement agreed upon after the client's balance sheet date. Certain cut-off procedures, physical examination of inventory, and other important procedures may not be possible under those circumstances. When the auditor cannot perform desired procedures but can be satisfied with alternative procedures that verify the information is fairly stated, an unqualified report is appropriate. If alternative procedures cannot be performed, a scope qualification and, depending on the materiality and pervasiveness, either an opinion qualification or a disclaimer of opinion, is necessary. A reservation paragraph would describe the restriction.

For example, the report in Figure 22-3 would be appropriate for an audit in which the amounts were material but not pervasive, and the auditor was unable to audit the financial statements of a company's foreign affiliate and could not satisfy himself or herself by alternative procedures. The introductory statement, management responsibility paragraph, and the bulk of the auditor responsibility section are omitted from the example because they contain standard wording. The final sentence of the auditor responsibility section is included, as it has changed.

When the amounts are so material that a disclaimer of opinion is required, the introductory statement is modified to indicate that the auditors were engaged to audit (rather than conducted the audit). The management responsibility paragraph could remain the same. The auditor's responsibility section would be severely truncated, reflecting the fact that an audit could not be conducted, while an explanatory basis paragraph would be included prior to the renamed disclaimer of opinion paragraph as shown in Figure 22-4.

STATEMENTS ARE NOT IN CONFORMITY WITH GAAP, OR OTHER KNOWN MISSTATEMENTS

When the auditor knows that the financial statements may be misleading because material misstatements have been quantified or the statements were not prepared in conformity with generally accepted accounting principles, he or she must issue a qualified or an adverse opinion, depending on the materiality and pervasiveness of the item in question. The opinion must clearly state the nature and the amount of the misstatement, if it is known. Figure 22-5 on page 730 shows an example of a qualified opinion when a client did not capitalize leases as required by GAAP. The introductory statement, management's responsibility paragraph, and first two paragraphs of the auditor responsibility section in the example are omitted because they include standard wording.

Figure 22-3 Qualified Scope and Opinion Report Due to Scope Restriction

INDEPENDENT AUDITOR'S REPORT

(Same addressee, introductory statement, and management responsibility paragraph as the standard report)

(First two paragraphs of the auditor's responsibility section are unchanged.)

We believe that the audit evidence that we have obtained is sufficient and appropriate to provide a basis for our qualified audit opinion.

Basis for Qualified Opinion

We were unable to obtain audited financial statements supporting the Company's investment in a foreign affiliate stated at $475,000, or its equity in earnings of that affiliate of $365,000, which is included in net income, as described in Note X to the financial statements. Because of the nature of the Company's records, we were unable to satisfy ourselves as to the carrying value of the investment or the equity in its earnings by means of other auditing procedures.

Qualified Opinion

In our opinion, except for the effects of such adjustments, if any, as might have been determined to be necessary had we been able to examine evidence regarding the foreign affiliate investment and earnings, the financial statements present fairly, in all material respects, the financial position of Laughlin Corporation as of December 31, 2010, and the results of its financial performance and cash flows for the year then ended in accordance with Canadian generally accepted accounting principles.

Side notes:
- Addressee, Introductory statement, Management responsibility
- Auditor's responsibility
- Last sentence—changed
- Basis for Qualified Opinion paragraph—added
- Opinion paragraph—qualified

When the amounts are so material and pervasive that an adverse opinion is required, the introductory statement, management's responsibility, and auditor's responsibility are fully described. The basis for the changed opinion could remain the same, but the opinion paragraph would be adverse as shown in Figure 22-6 on the next page.

When the client fails to include information that is necessary for the fair presentation of financial statements in the body of the statements or in the narrative disclosures in the notes, it is the responsibility of the auditor to explain how these

---

Figure 22-4 Disclaimer of Opinion Due to Scope Restriction

INDEPENDENT AUDITOR'S REPORT

(Same addressee)

We were engaged to audit the accompanying financial statements of XiaPlus Company, which comprise the balance sheet as at December 31, 2010, and the statement of revenue and expenses, statement of changes in accumulated surplus, and cash flow statement for the year then ended, and a summary of significant accounting policies and other explanatory notes.

(Management responsibility paragraph same as the standard report)

Our responsibility is to express an opinion on these financial statements based on conducting an audit in accordance with Canadian generally accepted auditing standards. Because of the matter described in the Basis for Disclaimer paragraph, however, we were not able to obtain sufficient appropriate evidence to provide a basis for an audit opinion.

Basis for Disclaimer of Opinion

Our examination indicated serious deficiencies in internal control of general fund transactions. As a consequence, we were unable to satisfy ourselves that all revenues and expenditures of the organization had been recorded nor were we able to satisfy ourselves that the recorded transactions were proper. As a result, we were unable to determine whether adjustments were required in respect of recorded and unrecorded assets, recorded and unrecorded liabilities, and the components making up the statements of revenue and expense, accumulated surplus, and changes in cash flow.

Disclaimer of Opinion

In view of the possible material effects on the financial statements of the matters described in the Basis for Disclaimer of Opinion paragraph, we have not been able to obtain sufficient appropriate audit evidence to provide an audit opinion. Accordingly, we do not express an opinion on the financial statements.

Side notes:
- Addressee
- Introductory statement—modified
- Management responsibility—unchanged
- Auditor's responsibility—curtailed and modified
- Basis for Disclaimer of Opinion paragraph—added
- Disclaimer of Opinion

Figure 22-5   Qualified Opinion Report Due to Non-GAAP

INDEPENDENT AUDITOR'S REPORT

Addressee, Introductory statement, Management responsibility

(Same addressee, introductory statement, and management responsibility paragraph as the standard report)

Auditor's responsibility

(First two paragraphs of the auditor's responsibility section are unchanged.)

Last sentence—changed

We believe that the audit evidence that we have obtained is sufficient and appropriate to provide a basis for our qualified audit opinion.

Basis for Qualified Opinion paragraph—added

Basis for Qualified Opinion

The company has excluded from property and debt in the accompanying balance sheet certain lease obligations that, in our opinion, should be capitalized in order to conform with Canadian generally accepted accounting principles. If these lease obligations were capitalized, property would be increased by $4,600,000, long-term debt by $4,200,000, and retained earnings by $400,000 as of December 31, 2010, and net income and earnings per share would be increased by $400,000 and $1.75, respectively, for the year then ended.

Opinion paragraph—qualified

Qualified Opinion

In our opinion, except for the effects of not capitalizing lease obligations, as discussed in the Basis for Qualified Opinion paragraph, the financial statements present fairly, in all material respects, the financial position of Tonah Company as at December 31, 2010, and of its financial performance and cash flows for the year then ended in accordance with Canadian generally accepted accounting principles.

Figure 22-6   Adverse Opinion Due to Non-GAAP

INDEPENDENT AUDITOR'S REPORT

Addressee, Introductory statement, Management responsibility

(Same addressee, introductory statement, and management responsibility paragraph as the standard report)

Auditor's responsibility

(First two paragraphs of the auditor's responsibility section are unchanged.)

Last sentence—changed

We believe that the audit evidence that we have obtained is sufficient and appropriate to provide a basis for our adverse audit opinion.

Basis for Adverse Opinion paragraph—added

Basis for Adverse Opinion

(Same as contents of Basis for Qualified Opinion in Figure 22-5)

Opinion paragraph—adverse

Adverse Opinion

In our opinion, because of the significance of the matter discussed in the Basis for Adverse Opinion paragraph, the financial statements do not present fairly the financial position of Tonah Company as at December 31, 2010, and of its financial performance and cash flows for the year then ended in accordance with Canadian generally accepted accounting principles.

---

disclosures are misstated in a Basis paragraph in the auditor's report and to issue a qualified or an adverse opinion. Figure 22-7 shows an example of an auditor's report in which the auditor considered the financial statement disclosure inadequate. As it is qualified, it follows a format similar to that of Figures 22-3 and 22-5.

EXISTENCE OF MORE THAN ONE CONDITION REQUIRING A QUALIFICATION Auditors may encounter situations involving more than one of the conditions requiring modification of the unqualified report. In these circumstances, the auditor should qualify or modify his or her opinion for each condition. CAS 705 (previously Section 5510) requires a description of the basis for any modifications, the reasons why the auditor is including the information, and the material included in the Basis Paragraph. An example is presented in Figure 22-8.

REPORTS INVOLVING RELIANCE ON ANOTHER AUDITOR OR A SPECIALIST In Canada, although the main or primary auditor may rely on another auditor or a specialist in determining the appropriate opinion to issue on the financial statements, the primary

Figure 22-7 Qualified Opinion Due to Inadequate Disclosure

INDEPENDENT AUDITOR'S REPORT

(Same addressee, introductory statement, and management responsibility paragraph as the standard report)

(First two paragraphs of the auditor's responsibility section are unchanged.)

We believe that the audit evidence that we have obtained is sufficient and appropriate to provide a basis for our qualified audit opinion.

Basis for Qualified Opinion

On January 15, 2011, the company issued debentures in the amount of $3,600,000 for the purpose of financing plant expansion. The debenture agreement restricts the payment of future cash dividends to earnings after December 31, 2012. In our opinion, disclosure of this information is required to conform with Canadian generally accepted accounting principles.

Qualified Opinion

In our opinion, except for the effects of not disclosing future dividend payment restrictions, as discussed in the Basis for Qualified Opinion paragraph, the financial statements present fairly, in all material respects, the financial position of Tonah Company as at December 31, 2010, and of its financial performance and cash flows for the year then ended in accordance with Canadian generally accepted accounting principles.

Annotations:
- Addressee, Introductory statement, Management responsibility
- Auditor's responsibility
- Last sentence—changed
- Basis for Qualified Opinion paragraph—added
- Opinion paragraph—qualified

Figure 22-8 Qualified Opinion (Departure from GAAP and a Scope Limitation)

INDEPENDENT AUDITOR'S REPORT

(Same addressee, introductory statement, and management responsibility paragraph as the standard report)

(First two paragraphs of the auditor's responsibility section are unchanged.)

We believe that the audit evidence that we have obtained is sufficient and appropriate to provide a basis for our qualified audit opinion.

Basis for Qualified Opinion

Management has advised us that the company may become liable with respect to guarantees given for indebtedness of a subsidiary located in another country. However, management has declined to provide us with further information and will not permit us to contact the subsidiary as management believes disclosure is not in the company's best interests. As a result, we have been unable to obtain sufficient audit evidence to form an opinion with respect to the possible liability. Furthermore, the matter has not been disclosed in the notes to the financial statements. In our opinion, such disclosure is required under Canadian generally accepted accounting principles.

Qualified Opinion

In our opinion, except for the effects of not disclosing the potential contingent liabilities with respect to the subsidiary, which we could not determine, as described in the Basis for Qualified Opinion paragraph, the financial statements present fairly, in all material respects, the financial position of Tonah Company as at December 31, 2010, and of its financial performance and cash flows for the year then ended in accordance with Canadian generally accepted accounting principles.

Annotations:
- Addressee, Introductory statement, Management responsibility
- Auditor's responsibility
- Last sentence—changed
- Basis for Qualified Opinion paragraph—added
- Opinion paragraph—qualified

auditor takes responsibility for that opinion, and only the name of the primary auditor appears on the auditor's report. CAS 600 (formerly Section 6930) and CAS 620 (formerly Section 5049) deal with the (primary) auditor's reliance on another auditor and on a specialist, respectively. Inability to rely on the work of another auditor or a specialist is a scope limitation issue.

The auditor may rely on another auditor because the client's business is either too complex or widespread and the primary auditor either does not have the personnel or the proximity to all the client locations to do the audits with his or her own personnel. For example, the primary auditor, a public accounting firm located in Halifax, may

CAS rely on another public accounting firm located in Regina as the secondary auditor to audit the Halifax client's subsidiary located in Regina.

CAS 600 requires the primary auditor to assess the secondary auditor's professional qualifications, compliance with ethical requirements, quality control systems, and whether necessary access to documentation will be provided when determining whether or not to rely on the secondary auditor. As we explained in Chapter 4, the primary auditor who does rely on a secondary auditor is responsible for any deficiencies in the secondary auditor's work. The decision on whether or not to rely on that work is based on the primary auditor's judgment.

If the primary auditor decides that an unqualified opinion is appropriate, the name of the secondary auditor is not mentioned. If, however, the primary auditor decides that a qualified or disclaimer of opinion is appropriate and the qualification arises because of inability to rely on the work of the secondary auditor, the explanation of the qualification in the Basis for Disclaimer paragraph could mention the name of the secondary auditor in explaining the reason for the qualification (scope limitation).

The auditor may have to rely on a specialist, such as an actuary, in completing the audit. Normally the auditor would not mention the specialist or reliance on the specialist. However, if the auditor believes that a qualified or disclaimer of opinion is appropriate and the qualification arises because of inability to rely on the work of the specialist, the explanation of the qualification in the Basis paragraph would mention the name of the specialist in explaining the reason for the qualification.

Negative Assurance

It is inappropriate to include in the auditor's report any additional comments that counterbalance the auditor's opinion. For example, the use of such terminology as "However, nothing came to our attention that would lead us to question the fairness of the presentations" as a part of a disclaimer of opinion is inappropriate and a violation of the standards of reporting. A statement of this kind, which is referred to as negative assurance, tends to confuse readers about the nature of the auditor's examination and the degree of responsibility he or she is assuming.

The use of negative assurance is considered appropriate only in the case of review engagements and prospectuses (Sections 7110 and 7115). Review engagements are considered in Chapter 23.

Including Internal Control Attestation, Electronic Audit Report Inclusion, and Subsequent Matters

COMBINED REPORTS ON FINANCIAL STATEMENTS AND INTERNAL CONTROL OVER FINANCIAL REPORTING The Sarbanes–Oxley Act of 2002 requires the auditor of a public company that is registered with the SEC to attest to management's report on the effectiveness of internal control over financial reporting. The audit of internal control integrated with the audit of the financial statements is discussed further in Chapter 23. The auditor may choose to issue separate reports on the financial statements and internal control over financial reporting or issue a combined report. Figure 23-2 in the next chapter provides an example of a separate report, and a combined report is included with the financial statements of Hillsburg Hardware Ltd. at the end of Chapter 5.

IMPACT OF E-COMMERCE ON AUDIT REPORTING Most public companies provide access to financial information through their webpages. Visitors to a company's website can view the company's most recent audited financial statements, including the auditor's report. In addition, it is common for the company to include such information as unaudited quarterly financial statements, other selected financial information, and press releases often labelled as "About the Company" or "Investor Relations."

Even before the widespread use of the internet, companies often published documents that contained information in addition to audited financial statements and the independent auditor's report. The most common example was and still is the company's annual report. Under generally accepted auditing standards, the auditor has no obligation to perform any procedures to corroborate the other information. The auditor is, however, responsible for reading the other information to determine whether it is materially consistent with information in the audited financial statements.

However, under current auditing standards, auditors are not required to read information contained within electronic sites, such as the company's website, that also contain the company's audited financial statements and the auditor's report. Auditing standards note that electronic sites are a means of distributing information.

SUBSEQUENT DISCOVERY OF FACTS VERSUS SUBSEQUENT DEVELOPMENTS

Subsequent discovery of facts If the auditor becomes aware after the audited financial statements have been released that some information included in the financial statements is materially misleading, the auditor has an obligation under CAS 560 (previously Section 5405) to make certain that users who are relying on the financial statements are informed about the misstatements. These events are known as **subsequent facts**.

CAS

Subsequent facts—additional information that the auditor becomes aware of after the audited financial statements have been released that indicates that some information included in the financial statements is materially misleading.

The *CICA Handbook* requires the auditor first to discuss the matter with management and, if required or appropriate, with the board of directors or the audit committee. The auditor may also have an obligation, under the Canada Business Corporations Act (Section 171[7]) to notify each of the directors. The directors and those charged with governance must also inform the appropriate regulatory agencies, such as the Corporations Branch of the Department of Consumer and Corporate Affairs.

If a director or officer discovers a misstatement of any size, he or she is required to notify the audit committee and the auditor. The auditor would then need to assess the misstatement to consider whether it is material. Possible causes of misstatements are the inclusion of material fictitious sales, the failure to write off obsolete inventory, and the omission of an essential footnote. Regardless of whether the failure to discover the misstatement was the fault of the auditor or the client, those who rely upon the financial statements ultimately need to be informed. If additional audit work is required, the audit work would need to be completed and a revised audit opinion issued.

If it is the auditor who discovers the subsequent fact, then the auditor would request management to revise the financial statements if the subsequent fact is material. If management will not revise the financial statements, and the auditor believes that a revised audit report would be required, then the auditor will need to ensure that those charged with governance are informed. The auditor would consult legal advice as to the next step to help ensure that the users of the financial statements are informed, so that reliance on the now incorrect auditor's report will be prevented.

Distinguishing subsequent developments from subsequent facts In the previous section, we described events that already existed at the auditor's report date. **Subsequent developments** arise after the date of the audit report. For example, if an auditor believes that an accounts receivable is collectable after an adequate review of the facts at the date of the auditor's report but the customer subsequently files for bankruptcy, a revision of the financial statements is not required. The statements must be recalled or reissued only when information that would indicate that the statements were not fairly presented already existed at the auditor's report date. If, for example, the customer had filed for bankruptcy before the audit report date, there would be a subsequent discovery of facts.

Subsequent developments—information that becomes available or events that occur after the date of the audit report.

The auditor's responsibility for subsequent events review begins on the balance sheet date and ends with the approval of the financial statements. Any pertinent information discovered as part of the review can be incorporated into the financial statements before they are issued. Note that the auditor has no responsibility to search for subsequent facts of the nature discussed in this section, but if the auditor discovers

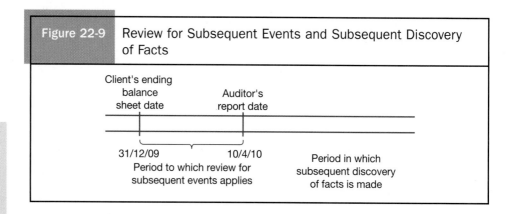

| Figure 22-9 | Review for Subsequent Events and Subsequent Discovery of Facts |

Client's ending balance sheet date — Auditor's report date

31/12/09 — 10/4/10
Period to which review for subsequent events applies

Period in which subsequent discovery of facts is made

concept check

C22-5 What is the relationship among materiality, pervasiveness, and a qualified audit report?

C22-6 What type of audit report is issued when the only errors found during the audit are immaterial? Why?

C22-7 Why is a report that contains a disclaimer of opinion normally shorter than other reports?

that financial statements are improperly stated, he or she must take action and request that management correct them. Typically, an existing material misstatement is found as part of the subsequent year's audit, or it may be reported to the auditor by the client.

Figure 22-9 shows the difference in the period covered by the review for subsequent events and that for the discovery of facts after the auditor's report date. If the auditor discovers subsequent facts after the audit report date but before the financial statements are issued, he or she would require that the financial statements be revised before they are issued.

Summary

1. *When can the public accountant issue a standard unqualified audit report?* It can be issued for an audit engagement where sufficient evidence has been collected using GAAS, and where the financial statements are fairly presented in accordance with GAAP.

   What parts are there in this report and why are they significant? Figure 22-1 on page 717, shows the nine parts to the audit report: (1) the report title describes the document; (2) the addressee is identified; (3) the introductory statement provides a context for the report; (4) the management responsibility paragraph describes the responsibilities of management; (5) the auditor responsibility section describes the auditor's responsibilities, the criteria used to conduct the audit, and the nature of an audit engagement and states that the auditor has gathered enough high-quality evidence to state an opinion on the financial statements; (6) provides an opinion on the financial statements; (7) identifies the audit firm, (8) identifies the date of the report; (9) identifies the place of issue.

   How is the date of the audit report decided? The audit report date is the date that management approves the financial statements, after the audit field work has been completed.

   When might dual dating of the audit report occur? If a significant event occurs after the audit report has been completed but not yet released, audit work could be completed with respect to that event only (disclosed in a note), and then the audit report would have two dates, with the second, later date pertaining only to the note with respect to the significant event.

2. *How can we categorize the auditor's report when there are variations in wording?* In addition to the standard unqualified report, there is (1) the unqualified report with an explanatory paragraph or modified wording, (2) a qualified, (3) adverse, or (4) disclaimer of opinion.

   Under what conditions would modified wording occur or an additional explanatory paragraph be added? Such a report would be issued when a complete audit with satisfactory results has been completed, but the auditor believes it is necessary to provide additional information.

3. *What two types of situations would cause problems with issuing an opinion on financial statements?* When either the scope of the auditor's examination has been restricted or the financial statements have not been prepared in accordance with GAAP, the auditor may be unable to issue a standard unqualified report. A disclaimer is associated with a scope restriction, and an adverse report is used when there is a known material misstatement.

   How is materiality related to the wording changes used for these departures in audit opinion? A qualified report is likely to be used when the issue is material but does not overshadow the financial statements as a whole (pervasiveness). If problems are material and pervasive, then a disclaimer of opinion or an adverse opinion would result.

   What type of report is issued when the auditor provides an opinion on management's report on internal control? The auditor can provide a report that is a combined report on the financial statements and on management's report on internal control over financial reporting.

Review Questions

22-1 Explain why auditor's reports are important to users of financial statements.

22-2 What five circumstances are required for a standard unqualified report to be issued?

22-3 List the nine parts of an unqualified auditor's report and explain the meaning of each part. How do the parts compare with those found in a qualified report?

22-4 What is the purpose of the introductory statement in the auditor's report? Identify the most important information included in the introductory statement.

22-5 What are the purposes of the management responsibility paragraph in the auditor's report? Identify the most important information included in the paragraph.

22-6 What are the purposes of the auditor responsibility section in the auditor's report? Identify the most important information included in the section.

22-7 What are the purposes of the opinion paragraph in the auditor's report? Identify the most important information included in the opinion paragraph.

22-8 What is meant by the term "appropriate disclosed basis of accounting"? How does such a basis differ from GAAP? When is such a basis acceptable?

22-9 On February 17, 2010, a public accountant completed the examination of the financial statements for Buckheizer Corporation for the year ended December 31, 2009. The audit is satisfactory in all respects. On February 26, the auditor completed the tax return and the pencil draft of the financial statements. Management approved these financial statements on March 1. The final auditor's report was completed, attached to the financial statements, and delivered to the client on March 7. What is the appropriate date on the auditor's report?

22-10 Explain what is meant by "contingencies." Give an example of a contingency, and discuss its appropriate disclosure in the financial statements.

22-11 List the conditions requiring a departure from an unqualified opinion, and give one specific example of each of those conditions.

22-12 Distinguish between a qualified opinion, an adverse opinion, and a disclaimer of opinion, and explain the circumstances under which each is appropriate.

22-13 Define "materiality" as it is used in audit reporting. What conditions will affect the auditor's determination of materiality?

22-14 Distinguish between the levels of materiality and pervasiveness an auditor considers when assessing how to deal with a non-GAAP condition or known material error in the financial statements.

22-15 How does an auditor's opinion differ between scope limitations caused by client restrictions and limitations resulting from conditions beyond the client's control? What is the effect of each on the auditor's work?

22-16 Munroe Corp. had a bad year financially and the president, Jan de Boer, instructed the controller not to amortize the capital assets so that the company would show a small profit. The controller argued that GAAP required Munroe to amortize the capital assets on a regular basis and a qualified auditor's report would likely result. Jan told the controller to disclose the failure to record amortization in the notes to the financial statements. You are the auditor in charge on the Munroe audit. Write a memo to Jan in response to the controller's comments.

22-17 At times, for a variety of reasons, an auditor must rely on another firm of auditors to perform part of an audit. What reference does the primary auditor make to the secondary auditor in the auditor's report? Justify your response.

22-18 What responsibility does the auditor have for information on the company's website that may be linked to electronic versions of the company's annual financial statements and auditor's report? How does this differ from the auditor's responsibility for other information in the company's annual report that includes the financial statements and auditor's report?

Discussion Questions and Problems

22-19 A careful reading of a standard unqualified auditor's report indicates several important phrases. Explain why each of the following phrases or clauses is used rather than the alternative provided.

a. "In our opinion, the financial statements present fairly" rather than "These financial statements present fairly."

b. "We conducted our audit in accordance with Canadian generally accepted auditing standards" rather than "Our audit was performed to detect material misstatements in the financial statements."

c. "The financial statements present fairly, in all material respects, the financial position" rather than "These financial statements are correctly stated."

d. "In accordance with Canadian generally accepted accounting principles" rather than "are properly stated to represent the true economic conditions."

e. "We believe that the audit evidence we have obtained is sufficient and appropriate" rather than "we have checked the transactions and account balances."

f. "Brown & Phillips, CAs (firm name)," rather than "James E. Brown, CA (individual partner's name)."

22-20 Roscoe, a public accountant, has completed the examination of the financial statements of Excelsior Corporation as of and for the year ended December 31, 2010. Roscoe also examined and reported on the Excelsior financial statements for the prior year. Roscoe drafted the following report for 2010:

We have audited the balance sheet and statements of income and retained earnings of Excelsior Corporation as of December 31, 2010.

MANAGEMENT'S RESPONSIBILITY

Management prepared the financial statements and is responsible for risk assessment and designing systems of internal control in response to those risks. It also selects and implements the accounting policies embedded in these financial statements.

AUDITOR RESPONSIBILITY

We were engaged to conduct an audit for the above-mentioned financial statements. We conducted our audit in accordance with Canadian generally accepted auditing standards. Those standards require that we plan and perform the audit to obtain reasonable assurance about whether the financial statements are free of misstatement.

We believe that our audit provides a reasonable basis for our opinion.

OPINION

In our opinion, the financial statements referred to above present fairly the financial position of Excelsior Corporation as of December 31, 2010, and the results of its operations for the year then ended in conformity with Canadian generally accepted auditing standards, applied on a basis consistent with those of the preceding year.

(Signed)
Roscoe, Public Accountant

OTHER INFORMATION:
- Excelsior is presenting comparative financial statements.
- Excelsior does not wish to present a cash flow statement for either year.
- During 2010, Excelsior changed its method of accounting for long-term construction contracts, properly reflected the effect of the change in the current year's financial statements, and restated the prior year's statements. Roscoe is satisfied with Excelsior's justification for making the change. The change is discussed in footnote 12.
- Roscoe was unable to perform normal accounts receivable confirmation procedures, but alternate procedures were used to satisfy Roscoe as to the existence of the receivables.
- Excelsior Corporation is the defendant in a lawsuit, the outcome of which is highly uncertain. If the case is settled in favour of the plaintiff, Excelsior will be required to pay a substantial amount of cash, which might require the sale of certain capital assets. The litigation and the possible effects have been properly disclosed in footnote 11.
- Excelsior issued debentures on January 31, 2008, in the amount of $10,000,000. The funds obtained from the issuance were used to finance the expansion of plant facilities. The debenture agreement restricts the payment of future cash dividends to earnings after December 31, 2009. Excelsior declined to disclose these essential data in the footnotes to the financial statements.

REQUIRED
a. Identify and explain any items included in "Other Information" that need not be part of the auditor's report.
b. Explain the deficiencies in Roscoe's auditor's report as drafted.

(Adapted from AICPA)

22-21 For the following independent situations, assume you are the audit partner on the engagement.

1. During your examination of Debold Batteries Ltd., you conclude there is a possibility that inventory is materially overstated. The client refuses to allow you to expand the scope of your examination sufficiently to verify whether the balance is actually misstated.

2. You are auditing Woodcolt Linen Services, Inc. for the first time. Woodcolt has been in business for several years but has never had an audit before. After the audit is completed, you conclude that the current year balance sheet is stated correctly in accordance with GAAP. The client did not authorize you to do test work for any of the previous years.

3. You were engaged to examine Cutter Steel Corp.'s financial statements after the close of the corporation's fiscal year. Because you were not engaged until after the balance sheet date, you were not able to physically observe inventory, which is very material. On the completion of your audit, you are satisfied that Cutter's financial statements are presented fairly, including inventory about

which you were able to satisfy yourself by the use of alternative audit procedures.

4. Four weeks after the year-end date, a major customer of Prince Construction Ltd. declared bankruptcy. Because the customer had confirmed the balance due to Prince at the balance sheet date, management refuses to charge off the account or otherwise disclose the information. The receivable represents approximately 10 percent of accounts receivable and 20 percent of net earnings before taxes.

5. You complete the audit of Johnson Department Store Ltd., and, in your opinion, the financial statements are fairly presented. On the last day of the examination, you discover that one of your supervisors assigned to the audit had a material investment in Johnson.

6. Auto Delivery Company Ltd. has a fleet of several delivery trucks. In the past, Auto Delivery had followed the policy of purchasing all equipment. In the current year, it decided to lease the trucks. This change in policy is fully disclosed in footnotes.

For each situation, state the type of auditor's report that should be issued. If your decision depends on additional information, state the alternative reports you are considering and the additional information you need to make the decision.

22-22 For the following independent situations, assume you are the audit partner on the engagement.

1. Kieko Corporation has prepared financial statements but has decided to exclude the cash flow statement. Management explains to you that the users of its financial statements find that particular statement confusing and prefer not to have it included.

2. HardwareFromHome.com is an internet-based start-up company created to sell home hardware supplies online. Although the company had a promising start, a downturn in e-commerce retailing has negatively affected the company. The company's sales and cash position have deteriorated significantly, and you have reservations about the ability of the company to continue in operation for the next year.

3. Approximately 20 percent of the audit for Furtney Farms, Inc. was performed by a different public accounting firm, selected by you. You have reviewed its working papers and believe it did an excellent job on its portion of the audit. Nevertheless, you are unwilling to take complete responsibility for its work.

4. The controller of Fair City Hotels Co. Ltd. will not allow you to confirm the receivable balance from two of its major customers. The amount of the receivable is material in relation to Fair City's financial statements. You are unable to satisfy yourself as to the receivable balance by alternative procedures.

5. In the last three months of the current year, Oil Refining Corp. decided to change direction and go significantly into the oil-drilling business. Management recognizes that this business is exceptionally risky and could jeopardize the success of its existing refining business but that there are significant potential rewards. During the short period of operation in drilling, the company has had three dry wells and no successes. The facts are adequately disclosed in footnotes.

REQUIRED

a. For each situation, identify which of the conditions requiring modification of or a deviation from an unqualified standard report is applicable.
b. State the level of materiality as immaterial, material, or material and pervasive. If you cannot decide the level of materiality, state the additional information needed to make a decision.
c. Given your answers in parts (a) and (b), identify the appropriate auditor's report from the following choices:
   1. Unqualified—standard wording.
   2. Qualified opinion—GAAP departure or material misstatement.
   3. Qualified opinion—scope limitation.
   4. Disclaimer.
   5. Adverse.

22-23 The following are independent situations for which you will recommend an appropriate auditor's report:

1. Subsequent to the date of the financial statements as part of the post–balance sheet date audit procedures, a public accountant learned of heavy damage to one of a client's two plants due to a recent fire; the loss will not be reimbursed by insurance. The newspapers described the event in detail. The financial statements and appended notes as prepared by the client did not disclose the loss caused by the fire.

2. A public accountant is engaged in the examination of the financial statements of a large manufacturing company with branch offices in many widely separate cities. The public accountant was not able to count the substantial undeposited cash receipts at the close of business on the last day of the fiscal year at all branch offices.

   As an alternative to this auditing procedure used to verify the accurate cut-off of cash receipts, the public accountant observed that deposits in transit as shown on the year-end bank reconciliation appeared as credits on the bank statement on the first business day of the new year. The public accountant was satisfied as to the cut-off of cash receipts by the use of the alternative procedure.

3. On January 2, 2010, the Retail Auto Parts Company Limited received a notice from its primary supplier that effective immediately all wholesale prices would be increased by 10 percent. On the basis of the notice, Retail Auto Parts revalued its December 31, 2009, inventory to reflect the higher costs. The inventory constituted a material proportion of total assets; however, the effect of the revaluation was material to current assets but not to total assets or net income. The increase in valuation is adequately disclosed in the footnotes.

4. E-lotions.com, Inc. is an online retailer of body lotions and other bath and body supplies. The company records revenues at the time customer orders are placed on the website, rather than when the goods are shipped, which is usually two days after the order is placed. The auditor determined that the amount of orders placed but not shipped as of the balance sheet date is not material.

5. During the course of the examination of the financial statements of a corporation for the purpose of expressing an opinion on the statements, a public accountant is refused permission to inspect the minute books. The corporate secretary instead offers to give the public accountant a certified copy of all resolutions and actions relating to accounting matters.

REQUIRED

a. For each situation, identify which of the conditions requiring a deviation from or modification of an unqualified standard report is applicable.

b. State the level of materiality as immaterial, material, or material and pervasive. If you cannot decide the level of materiality, state the additional information needed to make a decision.

c. Given your answers in parts (a) and (b), identify the appropriate auditor's report from the following alternatives:

1. Unqualified—standard wording.
2. Qualified opinion—GAAP departure or known material misstatement.
3. Qualified opinion—scope limitation.
4. Disclaimer.
5. Adverse.

(Adapted from AICPA)

22-24 You are in charge of the audit of Saskatoon Building Products Limited (SBP), a company listed on the Vancouver Stock Exchange. In the course of your audit, you discover that SBP's working capital ratio is below 2:1 and that, therefore, the company is in default on a substantial loan from Prairie Bank. Management announces to you its intention to sell a large block of provincial bonds, which were included in long-term investments, and some land that had been purchased for expansion, which was included in capital assets. Management proposes including the bonds and land as current assets pending disposition. Such inclusion would increase the current ratio to 2.2:1.

Prairie Bank and your client have not enjoyed cordial relations of late, and you have been advised by Avril Chui, the manager of the Saskatoon branch, that the bank is "looking forward to receiving the audited statements because we are concerned that SBP has been having problems."

REQUIRED

a. Draft the memo to your partner outlining the problem.
b. Draft the auditor's report.

22-25 The following tentative auditor's report was drafted by a staff accountant and submitted to a partner in the public accounting firm of Bettrioni & Bee.

AUDITOR'S REPORT

TO THE AUDIT COMMITTEE OF ATHABASCA WIDGETS, INC.

We have examined the consolidated balance sheet of Athabasca Widgets, Inc., and subsidiaries as of December 31, 2010, and the related consolidated statement of income, equity, and cash flow for the year then ended.

MANAGEMENT'S RESPONSIBILITY FOR THE FINANCIAL STATEMENTS

These financial statements are the responsibility of the company's management and have been prepared in accordance with GAAP. Management designed, implemented, and monitored internal controls in accordance with the COSO framework. This was done in response to assessed risks of fraud and error. Management also selected and used accounting estimates in the development and preparation of the financial statements.

AUDITOR RESPONSIBILITY

Our responsibility is to express an opinion on these financial statements based on our audit.

Our examinations were made in accordance with Canadian generally accepted auditing standards as we considered necessary in the circumstances. Other auditors examined the financial statements of certain subsidiaries and have furnished us with reports thereon containing no exceptions. Our opinion expressed herein, insofar as it relates to the amounts included for those subsidiaries, is based solely upon the reports of the other auditors.

We conducted the tests that we felt were necessary, based upon our assessment of risks using the audit risk model. We have gathered enough evidence to justify the audit opinion stated below.

BASIS FOR OPINION INFORMATION

As discussed in note 4 to the financial statements, on January 8, 2011, the company halted the production of certain medical equipment as a result of inquiries by the Alberta Medical Association, which raised questions as to the adequacy of some of the company's sterilization equipment and related procedures. Management is not in a position to evaluate the effect of this production halt and the ensuing litigation, which may have an adverse effect on the financial position of Athabasca Widgets, Inc.

As fully discussed in note 7 to the financial statements, in 2010 the company extended the use of the average cost method of accounting to include all inventories. In examining inventories, we engaged Dr. Irwin Same to test check the technical requirements and specifications of certain items of equipment manufactured by the company.

OPINION

In our opinion, except for the effects, if any, on the financial statements of the ultimate resolution of the matters discussed in the second paragraph, the financial statements referred to above present fairly the financial position of Athabasca Widgets, Inc., as of December 31, 2010, and the results of operations for the year then ended, in conformity with Canadian generally accepted accounting principles.

To be signed by
Bettrioni & Bee

March 1, 2011, except for note 4 for which the date is January 8, 2011

REQUIRED
Identify deficiencies in the staff accountant's tentative report that constitute departures from the generally accepted standards of reporting.

(Adapted from AICPA)

Professional Judgment Problem

22-26 Jeffrey Simms, a qualified accountant, is a supervisor with a public accounting firm, and is a close friend of yours. You regularly have lunch together and share both personal and business information.

Today, you ask Jeffrey why he looks so tired, even when it is not busy season. Jeffrey responds, "Well, it's great to be a qualified accountant right now. Not only is there work for my own firm, but because I have so much experience designing internal control systems, I can provide consulting for clients advising them how to beef up their internal controls before the auditors come in. Everyone wants to get a clean combined audit report. With a consulting company that a few of us have set up, I can work through my holidays and my weekends while the going is hot!"

Your mind in a turmoil, you make some non-committal remark and change the subject.

REQUIRED
What should you do?

Case

22-27 Materia Blues Inc. is a company that manufactures and distributes books internationally. The company has proposed that the following comments be included in the company's 2010 annual report to the shareholders:

"The integrity of the financial information reported by Materia Blues Inc. is the responsibility of the company's management. Fulfilling this responsibility requires the preparation of financial statements in accordance with Canadian accounting principles.

Materia Blues Inc. has established an excellent system of accounting and internal controls, used to gather and process financial data. Management believes that the role of the internal audit department is sufficient to ensure the high quality of the business practices and monitoring activities that are used to keep operations functioning smoothly at the company.

Our public accounting firm is engaged to provide an independent opinion on our financial statements. Together with our audit committee, they provide high-quality oversight over the financial accounting processes at Material Blues Inc. The audit committee has checked the audit report prepared by the auditors and believes that it is sound. The external auditors have had free and clear access to the audit committee and to management and employees of the company during the conduct of their audit engagement."

REQUIRED
Describe the incorrect assumptions that are implicit in the above comments. For each incorrect assumption, provide an example of more appropriate wording that might be included in the annual report to more accurately reflect healthy business practices.

23

Assurance services: Review and compilation engagements

In addition to financial statement audits, a public accountant performs a variety of services for clients with respect to financial information or business operations. This chapter begins by reviewing the nature of assurance engagements, then describes examples of specific engagements. Management accountants can use this information to determine alternative types of reporting, while potential auditors learn about the types of services they can offer.

LEARNING OBJECTIVES

1 Describe how the assurance engagement general standard is different from and similar to the audit standard. Provide examples of special reports that provide (i) high assurance and (ii) no assurance.

2 Explain the importance of review and compilation services. Explain how the evidence collection procedures are related to the assurance level provided for audits, reviews, and compilations.

3 Describe the type of report that the public accountant provides for interim financial information. State the alternatives for public accounting reporting on future-oriented information.

STANDARDS REFERENCED IN THIS CHAPTER

CICA Standards

CAS 800 – Special considerations: audits of financial statements prepared in accordance with special purpose frameworks (previously Section 5805 – Special Reports: Audit reports on financial information other than financial statements)

Section 4250 – Future-oriented financial information

Section 5020 – Association

Section 5025 – Standards for assurance engagements.

Section 5815 – Special reports: audit reports on compliance with agreements, statutes, and regulations

Section 5925 – An audit of internal control over financial reporting that is integrated with an audit of financial statements

Section 7050 – Auditor review of interim financial statements

Section 8100 – General review standards

Section 8200 – Public accountant's review of financial statements.

Section 8500 – Reviews of financial information other than financial statements

Section 8600 – Reviews of compliance with agreements and regulations

Section 9100 – Reports on the results of applying specified auditing procedures to financial information other than financial statements

Section 9200 – Compilation engagements

AuG-6 – Examination of a financial forecast or projection included in a prospectus or other public offering document

AuG-16 – Compilation of a financial forecast or projection

AuG-20 – Performance of a review of financial statements in accordance with sections 8100 and 8200

Skepticism Applies to All Types of Engagements

Menard Construction Ltd. was a contractor specializing in apartment complexes in Alberta. The owner of the construction company, Tony Menard, reached an agreement with a promoter named Alice Mayberry to serve as contractor on three projects that Alice was currently marketing. One problem with the agreement was that Tony would not receive final payment for the construction work until all partnership units in the complexes were sold.

The first partnership offering was completely sold and Tony was paid. Unfortunately, the next two partnerships were not completely sold. To solve this problem, Tony loaned money to relatives and key employees who bought the necessary interests for the partnerships to close so that Tony would receive the final payment.

When Menard Construction Ltd. had a review service performed by Renée Fortin, a public accountant and sole practitioner, the accounting records showed loans receivable from a number of employees and individuals with the last name Menard. Fortin observed that the loans were made just before the second and third partnerships closed, and they were for amounts that were multiples of $15,000, the amount of a partnership unit. Renée asked Tony to explain what happened. Tony told her, "When I received the money from the first partnership escrow, I wanted to do something nice for relatives and employees who had been loyal to me over the years. This is just my way of sharing my good fortune with the ones I love. The equality of the amounts is just a coincidence."

IMPORTANCE TO ACCOUNTANTS*

Accountants need to consider the reasonableness of the information they receive. In this case, the timing was odd. Second, the identical amounts are an unusual coincidence. Third, if Tony really had wanted to do something special for these folks, why didn't he give them something, rather than loaning them money? When information does not match or seems unreasonable, it is important to ask for additional evidence. Fortin asked that the promoter, Alice, send her detailed information on the subscriptions to each partnership. Alice refused, stating that she was under legal obligation to keep all information confidential. When Renée pressed Tony, he also refused further cooperation, although he did say he would "represent" to her that the loans had nothing to do with closing the partnerships so he could get his money. At this point, Renée withdrew from the engagement. The appearance of Tony hiding something threw the rest of the financial information into question.

WHAT DO YOU THINK?

1. Why is Tony hiding the purchases made by his relatives? What adjustments or disclosures would need to be made to the financial statements?

continued >

2. What other financial information could be incorrect? Could review procedures compensate for these potential errors?

IT is difficult to resign from an engagement. As a professional accountant, to maintain your professional integrity and protect your business, you may have to resign from high-risk engagements at some time in your professional career. Think about difficult decisions that you have made in your life. How have they enhanced your ability to act with integrity?

In this chapter, we talk about engagements that work with financial information as well as other types of engagements. Currently, international standards on auditing are being adapted as CASs (Canadian Auditing Standards) for audits of financial information only. After those standards have been finalized, Canadian standard setters will turn to the remaining standards to determine the changes that are required. Accordingly, this chapter contains a mix of both *CICA Handbook* and CAS references which will change. Please check current *CICA Handbook* references when you are working with these topics.

*As Renée Fortin is conducting a review engagement rather than an audit, Fortin would be referred to as the accountant rather than the auditor.

 ## Attest and Assurance Engagements

In addition to being involved with audits of historical financial statements prepared in accordance with generally accepted accounting principles, public accountants commonly deal with situations involving other types of information, varying levels of assurance, and other types of reports.

This chapter describes some of the services that a public accountant can provide. It is very important that the public accountant properly communicate to users of information with whom he or she is associated both the nature and extent of the association as described in *CICA Handbook* Section 5020. There are a number of figures in this chapter that illustrate the various forms of communication that the public accountant may issue. In studying them, you should note similarities and differences between the auditor's report discussed in Chapter 22 and the communications in this chapter.

Engagement letters were discussed in Chapter 5; an illustration of an engagement letter appears in Figure 5-2 on page 118. The various topics discussed below suggest the need for an engagement letter describing exactly what work the public accountant, acting as auditor or accountant, will do for the client and the proposed communication that will describe the work done (e.g., providing assurance as shown in Figure 23-2 on page 745). The need for an engagement letter that is tailored to reflect the circumstances of the engagement cannot be overemphasized.

Assurance Engagements

Public accountants have increasingly been asked to perform a variety of audit-like or assurance services for different purposes. For example, a public accountant might be asked to provide assurance on the reliability of computer software or with respect to the meeting of environmental standards by an entity. Existing standards dealt separately with historical financial statements prepared according to generally accepted accounting principles, whereas the new services often dealt with other types of information. Accordingly *CICA Handbook* Section 5025, Standards for asssurance engagements, provides a combined standard for all assurance engagements (which will be revised to take account of CASs) and applies to the following:

- Public and private sector engagements.
- Attest engagements and direct reporting engagements.
- Engagements such as audits that provide a high level of assurance and engagements such as reviews that provide a lower level of assurance.

The section defines an **assurance engagement** as an engagement where there is an accountability relationship between two or more parties, and the practitioner is engaged to issue a written communication expressing a conclusion about subject matter for which the accountable party is responsible. There are three parties to the relationship: (1) the practitioner, (2) the user(s), and (3) the person who is accountable (usually management). Figure 23-1 (based on Section 5025.07) illustrates this relationship. The user could be any stakeholder who will use the information on which the assurance is provided.

The section was designed to provide guidance for a broad range of services. For example, the new section considers both attest engagements and direct reporting engagements. **Attest engagements** are engagements where the auditor expresses a conclusion on a written assertion about a subject prepared by the accountable party, such as management. The assertion measures the subject matter using appropriate criteria. For example, a review engagement and a financial statement audit are both attest engagements, since management prepared the report (the financial statements), and specified criteria (such as Canadian GAAP) are used to measure the financial statements (the subject matter).

A **direct reporting engagement** is an engagement where the auditor directly expresses a conclusion on his or her evaluation of subject matter using criteria; management does not report in a direct reporting engagement. Perhaps the best example of a direct reporting engagement is the communication by the Auditor General to Parliament. In her report, the Auditor General, Sheila Fraser, describes what was found as a result of audits performed by her office. Public sector auditing is discussed further in Chapter 24.

The general standard in Section 5025.16 requires that the practitioner have sufficient information to decide whether the engagement can be completed in accordance with the assurance standards. The practitioner and all others involved with the assurance engagement should have adequate proficiency to perform the

Assurance engagement—an engagement where there is an accountability relationship between two or more parties, and the practitioner is engaged to issue a written communication expressing a conclusion about subject matter for which the accountable party is responsible.

Attest engagement—an engagement where the auditor expresses a conclusion on a written assertion about a subject prepared by the accountable party, such as management; the assertion measures the subject matter using appropriate criteria.

Direct reporting engagement—one where the auditor directly expresses a conclusion on his or her evaluation of subject matter using criteria; management does not report.

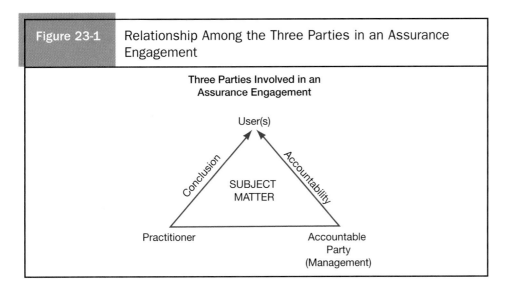

| Figure 23-1 | Relationship Among the Three Parties in an Assurance Engagement |

Three Parties Involved in an Assurance Engagement

User(s)

Conclusion

Accountability

SUBJECT MATTER

Practitioner

Accountable Party (Management)

engagement and should collectively possess adequate knowledge of the subject matter. In addition, the engagement should be performed with due care and an objective state of mind.

The practitioner should obtain some form of evidence that an accountability relationship exists (i.e., that management is responsible for the subject matter). The evidence will normally be an acknowledgment from management but may be in some other form.

The section requires the practitioner to identify or develop criteria that can be used to evaluate the subject matter. The importance of this requirement cannot be overemphasized. If the criteria are not suitable, the value of the assurance engagement is doubtful. The section suggests that the necessary characteristics are relevance, reliability, neutrality, understandability, and completeness. The section lists sources of criteria that may be considered generally accepted and suggests that they are preferred. Criteria that could result in the report being misleading should not be used.

There are three performance standards outlined in Section 5025:

- The work should be adequately planned, and there should be proper supervision.
- The practitioner should consider both significance (similar to materiality) and engagement risk (similar to audit risk) when planning and performing the engagement.
- Sufficient evidence should be gathered to support the conclusion the practitioner expresses in his or her report.

The reporting standards (extracted from 5025.64) indicate that, as a minimum, the report should satisfy these requirements:

1. Identify to whom the report is directed.
2. Describe the objective of the engagement.
3. Identify management's assertion in an attest engagement.
4. Distinguish between the responsibilities of management and those of the practitioner.
5. Identify the applicable standards in accordance with which the engagement was conducted.
6. Identify the criteria against which the subject matter was evaluated.
7. Provide a conclusion that states the level of assurance being conveyed and/or any reservation that the practitioner may have.
8. State the date of the report.
9. Identify the practitioner.
10. Identify the place of issue.

Note that the reporting standards are much like those of the GAAS discussed in Chapter 22.

There can be scope limitations leading to a qualification or a denial of opinion with an assurance engagement. There can also be a qualification or an adverse opinion with an assurance engagement when the following are true:

- In a direct reporting engagement, the subject matter does not conform to the criteria.
- In an attest engagement, the assertion made by management does not present fairly the criteria used or conformity of the subject matter with the criteria, or if essential information has not been presented or is presented in an inappropriate manner.

These standards for assurance engagements apply to other engagements, such as the audit of internal controls over financial reporting that is integrated with the financial statement audit (covered in Section 5925, and required by Section 404 of the Sarbanes–Oxley Act). Figure 23-2 illustrates the form of communication that would be issued under Section 5925 if the report is provided as a stand-alone report, separate from the auditor's report on the financial statement. The Hillsburg Hardware Ltd. financial statements at the end of Chapter 5 provide an example of an integrated report. These reports are attest reports providing a high level of assurance. Note that the report in Figure 23-2 has the following features:

- An introductory paragraph describing the purpose of the engagement (the subject matter), the responsibilities of management (the accountable party) and the auditor, and the criteria used (the criteria for the engagement are COSO standards, from the Committee of Sponsoring Organizations of the Treadway Commission; see **www.coso.org**).
- A scope paragraph that summarizes standards used to conduct the field work.
- A definition paragraph that defines the nature of internal control over financial reporting and the general purposes of such controls.
- An opinion paragraph that provides a conclusion.
- An inherent limitations paragraph.
- A final paragraph that provides a cross reference to the audit opinion with respect to the financial statements (see also Chapter 22).

Figure 23-2	Example of an Assurance Report: Report on Internal Control over Financial Reporting

AUDITOR'S REPORT

To: The Shareholders of Gaa Corp.

We have audited the effectiveness of Gaa Corp.'s internal control over financial reporting as at December 31, 2009. The entity's management is responsible for maintaining effective internal control over financial reporting. Our responsibility is to express an opinion, based on our audit, on whether the entity's internal control over financial reporting was effectively maintained in accordance with criteria issued by the Committee of Sponsoring Organizations of the Treadway Commission (COSO).

We conducted our audit in accordance with standards established by the Canadian Institute of Chartered Accountants (CICA) for audits of internal control over financial reporting. Those standards require that we plan and perform the audit to obtain reasonable assurance about whether effective internal control over financial reporting was maintained in all material respects. Our audit of internal control over financial reporting included obtaining an understanding of internal control over financial reporting, assessing the risk that a material weakness exists, testing and evaluating the design and operating effectiveness of internal control based on the assessed risk, and performing such other procedures as we considered necessary in the circumstances.

An entity's internal control over financial reporting is a process designed to provide reasonable assurance regarding the reliability of financial reporting and the preparation of financial statements for external purposes in accordance with generally accepted accounting principles. An entity's internal control over financial reporting includes those policies and procedures that (1) pertain to the maintenance of records that, in reasonable detail, accurately and fairly reflect the transactions and dispositions of the assets of the entity; (2) provide reasonable assurance that transactions are recorded as necessary to permit preparation of financial statements in accordance with generally accepted accounting principles, and that receipts and expenditures of the entity are being made only in accordance with authorizations of management and directors of the entity; and (3) provide reasonable assurance regarding prevention or timely detection of unauthorized acquisition, use, or disposition of the entity's assets that could have a material effect on the financial statements.

In our opinion, the entity maintained, in all material respects, effective internal control over financial reporting as at December 31, 2009, in accordance with criteria issued by the Committee of Sponsoring Organizations of the Treadway Commission (COSO).

Because of its inherent limitations, internal control over financial reporting may or may not prevent or detect misstatements. Also, projections of any evaluation of effectiveness to future periods are subject to the risk that controls may become inadequate because of changes in conditions or that the degree of compliance with the policies or procedures may deteriorate.

We have also audited, in accordance with Canadian generally accepted auditing standards, the balance sheet and the statements of income, retained earnings, and cash flows of Gaa Corp. and issued our report dated February 7, 2010, which is the same as the date of the report on the effectiveness of internal control over financial reporting.

Edmonton, Alberta

February 7, 2010

Brunkof & Makepeace

Chartered Accountants

These paragraphs are examples of additional information that the practitioner includes to make the auditor's report more informative.

You should compare Figure 23-2 to Figure 22-1 on page 716 in order to understand the differences and similarities between a standard auditor's report and a report issued in connection with an assurance engagement.

Figure 23-2 is the current Canadian standard with respect to reporting on the effectiveness of the system of internal control over financial reporting. The Canadian Securities Administrators (CSA) have proposed that management of certain Canadian public companies be required to report on the effectiveness of internal control over financial reporting, but these reports do not have to be audited. Hillsburg Hardware Ltd. requires an audit of effectiveness of internal control over financial reporting because it sells its shares via the TSX.

REPORTS ON THE RESULTS OF APPLYING SPECIFIED AUDITING PROCEDURES TO FINANCIAL INFORMATION OTHER THAN FINANCIAL STATEMENTS (SECTION 9100) At the opposite end of the assurance spectrum, we have an engagement that includes audit procedures but provides no assurance, covered by Section 9100. This section is concerned with an accountant's application of prespecified auditing procedures to financial information. The engagement is not an assurance engagement and an expression of an opinion is not expected. Since the client specifies what auditing procedures are to be applied (condition 1) and the form of report that is to be issued (2), distribution of the report is normally restricted (3). The accountant reaches an agreement with the client with respect to all three issues before beginning the engagement. In this situation, the accountant should comply both with the general assurance standard and the first examination standard.

The report should specify the following:

- The financial information to which the procedures were applied.
- The procedures applied.
- The factual results of the procedures; negative assurance should not be expressed.
- That an audit was not performed; there should be a disclaimer of opinion.
- Any restrictions on circulation of the report.

Figure 23-3 is an illustration of such a report. It was prepared in the situation where the financial statements were audited, but gross sales were not audited on a store-by-store basis.

Figure 23-3	Example of a Report Under Section 9100

ACCOUNTANTS' REPORT IN CONNECTION WITH GROSS SALES

To Garner Limited:

As requested by Okanagan Stores Limited, we report that the gross sales of the company's store at King Street, Kelowna, B.C., for the year ended June 30, 2009, are recorded in the amount of $790,000 in the general ledger sales account of the company and form part of the company's gross sales in its financial statements for the year then ended, on which we reported on August 3, 2009.

Our examination of the company's financial statements for the year ended June 30, 2009, was not directed to the determination of gross sales or other financial information of individual stores. We have not performed an audit of and accordingly do not express an opinion on the amount of gross sales referred to in the preceding paragraph.

It is understood that this report is to be used solely for computing percentage rental and is not to be referred to or distributed to any person who is not a member of management of Garner Limited or Okanagan Stores Limited.

Kelowna, B.C.
August 8, 2009

Carter & Wilhelm

Certified General Accountants

Review and Compilation Services

Many public accountants are involved with non-public clients that do not have audits. A company may believe an audit is unnecessary due to the active involvement of the owners in the business, lack of significant debt, or absence of regulations requiring the company to have one. Common examples are smaller companies and professional organizations such as partnerships of physicians and lawyers.

These organizations often engage a public accountant to provide tax services and to assist in the preparation of accurate financial information without an audit. Providing these services is a significant part of the practice of many smaller public accounting firms. When a public accountant provides any services involving financial statements, certain requirements exist. The requirements for review engagements are covered in *CICA Handbook* Sections 8100, 8200, 8500, and 8600. Requirements for compilation engagements appear in Section 9200.

The assurance provided by reviews and compilations is considerably below that of audits, and the practitioners' reports are intended to convey that difference. Similarly, the extent of evidence accumulation differs among the three types of engagements (i.e., audit, review, and compilation). Figure 23-4 illustrates the difference in both the evidence accumulation and the level of assurance provided. The amount of assurance and extent of evidence accumulation, shown in Figure 23-4, are not well defined by the profession. This is because both evidence accumulation and assurance are subjective. Only a practitioner in the circumstances of an engagement can judge how much evidence is sufficient and what level of assurance has actually been attained.

Table 23-1 on the next page compares audits, reviews, and compilations on a number of dimensions and, as such, is helpful in understanding the differences among the three types of engagement.

TERMS OF ENGAGEMENT While the *Handbook* sections covering review and compilation engagements do not require an engagement letter, they do require that the public accountant and the client reach an understanding and agreement regarding the services to be provided. A written agreement as to the nature and extent of services is most appropriate. The engagement letter would include such items as follows:

- A description of the services to be provided.
- A discussion of the client's responsibility for providing complete and accurate information.
- A statement that an audit is not to be performed and that, consequently, no opinion will be expressed. In the case of a compilation engagement, the fact that no assurance results should be stated.

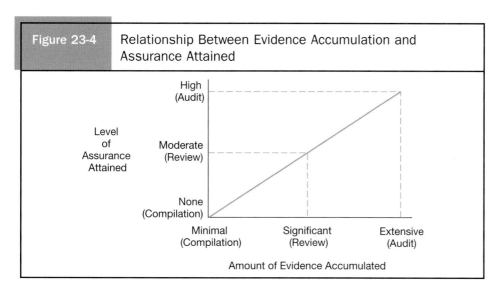

Figure 23-4 Relationship Between Evidence Accumulation and Assurance Attained

Table 23-1 Comparison of Audit, Review, and Compilation Engagements

	Amount of Evidence to Be Collected	Procedures Used to Collect Evidence	Levels of Assurance Provided	Relative Cost of Engagement	Communication Title	Engagement Letter Desired	Area Proficiency Required in	Public Accountant Required to Be Objective?	Knowledge of Business Required?	Understanding of Internal Control Required?	Documentation Required?
Audit	Extensive	Inspection, Observation, Inquiry, Confirmation, Recalculation, Reperformance, Analytical review	High	High	Auditor's Report	Yes	Auditing	Yes	Yes	Yes	Yes
Review	Significant	Inquiry, Analytical review, Discussion, Others if necessary	Moderate	Moderate	Review Engagement Report	Yes	Review	Yes	Yes	No	Yes
Compilation	Minor	Computation	None	Low	Notice to Reader	Yes	Accounting	No	No	No	Not specifically stated but desirable

Small Business Risks

A review engagement focuses on plausibility, or reasonableness, of financial information. This includes assessing the likelihood of fraud, and of the entity's compliance with laws and regulations.

Small business systems may be basic. For example, what would an organization do to comply with privacy legislation? It would need to have clear procedures when dealing with client information, and use a very powerful tool—the shredder! Combined with owner vigilance over employees and access to information, the shredder is important in destroying paper records that may contain private data.

Even small businesses may use electronic means to transmit and receive funds via intermediate organizations such as PayPal,

an electronic payment service. The business would need to monitor the service to ensure that it is not hacked—one convenient method is to have a separate bank account or credit card with a relatively low limit to mitigate the likelihood of loss. A small business that has had its electronic payment systems "hijacked" could literally close its doors if large amounts of funds are taken.

Sources: 1. Kandra, Anne, "The problem with PayPal," *PC World*, January 3, 2005.
2. Perkins, Tara, "Information theft: security firms boom," *Toronto Star*, January 20, 2007, p. D1, D4.

- A note on any restrictions on the distribution of the statements.
- A statement that each page of the statements should be clearly marked "unaudited."
- The probable content of the communication, to be appended by the accountant.
- The fact that the engagement cannot be relied on to detect error or fraud and other irregularities.
- Possibly a comment to the effect that the statements do not satisfy any statutory requirements.

Figure 23-5 on the next page provides an example of an engagement letter for a review of annual financial statements.

REVIEW A **review engagement** is described by the *CICA Handbook* (Section 8100.05) by means of the procedures used to conduct it. The accountant would use inquiry, analytical procedures, and discussion during the engagement. Rather than providing reasonable assurance, the accountant's objective is to provide an opinion on "plausibility" of the information using appropriate criteria. Plausible can be defined as being worthy of belief.

GENERAL REVIEW STANDARDS Section 8100, General review standards, discusses the acceptance of an engagement and the standards applicable to review engagements. These include knowledge of the client's business, review procedures, documentation, and reporting. Review engagements should be accepted by a public accountant only if the accountant believes that he or she has the necessary competence in the subject matter to be reported on and is independent of the client.

Procedures suggested for reviews Reviews imply a level of assurance somewhere between that of an audit and the absence of assurance provided by a compilation. A review does not include obtaining an understanding of internal controls or tests of controls, independent confirmation, or physical examination. The emphasis in reviews is on four broad areas:

- *Obtain knowledge of the client's business.* The information should be about the nature of the client's organization and business transactions; its accounting records and employees; the basis, form, and content of the financial statements; and accounting matters peculiar to the client's business and industry.
- *Make inquiries of client personnel.* The objective of these inquiries is to determine whether the financial statements are fairly presented, assuming that management does not intend to deceive the accountant. The CICA Assurance and Related Services Guideline AuG-20, Performance of a review of financial statements in

> **Review engagement**—one that consists primarily of inquiry, analytical procedures, and discussion with the limited objectives of assessing whether the information being reported on is plausible within the framework of appropriate criteria.

Figure 23-5	Example of an Engagement Letter for a Review Engagement

September 23, 2009

JOSEPHINE LIMITED
677 PETER STREET
WIINNIPEG, MANITOBA
R3Y 1Z6

Attention: Josephine Collins, President

Dear Ms. Collins:

The purpose of this letter is to outline the nature of our involvement with the financial statements of Josephine Limited for the year ending December 31, 2009. As agreed, we will conduct a review, consisting primarily of inquiry, analytical procedures, and discussion in accordance with the generally accepted standards for review engagements.

Unless unanticipated difficulties are encountered, our report will be substantially in the following form:

> We have reviewed the balance sheet of Josephine Limited as at December 31, 2009, and the statements of income, retained earnings, and cash flows for the year then ended. Our review was made in accordance with Canadian generally accepted standards for review engagements and accordingly consisted primarily of inquiry, analytical procedures, and discussion related to information supplied to us by the company.
>
> A review does not constitute an audit, and consequently, we do not express an opinion on these financial statements.
>
> Based on our review, nothing has come to our attention that causes us to believe that these financial statements are not, in all material respects, in accordance with Canadian generally accepted accounting principles.

This review does not constitute an audit. For example, it does not contemplate a study and evaluation of internal control, tests of accounting records, and responses to inquiries by obtaining audit evidence through inspection, observation, or confirmation and other procedures ordinarily performed during an audit. Accordingly, this review is not intended to, and will not, result in the expression of an audit opinion or the fulfilling of any statutory or other audit requirement. Since we are not accepting this engagement as auditor, we request that you do not record this as an auditing engagement in the minutes of your shareholders' meetings. You may wish to obtain legal advice concerning statutory auditing requirements.

It is understood that:

(a) you will provide the information required for us to complete this review;

(b) the responsibility for the accuracy and completeness of the representations in the financial statements remains with you;

(c) if our name is to be used in connection with the financial statements, you will attach our review engagement report when distributing the financial statements to third parties; and

(d) each page of the financial statements will be conspicuously marked "Unaudited."

This engagement cannot be relied on to prevent or detect error or fraud and other irregularities. We wish to emphasize that control over and responsibility for the prevention and detection of error or fraud and other irregularities remains with management.

The arrangements outlined in this letter will continue in effect from year to year unless evidenced by a new engagement letter.

If you have any questions about the contents of this letter, please raise them with us. If the services outlined are in accordance with your requirements and if the above terms are acceptable to you, please sign the copy of this letter in the space provided and return it to us. We appreciate the opportunity of continuing to be of service to your company.

Yours very truly,

Simunic & Stein
Chartered Accountants

The services and terms set out are as agreed.
Josephine Limited
Per

Valerie Mann

accordance with sections 8100 and 8200, provides a thorough list of questions that can be asked.

- *Perform analytical procedures.* These are meant to identify relationships and individual items that appear to be unusual. Analytical procedures performed during a review engagement would normally be less extensive than those performed during an audit. The appropriate analytical procedures are the same as the ones already studied in Chapter 6 and in those chapters dealing with substantive procedures. Explanations for relationships and items that appear to be unusual would be obtained by inquiry of appropriate client personnel.
- *Have discussions with management concerning information received and the information being reported on.*

Generally accepted review standards The standards for review engagements are similar to generally accepted auditing standards, except that they deal with reviews and not audits. Based on Section 8100.15, these standards comprise the following:

- A *general standard* indicating that the engagement and its resulting report should be completed by individuals with sufficient training and competence, who are independent and conduct the work with due care.
- *Review standards* that cover similar areas as GAAS. These are as follows:

  (i) The engagement should be properly planned and executed, with any assistants adequately supervised.
  (ii) Adequate knowledge of the business is gathered as the basis for the completion of the engagement.
  (iii) Techniques used should be used to measure the plausibility of the subject matter against specified criteria (e.g., GAAP). Techniques would normally be limited to inquiry, analytical procedures, and discussion. Only if there were uncertainty with respect to the plausibility of the subject matter would the accountant conduct additional procedures.

- *Reporting standards* describe the required contents of the report, as illustrated in Figure 23-6.

The requirement that the accountant have sufficient knowledge of the client's enterprise and type of business is made so that the accountant can assess whether the

---

Figure 23-6	Example of a Report Under Section 8200

REVIEW ENGAGEMENT REPORT

To R. Fortin:

I have reviewed the balance sheet of Leger Inc. as at December 31, 2009, and the statements of income, retained earnings, and cash flows for the year then ended. My review was made in accordance with Canadian generally accepted standards established for review engagements and accordingly consisted primarily of inquiry, analytical procedures, and discussion related to information supplied to me by the company.

A review does not constitute an audit, and, consequently, I do not express an audit opinion on these financial statements.

Based on my review, nothing has come to my attention that causes me to believe that these financial statements are not, in all material respects, in accordance with Canadian generally accepted accounting principles.

Montréal, Québec
February 18, 2010

a. Vachon

Certified General Accountant

Not-for-profit organizations (NPOs) do not have shareholders, but they do have a board of directors. These directors are elected by members, rather than shareholders, so the accountant needs to find out how membership is determined. If the accountant is a member (such as of a golf club), his or her independence might be questioned. One possibility is to ask for a bylaw stating that the accountant cannot vote for board members. This is particularly relevant, since the accountant must report a number of issues to the audit committee (a subcommittee of the board).

Important issues for NPOs include the following:

- Awareness of fraud risks: Is leadership organized, rather than chaotic, and aware of the risks of fraud? Are random supervision and volunteer/staff rotation used to encourage early detection? Does the environment make it easy to report suspicious behaviour?

- Completeness of revenues: Are numbered receipts issued? How is fundraising handled? What is the mix between government grants and fundraising?
- Valuation of donated assets or services: How are donated services or donated assets valued? Are charitable donation receipts given for these items and services? Are valued amounts defensible for tax purposes? Is volunteer time recorded at nil?
- Existence of donated assets: Are these items added to a capital assets ledger, even if they were donated and have been recorded at a nil value?
- Compliance with regulations: Are funds disbursed in accordance with their intended purpose? Is an accounting system in place that properly tracks and distributes restricted funds? How does the NPO ensure that directors do not receive any funds or benefits?

information to be reported on is plausible in the circumstances. The accountant would not be able to make the required inquiry and assessment of the information obtained without such knowledge. For instance, the accountant would not be able to assess the plausibility of manufactured inventory unless he or she had knowledge of the company's product and manufacturing processes.

The review standards should be appropriate to the particular engagement; for example, it is likely that procedures would differ between a review of financial statements and financial information. The review procedures do not preclude audit procedures if the accountant believes that more extensive procedures are required to assess plausibility. However, once the accountant decides to use more extensive procedures, such as audit procedures, the particular procedure must be carried out to completion. The accountant should not carry out an audit procedure to partial completion simply because the engagement is a review.

Materiality would be measured in the same manner as with an audit.

Negative assurance should be expressed only when the standards applicable to a review engagement described above have been met.

As illustrated in Figure 23-6, the report first indicates the type of engagement, then identifies the information presented (a set of financial statements as of a specific date) and the criteria used (Canadian GAAP). The report states that a review does not constitute an audit after clearly indicating the procedures used (primarily inquiry, analytical procedures, and discussion) were performed in accordance with generally accepted standards for review engagements. The purpose of stating that a review does not constitute an audit is to ensure that financial statement users are aware that a review provides a lower level of assurance than an audit. As illustrated in the last sentence of the report, the accountant should also state, except when a reservation is required, that nothing has come to his or her attention as a result of his or her review that causes him or her to believe that the information is not, in all material respects, in accordance with an appropriate disclosed basis of accounting. The appropriate disclosed basis of accounting should be generally accepted accounting principles, except in special circumstances or, in the case of non-financial information, other appropriate criteria. This is called "negative assurance." In addition, each page of information reported on would be marked "unaudited."

Reservations may be required in the accountant's report when the review cannot be completed, when there is a departure from the appropriate criteria, or when the accountant concludes that the client's interpretation of an agreement or regulation is not reasonable. The reservation would be disclosed in a reservation paragraph in the review engagement report, which would appear immediately preceding the negative assurance paragraph. The reason for the reservation and the effect of the reservation on the information reported on should also be disclosed.

The discovery of a misstatement after the release of the report by the accountant should be treated in the same way as the discovery of a misstatement by an auditor after the release of audited financial statements.

Reviews of financial statements Section 8200 provides guidelines that apply to a review of financial statements (in addition to those in Section 8100) when the accountant is reporting on interim or annual financial statements. An example of a report that the accountant would issue is shown in Figure 23-6.

Financial information other than financial statements Section 8500 describes the sorts of financial information that might be included under this grouping. This section is parallel to CAS 800 (previously Section 5805) and refers the accountant to Section 5805 for further guidance in this matter. When the information is prepared in accordance with an agreement or a regulation and that agreement requires interpretations, the report should refer to such interpretations. Figure 23-7 shows the form a communication might take when the auditor is reporting on financial information other than financial statements.

CAS

Reviews of compliance with agreements and regulations Section 8600 is parallel to Section 5815. The accountant should read the relevant provisions of the agreement or regulation, inquire about how the client monitors its compliance with the provisions, and consider whether the provisions have been consistently applied. In the review engagement report, the public accountant should identify the provisions of the agreement or regulation that establish the criteria on which his or her assessment of compliance is based. As well, any significant interpretations of the criteria made by the accountant when the criteria were non-specific and any significant changes in interpretations from the previous year should be identified. Figure 23-8 on the next page presents an example of a report that the accountant might issue.

Figure 23-7	Example of a Report Under Section 8500

REVIEW ENGAGEMENT REPORT

To Kamloops Limited:

At the request of Pacific Limited, I have reviewed the plant and equipment of Pacific Limited as at March 31, 2009 (calculated in accordance with the provisions of section 10 of the mortgage agreement with Kamloops Limited dated May 5, 2006, and the interpretations set out in note 1). My review was made in accordance with Canadian generally accepted standards for review engagements and accordingly consisted primarily of inquiry, analytical procedures, and discussion related to information supplied to me by the company.

A review does not constitute an audit, and, consequently, I do not express an audit opinion on this plant and equipment.

Based on my review, nothing has come to my attention that causes me to believe that this plant and equipment are not presented fairly in accordance with the provisions of section 10 of the mortgage agreement with Kamloops Limited dated May 5, 2006, and the interpretations set out in note 1.

Vancouver, B.C.

June 7, 2009

L. Daryl

Chartered Accountant

Figure 23-8 | Example of a Report Under Section 8600

REVIEW ENGAGEMENT REPORT

To J. O'Sullivan:

I have reviewed Separate Limited's compliance as at December 31, 2009, with covenants to be complied with described in sections 8 to 10 inclusive of the agreement dated November 3, 2007, with Waterloo Inc. My review was made in accordance with Canadian generally accepted standards for review engagements and accordingly consisted primarily of inquiry, analytical procedures, and discussion related to information supplied to me by the company.

A review does not constitute an audit, and, consequently, I do not express an audit opinion on this matter.

Based on my review, nothing has come to my attention that causes me to believe that the company is not in compliance with covenants to be complied with as described in sections 8 to 10 inclusive of this agreement.

Calgary, Alberta

January 18, 2010

G. On

Certified General Accountant

Compilation Compilation services are bookkeeping services that lead to the completion of financial statements. It is common for smaller public accounting firms to own one or more microcomputers and provide bookkeeping services, monthly or quarterly financial statements, and tax services for smaller clients.

In **compilation engagements**, discussed in Section 9200, the public accountant provides assistance in compiling financial statements but is not required to provide any assurance about the statements; the engagement is not an assurance engagement. The statements may be complete (i.e., include balance sheet, income statement, and statement of cash flows); they may be part of a complete set of financial statements; or they may be for the whole enterprise or for a part of the enterprise. The accountant assembles the information supplied by the client and ensures that it is arithmetically correct; the accountant is concerned with neither the accuracy or completeness of the information nor whether the financial statements comply with GAAP. Although the accountant should not be associated with false or misleading financial statements, determining whether the statements are false or misleading can be difficult because of his or her limited involvement.

Section 9200.10 sets out the criteria for accepting a compilation engagement: the accountant must have no reason to believe that the statements are false or misleading, and the client clearly understands the nature and scope of the engagement, including its limitations.

Professional standards The compilation services should be performed and the report prepared by individuals who have adequate technical training and proficiency in accounting, and who completed their work with due care. As for other engagements, planning and proper conduct of the work is required. Any assistants should be properly supervised.

If something comes to the attention of the public accountant that could indicate that the financial statements may be false or misleading, additional information must be obtained and the statements amended, or the accountant should resign from the engagement.

Form of report The communication from the public accountant in a compilation engagement is entitled "Notice to Reader." Each page of the statements should include either the "Notice to Reader" heading itself or the statement "Unaudited— See Notice to Reader." An example of a "Notice to Reader" appears in Figure 23-9. The example illustrates key aspects of the report: it is clearly labelled, with the work and the financial statements (including period covered) described. The report states that the accountant has not audited or otherwise checked the information that was

> **Compilation engagement—** non-audit engagement in which the public accountant provides assistance in compiling financial statements but is not expected to provide assurance about the statements.

NOTICE TO READER

I have compiled the balance sheet of New B Ltd. as at March 31, 2009, and the statements of income, retained earnings, and cash flows for the year then ended from information provided by management. I have not audited, reviewed, or otherwise attempted to verify the accuracy or completeness of such information. Readers are cautioned that this statement may not be appropriate for their purposes.

Halifax, N.S.

June 12, 2009

R. Fundy

Chartered Accountant

provided by management. Because the statements might not be in accordance with GAAP, the report also includes a warning with respect to the use of the financial statements.

Departures from generally accepted accounting principles should not be referred to in the report as this may suggest that the public accountant has a responsibility to detect and report all such departures.

Compilation standards also apply to the financial information included in a client's tax return. Thus, accountants should include a "Notice to Reader" with financial information included with personal tax returns prepared on behalf of clients.

concept check

C23-3 What is an important difference between a compilation engagement and a review engagement?

C23-4 Evaluate the following statement: "For a compilation engagement, the accountant does not check the financial statements, so they are very likely to contain material misstatements."

Interim Financial Information and Future-Oriented Information

Interim Financial Information

Interim financial information may be audited, reviewed, or compiled by a public accountant. The decision depends on how much assurance is desired from the accountant's involvement and how timely the information must be. Estimates normally have to be made in order to prepare the information on a timely basis. Therefore, the information may not be as reliable as annual financial information. Since the objective of producing interim financial information is to provide up-to-date information to users of the statements, such information is usually not audited. Section 7050, Auditor review of interim financial statements, provides thorough guidance for review of financial statements for a financial reporting period that is shorter than the fiscal year. Sections 8100, 8200, 8500, and 8600 can also be consulted when interim financial information is reviewed. If the information is compiled, Section 9200 is relevant.

Future-Oriented Financial Information

Future-oriented financial information (FOFI) is prospective information about results of operations or other financial information that is based on assumptions about future economic conditions and courses of action. It may be presented either as a forecast or a projection. Section 4250 establishes accounting standards for such information. The CICA also issued Assurance and Related Services Guideline AuG-6, Examination of a financial forecast or projection included in a prospectus or other public offering document. This Guideline is directed at prospective information included in offering documents.

Assurance and Related Services Guideline AuG-16, Compilation of a financial forecast or projection, indicates the standards that the public accountant should follow when compiling a forecast or projection for a client who does not require the public accountant to provide any assurance.

Future-oriented financial information (FOFI)—information about prospective results of operations, financial position, and/or changes in financial position based on assumptions about future economic conditions and courses of action; may be presented either as a forecast or projection.

Chapter 1 has pointed out that Assurance and Related Services Guidelines do not have the force of Recommendations. Their intent is to provide guidance in the absence of Recommendations.

FORECASTS AND PROJECTIONS Future-oriented financial information deals with the future, not with the past. Section 4250 describes two general types of future-oriented financial information: forecasts and projections. A **forecast** is prospective financial information prepared using assumptions reflecting management's judgment as to the most probable courses of action for the entity. The information is presented to the best of management's knowledge and belief. A **projection** is prepared using one or more assumptions (hypotheses) that do not necessarily reflect the most likely course of action in management's judgment.

USE OF PROSPECTIVE FINANCIAL STATEMENTS **Prospective financial statements** are financial statements that deal with expected future data rather than with historical data, for either general use or special use. General use refers to use by any third party. An example of general use would be inclusion of a financial forecast in a prospectus for the sale of shares of a large public company. Special use refers to use by third parties with whom the responsible party is negotiating directly. An example of special purpose future-oriented financial information would be the inclusion of a financial projection in a takeover bid circular aimed at current shareholders of the company or in an entity's application for a bank loan.

ACCEPTANCE OF THE ENGAGEMENT The following discussion pertains to Assurance and Related Service Guideline AuG-6. As with other types of engagements performed by the public accountant, it is important to ensure that the nature and terms of involvement with future-oriented financial information are understood and agreed to by management, preferably in writing. Management should also acknowledge its responsibilities related to the financial information. AuG-6 identifies a number of matters that should be agreed to by management and the public accountant and included in an engagement letter:

- The anticipated form of the financial forecast.
- The period of time to be covered.
- The fact that management will prepare and present the forecast in accordance with accounting standards established by the CICA and in accordance with any applicable securities requirements.
- The fact that management is responsible for the forecast: its presentation, the process of preparation, and the assumptions used.
- The fact that management is responsible for obtaining or developing appropriate support for the assumptions sufficient to enable the public accountant to report without reservation.
- The need for the public accountant to have access to outside specialists and third-party reports obtained by management (e.g., a feasibility study).
- The anticipated form and content of the public accountant's report.
- The fact that the public accountant has no responsibility to update his or her report for events and circumstances occurring after the date of that report.

Before accepting such an engagement, the public accountant should ensure that management will act with integrity during the engagement, providing relevant information, and that sufficient evidence will be available to conduct the engagement.

Professional standards As with other types of reports, FOFI services should be performed by someone with adequate technical training and proficiency; the examination should be carefully supervised and properly performed; and the report should be prepared with due care. Enough evidence should be obtained about the assumptions and the underlying data to provide a reasonable basis for the report. Supporting documentation and evidence should be retained in a working paper file.

Forecast—prospective financial information prepared using assumptions as to the most probable courses of action for the entity.

Projection—prospective financial information prepared using assumptions reflecting management's judgment as to the most probable course of action for the entity; prepared using one or more assumptions (hypotheses) that do not necessarily reflect the most likely course of action in management's judgment.

Prospective financial statements—financial statements that deal with expected future data rather than with historical data.

EXAMINATION OF PROSPECTIVE FINANCIAL STATEMENTS An examination of future-oriented financial information involves evaluating the preparation of the future-oriented financial information and the underlying assumptions and assessing the plausibility of hypotheses. In addition, the public accountant would evaluate the presentation of the financial information for conformity with CICA presentation and disclosure guidelines (Section 4250) and ensure that accounting policies are consistent with those used in the historical financial statements. The public accountant would obtain a written letter of representation from management acknowledging its responsibility for preparing the forecast or projection and indicating that forecast figures are management's best estimate of the forecast results. Finally, the accountant would issue an examination report.

These evaluations are based primarily on accumulating evidence about the completeness and reasonableness of the underlying assumptions as disclosed in the prospective financial information. This requires the accountant to become familiar with the client's business and industry, to identify the significant matters on which the client's future results are expected to depend ("key factors"), and to determine that appropriate assumptions have been included with respect to these.

REPORTING The accountant's report on an examination of financial statements is illustrated in Figure 23-10. Like other examples in this chapter, the report is clearly identified, and the information that was examined is described. Then, the role of management and the accountants is stated. For FOFI, the auditor states an opinion about the underlying assumptions rather than the data presented in the financial statements themselves. Finally, the last paragraph in the report includes a warning that the results may not be achieved and that the accountant cannot provide any kind of opinion about such future events.

The date of the report would be the date of the completion of the fieldwork by the public accountant.

concept check

C23-5 What is the purpose of interim financial information?

C23-6 The difference between a forecast and a projection relates to the nature of the underlying assumptions. Describe that difference.

Figure 23-10	Example of a Report on a Financial Forecast

AUDITOR'S REPORT ON FINANCIAL FORECAST

To the Directors of Nomad Corp.:

The accompanying financial forecast of Nomad Corp. consisting of a balance sheet as at June 30, 2010, and the statements of income, retained earnings, and changes in financial position for the period then ending have been prepared by management using assumptions with an effective date of June 30, 2009. We have examined the support provided by management for the assumptions, and the preparation and presentation of this forecast. Our examination was made in accordance with Auditing Guideline AuG-6 issued by the Canadian Institute of Chartered Accountants. We have no responsibility to update this report for events and circumstances occurring after the date of our report.

In our opinion, as of the date of this report, the assumptions developed by management are suitably supported and consistent with the plans of the Company and provide a reasonable basis for the forecast; this forecast reflects such assumptions; and the financial forecast complies with the presentation and disclosure standards for forecasts established by the Canadian Institute of Chartered Accountants.

Since this forecast is based on assumptions regarding future events, actual results will vary from the information presented and the variations may be material. Accordingly, we express no opinion as to whether this forecast will be achieved.

Toronto, Ontario
August 15, 2009

McWhite & Kedwell

Chartered Accountants

Summary

1. *How is the assurance engagement general standard different from the audit standard?* The assurance standard requires that the public accountant believe it is possible to complete the engagement. The equivalent statement (i.e., having a reasonable basis to conduct an audit) is not present in the audit standard.

    How is it similar? Both general standards require adequate proficiency to perform the engagement, having knowledge of the business or subject matter, and that the engagement be completed with due care and an objective state of mind.

    Provide an example of a special report that provides the following:
    (i) *High assurance*—an auditor's report concerning the effectiveness of the system of internal control over financial reporting.
    (ii) *No assurance*—an accountant's report on gross sales that were not audited.

2. *Why are review and compilation services important?* Many businesses and other organizations do not require the assurance level that is provided by an audit. Even some banks require only moderate assurance (i.e., a review engagement) for bank loans. A key service that may not require assurance is the preparation of information included with a tax return.

    How are the evidence collection procedures related to the assurance level provided for audits, reviews, and compilations? Audits require the greatest amount of evidence collection, with the requirement that objective evidence be collected, where possible. This results in the audit providing the greatest assurance level of the three engagements. Reviews require less evidence, and the procedures are normally limited to inquiry, analysis, and discussion, while compilations provide no assurance—the accountant does not gather any evidence.

3. *What type of report does the public accountant provide for interim financial information?* Interim financial information can be audited, reviewed, or compiled. The type of report depends on the type of engagement.

    How does the public accountant report on future-oriented information? The public accountant evaluates the assumptions used by management and checks that the information has been compiled correctly (compilation engagement).

Visit the text's website at www.pearsoned.ca/arens for practice quizzes, additional case studies, and international standards information.

Review Questions

23-1 Distinguish between an "attest engagement" and a "direct reporting engagement."

23-2 Explain why criteria are so important with respect to assurance engagements.

23-3 Identify the three parties to an accountability relationship, and explain the roles of each.

23-4 Give three examples of the special reports that a public accountant may be asked to issue. Explain why these reports would be requested.

23-5 Why do public accountants prepare reports on the results of applying specified auditing procedures to financial information other than financial statements?

23-6 How do the general standards applicable to review engagements differ from generally accepted auditing standards?

23-7 Contrast the level of assurance provided by negative assurance discussed in Sections 8100, 8200, 8500, and 8600 of the *CICA Handbook* with the level of assurance provided by the opinion given in the auditor's report.

23-8 What is the intention of Section 9200, Compilation engagements, in the *CICA Handbook*?

23-9 Discuss the standards for compilation engagements, and explain why they differ from those for review engagements and audits.

23-10 The financial statements prepared for a compilation engagement may not be complete according to GAAP. Why is this exception permitted? Provide examples of information that might be excluded.

22-11 Explain how the review engagement for an NPO differs from the review engagement for a profit-oriented entity.

23-12 On what does the auditor comment in his or her report on financial forecasts? On what does the auditor disclaim an opinion and why?

Discussion Questions and Problems

23-13 Joseph, a public accountant, has been keeping the books for his father's business, JoPar Tech Ltd., in the evenings, while working with other clients during the day. Yesterday, Joseph's father proudly announced that he had negotiated a loan with the Federal Business Development Bank at favourable rates so that he could purchase $120,000 in new machinery and equipment. Upon reviewing the loan agreement, Joseph discovered that one of the requirements of the loan agreement is that JoPar Tech Ltd. submit financial statements that have been reviewed by a public accountant within 90 days of the fiscal year end.

a. Can Joseph complete a review engagement report for JoPar Tech Ltd.? Why or why not?

b. What type of engagement can Joseph complete with respect to the financial statements of JoPar Tech Ltd.?

c. What would you advise Joseph to do? Why?

23-14 You are doing a review engagement and the related tax work for Regency Tools, Inc., a tool and die company with $2,000,000 in sales. Inventory is recorded at $125,000. Prior-year unaudited statements, prepared by the company without assistance from a public accounting firm, disclose that the inventory is based on "historical cost estimated by management." You obtain the following facts:

1. The company has been growing steadily for the past five years.
2. The unit cost of typical material used by Regency Tools has increased dramatically for several years.
3. The inventory cost has been approximately $125,000 for five years.
4. Management intends to use a value of $125,000 again for the current year-end financial statements.

When you discuss with management the need to get a physical count and an accurate inventory, the response is negative. Management is concerned about the effects on income taxes of a more realistic inventory. The company has never been audited and has always estimated the historical cost of inventory. You are convinced, based upon inquiry and ratio analysis, that a conservative evaluation would be $500,000 at historical cost.

REQUIRED

a. What are the generally accepted accounting principle requirements for valuation and disclosure of inventory for unaudited financial statements with a review report?
b. Identify the potential legal and professional problems that you face in this situation.
c. What procedures would you normally follow for a review engagement when the inventory is a material amount? Be as specific as possible.
d. How should you resolve the problem in this situation? Identify alternatives, and evaluate the costs and benefits of each.

23-15 The following items represent a series of unrelated procedures that an accountant may consider performing in an engagement to review or compile the financial statements of a non-public entity. Procedures may apply to only one, both, or neither type of engagement.

1. The accountant should establish an understanding with the entity regarding the nature and limitations of the services to be performed.
2. The accountant should make inquiries concerning actions taken at the board of directors' meetings.
3. The accountant should obtain a level of knowledge of the accounting principles and practices of the entity's industry.
4. The accountant should obtain an understanding of the entity's internal control.
5. The accountant should perform analytical procedures designed to identify relationships that appear to be unusual.

6. The accountant should send a letter of inquiry to the entity's lawyer to corroborate the information furnished by management concerning litigation.
7. The accountant should obtain a management representation letter from the entity.
8. The accountant should make inquiries about events subsequent to the date of the financial statements that would have a material effect on the financial statements.
9. The accountant should perform a physical examination of inventory.

REQUIRED

a. Indicate which procedures are required to be performed on a review engagement.
b. Indicate which procedures are required to be performed on a compilation engagement.

23-16 Your public accounting firm is the auditor of Taylor Fruit Farms, Inc., a company located in Penticton, B.C., and incorporated under the laws of British Columbia. As part of your audit of Taylor Fruit Farms, Inc., you have been requested by the management of Taylor to issue an opinion under Section 5815 of the *CICA Handbook* with respect to Taylor's compliance under the terms of a chattel mortgage issued by J.L. Lockwood Corp., which is a supplier of irrigation equipment. Much of the equipment, including that supplied to Taylor, is sold on a secured contract basis. Unlike Taylor Fruit Farms, Lockwood is not an audit client of yours.

In addition to the present equipment, Taylor informs you that Lockwood is evaluating whether it should sell another $500,000 of equipment to Taylor Fruit Farms.

You have been requested to send Taylor the report under Section 5815 concerning the following matters:

1. The current ratio has exceeded 2.0 in each quarter of the unaudited statements prepared by management and in the annual audited statements.
2. Total owners' equity is more than $800,000.
3. The company has not violated any of the legal requirements of British Columbia's fruit-growing regulations.

4. Management is competent and has made reasonable business decisions in the past three years.
5. Management owns an option to buy additional fruit land adjacent to its present property.

REQUIRED

a. Define the purpose of a report under Section 5815.

b. Is it necessary to conduct an audit of a company before issuing a report on compliance under Section 5815?
c. Would you include all five matters listed above in your report? If not, explain why you would exclude any from the report.

23-17 It is now March 2010. Margaret Monson, the owner of Major Products Manufacturing Inc., a small, successful long-time audit client of your firm, has requested you to work with Major in preparing three-year forecast information for the year ending December 31, 2010, and two subsequent years. Margaret informs you that she intends to use the forecasts, together with the audited financial statements, to seek additional financing to expand the business. Margaret has had little experience in formal forecast preparation and counts on you to assist her in any way possible. She wants the most supportive opinion possible from your firm to add to the credibility of the forecast. She informs you that she is willing to do anything necessary to help you prepare the forecast.

First, Margaret wants projections of sales and revenues and earnings from the existing business, which she believes could continue to be financed from existing capital.

Second, Margaret intends to buy a company in a closely related business that is currently operating unsuccessfully. She states that she wants to sell some of the operating assets of the business and replace them with others. She believes that this will make the combined company highly successful. She has made an offer on the new business, subject to obtaining proper financing. She also informs you that she has received an offer on the assets that she intends to sell.

REQUIRED

a. Explain circumstances under which it would be and would not be acceptable to undertake the engagement.
b. Why is it important that Margaret understand the nature of your reporting requirements before the engagement proceeds?
c. What information will Margaret have to provide you before you can complete the forecasted statements? Be as specific as possible.
d. Discuss, in as specific terms as possible, the nature of the report you will issue with the forecasts, assuming that you are able to properly complete them.

23-18 O'Sullivan, a public accountant, has completed the audit of Sarawak Lumber Supply Co. Ltd. and has issued a standard unqualified report. In addition to a report on the overall financial statements, the company needs a special audit report on three specific accounts: sales, net fixed assets, and inventory valued at FIFO. The report is to be issued to Sarawak's lessor, who bases annual rentals on these three accounts. O'Sullivan was not aware of the need for the special report until after the overall audit was completed.

REQUIRED

a. Explain why O'Sullivan is unlikely to be able to issue the special audit report without additional audit tests.
b. What additional tests are likely to be needed before the special report can be issued?
c. Assume that O'Sullivan is able to satisfy all the requirements needed to issue the special report. Write the report, making any necessary assumptions.

Professional Judgment Problem

23-19 Ballantine Church has been located on a central downtown street in Toronto for over 120 years. Originally, the church was in the middle of farmland but is now surrounded by high-rise apartments and condominiums. The church has an active parish community that engages in fundraising in the neighbourhood, assisting the homeless, and providing drop-in housing during the winter. Francine, the parish priest, and the church board have decided it is time to have a review engagement completed for the church finances. In the past, this work has been done by church members on a part-time basis.

The church organizes its finances based on five funds: operating, endowment, youth, homeless, and music scholarship. Any transfers from the endowment fund to the operating fund must be approved by the board. The church has about $1.2 million in cash and marketable securities in the bank. The church is valued at zero on the balance sheet.

The church also owns a large house. Francine lives in a section of the house and the rest of the property is used for storage, as office space for three permanent church staff, and as meeting space.

REQUIRED

a. What should you do before you accept the review engagement?
b. Outline the process for conducting the review engagement and describe any analytical review procedures that you would conduct specific to the church. What types of questions would you ask that are specific to the church to address plausibility of financial information?

Case

23-20 Quality Review is the franchisor of a national accounting review course for candidates taking CA, CGA, and CMA examinations. Quality Review is responsible for providing all materials, including CDs and video material, doing all national and local advertising, and giving assistance in effectively organizing and operating local franchises. The fee to the participant is $1,500 for the full course if all parts of the examination are taken. Quality Review gets 50 percent of the total fee.

The materials for the review course are purchased by Quality Review from Ronnie Johnson, a highly qualified writer of review materials. Quality Review receives one copy of those materials from Ronnie and reproduces them for candidates. Quality Review must pay Ronnie a $60 royalty for each full set of materials used and 12 percent of the participant fee for partial candidates. The contract between Ronnie and Quality Review requires an audited report to be provided by Quality Review on royalties due to Ronnie. Recorded gross fees for the 2009 review course are $1,500,000.

Even before the audit was started, there was a dispute between Quality Review and Ronnie. Quality Review does not intend to pay royalties on certain materials. Ronnie disagrees with that conclusion but the contract does not specify anything about it. The table on the right lists the disputed sales on which Quality Review refuses to pay royalties:

1. Materials sent to instructors for promotion	$31,000
2. Uncollected fees due to bad debts	6,000
3. Candidates who paid no fee because they performed administrative duties during the course	16,000
4. Refunds to customers who were dissatisfied with the course	22,000
Total	$75,000

REQUIRED

a. Assume that you are engaged to do the ordinary audit of Quality Review and the special audit of royalties for Ronnie. What additional audit testing beyond the normal tests of royalties is required because of the special audit?

b. Assume that the financial statements of Quality Review are found to be fairly stated except for the unresolved dispute between Ronnie and Quality Review. Write the appropriate audit report.

c. Write the report for total royalties to Ronnie, assuming that the information as stated in the case is correct and the dispute is not resolved.

24

Assurance services: Internal auditing and government auditing

Many public accountants work in industry, in internal audit departments, or in government. Government auditors in the Auditor General's offices play important roles in providing accountability for government departments and programs. Management accountants' understanding of internal audit can help them coordinate with their own internal auditors, while financial and specialist auditors often work on internal audit teams.

STANDARDS REFERENCED IN THIS CHAPTER

CICA Standard

CAS 610 – Using the work of internal auditors (previously Section 5050 – Using the work of internal audit)

LEARNING OBJECTIVES

1 Describe the role of internal auditing. State the key differences between operational auditing and financial auditing. Provide an example of an audit criterion associated with each of effectiveness and efficiency.

2 Explain how the functions of an Auditor General's office differ from those of an internal audit office. Describe how independence is facilitated for government and internal auditors. Identify some sources of criteria for conducting an operational audit.

3 List the phases in operational auditing. Note where one can find sample reports of value-for-money audits.

What Do You Ask the Board?

Internal auditors can start working with the board of directors by asking them to do a self-assessment. However, such an assessment may be biased, as Joyce Drummond-Hill found when she worked with Prison Service board members in the United Kingdom. She found that there was no independent evaluation of the board and that there was lack of communication among sub-committees. This internal auditor's work led to an increase in the size of the board by adding three directors who were not members of the Prison Service executive.

Sarbanes–Oxley in the United States emphasizes the role of the board in providing independent governance of an organization. Yet such independent directors need assistance from those who directly look at the records, such as internal auditors. Perhaps a solid internal audit department would have prevented or detected the massive Satyam Computer Services Limited fraud in India, where the chair and co-founder of the company admitted to having placed about US$1 billion in fictitious assets on the balance sheet of the company, inflating income for several years.

At the present time, India and many other countries do not encourage public companies to have an internal audit department. Many organizations around the world may have an internal audit department that consists of one or two individuals, who could be subject to management pressure during the conduct of their work.

IMPORTANCE TO AUDITORS

Informing stakeholders of standards used by the board and by internal auditors can lead to a stronger, more supportive environment for internal auditors. The Institute of Internal Auditors regularly publishes a brochure titled "Tone at the Top," which is intended to provide suggestions to executive and board management to improve corporate governance. The February 2009 brochure described how an ethical corporate culture could be promoted, by listing steps that constitute ethical behaviour. It similarly talked about internal audit's role and new voluntary standards that state that every five years the internal audit department should have an external quality assessment. Such an assessment would help an internal audit department illustrate its own capacity to be independent and provide high-quality service to the organization.

WHAT DO YOU THINK?

1. Do you think that public awareness plays a role in the board's decisions for a large organization? Why or why not?

2. What type of information should management or the board provide to stakeholders about the role of internal audit at their organization?

Sources: 1. Harris, Trish W., "Doing the right thing," *Tone at the Top*, Institute of Internal Auditors, February, 2009. 2. McMullum, Tim, "On the road to good governance," *Internal Auditor*, October, 2006. 3. New York Times News Service, "India charges 9 after probe into outsourcing firm," *Toronto Star*, April 8, 2009, p. B8. *continued >*

WHAT kind of work would you like to do once you have received your accounting designation? Are you interested in public accounting or working in industry? You could become a financial officer, an internal auditor, or a public sector auditor—all of these positions provide the opportunity to get to know particular entities very well. Internal auditors use financial and non-financial skills to assist management to monitor the activities in the organization, as we will see in this chapter.

① The Nature of Internal Auditing

As discussed in Chapter 1, internal auditors are employed by entities to help improve the organization's operations. Internal auditors typically use a risk-based approach in consultation with the audit committee to determine the type of work that they will complete. This could include operational auditing, systems development auditing, fraud auditing, and providing assistance with the financial statement audit conducted by the external auditors. Their role in auditing has increased dramatically in the past two decades, primarily because of the increased size and complexity of many corporations, and the requirement of management in many countries around the world to certify the quality of internal controls.

In financial auditing, external auditors are responsible for evaluating whether their client's internal controls are designed and operated effectively and whether the financial statements are fairly presented. Because internal auditors spend all of their time with one company, their knowledge about the organization's operations and internal controls is much greater than the external auditors' knowledge.

Guidelines for performing internal audits for companies are not as well defined as for external audits. This occurs because of the wide variety of internal audits. Based on user requirements, the audit purpose, audit methods, and audit reports must be customized. Management of different companies may have widely varying expectations of the type and extent of financial system auditing to be done by internal auditors. For example, management of one company may decide that internal auditors should be extensively involved in systems development, whereas others may decide that their work should focus primarily on financial controls and fraud audits.

THE INSTITUTE OF INTERNAL AUDITORS Internal auditors look to **The Institute of Internal Auditors** (IIA, **www.theiia.org**) for professional guidance. The IIA is an organization that functions for internal auditors much as the CICA does for CAs, the CGAAC for CGAs, and the SMAC for CMAs; it establishes ethical standards and **standards for the practice of internal auditing**, provides education, and encourages professionalism of its approximately 103,000 members. The IIA has played a major role in the increasing influence of internal auditing. For example, the IIA has a highly regarded certification program resulting in the designation of Certified Internal Auditor (CIA) for those who meet the testing and experience requirements.

The Institute of Internal Auditors (IIA)—an organization for internal auditors that establishes ethical and practice standards; provides education, a professional exam, and a professional designation; and encourages professionalism of its members.

Standards for the practice of internal auditing—guidelines issued by the Institute of Internal Auditors, covering the activities and conduct of internal auditors.

The IIA standards include attribute standards (pertaining to the characteristics of internal auditors) and performance standards (about execution of field work, whether assurance or consulting), as detailed in Figure 24-1.

RELATIONSHIP OF INTERNAL AND EXTERNAL AUDITORS There are both differences and similarities between the responsibilities and conduct of audits by internal and external auditors. The primary difference is to whom each party is responsible. The external auditor is responsible to financial statement users who rely on the auditor to add credibility to the statements. The internal auditors are responsible to management, although, to improve independence, they should report to the audit committee. Even with this important difference, there are many similarities between the two groups. Both must be competent as auditors and remain objective in performing their work and reporting their results. They both follow a similar methodology in performing their audits, including planning and performing tests of controls and substantive tests. Similarly, they both use the audit risk model and materiality in deciding the extent of their tests of financial systems and evaluating results. Their decisions about materiality and risks may differ, however, because external users may have different needs from management's.

External auditors justify reliance on internal auditors through the use of the audit risk model. External auditors significantly reduce control risk and thereby reduce substantive testing if internal auditors are effective. The fee reduction of the external auditor is typically substantial when there is a highly regarded internal audit function. External auditors typically consider internal auditors effective if they are independent of the operating units being evaluated, competent and well trained, and have performed relevant audit tests of the internal controls and financial statements.

CAS 610, Using the work of internal auditors (formerly Section 5050, Using the `CAS` work of internal audit), permits the external auditor to use the internal auditor for direct assistance on the audit. (In fact, the CAS requires the external auditor to understand the functions of the internal audit department, even if the external auditor does not intend to rely upon the actions of internal audit, which was not required under

---

| Figure 24-1 | Institute of Internal Auditors Professional Practice Attribute and Performance Standards |

ATTRIBUTE STANDARDS

1000 Purpose, Authority, and Responsibility. The purpose, authority, and responsibility of the internal audit activity should be formally defined in a charter, consistent with the *Standards*, and approved by the board.

1100 Independence and Objectivity. The internal audit activity should be independent, and internal auditors should be objective in performing their work.

1200 Proficiency and Due Professional Care. Engagements should be performed with proficiency and due professional care.

1300 Quality Assurance and Improvement Program. The chief audit executive should develop and maintain a quality assurance and improvement program that covers all aspects of the internal audit activity and continuously monitors its effectiveness. The program should be designed to help the internal auditing activity add value and improve the organization's operations and to provide assurance that the internal audit activity is in conformity with the *Standards* and the *Code of Ethics*.

PERFORMANCE STANDARDS

2000 Managing the Internal Audit Activity. The chief audit executive should effectively manage the internal audit activity to ensure it adds value to the organization.

2100 Nature of Work. The internal audit activity evaluates and contributes to the improvement of risk management, control, and governance systems.

2200 Engagement Planning. Internal auditors should develop and record a plan for each engagement.

2300 Performing the Engagement. Internal auditors should identify, analyze, evaluate, and record sufficient information to achieve the engagement's objectives.

2400 Communicating Results. Internal auditors should communicate the engagement results promptly.

2500 Monitoring Progress. The chief audit executive should establish and maintain a system to monitor the disposition of results communicated to management.

2600 Management's Acceptance of Risks. When the chief audit executive believes that senior management has accepted a level of residual risk that is unacceptable to the organization, the chief audit executive should discuss the matter with senior management. If the decision regarding residual risk is not resolved, the chief audit executive and senior management should report the matter to the board for resolution.

Source: From the *International Standards for the Professional Practice of Internal Auditing*, Copyright © 2004 by The Institute of Internal Auditors, Inc., 247 Maitland Avenue, Altamonte Springs, FL 32701-4201. Reprinted with permission.

Section 5050.) If relied upon, the external auditor is permitted to treat internal auditors much like his or her own audit staff. The incentive for management is a reduced audit fee, whereas the incentive for the public accounting firm is retaining the client. The risk to the external auditor is the lack of competent and independent performance by the internal auditors. Before relying upon internal auditors, the external auditor must be confident of their competence, independence, and objectivity and must know whether there are any constraints placed on the internal audit function that restrict the ability of internal auditors to operate effectively. In addition, external auditors typically review the internal auditors' work to make certain that it was done correctly.

Operational Auditing

Operational auditing—the review of an organization for efficiency and effectiveness. The terms "management auditing," "performance auditing," and "operational auditing" are often used synonymously.

Although **operational auditing** is generally understood to mean the review of an organization for efficiency and effectiveness, there is less agreement on the use of that term than one might expect. Many people prefer to use the terms "**value-for-money auditing**" or "performance auditing" instead of "operational auditing" to describe the review of organizations for efficiency and effectiveness. Those people typically describe operational auditing broadly, including evaluating internal controls and even testing those controls for effectiveness. Others do not distinguish among the terms "performance auditing," "management auditing," and "operational auditing."

Value-for-money auditing—a public sector audit that considers the efficiency and effectiveness with which an entity's operations are conducted; see also "operational auditing."

Differences Between Operational and Financial Auditing

Three major differences exist between operational auditing and financial auditing: the purpose of the audit, the distribution of the reports, and the inclusion of non-financial areas in operational auditing. Due to the breadth of the services offered, many internal auditors provide internal consulting.

PURPOSE OF THE AUDIT The major distinction between financial and operational auditing is the purpose of the tests. Financial auditing emphasizes whether historical information was correctly recorded. Operational auditing emphasizes effectiveness and efficiency. The financial audit is oriented to the past, whereas an operational audit concerns operating performance for the future. An operational auditor, for example, may evaluate whether a type of new material is being purchased at the lowest cost to save money on future raw material purchases.

DISTRIBUTION OF THE REPORTS For financial auditing, the report typically goes to many users of financial statements, such as shareholders and bankers, whereas operational auditing reports are intended primarily for management. As indicated in Chapter 22, well-defined wording is needed for financial auditing reports as a result of their widespread distribution. Because of the limited distribution of operational reports and the diverse nature of audits for efficiency and effectiveness, operational auditing reports vary considerably from audit to audit.

INCLUSION OF NON-FINANCIAL AREAS Operational audits cover any aspect of efficiency and effectiveness in an organization and can therefore involve a wide variety of activities. For example, evaluating the effectiveness of an advertising program or the efficiency of factory employees could be part of an operational audit. Financial audits are limited to matters that directly affect the fairness of financial statement presentation. Operational audits also differ from financial audits in that financial audits are done on an annual basis. Operational audits are done cyclically, in that parts of the organization are audited each year based upon a risk assessment process.

Effectiveness Versus Efficiency

Effectiveness—the degree to which the organization's objectives are achieved.

Efficiency—the degree to which costs are reduced without reducing effectiveness.

Effectiveness refers to the accomplishment of objectives, whereas **efficiency** refers to the resources used to achieve those objectives. An example of effectiveness is the production of parts without defects. Efficiency concerns whether those parts are

Major Changes Seen in Role of Internal Auditors

The control environment of major financial institutions has changed dramatically in the face of shifting regulations, complex financial instruments, technological breakthroughs, and accelerating customer and stockholder demands. Crippling losses resulting from control failures are prompting far-reaching changes in the internal audit function. Some major changes are discussed below.

Tension Between Roles: Traditionally, internal auditors have been the organization's "control conscience," but they are now being asked to provide strategic and operational input. These conflicting roles of both creating and enforcing rules have resulted in tension that must be effectively managed. They also demand new types of skill sets, requiring that auditors have not only technical expertise but also "live" skills such as communication, decision making, and business analysis.

Risk Management: Two major interrelated trends are affecting the area of risk management. One is the need for more audit attention to control operational risk. The second is the movement toward integrated financial risk management, a central component of which is "value at risk"—the potential loss from adverse changes in market factors for a specified period and confidence level. In response, internal auditors plan their audits and link their testing to the risks assessed at the organization under audit.

Electronic Commerce: Conducting financial activity in a "paperless" electronic environment poses a major concern. As reliance on computer networks increases, institutions must design and implement control systems that can adequately manage risk, particularly in areas such as data security and integrity, and vulnerability to viruses. Internal auditors need to be involved early in designing and developing new data systems and products, allowing institutions to build internal controls into new procedures and systems instead of controlling them after the fact.

Sources: 1. Aerts, Luc, "A framework for managing operational risk," *Internal Auditor*, August 2001, p. 53–59. 2. "Major changes seen in role of internal auditors," *Deloitte & Touche Review*, February 5, 1996, p. 2. 3. Pelletier, Jim, "Adding risk back into the audit process," *Internal Auditor*, August 2008, p. 73–77.

---

produced at minimum cost. **Economy**, which may be defined as acquiring goods or services of suitable quality at the best price, is often included with efficiency.

EFFECTIVENESS Before an operational audit for effectiveness can be performed, there must be specific criteria for what is meant by effectiveness. An example of an operational audit for effectiveness would be to assess whether the elevator maintenance department of a hotel chain has met its assigned objective of achieving elevator safety in the chain's many hotels. Before the operational auditor can reach a conclusion about the department's effectiveness, criteria for elevator safety must be set. For example, is the objective to see that all elevators in the chain's hotels are inspected at least once a year? Is the objective to ensure that no fatalities occurred due to elevator breakdowns, or that no breakdowns occurred?

EFFICIENCY As with effectiveness, before operational auditing can be meaningful, there must be defined criteria for what is meant by doing things more efficiently. It is often easier to set efficiency than effectiveness criteria if efficiency is defined as reducing cost without reducing effectiveness. For example, if two different production processes manufacture a product of identical quality, the process with the lower cost is considered more efficient.

Table 24-1 on the next page outlines several types of inefficiencies that frequently occur and often are uncovered through operational auditing.

RELATIONSHIP BETWEEN OPERATIONAL AUDITING AND INTERNAL CONTROLS In Chapter 9, it was stated that management establishes internal controls to help it meet its own goals. Certainly, two important goals of all organizations are efficiency and effectiveness. The following four concerns in setting up good internal controls were identified and discussed in Chapter 9:

- Maintain reliable systems.
- Safeguard assets including records.
- Optimize the use of resources.
- Prevent and detect error and fraud.

Economy—the degree to which goods and services of suitable quality are acquired at the lowest price.

Table 24-1	Types of Inefficiencies	
Types of Inefficiency	**Example**	
Acquisition of goods and services is excessively costly.	Bids for purchases of materials are not required.	
Raw materials are not available for production when needed.	An entire assembly line must be shut down because necessary materials were not ordered.	
There is duplication of effort by employees.	Identical production records are kept by both the accounting and production departments because they are unaware of each other's activities.	
Work that serves no purpose is being carried out.	Copies of vendor's invoices and receiving reports are sent to the production department where they are filed without ever being used.	

Each of these four concerns can be part of operational auditing if the purpose is to achieve efficient and effective operations. For example, reliable cost accounting information is important to management in deciding such things as which products to continue and the selling price of products. Similarly, failure to safeguard assets such as accounts receivable files on a computer could result in the company being unable to collect money owing when it is due.

There are two significant differences in internal control evaluation and testing for financial and operational auditing: (1) the purpose of the evaluation and testing of internal controls, and (2) the normal scope of internal control evaluation.

The primary purpose of internal control evaluation for financial auditing is to determine the extent of substantive audit testing required. The purpose of operational auditing is to evaluate efficiency and effectiveness of internal control and make recommendations to management. Although control procedures might be evaluated in the same way for both financial and operational auditing, their purposes differ. To illustrate, an operational auditor might determine if internal verification procedures for duplicate sales invoices are effective to ensure that the company does not offend customers but also receives all money owed. A financial auditor often does the same internal control evaluation, but the primary purpose is to reduce confirmation of accounts receivable or other substantive procedures. A secondary purpose, however, of many financial audits is to make operational recommendations to management.

The scope of internal control evaluation for financial audits is restricted to matters affecting the financial statements, whereas operational auditing concerns any control affecting efficiency or effectiveness based on risks. Therefore, for example, an operational audit could be concerned with policies and procedures established in the marketing department to determine the effectiveness of catalogues used to market products.

Who Performs Operational Audits?

Operational audits are usually performed by one of three groups: internal auditors, government auditors, or consulting firms.

INTERNAL AUDITORS Many internal audit departments do both operational and financial audits as well as compliance audits. Often, operational and financial audits are done simultaneously. An advantage that internal auditors have in doing operational audits is that they spend all their time working for the company they are auditing. They thereby develop considerable knowledge about the company and its business, which is essential to effective operational auditing.

To maximize their effectiveness, the internal audit department staff should report to the audit committee of the board of directors. This organizational structure helps internal auditors remain independent. For example, if internal auditors report to the controller, it is difficult for them to evaluate independently and make recommendations to senior management about inefficiencies in the controller's operations.

Government Auditors

The Auditor General offices conduct both financial statement audits where mandated by legislation (e.g., for Crown corporations and government financial statements) and program (or operational) audits at government departments, universities, school boards, and other government-funded institutions such as hospitals and municipal governments. They are also given resources to subcontract the financial or program audits to public accounting or consulting firms.

There are other auditors employed by governments, such as Canada Revenue Agency auditors and provincial tax auditors. However, the discussion in this chapter focuses on government auditors who do operational and financial statement audits.

PUBLIC ACCOUNTING FIRMS When public accounting firms do an audit of historical financial statements, part of the audit usually consists of identifying operational problems and making recommendations that may benefit the audit client. The recommendations can be made orally, but they are typically made by use of a management letter. Management letters were discussed in Chapter 21.

The understanding of a client's operations that an external auditor must obtain in doing an audit often provides information useful for giving operational recommendations. For example, suppose the auditor found that inventory turnover for a client slowed considerably during the current year. The auditor is likely to determine the cause of the reduction to evaluate the possibility of obsolete inventory that would misstate the financial statements. In determining the cause of the reduced inventory turnover, the auditor may identify operational causes, such as ineffective inventory acquisition policies, that can be brought to the attention of management. An auditor who has a broad business background and experience with similar businesses is more likely to be effective at providing clients with relevant operational recommendations than a person who lacks those qualities.

Independence and Competence of Operational Auditors

The two most important qualities for an operational auditor are independence and competence.

auditing in action 24-2
Examining the Issuance of Passports and Border Security

The Auditor General of Canada reported in 2004 with respect to various initiatives that affected Canada's national security. One of the points raised in the report was the inability of the passport office to provide accurate and timely data in "watch lists," lists of individuals who were suspected terrorists or who were wanted for criminal activities.

The 2005 report expanded on these findings. The passport office does meet targeted performance levels for its clients, balancing cost, service, and security of new passports issued. The issuance of passports is a large part of the service provided by this office (98 percent). However, reliable cost information is absent, which makes it difficult to assess the cost of the new security demands (e.g., digital photographs). This 2005 report repeated that the watch lists were out of date because the passport office is unable to obtain data in electronic form from other government offices.

Not only passports but also physical goods require greater attention. In continuing to focus on security in 2007, the Auditor General's staff found that potentially dangerous people and goods were entering Canada. There are criteria to determine which people and products should be further examined at the border, but apparently about 13 percent of containers and about 21 percent of persons identified as high risk were not further examined (in the period under audit, January through March 2007).

Sources: 1. Brennan, Richard, "Border security flawed, auditor reports," *Toronto Star*, October 31, 2007, p. A5. 2. "National security in Canada—The 2001 anti-terrorism initiative," Report of the Auditor General of Canada to the House of Commons, 2004, Chapter 3. 3. "Passport office—passport services," Report of the Auditor General of Canada to the House of Commons, 2005, Chapter 3.

To ensure that investigation and recommendations are made without bias, whom the auditor reports to is important. Independence is evaluated by auditors in public accounting firms using threat analysis (see Chapter 3) and is normally considered good because they are not directly employed by the organization being audited. As stated earlier, independence of internal auditors is enhanced by having the internal audit department report to the audit committee. Similarly, government auditors should report to a level above the operating departments. The Auditor General of Canada, for example, reports to an all-party committee of Parliament as a means of enhancing independence.

The responsibilities of operational auditors can also affect their independence. The auditor should not be responsible for performing operating functions in a company or for correcting deficiencies when ineffective or inefficient operations are found. For example, it would negatively affect their independence if auditors were responsible for designing an automated information system for acquisitions or for correcting it if deficiencies were found during an audit of the acquisitions system.

It is acceptable for auditors to recommend changes in operations, but operating personnel must have the authority to accept or reject the recommendations. If auditors had the authority to require implementation of their recommendations, they would actually have the responsibility for auditing their own work the next time an audit was conducted. Independence would therefore be reduced.

The Institute of Internal Auditors considers independence of internal auditors critical and has guidelines for independence as part of its attribute standards. International standards specific to government auditors are available from International Standards of Supreme Audit Organizations (**www.issai.org**), which also stresses the importance of organizational independence of government auditors.

Competence is, of course, necessary to determine the cause of operational problems and to make appropriate recommendations. Competence is a major issue when operational auditing deals with wide-ranging operating problems. For example, imagine the difficulties of finding qualified internal auditors who can evaluate both the effectiveness of an advertising program and the efficiency of a production assembly process. The internal audit staff doing that type of operational auditing would presumably have to include some personnel with backgrounds in marketing and others with backgrounds in production.

Criteria for Evaluating Efficiency and Effectiveness

A major difficulty found in operational auditing, as with assurance services discussed in Chapter 23, is determining specific criteria for evaluating whether operations have been efficient and effective. In auditing historical financial statements, GAAP, international financial reporting standards (IFRS), are the broad criteria for evaluating fair presentation. Audit objectives are used to set more specific criteria in deciding whether GAAP have been followed. In operational auditing, no such well-defined criteria exist.

One approach to setting criteria for operational auditing is stating that the objectives are to determine whether some aspect of the entity could be made more effective or efficient, and to recommend improvements. While perhaps adequate for experienced and well-trained auditors, this poorly defined approach would be difficult for most auditors to follow.

SPECIFIC CRITERIA More specific criteria are usually desirable before operational auditing is started. The auditor considers risks when setting such criteria. For example, suppose you are doing an operational audit of the equipment layout in plants for a company to address the issues of quality control and efficient production. The following are some specific criteria, stated in the form of questions, that might be used to evaluate plant layouts:

- Were all plant layouts approved by home office engineering at the time of original design?

- Has home office engineering done a re-evaluation study of plant layout in the past five years?
- Is each piece of equipment operating at 60 percent of capacity or more for at least three months each year?
- Does the layout facilitate the movement of new materials to the production flow?
- Does the layout facilitate the production of finished goods?
- Does the layout facilitate the movement of finished goods to distribution centres?
- Does the plant layout effectively utilize existing equipment?
- Is the safety of employees endangered by the plant layout?

SOURCES OF CRITERIA There are several sources that the operational auditor can utilize in developing specific evaluation criteria. These include the following:

Historical performance A simple set of criteria can be based on actual results from prior periods (or audits). The idea behind using these criteria is to determine whether things have become better or worse in comparison. The advantage of these criteria is that they are easy to derive; however, they may not provide much insight into how well or poorly the audited entity is really doing.

Benchmarking Most entities subject to an operational audit are not unique; there are many similar entities within the overall organization or outside it. In those cases, the performance data of comparable entities are an excellent source for developing criteria for benchmarking. For internal comparable entities, the data are usually readily available. When the comparable entities are outside the organization, they are often willing to make such information available. It is also often available through industry groups and governmental regulatory agencies.

Engineered standards In many types of operational auditing engagements, it may be possible and appropriate to develop criteria based on engineered standards—for example, time and motion studies to determine production output rates. These criteria are often time-consuming and costly to develop as they require considerable expertise; however, they may be very effective in solving a major operational problem and well worth the cost. It is also possible that some standards can be developed by industry groups for use by all their members, thereby spreading the cost and reducing it for each participant. These groups may be within the industry of the subject organization or may be functional, such as an application system's users' organization.

Published standards or criteria There are ISO (International Organization for Standardization) standards for a variety of management processes such as quality control management and environmental management. Published best practices for the development of automated information systems are available from the Software Engineering Institute (SEI, **www.sei.cmu.edu**) at Carnegie Mellon University.

Discussion and agreement Sometimes objective criteria are difficult or costly to obtain, and criteria are developed through simple discussion and agreement. The parties involved in this process should include management of the entity to be audited, the operational auditor, and the entity or persons to whom the findings will be reported.

concept check

C24-3 What is the purpose of operational audit criteria?

C24-4 What are the advantages and disadvantages of developing operational audit criteria by means of discussion and agreement with the audit client?

❸ The Operational Audit Process

Phases in Operational Auditing

There are three phases in an operational audit: (1) planning, (2) evidence accumulation and evaluation, and (3) reporting and follow-up.

PLANNING The planning in an operational audit is similar to that discussed in earlier chapters for an audit of historical financial statements. Like auditors of financial statements, the operational auditor must determine the scope of the engagement, assess risks, and communicate with the organizational unit. It is also necessary to staff the engagement properly, obtain background information about the organizational unit, understand internal control, and decide on the appropriate evidence to accumulate.

The major difference between planning an operational audit and planning a financial audit is the extreme diversity in operational audits. Because of this diversity, it is often difficult to determine specific objectives of an operational audit. The objectives will be based on the criteria developed for the engagement. As discussed in the preceding sections, these will depend on the specific circumstances at hand. For example, the objectives for an operational audit of the effectiveness of internal controls over petty cash would be dramatically different from those of an operational audit of the efficiency of a research and development department.

Another difference is that staffing is often more complicated in an operational audit than in a financial audit. This, again, is because of the breadth of the engagements. Not only are the areas diverse—for example, production control, advertising, and strategy planning—but the objectives within those areas also often require special technical skills. For example, the auditor may need an engineering background to evaluate performance on a major construction project.

Finally, it is important to spend more time with the interested parties reaching consensus on the terms of the engagement and the criteria for evaluation in an operational audit than in a financial audit. Regardless of the source of the criteria for evaluation, it is essential that the auditee, the auditor, and the sponsor of the engagement (e.g., the audit committee) be in clear and complete agreement on the objectives and criteria involved. This agreement will facilitate effective and successful completion of the operational audit.

EVIDENCE ACCUMULATION AND EVALUATION The seven types of evidence studied in Chapter 6 and used throughout the book are equally applicable to operational auditing. Because internal controls and operating procedures are a critical part of operational auditing, it is common to extensively use documentation, client inquiry, and observation. Confirmation and reperformance are used less extensively for most operational audits.

To illustrate evidence accumulation in operational auditing, we return to the example discussed earlier about evaluating the safety of elevators for a chain of hotels. Assume there is agreement that the objective is to determine whether an inspection is made annually of each elevator in every hotel in the chain by a competent inspector. To satisfy the completeness objective, the auditor would, for example, examine blueprints of the hotel buildings and elevator locations and trace them to the head office's master list to ensure that all elevators are included in the population. Additional tests on newly constructed hotels would be appropriate to assess the timeliness with which the central listing is updated.

Assuming that the head office list is determined to be complete, the auditor can select a sample of elevator locations and evidence can be collected as to the timing and frequency of inspections. The auditor may want to consider inherent risk by doing heavier sampling of older elevators with previous safety defects. The auditor may also want to examine evidence to determine whether the elevator inspectors were competent to evaluate elevator safety. The auditor may, for example, evaluate inspectors' qualifications by reviewing résumés, training programs, competency exams, and performance reports. It is likely that the auditor would want to reperform the inspection procedures for a sample of elevators to obtain evidence of inconsistencies in reported and actual conditions.

In the same manner as for financial audits, operational auditors must accumulate sufficient appropriate evidence to afford a reasonable basis for a conclusion about the objectives being tested. In the elevator example, the auditor must accumulate sufficient evidence about elevator safety inspections. After the evidence is accumulated, the auditor must decide whether it is reasonable to conclude that an annual inspection is made by a competent inspector of each elevator in each hotel owned by the chain.

REPORTING AND FOLLOW-UP Two major differences between operational and financial auditing reports affect operational auditing reports. First, in operational audits, the report is usually sent only to management and to the audit committee, with a copy to the unit being audited. The lack of third-party users reduces the need for standardized wording in operational auditing reports. Second, the diversity of operational audits requires a tailoring of each report to address the scope and objectives of the audit, findings, and recommendations.

The combination of these two factors results in major differences in operational auditing reports. Report writing often requires a significant amount of time to communicate audit findings and recommendations clearly, particularly as management responses or action plans to address the auditor's recommendations are included in the report.

Follow-up is important in operational auditing when recommendations are made to management. The purpose of follow-up is to determine whether management has implemented the actions that it said it would: Have the recommended changes been made, and if not, why?

Examples of Operational Audit Findings

A broad variety of documents discussing existing internal audits and operational audits is generally available. Often, these articles show up as "how to" articles where internal auditors take the experience gained during audits and share this experience with the broader community.

The *Internal Auditor* is a bimonthly publication of the Institute of Internal Auditors. Following is a selection of recent articles:

- *Making Integrated Audits Reality*, by Anita Helpert and John Lazarine (April 2009). This article looks at the conduct of audits, and how manual-based and information technology–based teams can integrate their work, with the experience at Raytheon Inc. as the focus.
- A *Risk-Centric Approach That Works*, by Daniel Clayton (February 2009). Clayton uses the experiences of a health-care audit group to explain how risk assessment can be integrated into the conduct of operational audits.
- *Elementary Fraud*, by Andrew Medina (February 2009). An office manager of an elementary school stole $15,000 using several different fraud schemes, which were detailed by an internal auditor who discovered the fraud during a surprise cash count.
- *The Risk of Rogues*, by Louis Slifker, Jr. (December 2008). Slifker was an internal auditor who helped itemize the extent of the US$691 million fraud at Allfirst Financial executed by John Rusnak. Slifker uses that experience to analyze controls over trading and to discuss the US$6.2 million fraud at the Société Générale Bank in France.
- *Entity-Level Controls*, by Jaap Gerkes, Wilbert JanVan Der Werf, and Heiko Ven Der Wijk (October 2007). Using examples from several large Dutch corporations, the authors provide a framework for examining and auditing entity-level controls, with several detailed examples.

Auditor General reports are available at the following websites:

- Canada: **www.oag-bvg.gc.ca** (also the Auditor General for Northwest, Nunavut, and Yukon Territories)
- Alberta: **www.oag.ab.ca**
- British Columbia: **www.bcauditor.com**
- Manitoba: **www.oag.mb.ca**
- New Brunswick: **www.gnb.ca/oag-bvg/index-e.asp**
- Newfoundland and Labrador: **www.ag.gov.nl.ca/ag/**
- Nova Scotia: **www.gov.ns.ca/audg/**
- Ontario: **www.auditor.on.ca**
- Prince Edward Island: **www.assembly.pe.ca/auditorgeneral/index.php**
- Quebec: **www.vgq.gouv.qc.ca/default-EN.aspx**
- Saskatchewan: **www.auditor.sk.ca**

The Auditor General reports cover a broad range of diverse audits. As these reports are public, you can see the risk assessments, objectives of the audit, how the audit was conducted, and the findings in great detail. For example, the spring 2009 Annual Report of the Office of the Auditor of Canada (May 2009) has seven value-for-money (operational or program) audits. The topics are diverse, including gender-based analysis to support pay equality obligations, health and safety in federal office buildings, and financial management and control of national defence spending. The Auditor General of Canada also publishes an annual status report that follows up prior audits to assess whether recommendations have been acted upon. For example, in March 2009, the Status Report considered seven prior audits. Five were considered as having made satisfactory progress, while unsatisfactory process was described for two of the audits: (1) Governor in Council Appointments Process and (2) Auditing Small and Medium Enterprises—Canada Revenue Agency.

This follow-up is important for all types of auditors. Management, the audit committee, or the legislature is concerned that operations are handled effectively.

concept check

C24-5 What are the major differences between planning an operational audit and planning a financial statement audit?

C24-6 Why are operational audit reports more difficult to prepare than financial statement audit reports?

Summary

1. *What is the role of internal auditing in many organizations?* Internal auditors help improve an organization's operations—they perform operational auditing, systems development auditing, and fraud auditing and provide assistance with the financial statement audit.

   What are the key differences between operational auditing and financial auditing? The differences are driven by the objectives. The results of a financial statement audit are an opinion on the financial statements, whereas operational audits are based upon the risks and criteria for that particular audit, normally related to effectiveness or efficiency.

   Provide an example of an audit criterion associated with each of effectiveness and efficiency. Effectiveness: Are the elevators adequately maintained to ensure safety of passengers? Efficiency: Are raw materials purchased at the best quality for the best possible price?

2. *How are the functions of an Auditor General office different from those of an internal audit office?* An Auditor General office also conducts financial statement audits, which are outside the scope of an internal audit office.

   How is independence facilitated for government and internal auditors? Government auditors report to an all-party legislative group or to the legislature. Internal auditors report to the audit committee to help improve independence.

   What are some sources of criteria for conducting an operational audit? Criteria can be obtained based upon historical performance, from benchmarking with comparable organizations, from engineered or published standards, or from discussion and agreement with the clients.

3. *List the phases in operational auditing.* The phases are planning, evidence accumulation and evaluation, and reporting and follow-up.

   Where can one find sample reports of value-for-money audits? Publicly available operational audit reports (also known as value-for-money reports) can be obtained from the websites of the Auditors General for Canada and the provinces. Information about results of operational audits can also be obtained from written publications such as the *Internal Auditor* journal.

Visit the text's website at www.pearsoned.ca/arens for practice quizzes, additional case studies, and international standards information.

Review Questions

24-1 Explain the role of internal auditors for financial auditing. How is it similar to and different from the role of external auditors?

24-2 Explain the difference in the independence of internal auditors and external auditors in the audit of historical financial statements. How can internal auditors best achieve independence?

24-3 Describe what is meant by an "operational audit."

24-4 Identify the three major differences between financial and operational auditing.

24-5 Distinguish between efficiency and effectiveness in operational audits. State one example of an operational audit examining efficiency and another examining effectiveness.

24-6 Identify the four concerns that management has in establishing internal controls. Explain how each of those four concerns can be part of operational auditing.

24-7 Explain why many people think of internal auditors as the primary group responsible for conducting operational audits.

24-8 Explain the role of public accountants in operational auditing. How is this similar to and different from the role of internal auditors?

24-9 Under what circumstances are external auditors likely to be involved in operational auditing? Give one example of operational auditing by a public accounting firm.

24-10 Explain what is meant by the "criteria for evaluating efficiency and effectiveness." Provide five possible specific criteria for evaluating effectiveness of an automated information system for payroll.

24-11 Identify the three phases of an operational audit.

24-12 Explain how planning for operational auditing is similar to and different from that for financial auditing.

24-13 What are the major differences between reporting for operational auditing and reporting for financial auditing?

24-14 Explain why the Auditor General of Canada performs value-for-money audits rather than simply performing financial audits of the various government departments.

Discussion Questions and Problems

24-15 Lajod Ltd. has an internal audit department consisting of a manager and three staff auditors. The manager of internal audit reports to the corporate controller. Copies of audit reports are routinely sent to the audit committee of the board of directors as well as to the corporate controller and the individual responsible for the area or activity being audited.

The manager of internal audit is aware that the external auditors have relied on the internal audit function to a substantial degree in the past. However, in recent months, the external auditors have suggested that there may be a problem related to objectivity of the internal audit function. This objectivity problem may result in more extensive testing and analysis by the external auditors.

The external auditors are concerned about the amount of non-audit work performed by the internal audit department. The percentage of non-audit work performed by the internal auditors in recent years has increased to about 25 percent of their total hours worked. A sample of five recent non-audit activities are as follows:

1. One of the internal auditors assisted in the preparation of policy statements on internal control. These statements included such things as policies regarding sensitive payments and standards of internal controls.

2. The bank statements of the corporation are reconciled each month as a regular assignment for one of the internal auditors. The corporate controller believes that this strengthens internal controls because the internal auditor is not involved in the receipt and disbursement of cash.

3. The internal auditors are asked to review the budget data in every area each year for relevance and reasonableness before the budget is approved. In addition, an internal auditor examines the variances each month, along with

the associated explanations. These variance analyses are prepared by the corporate controller's staff after consultation with the individuals involved.

4. One of the internal auditors has recently been involved in the design, installation, and initial operation of a new computer system. The auditor was concerned primarily with the design and implementation of internal accounting controls and the computer application controls for the new system. The auditor also conducted the testing of the controls during the test runs.

5. The internal auditors are frequently asked to make accounting entries for complex transactions before the transactions are recorded. The employees in the accounting department are not adequately trained to handle such transactions. In addition, this serves as a means of maintaining internal control over complex transactions.

REQUIRED

a. Define "objectivity" as it relates to the internal audit function.

b. For each of the five situations outlined, explain whether the objectivity of Lajod Ltd.'s internal audit department has been materially impaired. Consider each situation independently.

c. The manager of internal audit reports to the corporate controller.
   (1) Does this reporting relationship result in a problem of objectivity? Explain your answer.
   (2) Would your answer to any of the five situations in requirement (b) have changed if the manager of internal audit reported to the audit committee of the board of directors? Explain your answer.

(Adapted from CMA)

24-16 Superior Co. manufactures automobile parts for sale to the major U.S. automakers. Superior's internal audit staff is to review the internal controls over machinery and equipment and make recommendations for improvements where appropriate. The internal auditors obtained the following information during the assignment:

- Requests for purchase of machinery and equipment are normally initiated by the supervisor in need of the asset. The supervisor discusses the proposed acquisition with the plant manager. A purchase requisition is submitted to the purchasing department when the plant manager is satisfied that the request is reasonable and that there is a remaining balance in the plant's share of the total corporate budget for capital acquisitions.

- Upon receiving a purchase requisition for machinery or equipment, the purchasing department manager looks through the records for an appropriate supplier. A formal purchase order is then completed and mailed. When the machine or equipment is received, it is immediately sent to the user department for installation. This allows the economic benefits of the acquisition to be realized at the earliest possible date.

- The property, plant, and equipment ledger control accounts are supported by lapse schedules organized by year of acquisition. These lapse schedules are used to compute depreciation as a unit for all assets of a given type that are acquired in the same year. Standard rates, amortization methods, and salvage values are used for each major type of capital assets. These rates, methods, and salvage values were set 10 years ago during the company's initial year of operation.

- When machinery or equipment is retired, the plant manager notifies the accounting department so that the appropriate entries can be made in the accounting records.

- There has been no reconciliation since the company began operations between the accounting records and the machinery and equipment on hand.

REQUIRED

Identify the internal control weaknesses, and recommend improvements that the internal audit staff of Superior Co. should include in its report regarding the internal controls over capital assets. Use the following format in preparing your answer:

Weaknesses	Recommendations
1.	1.

24-17 Haskin Inc. was founded 40 years ago and now has several manufacturing plants in Central and Western Canada. The evaluation of proposed capital expenditures became increasingly difficult for management as the company became geographically dispersed and diversified its product line. Therefore, the Capital Budgeting Group was organized in 2000 to review all capital expenditure proposals in excess of $50,000.

The Capital Budgeting Group conducts its annual planning and budget meeting each September for the upcoming calendar year. The group establishes a minimum return for investments (hurdle rate) and estimates a target level of capital expenditures for the next year based on the expected available funds. The group then reviews the capital expenditure proposals that have been submitted by the various operating segments. Proposals that meet either the return-on-investment criterion or a critical-need criterion are approved to the extent of available funds.

The Capital Budgeting Group also meets monthly, as necessary, to consider any projects of a critical nature that were not expected or requested in the annual budget review. These monthly meetings allow the Capital Budgeting Group to make adjustments during the year as new developments occur.

Haskin's profits have been decreasing slightly for the past two years in spite of a small but steady sales growth, a sales growth that is expected to continue through 2010. As a result of profit stagnation, top management is emphasizing cost control, and all aspects of Haskin's operations are being reviewed for cost reduction opportunities.

Haskin's internal audit department has become involved in the company-wide cost reduction effort. The department has already identified several areas where cost reductions could be realized and has made recommendations to implement the necessary procedures to effect the cost savings. Tom Watson, internal audit director, is now focusing on the activities of the Capital Budgeting Group in an attempt to determine the efficiency and effectiveness of the capital budgeting process.

In an attempt to gain a better understanding of the capital budgeting process, Watson decided to examine the history of one capital project in detail. A capital expenditure proposal of Haskin's Regina plant that was approved by the Capital Budgeting Group in 2008 was selected randomly from a population of all proposals approved by the group at its 2007 and 2008 annual planning and budget meetings.

The Regina proposal consisted of a request for five new machines to replace 20-year-old equipment, for which preventive maintenance had become very expensive. Four of the machines were for replacement purposes, and the fifth was for planned growth in demand. Each of the four replacement machines was expected to result in annual maintenance cost savings of $10,000. The fifth machine was exactly like the other four and was expected to generate an annual contribution of $15,000 through increased output. Each machine cost $50,000 and had an estimated useful life of eight years.

REQUIRED

a. Identify and discuss the issues that Haskin Inc.'s internal audit department must address in its examination and evaluation of the Regina plant's 2008 capital expenditure project.

b. Recommend procedures to be used by Haskin's internal audit department in the audit review of the Regina plant's 2008 capital expenditure project.

(Adapted from CMA)

Professional Judgment Problem

24-18 Projections indicated that there would be record numbers of homeless over the next few years, so the city decided that it was important to make shelters available. Accordingly, contracts were signed with two hotels in the downtown area over a three-year period. The hotels committed to have rooms available in the two coldest months of the year, and the city agreed to pay for the rooms at the rate of $40 per night. The hotel rooms were intended for homeless families.

At the same time, local churches got together and arranged to have volunteers staff the churches and provide hot meals so that the churches could be used as shelters by single individuals. The result was that the hotel rooms were not used, and over a period of three years, the city paid almost $850,000 for empty rooms. This was publicized when the Auditor General for the city published his annual report.

REQUIRED

a. What objectives and criteria would the city Auditor General have used when conducting his audit of expenditures for the homeless?
b. Draft a section of the value-for-money report that would explain how the audit was conducted as well as the findings.
c. What recommendations for improvement might be included in the audit report?

Case

24-19 Mont Louis Hospital, which is affiliated with a leading university, has an extremely reputable research department that employs several renowned scientists. The research department operates on a project basis. The department consists of a pool of scientists and technicians who can be called upon to participate in a given project. Assignments are made for the duration of the project, and a project manager is given responsibility for the work.

All major projects undertaken by the research department must be approved by the hospital's administrative board. Approval is obtained by submitting a proposal to the board outlining the project, the expected amount of time required to complete the work, and the anticipated benefits. The board also must be informed of major projects that are terminated because of potential failure or technological changes that have occurred since the time of project approval. An overall review of the status of open projects is submitted to the board annually.

In many respects, profit-making techniques utilized by business firms are applied to the management of the research department. For example, the department conducts preliminary research work on potential major projects that it has selected prior to requesting the board to approve the project and commit large amounts of time and money. The department also assesses the potential for grants for and future revenues of the project. Financial reports for the department and each project are prepared periodically and reviewed with the administrative board.

Over 75 percent of the cost of operating the department is for labour. The remaining costs are for materials utilized during research. Materials used for experimentation are purchased by the hospital's central purchasing department. Once these materials are delivered, the research department is held accountable for their storage, their utilization, and the assignment of their costs to the projects.

In order to protect the hospital's right to discoveries made by the research department, staff members are required to sign waiver agreements at the time of hire and at certain intervals thereafter. The agreements relinquish the employees' rights to patent and royalty fees relating to hospital work.

The excellent reputation of Mont Louis is due, in part, to the success of the research department. The research department has produced quality research in the health-care field and has always been able to generate revenues in excess of its costs. The administrative auditing board believes that the hospital's continued reputation depends on a strong research department, and therefore the board has requested that the university's internal auditors perform an operational audit of the department. As part of its request for the operational audit, the board has presented a set of objectives that the internal audit is to achieve.

The operational audit to be conducted by the university's internal audit department should provide assurances as follows:

- The research department has assessed the revenues and cost aspects of each project to confirm that the revenue potential is equal to or greater than estimated costs.

- Appropriate controls exist to provide a means to measure how projects are progressing and to determine if corrective actions are required.

- Financial reports prepared by the research department for presentation to the administrative board properly reflect all revenues (both endowment and royalty sources and appropriated funding) and all costs.

REQUIRED

a. Evaluate the objectives presented by the administrative board to the university's internal audit department in terms of their appropriateness as objectives for an operational audit. Fully discuss the following:
   (1) The strengths of the objectives.
   (2) The modifications and/or additions needed to improve the set of objectives.
b. Outline, in general terms, the basic procedures that would be suitable for performing the audit of the research department.
c. Identify three documents that members of the university's internal auditing staff would be expected to review during the audit, and describe the purpose that the review of each document serves in carrying out the audit.

(Adapted from CMA)

Index

Note: *f* indicates a figure, *t* indicates a table, *n* indicates a note

A

absence
  of causal connection, 85–86, 90–91
  of misstatement, 83, 90
  of negligence, 85
AC Group, 26
acceptability of population, 432–433, 484–485
acceptable risk of assessing control risk too low
    (ARACR), 423–426, 424t, 425t, 432
acceptable risk of incorrect acceptance (ARIA), 424t,
    425–426, 426t, 427t
access controls, 300, 339
access rights change form, 571
access rights management, 570–572
  access rights change form, 571
  code of conduct statement, 571
  described, 570–571
  employee rights approval form, 571
  importance of, 570–571
  internal controls, 571–572
account balances
  analysis of, 630
  entity-level controls, 339–340
  internal controls, 471–472
accountants. *See* professional accountants (PAs);
    public accountants
accounting
  see also professional accountants
  attestation services, 9–11
  vs auditing, 5–7, 8
  bookkeeping services, 13
  compilations, 12
  defined, 6
  estimates, review of, 365
  generally accepted accounting principles, 6
  management advisory services, 12
  practice of, 56
  separation of duties, 280–281
  tax services, 12
  unique requirements, 244
"Accounting and Auditing Enforcement Releases"
    (SEC), 40
accounting and auditing standards
  audit sampling, 427
  auditing organizations, 15–16
  Canadian Auditing Standards (CASs), 8, 29, 36–37
  changes in, 8, 29
  financial reporting frameworks, 8, 32, 109
  general standards of quality control, 39
  generally accepted auditing standards, 34–36
  International Financial Reporting Standards
    (IFRS), 315–316
  international standards, 37–38, 315–316
  published standards or criteria, 771
  qualifications, 35–36
  quality control, 38–43
  standards for the practice of internal auditing,
    764–765, 765f
  in the U.S., 36–37
accounting control activities, 279–280
accounting firm surveys, 27
accounting information and communication system,
    283–284
accounting organizations. *See* professional
    accounting/auditing organizations
accounting principles, shopping for, 61–62
accounting systems
  control activities, 279–280, 279t
  defined, 279
  general controls and, 278t
  understanding, 288
accounts payable
  analytical procedures, 609, 609t
  balance-related audit objectives, 609, 610t
  confirmation request, 613f
  cutoff tests, 611–612
  described, 607

existence, 135
fraud risks, 371
internal controls, 608–609
methodology for designing tests of details of
    balances, 608, 608f
out-of-period liability tests, 610–611
reliability of evidence, 612–614
sample size, 614–615
substantive testing of, 607–614
systems conversions, 605–607
tests of details, 609–610, 610t
accounts payable trial balance, 599
accounts receivable
  accuracy of, 505
  aged trial balance, 507, 507f
  agreement with customer master file and general
    ledger, 507–508
  allowance for uncollectible accounts, 505–506
  bad-debt expense, 506
  balance-related audit objectives, 499–502
  classification of, 506–507
  client's rights to, 505
  confirmation decisions, 512–517
  confirmation of, 510–512
  correct addition of, 507–508
  cutoff for, 508–509
  cutoff misstatements, 508
  detail tic-in, 507–508
  disclosure-related audit objectives, 499
  existence of recorded receivables, 505
  fraud. *See* revenue and accounts receivable fraud
  lapping of accounts receivable, 471
  presentation and disclosures, 509–510
  tests of details of balances. *See* tests of details of
    balances for accounts receivable
  timing difference (in accounts receivable
    confirmation), 509
  trial balance, 451
  typical information in data sales, 447t
  uncollectible accounts receivable, 453
  valid, inclusion of, 505
  valuation, 505–506
accounts receivable audit case illustration, 517–529
  acceptable risk of incorrect acceptance
    (ARIA), 521
  adjusted misstatement bound, calculating,
    526–527, 528t
  adjustment for offsetting amounts, 526–527
  adjustment misstatement bounds with offsetting
    amounts, calculating, 528t
  analysis of misstatements, 527–528
  analytical procedures, 518t
  appropriate percent of misstatement
    assumption, 524–525
  assumption re: average percent of misstatement,
    521–522
  assumptions, 524–525
  assumptions and facts for accounts receivable
    sample, 522t
  audit procedures, performance of, 523
  balance-related audit objectives, 520t
  estimated population exception rate, 521
  evidence planning spreadsheet, 518f
  generalization, misstatements found, 525–526, 525t
  generalization, no misstatements found, 523–525
  generalization, sample to population, 523–529
  judgmental sampling, 529
  materiality, 520–521
  misstatement bounds, calculating, 525–526, 527t
  misstatements bounds, percent, 526t
  monetary unit sampling, use of, 519–529
  objectives, 519
  overview of, 517–519
  population, 519
  population, acceptability of, 527–529
  population, rejection of, 529
  sample selection, 523

sample size calculation, 522t
sampling, applicability of, 519
sampling unit, 519
selected comparative information, 517t
tainting, 521
tests of details of balances audit program, 521t
accounts receivable balance-related audit objectives,
    499–502, 501f
accounts receivable disclosure-related audit
    objectives, 499
accounts receivable turnover, 192f
accrued benefits, 585
accrued bonuses, 585
accrued commissions, 584
accrued liabilities, 626–627
accrued payroll expenses, 582–583
accrued property taxes, 627–628, 627f
accrued salaries and wages, 583–584
accrued sick pay, 585
accrued warranty costs, 627
accumulated amortization, 622
accuracy
  of accounts receivable, 505
  acquisitions, 602
  audit objective, cheque printing application, 340
  capital stock audit, 679
  dividend declaration, 680
  general balance-related audit objective, 138
  general transaction-related audit objective, 137
  management assertions, 134
  prepaid insurance, 626
achieved audit risk, 230–231
achieved detection risk, 231
acquisition and payment cycle
  accounting information flows, 595, 596f
  accounts in, 595, 596f, 615
  accounts payable. *See* accounts payable
  accrued liabilities, 626–628
  audit tests, types of, 614f
  business function, 597t
  capital assets, 615
  cash disbursements, processing and recording, 600
  defined, 595
  goods and services, receipt of, 597–598
  and inventory and warehousing cycle, 659, 659f
  liability recognition, 598–600
  manufacturing assets acquisition, 615–622
  misstatements, 542
  nature of, 595–600
  operations audit, 628–631
  prepaid assets and intangibles, 622–626
  purchase orders, processing of, 595–597
  purchase requisition, 595–596
  receiving report, 597–598
  related documents and records, 597t
  related-party transactions, 632
  systems conversions, 605–607
  tests of controls for sales, 600–605
  transaction classes, 597t
acquisitions
  accuracy, 602
  classification, 602
  completeness, 602
  occurrence, 602
  verification of, 602, 603t
acquisitions journal, 598
adhocracy, 316, 318t
adjusting entries, 256–257
adjustments
  to customer accounts, 369
  to financial statements, 364–365
  prior-period adjustments, 680
  to revenues, 368
  summary of possible adjustments, 702
advanced information systems
  and audit phases, 329, 330t
  and the audit process, 329–336

Chung, Andrew, 324*n*
CIBC's Amicus unit, 172
CICA. *See* Canadian Institute of Chartered
    Accountants (CICA)
CICA Accounting Handbook, 315
CICA Assurance Handbook, 29
    see also CICA Handbook
CICA Handbook
    see also CICA Standards
    Assurance and Related Services Guidelines, 31
    Assurance Recommendations, 30, 34
    adherence to ethical standards, 32
    auditing requirements, 33–34
    auditor qualifications, 33
    auditor statutory rights and responsibilities, 33
    described, 28, 30
    generally accepted accounting standards
        (GAAS), 31
    negligence, 85
    public accountant's involvement with enterprise, 79
    standards set out in, 8, 28, 31, 36–37
CICA Standards
see also Assurance and Related Services Guidelines
    accounting estimates, review for bias, 365
    accounts receivable, disclosure, 509
    accuracy of information, 169
    analytical procedures, 163, 176–177, 181, 184,
        362–363, 389, 398, 697
    association, 79, 742
    assurance engagement, standards, 271, 743–744
    attest engagements, 743–744
    attributes, defining, 421
    audit documentation, 253, 254
    audit engagements, 2, 8
    audit evidence, 106, 168, 169, 171–172, 421
    audit evidence collection, 171–172
    audit evidence regarding financial statement
        account balances and disclosures, 651–652,
        693, 694–695, 699
    audit of internal control over financial reporting
        integrated with audit of financial statements,
        271, 303–304, 744
    audit objective, 106, 108, 109, 208
    audit planning, 241–242
    audit procedures to address fraud, 364
    audit report date, 719
    audit risk, 203, 208
    auditor's report, unqualified, 715–720
    auditor's report, unqualified with modified
        wording, 721–722
    auditor's responsibilities, 111
    business rationale for unusual transactions, 365
    business risk, 210
    client, written representation, 699
    commitments, 692
    communication with audit committee, 361–362, 705
    communication among audit team, 360–363
    communication with law firms, 694–695
    communication with management, 361–362, 705
    comparative financial statements approach, 722
    comparative information, 712, 722
    compilation engagements, 85, 747, 754, 755, 755*f*
    completeness of information, 169
    compliance with provisions, 753
    confirmation, refusal to permit, 514
    confirmations, 174, 511, 513
    consistency, 169
    contingent liabilities, 690
    contractual obligations, disclosure of, 692
    corresponding figures approach, 722
    date of auditor's report, 719
    deficiencies in internal control, communication of,
        267, 298
    direct reporting engagement, 743–744
    disclosure of commitments, 692
    disclosure of information in auditor's report, 715
    disclosure of unlikely events, 690
    documentation, 253, 254
    dual dating, 720
    examination of prospective financial statements, 757
    ethical standards, 35
    external confirmations, 163, 174, 511, 513, 514
    file freeze, 254
    final analytical procedures, 697
    financial information other than financial
        statements, 746, 753
    forecast, 756
    fraud assessment, documentation, 363

fraud, auditor responsibilities, 106, 111, 348–349,
    360–366, 699
fraud inquiries, 361–362
fraud risk, 358–359, 360–363
fraud risk factors, 362, 366
fraudulent financial reporting, 366
future-oriented financial information, 755–757
GAAP, changes in, 722
GAAP departure, 723
general review standards, 747, 749–755
generally accepted review standards, 751–753
going concern, 698
illegal acts, 113–114, 699, 705–706
independence, 32, 35
inquiries of management and audit committee,
    361–362
interim financial information, 753, 755
internal audit function, consideration of, 267, 277,
    765–766
internal audit, using work of, 277, 765–766
internal control over financial reporting,
    agreed-upon procedures, 272, 303
internal control conditions, communication of,
    267, 298, 707
inventory audit, 651–652
journal entries, examination of, 364–365
law firms, communication with, 694–695
laws and regulations in audit, 106, 113–114
letter of representation, 693
listed entity, 59
management assertions, 110
management bias, 365
management discussion and analysis (MD&A), 701
management, written representation, 699
materiality, 203, 217–218, 219
matter paragraphs, emphasis on, 712, 721
misstatements, evaluation of, 217–218, 705
misstatements, illegal acts, 106, 113–114, 699,
    705–706
misstatements, risks of, 178, 244, 271, 273, 398
negative assurance, 732
negative confirmations, 513
other information in annual reports, 700, 701
planning of audit, 241–242
precision of evidence, 169
professional skepticism, 358–359
projection, 756
quality control for financial statement audit, 39, 51
quality control for firms, 39, 51
quality control standards, 39, 39–41, 51
reasonable assurance and audit risk, 203, 208
regulatory environment, understanding of, 705–706
related party transactions, 239, 247, 632, 699
reliance on another auditor, 731–732
reliance on specialist, 731–732
reports on the results of applying specified audit
    procedures to financial information other than
    financial statements, 746
response to assessed risks, 163, 166, 180–181,
    184, 330
revenue recognition and fraud, 366, 386
review engagements, 747, 749–751
review of financial statements, 753
reviews of compliance with agreements and
    regulations, 753
risk assessment, 178, 184
risks, response to, 163, 166, 180–181, 184, 330
scope restriction, 727–728
service organization, 566, 582
service organization controls, 582
specialists, use of, 731–732
substantive tests, 330
subsequent discovery of misstatement, 700
subsequent events, 695, 699, 719, 720
subsequent facts, 733
sufficiency of evidence, 168
terms of engagement, 2, 8, 109, 110, 747–748
third-party service organization, 566, 582
timing, 184
unpredictability in audit plan, 364
unqualified auditor's report, 715–722
written representation, 698–699
Cineplex Odeon v. Ministry of National Revenue, 81
civil action, 82*t*
civil liability (Ontario), 80, 99
claim
    asserted claim, 692
    outstanding claim, 692

possible claim, 692
unasserted, 692
classes of transactions. *See* transaction classes
classification
    accounts receivable, 506–507
    acquisitions, 602
    general balance-related audit objective, 139
    general transaction-related audit objective, 137
    management assertions, 134
    prepaid insurance, 626
    as presentation and disclosure-related audit
        objective, 140
    recorded sales, 466
classification errors, 282, 579
Clayton, Daniel, 773
clerical errors, 516
client acceptance or continuance
    continuing clients, 116
    importance of, 115
    new client investigation, 115–116
    and quality control, 40*t*
client business risk
    see also client risk profile
    assessing, 250–251
    assessment methods, 213*t*
    defined, 210
client data
    vs auditor-determined expected results, 189, 190*f*
    budgets, 188–189
    vs client-determined expected results, 188–189
    vs industry data, 185–186, 185*t*
    security of, 180
    vs similar prior-dated data, 185
client motivation, 216
client objectives and strategies, 249–250
client personnel inquiries, 291–292, 749–750
client representation letter, 698–700
client risk profile, 121–122
    analytical procedures, 252
    articles of incorporation, 248
    business environment, knowledge of, 121
    business operations and processes, 245–247
    bylaws, 248
    client business risk, assessment of, 250–251
    client objectives and strategies, 249–250
    client's business and industry, 121, 242–244, 243*f*
    code of ethics, 248
    contracts, 249
    corporate governance, 249
    corporate governance processes, documentation
        of, 121–122
    corporate minutes, 248
    development of, 242–251
    entity-level controls, 122
    entity-wide controls, 121–122
    entity's ability to continue, 183
    evidence gathering, 251–252
    external environment, 244–245
    fraud risks, assessing, 122
    high-risk transactions/ accounts, 122
    industry knowledge, 121, 243*f*, 244, 244–245
    inquiries of management and others, 251
    inspection, 251
    internal controls, 122
    management and governance, 247–249
    measurement and performance, 250
    observation, 251
    operational and reporting structure, 245–246
    preliminary analytical review, 252–253, 252*t*
    related parties, identification of, 246–247
    related party-transaction, 247
    relevance of, 241
    risk assessment, 121
    technology infrastructure, 246
    tour of plant and offices, 246
clients
    acceptance and continuance, 115
    accounts receivable, rights to, 505
    auditors and external users, relationships among, 10*f*
    business. *See* client's business
    continuing clients, 116
    correspondence review, 516
    definition, 56
    integrity of, 96
    internal control perspectives, 270
    internal controls, effectiveness of, 169–170, 179
    liability to, 82–86
    motivation, 216

likely misstatements, 218, 225
limitations of internal controls, 273
limited liability partnerships (LLPs), 80, 96
Lineberry, Stephen, 180n
liquidity position, 211
liquidity ratios, 192–193
listed entity, 58, 59
listeria outbreak, 641
litigation. *See* legal liability
litigation risk, 28
Livent case, 366
loan agreements, 668–669
lobby for changes in law, 96
local firms, 25–26
lockbox systems, 452
long-term credit transactions, 677
long-term debt and preferred dividend ratios, 193, 193f
Lowe, D. Jordan, 255n
Lu, Vanessa, 642n
Lysecki, Sarah, 417

M
MacDonald Commission, 698
Macdonald, Jim, 215n
maintaining control (of confirmations), 514–515
Major Financial Inc., 444
Making Integrated Audits Reality (Helpert & Lazarine), 773
Maloney, Paul, 352n
management
    authority, assignment of, 276
    and client business risk, 251
    communication with, 705–707
    competence of, 212
    and control environment, 274, 275
    control methods, 276
    control systems, maintaining reliable, 270
    error prevention and detection, 270
    external influences, reaction to, 276
    fraud prevention and detection, 270, 364
    fraud-related inquiries, 361–362
    importance of understanding, 247–249
    inquiries of management, 251, 696–697
    integrity of, 213–214, 215–216
    internal control perspectives, 270, 271, 303
    internal control responsibilities, 273
    judgment of, 216–217, 243
    management fraud, 79
    National Policy requirements, 317t
    officers' compensation, 585
    operating style, 275
    override of controls, 357, 364–365
    philosophy, 275
    refusal to permit confirmation, 514
    regulatory influences on, 315–316
    resource optimization, 270
    responsibilities, in audit, 28f, 110, 718
    risk assessment, 277
    safeguarding assets, 270
    tone at the top, 352–353
management accountants, 76f
management advisory services, 12
management assertions, 133–135
    accuracy, 134
    allocation, 134
    and audit objectives, relationships among, 140–141
    classification, 134
    completeness, 134
    defined, 133
    development of, 126, 126f
    examples of, 136t
    existence, 133–134
    financial statement presentation and disclosure, 134–135
    high-risk, identification of, 399–400
    measurement, 134
    occurrence, 133–134
    and risk of material misstatements, 290
    valuation, 134
management control methods, 276
management controls. *See* organization and management controls
management corruption, 347
management discussion and analysis (MD&A), 700–701
management fraud, 79, 111–112, 112–113

management information systems (MIS), 323–324
management inquiries, 251
management letters, 435, 707, 769, 299
management representation letter, 83n, 96, 698–700
"Management's Discussion and Analysis: Guidance on Preparation and Disclosure", 701
manager and partner review, 689
"Managing the Business Risk of Fraud: A Practical Guide", 355
mandatory rotation of senior personnel, 60
manual controls, 299
manual information system, 278t
manual systems, for transaction flow, 126, 127f
manufactured inventory, 658
manufacturing assets acquisition, 615–622
    accounts, overview of, 616, 616f
    accumulated amortization, verification of, 622
    allocations, 621
    amortization expense, verification of, 621–622
    analytical procedures, 617, 617t
    asset balance, verification of, 620–621
    auditing manufacturing equipment, 616–617
    balance-related audit objectives, 618t
    capital asset master file, 616
    current-year acquisitions, verification of, 617
    current-year disposals, verification of, 619–620
    supporting documentation, examination of, 617–619
    tests of details of balances, 618t
manufacturing equipment. *See* manufacturing asset acquisitions
Maple Leaf Foods, 641
Maremont, Mark, 468n
material and pervasive amounts, 726
material but not pervasive amounts, 725–726
material misstatement
    absence of causal connection, 90
    accrued bonuses, 585
    assertion level, 290
    audit failure, 78
    and auditor's report, 32
    auditors' responsibilities, 718
    client business risk, 250
    client risk profile, 242
    control risk and, 296–298
    defined, 725
    final analytical procedures, 697
    financial statement level, 290
    fraud, 359, 363, 373, 374
    GAAP departure, 724, 726
    high-risk assertions, 399–400
    identification and assessment of risk of, 290, 461–462
    immaterial misstatements, 702, 724, 725
    inherent risk, 209
    internal control weaknesses, 295
    management and governance, 247
    management's responsibilities, 718
    planned detection risk, 209
    and relevant controls, 287
    risk assessment procedures, 387
    risks of, 123, 181, 214
    sales and collection cycle, 461
materiality, 724–727
    accounts receivable audit case illustration, 520–521
    allocation to segments, 223–224
    application of, 222–223
    and audit performance, 226–231
    audit sampling and, 423
    bases required for evaluating, 220
    client business risk and, 250
    comparison of estimated misstatement, 224–226
    current files, 256
    decisions, GAAP departure, 726–727
    decisions, scope limitations, 727
    defined, 217
    direct projection method of estimating misstatement, 225
    dollar amounts compared with base, 726
    estimate of misstatement, 224–226
    factors affecting judgment about, 220–221
    illustrative guidelines, 221, 221f
    immaterial amounts, 725
    immaterial misstatements, 725
    importance of, 217–226, 724–725
    material and pervasive amounts, 726

material but not pervasive amounts, 725–726
material misstatements, 735
    maximum possible misstatements and, 226, 226t
    measurability of dollar error, 726–727
    measurement limitations, 227–228
    nature of item, 727
    planning materiality, 218
    qualitative factors, impact of, 221
    relative rather than absolute concept, 220
    and risk, and audit evidence, 230
    sampling error, 225
    scope limitations, 727
    setting planning materiality, 219–223, 398, 499–500
    and significance, 725t
    steps in applying, 219f
    total dollar misstatement, 726
    and type of opinion, 725t
Mathias, Philip, 89n
Mattamy Homes, 698
Mavin, Duncan, 324n
maximum possible misstatements, 218
McConnell, Donald K., 510n
McKesson & Robbins Company, 651
McMillan, Robert, 648n
McMullum, Tim, 763n
MD&A (management discussion and analysis), 700–701
mean-per-unit estimation, 419
measurability of dollar error, 726–727
measurement
    of client's performance, 250
    management assertions, 134
    statistical measurement, 433–434
Medina, Andrew, 773
Mejri, Sofiane, 78n
member, 15–16, 56
Merrill Lynch, 573
MERX, 598, 598n
Messier, Nixon, & Royce, 688
Meyers Norris Penny, 28, 28n
Microsoft Corporation, 3
Miles, William, 451n
Millan, Luis, 73n
Milman & Company, 244, 244n
Ministry of Health and Long-Term Care, 642n
Ministry of Small Business and Revenue (MSBR), 6, 6n
minutes of meetings, 248
misappropriation of assets, 347–348
    accounts payable, 371
    acquisition and payment cycle, 371
    attitudes, 351
    defined, 347
    failure to record a sale, 369–370
    incentives/ pressures, 350
    inherent risk assessment, 348
    inventory fraud, 370–371
    management corruption, 347
    opportunities, 351
    prevention of, 370
    procurement fraud, 348
    purchases and accounts payable, 371
    rationalization
    receipts involving revenue, 369–372
    risk factors for, 350–351, 351t
    susceptibility of, 217
    theft of cash receipts after sale is recorded, 370
misstatement of fact, 700
misstatements
    absence of misstatement, 83, 90
    adjusting entries, 257
    anomaly, 431
    assessment of, 461–462
    bank reconciliation, 542–544
    bonuses, 462
    cash-related, 542
    client business risk and, 250
    communication of, 705
    comparison of estimated, 224–226
    control risk and, 296–298
    direct projection method of estimating misstatement, 225
    estimate of, 224–226
    example of, 365
    fraudulent financial reporting, 364–365
    fraudulent, responding to, 372–373